QM
23
D1757857

THE OXFORD HANDBOOK OF

GRAMMATICALIZATION

OXFORD HANDBOOKS IN

LINGUISTICS

The Oxford Handbook of Applied Linguistics
Edited by Robert B. Kaplan

The Oxford Handbook of Case
Edited by Andrej Malchukov and Andrew Spencer

The Oxford Handbook of Cognitive Linguistics
Edited by Dirk Geeraerts and Hubert Cuyckens

The Oxford Handbook of Comparative Syntax
Edited by Guglielmo Cinque and Richard S. Kayne

The Oxford Handbook of Compounds
Edited by Rochelle Lieber and Pavol Štekauer

The Oxford Handbook of Computational Linguistics
Edited by Ruslan Mitkov

The Oxford Handbook of Grammaticalization
Edited by Heiko Narrog and Bernd Heine

The Oxford Handbook of Japanese Linguistics
Edited by Shigeru Miyagawa and Mamoru Saito

The Oxford Handbook of Linguistic Analysis
Edited by Bernd Heine and Heiko Narrog

The Oxford Handbook of Linguistic Interfaces
Edited by Gillian Ramchand and Charles Reiss

The Oxford Handbook of Linguistic Minimalism
Edited by Cedric Boeckx

The Oxford Handbook of Linguistic Typology
Edited by Jae Jung Song

The Oxford Handbook of Translation Studies
Edited by Kerstin Malmkjaer and Kevin Windle

THE OXFORD HANDBOOK OF

GRAMMATICALIZATION

Edited by

HEIKO NARROG

and

BERND HEINE

OXFORD
UNIVERSITY PRESS

OXFORD
UNIVERSITY PRESS

Great Clarendon Street, Oxford OX2 6DP

Oxford University Press is a department of the University of Oxford.
It furthers the University's objective of excellence in research, scholarship,
and education by publishing worldwide in

Oxford New York

Auckland Cape Town Dar es Salaam Hong Kong Karachi
Kuala Lumpur Madrid Melbourne Mexico City Nairobi
New Delhi Shanghai Taipei Toronto

With offices in

Argentina Austria Brazil Chile Czech Republic France Greece
Guatemala Hungary Italy Japan Poland Portugal Singapore
South Korea Switzerland Thailand Turkey Ukraine Vietnam

Oxford is a registered trade mark of Oxford University Press
in the UK and in certain other countries

Published in the United States
by Oxford University Press Inc., New York

First published by Oxford University Press 2011

British Library Cataloguing in Publication Data
Data available

Library of Congress Cataloging in Publication Data
Data available

Typeset by SPI Publisher Services, Pondicherry, India
Printed in Great Britain
on acid-free paper by
CPI Group (UK) Ltd, Croydon, CR0 YY

ISBN 978–0–19–958678–3

3 5 7 9 10 8 6 4 2

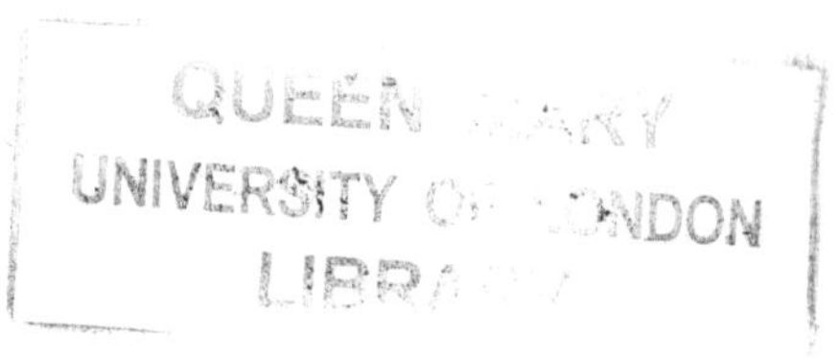

To our friends in Japan and Korea

Contents

PART I GRAMMATICALIZATION AND LINGUISTIC THEORY

PART II METHODOLOGICAL ISSUES

PART III DOMAINS OF GRAMMATICALIZATION

PART IV GRAMMATICALIZATION OF FORM CLASSES AND CATEGORIES

PART V THE DIFFERENT FACES OF GRAMMATICALIZATION ACROSS LANGUAGES

Acknowledgements

Heiko Narrog wishes to thank Elly van Gelderen and Elizabeth Traugott, who contributed invaluable advice in the planning stages of this volume, and Werner Abraham, for his precious advice in the finishing stages. His research activities during the period while working on this book were partly sponsored by grant no. 20520346 of the Japanese Society for the Promotion of Science. In the academic year 2010/11 the Harvard-Yenching Institute and Maria Polinsky enabled him to spend an extended period of research at Harvard University.

Bernd Heine expresses his gratitude to a number of colleagues who have been of help in working on this volume, in particular to Tania Kuteva and John Haiman. Most of this work was carried out while he was staying in Japan and Korea. He wishes to thank in particular Professor Osamu Hieda and the Tokyo University of Foreign Studies for their hospitality during the academic year 2008/9, and Professor Kyung-An Song and the Korean Ministry of Education, Science and Technology for generously having sponsored the research leading to the handbook within its World Class University program (Grant No. R33–10011), as well as Seongha Rhee of Hankuk University of Foreign Studies, Seoul, and Hyun Jung Koo for all their care and encouragement, and finally also to Haiping Long, Shenzhen Polytechnic, China for inspiring discussions and his hospitality.

The contributors

Alexandra Y. Aikhenvald is Professor and Research Leader, People and Societies of the Tropics, in the Cairns Institute of James Cook University. She has worked on descriptive and historical aspects of Berber languages and has published, in Russian, a grammar of Modern Hebrew (1990; 2nd edn 2009). She is a major authority on languages of the Arawak family from northern Amazonia, and has written grammars of Bare (1995, based on work with the last speaker, who has since died) and Warekena (1998), plus *A Grammar of Tariana, from Northwest Amazonia* (Cambridge University Press, 2003; paperback 2007), in addition to essays on various typological and areal features of South American languages. Her lengthy grammar, *The Manambu Language from East Sepik, Papua New Guinea*, was published by Oxford University Press in 2008. Other monographs with OUP are *Classifiers: Devices* (2000; paperback 2003), *Language Contact in Amazonia* (2002), *Evidentiality* (2004; paperback with revisions 2006) and *Imperatives and Commands* (2010).

Walter Bisang studied General Linguistics, Chinese, and Georgian at the University of Zurich. He has been Professor of General and Comparative Linguistics (Typology) in Mainz (Germany) since 1992, and director of the Collaborative Research Center on 'Cultural and Linguistic Contact' from 1999 to 2008. His research interests include linguistic typology/language universals, formal vs. functional linguistics, grammaticalization, language contact/areal typology. His languages of interest are: East and mainland Southeast Asian languages, Caucasian languages (Georgian and others), Austronesian languages (Bahasa Indonesia, Tagalog, Yabêm, Paiwan), and Yoruba (together with Remi Sonaiya).

Kersti Börjars is Professor of Linguistics at the University of Manchester. She has published on linguistic change in general and also more detailed studies of Germanic languages, in particular the Scandinavian languages and Pennsylvania German. She is the author of *Feature Distribution in Swedish Noun Phrases*, and with Bob Borsley she has edited *Non-transformational Syntax: Formal and Explicit Models of Grammar.* She has led funded projects on 'Modelling syntactic change in Pennsylvania German' (ESRC) and 'Germanic possessive *s*: an empirical, historical and theoretical study' (AHRC).

Kasper Boye is postdoctorate member of the Department of Nordic Languages and Linguistics at the University of Copenhagen. His PhD dissertation (2006) was a cross-linguistic study of epistemic meaning. His research interests include grammar and semantics in a functional and cognitive perspective, with modality and grounding as focal areas. He has also published articles about semantic mapping and complementation constructions.

Laurel Brinton is Professor of English Language at the University of British Columbia. Her areas of research include tense/aspect, diachronic discourse analysis, pragmatic markers, grammaticalization, lexicalization, and linguistic stylistics. She is the author of *The Development of English Aspectual Systems* (Cambridge University Press, 1988; reissued 2009), *Pragmatic Markers in English* (Mouton, 1996), and *The Comment Clause in English* (CUP, 2008). With Elizabeth Closs Traugott, she has co-written *Lexicalization in Language Change* (CUP, 2005), and with Alexander Bergs she is co-editing the two-volume *Handbook of Historical English Linguistics* (Mouton).

Joan L. Bybee was on the faculty at the State University of New York at Buffalo from 1973 to 1989 and is now Distinguished Professor Emerita of the Department of Linguistics at the University of New Mexico. Her work utilizing large cross-linguistic databases, e.g. *Morphology* (1985), and *The Evolution of Grammar* (with Revere Perkins and William Pagliuca, 1994), provide diachronic explanations for typological phenomena. In addition, her books presenting a usage-based perspective on synchrony and diachrony include *Phonology and Language Use* (2001), *Frequency of Use and the Organization of Language* (2007), and *Language, Usage and Cognition* (2010).

Rena Torres Cacoullos is Associate Professor of Spanish and Linguistics at Penn State University. Her research addresses how to establish grammatical change diachronically and grammatical difference synchronically, including in language contact situations, by comparing patterns of linguistic variation.

Anne Carlier is Professor of Linguistics at the University of Lille 3 (France). Her research interests include grammaticalization, typological perspectives on Romance languages, and word class formation. Her current research topics are the early stages of development of the articles and their integration into a paradigm, nominal and verbal quantification, and the interaction between aspect and argument structure, mainly in the different language stages from Latin to French. She is involved in the development of an electronic corpus for the study of the transition between Late Latin and early Old French.

Maria Maura Cezario is Professor at the Universidade Federal do Rio de Janeiro (UFRJ). She holds a Master's Degree and a PhD in Linguistics from that university, and is coordinator of the Discourse and Grammar Research Group at UFRJ with Professor Mário Martelotta. Her publications include the books *Manual de linguística* (Contexto, 2008), *Linguística funcional* (DP&A, 2003), with other

Brazilian professors, and articles on linguistic change, grammaticalization, word order, and Portuguese adverbs and verbs.

Hilary Chappell is currently Chair Professor in Linguistic Typology of East Asian Languages at the École des Hautes Études en Sciences Sociales (EHESS) in Paris, an appointment she took up in 2005. Since the 1990s, she has been engaged in opening up the new domain in Chinese linguistics of typology and the comparative grammatical description of Sinitic languages (or 'Chinese dialects'), with the aim of gauging the extent of their diversity. More recently, she has also begun research on the diachronic syntax of Southern Min (Hokkien) with Professor Alain Peyraube, using a corpus of late 16th- and early 17th-century materials compiled by Spanish missionaries.

Elizabeth Couper-Kuhlen has held professorships at the University of Konstanz and the University of Potsdam in Germany, and is currently Finland Distinguished Professor for Interactional Linguistics at the Department of Finnish, Finno-Ugrian, and Scandanavian Studies at the University of Helsinki. She has published widely on prosody and syntax in conversation. (Among her best-known publications are *An Introduction to English Prosody* (1986), *English Speech Rhythm* (1993), and the co-edited volumes *Prosody in Conversation* (1996) and *Sound Patterns in Interaction* (2004).)

Östen Dahl has been Professor in General Linguistics at Stockholm University, Stockholm, since 1980. Among his research interests are language typology, in particular tense and aspect, semantics, grammaticalization, and language complexity. He is the author of *Tense and Aspect Systems* (1985) and *The Growth and Maintenance of Linguistic Complexity* (2004) and co-author of *Logic in Linguistics* (1977), in addition to publishing a large number of articles in journal and collective volumes. He holds an honorary doctorate from the University of Helsinki.

Scott DeLancey is a Professor of Linguistics at the University of Oregon, where he has taught since 1982. His primary research area is the descriptive and comparative study of Tibeto-Burman and Southeast Asian languages and languages of western North America. He has also contributed to the study of grammaticalization theory, case theory, and several areas of typology, including ergativity, evidentiality, and inverse systems, and works with community language documentation and development projects in the northwestern US and northeast India.

Walter De Mulder is Professor of General and French Linguistics at the University of Antwerp. His research interests include usage-based approaches to grammaticalization and cognitive approaches to meaning and reference. He has worked intensively on the semantics and pragmatics of tense, aspect, and mood markers, referential expressions, and prepositions, mainly in French, but occasionally also in other languages.

Guy Deutscher received his PhD in Linguistics from Cambridge University. He was Research Fellow in Historical Linguistics at St John's College, Cambridge, later at the Department of Languages of the Ancient Near East in Leiden University. He is now Honorary Research Fellow in the Department of Linguistics at the University of Manchester. He has published three books, *Syntactic Change in Akkadian* (2000), *The Unfolding of Language* (2005), and *Through The Language Glass* (2010).

Holger Diessel is Professor of English linguistics at the University of Jena. His research interests include linguistic typology, grammaticalization, language acquisition, and the usage-based model of grammar. He has conducted cross-linguistic research on demonstratives and subordinate clauses and has worked intensively on the acquisition of relative clauses and other complex sentence constructions.

Gabriele Diewald has been full Professor of German Linguistics at the German Department of Leibniz Universität Hannover since 2001. Previously she was Professor of German Linguistics at the German Department of the University of Hamburg (2000–2001), and Assistant Professor at the German Department of the Friedrich-Alexander Universität Erlangen-Nürnberg (1998–2000). Her Habilitation thesis was published as *Die Modalverben im Deutschen* (Niemeyer, 1999). Other book publications include *Deixis und Textsorten im Deutschen* (Niemeyer, 1991) and *Grammatikalisierung* (Niemeyer, 1991). She works in the fields of grammaticalization, language change, modality, evidentiality, verbal categories, pragmatics, discourse, and semiotics.

Regine Eckardt holds a doctorate from Stuttgart, and is now Professor of Linguistics in the Department of English Language and Literature at Göttingen University. Building on her early research topics in synchronic semantics, and pragmatics, she has been working on meaning change and grammaticalization since 2000. Specifically, she pursues the hypothesis that the paradigm of truth-conditional, compositional semantics and pragmatics is particularly suited to analyse the shifts and changes of semantic composition in grammaticalization.

Olga Fischer is Professor of Germanic Linguistics at the University of Amsterdam, where her PhD thesis, 'Syntactic change and causation: developments in infinitival constructions in English', was accepted in 1990. She is a contributor to the Cambridge History of the English Language (1992), co-author of *The Syntax of Early English* (Cambridge University Press, 2000), author of *Morphosyntactic Change* (Oxford University Press, 2007), and has edited a number of books on iconicity in language and literature and on grammaticalization.

Zygmunt Frajzyngier is Professor of Linguistics at the University of Colorado in Boulder. His research interests include: discovery and proofs of meaning; cross-linguistic study of syntax; grammaticalization; discoveries of forms and functions of hitherto undescribed languages; and typological and comparative Afroasiatic and Chadic linguistics. His recent books include: *Grammar of Wandala* (in press); *Grammar of Gidar* (2008); *Grammar of Mina* (with Eric Johnston and Adrian Edwards, 2005); *Grammatical and Semantic Relations in Hausa* (with Mohammed Munkaila, 2004); *Explaining Language Structure through Systems Interaction* (with Erin Shay, 2003).

Elly van Gelderen is a syntactician interested in language change. Her current work shows how regular syntactic change (grammaticalization) can be accounted for by (Minimalist) Economy Principles that help a child acquire a language and analyse it in a different way from previous generations. She has taught at Arizona State University since 1995. Related interests are the evolution of language, biolinguistics, prescriptivism, authorship debates, and code switching.

Anna Giacalone Ramat is Professor of Linguistics at the University of Pavia. Her areas of research include theoretical issues of grammaticalization, linguistic change in typological perspective, language obsolescence, and second language acquisition of tense/aspect relations. She is the author of *Lingua, dialetto e comportamento linguistico: la situazione di Gressoney, Aosta* (Musumeci, 1979). She has also published articles on diachronic developments of Indo-European languages and on semantic change of interclausal connectives. She is the editor of *Typology and Second Language Acquisition* (de Gruyter, 2003) and (with Paul J. Hopper) of *The Limits of Grammaticalization* (Benjamins, 1998). She has served as President of the 'International Society for Historical Linguistics' (1983–85), as President of the Società Italiana di Glottologia (1991–2), and as President of the Societas Linguistica Europaea (1999–2000).

Nikolas Gisborne teaches Linguistics and English Language at the University of Edinburgh. He is the author of *The Event Structure of Perception Verbs* (Oxford University Press, 2010) and is currently writing a book on constructional change and predicative constructions called *English Predicative Constructions* for Cambridge University Press.

John Haiman has done fieldwork on Romansch, Hua, and Khmer. He is the author of *Natural Syntax* (Cambridge University Press, 1985), *Talk is Cheap* (Oxford University Press, 1998), and other books.

Peter Harder is professor in the Department of English, Germanic, and Romance Studies at the University of Copenhagen. His research interests focus on the relations between functional (including cognitive) and structural properties of language, and he has published on areas such as tense, determiners, and subordinators. His main work is *Functional Semantics* (1996); *Meaning in Mind and Society* appeared in 2010.

Martin Haspelmath is a researcher at the Max-Planck-Institut für evolutionäre Anthropologie, Leipzig. He received degrees from the Universität zu Köln, University at Buffalo, and the Freie Universität Berlin. He taught at the FU

Berlin, the Universität Bamberg, the Università di Pavia, the Universität Leipzig, and at summer schools in Albuquerque, Mainz, Düsseldorf, Cagliari, Campobasso, MIT, and Berkeley. His research interests are primarily in the areas of broadly comparative morphosyntax and general and diachronic linguistic theory. He is one of the editors of *The World Atlas of Language Structures* (2005), and of the forthcoming *Atlas of Pidgin and Creole Language Structures.*

Bernd Heine is Emeritus Professor at the Institute of African Studies (Institut für Afrikanistik), University of Cologne. His 33 books include *Possession* (Cambridge University Press, 1997); *Auxiliaries* (Oxford University Press, 1993); *Cognitive Foundations of Grammar* (OUP, 1997); with Derek Nurse, *African Languages* (CUP, 2000); *A Linguistic Geography of Africa* (CUP, 2008); with Tania Kuteva, *World Lexicon of Grammaticalization* (CUP, 2002); *Language Contact and Grammatical Change* (CUP, 2005); *The Changing Languages of Europe* (OUP, 2006).

Kees Hengeveld has been Professor of Theoretical Linguistics at the University of Amsterdam since 1996. Before that, he taught Spanish linguistics at that same university. His research focuses on Functional Discourse Grammar and linguistic typology, and often on the combination of the two. With J. Lachlan Mackenzie he published *Functional Discourse Grammar* (Oxford University Press, 2008). Before that, he edited Simon C. Dik's posthumous *The Theory of Functional Grammar* (Mouton de Gruyter, 1997) and many collections of articles, and authored *Non-verbal Predication* (Mouton de Gruyter, 1992), as well as numerous articles.

Martin Hilpert is a junior research fellow at the Freiburg Institute for Advanced Studies (FRIAS). His interests include the corpus-based study of grammaticalization, construction grammar, and cognitive linguistics. He has worked on the grammaticalization of future constructions in the Germanic languages, and is currently exploring the interrelations between construction grammar and grammaticalization theory.

Brian D. Joseph is Distinguished University Professor of Linguistics and Kenneth E. Naylor Professor of South Slavic Linguistics at The Ohio State University, where he has taught since 1979. He received his PhD from Harvard University in 1978, writing his dissertation on syntactic change between Medieval and Modern Greek. He specializes in historical linguistics, Greek linguistics, and Balkan linguistics, and has published extensively in these areas. He served as editor of *Diachronica* from 1999 to 2001 and as editor of *Language* from 2002 to 2008.

Lars Johanson is Professor of Turcology at the Oriental Institute of the University of Mainz. He has published extensively on synchronic and diachronic linguistics, especially in the domains of aspect–mood–tense, language contact, and language typology. Most of his publications focus on the Turkic language family. He is the Editor-in-Chief of the journal *Turkic Languages* and the book series Turcologica.

Christa König is a Lecturer in African Cultures and Languages at the Centre for African Studies, University of Frankfurt. She has taught at the Universities of Cologne, Zurich, Graz, Gwangju, and at the Tokyo University of Foreign Studies, and has carried out field research in East Africa and Namibia. She is presently working on the Khoisan language !Xun. Her main book publications are *Aspekt im Maa* (AMO, 1994), *Kasus im Ik* (Köppe, 2002), and *Case in Africa* (Oxford University Press, 2008).

Bernd Kortmann is Full Professor of English Language and Linguistics at the University of Freiburg, Germany. His publications include four monographs, six edited volumes (with four more volumes currently in preparation), a two-volume handbook-cum-CD-ROM on the phonology and morphosyntax of the varieties of English around the world (2004), and about 80 articles and reviews in journals and collective volumes. His main research interest over the last decade has been the grammar of non-standard varieties of English around the world, especially from a typological perspective. Currently he is editing a 'World Atlas of Variation in English' which will be published in 2011/12 both electronically (interactive maps) and in print (by Mouton de Gruyter).

Manfred Krug is Chair of English and Historical Linguistics at the University of Bamberg. In his research, he focuses on frequency-driven approaches to language variation and change, typically from a grammaticalization perspective. He holds an MA in Applied Linguistics from Exeter University and studied Latin, English, and German at Freiburg University, where he completed his PhD and postdoctoral research project (Habilitation). He was a visiting professor at Portland State University (Oregon), and held the Chair of English Historical Linguistics at the University of Mannheim.

Tania Kuteva is a Full Professor of English Linguistics at the Heinrich-Heine-University of Düsseldorf, Germany. Apart from a number of articles in international journals, she has also published two books with Cambridge University Press and three with Oxford University Press on grammaticalization, language contact, grammatical typology, and language evolution, of four of which she is co-author with Bernd Heine. She is on the Editorial Board of *Studies in Language*.

Béatrice Lamiroy is Professor of General and French Linguistics at the University of Leuven. Her research interests include comparative linguistics, syntax of Romance languages, grammaticalization, and lexicalization. She has worked intensively on Romance auxiliaries, case and grammatical relations, and French idiomatic expressions.

Ronald W. Langacker is Professor Emeritus and Research Professor at the University of California, San Diego. Early in his career, major areas of research included generative syntax and the comparative-historical grammar of the

Uto-Aztecan family of Native American languages. Over the last three decades, his main concern has been to develop and progressively articulate the theory of Cognitive Grammar, a radical alternative to generative theory. He has published numerous books and articles dealing with a broad array of issues in cognitive linguistics.

Adam Ledgeway. Since completing his PhD at the University of Manchester in 1996 and a Research Fellowship at Downing College, Cambridge (1996–97), Adam Ledgeway has been Lecturer in Romance Philology at the University of Cambridge, where he is currently the Head of the Department of Italian. His research interests include Italian dialectology, the comparative history and morphosyntax of the Romance languages, syntactic theory, and linguistic change, and he has worked on such topics as complementation, auxiliary selection and split intransitivity, word order, cliticization, clause structure, verb movement, finiteness, and the development of demonstrative systems. Recent books include *A Comparative Syntax of the Dialects of Southern Italy* (Blackwell, 2000), *Sui dialetti italoromanzi* (Biddles, 2007 co-edited with D. Bentley; *Didattica della lingua italiana* (Guerra, 2008, co-edited with A. L. Lepschy); *Syntactic Variation* (Cambridge University Press, 2009, co-edited with R. D'Alessandro and I. Roberts); *Grammatica diacronica del napoletano* (Niemeyer, 2009). Currently, he is writing a book for OUP entitled *From Latin to Romance*, and is co-editing the two volumes of *The Cambridge History of the Romance Languages* (CUP, with M. Maiden and J. C. Smith).

Douglas Lightfoot is Associate Professor of German Linguistics at the University of Alabama. His interests include the lexicalization and grammaticalization interface, synonymous compounding in German, German derivational suffixation, affixoids, and gestalt linguistics. He is also a language programme director and further interested in the teaching and learning of foreign languages. A recent publication on incorporating language history into the instruction of German won the Article of the Year prize from the American Association of Teachers of German.

Christian Mair was Assistant and, subsequently, Associate Professor in the English Department of the University of Innsbruck, before being appointed to a Chair in English Linguistics at the University of Freiburg in Germany in 1990. He has been involved in the compilation of several linguistic corpora (among them F-LOB and Frown, updates of the classic LOB and Brown corpora designed to make possible real-time studies of change in progress). His research over the past two decades has focused on the corpus-based description of modern English grammar and regional variation and ongoing change in standard Englishes world-wide, and has resulted in the publication of several monographs (most recently *Twentieth-Century English* (2006) and more than 60 contributions to scholarly journals and edited works. In addition he has produced several popular introductions to the field of English.

Mário Eduardo T. Martelotta* was Professor at the Universidade Federal do Rio de Janeiro (UFRJ) until his untimely death in April, 2011. He had a Master's Degree and a PhD in Linguistics from that university, and was coordinator of the Discourse and Grammar Research Group at UFRJ with Professor Maria Maura Cezario. His publications include editing the Manual de linguística (Contexto, 2008) and Linguística funcional (DP&A, 2003), as well as numerous articles in linguistic change, grammaticalization, word order, and Portuguese adverbs.

Yaron Matras is Professor of Linguistics at the University of Manchester, where he has been working since 1995. His areas of interest include linguistic typology, dialectology, language documentation, sociolinguistics, and discourse pragmatics, and he has written descriptive investigations of Romani dialects, Kurdish, Domari, Arabic, Turkish, and German dialects. He is best known for his work on Romani, including *Romani* (Cambridge University Press, 2002), *Markedness and Language Change* (with Viktor Elšík, Mouton, 2006), and an online database of Romani dialects (http://romani.humanities.manchester.ac.uk/rms), and for his theoretical work on language contact, including the edited volumes *The Mixed Language Debate* (with Peter Bakker, Mouton, 2003), *Grammatical Borrowing in Cross-Linguistic Perspective* (with Jeanette Sakel, Mouton, 2007), and the monograph *Language Contact* (CUP, 2009).

Caterina Mauri has a post-doc fellowship at the University of Pavia, and is involved in both historical and typological research projects, concerning the cross-linguistic coding and the grammaticalization of coordinating constructions, directives, and reality status. In her PhD (2003–7, University of Pavia), she carried out a typological research on coordination, which was published in 2008 by Mouton de Gruyter with the title *Coordination Relations in the Languages of Europe and Beyond*, and for which she received the ALT Greenberg Award 2009.

Marianne Mithun is Professor of Linguistics at the University of California, Santa Barbara. Her interests include morphology, syntax, discourse, prosody, and their interactions, language change, language contact, and language documentation and description. She has worked with a variety of languages, particularly those of the Iroquoian, Pomoan, Eskimo-Aleut, Siouan, Athabaskan, and Austronesian families.

Maj-Britt Mosegaard Hansen obtained her PhD from the University of Copenhagen in 1996. She has been Professor of French Language and Linguistics at the University of Manchester since 2007. She is the author of two monographs and numerous journal articles and book chapters. Her principal research interests are language change, semantics, pragmatics, and functional-cognitive linguistics.

Heiko Narrog is Associate Professor at the Graduate School of International Cultural Studies of Tohoku University. He holds two PhDs in linguistics in Germany and Japan, and his publications include *Modality in Japanese*

(Benjamins, 2009) and *The Oxford Handbook of Linguistic Analysis* (Oxford University Press, 2010), coedited with Bernd Heine.

Terttu Nevalainen is Professor and Chair of English Philology at the University of Helsinki and the Director of the Research Unit for Variation, Contacts and Change in English (VARIENG). Her research interests include historical sociolinguistics, language change, and corpus linguistics. She is the author of 'Early Modern English lexis and semantics' in *The Cambridge History of the English Language* (vol. 3, Cambridge University Press, 1999), *Historical Sociolinguistics* (with H. Raumolin-Brunberg, Pearson Education, 2003) and of *An Introduction to Early Modern English* (Edinburgh University Press, 2006) and a co-editor of e.g. *Types of Variation* (Benjamins, 2006) and *The Dynamics of Linguistic Variation* (Benjamins, 2008). She is one of the compilers of the Helsinki Corpus of English Texts and the director of the research project 'Sociolinguistics and Language History', which has produced the Corpus of Early English Correspondence, and over 100 publications on English historical sociolinguistics.

Steve Nicolle has lived in Kenya since 1999, during which time he has published on grammaticalization, pragmatics, translation, Bantu languages, and ethnobotany. He currently coordinates SIL's linguistic work in Africa, teaches linguistics and translation at Africa International University (Nairobi), and works as an SIL linguistics and translation consultant in Kenya and the Democratic Republic of Congo.

Muriel Norde is Professor of Scandinavian Languages and Literature at the University of Groningen. She was previously a research fellow at the University of Amsterdam. Her 1997 University of Amsterdam PhD was awarded for a study of the history of the Swedish genitive. She has published extensively on grammaticalization and related phenomena, including articles in *Nordic Journal of Linguistics* and *Language Sciences*. She is also the author of *Degrammaticalization* (Oxford University Press, 2009), and the co-editor, with Olga Fischer and Harry Perridon, of *Up and Down the Cline* (Benjamins, 2004).

Arja Nurmi is an Academy of Finland Research Fellow and a Domain Co-ordinator for the Research Unit for Variation, Contacts and Change in English at the University of Helsinki. She works in the field of historical sociolinguistics, currently studying the history of English modal auxiliaries. She is also carrying out research on the multilingual practices found during the history of English. Her doctoral dissertation was 'A social history of periphrastic *do*', and she has edited several volumes, most recently *The Language of Daily Life in England (1400–1800)* with Minna Nevala and Minna Palander-Collin and *Annotating Variation and Change* with Anneli Meurman-Solin. She is one of the compilers of the Corpus of Early English Correspondence.

Toshio Ohori graduated from the University of California at Berkeley in 1992, and is currently an Associate Professor at the University of Tokyo. His main areas of interest are semantics, linguistic typology (with special focus on complex sentences), grammaticalization, and discourse analysis. His publications include *Studies in Japanese Grammaticalization* (1998, editor), *Cognitive Linguistics* (2002, in Japanese), 'Coordination in Mentalese' (2004), and 'Pragmatic factors in the development of a switch-adjective language' (2008, with Julia Koloskova). More information can be obtained at: http://gamp.c.u-tokyo.ac.jp/~tohori/ohori.html

Noriko O. Onodera (PhD, Georgetown University, 1993) is Professor of Linguistics in the Department of English at Aoyama Gakuin University, where she teaches pragmatics, sociolinguistics, and discourse studies. She is the author of *Japanese Discourse Markers* (Benjamins, 2004) and co-editor of *Journal of Historical Pragmatics* 8.2 (2007), *Historical Changes in Japanese* (with Ryoko Suzuki). Her research interests centre on pragmatics and historical pragmatics, more specifically, discourse markers, modality, subjectification, and intersubjectification, especially in English and Japanese.

Minna Palander-Collin is currently Professor of English Philology at the Department of Modern Languages and Senior Researcher at the Research Unit for Variation, Contacts and Change in English (VARIENG), University of Helsinki. Her main research interests include historical sociolinguistics, historical pragmatics and corpus linguistics, and her latest project focuses on 'language and identity: variation and change in patterns of interaction in the history of English'. She has published several articles on these topics and co-edited *The Language of Daily Life in England (1400–1800)* (Benjamins, 2009) and *Social Roles and Language Practices in Late Modern English* (Benjamins, 2010). She is also one of the compilers of the Corpus of Early English Correspondence.

Amanda Patten is a Lecturer in Language and Linguistics at Northumbria University. She has recently completed a PhD at the University of Edinburgh, 'Cleft sentences, construction grammar and grammaticalization', in which she undertakes a synchronic and diachronic study of the structure and function of the English *it*-cleft. She has published on the development of the Early Modern English *it*-cleft as an example of constructional change.

Alain Peyraube is currently Directeur de Recherche at the Centre National de la Recherche Scientifique (CNRS, Paris, France) and Chair Professor of Chinese Linguistics at the École des Hautes Études en Sciences Sociales (EHESS). He has been a corresponding member of the Academia Sinica of Taiwan since 2002, Adjunct Professor at the University of Science and Technology of Hong Kong since 2005, Honorary Professor at the University of Beijing since 2007, and member of the Academia Europaea (European Academy of Arts and Sciences) since 2006. His main research interests concern Chinese diachronic syntax and semantics, typology of East Asian languages, cognitive approaches to the diversity of languages, and the origin and evolution of languages. His most recent research has treated the mechanisms of syntactic and semantic change in Chinese from the period of the first recorded inscriptions (14th century BC) to the modern period (18th century): this includes problems of analogy, of reanalysis (grammaticalization), and of external borrowing through language contact.

Roland Pfau is Assistant Professor at the Department of General Linguistics at the University of Amsterdam, where he teaches in the sign linguistics programme. His main research interests are the morphological and syntactic structure of sign languages and language typology. One of the questions that guides his research, therefore, is whether typological patterns that have been described for spoken languages also hold for signed languages. Also, he is interested in typological variation across sign languages. Besides that he is fascinated by morphosyntactic properties of spontaneous speech errors. He is editor of the journal *Sign Language and Linguistics.*

Shana Poplack is Distinguished University Professor of Linguistics, Canada Research Chair and Director of the Sociolinguistics Laboratory at the University of Ottawa. An expert in variation theory and its application to diverse areas of language inquiry, she has published widely on language variation and change, linguistic consequences of language contact, and morphosyntactic variability in Spanish, French, Portuguese, and African American English.

Paolo Ramat was Professor of Linguistics at the University of Pavia and is now responsible for the Humanities Class of the Istituto Universitario di Studi Superiori (IUSS) in Pavia. His research interests include historical (especially Indo-European) linguistics, typology, and history of linguistics. He was one of the four initial proposers of the large European Science Foundation research project 'Typology of Languages in Europe' (EUROTYP). Among his books there are *Grammatica dell'antico sassone* (Mursia, 1968); *Das Friesische* (Innsbruck, 1976); *Introduzione alla linguistica germanica* (Il Mulino, 1986); *Linguistic Typology* (Mouton de Gruyter, 1987); (with Giuliano Bernini) *Negative Sentences in the Languages of Europe* (Mouton de Gruyter, 1996); *Pagine linguistiche* (Laterza, 2005). He is the editor (with A. Giacalone Ramat) of *The Indo-European Languages* (Routledge, 1997); (with Th. Stolz) of *Mediterranean Languages* (Brockmeyer, 2002); (with E. Roma) of *Europe and the Mediterranean as Linguistic Areas* (Benjamins 2007).

Helena Raumolin-Brunberg is a senior scholar in the Research Unit for Variation, Contacts, and Change in English at the University of Helsinki. Her research interests include historical sociolinguistics, language change, and corpus linguistics, on which she has published over 50 articles. Her books include *Sociolinguistics and Language History* (1996) and *Historical Sociolinguistics* (2003) (both with Terttu Nevalainen). She was one of the compilers of the Early Modern English section of the Helsinki Corpus of English Texts and the Corpus of Early English Correspondence.

Seongha Rhee obtained his PhD in linguistics from the University of Texas at Austin in 1996. He has been Professor of Linguistics at Hankuk University of Foreign Studies in Seoul since 1997. He taught at Stanford University in 2003–4 as a Fulbright scholar. His major interests are grammaticalization, typology, cognitive semantics, language and culture, and language education.

Agnes Schneider studied modern languages and literatures (English, Romance, and German) at the University of Freiburg, and completed her MA in 2007. She is a part-time Assistant Professor at the English Department at the University of Freiburg, and is currently working on her PhD, exploring morphosyntactic variation in West African varieties of English.

Andrew D. M. Smith is Lecturer in Language Studies at the University of Stirling, having previously worked as a postdoc in the Language Evolution and Computational Research Unit at the University of Edinburgh. He studies the cognitive and cultural foundations of human language, to investigate how language evolved and became complex. His current research interests include cross-situational learning, the ostensive-inferential nature of human communication, grammaticalization, and the cultural evolution of systematicity.

Markus Steinbach is Professor of German Linguistics at the University of Göttingen. His research focuses on the influence of modality (spoken vs. sign languages) on language structure, the interfaces between syntax, semantics, and pragmatics, theoretical and experimental linguistics, and linguistics in schools. In 2007 and 2008, he was Visiting Professor at the University of Frankfurt am Main for two semesters. From 2004 to 2007, he was the Vice-President of the German Linguistic Society (Deutsche Gesellschaft für Sprachwissenschaft). He is a member of the editorial boards of the journals *Sign Language and Linguistics* and *Zeitschrift für Sprachwissenschaft.*

Chaofen Sun is Professor of East Asian Languages and Cultures at Stanford University. He did his undergraduate work at East China Normal University, and received his MA from the University of Oregon and PhD from Cornell University (1988), both in linguistics. Among his books are *Word-Order Change and Grammaticalization in the History of Chinese* (1996), and *Chinese* (2006). He specializes in grammaticalization in the history of Chinese, discourse/pragmatics, and the history of Chinese.

Ryoko Suzuki is Associate Professor at Keio University, Japan, and was a Visiting Scholar at UC Santa Barbara (2008–10). Her major research area is grammaticization patterns in Japanese, using diachronic and contemporary conversational data, especially of quotative forms and abstract nouns becoming pragmatic particles.

Sandra A. Thompson is Professor of Linguistics at the University of California at Santa Barbara. She specializes in usage-based linguistics, considering the role of patterns of conversational discourse in shaping morphosyntactic and prosodic regularities, her published work drawing on interactional data from English, Chinese, and Japanese.

Elizabeth Closs Traugott is Professor of Linguistics and English Emerita at Stanford University. She did her undergraduate work at Oxford University, and received her PhD from the University of California at Berkeley (1964). Among her books are *Grammaticalization* (with Paul Hopper, 2003, 2nd edn), *Regularity in Semantic Change* (with Richard Dasher, 2002), and *Lexicalization and Language Change* (with Laurel Brinton, 2005). Her current research is on accounting for grammaticalization and lexicalization in a constructionalist framework. She specializes in discourse/pragmatics and grammaticalization in the history of English.

Johan van der Auwera is Professor of General and English Linguistics at the University of Antwerp in Belgium. He holds undergraduate degrees in Germanic philology and in philosophy (1975). His PhD was on the philosophy of language (1980), and his Habilitation on the structure of the noun phrase (1990). His student days were spent in Antwerp, Berkeley, and Stockholm, and longer research appointments took him to Hannover, Nijmegen, Paris, and Princeton. Current research focuses on grammatical semantics and typology (including areal typology and dialectology), with special reference to mood, modality, and negation. He is the editor-in-chief of *Linguistics.*

Nigel Vincent is Mont Follick Professor of Comparative Philology at the University of Manchester. He is the author of numerous articles on the categories and mechanisms of linguistic change, and has published on aspects of the structure and evolution of Italian and on the historical syntax of Latin. With Martin Harris he co-edited *Studies in the Romance Verb* and *The Romance Languages.* He has held British Academy-funded projects on 'Archaism and innovation in the linguistic history of Europe' and 'Morphosyntactic change: from Latin to Romance'.

James A. Walker is Associate Professor of Linguistics at York University (Toronto). He specializes in sociolinguistic variation and change, with interests in multilingualism, ethnicity, language contact, phonology, and morphosyntax. He has worked on variation in English (including African American English, Canadian English, and Caribbean English) and Sango (the national language of the Central African Republic).

Richard Waltereit is Reader in French and Romance Linguistics at Newcastle University. He earned his PhD at the Free University of Berlin in 1997.

Subsequently he moved to Tübingen and in 2006 to Newcastle. He has published on reanalysis, grammaticalization, and the diachronic rise of discourse markers in French and other Romance languages.

Anne Wichmann is Emeritus Professor of Speech and Language at the University of Central Lancashire, Preston. Her research focuses on speech prosody, particularly intonation, and is concerned chiefly with the way in which speech melody constructs, negotiates, and maintains spoken discourse. Her monograph *Intonation in Text and Discourse* (Longman, 2000), represents a detailed study of the use of speech melody in reading aloud. She has a long-standing interest in how emotions and attitudes are expressed by tone of voice, claiming that so-called 'attitudinal intonation' is not inherent in the intonation itself but the result of pragmatic inference in a given context. Her work at the interface between prosody and pragmatics is reflected most recently in *Where Prosody Meets Pragmatics* (Emerald, 2009) co-edited with Dagmar Barth-Weingarten and Nicole Dehé. She has recently investigated the relationship between contemporary speech patterns and historical change in relation to discourse markers. Professor Wichmann bases her work on speech corpora, and she is active in the corpus linguistics community.

Björn Wiemer studied Slavic and general linguistics in Hamburg and Leningrad (MA 1992, Hamburg). Before his PhD (1996, Hamburg) he was a postgraduate student for two years in Warsaw. From 1996 to 2007, he was Chair of Slavic Languages at the University of Constance (Germany), where he finished his post-doctoral thesis in 2002. Since 2007, he has been Professor at the Institute of Slavic Languages and Literatures at the Johannes-Gutenberg University Mainz. His particular interest in grammaticalization developed during his work in Constance. Further research fields include aspectology, evidentiality, modality, language contact, areal linguistics, diachronic semantics, and discourse pragmatics.

Ilse Wischer is Professor of English Linguistics at Potsdam University. She studied English and Russian at the former Pedagogical College of Potsdam (since 1991 University of Potsdam), where she received her PhD in 1986 and her Habilitation in 1996. She held teaching positions at the universities of Potsdam, Düsseldorf, Oldenburg, and Berlin. Her research interests lie mainly in the domain of English historical linguistics and grammaticalization studies. She has published on various topics of language change with a focus on the history of English. Together with Gabriele Diewald she edited the conference volume *New Reflections on Grammaticalization* (2002).

Debra Ziegeler has been working on modality, on the topic of hypothetical and counterfactual modality, since before attaining her PhD in 1997. Her publications include a range of papers on modal verbs and counterfactual adverbs in English, in journals such as *Studies in Language*, *Language Sciences*, *Journal of Historical Pragmatics*, and *Journal of Pragmatics*, and two books published by Benjamins: *Hypothetical Modality* (2000) and *Interfaces with English Aspect* (2006), which looked at the crossover between aspect and modality. She is now attached to the University of Montpellier, France, as a Visiting Scholar.

Abbreviations

=	cliticized to
*	unattested form or usage; reconstructed form
**	ungrammatical form or usage
Ø	empty element or position; zero
1	1st person
2	2nd person
3	3rd person
A	adjective; subject of a transitive clause
ABL	ablative
ABS	absolutive
ABSL	Al-Sayyid Bedouin Sign Language
ACC	accusative case
AD	After Death
ADJ	adjective
ADN	adnominal
ADP	adposition
ADV	adverb
ADVR	adverbializer
AFF	affix
AGR	agreement
AN	animate
ANAPH	anaphor
AND	andative
ANT	anterior
Ant.	anticipatory agreement marker
AOR	aorist
APPL	applicative
ARCHER	A Representative Corpus of Historical English Registers
ASL	American Sign Language
ASP	aspect
ASSC	associative
ASSOC	associative
AUX	auxiliary

AVS	adversative
Bal.	Balearic Catalan
BC, BCE	Before Christ, before Common Era
BEN	benefactive; beneficiary
BNC	British National Corpus
BP	backgrounding passive
C	complementizer, complementizer position
C1, C2, etc.	noun class 1, 2, etc.
Cal.	Calabrian
Cat.	Catalan
CAUS/PASS	causative-passive
CERT	certainty
C. FOC	contrastive focus
CG	Cognitive Grammar
CI	Conceptual Intentional
CL	classifier
CLF	classifier
CLFR	classifier
CLMET	Corpus of Late Modern English Texts
COCA	Corpus of Contemporary American (English)
COMP	complementizer
COMPAR	comparative
ComPred	complex predicate
CON	conditional
CONJ	conjunction
CONN	connective
CONT	continuative; contemporative
COP	copula
CP	complementizer phrase; complex predicate
CS	Common Slavic
CUS	colloquial Upper Sorbian
D	determiner; determiner position
DAT	dative
DECL	declarative
DED	deduced reference
DEF	definite (marker)
DEM	demonstrative
DET	determiner
DGS	Deutsche Gebärdensprache
DIMIN	diminutive
DISP	disposal form

DIST	distal
DISTR	distributive
DOEC	Dictionary of Old English Web Corpus
DP	determiner phrase
DS	different subject
DU	dual
E	event time; event; English
EE	end of event
EEPF	Early English Prose Fiction
EMPH	emphatic marker
END	sentential ending
ERG	ergative
EX	existential
EXCL	exclusive
F	feminine; feature
F.	Fula
FE	Feature Economy
FEM	feminine
FIN	finite element
Fin	finiteness
FOC	focus (marker); focus position
FP	sentence-final particle; foregrounding passive
Fr.	French
Frl.	Friulian
FUT, fut	future
GEN	genitive
Gen.	Genoese
GER	gerund
GIIN	generalized invited inference
GND	gerund
GO	goal
GRAM	grammatical
Gsc.	Gascon
GSL	Greek Sign Language
GT	grammaticalization theory
HAB	habitual
HON	honorific
HORT	hortative
HP	*haver*-periphrasis
hs	headshake
HYP	hypothetical

IbR.	Ibero-Romance
ICE-GB	International Corpus of English–Great Britain
i-F	interpretable feature
IIN	invited inference
ILL	illocutionary modification
IMP	imperative
IMPERS	impersonal
IMPF	imperfective
INCL	inclusive
IND	indicative
INDEF	indefinite
INF	infinitive
Infl	(verbal) inflection
INGR	ingressive
INJ	interjection
INSTR	instrumental
INT	interrogative
INTERJ	interjection
IO	indirect object
IP	inflectional phrase; intonational phrase
IPFV	imperfective
IR	internal reconstruction
IRR	irrealis
It.	Italian
ItR.	Italo-Romance
ITR	iterative
JUNC	juncture
Lec.	Leccese
LEX	lexical; lexical verb
LF	Logical Form
LIG	ligature
LIS	Italian Sign Language
lit.	literally
LK	linking article
LOC	locative
M	masculine; male
Maj.	Majorcan Catalan
MASC	masculine
ME	Middle English
MED	*Middle English Dictionary*
Med.	medial agreement marker

MHG	Middle High German
MODE	mode connective
ModHG	Modern High German
MP	modal particle
MSL	Molise Slavic
MW	measure word
N	noun; neuter gender
N3	noun class 3
NAR	narrative
NEG, Neg	negation
NegP	negative phrase
NEUT	neutral
NF	non-final; non-finite; non-future
NGT	Sign Language of the Netherlands
NMZ	nominalizer
NOM	nominative (case); nominal
NOMIN	nominalizer
NONVIS	nonvisual
NP	noun phrase
NPI	negative polarity item
NPS	non-past
NR	nominalizer
NSL	Nicaraguan Sign Language
O	object of transitive clauses; Old
OBJ	object
OBL	oblique
Occ.	Occitan
OChS	Old Church Slavonic
OE	Old English
OED	*Oxford English Dictionary*
OFr.	Old French
OHG	Old High German
OM	direct object marker
OT	Optimality Theory
OV	object-verb order
P	plural (in gloss); particle; futurate present
PAM	person agreement marker
PART	particle; participle
PASS	passive
PAST.PART	past participle
PB	phrasal boundary

P/C	pidgins and creoles
PEE	possessee
PERF	perfect; perfective
PF	Phonological Form; perfect; periphrastic future
PFV	perfective
phi-	person and number features
PII	privileged interactional interpretation
PL	plural
PLUR	plural
PM	predicate marker; previous mention
PN	proper name
POL	polite; politeness
POSS	possessive
POST	postposition; posterior
PP	prepositional phrase; postposition
PPART	past participle
PRED	predicator
PREP	preposition
PRES	present tense
PRES.PART	present participle
PREV	preverb
PRF	perfective
PRO	pronoun
PROS	prospective
PRS	present
PRT	particle
PS	past simple
PST	past
Pt.	Portuguese
PT	past
PTCP	participle
Q	question; interrogative (pronoun)
QM	quotative marker
QUE	interrogative
QUOT	quotation particle; quotative
R	reference time
REC	reciprocal
RECIP	recipient
REF	reflexive
REFL	reflexive
REL	relative (clause marker)

REM	remote
REP	reported speech
REV	revisionary
RM	reflexive marker
RN	relator noun
Ro.	Romanian
S	subject of intransitive clauses; singular; Southern; speech time
Sal.	Salentino
SBJ	subject
SBJV	subjunctive
SEC	sequential
SEQ	sequential
SF	sentence-final; synthetic future
SG	singular
SIC	speech introducing clause
Sic.	Sicilian
SL	sign language
SM	sensory motor
SMI	semeliterative
SOV	subject-object-verb order
Sp.	Spanish
SPEC	specific
Srd	Sardinian
Srs.	Surselvan
SS	same subject
STA	stative
STAT	stative
SU	subject
SUBJ	subjunctive; subject
SUPL	superlative
SVO	subject–verb–object order
T	Tense
t	trace (of moved element)
T&A	tense and aspect
TAM	tense–aspect–modality
THM	thematic
TM	tense/mood
TMA	tense–modality–aspect
TOP	topic (position)
TP	Tense Phrase
TR	transitive

TSL	Taiwan Sign Language
u-F	uninterpretable feature
UG	Universal Grammar
V	verb
V2	Verb second
V/v	Verb/light verb
V(P)	verb (phrase)
VBZ	verbalization
VENT	ventive
VIR/NONVIR	virile/non-virile (gender)
VIS	visual
VN	verbal (action) noun
Vnz.	Venetian
VP/vP	Verb Phrase/(light) verb phrase
VSO	verb–subject–object order
VT	variation theory
WAVE	World Atlas of Variation in English
WL	Watkins' Law
WFR	word formation rule

CHAPTER 1

INTRODUCTION

HEIKO NARROG

BERND HEINE

Grammaticalization is believed to be a young sub-field of linguistics. As a matter of fact, however, it is almost as old as linguistics, even if the term was presumably coined only in 1912 by Meillet.[1] Many of the issues figuring in contemporary discussions on grammatical evolution were already discussed by German 19th-century linguists such as Bopp (1816; 1833), Wüllner (1831), or von der Gabelentz (1961[1891]).

Modern studies in grammaticalization began in the early 1970s with the work of Givón, who argued that in order to understand language structure one must know how it has evolved. With his slogan 'Today's morphology is yesterday's syntax', he opened a new perspective for understanding grammar (Givón 1971: 12; 1979; see below). The first monographic treatments of grammaticalization were Lehmann (1995a[1982]) and Heine and Reh (1982). But perhaps a milestone in the history of modern grammaticalization studies can be seen in the symposium that Givón organized at the University of Oregon in 1988, resulting in two volumes on the topic (Traugott and Heine 1991a; 1991b). The two textbooks by Heine, Claudi, and Hünnemeyer (1991) and Hopper and Traugott (1993) then cemented the status of grammaticalization as an independent field of study within linguistics. Of similar importance to the Oregon symposium is the series of bi-annual conferences that Wischer initiated in Potsdam in 1999 and the publications resulting from this

[1] For accounts on the history of grammaticalization studies, see Lehmann (1995a[1982]); Heine, Claudi, and Hünnemeyer (1991); Hopper and Traugott (2003).

meeting (Wischer and Diewald 2002), as well as from subsequent meetings (Fischer, Norde, and Perridon 2004; López-Couso and Seoane 2008).

Since roughly the beginning of this century, grammaticalization studies have entered a new phase of development. On the one hand, they were subject to serious criticism (especially Newmeyer 1998; Campbell 2001a; Joseph, Chapter 16 below); on the other hand, they experienced an enormous expansion. Having been restricted primarily to core grammatical, semantic, and pragmatic analysis in the 20th century, they now attract interest in a wide array of related fields of linguistics, such as corpus linguistics, phonology, language acquisition, and sociolinguistics. Furthermore, while grammaticalization was initially practically exclusively the domain of functionally oriented scholars, it has increasingly been recognized as an important research topic by formal linguists as well. Moreover, grammaticalization research has spread beyond the traditional centres of linguistics to regions such as East Asia and South America. Facing this increasing expansion and diversification, we as editors believed that now would be a good point in time to take stock of the current state of grammaticalization studies, and simultaneously uncover possible directions for future research in this field.

1. Definitions

Currently a wide range of approaches and theoretical orientations are in some way or other based on a grammaticalization perspective. This diversity is associated with a variety of different views on how this phenomenon should be defined. Going through the chapters of this volume, the reader will notice that grammaticalization is far from being a uniform concept, and various definitions have been proposed.

One kind of definition relies on pragmatic functions of linguistic material. Harder and Boye, for example, invoke the notion of competition for discourse prominence, and propose to define grammaticalization as 'diachronic change which gives rise to linguistic expressions which are coded as discursively secondary' (Chapter 5). And Nicolle concludes that what defines grammaticalization is the addition of procedural information to the semantics of an expression. In his approach, lexical items encode conceptual information, while discourse markers, pronouns, and tense, aspect, and modality markers encode procedural information (Chapter 32). Another aspect of grammaticalization concerns the frequency of use of linguistic material. In some of the definitions provided, frequency is portrayed as one of the driving forces, or *the* driving force of grammaticalization (see especially Chapter 6 by Bybee). We will return to this issue below.

On the other hand, there is also the view that grammaticalization concerns anything that relates to grammar. For Frajzyngier, for example, the term stands simply for any coding of a function within the grammatical system of a language (Chapter 51). Depending on which definition is employed, there are great differences with respect to the phenomena to be considered. In extremely general definitions, such as that proposed by Frajzyngier, for example, diachrony is not a major issue, and the 'sources' of grammaticalization are not restricted to lexical and other form–meaning units but also include tone, intonation, phonological changes affecting segments, linear order, and position. Still, when controversies arise many scholars agree in draw attention to the classic definition by Kuryłowicz to help settle the issue of what should be subsumed under the rubric of grammaticalization:

> Grammaticalisation consists in the increase of the range of a morpheme advancing from a lexical to a grammatical or from a less grammatical to a more grammatical status, e.g. from a derivative formant to an inflectional one. (Kuryłowicz 1975[1965]: 52)

For most students of the field, grammaticalization is understood to be a diachronic process and, hence, findings can be verified or falsified by means of historical evidence. But it is also possible to analyse grammaticalization phenomena within a synchronic framework. This is demonstrated in particular by Langacker in his Cognitive Grammar account of a range of instances of grammaticalization (Chapter 7). As this volume suggests, there is no single approach or model that is predestined more than others to deal with grammaticalization phenomena, or that would account for all phenomena better than any other approach. To be sure, the questions asked differ from one approach to another and the answers given to central questions are not the same across the different approaches; but these answers are in most cases compatible with one another.

2. Delimiting the field

Each approach or 'school' of linguistics has its preferences as to the kind of linguistic phenomena that it is concerned with, and with respect to the way that it demonstrates its strengths and the advantages it offers over alternative approaches. Studies in grammaticalization also have their preferences. One noteworthy preference appears to be working on English and employing the English *be-going-to* future as a paradigm case of grammatical change. In a number of chapters, especially that by Bisang (Chapter 9), it is argued, implicitly or explicitly, that there is a need to take account of the typological diversity of the world's languages, more so than has been done in the past. This call for more diversity in the object of research is partially reflected in the design of this handbook, especially in Part V, which contains articles on a wide variety of languages, also outside the Indo-European area.

The flip side of the question of how to define the phenomenon is of course: what counts as an instance of grammaticalization and what does not? One of the areas where this question has been hotly debated is that of discourse markers or particles (see e.g. Onodera in Chapter 50). Can they, or at least part of them, be described exhaustively within the framework of grammaticalization theory? Or, is a separate framework of 'pragmaticalization' required, as has been argued ever since Erman and Kotsinas (1993; Aijmer 1997: 2) proposed this term? Is it desirable to draw a boundary between 'sentence-grammatical phenomena', to be treated under the rubric of grammaticalization, and 'discourse-pragmatic phenomena', which are the subject matter of pragmaticalization studies (Günthner and Mutz 2004)? Diewald (Chapter 36) argues that it is possible to treat pragmaticalization as a sub-process of grammaticalization. Note that already in 2000, Wischer (2000: 359) had proposed to treat the two as subtypes, referring to pragmaticalization as 'grammaticalization on the text or discourse level' and to orthodox grammaticalization as 'grammaticalization on the propositional level'. Both processes have in common that language material undergoes recategorialization by changing from a more open to a closer categorial system. It is therefore obvious that grammaticalization theory provides a principled tool to bridge the boundary between two domains of linguistic analysis that tend to be treated as distinct, namely grammar and pragmatics. This is a point also brought home in much detail in a recent book publication by Ariel on the topic (2008).

More general, and this is an issue that comes up in a number of chapters, is the question of where the limits of grammaticalization lie. For example, is grammaticalization restricted to oral and written languages, or does it show up in other modalities of human communication as well? As Pfau and Steinbach show in Chapter 56, the behaviour of grammaticalization in sign languages is largely similar to that in oral languages. To be sure, there are modality-specific differences. For example, in both kinds of modalities there are auxiliaries. However, whereas in spoken and written languages there is a major pathway from lexical verbs to the functional categories of tense, aspect, and modality (Bybee, Pagliuca, and Perkins 1994), in sign languages it is not only verbs but also nouns and pronouns that may give rise to auxiliaries.

There is reason to assume that grammaticalization most commonly arises in spoken, rather than in written language use. However, as Narrog and Ohori show Chapter 64, Japanese provides a number of examples where grammaticalization was triggered by the written rather than the spoken language, especially via translation.

Strikingly similar developments have also been reported from European languages (see Heine and Miyashita 2008b).

On a more fundamental perspective, there are general human strategies, or mechanisms, that have been invoked for describing, delimiting, and understanding grammaticalization, such as analogy, reanalysis, generalization, or creativity; see especially Traugott (Chapter 2) and Fischer (Chapter 3). Among these conceptual mechanisms, reanalysis is one of the most frequently cited. But the significance of this notion has been challenged. Fischer, for example, argues that reanalysis is not something that speakers or hearers do. Rather, it is a concept of the analyst that is, at least with reference to language processing, being based on our ability to analogize (Chapter 3). Humans are analogical animals, as Anttila (2003: 438) puts it, but they also reanalyse the material they dispose of. They generalize, and they use linguistic forms and constructions creatively for novel purposes. The question then is: to what extent are these notions helpful for understanding or for defining grammaticalization, and, is any of these more relevant than others? Many different answers are volunteered in the following chapters, reflecting the conceptual diversity that characterizes the field of grammaticalization.

3. Central issues

Since the late 1990s, studies in grammaticalization have been the subject of critical discussions. Perhaps the most serious claim, first made by Newmeyer (1998) and taken up in this volume by Joseph in Chapter 16, is that grammaticalization is not a distinct process but merely represents a combination of independent linguistic processes (see also Campbell and Janda 2001, as well as the other contributions to *Language Sciences* 23.2–3). Another problem concerns what is most commonly referred to as 'degrammaticalization'. Central to the problems of defining and delimiting grammaticalization is the question of what to do with what Hilpert calls 'developmental U-turns' and other cases of degrammaticalization (Chapter 58); for some examples, see Narrog and Ohori's analysis of Japanese (Chapter 64). On the basis of detailed analysis, Norde concludes that while changes classified as degrammaticalization challenge the unidirectionality hypothesis, they also lend support to it in affirming it as a strong directional tendency in grammatical change as quantitatively limited exceptions (Chapter 38; see Norde 2009a for more details). That there is need for much further analysis of cases of suspected degrammaticalization, and more generally of degrammaticalization as such, is shown convincingly in Chapter 14 by Börjars and Vincent.

It may be useful to distinguish between two kinds of approaches to grammatical evolution. On the one hand there are approaches that focus on the initial phase leading from non-grammatical, lexical structures to grammatical, non-lexical structures. On the other hand there are also approaches that concentrate on a more advanced phase of the process relating to bound, typically inflectional structures, and the development of further advanced and abstract grammatical functions. An overview of the findings presented in this volume suggests that the kind of generalizations proposed are not the same, depending on which of the phases is highlighted by a given author (see e.g. the discussion in Chapter 5). Another issue that comes up in many chapters concerns the motivation(s) of grammatical change, and here a wide spectrum of views are voiced. At one end are adherents of schools of functional linguistics invoking discourse pragmatic and/or semantic principles. At the other end are students of generative models who tend to hold innate principles in children responsible for grammaticalization (see especially Chapter 4 by van Gelderen). What the two have in common is that both assume that, across languages, grammatical change is directional, leading, for example, from lexical to functional categories or structures, Hence there must be universal principles underlying them. Grammaticalization and generative grammar have had, as van Gelderen observes, 'an uneasy relationship', but due to the introduction of functional categories in the late 1980s and features in the 1990s, it has become possible to account for gradual unidirectional change in a generative framework.

Another central topic of linguistic theory concerns the nature of linguistic categories, and this is an area where the contribution of grammaticalization studies may have been of particular importance. When Ramat observes in Chapter 40 that it is not always easy to distinguish morphologically between adverbs and nouns or adjectives, or between adverbs, prepositions, and conjunctions, this points to an area where work on grammaticalization has come up with a range of new findings: clines (Hopper and Traugott 2003) or chains of grammaticalization (Heine 1992) are some of the constructs that have been proposed to describe and account for the overlapping nature of syntactic or morphological categories. That grammatical forms and constructions are best analysed as gradient categories is suggested in a number of chapters; Brinton, for example, presents evidence for a gradience view of lexicality and grammaticality in her discussion of English complex predicates (Chapter 45), and Krug concludes in his analysis of auxiliation and categorization in the domain of tense, aspect, and modality that ambiguous cases are the norm rather than the exception and that the borderline between lexical and grammatical items will always remain arbitrary to some extent (Chapter 44).

Syntax and morphology are in many theoretical frameworks of linguistics treated as phenomena belonging to distinct domains of analysis; still, it is well known to students of grammaticalization that it is hard to trace a clear boundary between the two. But the problem is even more serious than has previously been thought.

Haspelmath argues in Chapter 27 that, 'the non-coincidence of the various criteria for syntactic vs. morphological status makes the very idea of a syntax/morphology distinction highly doubtful. Combinations of signs have different degrees of tightness, and it is not at all clear that this continuum can usefully be divided into two parts (syntax vs. morphology) or three parts (free words vs. clitics vs. affixes).' One of the issues raised by Haspelmath, the categorial status of case marking in Hungarian, is also highlighted in König's discussion (Chapter 41): is Hungarian a language without case system or with an extremely rich case system?

This raises the question of whether students of linguistic analysis should decide on models that aim at accounting for the gradual nature of grammatical categories rather than insisting on classical models of discrete categorization in terms of necessary and sufficient criteria. Even if one were to decide on answering this question in the negative, Krug maintains in Chapter 44 that grammaticalization studies are helpful in improving the basis for decisions on where to draw relevant lines between categories.

Two other issues have figured prominently in earlier studies. One concerns the role of iconic coding, which is discussed by Haiman in Chapter 37, leading to the question: does iconicity influence grammaticalization processes? The second issue, one that has now attracted renewed attention, concerns what is commonly known as 'the linguistic cycle'. That certain linguistic developments are cyclical has been claimed by scholars almost as long as linguistics exists as an independent discipline. In the history of grammaticalization studies, this claim has been put forward in various formats, perhaps the best-known being Givón's cycle (1971; 1979: 209), reproduced in (1).

(1) Discourse > Syntax > Morphology > Morphophonemics > Zero

To what extent is grammatical evolution cyclical? This question is addressed in several of the chapters. A much-debated case of cyclicity relates to negation and concerns what is widely known as Jespersen's Cycle; an analysis of this phenomenon, as well as that of a negative-existential cycle, is discussed by Mosegaard Hansen in Chapter 46. Another kind of cycle concerns the rise and fall of grammatical subject and object agreement, which is van Gelderen's topic in Chapter 39. The same author has recently edited a whole volume on the topic of cyclicity (van Gelderen 2009).

Another feature that has received some attention concerns the behaviour of scope. Does grammaticalization entail a decrease in the scope that the entities concerned experience—hence, can scope be taken to be adopted as a definitional property (cf. Lehmann 1995a[1982])? This issue is addressed in some of the chapters; Hengeveld in particular maintains that the diachronic development of expressions for tense, aspect, and mood leads from lower to higher scope (Chapter 47). The same stance is basically taken in generative grammar, which conceives of grammaticalization as 'category climbing', or in terms of Late Merge (cf. Roberts and Roussou 2003; van Gelderen 2004; Chapter 4 below). As has been pointed out however by some authors, for example by Norde in Chapter 38, scope is a problematic parameter. After all, the directionality of change with respect to scope largely depends on the particular notion of scope, and on the domain of grammar that it refers to.

Among the general questions that have so far not received the kind of attention they deserve is the following: how long does a grammaticalization process need to take its course? That such a process does not happen overnight is beyond any reasonable doubt. But what is the minimum and the maximum time required? Studies of pidgins and creole languages suggest that new grammatical categories can arise within less than a century. At the other end, however, there are also examples to show that the evolution of a category can extend over more than a thousand years. As Deutscher shows in Chapter 53, it took nearly two millennia for a fully independent speech-introducing clause ('this is what X said') to grammaticalize into an obligatory quotative marker in Accadian. Furthermore, there is the question of how human languages evolved. Once an issue that was ignored or avoided by linguists for over a century, language evolution has recently become a hotly contested subject matter in some schools of linguistics. Smith in Chapter 12 argues that studies in grammaticalization can make a significant contribution to reconstructing the genesis and development of human language (see also Heine and Kuteva 2007). This is also a central issue in Dahl's discussion of how grammatical change relates to linguistic complexity. Approaching grammaticalization from the vantage point of complexity studies and distinguishing between system complexity and structural complexity, he is able to establish a number of correlations, for example between non-linearity and high degree of grammaticalization (Chapter 13).

Finally, the volume is also concerned with a question that some might consider central in understanding grammatical change, but one that has also been discussed controversially: how does grammaticalization relate to first language acquisition? Does language acquisition recapitulate the diachronic evolution of grammar, as some have argued, or does grammaticalization originate in changes in child language? As Diessel argues on the basis of solid evidence from both domains, both questions have to be answered in the negative (Chapter 11). The two developments are in principle independent of each other. There is no causal link between them. Children seek to uncover the meanings of existing expressions. Grammaticalization, by contrast, involves the creation of novel meanings. Nevertheless, Diessel concludes that, while morphosyntactic and phonological changes in particular are different in language acquisition and in grammaticalization, the semantic and pragmatic developments of grammatical markers are based on the same mechanisms of categorization. In both cases, they are grounded in general perceptual and cognitive principles of the human mind.

4. Domains and structures

What is the primary target of grammaticalization processes: meaning, form, or structure? Are the units to which grammaticalization applies lexical or non-lexical items, constructions, or more generally, collocations of meaningful elements? These questions cannot be decided a priori but are necessarily linked to the particular theoretical framework within which they are raised. The issue of form vs. function is perhaps most relevant when grammatical change is viewed from the perspective of construction grammar. As Gisborne and Patten argue convincingly, the 'constructional change' of two constructions looked at in their Chapter 8 shares a number of properties with canonical processes of grammaticalization involving lexical items. Note that, like many (though not all) versions of grammaticalization theory, constructional models assume that lexicon and grammar form a continuum, and that grammatical change is gradual and incremental and leads to an increase in productivity and schematicity. It would seem that one either follows Noël (2006) in maintaining that schematization in constructions and grammaticalization are two different types of change, or one searches for an overarching theoretical framework that encompasses both. The case of the grammaticalization of quotative markers, as presented by Deutscher (Chapter 53) seems to provide support for the second approach. Deutscher suggests that speech-introducing clauses rather than verbs such as 'say' or particles such as 'like' are the source material on which the path to the development of quotative markers is constructed. The lexical sources are only relevant in as far as they are used inside such a clause.

The nature of the process from lexical or less grammaticalized to more grammaticalized structures is a topic in many of the following chapters. One salient direction in grammaticalization leads from more concrete to more abstract meanings, as shown, for example, by Eckardt with reference to the emergence of scalar degree modifiers (Chapter 31). That such semantic processes need not be confined to one particular morphological category, such as the verb, is demonstrated by Ziegeler in her analysis of modality, where she argues in favour of what she calls a "more holistic semantic approach" to the study of modality (Chapter 48).

There are certain grammatical categories that time and again can be traced back mainly to one particular conceptual source only, while others derive from multiple conceptual sources. Both kinds of process are represented in this volume. The evolution of definite articles is of the former type, as De Mulder and Carlier show in Chapter 42. Many contributions to this volume observe that for most functional categories there is not just one source but an entire pool of different sources of grammatical development. Evidentials, for example, may not only come from grammaticalized verbs but may also go back to locative and deictic markers or members of other word classes (Chapter 51). The genesis of passive markers and constructions can be due to an even larger range of pathways (see Chapter 43 by Wiemer; see also Haspelmath 1990).

Grammaticalization takes place in discourse, and its most obvious outcome is to be found in morphology. Syntax, by contrast, is a domain that some do not centrally associate with grammaticalization theory. That such a view is in need of revision is demonstrated in a number of chapters. One of them is DeLancey's Chapter 29, where it is shown that grammaticalization theory is one of the two essential components of the functional-typological approach to syntax. Grammaticalization, DeLancey states, 'is not simply a mechanism by which morphological structure develops, it is the constant, universal tendency of language out of which all structure arises'. And in fact, for quite a number of students of grammaticalization, syntax is a central field of research. Therefore it is hardly surprising that there is a range of chapters in this volume analysing syntactic phenomena, like word order in Chapter 30 by Sun and Traugott.

A large part of research on grammaticalization relates to the interface area between semantics and pragmatics, and even approaches that focus on semantic issues tend to include a pragmatic component in addition, as can be seen for instance in Chapter 31 by Eckhardt. Of central importance for this issue is the following question, raised especially by Nicolle (Chapter 32): What is the contribution of context as opposed to inferential mechanisms in the rise of new grammatical meanings and constructions?

Another issue raised in a number of chapters concerns the question of whether a given phenomenon really qualifies as an instance of grammaticalization. Otherwise it may be more appropriately treated within some alternative field of analysis, or it may be best analysed as being located at the interface of two or more different fields of study. A paradigm example of an interface area concerns the relationship between grammaticalization and lexicalization. Having long been neglected as a distinct research field, lexicalization attracted considerable research between 2002 and 2005, where the central question was one of delimitation: where does grammaticalization end and lexicalization begin? We now know much more about the different manifestations of lexicalization processes, but, as Lightfoot observes in Chapter 35, the challenge remains for examining lexicalization in relation to grammaticalization.

Another interface area relates to the structure of predication. One of the test cases analysed in this volume concerns complex predicates in English, such as *have a drink*, *make a call*, *give advice*, which have been discussed in terms of lexicalization and idiomaticization. As Brinton shows convincingly, one type of complex predicates that involves the English light verbs *make*, *take*, *give*, *have*, and *do* exhibits changes that are characteristic of grammaticalization, being instances of grammaticalized phrasal constructions (Chapter 45).

Clause combining has attracted considerable attention in studies of grammatical change, and most aspects of combining are treated in the present volume.

Clause subordination is discussed most of all by Ohori (Chapter 52), but coordination of clauses is also well represented, being in particular the subject of Giacalone Ramat and Mauri's Chapter 54. While there is the issue of how conjunctions and other elements of clause combining may arise, there is also the issue of what can happen further to such elements. Some new lines of research have shown that complementizers and other clause connectives can become final particles, for example, of utterances. Thompson and Suzuki demonstrate in Chapter 55 that this is potentially a cross-linguistically regular process.

One domain that has, conversely, been somewhat neglected in past work is that of personal deixis. Personal pronouns, and more generally person markers, belong to the most conservative parts of grammar. Most of them are etymologically opaque. That speakers may create more than one new category of personal deixis is shown by Martelotta and Cezario in Chapter 60 on Brazilian Portuguese. Another domain that so far has perhaps not received the kind of attention it deserves is parenthetical constructions. This fairly new research topic appears to have many implications for the study of grammaticalization phenomena. Processes such as the rise of new discourse markers or particles are considered by some to be a test case for defining the limits of grammaticalization. Among the phenomena discussed by Hilpert (Chapter 58) are conjunctions in Germanic languages that come to be used outside their typical syntactic context, and undergo decategorialization. This is manifested in the development of independent intonation, strong restrictions on the initial or final position, and a replacement of earlier grammatical meanings with discourse-pragmatic functions.

There are many different ways of explaining linguistic phenomena. Yet, when it comes to finding answers to the question of why languages are structured the way they are, grammaticalization studies provide insights that are indispensible for providing a satisfactory explanation. Mithun (Chapter 15) demonstrates how they help in understanding the morphosyntactic structure of extremely complex languages such as Navajo and other Athapaskan languages. Showing that the ordering structure of the Navajo verb structure was built up in stages over time via principles of grammaticalization, she is able to account for a number of morphosyntactic issues that have plagued preceding analyses of this language for decades. She rightly emphasizes that work on grammaticalization cannot replace synchronic language description. At the same time, she also points out that this work may, for example, lead to the conclusion that it is no longer necessary to decide whether a given morpheme is actually 'lexical' or 'grammatical', or whether subject and objects prefixes are 'really agreement' or 'really pronouns'.

Grammaticalization theory can also shed light on the distinction between polysemy and homonymy. For example, there are languages where one and the same item serves on the one hand as both a passive and a causative marker and on the other hand as a lexical verb for 'to give'. As Chappell and Peyraube show in Chapter 65, this situation is in no way odd or peculiar. Rather, it can be accounted for with reference to the grammaticalization processes that gave rise to it. Whether such situations should be treated as instances of polysemy or homonymy is a question that is notoriously controversial in linguistics. It is obvious, however, that from the perspective of grammaticalization theory they qualify as instances of *heterosemy* (Lichtenberk 1991), being the result of polygrammaticalization (Craig 1991), where there was one lexical structure that has given rise to different lines of development. Polysemy, or heterosemy, is in fact an area where grammaticalization studies provide both an important tool of analysis and some explanatory potential, and polysemy is also the focus of research on semantic maps. The question of how grammaticalization paths relate to (synchronic) polysemy as represented in semantic maps is a main topic of Chapter 25 by Narrog and van der Auwera.

In addition to the question of how grammaticalization can contribute to understanding the nature of language structure, there is also the question of what explains grammaticalization itself. While a range of different stances is voiced in this volume, two of them appear to be particularly prominent. On the one hand, there are explanatory approaches associated with what may be called the construction grammar paradigm that invoke frequency of use as one of the main forces, or the main force, driving grammaticalization, if not linguistic change in general. In the tradition of Bybee and Hopper (2001; see also Chapter 6), Torres Cacoullos and Walker, for example, define grammaticalization as the set of gradual semantic and structural processes by which constructions involving particular lexical items are used with increasing frequency and become new grammatical constructions, following cross-linguistic evolutionary paths (Chapter 18). On the other hand, there are also approaches that highlight the speaker's communicative motivations and the way in which linguistic material is manipulated for finding optimal rhetorical solutions (see Chapter 33 by Waltereit).

One of the main challenges facing students of grammaticalization is the question why grammatical development is, at least to a large extent, unidirectional. Various ways have been proposed to explain unidirectionality. In generative linguistics, unidirectionality has been explained with reference to universal principles such as Late Merge, ultimately relating to the principle of Economy (van Gelderen 2004; Chapter 4). On the other hand, it is argued by Fischer (Chapter 3) that unidirectionality is not something necessarily intrinsic to grammaticalization on the speaker–listener level. In the usage-based model of Bybee (Chapter 6), it is frequency of use that plays a central role. It is only when increases in frequency spur all the mechanisms to work together, she maintains, that we recognize an instance of grammaticalization: 'Changes related to increases in frequency all move in one direction and even decreases in frequency do not condition reversals: there is no process of de-automatization or de-habituation, subtraction of pragmatic inferences, etc. Once phonetic form and semantic properties are lost, there is no way to retrieve them. Thus grammaticization is unidirectional.'

Rather than simply frequency of use, some students of discourse analysis see conversational routines as being central for the development of unidirectionality. Such routines have the effect that, for example, two or more independent units of language structure or meaning grow together into a single grammatical construction with interdependent, integrated components (see Couper-Kuhlen in Chapter 34).

5. Studies across the world

Principles of grammaticalization have been claimed to apply to languages across the world irrespective of genetic or areal affiliation, and the question is whether this is appropriately reflected in the present volume. Unfortunately, the answer is not an unequivocal 'yes'. As in grammaticalization studies in general, there is clearly a bias towards the major languages of the world. English in particular enjoys a privileged status, both in the discussions and in the exemplifications to be found in the chapters. While a number of chapters are devoted primarily to languages of European origin, the linguistically most complex regions of the world are clearly under-represented. There is only one chapter devoted to the 2,000-odd African languages (Chapter 57 by Heine), but other regions also showing a remarkable linguistic diversity, such as New Guinea, South America, or Australia, have not found the kind of attention they deserve. The reasons for this are obvious. Grammaticalization studies have traditionally focused on European languages, and to a lesser extent also on languages of Eastern Asia, i.e. Chinese (Chapter 65 by Chappell and Peyraube), Korean (Chapter 63 by Rhee), and Japanese (Chapter 64 by Narrog and Ohori). With respect to research on grammaticalization, languages in these areas are naturally at an advantage in the sense that they are historically relatively well documented. In contrast, relatively little information is available on grammaticalization processes, for example, in Papua New Guinea or Australia.

Work on grammaticalization thus shows a strong bias in favour of a few languages, while in most regions of the world this is a recent and yet underexplored field of study. On the other hand, there are also earlier academic traditions dealing with issues of grammatical development under a different heading, or under different theoretical premises. This is especially, but not only, the case in countries having a long tradition of written language use. In Korea, for example, such studies can be traced back to the 1960s (see Chapter 63). But even on a continent like Africa, studies in grammaticalization meanwhile have a history of roughly thirty years (Chapter 57). A large number of scholars around the globe now devote their work to issues of grammaticalization, thereby contributing to our knowledge of the typological diversity of grammatical change. This is reflected in particular in chapters such as that of Johanson on Turkic languages (Chapter 62), Wiemer on Slavic languages (Chapter 61), or Martelotta and Maura Cezario on Brazilian Portuguese (Chapter 60).

Note that grammaticalization processes usually concern individual categories or constructions of a language rather than languages as a whole. That it is nevertheless possible to determine the profile of grammaticalization for entire languages is claimed by De Mulder and Lamiroy in their comparative study of Romance languages (Chapter 24).

6. New topics and fields

As observed above, grammaticalization has more recently become the target of new fields of analysis. One of those new and promising fields can be seen in prosody. As Wichmann points out in Chapter 26, segmental attrition tends to be seen as a typical feature of grammaticalization, but she finds that it is a partial and secondary phenomenon, while the primary phenomenon is prosodic. The primary effect of frequency and habituation, she suggests, is not segmental attrition, but prosodic erosion or loss of prominence.

Grammatical change begins with individual speakers and affects specific social groups before it spreads to other individuals and social categories of speakers. While this is intuitively clear to students working in this field, work on the individual and the social dimension of grammaticalization has so far not received the attention it deserves. We are therefore glad that both dimensions are being considered in the present volume. That individuals provide the very first occurrences of phenomena that eventually develop into changes in language is pointed out above all in Chapter 20 by Raumolin-Brunberg and Nurmi. At the same time, these authors observe that processes of grammaticalization tend to be slow, making it difficult to observe them in an individual's linguistic practices over her or his lifetime.

Much of the information on grammaticalization that is available is based on the analysis of standard languages or linguistic systems that are portrayed as being fairly uniform, while there is little information on how grammatical evolution relates to dialectal and demographic variation. Impressive insights into this issue can be found in recent sociolinguistic work, as discussed by Nevalainen and Palander-Collin in Chapter 10, or in the treatment of English non-standard varieties by Kortmann and Schneider (Chapter 21).

A question that is of interest in any academic discipline but that appears to be particularly relevant to grammaticalization studies is the following. What counts as evidence to support one's hypotheses and generalizations? Since grammaticalization is a diachronic process, evidence should first and foremost consist of historical 'facts'. In this respect, students working on languages for which substantial written records on their earlier stages of development exist are in an ideal position. This becomes especially clear in the contributions on languages such as Chinese, as Chappell and Peyraube show in Chapter 65, or Ledgeway in his contribution on Latin and the Romance languages (Chapter 59). Languages without any written documents offer a less enviable prospect for finding appropriate empirical evidence.

Larger text samples and quantitative approaches are increasingly valued in the search for appropriate evidence. This development is reflected in many of the chapters. Clearly, research in grammaticalization increasingly relies on methods of analysis that allow for quantitative generalizations, most of all on corpus linguistics. Here the motto is: the larger the corpus is, the more likely that it will allow for a comprehensive analysis of the dynamics of linguistic change. Mair observes, for example, that small corpora may be sufficient to study grammaticalization of high-frequency core-grammatical categories, but they are insufficient when it comes to rarer phenomena, such as certain types of clausal subordination (Chapter 19).

Use of quantitative data, though, already has a distinguished tradition outside grammaticalization studies, concerning topics that are nevertheless relevant to grammaticalization. This is the case, for example, in work carried out by students of variation theory that seek to explain why one form is chosen over another to signal the same meaning or function in a given context. As Poplack shows in Chapter 17, variation theory can shed light on ongoing processes that are not within the scope of orthodox grammaticalization theory. Language change is commonly classified into whether it takes place entirely within a given language (i.e. internal change) or is influenced or caused by contact with other languages (external change). Grammaticalization, then, tends to be viewed as a paradigm case of internal language change. As more recent research has demonstrated, however, this view is in need of reconsideration. A large body of data shows that grammaticalization can be induced by language contact. A striking example is provided by the domain of evidentiality. For example, Aikhenvald observes that language contact and areal diffusion provide a major motivation for developing an evidentiality system and, consequently, grammaticalized evidentials are a feature of many linguistic areas (Chapter 49).

As is argued by Heine and Kuteva (2005; see also Chapter 23), cases of contact-induced grammatical change are shaped essentially by the same mechanism as grammaticalization processes not affected by language contact. While grammaticalization exhibits the same kind of unidirectional behaviour irrespective of whether or not language contact is involved, Matras rightly insists that there is need for an overriding framework of language convergence, where grammatical change is viewed as internal to the individual speaker's language processing. In such a framework, he argues, contact-induced grammaticalization is merely a subcategory, even if an indispensable one (Chapter 22).

PART I

GRAMMATICALIZATION AND LINGUISTIC THEORY

CHAPTER 2

GRAMMATICALIZATION AND MECHANISMS OF CHANGE

ELIZABETH CLOSS TRAUGOTT

Debates concerning the relationship between grammaticalization and three mechanisms of change that are often associated with it are discussed: reanalysis, analogy, and repetition. It is argued that although reanalysis requires discreteness, it does not necessarily involve a 'saltation', and that a distinction should be made between mechanisms and motivations, hence analogical thinking should be distinguished from analogical change.

1. Introduction[1]

Research on 'mechanisms' of change seeks to answer the question how one gets from one mental representation of a given expression to a different one.[2]

[1] Parts of this paper draw on Traugott and Trousdale (2010). Thanks to Chaofen Sun and an anonymous reviewer for comments on earlier drafts.

[2] While the hypothesis that mechanisms, especially reanalysis, operate on abstract mental representations is the most widely held one, it has also been proposed that reanalysis can operate on surface ambiguity (Garrett forthcoming) and analogy on surface similarity (Fischer 2007).

'Mechanisms of change are processes that occur while language is being used, and these are the processes that create language' (Bybee 2001: 190). The search has been for a small set of such mechanisms:

> By postulating a finite set of mechanisms attributable to human neuromotor, perceptual, and cognitive abilities, which interact with linguistic substance in acquisition and in language use, a range of possible language structures and units will emerge. (Ibid.)

Among proposed taxonomies, the best known is probably Harris and Campbell's (1995: 50) claim that there are 'only three basic mechanisms: reanalysis, extension, and borrowing'. These are mechanisms of (morpho)syntactic change, but reanalysis has been extended to semantic change as well (Eckardt 2006). Among other mechanisms discussed in the literature are sound change and metaphoric extension (Joseph 2004: 51), and repetition leading to frequency (Bybee 2003).

The agenda for work on mechanisms of morphosyntactic change, later thought of as grammaticalization, was largely set in Li (1977). Two articles in the volume in particular have proved seminal for concepts of reanalysis: Langacker (1977) and Timberlake (1977). Reanalysis was the mechanism most frequently associated with grammaticalization for the following three decades. However, as 'analogy' and extension have come to be better understood, interest in usage-based grammars has increased, and large electronic corpora have become major sources of evidence for change, the role of analogy vis-à-vis reanalysis is being rethought. So is a distinction between 'mechanism' as the 'how' of change, and 'motivation' as the 'why' of change. Croft (2000: 63) refers to 'casual mechanisms', which include analogy but also conversational maxims and discursive practices, and, arguing for the importance of analogy, Fischer (2007: 324) refers to analogy as 'one of the main mechanisms or motivating factors' in change.

Here I limit discussion to issues in reanalysis (section 2), analogy (section 3), and repetition (section 4). Debates about whether there are mechanisms specific to grammaticalization are briefly mentioned (section 5).

Views about mechanisms presuppose certain stances and developments elsewhere in linguistic theorizing. These have to do with directionality, abruptness, and the status of grammaticalization in theories of language change. Briefly, unidirectionality (e.g. from contentful lexical structure > schematic, abstract grammatical structure, from complex > simple clauses) has been central to much thinking on grammaticalization. It is a strong hypothesis that has been extensively debated and refined (see Börjars and Vincent, Fischer, Joseph, and Norde, Chapters 14, 3, 16, and 38 below).

Regarding abruptness, all change is discontinuous ('discrete') to the extent that change depends on acquisition: each individual has to learn a language so there is discontinuity from generation to generation. Acquisition during lifetime is also discrete, whether it involves restructuring of what the speaker knows, or borrowing. There is nothing in the concept of abruptness that inherently requires it to be understood as a large jump or 'saltation'. It can be thought of terms of tiny micro-steps. However, in the 1980s, especially in generative circles, macro-changes that affect the system as a whole were privileged over the micro-steps that may lead to such changes. What Lightfoot (1979 and later) termed 'catastrophic' or 'cataclysmic' changes were identified with abrupt reanalysis. Later, reanalysis was construed in terms of parameters, which were themselves initially conceived in large-scale terms. However, with the development of micro-parameters and feature analysis within Minimalism (see Roberts and Roussou 2003; van Gelderen 2004), reanalysis has been rethought in terms of small (though abrupt) steps. This is in keeping with thinking among constructionalists, who focus on small differences between constructions rather than on major ones (e.g. Trousdale 2010). The issue of the 'size' of an abrupt change, then, is ultimately a question of the linguist's search for 'diachronic correspondences'; for the individual innovation is usually only a very minor adjustment (Andersen 2008: 31–2).

With regard to the status of grammaticalization, two related proposals are relevant here. One is that grammaticalization is itself a mechanism (see e.g. 'the main mechanism of syntactic change is grammaticalization', Haspelmath 1998: 344). This proposal has been sharply criticized (see e.g. Joseph 2004; Fischer 2007; Chapter 3 below), although it has barely been addressed in practice by researchers in grammaticalization, and it is hard to see how it could be, considering that grammaticalization interacts with different types of processes. The proposal does, however, resonate with another idea: that grammaticalization is a uniquely distinct type of language change. While some of Haspelmath's and Heine's earlier writing suggest this position, the more widely held view is that grammaticalization is a subset of types of language change in which form and meaning pairings change, i.e. of morphosyntax and morphophonology. It is distinct from semantic and phonological change, as well as from some types of syntactic change, e.g. word order, but is closely interdependent with them.

2. Reanalysis

Langacker identified reanalysis as 'change in the structure of an expression or class of expressions that does not involve any immediate or intrinsic modification of its surface structure' (Langacker 1977: 58). He went on to specify two subtypes of reanalysis: (a) 'resegmentation', i.e. boundary loss, boundary creation, and boundary shift, and (b) 'syntactic/semantic reformulation' (p. 64). A standard kind of example which involves both types of reanalysis is from Hungarian (Anttila 1989 [1972]: 149, 256):

(1) Old Hungarian *vila béle* 'world core/guts:directional' > *vilagbele* 'world into' > Modern Hungarian *világba* 'into the world'

Here a phrase with two originally independent words that could occur in a different order has been restructured as a single word with an affix, and *béle* has been reduced to the case marker *ba*. There has been semantic reanalysis (of *béle*), and change in boundaries (from phrasal to morphological).

Drawing on Langacker (1977) and Timberlake (1977), and assuming a version of Government and Binding syntax, Harris and Campbell similarly defined (morpho) syntactic reanalysis as involving change in constituency, hierarchical structure, category labels and grammatical relations in underlying structure (1995: 50) without change in surface structure. Some researchers have taken the assumption of absence of change in surface structure as criterial for reanalysis, and as evidence that it takes place in child language acquisition (see e.g. Faarlund 2000 on changes involving word order in Northern Scandinavian languages). A striking example of the potential stability of ambiguity is provided by the development of *wh*-pseudo-clefts with *do*; they have allowed ambiguities such as are illustrated by (2) for over 250 years (Traugott 2008a). (2) is potentially ambiguous between the original purposive meaning (i) and what was to crystallize as a new pseudo-cleft structure a couple of generations later (ii):

(2) What I did was to deceive the pagans (1612)
   (i) 'What I did was in order to deceive the pagans': what was done may refer to an act separate from and temporally prior to the deception; *to* is purposive
   (ii) 'I deceived the pagans': *do* is a proverb for *deceive*, and therefore the temporality of *do* and *deceive* is the same; *to* is an infinitive marker

When the *wh*-pseudo-cleft arose, *c.*1660, there was semantic reanalysis and syntactic restructuring of constructions like (2i). Pragmatically an originally unmarked Focus became a marked Focus (2ii).

Harris and Campbell (1995) and Andersen (2001), among others, rightly caution that one can only 're-analyse' something that pre-exists. If an adult knew the structure (2i) and reinterpreted it as (2ii), either in production or perception, this would be reanalysis, but if a child learning the language parsed (2i) as (2ii), no 're-analysis' would have occurred from the point of view of the learner. Like many metalinguistic terms, including 'language change', the term 'reanalysis' is therefore not accurate in a compositional semantic sense, except in the case of language users who reanalyse their own structures.

The following four main positions have been taken regarding the relationship between grammaticalization and reanalysis (discussed in far more detail in Campbell 2001a; Fischer 2007):

(i) Grammaticalization and reanalysis intersect but are independent. Arguments put forward for their independence include the fact that: (a) grammaticalization is unidirectional but reanalysis is not, (b) reanalysis does not imply loss of autonomy or of information, (c) reanalysis consists of two stages, whereas grammaticalization is a sequence S1, S2 . . . Sn, and (d) reanalysis is not gradual (C. Lehmann 2004). As mentioned above, the last argument assumes a definition of reanalysis as saltation, which is not necessary since reanalysis can, and typically does, occur by micro-steps.

(ii) Grammaticalization is a subtype of reanalysis (i.e. an epiphenomenon of it), and reanalysis itself is an epiphenomenon of child language acquisition: 'the notion of Diachronic Reanalysis is derivative of aspects of the process of language acquisition. Since grammaticalization is derivative of Diachronic Reanalysis, we see that this is a doubly derivative notion' (Roberts 1993a: 254). However, while Roberts (p: 252) conceptualizes parametric change as 'a random "walk" through the space defined by the set of possible parameter values', Roberts and Roussou (2003: 201) suggest grammaticalization can be 'reduced . . . to an instance of parameter change', upward 'along the functional hierarchy' (p. 202). This upward reanalysis accounts for unidirectionality, in their view, and can give rise to new functional material (p. 209); in this sense, grammaticalization is identifiable with a subset of types of reanalysis.

(iii) Reanalysis is largely irrelevant to grammaticalization because it has properties inconsistent with it (Haspelmath 1998: 315). Haspelmath makes essentially the same arguments as Christian Lehmann (2004) cited above in (i), but in addition argues that reanalysis is distinct from grammaticalization because reanalysis requires ambiguity in the input structure. For example, Harris and Campbell (1995: 51) considered reanalysis to depend on 'a pattern characterized by surface ambiguity or the possibility of more than one analysis'. Despite Haspelmath's remark, researchers often associate ambiguity with the onset of grammaticalization (see (2) above). Indeed, Heine (2002) hypothesized that 'bridging contexts', i.e. contexts in which there is unresolved pragmatic ambiguity, are a necessary 'stage' in grammaticalization. Diewald (2002) also hypothesized that there is a necessary stage of ambiguity as 'critical contexts' develop. Critical contexts are not only ambiguous but display morphosyntactic and constructional restrictions that eventually lead to grammaticalization. Corpus data show that in many cases of lexical to grammatical change examples in which the new structure is only potentially inferrable clearly do precede unambiguous ones (e.g. *be going to*), but whether a 'stage' is always necessary is questionable on the assumption that 'stage' implies a period of time when a community of speakers can use the structure ambiguously (Traugott forthcoming).

(iv) Reanalysis is actually largely irrelevant to language change, and therefore to grammaticalization, as it has 'no reality from the point of view of speaker-listener processing' (Fischer, Chapter 3 below). However, since speakers parse their output and hearers parse input, reanalysis does appear to have reality for language users. Reanalysis does not require, as Fischer supposes, that speakers see the connections between variants in a historical light (though they might have some access to recent changes owing to age grading).

Among types of reanalysis that interact with grammaticalization and that have received considerable attention is semantic reanalysis associated with the semanticization of pragmatic implicatures or invited inferences (see Eckardt 2006; Traugott and König 1991). Heine, Claudi, and Hünnemeyer (1991) conceptualize these as 'context-induced reinterpretations'. The implicatures are metonymic within the flow of speech, and may result in subjectification, understood as the development of meanings that encode speaker attitude or viewpoint.

3. Analogy, extension

Following Timberlake (1977), it has become standard in much of the grammaticalization literature to think of reanalysis followed by actualization, in other words of 'the formulation of a novel set of underlying relationships and rules', followed by 'the gradual mapping out of the consequences of the reanalysis' (Timberlake 1977: 141; developed further in e.g. Lichtenberk 1991a; Harris and Campbell 1995; Andersen 2001; 2008). In the functionalist literature, a distinction is made between actualization and extension that occurs within the linguistic system and actualization across speakers, spaces, and time (often called 'social gradualness': see Trask 1996: 295). Only the former is addressed here.

Meillet explicitly distinguished grammaticalization from analogy when he proposed that grammaticalization introduces new categories, and 'transforms the system as whole', while analogy 'can renew details of forms' (1958[1912]: 133). However, most changes involve extant (sub)systems, and what we most often see is an intertwining of reanalysis and analogy (Hopper and Traugott 2003: ch 3). Christian Lehmann (2004: 161) comments that the grammaticalization of forms of Latin *habere* 'have' to Romance conjugation suffixes, as in Italian *canterò* 'I will sing', presupposes fixing of the verb-final order *cantare habeo*. This was not the dominant word order, so by hypothesis the co-presence of a productive conjugation system, including imperfect and the subjunctive, both expressed by partly agglutinative verb suffixes, served as an analogical model for *canterò*. He called this kind of change 'analogically-oriented grammaticalization' (p. 162) and distinguished 'pure grammaticalization without analogy' (p. 161), which he considered the norm. However, as Kiparsky (forthcoming) argues, interactions between analogy and reanalysis are actually the norm.

In morphology two kinds of analogy are often mentioned (McMahon 1994; Croft 2000). These illustrate the kinds of general principles that underlie much current thinking on analogy. One is analogy as levelling, specifically reduction of stem allomorphs (e.g. the levelling of the singular/plural distinction in the past tense of strong verbs in English except for *be*, where *was/were* retain the distinction). The other type of analogy is extension or generalization, e.g. the spread of the plural *-s* marker to most nominals. With advances in work on analogy, its role in change in general and in grammaticalization in particular began to be reassessed. But until recently most researchers probably agreed with Givón's (1991) conclusion that analogy was too weak a concept to be useful in thinking about directionality.

A distinction can be made between exemplar-based analogy and constraints-based analogy (Kiparsky forthcoming). Work on exemplar-based analogy focuses on pattern match. Viewed this way, the question arises whether analogy should be thought of as following on from reanalysis or as also preceding it. The actualization model suggests that analogy follows on from reanalysis, and indeed it has often been noted that reanalysis can normally be detected only via evidence from analogical extension—for example, we know that *be going to* has been grammaticalized only when we find it occurring with a verb that is semantically incoherent with 'motion-for-a purpose', e.g. a stative verb like *know*. But analogy also appears to drive change. It seems plausible that the development of binominal quantifiers like *a lot of* 'much', *a shred of* 'little' from partitives of the same form was enabled by the prior existence of e.g. *a heap of*.

This brings us to the question whether analogy is a mechanism and/or a motivation. Anttila proposed that 'Humans are simply analogical animals' (2003: 438), and that analogies operate on a 'grid' that functions as 'warp and woof', i.e. on the two dimensions of similarity (paradigmatic) and indexicality (syntagmatic) (see also Itkonen 2005). Insofar as humans engage in analogical thinking, one can think of analogy as a motivation for change. Insofar as particular changes are exemplar-based, one can think of analogy as a mechanism of change. If so, the same term is being used for two different processes. The distinction is necessary because much analogical thinking never results in change, understood as innovation that is taken up within a community. Furthermore, not all that can be conceptually analogized becomes grammaticalized in language; for example Talmy (1983) suggested *corner in time* is not grammaticalized in any language because only topological relations grammaticalize. It is therefore useful to distinguish 'analogy' (analogical thinking) from 'analogization' (the mechanism).

Drawing on Anttila's and Itkonen's primarily linguistic views of analogy and on converging views that are primarily psychological (Tomasello 2003) and neurological (Pulvermüller 2002), and regarding analogy as both motivation and mechanism, Fischer (2007; Chapter 3 below) proposes that analogy should be given far more theoretical prominence in work on morphosyntax than it has been in the past. While much work on grammaticalization has been focused on structural differences between earlier and later stages, Fischer's focus is on processing. She proposes that analogy can operate on form alone, but no criteria are given as to how strong or weak the formal match needs to be. Discussing the development of *be going to* (Fischer 2007: 145), she points out that the category Aux already existed, including several periphrastic auxiliaries. It may be noted that the periphrastic auxiliaries available at the time (mid-17th century), *have to, be to, ought to,* had no *-ing,* and therefore the formal match is weak. The view that *be going to* changed by analogy to form alone takes no account of future orientation of *be going to* that is by hypothesis derived from the original meaning of the purposive motion construction, or of the 150 years of examples in corpora in which two readings are pragmatically possible in contexts such as passive (e.g. 1477 *was goyng to be hanged*) or with verbs that do not necessarily require intentional motion (e.g. 1630 *going to bid* ('summon') *gossips*) (see Traugott forthcoming). While analogical thinking may well have played a part and contributed to the development of *be going to* (and many other examples of grammaticalization), it would appear to have been a motivation for, not the chief mechanism of, this particular change.[3]

The broader concept of extension draws attention to ways in which the range of a newly grammaticalizing item is expanded. Himmelmann (2004) has suggested that grammaticalization involves three kinds of extension. His examples are taken from the development of articles in German. Here I use the example of *be going to.*

(i) Semantic-pragmatic extension: pragmatic meanings become conventionalized in specific contexts and may eventually be semanticized as polysemies—cf. the two meanings of *be going to* at the time of grammaticalization (such polysemies may persist, cf. partitive and quantifier meanings of *a bit of,* or may become homonymies as in the case of *be going to*).

(ii) Syntactic expansion; although grammaticalization occurs in restricted syntagmatic contexts, the coexistence of both main and auxiliary verb uses of *be going to* permits a wider range of syntactic uses than was available before the development of the auxiliary, cf. use in raising constructions (*It's going to rain tonight*).

[3] Garrett (forthcoming) proposes that the inceptive *go to V(ing)* as in *I goe to writing* (1577), as *he was going to make a nooze* ('noose') (1611) is a more plausible source than motion with a purpose. Garrett's focus is on pivotal contexts (akin to Diewald's critical contexts) and again points to reasons for rather than mechanisms of change.

(iii) Host-class expansion; the range of collocations is expanded, e.g. *be going to* as an auxiliary can occur with stative verbs, but the motion construction cannot.

According to Himmelmann (2004), host-class expansion is criterial for grammaticalization as opposed to lexicalization (this observation applies to early and sustained grammaticalization; if a competing grammatical expression is in decline, retraction and possibly loss is expected). Hilpert (2008) demonstrates how detailed 'collostructional' work on historical corpora can reveal the path of host-class expansion in detail, as well as significant differences in trajectories between languages. Collostructional analysis is a data-driven statistical analysis of collocations practiced within the Construction Grammar framework (e.g. Goldberg 1995). Hilpert shows how, for instance, in English the verbs with which *be going to* collocates are typically, though by no means always, transitive and agentive (*fight*, *tell*) and/or punctual (*happen*). However, the cognate *gaan* in Dutch typically collocates with non-punctual intransitives (*lopen* 'walk', *spreken* 'speak'). The micro-shifts in distribution over time can be considered to be reanalyses of the constructional sets in which form–meaning paired expressions may be used, as well as analogizations in the sense of extensions and in some cases matches with other expressions undergoing similar shifts.

Unlike exemplar-based approaches to analogy, the constraints-based approach relies on concepts of UG and general principles of language optimization, 'the elimination of unmotivated grammatical complexity or idiosyncrasy' (Kiparsky forthcoming). Reconceptualizing his (1968) proposal that sound change involves rule-generalization in terms of OT constraints, Kiparsky develops an account of unidirectionality in grammaticalization that appeals to structural economy and embraces both pattern match and pattern extension. From this perspective, 'grammaticalization is analogy, albeit a special kind'. At the same time, it is reanalysis: '[g]rammaticalization is unified with ordinary analogy—not just in the trivial sense of classifying them both as instances of reanalysis, but within a restrictive theory of analogical change.' Kiparsky argues, contrary to Meillet, that new categories can be derived by analogy/optimization. His example is from Finnish (see Table 2.1). Here the case paradigm involved triplets of locative cases and a partly corresponding pair of predicational cases:

Table 2.1.

	Place/State	End point	Source
External Location	Adessive	Allative	Ablative
Internal Location	Inessive	Illative	Elative
Predication	Essive	Translative	–

The gap in the paradigm would mean 'cease to be'. Kiparsky argues that in some southern dialects this gap has been filled by an Exessive (Source) case derived from the Partitive ('from X'), which otherwise has no locative functions. In traditional terms, this optimization of the system has involved reanalysis of the Partitive in specific contexts on analogy with other Locative cases.

Meaning changes of analogical nature that interact with grammaticalization are metaphorizations. Metaphor has often be thought to be the major semantic factor in grammaticalization, but close inspection of corpora suggests that in many cases the metaphorical interpretation is the outcome of non-analogical metonymic, contextually derived changes (e.g. *be going to*; see also Heine et al. 1991).

4. Repetition resulting in frequency

As a mechanism, repetition, which leads to frequency, is different from reanalysis and analogy, as it is derived primarily from online speaker production rather than from hearer interpretation. Frequency often appears in the context of recent discussion of mechanisms (Bybee 2001; 2003; Smith 2001). Bybee proposed a definition of grammaticalization that privileges frequency: 'the process by which a frequently used sequence of words or morphemes becomes automated as a single processing unit' (2003: 603). She distinguishes token frequency (the number of times an expression appears in text) and type frequency (the number of expressions of a particular category available). She hypothesizes that token repetition leads to a number of characteristics of grammaticalization that Haiman (1994) associates with grammaticalization: habituation and depletion of speech act or contentful force, automatization as a chunk, and use with a schematic function. Effects of high token frequency lead to (a) phonological reduction, e.g. *be going to* > *be gonna, isn't it* > *innit*; (b) entrenchment that allows for retention of old properties, e.g. core auxiliaries in English maintain earlier English patterns of interrogative inversion, and have not been generalized to patterns requiring *do*-support; and (c) storage in memory (see also Smith 2001 on the development of anterior or perfects in English). While some cases of grammaticalization do not show evidence of having arisen through high frequency (see Hundt 2001 on the rise of the *get* passive), or even of resulting in it (Hoffmann 2005), the majority of examples of grammaticalization investigated so far do show increased frequency at inception.

5. Are there mechanisms specific to grammaticalization?

Reanalysis, analogy, and repetition are common not only to language change but to cognition and human behaviour in general. Recently there has been an effort to identify mechanisms that are specific to grammaticalization. For example, Heine (2003: 579) identifies four mechanisms. Of these, three are associated with the view of grammaticalization as loss of features and as increased dependency (see Lehmann 1995a[1982] Haspelmath 1998): (a) desemanticization or bleaching, (b) decategorialization or loss of morphosyntactic properties, (c) erosion/phonetic reduction, and (d) extension or context generalization. Heine points out that none of these is confined to grammaticalization, but 'to the extent that jointly they are responsible for grammaticalization taking place, they can be said to constitute different components of one and the same general process' (Heine 2003: 579). He regards the set of mechanisms identified by Harris and Campbell: reanalysis, extension, and borrowing, as an 'entirely different catalog of mechanisms' (p. 600, fn. 6), but in fact his (a–c) are particular subtypes of reanalysis resulting from increased token frequency (i.e. analogical extensions), and (d) is a subtype of extension/analogy (host-class expansion).

6. Conclusion

Kiparsky (forthcoming) suggests that all analogy is reanalysis (though not all reanalysis is analogy), because local (micro-)restructuring results from optimization. Christian Lehmann (2004: 162) defined 'reanalysis of a construction' generally as 'the assignment of a different grammatical structure to it'. It may be objected that generalizations of this type are too broad, since it would follow that all change is the result of reanalysis. However, one way of thinking of this is that the formulation of language change A > B/A (> B) is a shorthand for the development of B in variation with A as a result of reanalysis, and for the possible subsequent loss of A (another reanalysis). What is of interest to the researcher on grammaticalization is whether the change A > B/A (> B) is a subpart of a sequence of changes S1, S2 . . . Sn of the type Lehmann (2004) associates with grammaticalization. More importantly, precisely what kind of mechanism does the '>' in any particular case of change represent: an instance of resegmentation, of recategorization or of extension?

'Perceptual and neuromotor systems make language possible' (Bybee 2001: 206). They are the language-internal sources for changes as speakers and hearers acquire language and engage in language use. Advances in neuro-imaging and in articulatory and acoustic phonetics should eventually lead to a better understanding of mechanisms and of their role in language change. They should help clarify the extent to which early acquisition by children and later throughout life play a role in reanalysis, and also help distinguish mechanisms from the motivations that speakers and hearers have in activating these mechanisms, consciously or not.

CHAPTER 3

GRAMMATICALIZATION AS ANALOGICALLY DRIVEN CHANGE?

OLGA FISCHER

> One of the ubiquitous principles of the psycholinguistic system is its sensitivity to similarity. It can be found in the domains of perception and production (as well as learning).
>
> The more similar any two sets are, the more likely the wrong rule is applied.
>
> (Berg 1998: 185; 236)

1. Introduction

Since the 1980s, grammaticalization has been a popular research topic in diachronic linguistics, with its field of application widening considerably over time so that the phenomenon of grammaticalization came to be elevated to theoretical status: a model to understand how language is used and structured, and develops through time. Gradually, grammaticalization also began to include the development of grammatical constructions in general, without the kernel of substantive elements, so that word-order restrictions, clause combining, or the creation of new syntactic patterns also became part of it (cf. Givón 1979; Hopper and Traugott 2003; Bybee 2003). Its spreading popularity has led to increasing concern about quite a number of aspects related to the model. In this chapter I will address a number of questions that are related to the nature of grammaticalization in order to find out what its status is in change. In this context I will be especially interested in the role played by analogy.

(i) What is the relation between the synchronic speaker-listener and the essentially diachronic nature of grammaticalization? What role is played by the synchronic system that the grammaticalizing structure is part of?
(ii) What empirical evidence do we have for grammaticalization, and, perhaps more importantly, where should we look for evidence?
(iii) What causes grammaticalization and language change in general? Should the mechanisms that apply in language learning also apply in language change? And more particularly, what is the role of analogy, reanalysis, frequency, unidirectionality, to mention some of the more important factors/mechanisms?

These questions will be addressed in section 2, where I will also highlight the position of analogy. In section 3, I will explore the nature of analogy further in order to find out how far grammaticalization can be understood as an instance of analogically driven change.

2. The nature of grammaticalization: synchronic and diachronic considerations

The widening of the field involved in the phenomenon called grammaticalization has led to a weakening of the power of grammaticalization as a clearly circumscribed process of change. This can easily be seen from the fact that the parameters originally set up by Lehmann (1982: 306) to characterize the canonical type no longer all neatly apply in each case. Lehmann's parameters give the process a unity in that they all involve reduction or loss on both the paradigmatic and the syntagmatic plane, i.e. loss of weight (phonetic attrition, semantic bleaching, and scope decrease), loss of choice (paradigms of possibilities become reduced and elements become bonded together), and loss of freedom (elements become obligatory in the clause and fixed in position). Obviously, the development of fixed word order or new syntactic patterns doesn't involve phonetic attrition (unless one thinks of this as whole elements being elided—but note that this would disrupt the widely accepted notion of grammaticalization being gradual) or bleaching.

Furthermore, it has been suggested that in many cases, especially those involving subjectification, there is scope *in*crease rather than *de*crease. Similarly, in the case of clause fusion or syntacticization discussed by Givón (1979: 214)—he suggests that complement clauses with non-finite verb forms and PRO subjects, may have developed from paratactic clauses with finite verbs and lexical subjects—there is no question of Lehmann's parameter 'increase in paradigmaticity' applying, since such constructions usually remain in use side by side.

For many grammaticalizationists, grammaticalization is a unified, unidirectional development that guides, and hence explains, change. On the other hand, linguists with formal, functional, as well as more philological backgrounds (who combined their voices in the critical volume of *Language Sciences* 23, and cf. also Janda and Joseph 2003; Joseph 2004) stress the fact that all the changes occurring in grammaticalization may also occur independently, thereby querying the nature of the unity of Lehmann's parameters. These linguists generally stress that more attention should be paid to the speaker-listener, and the synchronic language system used to produce or interpret language utterances. This is not to say that in grammaticalization theory no attention is paid to the speaker-listener level, but this is mainly confined to the immediate pragmatic-semantic context, while the shape of the (formal) system also guiding the speaker-listener is ignored (cf. Mithun 1991; Fischer 2007). In general, supporters of grammaticalization see the process as being driven by pragmatic-semantic forces only, a 'product of conceptual manipulation' with changes in form *resulting* from this (Heine, Claudi, and Hünnemeyer 1991: 150; 174; and cf. Hopper 1991: 19; Rubba 1994; Hopper and Traugott 2003: 75–6). In other words, they would not admit the possibility of form also driving a change.

Looking at grammaticalization from a purely synchronic, speaker-listener point of view rather than a diachronic one may shed a different light on the process or mechanism called 'grammaticalization'. Even though diachrony is present in synchrony in the form of variation, it is not the case that a 'pure' synchronic system does not exist, as Lehmann (2004: 153) maintains. For the speaker-listener, there *is* only the synchronic system at any moment of speech. The point is that the speaker-listener has no panchronic sense: he doesn't necessarily see the connections between the grammaticalization variants in a *historical* light. In other words, in order to prove the existence of grammaticalization as an *actual* mechanism of change linked to human processing, one cannot fall back on the historical process itself. However, this is what is typically done in grammaticalization studies. These attempt to empirically prove the 'reality' of grammaticalization as a mechanism by showing its universal pathway (cf. Haspelmath 1989; 1998; Heine 1994; Bybee 2003): the 'diachronic identity' or 'continuity of two forms or constructions F_1 and F_2, at $T(ime)_1$ and T_2' (Lehmann 2004: 156ff.).

Now this may constitute empirical evidence if one looks at change on the *language output* level: the diachronic stages may be seen as connected, with the constructions at each stage changing gradually, almost imperceptibly, by pragmatic inferencing, analogical extension, and reanalysis. However, this scenario need not have any reality at the *processing* level, where the same constructions need not be connected at all. The following question should be raised: is there an actual reanalysis in psycho/neurolinguistic terms? This point is important considering the fact that it is ultimately the speaker-listener who causes the change.

The 'grammaticalization' of constructions, or the way (diachronically connected) forms are stored in our brains, could be said to resemble the process of conversion and storage. What is involved here is analogy. When a noun like *table* is used as a verb, the two items are stored in different paradigms or categories, both formally and semantically, and, once there, they may drift further apart. There is no question of reanalysis here for the speaker-listener; he is simply making use of the (abstract) grammar system of English that allows such an option (and with increasingly greater ease after most inflections were lost in the Middle English period). Since there are many such hybrid items in the language, he analogizes, on the basis of an existing pattern, that *table* belongs to this pattern too. How is he to know that *table* had not been used as a verb before, when the verb=noun scheme is such a common pattern in his language?

In a similar way, with the construction *going to*+infinitive (an often-quoted example of grammaticalization), a present-day speaker-listener identifies it in any actual speech situation as either a full lexical verb followed by a purposive *to*-infinitive or an auxiliary (with *to* incorporated) followed by a bare infinitive, according to the patterns of the full verb and the auxiliary paradigms that he has mastered in the course of language acquisition. As with conversion, the speaker-listener doesn't reanalyse, he categorizes holistically, whereby he may apply the 'wrong rule'. How he categorizes in each case depends on the present state of his grammar as well as the context, just as he can recognize whether *table* is a noun or a verb from the (syntagmatic) context and the paradigmatic inventory of patterns present in his grammar. The context is characterized by formal (i.e. position, word order, the presence of a determiner, inflections, etc.) as well as semantic-pragmatic information. The very first time a historical speaker-listener identified *going to* as auxiliary, therefore, did not constitute an actual reanalysis of *going*(full verb)+*to*-infinitive but a category mistake—a mistake that he could make because the *going to* form fitted both the V-*to*-V as well as the Aux-V pattern. (For a different interpretation of the role of reanalysis, see Traugott, Chapter 2 above.)

Analogical 'extension' is similar, too, in terms of speaker-listener processing: like grammaticalization and conversion it is also based on pattern recognition and categorization. When a speaker uses *brung* rather than *brought*, or *shaked* rather than *shook*, there is no question of reanalysis. He uses past tense *brung* because it fits another past tense pattern: *rung*, *stung*, etc., which happens to be far more frequent than the pattern of *brought*. The important point about analogical extension is that it occurs proportionally. It doesn't simply involve the 'expansion of contexts in which a construction can occur', 'adding new peripheral members [e.g. new infinitives, inanimate subjects] to a category [e.g. *going-to*]' (Bybee 2003: 158); it happens because, once *going to* is taken for the Aux-category, it will follow the behaviour of other members of this new category.

In all three cases, we can thus provide a *historical* explanation for the new forms. However, although a certain overall continuity or development (unidirectionality) may be ascertained—especially with surface forms connected by 'grammaticalization', and, on a more abstract level, with strong verbs becoming weak (rather than vice versa)—such unidirectionality need not be the case, as we can see in the case of *brung*. In terms of *synchronic processing*, the choice is not guided by any historical development but by the strength of the patterns that the form can be seen to belong to, and this strength depends in turn on the frequency of the patterns themselves. If one of the variant forms is more of a grammatical function word (as with *going to*) or a more basic vocabulary item, then that variant will be more frequent, and may become the norm, often followed by the loss of the older form if there is not enough distinction in meaning to preserve both. It could also be said that this type of processing is in fact no different from our ability to fill a sentence pattern like SVO with different lexical elements chosen from the NP and VP categories. That too is a choice, not a reanalysis each time of the SVO pattern.

If we follow this line of argument and try to understand what grammaticalization entails from the synchronic speaker-listener aspect, then it is not necessarily the case that the 'cline' (which has reality only on the level of the historical development of language-output data) has to continue inexorably in the same unidirectional way. Quite possibly, it may, and it often does (due to the fact that the more grammatical variants also happen to become more frequent over time), but it does not always, as shown by attested cases of degrammaticalization, or in cases where weak verbs become strong. Sometimes also processes stop halfway, and similar processes with the same starting point may develop differently in different languages, as has happened, for instance, with the modals and the infinitival marker in Germanic languages.

What may stop a process or what may cause degrammaticalization? It could be a drop in frequency, for whatever reason. But in cases of degrammaticalization, it may be a change elsewhere in the system which affects the pattern that the grammatical element belongs to (cf. Norde, Chapter 38 below). If indeed an important driving force in the grammaticalization of a particular construction is the availability of a grammatical category or pattern that it could fit into, then in a similar way, but with the opposite effect, the non-availability of a pattern may drive *de*grammaticalization. Plank (1995) has shown, in the case of the English genitive inflection becoming a clitic, that this follows from the fact that the inflectional system of nouns had been eroded so that the genitive ending had become isolated, no longer fitting the new, inflectionless noun pattern. A similar situation existed in the case of the Irish 1st plural verb ending *-mid*, which had become the only inflected pro-form. The fact that *-mid* was upgraded to an independent pronoun, *muid*, is not surprising considering that the pronoun pattern was available in the rest of the verbal paradigm (cf. Kiparsky forthcoming: 28). In such cases, as Plank makes clear, there is a *Systemstörung*, which asks for drastic methods on the part of the speaker-listener to keep the language system manageable.

The hypothesis, then, is that in both grammaticalization and degrammaticalization (and in conversion too) the driving force, next to (syntagmatic) context and frequency, is the availability of a (paradigmatic) category or construction pattern that shows formal and/or semantic similarities so that the new variant may fit the synchronic system of the speaker-listener. If this is correct, analogical thinking plays a role in all the above cases. Analogy only happens on the basis of an exemplar, which may be a concrete lexical form or a more abstract morphosyntactic pattern.

Kiparsky (forthcoming: 6) agrees that both degrammaticalization and grammaticalization are forms of analogical change, which he calls 'grammar optimization'. At the same time, however, he makes a distinction between the two: degrammaticalization is based on exemplar-based analogy, while grammaticalization is not. The analogy in the latter case follows 'constraints, patterns and categories... provided by UG' (p. 6), and only arises 'under a reduced input' (p. 11). In this way, Kiparsky can preserve Meillet's idea that only grammaticalization can create *new* categories, and he can also save the principle of unidirectionality because degrammaticalization is now seen as different in nature and is therefore no longer the opposite of grammaticalization.

There are, however, a number of problems connected with Kiparsky's proposal. First of all, it is almost too clever: grammaticalization and degrammaticalization are said to be the same because they are based on analogy, but are different as far as unidirectionality is concerned. Secondly, it relies on the idea of an innate grammar—of which we do not know the contours—so that the notion of non-exemplar-based analogy is not falsifiable, and indeed not explanatory outside its own linguistic model (cf. Fischer 2007: 67–74, and references there). Thirdly, the idea of non-exemplar-based analogy creating new categories is difficult to distinguish from reanalysis, which is seen by many as primary in grammaticalization (cf. Harris and Campbell 1995; Hopper and Traugott 2003: 39, 63–9; Roberts and Roussou 2003). Since Kiparsky's facilitator for grammaticalization is not based on an existing pattern but on an innate one, it would have to be called 'reanalysis' by anyone whose model doesn't include UG. Thus, Kiparsky is only able to downgrade or 'go beyond' (forthcoming: 19) reanalysis by proposing empirically invisible UG patterns to base his analogy on. He rejects reanalysis because it doesn't provide an explanation: 'labeling a change as a reanalysis, innovative or otherwise, doesn't get at its nature or motivation. For now the claim that grammaticalization is reanalysis remains virtually a tautology' (p. 19). In other words, he does not reject reanalysis because it has no reality from the point of view of speaker-listener processing, as I have done above. Fourthly, we end up with two types of analogy, even though ultimately they are both said to fall under grammar optimization (p. 6). This, however, is also a problem because it is well known that exemplar-based analogy is often very local (cf. McMahon 1994: 70–76); such local cases cannot be said to lead to the same form of grammar optimization as that driven by the much more global rules and constraints of UG. It would therefore be simpler if it could be shown that analogy works in the same way in all cases.

The positive aspect of Kiparsky's proposal is that it rejects the process of grammaticalization *itself* as a cause or mechanism for change. He emphasizes that the definitions of grammaticalization given in the literature do not work because the different aspects of grammaticalization 'do not have to march in lockstep', and because one aspect is not 'a necessary consequence' of another; rather, grammaticalization as described 'pick[s] out separate and more or less loosely parallel trajectories of change' (p. 4).

It is time to look at analogy in more detail. In section 3, attention will be paid to analogy as a deep-seated cognitive principle that is relevant not only to language processing and language change but also to learning processes outside language. I will stress that analogy is used to categorize, and that categorization involves both concrete and abstract linguistic signs. In addition, the ability to analogize is evolutionarily old and present in other mammals too. Finally, it is an important mechanism in language acquisition (cf. Slobin 1985; Tomasello 2003) and in the processing of language in general (cf. Berg 1998). If we accept that the system of grammar that each of us acquires in life should be an empirical psychological/biological model, and not some abstract linguistic model that has no relation to our psychobiological make-up, then this system should reflect human processing, and the key to this should be found with the help of advances in neuro- and psycholinguistics. Berg (1998: 278) writes: 'The structure of the language is shaped by the properties of the mechanism which puts it to use.' The more the same mechanisms are seen to operate elsewhere, the more persuasive they become.

3. Analogy: its nature and the role it plays in linguistic modelling and change

Analogies can be very concrete or quite abstract; that is, an analogy may be based on concrete lexical items as well as more abstract schemas. Analogy is also a highly fluid concept, and therefore works quite differently from the type of global rules favored by generative linguists. Hofstadter (1995: 198ff.) discusses the fluidity of analogical thinking at the very concrete level of language use. He shows how an individual can mistake one word for another (so-called substitution errors) because the words in question are associated in that individual's experience (either indexically or iconically), or the words are used elsewhere in similar constructions. He describes analogy as 'conceptual slippage', and argues that this slippage is important in order to keep language workable and flexible. It is to be preferred to a rigid system. As will be seen below, this 'conceptual mismatch' may also take place on a more abstract level, that of the system, once patterns have been formed.

Analogical rules are typically not across the board but work in local areas. Analogical learning starts with concrete situations and is based on experience, both linguistic and situational. In learning, the analogies may become more and more abstract by means of what Slobin (1985) has called 'bootstrapping'. That means that abstract patterns deduced from concrete tokens begin to form a system provided these tokens occur frequently enough. The most frequent concrete and abstract patterns (i.e. idiomatic phrases, such as *He kicked the bucket*, and grammatical schemas, such as the English NP consisting of [(Det) (Adj) Noun]) become automatized and will become part of our lexical and grammatical knowledge.

The advantage of a usage-based grammar (i.e. a grammar that is the result of actual learning), such as the one indicated here, is that no distinction is made between lexical items/phrases and grammatical words/schemas (as in Construction Grammar). Lexical items are learned first; patterns, both concrete and abstract, follow from that. The learning itself takes place by what Slobin (1985) and Peters (1985) have called 'operating principles'. These are general strategies, based on analogy, on recognizing what is same and what is not-same, and drawing conclusions from that. These same/different operations are performed on linguistic utterances in context, on the form as well as the situated meaning of the utterance, in which frequency plays an important role. The same analogical procedures also provide us with the ability to build up categories (like Noun, Verb) and syntactic structures (cf. Itkonen 2005; Wanner 2006).

In analogy, both iconic and indexical forces are important. The strong interconnections between the indexical and the iconic are clearly indicated in Anttila's (2003) 'analogical grid', whose paradigmatic and syntagmatic axes represent the 'woof and warp of cognition'. Anttila emphasizes that all linguistic signs (which include both concrete lexical items and structural patterns) are double-edged: they are combinations of form and meaning. Even more importantly, in view of the force of analogy, he stresses that similarity relations exist in both form and meaning. Meaning is related to the function an object/sign has. It is clear that signs may end up in the same paradigmatic set because their referents are seen to be similar in function. For instance, items like *apple, pear, banana* do not form the set (sign) *fruit* so much on the basis of similarity of form/colour, but on the basis of similarity of function, i.e. they are all plucked, eaten, peeled, enjoyed in similar ways. The analogical grid implies a close bond between the form and the function of a sign; it applies to all meaningful units, from the smallest morphemes to complex words, but also to larger and more abstract (morpho)syntactic structures. Because form and meaning constitute a whole, a meaning change may affect the form, but change may also be driven by lexical items similar in form or by the more abstract formal requirements of the system. That form may drive meaning is nicely illustrated on a lexical level by Coates (1987), who shows how folk-etymological changes are often shaped by similarities in form.

Analogy is a basic force not only ontogenetically but also phylogenetically. Deacon (1997) shows that the grammatical, symbolic (i.e. abstract/arbitrary) system that became part of human language in the course of evolution was built up incrementally on the basis of iconic and indexical modes of thinking, guided by evolutionary old cognitive principles (i.e. the ability to see similarities and differences, the ability to categorize), which are also at work in other (non-linguistic) domains.

Iconic relationships are the most basic means by which things can be represented, and are the foundation on which all other forms of representation are built. What is important here is that iconicity depends on recognition, and recognition depends on the interpreter. When we interpret the world around us in terms of similarities and differences, we learn to see only differences which are functional or relevant, gradually ignoring non-functional ones. In other words, we don't learn and remember more than is absolutely necessary. This is what Hawkins has called the principle of 'Minimize Forms':

> Minimizations in unique form-property pairings are accomplished by expanding the compatibility of certain forms with a wider range of properties [meanings]. Ambiguity, vagueness, and zero specification are efficient, inasmuch as they reduce the total number of forms that are needed in a language. (Hawkins: 2004: 40)

Hawkins goes on to say that this minimization is connected with the frequency of the form and/or the processing ease of assigning a particular property to a reduced form. The ambiguity that arises is no problem, since '[t]he multiple properties that are assignable to a given form can generally be reduced to a specific P[roperty] in actual language use by exploiting "context" in various ways' (p. 41). For example, we learn to recognize phonemic and ignore phonetic distinctions in the course of language acquisition because the latter are not functional. In other words, it is more economical to ignore these differences.

What I am suggesting is that in the course of both language evolution and language learning, and hence also in language change, the same analogical reasoning keeps playing a role, whereby abstract items/structures gradually evolve from concrete (lexical) items constituting what Holyoak and Thagard (1995) have called 'system mapping'. System mapping led to the evolution of grammar; it is still basically followed by children when they build up their grammar; and it guides language processing all through our lives. The exact path is not the same in all three fields because the input is different and keeps changing, but the same analogical principles are at work each time. An additional advantage of the analogical learning system is that there is only one system to begin with, i.e. a lexical one. It is therefore more parsimonious from an evolutionary point of view, and it better fits present neurological findings and the ideas developed about neural networks by, for instance, Pulvermüller (2002).

In a framework like the above, analogy is both a mechanism and a cause. By means of analogy we may arrange linguistic signs (both concrete and abstract) into (other) paradigmatic sets, but it is also analogy that causes the learner to build up more abstract schemas, and to keep the number of these to a minimum (so a form of 'grammar optimization', but more local than suggested by Kiparsky forthcoming, and always exemplar-based). In this learning model, analogy is the primary force, and not reanalysis. 'Reanalysis' is what a linguist may see from the point of view of what changes in the system between generations or in the language output in the course of time, but it is not something that speakers actually do. Speakers do not reanalyse, they substitute one pattern holistically for another.

Analogy is often seen as too loose, and therefore impractical or unworkable as a principle within a linguistic model. But, indeed, it is not a principle of the system or a principle of language (change), it is a faculty of language users. As Hofstadter emphasized, the conceptual mismatch represented by analogy is in fact its strength: its flexibility keeps the system oiled. This is not to say that our analogizing capacities are not controlled. They are. The 'looseness' of analogy will be much constrained if one thinks of analogizing as taking place on different levels, and in relation to concrete as well as abstract categories, all connected in tight networks. The possibilities are also constrained by the fact that the patterns and the paradigms are organized both semantically and structurally, since each linguistic sign or token, be it single or complex, is, because of its binary nature, part of formal (sound-shape, structure, position) as well as semantic categories.

This means that, in order to discover how exactly analogy plays a role in grammaticalization processes or in change in general, one cannot concentrate only on the development of one particular structure or (combination of) lexical item(s). One has to consider the change in terms of the network that the construction/item operates in. To get an idea of how this works, it is useful to consider what happens in actual processing. Berg (1998) has looked at processing errors (and what causes them) as a way of determining the structure of the grammatical system.

Berg makes a distinction between contextual and non-contextual errors. He shows how errors depend on 'similarity constraints "elsewhere"' (1998: 173). Thus, an error like *cuff of coffee* is much more likely to occur than *hit the roop.* In both cases there is a [p]/[f] interchange, but in the first case the error is caused syntagmatically (by *coffee*), and in the second paradigmatically (i.e. [p] and [f] belong to the feature set of voiceless labials). Interestingly enough, with higher-level errors involving meaningful elements, *non*-contextual errors are much more likely to occur. Berg (p. 165) gives the following German example: *Muß sie es noch mal ticken—tippen?* ('does she have to retype it?'), which he describes as an error that is 'neutral with respect to the similarity scale, as there is nothing to compare [it] with' (p. 166), i.e. there is no [k] around in this case to cause the [p] in *tippen* to change to [k]. The interesting thing, however, is that both *ticken* and *tippen* are possible words in German. Moreover, semantically and formally they are very similar: both are verbs, they look alike phonetically, and both refer to a light, repetitive ticking sound. Quite clearly, here, the error is of a paradigmatic kind, showing similarity on a deeper level of mental organization.

I would suggest that processing errors of the paradigmatic, non-contextual kind are more likely than are contextual ones to be innovations that could result in actual change, because the influence of paradigms in the grammar system is likely to be stronger than the influence of context. The latter is bound to be variable, being part of the actual discourse, while the former is much more stable, paradigms having become part of the system through learning and repeated use. It has been shown in Analogical Modelling that changes in the morphological system are heavily constrained by the different paradigmatic sets that an item is part of (cf. Chapman and Skousen 2005).

Although such constraints are much more difficult to establish in the area of syntax (because the paradigmatic choices are so much wider), promising work has been done here too, showing that the development of constructions is not a linear affair (affecting only the particular construction under discussion) but 'starlike', influenced by other constructions that resemble them formally and/or semantically. De Smet (2009; forthcoming) argues convincingly that certain cases which traditionally were seen as instances of reanalysis are better explained (in terms of the available data) as being driven by the presence of analogical forms elsewhere. Looking at the spread of the 'new' *for*-NP-*to*-V construction (with *for* functioning as complementizer and NP as subject) in English, he shows that this new construction became available because it was cast into the mould of an older but formally identical *for*-NP-*to*-V construction, where *for* was part of the infinitival marker *for*... *to* and the NP the *object* of the infinitive. The latter disappeared because the OV pattern itself was cast into the mould of the (by then) more regular Middle English clause pattern, SVO, so that any NP before a verb came to be interpreted as subject rather than object. This explains better than the reanalysis story why the new construction doesn't first appear as extraposed subject (as one would expect with reanalysis), and why there is an early predominance of passive infinitives. Another paradigmatic factor that facilitated the spread of the 'new' construction to more and more verbs was the analogy i.e. (the close *formal* similarity) between the *for*-NP (in the subject construction) and the *for*-NP found as a prepositional object with the same verbs, causing the spread of the new subject-construction to other verbs taking a *for*-PP.

Other cases investigated show that grammaticalization doesn't necessarily follow a gradual linear path but constitutes an abrupt process by analogy (Bisang 1997;

Noel 2005). Fischer (2007: 274ff.) shows that in the cline from adverbial adjuncts to pragmatic markers in English, some of the pragmatic markers were attracted to the pattern directly via analogy, or via another pattern—that of reduced modal clauses. Similarly, she argues that in the development of English epistemic modals, there was no direct path from deontic to epistemic use. Epistemic meaning arose through functional and formal analogy with pairs of constructions like *he seems to be... / it seems that he...*, which enabled the *it must be that he...* to be replaced by *he must be...* These solutions are more commensurate with the philological facts and, as a further bonus, obliterate the problem that they do not neatly follow Lehmann's parameters in terms of scope.

4. Concluding remarks

Grammaticalization as a process only 'exists' on the language-output level. It may involve universal paths and look unidirectional, but this is not something intrinsic to the process on the speaker-listener level. As a process, it is an analyst's generalization, a convenient summary but not something that has actually 'happened' (cf. McMahon 2006: 173). Its apparent universality and directionality is caused by the fact that the lexical source items which are involved in it are (i) part of the basic vocabulary, (ii) as such are relatively frequent, (iii) are therefore likely to be phonetically and semantically reduced, which in turn (iv) makes them more eligible than other linguistic signs to function in abstract structural patterns. There is, however, no necessity about the development.

Language change can therefore not be *explained* in terms of grammaticalization. Grammaticalization occurs, and often as a homogeneous 'type' especially when a form/construction through frequency has eroded so much that it becomes part of a drift; but what ultimately decides whether a linguistic sign becomes part of a user's grammatical system is whether it resembles in some way (semantically, formally or both) an already existing category. Grammaticalization does not lead to new grammatical structures in any general sense (*pace* Meillet 1912; Bybee 2003; Kiparsky forthcoming; Traugott 2008a: 154), except perhaps in cases of substratum or long-term contact, where new structures may enter through bilingualism or imperfect learning. This may introduce genuinely new structures (although they would still be based on the analogy of contact/substrate structures), which may then be used as a pattern. I have tried to show that reanalysis is an analyst's concept; in terms of language *processing* it is based on our ability to analogize. This ability is steered by frequency, and includes analogical expansion, thus covering all the important factors mentioned under (iv) in section 1.

CHAPTER 4

GRAMMATICALIZATION AND GENERATIVE GRAMMAR: A DIFFICULT LIAISON

ELLY VAN GELDEREN

Grammaticalization is relevant in all areas of grammar. For instance, how does one label the prepositions *like* and *after* when, as a result of grammaticalization, they function as complementizers, and how does a grammar deal with pronouns that have been reanalysed as agreement markers? Different grammatical approaches look at these issues differently. For some, gradient and fuzzy categories are typical of language; for others, there are a small number of categories and the boundaries are absolute. For some approaches, the more distinctions made, the better the grammar, while others allow fairly abstract representations. This outlook affects views on grammaticalization as well.

Generative grammar had its beginnings in the late 1950s with the work of Noam Chomsky emphasizing the innate linguistic knowledge. It focused then and now on the generative capacity of native speakers to form grammatical sentences. As a result of the emphasis on native speaker intuitions, mainstream generative grammar has been very negative towards historical linguistics, notwithstanding important work by Elizabeth Traugott,[1] Paul Kiparsky, and David Lightfoot. If language

[1] I include the early work by Traugott, e.g. Closs (1965) and Traugott (1972), since that was generative in nature unlike her later work.

change is where one encounters grammaticalization the most, the uneasy relationship between generative grammar and grammaticalization is not surprising. However, even among the relatively few generative historical linguists, grammaticalization has been ignored.

One reason for this lack of interest is that grammaticalization is about small-scale changes in the E-language (i.e. the language we see and hear in the world) whereas the focus of generative grammar is on I-language (i.e. the linguistic knowledge in the mind of a native speaker). Native speakers of extinct languages are unavailable, and that makes it hard for generativists to study their I-language. A second reason is, of course, that grammaticalization involves phonological and syntactic as well as semantic and pragmatic changes. This emphasis on pragmatics-semantics was another reason for the early tension, since generative grammar, in common with other formal approaches, assumes the independence (autonomy) of syntax. All this makes Newmeyer (1998: 226) exclaim that 'there is no such thing as grammaticalization' (italics omitted) and that grammaticalization is an epiphenomenon. A major argument used by Newmeyer against positing a grammaticalization theory is the unidirectionality assumed by most linguists working on grammaticalization. If a learner just reacts to a certain input, there should not be unidirectional changes, according to Newmeyer (1998), Lightfoot (2006), and others. This is a serious objection, one I discuss below as a third major generative argument against taking grammaticalization seriously. A fourth reason is that grammaticalization is seen by some as belonging to typology. Currently, typology and generative grammar are also coming together more, especially in the work of Mark Baker.

In section 1, I first sketch the generative attitude towards historical linguistics in general and then to grammaticalization in particular, focusing on the four problematic areas just mentioned. I also discuss what the locus of change is in a generative model. There are a number of generative models; here I focus on two: the Principles and Parameters model of the 1970s and 1980s and the Minimalist Program of the 1990s to the present. Then, in section 2, I briefly review some early work on historical linguistics within generative grammar, e.g. Traugott (1965; 1972), Kiparsky (1965), Allen (1977), and Lightfoot (1979). This early work does not mention grammaticalization although Traugott (1972) mentions (de)segmentalization, gradualness, and subjectivization.

Since the 1990s, there has been a considerable switch in generative attitudes towards grammaticalization and in the recognition that it is an area to be dealt with. Werner Abraham was crucial to this endeavour (and later Ian Roberts and others). I discuss that change in attitude in section 3. At this stage, the 1990s, grammaticalization is seen as a change in the input learners are presented with rather than as an issue on its own. Currently, many generative, formal linguists working in historical linguistics are taking the insights from grammaticalization more seriously. I think this shift became possible with the introduction of functional categories such as D(eterminer), T(ense), and C(omplementizer) in the mid-1980s and the emphasis on features in the 1990s. Especially since the beginning of the 21st century, there has appeared a large quantity of work, the most relevant of which I will discuss in section 4 (although such a review cannot cover everyone working on grammaticalization as a generative linguist). I will end by arguing that the child's innate principles are in fact responsible for grammaticalization, and that generative grammar can therefore gain much insight from grammaticalization processes.

1. Generative grammar, historical linguistics, and grammaticalization

In this section, I first discuss the generative attitude towards historical linguistics and grammaticalization. Then, I outline the aspects of generative grammar that will be relevant for an account of grammaticalization and language change: principles, parameters, and features.

There are of course many ways in which language change can provide insights into the language faculty. For instance, if certain changes never occur, this could be due to restrictions imposed by Universal Grammar. However, possibly because of the early emphasis on introspection and grammaticality judgements by a native speaker, work in historical generative syntax was not encouraged. In his own writings, Chomsky certainly has never been interested in language change—except in Chomsky and Halle (1968), and that was most likely due to Halle's interests (as evidenced in Halle 1962). Since Chomsky has set the agenda for generative linguists for at least 50 years, it has been 'less popular' to pursue historical linguistics using that framework. Historical linguistics was one of the first subfields to enthusiastically use corpora, and that too might have kept generative grammar from going into historical linguistics. Even now, there are leading historical formal linguists who do not themselves use corpora. Here I will just return in more detail to the four reasons I mentioned above as to why grammaticalization was not popular among generative linguists.

First, generative grammar is interested in how a child acquires a grammar on the basis of the available language the child is exposed to. If the language the child hears has changed or is changing from that which the parents grew up with, the child will have a different input and will come up with a grammar (I-language) different from that of its parents/caregivers. Generative grammar studies the cognitive processes that allow a child to construct a grammar. It isn't interested in grammaticalization if grammaticalization is seen as something that 'happens' away from the learning process. Grammaticalization changes the linguistic input, the E-language, available to the child, but the real interest is in how the child deals with this, for example in terms of parameter resetting or, in later Minimalism, in terms of the features posited for certain lexical items.

Secondly, if grammaticalization is formulated as 'that part of the study of language change that is concerned with such questions as how lexical items and constructions come in certain linguistic contexts to serve grammatical functions or how grammatical items develop new grammatical functions' (Hopper and Traugott 2003: 1), a prominent place is given to semantics and pragmatics: pragmatically marked items and constructions lead the way in grammaticalization. Generative grammar always emphasized the centrality of syntax, and thus there was a problem. Allowing (formal) features into the picture, as in current Minimalism, makes it possible to overcome that obstacle.

A third reason has to do with unidirectionality. Newmeyer (1998: 263–75) and Lightfoot (2006: 38, 177) are adamant about change not being unidirectional. They rely on the well-known instances of degrammaticalization. I will not go into that in much detail, but take the approach by Traugott and Dasher (2002: 87), who claim that the number of counterexamples to unidirectionality is small and not systematic.

A fourth reason is that generative grammar did not always have a good relationship with typology, the study of structural features such as causatives and word order across languages initially pioneered by Joseph Greenberg. Grammaticalization was seen as part of that focus. In Lightfoot's words, '[c]ommitment to the gradualness of change has a long pedigree... It was a crucial element in the "typological" view of language change, which dominated discussion of diachronic syntax in the 1970s' (1991: 158). Lightfoot avoids grammaticalization in the above quotation, and uses 'gradualness' instead. Lightfoot's (2006: 37–8; 177–8) book has a short section entitled 'Drift, typologists, and grammaticalization' in which he criticizes the view of language as an external object in these three related concepts. He acknowledges that grammaticalization exists as a phenomenon, 'not an explanatory force'. I come back to Lightfoot's views in the next section.

I'll now turn to the areas in the generative framework that are perhaps most relevant to historical linguistics and grammaticalization: principles and parameters. These have been used in generative grammar since the so-called 'Principles and Parameters' approach of the 1970s. Principles are valid for all languages and have mostly been attributed to Universal Grammar. At the moment, however, the emphasis in the Minimalist Program is on principles not specific to the language faculty, but to 'general properties of organic systems' (Chomsky 2004: 105), 'third factor principles' in Chomsky (2005; 2007). As I will briefly mention in section 4, one can argue that principles are responsible for similar changes across languages.

Parameters are seen as responsible for variation among languages and are therefore also the locus of change. Since (the early) parameters have +/– settings, they are unlikely to account for gradual unidirectional change. Early examples of parameters include determining if a language is pro-drop (Rizzi 1982), its headedness, and whether it moves its *wh*-elements. 'Pro-drop' is the cover term for a set of related phenomena, but mainly indicates the possibility of not expressing the subject through a separate (pro)noun. Pro-drop languages include Italian, Spanish, Japanese, and Korean. Headedness is a way to characterize a language, with Arabic being head-initial and Japanese head-final. Following work by Kayne (1994), headedness has been abandoned as a formal parameter. In Kayne's framework, the basic word order is SVO and other word orders come about through movement (e.g. the object preposes in an SOV language). This movement is possibly due to feature strength attracting the object to a higher functional category. The +/– setting of the *wh*-movement parameter determines whether or not *wh*-movement occurs (as in English) or does not occur (as in Chinese). This parameter is now also seen as dependent on strength of the features in a higher functional category. For historical syntax, the changing view of parameters means that what was originally seen as a parameter switch, for example from head-first to head-last, is now a change in whether or not a feature on a functional head triggers movement.

Within the Minimalist Program, there is currently a movement to eliminate parameters. For instance, Chomsky (e.g. 2004; 2007), Lohndal (2009), and Richards (2008) attribute as little as possible to the role of parameters and to Universal Grammar in general. Minimalist parameters consist of choices of feature specifications as the child acquires a lexicon, dubbed the Borer–Chomsky Conjecture by Baker (2008). All parameters are lexical; therefore, they account for the variety of languages. As Pintzuk, Tsoulas, and Warner (2000: 7) put it, 'the lexicon . . . must be the locus of syntactic change'. Seeing language change in terms of small changes in the features makes it easier to account for grammaticalization.

Both developments just sketched—the move towards general principles and that towards parametric features—make it easier to account for grammaticalization. I return to this in the last section.

2. Early historical generative work

In this section, I discuss some early generative approaches to language change. These involved both phonological change and syntactic change. King (1969) provides a good overview.

Closs (1965), Klima (1965), Kiparsky (1965), and Chomsky and Halle (1968) emphasize learning as the cause of change. The latter authors state that 'speakers

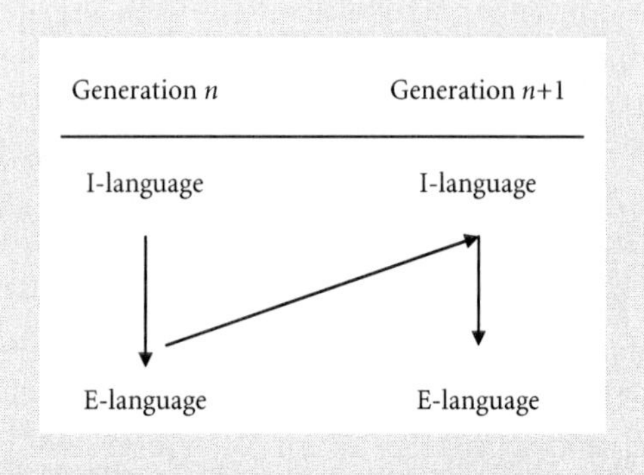

Fig. 4.1. Model of language acquisition (based on Andersen 1973)

are by and large unaware of the changes that their language is undergoing' (1968: 250), but that adults can only add or delete minor rules; children can reorganize the system. This view goes back to Halle (1962: 64, 66–7). Closs (1965: 415) concludes: 'language changes by means of the addition of single innovations to an adult's grammar, by transmission of these innovations to new generations, and by the reinterpretation of grammars such that mutations occur'.

Klima (1965: 83) formulates a model of generative language change emphasizing the discontinuous nature of change and reanalysis by the learner.[2] I reproduce it as Figure 4.1 based on Andersen (1973), since that is slightly simpler than Klima's.

Closs (1965), Kiparsky (1965), Lakoff (1969), Traugott (1972), and Lightfoot (1974; 1979) in various forms use this model. Their explanations depend on the then current model of phonology and syntax. The phonology is fairly abstract, with lots of rules in a particular order (e.g. devoicing, palatalization, spirantization), and the syntax has a phrase structure component and a set of ordered transformations. Most change is seen as change in the phonological and transformational rules, either by rule loss, addition, or restructuring/simplification. Early work on syntactic change examines modals, complementizers, and subjunctives. Closs (1965) presents a groundbreaking study of the changes from verbs to auxiliaries in English. Lakoff (1969) focuses on complementation in Latin. The changes are phrased in terms of the then current model and are termed innovations; change comes about through additions of single rules to the grammar of the adult speaker and then reanalysis by the learner in the next generation. Intelligibility has to be preserved.

Closs (1965) is of course the basis of much later work on auxiliaries, in terms both of data and of analysis. She is concerned with the phrase structure rules and how the shape of AUX is different in Old English, and suggests ways to account for

[2] Since generative grammar takes a purely synchronic approach, there is no reanalysis in the strict sense. A child acquires a language based on the available data and does not reanalyse. It is just a convenient term.

the difference. Lightfoot (1974), also focusing on modals, formulates the phrase structure rules for the modals in fairly similar ways to Closs (1965), namely as in (1), which sets apart the modals as a separate category.

(1)	S	→	NP	AUX	VP	
	AUX	→	T	(M)		
	VP	→	(have-en)	(be-ing)	V	...

One of the main concerns for Lightfoot is whether modals are main verbs or auxiliaries, and this remained a huge debate. He argues they are not full verbs in Modern English, and that this is due to a 'radical restructuring' (1974: 234). Around the same time, Canale (1978) suggests a (radical) reanalysis of OV to VO in the English of around 1200.

Thus, the motivation in much of this early work on historical syntax lies in testing certain aspects of the generative model, in particular the phrase structure rules. For instance, Closs (1965) examines the levels/boundaries between which the changes take place. Allen (1977: 1) justifies her study on the history of *wh*-questions and relative clauses as follows: 'The complementizer has become a focal point of the so-called Extended Standard Theory, as developed by Chomsky in his works from around 1970 to the present... Because of this, the history of the system of complementation in English is of great potential interest... ' In this period, i.e. the 1960s and 1970s, there is no mention of grammaticalization, even though of course Closs Traugott's data present prototypical examples of grammaticalization. Since acquisition is crucial, historical change is seen as reanalysis by the child acquiring the language.

3. The 1990s: Acknowledging Grammaticalization

In the 1980s, functionalist approaches rediscover grammaticalization (e.g. Lehmann 1982; Heine and Reh 1984) after many years of neglect of the topic in linguistics as a whole. (See Hopper and Traugott 2003 for a short history of the varying interest in grammaticalization in the last few centuries.) In this section, I first look at how grammaticalization was initially regarded and accounted for by generativists and then at which phenomena were studied.

An early effort to confront generative grammar with grammaticalization was a workshop, the Groningen Grammar Talks, organized by Werner Abraham in November 1990. Its title, 'Explanation in Historical Linguistics: Grammaticalization vs. Reanalysis', seems to suggest conflict rather than compatibility. Other early treatments of grammaticalization are Abraham (1991; 1993), van Gelderen (1993), and Roberts (1993a). Although Abraham and van Gelderen acknowledge the existence of grammaticalization, they see it as something happening externally, so to speak, which speakers have to react to by means of reanalyses: 'As a reaction to grammaticalization, a reanalysis must take place in the grammar internalized by the speaker' (van Gelderen 1993: 193). Roberts (1993a) is the first to give a formal account of the grammaticalization of the future in Romance. He argues that grammaticalization involves 'the loss of thematic structure [of the V] and a related shift in category from V to I' (1993a: 227). This is due to a parametric shift, but the motivating factor is a strategy of least effort that eliminates movement.

The year 1990 sees the first Diachronic Generative Syntax conference (DIGS) in York. Selected papers from this conference were published in Battye and Roberts (1995). Other DIGS volumes appeared in van Kemenade and Vincent (1997) and in Pintzuk et al. (2000), including some work on grammaticalization. The tone in Battye and Roberts (1995) is still quite negative: 'This approach can explain many cases of what has been referred to in the typological literature in diachronic syntax as "grammaticalization"' (1995: 9)—the only reference in the book, it seems, to grammaticalization.

Typical topics addressed in the 1990s are the modals and the auxiliary *do*, the infinitival marker *to*, demonstratives, and articles. These topics are all prime instances of grammaticalization. With the shift towards an emphasis on functional categories in the late 1980s, these changes could be discussed in structural terms, as Roberts (1993b) and van Gelderen (1993) do. This will lead to the insight that grammaticalization is a reanalysis from lexical category to grammatical category. Roberts (1993b) doesn't mention grammaticalization, and no account is provided for the regularities seen in the grammaticalization processes, i.e. volition verbs grammaticalize as future markers and spatial prepositions turn into temporal and causal markers. Van Gelderen also discusses grammaticalization, as mentioned, but as something to be responded to by the learner, not accounted for by the model of syntax used.

4. Features and principles: embracing grammaticalization

From about the year 2000 on, there has been much generative interest in grammaticalization (see e.g. the special issue of *Linguistics* edited by Ans van Kemenade in 1999). Simpson and Wu (2002), Wu (2004), Roberts and Roussou

(2003), and van Gelderen (2004) all use a mechanism that the latter calls Late Merge, and that results in what has been expressed as 'grammaticalization is up the tree'. Before going into the explanations, I'll first discuss the current syntactical model very briefly.

As mentioned in section 1, in the Minimalist Program all parameters are encoded in the lexicon, with the consequence that linguistic variation falls out from the morphological properties of the lexical items. Lexical items have features that vary across languages, but can be divided into phi-features (number, person, and gender), case features (dependent marking of DPs by the T and the (light) v), and EPP features. The latter features are responsible for movement (for example) of the subject from a VP-internal position, where it gets its semantic role, to a higher position to become the grammatical subject. In this model, language change is due to the reanalysis by the learner of the features of the lexical items.

In Chomsky (e.g. 1995; 2004), phrase structure rules, as in (1), are abandoned in favour of a general rule Merge. Merge combines two bundles of features taken from the lexicon. Chomsky (2004: 4) suggests the lexicon has 'atomic elements, lexical items LI, each a structured array of properties'. Merging the lexical items could look like (2).

(2)

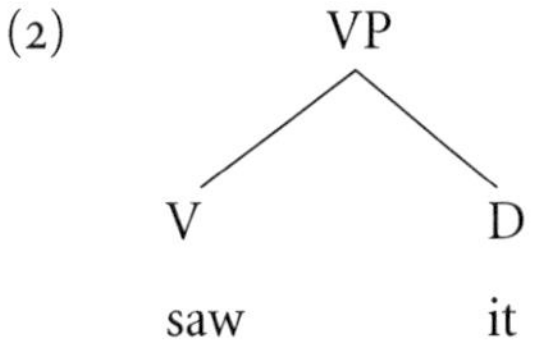

To this, a (small) v is added, as in (3), which is responsible for case assignment (checking) to the object. The v comes with uninterpretable person and number features that look down the tree for something to agree with. The object *it* has interpretable phi-features that can value those of v, and in turn gets accusative case from v. The features that are not relevant to the interpretation (at LF) are deleted, i.e. struck through.

(3)

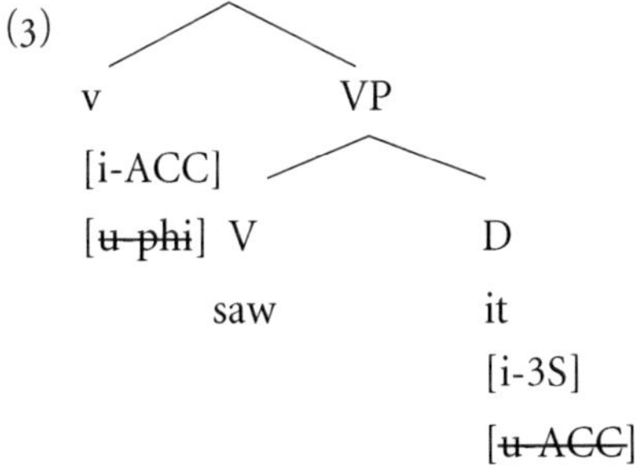

After adding a finite T(ense), responsible for licensing the subject, the structure looks like (4). The subject *sparrows* moves to Spec TP.

(4)

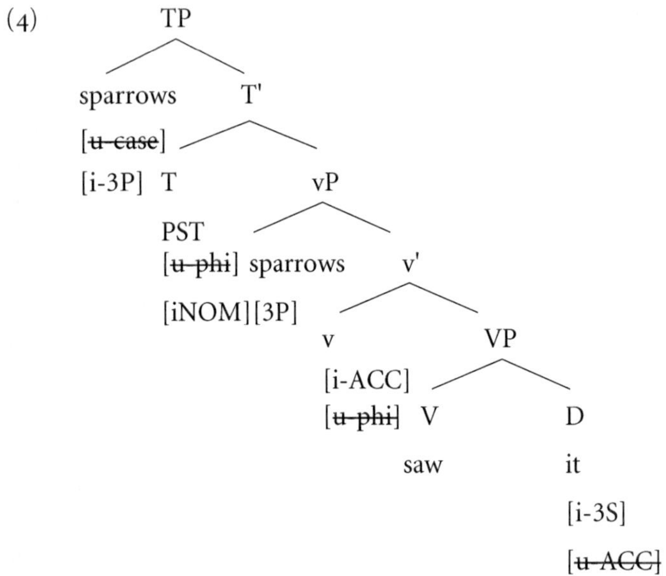

In (4), both v and T find an appropriate noun with interpretable phi-features. Clearly, there is much interaction, and only if the features match will the uninterpretable features be valued.

At some point, the derivation has to be handed over to the Sensorimotor (SM) and Conceptual-Interpretative (CI) systems external to the syntax. This is done through the interfaces PHON and SEM, corresponding to PF and LF in older frameworks. Thus, crucial to Minimalism are merge, move, and feature checking. Let's see how these concepts are relevant to change.

Simpson and Wu (2002) analyse the changes in negation in the history of French. As is well known, the original negative *ne* weakens and is reinforced by objects, e.g. the minimizer *pas* 'step'. Simpson and Wu analyse the negative *ne* as selecting a Focus projection below NegP but above the VP to which the negative

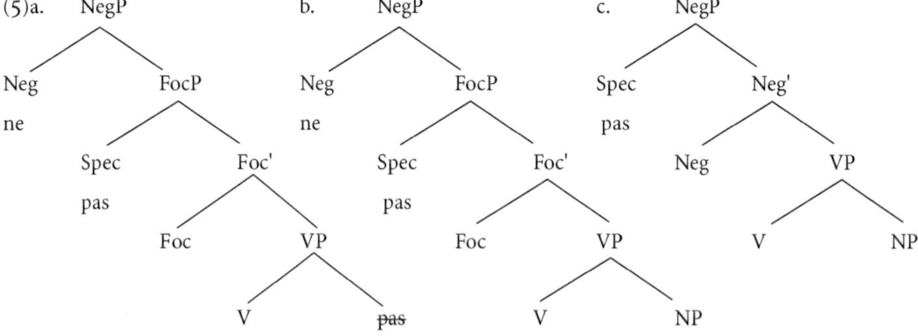

object *pas* moves, as in (5a). This object is then reanalysed in the Spec(ifier) of FocP, as in (5b), and subsequently in the Spec of NegP, as in (5c), which represents colloquial French.

Simpson and Wu argue that a FocP may be selected by certain functional categories, and that over time the focus interpretation may be lost, in which case the FocP is reanalysed as an AGR(eement) Phrase. They analyse Chinese relatives, Chinese aspect, and Thai modals in the same way. Wu (2004) works on the development of functional elements in Chinese, such as classifiers, aspect markers, and complementizers, and argues they were reanalysed in higher position after first moving there.

Roberts and Roussou (2003: 2) state that 'grammaticalization is a regular case of parameter change... [and] epiphenomenal'. The authors' 'main theoretical goal ...is to provide an understanding of the nature of functional categories, using grammaticalization as our tool, since it creates new functional material'. This creation of new functional material happens through structural simplification. The deeper question they ask is how to reconcile 'the clear evidence for pathways of change at the descriptive level with the fact that an explanatory account of change must involve parameter change' (2003: 4). They attempt this by creating basins of attraction within the parameter space.

The mechanisms, i.e. possible parameter settings, that Roberts and Roussou suggest are not so different from those used by other historical generativists; especially 'merge over move' (choosing a feature F^*_{merge} is preferable over a feature F^*_{move}[3]) resembles Simpson and Wu, van Gelderen, and others. For instance, for the changes involving negatives, Roberts and Roussou (2003: 195) invoke the parametric change of T^*_{merge} over T^*_{move} and argue that this is due to the loss of the infinitive marker. The changes in negatives, described in (5), involve loss of movement, loss of features, and structural simplification, according to Roberts and Roussou (2003: 157).

Van Gelderen (2004) proposes two principles that the child uses to acquire its language. If the linguistic input is ambiguous between postulating a head or a phrase, the child will select a head, i.e. the head preference principle (and this is the reason why full negative objects reanalyse as negative heads), and if a lexical item is checking a number of features in several positions, it can be reanalysed in a higher position (e.g. the modals). The emphasis in this account is on the inevitability of grammaticalization (and renewal). It is not something that happens in the E-language that the learner responds to but it is 'caused' by the innate principles.

Van Gelderen (e.g. 2008; 2011) reformulates her earlier principles and argues that it is economical for an item to be reanalysed with uninterpretable features, since these features keep the derivation going. Feature Economy might look like (6). Roberts and Roussou also have feature loss as part of the simplification.

[3] The F* stands for 'a feature requiring phonological spell out'.

(6) Feature Economy

Adjunct/Argument		Specifier (of NegP)		Head (of NegP)		affix
semantic	>	[iF]	>	[uF]	>	—

Let's take the example of negatives again. An object that is semantically negative, for example a small step (e.g. *pas* in French), is reanalysed in a higher position with grammatically negative features. It can then be reanalysed as having uninterpretable features, i.e. as a probe looking for an element to value its features. Some elements are straightforward renewers: negative indefinites renew negatives, demonstratives have phi-features and can renew agreement, and adverbs have temporal or spatial features and renew prepositions and complementizers.

5. Conclusion

Grammaticalization and generative grammar have had an uneasy relationship. Proponents of generative grammar see syntax as autonomous (see e.g. Chomsky 1957), whereas advocates of grammaticalization see meaning and function as the determining factors behind syntactic structure and, of course, behind change. The emphasis on function and meaning has prompted one side to say there are no structural representations (e.g. Hopper 1987, cited in Newmeyer 1998) and the

Table 4.1. Grammaticalization phenomena dealt with by generativist historical linguists

Modals	Roberts and Roussou (2003)
Negation	Simpson and Wu (2002); van Gelderen (2004)
Definiteness	Roberts and Roussou (2003)
Mood particles	Abraham (1991)
Demonstrative to C	Simpson and Wu (2002); van Gelderen (2004); Wu (2004)
Aspect	Simpson and Wu (2002); Wu (2004)
Full pronoun to agreement	van Gelderen (2004); Fuß (2005)
Future	Roberts (1993a: 1993b); Roberts and Roussou (2003)
Infinitival marker	Abraham (2004); van Gelderen (2004); IJbema (2002)
P(P) to C	van Gelderen (2009)
N to P	Longobardi (2001)

other that there is no grammaticalization (Newmeyer 1998: 226). Lightfoot (1999: 83) argues that languages change gradually but that grammars change abruptly.

In this chapter, I have chronicled the initial reluctance of generative grammar to work on historical linguistics in general and grammaticalization in particular. This is currently no longer the case. Due to the introduction of functional categories in the late 1980s and features in the 1990s, it has become possible to account for gradual unidirectional change in a generative framework. There is generative work that sees the (unidirectional) pathway as determined by language learning and cognitive principles that the child applies. Table 4.1 summarizes some recent work.

CHAPTER 5

GRAMMATICALIZATION AND FUNCTIONAL LINGUISTICS

PETER HARDER
KASPER BOYE

1. Introduction[1]

Functional linguistics is a multi-stranded phenomenon, also from the point of view of grammaticalization; and many other chapters in this volume will demonstrate the breadth of functional contributions to the study of grammaticalization. The central motif here is the element of tension between the two keywords in the title: grammaticalization is about structure, while function is about what language is used for. An adequate theory of grammaticalization based on function has to reflect a function-based theory of what grammar is. We begin by discussing why there have been problems in clarifying what such a theory must be like, and then focus on what we see as the functional nucleus of grammaticalization.

[1] Kasper Boye's work on this paper was made possible by a grant from the Carlsberg Foundation.

2. Functional linguistics

The term 'function' is slippery because it has an ambiguous relation with 'structure'. From one perspective, function and structure are opposites, because structure looks inward (what is the anatomy of the object?), while function looks outward (what can it be used for?). From another perspective, function and structure share an agenda focusing on *relations* as opposed to substantive, non-relational properties: in the early days of cognitive science, 'computational functionalism' referred to the belief that it does not matter whether processing is performed by brain matter or silicon chips, as long as the elements have the right relational complexity. Broadly speaking, the two perspectives can be captured by a distinction between internal function (which is closely associated with 'structural role') and external function (which contrasts with internal anatomy).

Ramifications of this ambiguity pervade the understanding of 'function' as a linguistic topic. Traditional word-based grammar began with form and meaning, where the formal properties were more or less equal to morphology and meaning was 'notional'. Functional properties typically came third in line, covering everything else apart from the properties of the element viewed in isolation. As such, functional properties included both syntactic properties (e.g. linguistic expressions 'function' as subjects) and pragmatic properties (the vocative served to mark the 'function' of addressing someone).

This perspective, where function and structure go together, remains the predominant understanding in European linguistics. The structuralist revolution highlighted the privileged status of internal structural relations, and the more rigorous structuralists (including Hjelmslev, cf. 1966[1943]) regarded only these as being part of linguistics, but nevertheless structural relations were generally understood as manifesting functional properties. This association earned this general approach the epithet 'structural-functional' theories (cf. Butler 2003).

More recently, in relation to generative grammar, 'functional' increasingly came to be used as the antithetical term to 'structural' or 'formal'. When the sentence (rather than the word) became the object of structural description, the word 'function' became associated primarily with external function, especially 'use in communication'. In this perspective, rather than being associated, structure and function come to be viewed as competing sources of explanation. The disagreement goes beyond conflicting hypotheses: because there is no shared view of what structure is, it has been difficult even to agree on where the precise disagreements are (cf. the efforts by Croft 1995; Newmeyer 1998 to map out the territory). As stressed in various contexts by Tomlin (e.g. 1990), functionalists have not always been very clear about what precisely a functional approach entails, including how it differs from what Givón (2002) calls 'naïve functionalism': the assumption that structure can be explained directly by reference to external function.

From the traditional European perspective, it is not surprising that (internal) grammar should arise gradually out of (external) usage and reflect the functions served by words in changing patterns of language use. However, when the modern discussion on grammaticalization arose, the existence of recurrent pervasive paths of grammaticalization constituted a striking argument against the radical separation between grammar and language use that was a prominent feature of the generative revolution. The generative dominance thus gave rise to what may be called usage functionalism, in which the role of structural generalizations that abstracted from actual usage was kept to a minimum.

This issue has determined the approach of 'classic' grammaticalization theory (as found in Bybee, Perkins, and Pagliuca 1994; Hopper and Traugott 1993/2003), in which great emphasis was assigned to a gradual as opposed to a dichotomous view of grammar vs. lexicon. The aim of eliminating the radically autonomous status of grammar is clearly a functionalist feature, and is shared with the views expressed below—but it became associated with a slightly different purpose: to tone down the distinction between grammar and the rest of language. Hopper thus rejects the idea that grammaticalization can be viewed as a form 'entering the grammar'—rather, one and the same form can be sometimes lexical and sometimes grammatical (cf. Hopper 1991: 33, who understands this as Meillet's view as well).

In our view, however, a proper understanding of grammaticalization depends on a version of functionalism that is neither structural-functional in the sense that takes structure to be the bottom line, nor strictly usage-functional in the sense that it rules out the idea of a linguistic feature 'entering the grammar'. Another way of formulating our position is to say that we believe in a usage-*based* theory of grammar, and also in a clear *distinction* between usage and grammar. Grammaticalization has a central position in such a theory, because it is the process whereby grammar emerges out of usage. A satisfying account of grammaticalization can thus demonstrate both how the two levels are distinct and simultaneously how they are linked.

We take the basic framework for such a functionalism to include a form of evolutionary dynamics (cf. Croft 2000). This entails a panchronic approach (as suggested by Heine, Claudi, and Hünnemeyer 1991), rather than one that prioritizes either the synchronic or the diachronic dimension. In such a panchronic perspective, functions are defined in terms of selection–adaptation relations that create 'lineages', i.e. successive reproductions of linguistic forms that are shaped by their contribution to overall communicative success. Both lineages that go on essentially unchanged and lineages that undergo change are shaped by degrees of success or failure in actual usage, i.e. by functional relations with the context of communication. The difference is that selection pressures in one case favour the usage range of the linguistic form as it is, while in another case some parts of the usage range are more selectionally favoured than others, yielding a gradually changed usage profile in successive reproductive cycles—which includes the extinction of some types of usage from time to time (cf. Keller 1990 on the German word *englisch* in the sense of 'angelic', which gave way to *engelhaft* and thus left *englisch* with only the 'English' sense). The relation between function and selection is basically the same as in evolutionary biology: 'function' is defined as the success-promoting (i.e. selection-promoting) effects(s) of the form: roughly speaking, powers of flight in the case of bird wings, sonority in the case of the vowel category, and 'informal greeting' in the case of words like *hi*.

Apart from the panchronic perspective, the significance of the evolutionary account is that it views change and functionality as a result of a constant interplay between two levels: the level of the individual, and the level of the whole population.[2] The human individual selects a linguistic form based on personal experience, intentions, and preferences, but the population-level effects operate on the whole collective output, promoting some features but not others. Among the effects that can only be captured at the collective level is extinction: there is no individual act or event which constitutes the extinction of a linguistic form.

The same applies to grammaticalization: there is no individual usage act or event which constitutes the grammaticalization of a linguistic form. Like other forms of language change, grammaticalization is the outcome of selection processes that operate at Keller's 'invisible hand' level, changing the potential of a linguistic element across replicative cycles. As a result, individual language users at time t+1 have different options available than language users at time t. A functional account of grammaticalization, from this point of view, has to specify (1) what type of change constitutes grammaticalization and (2) what type of functional pressures bias replication towards (more) grammaticalized potentials.

This means that functional explanation always refers to two levels that cannot be reduced to one: the function of an utterance in the individual context—and functional pressures at the collective level that bias successive reproduction towards certain forms and meanings. Grammaticalization must be understood as the outcome of such a selection process—not as the result of individual intentions. The functional account of grammaticalization that we propose demonstrates how the rise of new grammatical structure can be understood as a fundamental part of the interaction between the level of actual utterances in context and the winnowing processes that shape the potential available to tomorrow's language users.

[2] Croft (2000) views the analogy as applying to a population consisting of utterances, but the evolutionary mechanism does not depend on that precise interpretation.

3. A functionalist view of grammatical status

Any understanding of grammaticalization as the creation of grammar presupposes an understanding of what grammar is. In spite of its central role in most linguistic theorizing, however, the notion of grammar is often left undefined, and typical definitions are circular—for instance, grammatical expressions are defined as expressions that have grammatical meaning, but grammatical meaning is then defined ostensively in terms of examples of expressions that most linguists would intuitively agree are grammatical. The problem is that none of the prominent properties of linguistic expressions—phonological, semantic and distributional—can be used to define grammatical status in a concise way (e.g. Campbell 2001b; Boye and Harder submitted.). For instance, phonological reduction is often found with standard examples of grammatical expressions (e.g. the English auxiliary *gonna*), but can be found also with expressions that are considered lexical as opposed to grammatical (cf. the fact that haplology may affect clear-cut cases of lexical expressions). Likewise, semantic generality is a feature not only of grammatical expressions but also of abstract nouns (e.g. *element*), and closed-class membership can be shown to be a property of lexical as well as grammatical expressions provided the distributional context that defines a given closed class is itself defined narrowly enough.

In continuation of the type of functional perspective outlined above, we suggest that the familiar properties of grammatical items can be seen as a consequence of a functional relationship that becomes part of the conventional code. What defines grammatical expressions is that they are *coded as discursively secondary in relation to one or more syntagmatically related expressions.* Grammatical expressions thus serve an ancillary communicative purpose in relation to syntagmatically related expressions. This ancillary status is a structural phenomenon (a dependency relation), but at the same time it gives grammatical items a particular functional role: they express secondary or backgrounded information (cf. e.g. Talmy 2000) and cannot under normal circumstances be used to convey the main point of a linguistic message.[3]

As an example, the English genitive marker *-s* cannot under normal circumstances be brought into focus or addressed in subsequent communication. A pronunciation of *-s* with focal stress as in (1) is highly unusual, and the question

[3] A discussion of what 'normal circumstances' entail, including the relation with intonation, would take us beyond the scope of this paper, but cf. Boye and Harder (submitted).

what in (2) can hardly be interpreted as addressing the genitive marker in the preceding utterance.[4]

(1) ?John'S mother married once again last week.

(2) – John's mother married again last week.
– What?

The proposed conception of grammatical status has three important features. First, it allows a strict distinction between grammatical expressions and non-grammatical or lexical expressions while at the same time highlighting the link between the two.[5] Lexical expressions can be defined as expressions that are coded as potentially discursively primary in relation to one or more syntagmatically related expressions.[6] As opposed to grammatical expressions, they can express primary or foregrounded information and can thus be used to convey the main point of a linguistic message. Alternatively, however, just like grammatical expressions, they can be discursively secondary: since there may be several lexical elements in an utterance, not all of them can be the most important one. Thus, lexical and grammatical expressions differ from each other in that only the former has the possibility of being used as discursively primary, but they have a shared feature in that both have the possibility of being used as discursively secondary.

Secondly, the proposed conception goes naturally with a conception of linguistic structure as rooted in usage and function. Discursively secondary status is basically a usage phenomenon, but when it becomes a coded property (i.e. when an expression becomes 'selected for' secondary rather than primary status at the level of the invisible hand; see above), a new structural relation comes into being. In order for a given grammatical expression to figure with secondary status in actual usage, there has to be an expression with respect to which the grammatical expression at hand can be secondary. Even with its structural status and its structural consequences, however, coded secondary status can only be understood as usage-based: it is the result of conventionalization of a set of values belonging in actual usage.

Third, while the proposed conception of grammatical status entails a distinction between lexical and grammatical, it simultaneously leaves room for expressions with lexical constituents within grammar. It does so by including under

[4] Grammatical expressions can be focused or addressed only in cases such as metalinguistic contexts where they are considered in relation to a paradigmatically related element, as in I said 'emergED', not 'emergENT' (cf. Boye and Harder 2007). Even in such cases, grammatical expressions are arguably still secondary in relation to one or more syntagmatically related elements.

[5] A strict distinction between grammatical and non-grammatical expressions is fully compatible with a conception of both classes of expressions as being organized around prototypes, as well as with the idea of grammatical expressions as entering into diachronic continua with non-grammatical expressions.

[6] We do not discuss criteria for lexical status in detail, partly because our group is wider than standard notions, including e.g. proper names and numerals.

grammatical expressions not only morphologically simple expressions like affixes, clitics, and grammatical words but also morphologically complex expressions with abstract constructions as the extreme pole. Just like affixes, clitics, particles, and auxiliaries, constructions straightforwardly qualify as grammatical by virtue of being inherently secondary. Consider, for instance, the English declarative construction. As what Searle calls an 'illocutionary-force indicating device' it has the meaning of 'assertion', but it cannot be used to convey this meaning as the main point of a linguistic message. For instance, the main point of uttering (3) couldn't possibly be to convey: 'I now make an assertion.'

(3) Federer is the best tennis player.

Rather, the main point necessarily has to do with one or more of the lexical elements *Federer*, *best*, and *tennis player*. Just as the genitive marker *-s* is dependent on a noun phrase in order to convey its meaning of 'possession' (or whatever else its meaning might be) as secondary, the declarative construction is dependent on the lexical material which fills it in order to express its secondary meaning of assertion.

The definition in terms of coded discursively secondary status, we believe, captures most of the standard examples of grammatical expressions discussed in the literature. Affixes, clitics, particles, auxiliaries, and constructions are all inherently discursively secondary. There are exceptions, however. A case in point is demonstratives like English *that* and *this*. They are semantically general and make up a closed class, and because of this they are often thought of as grammatical. The theory advocated here suggests that this is wrong. Demonstratives can be addressed, as illustrated in (4), and brought into focus, as illustrated in (5), where *this* appears as the focused part of a focus construction.

(4) – Give me that book!
– Which?

(5) What I don't get is this.

By these criteria, demonstratives are clearly not grammatical (cf. also Diessel 1999).

4. A functionalist view of grammaticalization

The conception of grammatical status outlined above makes possible a definition of grammaticalization as covering a distinct class of language changes.

(6) *A functional definition of grammaticalization*
Grammaticalization is the diachronic change which gives rise to linguistic expressions which are coded as discursively secondary.

With this definition, at least three subtypes of grammaticalization may be distinguished. One type of grammaticalization consists in an originally lexical and thus potentially primary expression becoming coded with secondary status. This is the type focused on in much grammaticalization literature. It comprises cases like the familiar development of Latin *habere* in construction with an infinitival complement into Romance future tense suffixes. We suggest that this development takes its point of departure in uses of lexical *habere* with discursively secondary status and consists in a coding of this status, as illustrated in (7).

(7) *The grammaticalization of Latin* habere

amare	**habeo**(LEX)	Competition for discourse prominence, and *habere* wins the competition: *amare* is secondary
	<>	Usage alternation
amare	habeo(LEX)	Competition for discourse prominence, and *amare* wins the competition: *habere* is secondary
	>	Grammaticalization: coding (=conventionalization) of *habere* as secondary
amare	habeo(GRAM)	Result of grammaticalization: a grammatical descendant of lexical *habere* which is coded as secondary

In another type of grammaticalization an already existing grammatical expression gives rise to a new grammatical expression which is more grammatical than its source either in the sense of being inherently less discursively prominent than its source or in the sense of showing more symptoms of grammatical status (see Boye and Harder submitted for details). This type comprises the development of grammatical *habere* into, ultimately, the Romance future tense suffix (in Andersen's terms (2006), a type of regrammation).

The third type consists in a conveyed meaning with secondary status becoming coded in (i.e. conventionally associated with) a new linguistic expression. This type covers cases of what have been called 'syntacticization'—for instance, the change from topic to subject in 'noneducated American English' (Givón 1979: 209):[7]

(8)
My ol' man,	he rides with the Angels	>
TOPIC	PRO	
My ol' man	he-rides with the Angels	
SUBJECT	AGR-	

[7] According to Givón, the change is accompanied by the development of a pronoun into an agreement marker. This development will be left out of consideration here.

In accordance with the description given by Givón, the change may be seen as originating in a motivated but non-conventional association of initial clause position with 'topic status', and as having as its output a conventional—i.e. coded—association of initial clause position with 'subject status'. Both 'topic' and 'subject' status obviously constitute secondary information. Thus, the change essentially consists in the rise of an expression (an abstract word-order construction) that codes the secondary information at hand.

Like the first type, the third type of grammaticalization gives rise to a new construction in the sense that new dependency relations come into being. As a result of (7), a dependency is formed between grammatical *habere* and the infinitival companion it requires in order to be used with secondary status. As a result of (8), a dependency is formed between the word-order construction which identifies the subject and all the lexical material the construction needs to be filled with in order to be used with secondary status (and at all). All cases of grammaticalization thus go together with constructionalization (i.e. the formation of a larger grammatical construction of which the grammatical element forms part). The distinction between the two types may thus be seen as a distinction between constructionalization with and without grammaticalization of lexical expressions.

Kiparsky (forthc.) points at 'two principal competing families of definitions' of grammaticalization in the literature. One family takes a structural approach and, for instance, sees grammaticalization as a change 'by which the parts of a constructional schema come to have stronger internal dependencies' (Haspelmath 2004b). The other takes a functional approach and, for instance, sees grammaticalization as a change 'where a lexical unit or structure assumes a grammatical function, or where a grammatical unit assumes a more grammatical function' (Heine, et al. 1991). The theory advocated here follows neither of these, but stresses the importance of a combined approach.

5. Functional and structural prerequisites for grammaticalization of lexical expressions

The same thing goes for the question of what qualifies a lexical expression for grammaticalization (Boye and Harder submitted). In the literature there seems to be general agreement that the answer is functional or conceptual. It has often been observed, for instance, that there is a limited set of what Slobin (1997) calls 'grammaticizable notions', and it is reasonable to assume that the engine that drives grammaticalization is some feature of this set. Bybee (1994) hypothesizes that 'it is the reference plane of basic, irreducible notions—whether they concern existence or movement in space or psychological or social states, perspectives, and events—which serves as the basis for grammatical meaning in human languages' (p. 10). The functionalist view advocated here offers a supplementary characterization.

The crucial functional prerequisite for grammaticalization is that the expression is functionally useful in a discursively secondary role. Only such expressions will be used with sufficient frequency (absolute frequency as well as frequency relative to primary uses) for them to become conventionalized in their secondary capacity—and this conventionalization is what we understand by grammaticalization. Since secondary status goes with an ancillary role, and since the ancillary role of a grammatical expression must ultimately be understood in relation to a lexical expression, it follows that lexical candidates for grammaticalization must have some property that makes them useful as 'assistants' of lexical 'host' expressions. That is, they must have some property which enhances the usefulness—the information value, the functional potential—of accompanying lexical expressions. We see this requirement as an essential functional prerequisite for grammaticalization of lexical expressions. In other words, although expressions are 'weakened' when they become grammatical, the resulting combination (i.e. construction) is more 'functionally powerful' than the 'host' expression would be on its own.

But there is also a structural prerequisite, which follows from what we see as the central development in all grammaticalizations of lexical expressions: the conventionalization of secondary status. In order to become coded with secondary status a lexical grammaticalization candidate must occur with secondary status in linguistic communication. Just like grammatical expressions, which are inherently secondary, secondary lexical expressions are dependent upon some other expression relative to which they can be secondary in actual communication. It follows that in order for a lexical expression to qualify for grammaticalization, it needs to co-occur with some other lexical expression with which it can compete for discourse prominence. And in order to actually undergo grammaticalization, it also needs to *lose* the competition.

Consider again Latin *habere*. The verb could not possibly have undergone grammaticalization to an auxiliary in constructions like (9).

(9) amicu-m habe-o.
Friend-ACC have-1SG
'I have a friend'.

The reason is that *amicum* is not a relevant competitor for discourse prominence. In (10), by contrast, *habere* is accompanied by another verb, *amare*.

(10) amare habe-o.
love have-1SG
'I have to love'.

As a verb, *amare* is an appropriate competitor of *habere*, itself a verb. A competition can and did arise, and as discussed in section 4, *habere* eventually lost the competition so often that it gave rise to a grammatical, inherently secondary and ancillary, variant.

6. The phylogenetic perspective

We have tried to show that the understanding we have proposed of grammatical status captures the type of expressions that are generally recognized as core cases of grammatical elements: auxiliaries, clitics, and affixes, plus the grammatical patterns that arise from syntacticization rather than de-lexicalization (syntactic roles and constructions). We now want to suggest that this account has the additional merit of linking up with a theory of why grammatical structure is an evolutionarily significant feature of human languages as opposed to all other forms of communication.

As frequently pointed out, the classic cline that begins with a lexical expression and moves 'downwards' is also the path towards annihilation; and the association between grammaticalization and gradual attrition seems on the face of it to run counter to a claim that grammatical aspects of language are terribly important. This is where the conception that we propose may offer a crucial link: it is not the expression in itself that is terribly important, but the fact that it becomes attached to a 'host' expression, whose functional potential is thereby strengthened, that is the functional key to understanding grammaticalization of lexical expressions. By assuming secondary status, the grammatical expression sacrifices itself for the greater good of the whole construction, anthropomorphically speaking.

This story makes explicit the inherent link between grammaticalization and complexification (cf. Dahl 2004; Heine and Kuteva 2007: 24, assumption 10d), and thereby constitutes a type of change that can naturally be associated both with the step from pre-grammatical to grammatical language and with diachronic change that brings about new structural relations. More specifically, the theory we have proposed goes with a scenario that is closely analogous to a familiar aspect of the language acquisition process, i.e. the ontogenetic step into grammatically structured language. The scenario involves two canonical phases.

The first step involves the transition from a holophrastic code, where each simplex expression constitutes a whole utterance, to the multi-word stage. At the one-word, holophrastic stage a speaker can invoke meanings in isolation from each other, such as *daddy* and *bed*. What is meant on a particular occasion by a child saying *daddy* is not exhausted by the adult conventional meaning, of course, but there is no internal structure in the linguistic expression to cue the hearer's interpretation. This changes with the rise of combinations of the 'pivot-grammar' type, (cf. Braine 1963). An example is *daddy bed* (cf. Karmiloff and Karmiloff-Smith 2001: 100); although one should still be careful not to ascribe adult grammar to such combinations (cf. Tomasello 2003), it constitutes a step into grammar if the combination means something more than the sum of its parts (however vague and general the extra element may be). We may suppose that 'Daddy' is the topic/subject of the utterance, and 'bed' expresses the place he is at or should move to, for instance. This is the difference in relation to complex but unstructured sequences produced by chimpanzees (such as *Drink eat me Nim*; cf. Pinker 1994: 339 on the 'Nim Chimpsky' debate).

A systematicity in the use and understanding of sequences like *daddy bed*, however embryonic, such that *daddy* is a 'subject/topic', and bed has a 'comment/predicate' status, means that there is now something extra provided by the linguistic utterance, namely a relation between the two meanings. This extra element, of course, cannot be discursively primary, but it is inherently a secondary companion to other expressions—hence it qualifies as grammatical by our definition. Only when this first step has occurred does the possibility arise of actual lexical expressions getting secondary status in relation to other lexical expressions (the standard grammaticalization path). As argued above, there has to be a syntagmatic relation between two expressions which makes them compete for discourse prominence. Such competition cannot arise at the stage where all utterances are holophrastic. The patterns established by Heine and Kuteva (2007) strongly suggest that the layer where we find nouns and verbs is the basic layer of the evolutionary process, and that would fit naturally into the scenario described above.

7. Conclusion

The theory we have outlined above is usage-based and functional. It assumes that structure arises out of regularities in usage, selected and systematized through invisible-hand type feedback mechanisms: what works is what gets entrenched. However, it has sometimes been understood as an inherently structural (rather than functional) approach to grammaticalization, because it attaches so much importance to the formation of a combination (and a dependency relation) between a secondary, 'assisting' element and a 'host' element as the defining feature of what counts a grammaticalization. From our point of view, this constitutes the bare minimum of structure that must be present in order to talk meaningfully of grammar and grammaticalization at all. A wholly functional definition would only be possible if you could define grammar in purely functional terms ('grammar without structure'), i.e. naïve functionalism.

Non-naïve functionalists, in our view, thus have to provide an account of what they take to be the structural characteristics that functional elements have to take on in order to fall within the purview of grammaticalization. The difference between the proposal we have argued for and most other accounts is that they tend to focus on properties that arise at the later and more sophisticated stages (such as paradigms of bleached, phonetically reduced, closed-class elements), while we have tried to provide a theory that focuses on the most basic step in the process.[8]

[8] What we have outlined is therefore only part of a full theory, which must include the more advanced and complex stages of the process. Nørgård-Sørensen, Heltoft and Schøsler (2011) demonstrate how an account based on the same understanding of function and structure accounts for the role of paradigm formation in grammaticalization.

CHAPTER 6

USAGE-BASED THEORY AND GRAMMATICALIZATION

JOAN L. BYBEE

1. Introduction

This chapter treats grammaticalization in the context of usage-based grammar. Setting the topic in this way, however, does not accurately reflect the relationship between the phenomenon and the theory. It is not so much that usage-based theory offers a particular perspective on grammaticalization, but more that our understanding of usage effects on grammar has been greatly informed by research on grammaticalization. In other words, research on grammaticalization more than any other phenomenon has led researchers to a usage-based approach to grammar.

The basic tenet of usage-based theory is that language structure is created as language is used (Barlow and Kemmer 2000; Bybee and Beckner 2009; Bybee 2010). The mechanisms that create grammar, which will be discussed below, are all in operation in language use. The use of the same sounds, words, and patterns over thousands of usage-events has an impact on the cognitive storage and processing of linguistic experience that gives language its structure. As a result, then, linguistic structure is emergent from language use (Lindblom, MacNeilage, and Studdert-Kennedy 1984; Hopper 1987). Some of the sources of data and factors that are considered in usage-based theory that are often neglected in more structural approaches are the effects of frequency of use, the patterning of linguistic structures within the discourse context, and the pragmatic inferences that accompany language used in interaction. Because language change and, in particular, grammaticalization, is traced back to small changes that take place in actual usage-events, the theory provides a natural account of the gradualness of change. This chapter surveys how usage effects propel grammaticalization on the phonetic, semantic, and syntactic dimensions, focusing on structural changes. By understanding how structure, such as constituent structure, emerges from cognitive representation, we are able to demonstrate that seemingly discrete grammatical features can change gradually in grammaticalization.

The mechanisms to be treated in this chapter are chunking of contiguous units, phonetic reduction due to neuromotor automatization, semantic generalization, pragmatic inferencing, and growing autonomy with its loss of compositionality and analysability. It will be shown that the loss of analysability is the mechanism behind decategorialization and reduction in constituent structure. In connection with this proposal, it is argued that reanalysis in grammaticalization is unidirectional, and results in a loss of constituent structure.

2. Chunking and phonetic reduction

Speaking is at least in part a neuromotor activity. As a consequence, repetition or practice leads to increases in fluency. Sequences of units or word strings that are often produced together, such as *going to*, *have to*, *want to*, *in spite of*, *in back of* become units or chunks in their own right. They are stored and processed together (Boyland 1996; Ellis 1996). Another consequence of speech as a neuromotor activity is that repeated sequences—either within a word or across words—become more efficient, and the individual articulatory gestures reduce in magnitude and also increase their degree of temporal overlap (Browman and Goldstein 1992; Mowrey and Pagliuca 1995). As a result, frequent phrases, including those that are grammaticalizing, undergo phonetic reduction, as seen in such phrases as *gonna*, *wanna*, and *hafta* (Krug 2000). The cases just cited are rather salient cases in which alternate spellings have arisen, but there is also reduction in other cases, such as in the pronunciation of the modal *can* in English, which is often reduced to a velar with a syllabic nasal (Bybee 2003).

The evidence that chunking is the result of co-occurrence and that phonetic reduction is more extreme under high frequency is that both processes occur independently of grammaticalization. Chunks can be formed from items that are not semantically or grammatically related, as when prepositions fuse with determiners: for example, Spanish *a* 'to' + *el* 'the, masc. sg.' becomes *al* (similar examples are found in German and French). These function words frequently occur together in the same order, and this is what leads to their fusion. Other examples are the contraction of the English auxiliary elements with the subject, as in *I'm*, *I'll*, and *I've* and the contraction of *not* with the preceding auxiliary. Such sequences can be shown to be of very high frequency, and the higher the frequency the greater likelihood of reduction (Krug 1998; 2000; Bybee 2002). Thus frequency of use is a major factor in phonetic reduction in grammaticalization. (For proposals about how this reduction is modeled in a usage-based framework, see Bybee 2000; Pierrehumbert 2001.)

3. Loss of compositionality and analysability leading to semantic/pragmatic change

Once word sequences such as *be going to* or *in spite of* have become frequent enough to be accessed from cognitive storage and produced as units, they begin to become autonomous from the words or morphemes that compose them. Both chunking and increase in autonomy are gradual processes, and the formation of a chunk (a storage and accessing unit) does not necessarily mean that speakers are no longer aware of the component parts and their meanings. That is, a sequence of words can become automated as a chunk through usage while a transparent relationship with the words in other contexts is maintained. Thus transparent prefabricated expressions or collocations that are not highly frequent, such as *it is interesting to note*, *bright daylight*, or *several times*, constitute chunks while still maintaining strong connections to component words. Over time, however, increases in frequency strengthen the sequential relations within the chunk while weakening the relations of component members to cognates elsewhere (Hay 2001; Beckner and Bybee 2009; Bybee 2010).

The more holistic processing of a chunk, then, leads to the assignment of pragmatic function and meaning to the whole unit, downgrading the contribution of meaning from the components. For example, a phrase such as *in spite of* has a meaning as a whole expression, of 'overcoming obstacles' (1) or 'concessive or counter expectation' (2) (and sometimes both), which cannot be assembled by accessing the meaning of its parts.

(1) Michelle and I have a different kind of a marriage, for today, like we always do, *in spite of* the obstacles, regardless of the circumstances, we move forward. (COCA 2008)

(2) And that's pretty pervasive in the United States, *in spite of* what you hear. (COCA 2008)

The original meaning of *spite* 'defiance, contempt' is not appropriate to the contexts of its modern use within the phrase. Originally, the object of *in spite of* was a person, such as an enemy, but later the meaning generalized to obstacles of various sorts—people, laws, cultural conventions, physical obstacles. Semantic generalization leads to extension to new contexts of use and further bleaching of the original meanings. With so much of the original meaning depleted, the expression is open to reinterpretation in context. An inference that is often available is that given an obstacle, one would not expect the statement to be true (Hoffman 2005; Beckner and Bybee 2009). Consider this example where both meanings are available:

(3) Some would say he's done very well *in spite of* being black. (COCA 2008)

That is 'being black' is both an obstacle and a counter-indication. As pointed out by Traugott in various publications (Traugott 1989; Traugott and Dasher 2002) sentences such as (3) with the obstacle meaning also convey by inference the counter-expectation meaning. If such inferences are frequently made, they become part of the meaning of the phrase, allowing sentences such as (2) which have only the counter-expectation meaning. Note again that frequency or repetition is important to this process of meaning change, not because it causes it, but because only by repetition can the change be implemented.

4. Gradual constituent structure and category change

In terms of grammatical change, a number of researchers have defined grammaticalization as 'reanalysis'—a change in constituent organization or category membership. A major paradox that has arisen in studies of grammaticalization is the apparent gradualness of change in the face of before-and-after comparisons that show major changes in grammatical structure. Since structural categories and constituents are assumed in most theories to be discrete, it is difficult to explain how they could change gradually. However, if we acknowledge the robust facts that languages are always changing and that grammaticalization is gradual, we must admit that even synchronic categories are not discrete (Heine 1993; Haspelmath 1998). Categories are not discretely distinct from one another; for instance, auxiliaries are not always separable from verbs, and items within categories can have different features—one verb might become an auxiliary earlier than another.

Change in category membership is referred to by Hopper (1991) as 'decategorialization' because it is typically the case in grammaticalization that nouns and verbs are the lexical items that change their category within constructions and move into or create new, more grammaticalized categories. For example, when the noun *spite* loses its noun features, it becomes part of a complex preposition. A noun within a complex preposition in English tends to lose the ability to be pluralized, to be modified with an adjective, to take a range of determiners, and to occur freely with other prepositions. Another way of thinking about this is to say that as the phrase *in spite of* becomes more autonomous from its component parts, it loses its association with them, or it loses analysability (Langacker 1987). Earlier when the phrase *in spite of* was used it would activate other instances of the three component words. However, as a chunk such as this is used more, the activation of the independent noun *spite* becomes weaker until a point is reached in which the new chunk *in spite of* is completely autonomous from *spite*. At this point, there would be no reason for *spite* to maintain any of its noun properties.

With *spite* having lost its noun properties, then, the constituent structure of the phrase has also changed. *Spite* would no longer be the object of the preposition *in* nor the head of the phrase that *of* + NP modifies. Beckner and Bybee (2009) and Bybee (2010) argue that loss of analysability is the same as loss of constituent structure. That is, in a usage-based grammar, constituent structure is the result of chunking (Bybee 2002) and constituent structure internal to a chunk is maintained by the cognitive association of the words or morphemes in a chunk to other instances in cognitive storage of the same words or morphemes. Since these associations can be weaker or stronger, depending upon the frequency of use of the chunk, contexts of use and meaning, constituent structure can change gradually.

Various syntactic tests for decategorialization or collapsing of constituent structure can be applied. Besides the tests for the categoriality of a noun in a complex preposition mentioned above, there are tests for degree of unit-hood of the chunk (Bybee and Torres Cacoullos 2009; Torres Cacoullos and Walker, Chapter 18 below). Some of these overlap with categoriality tests. For example, the adjacency measure of Bybee and Torres Cacoullos (2009) and Torres Cacoullos and Walker (Chapter 18) takes into account the ability of the elements in the chunk to be separated by intervening words. In their examples, the ability of a subject to follow *estar* 'to be (located)' in the Spanish Progressive construction is taken to indicate a lower degree of unithood for *estar* + participle. It could also be taken to indicate the continued categoriality of *estar* as a verb whose subject can follow it.

Another series of tests involve coordination. Torres Cacoullos and colleagues show in the papers cited above that the ability of *estar* in the Spanish Progressive construction to occur with conjoined participles declines gradually from the 13th to the 19th centuries. Beckner and Bybee (2009) look for evidence of coordination with *in spite of* in the 360 million-word Corpus of Contemporary American English (COCA). One type of conjoining would give evidence for internal structure for *in spite of*: if this phrase could share its *of* with another such phrase, that would show that the phrases are still analysable. A search of the corpus turned up seven such examples, all from written sources.

(4) Last July after she beat out a field of 67 applicants in a nationwide search, President Anderson feels that she was chosen for the job, not *because* or *in spite of* the fact that she is Black and a woman, but simply because she was the most qualified applicant. (1992)

However, the same corpus yielded thirty-five cases in which *of* is repeated, arguing for the lack of analysability of this phrase.

(5) the dogma of self-expression says that the gifted child can flower *in the absence of* or *in spite of* art education. (1995)

Also we find that multiple instances of *in spite of* are frequently conjoined by repetition of the whole phrase. (6) is one characteristic example:

(6) *In spite of* motorbikes, *in spite of* karaoke music, *in spite of* the stink of gasoline fumes that seeps into each kitchen. (2005)

In the COCA, there are thirty-eight examples of this type, with no counterexamples in which only subparts of *in spite of* are conjoined. In addition, the fact that *in spite of* can be conjoined with simple prepositions as in (7) suggests that it is functioning as a unit.

(7) Commitment is healthiest when it is not *without* doubt, but *in spite of* doubt. (1991)

The conjoining of *in spite of* with a simple preposition indicates that another type of analysability is coming into play—the association of the phrase *in spite of* with the preposition construction. Having become autonomous from the noun *spite*, the phrase it occurs in cannot be analysed as two prepositional phrases; now it is analysed as one.

The important point about the corpus data, however, is that they show variation: a few examples show the analysability or separability of *spite* from *of*, while the majority of examples show that *in spite of* is a single unit, functioning as a preposition. Thus the change in constituent structure, which is a result of the loss of analysability, is gradual and still ongoing in contemporary English.

Finally, another contribution to the gradual changes that result in reanalysis is the fact that different collocations involving a grammaticalizing construction can change at different rates. It is well known that constructions with specific items in them change at different rates for different items. For example, the English modal auxiliaries grammaticalized at different times, with *shall* and *may* leading *will* and *can* (Plank 1984) and English complex prepositions such as *in spite of*, *in back of*, *in front of* have different properties (Hoffman 2005). More recently, Bybee and Torres Cacoullos (2009) argue that certain frequent prefabs (conventionalized word sequences) formed on grammaticalizing constructions lose their analysability earlier than less frequent uses. For instance, in Middle English *can* was still used to express mental ability or knowledge. With a verb such as *seye/sayn* 'to say', *can* would mean having the knowledge to say. However, a collocation frequently used by Chaucer in the *Canterbury Tales*, the sentence *I kan sey yow namoore*, has *can* expressing root possibility. This sentence is used as a rhetorical device to end a description, not because the narrator has exhausted his/her knowledge, but because s/he does not want to hold up the tale with further description.

5. Is reanalysis in grammaticalization unidirectional?

Heine and Reh (1984) and Haspelmath (1998) have made the point that reanalysis is not unidirectional, while grammaticalization is. A simple example of a reanalysis that goes in both directions is the change of the assignment of the /n/ in English *a naperon* to *an apron* vs. *an ekename* to *a nickname*. However, when change in constituent structure occurs in grammaticalization, it appears to always reduce the number of constituents in the grammaticalizing construction. This follows from the principles just discussed: the more a sequence is used as a unit the more its internal structure is reduced, or as Hawkins (2004) puts it: frequency reduces complexity. The reduction in constituent structure combined with the oft-noted directionality in category change, as when the more lexical nouns and verbs become the more grammatical prepositions, auxiliaries, etc., provides the means of viewing reanalysis within grammaticalization as unidirectional.

In the example of *in spite of* discussed above, as *spite* loses its status as a noun, the whole sequence becomes a preposition. Its internal structure will eventually be lost (cf. the prepositions *behind* and *beyond* which developed in an analogous way)—a reduction of constituent structure. When a lexical verb becomes an auxiliary within a construction in which another lexical verb served as the complement to the finite verb, the complement verb becomes the main verb of the clause. The change is from a structure with two verb phrases to a single verb phrase containing an auxiliary and a lexical verb. This is a reduction in the number and status of the constituents. When a verb becomes a preposition, as for example *during* has, a verb phrase becomes a prepositional phrase; there may be the same number of constituents, but the change is from a more lexical constituent to a more grammatical one.

Heine and Reh (1984) and Heine, Claudi, and Hünnemeyer (1991) see reanalysis in grammaticalization as failing the unidirectionality test, based on examples in which it is argued that a main clause becomes a subordinate clause in comparison to examples in which a subordinate clause becomes a main clause. I would argue in contrast that if we consider the entire construction that has grammaticalized, both types of cases result in a reduction of constituent structure. Consider an example of the first type, which occurs in the well-known development of complementizers. Heine et al. (1991: 180) give the example of the Faroese demonstrative *tadh* which can be used as in (8) as the object of the main verb or as in (9) introducing a subordinate clause.

(8)	eg	sigi	tadh:	hann	kemur
	I	say	that:	he	comes

(9)	eg	sigi	at	hann	kemur
	I	say	that	he	comes

Hopper and Traugott (2003) provide evidence that English *that* became a complementizer in a comparable way, leading to the change of a main clause to a subordinate clause. Examples such as (8) have two independent main clauses; in (9) that structure is reduced such that the second clause functions as the object complement to the first verb. In these cases, it is not so much that a main clause becomes a subordinate clause as that two main clauses reduce to a main clause cum subordinate clause.

The second type of example—in which a subordinate clause becomes a main clause in Heine et al.'s analysis—can perhaps more realistically be seen as cases in which a main clause reduces to a modifier of the erstwhile subordinate clause. This can also be analysed as a reduction in constituent structure, as the 'before' state has two clauses while the 'after' state has one. That is, if one takes into account the entire construction, the change is a reduction. Heine et al.'s example (1991: 217f., also cited in Heine and Reh 1984) from Teso (Eastern Nilotic) involves negation as in (10):

(10)	mam	petero	e-koto	ekiŋok
	not	Peter	3SG-want	dog
	'Peter does not want a dog'			

Heine et al. (1991) point out that this sentence is derived from **e-mam petero e-koto ekiŋok* 'It is not Peter who wants a dog' in which the main clause is *e-mam petero* where *mam* means 'not to be'. Teso is usually VSO, but (10) is SVO because *mam* was originally a verb which was followed by the subject. As *mam* is now the negative marker and no longer inflected for 3SG, the construction has only one clause. Another example of a similar change occurs in English when earlier main clause verbs such as *I think* and *I guess* become epistemic markers modifying a main clause (Thompson and Mulac 1991).

Thus it appears that the fact that some main clauses can become subordinate and some subordinate clauses become main clauses does not provide an argument against the unidirectionality of reanalysis when it accompanies grammaticalization. Rather, if we take into account the whole construction that is undergoing change and argue that the change in grammaticalization is the loss of constituent structure, then we can see the syntactic changes in grammaticalization as reductions in parallel with the phonetic and semantic reduction that are characteristic of grammaticalization (Bybee, Perkins, and Pagliuca 1994).

6. Unidirectionality in Grammaticalization

There has been much discussion of whether or not grammaticalization is unidirectional, with the conclusion being that, with a few relatively well-defined exceptions, it is. In contrast, there has not been a consensus on why grammaticalization is unidirectional. The unidirectionality occurs at all levels: phonetic change in grammaticalization is reductive, as mentioned above; semantic change follows certain well-defined paths from lexical to grammatical, losing features of meaning or adding certain inferences; and, as I argued above, morphosyntactic change follows a course of decategorialization, loss of analysability, and gain in autonomy, leading to a reduction in constituent structure.

In the preceding I have shown how frequency of use figures in the operation of all of the mechanisms of change. Thus as long as frequency is on the rise, changes will move in a consistent direction. In Bybee (2008: 348), I explain it as follows:

> The inherent directionality of grammaticization is directly related to the mechanisms of change that propel the process and these mechanisms are all a part of language use. Changes related to increases in frequency all move in one direction and even decreases in frequency do not condition reversals: there is no process of de-automatization or de-habituation, subtraction of pragmatic inferences, etc. Once phonetic form and semantic properties are lost, there is no way to retrieve them. Thus grammaticization is unidirectional.

When a grammaticalizing construction ceases to rise in frequency, various things happen, but none of them is the precise reverse of the process. For example, when *shall* decreased in frequency due to the rise of *will* and *be going to* as indicators of future in American English, it was for a time frozen in certain phrases, particularly questions, *shall we go?* or parentheticals, *shall we say*, and eventually used very little in the speech of the young generation, but there are no mechanisms that would cause it to retrace its path of change. As Greenberg (1991) points out, old affixes, which have been bleached of meaning and lost their analysability, become part of lexical items. Again, there are no mechanisms of change that would cause them to run backwards on a grammaticalization path.

Thus the explanation for unidirectionality can be found in the mechanisms of change. As I emphasized above, these mechanisms of change are operative in language use and applied repeatedly to frequent items and constructions.

7. Language as a complex adaptive system

The emphasis on mechanisms of change has several consequences. First, the mechanisms provide the explanation for the way grammatical structures and meanings come into existence and therefore provide an explanation for why languages have grammar and why grammar takes the shape it does. Second, since the mechanisms of change have their basis in the processing mechanisms that are operating as language is used, they provide a level at which universals may be formulated: the mechanisms are common to all languages and they are operating whenever people are speaking the world over. Third, the view of linguistic structure as emergent from the repetitive operation of a few mechanisms (all of them domain-general: see Bybee 2009; 2010) allows us to view language as a complex adaptive system (Larsen-Freeman 1997). In this view, linguistic structure is not universal, nor is it given in advance in any way. Rather, the mechanisms of change are universal and their application creates common paths of change (grammaticalization paths are one example). As I have argued here, the mechanisms of change can operate independently of one another; thus grammaticalization itself is an emergent phenomenon—only when increases in frequency spur all the mechanisms to work together do we recognize an instance of grammaticalization. In this view, too, language is dynamic and ever-changing; each time period and each language is unique, but each one shares many properties with other languages because it has been created by the same forces operating in similar contexts.

CHAPTER 7

GRAMMATICALIZATION AND COGNITIVE GRAMMAR

RONALD W. LANGACKER

COGNITIVE GRAMMAR (CG) has a natural affinity with grammaticalization owing to some basic features of the framework (Langacker 1987; 1991; 2008a). In line with its functional orientation, factors like processing, discourse, communication, and social interaction are regarded as foundational rather than subsidiary (Langacker 1999a). And since a language is continually adapted through usage, its structure at any moment being the product of ongoing change, there is no sharp distinction between synchrony and diachrony. The usage-based perspective of CG (Langacker 2000; 2008a: ch. 8) is further evident in its recognition of frequency effects (Bybee and Hopper 2001), the coexistence of multiple variants (Heine 1992), and the importance—if not the primacy—of specific forms (in addition to general patterns). As a kind of construction grammar, CG maintains that lexicon and grammar form a gradation, and that lexical items cannot be clearly separated from the structural frames they occur in (Langacker 2005a; 2009b). It is thus anticipated that grammaticalization should affect lexical items in the context of particular constructions. Moreover, its semantic characterization is most straightforward given the CG view that all grammatical elements are meaningful.

An in-depth account of grammaticalization requires explicit characterizations of the meanings and constructions involved at every stage. CG's identification of meaning with conceptualization does not exclude the interactive, communicative, and discourse import of linguistic elements: after all, language is used and meanings are negotiated by cognizing individuals engaged in assessing the knowledge, intentions, and mental state of their interlocutors. Nor does recognizing the variability and functional shaping of grammar excuse us from actually describing the specific forms it assumes, including the meanings of grammatical elements. Grammatical structure does exist. And while it is not autonomous, monolithic, static, universal, or innate, neither is it epiphenomenal: it emerges from usage and serves as the basis for subsequent usage (Langacker 1981; 2010; cf. Hopper 1998).

A speaker's linguistic ability resides in established patterns of processing activity, called **units**, emerging from interactive language use by the reinforcement of recurring features. CG posits only three broad types of units: **semantic** (pertaining to any aspect of conception), **phonological** (any aspect of expression), and **symbolic** (comprising links between the other two). Units differ greatly in terms of granularity (specific vs. schematic) and complexity (the incorporation of smaller units). Lexicon and grammar consist in **symbolic assemblies**, where **component** symbolic structures are linked by correspondences indicating their semantic and phonological integration ('unification') to form **composite** symbolic structures. A lexical assembly constitutes a specific, fixed expression. Being wholly or partially schematic, a grammatical assembly (construction) represents a pattern invoked in forming new expressions.

Basic to conceptual semantics is the asymmetry between the **subject** and the **object of conception**. The subject engages in conception, whereas the object comprises its content. In its role as such, the subject remains implicit—a conceptualizing agent that is not itself conceived. Maximally opposed to the subject in this respect is the entity made salient as the focus of attention. The entity focused by an expression (the one it refers to) is called its **profile**. Centred on the profile, the situation described subsumes a range of content extending to the periphery of awareness. Any facet of our mental universe can fall within this **objective scene**, including the conceptualizer, who then has a dual role as both subject and object of conception. But even when external to the scene, the subject shapes its apprehension by imposing a particular **construal**—e.g. by selecting the content, viewing it at a certain level of specificity, and deciding what to profile.

A central claim of CG, indicated in Table 7.1, is that fundamental grammatical notions have both schematic characterizations, involving **basic mental capacities**, and prototypes, involving experientially grounded **conceptual archetypes** (Langacker 2008a). The capacities make structured experience possible and are first manifested in archetypal conceptions. For instance, the capacity for apprehending relationships and tracking them through time is inherent in the verbal archetypes of an object moving through space or an agent affecting a patient. Likewise, grouping and reification are inherent in the conception of an object, the prototype for nouns. An object exemplifies 'reification' by moving as a unit with respect to its surroundings. And while the grouping inherent in object conceptions

Table 7.1.

Grammatical notions	Conceptual archetypes (prototypes)	Basic mental capacities (schematic characterizations)
noun	(inanimate) object, person, substance	grouping, reification (treating a group as a single entity for some purpose)
verb	person acting on object, object moving through space	apprehending a relationship, tracking a relationship through time
subject	agent, mover	focusing a relational participant
possessive	physical control, access	reference point ability (invoking one entity to mentally access another)

lies below the threshold of awareness, its role is evident with less typical nouns like *flock*, *orchestra*, and *constellation*.

Conceptual archetypes are instantiated in early vocabulary and function as category prototypes. As lexical learning proceeds, reflecting conceptual development and more varied experience, the capacities inherent in the archetypes apply to more and more diverse content. The end result is the absence of any specific content shared by all category members, leaving only the basic capacities as a general characterization. Accordingly, CG proposes schematic definitions based on these mental operations: a noun profiles a **thing**, i.e. any product of grouping and reification; a verb profiles a **process**, i.e. a relationship tracked in its evolution through time.

As a general matter, the gradation from 'lexical' to 'grammatical' elements reflects this conceptual progression from specific content to mental operations applicable to any content. For example, auxiliary *do* is usually considered a meaningless grammatical marker because it lacks specific content. It is however meaningful: it profiles a maximally schematic process (Langacker 1987: 354–5; 2005b; 2009a: ch. 8). That is, its conceptual import resides in the basic capacities characteristic of verbs as a class (apprehending a relationship and tracking it through time). We might also compare the lexical meaning of *thing* with its grammatical meaning as part of the indefinite pronoun *something*. In (1a), *thing* designates an inanimate physical object. But in its pronominal use, *thing* can refer to anything labeled by a noun: concrete or abstract; count, mass, or even plural, as in (1b). (The apparent exception of *something* not being used for people or places is simply a matter of its being preempted by the more specific *someone* and *someplace*.) The pronoun *thing* is thus schematic for the class of nouns, designating any product of grouping and reification.

(1) a. *I found this* ***thing*** *in the attic.*
b. *Complaints are some****thing*** *we can do without.*

The relation between these senses illustrates some common features of grammaticalization. The lexical source represents a conceptual archetype. From this, the grammatical meaning develops by **schematization** or a general loss of content. It is also a case of **subjectification**, defined in CG as the operation of basic mental capacities independently of the domain or conceptual content in which they are initially manifested (Langacker 2008a; for comparison with how the term is used by Traugott (e.g. 1989), see Langacker 2006). An example not involving grammaticalization is 'fictive motion', for example *A hedge runs along the property line* (Talmy 1996; Matlock 2001; Langacker 2005c). Here, the spatial scanning inherent in conceptualizing motion occurs independently of change through time (hence the 'motion' inheres in the subject rather than the object of conception). In the case of *thing*, the archetypal conception reflects the application of basic capacities—grouping, reification, and bounding—in the realm of space and physical substance. But in its pronominal use, the capacities of grouping and reification apply in any realm.

Despite the absence of a definite boundary, lexicon and grammar serve different primary functions. Lexical items have a descriptive function: their conceptual content serves to specify some portion of the objective situation. The role of grammar is to abet and supplement their description. Grammatical constructions sanction and symbolize the integration of lexical content to form more complex conceptions. Some grammatical elements (e.g. conjunctions, case markers) indicate how these conceptual 'chunks' fit together. Others (aspect, voice) impose a particular perspective for viewing them. Still others pertain to factors external to the objective scene, such as the speaker–hearer interaction (illocutionary force) and how described entities relate to the speech event and the ongoing discourse (deixis, information structure). This supplementary function corresponds to what Boye and Harder (2009; see also Harder and Boye, Chapter 5 above) identify as the basic feature distinguishing grammar from lexicon, namely the 'coding of secondary information status'.

Their secondary status translates into a tendency for grammatical elements to be allocated fewer processing resources, resulting in their conceptual and phonological **compression.** Consider (2a), where small caps represent unreduced stress and boldface indicates profiling. As is typically the case, only the lexemes bear stress. Grammatical markers are either affixal or unaccented and given to cliticization.

(2) a. [*The* PRESIDENT ***ANNOUNCED***] / [*that* SPENDING *will* ***INCREASE.***]
b. [*I think* SPENDING *will* ***INCREASE.***]
c. [SPENDING *will* ***INCREASE***, *they say.*]

Moreover, in (2a), the matrix and complement clauses are fully manifested. They constitute what Chafe (1994) calls 'intonation units', appearing in separate windows of attention (marked by brackets) set off by a slight hesitation (/). But in

(2b, c) a multi-clause construction appears in a single window of attention. It all fits because the matrix clause is reduced to secondary status. Semantically, the thinking or saying is no longer part of the situation described, but rather an assessment relating it to speaker knowledge (Diessel and Tomasello 2001; Thompson 2002; Verhagen 2005). It thus remains unprofiled, an expression's profile being the focus of attention within the objective scene (Langacker 2009a: ch. 11). Signaling this conceptual compression, in the guise of diminished attention and salience, is a phonological compression whereby *I think* or *they say* is manifested in a shorter time span, with less amplitude, and at a lower pitch level. This reduction in form, meaning, and status constitutes incipient grammaticalization. The further evolution of *I think* or *they say* into a simple grammatical marker (a modal or an evidential) is not inconceivable.

Over its long trajectory, grammaticalization can be viewed as a multi-faceted reductive process whose facets are intertwined and mutually reinforcing. Reducing the allocation of time, attention, and bandwidth brings about not just the compressed manifestation of semantic and phonological content but its actual erosion. Phonologically, it leads to an overall reduction in the number, complexity, and distinctiveness of words, syllables, and segments (e.g. *going to* > *gonna* > *gn*). There can be an equally drastic loss of semantic content (e.g. the motion component of *gonna*). These developments result in component morphemes no longer being recognized, which in turn entails a grammatical reorganization. The parallel reduction of semantic and phonological content has both iconic and economic motivation (Haiman 1983): not only is less meaning analogous to less form, but since fewer notions need to be distinguished, phonological cues can be more subtle. We can also note a cycle of reinforcement involving frequency effects: less distinctive semantic content results in broader applicability, which leads to greater frequency, encouraging further phonetic reduction, hence a further erosion of meaning, which reinforces secondary status.

This basically reductive view is consistent with Traugott's insight that early stages of grammaticalization are characterized by semantic enrichment (Traugott 1988). Schematization is driven by the extension of source elements to wider ranges of uses, thereby reinforcing the shared features invoked as its basis. Early stages of extension often involve metonymy or metaphor. But through the gradual loss of analysability affecting complex expressions (Langacker 2009b), the original motivation fades away, as one facet of the reductive process.

Consider the grammaticalization path whereby a posture verb—SIT, STAND, or LIE—evolves into a BE-type predicate indicating the continuation through time of the relationship specified by its complement, e.g. in a locative, progressive, or durative construction (Newman 2002). It is natural for these archetypal human postures to be projected metaphorically onto objects, as shown for SIT in Fig. 7.1. SIT profiles a relationship, stable through time, in which a person both occupies some location and exhibits a relatively compact arrangement of limbs and torso. Its

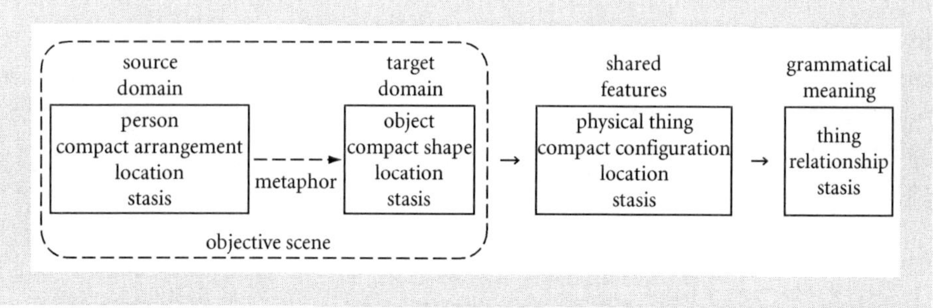

Fig. 7.1.

metaphoric extension to objects hinges on the shared configurational property of being compact (rather than extended). Initially, while this is still a 'live' metaphor, the source is actively invoked as a basis for apprehending the target; their co-activation constitutes the blended conception (Fauconnier and Turner 2002) of an object with human-like properties. At this stage the source and its correspondence to the target are part of the situation described, an imaginative aspect of the objective scene. The subsequent 'fading' of the metaphor is a matter of their gradually receding into the background, until SIT applies directly to objects as such.

By invoking and reinforcing their coarse-grained commonality, the extension from source to target begins the abstractive process. Applied to either people or objects, SIT designates a stable relationship in which a physical thing both occupies some location and exhibits a compact spatial configuration. Further extensions contribute to the emergence of more schematic conceptions. If this runs its course, the end result will be a highly schematic conception specifying only that a thing (of any sort) participates in a static relationship (of any sort). This is in fact the meaning proposed in CG for English *be*: it profiles the continuation through time of a stable relationship. Devoid of specific content, it has a 'grammatical' meaning comprising basic mental capacities (apprehending a relationship, tracking it through time, comparison revealing identity through time). It is thus schematic for the class of stative (or 'imperfective') verbs, combining with its complement to derive a specific imperfective process.

Schematization is just one dimension of the conceptual attenuation characteristic of grammaticalization. Others are evident in the evolution of general possessive predicates, like English *have*, from verbs of physical manipulation, e.g. GRASP (Heine 1997b: 91). There is first a 'diffusion' in the locus of activity (Langacker 1999b: ch. 10). Even when direct physical control is still involved, as in (3a), *have* is imperfective: rather than a specific bounded action of taking or exercising control, it designates a situation construed (in local terms) as being stable and continuous. Diffusion goes one step further in (3b), where the control conveyed by *have* is more social than physical, involving the privilege of access and use rather than any actual instance of it. This shift from actual to potential occurrences represents another dimension of attenuation, as does the transfer to a non-physical domain. Expressions like (3c), where *have* is used for social and experiential relationships, are now quite typical.

(3) a. *OK, I have a hammer. Where's the protruding nail?*
b. *I have an axe, but I seldom use it.*
c. *She has a lot of {children/cats/money/fun}.*
d. *This table has a rough surface.*
e. *The company's decline has analogs in the collapse of other corporations.*

Even these relationships—abstract counterparts of physical access and control—fade from the picture in cases like (3d, e). The table neither experiences the surface nor actively engages it, nor does the company's decline interact with its analogues. Within the objective scene (the situation described), these entities are inert. While they still anchor an experiential path leading to a target (the surface or the analogues), their role in it is wholly passive; they are merely invoked as **reference points** enabling the conceptualizer to locate the target entity. This path of mental access by the subject of conception, who apprehends the objective scene without being part of it, is proposed in CG as the schematic characterization of possessives. Moreover, the capacity for invoking one entity by way of mentally 'reaching' another is inherent in the conception of one entity manipulating, controlling, or experiencing another, as in (3a–c). The use of *have* in (3d, e) thus illustrates subjectification: the original objective content having been eliminated, the mental operations occur independently (Langacker 2009a: ch. 4).

A striking case of subjectification is the common evolution of a GO-type verb into a marker of future tense (Givón 1973). In the case of English *gonna*, it begins with expressions describing purposive spatial movement, e.g. *She's going to gather firewood.* This is shown in Fig. 7.2(a), with the profiled event in bold: the focused participant—the **trajector** (tr) in CG terms—moves through space with the purpose of carrying out some action upon reaching the destination. Since movement consists in occupying spatial positions successively through time, the temporal dimension has a significant role in the objective scene. This is **conceived time** (t), i.e. time as an aspect of the situation described. It has to be distinguished from **processing time** (T), the role of time as the medium of conception. The dashed arrows in Fig. 7.2(a) indicate that the conception of spatial motion requires the conceptualizer (C) to evoke the mover's spatial positions in the order of their temporal manifestation. Through processing time, the conceptualizer tracks the evolution, through conceived time, of the profiled spatial relationship.

Hence the conceptualizer scans mentally along the same spatial path that the mover traverses physically, and also through the span of time (t) over which the movement occurs. This subjective scanning through time, with an onstage event at its endpoint, is all that remains when grammaticalization runs its course and

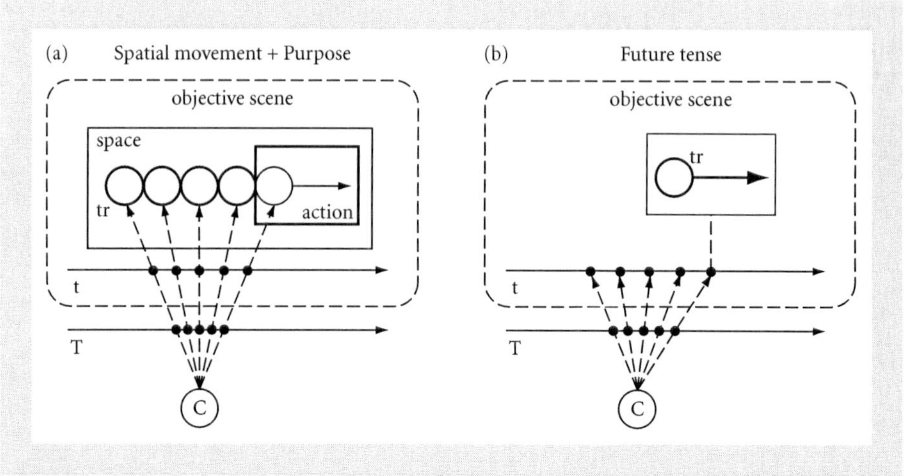

Fig. 7.2.

produces a true future tense marker. It specifies the temporal location of a process relative to a reference time by default identified as the time of speaking. Note that Fig. 7.2(b) is obtained from 7.2(a) just by erasing all reference to space and physical motion (so that only the original purpose is left onstage as the profiled occurrence). It represents subjectification in that the mental operation of scanning through time, inherent in the conception of spatial motion, comes to be applied independently of that content.

However, this change does not come about in a single step, but through a long process of attenuation involving conceptual factors not yet considered. Though well along this path, English *gonna* has not yet developed into a fully grammaticalized tense marker; indeed, it still bears tense itself: *{is/was} gonna*. Needed, then, is a finer-grained description of this developmental path, based on more detailed semantic characterizations of the construction at each stage. In particular, Fig. 7.2(a) omits a crucial feature of the source construction: that the trajector moves through space with the specific **intention** of carrying out the action in question. An aspect of constructional meaning, this mental relationship between mover and projected action is represented in Figure 7.3(a) with a double dashed arrow. Thus the profiled process has both a spatial and a mental component, both tending toward the action's execution. And with this fuller semantic description, the role of metaphor becomes apparent, so that GO > FUTURE is no longer a purely reductive change.

The coexistence of spatial and mental components does not itself make the conception metaphorical, since actual motion is involved. These do however figure in the 'event structure' metaphor (Lakoff 1990), whereby activity leading toward a goal is understood in terms of spatial movement toward a destination. Hence the

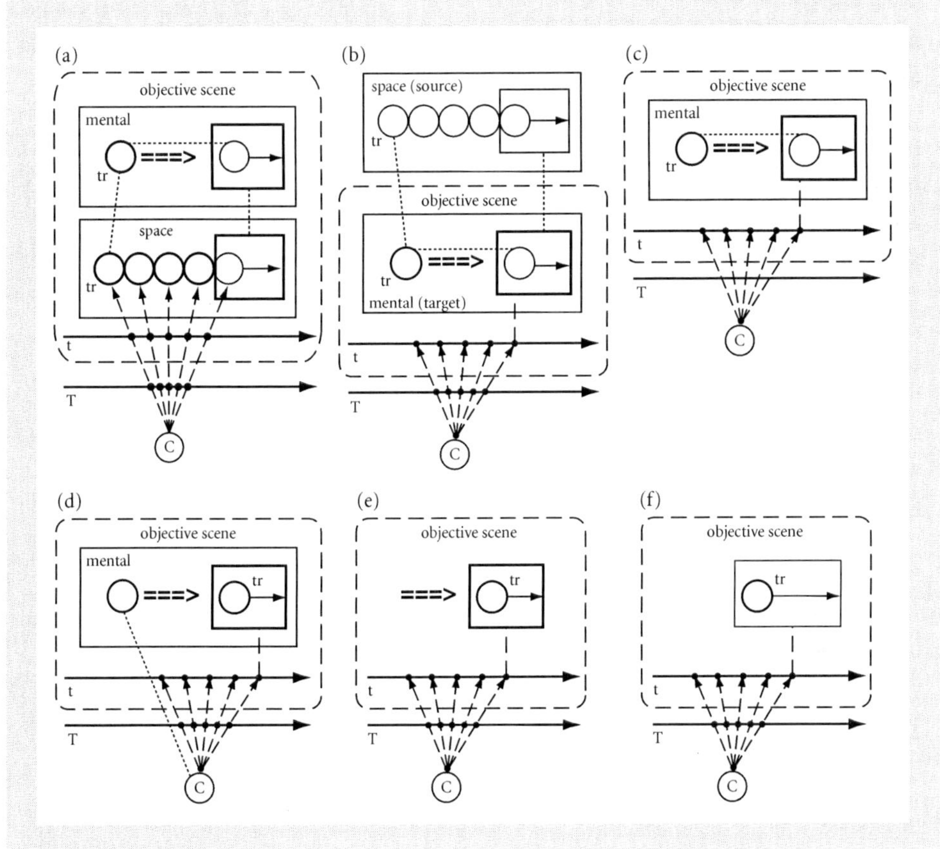

Fig. 7.3.

original construction lends itself to metaphorical construal, such that spatial motion is merely invoked as the source domain for apprehending the mental target. When this is still a 'live' metaphor, both domains are facets of the situation described. But gradually the spatial component fades from the objective scene, becoming part of the interpretive background, as indicated in Fig. 7.3(b). It may eventually disappear altogether, as in Fig. 7.3(c), in which case expressions like *Sean is going to graduate* are purely descriptions of intention. This represents one current use of the English construction.

So far, the trajector—the subject of *be going to*—has the dual role of both intending for the action to occur and being the one who carries out that action. This is shown in Figs 7.3(a)–(c) by the dotted correspondence line equating GO's trajector with the actor. The line's absence in Fig. 7.3(d) represents an important step along this evolutionary path: the trajector need no longer provide the impetus for the action's occurrence; its participation in that event may well be its only role in the overall situation. So interpreted, *Sean is going to graduate* still conveys an intention for Sean to graduate, but an intention on the part of someone else. By default this is the speaker, in the tacit role of offstage conceptualizer, as indicated in Fig. 7.3(d).

This development illustrates diffusion in the locus of activity, specifically in its force-dynamic aspect: the impetus toward the target event's occurrence undergoes diffusion in regard to both its source and its nature. As for its source, the intention shifts from an explicitly mentioned participant to the offstage speaker, who remains implicit; indeed, the speaker may simply be reporting someone else's intent, as in (4a). As for its nature, the impetus is not necessarily an intention. It might just be that some circumstance allows one to project the event's occurrence, as in (4b). Nor is it always possible to pinpoint a specific basis for projection. In that case the source is maximally diffuse, being indistinguishable from the objective situation as a whole, as indicated in Fig. 7.3(e). At the extreme, the notion of force or impetus fades away altogether, so that the projection is purely temporal, as in (4c). The final step—not yet reached by the English *gonna* construction—consists in shifting the profile to the projected event *per se* (it being the only substantial content left in the objective scene). At that stage, shown in Fig. 7.3(f) [=Fig. 7.2(b)], it will be a true future tense construction.

(4) a. *Sean is going to graduate—his mother is determined.*
b. *Sean is going to graduate—he got the loan he needs to finish.*
c. *Sean is going to graduate on Sunday, I hear.*

While individual semantic developments may not be evident through any change in form, they may still have observable grammatical consequences. The shift from (c) to (d) in Fig. 7.3 need not entail any difference in form—the overtly specified participant is still the trajector of *be going to*, and thus the subject of the overall expression. It simply has a diminished role in the objective situation; no longer the source of impetus, its actual participation is confined to the target occurrence. As a consequence, *be going to* exhibits 'transparency': as shown in (5), it allows as its own subject anything which could be the subject of the following verb, including 'dummy' elements like *there*, *it*, and idiom chunks. In the transformational era, this was taken as evidence for the rule of 'subject-to-subject raising'. However, in the CG account (Langacker 1995) it is simply a matter of *be going to* not imposing any significant semantic requirements on its subject (in particular, it need not be capable of intention).

(5) a. ***There** are going to be fireworks after the game.*
b. ***It**'s gonna rain tonight.*
c. ***Umbrage** is going to be taken at those remarks.*

Let me note in passing that English modals have followed a similar path of attenuation and diffusion in the nature and source of the impetus toward an occurrence. Their force-dynamic character has long been argued in cognitive linguistics (Sweetser 1982; Talmy 1988; Langacker 1991: §6.3). In the modern language, the modal force is mostly non-physical, pertaining to either social interaction (for root modals) or mental assessment (for epistemic modals). With respect to prominence, the force is intermediate between the status it has in Figs 7.3(e) and 7.3(f): though crucial to the modals' semantic value, it is no longer profiled and is at best peripheral to the objective scene, residing in either the speaker-hearer interaction or the speaker's epistemic judgment. But in either case the modals are transparent, as seen in (6), since the trajector's only specified role is the one it has within the target occurrence.

(6) a. ***There*** *must be beer at this party!*
b. ***It*** *may rain tonight.*
c. ***Umbrage*** *will certainly be taken at those remarks.*

The transparency of *gonna* and the modals is thus a consequence of particular semantic developments that are evident given reasonably explicit characterizations of the conceptual structures involved. Such interplay between conceptual and grammatical phenomena is of course expected in CG. Two factors are especially relevant for grammaticalization: adjustments in profiling, which determines grammatical category; and degree of conceptual overlap among component elements. Both contribute to the full grammaticalization of tense and modals, producing the arrangement in Fig. 7.3(f). With the loss of other objective content, these profile only the schematic target process. This is identified with the specific process designated by the complement verb, so there is full conceptual overlap in their profiles. And having just one processual profile is pivotal to the composite expressions being reanalysed as comprising a single clause.

As seen in (7), profile shift figures in the ongoing grammaticalization of *a bunch of* and *a lot of* into nominal quantifiers (Langacker 2009a: ch. 3). When *bunch* retains its concrete sense, designating multiple things forming a spatial cluster, it functions as the head within its phrase (as indicated by verb agreement). With the loss of spatial content, it has only the scalar value of designating a substantial quantity. This vaguely specified amount is too abstract and tenuous to be commonly invoked as a nominal referent, hence the profile for the phrase as a whole is shifted to the quantified mass. For *a lot of*, which is further along the grammaticalization path, the shifted version is the only one available, as the concrete sense of *lot* (set of articles for sale) is lost for all intents and purposes.

(7) a. *[A* ***bunch*** *of grapes] was sitting on the counter.*
b. *[A bunch of* ***marbles****] were scattered around on the floor.*
c. *[A lot of* ***marbles****] {*was/were} on the floor.*

Conceptual overlap is crucial for the grammaticalization of GIVE-type verbs into recipient or benefactive markings, as exemplified by Mandarin (Newman 1996). In

(8a), *gěi* is the lexical verb in its clause. By contrast, in (8b, c) it functions like a preposition, marking its single object as either a recipient or a beneficiary. Presumably the latter uses originate in paratactic or serial verb constructions, in which both verbs retain their profile in the composite conception. The deverbalization of GIVE is then a consequence of it no longer being focused at that level, instead being apprehended only in relation to the other process. In the CG account, the sequentiality ('tracking through time') characteristic of a verb requires focusing. So when a process is backgrounded, it undergoes a conceptual compression whereby the profiled relationship is apprehended holistically (in summary fashion) in the manner of nonverbal elements like prepositions (Langacker 2008b). If the processual nature of GIVE is consistently overridden within the composite whole, it may eventually be reanalysed as such an element.

(8)	a.	*Wǒ*	***gěi***	*tā*	*yì-fen*	*lìwù.*	
		I	give	him	one-CL	present	
		'I gave him a present.'					
	b.	*Wǒ*	*sòng-le*	*yì-fen*	*lìwù*	***gěi***	*tā.*
		I	present-ASP	one-CL	present	RECIP	him
		'I presented a present to him.'					
	c.	*Tā*	***gěi***	*wǒ*	*zào-le*	*yì-dōng*	*fángzi.*
		he	BEN	me	build-ASP	one-CL	house
		'He built a house for me.'					

Why, then, does GIVE have secondary status? It is a consequence of extensive conceptual overlap, represented by dashed lines in Fig. 7.4(a). GIVE profiles the event of its trajector inducing (double arrow) a certain situation: that in which its landmark (lm)—the focused participant coded by its object—controls or experiences (dashed arrow) another entity (small box). In expressions like (8b,c), the act of giving is not construed as a separate event, nor even a distinct phase within an overall occurrence, but as a temporally coextensive facet of the event coded by the other verb (Langacker 2003). Note that correspondences equate the trajectors of V and GIVE, as well as the causal components of these actions. In other words, the

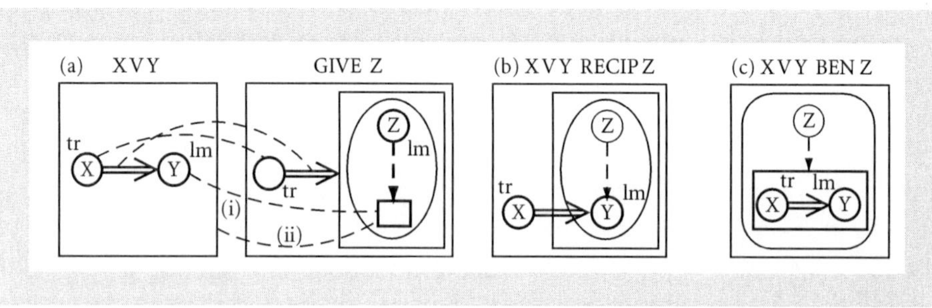

Fig. 7.4.

action described by V **constitutes** the giving. Hence adding GIVE and its object serves only to make the induced situation explicit and identify Z as the controller/experiencer. The difference between a recipient and a beneficiary is a matter of what it is that Z controls or experiences: either the landmark of V, as indicated by correspondence (i); or else the event it designates, with correspondence (ii). The composite meanings are thus as shown in Figs. 7.4(b, c). In the former, where the giving may be literal, Z is a recipient who gains possession of Y. In the latter, where the giving is metaphorical, Z is a beneficiary in the sense that the action (X V Y) occurs in the realm of Z's experience (Fagerli 2001).

At least initially, elements like Mandarin *gěi* retain their verbal character when pressed into service to introduce a recipient or beneficiary: the summary view of the profiled process is not intrinsic, but a function of the conceptual compression induced by being backgrounded to the other verb in the context of the overall construction. Their eventual reanalysis as adpositions or case markers is no doubt facilitated by the prior existence of categories and constructions into which they can be assimilated. It is in fact quite common for grammaticalization to be abetted, if not guided, by antecedent structures serving as 'attractors'. They offer alternative ways of analysing source expressions, with the result that competing analyses (e.g. *[a lot [of N]]* vs. *[alotta N]*) coexist for long periods of time. The other side of the coin is that existing lexical and grammatical resources allow the periphrastic expression of notions which subsume the conceptual import of grammatical markers and constructions and can therefore serve as source expressions. For instance, *a **bunch** of grapes* is also *a bunch of **grapes*** (= *many **grapes***). Likewise, complement constructions involving matrix predicates like THINK, SAY, WANT, GO, FINISH harbour the conceptual import expressed grammatically by modals, evidentials, tense, and aspect. This illustrates the 'fractal' nature of linguistic structure, such that comparable patterns are observed at multiple levels of organization (Langacker 2008a: §13.3.2).

I conclude by once more emphasizing that a full account of grammaticalization requires explicit descriptions of the conceptual structures and grammatical constructions involved at every stage. My own discussions of grammaticalization have at best been exploratory; even the most detailed description (Langacker 2009a: ch. 3) merely hints at what is needed. Importantly, I do not confuse these preliminary efforts with serious historical investigation carried out in its own terms based on extensive and reliable data. I do however believe that CG provides an appropriate and revealing framework for investigating grammaticalization and other diachronic phenomena.

CHAPTER 8

CONSTRUCTION GRAMMAR AND GRAMMATICALIZATION

NIKOLAS GISBORNE

AMANDA PATTEN

1. Introduction

The grammaticalization literature has often presupposed the existence of 'constructions', generally in a pre-theoretical way, as the context in which grammaticalization takes place. For example, Hopper and Traugott (1993: 2) explain that the grammaticalization of *be going to* into *be gonna* takes place in the context of 'purposive directional constructions with non-finite complements'. Hopper and Traugott explore which features of this construction make it possible for *gonna* to grammaticalize a future-time meaning, looking at (for example) the implicature of futurity inherent in purposives.

More recently, the role of the context has been recognized as fundamental to the definition of grammaticalization. For example, Traugott (2003: 645) defines grammaticalization as the 'process whereby lexical material in highly constrained pragmatic and morphosyntactic contexts is assigned grammatical function'. This raises some important theoretical questions. If changes to the grammaticalizing element are governed by a particular linguistic context, can grammaticalization cause this context (or 'construction') to change? How? What is the proper unit of study in grammaticalization? Is it the grammaticalizing element or the surrounding construction?

In response to such questions, a handful of grammaticalization theorists have redefined grammaticalization as a process affecting constructions (for now, we can define constructions as multi-word linguistic patterns) rather than individual lexical items. For example, Himmelmann (2004: 31) argues that 'the units to which grammaticization properly applies are *constructions*, not isolated lexical items' (see also Bybee 2003). Himmelmann (p. 32) defines grammaticalization as 'a process of context-expansion' whereby the construction allows a wider range of components to enter into it (called 'host-class expansion') and occurs in a broader variety of larger syntactic and/or semantic and pragmatic contexts. However, within this definition, the notion of the grammaticalizing lexical item is still important; Himmelmann (pp. 32–3) notes that 'grammaticization applies only to the context expansion of constructions which include at least one grammaticizing element'.

In the analysis of grammaticalization processes, the role of the surrounding context (or construction) has therefore become increasingly important to definitions of grammaticalization. However, if we assume a construction grammar model of language structure, then the definition of grammaticalization must change yet again: within this framework, larger and less substantive linguistic patterns (i.e. *constructions* defined as symbolic form–meaning pairings) are recognized to be as fundamental a unit of linguistic knowledge as lexical items. This raises a number of new questions which are important to those working on grammaticalization. How do new constructions emerge? How do existing constructions change? And how does the organization of the constructional taxonomy change?

In this chapter, we review some of the literature on constructional change and its integration with grammaticalization theory. We also highlight a number of issues that are relevant to work on grammaticalization, and along the way we ask the following questions, which fall out from a constructional view of grammaticalization.

- To what extent can we say that constructions actually *grammaticalize* in the traditional sense of the word? Does constructional change show evidence of traditional diagnostics of grammaticalization?
- Is the construction grammar framework useful to linguists examining grammaticalization changes to lexical items? What can a construction grammar approach offer them?
- What is the relationship between changes affecting the larger construction and changes to its components (i.e. to lexical items or classes of lexical items)? Can these changes be subsumed under the single rubric 'grammaticalization' or are they two separate, albeit related, types of change?

This chapter has five sections in addition to this introduction: section 2 introduces construction grammar; section 3 explores a constructional approach to grammaticalization and the question of how constructions change; section 4 looks at whether construction grammar is useful to linguists examining grammaticalization changes to lexical items; section 5 looks at the relationship between constructional change and the grammaticalization of lexical items; section 6 presents the conclusions.

2. Construction grammar

The defining property of construction grammar is the assumption that larger linguistic patterns are not simply the epiphenomenal products of syntactic and semantic composition and highly general grammatical rules. In construction grammar, constructions are given a theoretical status as symbolic form–meaning pairings: the entirety of the construction's form is related to its conventional meaning via a symbolic link. Lexical items are smaller, atomic constructions which have their own form–meaning mappings, and which make up the larger constructions, so the form–meaning mappings of atomic constructions are represented as internal to the larger construction (Croft and Cruse 2004: 255).

This means that in construction grammar, both grammatical constructions and lexical items are treated as symbolic, which is useful for two reasons. First, it allows for a complex construction to have meaning which need not be compositional or attributed to its component parts; second, it allows us to represent the phenomenon whereby lexical items acquire functions which are construction specific. There is a simple example in (1).

(1) He laughed his way into the room.

There are two points to note about (1): (i) the verb *laughed* is intransitive, but here it occurs with a direct object; and (ii) the verb *laughed* is not a verb of motion, but here it is interpreted as a verb of manner of motion. These facts are located in the construction itself, which is known as the *way*-construction (Goldberg 1995: 199–218). This is what coerces *laughed* into a verb of motion with a direct object.

The verb *laughed* in (1) therefore behaves in a non-default way because of how it is affected by its context. In this way, variability in the grammatical behaviour of lexical items is predicted in construction grammar, and consequently language change is built into this model. In particular, (1) shows how atomic items can have, or acquire, distinct functions in specific constructional environments.

In addition to the conception of the construction as a linguistic sign, the other fundamental aspect of construction grammar is the organization of the language system as a structured inventory of constructions which makes up the speaker's knowledge of language. This inventory is represented as a taxonomic network of constructions with each construction constituting a separate node (Croft and Cruse 2004: 262). The network is hierarchical in that some constructions are more basic or general than others and lower-level constructions inherit attributes from higher-level constructions.

Most versions of construction grammar make use of 'default' inheritance: by default, lower-level constructions in the taxonomy inherit the attributes of higher-level constructions, but it is possible for them to override attributes.[1] That is, a crucial property of the default inheritance model is that conflict between the information specified in inheriting constructions and information specified in dominating constructions is permitted. This means that categories defined by inheritance hierarchies are non-classical, containing more and less prototypical members. Hudson (2007: 25) says that classification is by the 'best fit' principle: an item is assigned to the category it most closely matches.

In terms of the modelling of grammaticalization, default inheritance is an essential feature of construction grammar because it allows us to show how the speaker can create novel instances (by extension from the prototype) which override inheritance from the more basic construction. It also allows us to model both the creation of new categories, and category strengthening. Most versions of construction grammar, including Radical Construction Grammar (Croft 2001), Cognitive Construction Grammar (Lakoff 1987; Goldberg 1995; 2006) and Cognitive Grammar (Langacker 1987; 1991) are usage-based. The assumption here is that language learning and language change originate in language use, and involve general cognitive processes such as categorization: the speaker-hearer inductively generalizes over instances to form schemas which are represented in the language system. Default inheritance, as understood in construction grammar, is a way of modelling the kinds of categorization that are found in usage-based theories.

3. How do constructions change?

In this section, we set out to answer the first set of questions we raised at the end of section 1: how do constructions change; do constructions grammaticalize; and do

[1] Unification construction grammar, as represented in Kay and Fillmore (1999), does not exploit default inheritance, although Goldberg (2006: 215) shows that current versions do adopt default inheritance as well.

they show traditional diagnostics of grammaticalization? We shall show that constructional change often involves a process of schematization.[2]

A reasonable assumption is that as a complex construction grammaticalizes, it will undergo both a process of semantic fixing of regular collocational patterns, and a process of abstraction so that the construction is thought of as increasingly schematic. Croft and Cruse (2004: 326) cite Israel (1996) as an example of how constructional change often happens: 'A new construction emerges from an often highly specific instance of an existing construction schema and then expands in its own direction.' They say that the entrenchment of the instance creates an 'island' from which the 'new construction grows'. We look first at Israel (1996), then explore a more grammaticalization-oriented analysis of constructional change, before considering how similar to grammaticalization this process is.

Israel (1996) introduces examples like those in (2) below.

(2) a. The wounded soldiers limped their way across the field.
 b. She pushed her way through the crowd.

In the examples in (2), the construction imposes a new argument structure on the verb, giving them both a direct object which they do not ordinarily have.[3]

In exploring the history of the *way*-construction, Israel looks at two sources which were 'independently motivated by the lexical semantics of *way*, and [which] formed the basis for an independent thread of analogical extensions'. These are the 'manner' thread, where *way* occurs in direct object position with verbs of motion, and the 'means' thread, where it occurs as the direct object of verbs of path creation.

Israel shows how in early examples of manner constructions with *way* direct objects, the verbs were usually high-frequency motion verbs such as *go* or *ride*: 'up to 1700 only sixteen distinct verb types are attested in this thread, and most of these are common basic-level words.' However, the construction gradually expanded to include manner of motion verbs, until by the end of the 19th century the construction includes verbs such as *crunch*, *crash*, and *sing*, verbs that encode 'not motion per se, but rather the noise that inevitably accompanies certain forms of motion'.

The other usage that Israel describes is the 'created path usage' which sets up the 'means' variety of the proto-construction. He says that by 1650, verbs such as *pave*, from the lexicon of road-building, and *furrow out*, from the lexicon of path-clearing, started to appear with *way* direct objects. This variant of the construction also grows in the 19th century as the verbs which appear in the construction

[2] Of course, not all types of constructional change involve schematization. Constructions can become less schematic (i.e. more substantive) over time. Trousdale (2008a) suggests that this type of constructional change has more in common with lexicalization than grammaticalization.

[3] The example in (1) above is also an example of the *way*-construction, known as the 'incidental activity' usage.

become more abstractly associated with the creation of a path. Both variants involve the encoding of some sense of difficulty. Israel notes that the 'manner' variant frequently appears with verbs of difficult or laborious motion, and the 'means' variant inherently encodes some difficulty of motion, otherwise why should a path be needed?

For our purposes, the interesting facts that emerge in Israel's paper are that a regularly occurring collocation can become entrenched, conventionalized, and constructional, so that it licenses an increasing range of verbs (this is Himmelmann's 2004 'host-class expansion', or increased schematicity), and so that the emerging construction affects the argument structure of the verbs that occur in the construction. We can also see that the new construction has undergone category strengthening.

Patten (2010a; 2010b) presents another example of constructional change which she more explicitly identifies with grammaticalization. She describes the growth of the *it*-cleft construction, shown in (3) below, and analyses some of the changes it went through. Patten shows that originally there were two specific restrictions in the *it*-cleft construction. Historically, it was only possible to focus an NP in the post-copular position (underlined in the example), and the cleft relative clause[4] could only express given information (see also Ball 1991; 1994). In the example below, the focused element (*the therapist*) is a Noun Phrase and the proposition expressed in the cleft clause *that someone killed her* is already established in the prior discourse.

(3) A: Is he the murderer?
B: No. It was the therapist [that killed her].

Patten claims that this type of example represents the prototypical use of *it*-clefts. In her synchronic analysis of *it*-clefts, she argues that the focus position is a semantically referential position and that the cleft clause (which restrictively modifies the initial *it*) forms part of an inherently presuppositional definite-like description. Since noun phrases typically denote objects, they are the phrasal category most suited to performing a referring function (see Croft 1991a: 67). Likewise, information which is presupposed is typically also known to the hearer because in order to successfully presuppose the existence of some entity, the speaker usually has to assume that the hearer is familiar with the description given. Therefore, early examples of the *it*-cleft construction conform to more general, broadly compositional patterns in the language system.

Over time, two changes take place in the *it*-cleft construction as it undergoes category strengthening and becomes a constructional category type in its own right. First, the focus position can accommodate a range of phrasal categories, not

[4] We call this constituent the 'cleft clause' in the rest of this paper; it is enclosed by square brackets.

just NPs; secondly, information which is hearer-new can be presented in the cleft clause. Both of these accommodations initially take place via coercion. These new instances involve mismatch: that is, non-nominal phrasal categories perform a referring function in the focus position, and new information is marked as presupposed or 'assumed to be true' when it occurs in the cleft clause. For instance, in the example in (4), the proposition that *someone once said 'laws are silent at times of war'* is not already known to the intended audience but is nevertheless presupposed as an established fact (see Patten 2010a).

(4) (Start of lecture)
It was Cicero [who once said, 'Laws are silent at times of war'].

Over time, this gives us two new subtypes of cleft: (i) clefts with non-nominal elements in focus position; (ii) clefts with new information in the cleft clause. Both of these new subtypes of *it*-cleft involve a kind of extension from the prototype, which therefore overrides the inheritance of certain properties from the existing *it*-cleft schema. This process is gradual since, as Goldberg (1995: 159) observes, coercion is governed by the extent to which there is relationship between the inherent meaning of the coerced item and the interpretation which it is given by the construction. As a result, changes to the *it*-cleft proceed in incremental steps, with instances deviating increasingly from the prototype over time.

According to a usage-based model, as prototypical and non-prototypical instances of *it*-cleft coexist, the speaker forms an inductive generalization (or abstraction) which states only those characteristics shared by all of its members. This abstraction is represented in the taxonomic hierarchy. As a result, the overarching *it*-cleft schema becomes a more basic and general construction over time, sanctioning an increasingly wide range of instances.

The question that follows from these two case studies is whether these examples of constructional change can really be called 'grammaticalization' and, therefore, whether they show evidence of the traditional diagnostics of grammaticalization. There are six reasons why we want to suggest that this kind of constructional change looks similar to grammaticalization.

First, both the development of the *way*-construction and the *it*-cleft show evidence of a directional change: both overarching constructions become increasingly schematic (or open) and productive (sanctioning more instances) over time. This is a categorical change of a particular kind: one that results in change to the categorical inventory.

Second, both changes are gradual, occurring in incremental stages. In the case of the *way*-construction, the incremental stages are verb by verb; in the case of the *it*-cleft the development works in terms of phrasal categories: the cleft position initially sanctions categories that are inherently suited to performing a referring function, and over time it sanctions further categories that are less suited to performing a referring function. Also, there are changes to the *it*-cleft's information structure. Over time, the cleft clause changes (in incremental steps) from expressing given information, to expressing non-salient but shared information, to expressing information that is factual or known to a third party, before it finally accommodates the speaker's opinion (see Patten 2010a).

Third, these processes involve analogy. In the case of the *way*-construction, verbs from similar semantic fields are accommodated to the construction first, with verbs from more distal semantic fields being added later. With each new verb that is added to the list of verbs that can occur in the construction, the speaker-hearer exploits analogical reasoning to make the categorization. With clefts, the processes described in the paragraph above involve analogy too.

Fourth, it is possible to argue that the development of the *way*-construction involves reanalysis. First, the direct object *the way* is reanalysed as part of the construction; secondly, in this construction verbs gain a new argument structure. Furthermore, we could take the view that the categorical change involved in both constructions becoming more schematic involves a kind of reanalysis, as the constructions are reanalysed into new construction types.

Fifth, both processes of constructional change involve the development of constructional polysemy. For the *way*-construction, the incidental activity interpretation, as in *he laughed his way into the room*, could be analysed as an extension from the more basic means usage. Although Israel says that this is a somewhat simplistic account, it is a proposal which Goldberg (1995: 210) supports. Goldberg takes the view that the manner interpretation (which includes the incidental activity usage) is a development of the means interpretation resulting in a polysemous construction type.

With clefts, pragmatic accommodation becomes a conventionalized feature of the construction, and so the construction becomes polysemous, with different types of instance conveying subtle yet distinct nuances of meaning. For instance, in the example below, the speaker's opinion is expressed in the sentence-final clause. Patten (2010a) says, 'This example is particularly interesting, since *I fear* does not qualify the assertion that *others are led astray* **here**, but the presupposition that *she risks leading others astray*.' This now conventional use for the *it*-cleft has the unique discourse function of providing an indirect way of communicating or asserting the proposition expressed in the cleft clause (see also Lambrecht 1994: 71).

(5) And it is here, I fear, that my right honorable friend increasingly risks leading herself and others astray in matters of substance as well as of style. (S2B-050 036) [example from ICE-GB corpus]

Tellingly, the coexistence, or *layering*, of original and emergent functions is a common outcome of the grammaticalization of lexical items, at least in its early stages (Hopper and Traugott 2003: 124–6).

Sixth, there is evidence of subjectification. We said above that the *it*-cleft has developed from a purely specificational function (identifying the referent that matches a familiar description) to ultimately acquiring an additional meaning where it is an indirect way of communicating the speaker's opinion. It would also be possible to argue that the incidental activity use of the *way*-construction, in (1) above, involves subjectification, because it allows the speaker to use an emotive or evaluative word in a position originally restricted to simple movement. As Traugott (1982; 1989) observes, grammaticalization often involves a shift towards increasingly subjective meanings; that is, the grammaticalized word or string of words comes to express the speaker's beliefs and attitudes.

These six points do not necessarily entail that the changes we observe in these constructions are grammaticalization changes. But we can see that the kinds of development reported in these two constructions share a lot with the more commonly analysed processes of grammaticalization involving lexical items, which supports the idea that constructional change is relevant to grammaticalization theory.

4. How useful is construction grammar to grammaticalization research?

In section 3, we saw that the emergence of new constructions looks very like grammaticalization. Here we explore the questions in our second bullet point in section 1: (how) is construction grammar useful to linguists examining grammaticalization changes to lexical items?

According to Traugott (2007), Trousdale (2008b), and Fried (2008), the hierarchical network of constructions provides a useful means of identifying and accounting for directional changes. Within the constructional network, specific linguistic patterns inherit properties from more basic constructions. As we have seen, constructional change originates in language use with actually occurring utterances. As new tokens emerge, the speaker generalizes over these instances (or constructs) to create a new level of abstraction. This in turn can have repercussions higher up in the taxonomy as existing schemas become more abstract in order to accommodate (or sanction) these new lower-level constructions (Trousdale 2008b: 55).

Within the framework of construction grammar, grammaticalization is therefore a process of schematization, in which the construction becomes a more abstract, higher-level category. Therefore, the cline from lexical to grammatical status is re-envisaged as a hierarchy from more substantive to more schematic constructions. As Trousdale (2008a: 170–71) comments, 'The more schematic the construction, the more productive it will be (thus such constructions become aligned with what is usually called "syntax" and "productive morphology"); the more substantive the construction, the less productive it will be (i.e. it will become more associated with the "unproductive morphology" and the "lexicon").'

So how do construction grammars help with understanding these processes? Grammaticalization of lexical items does not occur in a vacuum: as lexical items undergo grammaticalization, they can affect the constructional inventory that they inhabit. A simple example is the development of the English modal auxiliary system (Warner 1993). The English auxiliary construction historically involved the aspectual auxiliary verbs BE and HAVE, and the passive construction; as the modal auxiliaries evolved from the Old English preterite present verbs, so the auxiliary construction itself had to change.

Trousdale (forthcoming) says that, viewed from the perspective of the atomic lexical items, the English modals are the product of individual changes which conform to the well-established grammaticalization cline: lexical verb > modal verb. However, a constructional approach treats the grammaticalization of each verb as the creation of a new 'micro'-construction.[5] As more and more verbs develop modal uses, a new 'meso'-construction emerges: the modal construction. As the modal category expands, sanctioning new micro-constructions, this in turn has implications for the higher-order auxiliary construction, which becomes a more basic and distinctive 'macro'-construction.

For Trousdale, then, the constructional approach provides us with a means of representing changes to the language system (or the constructional taxonomy) in a uniform way. He notes that while 'the standard conceptualization of the cline' is itself a generalization, it focuses on the development of the atomic lexical item, and so 'fails to consider the larger constructional changes within which such micro-changes are embedded' (Trousdale forthcoming).

Another way to think about this set of changes is in terms of subjectivity and subjectification: the auxiliary construction has to instantiate the aspectual and passive constructions which are not inherently subjective, as well as the modal ones. Traugott (1989) shows that the modals develop subjective senses as they develop their epistemic senses which, on the whole, follow their deontic senses. Gisborne (2010: 97, 252) shows that subjectivity is not only a lexical property but is also constructional because it involves argument linking: subjectivity involves an argument-linking arrangement where there is a force-dynamic linking to the speaker (see also Sweetser 1990 for similar arguments). Argument linking is

[5] Traugott (2007) and Trousdale (2008b; forthcoming) use the terms *micro-*, *meso-*, and *macro-construction* as annotations on different levels in the taxonomic hierarchy. *Micro-constructions* are at the most substantive level in the hierarchy; *macro-constructions* the most schematic.

constructional: lexical items supply their arguments, constructions link them. In this case, the auxiliary construction had to change over time in order to accommodate the new argument-linking patterns associated with the modals as they grammaticalized and developed subjective senses. Gisborne's analysis of the argument linking of the modals supports the view that subjectification is not just a lexical phenomenon, but is involved in changes to the construction, as we say earlier in our discussion of *it*-clefts.

We can see, then, that a further advantage to the constructional approach is that it allows us to be more precise about what we mean by the terms 'more lexical' or 'more grammatical'. Grammaticalization theorists often find it difficult to draw a sharp line between items that are properly in the lexicon and items that are located in the grammar (Himmelmann 2004: 25). Indeed, the very concept of grammaticalization as a change which makes lexical items more grammatical argues against a theory of language structure which rigidly separates the lexicon from the grammar. Construction grammar is consistent with this idea; in this theory, grammar and lexicon are a continuum, both involving symbolic units of form and meaning. Within the constructional taxonomy, 'more lexical' and 'more grammatical' are measured in degrees of productivity and schematicity. This more accurately corresponds with the notion that change is gradual and progresses in incremental, unidirectional stages along a continuum.

In summary, the constructional framework offers a new perspective from which to view grammaticalization changes—even to atomic lexical items. The construction grammar framework allows us to model the changes predicted in grammaticalization theory, while being very precise about where change happens, and what its nature is.

5. What is the relationship between constructional change and the grammaticalization of lexical items?

In the previous section we showed that once we examine grammaticalization changes in relation to the constructional taxonomy, the process is reinterpreted as schematization (or 'expansion') which accommodates the examples of the *way*-construction and the *it*-cleft discussed in section 3. This constructional model of change overlaps considerably with the accounts of grammaticalization provided by Bybee (2003) and Himmelmann (2004).

As we explained in section 1, for these authors, grammaticalization properly applies to constructions rather than individual lexical items. However, while the organization of grammatical knowledge in construction grammar predicts that both atomic and complex constructions can undergo grammaticalization processes, Bybee (2003) and Himmelmann (2004) maintain that the expansion of the complex construction functions as the contextual change necessary for the grammaticalization of a particular lexical item within that construction.[6]

As a result, in this section we ask: what is the relationship between changes affecting the larger construction and changes to the components (i.e. the lexical items) within this construction? Should both of these changes be subsumed under the rubric of 'grammaticalization' or are these two separate, yet related, types of change?

Noël (2007) argues that while the processes of schematization (or constructionalization) and grammaticalization often intersect, they should be treated as separate developments. To illustrate the reasoning behind this claim, Noël (p. 183) discusses Bisang's (1998) work on serial unit constructions.

A serial unit construction consists of a main verb as well as positions for marking tense, aspect, and modality (filled by TAM verbs). Bisang (1998: 36) argues that each of these slots '*attract* linguistic items in order to grammaticalize them'. In other words, as the construction undergoes host-class expansion, it accommodates (or coerces) a wider range of verbs into the TAM positions. Even if a verb has never been used as a TAM marker before, it will automatically be interpreted as such simply as a result of its appearance in the construction, resulting ultimately in the grammaticalization of this item. As Noël (p. 184) puts it, 'the verb grammaticalizes by analogy to other verbs occurring in this position in the construction'.

For Noël, then, the schematization of the larger construction can lead to the grammaticalization of simple atomic elements, but these are two different types of change. He notes, 'Constructions of a higher level of abstraction can play a role as an analogical force behind grammaticalization . . . but there is no consensus in GT [grammaticalization theory] that they can also be grammaticalizing/grammaticalized constructions' (p. 184).

At the very least, studying changes to larger constructions is useful for identifying the cause, and also the context, of particular instances of grammaticalization. The important thing here is the observation that constructions can be coercion environments. As we saw in section 3, this is also true of the *way*-construction (involving the coercion of new verbs) and the *it*-cleft construction (involving the

[6] Himmelmann considers the grammaticalization of the individual element to be dependent upon the schematicity (or generality) of the surrounding construction. As a result of context-expansion, the fixed grammaticalizing element occurs alongside 'a growing class of items which enter into this construction'. Consequently it becomes 'the increasingly general construction marker' (Himmelmann 2004: 38). Therefore, Himmelmann thinks that traditional diagnostics of grammaticalization, including semantic bleaching, phonological erosion, and so on, are epiphenomena.

coercion of non-nominal phrases into the postcopular referring position). However, unlike the grammaticalization of Bisang's TAM markers, these coercions do not result in wholesale category change for the individual items. Why should there be this difference? One possible reason would be frequency: the *it*-cleft and *way* constructions are low-frequency. They are very specialized linguistic patterns (respectively an information-packaging construction and an idiom), and so the elements which obtain construction-specific, coerced interpretations have a restricted distribution. As a result, coercion within these constructions does not affect the speaker's conceptualization of the coerced individual lexical items in the hierarchy.

The question of whether grammaticalization theory should be entirely subsumed by a constructional model of change or whether the term 'grammaticalization' should be reserved for changes affecting only atomic elements remains an open issue. Nevertheless, it is clear that there is a bidirectional relationship between constructional change and traditional grammaticalization phenomena.

6. Conclusions

We have discussed several ways in which constructions emerge and change, and have identified traditional diagnostics of grammaticalization in these changes. This supports the idea that larger constructions can undergo grammaticalization, not only as the surrounding context for a grammaticalizing lexical item or morpheme but as the actual grammaticalizing element (Trousdale 2008b: 33–4). We have also shown that viewing grammaticalization changes from the perspective of the constructional model of language structure (as a change which proceeds upwards throughout the hierarchy, leading to the creation of new constructions and the reconfiguration of existing ones) offers a fresh approach to well-known cases of grammaticalization and allows us to be very precise, as we have said, about where change happens, and what its nature is. Finally, we saw that, since the grammaticalization of constructions involves coercion, such changes can (depending upon frequency) result in the grammaticalization of the construction's components.

CHAPTER 9

GRAMMATICALIZATION AND LINGUISTIC TYPOLOGY

WALTER BISANG

1. Introduction: From Typological Studies on Grammaticalization to a Typology of Manifestations of Grammaticalization

Grammaticalization is part of the study of language change, and is concerned with the question of how a lexical item develops into a marker of a grammatical category or how a marker representing a less grammatical function takes on a more grammatical one (for similar definitions, see. Kuryłowicz 1975[1965]; Hopper and Traugott 2003). For that purpose, linguists dealing with grammaticalization look at how grammatical categories are marked and how their marking changes over time in individual languages and, what is crucial for generalizations, across languages. The cross-linguistic typological study of grammaticalization led to a number of generalizations in terms of clines, pathways, continua, chains, or channels (for the terminology, see Hopper and Traugott 2003: 6–7).

This diachronic scenario of grammaticalization consists of certain pragmatic processes and certain formal (morphophonological and morphosyntactic) processes which interact with existing constructions and their semantic and formal structures (see section 2). The pragmatic side of the scenario is characterized by such processes as invited inferences (Traugott 2002a) or metaphor and metonymy (subsection 2.1). The formal side is represented by processes like erosion, cliticization, or affixation (subsection 2.2). The input to these processes comes from the lexicon that provides certain source concepts that frequently undergo grammaticalization (cf. e.g. Heine, Claudi, and Hünnemeyer 1991; Bybee, Pagliuca, and Perkins 1994) and from the inventory of grammatical morphemes of a language.

Classical typological studies on grammaticalization that are based on large numbers of languages (Bybee 1985; Bybee and Dahl 1989; Bybee et al. 1994; Lehmann 1995a) generally take it for granted that there is a certain interdependence between the meaning-side and the form-side of grammaticalization, i.e. that there is coevolution of meaning and form. How this works is very briefly illustrated by a short description of Lehmann's (1995a) approach. He presents a theory for measuring the degree of grammaticalization of linguistic signs in terms of their autonomy, i.e. the freedom the language user has in forming them. The parameters that determine the autonomy of a sign are its weight, its cohesion, and its variability, each with its paradigmatic and its syntagmatic side. The lower the autonomy of a linguistic sign, the higher is its degree of grammaticalization. 'Therefore the autonomy of a sign is converse to its grammaticality, and grammaticalization detracts from its autonomy' (Lehmann 1995a: 122).

A corollary of the assumption that there is coevolution of meaning and form is that at a certain stage of grammaticalization what was a former pragmatic inference is encoded as a new grammatical meaning and becomes part of the semantics of a lexical item or a construction (on the distinction of pragmatics vs. semantics, cf. Nicolle, Chapter 32 below). This change from pragmatics to semantics is generally supposed to be paralleled by concomitant changes on the form-side of the construction and/or its components. As will be pointed out in this chapter, processes of grammaticalization are not cross-linguistically homogeneous—there is a certain degree of cross-linguistic variation concerning the interaction between pragmatics and form. Instead of presenting typological studies on processes of grammaticalization as discussed above, this chapter will thus address the question of how grammaticalization is realized, a question that ultimately entails a typology of manifestations of grammaticalization. Since such an approach needs a lot of future research on a broad range of different languages from different geographic areas, this chapter will illustrate only one type that is manifested in East and mainland Southeast Asian (EMSEA) languages and is characterized by a considerably higher impact of pragmatics in contexts for which research in grammaticalization generally predicts a higher degree of grammaticalization that blocks pragmatic inference. For that purpose, it will be necessary to describe the elements of the above diachronic scenario of grammaticalization in section 2 and to see how they can be used for cross-linguistic comparison. Section 3 will present some empirical examples from EMSEA languages ('come to have'-verbs, numeral classifiers) and will show what restrains the coevolution of meaning and form. A short conclusion will be presented in section 4.

2. The elements of the grammaticalization scenario

2.1. Pragmatics and grammaticalization

Approaches to pragmatics from the perspective of grammaticalization must account for how meaning inferred from context can become conventionalized meaning that is part of the linguistic code. In the present subsection, I will briefly discuss two approaches (for a more detailed presentation of pragmatics see Nicolle, Ch. 32 below).

A well-known approach is Traugott's (2002a) Invited Inference Theory of Semantic Change. In her view, grammaticalization begins when a construction is used in a specific context that is designed in such a way that the addressee is invited to draw a particular inference, the invited inference. If the invited inference associated with that construction gets conventionalized in the same context, it becomes a generalized invited inference. At the final stage of grammaticalization, the generalized invited inference is coded as a new meaning of the construction. The old meaning of the construction may have disappeared during the process of grammaticalization or it may still be available and thus lead to ambiguity.

There are two approaches that are more explicit in terms of contexts: one of them is Heine (2002), the other is Diewald (2002). I will briefly summarize the latter. Diewald (2002) starts out from the hypothesis that processes of grammaticalization can be divided into three successive stages which correlate with particular contexts. The first stage is characterized by untypical contexts. A construction appears in contexts or combinations of constructions that are unusual but can be easily interpreted because of their compositional structure. The second stage depends on the emergence of a very specific type of context, the critical context, which is characterized by multiple structural and semantic ambiguities and thus 'invites several alternative interpretations, among them the new grammatical meaning' (Diewald 2002: 103). Finally, there are specific linguistic contexts that favour one interpretation to the exclusion of the other(s), the isolating contexts. This leads to an advanced stage of grammaticalization with oppositions between mutually exclusive contexts. Each of the constructions involved shows its unique form–meaning correspondence.

The above approaches cover a number of pragmatic processes. Two of them, metaphor and metonymy, will be briefly discussed here. Both notions are subject to quite different definitions in the literature (cf. Bisang 2008: 26–30). For the discussion of data from EMSEA languages in section 3, a short description of Hopper and Traugott's (2003) approach will be sufficient.

The core function of metaphor is defined in terms of 'experiencing one kind of thing in terms of another, and directionality of transfer from a basic, usually concrete, meaning to one more abstract' (Hopper and Traugott 2003: 84). Metonymy depends on transfer through (morpho)syntactic contiguity (Hopper and Traugott 2003: 88). It does not operate on individual words or grammatical markers but on the wider linguistic context, i.e., it 'points to . . . relations in contexts that include interdependent (morpho)syntactic constituents' (Hopper and Traugott 2003: 88).

The two pragmatic processes of metonymy and metaphor are associated with two mechanisms of grammaticalization: reanalysis and analogy. Reanalysis is basically an instance of constituency change or rebracketing that takes place without any concomitant change of the phonological surface of an utterance. Reanalysis and metonymy both operate on the syntagmatic level, whereby the pragmatic process of metonymy motivates the reanalysis of the phonological surface of an utterance through a conversational implicature. Metaphor and analogy take the paradigmatic axis. The pragmatic process of metaphor instigates processes of inference through conventional implicatures across conceptual boundaries and paves the way for analogy, i.e. the placement of a linguistic item into a functional slot it was not allowed to fill before.

2.2. The formal side of grammaticalization

The formal side of grammaticalization is usually described along clines that lead from syntax to phonetic reduction as illustrated by (1):

(1) Givón (1979: 209):
discourse > syntax > morphology > morphophonemics > zero

In their classical work on grammaticalization and reanalysis, Heine and Reh (1984) distinguish four types of processes:

(i) phonetic processes: adaptation, erosion, fusion, loss;
(ii) morphosyntactic processes: permutation, compounding, cliticization, affixation, fossilization;
(iii) functional processes: desemanticization, expansion, simplification, merger;
(iv) complex processes: verbal attraction, infixation, split, shift.

The first two processes are relevant for the formal side of grammaticalization as discussed here. It covers changes in the phonetic substance of constructions and is directly linked to the cline presented in (1). The processes in (i) and (ii) can thus safely be associated with what makes the formal part of grammaticalization. Since most of these processes are well known in the literature, no examples will be provided.[1]

2.3. The role of constructions in grammaticalization

Most linguists working in the framework of Construction Grammar define constructions as pairings of form and meaning which have their own meaning that cannot be described exclusively from their components (Goldberg 1995; 2006; Croft 2001). Since grammaticalization crucially depends on the interaction between the syntactic and the semantic properties of constructions, it is necessary to look for those elements within constructions that can instigate pragmatic processes of metonymy and metaphor and their corresponding mechanisms of reanalysis and analogy, respectively. A good framework for describing this interaction is the concept of coercion in terms of Michaelis (2004), who understands syntactic structures as patterns that have the power to coerce a lexical item into a particular grammatical function. A very important syntactic element for understanding processes of grammaticalization are syntactic positions or slots within constructions that are associated with certain functions. As will be shown in subsection 3.1, such slots often provide the only instrument for determining the grammatical function of a lexical item in EMSEA languages. As soon as a surface structure is associated with a certain construction, its syntactic components will get their function from taking specific syntactic slots within that construction.

Constructions with their coercive power form the basis of metonymy and metaphor. In the case of metonymy, a given surface structure that used to be analysed in terms of construction X is now interpreted in the framework of construction Z. Thus, a structure like *[[front]$_N$ of the house]$_{NP}$*, in which *front* is the head of an NP, may be reanalysed as a preposition in a PP with the structure *[[front]$_P$ of the house]$_{PP}$*.

[1] The only term that may need a short definition is permutation—a process which 'changes the basic arrangement of linguistic units (morphemes, words, or constituents)' (Heine and Reh 1984: 28).

3. Grammaticalization with limited coevolution of meaning and form

3.1. Examples from EMSEA languages

The area of EMSEA languages comprises the five language families of Sinitic (branch of Sino-Tibetan), Mon-Khmer (branch of Austro-Asiatic), Tai (branch of Tai-Kadai), Miao-Yao or Hmong-Mien, and Austronesian (Chamic in Vietnam) (Bisang 2006). The languages belonging to that area are characterized by the prominence of pragmatic inference and the lack of obligatory categories (Bisang 1996) and by a relative resistance of their phonology to the impact of the meaning–form coevolution.

A good example is the verb 'come to have', which is *ba:n* in Khmer, *dây* in Thai, *tau* in Hmong, and *dé* in Chinese. In their grammaticalized form, 'come to have'-verbs occur preverbally and postverbally and can express an impressive number of functions which are described in detail by Enfield (2003). In the preverbal position alone, they can have maximally four functions that cover three rather different grammatical domains: modality in (3a, b), tense in (3c), and truth in (3d). The meaning of these markers in a concrete context depends on pragmatic inference from context. The first line in (3a–d) presents the context, the second line the pragmatic inference represented by an arrow (→).

(3) Possible inferences of 'come to have'-verbs (Bisang 2009: 39):
   a. The event E is [+desired]:
      → modal interpretation: 'can' (potential meaning: abilitative or permissive)
   b. The event E is [–desired]
      → modal interpretation: 'must, to have to' (obligation)
   c. In order for X to come to have E, E must have taken place:
      → Past (E) (particularly if E is negated)
   d. In order for X to come to have E, E must be true:
      → truth, factuality, in contrast to a given presupposition

In Khmer, the verb *ba:n* 'come to have' in the preverbal TAM position can have the functions of (3a,c,d). The function of obligation in (3b) is marginally possible. Depending on context, a simple clause like the one in (4) can thus be interpreted as follows:

(4) *Khɲom ba:n tɤ̀u phsa:(r).*
    I TAM go market

a. 'I was able/allowed to go to the market.' (3a)
b. 'I went to the market.' (3c)
c. 'I WAS at the market.' (3d) [Against the presupposition that I was not.]

Even in texts such as (5) from a novel, *ba:n* is sometimes open to more than one interpretation. The example is uttered in a context in which everyone expects the protagonist to ask for the hand of a woman. In its first use, *ba:n* denies the fact that such an event took place at any time in the past (3c). At the same time, *ba:n* may express that he was not able (3a) to find a suitable woman. The second instance of *ba:n* can be interpreted in two ways which are again not mutually exclusive. (i) The marker *ba:n* is used against the presupposition that the protagonist does not meet a woman (because he did not ask to marry one) and focuses on the fact that he actually sees a woman (3d). (ii) The second interpretation is related to the temporal expression 'since seven months' and situates the action expressed by the verb in the past (3c):

(5) Khmer *ba:n* in preverbal position: past, factual (Sophat 1.7):

Lò:k *mùn* ***ba:n*** *dɔndɤŋ* *strɤy* *na:-mù:əy*
mister/he NEG TAM ask.for.the.hand.of woman anyone

thvɤ̀:-cì:ə kù: *kɔ̀əp cɤt(t) sɔh.* *Pontae rì:əs(tr) tɛ̀əŋ-pù:əŋ dɤŋ*
become pair/partners suitable at.all but people all.of.them know

cɛ̀ək *tha:* *lò:k* ***ba:n*** *tɤ̀u* *rù:əm-rɔ̀:k* *daoy* *lɛ̀ək-kombaŋ*
clearly QUOT he PST:get go join.together according hidden/secret

nɯ̀ŋ strɤy-kɔmprì:ə *m-nɛ̀ək* *chmùəh* *nì:əŋ so:pha:t cɔmnù:ən pram-pɯ̀l*
with woman-orphaned one-CL be.called Mrs Sophat number seven

khae *haəy.*
month PF

'He had not asked for the hand of any woman to become [his] suitable partner at all. But everybody knew clearly that he went to join secretly an orphaned woman called Sophat since seven months.'

The case of 'come to have'-verbs shows the following three properties that are characteristic of processes of grammaticalization in EMSEA languages:

(i) Even though these verbs allow the inference of grammatical categories that are highly abstract, they show comparably small changes in phonology. What may change is tonality and the quality/quantity of the vowel. What is preserved is the syllabic form. Khmer *ba:n* shows no phonological change.
(ii) They follow rigid word-order rules, i.e. their interpretations in (3a–d) depend on the preverbal position. Reduction of mobility is a strong indicator of grammaticalization in terms of Lehmann (1995a; syntagmatic variability; *see*

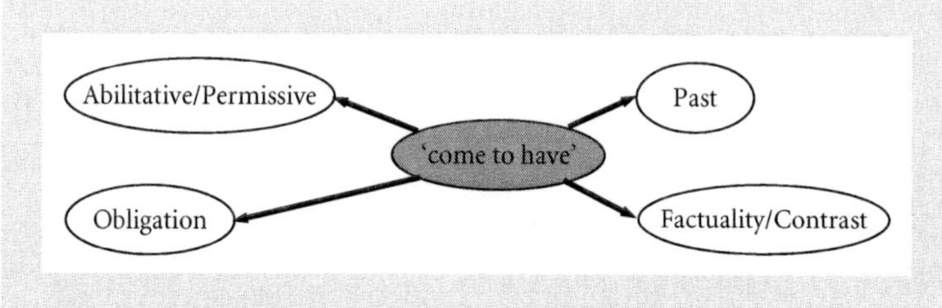

Fig. 9.1. Four radiating functions of 'come to have'

section 1). In fact, it is often the only parameter for the formal measuring of grammaticalization in EMSEA languages.

(iii) The functions in (3a–d) do not follow one from the other in terms of a cline, they are all inferred equally from the basic meaning of 'come to have'. For that reason, Fig. 9.1, with four possible functions that radiate from the source concept in the centre, is a more adequate representation.

If word order is an indicator of strong grammaticalization, 'come to have'-verbs represent a paradoxical situation in which a high degree of grammaticalization still allows for a vast number of inferences that belong to different domains (modality, tense, factuality/contrast). To state this situation in terms of Diewald (2002; see subsection 2.1 above), 'come to have'-verbs are still at the stage of critical context with 'several alternative interpretations' even though the degree of grammaticalization has reached a stage that can be compared to isolating contexts.

A second example is numeral classifiers (Aikhenvald 2000; Bisang 1999). As is well known, nouns are neutral with regard to number. For that reason, nouns must be individualized if they are counted by numerals in most EMSEA languages. The markers that do this are numeral classifiers. What is less known is that numeral classifiers can have a plethora of other functions, at least in some languages. In Thai, classifiers are not only used to individualize a concept expressed by the noun; in specific slots of certain clearly defined constructions they can express definiteness, singulative and contrastive focus (Bisang 2008: 21). The impact of these functions on the form side is again rather minimal (loss of tonality, sometimes loss of vowel quality/quantity).

Of particular interest for the functional range of classifiers beyond their individualizing function is the classifier+noun construction [Cl+N] in various Sinitic languages. In Mandarin Chinese, this construction is basically limited to the postverbal position,[2] in which it expresses indefiniteness. In other Sinitic languages, the situation is more interesting. In Wu Chinese, the classifier marks definiteness, if the [Cl+N] construction occurs preverbally (6) and indefiniteness

[2] In some instances, it seems possible to use [Cl+N] with the *ba*-construction. But this is subject to divergent native-speaker judgements.

if it is postverbal (7) (Li and Bisang forthcoming). As can be seen from (6b), [Cl +N] also occurs after the marker *ke*. This marker has the same function as Chinese *ba* 'take, hold' in the disposal construction, in which postverbal objects are moved into the preverbal position and become definite (see Li and Thompson 1976).

(6) Preverbal use of [Cl+N]:

a. [Cl+N] in preverbal position:

zeq	*giu*	*si-niao*	*die.*
CL	dog	die-finish	PART

'The dog died.'

b. [Cl+N] in the disposal construction:

yii	*ke*	*zeq*	*giu*	*teq*	*leh*	*yeq*	*jia.*
he	DISP	CL	dog	kick	PFV	one	foot

'He gave a kick to the dog.'

(7) [Cl+N] in the postverbal position:

ngooh	*shang*	*geh*	*you*	*maa*	*leh*	***bu***	***couzi.***
I	last	CL	month	buy	PFV	CL	car

'I bought a car last month.'

Word order is associated with information structure in many Sinitic languages. Li and Thompson (1976) claim that Chinese is a 'topic-prominent' language, in which the subject is the unmarked topic. More recently, Xu (2004) argues that the sentence-final position is a default position for focus in Chinese. According to the Topic Accessibility Hierarchy (Lambrecht 1994: 165), topics are preferably definite. In contrast, NPs in the focus position are indefinite by default. It is thus word order as it reflects information structure that determines the interpretation of the classifier in [Cl+N] in Wu Chinese.

As a consequence, the classifier only points to the relevance of referential status as a whole, but it is underspecified for [±definiteness]. The concrete referential value must be inferred from the position of [Cl+N] within the clause construction. The use of [Cl+N] in Wu Chinese is thus another example in which a linguistic item with a high degree of grammaticalization (cf. its dependence on word order) is still subject to pragmatic inference.

3.2. What contributes to the relative independence of form

The relative morphophonological stability of grammaticalized items in EMSEA languages is in line with some general typological findings presented by Schiering (2006), and is due to two specific properties discussed by Ansaldo and Lim (2004):

(8) Specific phonological properties of EMSEA languages:
- discreteness of syllable boundaries;
- phonotactic restraints.

Schiering (2006) shows that from a general typological perspective the loss of phonological substance (erosion) is not a defining property of grammaticalization. In his rhythm-based typology, he defines a continuum characterized by the following three rhythmic types:

(9) Schiering's (2006) three types of phonologies:
a. stress-based phonologies;
b. syllable-based phonologies;
c. mora-based phonologies.

These types are defined on the basis of six parameters:

(10) Schiering's (2006) six parameters:
a. phonetic realization of stress (pitch, quantity, intensity);
b. segmental effects of stress;
c. distribution of tone;
d. syllable complexity;
e. phonemic length;
f. word-demarcating vowel harmony.

As Schiering (2006) clearly shows, there is a correlation between erosion (cf. subsection 2.1) and grammaticalization only in the stress-based type (9a). 'The data suggests that grammaticalization will be accompanied by erosion in languages of stress-based rhythm only, which casts doubt on the intrinsic status of erosion in grammaticalization' (Schiering 2006: 215).

Ansaldo and Lim (2004) show that due to the two properties mentioned in (8), grammaticalization is mainly expressed by phonetic erosion in terms of syllable duration and vowel quality, while morphological reduction is only marginal. Since the syllable as such tends to be maintained, instances of subsyllabic morphology are very rare. There are at best some tendencies, such as the pronominal plural form in Mandarin Chinese, which develops from a bisyllabic word (*tā-men* [3.PERSON-PL] into a monosyllabic word (*tā-m*). What is not reduced or only slightly reduced is pitch. In Cantonese and in Hokkien, there is no significant pitch reduction. As Ansaldo and Lim (2004) point out, this is due to the necessity of maintaining tonal contrast for keeping up lexical contrast, particularly in languages like Cantonese and Hokkien with their system of three tonal registers. In Sinitic languages with only one tonal register like Mandarin, reduction of pitch does not produce the same strong effect of blurring distinctive features. For that reason, there are certain grammatical markers such as verb-final *-le* (derived from *liǎo* 'finish') and verb-final *-zhe* (durative marker, derived from *zhù* 'live, reside, stay'), which reduced their vowels to a toneless [ə].

The above discussion has shown that there must be certain phonological factors that provide the domain of form with a degree of resistance against the coevolution of meaning and form that is stronger than it is generally assumed in most approaches to grammaticalization.

Once syllabicity has become an areal property, even languages with subsyllabic morphology can reduce its use in situations of contact. A good example is Khmer (cf. *ba:n* in subsection 3.1) with its rich subsyllabic morphology (Jenner and Pou 1980/81; Bisang 1992: 447–72). In principle, this morphology can be used for derivational word formation as with the infix *-m-*, which marks agentive nouns: *sò:m* 'ask, ask a favor' > *smò:m* 'beggar', *cam* 'wait for, guard, keep' > *chmam* 'guard, n.', *cù:əɲ* 'do business' > *chmù:əɲ* 'business-man', etc. In contemporary Khmer, however, morphology is no longer productive and is replaced by non-morphological alternatives. Thus, agentive nouns are formed by the noun *nѐək* 'person' in the head position, as in *nѐək-daə(r)* [person-walk] 'pedestrian', *nѐək-taeŋ* [person-compose/write] 'author, composer, writer', and *nѐək-chlɔ̀:p* [person-go stealthily to watch someone] 'spy, snoop'.

3.3. What contributes to the relative independence of pragmatics

The factors that prevent a relatively strong correlation between the domain of form and the domain of pragmatics become evident from a look at the properties of instances of high degrees of grammaticalization that are formally manifested. Good examples are morphological paradigms (cf. paradigmaticity in terms of Lehmann 1995a; section 1 above). As I argued in Bisang (2008: 33), the absence of inflectional paradigms in EMSEA languages is due to two factors that are the preconditions for the emergence of such patterns:

- frequency and obligatoriness;
- existence of clearly determined semantic domains.

Morphological paradigms develop from categories that are frequently used. Frequency in turn is enhanced by semantic generality (Bybee 1985), which grants the compatibility of a marker with a large number of lexical items. As soon as a grammatical category is semantically general enough to be coextensive with a certain other grammatical category (e.g. with the categories of nouns or verbs) its co-occurrence with that category may become obligatory—a fact that additionally contributes to its frequency.

A paradigm consists of a certain category (e.g. tense) with its values or subcategories (e.g. present, past, future). These categories are semantically clearly defined, and thus stand for a high degree of categorial homogeneity within the paradigm as a whole.

Both factors that support the development of paradigms are comparatively weak in EMSEA languages. First, the lack of obligatoriness systematically undermines the emergence of a situation that would be necessary for a marker to become part of a paradigm even if that marker can be associated with highly generalized grammatical concepts. Second, the markers used to express grammatical categories often do not satisfy the condition of clearly determined semantic domains because the pragmatic inferences that can be drawn from them may cover several rather divergent grammatical categories (cf. Figure 9.1). As a consequence, it is not easy to integrate them into a clearly defined system of categories with their subcategories, as is needed in morphological paradigms.

4. Conclusion

EMSEA languages represent a type of grammaticalization that is characterized by its limited coevolution of meaning and form. As was shown in subsections 3.2 and 3.3, this is due to phonological properties (discreteness of syllable boundaries, phonotactic restraints) and to the lack of obligatoriness and clearly determined semantic domains. The core of grammaticalization in these languages thus consists in constructions with their slot structures which provide the basic syntactic framework for processes of reanalysis and analogy. Since rigid word-order patterns are the most important indicators of a high degree of grammaticalization in EMSEA languages, it does not come as a surprise that slot structures within constructions are of central importance for these processes.

These properties of grammaticalization are characteristic of the whole area of EMSEA languages (Bisang 2006)—an area that is characterized by complex contact situations over several millennia (Enfield 2003; Bisang 1996). Thus, a typology of manifestations of grammaticalization is not necessarily a matter of individual languages and their structural properties, it can also be a matter of areality (Heine and Kuteva 2005). In fact, areal influence can override language-internal structural properties. This has been shown by the case of Khmer, a language with subsyllabic morphology that follows the grammaticalization patterns of EMSEA to the detriment of its morphological potential (cf. subsection 3.2).

A situation in which pragmatics (metaphor, analogy) and phonology are relatively independent calls to mind Newmeyer's (1998: 295) criticism that 'grammaticalization appears to be no more than a cover term for a conjunction of familiar developments from different spheres of languages, none of which require or entail any of the other'. From such a perspective, grammaticalization is only an epiphenomenon that results from the interaction of morphosyntactic reanalysis, semantic change, and phonetic reduction. However, this view is not necessarily supported by this chapter. The way in which processes of grammaticalization develop in individual languages and in larger areas such as the one covered by the EMSEA languages is determined by specific factors that are responsible for the degree of (in)dependence with which the domains of pragmatics and phonology interact. This opens a new typological perspective in grammaticalization research, a perspective that may be able to account for different manifestations of grammaticalization. From such a typological perspective, research on grammaticalization is anything but irrelevant.

CHAPTER 10

GRAMMATICALIZATION AND SOCIOLINGUISTICS

TERTTU NEVALAINEN
MINNA PALANDER-COLLIN

1. Introduction

Grammaticalization and sociolinguistics is still a rare combination of research perspectives. Grammaticalization studies have primarily been concerned with language-internal issues like the directionality and pathways of grammatical change and the layered nature of linguistic forms and meanings undergoing change from lexical items to grammatical structures, or from less to more grammatical and routinized constructions. Sociolinguistic studies, on the other hand, have been interested in the social evaluation and embedding of language change in speech communities but have not usually specified research questions in relation to grammaticalization theory, even if the changes studied were grammatical.

Sociolinguistics has a strong tradition in exploring phonological rather than grammatical variation and change and many sociolinguistic generalizations concerning language change are based on phonological change, especially in languages like English (e.g. Labov 1994; 2001). The phonological focus in sociolinguistics perhaps partly explains the relative scarcity of sociolinguistic studies on grammaticalization. Another issue that has probably discouraged the sociolinguistic study of grammatical variation and change is the relative complexity of the linguistic variables to be studied. While it may be easy to observe and analyse the 'different ways of saying the same thing' in phonological terms, this is less straightforward in grammar, at least beyond low-level morphological variants. This also has implications for data collection: much more primary data are needed for the study of variation in grammar than in phonology.

In historical research the obstacles to combining sociolinguistics and grammaticalization studies are not only methodological—lack of systematic materials in sufficient quantities—but also conceptual. While lamenting the absence of individuals and their collective social groups from grammaticalization studies, Janda (2001: 266, 272), for one, dismisses grammaticalization as a primitive process needed for studying long-term diachrony. He regards it rather as an epiphenomenon that historical linguists reconstruct from diachronic correspondences of linguistic phenomena without paying attention to discontinuities in the transmission of linguistic changes across generations. According to Janda, the way forward would be 'sociolinguistically oriented studies which would compare the ways in which elements apparently undergoing grammaticalization are used by speakers vis-à-vis those on whom they model their behavior' (p. 318).

Comparing changes in apparent and real time provides us with a transition from currently ongoing processes of grammaticalization into those of the past. However, the discussion cannot be limited to a strictly generational perspective because both generational and communal processes of change can be observed in present-day language communities. Labov (1994: 84), in fact, expects phonological and morphological changes to follow the generational pattern, but syntactic and lexical changes to diffuse communally as 'all members of the community alter their frequencies together, or acquire new forms simultaneously'. As grammaticalization processes cut cross the morphology–syntax divide, Labov's suggestion would imply that both modes of diffusion are relevant to grammaticalization research. Historical studies similarly suggest that the dichotomy is too strict and that both modes can be attested, for example, in morphological changes (Nevalainen and Raumolin-Brunberg 2003: ch. 5).

Our aim in this chapter is to discuss the diffusion of grammaticalization processes of varying time depths and complexity across language communities. We will argue that a process of grammaticalization need not differ from other types of linguistic change in terms of its social embedding and evaluation. This uniformitarian generalization is supported by studies of current processes of change (see 2.1) as well as the historical sociolinguistic work carried out on English and other languages (2.2–2.4). The empirical work we will discuss draws mostly on the variationist, quantitative paradigm, although relevant prescriptive and discourse-based frameworks will also be introduced. For other related topics and approaches, see the contributions to this volume by Heine and Kuteva (Chapter 23), Kortmann and Schneider (21), Poplack (17), and Raumolin-Brunberg and Nurmi (20).

2. Sociolinguistic perspectives on grammaticalization

Our working definition of grammaticalization makes a distinction between grammar and lexis. Where grammar consists of functional forms and categories whose membership is more or less fixed, lexical forms constitute open classes, which can be freely expanded by means of word-formation processes. As a result of grammaticalization processes, lexical forms and constructions come to serve grammatical functions and, once grammaticalized, develop new grammatical functions (Hopper and Traugott 2003: 18). Grammaticalization is hence viewed as a gradual historical process of varying complexity. In this chapter we are concerned with the diffusion of grammaticalizing or newly grammaticalized forms or constructions in the community. The diffusion of linguistic changes usually follows an S-shaped curve. The incoming pattern spreads slowly in its initial stages, rapidly in mid-range, and slowly again when the change is reaching completion. Labov (1994: 65–6) suggests that this process reflects the frequency of contact between users of the incoming and the recessive forms, and the subsequent adoption of the incoming form.

2.1. Diffusion in apparent vs. real time

In most cases language change takes several generations to be completed, i.e. to reach the frequency of over 85 per cent of the competing variant forms (Nevalainen and Raumolin-Brunberg 2003: 55). Real-time data following the course of change provides the most authentic material for observing the progression of change, but as it requires longitudinal panel or trend studies, real-time data is often difficult or impossible to obtain. Real-time studies of ongoing change in contemporary communities are therefore understandably scarce, and their time depths are usually a couple of decades (for real-time phonological and morphophonological studies, see Labov 1994: ch. 4; Sundgren 2009: 98–9; Tagliamonte and D'Arcy 2009: 61–2). To overcome the difficulties of sampling real-time data, sociolinguistic studies dealing with ongoing language change employ the apparent-time method, which interprets the different age groups of language users at a certain point in time as representing the different historical stages of the change (for apparent time and real time, see Labov 1994: chs 3 and 4; Chambers 1995: 185–206). The apparent-time method thus relies on the assumption that once individuals have acquired the language during their formative years, their vernaculars remain more or less constant for the rest of their lifespans. This pattern results in generational change, where successive generations enter the community with a characteristic frequency of a linguistic form but also increase their frequencies in comparison to the previous generation.

However, accumulating empirical evidence shows that adult speakers are linguistically unstable, and the whole community may participate in language change at the same time. Thus, apparent-time studies underestimate the degree of change (Labov 2001: 446). Participation in ongoing changes, nevertheless, seems to be more restricted in later life as compared to (pre-)adolescent years. Nahkola and Saanilahti (2004), for example, argue on the basis of a panel study of Finnish morphophonological changes that it is easier for adults to change their language if forms were originally adopted as variables. Similarly, Tagliamonte and D'Arcy's (2009) findings on ongoing changes in the quotative *be like* in Toronto English suggest that changes in adulthood tend to be quantitative increases in frequencies rather than qualitative restructurings of the language system. Sundgren (2009) concludes that where there are changes towards a more standard use in Swedish morphophonological variables compared between 1967 and 1996, they can be observed both as individual change and as generational change. Although the apparent time model clearly has its limitations, it helps us understand the incrementation of language change in the shape of an S-curve over successive generations of users.

Labov's (2001: 446–65) logistic incrementation model sets out to explain (1) how phonological change advances in a step-by-step fashion across successive generations of speakers, showing a peak in apparent time near the age of stabilization, and (2) why in prototypical new and vigorous changes women are a generation ahead of men in the progress of change. In a nutshell, this model sets the age of stabilization of the linguistic system (*vernacular reorganization*) at 17(–20). Until that age, the increment is continuous from the time when children first enter the wider linguistic community and move away from the domination of their parents. To explain the gender difference, it is suggested that both boys and girls pick the level of their primary caretaker, the mother, but girls continue to add increments until vernacular reorganization, while boys do not. The applicability of the logistic incrementation model beyond phonology has been tested by Tagliamonte and D'Arcy (2009), who focus on six ongoing morphosyntactic(-semantic) (3–5 below) and discourse-pragmatic (1, 2, 6) changes in Present-day Toronto English, including the following forms:

(1) quotative *be like* (*And I'm* ***like****, 'Yeah'*);
(2) discourse marker *like* (*You know,* ***like*** *the people were very friendly*);
(3) stative possessive *have* (*It* ***has*** *some strength*);
(4) modal *have to* (*You* ***have*** *to like run to the other side*);
(5) future temporal *going to* (*Like if I'm* ***gonna*** *go downtown*);
(6) intensifier *so* (*She was like* ***so*** *sure and* ***so*** *careful*).
(Tagliamonte and D'Arcy 2009: 75–9)

The time depth and the pace of these changes varies enormously, as the quotative *be like* was first attested only in the 1980s and has already reached the maximum frequency of 63 per cent in the age group that uses it most frequently. Similarly, the discourse marker *like* and the intensifier *so* date to the 19th and early 20th centuries, with the current frequencies at 26 and 12 per cent, respectively. The modal *have to*, on the other hand, dates to the 15th century, with the current top frequency at 94 per cent, while the future *going to* also has its first attestations in the 15th century, with a contemporary frequency at a mere 53 per cent (Tagliamonte and D'Arcy 2009: 80). All these ongoing changes are not necessarily instances of grammaticalization, but (4) and (5) in particular have been discussed as such in earlier literature. The current stage of these two changes in Toronto English is nearing completion, as *have to* is almost completely specialized to express obligation and necessity with fairly limited variation with the other modal equivalents *must*, *have got to*, and *got to* (Tagliamonte and D'Arcy 2009: 78). The frequencies of the variants *be going to* and *will* are around 50 per cent, which Tagliamonte and D'Arcy (2009: 79) interpret to indicate that the progression of *be going to* might be very slow or be slowing down, or the two forms have already become specialized within certain contexts.

The apparent-time trajectories of the six changes confirm that the logistic incrementation model has validity beyond phonological change, but the emerging patterns are not straightforward, as the stage and duration of the change seem to have clear implications for the adolescent peak and gender differences. They are the most visible in new and vigorous changes such as quotative *be like*, but very weak or not visible at all at a later stage of the change, which is the case with *have to* and *be going to*. All the changes studied by Tagliamonte and D'Arcy are led by women (except *be going to*), but contrary to expectations the results show that both men and women have adolescent peaks in apparent time (except modal *have to*). They therefore suggest that 'men are full participants in incrementation; they simply do so, all other things being equal, at a slower rate than women do' (Tagliamonte and D'Arcy 2009: 98).

2.2. Time depth of change

The duration of a change also has implications for its sociolinguistic reconstruction in real time. Jespersen's Cycle serves to illustrate the point. It refers to a grammaticalization process whereby sentential negation, which is marked by a single preverbal negator, comes to involve two simultaneous morphemes, one preceding the verb and the other following it. Finally, the construction is reduced to one postverbal negative marker. Linguists argue about the Cycle's theoretical status and typological interpretation, but the following stages are traditionally distinguished (using English morphemes):

stage I: *ne* > stage II: *ne... not* > stage III: *not*

Altogether 66 of the 1,011 languages described by Dryer (2008) currently have a two-part negative construction. Many have lost the first negative element in the course of their history, while others, like French, are currently in the process of losing it. As Jespersen's Cycle characterizes the history of negation in a variety of language families, it is not plausible that it would constitute a single contact-induced phenomenon. Something like 'gram families' may nevertheless have been formed (Heine and Kuteva 2005: 183–85). For example, Dutch, English, and German largely underwent Jespersen's Cycle during the Middle Ages. However, the research on the duration of the Cycle in these languages also suggests varietal differences. In the absence of sufficient historical evidence, the entire Cycle cannot be accounted for in any sociolinguistic detail. We will therefore concentrate on the transition from stage II to stage III.

A comparison of West Germanic languages shows that the transition from stage II to III took longest in Dutch, where it progressed gradually from the early 14th century to the middle of the 17th century (Burridge 1993: 190–94). Moreover, dialectal variation was considerable throughout the period in the multi-genre corpus Burridge analysed. The process towards stage III was led by Hollandish in the north, where the deletion of the preverbal negator was well under way around 1300. By contrast, stage II prevailed in Brabantish in the south throughout the 350-year period studied in almost all sentence types. Breitbarth (2009: 109) suggests that Low German varieties also transferred from stage II to stage III quite late, between 1450 and 1500. Up until the third quarter of the 15th century, the bipartite *en... nicht* dominated but was outnumbered by plain *nicht* in the first quarter of the 16th century. Breitbarth's corpus consisted of official documents from different northern German cities, and she does not report any regional variation.

Stage II was shorter in Middle High German and Middle English. On the basis of her quantitative evidence, Jäger (2008: 143–4) suggests that Middle High German (1050–1350) was already predominantly a stage-III language with *niht* as the principal negator. Her corpus of three texts is, however, too limited for regional comparisons. The more ample corpus data presented by Wallage (2008: 645) for English indicate that English transferred rapidly from stage II to stage III in the late 14th century: while *ne... not* dominated in 1250–1350 (68 per cent of the cases), the single postverbal *not* was attested in 87 per cent of the cases in the next period, 1350–1420. Table 10.1 presents an overview of these corpus findings.

One of the reasons for what looks like an extraordinarily rapid change from one Middle English period to the next may be partly a corpus artefact, a reflection of the low number of texts produced in the period 1250–1350. In this period French and Latin were the dominant written languages in England. The transition may in fact have been much smoother, especially if the substantial regional variation reported in Middle English is taken into account (Mazzon 2004: 18–90). Many

Table 10.1. Periods of transition (x) from stage II to stage III in Jespersen's Cycle

Language/ variety	-1350	1350–1450	1450–1550	1550–1650	1650–1800	1800–1950	1950–
High German	x						
English		x					
Dutch		x	x	x			
Low German			x				
French						x	x

linguistic changes diffused from the north to the south in Middle English. Those involving simplification are often attributed to contacts of the English with speakers of Old Norse, a North Germanic language, where the first negator had probably disappeared from speech by the Viking period (Haugen 1982: 164–5).

Diachronic and cross-varietal comparisons become considerably easier when we move on to the Romance languages, and French in particular, where the process is still under way. Stage I dominated in French from the 9th to the 13th century when *ne* was the sole negator. Stage II (*ne... pas*) was established between the 14th and 16th centuries, and remained stable until the end of the 18th century. It was not until the 19th and 20th centuries that the transition from stage II to stage III properly began in both European and North American French (Martineau and Mougeon 2003: 146).

Williams (2009) provides a survey of some dozen studies, which suggest that the process is more advanced in Canadian French than in the European varieties studied. Martineau and Mougeon (2003: 145), for example, note that in contemporary Quebec speech *ne* deletion is almost categorical. Real-time studies on European French show that the change is progressing in speech at different rates in different localities. Space allows only a discussion of the trend and panel studies Ashby conducted in the mid-1970s and mid-1990s on the metropolitan French dialect of Tours (Ashby 1981; 2001), with a comparison with *ne* deletion in Parisian French (Hansen and Malderez 2003/4).

Ashby's 1975 data from 35 speakers show a significant apparent-time pattern suggestive of a change in progress. While the overall rate of *ne* use in the sample was 37 per cent, the older age group used *ne* in half of the cases in which it could occur, but the younger only in one fifth. The observed gender difference proved statistically significant: women were found to lead the process. Moreover, *ne* deletion was shown to be socially stratified: lower-middle-class speakers had the highest deletion rate and upper-middle-class speakers the lowest. Ashby (1981: 684) interprets this pattern in social terms as a 'change from below'. His 1996 follow-up study of 29 speakers indicates that *ne* use had dropped in real time from the average of 37 per cent to 18 per cent. The age difference was now much reduced and gender difference no longer significant, while social stratification still persisted, with the lowest-ranking speakers leading the change. However, when age difference was taken into account, social stratification hardly played any role among the younger speakers, although individual variation could be observed. In order to find out whether individuals changed over time, a panel component was added to the trend study, and ten speakers from the 1975 study were re-interviewed in 1996. Six of them were quite stable in their usages, and three of those whose use of *ne* had decreased were over 65 years of age. Ashby (2001: 19) accounts for this unexpected finding in terms of lifecycle patterns, elderly people adopting a more relaxed style than those still active in the working life.

Real-time studies on the transition from stage II to III in Paris similarly suggest a steady overall decline, from about 16 per cent of *ne* in the early 1970s to 8 per cent in the early 1990s. The three speech corpora discussed by Hansen and Malderez (2003/4) show apparent-time differences similar to those found by Ashby: in the early 1970s, the oldest age group used *ne* in one third of the cases, and their average dropped to one fifth in the later data. In the 1990s those under 14 did not use *ne* at all, which suggests that the change had run its course in the French capital. It remains to be seen how long the written word will take to follow suit. Discussing *ne* deletion in computer-mediated conversation, Williams (2009: 472) concludes that, as a result of editorial policy, all major newspapers and magazines can still be expected to show a *ne* retention rate close to 100 per cent in any francophone country.

2.3. Social evaluation

It is a commonplace in sociolinguistics that social value is attached to linguistic variation and change, although not necessarily to all processes of change (Labov 2001: 28–9). Our next set of studies shows how the diffusion of the suffix *-ly* became subject to social evaluation in English. Standard English stands out as an 'adverbial language' among its Germanic relatives in that overt adverbial marking by means of *-ly* has spread to all adverbial functions at both clause and constituent levels (Swan 1988; 1997; Nevalainen 1997; 2008). Brinton and Traugott (2005: 93) place this suffix at the productive end of their cline of grammaticality, which is defined in terms of degrees of fusion of the units of grammaticalization with other, external unit types. The increasing productivity of the *-ly* suffix has significantly expanded its host classes over time. Today they also include intensifiers that modify adjectives and other adverbs.

Nevalainen (2008) analysed the use of six dual-form intensifiers in the Corpus of Early English Correspondence (*exceeding/-ly, excellent/-ly, extraordinary/-ly, extreme/-ly, full/-ly*, and *marvellous/-ly*). The results indicate that *-ly* adverbialization accelerated among the literate social ranks between the 15th and 17th centuries. The frequency of suffixless intensifiers fell from almost categorical use in the fifteenth century to 72 per cent in the 17th century in the adjective/adverb-modifier function, and from 20 per cent to 7 per cent in the verb-modifying function. These results support Swan and others who find a marked increase in the overt marking of the English adverbial category well before the appearance of normative grammars in the 18th century.

As the process spread by lexical diffusion, considering the use of the individual adverb pairs throws light on their social embedding. It is particularly relevant to intensifiers, whose turnover is remarkably rapid as new items replace older ones in the community grammar (e.g. Ito and Tagliamonte 2003). This was also borne out by the historical data. *Full* lost momentum after the 15th century, and *fully* never became as popular across the literate population. The less frequent *exceeding/ly* and *extreme/ly* came into general use in the 17th century (7–10). Both suffixless and suffixed forms could be employed by one and the same person.

(7) I am **exceeding sorry** the strangurie is become soe afflictive unto you. (CEEC 1653, Thomas Browne; 285)

(8) Butt I am **exceedingly sorry** for the death of that worthy honest gentleman Dr Jaspar Needhame, (CEEC 1679, Thomas Browne; 136)

(9) . . . a cuntry so **extreame foule**, that I think winter is to be found heer at Midsummer. (CEEC 1615, John Holles; I,61)

(10) I am **extreamly sorry** that your letter miscaryed (CEEC 1653, Dorothy Osborne; 117)

The patterns of diffusion that emerged reveal varying input from different social strata. While the modifier *exceeding* was to a large extent shared by all the literate social ranks and both genders alike, *extremely* was clearly promoted by the highest ranks, and by women rather than men. The pattern of social stratification was consistent: the lower gentry used *extremely* only rarely, and merchants and other ranks below the gentry hardly at all. The same groups of people were analysed in both cases.

Variation between suffixed and suffixless forms began to attract social comment in the following centuries. The suffixless forms of the six intensifier pairs were all among those stigmatized by 18th-century prescriptive grammarians. Labels such as 'improper' and 'inelegant' imply that they were associated with the lower social ranks by second-order indexicality, i.e. attaching to the use of these forms a social evaluation of their users (Milroy 1999). However, social evaluation is not governed by logic, and a suffixless form could transcend censure by virtue of its frequency.

Very has preserved its great popularity from the 16th century to the present-day without becoming stigmatized or acquiring a suffixed variant.

Despite the generalization of the *-ly* suffix over time, suffixless adverb types continue to be frequently used in nonstandard varieties and in common colloquial speech (Biber et al. 1999: 542–4; Kortmann and Schneider 2006). In his studies of Scottish English, Macaulay (2005: 112–28) found that *-ly* adverbs, types as well as tokens, were used by middle-class speakers much more frequently than by lower-class speakers. This pattern was repeated in both adults and adolescents, and the gender variation observed was minor in comparison with class differences. Macaulay takes these differences to reflect socially stratified discourse styles. Variation in discourse styles may also hold the key to understanding the social layering in adverbialization in the past.

2.4. Social complexity of pragmaticalization

The development of 'comment clauses', 'parentheticals', or 'pragmatic markers' in English has attracted considerable attention both diachronically (e.g. Brinton 2008b; Palander-Collin 1999) and synchronically (Aijmer 1997; Kärkkäinen 2003; Thompson and Mulac 1991). The studies discussing the development of pragmatic items do so mostly in terms of grammaticalization, as many of the criteria associated with grammaticalization like decategorialization, phonological reduction, and generalization, as well as subjectification and pragmatic strengthening, are fulfilled even though decrease of syntactic scope and bonding were not (Traugott 1995b). One of the controversies, however, is what status should be assigned to the development of items like *I think*, *methinks*, *I guess*, *as you see*, *you know*, *indeed*, or *in fact* as routinized ways of expressing subjective point of view or discourse organization. As an alternative model, pragmaticalization, has been posited, since the developing items serve pragmatic rather than 'core' grammatical functions (e.g. Aijmer 1997). However, Traugott (1995) argues that syntactic restriction should not be a central criterion of grammaticalization, as different parts of grammar—like speaker attitude and tense—serve different purposes, which again may lead to different morphosyntactic results. (For a discussion of the treatment of comment clauses in earlier research, see Brinton 2008: 58–61.)

We shall focus on *I think* and *methinks* as an example of grammaticalization of a pragmatic item, as these phrases have been studied within a sociolinguistic framework from the 12th century to 1680 (Palander-Collin 1999). The grammaticalization of *I think* as a subjective marker expressing certainty and doubt or deliberativeness and tentativeness appears to have started in the 16th century when the relic *methinks* became increasingly rare. *Methinks* has its origins in the Old English impersonal construction, which was gradually replaced by the personal verb *think* and other verbs with a similar meaning, including *seem*. The 1st person experiencer *me* was overwhelmingly used with the verb even earlier, but in the 16th-century data the phrase appears only in the 1st person (Palander-Collin 1999: 134). To our knowledge, there are no studies mapping the diachronic history of *I think* from the 18th century up to the present, but in Present-day English *I think* seems to be developing even more grammaticalized functions as a discourse marker: Kärkkäinen (2003) has noted that *I think* often performs a routine organizational task in contemporary discourse rather than merely conveying certainty or uncertainty.

In studies dealing with *I think* and *methinks*, increasing frequencies and the position of the phrase have been used as the central indicators of ongoing grammaticalization (e.g. Palander-Collin 1999; Thompson and Mulac 1991). Sentence-initial position without the subordinator *that* is seen as more grammaticalized than *I think that*..., and the parenthetical use shows the most grammaticalized context. In studies on spoken language, accelerated tempo, reduced accent, and reduced form are further signs of more grammaticalized uses (Kärkkäinen 2003). Although many studies are concerned with pragmatic factors in the use and development of parentheticals, diachronic sociolinguistic studies of grammaticalization processes are infrequent. Palander-Collin's (1999) study on *I think* and *methinks* in the socially stratified Corpus of Early English Correspondence (1410–1680) shows that as far as the development of *I think* and *methinks* is concerned, grammaticalization is a socially embedded language change, although the patterns are not necessarily straightforward, and discourse pragmatic factors also affect the development.

For instance, the frequencies of *I think* in general increase in the 16th century with the gentry using *I think* the most, but merchants seem to be leading the use of the most grammaticalized parenthetical forms. *Methinks*, on the other hand, is used most frequently by the gentry in the 15th and 16th centuries (Palander-Collin 1999: 214–16). These tendencies suggest that the new point-of-view marker *I think* was a change from below, emerging first in the vernacular, while the older form *methinks* was maintained longest in more conscious styles. In addition to the social-group perspective, it may be an important factor in the spread of more routinized uses that frequent 1st person mental verb expressions (e.g. *I think, I know, I hope, I wish*) were not only used to express the writer's position as regards the epistemic or evidential stance, but also convey meanings that relate the writer to the addressee in various ways and hence contribute to the writer–addressee relationship (Palander-Collin 2009).

The development of *I think* and *methinks* can also be viewed within paradigms other than that of parentheticals, such as the semantically oriented paradigm of epistemic expressions (Bromhead 2009; Wierzbicka 2006) or stance markers implying involvement and subjectification (Biber 2004). In terms of diachronic frequencies, the importance of these paradigms seems to have increased in Modern English, which may link a linguistic change to cultural change. Wierzbicka (2006: ch. 7) claims that 1st person epistemic phrases (*I think, I suppose, I guess*, etc.)

started to be used 'on a large scale in the first half of the eighteenth century, that is, some time after the publication of Locke's *Essay Concerning Human Understanding*' (2006: 207). Her hypothesis is that the rise of epistemic phrases relates to the Anglo cultural scripts that shifted in the Enlightenment period from certainty to doubt, and reflect the need to distinguish between 'knowledge' and 'judgement' (Wierzbicka 2006: 35). The hypothesis, whether tenable or not, highlights the importance of usage in the spread of change across speech communities, as specific linguistic items may be more relevant for some social practices than others, such as the intellectual debate of the Enlightenment period, and specific social groups may then be more likely to become involved in these practices and ongoing language change.

3. Conclusion

The evidence we have discussed suggests two conclusions. First, grammaticalization processes can be described using the same sociolinguistic frameworks as other processes of linguistic change. Secondly, the present can be used to explain the past, in that similar social factors are found to correlate with ongoing changes in both real- and apparent-time studies. This is of theoretical relevance because the real-time study of the social dynamics of grammaticalization naturally becomes more elusive the further back in time we go, even in languages with extensive written records. The surviving evidence is nonetheless often sufficient for charting the time courses of grammaticalization processes, showing that they may range from a few decades to several centuries or even longer.

CHAPTER 11

GRAMMATICALIZATION AND LANGUAGE ACQUISITION

HOLGER DIESSEL

1. Introduction

There are extensive parallels between language acquisition and diachronic change that have intrigued historical linguists for many decades (see Baron 1977 for an overview of the older literature). The parallels are particularly striking in morphology. When children begin to produce inflected word forms, they often create novel forms that correspond to diachronic innovations. For instance, Bybee and Slobin (1982) showed that children's errors in the formation of the English past tense are similar to novel past tense forms in language change. There are also similarities between children's phonetic errors and patterns of sound change. For instance, Stampe (1969) observed that there is a similar tendency in ontogeny (i.e. child language development) and diachrony (i.e. historical language change) to simplify consonant clusters and to devoice final obstruents; however, other aspects of historical sound change do not have any parallels in child language (e.g. the tendency to weaken strong consonants, i.e. lenition; see Drachman 1978 and Vihman 1980).

The similarities between diachrony and ontogeny play an important role in certain theories of language change (see Croft 2001: §3.2 for an overview). However, there is no consensus among historical linguistics as to how the two developments are related. Some scholars have argued that language change results from errors and misanalyses in child language (e.g. Andersen 1973); other scholars have claimed that children recapitulate the diachronic development (or phylogenetic evolution) of language in the process of language learning (e.g. Bickerton 1981; see also Givón and Malle 2002); and yet other scholars have argued that ontogeny and diachrony are often parallel because they involve similar mechanisms of change (e.g. Ziegeler 1997) or similar adaptive behaviours (e.g. Givón 2009).

The previous literature on the relationship between ontogeny and diachrony has been mainly concerned with parallels in morphology and phonology, but there are also intriguing parallels in the development of grammatical markers, suggesting that grammaticalization is not only a historical phenomenon but can also be found in child language (cf. Givón 1979; 2009; Givón and Shibatani 2009; Schmidtke-Bode 2009; Slobin 1994; Ziegeler 1997). On this view, the notion of grammaticalization refers to a general developmental process that is instantiated in both language acquisition and diachronic change (cf. Ziegeler 1997).

This chapter compares several cases of grammaticalization to the development of grammatical markers in child language. The review of the literature reveals some striking parallels in the semantic development of grammatical markers in ontogeny and diachrony. There is a general developmental pathway leading from relatively concrete meanings to meanings that are more abstract. However, the phonological and morphological changes of grammaticalization do not have parallels in child language, suggesting that the two developments are in principle independent of each other. There is no evidence that the acquisition of grammatical markers repeats the process of grammaticalization or that the historical development of grammatical markers originates from changes in child language.

2. Case studies

2.1. Adpositions

A classical case of grammaticalization is the development of adpositions from nouns and verbs (cf. Heine, Claudi, and Hünnemeyer 1991; Lehmann 1995a). Historically, adpositions are derived from relational nouns, serial verbs, and various other lexical expressions. For instance, in some languages adpositions are derived from body part terms such 'head' (> 'on'), 'belly' (> 'in'), or 'buttock' (> 'under') (cf. Heine et al. 1991: 126). In contrast to the diachronic evolution, the ontogenetic development does not originate from lexical expressions; there is no evidence that children's early adpositions are derived from nouns and verbs. But, interestingly, there are far-reaching parallels in the semantic developments of adpositions in language change and acquisition.

Adpositions denote spatial, temporal, causal, and various other semantic concepts. There is abundant evidence that the spatial sense of adpositions is the most basic meaning from which all other senses are historically derived. Across languages, spatial adpositions provide the diachronic source for adpositions with abstract meanings; notably, temporal adpositions are commonly derived from adpositions with spatial meanings (cf. Haspelmath 1997; see also Heine et al. 1991).

The same development from space to time occurs in child language (cf. Ziegeler 1997). The earliest prepositions that English-speaking children produce have usually a spatial meaning. A notable exception are prepositions in fixed expressions such as *on Christmas* or *come on*, which often appear prior to all other uses because they are more frequent in the ambient language (cf. Hallan 2001). However, if we limit the view to the productive use of prepositions, the earliest uses usually have a spatial meaning, which is later often extended to more abstract meanings. Since many adpositions are ambiguous between several meanings, semantic extensions are often difficult to recognize. However, sometimes children extend the use of spatial adpositions to non-spatial meanings that are not conventionalized, as in example (1), in which the spatial preposition *behind* is used with a temporal meaning (example adopted from Bowerman 1985: 1292):

(1) Can I have any reading *behind* the dinner? (= after)

Examples of this type suggest that children do not simply imitate the various senses they encounter in the ambient language; rather, they actively construe the mappings between space and time. Clark and Carpenter (1989) argue that children's semantic errors with adpositions reflect the existence of 'emergent categories' that underlie the use of adpositions in child language. Using data from several English-speaking children, they compared the development of the preposition *from* in early child language to its development in language change. In Present-day English, *from* is primarily used with spatial and temporal meanings, but can also mark the oblique agent of the verb *get* (cf. examples 2–4).

(2)	That vase comes *from* Lugano.	spatial
(3)	*From* World War II on, their fortune failed.	temporal
(4)	He got a book *from* Jill.	agent

In Old English *from* occurred in a broader range of contexts, indicating not only spatial and temporal meanings and animate agents but also natural forces such as rain and wind. Clark and Carpenter argue that the various uses of *from* are conceptually related through a general 'notion of source'. Like a location and a point in time, an agent can be conceived of as a metaphorical source denoting the origin of an action. Interestingly, this notion of source plays an important role in the ontogenetic development of *from* in early child language. In addition to the spatial and temporal uses, children make extensive use of *from* with animate instigators and natural forces that are reminiscent of certain uses of *from* in Old English (cf. examples 5 and 6 adopted from Clark and Carpenter 1989).

(5) This fall down *from* me. animate instigator
(6) Look at that knocked down tree *from* the wind. natural force

Moreover, children use *from* to mark abstract causes and instruments (cf. examples 7–9) as well as possessors (cf. example 21 adopted from Clark and Carpenter 1989).

(7) I am tired *from* my games. cause
(8) I drawed the lines *from* the pencil. instrument
(9) That's a finger *from* him. possessor

Like animate instigators and natural forces, causes and instruments can be construed as the source of an action. The use of *from* with a possessor involves a further extension. Clark and Carpenter argue that a possessor can be seen as the source or origin of the possessed object, which is reflected in the fact that in some languages possessors are marked by the same adposition as a spatial source (e.g. German *Das Auto von dir* 'The car from you').

In accordance with the historical development, children acquire the spatial sense of *from* prior to the temporal sense and the use of *from* with animate agents, which in turn appear prior to all other uses. While the ontogenetic development of *from* does not directly correspond to its diachronic evolution, it is consistent with the frequent mapping from space to time and other non-spatial meanings.

2.2. Future tense auxiliaries

A similar mapping from space to time is involved in the development of the motion verb *go* into a future tense marker (cf. Bybee, Pagliuca, and Perkins 1994). The development is well known from the *be-going-to* future in English (cf. Hopper and Traugott 2003: 1–3). In the source construction, *go* denotes a motion event, involving an agentive subject and an allative prepositional phrase that indicates the (physical) goal of the motion event (cf. example 10a). This construction was transformed into a future tense construction in which *go* functions as an auxiliary. One important stage of the development involves the use of *go* in a biclausal structure in which the motion event is combined with an infinitive denoting a metaphorical goal, i.e. a purpose, of the motion event (cf. example 10b). In the context of this construction, the motion sense of *go* is backgrounded in favour of the semantic feature of intention. The semantic shift is evoked by the purposive infinitive emphasizing the metaphorical goal of the activity. If *go* is routinely used in this context, the motion sense is gradually reduced to the point that it is eventually no longer perceived as a separate activity. At this point, *go* assumes the function of an auxiliary and the biclausal structure is reanalysed as a simple sentence denoting a single future event (cf. example 10c). Parallel to these developments, the expression *be going to* is phonetically reduced to *gonna.*

(10) a. Peter is going to school. motion
b. Peter is going (in order) to help John. intention
c. Rain is going to fall. future

The ontogenetic development of the *be-going-to* future takes a similar path. Drawing on comprehensive corpus data from several English-speaking children, Schmidtke-Bode (2009) found that the earliest utterances in which *go* occurs with an implicit future meaning denote a motion event that is combined with some other activity, as in the following example from a two-year old boy (adopted from Schmidtke-Bode 2009: 526).

(11) Child: Going wash a hands.
Comment: [Child goes into the kitchen to wash a towel]

These early motion-cum-purpose clauses are semantically similar to the diachronic source of the *be-going-to* future. They include the verb *going* with its literal meaning, combined with an activity that is conceptualized as the purpose of the motion event. The motion sense is dominant in the early uses, but it does not take long until the auxiliary use of *going* outnumbers the motion-cum-purpose sense. Interestingly, although the children's production of *be going to* changed from the literal to the metaphorical sense, the children's parents produced the two senses of *be going to* with the same frequency throughout the time of the study, suggesting that the changes in the children's speech cannot be attributed to changes in the ambient language.

The semantic development of the construction is accompanied by morphosyntactic changes. The earliest instances of the *be-going-to* future occur in very simple constructions: They include the verb *going*, or the reduced from *gon*, without the auxiliary *be* and the infinite marker *to*, and often lack on overt subject (e.g. *Gon play outside*) (cf. Schmidtke-Bode 2009). Formally reduced clauses of this type differ from the historical source of the *be-going-to* future, in which *go* is accompanied by an overt subject and the auxiliary *be*, the *-ing* suffix, and the infinitive marker *to*. In fact, one could argue that the ontogenetic development of the *be-going-to* future proceeds in the opposite direction from the development of the *be-going-to* future in language change. Historically, the development of the future tense marker originated from a biclausal construction that was reduced to a simple sentence in which *be going to* is often phonetically reduced to *gonna*; but ontogenetically the future tense marker evolves in the context of morphologically deprived clauses that are gradually expanded into more complex structures (cf. Diessel 2004: §4). Thus, while the semantic acquisition of the *be-going-to* future takes the same path as in diachronic change, the morphosyntactic development of the future tense marker does not correspond to the diachronic path.

2.3. Modal verbs

One of the most intensively studied phenomena of grammaticalization is the development of modal verbs (cf. Lightfoot 1979; Plank 1984; Krug 2000; Fischer 2007). The bulk of the literature is concerned with the emergence of modal auxiliaries in English, but there are also cross-linguistic studies on the development of modal verbs (e.g. Bybee et al. 1994). Across languages, modal verbs are commonly derived from lexical verbs such as *owe*, *need*, *know*, or *get* that take a nominal complement. When these verbs are routinely used with a deverbal noun (e.g. an infinitive) they may be reanalysed as modal auxiliaries, which at first occur in performative contexts expressing 'obligation', 'permission', and 'ability'. These early deontic uses are later extended to epistemic uses expressing 'possibility' and 'necessity'. The development constitutes a unidirectional cline of modality with three major stages (cf. Bybee et al. 1994: 240–41):

(12) lexical verb > deontic modal verb > epistemic modal verb

The three stages can be identified in the history of the English language. In Old English, the demotic use of modal verbs was prevalent. Some Old English modal verbs were still commonly used as lexical verbs that could take a nominal complement (e.g. *cunnan*), and some modal verbs could already be used with an epistemic meaning; but the majority of the Old English modal verbs occurred in the deontic use and developed the epistemic use only later as a secondary meaning (cf. Fischer 2007: 188–90). In Old English, modal verbs were primarily defined by semantic criteria; since most modal verbs were based on preterite-present tense forms, they had some morphological features that distinguished them from other (i.e. non-modal) verbs; but it was only in Early Modern English that the English modal verbs were established as a particular grammatical class. At that time, some general syntactic changes led to the formal division between lexical verbs and modal auxiliaries. The most important change involved the emergence of the dummy auxiliary *do*, which became obligatory with lexical verbs in negative contexts and questions, whereas sentences with modal verbs preserved the old grammatical forms (cf. Plank 1984).

In parallel to the diachronic evolution, the ontogenetic development of modal verbs originates from the deontic use. Children begin to use modal verbs in negative sentences, questions, and imperatives (i.e. in 'performative contexts') that are concerned with different aspects of deontic modality (cf. Stephany 1986). The epistemic use emerges only several months later, and is initially restricted to specific verbs (e.g. *can*, *could*, *may*) (cf. Stephany 1986). However, the similarity between the ontogenetic and diachronic development of modals concerns only their semantic features; the morphosyntactic developments are different. There are several aspects that distinguish them. First, there is no evidence that the acquisition of modal verbs involves a categorical change from lexical verbs to auxiliaries. Second, the morphosyntactic changes that led to the development of a particular grammatical class of modal auxiliaries in Early Modern English have no parallels in child language. Third, among the earliest modal verbs that English-speaking children produce are contracted negative forms such as *can't* and *won't*, which are historically derived from two separate words through univerbation. And finally, the English modals have undergone a process of phonetic reduction (e.g. *cunnan* > *can*) that does not occur in child language.

2.4. Present perfect

Another grammatical construction that takes the same conceptual pathway in language acquisition and diachronic change is the English present perfect, which Slobin (1994) investigated in one of the earliest studies on the parallels between grammaticalization and child language. In diachrony, the present perfect originated from an attributive construction including the verb *habban* 'have' denoting possession and an attributive participle that modified the possessed noun (cf. example 13 from Traugott 1992: 191).

(13) Old English (ÆC Hom 1, 31, 458.18)

[Ic	hæbbe	[gebunden	þone	feond]]	þe	hi	drehte.
I	have	bound	that.ACC	enemy	DEM	them	afflicted

'I have bound the enemy who afflicted them.'

In example (13) the participial verb form is uninflected, but in other contexts it agreed in gender, number, and case with the direct object, indicating that the participle was originally a noun modifier rather than an element of the verb phrase. However, in the course of development the participle lost its inflectional categories and became associated with the verb *habban*, resulting in an analytical verb form in which *habban* was downgraded to an auxiliary and the participle promoted to the main verb (cf. example 14):

(14) Ic hæbbe [gebunden [þone feond]] -> Ic [hæbbe gebunden] [þone feond]

The development was crucially motivated by semantic aspects of the source construction. Slobin argues that the construction in (13) is semantically ambivalent; it can be construed in two ways. If the focus is on the state of the bound enemy, the construction has its original attributive meaning, which can be paraphrased as 'I have that enemy bound that afflicted them'. However, if the focus is on the action of the subject, the construction invites the perfect meaning, i.e. 'I have bound that enemy that afflicted them'. In this interpretation, the sentence expresses the possession of a current state that is construed as the result of a past event. In this use, the present perfect occurred at first only with telic verbs denoting a resultant state with an (implicit) consequence for the present and/or future. However, later the *habban*-perfect was extended to iterative and non-telic verbs in which the result interpretation of the original perfect was backgrounded. In these novel uses, which Slobin calls the 'perfect of experience' and the 'continuative perfect' (cf. examples 15b,c), the present perfect does not imply a consequence as in the original 'resultant state perfect' (cf. example 15a).

(15) a. I have eaten lunch [and am therefore not hungry]. resultant state perfect
b. I have been abroad several times. perfect of experience
c. He has sung in the choir for years. continuative perfect

A parallel development from the resultant state perfect to the perfect of experience and the continuative perfect occurs in child language. The first present perfect forms that children produce involve telic verbs 'in contexts in which the completion of one action provides the grounds for a subsequent action' (cf. Slobin 1994: 122). Two subtypes of this use can be distinguished. Either the present perfect occurs in sentences that children use to 'negotiate sequences of activities' (cf. example 16), or it occurs in sentences that function to 'draw the hearer's attention to a result' (cf. example 17) (examples adopted from Slobin 1994: 122–3).

(16) Mother: Pick the bricks up, and then you go to bed.
Mother: No more pies this morning.
Child: Only one?
Mother: No
Child: When I'*ve picked* the bricks up? [I want more pie]

(17) Mother: You draw a letter for me.
Child: [draws letter] I'*ve drawed* a letter for you. [thus I want immediate attention]

In both uses, the construction invites the inference that the situation described by the verb in the present perfect has important consequences for the future. In example (16) it is implied that the child, a 4-year-old boy, wants more pie after he has picked up the bricks, and in example (17) it is implied that the boy expects to receive immediate attention from his mother because he has already completed the task. Starting from these early uses, children gradually extend the present perfect to sentences with iterative and non-telic verbs that are pragmatically less constrained than the early uses with telic verbs.

3. Discussion

The previous discussion has shown that the developments of grammatical markers in child language are often parallel to their developments in language change. However, the parallels are restricted to semantic and pragmatic features; the developments of morphosyntactic and phonological features are different. If the acquisition of grammar recapitulated its diachronic evolution, one would expect that the parallels between the two developments comprise all aspects of language; but the evidence reviewed in this chapter suggests that the morphosyntactic and phonological features of grammatical markers evolve along different pathways in language acquisition and diachronic change. The following differences have been observed:

1. First, grammaticalization involves categorical changes that do not occur in child language. According to grammaticalization theory, all grammatical markers are eventually derived from a lexical source, notably from nouns and verbs; but the acquisition of grammatical markers does not generally originate from a lexical source. Most grammatical markers are learned without a prior lexical term, and even if there is a related lexical expression, it is not generally the noun or verb that is learned first (e.g. the conjunction *[be]cause* appears prior to the noun *cause*).
2. Second, grammaticalization involves syntactic reanalyses that do not have parallels in child language. There is, for instance, no evidence that the acquisition of the English present perfect originates from an earlier attributive construction with a participial verb form, or that the acquisition of the *be-going-to* future presupposes the acquisition of an earlier complex sentence construction that is later reduced to a simple sentence as in diachronic change.
3. Third, grammaticalization processes often involve phonetic and morphological changes that do not occur in child language. In diachrony, grammatical markers are commonly derived from complex expressions that are phonetically reduced; but in language acquisition, children often learn the reduced forms (e.g. *don't, gonna, hafta*) prior to the analytical expressions (e.g. *do not, going to, hafta*) from which they are historically derived.

The formal differences between child language and diachronic change suggest that the two developments are in principle independent of each other; there is no direct link between them. Language acquisition does not recapitulate the diachronic evolution of grammar, nor does grammaticalization originate from changes in child language. It is striking, however, that the acquisition of grammatical markers often proceeds along the same conceptual paths as the development of grammatical markers in language change. Some well-known grammaticalization clines are paralleled by semantic developments in child language:

(i) space > time
(ii) motion > future
(iii) deontic modality > epistemic modality
(iv) resultant state perfect > perfect of experience/continuative perfect

However, not all grammatical phenomena take the same conceptual route in language acquisition and diachronic change. Consider for instance the development of finite complement clauses in English. The historical development originated from two independent sentences that were combined into a biclausal construction consisting of a main clause and a subordinate clause (cf. Hopper and Traugott 2003: 190–94; see Fischer 2007: §4 for a critical discussion of this analysis). Thompson and Mulac (1991) showed that in conversational English the main clause is often demoted to an epistemic marker with no referential meaning. Specifically, they argued that clauses such as *I think* or *I guess* do not denote an independent state of affairs, but function to indicate the speaker's attitude towards the proposition in the complement clause (cf. examples 18a,b).

(18) a. I think you are right.
b. I guess she will come.

Interestingly, the first complement clauses in language acquisition are similar to the formulaic main clauses that Thompson and Mulac characterized as the result of grammaticalization. As Diessel and Tomasello (2001) have shown, the earliest complement clauses that English-speaking children produce are accompanied by parenthetical main clauses functioning as epistemic markers, attention getters, or markers of the illocutionary force (cf. example 19 adopted from Diessel 2004: §5).

(19)	I think I'm go in there.	I guess I better come.	See these are stamps.
	I think I play jingle bells.	(I) guess I lay down it.	See the peoples going.
	I think he's gone.	I guess I have one more.	See I'm writing.

As children grow older, the main clauses become increasingly more complex and diverse, occurring with different types of subjects, inflected verbs forms, and a greater variety of complement-taking verbs, including verbs of saying such as *say* or *tell*, which in contrast to the mental state verbs of children's early formulaic main clauses are referential (cf. examples 20a,b).

(20) a. The kitty says he wants to come in.
b. She telled me she forget the doll carriage for me.

Thus, while the diachronic development of complement clauses originates from two independent sentences, which are later reduced to a monoclausal construction with a parenthetical main clause, the ontogenetic development originates from a simple sentence including a formulaic main clause that is gradually expanded into a fully developed clause (see Givón 2009: §7 for a somewhat different analysis). In other words, the two developments proceed in opposite directions, suggesting that they are driven by different forces. The historical development involves semantic bleaching and subjectification (cf. Traugott 1989), whereas the ontogenetic development is motivated by the fact that sentences with parenthetical main clauses are more frequent and simpler than complex sentences with referential main clauses (see Diessel 2004: §5 for discussion).

What this example demonstrates is that the conceptual developments of language acquisition are not predetermined by conceptual changes of grammaticalization—the two developments do not *have* to coincide. However, as we have seen, very often they *do* proceed along similar conceptual paths leading from relatively concrete meanings to meanings that are more abstract. Slobin (2002) argues that the conceptual parallels between language acquisition and diachronic change are 'spurious' because children and adults are engaged in different communicative tasks. Children seek to 'discover' meanings that are present in the ambient language, whereas adult speakers sometimes extend the meaning of existing expressions to novel meanings by pragmatic inference. Slobin's analysis draws our attention to an important difference between child language and diachronic change; but it disregards the creative and innovative aspects of child language. As we have seen above, children do not simply uncover existing meanings in the ambient language; rather, they actively construe novel forms and novel senses in ways that are similar to the creation of novel expressions in adult language. The occurrence of 'emergent categories' suggests that the acquisition of grammatical markers involves the same creative mappings between conceptual domains as pragmatic inferences involved in diachronic change; and thus we may hypothesize that the semantic parallels between the two developments are based on similar cognitive processes. Child language and language change occur under different circumstances, but the semantic parallels between them are not spurious because they involve the same mechanisms of categorization (cf. Ziegeler 1997).

4. Summary

We have seen that there are striking parallels between grammaticalization and language acquisition, but the parallels are not without exception. There are developments that take a different path in language acquisition and diachronic change. Moreover, we have seen that the parallels between the two developments are restricted to semantic features; the phonological and morphosyntactic aspects of grammaticalization do not occur in child language, suggesting that diachrony and ontogeny are in principle independent of each other. There is no evidence that grammaticalization and language acquisition are directly related. However, the two developments often proceed along similar conceptual paths because they involve the same mechanisms of categorization.

CHAPTER 12

GRAMMATICALIZATION AND LANGUAGE EVOLUTION

ANDREW D. M. SMITH

1. Introduction

1.1. The evolution of language

Our ancestors had no linguistic communication system, yet modern humans do. Evolutionary linguists aim to explain how language, this singular, species-defining phenomenon, emerged from the preceding, nonlinguistic state. Unfortunately, the genesis of language cannot be directly observed, which leads to a crucial methodological problem: it is unclear what evidence can provide convincing support for any hypotheses being evaluated (Botha 2003). Even worse, there is major disagreement over the fundamental nature of language, and thus what evolutionary linguists need to explain.

The dominant nativist account (Chomsky 1965) regards language as a domain-specific, genetically-encoded, autonomous module in the brain, dedicated to language acquisition. Language is thus biologically determined, and language learning consists of setting parameters in response to exposure to linguistic data; these parameter settings determine the rules in the language module, control its output, and dictate the specific language produced. Under this account, the language module contains arbitrary components, and the differences between individual languages are considered relatively superficial. This has led to the near-axiom of uniformitarianism in linguistics: that all languages are equivalently complex (although see Sampson, Gil, and Trudgill (2009) for recent challenges to this). Pinker and Bloom's (1990) major contribution to the nativist perspective was to point out that language shows clear signs of having been designed for communication; as natural selection is the only known source of the appearance of design, language must therefore have evolved through natural selection. A plausible account of relevant language-specific selection mechanisms, however, has so far proved elusive, leading some nativists to invoke non-adaptationist accounts (Chomsky 1988; Piattelli-Palmarini 1989; Lightfoot 2000), either suggesting that the language faculty originally evolved for another unspecified function and was then used by language, or that language was a dramatic saltation, emerging by chance through random mutations, and that its evolution is intrinsically inexplicable, and even uninteresting, as suggested by Chomsky:

> We know very little about what happens when 10^{10} neurons are crammed into something the size of a basketball, with further conditions imposed by the specific manner in which this system developed over time. It would be a serious error to suppose that all properties, or the interesting properties of the structures that evolved, can be 'explained' in terms of natural selection. (Chomsky 1975: 59).

All non-adaptationist accounts, however, come up against what Christiansen and Chater term the nativist dilemma:

> If language can emerge from general physical, biological, or cognitive factors, then the complexity and idiosyncrasy of U[niversal] G[rammar] is illusory; language emerges from general non-linguistic factors... If, by contrast, UG is maintained to be sui generis and not readily derivable from general processes, the complexity argument bites: the probability of a new and highly complex adaptive system emerging by chance is astronomically low. (Christiansen and Chater 2008: 497).

In contrast to the nativist account, others view language as a developing set of societal cultural conventions (e.g. Langacker 1987; Croft 2000; Tomasello 2008). From this perspective, evolutionary linguists seek to identify the minimal set of cognitive capacities needed to allow cultural conventions to be shared in a community, and to document how processes of cultural evolution can allow language to evolve from these underlying mechanisms (K. Smith and Kirby 2008). Importantly, the relevant cognitive capacities need not be dedicated to language alone, but could have evolved for a different purpose, and the way language is acquired, used, and transmitted is relevant to its structure. These cultural processes of acquisition, use, and transmission introduce selective pressures on language, which lead to its *cultural evolution*: linguistic structures which are easy to acquire, or are communicatively effective, will persist and increase in the language; those which are difficult to learn or hinder communication will be dispreferred and disappear from the language (Croft 2000; A. D. M. Smith forthcoming).

This proposed cultural origin for linguistic structure shifts the explanatory burden considerably, as only the existence of the underlying cognitive capacities need now be explained biologically:

> [C]ultural transmission potentially offers a uniform mechanism that explains both the genesis of language (a qualitative shift from a nonlinguistic system to a linguistic system) and language change (subsequent quantitative shift), at whatever temporal granularity is required. (K. Smith 2006: 316)

Non-nativists are also committed to uniformitarianism, but in the sense of *uniformity of process*: the mechanisms of cultural evolution which yielded linguistic change in early language are the same as those yielding linguistic change in modern language, and investigations of these mechanisms can provide insights into prehistorical qualitative linguistic change; it is in this respect that the study of grammaticalization is most relevant for evolutionary linguists.

1.2. The nature of grammaticalization

In historical linguistics, grammaticalization is a specifically *linguistic* process, through which a discourse strategy, syntactic construction, or word loses some of its independence of use, and becomes more functional in meaning (Givón 1979; Haspelmath 1998). Two major explanations have been suggested for this process in the literature: one identifying metaphorical extension as the driving force (Heine, Claudi, and Hünnemeyer 1991; Heine 1997b), the other reanalysis (Hopper and Traugott 2003). In evolutionary linguistics, however, grammaticalization is frequently invoked as a potential explanation for the emergence of language (Heine and Kuteva 2007; Hurford 2003; A. D. M. Smith 2006; Tallerman 2007; Hoefler and Smith 2009), though not without disagreement over whether its study can provide useful insights (Newmeyer 2006). A specifically linguistic process, however, cannot provide a satisfactory account of how language evolved, as we would be invoking language to explain its own origin. We must therefore abstract away from the linguistic process somewhat, concentrate on the underlying cognitive mechanisms which are necessary for grammaticalization to take place, and consider how these mechanisms can illuminate the processes of cultural evolution which may have led to the genesis of language.

Assuming that pre-linguistic communication and modern linguistic communication had the same foundations and motivations allows us to use grammaticalization theory as a tool to reconstruct the development of grammatical categories (Heine and Kuteva 2007). Section 2 below summarizes the attested pathways of grammaticalization; the striking directionality therein permits a tentative reconstruction of the order in which grammatical phenomena are likely to have arisen, and leads to the suggestion that the earliest lexical items were entities referring to conceptually autonomous things. In section 3, the mechanisms of grammaticalization are investigated from a cognitive perspective, showing how different accounts of grammaticalization based on metaphor and reanalysis can be unified through the domain-general mechanisms underlying ostensive-inferential communication (Hoefler and Smith 2009). In section 4, these are projected back to the 'protolanguage' debate, demonstrating that ostensive-inferential mechanisms can account for the initial emergence of arbitrary symbolic conventions and for the emergence of linguistic structure and its continuous development and renewal.

2. Pathways of Grammaticalization

The reader of Heine and Kuteva's (2002) detailed list of attested grammaticalization processes in modern language is immediately struck by the repeated similarities: not only that the same changes appear in multiple unrelated languages, but also that they can be grouped into higher-level categories of change. For example, Heine and Kuteva show that forms meaning BACK have independently developed into adpositional markers denoting location BEHIND in multiple languages as diverse as Icelandic, Halia, Moré, Kpelle, Baka, Aranda, Welsh, Imonda, and Gimira, and that this development 'appears to be an instance of a more general process whereby certain body parts, on account of their relative position, are used as structural templates to express deictic location' (Heine and Kuteva 2002: 48), presenting examples from a wide range of languages where adpositions have developed from other body parts, such as BELLY, BOWELS, BREAST, BUTTOCKS, EYE, FACE, FLANK, FOREHEAD, HEAD, HEART, MOUTH, NECK, SHOULDER, and SIDE. More generally, these changes from body part to location marker are instances of a categorical change in which nouns grammaticalize into adverbs and then adpositions.

The changes are overwhelmingly unidirectional; nouns are transformed regularly into adverbs, yet the reverse is exceedingly uncommon. With this in mind, Heine and Kuteva (2007) undertook a detailed analysis of the changes documented in their lexicon, producing an 'evolutionary network' (Fig. 12.1), which links clusters of commonly recognized grammatical categories into relative developmental layers. This analysis shows that all the major word classes in the world's languages can be derived ultimately from nouns and verbs, through a gradual process of cultural evolution, via grammaticalization. Heine and Kuteva consider both nouns and verbs to be evolutionarily primitive, because both categories regularly develop into categories on lower layers, yet neither is productively derived from other categories. The distinction between nouns and verbs as categories is initially

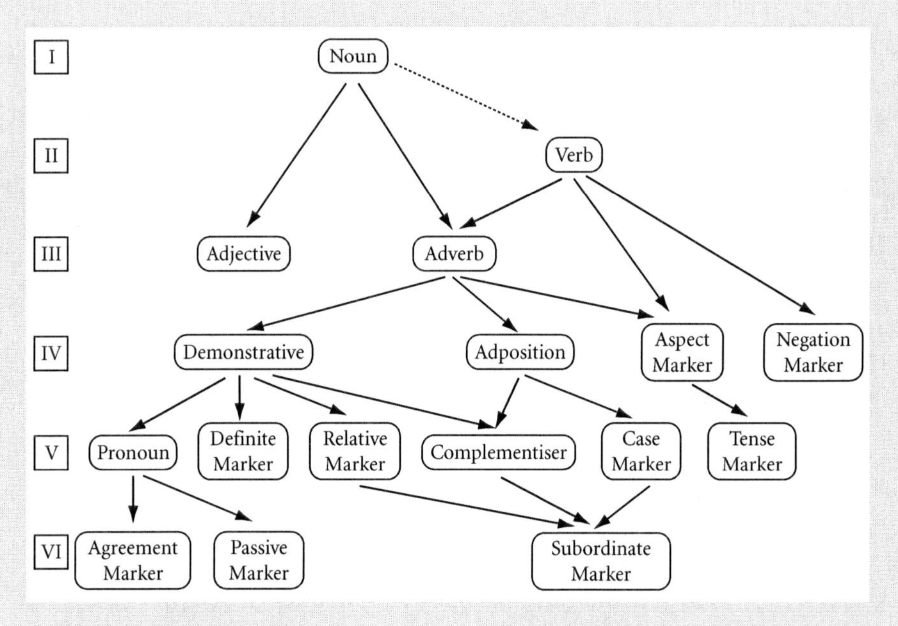

Fig. 12.1. Layers of grammatical evolution via pathways of grammaticalization, after Heine and Kuteva (2007). Pathways denoted by arrows; higher-numbered layers indicate increased levels of grammaticalization relative to other categories on the same pathway.

primarily conceptual, not syntactic: 'nouns' are prototypically objects, fixed in space and persisting indefinitely in time, which can be conceptualized independently, while 'verbs' are prototypically events, bounded in time, conceptualizable only by presupposing the existence of their participants (Langacker 2008a). This asymmetry leads to the reasonable conclusion that nouns probably emerged earlier than verbs; a language containing only nouns is more plausible than a verb-only language, although there is no clear directionality between nouns and verbs in the attested pathways of grammaticalization.

3. The cognitive basis of grammaticalization

Linguistic communication is characterized by the meaning of a sentence not simply being the logical meaning suggested by the words, but also containing components from the conversational context (Grice 1957; 1975). Communication between interlocutors is only made possible by the existence of common ground—the knowledge which the interlocutors recognize (or assume) that they share about the situation (Clark 1996; Sperber and Wilson 1995). Two crucial aspects of common ground are: (i) a shared understanding of the goal of the interaction, which requires them to understand each other's intentions (Tomasello et al. 2005); (ii) an awareness of their shared linguistic conventions, or form–meaning associations. Understanding the interactional goal is vital to successful communication, because it allows the interlocutors to work out what information is relevant in the current context—what information would bring about the achievement of the goal, if it were communicated.

3.1. Ostensive-inferential communication

Common ground allows communication to be established through an *ostensive* act performed by the 'speaker' and an *inferential* act performed by the 'hearer'. An ostensive act is any modification of the environment which enhances the common ground shared by the interlocutors; a prototypical ostensive act might be pointing at an object to draw the hearer's attention to it. By its deliberate, unusual nature, the ostensive act communicates the speaker's communicative intention (the fact that the speaker wishes to communicate) to the hearer, and thereby triggers the inferential act, the hearer's attempt to infer the speaker's informative intention (what the speaker is trying to communicate). The hearer uses their discourse world knowledge (Kuteva 2001), including their perception of the external environment, their pragmatic insights, and aspects of their models of cultural and social knowledge, to infer the meaning of the speaker's ostensive act from the current context (LaPolla 2006). This process of semantic reconstruction is fundamentally approximate and uncertain (Hurford 2007): the speaker's ostensive act serves merely as evidence on which the hearer's inferential act is based, and the hearer does not decode the meaning from the signal, but rather infers the meaning they think the speaker intended, given the current context and their assumptions about the shared common ground (A. D. M. Smith 2008). Such uncertainty yields two important characteristics of ostensive-inferential communication: (i) the speaker's original meaning and the hearer's reconstructed meaning can differ; (ii) there is a selective pressure on utterances that their meanings be reconstructible from context.

An individual's discourse world knowledge and their understanding of a particular context are highly idiosyncratic; it is extremely unlikely that the interlocutors in a communicative episode will represent the situation in the same way. These differences are not necessarily problematic, however, as successful communication depends not on sharing an identical representation, but on the perlocutionary effects of the communicative episode (Hoefler and Smith 2008). Ostensive-inferential communication is therefore itself an important source of linguistic variation, an essential requirement for evolutionary systems (Darwin 1968[1859]). Following Croft's (2000) evolutionary model of language change, we can view the hearer's reconstruction of the meaning, together with the way in which it maps to the form, as a replication of the speaker's original meaning. The replication is not completely faithful, but nevertheless the reconstruction of meaning is the mechanism through which form–meaning mappings, or constructions (Croft 2001), survive or die. Constructions whose meanings can be easily, and repeatedly reconstructed will be preferentially replicated, while those difficult to reconstruct will perish; the semantic reconstructibility of a construction is effectively the fitness function to which the language adapts (A. D. M. Smith forthcoming; Hruschka et al. 2009). Both the environment in which linguistic constructions are used and the fitness function against which they are selected, however, are in a constant state of flux; hence the adaptation of linguistic constructions is never-ending, and language is forever changing.

3.2. Metaphor and reanalysis

Ostensive-inferential communication forms the foundation of Hoefler and Smith's (2009) analysis of grammaticalization. Both metaphor- and reanalysis-based approaches to grammaticalization can be viewed in terms of the same underlying cognitive mechanisms, and the differences between them can be effectively captured by differences in the interlocutors' understanding of their shared common ground.

Metaphor is a cognitive process through which an existing form is used to express a meaning which is similar, but not identical, to its conventional meaning (Kövecses 2002; Lakoff and Johnson 1980; Hopper and Traugott 2003). The speaker draws an analogy between the conventional meaning and the novel meaning, and the analogy can succeed communicatively because some semantic components of the form's conventional meaning are irrelevant in the context and can thus be ignored; the remaining relevant components are shared with the novel meaning, which can therefore be inferred as the meaning of the form. The more obviously the ignored parts of the conventional meaning would conflict with the actually communicated meaning, the more figurative and conspicuous the metaphor is, but there is no clear-cut distinction between literal and metaphorical use; instead they fall on a continuum of 'loose talk' (Sperber and Wilson 1995) or 'partial sanction' (Langacker 1987), defined by the degree of similarity between the conventional meaning and the novel meaning (Hoefler and Smith 2009). Metaphor therefore includes any deviation from convention, which is inferable in context, and is as such ubiquitous in ordinary language use (Deutscher 2005: 117ff.). Notably, metaphor has great creative potential, as it allows a speaker can to express a novel meaning with no conventionalized form, and which has potentially never been expressed before.

Reanalysis is concerned with changes in linguistic structure, but has been understood in many different ways in the literature (Langacker 1977; Harris and Campbell 1995; Haspelmath 1998; Trask 2000). Hoefler and Smith (2009) define it very broadly as any difference in the (arbitrarily complex) form–meaning mappings of two constructions with the same form, including differences in (a) the holistic meaning associated with the utterance; (b) whether particular components of the meaning are pragmatically inferred or semantically encoded (Traugott and Dasher 2005); (c) how the components of the form are mapped to components of the meaning (Croft 2001), including both sides of the traditional division between morphological and syntactic change. Under this view, reanalysis too is an inevitable and ever-present consequence of ostensive-inferential communication (Detges and Waltereit 2002), though it is not always noticeable until it is actualized through the production of utterances which are no longer consistent with an earlier analysis: in English, for example, *be going to* can clearly not have the historical meaning MOTION in a sentence like *We are going to stay at home tonight*, as this conflicts directly with the meaning of *stay*.

A form–meaning association can become a linguistic convention if the interlocutors remember the association and add it to their shared common ground. The more frequently a form is used to express a meaning, the more deeply the form–meaning association becomes entrenched in the user's linguistic knowledge (Evans and Green 2006; Langacker 2008a), making the form polysemous. Once the association is sufficiently entrenched, the form may be used to convey the meaning independently of the original context. In linguistic terms, the context-specific, pragmatically inferred meaning has become semantically encoded and conventionalized (Kuteva 2001; Levinson 2000; Traugott and Dasher 2005).

Hoefler and Smith (2009) show that both metaphor- and reanalysis-based accounts of grammaticalization rely on the same cognitive mechanisms: (i) the assumption of common ground, including the knowledge of shared linguistic conventions and the recognition of what is relevant in the given context; (ii) the memorization of usage and the subsequent entrenchment of form–meaning associations. In both metaphor- and reanalysis-based accounts of grammaticalization, the hearer's reasoning is identical: the conventional meaning of the form is assumed to be irrelevant in context, and a novel meaning is inferred. The difference lies in the speaker's intentions, and in whether these coincide with the hearer's assumptions. In metaphor-based change, common ground is successfully established: the speaker innovates and the hearer infers the innovative meaning. In reanalysis, however, there is a mismatch between their assumptions: although the speaker is acting conventionally, the hearer infers an innovative meaning.

The semantic changes underlying grammaticalization are thus an inevitable result of ostensive-inferential communication. Yet ostensive-inferential communication is not necessarily linguistic; it can use gestures, sounds, or any behaviour interpretable as communicative by an observer. Importantly, there is no reason to doubt that pre-linguistic communication was also based on ostension and inference.

4. Protolanguage and pre-linguistic communication

A major debate in evolutionary linguistics is concerned with the nature of early language (often called protolanguage) and its transformation into complex language. Two major camps have become established: the synthetic account (Bickerton 1990; 1995; Tallerman 2007), in which word-like units are composed into sentences, and the analytic account (Wray 2000; Arbib 2005), in which sentence-like units are broken apart into words. The fundamental distinction between the two accounts lies in their initial conditions, in the nature and complexity of the meanings associated with the protolinguistic form units (A. D. M. Smith 2008). In the synthetic account, these are simple representations of easily accessible things and actions, such as 'eat' or 'water'; in the analytic account they are much more complex, ranging from 'give that to her' (Wray 2000), to exceedingly elaborate suggestions like 'go and hunt the hare I saw five minutes ago behind the stone at the top of the hill' (Mithen 2005: 172).

In a pre-linguistic situation, there are no shared linguistic conventions, so the meaning must be inferred solely from context; the cue which triggers the inferential process must be clear enough for the meaning to be inferred without assistance from pre-existing conventions. Importantly, if the association is to become conventionalized, this process must be reliably repeatable. This constraint of repeated reconstructibility strongly suggests that the meanings in the earliest form–meaning associations are likely to have been relatively simple, basic-level categories (Rosch et al. 1976), grounded in the context; such categories are cognitively salient, maximally informative, and more easily and quickly learnt by children (Taylor 1995). Even if a more complex meaning were reconstructed occasionally, from a very rich context, it would have almost no chance of being repeatedly replicated, and could never become entrenched.

Consider a pre-linguistic individual wanting to warn another of the presence of a predator, with no conventional way of signaling danger. An ostensive action which grabs the other's attention (shouting, waving, pushing, etc.), may provide a stimulus for them to infer the intended meaning. Importantly, the action must be deliberate and unexpected, so that the hearer is stimulated to work out why it took place. To interpret this behaviour as a communicative cue, the 'hearer' uses the same reasoning which underlies grammaticalization, including the capacity to recognize shared common ground, and a recognition of what is relevant in the current situation; both are based on the underlying ability to interpret the intentions of other individuals (Tomasello 2008). The development of a successful communicative episode into a shared convention depends on the episode being remembered by the participants, and the behaviour being entrenched and conventionalized through repeated use (Croft 2000; Tomasello 2003).

4.1. The emergence of symbols

One of the most important properties of linguistic constructions is their symbolic nature, or the arbitrariness of the relationship between form and meaning (Saussure 1916). It has been claimed (Hurford 2003) that this arbitrariness is connected to the fact that associations are learnt culturally rather than being specified genetically. The ostensive-inferential account suggests, however, that the earliest pre-linguistic associations could not have been completely arbitrary, else the meaning would *not* be inferable from the context. Nevertheless, non-arbitrary associations can *become* arbitrary through a change in the form–meaning association which obscures the original iconic link, using the same cognitive capacities which underpin grammaticalization.[1]

4.2. The complexification of language

The evidence from both the attested pathways of grammaticalization, and the nature of ostensive-inferential communication suggests that early language consisted of unitary utterances representing simple, grounded meanings which could be repeatedly reconstructed from context. The complexification of this early language requires the stable introduction of both semantic and syntactic complexity.

Semantic complexity can be maintained only when additional meaning components are sufficiently salient and important to be reliably and repeatedly inferred from context, so that the complex meaning becomes conventionalized through entrenchment. Syntactic complexity, however, can arise from concatenation in the normal course of communicative discourse. If two 'words' are uttered

[1] Note that this implies that all form-meaning associations could in theory be traced back to a non-arbitrary origin, if we could find enough historical information to do so.

consecutively within a short period of time, a hearer may interpret them as a single utterance (Burling 2005). The newly interpreted utterance is no longer unitary, but is composed of two sub-units (the original forms), with an inherent linear ordering (Jackendoff 2002). Concatenated elements can then become grammaticalized through the mechanisms of ostensive-inferential communication, through the layers of grammar proposed by Heine and Kuteva (2007): two individual items can be reinterpreted as verb and noun ('EAT ANTELOPE'), leading to rudimentary mono-clausal propositions, or as a head and its modifier ('DEAD ANTELOPE'), leading to the emergence of hierarchical syntactic organization. As more items become conventionalized, the increased common ground allows greater complexity in the propositions which can be communicated, and both semantic and syntactic complexity can increase. Complex and abstract concepts can be communicated, scaffolded by existing conventions and the knowledge of what is relevant in the context, while syntax becomes increasingly elaborate to reflect the complex semantics: the elaboration of phrase structure leads eventually to clause subordination and the obligatory marking of functional categories (Johansson 2005).

5. Conclusions

The cognitive mechanisms underpinning grammaticalization are not specifically linguistic, but derive from the principles of ostensive-inferential communication. It is reasonable to assume that pre-linguistic communication was based on these same principles, which allows us to gain insights into how language evolved from a non-linguistic state by studying grammaticalization.

Evidence from the nature of ostensive-inferential communication suggests that early language was initially lexical in nature, with units referring to simple, grounded, basic-level categories. Attested pathways of grammaticalization, moreover, demonstrate that all linguistic categories can be traced back to noun-like and verb-like categories; it is likely that noun-like items would have been conventionalized before verb-like items, because the latter are more complex conceptually. The complexification of early language into modern language was probably not abrupt but gradual, and took place via the same cultural processes of metaphor and reanalysis which yield grammaticalization.

CHAPTER 13

GRAMMATICALIZATION AND LINGUISTIC COMPLEXITY

ÖSTEN DAHL

1. General

Interest in the application of the notion of complexity to linguistic issues has increased markedly in recent years. Two questions that have been in focus are (i) whether cross-linguistic comparisons between languages makes sense and whether differences in complexity between languages exist (see e.g. McWhorter 2001 and the responses in the same issue of *Linguistic Typology*; further, the papers in Miestamo, Sinnemäki, and Karlsson 2008; Sampson, Gil, and Trudgill 2009; Givón and Shibatani 2009), and (ii) the role of recursion in human languages.

The relationship between complexity and grammaticalization is not a straightforward one, partly because both notions can be understood in several different ways. In the following, I will assume that grammaticalization is understood in a relatively broad sense, as the processes by which grammatical structures and grammatical markings arise and evolve, including but not restricted to the development from lexical to grammatical morphemes. As for the notion of complexity, the following sections aim to clarify some of the interpretational possibilities.

2. The notion of complexity

Complexity is often confounded with difficulty: a complex language would be one that is difficult to learn. But in information theory and the theory of complex systems, complexity is understood as an objective property of an object or a system. Admittedly, it is notoriously difficult to give a rigid definition of complexity in this sense, although the general idea is clear: the complexity of an object is related to the amount of information needed to re-create or specify it (or alternatively, the length of the shortest possible complete description of it). I shall give a simple example to show how this idea could be applied in practice. Suppose we have three strings of characters: *hahaha*, *byebye*, and *pardon*. Although these all consist of six characters, they differ in that the two first strings can in fact be represented in a more compact way, e.g. as *3*ha* and *2*bye*, whereas there is no way of compressing the string *pardon* in a similar way. We might therefore say that *hahaha* is the least complex string, since it can be reduced to four characters, while *byebye* takes minimally five and *pardon* six characters. As applied to strings, this notion of complexity, which is sometimes called 'Kolmogorov complexity' or 'algorithmic information content', comes out as an inverse of compressibility: the most complex string is one which cannot be compressed at all. If we implement this idea in the most straightforward way, we obtain what Gell-Mann (1994) calls 'effective complexity', which differs from Kolmogorov complexity in that it does not measure the length of the description of an object as a whole, but rather the length of the description of the 'set of regularities' or structured patterns that it contains. A random string of characters, such as 'w509mfowr6435217r00l71734', will have maximal Kolmogorov complexity (the string is its own shortest description), but no effective complexity, since it contains no structured patterns.

This corresponds better to an intuitive understanding of the notion of complexity. We also come close to a notion which may feel more familiar to linguists: the set of patterns that an object contains can be said to equal its structure, so the complexity of an object is really a measure of the complexity of its structure. In linguistics, such a complexity measure could apply to different things. Most importantly, it could apply on the one hand to a language seen as a system—what I call system complexity—and on the other to the structure of utterances and expressions—what I call structural complexity.

The first of these two notions—system complexity—could be seen as a measure of the content that language learners have to master in order to be proficient in a language—in other words, the content of their competence. It does not as such tell us anything about the difficulty they have in learning, producing, and understanding the language. In my view, it is better not to use the term 'complexity' in an agent-related sense, i.e. relativizing it to a user.

Turning now to the notion of structural complexity, it can of course be applied to one and the same expression at different structural levels—syntax, morphology, etc.—and there are also various measures that could be used. For instance, we could consider the depth of the maximal sentential embedding in a sentence. On this measure, a sentence such as *John said [that Mary said [that she was coming]]* is more complex than *John said [that he was coming]]*. A more general measure would be the number of nodes in a structural representation.

Although system complexity is often accompanied by structural complexity, this is not necessarily always the case. For instance, the rules for plural formation in nouns are more complex in Swedish than in English, since there are a number of different plural suffixes to choose from (e.g. *hund-ar* 'dogs' vs. *katt-er* 'cats'), while in English there is only one (*-s*) except for a limited number of irregular nouns, but Swedish plural nouns are not structurally more complex than the English ones (cf. *hund-ar* vs. *dog-s*).

Another way of viewing the system/structure distinction is to say that while system complexity concerns competence/langue, structural complexity pertains to performance/parole, since it is about properties of individual utterances. However, in a given system, there may be a limit on how complex an utterance can be, and this maximal structural complexity would be a property or at least a consequence of the language system. In fact, this seems to be what is usually meant by 'complexity' in the debate about recursion in natural language.

In Dahl (2004), I focused on the complexity of rules that relate meaning to form—asking the question: Given a certain content, how complex are the rules that allow you to express that content in a language? This question makes more sense for grammar proper than for components of the language such as phonology and lexicon. One often-heard reason for scepticism towards using complexity measures that build on length of descriptions is that they seemingly make a language with a large vocabulary more complex than one with a small vocabulary. A similar objection is that the complexity of a language would be dependent on the average length of words. It seems to me that these objections can be met by going up one level: we are not so much concerned with the actual length of the lexicon as with the specification of the form of a lexical item, that is, what we ask is how complex is the format of a lexical item—this could be termed 'lexical meta-complexity'. This means among other things that the length of lexical items would not be essential, since adding another phoneme to a word just gives you 'more of the same'—the format of the lexical item is not affected. If, on the other hand, one adds information of a different kind—such as lexical tones—that complicates the format and adds to the lexical meta-complexity of the language.

Returning now to the issue of the relationship between complexity and grammaticalization, it may be said that if we understand grammaticalization in the way suggested above, i.e. as the processes that give rise to grammatical structures and markings, it could be expected to be connected with an increase in system complexity, since it would entail that there would be 'more grammar' in the language. However, comparisons of system complexity are often only possible with a 'ceteris paribus' clause—that is, we can say that the introduction of a certain element increases complexity if everything else remains the same, but if, for instance, one construction replaces another, it may not always be possible to say unequivocally which of the constructions is most complex. We will consider below some cases where the relation between grammaticalization and complexity is not straightforward.

3. Complexity of the meaning–form relation

One reason why human languages have to be complex is that they are capable of expressing complex thoughts and conveying complex messages. This, of course, distinguishes human languages from most other communicative systems. In Bertrand Russell's words, 'A dog cannot relate his autobiography; however eloquently he may bark, he cannot tell you that his parents were honest though poor.' However, complexity of thought does not always correspond to complexity in expression. A person standing in front of a picture in a museum might utter the single word *Picasso* to express the proposition 'this picture was painted by Picasso' involving (at least) three entities, two individual objects and one action; but of these three entities only one gets expressed in the utterance: the rest are supplied from the situational context. What is most interesting from our point of view here is that there is no indication of what role the referent of the expression *Picasso* has to the action of painting; in fact, if the painting is a portrait, there is nothing to reveal whether Picasso is the painter or the person represented in the painting. Still, of course, the person uttering *Picasso* would normally intend the listener(s) to understand which of these is meant.

We may imagine a language in which the intended structural relationships between elements in the conceptual structure are never indicated or reflected in any systematic way in the expression. According to Gil (2009), Riau Indonesian is a language which comes close to this ideal. Thus, the expression *ayam makan*, consisting of the uninflected words *ayam* 'chicken' and *makan* 'eat', could mean, among other things, both 'the chicken is eating' and 'someone is eating the chicken'. In actual usage, there is a preference for the former interpretation, so the ideal is not quite attained. Still, Riau Indonesian as described by Gil may serve as an illustration of what it would mean for a language to be able to express complex thoughts but not having any grammar in the sense that the expression of these thoughts is wholly specified by enumerating a set of lexical items (what generativists tend to call a 'numeration'). Such a language could be said to have minimal complexity with respect to the relationship between content (conceptual structure) and expression, and everything that goes beyond that would count as contributing to grammatical complexity.

Consider now how Riau Indonesian could be changed in a way that would let the roles of noun phrases be reflected in the expression of a sentence. One way would be to introduce a fixed word order which would differentiate between agent and object. Another would be to use consistent markers such as adpositions to distinguish them. Both these methods have one thing in common: the result can be described in terms of a sequence of elements that are independent of each other, which is the same as saying that it can be generated by a context-free phrase structure rule without complex symbols. Constructions that obey this condition—sometimes referred to as 'juxtaposition'—can be called linear, and can in general be said to represent the lowest degree of grammatical complexity above the minimum, since they do not necessitate a specification of how the construction is expressed beyond what fits into the context-free format. Any such specification will involve non-linearity of some sort at the same time as it adds to the complexity of the system.

4. Non-linearity

Linearity means, among other things, that the input elements are realized independently of each other in the output. Linearity thus excludes such phenomena as grammatical agreement, in which the form of one element depends on some property of another element (such as its grammatical gender). But also any form of integration between the components of the output expression can be seen as providing non-linearity. In practice, this means that almost any linguistic pattern in which expressions are combined deviates from linearity to some extent. The term 'juxtaposition' is strictly speaking misleading, in that the parts of complex expressions in spoken language are not simply juxtaposed but integrated into a prosodic pattern. Even in written language, complex expressions are usually not strict concatenations of their components, but involve formatting such as capitalization and punctuation.

The term 'non-concatenative' is sometimes used for more advanced forms of non-linearity, such as cumulative ('portmanteau') expression, and stem alternations. Classic examples are Indo-European ablaut as manifested, for instance, in the strong verbs of Germanic languages, or the Semitic verb systems with their combination of three-consonant roots, consonant gradations, and bisyllabic vowel alternation patterns. Non-linearity, however, is a wider notion, in that it involves anything that goes beyond strict juxtaposition.

What is the relation between non-linearity and grammaticalization? It is often suggested that grammatical forms undergo a development which can be summarized as follows (Dahl 2004: 106):

free > periphrastic > affixal > fusional

This schema, with roots in the 18th century, was originally seen as characterizing languages as wholes rather than individual grammatical markers. The schema is readily reinterpreted as a general trend towards increased non-linearity and, given that the introduction of non-linearity involves additional grammatical complexity, as a trend towards greater complexity. It also embodies the insight that certain types of grammatical structures—called 'mature' in Dahl (2004)—presuppose a prehistory; they do not come about through simple changes but are the result of a longer evolution in several stages. We do not expect Riau Indonesian to acquire anything like the Semitic system of verb morphology in one generation; it stands to reason that such a process of 'maturation' would take a much longer time. In general, non-linearity of expression can be taken as an indication of maturity, in that non-linear structures typically arise from linear ones. Non-linearly expressed constructions or expressions will also coincide with the ones that have been said to be 'highly grammaticalized'— in other words, items that have advanced far on a grammaticalization path.

Which are the processes in grammaticalization that lead to non-linearity? Clearly, phonological change plays an important but not quite straightforward role. Thus, it is well known that a grammaticalizing morpheme often undergoes reductive sound change which may lead to fusion with other elements. In Dahl (2004), a distinction is made between 'Neo-grammarian' and 'adaptive' sound change. Famously, the Neo-grammarian school claimed that 'sound laws' have no exceptions, meaning that they apply as soon as the phonological conditions are fulfilled, disregarding grammatical and lexical factors. This, however, clearly does not apply to the kind of reductive change that is a result of the reduction of the informational value of an element, something that necessarily happens when a lexical element is grammaticalized. An extreme example would be the development from Spanish *Vuestra Merced* 'Your Grace' into a 2nd person pronoun *usted* or even (in certain varieties) *te*. This, then, would be a case of 'adaptive' change. Both these kinds of change may play a role in the rise of non-linearity, however, by obscuring the borders between morphemes and creating irregularities in paradigms but also by contributing to the 'morphologization' of both segmental and suprasegmental (prosodic) features. For instance, vowel alternations in stems may arise due to sound changes that are sensitive to differences in stress.

The kind of adaptive process of change just mentioned, when a lexical expression such as *Vuestra Merced* is grammaticalized and ends up as *te*, is often seen in the literature on grammaticalization as the result of a striving towards economy or efficiency, whose final result is the weakening or 'wearing out' of the expression to such an extent that it is no longer usable (for a recent formulation of this idea, see Geurts 2000a; 2000b). It then comes into conflict with the need for effectiveness and clarity, which motivates the creation of a new pattern which satisfies this need—and these counteracting tendencies give rise to an eternal cyclical process. I argue in Dahl (2004) that this picture is inadequate in several ways. Thus, there is little evidence that there is a natural tendency for grammatical expressions to be worn out, or that this would be the motivation for the creation of new grammatical patterns. What is clear is that maturation involves processes that remove excessive redundancy. On the other hand, the structures that arise through maturation are often very stable—the Indo-European and Afro-Asiatic systems of vowel alternations, for instance, have existed for several millennia. In addition, there is in fact some evidence that inflectional morphemes are shielded to some extent from ongoing reduction processes in speech, although from the informational point of view, they ought to be redundant. Thus, arguably, maturation processes tend to lead to stable states in which a certain redundancy is preserved. It is plausible that this redundancy helps the listener to recover the structure of the utterance even in the presence of noise in the channel. The advantage of non-linear features of expressions is that they make it possible to add keep this kind of 'smart' redundancy in expressions even though their phonetic weight has been reduced.

How does the rise of non-linearity affect structural complexity? This depends on what kind of structure we are speaking of. A fused form, such as the past tense of a Germanic strong verb (*sang*), does not contain any internal morpheme boundary and could thus be said to be structurally simple; on the other hand, at a 'deeper' level of analysis, it could be claimed that it contains the same kind of elements (lexical verb + past tense) as a weak verb form such as *call-ed*. Reductive processes thus have an effect at the surface while the underlying structure may be untouched.

An important source of grammatical complexity is the competition between different grammatical patterns that is typical of ongoing grammaticalization. In many European languages, older synthetic comparative forms of adjectives have been replaced by periphrastic constructions involving an adverb 'more'. In some languages, such as English, this process has not been completed but appears to have stopped half-way, and the choice between the old and the new way of forming comparatives involves more or less complex rules. These languages, then, have a more complex system of comparatives than both languages where the change has not at all taken place and languages where it has been fully implemented – in other words, a grammaticalization process can lead first to an increase and then to a decrease in grammatical complexity.

5. Differences between languages

Global between-language comparisons of complexity are a notoriously difficult issue. In principle, it should be possible to apply the criterion of description length, but in actual practice it is not at all clear, for example, how much syntactical complexity is needed to compensate for a difference in morphological complexity. In spite of this, it has often been assumed that all languages are equally complex. If this were true, it would lead us to expect that a significant difference in complexity in one component ought to be matched by a similar difference (although going in the opposite direction) in another component. This invariance assumption has recently been challenged by various scholars (e.g. by McWhorter 2001) and by several authors in Sampson et al. (2009).

The recent discussion of differences in grammatical complexity between languages has to a large extent focused on the claim that creole languages are less complex than other languages. What is apparent is that creole languages, but also other languages that have been classified as isolating (such as the majority of the languages spoken in mainland Southeast Asia), lack many or even all the features that can be characterized as mature, most notably inflectional morphology. The genesis of creole languages is not uncontroversial, but it is natural to regard them as extreme cases of what is referred to in Dahl (2004) as 'suboptimal transmission'—that is, at some stage there has been a break in the transmission chain by which children learn their native language from other native speakers. It appears that mature language features generally belong to the ones that are hard to learn for adult second-language learners, and which thus tend to be filtered out in language contact situations or, more properly expressed, in situations of suboptimal transmission of languages. (It is no accident that Riau Indonesian, which was discussed above, is a language with a high proportion of non-native speakers.) For grammaticalization, it is also relevant that these features also seem to be hard to borrow, and that areal pressure is most clearly visible in the early stages of grammaticalization processes—strong verbs are usually not a popular export item.

6. Tightness and complexity

As constructions and expressions develop over time, they tend to become tighter, or more condensed—this is an important component of grammaticalization. A topic–comment construction with a dislocated noun phrase and a free pronoun referring back to it (*John, he comes*) may turn into a tighter subject–predicate construction where the pronoun eventually becomes a bound agreement marker on the verb, perhaps at a later stage fusing with other markers and the verb stem, creating a non-linear structure (Givón 1979). Increase in tightness means that structural complexity shifts downwards, from a higher level to a lower one. It may also be accompanied by an increase in system complexity, especially if non-linearity increases. In fact, both syntactic and morphological complexity largely depends on this kind of downshifting process, in which material taken from higher levels is condensed on a lower one.

The relationship between tightness and complexity is not entirely straightforward. Inflectional grammatical marking such as subject–verb agreement and cases on nouns arises when syntactic constructions are condensed. But a combination of a verb and a noun phrase may be further condensed through the incorporation of the noun phrase (usually a single noun) into the verb. However, incorporating constructions do not usually involve any internal grammatical marking; rather, the elements tend to be simply joined together in one phonological word. Cf. the following example from Southern Ute (Givón 1995: 189):

(1) a. kwana-ci ʻuway paqa-pu̯ga
eagle-AN.OBJ DEF.OBJ kill-REM
'He killed the eagle'

b. kwana-paqa-pu̯ga
eagle-kill-REM
'He did some eagle-killing' or 'He killed eagles'

In (1a), there is an object noun phrase *kwana-ci ʻuway*, which contains both a case-marking suffix *-ci* and a determiner *ʻuway*. In (1b), there is no independent object noun phrase; rather, the stem *kwana* 'eagle' shows up as an incorporated part of the verb, without any grammatical marking accompanying it. Thus, inflections are morphological elements that reflect the external connections of a word rather than its internal structure (see further Dahl 2009). It might seem that (1) is an exception to the generalization that complexity is shifted downwards when a construction is condensed, but it is rather the case that the referential character of the object noun phrase in (1a) both motivates the additional grammatical marking and shields it from incorporation.

An interesting issue concerns the relationship between tightness and expressivity. A tighter construction often seems to be able to express the same content as a looser one, but it allows the speaker to use more restricted means, as is illustrated by the following examples:

(2) a. I see a cat. It is white.
b. I see a cat that is white.
c. I see a white cat.

Languages vary as to what kinds of tight constructions they offer their speakers. In Dahl (2008), it is argued that the Tupían language Sirionó lacks syntactic NP coordination, and that coordinate NP's are replaced by constructions of the kind illustrated by the following quotation from the Sirionó New Testament, which in the original contains a coordinate NP:

(3) Josías rei Jeconías ru. Jeconías nongue abe ru.
Josias COP Jechonias father Jeconias brother also father
'(Lit.:) Josias was the father of Jechonias. Jechonias' brothers' father, too.' (King James' Version: *And Josias begat Jechonias and his brethren*)

In (3), the content of what is one sentence in the original text is broken up into two units with a full stop between them in the written text—this would correspond to two intonational units in the spoken language. A language with syntactic coordination is able to express the same content in one sentential unit. It is argued in (Dahl 2008) that constructions involving words meaning 'also' may be diachronic sources of coordinate structures with 'and' (cf. Norwegian *og* which means both 'also' and 'and'), and that this is a grammaticalization path by which a language like Sirionó could develop syntactic coordination, and thus enrich its range of syntactic constructions.

CHAPTER 14

GRAMMATICALIZATION AND DIRECTIONALITY

KERSTI BÖRJARS
NIGEL VINCENT

1. Introduction

One of the most interesting and challenging hypotheses to emerge from the literature on grammaticalization has been the unidirectionality hypothesis: the claim that the changes which fall under the rubric of grammaticalization always move in the direction from more to less lexical or from less to more grammatical.[1] Givón (1971), who is commonly taken to have sparked the modern discussion of the phenomenon, postulates a clear diachronic sequence leading from full form to reduced form (and ultimately to zero). Lehmann (1995a[1982]: 16) takes change of this type to be unidirectional and is thus led to claim that degrammaticalization does not exist. More recently, work by for instance Hopper and Traugott (1993: ch. 5), Traugott (2001), Heine (2003), and Brinton and Traugott (2005: ch. 4.3) is characterized by caution about the existence of degrammaticalization, though they generally recognize that there may be some genuine examples of grammaticalization reversed. Traugott (2001) makes the point that languages should be

[1] Some researchers do not recognize grammaticalization as a separate phenomenon, but consider it as at best an epiphenomenonal effect of the interaction of other more basic mechanisms of change (Campbell 2001b; Harris and Campbell 1995). We will not enter into this discussion here.

understood to be subject to statistical and not absolute generalizations, and that therefore a small number of counterexamples need not be a matter of great concern. Even Newmeyer (2001: 13) agrees that 'unidirectionality is almost true'.

In the hands of some scholars, unidirectionality has been vested with even greater significance since it is argued that the existence of these paths underpins a cognitive-semantic view of the ontology of natural language which presents a challenge to the post-Saussurean understanding of language as structure. Not all those who work on grammaticalization draw such radical conclusions, but for most, the data of grammaticalization challenge the dichotomy of synchrony and diachrony which has characterized mainstream structuralist and generativist linguistics for almost a century (see in this connection Matthews 2001: esp. 52–73, 113–17). Conversely, until recently, most researchers working within formal frameworks have given even the basic descriptive data of grammaticalization, let alone so-called 'grammaticalization theory', fairly short shrift. This changed with the ideas developed by Roberts and Roussou (1999; 2003), on whose view the directionality of grammaticalization is not necessarily incompatible with the autonomy of syntax as standardly conceived within the Chomskyan framework (see section 4).

Some of the early work—notably Givón (1971) and Vincent (1980)—also saw in the apparent unidirectionality of grammaticalization a valuable tool for reconstruction in a domain, morphosyntax, where reconstruction has been frequently argued to be difficult if not impossible (and not simply for the ideological reasons expressed repeatedly since Lightfoot 1979: 154–66).

Though unidirectionality has been seen as a core property of grammaticalization in most of the literature, it has also been called into question. Ramat (1992) recognized the evidence of grammaticalization as demonstrating valid cross-linguistic patterns of change, but claimed that there was also evidence of degrammaticalization. The latter has been seized on by those sceptical of the existence of directed mechanisms of change that linguistic theory needs to account for (Janda 2001; Joseph 2001; Newmeyer 2001), although this was very far from Ramat's original intent.

2. Defining unidirectionality

One major issue for this debate has been that the key term in the debate has been poorly defined. Degrammaticalization is intuitively understood as an item going from more to less grammatical or in the limit from grammatical to lexical. Newmeyer (2001: 205) writes: 'I take any example of upgrading as sufficient to refute grammaticalization', where upgrading equals increase in lexical content or increased morphological independence. Unlike Newmeyer, we concur with Willis's (2007: 272) conclusion: 'in order to be theoretically interesting, degrammaticalization must be parallel to and linked to grammaticalization. That is, the nature of the mechanisms involved must, in some sense, be the same in both cases, but they must lead to opposite results.'

One characteristic of grammaticalization is that it operates at different linguistic levels. We should then expect the same to be true of degrammaticalization. Willis (2007: 273) posits five processes relating to different dimensions that could justifiably be described as degrammaticalization:

(i) phonological 'strengthening';
(ii) change rightwards along the cline: affix > clitic > independent word;
(iii) category reanalysis from grammatical to lexical;
(iv) metaphorical shift from abstract to concrete;
(v) pragmatic inferencing from abstract to concrete.

Willis points out that there are problems with (i) and (iv), and argues that (ii) and (iii) are central to arguments for degrammaticalization. Norde (2009a: 120) uses similar distinctions in her definition: 'Degrammaticalization is a composite change whereby a gram in a specific context gains in autonomy or substance on more than one linguistic level (semantics, morphology, syntax, or phonology).'

Though these attempts at restricting degrammaticalization have made the notion more interesting, we believe the distinctions need to be refined further. At the heart of most, if not all, definitions of both grammaticalization and degrammaticalization lies the cline in (1) (cf. e.g. Hopper and Traugott 1993: 7).

(1) content item > grammatical word > clitic > affix

As Andersen (2005) has pointed out, this cline is defined in a mixture of formal and semantic categories. In addition to this, we would argue that the categories 'clitic' and 'affix' conflate a number of distinctions in a way that obscures certain types of change (see Börjars 2003). Both Willis's and Norde's definitions of degrammaticalization involve reference to these categories, and to our mind this is a weakness. Instead, further dimensions should be distinguished.[2] We will return to this issue in 3.2.

With respect to semantic changes from functional to lexical, it is crucial that there should have been discontinuity between the new lexical meaning and any earlier lexical meanings the word may have had so that it is clear that the new

[2] Norde (2009a: 133) actually defines degrammaticalization as a change from 'bound (affix, clitic) to free', but it is clear from her analysis of the Swedish possessive *s* that she sees a change from affix to clitic as a case of degrammaticalization.

meaning is not just a development from an earlier lexical meaning.[3] Similarly, changes in frequency between two forms which have existed side by side, leading to a decrease and disappearance of a functional form and the maintaining of a lexical form, should not be considered degrammaticalization unless it can be shown that there was a time when only the functional form existed and there is evidence that the lexical one developed from it. We will illustrate this in section 3.3.

It should also be emphasized that to qualify as degrammaticalization, changes should be gradual, just as grammaticalization is recognized as a gradual process. This rules out the examples we discuss in 3.1.

3. Potential examples of degrammaticalization

3.1. Synchrony rather than diachrony

The enthusiasm for finding instances of degrammaticalization that followed the reawakened interest in the notion in the early 21st century catalogued a number of examples that to our minds do not impact on the unidirectionality debate. This is true of examples such as the English *to down a beer*, where a verb is derived from a preposition. However, whereas the developments from verb to preposition such as Latin *adire* 'to go to' > Sicilian *aggiri* 'towards' take place gradually over a period of time, formations like *to down* are the immediate result of applying a synchronic rule of conversion, and hence do not impinge on the debate around unidirectionality.

This argument can be generalized, so that any cases that involve productive word formation rules can be excluded from discussion. Even more generally, we should be very cautious about citing as a case of degrammaticalization anything that can be attributed to the myriad ways in which new lexical items can be coined or derived.

An example is what Benveniste (1958) referred to as delocutives.[4]

(2) I heartily wish I could, but
Nay, but me no buts I have set my heart upon it. (Scott, *The Antiquary* xi)

(3) Physician: Yes, you may live, but—
Leo: Finely butted, doctor! (Fletcher, *The Humorous Lieutenant*)

[3] This is similar to Norde's (2009a: 120–21) 'novelty' and different from her use of 'discontinuity'.

[4] We are grateful to Sylvia Adamson for bringing some of these examples to our attention.

Here, the new word form is created not from the linguistic item itself but from the utterance in which it occurs. In other words, the context is metalinguistic rather than simply linguistic. Conversion facilitates this process in English but is by no means essential, as Plank (2005) shows. The verbs to describe the different forms of address in many languages also fall into this category, e.g. German *duzen* and *siezen* 'to use *du*/*Sie*'.

An extension of the same argument is used by Haspelmath (1999) to defuse another category of alleged degrammaticalization, namely derivational affixes like *-ism* and *-teens*, which end up as independent words or indeed as input to word formation processes, as in German *zigmal* 'umpteen times' (← *zig* as in *zwanzig* 'twenty' etc. + *mal* 'times'). Haspelmath (1999: 1048) comments on *-ism*: 'it seems to be another case of a citation form of a word taken out of its constructional context rather than degrammaticalization.'[5]

3.2. A question of categorization: English and Swedish possessive *s*

As we saw in section 2, both Willis (2007) and Norde (2009a), after having discarded dubious examples of degrammaticalization, include the change from affix to clitic, as allegedly exemplified by the English or Swedish possessive *s*, as a proper example of degrammaticalization. A development from an affix to a clitic would indeed be a reverse change on the grammaticalization cline. However, we have argued elsewhere (Börjars 2003; Vincent and Börjars 2010) that this view of the change to the possessive *s* is misguided in that it is an oversimplification to describe the change as essentially one-dimensional, from the simple category of affix to the simple category of clitic. It is more appropriate to describe it in terms of at least four separate changes: (i) paradigm reduction to one form; (ii) agreement > once only marking; (iii) degree of boundedness reduced; (iv) head marking > head and right edge marking. When the subtlety of the change and the current nature of the possessive *s* is done justice, it cannot be described as a straightforward case of degrammaticalization. Indeed, according to Lehman's (1995a[1982]) criteria, (i) would even be a sign that grammaticalization, not degrammaticalization, has taken place.[6]

[5] It is interesting to see that Norde (2009a: 213–20) still includes the Dutch *-tig* as an example of degrammaticalization.

[6] Another example of how an argument for degrammaticalization can in fact be construed as involving grammaticalization involves van der Auwera's (2002) argument that the apparent reinforcement in pairs such as *keep V-ing* vs. *keep on V-ing* exemplifies degrammaticalization. For this argument to hold, however, would require evidence, which the author does not provide, that the *keep* and *keep on* constructions are not independent developments. In fact, reinforcement is a natural

3.3. Discontinuity of historical trajectory

In arguing for degrammaticalization, it is not sufficient to show that there is a historical stage at which the less grammatical form exists and that there was an earlier stage at which the more grammatical form existed. It is crucial that the intervening historical trajectory supports a degrammaticalization analysis; the less grammatical form must be shown to have developed from a more grammatical form.

The development of the English infinitival marker *to* is argued by Fischer (2000) to be an example of degrammaticalization (see also Fitzmaurice 2000). Norde (2009a: 190–99) accepts it as such, and Traugott (2001: §4) describes it as a 'probably legitimate counterexample'.

Fischer argues that a major force behind grammaticalization is iconicity. In the early stages of grammaticalization, a form corresponds to one function (4a), but as a new grammaticalized meaning develops, the form comes to represent two functions (4b). The non-isomorphism of the second stage makes it non-iconic and Fischer (2000: 155) argues that this is dispreferred. A language should move away from this situation and a third stage, where a new form develops for the new function, should be expected (4c). The new function is grammaticalized, 'weakened', and hence the form which develops to recreate isomorphism can be expected to be a weakened form. This is then essentially a picture of grammaticalization where semantic change drives form change.

(4) a. $\frac{\alpha}{\text{x}}>$ b. $\frac{\alpha}{\text{xy}}>$ c. $\frac{\alpha}{\text{x}}\ \frac{\beta}{\text{y}}$

$\alpha\ \beta$ are forms; x, y functions ('goal', 'infinitival marker')

As Fischer shows, Dutch and English 'to' develop through processes associated with grammaticalization to (4b). Dutch behaves the way Fischer's assumptions about iconicity and isomorphism would lead us to expect: there are three forms for the three functions—the preposition *toe*, the strengthened purposive *om te*, and the infinitival *te*.[7]

Fischer (2000: 156) shows that examples of a weakened form, *te*, can be found in Middle English, which for her means that the distribution in (4c) has been achieved. The weak form ceases to be attested in the mid-14th century; under the view illustrated by (4), this is a return to an earlier stage (4b) and hence a reversal of the grammaticalization process. Fischer (p. 158) states: '*to* went back to its original meaning, again strongly expressing goal or direction.' The evidence for a reversal provided by Fischer (pp. 158–62) is largely based on a comparison with the further

consequence of grammaticalization, and one of the mechanisms of what Hopper and Traugott (1993: 121–2) call renewal.

[7] Fischer (2000: 159) states that *om te* expresses 'goal' or 'direction'. This inaccuracy may arise because she lumps the original prepositional meaning in with the later purposive use.

development of the corresponding Dutch element and the failure of certain developments to take place in English.[8]

Even under Fischer's interpretation of the data, the infinitival *to* would be an example of degrammaticalization only if there had been a stage in English when only the more grammaticalized form existed, so that the less grammaticalized form would truly have developed out of it. As Hollmann (2003: §4.1) points out, (4) represents an oversimplified view of how grammaticalization progresses. A condition for change of this type is that there is a period where two form–function combinations exist side by side; in order for speakers to get from one stage to the next, there would have to be an intermediate stage of variation. This means that the development is more accurately represented as in (5).

(5) a. $\frac{\alpha}{\mathrm{x}} >$ b. $\frac{\alpha}{\mathrm{x}} \sim \frac{\alpha}{\mathrm{xy}} >$ c. $\frac{\alpha}{\mathrm{xy}} >$ d. $\frac{\alpha}{\mathrm{xy}} \sim \frac{\alpha}{\mathrm{x}} \quad \frac{\beta}{\mathrm{y}}$

In (5d), two distinct forms are sometimes used to refer to the two distinct functions, but not always. On this view then, there is a stage where there is variation between the original form representing both meanings and a grammaticalized form representing the grammaticalized meaning *y*. What happens is that the latter option ceases to exist, whereas the former is maintained. The change from the state in (d) to that in (c) is then not a reversal to an earlier stage, but the disappearance of one variant distribution (cf. Haspelmath's 2004b term 'retraction'). As Hollmann (2003: 162) puts it, under this interpretation of the data: 'It is simply a case where more grammaticalized structures cease to be used, leaving behind the earlier form-function pairing.'

One initially plausible type of degrammaticalization which has been put forward in the literature involves a putative change from modal to lexical verb, and can hence be referred to as demodalization. For these to be genuine examples of degrammaticalization, there would need to be a first stage in which a given item had only a modal meaning, so that it can be shown that the lexical meaning must have developed from the grammatical meaning. Lexical splits are common, so that it is not unusual for an original lexical meaning to persist even after a new modal verb has developed from it. Discontinutity between the new lexical item and earlier lexical elements must be demonstrated.

The Swedish verb *må* is one of the examples van der Auwera and Plungian (1998) provide, but Andersson (2007; 2008) has shown that the lexical meaning is present

[8] It should be said here that with this importance assigned to iconicity and isomorphism it is surprising that (4b) arises in the first place. While we would not want to deny that iconicity and the striving for isomorphism has some explanatory power in linguistics, stable non-isomorphism is not uncommon in language. In fact, this very development would seem to illustrate this. In Modern English, the form *to* would appear to express three separate functions; the direction/goal preposition, the purposive, and the infinitival marker.

as far back as the earliest remaining documents, and though it has developed over time, the modern lexical meaning can be shown clearly to have developed from the original lexical meaning, not from a more recent functional meaning. Beths's (1999) claim that English *dare* exemplifies demodalization is problematic in many ways, but the major problem is that a lexical meaning existed already in Old English (see Traugott 2001). Another example frequently quoted in the literature is the Pennsylvania German *wotte* (Burridge 1998). However, given the impact of detailed historical evidence on the other cases and the unavailability of information about earlier stages of this variety, we remain sceptical about this example.

Van der Auwera and Plungian (1998: 106) also cite the history of the Latin *posse* 'to be able' as an example of demodalization. Once again the crucial point is the chronology of developments that their case requires. Their (admittedly brief) discussion implies the following sequence:

Stage 1: there exists a periphrasis made up of the adjective *potis* 'able' plus the copula *esse* 'be', which has only a modal meaning, as in the following example:

(6)	Potin	es	mihi	verum	dicere?
	able.INT	be.2SG	1SG.DAT	truth.ACC.N	say.INF

'Are you able to tell me the truth?' (Terence, *Andria* 437)

Stage 2: univerbation produces the modal verb *posse* 'be able, can', attested classically with a full paradigm based on *esse* 'be';

Stage 3: only after univerbation has taken place does *posse* develop non-modal meanings such as 'have influence, avail, be strong', as evidenced in the following example which they adduce from Cicero:

(7)	plus	apud	te	pecuniae	cupiditas
	more	at	2SG.ACC	money.GEN.SG	desire.NOM.SG
	quam	judicii	metus	potuit[9]	
	than	law.GEN	fear.SG.NOM	*posse*.PF.3SG	

'desire for money is stronger in you than fear of justice'

The transition from Stage 2 to Stage 3, if genuine, would certainly be a case of degrammaticalization even in the strict sense in which we suggest the term should be applied. It would, in fact, be parallel to the scenario for Swedish *må* envisaged by van der Auwera and Plungian. However, it turns out that this case can be deconstructed in much the same way as Andersson (2007; 2008) has done for the Swedish verb.

Consider again van der Auwera and Plungian's (1998) example of Stage 3, given here as (7). It is crucial to their argument that the non-modal meaning of this

[9] We use the gloss *posse* here, so as not to prejudice the discussion of its meaning.

example was not available in the pre-classical language. However, instances in which *posse* is constructed with *plus* are already common a century and a half earlier in Plautus (254–180 BCE). Examples are cited by Lewis and Short (1879) in the same entries from which van der Auwera and Plungian draw (7), for example:

(8) plus potest qui plus valet
more *posse*.3SG REL more be powerful.3SG
'he who is strongest has most power' (*Truculentus* 4.3.38)

Note too that van der Auwera and Plungian's preferred translation of *potuit* in (7) as 'was stronger' tends to exaggerate the semantic distance between uses like this and the core modal uses in which *posse* is constructed with an infinitive. Nearer the literal meaning of the Latin would be a translation like 'had more power', which in turn suggests that we reconstruct from the earliest stages of its existence as a verb a monosemous verb with slightly different interpretations according to whether the context is a measure phrase or an infinitival complement. This appears too to be the view of the *Oxford Latin Dictionary* (Glare 1977), which gives as one of the submeanings for *posse* 'to have (a specified) power, influence, importance, efficacy, force, meaning, value, worth'.

A further argument for the full lexical status of *posse* in early Latin is that it could take a direct object as in the following example from the poet Lucilius (180–102 BCE):

(9) non omnia possumus omnes
NEG all.ACC.N.PL. *posse*.PRS.3SG all.NOM.PL
'we cannot all (do) everything' (Lucilius 21)

In sum, in Plautus and other early writers what we find is both the periphrasis *potis esse* and the verb *posse*, and both have modal and non-modal meanings, or (perhaps better) have a meaning which encompasses both modal and non-modal sense. There is certainly no evidence for the chronological sequence of form and meaning developments that van der Auwera and Plungian's argument requires, and therefore no support here either for demodalization.

3.4. Syntactic lexicalization

As discussed in section 2, Willis (2007) takes a restrictive view of what would constitute degrammaticalization. Like us, he does not, for instance, recognize the examples discussed in section 3.1 as being a mirror image of grammaticalization. He does, however, discuss a type of change that is superficially similar to lexicalization, but differs from it in that there is evidence of processes similar to those of grammaticalization, but reversed in directionality. These examples show a historical continuity between the earlier, more grammatical element and a later, less grammatical element, and they involve category reanalysis from functional to lexical and pragmatic inferencing from abstract to concrete.

One of the examples Willis provides involves the Bulgarian *nešto*, which has two roles in Modern Bulgarian: a noun meaning 'thing' and an indefinite pronoun meaning 'something'. The two can be distinguished on morphosyntactic grounds. Willis shows that in Old Church Slavonic, its ancestor form *něčĭto* has all the morphosyntactic hallmarks of an indefinite pronoun with the meaning 'something', and there is no evidence of any other use of the same (or a related) word. Whereas the original grammatical use of the word has remained, a new lexical form has developed. The development from a noun meaning 'thing' to an indefinite pronoun is a common one typologically (cf. Heine and Kuteva 2002: 209–19), and hence it may be reasonable to characterize the Bulgarian development as degrammaticalization. It is distinct from the lexicalization examples in section 3.1 in that the historical changes genuinely appear to mirror grammaticalization. Semantically, as Willis (2007: 282) points out, it seems reasonable to assume that speakers may reinterpret the meaning 'something' in the sense of 'some thing known to exist, but whose actual identity is not known' as '"a thing", the identity of which is known to one or both participants'. This would be 'reversed pragmatic inferencing', from abstract to concrete. Willis (2007: 283) then argues that each new generation of language learners will use formal cues to determine whether it is a noun or a pronoun. The Old Church Slavonic form has some formal properties that mark it out as different from nouns and connect it with pronouns, but in its nominative form it resembles a nominative neuter noun. This latter fact is not sufficient to override its pronominal characteristics for the Old Church Slavonic language learner. However, general changes to the language mean that the connection to pronouns disappears over time and hence the road to reinterpreting it as a noun is open. This, then, seems a genuine example of the reversal of the grammaticalization process.

4. Explanations for unidirectionality

About ten years ago, Haspelmath (1999: 1049) wrote: 'Quite generally, the most striking fact about the previous explanations of unidirectionality is that there are so few of them.' Since then, a range of explanations have been offered, also by Haspelmath himself, but there is no obvious convergence between them and it is not clear that our understanding has increased of why grammaticalization is overwhelmingly more frequent than degrammaticalization.

Haspelmath's (1999) explanation of unidirectionality involves traditional usage-based assumptions about grammaticalization, but also reference to social factors.

He follows in the tradition of 'the invisible hand' (Keller 1990) in assuming that 'language change is shown to result from the cumulation of countless individual actions of speakers' (1999: 1043). Following Keller, he assumes five maxims of action which refer not just to notions such as economy and clarity, but also to speaker choice being influenced by the desire to be socially successful. One of the maxims referred to by Haspelmath in his account of the directionality of grammaticalization is EXTRAVAGANCE: 'talk in such a way that you are noticed' (1999: 1055). This essentially accounts for the 'reinforcement' which forms the starting point of grammaticalization, as discussed above in relation to van der Auwera (2002), and contrasts with standard accounts which assume it is linked to the communicative goal of expressiveness, in having instead a social motivation. Once speakers have been extravagant and creative in this way, others will adopt the new element following the maxim of CONFORMITY. As the element is used more frequently, it undergoes the processes commonly associated with grammaticalization—for instance, phonological reduction and routinization leading to elements becoming more fixed, more predictable, and possibly obligatory. At the end of this process, extravagance comes into play again and an innovative form is introduced. The unidirectionality is then due partly to the standard assumptions of reduction and routinization, but also to the fact that extravagance can never lead to a functional element being introduced to replace a lexical one; this would violate the maxim of CLARITY, since the functional element would be less explicit. It would also go against the assumption that lexical elements are freely manipulable by speakers, whereas functional elements are not. Haspelmath's analysis has been called into question by Geurts (2000a; 2000b) with a response from Haspelmath (2000).

Kiparsky (forthcoming) argues that unidirectionality is, in fact, exceptionless. This is based on a redefinition of grammaticalization. According to Kiparsky, analogy and traditional grammaticalization are both examples of the same, more general principle of GRAMMAR OPTIMIZATION, i.e. a striving towards an improved, more regular grammatical system.[10] As in more traditional accounts, analogy will often be based on exemplars, but Kiparsky also assumes that analogy can be driven by constraints and patterns which form part of Universal Grammar or other associated principles: 'Analogy can then give rise to patterns which are not instantiated in a parallel exemplar, or even patterns which are not yet instantiated at all. These patterns reflect preferences grounded in UG and/or in pragmatics or perception/production factors' (forthcoming: 6).[11] To Kiparsky, this non-exemplar-driven analogy is grammaticalization, and since it is driven by invariant

[10] Though Kiparsky (forthcoming) recognizes that such optimization processes, when happening in a particular combination or when not completed, can 'accidentally' lead to a less optimal system.

[11] It is interesting to note that Kiparsky is open to the idea that non-analogy based grammaticalization can find its explanation either in the properties of UG or in pragmatic or cognitive factors.

non-language-specific principles and constraints on language which aim to optimize the system, they are always striving in the same direction and hence unidirectionality is absolute. Degrammaticalization must then always be driven by exemplar-based analogy, and examples such as the English and Swedish possessive *s* or the infinitival *to*, which have been claimed as counterexamples to unidirectionality, are included under analogical change (cf. Plank 1993). Kiparsky (forthcoming) focuses on formal rather than functional grammaticalization in the exemplification of his analysis. In formal terms, optimization is closely connected to morphological blocking—essentially the idea that one word is better than two. When grammaticalization in the form of univerbation, or of prepositions becoming case markers, occurs, this is then driven by general principles which prefer less syntactic structure. These principles can never give rise to degrammaticalization in the form of words splitting into two, and hence such examples must always be formed by exemplar analogy; and because of this they are rare.

Within Chomskyan linguistics, the only possible locus of change is the intergenerational transmission of language. This led to the assumption of non-directionality; since the learner cannot have any knowledge of previous stages of the language, the argument ran, change must be directionless (see e.g. Hale 1998; Lightfoot 1999).[12] Empirically, however, even under the broader interpretations of degrammaticalization, there is an overwhelming tendency for the change to go in one direction, and this has been recognized in more recent work within the Minimalist Program. In this work, the asymmetry characteristic of grammaticalization is linked to an asymmetry inherent in the theoretical model. This is the strategy of argumentation followed by Roberts and Roussou (1999; 2003), who relate the directionality of change to the directionality of syntactic movement (see also van Gelderen 2004). Within this theory, movement is asymmetric in the sense that it can only be 'upwards' in the tree structure. Assumptions about structure mean that heads with grammatical content occur higher in the tree than associated ones with lexical content; movement is then always from a lexical category to a grammatical one. Elements which in the grammar of one generation are generated in a lexical category but moved to a grammatical one may be analysed by the next generation of language learners as having originated in the higher grammatical category. To the new generation, the formerly lexical element has then grammaticalized. Under this approach, a change in the other direction—degrammaticalization—would require a generation of speakers to have a rule which moved an item from a higher to a lower position, but this is ruled out a priori by UG. Though this explanation appeals to the principles of UG, it does so in a more specific and theory-dependent way than Kiparsky's (forthcoming). A serious concern for this account is that its technical instantiation appears to involve a fundamental circularity in that it

[12] This ignored the possibility that the principles of UG itself might be responsible for the directionality, as we have just seen in the discussion of Kiparsky (forthcoming).

requires the postulation of a feature which is not independently predictable, and thus is in effect a grammaticalization feature.

The idea of seeking the explanation for unidirectionality by linking the directional asymmetry of grammaticalization with another form of asymmetry associated with language is also explored by Jäger and Rosenbach (2008a), though in a profoundly different way from Roberts and Roussou (1999; 2003). Rather than appeal to a structural asymmetry that is essentially an artefact of the particular framework of analysis, Jäger and Rosenbach explore a psycholinguistic explanation in terms of priming. Priming refers to the process whereby the choice between linguistic elements in a particular environment can be influenced by elements occurring immediately preceding it. In an experimental study, Boroditsky (2000) tests the priming relation between spatial and temporal interpretations of prepositions. She shows that pictorial spatial cues can prime a temporal interpretation of linguistic elements, while temporal cues could prime only temporal interpretations, not spatial ones. Grammaticalization from spatial to temporal interpretation is a common change and Jäger and Rosenbach (2008a) attempt to link this to the priming direction. In order to link the local priming effects to diachronic change over time, they appeal to the idea of repeated priming as a learning process, referred to as implicit learning. In this way, priming effects can become entrenched in grammar. Though this link appears potentially more explanatory than the structural one appealed to by Roberts and Roussou (1999; 2003), the work is, by the authors' own admission, in its early stages. For instance, the possibility that unidirectionality is not the result of priming but that they are both epiphenomenal needs to be investigated (for further discussion of the proposals see also Chang 2008; Eckardt 2008; Jäger and Rosenbach 2008b; Traugott 2008b). Jäger and Rosenbach's general approach fits within a usage-based and cognitive approach to language change, and though they are unique in using priming specifically, there is currently work in applying usage-based assumptions to language change that by its nature will aim to offer cognitive explanations (see e.g. Croft 2010; Hilpert 2007).

In the descriptive literature and also in some of the theoretical literature, grammaticalization is generally seen as loss: loss of phonology, loss of meaning, and loss of independence. In sharp contrast to this, von Fintel (1995) sets out an interesting alternative in which grammaticalization is seen as a process that enriches the language, and does so by enriching the inventory of functional categories in the language. Using formal semantics, von Fintel argues that functional elements are by no means devoid of meaning; they just have a different kind of meaning from lexical elements. This meaning may possibly be innate, unlike lexical meaning, which has to be learnt. He also argues that this functional meaning is crucial to a language, so that developing functional elements to be associated with this functional meaning is a driving force behind grammaticalization. As he puts it, when an element has grammaticalized, 'Functional meanings that before were just floating around without an overt foothold can get one this way' (von Fintel 1995: 185).

Though the explanations discussed here all have something to recommend them, each also has its limitations. We have reviewed explanations in terms of social behaviour, general cognitive properties, and specific theoretical assumptions. One's preference for a particular account is likely to be related to one's general assumptions about language, its structure, its function, and how it is acquired. We do believe that there is a question to answer in relation to the overwhelming asymmetry between the frequency of grammaticalization and the occurrence of degrammaticalization, but we do not believe that at this stage a definitive answer to the question has been found.

CHAPTER 15

GRAMMATICALIZATION AND EXPLANATION

MARIANNE MITHUN

A goal of linguistics is discovering what kinds of structures occur in languages and why. We see progress in ever-evolving theoretical models of phonology, morphology, syntax, and semantics, but intriguing puzzles remain. These can be approached from several directions. One is to refine existing models to account for them. Another is to deem them outside theoretical interest. A third is to step back from a purely synchronic viewpoint to consider additional sources of explanation, including the forces that create and shape the structures in question. This chapter illustrates the last approach.

One language notorious for theoretical puzzles is Navajo. Much of what is expressed syntactically in European languages is expressed within a Navajo word. The word in (1) corresponds to a multi-word English sentence.[1]

[1] For assistance with the Navajo material cited here, I am grateful to speakers Jalon Begay, Dolly Hermes Soulé, and Marilyn Notah. Any mistakes are my own.

The material is cited in the standard Navajo orthography. The vowels, *a*, *e*, *i*, and *o* have nearly their IPA values. Vowel length is indicated by a doubled vowel (oo), high tone by an acute accent (ó), and nasalization by a Polish hook (ǫ). Plain stops are written *b*, *d*, *g*, and aspirated stops *t*, *k*. Fricatives *s*, *z* have their usual values. Alveopalatal fricatives are *sh*, *zh*. The voiceless fricative lateral is *ł*. The digraph *gh* is a voiced velar fricative. Voiced affricates are *dz*, *dl*, and *j*, and voiceless affricates *ts*, *tł*, and *ch* [tʃ]. Ejectives are *t*, *ts'*, *tł'*, *ch'*, and *k'*. There are nasals *m* and *n*; glides *y* [IPA j] and *w*; and laryngeals *h* [x, h] and glottal: stop' [ʔ].

(1) Navajo (Dolly Hermes Soulé, speaker, p.c.)
Baayádiiłti'.
b-aa-yá-d-iid-ł-ti'
3-about-talking-DISTR-1DU.SBJ-CL-speak.CONT.IPFV
'We were talking about a lot of things.'

Such sentences have raised the issue of whether words in polysynthetic languages should be accounted for by syntactic theory.

1. The Navajo verb

Navajo is spoken by perhaps 140,000 people in Arizona, New Mexico, Utah, and beyond. It is a member of the Athabaskan–Eyak–Tlingit family of languages, spoken over a wide area from Alaska into the Southwest. The structures of the languages are quite similar, particularly those of the Athabaskan group.

Most research on Navajo has focused on the verb. Verbs are usually described in terms of a templatic model, as a sequence of position classes or slots (e.g. Hoijer 1945; 1971; Kari 1975; 1989; Young and Morgan 1987[2]). The most frequently cited version is given in Figure 15.1. The prefixes furthest from the stem, in positions 0–III at the beginning of the verb, are referred to as 'disjunct' prefixes, and those closer to the stem, in positions IV–IX, as 'conjunct' prefixes. The two groups are distinguished by certain phonological characteristics.

The categories are given in (2). (Athabaskanist terminology does not always correspond to general linguistic usage.)

0	Ia	Ib	Ic	Id	Ie	II	III	IV	V	VI	VII	VIII	IX	X
PP	Ø	PP	REFL	REV	SMI	ITR	DISTR	OBJ	3	THM	MODE	1,2	CLF	STEM
OBJ	PP	ADV					PL		SBJ	ADV		SBJ		
		NOM												
Disjunct prefixes								*Conjunct prefixes*						

Fig. 15.1. Navajo verb template (YM 37–8)

[2] The following abbreviations are used in this chapter: Y = Young (2000); YM = Young and Morgan (1987); YMM = Young, Morgan, and Midgette (1992).

(2) Position classes (Y)

0	Object of a postposition [applied objects]
Ia	Null postposition
Ib	Postpositions [applicatives], Adverbial–Thematic, Nominal prefixes
Ic	Reflexive
Id	Reversionary: 'returning back'
Ie	Semeliterative 'once more'
II	Iterative
III	Distributive plural
IV	Object pronominals
V	Subject pronominals: 3rd person
VI	Thematic and adverbial prefixes [three slots]
VII	Mode [modality, aspect]
VIII	Subject pronominals: 1st and 2nd persons
IX	Classifiers [valency]
X	Stem

The contents of the slots vary: YM list 171 prefixes for position Ib, but just one for III. Some prefix meanings are common cross-linguistically, such as the reflexive *á-* (Ic). Some are rare, such as *da-* (Ib) 'death' (YM 38). Some are nearly impossible to define in isolation, such as *dee-* (VIa) 'a compound prefix, the components of which are not identifiable at present' (e.g. *bídéé yá* 'I brushed against him', *náhi-déélts'id* 'it capsized', *na'ídéétkid* 'I inquired' YM 38).

Athabaskanists distinguish several layers of verb structure.

(3) The Navajo verb

Stem	Single morpheme (fused root + aspect)
Theme	Basic lexical entry
Base	Theme + additional derivation
Word	Base + inflection

The layers in (1) *baayádiiłti'* 'we were talking about a lot of things' are in (4).

(4) Navajo verb *baayádiiłti'*

Stem	*-ti'*	speak.DURATIVE.IMPERFECTIVE
Theme	*-yá-ł-ti'*	Stem + *yá-* 'talk', *-ł-* CLASSIFIER
Base	*-aa-yá-d-ł-ti'*	Theme + *-aa-* 'about', *d-* DISTRIBUTIVE
Word	*baayádiiłti'*	Base + *b-* 'it', *iid-* 'we'

Navajo verb structure violates a number of generally held assumptions.

(i) Languages with verb-final syntactic structure are expected to be suffixing. Navajo shows strong verb-final order in clauses, but it is uniquely prefixing.

(ii) Mutually-dependent morphemes are often expected to be contiguous, but many Navajo lexical entries consist of parts scattered throughout the verb, like *yá-...łti'* 'speak...talk' in (1). Also, mode–aspect categories are expressed by combinations of non-contiguous prefixes and stem shape.

(iii) Inflectional affixes are expected to occur outside of derivational affixes, but in Navajo, derivational and inflectional prefixes are intercalated: in *baayádiiłti'*, the 1st person plural subject prefix *-iid-* 'we' is in position VIII, in the middle of the base: *baayád-iid-ti'*.

(iv) Paradigmatically related affixes, usually mutually exclusive, typically all occur in the same position in a template. In Navajo, 3rd person subject prefixes occur in position V, while 1st and 2nd occur in VIII.

Navajo presents more puzzles, but the discussion here will focus on these and the major theoretical approaches that have been taken to solving them.

2. A syntactic approach: the Mirror Principle

A number of authors have argued that word formation is essentially a syntactic process. Baker links the two with his 'Mirror Principle'.

> The way in which a complex word is built up will be related to the relative embeddings of its parts in syntax, which in turn represents aspects of their semantic scope and interpretation ... It therefore follows from the theory that the order of morphemes on a verb will reflect aspects of the syntax of the clause that the verb is the pivot of—which is the essential content of the Mirror Principle. (Baker 1988: 422)

Baker locates word formation squarely within the syntax. A syntactic approach is appealing for polysynthetic languages like Navajo, where a word can constitute a complete sentence. But non-contiguous dependencies like those making up lexical entries, and the fact that paradigmatically related markers occur in different positions, present challenges to the Mirror Principle. Baker himself recognized these problems (1985: 402).

3. A syntactic/semantic approach: scope

In a carefully argued book-length study of the Athabaskan template, Rice (2000) similarly presents word formation as a syntactic process. She considers the leftmost prefixes (Navajo 0–III), along with the rightmost elements (IX valency, X stem), all to be lexical items. Prefixes between these two (IV–VIII) are labelled functional items.

Following Baker, she proposes that in Athabaskan, 'morpheme order follows largely from scopal relations' (2000: 18). Each morpheme has within its scope everything to its left. As Rice observes, the position of the stem at the right end of the verb presents a problem for a scope analysis, since affixes are assumed to have scope over the stems they modify, but the stem is to their right. Her solution is to generate the stem at the beginning of the verb in a left-branching syntactic structure, then move it up and rightward over the prefixes.

A primary idiosyncrasy of the Athapaskan verb is that the verb stem is located in the 'wrong' place in the surface string. In the remainder of this book, I assume a movement-based account along the lines proposed in Speas 1990, 1991, Rice 1993, 1998. (Rice 2000: 78)

The position of the valency classifiers immediately before the stem at the end of the verb also presents a challenge for a scope account. These prefixes (*-ł-*, *-l-*, *-d-*) are usually lexicalized with the stem, though they can reflect transitivity. Rice proposes a syntactic solution for these as well. She considers them 'syntactically verbs that require a verb phrase complement' (2000: 126).

The stem raises to the voice/valence markers, and this unit in turn raises to the right edge of the verb phrase. This assumption is required to place the verb and voice/valence markers, a phonological constituent, in the correct position on the surface. (p. 171)

The positions of the subject prefixes pose still another challenge. As Rice notes, the formal status of these prefixes as arguments or agreement has long been a topic of discussion. The puzzle here is that 1st and 2nd person prefixes appear immediately before the valency–stem complex (VIII), but 3rd person prefixes appear several positions to their left (V), separated by three groups of adverbial and thematic prefixes, and mode–aspect prefixes. Rice's explanation is that while the 1st and 2nd person prefixes are Agreement, with features of person, number, and gender, the 3rd person prefixes are Number, with only number and gender features.

These are not the same sorts of items, but represent two distinct functional categories, Agreement and Number. Thus, one part of the ordering problem is solved: subject inflection is in two places in the verb because subject inflection is not homogenous, but rather involves two types of functional elements. (p. 191).

Her reasoning is based on the fact that one 3rd person prefix, the generic 'one', is used on occasion to refer obliquely to the speaker or the listener, and in some of the languages (though not Navajo) it is also used for 1st person plurals.

4. A SYNTACTIC/PHONOLOGICAL APPROACH

Hale (2001) explains Navajo order by a combination of syntactic and phonological principles. He begins with the now familiar puzzle that Navajo lexical items often consist of non-contiguous parts, as in (5).

(5) Lexical item 'jerked me outdoors' (YM 283, cited in Hale 2001: 283)
Silao t'óó'góó ch'íshidiniłdą̨zh.
'The policeman jerked me outdoors.'

The verb is based on the lexical item *ch'í-... dą̨zh.*

(6)	ch'í-	sh-	d-	n-´-	ł-	dą̨zh
	Ib	IV	VIa	VII–VIII	IX	X
	out.horizontally-	1SG.OBJ-	arm.movement-	ASP	TR	move.jerkily

Hale proposes an underlying left-branching tree structure for the verb, with the stem *-dą̨zh* at the lowest, rightmost V node.

He accounts for the positions of the inner, conjunct prefixes phonologically, based on analyses developed by Speas (1984) and McDonough (2000) of the Navajo verb as a minimal disyllabic phonological skeleton CVC-<u>CVC</u>. The process of creating a verb consists of filling out the skeleton. The right <u>CVC</u> half of the skeleton receives the verb stem. The left CVC half, termed the 'receptor', is filled in with phonetic features of the functional heads (Qualifier, Mode/Subject, Voice, V).

> The phonetic features of the functional heads are transferred successive-cyclically to the receptor within the verbal skeleton, satisfying the coda requirement first, if possible. (Hale 2001: 682)

The skeleton is filled in from right to left. The heads occupy one plane, in this example the Qualifier or thematic *d-* 'arm movement', the Mode/Subject *n -´-*, the transitivizer *-ł-*, and the stem *-dą̨zh* 'jerk'. The non-heads occupy another plane, here the preverb *ch'í-* 'out' and object *sh-* 'me'. First the stem is inserted into the CVC-<u>CVC</u> skeleton, yielding CVC-**<u>dą̨zh</u>**. Next, the transitive classifier *-ł-* assumes the coda position in the CVC receptor: CV-**<u>ł</u>**-dą̨zh. Then the mode-subject is added, with an epenthetic *i* that assumes the floating tone: **<u>ní</u>**-łdą̨zh. There is no position left for the prefix *d-* 'movement of arms or legs', but since the skeleton is only a minimal structure, further prefixation is allowed. The conjunct prefix *d-* is attached to the left with an epenthetic *i* added to complete the syllable: **<u>di</u>**-níłdą̨zh. Finally, the two planes are collapsed, with elements ordered as in the underlying tree: *ch'í-shi-diníłdą̨zh.*

Hale then turns to the subject prefixes. Basic 3rd person subjects are unmarked or zero. These he groups with the 1st and 2nd person prefixes. The subject prefixes remaining in position V are the generic *j-* 'one', the indefinite *'-* 'someone, something', and the spatial *hw-* 'area, space'. Hale notes that their position between the object and verb stem is problematic: they have scope over the object–verb complex. He addresses this problem by classifying them with lexical noun phrases.

> The so-called deictic prefixes of position V belong grammatically to the same category of elements as full DP (or NP) arguments, like *ashkii* 'boy'. They are, in some fundamental sense, 'adjuncts' to the clause. (Hale 2001: 691)

They are moved into the verb by a process of infixation.

> To account for the *actual* surface position of the deictic subjects, I will assume that… inflectional morphology, originating in positions external to the verb, is 'infixed' to the verb. (Hale 2001: 691)

5. An approach from grammaticalization

An awareness of processes of grammaticalization suggests another approach to the puzzles, one taken by Givón (2000) in his discussion of Tolowa, an Oregon Athabaskan language. With this, the Athabaskan verb can be understood as the result of successive developments over time.

The development of grammatical structures and the markers that constitute them can involve a constellation of changes, most of them gradual. Among these may be an extension of morphemes to new contexts of use, resulting in more diffuse and general or grammatical meanings; increasing abstraction; decategorialization or loss of properties characteristic of specific lexical categories; and reduction in phonetic independence and substance (Heine and Kuteva 2007: 34). The Navajo verb exhibits ample evidence of all of these effects.

Phonologically, the picture is striking. The outer (leftmost) prefixes (0–III) have the most phonological substance. They show a variety of shapes. Their onsets are drawn from the full consonant inventory of the language, and their nuclei represent nearly all the vowels: *tsístł'a-* 'cornered, trapped, blocked, baffled', *hasht'e-* 'in order, ready, prepared', *k'eh-* 'overcome'. Most of the inner prefixes (IV–IX) consist of a single consonant, drawn from just a subset of the Navajo inventory (plain coronals, glides, laryngeals), augmented in some contexts by the epenthetic vowel *i* descended from Proto-Athabaskan schwa: *n-/ni-* terminative, *sh-/s-* 'I'. The prefixes closest to the stem, the valency classifiers, consist of at most a single consonant, or only a phonetic effect on the following consonant, or nothing at all. Phonological substance thus shows increasing reduction with proximity to the stem.

There is similar semantic progression. Outer prefixes often show quite specific meanings, many typical of lexical items in other languages: *-chá:-* 'bunched, huddled', *chą́-* 'crave, be addicted to', *-ch'o-* 'support, help', *cha-* 'darkness', *di-* 'into or near fire', *ka-* 'chronically ill, invalid', *k'e-* 'loosen, untie, take down (loom or hair)', *łi-* 'flattery, cajolery, cheating', *tso-* 'prayer', *soh-* 'hardship', *tii-* 'tackle, attack', *tsi-* 'startle, fright'. Many of the inner prefixes serve more grammatical functions, such as the subject and object pronominals and the various mode/aspect markers. The valency prefixes adjacent to the stem are highly grammatical, sometimes with barely identifiable functions.

While many outer prefixes have clear concrete meanings, such as *-níká-* 'through an opening' (Ib), many inner prefixes show effects of extension in their diffuse meanings. Young and Morgan distinguish 14 prefixes in position VIa of the shape *d-/di-* on the basis of their meanings (YM 38). Most definitions begin: 'occurs as a component of some verb bases that involve . . .'. The definitions continue 'movement of the arms or legs', 'relinquishment, relaxation, opening or closing and addition or reduction', 'an elongated object', 'refuge, relief, succor', 'fire or light', 'the mouth, stomach, throat, oral action, food, smell, noise', 'pain, hurt', 'holiness, faith, respect, immunity from the effects of a ceremony, prayer', tilting, slanting, placing on edge, leaning, dangling', 'sound, hearing'. Some have more grammatical definitions: 'occurs in combination with *ni-* (VIb) in certain Neuter Imperfective Adjectivals', 'occurs in certain Active and Neuter verb bases that are concerned with color', 'the Inceptive marker that, in combination with *yi-* (VII) Progressive mode marker produces the future paradigms'. One is defined as 'a catch-all for *di-* prefixes that, even speculatively, cannot be assigned to one of the foregoing categories'. They mention possible associations between some of the prefixes: the *d-/di-* prefix used with verbs of 'refuge, relieve, succor' is said to probably be cognate with the *d-/di-* prefix in verbs of 'relinquishment, relaxation, opening or closing and addition or reduction' and with the *d-/di-* prefix in verbs 'concerned with the mouth, stomach, throat, oral action, food, smell, noise, speech', and perhaps with that in verbs of 'sound, hearing'. Some of the homophony could be the result of phonological erosion, but some appears to be the result of semantic extension.

The coincidence of increasing phonological reduction, generality, abstraction, and diffuse meaning with increasing proximity to the stem suggests that the positions of prefixes in the verb correlate with their age: those closest to the stem are the oldest, and those furthest the youngest.

5.1. Comparative evidence

A comparison of verb structures across the family corroborates this scenario. Relations within the Athabaskan–Eyak–Tlingit family are illustrated in Fig. 15.2.

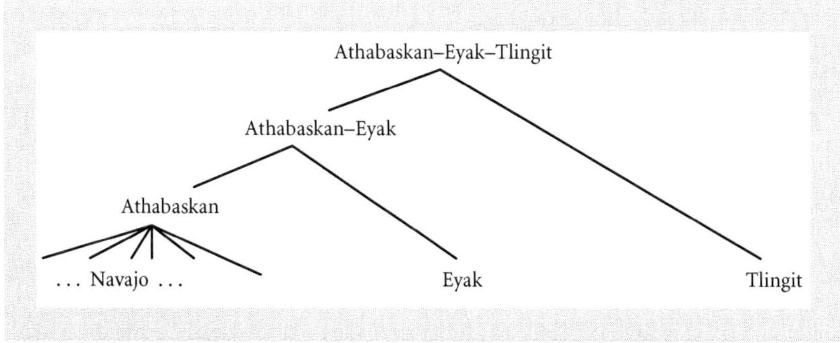

Fig. 15.2. The Athabaskan–Eyak–Tlingit family (Krauss 1973)

17	16	15	14	13	12	11	10-9	8	7-4	3	2	1	0	
PREVB	DST	PL	OBJ	AREA	NOUN		LOC	BEN	MODE/ASP	DST	**SBJ**	**CLF**	**STEM**	SUF

Fig. 15.3. Tlingit verb template (Crippen 2010: 105)

I	II	III	IV	V	VI	**VII**	VIII	**IX**	**X**	
OBJECT	MODE/ASP		PL	CLF	MODE/ASP	**SUBJECT**	MODE/ASP	**CLF**	**STEM**	SUFFIXES

Fig. 15.4. Eyak verb template (Krauss 1965: 171)

0	Ia	Ib	Ic	Id	Ie	II	III	IV	V	VI	VII	**VIII**	**IX**	**X**
PP OBJ	0 PP	NOM	REFL	REV	SMI	ITR	DISTR PL	OBJ	3 SBJ	THM	MODE	**1,2 SBJ**	**CLF**	**STEM**
		ADV								ADV				
		PP												

Fig. 15.5. Navajo verb template (Young and Morgan 1987)

All of the languages share a core: SUBJECT–VALENCY–STEM. Templates for Tlingit and Eyak are in Figs 15.3 and 15.4. Those for the Athabaskan languages are largely as in Navajo, repeated in Fig. 15.5, with some differences particularly in the leftmost sections.

Valency classifier (CLF) and subject prefixes are cognate across the three branches, suggesting that the SUBJECT–VALENCY–STEM core was already in place in their common parent.

5.2. Navajo-internal evidence

It is no longer possible to trace the origins of the oldest prefixes, such as the valency classifiers. Likely sources of some younger prefixes, however, can still be identified even within Navajo. Position Ib contains three types of prefixes, grouped by Young (2000) as 'nominal', 'adverbial', and 'postpositional'.

In the nominal prefix category, twenty-five forms are listed, many with lexical counterparts: *a'ą́-* 'into a hole or burrow', *a'áán* 'hole, burrow'; *dá'ák'e-*'into the field', *dá'ák'eh* 'cornfield, field'; *dį́-* 'foursome', *dį́į́'* 'four'; *jé-* 'carefully'; *jéí* 'pleura, heart'; *łe-* 'into the ashes (to cook)', *łeezh* 'dirt, soil'; *naa-* 'war, enemy', *'anaa'* 'war'; *n-/ni-* 'pair, couple, by two's', *naaki* 'two'; *tá-* 'threesome', *táá'* 'three'; *tó-* 'water, fluid', *tó* 'water'; *t'á-* 'wing(s)', *t'á'* 'wing'. A number are based on body parts or object parts, inalienable possessions that require a possessive prefix when used as independent nouns: *-'lák'ee-* 'into hand', *-'ák'ee* 'hand'; *-láta-* 'at the tip', *-látah* 'tip, end, extremity'; *-nák'ee-* 'in(to), on the eye', *-nák'ee* 'ocular area, eye place' (*-k'ee* 'place'); *-niik'i-* 'on the face', *-nii'* 'face' with *-k'i-* 'on'); *-tsą́-* 'belly, in the belly, food', *-tsą́* 'belly'; *-zá-/-zé-* 'neck, throat', *-zéé'* 'mouth, neck'; *alkéłk'e-* 'in agreement, in each other's footsteps', *á-* REFLEXIVE + *-k'eh* 'footprint, footstep'.

These prefixes appear to be descendants of incorporated nouns. Incorporation is no longer productive in Navajo, but it persists in some Northern Athabaskan relatives and Tlingit. The prevalence of prefixes pertaining to body parts is not surprising: body part terms are among the first to be incorporated when such constructions develop in languages. The prefixes already differ from their lexical counterparts. They have been decategorialized, no longer appearing with possessive prefixes. They are often slightly reduced phonologically. They occur as elements of lexicalized verb themes. Uses of the lexical noun *tó* 'water' and the prefix *tó-* can be compared in (7) and (8). (The 'water' prefix often appears as *ta-*.)

(7) Noun *tó* 'water' (Dolly Soulé, speaker, p.c.)
Tó bíká níyá.
'I've come after water.'

(8) Prefix *tó-* 'water' (YM 707)

Shikee'	bąąh	tó'diisóół
shi-kee'	bąąh	tó-'-di-yi-ł-yóól
1SG.POSS-foot	on	water-something-pain-y.PFV-TR-cause.to.inflate.PFV

'A water blister formed on my foot.'

The prefixes do not specify a grammatical relation. Role is simply inferred from the situation.

(9) Navajo nouns and nominal prefixes (YM 488, 516, 517, 302, 84)

a. jéi — 'pleura, heart'
Baa jé'ííníshná — 'I handle it carefully' — *-l-ná* 'do right.handedly'

b. łeezh 'soil, ground, earth, dust, dirt, land'
Łe-'doolch'il 'It struck the ground (a bolt of lightning)' *-l-ch'ííł* 'flash'
Łe-'ashgééd 'I'm digging a cellar, pit' *-Ø-gééd* 'dig'

In the adverbial category, Young lists 101 prefixes (Y 21–2). Lexical sources of many of these are also identifiable. Some directionals have sources in adverbs: *a-* 'away out of sight', *áá* 'there, remote'; *ada-* 'downward from a height', *adah* 'down'; *da-* 'up at an elevation, off', *dah* 'up'; *na-/n-/ni-* 'across, crosswise', *naa, naanii* 'crosswise, across, over'. Some were nouns: *yá-* 'up into the air', *yá* 'sky'. It is easy to see how these prefixes could develop. Lexical adverbs often appear immediately before the verb. When particular adverb–verb combinations co-occur frequently, speakers can process them as chunks, and the adverbial constituent can lose its individual salience.

(10) Adverb *adáh* 'down' (Dolly Soulé, speaker, p.c.)
Adáh náánádá
down he sat again
'He came back down.'

(11) Prefix *ada-* 'down' (Dolly Soulé, speaker, p.c.)
Adanáátsaad ndę́ę́'
ada-náá-tsaad ni=dę́ę́'
down-again-scoot.MOMENTANEOUS.PFV that=from
'When he came down again ...'

The adverb and prefix coexist in the modern language, serving subtly different functions. (10) and (11) were from a Pear Film narrative. The story opened with a man picking pears in a tree. When he climbed down, the speaker used the adverb *adáh* 'down'. He emptied the pears into a basket and climbed back up. After a while, he climbed back down with more pears. This time the routine was familiar, and the speaker expressed it in a single word with prefix *ada-*.

Other adverbial prefixes in position Ib simply occur as parts of particular lexical items, thematically. Sources for a number of these are identifiable as well, some adverbs, some verbs, some nouns: *cha-* 'crying', *-cha-* 'cry (verb stem)'; *k'a-* 'wound, blemish'; *k'aa'* 'arrow'; *k'é-* 'peace, friendliness, amicable relations', *-k'éí* 'kinsman, *literally* friendly one'.

(12) Thematic prefix *kéé* 'living, residing' (YM 493)
kéyah 'land, country, nation'
K'ad dził ghą́ą́'di kééhasht'į́.
k'ad dził ghą́ą́'=di kéé-ha-sh-t'į́
now mountain top=at residing-area-1SG.SBJ-animate.at.rest.NEUTER.IMPV
'I live on top of the mountain now.'

Prefixes in the third group are applicatives, derivational prefixes which add an argument to the verb. Many have surprisingly grammatical meanings for recent additions: *-á'-* 'for, on behalf of', *-aa-* 'to, about, concerning, on, off, by', *-í-/-é-* 'against', *-gha-* 'away from', *-ghá-* 'through', *-'ká-* 'for, after', *-k'i-* 'on, on top of, off of', *-ná'* 'beside', *-ta-* 'among', *-ts'á-* 'away from', *-ya-* 'under, beneath'. The applicative *ká-* 'after' can be seen in (13). Prefixed to the intransitive verb *-'į́į́'* 'look', it derives transitive verbs meaning 'look for'.

(13) Applicative prefix *-ká-* (Dolly Soulé, speaker, p.c.)
Shiyostsah bíkádésh'į́į́'
shi-yostsah bi-ká-dé-sh-'į́į́'
my-ring 3-after-thematic-1SG.SBJ-look.IMPV
'I'm looking for my ring.'

The applicative prefixes are referred to as 'postpositions' by Young and Morgan. The sources of many of them still survive as genuine postpositions, independent forms inflected for their objects with prefixes. The postposition *-ká* 'after' occurred in (7) above.

(7) Postposition *-ká* 'after' (Dolly Soulé, speaker, p.c.)
Tó bíká níyá.
tó bi-ká ni-yá
water it-after TERMINATIVE.1SG.SBJ-one.walk.PFV
'I've come after water.'

When the postpositions fused with a following verb, they brought their pronominal objects with them. The relatively grammatical meanings of these prefixes now make sense. They had already undergone some grammaticalization as postpositions, before attaching to the verb.

The Navajo postposition > applicative development provides a snapshot of a construction in the process of grammaticalization. There is a large set of forms that serve only as postpositions: forty-seven are listed in YM. A smaller set occur both as postpositions and as applicative prefixes: YM list twelve. For many of these new prefixes, the bond to the verb is still loose; speakers generally feel they form a single word together, but are sometimes somewhat unsure. The speaker cited above, Mrs Soulé, felt confident that *bíká-* in (13) was part of the verb, but there is a convention in the practical orthography for writing them separately. Some of the applicatives have begun to lose phonological substance in their new prefix positions. The postposition *-'ąą* 'over', for example, is the source of the applicative prefix *-'ą-*. The postposition *-lááh* 'beyond' is the source of the prefix *-lá-* (YM 27). Finally, some forms now occur only as prefixes, though they can be seen to be descended from earlier postpositions: YM list twenty-seven. This process of reanalysis, described for a number of genetically unrelated languages in Craig and Hale (1988), is not very different from that behind English verbs like *oversee* and *overlook*.

Though the applicative prefixes are historically related to postpositions, they are not equivalent. Postpositions can in principle follow any noun which could designate a potential object. The applicative prefixes are derivational: they create new lexical verbs. They develop through the repeated use of certain postposition–verb collocations that ultimately become routinized, so that the boundaries between the parts are dimmed. The reanalysis occurs postposition by postposition, and lexical item by lexical item. On occasion, speakers innovate, but for the most part, derived expressions containing postpositions are learned, stored, and retrieved as lexical units. Speakers know which ones exist and which do not, and know their particular, often idiosyncratic meanings.

5.3. Converging evidence

These facts taken together provide evidence that Navajo verb structure was built up in stages over time, beginning with the verb stem, with successive prefixation of what are now the valence classifiers, then the subject prefixes, etc. This understanding of the development of the system provides explanations for the issues raised at the outset.

Discontinuous lexical entries are no longer baffling. Languages are full of lexicalized idiomatic expressions formed from a noun, adverb, or adpositional phrase plus an inflected verb. The marking of mode–aspect categories with combinations of morphemes in different positions is understandable. Finer distinctions may be added to existing systems with additional adverbs or auxiliaries, which again may fuse to full inflected forms.

The verb stem is no longer in the 'wrong' place. The positions of affixes depend on their individual source constructions. The Navajo prefixes whose sources are still identifiable developed from words that still occur syntactically before the verb: subject and object pronouns, nouns, adverbs, and postpositions.

It is not surprising that 1st and 2nd person subjects should appear in one position and 3rd in another. The original pronominal paradigm apparently consisted of independent pronouns for 1st and 2nd persons, singular and plural. Basic 3rd persons might have been unmarked, a common pattern cross-linguistically, or marked with a pronoun that subsequently eroded to almost nothing, mentioned by Hale. The generic, indefinite, and spatial categories were added later. It is no surprise that the subject prefixes occur closer to the verb stem than the objects. As highly topical, frequent, unstressed morphemes in a relatively fixed position before the verb, they were likely candidates for grammaticalization, more likely than objects. Studies of English spontaneous speech show that subjects are overwhelmingly given (so pronominal), while objects are given only around 50 per cent of the time (Chafe 1994: 85–6).

It is no longer necessary to decide whether morphemes are actually 'lexical' or 'grammatical', or whether subject and object prefixes are 'really agreement' or 'really pronouns'. There are Navajo morphemes that are highly lexical, separate words, such as *ashkii* 'boy', and prefixes that are highly grammatical, such as the detransitiver *d-*. But grammaticalization involves gradual processes, and there are many morphemes at stages of development between these two extremes. Recognizing the clines allows us to ask more interesting questions about the sequences in which individual pragmatic, semantic, syntactic, and phonological changes occur.

The view of the Navajo verb as the product of successive layers of development over time also explains some puzzles not addressed in the synchronic treatments. One is the surprising number of prefixes with similar forms. Such similarities are discussed by Givón (2000) for Tolowa. One Navajo set includes the Iterative *ná-/né-/ní-/ń-* (Position II in the template in Fig. 15.1); the Reversionary *ná-/né-/ní-/ń-* 'returning back, reverting to a previous location, state or condition' (Position Id); the Continuative *na-/naa-/ni-/n-* (Position Ib2), the thematic *ná-/ní-/ń-* 'sewing' (Position Ib2); the adverbials *na-/naa-/ni-/n-* 'around about, without defined direction' (Position Ib2), *ná-/ní-/ń-* 'around encircling, embracing' (Position Ib2), and *ná-/né-/ní-/ń-* 'repetition' (Position Ib2); and the applicatives *-na-/-naa-/-ni-/-n-*, 'around, around about, surrounding (it)' (Position Ib1), and *-ná-/-ní-/-ń-* 'around encircling, embracing (it)' (Position Ib1). For all of these prefixes, allomorphy is conditioned by the same phonological contexts. With thirty-four consonants in the language, the similarities are unlikely to be the result of chance.

Such constellations appear to be the result of multiple developments, at different times, from a single source. Perhaps the oldest prefix is the Iterative, part of the mode–aspect system. It is added to Usitative verbs to form a kind of Frequentative: Usitative *'ahbínígo gohwééh yishdlį́į́h łeh* 'I usually drink coffee in the morning'; Iterative *'ahbínígo gohwééh <u>ná</u>-shghlį́į́h* 'I drink coffee in the morning (repeatedly and customarily)' (Y 67–8). It is the closest of the *na-* prefixes to the stem, and has the most grammatical function. It is easy to see a semantic relationship among the somewhat abstract Reversionary prefix in Id 'returning to a previous location, state, or condition' (*<u>ná</u>-dzá* 'he returned' Y 43), the thematic prefix 'sewing' (*<u>ná</u>-shkad* 'I am sewing' YMM 285), and the somewhat more concrete adverbial prefix of Ib2 'around encircling, surrounding, embracing' (*<u>ná</u>-bał* 'to whirl <u>around</u>, gyrate, spin around' YM 521, *<u>ná</u>-zt'i'* 'it extends <u>around in a circle</u>, as a fence' Y 44). Also similar is the adverbial prefix 'around about, without defined direction' (*<u>naa</u>-gh'a* 'he's walking <u>around</u> here and there' Y 44), and applicatives 'around' (*bi-<u>ná</u>-shááh* 'I walk around it' YMM 665). It is likely that the various prefixes developed through extensions of existing markers to new contexts. Closer proximity to the stem can indicate earlier grammaticalization and longer opportunity for abstraction. But younger prefixes can also be exploited for new grammatical functions. The continuative aspect is formed by adding the Ib prefix *na-* to Imperfective verbs: *Dah naa-kaad* 'it hangs flapping or waving, as a flag on a flagpole' (*dah* 'up, at an elevation', *-kaad* 'be spread out') (YMM 306).

The story does not stop here. Navajo also contains a postposition *-naa* 'around about, in the vicinity of, surrounding': *Shighan bi-naa=góó hózhóní* 'it's pretty around my place' (*bi-naa-góó* 'it-around=along') (YMM 418). This postposition is a likely source of the applicative. Its own source persists in the lexical verb *na'/naad* 'move, stir, live', reconstructed for Pre-Proto-Athabaskan as **na* 'move, stir, live, work' (YMM 407). The tone variation seen among the prefixes is now explained by the array of aspectual forms of this stem: modern Navajo 'live, work', 'move' verbs appear as *-ná*, *-na'*, *-náá'*, *-naah*, etc.

6. Conclusion

The various theoretical approaches to the issues discussed here have been based on many of the same observations—about Navajo, about Athabaskan languages, and about language in general. They differ in how they relate these observations to each other.

Similarities between syntactic and morphological structure have been observed in many languages, but the resemblances are not evidence that the two are the same. The structures can be related diachronically: some syntactic constructions evolve into morphological structures over time. The Navajo verb did not develop instantaneously from a parallel syntactic structure: it evolved step by step, each time from a syntactic construction in frequent use at that moment. Once attached, morphemes continued to evolve, so that their modern forms and functions no longer necessarily match those of their lexical sources.

Relations between semantic scope and particular morpheme orders are certainly observable cross-linguistically, but this need not mean that speakers order their morphemes online by scope. Scope can be an effect of sequences of grammaticalization processes. When words evolve into affixes, they generally attach not just to a part of their host, but to the whole. Understanding the resulting structure as a historical product solves another problem encountered by synchronic scope analyses: the fact that corresponding markers may exhibit different relative orders cross-linguistically. Both Athabaskan and Eskimo–Aleut languages show clear SOV clause structure, but in the first, pronominal affixes precede the stem, and in the second, they follow. The two morphological structures apparently developed from different syntactic structures. The first continues earlier SOV clause order. The second developed from nominalized clauses with suffixed possessive pronominals (Mithun 2008).

Prefixes closer to the Navajo verb stem show more phonological erosion than those further from the stem, but their phonology need not be the cause of their relative order. Both phonological reduction and prefix sequence are the result of the histories of the morphemes.

Recognition of the processes involved in grammaticalization can provide valuable tools as we seek to explain the patterns that occur in languages, but of course it does not replace synchronic considerations. Each small change is a motivated synchronic event, stimulated and constrained by cognitive and communicative factors. Understanding how the system was built up does not tell us exactly how speakers produce Navajo words in speech. It does suggest that they do not generally order morphemes spontaneously online according to abstract syntactic, semantic, or phonological principles. If each word were created anew, the template could not have remained as stable as it has. An understanding of grammaticalization simply provides us with an additional tool for understanding and allows us to move on to yet more interesting questions.

CHAPTER 16

GRAMMATICALIZATION: A GENERAL CRITIQUE

BRIAN D. JOSEPH

1. Introduction

I start this contribution with a personal note: it is no secret that I have expressed critical views on the whole enterprise of grammaticalization, grammaticalization theory, and grammaticalization studies, as Joseph (2001; 2003; 2004; 2006) make abundantly clear. At the same time, though, I readily recognize that this enterprise has revealed some real aspects of language development that deserve attention. To be perfectly clear, I believe that there is a *phenomenon* that can be called 'grammaticalization', that one-time lexical material can certainly come to serve grammatical functions and to change regarding their lexical (content) vs. grammatical (function) status, and that such changes can correlate with changes in morphological status (e.g. word versus affix). Nonetheless, I do *not* believe all claims in the literature about this phenomenon. Therefore, I welcome this opportunity to address some issues I have with grammaticalization, in the spirit of intellectual inquiry.

Here are the major themes that inform this critique:

(1) a. grammaticalization as process or result (and terminology more generally);
  b. privileging one cluster of developments over others;
  c. alternative outcomes/results;

d. unidirectionality;
e. grammaticalization in language contact.

In what follows, I take these themes up one by one, and elaborate on each.

2. Process vs. result and terminology

This first theme centres on the very nature of grammaticalization, and whether it is a process/mechanism[1] of change, parallel to sound change, analogy, borrowing, reanalysis, and metaphorical extension, to name a few well-known and universally recognized ways in which change in language is effected. There are actually several questions here: first, is grammaticalization a process/mechanism, separate and distinct from other independently needed processes, or is it instead a label for the result of such processes? Second, if one adopts a process view, is grammaticalization a single process or are there several grammaticalization processes? The literature offers many ambiguous remarks on these points (see Campbell and Janda 2001 and the discussion in e.g. Janda 2001 and Joseph 2001).

Clarifying these issues is practical if all scholars can show uniformity in talking about grammaticalization. However, there is a deeper reason why they matter: it is hard to see how one can generalize about 'grammaticalization' if there are many processes of 'grammaticalization', all the more so if the overarching phenomenon is nothing more than the name for a particular kind of outcome of the operation of other processes are involved, rather than being a process/mechanism of change itself (see Janda 2001; Joseph 2001; Newmeyer 2001; Fischer, Chapter 3 above).

But even if one grants that the involvement of several processes does not preclude grammaticalization being its own process/mechanism of change (as opposed to a name for a result), there is a further problem. In some views, for example that of Lehmann (1995a[1982]), grammaticalization is determined by the clustering together of several processes/mechanisms, (e.g. semantic bleaching, phonetic reduction). This raises the question of how this clustering is accomplished by the speakers engaging in the particular changes, and how these various processes come to be coordinated. This is especially problematic since all interested parties accept that each of these effects can occur independently; that is, phonetic

[1] I am using these terms interchangeably, inasmuch as dictionary definitions (e.g. in the *OED*) treat them as quite similar (*process* as 'action or succession of actions occurring or performed in a definite manner, and having a particular result', *mechanism* as 'a means by which an effect or result is produced'); both definitions focus on the step or steps leading to a result, and thus treat those steps as distinct from the endpoint, the result itself.

reduction can occur without any concomitant semantic effect, as in numerous instances of reductive sound changes (e.g. Old Latin *stlocus* 'place' > Romanian *loc*, ancient Greek *ommation* 'eye' > Modern Greek *mati*, Old English *scīrgerēfa* 'shire-reeve' > Modern English *sheriff*), and conversely, semantic bleaching, and shift from lexical/content meaning to grammatical/function meaning, can occur without phonetic reduction, as in:

(2) a. Russian *davaj(te)* 'let's....' (hortative, from 2SG(PL) imperative of 'give' (possibly: 'permit' in Old Russian)).
b. English *let us* (hortative).[2]
c. English *concerning* (marking topic, etymologically a participle, but apparently a preposition now, no longer syntactically participle-like in not controlling an understood subject (cf. *Concerning the exam, you needn't take it*, with no 'controlled subject' with *concerning*, vs. Ø *Leaving the exam, you should take your belongings*, where *you* as the understood subject of *leaving*).
d. Medieval Greek *thelō* 'FUTURE' (a functional shift from a lexical verb meaning 'want' with, at first, no reduction; as shown below in section 3, there ultimately is reduction but the grammatical use of *thelō* occurs independently of the later reduction).
e. English *kind of/sort of* (originally *(a) kind/sort of*, a noun + preposition modifier, originally with other nouns (e.g. *John is (a) kind/sort of a fool*), but now with all kinds of words, e.g. *I only kind of (sort of) believe you;* importantly, even though reduced forms *kinda/sorta* occur, the more grammatical use occurs with the unreduced form (*kind of/sort of*) and the reduced form, so reduction does not correlate directly with grammatical use).

To some extent, this objection boils down to why one might decide to even call a phenomenon 'grammaticalization', thus touching on theme (1b)—see section 2—but also speaking to matters of terminology. It is therefore appropriate to address some concerns in this realm before treating the next theme. Of course, harping on terminology is perhaps the least productive kind of criticism, since, following Saussure, labels for concepts are arbitrary. Nonetheless, terminology is important; it assures consistency of interpretation across different authors, and terms *do* have meanings, invoking for readers and users certain images and notions, despite Saussurean arbitrariness. And some grammaticalization-related terminology has problematic aspects.

[2] That there is phonetic reduction in the contracted form *let's* is irrelevant here since both the full form *let us* and the reduced form *let's* can serve a hortative function; thus the grammatical use is independent of the reduction.

First, there is the very term 'grammaticalization'. Some linguists seem to use it very broadly almost as a synonym of 'change', as Fischer (Chapter 3 above) notes, yet surely not all changes are instances of grammaticalization; sound change, for instance, could hardly qualify.

Even more telling, the term is sometimes used in characterizing developments that have nothing to do with grammar. An extreme case of this sort is *phonogenesis*, a term Hopper (1994: 31) developed to characterize the addition of 'phonological bulk' to originally polymorphemic words through the elimination of concrete meaning for constituent morphemes, as in OE *hand-geweorc* 'collection of works done by hand', where *ge-* is a collective prefix, becoming *hand-iwork*, where, he says, the *-i-* has no concrete function but is simply there. Hopper terms phonogenesis an 'advanced stage of grammaticalization', but since he posits the complete effacement of morphemic status in such cases, it seems rather that such developments instantiate movement of an element totally *out* of grammar (see Joseph 2003). Subsuming them under a rubric of 'grammaticalization' seems to extend the term's sense term beyond utility. So too with cases where an element passes into discourse usage, as with English *say* coming to show equivocation, in that in many conceptions, discourse is not a part of grammar *per se*; discourse may well have a 'grammar' and it may feed into grammar *sensu stricto*, but those are different issues from saying that discourse *is* grammar.

Furthermore, there are presuppositions to confront underlying the use of the term 'grammaticalization'. For instance, if a linguist claims one adposition (A) is 'more grammaticalized' than another (B), based on one (say) showing more nominal traits (e.g. occurring with a possessive), is that a neutral statement? Maybe, if 'more grammaticalized' simply means having fewer nominal characteristics. But, by the process interpretation of grammaticalization, 'more grammaticalized' implies that A has moved further along the cline of grammaticalization than B has, i.e. that A has diverged from B by becoming less nominal. However, in principle, B could have diverged from A by becoming more nominal in nature.

One might say here that such an interpretation goes against unidirectionality (a topic discussed in section 4), but one should recognize that this statement is only as neutral as it is free of assumptions about grammaticalization as a process and about unidirectionality on the cline of grammatical status. Most advocates of grammaticalization surely would look at the situation described here and assume the nominal type reflects the older state of affairs.[3] I would advocate a more neutral labelling, e.g. 'adposition A is more grammatical [not: 'more grammaticalized'] than B.'

[3] As it often is; my point here is that if the reverse sort of development can occur, then the use of a characterization like 'more grammaticalized' implies a greater understanding of the historical facts than might be warranted.

3. Privileging one cluster of changes

Thus, in classic cases of grammaticalization as discussed in the literature, several different effects generally line up to give a particular result, even though it can be the case that only some of these characteristic effects occur, e.g. phonetic reduction without semantic bleaching, or vice versa. One interpretation that such cases invite is a recognition that there is much more besides grammatical change to worry about in historical linguistics. Indeed, a glance at the programme for a conference on historical linguistics or the table of contents of a historical linguistics journal makes it clear that historical linguists are concerned with sound change, spread of innovation, language relationships, rate of change, etc. One has to wonder, therefore, even restricting attention to just changes affecting or involving grammar, why one particular grouping of changes (semantic shifts of a certain type + phonetic reductions + extension of usage into novel realms, etc.) should be treated as special, deserving its own label, conferences, textbooks, and other compendia, and not just an accidental confluence of factors.

To take one concrete example, is the development of *thelō hina X* 'I want that X' at one stage of Greek to *thelō hina X* 'I will X' at a later stage, without any reduction, any more or less interesting than later developments of *thelō hina X* to *thelei ina X* 'it will that X' to *thel na X* to *thenna X* to *thana X* to *than X* to *tha X*, some by regular sound change, some by analogy, some perhaps with other motivations? Is each of these several developments an instance of 'grammaticalization', even though some, e.g. the degemination in *thenna* > *thena*, are fully regular and widely instantiated outside of this collocation? Or is the whole set of developments taken together a single instance of 'grammaticalization'? If so, since languages can stop at any point, there is nothing deterministic about this particular sequence of changes—Greek got along just fine for several decades (or more) with unreduced *thelō hina* for future, and with unreduced *theli na*, etc. Since nothing impels the collocation on to the next stage, how would we know when a suitable endpoint has been reached that justifies the label 'grammaticalization'? In fact, in a certain sense, as suggested in (2), it is the first development, by which *thelō hina X* with lexical meaning ('want that X') came to be employed—with no change in form—as a future, with grammatical meaning ('will X'), that was the grammaticalization, representing the entry of a lexical form into the grammatical realm, whereas the remaining developments did not alter the status of the collocation as a grammatical functor.[4]

[4] Admittedly, there might be a difference here between some of the stages in terms of the word-to-affix cline; so in that sense, these developments could be reckoned as some sort of grammaticalization.

To pick up further on the theme in section 2, just as there can be a shift in grammatical status without phonetic reduction, importantly also, there can be phonetic augmentation of grammatical material, even where that grammatical material has a lexical source. The expansion in form of *m(i)ente* in Old Spanish, from the Latin ablative of *ment-* 'mind' and used in forming manner adverbials, is such a case, since beside *miente*, there is also *mientre* in this use. The extra *-r-*, following Dyer (1972), is due to the influence of other adverbials, e.g. those in *-ter* or from *dum interim*.[5]

I call this intense interest in grammaticalization the 'privileging of one cluster of changes over others', because it gives undue attention to what even the grammaticalization literature recognizes as just one type of development. Traugott (1994: 1481), for example, says: 'From the diachronic perspective, grammaticalization is usually thought of as that subset of linguistic changes whereby a grammatical item becomes more grammatical'; the key word here is 'subset', presupposing that there is more to change than grammaticalization. In that case, it seems fair to ask why this subset should command such attention among linguists. This is not to say that it should be ignored, but only to query the intensity of the interest, as measured by conferences on the topic, textbooks, etc.

4. Alternative outcomes/results

A focus on just one cluster of changes means that other outcomes of change may not always be considered, or may not be accorded particular interest. Yet it should be obvious that much more goes on in language change than just the oft-cited movement of *lexical/somewhat-grammatical* to *(more) grammatical* that characterizes grammaticalization. For instance, to consider just a subset of changes involving grammar, there are four logical possibilities for developments involving movement between derivational and inflectional morphology, specified in (3).

[5] Such augmentation may counter the claim in Kiparsky (forthcoming) that 'grammaticalization is often accompanied by phonological *weakening* of the grammaticalized element, and never, it seems, by strengthening'. However, for Kiparsky, this would probably not be a case of grammaticalization, as it involves both existing grammatical material and an analogical model (whence the *-r-*). He rejects defining grammaticalization as movement towards (greater) grammatical function and sees it instead as 'non-exemplar-based analogical change [that] establish[es] new patterns in the language'. Still, if the introduction of *-r-* occurred as *miente* was becoming established as a new manner adverbial marker, then the augmentation would have co-occurred with the grammaticalization, even if only as an ephemeral effect.

(3) a. derivational morphology ⇒ inflectional morphology
b. derivational morphology ⇒ derivational morphology
c. inflectional morphology ⇒ inflectional morphology
d. inflectional morphology ⇒ derivational morphology

All of these are attested types of grammatical change, yet in measuring (3) against usual characterizations of 'grammaticalization', only (3a) would be 'classical' grammaticalization, involving movement from less grammatical (derivational) to more grammatical (inflectional), whereas the other outcomes would not fall under most notions of grammaticalization, even though they involve grammatical change. In particular, (3b) and (3c) involve no movement on the cline of grammaticalization (thus 'lateral movement' (Joseph 2006)), and (3d) would be counter-directional movement, from more grammatical to less grammatical.

Yet examples of each occur. Regarding (3a), there is the case of the High German *-er* plural (as in *Buch* 'book'/*Bücher* 'books') from a reanalysis of a Proto-Indo-European (and Proto-Germanic) neuter stem-forming suffix **-es-* (Proto-Germanic **-iz-*). The lateral shifts on the cline, with no alteration of grammatical status, are exemplified in the first instance, (3b), by the accretion of derivational suffixes to form larger suffixes via resegmentation or erasure of morpheme boundaries, e.g. Latin *-ānus* from the 1st declension noun suffix *-ā* + adjectival **-no-* suffix, or English *-ness* from *-n-* of an adjectival suffix + the noun suffixes **-ot-* + **-tu-*, cf. Gothic *ibnassus* / Old Saxon *eƀnissi* / Old English *efnes* 'equality', based on a *-no- stem adjective, cf. Modern English *even*. For the second type of lateral shift, (3c), a good example is the remaking in Greek of verb endings based on other endings: the 3PL non-active past imperfective *-ondusan* became *-ondustan*, with a *-t-* taken from the 1PL/2PL endings *-mastan/-sastan* and 2SG non-active past imperfective *-sun* resulted from earlier *-so*, augmented with material from the 1SG ending *-mun* (cf. Joseph 2006). These endings are equally inflectional—and equally grammatical, as to function and morphological status—before and after the augmentation.

Finally, (3d), where inflectional material develops into derivational material, is exemplified by the so-called Watkins' Law (WL) developments (see Arlotto 1972; Collinge 1985). In these developments, an inflectional ending, usually 3SG (prototypically functionally unmarked in a paradigm), is reanalysed as part of the verbal stem; an example is the passage from early Greek end-stressed present tense forms to forms marked with the stem-stressed endings, with the old 3SG form as the new stem:

(4)	1SG	rot-ó	'I ask'	⇒	rotá-o	(cf. 1SG kán-o 'I do')
	2	rot-ás	'you ask'	⇒	rotá-is	(cf. 2SG kán-is 'you do')
	3	rot-á	'(s)he asks'	⇒	rotá-i	(cf. 3SG kán-i'(s)he does')

Interestingly, although the new present (imperfective) stem is *rotá-*, the perfective stem is *rot-is-*, e.g. aorist *rót-is-a* 'I asked', so that even *rotá-* should be segmented as *rot-á-*, with the *-a-* as a stem formative, i.e. a derivational element.[6]

Since derivational material is generally considered less grammatical than inflectional material, (3d) raises the spectre of unidirectionality: the claim that grammaticalization changes always proceed from less grammatical to more grammatical.[7] This somewhat controversial claim is taken up in the next section.

5. Unidirectionality reconsidered

As implied in the WL example, counter-directional movement along clines of grammatical form and function, with more grammatical elements becoming less grammatical, grammatical elements becoming lexical, and/or bound affixes becoming free(r) forms, is not envisioned as typical or, in some formulations, even possible, as far as grammaticalization is concerned. This principle of unidirectionality is generally viewed as foundational for grammaticalization (see e.g. Hopper and Traugott 1993/2003: ch. 5; Haspelmath 1999; 2004b; Traugott 2001; 2002b; Ziegeler 2003; 2004).

There is reason to be dubious, however, about the empirical content of this claim. Newmeyer (1998), Lass (2000), Janda (2001), and others note that unidirectionality is built into most definitions of grammaticalization, and so is not a testable hypothesis; if grammaticalization is defined as movement in one direction, then any apparent counter-directional movement would not constitute a case of grammaticalization, and would thus not be a counter-example.[8] Moreover, a given change can only move in one direction at a time, so that finding examples showing movement towards greater grammatical status does not constitute a valid test of a principle of unidirectionality.

One solution to this definitional trap is redefine grammaticalization and take a stronger and more directly testable position. Haspelmath, for instance, has recast

[6] Other cases of WL may be similarly analysable; Modern Persian 1SG *hast-am* 'am' and 3SG *hast-Ø*, with a stem from earlier 3SG *as-ti*, may have *-t-* as a segmentable stem-deriving element, since there is an enclitic 3SG form with the shape [s]. I thank Kevin Gabbard for help here (though he bears no blame if my analysis is wrong).

[7] The claim is often made that counter-examples to unidirectionality are unsystematic and unpatterned, but since there are numerous instances of WL in the literature, this sort of development seems to represent a fairly systematic case of counter-directional movement.

[8] Janda likens grammaticalization to 'walking north', noting that this action too is 'unidirectional' but that any deviation from that direction is not 'walking north' and is thus not an instance of the action.

grammaticalization as 'a diachronic change by which the parts of a constructional schema come to have stronger internal dependencies' (2004b: 26), and states also (2002) that 'there is no degrammaticalization'. While Kiparsky (forthcoming) feels that this recharacterization does not eliminate the trap, it does allow for testing in that boundaries are well-recognized analytic units in linguistics with different types of boundaries, usually characterized as being of different 'strengths' (e.g. morpheme vs. word boundary), typically posited. That is, one can see if there are changes involving grammar that loosen rather than tighten 'internal dependencies'; such changes would constitute counter-examples to Haspelmath's view of grammaticalization.

Viewed this way, unidirectionality has numerous counter-examples. Kiparsky cites several, and Haspelmath himself acknowledges seven cases.[9] In actuality, there are many more: Norde (2009a) gives several, though perhaps not all are equally compelling, and in (5), I list cases not previously discussed in the literature, with some annotation, as needed.

(5) a. Standard (and earlier) English *The baby is hiccoughing* ⇒ colloquial American English *The baby is hicking up*, reanalyzing *hiccough* (phonetically [hɪkəp]) as a Verb+Particle combination, thus with a *weaker* (less fused) internal dependency, so that [əp] can move to phrase-final position

b. Colloquial American English *a whole nother area* (vs. Standard *another entire area*), with *another* resegmented so as to have weaker internal dependency, moving from a single (albeit polymorphemic) word to a discontinuous syntactic combination involving a closed class (grammatical) element, the indefinite article, as a separate word, and thus with less fusion rather than more

c. Various reanalyses, e.g., from the Ohio State University campus, *Mendenhall Laboratories* called *Menden*, as if 'Menden Hall', i.e. re-parsed in the direction of *weaker* internal dependency (since originally a proper name would be monomorphemic, even if perceivable as having internal structure)

d. Reversal, in acquisition, of *kinda/sorta* to fuller *kind of/sort of*; i.e. children are more likely to learn the reduced forms first, since reduced *kinda/sorta* are commoner in conversation and thus represent more likely input to early language acquisition than *kind of/sort of*. But once children realize

[9] This means of course that even the staunchest advocates of grammaticalization have recognized that there are 'anti-grammaticalizations' (alternatively, following different terminological conventions, 'counter-grammaticalization' or 'degrammaticalization'), so that at best one can talk about a strong tendency in the direction of fuller grammatical status. Haspelmath (2004b: 22), for instance, says that 'grammaticalization is overwhelmingly irreversible', implying that it *is* reversible. Kiparsky, as noted (see above), develops an approach wherein grammaticalization has a more restricted scope but is completely unidirectional.

that reduced forms have these equivalent fuller forms, possibly through exposure to written English through formal education, and connect the fuller and reduced forms, they are counter-directionally 'rebuilding' structure, reversing the putative unidirectional reduction.

Admittedly, if one rejects Haspelmath's characterization of grammaticalization,[10] then perhaps examples (5c, d) are problematic since they do not involve grammar *per se*. However, these examples all show that speaker behaviour resulting in counterdirectional outcomes is possible, and thus that speakers can loosen dependencies between fused elements by some means. In that sense they seem highly relevant to any discussion about putative unidirectionality and grammaticalization, even though there is certainly more to say on the matter.[11] Still, the discussion here shows where some of the potential problems with the notion lie.[12]

6. Grammaticalization and language contact

It has become common to see grammaticalization extended into situations involving not language-internal developments (as with all cases discussed so far) but rather language contact; Heine and Kuteva (2005; 2006) offer good examples of this extension of grammaticalization to externally motivated change. In this brief critique, I focus on just two aspects of this extension: degrammaticalization in language contact situations and Heine and Kuteva's notion of 'grammaticalization contact zones'.

[10] I note though that Norde (2009a: 6) accepts it as one of the current prevailing definitions available.

[11] See e.g. Joseph (2006) for one way of giving substance to unidirectionality, via the evidence of 'lateral shifts' (see section 4 above). For Kiparsky, those lateral shifts would not instantiate grammaticalization, being based on pre-existing analogical models (see footnotes 5 and 9 above).

[12] Kiparsky (forthcoming), following an entirely different approach (see also footnote 5 above), covers relevant cases of grammaticalization and claims to derive unidirectionality naturally. I find this approach intriguing, even compelling, but wonder about instances of univerbation that do not involve grammatical material, e.g. the oft-cited case of Old High German *hiu tage* '(on) this day' giving modern *heute* 'today', or the erasure of boundaries in original compounds, e.g. preverb + verb combinations that in Sanskrit typically had the prefixal past tense marker (the 'augment') occurring between the preverb and the verb (e.g. *sam-a-gacchan* 'they came together') but which sporadically positioned the augment outside the original preverb, e.g. *a-samgacchan* (Whitney 1889). Perhaps for Kiparsky such cases would indicate the independent need for recognizing movement towards single-word status for non-grammatical once-complex combinations, a process he then employs in his approach to grammaticalization.

Just as there are language-internal *lexical* developments that counter claims about unidirectionality, so too borrowings can show such developments. For instance, Klima and Bellugi (1979: 274) write:

To our knowledge there are no intrinsic segmental affixes in A[merican]S[ign]L[anguage]. Four such affixes are listed among the 2500 signs of the DASL [*Dictionary of American Sign Language*, 1965] but these are clearly loan translations from English and their usage in communication between deaf native signers has so evolved that they now have the status of independent lexical items.

Thus contact with English has led ASL to develop lexical forms from once-affixal material. While such 'lexicalizations' may not be problematic for unidirectionality if they are judged to be different in nature from the grammatical developments governed by grammaticalization,[13] the parallels are interesting. Similarly, Cypriot Greek *mishi mu* (where *mu* is a possessive pronoun) is a sentence adverb or discourse element marking evidentiality, as in *en' plusios mishi mu* 'he-is rich so-they-say', but appears to be from the Turkish suffix *-mIş-* marking unwitnessed/unconfirmed events.[14]

Moreover, borrowings themselves can serve to loosen tight bonds among elements in a word or phrase, countering Haspelmath's claims of unidirectional movement towards ever-stronger internal dependencies. Spanish *mente* adverbial formations, e.g. *claramente* 'clearly', offer a good example. *Claramente* was etymologically phrasal, *clara # mente* 'with a clear mind' (⇒ manner adverb 'clearly'), and note the free word *mente* 'mind' in Spanish. The adverbial use of the bound form is linked with the lexical use of the free form in a natural way, consistent actually with unidirectionality. As indicated in section 3, Old Spanish has not just phrases like *clara mente*, but also *clara miente*, *clara mientre*, among other variants. The diphthongal forms show the regular outcome in later Spanish from Latin *mente*; compare modern Spanish *pienso* 'I think' from earlier *pens-*. These Old Spanish facts mean that the *ment-* form, in the free word and the adverb, is not a straight-line development out of Latin *ment-*. Rather, *ment-* must represent a learned borrowing from Latin into Spanish that replaced the regularly developing form *(-)miente* (cf. Posner 1996; Karlsson 1981). Importantly, this means that the learned borrowing was reintroduced into the adverbial, and thus interrupted the 'flow' from the phrasal combination of Latin to the Spanish adverbial form; this reintroduction would have loosened the tightening bond between the adjectival base and the adverbializer, making the formation more like a phrase once again, and not a base + affix single word (note that the corresponding adverbial *-ment* in French is best taken as a suffix, there being no free noun **ment* in the language). In

[13] Not all linguists dismiss 'lexicalization' so readily as a problem for grammaticalization; see e.g. Newmeyer (2001) and Janda (2001).

[14] I thank Erma Vasileiou (La Trobe University) for alerting me to this form, and Marina Terkourafi of University of Illinois for important clarifications as to its use.

a sense this restarted the devolution from word to affix, via phrase, in the Middle Spanish period. Since Latin influence was responsible, this loosening of the internal bond, and the subsequent restarting of the development of the adverbial, would not have occurred but for the language contact that led to a Latinism entering Spanish secondarily; it thus fits the definition in Thomason (2001) of 'contact-induced change', since contact set the wheels of the loosening change in motion.

This argument about contact-induced loosening of internal bonds moves one step further when one considers code-switching, a shift by a speaker at certain points in an utterance to a different language shared with a conversational partner. A key question in code-switching research is the determination of the points where the switch can occur. Some linguists (e.g. Poplack 1980, with her 'Free Morpheme Constraint') have proposed that switches occur only at major breaks in constituency, which, interpreted in Haspelmath's terms, would mean only at points of *weaker* internal dependency among elements (assuming that words that form a phrase give a stronger internal dependency to the component parts of the phrase). Therefore, if code-switching occurs at points other than major boundaries, simply triggered perhaps, as Clyne (1967) has suggested, by similar-sounding *forms* ('homophonous diamorphs') in the two languages, then language contact as realized in this form (code-switching) will have caused a relaxing of tight dependencies, since one can move into an entirely different *grammar*, even. And there are such cases. Janse (2009) argues that some Cappadocian Greek forms show word-internal switching, citing forms such as (Semendere village) *cé-tun-misti-c* 'we were' with both a Greek ending (1PL *-misti*) and a Turkish ending (1PL *-k*), and he suggests that the similarity ('diamorphic homophony') between Greek *-misti* and Turkish past tense morphemes *-miş-ti-*, which occur together in the pluperfect tense, triggered a Clyne-ian code-switch, even though word-internally.

As for grammaticalization contact zones, Heine and Kuteva (2005; 2006) claim that there are 'zones' where parallel grammaticalizations occur due to language contact. The Balkans are an interesting test case, since there are numerous parallel grammatical features across Bulgarian, Macedonian, Greek, Albanian, and Romanian, among other co-territorial languages. All, for instance, share a future tense formation with an element based on a verb of volition (as in Greek: sections 2 and 3). In almost all such Balkan formations, there has been reduction from a fuller, inflected form of the verb of volition to a particle-like, possibly affixal, element (e.g. Greek *tha*, above, but also Macedonian *ḱe*, Romanian *o*, etc.). To the extent that reduction correlates with grammaticalization, this feature would thus appear to define a Balkan grammaticalization zone.

However, when one reviews the steps and processes needed to actually make this claim work, it is hard to maintain it as a meaningful account of what happened with the Balkan future. In particular, the use of WANT for the future could be calqued, i.e. imported into the various languages from one language (not necessarily the same language in each case), and the reduction to invariance of the future marker could be an internal set of developments in each language (as suggested for Greek above). In that case, in what sense is this a 'grammaticalization contact zone'? It is certainly a 'zone', and contact is involved, but the putative grammaticalization and the steps leading to the full embedding of the future marker in the grammar crucially do not involve contact. Alternatively, the use of WANT for the future was calqued, but the availability of reduced forms was calqued too (so that Romanian variation between a full form *va* and reduced *o* would have been calqued on, e.g. Greek *thel'na/than*, assuming both were competing in Greek in a way salient to non-Greeks learning/speaking Greek, even though different parts are reduced in each language). If so, then, one can again ask in what sense this is a 'grammaticalization contact zone'. In particular, the sort of 'grammaticalization' that passed from language to language then crucially is not a *process* of reduction but rather a *model* of reduction, i.e. a *result* of processes of reduction within individual languages; this therefore recalls the discussion in section 2 about the very nature of grammaticalization. Thus, to invoke grammaticalization in contact situations, one must be prepared to call it a result and not a process, as suggested earlier on independent grounds.

7. Conclusion

This wide-ranging critique has of necessity cut corners here and there, and it may well be that a fuller account of all that is discussed here would put grammaticalization in a better light. Still, even with my critical stance, I maintain my earlier stated view that our understanding of language and language change has been enriched by the consideration of grammaticalization over the past thirty years or so, despite those aspects of the enterprise that strike me as flawed. Insight can come from anywhere and in different shapes; one just needs to be open to the possibility of gaining it, wherever it might emanate from.

PART II

METHODOLOGICAL ISSUES

CHAPTER 17

GRAMMATICALIZATION AND LINGUISTIC VARIATION

SHANA POPLACK

1. Introduction

Grammaticalization theory (GT) and variation theory (VT) have traditionally made uneasy bedfellows, but in many ways they are natural allies. For one thing, they share a number of underlying assumptions that are not often made explicit. For another, GT furnishes strong hypotheses about change, many of which are amenable to empirical test. VT has a well-developed framework for the study of change in progress, powerful methods for deciding amongst competing hypotheses, and an incipient but growing tradition of applying them to major issues in grammaticalization (Aaron 2006; Poplack 2001; Poplack and Tagliamonte 1996; 2001; Schwenter and Torres Cacoullos 2008; Tagliamonte 2003; 2004; Tagliamonte and Smith 2006; Torres Cacoullos 1999; 2001; 2009; in press; Zilles 2005). In this chapter, I first detail the most pertinent of these shared assumptions, highlighting

The research on which this paper is based was generously supported by grants from the Social Sciences and Humanities Research Council of Canada. The author holds the Canada Research Chair (I) in Linguistics. I am grateful to Joan Bybee, Rena Torres Cacoullos, and students in LIN 7913 for comments that substantially improved this chapter.

similarities and differences in the two approaches. I then describe the variationist take on grammaticalization, and outline some of the ways in which VT can contribute to grammaticalization studies.

Finally, by way of illustration, I apply the variationist method to a paradigm example of grammaticalization cross-linguistically: the development of future markers from the motion verb *go*. I will show that this approach is particularly well-suited to tracking pathways of grammaticalization, through its capacity to elucidate the transition period between endpoints of change. In the process, I will argue that GT can be checked, modified, and subtly enhanced by taking account of the fine details of inherent variability and the empirical analysis of grammaticalization in progress.

2. Shared assumptions

The primacy of language use, the ubiquity of variability, and the gradualness of change are cornerstones of both GT and VT. The central assumption is that the fundamental object of study is language *use*, as opposed to some idealization of how language *should* be used (e.g. Brinton and Traugott 2005; Bybee 1998a; Hopper 1987). The careful observer of language use, especially as instantiated in speech, cannot help but be struck by its rampant *variability*. Thus, in recounting a series of past habitual actions, all with the same temporal reference and (ostensibly) meaning, the African Nova Scotian English speaker in (1) nonetheless alternates among the preterite, *used to*, *would*, and bare verb forms. This variation is present whether change is occurring or not.

(1) [4] How did you get your clothing? You know, you were small?
[066] When I was small, no, somebody ***give*** her something, we ***had*** it or else she ***took*** the flour bag. [4] Mhm. [066] ***Used to buy*** the flour bag and white bags with the Robin Hood on it. And she ***boiled*** it on the stove 'til she ***got*** the Robin Hood out of it. [4] Mhm. [066] And then she ***would*** uh- ***make*** us a pair of pants. (066.1227)[1]

Now, a key premise of GT is that on the path to achieving grammaticalization, a number of (more and less grammaticalized) forms may be simultaneously available to express the same meaning. Hopper (1991) calls this type of form–

[1] Codes refer to speaker number and line number in the *Corpus of African Nova Scotian English* (Poplack and Tagliamonte 2001). Examples are reproduced verbatim from speaker utterances.

function asymmetry *layering*; it is a subset of what variationists refer to as *inherent variability*. The existence of layering entails that alongside the grammaticalizing form, other variant forms will be jockeying for the same linguistic work. Yet grammaticalization is usually construed—and studied—as the set of changes involved in the association of *one* form with a new (presumably more grammatical) meaning or function, downplaying, or even ignoring, the role of other layers coexisting in that context. As I will show, without an understanding of how these layers accommodate to the incursion of the emergent form, we obtain only a very partial (and sometimes misleading) view of the grammaticalization process.

The standard structural linguistic view of language *change* (A > B) suggests that it (1) is abrupt, and (2) involves total replacement. In contrast, many grammaticalization theorists espouse the VT view that change is characterized (and preceded) by variation, proceeds gradually across time and linguistic contexts, and may never result in completion (Heine and Kuteva 2005; Brinton and Traugott 2005; Mair 2004). Contemporary usage data are in fact rife with residual forms which are highly restricted, fossilized, or endowed with entirely new discourse functions. Thus, although the grammaticalization of French *pas* 'step' into a postverbal negator—and the concomitant evanescence of preverbal *ne*—is uncontroversial, *ne* shows no signs of disappearing. This despite an infinitesimal rate of occurrence (0.2 per cent) in spoken Québec French over the last century and a half (Poplack and St-Amand 2007). It persists as a marker of highly formal speech (Poplack, Bourdages, and Dion 2009).

3. A variationist model of grammaticalization

3.1. The variationist perspective on change

The standard variationist construal of change involves the progressive increase of one of a set of variant expressions of a meaning or function until it ousts its competitors from the grammatical sector. It follows that the most straightforward way of tracing change is by rate, and this is what most grammaticalization studies do (e.g. Hundt 2001; Krug 2000; Macaulay 2006; Mair 2004, to name but a very few). But since grammaticalization involves a specific type of change (i.e. lexical to grammatical and grammatical to more grammatical), it is particularly instructive to examine what happens to the structure of the grammar during the course of the change, when a number of layers/variants are still extant. The idea is not just to record the grammaticalizing form, but to compare the structure of the *context* hosting it at each stage over as long a time frame as possible.

The variationist hypothesis is that *structure can be discerned from the distribution and conditioning of variant forms* (Poplack and Tagliamonte 1996; 2001; Torres Cacoullos 2009; in press). This structure, instantiated in the quantitative patterning of variants across elements of the context, can be converted into a diagnostic and compared over different stages of the language to yield a detailed view of the transition between endpoints of change. The more such stages there are, and the farther apart, the more revealing the picture of the trajectory. As illustrated in sections 4 and 5 below, this can illuminate many of the proposed mechanisms of grammaticalization. Variationists have been experimenting with ways to tap into diachronic benchmarks old enough to reveal the evolution of change, while at the same time reflecting the spoken language, the prime locus of change. Analysis of speech surrogates, which represent earlier stages without necessarily being oral themselves, have been quite revealing in this regard (Poplack and Malvar 2007; Elsig and Poplack 2009; Poplack and Dion 2009).

3.2. Method

3.2.1. The significance of context in the study of change

The key construct in VT is the *linguistic variable*, or 'different ways of saying the same thing' (Labov 1972a: 94). Identification of a linguistic variable rests on the possibility of circumscribing the specific domain in which variants alternate without change in representational meaning, or, as Sankoff (1988) puts it, where any differences in meaning embodied by competing forms have become neutralized in discourse. This is the *variable context*, whose discovery and definition is fundamental to the study of linguistic variation and change. (The variable context in (1), for instance, may be defined as the domain of habitual past.) Grammaticalization theorists also espouse the idea that grammaticalization proceeds in specific domains or constructions (e.g. Brinton and Traugott 2005; Bybee 2003; Heine 2003; Lehmann 1993; Traugott and Heine 1991a; 1991b), though these tend not to be as explicitly defined as the variable context in VT studies.[2]

[2] This at least partly a result of the fact that so many grammaticalization studies are form-based, obviating the need to circumscribe a context (beyond the 10 or 100,000 words used to normalize token frequencies).

As empirical endeavours, both GT and VT have a commitment to counting. Where VT studies of grammaticalization distinguish themselves is by their adherence to the *principle of accountable reporting* (Labov 1972b: 72). This requires that an analysis consider not only the cases in which the form of interest materialized but also all the cases where it could have occurred even when it did not. This is because, as Gillian Sankoff (1990) already pointed out, it is misleading to conclude that use of one form entertains associations with a particular meaning or function without also testing whether other forms do as well. This step is usually overlooked in reports of grammaticalization.

VT has the capacity to examine both the extent to which a given form, once selected, actually expresses a given function, and the extent to which it is associated with a given context. These measures need not be coterminous. For example, in their study of the grammaticalization of zero and other markers of past temporal reference in Nigerian Pidgin English, Poplack and Tagliamonte (1996) tested widespread claims (e.g. Bickerton 1984; Faraclas 1987) that the preverbal marker *bin* marks anterior/remote past in punctual verbs and simple past in stative verbs. Multivariate analysis (Rand and Sankoff 1990), the relevant parts of which are reproduced in Table 17.1, confirmed that while the probability that *bin* would be selected in anterior contexts was in fact very high relative to other contexts (.90), its absolute probability of occurring in that context (or any other) was extremely small.

Only once *bin* was situated with respect to the six other variants with which it competes (the cases where it 'could have occurred but did not'), and the combined effect of frequency and probability of occurrence taken into account (the shaded columns in Table 17.1), could it be seen to be less likely to occur in this context than every other variant but one! Although other quantitative approaches would undoubtedly also have detected the overwhelming propensity of *bin* to express anteriority, a narrow form-based focus on the grammaticalizing form alone would have missed the crucial fact that anteriority was overwhelmingly *not* expressed by *bin*. Accountable analysis of usage data often turns up such surprises.

3.2.2. *Operationalizing hypotheses*

VT seeks to explain why, in a given context, one form is chosen over another to express the same meaning or function. The choice mechanism is the product of the aggregate of the contribution of environmental factors, which may conspire or conflict in the production of the form, plus a degree of inherent variability. This process is modelled by operationalizing and testing hypotheses about selection constraints as *factors* in a multivariate (or 'variable rule') analysis. To the extent that these hypotheses/factors are relevant to theories of grammaticalization, they

Table 17.1. Twelve independent variable rule analyses of the contribution of *temporal relationship* to variant selection in Nigerian Pidgin English past temporal reference contexts (adapted from Poplack and Tagliamonte 1996)[a]

	kɔm		*dɔn*		*bin*		*finiš*		*de*		zero	
Corrected mean	.19	.19	.07	.07	.004	.004	.012	.011	.07	.07	.57	.57
(Total N = 4,692)												
Temporal relationship												
Anterior	.20	.06	.76	.20	**.90**	**.04**	[ ]	.01	.50	.07	.55	.62
Sequential	.70	.35	.28	.03	.21	.00	[ ]	.01	.40	.05	.47	.53
Non-anterior	.41	.14	.65	.12	.65	.01	[ ]	.01	.64	.12	.51	.58
Range	*50*		*48*		*48*				*24*		*8*	

[a] Values vary between 0 and 1; the higher the value, the greater the probability the variant in question (*kɔm*, *dɔn*, etc.) will be selected in each of the contexts listed on the left. Shaded columns display the combined effect of corrected mean and factor weight; this shows that the overall probability of occurrence in a context may differ greatly from the relative probability of occurrence (unshaded columns) compared to other contexts. Here and in subsequent tables, factors not selected as significant are indicated by [ ].

enable us to assess key proposals about the mechanisms of this process. Thus, variationists have been quite successful in measuring such widely invoked parameters as unidirectionality, decategorialization, loss of constituency, phonetic erosion, syntactic fixation, unithood, semantic bleaching, and persistence, as well as others which (with some ingenuity) can be identified and, crucially, *operationalized* from the linguistic context.

To be sure, for many, grammaticalization is primarily a semantic process, involving notions like context-induced reinterpretation, pragmatic inferencing, conventionalization of implicature, and metaphorical and metonymic shifts, among others (Brinton and Traugott 2005; Bybee 2003; Bybee, Pagliuca, and Perkins 1994; Heine 2003; Heine, Claudi, and Hünnemeyer 1991; Hopper and Traugott 2003; Traugott and König 1991; Sweetser 1990). For example, one common assumption is that forms are recruited to express and evaluate the grammatical relations the speaker *envisions*, in a process Traugott refers to as subjectification (Traugott 1982; Traugott and König 1991; Brinton and Traugott 2005). But despite growing interest in characterizing the semantic changes involved, there is as yet no real heuristic as to how they can be detected, let alone how they develop. Speaker intent or attitude and hearer inference are most often not directly recoverable from the available data. The VT commitment to operationalizing and testing hypotheses requires discovering objective criteria that can be applied to identify a given process in a systematic and, more important, replicable, way. This is an area that would benefit from increased dialogue between practitioners of GT and VT.

3.2.3. *Modelling variant choice*

Variable rule analysis helps determine if and how the choice process is affected by the factors constituting the environment in which the variants co-vary. Three lines of evidence contribute to measuring the extent of grammaticalization: the (statistical) significance of the effect, the magnitude of the effect, and the direction of the effect, or the ranking of constraints conditioning variant choice, the latter construed as the 'grammar' underlying the variable surface realizations. Together, they offer a snapshot of the structure of the system at a given period. By comparing these snapshots over time, we can trace not only the rise and fall of variant forms but also their entry points into the system and the trajectory of their functions, which is of particular interest to grammaticalization theorists. In its capacity to transcend frequencies to reveal the *patterns* of variability and change, this is perhaps where VT has the most to offer.

4. Elucidating the transition period: expression of the future in Brazilian Portuguese

By way of illustration, consider the trajectory of the expression of future temporal reference in Brazilian Portuguese studied by Poplack and Malvar (2007). This constitutes a useful heuristic, both because it involves a paradigm example of this process cross-linguistically (the conversion of a *go*-verb into a future marker) and because the Portuguese periphrastic form (PF) figures among the most highly grammaticalized of *go*-futures studied, if only because it is virtually the only remaining exponent of future temporal reference available, at least in the spoken language.

Figure 17.1 shows that a system made up of a synthetic future (SF; *cantarei* 'I will sing') and the *haver*-periphrasis (HP; ***hei de** cantar)* in the 16th and 18th centuries[3] was converted, by the 20th century, into one in which PF (***vou*** cantar) had virtually replaced all its competitors. Making use of the VT framework, Poplack and Malvar trace the transition between endpoints of this dramatic change, examining the state of the future temporal reference *sector* period by period by performing independent multivariate analyses of the factors contributing to variant selection in each. These are summarized in Table 17.2.

In Period I, the task of expressing future was largely divided between SF and HP. With a *corrected mean* (overall probability of occurrence) of .63, at this time SF was the majority and default variant. Consistent with this role, it was favoured in frequent, neutral or unmarked contexts (i.e. declarative affirmative sentences and with most lexical verbs), while HP mostly occurred elsewhere. Although the futurate present (P) was extremely rare at this time (corrected mean: .05), it had already staked out its preferred loci of occurrence, the most important of which was with motion verbs, which favoured P highly (probability of .87).

By Period II, the emergent PF had increased substantially, now accounting for 15 per cent of the data. Like other *go*-periphrases, PF appears to have entered the system via proximate future contexts (.87), the former domain of P. This effectively relegated both the older SF and HP to a new context: distal future eventualities. Interestingly, considering that PF was still so rare, this was its only 'specialized' context of occurrence. Elsewhere, it was already showing

[3] Few pertinent data were available for the 17th century (Poplack and Malvar 2007).

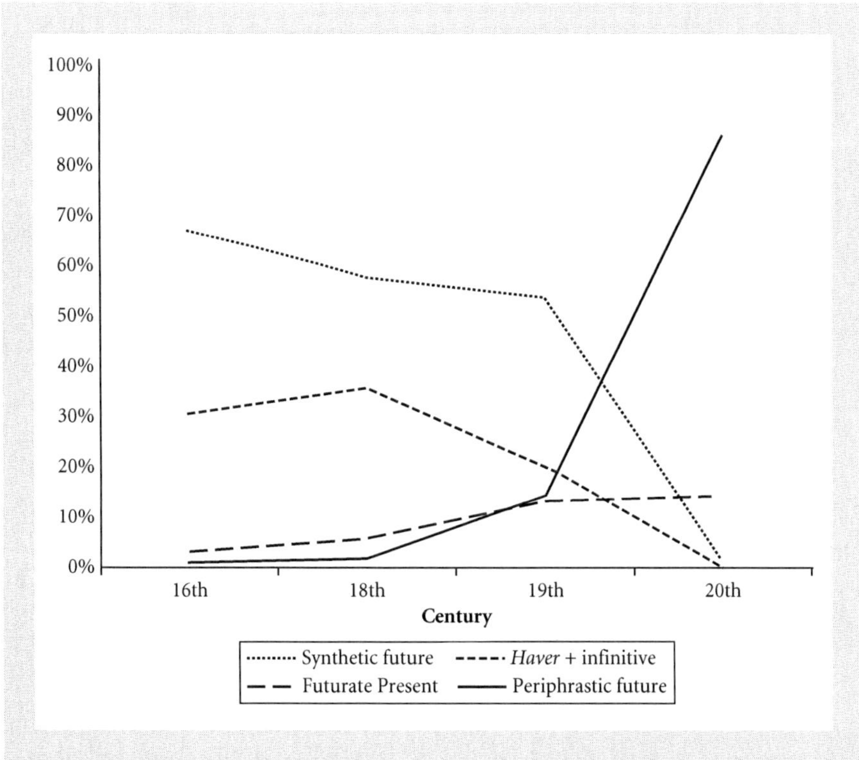

Fig. 17.1. Distribution of (Brazilian) Portuguese future temporal reference variants by century (adapted from Poplack and Malvar 2007)

harbingers of its current role as default future marker: it was preferred in the more frequent, less marked contexts of declarative sentences (which it usurped from SF), and those with no adverbial specification. Here it contrasted with both SF and P, associated with nonspecific and specific temporal adverbials respectively. Rates of P also doubled since the 16/18th centuries, but instead of spreading across the future temporal reference domain, it became more entrenched in the relatively infrequent, more specialized contexts of motion verbs, contingent contexts (*se* 'if' clauses) and specific adverbs, suggesting that it was still necessary to disambiguate its temporal reference.

By the 20th century, SF had receded dramatically (to 1 per cent of all future temporal reference), HP had disappeared, and PF had expanded into all the contexts formerly dominated by other variants, with the result that most of the factors once implicated in variant selection were no longer statistically significant. The only two barriers to the colonization by PF of the entire future reference sector

Table 17.2. Twelve independent variable rule analyses of the factors contributing to selection of future temporal reference variants in (Brazilian) Portuguese, over three time periods (adapted from Poplack and Malvar 2007)

	Period I: 16th and 18th centuries				Period II: 19th century				Period III: 20th century			
	SF	HP	P	PF	SF	HP	P	PF	SF	HP	P	PF
Corrected mean	*.63*	*.32*	*.05*	–	*.55*	*.21*	*.10*	*.15*	–	–	*.07*	*.93*
Total N	367	194	29	8	268	104	48	72	4	0	47	611
Sentence type												
Declarative	.55	.44	[]	–	[]	[]	[]	.59	–	–	[]	[]
Negative	.37	.62	[]	–	[]	[]	[]	.10	–	–	[]	[]
Interrogative	.31	.70	[]	–	[]	[]	[]	.31	–	–	[]	[]
Contingency												
Contingent	.68	.30	[]	–	[]	.26	.85	[]	–	–	.87	.13
Assumed	.48	.52	[]	–	[]	.52	.47	[]	–	–	.45	.55
Verb type												
Non-motion	.54	[]	.37	–	.52	[]	.44	[]	–	–	[]	[]
Motion	.35	[]	.88	–	.31	[]	.87	[]	–	–	[]	[]
Temporal distance												
Distal	[]	[]	.36	–	.56	.54	[]	.36	–	–	[]	[]
Proximal	[]	[]	.71	–	.38	.40	[]	.79	–	–	[]	[]
Grammatical person/animacy												
1st animate	[]	[]	.70	–	[]	[]	[]	[]	–	–	[]	[]
2nd animate	[]	[]	.21	–	[]	[]	[]	[]	–	–	[]	[]
3rd animate	[]	[]	.39	–	[]	[]	[]	[]	–	–	[]	[]
3rd inanimate	[]	[]	.58	–	[]	[]	[]	[]	–	–	[]	[]
Adverbial specification												
Nonspecific	[]	[]	[]	–	.70	[]	.46	.15	–	–	.57	.43
No adverbial	[]	[]	[]	–	.46	[]	.45	.62	–	–	.42	.58
Specific	[]	[]	[]	–	.43	[]	.89	.27	–	–	.80	.20
Factors not selected as significant												
Sentence type			X	–	X	X	X		–	–	X	X
Contingency			X	–	X			X	–	–		
Verb type		X		–		X		X	–	–	X	X
Temporal distance	X	X		–			X		–	–	X	X
Grammatical person/animacy	X	X		–	X	X	X	X	–	–	X	X
Adverbial specification	X	X	X	–		X			–	–		
Type of clause	X	X	X	–	X	X	X	X	–	–	X	X
Presence of clitics	X	X	X	–	X	X	X	X	–	–	X	X

are those in which P has remained entrenched: contingent contexts, and those modified by specific adverbs.

Focus on the variability inherent in the expression of future temporal reference shows how change comes about via a series of small adjustments made by both emergent and obsolescing variants. This change was driven by the gradual expropriation by the incoming PF of the preferred contexts of the older layers, culminating in the contemporary situation in which PF has become the default choice everywhere but in the remaining few bastions of P.

5. The universality of grammaticalization paths

The variationist apparatus can also be profitably applied to tracing grammaticalization paths cross-linguistically. Compare the evolution of the future temporal reference systems of two other closely related Romance languages, Spanish and French. They share the same three major variants (SF, PF, and P), all inherited from the same (Vulgar Latin) source. In each, the majority variant, PF, coexists with older layers, but is gaining ground, albeit at different rates (Fig. 17.2).

Despite this discrepancy, given the prediction that grammaticalizing forms deriving from the same source (a fortiori the same source *material*) will follow the same course of change (e.g. Bybee et al. 1994; Brinton and Traugott 2005), the languages should display parallel, if not identical, grammaticalization paths. Fortuitously, a series of replications of Poplack and Turpin's (1999) original study of French future temporal reference furnish comparable data and comparable analyses of the factors contributing to variant selection at the same two points in time. This affords a unique opportunity to assess this prediction empirically and, by extension, widespread claims for the universality of grammaticalization paths.

Table 17.3 displays six independent multivariate analyses of the factors contributing to the choice of PF in 19th- and 20th-century Spanish, French, and Portuguese. In 19th-century Spanish, two factors affected its selection. Most important is verb class; dynamic verbs (both motion and non-motion) favoured PF, with the exception of main verb *ir* 'go' (theoretically due to retention of its source lexical meaning: Bybee and Pagliuca 1987). The other is clause type, with subordinate clauses favouring PF. In Portuguese, neither of these factors was statistically significant. Instead, three other factors were

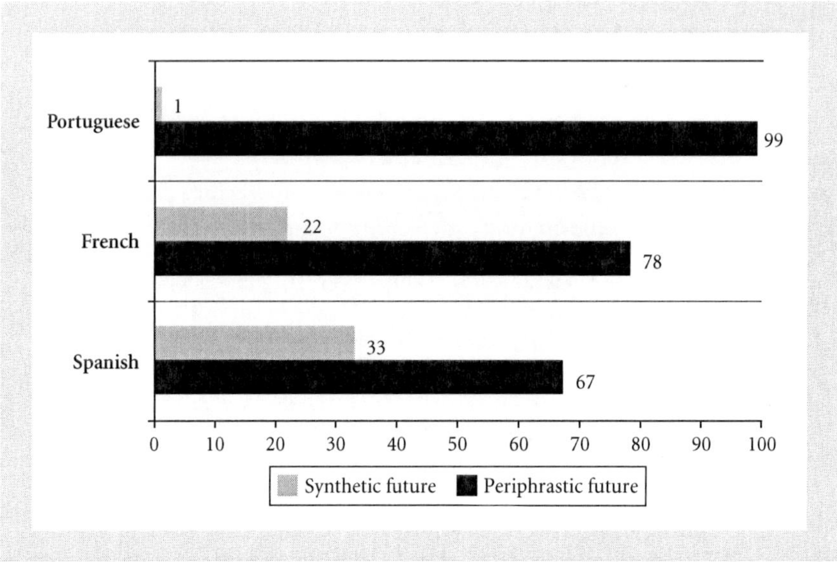

Fig. 17.2. Relative proportion (%) of synthetic to periphrastic future variants in three Romance languages (adapted from Aaron 2006, Poplack and Malvar 2007, Poplack and Dion 2009)

operative: sentence type, temporal distance, and temporal specification: temporally unspecified declarative sentences with proximal future reference all favoured PF. This despite the fact that at the time, the relative frequency of PF was the same (15 per cent) in both languages! In French, PF had already advanced much further along the grammaticalization path, occurring in fully two-thirds of all future temporal reference contexts. Here, the strongest constraint on variant choice by far is polarity: PF appears to be favoured in affirmative contexts, actually the flipside of the effect whereby negative contexts were (and are) almost categorically retentive of SF (Poplack and Turpin 1999; Poplack and Dion 2009). The factor of polarity is not operative in either of the other two languages. Unexpectedly, the closely related Spanish and Portuguese share no effects, although two robust constraints favouring PF in 19th-century Portuguese are echoed weakly in French.

The contemporary situation, displayed in the rightmost columns of Table 17.3, shows even fewer cross-linguistic correspondences. Dynamic verbs continue to favour PF in Spanish, as, at this stage, do negative and interrogative sentences. In Portuguese, assumed contexts, and in French, affirmative sentences, appear favourable, but both effects stem from the entrenchment of another variant elsewhere. Contrary to received wisdom, in none of the

Table 17.3. Six independent variable rule analyses of the factors contributing to the choice of PF in three Romance languages, 19th and 20th centuries (adapted from Aaron 2006: table 5.45; Poplack and Turpin 1999: table 3; Poplack and Malvar 2007: tables 3, 4, and 6; and Poplack and Dion 2009: table 8)[a]

	19th century			20th century		
	Sp.	Ptg.	Fr.	Sp.	Ptg.	Fr.
Input probability	.13	.15	.65	.69	.93	.73
Total N	75/ 507	72/ 492	2,630/ 4,293	768/ 1,147	611/ 662	2,627/ 3,357
Verb class						
Dynamic (non-motion)	**.65**	[]	[]	**.58**	[]	[]
Motion	.55	[]	[]	.53	[]	[]
Stative/percep./psych.	.32	[]	[]	.36	[]	[]
Range	*33*			*22*		
Adverbial specification						
No adverbial	[]	**.62**	**.52**	**.57**	**.58**	**.56**
Specific	[]	.27	.35	.42	.20	.23
Nonspecific	[]	.15		.22	.43	.19
Range		*47*	*17*	*35*	*38*	*37*
Sentence type/polarity[b]						
Interrogative	[]	.31	**.63**	.49	[]	**.65**
Declarative	[]	**.59**			[]	
Negative	[]	.10	.01	**.61**		.01
Range		*49*	*62*	*12*		*64*
Clause type						
Subordinate	**.63**	[]	[]	[]	[]	[]
Main	.47	[]	[]	[]	[]	[]
Range	*16*					
Temporal distance						
Proximal	–	**.79**	**.50**	–	[]	**.56**
Distal	–	.36	.40	–	[]	.43
Range		*43*	*10*			*13*
Speech style						
Less formal	–	–	**.51**	–	–	**.51**
More formal	–	–	.36	–	–	.22
Range			*15*			*29*
Contingency						
Assumed	–	–	–	–	**.55**	[]
Contingent	–	–	–	–	.13	[]
Range					*42*	

[a] Factor groups with the greatest magnitude of effect are shaded. Factors within each factor group most favourable to PF are bolded.

[b] Aaron analysed sentence type separately. For ease of comparison, we present her figures for polarity.

languages does temporal distance affect choice of PF. The only effect common to all three languages is the propensity of PF to appear in temporally unspecified contexts, a finding consistent with Schwenter and Torres Cacoullos' (2008) demonstration that grammaticalization advances in temporally indeterminate contexts. If there is any candidate for a grammaticalization universal in this context, this would be it.

This cross-linguistic comparison suggests that the pathways by which *go*-verbs grammaticalize into future markers are not parallel, even in closely related languages. The discrepancies in trajectories are perhaps most striking in the case of French and Portuguese, which, despite what their disparate overall rates of PF imply, are at appreciably the same level on the cline of grammaticalization. This is because in both languages, the process has stalled, an outcome which the variationist method is equally capable of detecting. In French the only context blocking PF from taking over the whole future temporal reference domain is the near-categorical association of SF with negative polarity (Poplack and Turpin 1999; Poplack and Dion 2009).[4] In Portuguese, barriers to the complete colonization of future temporal reference by PF are constituted by entrenchment of P in contingent and adverbially specified contexts and, inexplicably, with the motion verb *ir* 'go'. Despite the fact that it is basically the only variant remaining, PF remains (informally) inadmissible with main-verb *ir* (Poplack and Malvar 2007: 154). There is no restriction against PF co-occurring with *ir* in 20th-century Spanish (Aaron 2006), although grammaticalization is least advanced in that language, and lexical identity is not a factor in French either. This shows that the source meaning can persist further into the grammaticalization process than previously assumed, raising the question of why only some languages (and some forms) are affected and not other similar ones.

6. Discussion

GT has offered great insights into change based on strong but testable hypotheses, and supported a number of them with revealing studies of shifts in rates and distributions of grammaticalizing forms. What VT adds is a principled way of examining not only the grammaticalizing form, but also the other layers with which it competes. Extending the focus to the entire variable context confirms

[4] To be sure, Givón (1975) has characterized negative contexts as conservative. But why do they work this way only in French?

that forms do not grammaticalize in isolation, but are sensitive to the variants with which they alternate. The trajectory of future temporal reference in Portuguese is a case in point. As PF increases in frequency, it—and its competitors—lose, transfer, and acquire constraints, mostly as a reaction to the activity in the remainder of the sector. Thus, accompanying shifts in token frequency are shifts in conditioning of variant choice. These represent differences not just in *degree* of grammaticalization but in the *contour* of the grammaticalization pathways.

This is exemplified most convincingly by cross-linguistic comparison of three languages featuring the same lexico-grammatical material derived from the same source. In each, the *go*-future is apparently well en route to sweeping the entire future temporal reference system, though synchronically they are at different points along the cline. The GT prediction is that cross-linguistic recruitment of grammatical expressions from the same lexical sources, coupled with the coexistence of older and newer forms, repeatedly give rise to similar kinds of polysemies (inferable from the conditioning of variant choice) cross-linguistically (e.g. Brinton and Traugott 2005: 29). This was not borne out.

Analysis of variation suggests a number of reasons. Old distribution patterns may persist, even into the most advanced stages of grammaticalization, although they sometimes yield opposing results. Thus the early association of Portuguese P with motion verbs resolved itself in contemporary speech by near-categorical *avoidance* of the *go*-future with main verb *ir*, while the Spanish *andar* 'go around' auxiliary continues to be favoured with the verbs compatible with its source meaning (Torres Cacoullos 1999). Barriers to grammaticalization may arise, and these may also differ according to language: the overwhelming association of SF with negative polarity contexts blocks PF from colonizing the entire French future temporal reference system, while the entrenchment of P in contingent and temporally specific contexts plays the same role in Brazilian Portuguese. This suggests that with few exceptions, each language is following an independent trajectory to arrive at the same outcome, highlighting the risks of inferring grammaticalization paths from endpoints of change alone.

I have argued that VT is ideally suited to the study of grammaticalization in progress. Studying a form in its variable context allows us to distinguish evidence for a cross-linguistic grammaticalization path from effects that are reflexes of the forms with which it alternates in that context (Torres Cacoullos and Walker 2009b: 323–4; Poplack and Malvar 2007). The case of the Romance *go*-future shows that language-particular trajectories are contoured by variation with coexisting variants. More generally, VT provides the empirical tools necessary to scientifically test hypotheses central to GT, at least some of which enjoy the status of fact without the benefit of empirical proof.[5] The results I have presented may not constitute sufficient cause to retract claims for the universality of grammaticalization paths, but they certainly sound a clarion call for further cross-linguistic research using accountable methodology such as that outlined here.

[5] It also offers a check on promiscuous claims of grammaticalization, which have proliferated in the literature over the last decade.

CHAPTER 18

COLLOCATIONS IN GRAMMATICALIZATION AND VARIATION

RENA TORRES CACOULLOS
JAMES A. WALKER

1. Introduction: grammaticalization, collocations, and autonomy

Grammaticalization is the set of gradual processes, both semantic and structural, by which constructions involving particular lexical items are used with increasing frequency and become new grammatical constructions, following cross-linguistic evolutionary paths (e.g. Bybee, Pagliuca, and Perkins 1994; Givón 1979; Heine and Kuteva 2002; Traugott 2003). Grammaticalization may involve not only individual lexical items, but also *collocations* of items, or 'conventionalized word sequences' (Bybee 2006: 713), including 'prefabs' (Erman and Warren 2000), 'reusable fragments' (Thompson 2002: 141), or 'formulaic language' (Corrigan et al. 2009). Given this gradualness, collocations undergoing grammaticalization will vary in analyzability (or, conversely, what Bybee 2003 calls autonomy), which raises two questions:

1. To what degree do the sub-units composing the collocation retain individual independent associations with their cognates in other constructions?

2. To what degree do collocations retain an association with the (diachronically) related more general constructions?

For example, the phonetic reduction of future *(BE) going to* to *gonna* indicates decreased analysability (or increased autonomy): *go* is absorbed into a new fused single unit which is autonomous from other instances of the verb *go* and from the general purposive construction from which this future arose (Bybee 2006: 719–20). If collocations are ostensibly fixed, are they subject to variation? Do they play a role in grammaticalization and change more generally? If so, how?

In this chapter, we focus on collocations in grammaticalization. Using examples of grammaticalization in Spanish and English, we illustrate how patterns of distribution and co-occurrence can be used to demonstrate the variability and gradience of constituency. Furthermore, our quantitative analysis provides evidence that collocations may be viewed as particular instances of constructions that interact with their more general counterparts to shape grammatical structure.

We begin with two measures of collocation status: indices of unithood and relative frequency, in section 2. In section 3, we use multivariate models of variation between alternate forms to show that, despite their status as autonomous units, collocations retain the grammatical patterning of the more general construction with which they are associated. Finally, in section 4, we examine the role of collocations in contributing to apparent semantic effects in grammatical variation.

2. Measures of collocations: distributional analysis and relative frequency

2.1. Indices of unithood from distributional analysis

Distributional analysis examines the patterning of collocations across different contexts, that is, the proportion of occurrences (tokens) of that collocation in different contexts. For several grammaticalizing constructions, one measure of unithood, or degree of fusion, is *adjacency.* Over time, a decreasing proportion of tokens occur with other material intervening between sub-units of the collocation. For example, the Spanish construction [$ESTAR_{\text{Present}}$ + Verb-*ndo*]$_{\text{= present progressive}}$ is on its way to becoming an obligatory aspectual expression. In Old Spanish (12th–15th centuries), it began as a particular instance of a general gerund construction in which finite forms of spatial (locative, postural, or motion) verbs combined with another verb in gerund (*-ndo*) form to mean '*be*/*go* Verb-*ing*'. In evolving from a locative to a progressive, the construction underwent a change in constituency from a sequence of two independent parts (main verb *estar* 'be (located)' with a gerund complement) to a periphrastic unit, with an auxiliary (*estar*) and a main verb (the gerund). In the absence of observable phonetic reduction, what evidence can be assembled for such a change?

In addition to *adjacency*, that is, the absence of elements intervening between *estar* and the gerund (such as *ambos* 'both of them' in (1)), another measure of unit-hood emerging from changes in distribution is *association* between the finite form of *estar* and a single co-occurring gerund, as opposed to the co-occurrence of two or more gerund complements (e.g. *comiendo* 'eating' and *solazándo* 'sunning' in (1)). A third measure is *fusion*, the placement of object clitic pronouns before the emerging unit rather than attached to the gerund, or 'clitic climbing' (cf. Myhill 1988) (as with reflexive marker *se* 'themselves' in (1)) (Torres Cacoullos 2000: 33–55, 71–88).

(1) que tu marido está en la ribera de la mar et que ha por amigo un ximio; et **están** *anbos* **comiendo** et *solazandose.* (13th c., Calila e Dimna)
'that your husband is at the seaside and that he has befriended a monkey; and they **are (there)** *both of them* **eating** and *sunning themselves*'

Table 18.1, based on Spanish texts spanning six centuries, shows increasing unit-hood on all three measures. The proportion of occurrences without intervening material changes significantly across time, beginning with 36 per cent of all tokens in the 13th century and reaching 78 per cent in the 19th. Occurrences of single as opposed to multiple gerunds increase significantly, from 80 per cent in the 13th

Table 18.1. Increasing unithood [*estar* + Verb-*ndo*] progressive[a] (from Bybee and Torres Cacoullos 2009: table 4)

	13th c.	15th c.	17th c.	19th c.
Adjacency (lack of intervening material)	36% (104)	50% (134)	67% (217)	78% (217)
Chi-square:	4.950; p = 0.0261	9.799; p = 0.0017	9.324; p = 0.0023	
Association (absence of multiple gerunds)	80% (104)	86% (134)	88% (217)	92% (217)
Chi-square:	6.634; p = 0.01 (13th vs. 19th c.)			
Fusion ('clitic climbing')	63% (24)	50% (22)	82% (74)	70% (77)
	57% (46)	76% (151)		
Chi-square:	6.6827, p = 0.0097			

[a]All tense occurrences. Numbers within ( ) are Ns (tokens); % is proportion of tokens.

century to 92 per cent in the 19th. Finally, the rate of proclisis rises from 57 per cent in the combined 13th–15th centuries to 76 per cent in the combined 17th–19th centuries.

A different set of unithood measures emerge from Spanish *a pesar de X* 'in spite of X', which developed from a meaning of opposition by another person into a concessive, where the element 'X' is an NP, an infinitive, or a finite clause (Torres Cacoullos and Schwenter 2005). The strongest evidence for analysability appears in coordinated adnominal NPs, where repetition of *de* 'of' for each adnominal NP shows the relative independence of this component from the other subunit(s) of the collocation, *a* + *pesar*. In (2a), *de* is repeated with the coordinated NPs, but in (2b), one *de* suffices, or has scope over, both NPs. In fact, repetition of *de* in coordinated adnominal NPs declines from an average of 86 per cent (N = 23) in the 17th and 18th centuries to 60 per cent (N = 30) in the 19th and 20th centuries (Chi-square = 4.298, $p = 0.038$) (Torres Cacoullos 2006: 42).

(2) a. algo de atrevido y varonil en todo el ademán, **a pesar del** recogimiento **y de** la mansedumbre clericales (19th c., Pepita Jiménez)
'something bold and virile in his whole look, **in spite of** the withdrawal **and of** the tameness of the cleric'

(2) b. olía a lavanda y espliego, pero por debajo del perfume olía como yo, la fisiología nos igualaba **a pesar de** los potingues **y** las abluciones diarias (20th c., La tempestad)
'she smelled of lavender, but underneath the perfume she smelled like me, our physiologies making us equals **in spite of** the concoctions **and** the daily ablutions'

As erstwhile independent lexical item *pesar* 'sorrow' is absorbed into the fused unit *a pesar de*, it undergoes what Hopper (1991: 22) calls 'decategorialization', shedding its nominal trappings. This is measured by the loss of plural marking (from 6 per cent of all *pesar* tokens in the 12th–15th centuries to 1 per cent in the 17th–20th centuries), a drop in determiners (from 67 per cent to 7 per cent) and adjectival modification (from 10 per cent to 1 per cent), and a decline in coordination with other nouns (as in *mucho* ***pesar*** *y tristeza* 'much sorrow and sadness' (15th c., La Celestina), from 30 per cent to 5 per cent) (Torres Cacoullos 2006: 38–9). Thus, in both cases, the distributional analyses underscore the gradualness of decategorialization and the gradience of analysability.

2.2. Collocations and relative frequency

Increased frequency of use is integral in grammaticalization. Although text-based studies have profitably paid attention to token frequency (e.g. papers in Bybee and

Hopper 2001), relative frequency measures, which consider occurrences of subunits outside the collocation, may provide another gauge of analysability.

In the case of gerund (*-ndo*) periphrases (including the [*estar* + Verb-*ndo*] progressive mentioned above), token frequency rises in tandem with an increase in the proportion of gerunds in construction with an (emerging) auxiliary (in addition to *estar* 'be (located)', motion verbs *ir* 'go', *andar* 'go around', *seguir* 'follow, continue'): that is, an increased rate of gerunds preceded by an auxiliary relative to those gerunds that stand alone (as adverbials or relatives). Token frequency doubles between the 16th and early 20th centuries, from 8 to 16 occurrences per 10,000 words, as does relative frequency, from 14 per cent to 24 per cent. Such increased relative frequency means a greater probability that a gerund is tied to an auxiliary, leading to the growing identification of the auxiliary + Verb-*ndo* sequence as a unit (Torres Cacoullos 2000: 55–60).

In the development of concessive *a pesar de* 'in spite of', increased token frequency is accompanied by increased frequency of the collocation with respect to occurrences of lexical item *pesar* outside the collocation, which swells from 2 per cent to 96 per cent, a spectacular reversal (Table 18.2). As the collocation rises, other uses of *pesar* 'sorrow' (object, subject or adverbial phrases) decline steeply, to the point that *pesar* today occurs virtually always flanked by *a* and *de*.[1] Table 18.2 shows that the grammaticalization measures of decategorialization of *pesar* and fusion of the subunits in *a pesar de* (reviewed in section 2.1) shift in tandem with shifts in the relative frequency of the collocation.

Table 18.2. Grammaticalization and relative frequency: collocation *a pesar de* is increasing proportion of occurrence of *pesar* (from Torres Cacoullos 2006: tables 8–10)

Century	Unithood	Decategorialization	Token frequency	Relative frequency
	a pesar de (%)	*pesar* (%)	*a pesar de*	*a pesar de/pesar*
12th–15th	–	20	< 1	2% (4/199)
17th	73	5		72% (58/81)
19th	52	2	12 (17th–20th)	86% (169/196)
20th	30	0		96% (167/174)

Note: Unithood measure is repetition of *de* in coordinated adnominal NPs; decategorialization measure is use of definite article (see section 2.1); token frequency is normalized per 100,000 words.

[1] We do not expect that a decrease in the relative frequency of lexical use (with respect to a collocation) will necessarily correspond with a decrease in the absolute token frequency (e.g. per 10,000 words).

The cases reviewed here provide evidence that one measure of collocations is diachronically increasing relative frequency of the sequence of words with respect to the lexical component of the sequence. Such relative frequency may promote the absorption of the lexical constituent as the sub-units of the collocation fuse, as well as the autonomy of the collocation from its erstwhile lexical constituent (similar to the reduced compositionality and semantic transparency of morphologically complex words that are more frequent than their bases: Hay 2001).[2]

3. Collocations, from the Particular to the General: Evidence from the Linguistic Conditioning of Variants

We now move beyond simple measures of frequency to patterns of variation: that is, quantitative models of speaker choices between variant forms serving generally similar discourse functions. These patterns are observable in *linguistic conditioning*, probabilistic statements about the relative frequency of co-occurrence of linguistic forms and elements of the linguistic context (Labov 1969; Sankoff 1988). The methodological tool is a comparison of the linguistic conditioning of variants involving putative collocations and variants that do not (cf. Poplack and Tagliamonte 2001; Tagliamonte 2002). While different linguistic conditioning indicates collocational status, parallels in linguistic conditioning reveal shared grammatical patterning with other instances of more general constructions.

Consider the variable use of complementizer *that* to link two clauses, a widely attested feature of all varieties of English, illustrated in (3). Certain frequent collocations of main-clause subjects and verbs, such as *I think* and *I guess*, have been proposed as discourse formulas that function more as epistemic adverbials than as main clauses (Thompson and Mulac 1991).

(3) a. And I let it slip **that** Darth Vader was Luke's father. (071.468)
b. I can't even believe Ø I just said that. (059.1840)[3]

Examining a corpus of Canadian English (Poplack, Walker, and Malcolmson 2006), we note a remarkably skewed distribution of main-clause verb types in the variable complementizer construction: *think*, *know*, and *say* account for 63 per cent

[2] Relative frequency as the proportion of a lexical type in a particular construction has been shown to correlate with phonetic reduction (Alba 2008; Hollman and Siewierska 2007). Other measures of associations between words are tested in Krug (1998) and Jurafsky et al. (2001).

[3] Examples are taken from the *Quebec English Corpus* (Poplack et al. 2006).

of all the data, while five additional verbs (*guess*, *tell*, *remember*, *find*, and *realize*) account for a further 19 per cent. In other words, just eight lexical types make up 81 per cent of the data. Nevertheless, there is no one-to-one correlation between token frequency and the rate of *that* (vs. zero complementizer), which averages 21 per cent (N=2820) in the data examined. Among middle-frequency lexical types (50–200 tokens), the highest-frequency verb (*guess*) has a rate of *that* at 3 per cent, but the second-highest (*tell*) has a higher than average 43 per cent. Among high-frequency types, *know* and *say* occupy roughly the same proportion of the data (9–10 per cent), but *know* shows 34 per cent *that* while *say* has 27 per cent, both at rates higher than several much lower frequency predicates (Torres Cacoullos and Walker 2009a: 19–20).

However, if we adopt a relative-frequency view of collocations, examining main-clause subjects and verbs reveals a substantial difference between the three highest-frequency lexical types, *think*, *know*, and *say*, which present quite disparate rates of *that*. Unlike *know* and *say*, *think* is largely restricted to 1st-person singular present tense. As shown in the middle column in Table 18.3, seven subject–verb collocations make up an average of 80 per cent of their respective lexical types: *I think*, *I guess*, *I remember*, *I find*, *I'm sure*, *I wish*, *I hope*. In contrast, all other subject–verb combinations that make up a substantial proportion of their respective verb types present an average of only 19 per cent.

This sharp difference in relative frequency clearly correlates with rates of *that*. As shown in the right-most column in Table 18.3, the average rate of *that* for the seven high-relative-frequency subject–verb sequences is a bare 8 per cent (though the rate for individual collocations within this set ranges from 0 per cent to 24 per cent), in contrast to 31 per cent for the infrequent sequences. Are these high-relative-

Table 18.3. Main-clause subject–verb collocations by proportion of lexical type and rate of complementizer *that*

Collocations	N	% lexical type	% *that*
I think	734	61	5
I guess	163	99	3
I remember	90	96	4
I find	59	66	24
I'm sure	40	74	10
I wish	17	85	0
I hope	15	79	7
Total	1,118	80	8
Low-relative-frequency subject–verb sequences	216	19	31

frequency subject–verb sequences indeed discourse formulas, i.e. autonomous collocations? Beyond the correlation with lower rates of *that*, we seek evidence for their status as collocations by examining the patterns of *that*-variation, by comparing the linguistic conditioning of *that* in the putative collocations and in the other instances of the construction that do not involve collocations.

For each token, we noted whether *that* was present or not (the dependent variable) and coded for a number of factor groups (independent variables) to operationalize syntactic, semantic, or discourse-pragmatic hypotheses about the choice of variants (*that* or zero) based on contextual features. All of the factor groups were considered in multivariate analysis using GoldVarb X (Sankoff, Tagliamonte, and Smith 2005), to discover the set of factor groups that jointly account for the largest amount of variation in a statistically significant way.

We are interested in two lines of evidence from the multivariate analyses (cf. Tagliamonte 2006: 235–45). First, the *direction of effect* (or 'hierarchy of constraints': Labov 1969: 742) is instantiated in the order of the factors within a factor group, from most to least favourable, as indicated by the probability or *factor weight*: the closer to 1, the more likely, the closer to 0, the less likely that the variant of interest (here, *that*) will be chosen in the given environment. Second, the relative *magnitude of effect* is indicated by the *range*, the difference between the highest and lowest factor weight in the group.

Table 18.4 compares two multivariate analyses of factors contributing to choice of *that* in the subject–verb collocations identified by the relative frequency measure (Table 18.3) and in tokens not involving the collocations. The input, which indicates the overall likelihood that *that* will occur, is much lower in the collocations (.05) than in the other occurrences (.33), as expected.

Table 18.4. Two independent multivariate analyses of linguistic factors contributing to the occurrence of complementizer *that*: (a) excluding main-clause subject–verb collocations; (b) in main-clause subject–verb collocations (*I think, I guess, I remember, I find, I'm sure, I wish, I hope*)

	Non-collocations	Collocations
Total N:	1,552	1,118
Input:	.33	.05
Complement-Clause Subject		
Noun phrase (e.g. 3a)	**.65**	**.68**
Other pronoun	.52	.48
I (3b)	.42	.42
it/there	.38	.43
Range:	*27*	*26*

Adjacency: intervening material		
Present (*I remember on Saturday, my mother used to)*	**.72**	**.72**
Absent	.45	.47
Range:	*27*	*25*
Main-clause subject		
Noun phrase (*the teacher realized that...*)	**.68**	–
Pronoun	.45	
Range:	*23*	
Main-clause adverbial		
Post-subject (*they still think that...)*	**.65**	**.83**
Phrasal (*at the beginning, we told the guy that...)*	**.59**	.52
None	.47	.48
Pre-subject (*so already they think...)*	.45	**.77**
Range:	*20*	*35*
Adjacency: intervening verbal arguments		
Present (*we told the guy that...)*	**.60**	[ ]
Absent	.49	[ ]
Range:	*11*	
Main-clause verbal morphology		
Non-finite (*you would tell...)*	**.58**	–
Finite (*they tell me that...*)	.47	
Range:	*11*	
Complement-clause transitivity		
Transitive (*... find that they had a job*)	**.56**	[ ]
Intransitive	.47	[ ]
Range:	*9*	
Factors not selected as significant:		
Subject coreferentiality	X	X
Harmony of polarity	X	
Intervening verbal argument		X
Comp-clause mood/morphology	X	
Comp-clause transitivity		X
Cotemporality	X	

How does the linguistic conditioning compare? In the non-collocations (instances of the general complementizer construction, excluding *I think* and the other subject–verb collocations identified in Table 18.3), shown in the left-hand column, the greatest effects (range = 27) are exerted by the increasing referentiality of the complement-clause subject (full NP (3a) > other pronoun > *I* (3b) > *it/there*) and by the presence of intervening material between the two clauses. Also strong are the effects of main-clause NP subjects (range = 23) and of post-subject adverbials (range = 20). Complex main-clause verbal morphology and arguments in the main clause contribute lesser effects. This configuration of effects indicates that *that* serves to demarcate the boundary between two clauses which both have (lexical) content. In contrast, zero occurs when there is less semantic content and the two clauses behave more like a single proposition (cf. Fox and Thompson 2007).

If the collocations, such as *I think* and *I guess*, are fixed units, autonomous from other instances of the complementizer construction, the factors conditioning *that* should differ. As the right-hand column in Table 18.4 shows, the three factor groups with the greatest magnitude of effect for non-collocations are also significant for collocations: intervening material, complement-clause subjects, and main-clause adverbials. However, the relative *magnitude* of effect is not identical. The greatest contribution to *that* in the collocations is the main-clause adverbial (range = 35). This confirms their status as collocations, since the presence of a post- or pre-subject adverbial (4) nullifies the formulaic nature of the collocation.

(4) a. I personally think that it is well worthwhile. (027.737)
 b. Actually I- I think that those were the only two things they said in the entire skit. (071.737)

Nevertheless, it is important to note that the *direction* of effect is largely parallel. The choice of *that* is favoured most by full NP (and least by *it/there* and *I*) complement-clause subjects and by the presence of intervening material. Even though the absence of *that* is near-categorical (input = .05), frequent collocations retain traces of grammatical conditioning. The parallelism in linguistic conditioning shows that, despite their status as fixed collocations, these units are not completely autonomous from other instances of the complement construction. Patterns of variation thus demonstrate that collocations may maintain associations with more general constructions.

4. Collocations Shape Grammatical Variation

In the previous section, we compared the conditioning of linguistic variation by language-internal factors in collocations and in their associated general constructions. We provided evidence for formulaic or conventionalized collocations through differences in linguistic conditioning. In this section we discuss a slightly more complicated case, in which the collocational effects do not occupy the same proportion of the data. Nevertheless, we will demonstrate that these collocational effects can still be powerful (cf. Walker 2007). Specifically, we will show that apparent semantic effects are derived from, and shaped by, the influence of frequent collocations.

We take the example of the future in English, an area of grammar in which a number of variants coexist. Here we focus on variation between the two most robust future forms, *will* and *going to*, as shown in (5).

(5) a. And he*'ll* probably live 'til a hundred. (29:1480)
   b. My doctor tells me I*'m going to* live 'til a hundred. (29:341)

Semantic differences attributed to the two variants include proximity, certainty or willingness (see Torres Cacoullos and Walker 2009b for an overview). Table 18.5 shows the results of a multivariate analysis of the factors contributing to the

Table 18.5. Factors contributing to the choice of future *will* (vs. *going to*) in Quebec English

	Total N:	2,807
	Input:	.524
Sentence type		
Declarative		.54
Negative		.47
Yes/no question		.31
Wh-question		.09
Range:		*45*
Clause type		
Apodosis		.59
Other main		.53
Other		.36
Range:		*23*
Temporal adverbial		
Nonspecific/indefinite (*never*)		.67
Specific/definite		.48
No adverbial		.48
Range:		*19*

(continued)

Table 18.5. Continued

Total N:	2,807
Input:	.524
Grammatical person and animacy of subject	
1st person sg.	.56
1st person pl.	.50
3rd person, inanimate	.49
3rd person, animate	.47
2nd person	.38
Range:	*18*
Proximity	
Proximal (same day)	.49
Distal	.51
Range:	*2*

occurrence of *will*. There is no strong effect of proximity, but a more detailed breakdown (Figure 18.1) reveals that *will* tokens occur disproportionately in 'within a minute' and 'within an hour' contexts, most of which have 1st person singular subjects (e.g. *I'll tell you*). Although we might interpret this as a persistence of willingness in the use of *will* for offers, 1st person *will* (*'ll*) collocations (6) also

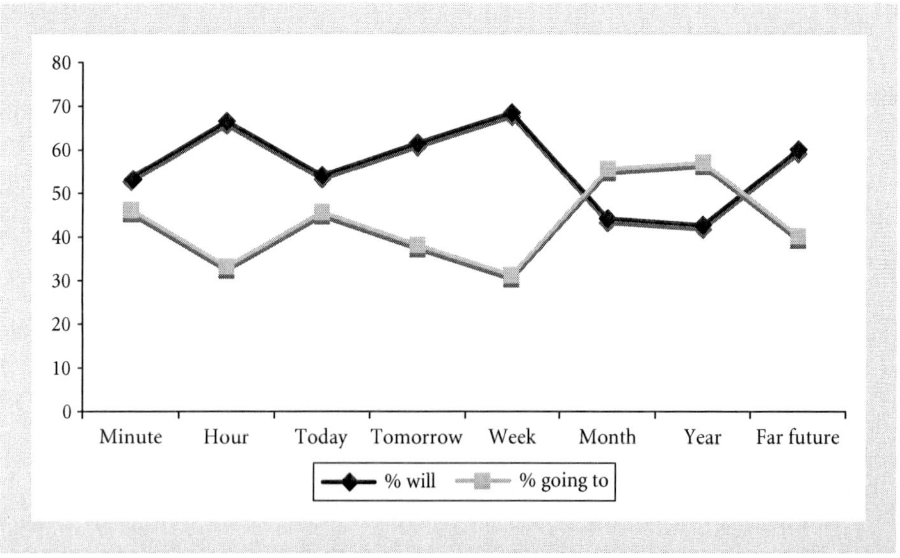

Fig. 18.1. Distribution of future variants by temporal proximity

make up substantial proportions of their corresponding lexical types. Taken together, these results suggest that perceptions of proximity and willingness may have more to do with fixed discourse formulas.

(6) *I'll tell...* 58% of *tell* (40/69)
I'll pay... 53% of *pay* (8/15)
I'll ask... 44% of *ask* (8/18)
I'll talk... 38% of *talk* (9/24)
I'll call... 35% of *call* (11/31)
I'll teach... 33% of *teach* (7/21)
I'll give... 33% of *give* (21/64)
I'll try... 29% of *try* (6/21)
I'll speak... 26% of *speak* (6/23)
I'll say... 20% of *say* (7/35)

The other effects shown in Table 18.5, although at first glance semantic, can in each case be shown to reflect (at least in part) the effects of collocations. The effect of indefinite adverbials is due in part to *never*, which constitutes a third (78/249) of these tokens and overwhelmingly (72 per cent (56/78)) occurs with *will*, largely in the collocation 'X *will/'ll never...*' (66 per cent (37/56)). Many of the non-main clauses, which disfavour *will*, are preceded by a frequent collocation of cognition verb and 1st person subject (7), such as *I think*. As we saw in the previous section, such collocations function more as epistemic phrases than as clauses. Rather than indicating degree of certainty, the effect may reflect early generalization of *go*-futures in contexts expressing speaker viewpoint (cf. Traugott 1995a), and thus retention of earlier distribution patterns rather than source-construction meaning (cf. Torres Cacoullos 2001).

(7) a. And <u>I think</u> she***'s gonna*** need uh- you know, she'll need that extra support. (48:865)
b. <u>I'm sure</u> today there***'ll*** be a lot of people at the movies. (67:1310)

The strongest effect, that of questions, can also be attributed to collocations. For example, *What am I going to do?*, *Is there gonna be...?*, and *What's gonna happen?* make up substantial portions (approximately one-fifth) of their respective grammatical persons in questions. The significance of grammatical person in Table 18.5 is also due (at least in part) to the disfavouring effect of 2nd person singular, which interacts with questions. Thus, general effects which at first glance appear to indicate semantic nuances may largely reflect particular constructions: nuances of proximity and willingness are due to formulas such as *I'll tell you*; the indefinite adverbial effect which operationalizes certainty is due to the *X'll never...* construction; rhetorical or formulaic questions contribute to the interrogative effect.

5. Conclusion

In this chapter, we have used various measures—token frequency, relative frequency, linguistic conditioning, and comparative analysis—to examine the role of collocations in variation and grammaticalization. These measures demonstrate that analysability in collocations (the converse of autonomy) is a gradient property. Collocations show retention of linguistic conditioning: they retain patterns associated with their more general cognate constructions. This retention indicates that, rather than being completely autonomous units, collocations can be viewed as particular instances of constructions which, while formulaic, interact with their associated general constructions. The patterns of future forms reviewed here also provide evidence for an interaction of collocations with general, productive constructions. Diachronic studies show that collocations constitute an important locus of grammatical development, since they may lead in changes and constitute subclasses that contour the grammaticalization of more general constructions (Bybee and Torres Cacoullos 2009). Thus, rather than being a peripheral part of the linguistic system, collocations may be considered an integral part of grammar.

CHAPTER 19

GRAMMATICALIZATION AND CORPUS LINGUISTICS

CHRISTIAN MAIR

1. Introduction[1]

A mere twenty years ago corpus linguistics and grammaticalization theory, while often focussing on similar kinds of empirical phenomena, tended to work in blissful ignorance of each other. Olofsson (1990), for example, working from a corpus-linguistic perspective, noted that the participle *following* was developing increasingly prepositional uses in contemporary English—without mentioning the term 'grammaticalization' even once in his argument. This is ironic not least because the diachronic move from nonfinite verbal forms to prepositions was identified as a well-travelled pathway of change in the literature on grammaticalization in English almost at the same time (Kortmann and König 1992). By the same token, there is no reference to Olofsson's work in Kortmann and König's theoretically orientated study.

[1] The present paper was completed while I enjoyed the extremely productive and congenial working environment provided by FRIAS, Freiburg University's Institute for Advanced Studies. I am grateful for this support.

In spite of such unpromising beginnings, the past two decades have seen a definite and mutually beneficial *rapprochement* between corpus linguistics and grammaticalization theory. Krug (2000), on English modals and semi-modals, or Hoffmann (2005), on English complex prepositions, have demonstrated the fruitfulness of cooperation in two comprehensive monographs, while further evidence is supplied in several collections of essays (Rissanen, Kytö, and Heikkonen 1997; Lindquist and Mair 2004a; Lenker and Meurman-Solin 2007). Recently, 'distinctive collexeme analysis' (Gries and Stefanowitsch 2004) has been applied to grammaticalizing English future and causative constructions to great effect by Hilpert (2006).

As corpus coverage is notoriously uneven for the world's languages, it is natural for much current corpus-based work on grammaticalization to focus on a few languages, and predominantly on English. However, the past few years in particular have seen promising beginnings of work on other languages, for example on the grammaticalization of connectives in Mandarin (Wang 2006), on compounding and grammaticalization in Thai and Chinese (Post 2007), on existential verbs in Korean (Kim 2003), or on adpositions and affixes in Lakota (Pustet 2008). It is safe to assume that, as suitable corpora become available for more and more languages, the current bias in favour of English and a few other European languages written in the Roman alphabet will be redressed.

While both parties stand to benefit from the cooperation between corpus linguistics and grammaticalization, they do so in rather different ways. The short history of computer-assisted corpus linguistics has often been characterized by a tendency for progress in data storage capacity, retrieval programs, and statistical software to outstrip the development of linguistically sophisticated usage-based models for the interpretation of the data. More and more data can be accumulated and profiled statistically in ever shorter periods and in ever more complex ways; however, the question of how much of the statistically significant patterning in the data is linguistically salient remains a contested issue. In this situation, a mature usage-based model of grammatical change such as grammaticalization theory is very helpful in framing research questions and interpreting the statistical findings which are fast accumulating. Grammaticalization theory, in its turn, profits greatly from cooperation with corpus linguistics because it has its 'data problem' solved—at least in the study of those few languages which, like English, German, French, or Spanish, boast a rich and pan-chronic corpus-linguistic working environment. While there is now almost universal agreement that frequency of use is relevant to grammaticalization in some ways, 'the exact nature of the interaction between frequency of use, context extension, and functional change is still largely unclear' (Heine and Kuteva 2005: 45), and in this situation large and generically stratified corpora afford an excellent opportunity to test claims at very advanced levels of granularity.

I will proceed as follows. Largely on the basis of the existing literature, I will show how corpora and the use of corpus-linguistic methods enrich the empirical basis of grammaticalization theory and, in some important instances, even help it to develop its theoretical foundations. I will then move on to discuss an incipient and hitherto unrecorded instance of grammaticalization in Present-day English to test the potential of the corpus-linguistic working environment for the investigation of such difficult empirical cases. The study example is the possible emergence of a new adverbial subordinator *(on) (the) basis (that)*, repeating a development previously attested for *because/cause*: prepositional phrase with apposition clause modifying the noun ('by cause + *that*-clause...') → reduced transparency through conventionalised omission of *that* ('by cause + clause') → univerbation/ loss of nominal status ('because') → further phonological attrition ('cause') (for further details of the process see Lee 2008).

2. Three reasons for using corpora in research on grammaticalization: convenience, context, quantification

A first and trivial reason why students of grammaticalization should turn their attention to corpora is that it will make their search for data more convenient, but also more systematic and efficient. Consider for illustration the following two scenarios. If the hunt is on for very early instantiations of well-documented grammatical innovations such as the *going to*-future in English (studied e.g. in Hopper and Traugott 1993: 82–4; 2003: 87–93), chances are that the 1482 attestation from the *OED* discussed by the two authors (2003: 89) will be pretty close to the actual period of origin of the new construction. However, if, as in the case of the 'candidate' subordinator *(on) (the) basis (that)*, the status of the form is still doubtful and the possible incipient process of grammaticalization has gone largely unnoticed, the following chance attestation from a written source is of questionable value:

(1) Taylor was also turned down for JSA **on the basis** his wife was earning and he had savings. 'I've paid taxes for over 20 years and have been sensible and frugal but now I'm told I can't claim anything while I'm out of work.' (*The Observer*, 31 May 2009, Cash: 11)

Whether this is an inconsequential performance 'slip' or evidence of stage 2 in the assumed grammaticalization process (reduced transparency through conventionalized omission of *that*) cannot be decided in the absence of large amounts of related data, systematically gathered and analysed (on which see section 4 below).

The second reason why students of grammaticalization stand to benefit from the use of corpora is that corpora are made up of authentic language data in their original syntactic and discourse contexts, which makes it possible to systematically study the 'bridging contexts' so important in early stages of grammaticalization (cf. Heine 2002). For example, in the development of possessive *have (got)* into semi-modal *have (got) to*, it is merely a first step to posit a decontextualized general semantic pathway of the development. To understand how the development actually came about it is essential to consider that, as Krug notes, 'almost all early contiguous HAVE GOT TO constructions [...] and almost all contiguous HAVE TO constructions in Shakespeare [...] occur in extracted environments like relative clauses or questions' (2000: 97) of the following type:

(2) Come, let me see what task I have to do. (Shakespeare, *Titus Andronicus*, I. i. 276; also discussed in Krug 2000: 97)

Of course, this particular insight could have occurred to anyone observing a number of early instances, with or without the benefit of corpora. Even so, the systematic evaluation of corpus data makes it possible to determine the precise impact of this factor, for example by tabulating extraction environments as a proportion of all relevant environments over time and, presumably, noting a reduction as entrenchment of the new use increases.

Even more important than the syntactic environment in which the grammaticalizing construction occurs is its discourse context, if only because the impact of the discourse factor is so much more difficult to assess objectively on the basis of impressionistically gathered collections of citations. Discourse factors potentially relevant for grammaticalization include 'micro' and 'macro' ones.[2] At the 'micro' end of the scale there are collocational preferences. With reference to the early stages of the grammaticalization of semi-modal *have (got) to*, for example, Krug points out the obtrusive frequency of HAVE TO *say/tell* (2000: 97) among the early attestations and plausibly argues that these forms had a trailblazing function in the establishment of the new semi-modals. On the 'macro' level of the social indexing of linguistic forms, for example, one might usefully ask how the grammaticalization of HAVE GOT TO is affected by the fact that this particular exponent of obligation/necessity is not just a new modal but also a prominent syntactic Briticism.

The third motivation for students of grammaticalization to turn to corpora is, finally, that only in this way can they resolve the central problem of the precise role

[2] These are frequently used concepts in contemporary pragmatics, discourse analysis, and sociolinguistics, usually employed in slightly different meanings by various authors. In 'micro' approaches, the focus is on the language structures implicated in contextualization and variation, whereas in 'macro' approaches the starting point is human orders of behaviour, among which communication in language is a central part (cf. similarly Mey 2001, with its well-known distinction between 'micro-pragmatics' and 'macro-pragmatics').

of frequencies and frequency effects in this particular usage-based model.[3] This is also the one aspect in which corpus-linguistic findings and methods may force grammaticalization theorists to reconsider the methodological underpinnings of their enterprise.

The general importance of frequency and repetition is taken for granted in most usage-based models of language acquisition, variation, and change, although different approaches may disagree about details. In the field as a whole, however, there is less consensus than ever before, with voices ranging from a wholesale dismissal of frequency as an explanatory factor to its endorsement as the prime force in grammaticalization. 'The "soul" of language does not use statistics' is the claim formulated in the title of Mehler et al. (2006), whereas in a paper published in the very same year Bybee (2006) regards the 'mind's response to repetition' as the chief shaping force in the emergence of grammatical structure. It should be obvious that systematic corpus-based analysis of specific problems is one way to come closer to an understanding of this big unresolved issue.

In a language rich in corpora such as English, and using state-of-the-art corpus-linguistic methodology, we are thus extremely well placed to address the following questions, among others:

(i) Does grammaticalization always lead to an increase in discourse frequency of the grammaticalized construction?

(ii) Is frequent use of a lexical pattern a precondition for grammaticalization, or do we have to make allowance for cases of 'low-frequency grammaticalization' (Hoffmann 2005; Brems 2007)?

(iii) What are the frequency measures most relevant to the grammaticalization process itself—absolute discourse frequency of the lexical starting point, or proportional frequencies of lexical and grammatical uses at successive stages, or a combination of both?

(iv) What is more important—frequency of the token (i.e. the concrete surface structure) or frequency of the type (i.e. a representation at more abstract levels)? To hark back to Olofsson's case study mentioned above: is the relevant measure the absolute frequency of *following*, or the frequency of the constructional type '*V-ing* with prepositional potential' (as instantiated e.g. by *regarding*, *concerning*, *assuming*, or maybe even *during* and *notwithstanding*), or—again—a combination of both?

[3] Let me emphasize from the start that there are several aspects of grammaticalization for which statistical considerations are of secondary importance at best. Discourse frequency is not the chief consideration in distinguishing between instances of grammaticalization and lexicalisation, for example (cf. Brinton and Traugott 2005). A rarely used counterexample to the unidirectionality hypothesis would still be a counterexample. And so on.

3. Bringing frequency into focus: the major current issues at the corpus–grammaticalization interface

There were probably no greater changes between the first (1993) and second (2003) editions of Hopper and Traugott's influential textbook on grammaticalization than with regard to the role of corpora and frequency. In the first edition, the term 'corpus linguistics' does not even rate a mention in the index. Where quantitative analyses are referred to, these generally do not involve the type of digitised text-base that we usually refer to by the name of 'corpus' today. What is mentioned (1993: 59–60) is classic pre-computational corpus work by Fries (1940), or work on frequency and grammaticalization produced by Joan Bybee (e.g. 1985). Kytö (1991), on Early Modern English modals, seems to be one of the very few corpus-based studies on the history of English which has made it into the bibliography of the first edition.

This is very different from what we see in the second edition. The term 'corpus linguistics' is now listed in the index, and 'the burgeoning of corpus linguistics in the 1990s' is explicitly invoked as one of the stimulants of innovative research on grammaticalization (Hopper and Traugott 2003: 36). The Helsinki Corpus, the 'Brown' family of corpora, the British National Corpus (BNC), or the Santa Barbara Corpus of Spoken American English are just some of the databases singled out in a discussion of the potential machine-readable corpora have in research on emergent constructions and grammaticalization past and present. Chapter 5 ('The hypothesis of unidirectionality') has a whole subsection 'Frequency' added to it (2003: 126–30). From these arguments (and similar ones presented elsewhere) we can draw the following conclusions as to current research priorities at the interface of corpus linguistics and grammaticalization theory.

The role of corpus findings as diagnostics is largely uncontroversial in the later stages of grammaticalization, where the chief task is to chart the way in which an already grammaticalized form or construction gradually spreads across textual genres, regional and social varieties and finally establishes itself in the core grammatical system. 'Synchronic' generically stratified corpora of a specific variety of a language (such as the BNC), 'synchronic' corpora documenting several regional and stylistic varieties of a language (e.g. ICE, the International Corpus of English), register-sensitive diachronic corpora (ARCHER—a Representative Corpus of Historical English Registers), or any combination of these (e.g. the 'Brown family', with its dual coverage of synchronic regional-stylistic variation and short-term diachronic change in standard Englishes) are all eminently suitable for this purpose.

With regard to the spread of a newly grammaticalized form in the community, the default assumption must be that grammaticalization will lead to an increase in corpus frequency, with expected time lags which are due to the fact that the material most likely to be collected in corpora, namely relatively standardized written sources, is not usually the type of genre in which grammaticalization typically occurs first. The default assumption is borne out by frequencies obtained for the *going to* future. While grammaticalization of this form was essentially complete by the end of the Early Modern English period (*c.*1750), we nevertheless observe drastic increases in frequency for example in the 19th- and 20th-century quotation corpus of the *OED* (cf. Mair 2004) or even in the Brown family of corpora (Mair 1997).

There is a small number of grammaticalization phenomena which originate in writing, for example some of the historically more recent English relativization strategies[4] or the emergence of certain complex prepositions (e.g. *notwithstanding*). Here, contact influence from Latin might have played an additional role. For these phenomena, genre-specific or medium-specific frequency differentials of the type observed for *going to* may never show up in corpora, either because their discourse frequency remains low overall even after grammaticalization or because they never make significant headway in speech.

On the other hand, there are intriguing cases of grammaticalization which almost certainly originate in the spoken medium but which, contrary to expectation, manifest themselves in written sources almost instantaneously. One such case is represented by specificational cleft sentences of the type *All I did was ask* (Traugott 2008a; Mair forthcoming), which have increasingly been replacing an earlier type with a marked infinitive (*All I did was to ask*) over the past 100 years or so. Real-time corpus data from the 'Brown family' (written English) and the Diachronic Corpus of Present-Day Spoken English (DCPSE, spoken British English) reveal American English to be in the lead of change but also show British English to change at parallel rates in speech and writing. The reason for this is probably that, unlike the *going to*-future, in particular in its realization as *gonna*, the new type of cleft sentence is not marked for informal style.

Finally, corpus data are apt to shed light on the contested phenomenon of 'low-frequency' grammaticalization. Krug (2000), for example, showed that the grammaticalization of semi-modal *have got to* proceeded much faster than the earlier grammaticalization of *have to*, in spite of the former form's relatively low discourse frequency. Hoffmann (2004) presented comparable data on complex prepositions of the *in* + noun + *of* type, showing that high-frequency forms such as *in view of* had apparently blazed the trail for *in fear of*, *in awe of*, *in point of*, *in celebration of*, etc. He was also apparently the first to take this observation as the starting point to explicitly posit a sub-type of 'low-frequency' grammaticalization proceeding at unusually high speed and involving analogical extension. The concept has recently

[4] Especially forms low on the hierarchy of accessibility (Keenan and Comrie 1977) such as relativization involving obliques or comparatives.

been taken up by others, for example Brems (2007), in a study of small size nouns such as *(not) a scrap/scintilla/skerrick of.*

4. (ON) (THE) BASIS (THAT)

As hinted at above, we will now turn to a concrete test case: the conjunction use of *(on) (the) basis (that)* briefly illustrated in example (1) above. It is, of course, not the only complex subordinator of its kind in Present-day English. Comparable cases, representing various stages of grammaticalization, include *the fact (that), on condition (that), in the event (that), for fear (that),* and *to the effect that.*

On the basis that happens to be well covered by Huddleston and Pullum (2002: 623), who point out that—unlike, for example, *the fact that*—the clause depends not on the noun phrase *the basis* but on the entire prepositional phrase. Thus, to paraphrase example (1) above: **the* ***basis*** *his wife was earning and he had savings* is not a legitimate phrase in itself. In addition, and in line with their new analysis of the category 'preposition', Huddleston and Pullum reject an analysis of *on the basis that* (and similar expressions such as in *the event that, on the grounds that,* or *to the effect that*) as complex prepositions, arguing instead that *on the basis* should be regarded as a prepositional phrase. They do not mention the possibility of omitting the subordinator *that,* and are not concerned with grammaticalization or the diachronic development of the construction in general.

To determine whether the construction has recently undergone or is undergoing grammaticalization at all, therefore, corpora need to be consulted, and the 'Brown family', with its coverage of (late) 20th-century British and American written English, would seem a good starting point.[5] The fact that the five corpora yield a total of seven relevant instances precludes a statistical analysis but it is nevertheless interesting to note that in addition to six *that*-clauses (see (3), (4), and (5)) there is one instance of the rarer type, with *that* omitted (6):

(3) In short, the procedure was not designed to accommodate a rehearing on the general merits of the cause or **on the basis that** the proceedings had been arbitrary or corrupt. (F-LOB, J 48)

[5] For readers not versed in the basics of English corpus linguistics: the 'Brown family' is a set of comparable one-million word corpora of written English documenting a broad range of written genres. The starting point was the Standard Corpus of Present-Day Edited American English, compiled at Brown University, Providence, RI, documenting American English in 1961, to which eventually the following four corpora were added: Lancaster-Oslo/Bergen (LOB, British English 1961), Freiburg update of Brown (Frown, American English, 1992), Freiburg update of LOB (F-LOB, British English 1991), 'before LOB' (B-LOB, British English, early 1930s).

(4) We play everything we do through them, working **on the basis that** if it sounds OK through them then it's going to sound OK anywhere! (F-LOB, E 31)

(5) **On the basis that** all citizens of the state are entitled to benefit equally in the development of its resources, plans for the provision of essential services (such as water) will be based on need regardless of arbitrary political boundaries [. . .] (Brown H 06)

(6) Until now, religious programmes gained a place in the schedules **on the basis** they were deemed an essential element of the balanced schedule demanded by previous legislation. (F-LOB G 66)

Similarly low figures are returned from small corpora of spoken English. The Diachronic Corpus of Present-Day Spoken English (DCPSE), a database matching components of the 1990s spoken material from ICE GB and the older London–Lund Corpus of spoken British English for real-time exploration of change in spoken English, attests *on the basis that* twice (in the 'new' material, as it happens), but the more interesting form without *that* is absent. Nor are the returns any more copious from the smaller standard historical reference corpora such as ARCHER—which, however, at least contains the following interesting structural variant (science, 1874):

(7) In the paper whose title is given above the author has shown upon experimental data, and **upon the acknowledged basis that** the amount of heat annually dissipated from our globe equals that evolved by 777 cubic miles of ice at 32° melted to water at the same temperature, what is the amount of heat that can be annually produced by the transformation of the mechanical work of mean rock when crushed [. . .]

The message from these exploratory investigations of small corpora is obvious. They may be sufficient in size to study grammaticalization of high-frequency core grammatical categories such as articles or the more common exponents of tense and aspect, but they are insufficient when it comes to rarer types of clausal subordination. And indeed, the findings from some of the larger corpora are far more encouraging. The 100-million-word British National Corpus (BNC), for example, contains 473 attestations for *on the basis that.*[6] On this broader basis of attestations, statistical profiling across genres becomes a possibility and, indeed, yields some interesting contrasts. At a normalized frequency of 11.3 occurrences per million words, the form is most common in academic writing, followed by spoken

[6] The raw total yield was 480 instances, from which were discounted 6 cases in which *that* introduces a relative clause rather than an apposition clause and one difficult-to-interpret anacoluthon.

language (7.1 p.m.w.), newspapers (3.1), and fiction (0.7). Similarly, it is now possible to produce reliable findings on the incidence of the *that*-less variant.

The BNC is part-of-speech tagged, and even allowing for the inevitable mistaggings, a search for *on the basis,* followed by any instance of the categories [pronoun], [article/determiner], and [noun], with manual post-editing, should identify most of the relevant constructions. The search yields six uncontroversial instances, which are spread across speech and writing, and thus show that the form without *that* is already in regular if rare use:

(8) [. . .] we were disappointed the licence was eventually approved **on the basis** it could be revoked if obsolete [. . .] (written, miscellaneous)

(9) [. . .] picked Fox and Steve Bachop as the fly-halves, very likely **on the basis** they are much more accurate punters than Little. (written, popular lore)

(10) Will you let me go again **on the basis** I made a cock-up the first time round? (spoken, meeting)

(11) [. . .] it should be **on the basis** the vendor acknowledges that in all circumstances [. . .] (written, academic)[7]

Of course, it is now also possible to determine genre-specific proportions of the long and short variants of *on the basis (that)*: for example 79 vs. 2 in the BNC spoken material.

Stronger entrenchment of a grammatical form may lead to structural and phonetic reduction, as can be seen in the development of *because* or, more recently, in the parallel case of *on (the) condition (that)*. Expectedly, the BNC attests a few instances of *on basis*—all, however, in the collocation *on basis of + NP.* The Corpus of Contemporary American English (COCA), roughly four times the size of the BNC, seems to represent the order of magnitude which is required to capture the conjunction use of *on basis.*

(12) OK. Hey, Karl. He came out **on basis** [filled pause] **that** she called me up and said don't talk about it (spoken, broadcast discussion)

(13) On the basis of what? **On basis of** it was getting tough. (spoken, broadcast discussion)[8]

In all, the corpus evidence presented thus seems to support our working hypothesis that we are dealing with a case of incipient grammaticalization in contemporary English. Thereby, the term 'incipient' is subtly ambiguous. On the one hand, it can refer to a diachronic development which got under way only recently and is gathering momentum. On the other, incipience can also refer to cases of

[7] The same text presents a similar example later on.

[8] Similar contaminations between the constructions *on the basis* of + NP and *on the basis* + clause are attested for *on account.* Note that *on account* also shares the broadly causal semantics of *on (the) basis.*

experimental or arrested grammaticalization, i.e. a diachronically stable situation in which the conjunction-uses of *on (the) basis* have been a minor option for centuries, occasionally used but never developed any further. To decide between the two options, it is necessary to consult larger historical databases in order to find out whether *on the basis (that)* has become more frequent in the recent past. In this connection it is interesting to note that none of the *c.*10 relevant attestations from the *OED* quotation base antedates the year 1959, which would support the first of the two interpretations offered above.

A final word is in order on the use of more sophisticated statistical techniques than the essentially descriptive corpus statistics provided above. In the case of *on the basis that*, the number of attested examples even in very large corpora was too low for the application of inferential statistical methods or more sophisticated analytical procedures such as multi-factorial analysis. This is not to be seen as a straightforward handicap. After all, there are two good reasons for using corpus data: first (the present case) because they are authentic records of performance systematically extracted from a known database and suitable for qualitative-discourse analytical interpretation within a relevant theoretical framework, and secondly, because they may be sufficient for quantitative statistical profiling.

In fact, it is doubtful that in cases of incipient grammaticalization the amount of data will ever be sufficient for purely quantitative analysis—and in any event individual examples are usually so complex that they usually need to be interpreted in their own terms. However, when it comes to charting the spread and layering of already grammaticalized forms in the core grammar of the languages, sophisticated quantitative analyses have demonstrated their usefulness—as is shown, for example, by Szmrecsanyi's (2006) study of the *will* and *going-to* futures, which integrates classic variationism with psycholinguistics and discourse analysis to develop a statistical model of observed variation and change.

5. Conclusion

In spite of more than a decade of mutually beneficial cooperation between corpus linguistics and grammaticalization studies, one is tempted to conclude these reflections with the prediction that the best is yet to come. The massive attention currently paid to frequency effects in grammaticalization makes it likely that we shall arrive at a clearer understanding of the frequency factor in grammaticalization in the foreseeable future. This represents a major step ahead in the refinement of the current model, and will make it better able to weather criticism. Progress will not be confined to the frequency question, however. In the concluding words to the second edition of their textbook, Hopper and Traugott point out some of the important aspects of grammaticalization which they have not addressed, and it is striking that most of them involve the use of corpora:

> Several other areas of work have not been considered here. They include patterns of grammaticalization across styles and genres; the involvement of institutions such as education, language planning, and literacy in initiating, establishing or deferring change; and the role of psychological factors such as short- and long-term retention and attention. A fuller understanding of all these issues suggests that it is necessary to coordinate historical work with sociolinguistics, psycholinguistics, and corpus studies; such coordination should lead to a better understanding of the extent to which the locus of change is to be found in changes in grammars of the speech community, to what extent in the mind/brain of speakers, and how changes in language use may lead to changes in the language system. (2003: 233)

The biggest challenge facing corpus-informed work on grammaticalization, however, is to take the approach beyond the study of a single language and thus link up to the cross-linguistic typological dimension of grammaticalization theory. There are very few cross-linguistic corpus-based studies of grammaticalization at the moment (but cf. e.g. Aijmer 2004 or Uchida 2002), and more would certainly be welcome in the future. Two types of approaches I would consider particularly promising. The first would focus on language contact between pairs of languages in particular historical periods. For example, many European vernacular languages were influenced by contact with Latin during the period of their standardization, and the comparison of historical vernacular corpora with suitable Latin corpus materials would clearly be useful in many cases. The second promising approach would be to establish usage-based generalizations through cross-linguistic comparisons of corpora representing a large number of typologically diverse languages. In this way, cross-linguistic evidence could be provided for claims about the assumed fundamental role of frequency in grammaticalization processes, and central theoretical notions of grammaticalization theory, such as the cross-linguistically valid 'pathway of grammaticalization', could be fleshed out in a way that befits a mature usage-based model.

CHAPTER 20

GRAMMATICALIZATION AND LANGUAGE CHANGE IN THE INDIVIDUAL

HELENA RAUMOLIN-BRUNBERG
ARJA NURMI

1. Introduction

The behaviour of the individual language user has not been among the key issues in the rapidly growing literature on grammaticalization. Nor has it been a popular topic in the general studies of language change. In the last few years, however, the issue of individual usage has been addressed in some publications within present-day and historical sociolinguistics. These studies have not only dealt with phonology, which is the traditional area in sociolinguistics, but also covered morphosyntax and discourse and thus discussed changes that evolve by processes which can be characterized as grammaticalization.

The research reported here has been supported in part by the Academy of Finland and the Research Unit for Variation, Contacts, and Change in English (VARIENG).

We would like to argue that the viewpoint of the individual deserves more attention than has been the case thus far because, to underline the obvious but often forgotten fact, it is in the communication between individuals that linguistic innovations come about and changes diffuse. This is, of course, especially true for grammaticalization processes in which the interlocutors' subjective views and involvement often act as instruments of change.

Section 2 will provide a general discussion of the linguistic behaviour of individuals under change in progress, from both the cross-sectional and the longitudinal angles. These case studies mostly deal with the history of English. Section 3 will deal with studies of language change in the individual from the viewpoint of grammaticalization. Section 4 will offer a detailed case study of three auxiliaries in the language of three English gentlemen around the turn of the 17th century.

2. Individuals under ongoing language change

This section will provide a brief presentation of the role that an individual language user plays in change in progress. If we follow the life of a linguistic change in a chronological order, the first factor to look at is a prerequisite of a change, namely speaker innovation (Milroy and Milroy 1985). This term refers to a new form or meaning used by an individual speaker, the innovator. It is often the case that speaker innovations remain individual idiosyncrasies and do not spread to anyone else's language, but sometimes they do. Once these innovations have become part of the language of a group of people, they can be considered to be linguistic changes. In other words, it is individuals who provide the very first occurrences of phenomena that eventually develop into changes in language.

As sociolinguistic research (e.g. Labov 1994; 2001) has shown, the progression of a linguistic change, i.e. the increased use of a new element or meaning, can be described with an S-curve: a slow beginning, fast in the middle, and slow again when nearing completion. As long as the change goes on, there is variation between the new and old ways of expressing the same thing. The main question for the present chapter is how individuals behave under ongoing change. We are interested in both inter- and intra-individual variability.

It has become a well-established fact in sociolinguistics that the adoption of new forms and/or meanings is often constrained by social factors such as gender, status, education, age, ethnic group, and region. To give a few examples of relevant findings, in many changes women are ahead of men, upwardly mobile people often for reasons of prestige try to copy the usage of people who are socially their superiors, and young people employ new forms more than old people. We cannot claim, however, that all changes would be socially conditioned or that even changes that have been found to be constrained by external factors would remain so during the whole of their operation.

It is also known that people vary their usage according to the situation of language use, so that new linguistic elements usually occur first in informal spoken language and only later in more formal genres. The availability of computerized corpora, covering either one or several genres from the past or present, has made it relatively easy to carry out research dealing with different types of spoken and written language.

What is especially interesting for this chapter is, however, that people with identical social backgrounds do not always behave linguistically in an identical manner in identical situations. One explanation for this type of variation can be found in the varying roles that people play in their social networks (e.g. Milroy and Milroy 1985; Labov 2001). The Milroys argue that linguistic changes diffuse via weak links in loose-knit social networks, which may of course explain the more advanced use by some people. On the other hand, Labov found that a number of central members of social networks led changes in Philadelphia at the time when the change was progressing vigorously. These findings suggest that the phase of change might also correlate with an individual's susceptibility to adopting new forms. Furthermore, individual variability has also been observed in historical data (e.g. Raumolin-Brunberg 2006; Nevalainen, Raumolin-Brunberg, and Mannila 2011).

Nonetheless, not all variation between people with identical backgrounds varies according to social networks. People tend to have their individual preferences, which in turn are so delicate and personal that they cannot be analysed by the research tools available today. As for the longitudinal aspects of adopting innovative forms or meanings, language acquisition and the early years of life have been shown to be crucial. On the basis of his study of sound changes in Philadelphia, Labov (2001: 415–97) argues that it is not the youngest generation but the next youngest, between 4 and 17 years old, that accounts for the largest increase in the use of the incoming variant. After this period, stabilization takes place in an individual's language. Nevertheless, it has been demonstrated that this stabilization is not absolute, and that people can change (and some do change) their language even later in life (e.g. Raumolin-Brunberg 2005; 2009). Further research is needed to find out whether this type of change only means quantitative increase in the use of the new forms, as Tagliamonte and D'Arcy (2007) have argued, or whether adults also change grammatical constraints. In any case, the main findings obtained from the studies of the linguistic behaviour of individuals across their lifespans show that age plays a significant role in their participation in ongoing linguistic changes.

3. Grammaticalization and the Individual

The main question we address here concerns the character of changes developed by grammaticalization. Do these changes diffuse in a way that is different from other changes, or are the trajectories similar? Does individual usage regarding grammaticalized changes diverge from that of other changes?

Nevalainen and Raumolin-Brunberg (2003) have demonstrated that the external factors that sociolinguists have found to constrain variation in present-day languages are also valid for changes in the past. Their study of fourteen English morphosyntactic changes covers over ten generations of language users. Their material consists of personal letters, compiled to form the 2.7-million-word *Corpus of Early English Correspondence*, from *c.*1410 to 1680, representing the literate sections of late medieval and early modern society.

Among the changes studied, there were processes of grammaticalization, including the development of the prop-word *one* (*Out of the two handbags we saw I would like to have the smaller* ***one***), the compound pronouns in *-body* and *-one* (e.g. *anybody, someone, nobody, everyone*; *There was* ***no man/none*** *to help us* → *There was* ***nobody/no one*** *to help us*),[1] periphrastic *do* in affirmative statements (*I went home* → *I* ***did*** *go home*), and periphrastic *do* in negative statements (*I knew it not* → *I* ***did*** *not know it*). (For further discussion on *do*, see section 4 below.) One of the changes, the loss of multiple negation or negative concord (*I didn't do* ***nothing*** →*I didn't do* ***anything***), represents one element in the chain of the grammaticalization of negation, a well-known phenomenon in several languages (see Nevalainen and Palander-Collin, Chapter 10 above).

Although every change seems to have a history of its own as far as details are concerned, the diffusion of these changes on the whole does not differ significantly from the changes that do not involve grammaticalization. For example, like these changes, gender variation is discernible in changes resulting from grammaticalization; women are ahead of men in the introduction of prop-*one* and the new compound pronouns in *-body* and *-one*, while men lead in the loss of multiple negation. As regards the periphrastic *do* in both uses, there is a switch from male to female advantage around 1600.

The regional background also plays a role: we can see, for instance, that the speakers in the north of England preferred the *-one* variants of the new compound pronouns in the first part of the 17th century, and it took a long time for the *-body*

[1] Until the 19th century one of the meanings of the lexeme *body* was 'a human being of either sex, an individual', which obviously forms the source for the compound pronouns in *-body*. The head morpheme *one* goes back to the numeral—not directly, however, but via the pronoun *one*, which also had the meaning 'a person'. It is noteworthy that the head morpheme of the compounds that were gradually rejected, *man*, also had the meaning 'person (irrespective of sex)'. (For the development of these pronouns, see Raumolin-Brunberg 1994.)

pronouns to make their way to the north. Moreover, there is geographical variation that can be characteristic of very small regions only. Macaulay (2006), for example, shows how the adjective *pure* has been grammaticalized into an adverb in the language of adolescents in Glasgow but not elsewhere (e.g. *She is a* ***pure*** *daftie. I* ***pure*** *like her trainers*).

Although changes involving grammaticalization seem to be socially embedded like other changes, we would like to emphasize that this is not the case for all changes. Consider, for example, anaphoric and cataphoric uses of common-number pronouns (such as the anaphoric reference to an antecedent using the pronouns *he* or *they*, e.g. *a person... he/they*, and cataphoric relative clause constructions *he that/who...*, *they that/who...*, and *those that/who...*) from the early 15th century to the end of the 17th. Studying the use of all these, Laitinen (2007: 203–41) found stable variation in the anaphora, conditioned by gender, so that women used the form *they* more than men. On the other hand, as to the cataphora, the change from *he that/who...* and *they that/who* to the present-day *those who...* seemed to progress without any social conditioning except genre variation, suggesting an origin in speech.

What the above suggests is that, under an ongoing grammaticalization process, the social and regional backgrounds of individual language users determine at least to some extent how each person uses the new form or meaning.

After discussing speaker variables, we shall turn to situational language use, i.e. register and genre variation. There is ample evidence of grammaticalization processes that have had their origin in the informal spoken language, such as the development of common-number pronouns introduced above.

The introduction of the above-mentioned compound pronouns in *-body*, studied in the multi-genre *Helsinki Corpus of English Texts* (Raumolin-Brunberg 1994), can serve as one example. The first occurrences of the *-body* pronouns were found in oral genres from 1500 to 1640, and only later did they spread into more literate types of writing. Even today, the pronouns in *-body* are more frequent in informal language. By contrast, the compounds in *-one* do not follow the same pattern but are used more in the more formal genres, which suggests that the origination in informal spoken language cannot be taken as a rule but a tendency.

As regards the mechanism of diffusion of grammaticalized forms, Moore (2007) argues in her article on the diffusion of grammaticalized forms, with the development of the semimodal deontic and epistemic meanings of *be* + *supposed to* as a case study, that ambiguity and frequency play important roles in the process. According to her, the semi-modal uses were first found in conversational genres, and at some point in the late 19th century some written genres began to use them, while other, more conservative ones, relied on the pregrammaticalized senses. She concludes:

> Because the process of writing allows the writer time to rethink and rephrase, it creates an environment in which the ambiguous forms can serve both initially as a stimulus for the

spread of a new grammatical sense and later as a deterrent for the use of the conservative sense. Such pragmatic impulses help us to see how our models of semantic change *be + supposed to* work. (Moore 2007: 129)

Regarding the behaviour of individual language users, it is likely that many people consciously or unconsciously select grammaticalized and pregrammaticalized senses for different types of text. This is, however, an area where further research is needed.

As mentioned in the previous section, Labov's arguments concerning the significance of adolescents in the progression of linguistic changes were based on research on sound changes. In a very thorough article, Tagliamonte and D'Arcy (2009) show that Labov's findings are not limited to phonology only, but in broad terms are also valid for other types of change. The objects of their investigation were six shifts currently ongoing in Toronto, representing morphosyntax and discourse pragmatics: *have to* for expressing deontic modality; *have* for marking stative possession; *going to* for encoding future temporal sense; *like* as a discourse marker; *be like* as a quotative complementizer; and *so* as an intensifying adverb (Tagliamonte and D'Arcy 2009: 71). Although the authors do not use the concept of grammaticalization, it is not difficult to place the changes in this framework.

The distributional analysis of the above changes indicates that the adolescent years are both decisive and foundational in the acquisition process, as was suggested by Labov (2001) for phonology. The adolescent peak manifests itself most clearly in high-frequency changes that are progressing at a fast rate. Gender asymmetry was also confirmed, with the consequence that men and women of the same age in the same community could represent different stages of change: women reflected a more advanced stage than men (Tagliamonte and D'Arcy 2009: 97). What these findings show is once more the fact that the social context and the speaker's background to a large extent determine the ways individuals participate in ongoing linguistic changes.

4. The auxiliaries *do*, *will* and *would* in the language of three individuals

Our case study deals with three auxiliaries in the late 16th and early 17th century: periphrastic *do* in negative statements and the modal auxiliaries *will* and *would*. We track the grammaticalization processes of each during the lifespan of three gentlemen, Sir Walter Ralegh (1554–1618), Philip Gawdy (1562–1617), and John Chamberlain (1553–1628). The material consists of personal letters included in the *Corpus of*

Early English Correspondence (CEEC) and its *Supplement* (CEECSU). The size of the personal data files are as follows: Ralegh *c.*40,000 words, Gawdy *c.*58,000 words, and Chamberlain *c.*69,000 words. Their letter-writing careers spanned several decades. More information on the corpora can be found in Nurmi, Nevala, and Palander-Collin (2009); background data on the informants can be found in e.g. Raumolin-Brunberg (2009).

During the Early Modern English period, periphrastic *do* was increasingly used as an operator in negated statements and imperatives, as well as in questions, leading eventually to the Present-day English obligatory *do*-support. In this study, we are concerned with the use of *do* in negated statements. The speed of development and timing of changes attested is divergent in different genres (Ellegård 1953; Nurmi 1999; Warner 2005), but in correspondence, the 16th century was a time of steady increase, with a notable drop in the frequency of usage in the first decade of the 17th century, and a further increasing trend after that. A constant in the spread of *do* to negated statements is the so-called *know* group (first identified by Ellegård), which consists of verbs averse to being combined with *do* in negation. The most frequent items in this group are *know* and *doubt*, which are tracked in this study. Examples (1)–(2) illustrate the use/non-use of *do* with the main group of verbs and (3)–(4) with the *know* group. At this point in its development, *do* is never used in the contracted form *don't* in our data.

(1) I *here not* from any part of the world as yet (Sir Walter Ralegh, 1602; Ralegh2 237)[2]
(2) I *do not here* how yow like the white stonn. (Sir Walter Ralegh, 1595; Ralegh 133)
(3) I *know not* whether any miscreant gready companion hath brought any thing to yowr handes agaynst me. (Philip Gawdy, 1602; Gawdy2 118)
(4) And now agaynst Christmas we thinke yow sholde remember olde Peter the tothe drawer for a Christmas man in the Chimneye corner but I *do not knowe* that euer he trauyled withe any mystris. (Philip Gawdy, 1600; Gawdy2 111).

Table 20.1 shows the spread of *do* in the usage of the three individuals. The table attests to clear inter-individual variation despite the relatively similar backgrounds of the three gentlemen, who lived most of their lives in the London area. In addition, apart from the difference between the main group and *know* and *doubt*, there seems little evidence to connect our findings with the general progression of this shift. For the main group of verbs, the decrease of *do* in the first decade of the 17th century found in correspondence in general is not clearly reflected in any of the men's usage. Ralegh shows a constant increase, Gawdy a fairly steady usage

[2] Examples from the corpus provide name of writer, year of writing, collection code and page number of the edition. See the appendix in Nurmi et al. (2009) for collection codes and details of editions used.

Table 20.1. *Do* in negative statements (excluding auxiliaries, *have, be, need, dare,* and *ought*)

	Age	Main group				*Know* and *doubt*			
		zero	*do*	%	Total	zero	*do*	%	Total
Walter Ralegh (Chi-square 6.40; p<0.025)									
1581–99	27–45	13	3	*19*	16	12	3	*18*	15
1600–18	46–64	23	28	*55*	51	9	0		9
Total[a]		36	31	*46*	67	21	3	*13*	24
Philip Gawdy									
1579–89	17–27	27	14	*34*	41	10	0		10
1590–99	28–37	16	7	*30*	23	10	0		10
1600–16	38–54	27	12	*31*	39	22	6	*21*	28
Total[a]		70	33	*32*	103	42	6	*13*	48
John Chamberlain									
1597–1609	44–56	12	4	*25*	16	13	0		13
1610–19	57–66	33	12	*27*	45	48	0		48
1620–25	67–72	12	2	*14*	14	8	0		8
Total[a]		57	18	*24*	75	69	0	*0*	69

[a] Comparison of the three totals: Chi-square 8.04; p<0.025.

level, and Chamberlain a decrease. In Chamberlain's case, it is possible to postulate that he is displaying a delayed reaction to the general decline of *do*, but there is no concrete evidence one way or the other. As far as the *know* group is concerned, all three men show a clear trend of avoidance. Chamberlain never uses *do* with these verbs, Ralegh only occasionally, and Gawdy only in the 17th century. Here the general trends in the order of grammaticalization seem somewhat evident.

The two modal auxiliaries studied, *will* and *would*, are part of two different processes of grammaticalization. On the one hand, they are changing from main verbs into auxiliaries. On the other, they are involved in a gradual semantic change. The process of change has again been tracked in various data sets (see e.g. Kytö 1991; Gotti et al. 2002; Nurmi 2002). During the 16th and 17th centuries, *will* and *would* both increase in frequency, although the rate of change seems more moderate for *would*. The semantic change has been differently described, depending on the models of modal meaning adopted, but e.g. Gotti et al. (2002) have presented corpus-based evidence to support the sequence suggested by Bybee, Pagliuca, and Perkins (1994): DESIRE > WILLINGNESS > INTENTION > PREDICTION.

The usage of both *will* and *would* as a main verb is already rare in our data, and the usage of *would* reflects its original function as the past tense form of *will*. Meanwhile, the main verb *will* has also a new past tense form, *willed*. Examples (5)–(7) illustrate the main verb usage of *will* and *would*.

(5) I will take my iorney to be with yow before the tyme apoynted, If God *will* and he gyveth me lyfe (Philip Gawdy, 1592; Gawdy 66)

(6) Sr Robert Jermin with bothe the Ladyes *willed* me to remember their commendacions bothe to my ffather and yow. (Philip Gawdy, 1581; Gawdy 6)

(7) at all adventures I *wold* her sister Jane were no worse bestowed. (John Chamberlain, 1624; Chamberlain II, 587)

Table 20.2 shows that main verb use of both *will* and *would* is fairly marginal in the language of all three informants. Minor differences occur, since Ralegh and Chamberlain use *would* more as a main verb, while Gawdy gives *will* a slight advantage. There is also no clear change in time; rather, the appearance of main verbs seems to be limited to certain contexts, and when these contexts appear, the main verb is also used. This can be described as the final tail of an S-curve. As with *do*, none of

Table 20.2. *Will* and *would* as main verbs and auxiliaries[a]

	Main verb			Auxiliary			% main verb	
	will	*would*	Total	*will*	*would*	Total	*will*	*would*
Walter Ralegh								
1581–99	2	2	4	130	40	170	1.5	5.0
1600–18	2	2	4	168	39	207	1.2	5.1
Total	4	4	8	298	79	377	1.3	5.1
Philip Gawdy								
1579–89	3	1	4	115	51	166	2.6	2.0
1590–99	5	0	5	128	28	156	3.9	0.0
1600–18	2	1	3	211	56	267	0.9	1.8
Total	10	2	12	454	135	589	2.2	1.5
John Chamberlain								
1597–99	0	0	0	13	7	20	0.0	0.0
1600–09	0	1	1	36	21	57	0.0	4.8
1610–19	2	1	3	137	64	201	1.5	1.6
1620–25	1	1	2	30	11	41	3.3	9.1
Total	3	3	6	216	103	319	1.4	2.9

[a] The frequencies of the main verbs are too low for statistical significance testing.

the three men use contracted forms of the auxiliaries, neither with subject pronouns nor in negations.

The meanings of *will* in this study have been analysed in terms of two major categories, volition and prediction. Volition (example 8) covers deontic senses, both external and internal obligation and the few dynamic uses indicating ability, while prediction (example 9) covers the expressions of likelihood and probability from neutral future to a handful of epistemic cases. The sense of future action is often present even in the volitional cases, but the strongest modal sense of each example has been taken into account.

(8) I *will* remayne yours before all the worlde (Sir Walter Ralegh, 1601; Ralegh 213)

(9) men doubt the chauncellor of Cambridge *will* scant follow his example (John Chamberlain, 1605; Chamberlain I,208)

The usage of *will* seems fairly stable throughout the lifespans of Ralegh and Gawdy. It could be argued that they have adopted a pattern of use in adolescence and are following it through their adult lives. The only notable fluctuation in the

Table 20.3. The senses of modal *will*

	Volition		Prediction		Total
	N	%	N	%	
Walter Ralegh					
1581–99	66	50.8	64	49.2	130
1600–18	89	53.0	79	47.0	168
Total[a]	155	52.0	143	48.0	298
Philip Gawdy					
1579–89	80	69.6	35	30.4	115
1590–99	89	69.5	39	30.5	128
1600–18	145	68.7	66	31.3	211
Total[a]	314	69.2	140	30.8	454
John Chamberlain (Chi-square 13.86; $p<0.01$)					
1597–9	1	7.7	12	92.3	13
1600–09	19	52.8	17	47.2	36
1610–19	69	50.4	68	59.6	137
1620–25	8	26.7	22	73.3	30
Total[a]	97	44.9	119	55.1	216

[a] Comparison of the three totals: Chi-square 42.86; $p<0.001$. Differences only statistically significant where so indicated.

pattern is in the letters of John Chamberlain. As far as the earliest subperiod goes, this is more than likely at least partly due to the small sample, but otherwise there seems to be a rising trend as evidence for the predictive uses and a decline in volition.

For the purposes of this study, the senses of *would* were divided into two major categories, volition (example 10) and hypothetical (example 11). The first is closer to the main verb sense of the verb, but also includes the various uses of *would* as the past tense form of *will.* The latter is the later development, which eventually includes epistemic senses. Roughly speaking, volition here stands for deontic *would*, while hypothetical includes dynamic and epistemic uses.

(10) but me thinckes they should have litle to do that *wold* adventure themselves so far with a man able to do them no more goode (John Chamberlain, 1604; Chamberlain I,198)

(11) I have thought yow *wold* have taken some order before this touching the buying of your lyveryes. (Philip Gawdy, 1587; Gawdy 13)

Table 20.4 shows that while Ralegh's usage could be interpreted as a gradual increase of the incoming, hypothetical uses, both Gawdy and Chamberlain show

Table 20.4. The senses of modal *would*

	Volition		Hypothetical		Total
	N	%	N	%	
Walter Ralegh					
1581–99	17	42.5	23	57.5	40
1600–1618	15	38.5	24	61.5	39
Total[a]	32	40.5	47	59.5	79
Philip Gawdy (Chi-square 6.83; p<0.05)					
1579–89	24	47.1	27	52.9	51
1590–99	18	64.3	10	35.7	28
1600–1618	40	71.4	16	28.6	56
Total[a]	82	60.7	53	39.3	135
John Chamberlain					
1597–9	3	42.9	4	57.1	7
1600–1609	12	57.1	9	42.9	21
1610–19	48	75.0	16	25.0	64
1620–25	8	72.7	3	27.3	11
Total[a]	71	68.9	32	31.1	103

[a] Comparison of the three totals: Chi-square 15.41; p<0.001.

the opposite pattern, using more of the volitional senses as time goes on. This might again reflect the varying contexts of usage, but could also be taken as evidence of individual preferences, which can oppose the general pattern of change.

5. Conclusion

The results of the above case study are in line with the findings of previous research testifying to a great deal of variation between individuals concerning their participation in ongoing linguistic changes. The patterns that arise from studies of large groups of people do not necessarily surface in the language of individuals. We can also see that even if a person's language shows lifespan changes with regard to a particular feature, here seen in Ralegh's use of negative *do* and Chamberlain's *will*, in other shifts, the same person goes on using the forms/meanings acquired in their youth.

It seems obvious that the rate of change, which indeed can vary greatly (e.g. Nevalainen and Raumolin-Brunberg 2003), provides unequal opportunities for observing ongoing changes. Rapid changes, such as replacing the English 3rd person singular suffix *-th* with *-s* around 1600, can be seen in the language of several individuals, even in that of the three gentlemen under investigation here (Raumolin-Brunberg 2009: 177–81). On the basis of our case study here, it would seem that the processes of grammaticalization tend to be rather slow, making it difficult to observe them in individuals' linguistic practices over their lifetime. Access to very large datasets that evenly represent the course of an informant's life would, of course, enhance the possibilities for idiolectal observations. On the whole, however, we would like to argue that there is no reason to believe that the diffusion of changes resulting from grammaticalization processes should in principle differ from that of other linguistic changes, with regard both to populations and to idiolects.

CHAPTER 21

GRAMMATICALIZATION IN NON-STANDARD VARIETIES OF ENGLISH

BERND KORTMANN
AGNES SCHNEIDER

1. Introduction

This chapter's focus is on grammaticalization phenomena in non-standard varieties of English which are not (or certainly not to the same degree) found in spontaneous spoken varieties of Standard English. Our overall aim is to draw a general, though by no means exhaustive, picture, and to point specifically to the wide range of interesting grammaticalization phenomena to be observed in the non-standard (including contact) varieties of English (and, no doubt, other languages). The basic assumption underlying the present chapter is this: spoken language is the primary motor of language change, and thus we take spoken language to be the natural habitat for most grammaticalization processes. This applies to first signs and traces of grammaticalization and/or to higher degrees of grammaticalization compared with the corresponding processes observable in written language.

Major questions to be addressed include the following. Are there markedly different grammaticalization patterns in spontaneous spoken non-standard varieties compared with what we know about (written and spoken) standard varieties of English? Are there instances of grammaticalization which operate on a global level in the Anglophone world, i.e. qualify as 'angloversals' (cf. Szmrecsanyi and Kortmann 2009 on the concept of and candidates for angloversals)? In which domains of non-standard grammars, in particular, can we observe such processes? Do different variety types (e.g. traditional, typically low-contact L1 dialects vs. high-contact L1 varieties vs. pidgins and creoles) display differences, or at least different preferences, concerning grammaticalization patterns, such as variety-type specific sources and targets, the nature (internal vs. contact-induced grammaticalization) or degrees of grammaticalization (e.g. rather early vs. (more) advanced stages)? Which of the observable grammaticalization processes are innovative in the history of English? Which ones rather represent continuations of or constitute, ultimately, 're-enactments' of internal grammaticalization processes known from the history of English? This leads on to the following two questions: For varieties with a pronounced contact history, are the relevant processes contact-/substrate-induced or perhaps rather induced by the superstrate? (Note that in the vast majority of historical contact scenarios it was a non-standard L1 variety which served as the superstrate leading to the contact varieties and pidgin and creole languages in our sample.) And where grammaticalization processes clearly seem to be substrate-induced, can we identify different grammaticalization patterns (again, in terms of sources, targets, or paths) depending on the Anglophone world region where the relevant variety is or the relevant varieties are spoken (e.g. Africa vs. Caribbean vs. Pacific)? The answers to all these questions will provide us with kind of a 'miniature world atlas of grammaticalization' on the basis of (largely non-standard) varieties of English and English-based pidgin and creole languages.

After a brief account of the data forming the foundation of this survey (section 2), the bulk of this chapter will be concerned with grammaticalization phenomena in individual variety types, zooming in on two domains of grammar: pronouns and tense and aspect (section 3). It is in the concluding section 4 where, among other things, the question will be addressed to what extent the relevant features observable in non-standard varieties of English and World Englishes can be interpreted as results of changes which have or have not been recorded in the grammaticalization literature before (either in the history of (Standard) English or maybe even in diachronic typology, i.e. across languages, as documented in Heine and Kuteva 2002). The focus of the following bird's-eye view on grammaticalization in the Anglophone world will clearly be on the outcomes of the relevant changes. Due to the nature of our data, the large number of varieties within the scope of our endeavour, and—not least—space constraints, it will be possible neither to discuss the contexts, steps, and mechanisms giving rise to these changes nor to provide fine-grained semantic or pragmatic observations.

2. Data

The two major data sources which the present chapter draws upon are the grammar sketches in the second volume (*Morphology and Syntax*) of the *Handbook of Varieties of English* (Kortmann et al. 2004) and, above all, the data collected as part of an ongoing research and publication project, the *World Atlas of Variation in English: Grammar* (henceforth *WAVE*; see Lunkenheimer in preparation; Kortmann in preparation). Out of a total of 74 varieties of English representing four basic variety types, data sets for 52 varieties from all Anglophone world regions have been selected for analysis here (see Table 21.1). Each data set consists of pervasiveness ratings by (often native speaker) specialist(s) on 235 morphosyntactic features from a dozen domains of morphosyntax.

In adopting a global perspective on variation in English, it is important to have representatives of different variety types in the sample, with the degree of dialect or language contact as the crucial underlying parameter for classification (cf. Trudgill 2009 and Kortmann and Szmrecsanyi to appear for details on this classification and the role of dialect and language contact in morphosyntactic simplification processes). In this context, it should also be remembered that Heine and Kuteva (2006: esp. 265–83) consider grammaticalization as the major type of grammatical replication, a process which in the case of English, for example, is not a one-way street (i.e. structures of English grammar serving as a model for another, replica language). Even a superficial look at the so-called World Englishes reveals, for example, that English has also been at the receiving, i.e. replica, end, with the grammatical structures of the relevant contact languages in different parts of the Anglophone world serving as models. Hence cross-varietal differences concerning the nature and degree of grammaticalization are expected to correlate with the differences in the nature and degree to which the individual varieties and English-based pidgin and creole languages in our sample have been exposed to and affected by dialect and/or language contact.

What is of particular interest in the present chapter is the distinction between internal and contact-induced grammaticalization. Thus it is in low-contact L1 varieties, i.e. traditional, regional dialects which are long-established non-standard mother tongue varieties, that the vast majority of all grammaticalization phenomena to be observed are the result of internal grammaticalization. It is for these varieties, too, that we might expect to find grammatical markers exhibiting a higher degree of (internal) grammaticalization than in any of the other varieties of English. A first indication of this is the fact that, of all variety types in English, traditional dialects exhibit clearly the highest degree of syntheticity in grammar (i.e. of bound grammatical markers; cf. e.g. Szmrecsanyi and Kortmann 2009; Kortmann and Szmrecsanyi to appear). The situation can be assumed to be similar for those high-contact L1 varieties with a dialect contact history, i.e. so-called

Table 21.1. Data sets for 52 varieties in the sample

Anglophone world region	Low-contact L1 (9)	High-contact L1 (13)	L2 (12)	P/C (18)
British Isles	Orkney and Shetland, North of England, SW of England, SE of England, East Anglia, Scottish E	Irish E, Channel Islands E, Manx E, Maltese E		British C
America	Newfoundland E, Appalachian E, Ozark E	Colloquial American E, Earlier African-American Vernacular E; Falkland Islands E	Chicano E	Gullah
Caribbean		Bahamian E	Jamaican E	Belizean C, Trinidadian C, Bahamian C, Eastern Maroon C, Guyanese C, San Andrés C, Vincentian C
Australia		Aboriginal E, Australian E		Torres Strait C, Roper River C (Kriol)
Pacific		New Zealand E	Colloquial Fiji E, Fiji E	Hawaiian C, Bislama, Norf'k
Africa		St. Helena E; Tristan da Cunha E	Cameroon E, Ghanaian E, Nigerian E, Kenyan E	Nigerian P, Cameroon P, Krio
South and Southeast Asia			Indian E, Pakistan E, Hong Kong E, Malaysian E	Butler E

C = Creole; E = English; P = Pidgin.

transplanted L1 Englishes or colonial varieties, such as New Zealand English. Other high-contact L1 varieties with a settlement history involving not just prolonged contact among speakers of different L1 dialects but of L1 (dialect) speakers and one or more other (typically typologically radically different) languages can be expected to feature a somewhat larger, if still moderate proportion of contact-induced grammaticalization phenomena, as in Bahamian English; or take language-shift Englishes like Irish English which shifted or are currently shifting from erstwhile L2 to L1 varieties.

At the other end of the continuum concerning contact-induced grammaticalization, we should expect to find English-based pidgins and creoles with their dramatic language contact histories. The reader may note that for the most part in this chapter, pidgins and creoles will be considered as belonging to the same variety type (P/C) since practically all pidgins in our sample, few as there are, qualify as expanded pidgins. As our specialist informants from the community of creolists have made amply clear it is difficult, and somewhat arbitrary from a synchronic perspective, to draw a clear line between expanded pidgins (such as the West African pidgins) and creoles, both structurally and socioculturally.

L2 varieties typically emerged in countries where English was introduced in the colonial era either in face-to-face communication or (more usually) via the education system. Their current status is that they qualify as non-native, indigenized varieties of English lacking significant numbers of native speakers, but that in some political communities they nonetheless enjoy prestige and important normative status. Thus although these varieties, too, clearly qualify as contact varieties, they often exhibit a morphosyntax which is closer to that of Standard Englishes than that of any of the other variety types.

3. Grammaticalization in different domains of grammar

Out of the 235 features contained in WAVE, almost a third qualify as instances of 'classic' cases of grammaticalization. In other words, they meet the definition(s) of grammaticalization given by Hopper and Traugott (1993; 2003): as the process [1993] or, more neutrally, 'the change whereby lexical items and constructions come in certain linguistic contexts to serve grammatical functions and, once grammaticalized, continue to develop new grammatical functions' (2003: xv). For the present survey, the following domains of morphosyntax have been explored in the search for instances of grammaticalization: pronouns, the noun phrase, the verb phrase (tense and aspect, modal verbs, verb morphology), negation, complementation, and relativization.

In sections 3.2 and 3.3 we will zoom in on two of these grammatical domains, tense and aspect and pronouns, concentrating on the results of grammaticalization rather than on the responsible mechanisms themselves, and only on the most widely found grammaticalization phenomena. Ultimately, we are trying to move some way towards a typology of grammaticalization phenomena (and the relevant paths leading to them) which will allow us to distinguish (a) continuations of grammaticalization processes documented in Standard English or earlier periods thereof from innovations, (b) regional (and thus possibly substrate-/ contact-triggered) features from global ones, and (c) variety-type specific features from features found across several or all of the variety types represented in our sample.

3.1. Survey

Table 21.2 gives an overview of the grammatical domains and grammaticalization-relevant features in each of these domains.

The tense and aspect (T&A) domain proves to be that domain of grammar in which we find the largest amount of grammaticalization-relevant features in our data set, with almost a third of all relevant features belonging to this category (see Table 21.3 below), followed by the domains of the noun phrase, pronouns (see Table 21.4), and verb morphology.

Table 21.2. Grammaticalization-relevant WAVE features per domain of grammar

DOMAIN	No. of features per domain of morphosyntax	% grammaticalization survey
Pronouns	9	12.5
Noun phrase	10	13.9
Verb phrase I: tense and aspect	22	30.6
Verb phrase II: modal verbs	4	5.6
Verb phrase III: verb morphology	9	12.5
Negation	5	6.9
Relativization	6	8.3
Complementation	7	9.7
TOTAL	72	100.0

With regard to the ranking of particular WAVE features according to their pervasiveness among varieties of English, it seems noteworthy that only two grammaticalization features are represented in more than 75 per cent of all 52 varieties in the sample and that only another two are attested in more than 50 per cent of them. The relevant features are the following: 'forms or phrases for the 2nd person plural pronoun other than *you*' (found in 77 per cent worldwide), '*never* as preverbal past tense negator' (found in 75 per cent worldwide), 'wider range of uses of the progressive: extension to stative verbs', and 'indefinite but specified article *one*' (found in 50 per cent and 52 per cent respectively). However, taking a closer look at the ranking of features for individual variety types, it becomes clear that many grammaticalization features are restricted either to a certain Anglophone world region or to a particular variety type, with the latter being definitely the stronger factor. The number of top features, i.e. features found in at least 75 per cent of the varieties of the relevant world region or representing a given variety type, is higher for individual variety types, with pidgins and creoles exhibiting the highest number of such top features (six in pidgins, five in creoles). This supports the assumption that many of the grammaticalization features discussed here represent typical developments in English-based pidgins and creoles. It is also noteworthy that in traditional L1 as well as in L2 varieties, more than half of the grammaticalization features in our data set do not exist at all. This shows that a large proportion of the grammaticalization features can be characterized as typical developments of (extreme) language contact situations, thus figuring prominently in pidgins and creoles and also, if to a lesser extent, in high-contact L1 varieties. Although L2 varieties, by their very nature, are contact varieties, too, most of them are rather standard(ized) varieties and thus cannot be expected to exhibit a large number of grammatical innovations. What we often encounter in their morphosyntax are rather regularizations and/or overgeneralizations as well as some innovations on the lexico-grammatical level. Moreover, as shown, for example, in Szmrecsanyi and Kortmann (2009), L2 varieties exhibit the lowest degree of grammaticity, i.e. overt morphosyntactic marking (be it synthetic or analytic), of all variety types of English.

3.2. Tense and aspect

Table 21.3 offers the complete list with a brief description of each of the relevant features and examples. Almost all of features 1–14 qualify as instances of internal grammaticalization (except for 4), whereas all of the other features can best be considered as the outcomes of contact-induced grammaticalization.

The first group of grammaticalization features (1–4) represents more advanced stages of grammaticalization processes than can be observed in Standard English. The extension of the progressive to stative contexts (1) is the most pervasive in this

Table 21.3. Grammaticalization in the domain of tense and aspect

1	Wider range of uses of the StE progressive: progressive with stative verbs	*She **is having** a child with a certain man from Ho* (Ghanaian E); *You **must be knowing** him* (Indian E)
2	Wider range of uses of the StE progressive: progressive to denote (non-delimited) habituals	*My holiday (Saturday, Sunday), I **am usually going** to library* (Hong Kong E)
3	Levelling of the difference between present perfect and simple past: present perfect for StE simple past	*I **have seen him yesterday*** (Pakistani E)
4	*would* for remote future	*I **would eat/would be eating** rice tomorrow* (Malaysian E)
5	*be sat/stood* with progressive meaning	*When you**'re stood*** ('are standing') *there you can see the flames* (Irish E)
6	*there* with past participle in resultative contexts	***There's something fallen** down the sink* (Scottish E)
7	Medial object perfect	*And you eat nothing till you **have the stations made**.* (Irish E)
8	Completive/perfect marker *slam*	*I **slam** told you not to mess up* (South Eastern American E)
9	Invariant *be* as habitual marker	*He **be** sick* 'He is always/usually sick' (African American Vernacular E)
10	*do* as habitual marker	*He **does** catch fish pretty* (Bajan)
11	Other non-standard habitual markers: *do be/ does be + V (+ -ing)*	e.g. combination of *do* and *be*: *He **do be** sick a lot* (Newfoundland E)
12	(Preverbal) completive/ perfect marker *done*	*Uh **done eat** dat one (already)* (Gullah)
13	Completive/ perfect *have/ be + done +* past participle	*He **is done gone*** (Earlier African American E)
14	*do* as a TA marker: *did* as (relative) past tense marker	*Ten tauzin yiers ago dem **did penichriet** all dem ting* 'Ten thousand years ago they already understood all those things' *(Jamaican C)*
15	*go*-based future markers	e.g. *Uh ain **ga** go nowhere* 'I won't go anywhere' (Gullah); *he **gon** build my house* (Turks Islands E)
16	perfect marker *already*	*We did move here a week **already*** 'We had moved here a week previously' (Cape Flats E)
17	*finish*-derived completive markers	*wakum gaden blong mifala **finis*** 'I have completed my work in our garden' (Solomon Islands P)

18	Volition-based future markers other than *will* (e.g. derived from *want* or *like*)	*a tel dem pipl da nobadi els* ***wan*** *de da kamp* 'I told them that nobody else will be at the camp' (Belize C); *em i* ***laik*** *go long gaden* 'he likes/is about to go to the garden' (Tok Pisin)
19	*come*-based future/ingressive markers	*I am* ***coming*** *to cook your meal* 'I am about to cook your meal' (Ghanaian E)
20a	Habitual marker *stap* or *stay*	*me* ***stap*** *ronron* 'I jog [every day]' (Bislama)
20b	Progressive marker *stap* or *stay*	*ol i wokabout i* ***stap*** 'they are walking'; *Hem i* ***stap*** *kaekae* 'He is eating' (Tok Pisin)
21	*ever* as marker of experiential perfect	*Last time I* ***ever bought*** *something on sale.* 'I have bought something on sale in the past' (Singapore E)
22	*after*-perfect	*She's* ***after selling*** *the boat* 'She has just sold the boat' (Irish E)

domain and one of the top candidates for a so-called angloversal. It can be found in more than half the varieties in our 52-varieties sample across all Anglophone world regions, but especially in L2 varieties. As the English progressive is widely acknowledged to be a category developing a more extended meaning range (ultimately resulting in a general imperfective marker; cf. Comrie 1976; Gachelin 1997), its extension to new meanings and uses in (spontaneous spoken) non-standard varieties could, in principle, be seen as a continuation of an ongoing process in the standard (especially in written Standard English). However, the extension of the progressive to habitual contexts (feature 2) seems to be less frequent among the varieties in our sample, and it is here that we can actually find different developments in high-contact and low-contact varieties. Whereas the extension of the progressive to stative contexts is a phenomenon that is pervasive in all variety types, its extension to habitual contexts seems largely restricted to L2 and high-contact L1 varieties (as well as to a few pidgins and creoles). Recently, Sharma (2009) has argued that while the extension of the English progressive seems to be a universal phenomenon, the way in which it is extended in the Anglophone world is heavily influenced by the way in which the respective substrate language of a variety deals with aspect. Thus an explanation merely based on explanations of universal tendencies of language change and language acquisition might well be premature.

The use of the present perfect as a narrative tense also belongs to the group of continuations of internal grammaticalization processes in English and, more broadly, Germanic (think especially of Dahl's 'perfect chain' from resultative to perfect to (narrative) past: 1985: 132f.). It is widespread among L2 varieties and L1 varieties across all world regions and is the second most pervasive feature in this domain. While the use of the perfect in narrative contexts has been observed to be common at a very advanced stage of the development of perfects across the languages of the world (cf. Dahl 1985; Bybee, Pagliuca, and Perkins 1994), its occurrence again seems to be more prominent among L2 and high-contact L1 varieties. This, of course, immediately leads on to the question whether intense contact with other languages simply triggers changes along typologically common paths or whether we are faced with a reinforcing influence from substrate languages in the individual cases.

The use of *would* as a remote future marker (feature 4) is largely restricted to high-contact L1 and L2 varieties. Possible reasons include the influence from substrate languages which distinguish degrees of remoteness via the use of certain tense markers. However, its use in Standard English as a conditional modal might have grammaticalized in these varieties as a marker of remote future, since an event in the distant future also usually carries a higher degree of uncertainty than events in the near future. After all, its distribution across varieties in the Caribbean, Africa, and Asia suggests that an explanation based on certain usage patterns in the superstrate equally needs to be considered in this case.

The remaining features in this domain represent grammaticalization processes that are non-standard in form. Features 5–8 belong to the group that represent processes primarily found in L1 varieties. They include the use of *there* with the past participle in resultative contexts, which is the most pervasive among them. The medial object perfect can be found in both low-contact and high-contact L1 varieties. Its development in Irish English dialects has been discussed in some detail by Pietsch (2009), who mentions the link to a functionally similar construction in Irish Gaelic but also to earlier constructions in Standard English. The use of *be sat/stood* with progressive meaning, by contrast, is largely restricted to traditional, low-contact L1 varieties (especially to the more conservative ones). Finally, the use of *slam* as a completive and perfect marker is a feature that has been reported only for dialects in the Southeast of the United States (cf. Wolfram 2004).

Features 9–13 form a group of 'transplanted' dialect features. They do exist in the so-called 'founder' L1 varieties (typically of former settlement colonies), but have reached a more advanced stage of grammaticalization, and are more pervasive and/ or more obligatory in pidgins and creoles and (to a lesser extent) in high-contact L1 varieties. The features in question are basically habitual/progressive and completive/perfect markers based on the verbs *be* and especially *do*. The use of *do* or *do/ does be* as habitual markers can be found in the dialects of the southwest of England and Irish English. These are exactly those dialects which are generally assumed to have had a great influence on the contact varieties in the Caribbean and North America. And it is exactly the fact that it is in these contact varieties that its use is obligatory, most pervasive, and most frequent which gives support to the so-called 'founder principle' in the formation of creoles suggested by Mufwene (e.g. 2008). The same applies to the use of *done* and *have/be done* (features 12 and 13) as completive/perfect markers. Again, we find some evidence of their use in traditional L1 varieties; however, the relevant grammaticalization processes seem to have proceeded further in high-contact L1 varieties and pidgins and creoles, especially in North America, the Caribbean, and Africa. The use of *do* as a T&A marker is discussed in Kortmann (2004a), who shows that while it is a typologically relatively rare phenomenon, the grammaticalization of *do* as T&A marker proceeds along typical grammaticalization paths found in the typological literature on T&A, with more advanced stages of these processes reflected in varieties with an extreme contact history.

The next T&A group (features 14–18) contains those features that are exclusive to pidgins and creoles and some high-contact L1 varieties. Since the relevant grammaticalization processes of these features are so widespread in the contact varieties across the Anglophone world, an explanation purely based on substrate influence seems rather unlikely in these cases. Even if we cannot find evidence of these grammaticalization features in the superstrate varieties, it is still possible that the frequent use of the lexical source items in the input varieties (e.g. the use of *finish* or *already* to express completion) has triggered the grammaticalization processes in the output varieties, with similar models in substrate languages possibly reinforcing this process. After all, the features in this group represent outcomes of typical grammaticalization processes found in the typological literature on tense and aspect (e.g. GO → future marker, verbs of volition → future marker, FINISH → completive/perfect marker; cf. Bybee et al. 1994; Heine and Kuteva 2002), so that the convergence of several factors seems to have shaped the processes in each case.

Features 19–21, on the other hand, are largely restricted to pidgins and creoles and L2 varieties and thus, not surprisingly, exclusive to certain world regions. The use of *come* as a future/ingressive marker, for example, clearly shows the importance of substrate models in grammaticalization processes: its use is restricted to varieties of English in Africa, and there is evidence from the Kwa languages and other African languages that COME is a common source for future markers. Also belonging to this group is the *after*-perfect (feature 22), which is typically associated with Irish English and shows clear substrate influence from Irish Gaelic. Irish English, as mentioned earlier, is one of the most important 'founder' varieties in many colonial settings in the Anglophone world, which of course explains the fact why a number of its features also figure in various 'transplanted' L1 varieties, or varieties of English with a dialect and/or language contact history that included Irish English (such as Newfoundland English).

3.3. Pronouns

The majority of the features in the domain of pronouns (see Table 21.4) relate to grammaticalized markers for the coding of number distinctions in pronouns.

Table 21.4. Grammaticalization in the domain of pronouns

23	Forms or phrases for the 2nd person plural pronoun other than *you*	e.g. *y'all* (Ozarks E); *yufela* (Tok Pisin); *you... together* (East Anglia); *all of you* (Indian E); *you guys* (New Zealand E); *you people* (Cameroon E)
24	Specialized plural markers for pronouns	e.g. *us-gang* (1PL.) (Fiji E); *as gaiz* (1PL), *yu gaiz* (2PL), *dem gaiz* (3PL) (Hawai'i C)
25	Plural forms of interrogative pronouns: using additional (free or bound) elements	e.g. *-all*: *Who-**all** did you say was gonna be there?* (Colloquial American E)
26	Alternative forms/phrases for referential (non-dummy) *it*	e.g. *the thing*: *When you on* ['switch on'] *the alarm system you press this button. When you off* **the thing** ['switch it off'] *you press that one* (Fiji E)
27	Emphatic reflexives with *own*	*Everybody took care of **their own self*** (Appalachian E)
28	Creation of possessive pronouns with prefix *fi-* + personal pronoun	e.g. *fi-mi* 'my', *fi-hoo* 'whose'; *Den no **fi-me** work me put yuh inna?* [lit.: Then no for-me job I put you into] 'Then wasn't it ***my*** job I got for you?' (Jamaican C)
29	Distinct forms for exclusive/ inclusive 1st person non-singular (plural)	e.g. *afla* (inclusive, i.e. 'we, including you') vs. *mifela* (exclusive, i.e. 'we, not including you') (Aboriginal E)
30	More number distinctions in personal pronouns than simply singular vs. plural (e.g. singular / dual / plural)	e.g. *hem* (3SG), *tufala* (3DU), *trifala* (3TRI), *ol(geta)* (3PL) (Bislama)
31	Plural forms of interrogative pronouns: reduplication	e.g. ***Who-who came?*** 'Who (of several people) came?'; ***What-what** they said?* 'What (different) things did they say?' (Indian South African E)

The formation of an alternative marker or phrase for the 2nd person plural (feature 23) is the only top feature in our sample (found in more than 75 per cent of the 52 varieties). As this feature is not restricted to specific variety types, it can be classified as an 'angloversal'. While this phenomenon as such is global and cross-varietal, the means by which it is created differ across the varieties, with regional and variety-specific factors playing a crucial role. The most widespread variant is the creation of the 2nd person plural marker via postposing additional elements, with *you-guys,* as for example in New Zealand English, Colloquial American English, Channel Island English, and *you-all (y'all),* as especially in the Caribbean as well as in the North American varieties, as the most pervasive patterns.

The postposing of a form related to *-people* is rather restricted to L2 varieties, especially in Africa (Cameroon English, Nigerian English, Kenyan English) but also in the Pacific (Colloquial Fiji English). The postposing of a form related to *-fellow*, on the other hand, is a feature exclusively found in Asian and Pacific varieties, which thus supports an analysis based on substrate influence. According to Heine and Kuteva (2002: 36, 230), the grammaticalization of lexical elements with a meaning related to 'people' or 'all' to a marker conveying the meaning of 'plural' is a well-attested phenomenon in the languages of the world. As Standard English is typologically uncommon in not distinguishing between 2nd person singular and plural personal pronouns, this is a likely process to occur in non-standard varieties.

In high-contact L1 varieties and L2 varieties as well as in pidgins and creoles in different Anglophone world regions we find that postposed elements like *-guys* are also used as general plural markers for personal pronouns, yielding forms like *us-gang, us-guys, you-guys, them-guys* (feature 24), as for example in the Australian creoles. The grammaticalization of affixes or pre- or postposed particles denoting 'plural' is more common than the creation of an element meaning 'singular', as the WAVE data reveal. This is in line with the typological tendency for the singular to be the unmarked member of the singular/plural opposition.

The same applies to the formation of plural interrogative pronouns via the postposing of elements such as *-all*, resulting in forms such as *who-all, where-all*, etc. (25). While this formation pattern can be found across all variety types, it is especially pervasive in the North American L1 varieties (e.g. Colloquial American English, Appalachian English, and Ozarks English), possibly triggered, at least reinforced, by the native dialects of German settlers (cf. as one option in Modern High German *Wer alles war da?* lit. who all was there? 'Who (plural) was there?'). It is in the L1 varieties of North America, too, that the pattern of forming the second person plural pronoun via the postposing of *-all* is most pervasive.

The use of alternative forms for referential (non-dummy) *it* (26) is the second most pervasive feature in the domain of pronouns. Half of the varieties in the sample across all variety types and world regions exhibit this feature. Variants range from different pronunciations and/or orthographic realizations of *the thing* (e.g. *di ting* in e.g. Guyanese Creole, *dar ting* in e.g. Norf'k) to different lexical items with the meaning of 'the thing' in pidgins and creoles (e.g. *da kain, da staf* in Hawaiian Creole). The grammaticalization of a lexical item meaning 'thing' into an indefinite pronoun is a well-attested path mentioned by Heine and Kuteva (2002: 295f.), and thus represents one of those many cases where non-standard varieties of English conform to typological paths of grammaticalization which cannot be observed in standard varieties of English.

The use of emphatic reflexives with *own* (27) is the only other member of the group of pronominal features which is pervasive across all variety types and world regions. The remaining features in this domain are restricted to high-contact varieties in different world regions and represent cases of contact-induced grammaticalization. These include: (i) the formation of possessive pronouns with the prefix *fi-* + PP (28), which is found among the Caribbean creoles; (ii) the use of distinct forms for inclusive/exclusive 1st person non-singular (29), and (iii) the distinction between more numbers in personal pronouns than simply singular vs. plural (e.g. singular/dual/plural (30)). The latter two features are restricted to varieties in the Pacific and Australasia. Finally, forming plural interrogative pronouns via reduplication (31) is most pervasive in the Asian varieties, but can also be found in Chicano English and in Cameroon Pidgin.

4. Major lessons (yet) to be learnt

Taking stock of English-internal morphosyntactic variation on a global scale, our chapter has provided a first survey and identified some first major tendencies from the point of view of grammaticalization. A first major lesson to be learnt from exploring data from non-standard and exclusively spoken varieties of English is this: the (hi)story of grammaticalization clearly needn't be rewritten. We did not observe any instances of grammaticalization, as defined in the classic text on this process, that run against accounts of similar phenomena in other languages. Neither did we—concerning all those features which qualify as the outcomes of (English- or Germanic-) internal grammaticalization—identify markedly different grammaticalization patterns in these varieties compared with what we know about (written or spoken) standard varieties of English. It should be noted that instances of internal grammaticalization are not restricted to low-contact L1 varieties. Frequently they can also be found in contact varieties, even though the majority of grammaticalization phenomena in these varieties, and especially in the English-based pidgins and creoles, do of course qualify as the results of contact-induced grammaticalization and are clearly unknown in (the history of) written and spoken standard varieties of English.

In general, the distinction between internal and contact-induced grammaticalization yields several interesting observations. Before we turn to these, two preliminary cautionary remarks are in place: (a) It is hard to prove that some change is exclusively internal; it is always possible that some (unknown) contact was also a triggering or accelerating factor. (b) When zooming in on the grammaticalization history of individual WAVE features, it may turn out, as it has elsewhere, that internal and contact-induced changes operated in tandem. A first rather surprising observation is that, given the large proportion of varieties in our sample with a contact history (altogether forty-three high-contact L1s, L2s, and P/Cs vis-à-vis only nine low-contact L1 varieties), internal grammaticalization goes considerably strong (37.5 per cent) among the total set of 72 grammaticalization-relevant features in the WAVE set. Instances of purely contact-induced grammaticalization (i.e. known neither in the history of English nor in low-contact L1 varieties) amount to 50 per cent of the entire feature set, with an additional 12.5 per cent of the features representing the outcomes of a contact-induced grammaticalization process using input material and/or undergoing a process also known from internal grammaticalization. It is also interesting to see how outcomes of internal and contact-induced grammaticalization are distributed in the eight large domains of grammar discussed here (recall Table 21.2): there is a fair balance in the domains of tense and aspect, pronouns, complementation, and relativization. Contact-induced grammaticalization accounts for the (sometimes vast) majority of features in the domains of verb morphology, the noun phrase, and negation. Only in one domain is it internal grammaticalization which dominates: in the domain of modal verbs, where in fact none of the features seems to be a candidate for contact-induced grammaticalization.

With regard to the distribution of internal vs. contact-induced grammaticalization phenomena across variety types, the following (predictable) picture emerges: internal grammaticalization predominates exclusively in the L1 varieties (most clearly, in a 4:1 proportion, in the traditional dialects, only by a margin in high-contact L1 varieties). In both L2 varieties of English and English-based pidgins and creoles, contact-induced grammaticalization accounts for about two-thirds of the relevant phenomena. Only a look at the absolute numbers of features makes clear the much higher extent to which the morphosyntax of pidgins and creoles is the result of grammaticalization processes (and especially of contact-induced grammaticalization), sometimes coupled with restructuring, compared with all other variety types (37 out of 54). Traditional dialects are located at the opposite end of the grammaticalization scale (only four instances of contact-induced grammaticalization out of twenty).

Given the fact that a clear majority of grammaticalization processes in pidgins and creoles is contact-induced, it is also to be expected that regional grammaticalization patterns (in terms of sources, targets, or grammaticalization paths) can be identified, i.e. depending on the Anglophone world region where the relevant variety or varieties are spoken. Thus it is possible to identify grammaticalization patterns which are characteristic of, or even exclusive to, e.g. the Pacific (feature 29, 'distinct forms for exclusive/inclusive 1st person non-singular') or Africa (feature 19, *come*-based future markers).

From the point of view of 'innovation vs. conservatism' in the realm of grammaticalization phenomena, what can be stated on the basis of our dataset is that the only clear cases of innovations in the grammaticalization history of English (or, more generally, Germanic) are those which are contact-induced. And even among those, about one-fifth can be considered either continuations of or, ultimately, 're-enactments' of internal grammaticalization processes known from the history of English and Germanic.

The following two features in the noun phrase, for example, qualify as features instantiating such 're-enactments'. Both the features are, however, restricted to contact varieties of English. The most pervasive feature in this domain (recurrent in >50 per cent of all varieties) is the use of the numeral *one/wan* as an indefinite article. This feature is pervasive in all world regions except for the Pacific and Australasia. The use of a numeral ('one') as the lexical source for the grammaticalization of indefinite articles is very common cross-linguistically (Heine and Kuteva 2002: 237f.), and is also well known from the history of Germanic and Romance languages in Europe.

Similarly, the grammaticalization of demonstratives to definite articles represents a development which is familiar from the typological literature (Heine and Kuteva 2002: 109f.) as well as from the development of definite articles in European languages (e.g. Latin demonstratives > definite articles in Romance languages). This feature is more pervasive in Africa, Asia, the Pacific, and Australasia than in the Caribbean and North America, but it is found equally in high-contact L1 varieties, L2 varieties, and pidgins and creoles. Similar to 'numeral *one/wan* as indefinite article', its presence is global, and not restricted to pidgins and creoles.

We interpret these instances of 're-enactment' as further nice illustrations of von der Gabelentz's idea of grammaticalization as a spiral process of language change. What is innovative of the outcomes of many internal grammaticalization processes in non-standard and contact varieties is that the relevant grammaticalized forms are taken further along a cross-linguistically widely attested grammaticalization path, thus yielding an even higher degree of grammaticalization than in (spoken or written) Standard English. Examples of such continuations include 'Progressive > Imperfective' (features 1 and 2), and 'Perfect > Past' (3).

Finally, it is especially in the verb phrase (above all in the domain of tense and aspect) that we find the largest number of grammaticalization features in non-standard and contact varieties of English, followed by the domains of pronouns and the noun phrase. Only two of the 72 grammaticalization-relevant WAVE features were found to operate on a truly global Anglophone level: 23, 'forms or phrases for the 2nd person plural pronoun other than *you*' and (not discussed in this chapter) '*never* as a preverbal negator'. Both features cross the 75 per cent threshold for true angloversals.

These are only some of the major lessons to be learnt from this chapter. Many more can be expected once we zoom in on individual grammaticalization phenomena and processes as found in non-standard and contact varieties of English as well as in pidgin and creole languages.

CHAPTER 22

GRAMMATICALIZATION AND LANGUAGE CONTACT

YARON MATRAS

1. Contact-induced internal change

Language contact and bilingualism are potential triggers of language change at various levels. These include changes that are internal to the language under scrutiny, in the sense that they involve an adaptation to the function, meaning, or distribution of an inherited structure. At the same time, they are triggered by replication of a model that is external to the language under scrutiny, one that is found in a contact language.

Consider Romani, the Indo-Aryan language of the Rom or 'Gypsies', which was brought to Europe in all likelihood sometime between the ninth and eleventh centuries CE. Romani has preposed definite articles that agree with the nouns they determine in gender, number, and case:

(1) Romani (Lovari/Kelderaš dialect)
e *dej* *akhar-d-as* *la* *raklj-a*
DEF.F.SG.NOM mother.NOM call-PAST-3SG DEF.F.SG.OBL girl.OBL
taj *le* *rakl-es*
and DEF.M.SG.OBL boy-OBL
'The mother called the girl and the boy'

Since Indo-Aryan languages typically do not have definite articles, nor are definite articles widespread in western Asia (an area through which the ancestors of the contemporary Romani-speaking population will have passed on their way to Europe), we can assume that this construction was acquired in contact with European languages, specifically with Byzantine Greek, which had an overall profound impact on the lexicon, morphology, and morphosyntax of Romani (cf. Matras 2002). In Greek, as in Romani, definite articles are preposed and agree with their head noun in gender, number, and case. Note that Greek is geographically isolated in its formation of definite articles. The Balkan languages to the north and west have postposed definite articles that appear to have derived from demonstratives (cf. Bulgarian *kuče-to* 'the dog', *kotka-ta* 'the cat'), while Serbian to the west and Turkish to the east lack definite articles altogether. This strengthens the assumption that Greek alone served as a model for the Romani article.

As can be seen in (1), some dialects of Romani retain article forms in *l-* in the oblique as well as in nominative plural forms. Such stems correspond to the oblique and plural nominative stems of Romani 3rd person pronouns (*les* 'him', *la* 'her', *le/len* 'them'), as well as to those of the oblique demonstratives (*-oles*, *-ola*, *-ole/-olen*).[1] The nominative forms of 3rd person pronouns are typically *ov* 'he', *oj* 'she', and *on* 'they' (with prothetic segments like *j-* or *v-* in some regions). There is therefore a likely historical reconstruction scenario for the Romani definite article (cf. Matras 2002: ch. 5): The Romani anaphoric demonstrative gave rise to both third person pronouns and definite articles. The forms were then subject to various analogies and processes of phonological erosion, so that nominative forms in particular have often been reduced to just single vowel words (*o*, *e*, *i*), while some dialects retain the more conservative, consonantal forms in the oblique and sometimes also in the nominative plural.[2] While the paradigm's inflection behaviour was carried over from its earlier referential function, its semantics and syntactic formation were modelled on those of the Greek definite article.

For cases like that of the Romani definite article, a theory of language change is called for that can answer the following questions. How and why does the need arise to replicate a construction that is present in a contact language using the inherited linguistic-structural material of the recipient language? How, precisely, does this replication proceed? What governs the choice of available item in the recipient language that is used in order to replicate the model? Which changes does this item undergo in order to replicate the model construction? What are the implications for the linguistic system of the recipient language?

[1] Romani demonstratives typically include a prefixed segment, thus *kod-oles*, *od-oles*, *ko-les*, etc.

[2] Oblique forms of the Romani definite article in *l-* are common in a central European area comprising Transylvania, Slovakia, southern Poland, Hungary, eastern Austria, and the Vojvodina regions. Forms of the plural nominative in *l-* are found the Romani dialects of central Slovakia. See Romani Morpho-Syntax Database online: http://romani.humanities.manchester.ac.uk/rms/

The notion of 'contact-driven grammaticalization' represents an attempt to address these questions within the framework of an overall theory of grammaticalization. In the following I refer to key stages in the development of the discussion on contact-induced grammaticalization and the questions it addresses, as well as some of the gaps that are left unanswered by this discussion.

2. Matter and pattern replication

The term 'borrowing' is probably the most common way of referring to the history of a structure that has been introduced into a language as a result of language contact. Borrowing presupposes some degree of bilingualism, but this can mean even just shallow exposure to another language, of the kind that brought about the import of words like *banana* or *mango* into English. Thomason and Kaufman (1988) and Thomason (2001), for example, speak of a 'borrowing scale' on which various types of contact-induced structures are accommodated: from the individual word form and morphs, through to phones and phonemes, and on to a wholesale inventory of syntactic-typological constructions.

But this general notion of 'borrowing' blurs an important distinction made in both earlier and contemporary works between the replication of what we might call linguistic *matter*—roughly defined as phonological word forms along with their meanings[3]—and *patterns*—the more abstract relationship between a form or sequence of forms and its meaning, or form–function mapping (cf. Matras 2009: ch. 9; Matras and Sakel 2007). Weinreich (1964[1953]) described pattern replication as a change in the function of morphemes in a 'replica language', inspired by a 'model language', referring to the process as 'convergent development' (see also Gołąb 1956). The phenomenon is also widely known by Haugen's (1950) label 'calque'. Later works refer to change in form–function mapping that is triggered by an external model as 'pattern transfer' (Heath 1984), 'metatypy' (Ross 1996; 2001), and 'partial or selective copies' (Johanson 2002). All these works identified processes of meaning extension, primarily at the lexical level, modelled on structures of a contact language.

[3] It is accepted that word-form replication is not always fully in harmony with the source. Changes to phonological form through phonological integration are extremely common (cf. Jordanian Arabic *banšer* from English *puncture*), but slight changes to meaning can also be found (cf. Romani *tajśa* 'tomorrow, yesterday', from Byzantine Greek *taixia* 'tomorrow', replacing the inherited Romani *kal-* 'tomorrow, yesterday'; or German *beamer* 'projector of digital images', based on English *beamer* 'an electronic device that projects a light').

Givón (1982) was one of the first works to interpret the emergence of grammatical categories from lexical material in creole languages in terms of grammaticalization processes. Typical creole aspectual markers like *ta*, *bi*, *go* were traced back to English lexical stems *stay*, *be*, and *go* respectively, and argued to have acquired secondary meanings as abstract modifiers of other verbs while at the same time undergoing an erosion of their original independent semantics ('bleaching') as well as their phonological form. Creoles were argued to undergo extensive processes of grammaticalization of this kind in order to compensate for the absence of grammatical markers, a state of affairs that was inherited from the simplified pidgin stage (see e.g. Heine 2005). But Keesing (1988; 1991) suggested that the process was not independent of external models. The expansion of complex grammar through grammaticalization in Melanesian Pidgin, he argued, was accelerated by a blueprint for the mapping of grammatical meanings onto word forms. This blueprint was inherited from the substrate languages and applied to the word forms of the lexifier language.

The notion of 'substrate' language had not been hitherto unknown, but it was often confined to speculative generalizations such as the viewpoint that attributed similarities among the contemporary languages of the Balkans to an extinct (and hardly documented) substrate language (cf. Solta 1980). Keesing's suggestion was that an existing model guided the natural tendency toward the formation of new categories in creoles. This and similar hypotheses expressed in connection with the influence of West African languages on the formation of Atlantic creoles (Boretzky 1983) led to the proliferation of substrate analyses in creoles studies (cf. Bruyn 1996; Plag 2002; Kouwenberg and LaCharité 2004; Migge and Winford 2007; and many more).

Creoles, however, remain particular in that there is an undeniable gap in the inventory of canonized grammatical expressions and constructions, one that drives users to seek solutions drawing on available resources. The substrate impact in creoles—the manner in which the model of a background, native language guides the speaker to construct grammatical devices in the new, expanding language—is comparable in many ways to that of the background languages of second language learners. 'Negative transfer'—in this case the employment of background (substrate) language blueprints by learners as a basis for the production of constructions in a target language—is often considered to be responsible for areal convergence in cases of language shift (Thomason 2001) and for the emergence of ethnolects, such as Chinese-influenced Singapore English (Bao 2005). The kind of mixtures that result from bilingual speakers' limited access to the full inventory of morphosyntactic constructions in the target language, namely the use of background-language construction templates with target-language lemmas, is well described in various works on bilingual speech and has been termed 'composite matrix language' (Jake and Myers-Scotton 1997; Bolonyai 1998).

3. Beyond creolization and second-language learning

Languages that already possess a full range of productive grammatical constructions may equally resort to processes of grammaticalization in order to rearrange their inventory of morphosyntactic devices or parts thereof, even in situations that do not involve fossilized learning of a target language. This point was highlighted in a series of works devoted to typological change in contact situations, which might be referred to as the 'Hamburg School' (Haase 1992; Matras 1994; 1996; Nau 1995). The shared assumption in these studies is that bilinguals are motivated on the one hand to make optimal use of their full repertoire of linguistic constructions irrespective of the constraints on situational language choice that apply in their multilingual speech community. On the other hand, language loyalty and the wish to comply with listener expectation on the appropriate selection of word forms motivates bilingual speakers to follow the constraints on word form selection. Speakers will therefore act in a creative manner in order to improvise matching constructions across the two languages—constructions that are, at least seemingly, licensed in the respective communication settings of both languages since they draw on word forms that are appropriate choices in the respective settings.

The basis for the creation of a new construction is the availability of a word form in the replica language the meaning of which can be exploited to replicate that carried by a key element in the model construction. Haase (1992) and Nau (1995) note that bilingual speakers wish to have equal constructions at their disposal in each language, but they can only do so if they are able to identify parallel items in the two languages as translation equivalents. This means that the grammaticalization process begins by matching lexemes to one another, and adapting the range of meanings expressed by the lexemes of the replica language to those expressed by the parallel lexemes in the model. The procedure exploits the polysemy of the word in the model, which usually has both a concrete meaning and a more abstract one. The process of grammaticalization therefore proceeds along a hierarchical scale from more concrete, lexical meanings to the more abstract, grammatical functions, a property that has been referred to as the 'unidirectionality' of the grammaticalization process.

Matras (1994; 1996) similarly emphasises the functionalization of existing internal meanings. He identifies a twofold process by which the bilingual speaker applies the very same mental processing procedure to matching items in both languages, leading to a transposition of the selected replica item from one functional field into another. Thus in the example in (2), the Macedonian dialect of Turkish exploits the inherited Turkish interrogative *ne* 'what' as an uninflected relativizer that follows the head noun in a postposed relative clause, replicating the construction of the contact language Macedonian, where the relative clause is introduced by a relativizer *što*, which also has the meaning of the interrogative 'what'. The new construction replaces the inherited preposed gerundial construction found in Modern Standard and in Ottoman Turkish. The grammaticalization path shows a shift from an interrogative, whose semantic-pragmatic meaning is fixed within a certain kind of illocution, to a conjunction/relativizer, which has a syntactic function within a complex clause:

(2) a. Modern Standard and Ottoman Turkish
gel-en adam
come-GER man
b. Macedonian Turkish
adam ne geldi
man REL came
c. Macedonian
čovek-ot što dojde
man-DEF REL came

Returning to the Romani definite article discussed above, the inherent meaning that makes the 'Early Romani' anaphoric demonstrative/3rd person pronoun a suitable candidate to take on the procedure instigated in the Greek model by the definite article is not polysemy *per se* (for the Greek definite article lacks pronominal-referential functions), but the referential potential of the Romani form, i.e. its semantic potential to act as determiner. The motivation to extract this abstract potential from the concrete meaning of the anaphoric element is triggered by the need to maintain matching organization procedures for referents in both languages, or in other words to syncretize linguistic–mental planning operations in both languages.

A further example is the development of finite modal complementation (or 'infinitive loss') in the Balkan dialects of Turkish, such as the variety spoken in Macedonia:

(3) a. Modern Standard and Ottoman Turkish
(o) git-mek istiyor
3SG go-INF want.3SG
b. Macedonian Turkish
(o) istiyor git-sin
3SG want.3SG go-3SG.SUBJ
c. Macedonian
toj sak-a da id-e
3SG want-3SG COMP go-3SG

Macedonian Turkish replicates the Macedonian model construction, replacing the inherited Turkish infinitive and postposed modal verb (*git-mek istiyor*) by a finite, postposed complement clause. Note, however, that the Macedonian and the Macedonian Turkish constructions are not isomorphic: Macedonian makes use of a subjunctive complementizer to introduce the non-factual complement clause, while the finite verb shows no distinction for mood. The Macedoinan Turkish construction is based on the historical optative inflection of the verb, with no complementizer. The 'pivotal' feature that is replicated is thus the order of constituent clauses—a main matrix clause followed by a complement clause—and the subjunctive marking of the complement clause. The means of achieving this marking are language-specific, and draw on language-specific resources and constraints. The historical change involves an extension of the meaning and environment of the historical, semantically conditioned optative, to serve as a syntactically conditioned subjunctive.

The tendency of languages in multilingual settings to develop similar constructions of this kind has been observed in various areas of the world, and for a variety of types of construction, ranging from lexicosemantic formations to the organization of clauses and even morphology (cf. Bisang 1996; 1998; Enfield 2003; Aikhenvald 2002; Bakker 2006). There is now widespread agreement that the process is not necessarily triggered by second language learners, but that native speakers of a language may equally import constructions into their own language based on a foreign model of imitation; thus, contact-induced grammaticalization can equally lead to a kind of 'borrowing', not just to 'negative transfer'.

Following the proposals made in Haase (1992), Nau (1995), and Matras (1998), Heine and Kuteva (2003; 2005) present a theory of contact-induced change that is intended to be fully reconcilable with grammaticalization theory. In the centre is the notion of a mental comparison between a model and a replica language, as a result of which a construction is identified in the replica with the potential to carry the same meaning as the target construction in the model. The candidate construction is then grammaticalized in order to take on the meaning conveyed in the model. The concrete changes may involve expansion of a construction from minor to major use patterns, including an increase in frequency, extension of its distributional context, extension across categories, and the emergence of new categories. Polysemy-copying is only one of several possible directions that the process of contact-induced grammaticalization may take. The unidirectionality of grammaticalization is manifested in the emergence of novel meanings, semantic bleaching, or blurring of existing meanings as lexemes take on more abstract grammatical functions, loss of morphosyntactic properties that are associated primarily with the content-lexeme (as in the case of nouns that are grammaticalized into location expressions, or interrogatives that are used as subordinators), and possibly also through an erosion or reduction of phonetic substance.

4. Problems with the grammaticalization model

The grammaticalization model accounts nicely for such developments as the evolution of the Macedonian Turkish relativizer from an interrogative (blurring of meaning of lexemes, acquisition of polysemy and an extended distribution context), the evolution of a subjunctive mood in Macedonian Turkish embedded clauses from an historical optative (through loss of the semantic-pragmatic properties of the optative and emergence of syntactic dependency), and the evolution of the Romani definite article from anaphoric pronouns (through bleaching of meaning, phonological erosion, and acquisition of a fixed distribution context). Nevertheless, there remain several issues with the grammaticalization model that justify the search for an overriding framework of language convergence, of which contact-induced grammaticalization is merely a sub-category.

Firstly, we have seen already that grammaticalization is only one aspect of the process, which often remains compliant with the morphosyntactic constraints of the replica language. We might refer to this as 'accommodated replication', as in the case of the Macedonian Turkish subjunctive, where an inherited inflection category of the verb is used to mark out modality rather than a non-factual complementizer as in the contact languages (cf. Macedonian *da*, etc.). Grammaticalization itself is partly constrained by both the word class or functional category and by the availability of other options for contact-induced adjustment of the recipient system. Categories such as personal pronouns, demonstratives, case markers, tense-aspect markers, and definite articles are usually highly resilient and rarely borrowed as word forms, but they are frequently subject to convergent development. We thus find that languages in contact tend to share the position and function of definite articles, the semantic setup of demonstratives or of pronouns (e.g. the presence of inclusive/exclusive distinction), or form–function mapping in the domain of nominal case. Arguably we are dealing in all these cases with highly abstract functional items; but the same can be said of relative pronouns, conjunctions, discourse markers, and modality markers, which in contact situations may undergo either pattern replication (i.e. some form of contact-induced grammaticalization) or matter replication (direct borrowing of word forms). In some societies, strong taboos on the borrowing of word forms is said to motivate the exploitation of inherited structures for new functions (cf. Aikhenvald 2002 on the Amazon and Ross 1996 on Melanesia). In other settings, one or the other procedure may be favoured based on the availability of resources for potential replication. For example, the German (Sinti) dialect of Romani replicates German Aktionsart modifications to the verb (so-called verbal particles). The calque *me kerav pre* 'I open', from *ich mache auf*, makes use of the inherited Romani preposition *pre* 'on', modelled on the polysemy of German *auf*. But in the case of *me džav hin* for 'I am going [there]' for German *ich gehe hin*, no adequate match is found for the German particle *hin*, which lacks such polysemy, and as a result the original word form of the German particle is replicated directly.

A further challenge facing the grammaticalization model is the fact that unidirectionality is a frequent tendency but not an absolute constraint. For a start, contact-induced change can lead to the loss of categories, such as the disappearance of the definite article in Romani dialects in contact with Polish and Russian, or the blurring of gender distinctions in Romani in contact with English. These developments do not occur as a result of structural erosion. Rather, they are the outcome of speakers taking on a less differentiated form–function mapping principle and applying it internally (i.e. to the replica language). Unidirectionality would normally predict that grammaticalization should lead to the continuous acquisition of greater differentiation within the system. As a further example, Dawkins (1916) reports on the generalization of the Greek M.SG.GEN ending *-yu* in the now extinct Anatolian Greek dialect of Fertek, copying the Turkish agglutinating marker *-ın*. The historical Greek endings F.SG.GEN *yinék-as* 'of the wife' and F.PL.GEN *yinék-on* 'of the wives' are thus replaced by *nék-a-yu* and *nék-es-yu* respectively, modelled on Turkish *kadın-ın, kadın-lar-ın*. This shift from greater inflectional abstractness to agglutinating transparency can similarly be argued to go against the grammaticalization cline. One would instead expect the product of a grammaticalization process to be the loss of semantic transparency and a fusion of functions within one abstract morph, rather than the replacement of an abstract morph through two semantically 'regular' morphs.

Finally—though according to some views this is outside the scope of a model of structural change—others argue that the model needs to cope with speakers' motivation to initiate change and the conditions under which structural innovations will be propagated across a speech community. Example (4) shows a spontaneous innovation by a German-Hebrew bilingual child. The child is at this age beginning to use German modality particles, a structure for which there is no equivalent in Hebrew. Aiming to make full use of the expressive means in his emerging overall repertoire of linguistic structures, and to avail himself of all expressive means, to an equivalent degree, in each and every conversational context irrespective of the language that is being spoken in that context or setting, the child is taking creative steps in order to improvise a construction in Hebrew that would parallel that of the German modality particle yet at the same time be acknowledged and accepted as a legitimate word form in the Hebrew conversation context. The procedure is, at first glance, similar to that identified above as (replica) grammaticalization. The child draws on the polysemy of German *aber*—which functions both as a conjunction 'but' and as a particle of accentuation. He selects the Hebrew equivalent of the conjunction, *avál*, and inserts it into an equivalent position, aiming at a meaning that is equivalent to that of the German modality particle:

(4) Bilingual (German-Hebrew) child
  a. Hebrew utterance
    ze aval yafe!
    this but pretty
  b. German model
    Das ist aber schön!
    this is PART pretty
    'How pretty [this is]'!

The directionality of the change remains an issue, as it is arguably less expected for a conjunction to become a modality modifier. Nonetheless, the child's creative engagement merely mirrors the pathway of development of the German word form itself, which has undergone an identical extension of meaning/function.

The point raised by (4) and numerous examples of comparable data shows that at the level of the individual speaker, pattern replication is a spontaneous, creative procedure. The likelihood of the innovative construction in (4b) being propagated throughout the speech community depends, of course, on the degree of normative authority exercised by the speech community, the degree of self-confidence of innovating speakers, and in this particular instance also the degree to which bilingualism is widespread in the community. In the specific case of (4), the construction is rather unlikely to gain further dissemination. But in a small community in which a large proportion of children are bilingual and parents (and institutions) exercise only lax normative control over speech habits, the construction would stand a fair chance of wide propagation, leading to language change.

An overall model of grammaticalization through contact that takes into account speakers' cognitive and conversational motivation to engage in creative pattern replication is presented in Matras (2009) (see Figure 22.1). The point of departure of the process is the speaker's aim to pursue a particular communicative goal, embedded into a particular communicative context. This is transposed into a concrete linguistic task for which an appropriate task schema (see Green 1998) needs to be assembled from within the linguistic repertoire. Scanning through the entire repertoire, the speaker identifies a construction that would serve this particular task most effectively. We assume that, when scanning the repertoire, the speaker has the entire repertoire at his or her disposal, and does not 'block' or 'deactivate' any particular language 'system'. But the speaker is also conscious of the need to meet certain expectations of the interlocutor in respect of the choice of word forms.

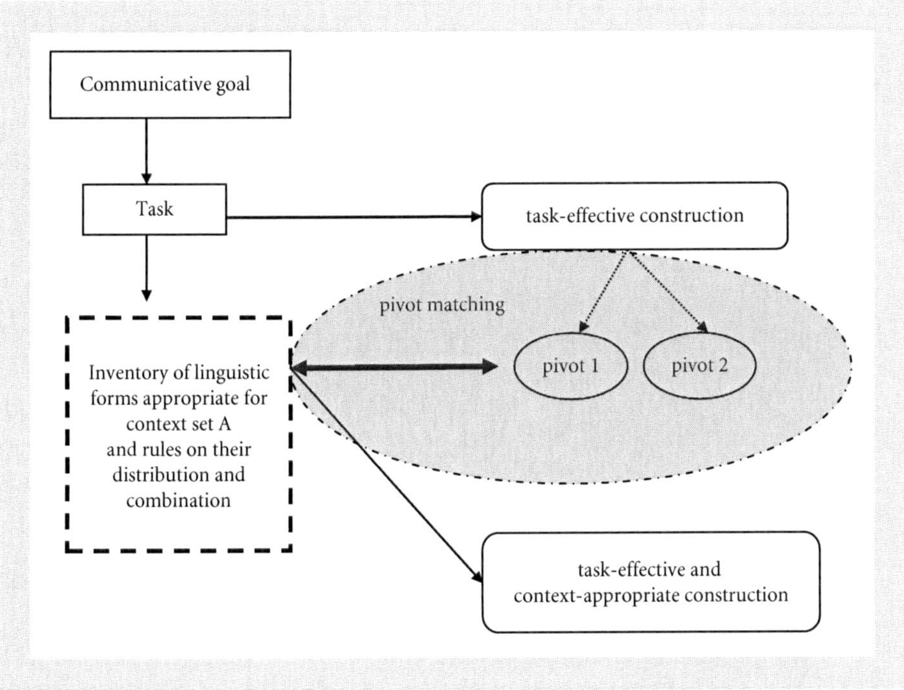

Fig. 22.1. Pivot-matching in pattern replication (from Matras 2009: ch. 9)

We assume that the optimal construction that was identified does not have an established structural representation that is appropriate for the present context. The speaker therefore tries to optimize communicative efficiency by combining the selected construction with context-appropriate word forms. In order to do this, the speaker deconstructs the construction by isolating its pivotal features, such as the reliance on a polysemic *aber* in example (4), or the reliance on finite complementation in example (3). This construction 'pivot' is then matched to the inventory of context-appropriate forms. The outcome is a creative, innovative construction that is both task-effective and, seemingly at least, context-appropriate.

5. Concluding remarks

Contact-induced change is often regarded as an *external* factor that motivates change, for it derives from outside the linguistic system that is under scrutiny. The explanation offered here questions this approach. It views change as internal to the individual speaker's language-processing mechanism, and so lends a communicative dimension to the process of grammaticalization. Speakers' engagement in innovating constructions is regarded as a creative process that is motivated by the wish to make full and exhaustive use of the expressive potential of the linguistic repertoire as a whole as well as to facilitate the syncretisation of mental planning operations in two or more languages, while at the same time honouring the principal demarcation among sub-inventories of the repertoire—or 'languages'—and their association with distinct contextual usage constraints. In this perspective, the fact that unidirectionality is observed with more than chance frequency can be explained by speakers' tendency to associate word forms most firmly and consistently with one language 'system' or another (i.e. with a particular set of communicative settings in which language 'X' is spoken). In other words, the kind of structures that can be referred to as linguistic 'matter' (as opposed to 'pattern') are more easily 'tagged' in the speaker's mental lexicon as belonging to a certain language rather than another; they are more 'contextually stable' in that their meaning tends to be more consistent and the extralinguistic conditions under which they are selected (and are therefore deemed to belong to one system rather than another) are more stable.

Pragmatic inferences, on the other hand, are drawn from the immediate conversational situation and the contextual environment. Inferences are the product of a creative process that allows the speaker to treat a form and the meaning associated with it with relative flexibility, and to adapt a meaning to the required context. The process of inferencing—the contextual extension of a form–meaning relationship—is less constrained and more universal than the permanent or stable association of a form with its meaning. Speakers therefore allow themselves to generalize pragmatic inferences across languages with relative ease. It is for this reason that so many instances of pivot-matching effectively result in deriving more subtle and abstract meanings from more concrete and transparent ones, thus resembling the process observed in grammaticalization and leading to the kind of developments identified by Heine and Kuteva (2003; 2005) as context extension, rise in frequency, and category renewal.

CHAPTER 23

THE AREAL DIMENSION OF GRAMMATICALIZATION

BERND HEINE

TANIA KUTEVA

1. Introduction

The main purpose of this chapter is to demonstrate, first, that grammaticalization is a ubiquitous process in language contact which may affect any part of language structure and exhibits the same format in all of its manifestations: speakers take a grammatical structure of language M (= the model language) as a model to design a functionally equivalent structure in language R (= the replica language) by using the resources available in R (see Heine and Kuteva 2003; 2005; 2006 for more detailed discussions). And second, this process has an areal dimension: it creates areas of structural relationship, in that—as a result of the process—M and R share a structural isogloss that was not there prior to language contact.

In section 2 we provide some examples of how languages have been influenced by other languages in developing new grammatical use patterns and categories. In accordance with the above characterization, our interest will be with what, following Weinreich (1964[1953]: 30–31), is called 'grammatical replication'. As Fig. 23.1 shows, this term relates to only one of the processes of transfer that can be observed

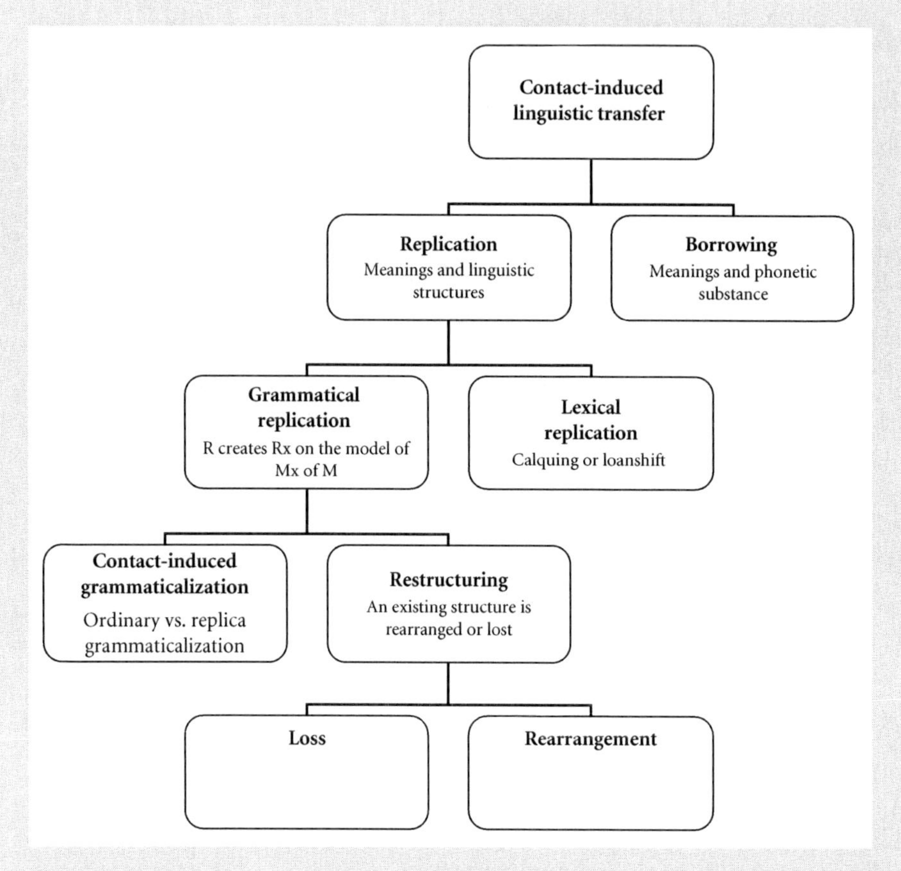

Fig. 23.1. Major types of contact-induced transfer of linguistic material in language-contact situations

in language contact. The term 'borrowing', by contrast, will be reserved for transfers involving phonetic material, either on its own or in combination with meaning. Furthermore, the terms model language and replica language are used for languages serving, respectively, as the source (or 'donor') and the target (or 'recipient') of transfer.

In section 3 we will look into the question of how grammaticalization leads to areal relationship among languages by highlighting the notion 'grammaticalization area', while in the final section 4 we draw some conclusions on areal relationship.

It is widely held that grammaticalization is a language-internal process, and that language-internal change and language contact are mutually exclusive phenomena. In the model that we propose, however, language contact and grammaticalization are not mutually exclusive; rather, they may complement one another. Grammaticalization theory aims at describing the way grammatical forms arise and develop through space and time, and to explain why they are structured the way they are.

Contact-induced grammaticalization is a grammaticalization process that is due to the influence of one language on another. Furthermore, there is a widespread assumption among linguists that grammatical structure, or syntax, cannot be 'borrowed', that is, transferred from one language to another. We consider this no longer to be an issue, given that there is now abundant evidence to demonstrate that grammar *can* be 'borrowed' or, as we will say here, replicated (see e.g. Ramisch 1989; Ross 1996; 2001; Johanson 1992; 2002; Aikhenvald 2002; Heine and Kuteva 2003; 2005; 2006; Aikhenvald and Dixon 2006), and this chapter will provide further evidence in support of this observation.

2. A survey of grammatical structures

In the present section we will look at two major domains of grammatical structure: the noun phrase and the verb phrase. For reasons of space, we cannot treat these domains in detail; rather, we will be restricted to exemplary categories characterizing each of these domains: markers of definite and indefinite reference within the noun phrase (section 2.1) and future tense markers within the verb phrase (2.2). The reader is referred to Aikhenvald (2002), Aikhenvald and Dixon (2006), Heine and Kuteva (2005; 2006), as well as other works cited below for similar generalizations on other kinds of grammatical categories.

2.1. Articles

A significant minority of the languages of the world have 'articles', that is, grammaticalized markers for definite and indefinite reference of nouns, while the majority of languages lack articles. That the presence of articles can be due to or be influenced by language contact has been established in a number of studies on contact situations in various parts of the world.

Slavic languages are well known for their lack of articles, but this does not hold true for some Slavic minority languages that have had a long history of contact with Germanic or Romance article languages. One of these minority languages is Upper Sorbian, spoken in Upper Lausitia (*Oberlausitz*) of eastern Germany (Breu 2003a; 2004). Prior to language contact, Upper Sorbian did not have any articles but, on the model of German, speakers have grammaticalized their proximal demonstrative ('this') to a definite article, to the extent that the two are now formally distinct; for example, the forms are *tón/te/ta* (masculine/feminine/neuter) for the nominative singular of the definite article but *tóne/tene/tane* for the demonstrative.[1] There is however a difference between the model and the replica languages: Whereas German has a semantically definite article (where the existence of a referent can be derived from world knowledge), Upper Sorbian has a less grammaticalized, context-definite article, illustrated in the following example, where the reference of 'smoke', expressed by the definite article *tón*, can only be derived from the preceding context. As the detailed comparison between German and Upper Sorbian shows (Breu 2004), there can be little doubt that this is a case of contact-induced transfer.

(1) Upper Sorbian (Breu 2004: 37ff.; the second line presents the corresponding German sentence; the definite article is printed in bold)[2]
Mó smó zade jeno Lkweja jě li. **Tón** kur bě šreklich.
'Wir sind hinter einem LKW hergefahren. **Der** Rauch war schrecklich.'
'We drove behind a truck. **The** smoke was terrible.'

A similar example of a development from demonstrative to definite article can be found in Pipil, an Uto-Aztecan language of El Salvador, belonging to the Nahua subgroup of Aztecan. The language is now nearing extinction; the remaining few hundred speakers are all Pipil-Spanish bilinguals, and for many of them Spanish is the dominant language. Accordingly, Pipil's more recent linguistic history is shaped primarily by its interaction with Spanish. Campbell (1987) notes that prior to language contact with Spanish, Pipil speakers did not dispose of conventionalized devices for marking definite reference on nouns; today, Pipil nouns occur with the definite article *ne* corresponding to the definite article of Spanish. What appears to distinguish the Pipil case from the Upper Sorbian one is that already before language contact, the Pipil demonstrative was weakly grammaticalized as an article, and contact had the effect that the erstwhile demonstrative developed into a fully-fledged article, becoming 'nearly a complete match' of the Spanish definite article (Campbell 1987: 272).

A third example concerns an Oceanic language. Ross (1996; 2001) describes a situation where two genetically unrelated languages spoken on Karkar Island off the north coast of Papua New Guinea have become semantically and syntactically largely intertranslatable while each of the two has retained its own lexical material. The model language is Waskia, a Papuan language of the Trans-New Guinea type, and the replica language Takia, a Western Oceanic language of the Bel family of the North New Guinea cluster. In an attempt to assimilate their language to the Papuan language Waskia, speakers of Takia largely replicated the syntax of the Papuan language. The development of a new postponed determiner on the model of the Papuan language was part of this process: Takia speakers created a new determiner *an*, which appears to act as a definite article, by grammaticalizing their deictic

[1] The present treatment is based entirely on Breu (2004), which provides a fine-grained analysis.
[2] No glosses are provided by the author.

morpheme **a* ('that', near speaker) in combination with a pronominal suffix agreeing in person and number with the head noun (Ross 2001: 142). Thus, once more we observe that language contact had the effect that a demonstrative, either on its own or in combination with some other element, developed into a marker for definite reference.

And much of what we observed above about definite articles[3] also applies to indefinite articles. The most detailed description of how a language acquires an indefinite article as a result of language contact is, once more, provided by Breu (2003a) on Upper Sorbian in eastern Germany and on Molisean of southeastern Italy. Molise Slavic, or Molisean, is the language of a community of Croatian speakers originating from the Herzegovinian Neretva Valley who emigrated around 500 years ago because of the Turkish invasion on the Balkans, settling in the Molise Region, Campobasso Province, of southeastern Italy. After contact both with the local varieties of Italian and with Standard Italian over a period of half a millennium, Molisean has been massively influenced by Italian (for a survey, see Breu 1998; see also Breu 1999; 2003a; 2003b; 2003c; 2004).

Upper Sorbian and Molisean are what Breu (2003a) calls Slavic 'micro-languages', having been surrounded for centuries by speakers of the dominant languages, German and Italian, respectively, and like other Slavic languages they lacked indefinite articles prior to language contact while the dominant languages have fully-fledged articles. As a result of contact, however, both 'micro-languages' created indefinite articles by grammaticalizing their numeral for 'one'. That language contact was the propelling force in these processes is suggested inter alia by the fact that the replica categories are associated with roughly the same kinds of context as the corresponding categories in the model languages; the reader is referred to Breu (2003a) for a detailed description of the situation in the two languages. Thus, Upper Sorbian has grammaticalized its numeral 'one' to an indefinite article *jen-* which, as Breu (2003a) shows convincingly, is equally grammaticalized as its German model category *ein-*: both are used as presentative (stage 2), specific indefinite (stage 3), and as nonspecific indefinite articles (stage 4);[4] consider the following example of the generic stage 4 article in Upper Sorbian and German.

(2) Upper Sorbian (Slavic; Breu 2003a: 46)

Upper Sorbian	**Jen**	Serb	nebči.	
	a	Sorbian	not.lies	
German	**Ein**	Sorbe	lügt	nicht.
	a	Sorbian	lies	not
	'A Sorbian never lies.'			

[3] Concerning the development in Molisean, see section 3.

[4] See Heine and Kuteva (2006: ch. 3) for the five-stage scenario of the grammaticalization of indefinite articles.

A similar example is provided by Basque (Haase 1992). As a result of centuries of intense contact with Gascon and later on with French, Basque speakers in south-western France introduced an indefinite article by grammaticalizing their numeral for 'one', *bat*. There are incipient uses as a non-specific marker as early as 1545, occasional uses of *bat* as a specific marker are attested already in 1782, but the grammaticalization as a nonspecific article is clearly a recent innovation of Basque. While the Basque article exhibits a high degree of grammaticalization, it is still less grammaticalized than its equivalents in the Romance model languages.

Another example can be found in the Uto-Aztecan language Pipil of El Salvador: In contact with the dominant language Spanish, Pipil-Spanish bilinguals developed their numeral *se:* 'one' into an indefinite article of the same kind as the corresponding article in Spanish, as Campbell (1987: 272) observes. Note that in pre-Conquest times—i.e. prior to language contact—*se:* was a numeral but not an article.

A further instance of this process is found in Mexico, involving the grammaticalization of the numeral *see* 'one' of another Aztecan language, Nahuatl, to an indefinite article as an equivalent of the indefinite article in the contact language, Spanish (cf. (3)), whereby the use of *see* was extended from the paradigm of numerals to a new paradigm of articles.

(3) Nahuatl (Aztecan, Uto-Aztecan; Flores Farfán 2004: 92)
see (∅)- pipitsah.
one 3.SG- kiss
'It's a kiss.'

These examples do not exhaust the number of cases where language contact, either as a propelling or an accelerating process, was responsible for the rise of new articles (see Heine and Kuteva 2006: ch. 3). Such observations suggest, first, that reference marking on nouns or noun phrases is a phenomenon that appears to be highly sensitive to contact: new structures for expressing definite and indefinite reference can easily develop in situations of contact. Second, these observations also suggest that this is a unidirectional process of grammaticalization. We are not aware of any language that has gone in the opposite direction by developing a definite article into a demonstrative or an indefinite article into a numeral for 'one', either in language contact or elsewhere.

And third, grammatical replication was responsible for the rise of areal relationship between the langugages concerned. For example, Upper Sorbian and Molisean now share areal isoglosses with German and Italian that did not exist prior to language contact; these Slavic languages have thereby joined the languages of the western half of Europe in having acquired an indefinite article via grammaticalization—a fact which sets them off from the many Slavic languages which lack articles—and the same applies to Basque in western Europe. In a similar fashion, via the contact-induced grammaticalization from demonstrative attribute to definite article, Upper Sorbian has become part of a large area characterized by the grammaticalization of a definite article that includes not only German but almost all the languages of western and central Europe.

2.2. Future tenses

In the same way as grammatical forms for discourse reference, new forms for tense, aspect, and modality constantly arise in situations of language contact; in the present section we will look at one particular grammatical function, namely future tense.

Work on grammatical categories of tense has shown that there is a limited spectrum of conceptual pathways of how markers for future tense may evolve. The main source is provided by motion schemas involving goal-directed verbs for 'come to' [X comes to Y] or 'go to' [X goes to Y], or a volition schema [X wants Y] using a verb for 'want' (Bybee, Pagliuca, and Perkins 1994); following Dahl (2000: 319ff.) we will refer to these schemas, respectively, as the de-venitive, de-allative, and de-volitive schemas or constructions. Most of this work has been done on what is presumably language-internal grammatical change, but, as has been shown in Heine and Kuteva (2005: sect. 3.3), the same kind of process can also be observed in situations of language contact, and below we present a selection of such cases.

De-allative futures are found, among others, in French (*aller faire*) and English (*be going to do*), and some languages that have been in close contact with these two languages appear to have replicated these tense forms. One example is reported from Luxembourgeois, where speakers of this German dialect are said to have replicated the French de-allative construction *aller faire* ('go to') by developing their verb *goen* 'go' into a future auxiliary (Alanne 1972); note that French is the second or primary language of these speakers.

A clearly more influential model was provided by English. One example has been reported from the Indo-Aryan language Romani. In the dialect spoken in Wales, Romani speakers developed a de-allative future on the model of English *be going to* (Boretzky 1989: 368), cf. (4).

(4) Romani of Wales (Boretzky 1989: 369)
brišindo **džala** te del.
(rain goes to give)
'It is going to rain.'

But more than British English, it was American English that provided a model for de-allative futures. In a number of situations where communities speaking other languages were in contact with English in the USA or Canada, some form of a future using a verb for 'go to' evolved, even if not always in a strongly grammaticalized form. One example is provided by Old Order Mennonites in Waterloo

County, Canada. In their variety of Pennsylvania German there is an emerging de-allative immediate future tense involving the verb *geh* 'to go' (Burridge 1995: 61ff.), and another example can be seen in the speech of a community of Yiddish speakers in Venice along the coast next to Los Angeles, which is strongly bilingual in English although Yiddish predominates in everyday conversations (Rayfield 1970). As a result of intensive contact with English, Yiddish speakers created a future tense on the model of the English *be-going-to* future, illustrated in (5).

(5) Yiddish of Venice, California (Germanic; Rayfield 1970: 69)
All right, **ge** ikh kum- en bald.
all right go 1.SG come- INF soon
'All right, I'm going to come in a minute.'

As a final example we return to the Pipil language of El Salvador. As we saw above, Pipil has been strongly influenced by Spanish, and one effect of this influence is that Pipil speakers developed a new 'go to'-future tense category, which Campbell (1987: 267–8) attributes to the influence of the local Spanish de-allative future (*lo voy a hacer* 'I'm going to do it'). That it is the conceptual schema of directed motion rather than the morphosyntactic structure of the Spanish future tense that provided the basis for replication is suggested by the fact that Pipil uses the main verb in its finite form, while in the Spanish model structure the main verb appears in the infinitive:

(6) Pipil (Aztecan, Uto-Aztecan; Campbell 1987: 268)
ti- **yu-** t ti- yawi- t ti- pa: xa: lua- t ne: pa ka ku: htan.
we- go- PL we- go- PL we- walk- PL there in woods
'We are going to go take a walk there in (the) woods.'

The second major pathway of future tenses whose growth was triggered or influenced by language contact is provided by de-volitive constructions, where a verb for 'want, wish' is grammaticalized to a future auxiliary, sometimes even further to a verbal affix. A paradigm case is provided by the languages of the Balkan Sprachbund, which we take up in the next section.

3. Grammaticalization areas

The data provided in section 2 were meant to show, first, that the rise of new grammatical categories such as articles and future tenses can be triggered or accelerated by language contact. Second, we saw that grammatical replication was generally unidirectional. For example, there were lexical verbs of physical motion ('go to') and of volition ('want, wish') that developed into future tense markers, and there does not appear to be any language where—with or without language contact—a future tense marker gave rise to a verb meaning 'go to' or 'want'. And third, these data also suggest that contact-induced grammaticalization has an areal perspective.

In fact, once there is a case of contact-induced grammaticalization, the result is a minimal areal grouping, consisting of the area where the model language and the replica languages are spoken. For this kind of grouping, the term 'grammaticalization area' has been proposed (Heine and Kuteva 2005: 5.2.1), which is defined as a group of geographically contiguous languages that have undergone the same grammaticalization process as a result of language contact. Upper Sorbian and German, Molisean and Italian, Basque and its Romance neighbours, or Pipil and Spanish each can be seen as forming a minimal grammaticalization area, since language contact was responsible for the grammaticalization from numeral 'one' to indefinite articles in each of the former on the model of the latter languages.

But it is also possible to propose a much larger grammaticalization area that includes all these languages. Neither Romance nor the Germanic languages had articles some two millennia ago, and, as has been argued by Heine and Kuteva (2006: ch. 3), in the diffusion of both indefinite and definite articles across Europe, contact-induced grammaticalization must have played an important role. The further diffusion of indefinite articles to the Slavic and other languages mentioned above is a younger process that took place in the course of the last centuries; note that this diffusion process was not confined to Europe, but extended across the Atlantic Ocean to regions where European languages spread as important dominant languages, such as Spanish in El Salvador and Mexico, thereby making the Aztecan languages Pipil and Nahuatl part of one and the same overall grammaticalization area.

What we just observed about indefinite articles applies in much the same way to definite articles, with one notable exception. Molisean acquired an indefinite but no definite article via grammaticalization.[5] Nevertheless, it is possible to include Molisean as well within the area of European definite-article languages, for the following reason. With the generalization of the new indefinite article, absence of this article tends to be interpreted by Molisean speakers as an equivalent of the definite article of Italian, and hence Molisean appears to have developed, at least with count nouns, a zeo definite article—one that is also due to language contact but not to grammaticalization.

[5] Breu (1994: 58, 64) suggests that this failure to grammaticalize is due to the fact that, unlike in the model language German in contact with Upper Sorbian, there was no polysemy pattern between the demonstrative (*quello* M, *quella* F) and the definite article (*il* M, *la* F) in the Italian model language, and that this could have prevented Molisean speakers from drawing on their demonstrative for developing a definite article.

Another grammaticalization area can be seen in the geographical region of de-volitive futures on the Balkans, where in one language after the other a verb for 'want, wish' was grammaticalized to a future auxiliary, sometimes even further to a verbal affix. While it remains unclear which of the languages provided the ultimate model for the Balkan futures, it is fairly uncontroversial that contact played a role in their spread. Evidence for this hypothesis is provided, among others, by Romani. As Boretzky (1989) shows, speakers of this Indo-Aryan language have as a rule replicated the future category of the dominant language that they were confronted with. For example, we saw above that for Romani speakers in Wales this was the English de-allative future; for speakers of Romani varieties in the Balkans this was the de-volitive future: They developed a future category marked with *ka(m)-*, which is derived from the verb *kam-av* 'want, love' (Boretzky 1989: 368).

To conclude, one is tempted to predict with a certain degree of probability that if speakers somewhere in southeastern Europe were to develop a new future tense they would do so by using a verb for 'want', since the de-volitive schema offers the primary conceptual choice that is most readily available to speakers on the Balkans. In a similar fashion, one will expect that immigrant speech communities in the USA are most likely to develop a de-allative future in their L1 (first language) because the English *be-going-to* future provides the most immediately available model for replication.

4. Conclusions

That contact-induced grammaticalization plays an important role in the growth of sprachbunds such as the Balkans, Meso-America, etc. has been demonstrated in Heine and Kuteva (2005): quite a number of properties characterizing these linguistic areas can in fact be described as areas of grammaticalization, which include all languages having undergone the same process of grammaticalization as a result of language contact. For example, of the following four 'uncontroversial' properties that have been proposed to define Meso-America as a linguistic area (Campbell, Kaufman, and Smith-Stark 1986: 555), all except one, (d), can be hypothesized to be the result of contact-induced grammaticalization (see Heine and Kuteva 2005: ch. 5).

(a) attributive possession of the type *his-dog the man*;
(b) relational nouns;
(c) vigesimal numeral systems;
(d) non-verb-final basic word order, to which absence of switch-reference is correlated.

In all examples provided in this chapter we were confronted with the same kind of constraint that has been described in more detail in Heine and Kuteva (2005; 2006): speakers in language contact observe principles of grammaticalization in much the same way as they do in situations not involving language contact: they draw on lexical material in order to form new functional categories, and they are unlikely to go in the opposite direction, even if such a possibility can never be entirely ruled out. The result of these processes is that the model and the replica languages become areally related: they form an area of grammaticalization.

Acknowledgements

The authors wish to thank Anna Giacalone Ramat and Caterina Mauri for valuable comments on an earlier version of this chapter. Bernd Heine also expresses his gratitude to Professor Osamu Hieda and the Tokyo University of Foreign Studies, as well as to Professor Kyung-An Song and the Korean Ministry of Education, Science, and Technology for having sponsored part of the research leading to this paper within its World Class University Program (Grant No. R33–10011). Tania Kuteva thanks the Alexander von Humboldt Foundation and the School of Oriental and African Studies (SOAS), University of London, for a generous fellowship within the framework of its Feodor-Lynen Program for Experienced Scholars.

CHAPTER 24

DEGREES OF GRAMMATICALIZATION ACROSS LANGUAGES

BÉATRICE LAMIROY
WALTER DE MULDER

1. Introduction

The central hypothesis of this chapter is that an essential property of grammaticalization, viz. its gradual character,[1] also applies within a genealogical family. Thus, several grammaticalization processes may be more advanced in one language than in the other languages of the same family. We will provide evidence for Romance, by comparing French to two other Romance languages, Italian and Spanish. The cline goes like this:

(1) French > Italian > Spanish

Various approaches have been proposed to account for grammaticalization phenomena, i.e. the development from lexical to grammatical items, and from

[1] The terminology differs according to the authors: grammaticalization is described as a 'continuum' (Brinton 1988), as a 'chain' (Heine and Kuteva 2002), as a 'cline' (Hopper and Traugott 2003), or as a 'pathway' (Bybee, Pagliuca, and Perkins 1994; Bisang 1996).

grammatical to more grammatical forms. We will assume here, following Heine and Narrog (2010), that grammaticalization results from the interaction between phonetic, morphosyntactic, semantic, and pragmatic factors, and that the following parameters can be used to uncover instances of grammaticalization:

- extension, both to new contexts and to other speakers of the linguistic community;
- desemanticization;
- decategorialization, i.e. the loss of the typical morphosyntactic properties of lexical items (or of less grammaticalized forms);
- phonetic reduction.

These parameters not only correspond to each of the above-mentioned linguistic components, but also reflect the diachronic order followed by a grammaticalization process. Phonetic erosion thus represents the final stage of the process, and is not a sine qua non for grammaticalization to occur. Most of the phenomena we will deal with are characteristic of grammaticalization which has already attained a fairly advanced stage in the process.[2]

As pointed out by Heine and Narrog (2010), the ultimate motivation behind any grammaticalization process is successful communication. This entails the development of simpler structures on the one hand (speaker's economy) and of more 'extravagant' structures (hearer's economy) on the other (Geurts 2000a; Haspelmath 2000). In both cases, frequent repetition by users is necessary for the propagation of the new form throughout the linguistic community (Bybee et al. 1994: 8; Krug 2001), a factor which is subsumed under the extension mechanism in Heine and Narrog (2010).

Although Heine and Narrog (2010) do not consider obligatorification, one of Lehmann's (1995a[1982]) parameters, as a central concept but rather as a predictable by-product of decategorialization, we tend to believe that it plays an important role in grammaticalization, along with paradigmatization,[3] because the constitution of paradigms is in part what grammar is about. We thus consider that a form which speakers can freely choose according to their communicative intentions is less grammaticalized than one for which their choice is limited in a systematic way. For this reason, for example, the French personal pronoun may be considered more grammaticalized than its Spanish and Italian counterparts, since its expression in

[2] They correspond to stages III and IV of Heine (2002).

[3] Obligatorification occurs when the choice of an item is 'systematically constrained and its use largely obligatory', as opposed to the free 'choice of items according to the communicative intentions' of the speaker (Lehmann 1995a[1982]: 164). 'The process of paradigmatic integration or paradigmaticization leads to a leveling out of the differences with which the members were equipped originally' (ibid. 135)

French, the only non-pro-drop Romance language, is no longer optional. We will come back to this point when we discuss the virtual disappearance of the 'past simple' and the decrease of the subjunctive in French.

A few remarks are in order here. First and foremost, the cline in (1) is not intended as a tool to measure the distance between the three languages and the mother language, Latin. Second, what we will show is a very robust tendency rather than an absolute principle. For example, in most cases, Spanish will be shown to be the most conservative language. Yet Spanish, just like Portuguese and French, but unlike Italian, developed a future auxiliary out of the motion verb *ir* 'go':

(2) Sp. Va a llover.
go.3SG.IND.PRS to rain.INF.PRS
'It is going to rain'.

Moreover, as is well known, a grammaticalization process may start without going all the way, and sometimes language seems to evolve in the opposite direction, i.e. there are also cases of degrammaticalization (Norde 2009a). However, as cases of degrammaticalization do not seem to amount to more than 10 per cent of all grammatical evolutions (Heine and Narrog 2010), they do not seriously threaten the unidirectionality hypothesis of grammaticalization. Likewise, there is significant evidence that clearly argues in favour of the hypothesis that, all in all, French is more grammaticalized than the other Romance languages under study. A well-known example is that of (late) Latin *casa* 'house', which grammaticalized into the French preposition *chez* 'at', whereas both Spanish and Italian have maintained *casa* as a noun meaning 'house'. Another case in point is the Latin noun *homo* 'man', which in French (and Occitan) grammaticalized into the indefinite pronoun *on* (e.g. Fr. *On ne vit qu'une fois* 'You live only once'): this happened in none of the other Romance languages. In addition, in French, the same pronoun *on* was the source of a second grammaticalization process, so that it now also functions as an equivalent of the 1st person plural pronoun *nous* (e.g. *on part* 'we are leaving').

The idea that French, Italian, and Spanish are grammaticalized to different degrees, with French being more grammaticalized than Italian and Spanish, and Italian more than Spanish (cf. (1)), will be illustrated here with data concerning central areas of the grammar: auxiliaries, tense and mood, existential sentences, and demonstratives. However, the same tendency also holds for other areas, which we will not be able to go into here, such as word order (Marchello-Nizia 2006a: 131; 2009), prepositions (Goyens et al. 2002; Lamiroy 2001), etc.

2. Auxiliaries

Auxiliaries are defined as TAM verbs (Heine 1993), i.e. they express tense, aspect, or mood, as in (3):

(3)

Fr.	Jean	commence	à	manger.
Sp.	Juan	comienza	a	comer.
It.	Gianni	comincia	a	mangiare.
	John	begin.3SG.IND.PRS	to	eat.INF.PRS

'John begins to eat.'

In all Romance languages, auxiliaries are the outcome of grammaticalization processes (Lamiroy 1999; Squartini 1998); however, French displays less lexical variation among its TAM verbs than Spanish and Italian, so its paradigmatic variability is more constrained. Spanish, for example, has at least six auxiliaries to express inchoative aspect, whereas French has only two, *commencer* and *se mettre*:

(4)
a. Sp. Ana empezó / comenzó a reir.
Ann begin.3SG.IND.PS / begin.3SG.IND.PS to laugh.INF.PRS
b. Ana se metió[4] / se puso a reir.
Ann herself put.3SG.IND.PS / herself put.3SG.IND.PS to laugh.INF.PRS
c. Ana se echó a reir.
Ann herself throw.3SG.IND.PS to laugh.INF.PRS
d. Ana rompió a reir.
Ann break.3SG.IND.PS to laugh.INF.PRS
'Ann began to laugh.'

The class of Spanish[5] and, to a lesser extent, of Italian[6] TAM verbs is also larger because certain iterative and habitual auxiliaries which did not survive in French are still in use in these languages. Paradigmaticization is thus more advanced in French:

[4] In contrast to the other Spanish inchoative verbs, *meterse, echar(se)*, and *romper* only take a [+hum] subject, which means that their extension to all contexts is not completed, as one would expect from fully grammaticalized auxiliaries: individual TAM verbs thus display different degrees of grammaticalization within the same language as well.

[5] These auxiliaries have again lexical variants, e.g. *acostumbrar* + infinitive is a synonym of *soler*.

[6] Renzi and Salvi (1991: 521) mention the Italian auxiliary with habitual meaning *solere* but say it is archaic. Note that *soloir* existed in old French (Tobler and Lommatzsch 1925–2002).

(5) Sp. Vuelve a llover.
go back.3SG.IND.PRS to rain.INF.PRS
It. ? Torna a piovere.
go back.3SG.IND.PRS to rain.INF.PRS
'It rains again.'

Sp. Solía verla cada día.
use.3SG.IND.IMPF see.INF.PRS=her.ACC.SG every day
'He used to see her every day.'

With respect to progressive aspect, Spanish and Italian respectively use *estar*, *stare* 'to be' and *ir*, *andare* 'to go' followed by the gerund:

(6) a. Sp. Está / va diciendo mentiras.
It. Sta / va dicendo bugie.
be.3SG.IND.PRS / go.3SG.IND.PRS say.GER lies
'He is lying.'

A similar construction used to exist in French, but gradually disappeared from the 17th century on, only surviving in semi-idiomatic expressions such as:

(6) b. Fr. Le problème va croissant.
the problem go.3SG.IND.PRS increase.GER
'The problem is increasing'.

Several accounts have been proposed in the literature for the disappearance of the gerund with progressive meaning in French, both external factors such as the criticism by normative grammarians, who consider it an Italianism, and internal factors, such as the competition with the imperfect, which can also express progressive meaning (Schoesler 2006). In our view, the emergence of the 'extravagant' infinitival structure *être en train de* and its gradual extension in French, which eventually made the progressive structure with gerund disappear, may be partly[7] due to the fact that the new structure enters the same paradigm as all the other TAM verbs, i.e. a verb necessarily followed by an infinitive. The infinitival structure thus has a 'magnetic' effect, attracting all TAM verbs into a similar formal pattern.[8] Whereas *être en train de* + infinitive only took [+hum] subjects and was followed by action verbs at first, its distribution progressively extended to all kinds of contexts (Mortier 2007).

In sum, not only are French TAM verbs more limited than their Spanish and Italian counterparts, but the class of auxiliaries is also more homogeneous since

[7] The official criticism by normative grammarians may of course have accelerated the spreading of the new construction.

[8] Note that the future auxiliary *aller* 'go' followed by the infinitive emerges around the same time, during the 17th century (Detges 1999).

they all display the same syntactic property, that of exclusively taking infinitival complements. Therefore paradigmaticization is more advanced in French than in the other languages.

3. The 'past simple'

In contemporary spoken French, the *passé simple* with aoristic meaning has disappeared and has been replaced by the present perfect (Grevisse-Goosse 2007: 882). In written and spoken Spanish in contrast, the equivalent tense, viz. *pretérito indefinido*, is not only common but is obligatory to indicate aoristic meaning[9] and in Italian, the *passato remoto*, still in use in the South, is disappearing in the North of the country:[10]

(7)	a.	Fr.	?*	Hier	il	vint.
				yesterday	he	come.3SG.IND.PS
		It.	?	Ieri		venne.
		Sp.		Ayer		vino.
				yesterday		come.3SG.IND.PS

b.	Fr.		Hier	il est venu.
			yesterday	he come.3SG.IND.PRF
	It.		Ieri	è venuto.
	Sp.	?*	Ayer	ha venido.
			yesterday	come.3SG.IND.PRF
			'He came yesterday.'	

The Romance present perfect, as is well known, is the result of a grammaticalization process of a resultative construction with the full verb *habere* + [past participle of a transitive verb + direct object], which was reanalysed as [*habere* + past participle] + direct object, before extending to intransitive verbs. In a seminal paper on the evolution of the Vulgar Latin periphrastic perfect, Harris (1982a) convincingly shows that its development consists of four stages, each of which can still be found in some Romance languages or dialects. Whereas the original value of the construction (stage I) is merely aspectual, expressing resultative meaning (which is still the case in Sicilian), in Stage II the perfect acquires a temporal

[9] This judgement holds for peninsular Spanish. In certain areas of South America, the present perfect is sometimes used with aoristic meaning (Scott Schwenter, p.c.).

[10] Interestingly, the simple past also survived longer in the south of France than in the north (Grevisse-Goosse 2007: 882).

value, indicating past events whose result lasts until the moment of speech (as in modern Portuguese). In stage III, it marks past events with relevance for the moment of speech (as in modern Spanish) and finally, in Stage IV, the perfect is simply used to encode past events, i.e. it has become a marker of aoristic value, thus replacing the 'past simple'. Although all four stages persist in French, of the three languages under analysis here, only French and northern variants of Italian have reached the last stage.

Interestingly, Detges (1999; 2000; 2006) argues that the evolution from stage I to IV should be accounted for in pragmatic terms, i.e. by subjectification.[11] While the resultative aspectual value is the starting point of the evolution of the Romance perfect (as is the case in many languages; cf. Heine and Kuteva 2006: 140–82), the present perfect was progressively used to mark past events with current relevance. As pointed out by Detges, there is a metonymic implicature between current knowledge and the previous experience by which it was brought about, which can be exploited for pragmatic reasons: by choosing the present perfect, a speaker coding himself as subject of this construction makes a strong commitment with respect to the current consequences of previous events. In other words, the function of the present perfect is to emphasize the subject's involvement in the state of affairs expressed by the verb. This metonymic implicature was conventionalized as part of the structure's temporal meaning. Finally, in stage IV, which French attained in the 18th century, the construction came to refer to the past event itself without necessarily implying its impact at the moment of speech. It is therefore the actual equivalent of what the simple past used to be. Detges (2006: 69) points out that the shift from stage I to II took place much later in Spanish than in French, which probably explains why Spanish still is at stage III and has not reached stage IV, as French has. The above mentioned ongoing evolution in the north of Italy suggests that the Italian perfect might be undergoing a similar grammaticalization process as the one that affected French in the 18th century.

4. Existential sentences

Whereas French and Spanish existential sentences take the form of an impersonal construction with the locative clitic *y* and *avoir/haber* respectively (*il y a* and *hay*), Italian uses *essere* in combination with the locative *ci*. *Essere* can occur in 3rd person singular or plural, *c'è* or *ci sono*:

[11] For an account of the English perfect also based on the notion of subjectification, see Carey (1995).

(8) Fr. Il y a beaucoup de monde ici.
it there have.3SG.IND.PRS a lot of people here
It. C' è molta gente quì.
there be.3SG.IND.PRS much people here
Sp. Hay mucha gente aquí.
have.3SG.IND.PRS much people here
'There are a lot of people here.'

Although Fr. *il y a*, It. *c'è* and Sp. *hay* are all three grammaticalized structures which originated either as an expression of possession (*avoir/haber*) or of existence (*essere*) combined with a now totally bleached locative pronoun *y/ci*, Meulleman (in press: 231ff.) argues that French *il y a* is far more grammaticalized than its Spanish and Italian counterparts. With respect to the four above-mentioned parameters of grammaticalization processes, French *il y a* shows the following results. As far as extension is concerned, three important facts can be pointed out. First, French *il y a* came to be used as an obligatory tool to restrict a subject in focus, e.g.

(9) Fr. Il n' y a que toi qui sais
it there have.3SG.IND.PRS only you who know.2SG.IND.PRS
où est la clé.
where be.3SG.IND.PRS the key
'Only you know where the key is.'

The Spanish and Italian counterparts here would use the adverb *sólo/solo*[12] respectively, since *hay* and *c'è* do not have a similar function. Secondly, with respect to the following NP, in existential sentences whose main discursive function is to introduce a (hearer-)new referent, the existential N is typically introduced by an indefinite determiner. Whereas this holds as a general rule for the Spanish examples in Meulleman's corpus, French and Italian allow all kinds of determiners, even proper names (Meulleman in press: 245), e.g.

(10) Fr. Ainsi à Roncevaux il y a Roland, son cor et
thus in Roncevaux it there have.3SG.IND.PRS Roland, his horn and
son épée, ça fait trois.
his sword, that make.3SG.IND.PRS three.
'Thus in Roncevaux there is Roland, his horn and his sword, that makes three.' (*Le Monde*, 28 Feb. 1994)

[12] French *seul* can also be used with restrictive meaning, but only in front of a full NP and its use is limited to written French.

It. Al fianco del regista ci sono Sienna Miller (. . .), il
next to the director there be.3PL.PRES.IND Sienna Miller (. . .), the
grande Jeremy Irons, . . .
great Jeremy Irons, . . .
'Next to the director there is Sienna Miller, the great Jeremy Irons, . . .'
(*Corriere della sera*, 4 Sept. 2005)

It should be noted, however, as pointed out by Meulleman (in press: 248), that the extension of the existential NP is more relevant for French than for Italian, since only the French construction is really an impersonal structure, whereas the Italian *c'è* also may appear as a plural and with a preposed subject, as in

(11) It. Però il disagio c' è e si sente lo stesso.
But the discomfort there be.3SG.IND.PRS and . . .
'But the discomfort is there and one feels it all the same.'
(*Corriere della sera*, 4 Sept. 2005)

And finally, French *il y a* has become extremely common in sentence initial position of a bi-clausal structure in which a non-topic NP appears postverbally in the first clause (Lambrecht 1994: 169):

(12) a. Il y a des garçons qui sont partis.
it there have.3SG.IND.PRS boys who go.3PL.IND.PRF
'Some boys left.'

b. Il y a ma mère qui est à l'hôpital.
it there have.3SG.IND.PRS my mother who be.3SG.IND.PRS at the hospital
'My mother is in the hospital.'

At the same time, the above examples show that *il y a* is the most desemanticized of all three existential structures, as it no longer has existential meaning in this case, but merely functions as a discursive tool for thetic sentences. In cases like (12), in Spanish and Italian, subject inversion would occur. In modern French, however, where subject inversion is highly constrained, *il y a* now functions as a device to obtain the same discursive effect (Béguelin 2000). Interestingly, whereas Spanish *hay* is never used in this context, specialists of spoken Italian (Aureli 2003; Fiorentino 1999) mention a non-standard use of a 'weak relative' with *c'è* that seems similar to the above indicated French structure, e.g.

(13) C' è un uomo che corre sulla spiaggia.
there be.3SG.IND.PRS a man who run.3SG.IND.PRS on-the beach
'A man is running on the beach.'

French *il y a* is also the most decategorialized of the three structures, since (as we have already mentioned) it no longer has the property of selecting indefinite NPs, which is a characteristic of impersonal existential sentences. Furthermore, *il y a* is a case of *polygrammaticalization*, since it also became a temporal preposition meaning 'ago'. This is neither the case for Sp. *hay* nor for It. *c'è*:

(14) Paul est arrivé il y a trois semaines.
Paul arrive.3SG.IND.PRF it there have.3SG.IND.PRS three weeks
'Paul arrived three weeks ago.'

Note finally that of the three existential structures, only the French one also shows phonetic erosion, *il y a* being often reduced to "*y a*" pronounced as [ja]. This form even occurs in written French, as the following press example testifies (Meulleman in press: 235):

(15) Rassurez-vous, y a un truc.
calm.2PL.IMP.PRS you, there have.3SG.IND.PRS a trick
'Don't worry, there is a trick.'
(*Le Monde*, 28 Jan. 1994)

5. Mood

That the French subjunctive is more grammaticalized than its Italian and Spanish counterparts was already pointed out by Harris (1978: 172), who considers the French subjunctive to be mainly a marker of subordination, in contrast with the remaining Romance languages, where mood alternation between the indicative and the subjunctive parallels a difference in meaning. The crucial difference between the two modes is based on the speaker's commitment with respect to a state of affairs in the case of the indicative and the avoidance of such a commitment in the case of the subjunctive (Dreer 2007: 24). Obviously it is not possible to treat all uses of the subjunctive in the three languages in the space allotted here. We will therefore only zoom in upon a certain number of significant facts.

First, although the French subjunctive obviously is still in use, there is no doubt that it is much less frequent than it used to be (Buridant 2000: 337; Dreer 2007: 201ff.; Lagerqvist 2009: 39). After verbs expressing hope or belief for example, the subjunctive could be used in Old French, but this is no longer the case now:

(16) OFr. Bien quident ce ait fait Tristan.
well think.3PL.IND.PRS this faire.3SG.SBJV.PST Tristan
(Dreer 2007: 209)

Fr. Ils pensent que Tristan a fait /
they think that Tristan faire.3SG.IND.PRF /
*ait fait cela
faire.3SG.SBJV.PST that
'They think Tristan did it.'

From the 17th century on, the indicative quickly spread as the normal mood after verbs expressing belief in French, at least in affirmative constructions. In the other two languages, verbs of belief still allow both moods, as exemplified by the Italian example in (17):

(17) a. Credo che ora è possibile difendermi
believe.1SG.IND.PRS that now be.3SG.IND.PRS possible defend.INF.PRS=me
da tutte le calunnie.
from all the slander
'I believe that I can protect myself against any gossip now.'
(Wandruszka 2001: 434)

b. Multi credono che la Borsa abbia toccato
Many think.3PL.IND.PRS that the Stock Exchange touch.3SG.SBJV.PST
il suo tetto.
its ceiling
'Many think that the Stock Exchange has touched the roof.'
(Wandruszka 2001: 434)

In general, both in the independent and in the subordinate clause,[13] the subjunctive is much less frequent in French than in contemporary Spanish and Italian, as shown by a large corpus study on the subjunctive in Romance languages (Loengarov 2006: 343).[14]

Second, even if the subjunctive in French, like the Latin *coniuntivus* (Pinkster 1990) can still signal non-factivity,[15] what has crucially changed is its status with respect to paradigmatic variability. Whereas speakers of Spanish (Ridruejo 2000:

[13] Adverbial clauses, object clauses, and indirect questions are all subsumed under this term.

[14] This observation has been confirmed by the results of a small corpus study of Antonio Tabucchi's novel *Sostiene Pereira* and its French translation. The Italian text contains 233 cases of the Italian *congiuntivo*, whereas its French translation only contains 111 cases of the *subjonctif*. A similar study of a small Spanish corpus, Isabel Allende's novel *De amor y de sombra*, and its French translation shows 434 forms in the *subjuntivo* in the original text against 147 forms in the *subjonctif* in the French translation.

[15] 'Non-factivity' means that the situation expressed in a clause is not presented as a fact by the speaker and thus is not asserted.

3229) and Italian (Brunet 2006: 162) often still have the choice between the two moods, according to their intention to present the denoted situation as a fact or not, mood selection in French is largely determined by lexical elements such as the valency of the main verb or a particular conjunction, i.e. mood has undergone what Lehmann (1995a[1982]) labeled 'obligatorification'. Thus a verb such as *espérer*, which allowed the subjunctive in former days to stress that the speaker did not ascertain the chances of the event hoped for, only takes the indicative now. The Spanish and Italian counterparts, *esperar* and *sperare*, allow both. Note that the phonetic and morphological evolution of French also led to a much higher degree of syncretism between verbal forms in the indicative and the subjunctive, so that the distinction between the two modes is also formally more blurred in French than in the other languages.

Interestingly, Wandruszka (2001: 422) signals that in some regions of Italy and in more informal popular language, the indicative is more frequently used than the subjunctive after verbs of hope and belief. On the other hand, Loengarov (2006: 195) argues that although the subjunctive is often found after verbs of belief in Italian, in many cases it does not seem to be clearly motivated by a semantic or discursive choice by the speaker. In other words, both moods after verbs such as *pensare* or *credere* seem to occur without a semantic difference, which could suggest that they are in an overlap stage (Heine 1993). Although of course more research is needed here, this could signal an ongoing evolution in Italian which parallels the history of French, something we have already observed with respect to the tense system in section 3.

A final point we want to make concerns the so-called thematic use of the subjunctive. In Latin, psych-verbs (i.e. verbs expressing a mental state or event, e.g. *to please*, *to disappoint*, *to frighten*) were followed by the indicative in the object clause (Pinkster 1990: 209), precisely because the situation indicated by the clause is presented as a fact:

(18) Lat. Sane gaudeo quod te interpellavi.
certainly be happy.1SG.IND.PRS that you interrupt.1SG.IND.PRF
'I am certainly happy to have interrupted you.'

Although the indicative remains more frequent in the oldest stages of all three Romance languages, the subjunctive after psych-verbs appeared in Late Latin and became the normal mood in cases such as:

(19) Fr. Je regrette qu' il soit parti.
I be sorry.1SG.IND.PRS that he leave.3SG.SBJV.PST
It. Mi dispiace che sia partito.
me.DAT not-please.3SG.IND.PRS that leave.3SG.SBJV.PST
Sp. Siento que se haya ido.
be sorry.1SG.IND.PRS that 3SG.RE. leave.3SG.SBJV.PST
'I am sorry that he left.'

The preference for the subjunctive in these contexts obviously cannot be accounted for by the non-factivity of the complement clause, since its content is presupposed. Its main function rather is to signal syntactic and discursive subordination: whereas the state of affairs indicated by the complement clause is thematic, the new information is expressed by the main clause. So the Romance subjunctive developed a new function which it did not have in Latin: that of signalling the theme of the sentence. This non-etymological or non-harmonic (Bybee et al. 1994: 218ff.) subjunctive now regularly appears in subject clauses in all three languages (Gsell and Wandruszka 1986: 87). However, it is revealing in this respect that the thematic subjunctive in subject clauses seems to have become the general rule in French: in a recent corpus study (Lagerqvist 2009: 423), not a single case was found in the indicative. Loengarov (2005) similarly underscores the extremely high frequency of the subjunctive after Fr. *le fait que* 'the fact that'. Although further research is needed here for Italian, it comes as no surprise that in Spanish the indicative appears to be not at all rare in this case, especially in its South American variants (Lope-Blanch 1990: 181). In other words, the new thematic function of the subjunctive seems to have attained a virtually complete extension in French, while this is not the case in Spanish.

6. Demonstratives

Classical Latin had an elaborate system of demonstrative pronouns and adjectives which contained, alongside the anaphoric *is*, three demonstratives that indicated the relation between their referent and the participants to the speech event in a straightforward way:

(20) Lat. *hic* meant 'this near to me; close to the first person'
iste 'that near to you; close to the second person'
ille 'that of some other person; close to third person'

This system was completed by the identity markers *ipse* 'self' and *idem* 'same'. It underwent several changes from Vulgar Latin to the modern Romance languages; most importantly, the original demonstratives weakened and had to be reinforced by *ecce* 'behold' or the equivalent form *accu*. Both forms lost their independence and became prefixes. In Spanish, *(accu+)iste*, *(accu+)ipse* and *(accu+)ille* evolved into *(aqu)este*, *(aqu)ese* and *aquel* respectively (Harris 1978: 71). These forms can be analysed as part of a 'person-oriented' system, as is the case in Latin, but also as part of a 'distance-oriented' system, as is illustrated by the two values of *ese* (Da Milano 2007: 28):

(21) a. Sp. *este*: close to the speaker
ese: at a middle distance from the speaker or near the addressee
aquel: far away

Of the reinforced forms, only *aquel* was maintained, probably because the corresponding simple form *el* developed other uses, as a definite article and as a pronominal (Harris 1978: 71).

In Italian, the Vulgar Latin system underwent different evolutions in different regions. The standard language developed three forms:

(21) b. It. *questo*: close to the speaker ('first-person oriented')
quello: away from the speaker
codesto: away from the speaker, near the addressee

However, whereas the three forms are still commonly used in Spanish, in modern Italian *codesto* has become obsolete. While Italian is thus on the way to reducing its system to a binary one,[16] Old French had already eliminated the demonstrative indicating the middle distance and retained only *cest* (from *ecce* + *istu(m)*) and *cel* (from *ecce+illu(m)*).[17] It had several other demonstrative forms (for an overview, see Marchello-Nizia 1995: 126–7), but these have been progressively eliminated, thus facilitating the creation of a more unified paradigm. *Cest* and *cel*, the precursors of the modern forms, marked a difference in distance:

(21) c. OFr. *cest*: close to the speaker
cel: farther away from the speaker

Moreover, both forms could be used either as a pronoun or as a determiner, as in Latin and in modern Spanish and Italian. Despite its clear structure, the system of demonstratives underwent a drastic change from Old French on (cf. Marchello-Nizia 1995; 2006b). The resulting modern French system differs from Italian and Spanish in two respects:

(i) Demonstrative pronouns and determiners are expressed by different forms: *ce* is mainly used as a determiner (it can be used as a neuter pronoun, but only in certain contexts), whereas *celui(-ci)*, *celui(-là)*, and *cela* are used as pronouns. In this way, French is the only one of the three languages under study that has created a formal distinction corresponding to the grammatical difference between determiner and pronoun.

[16] The distinction between three degrees of distance has been maintained in the south of Italy, with forms such as *stu*, *ssu*, and *ddu*, deriving from *istum*, *ipsum*, and *illum* respectively (Rohlfs 1966–9: §494; Harris 1978: 72).

[17] The masculine singular forms of Old French (*cest* and *cel*) and modern French (*ce*, *celui-ci* and *celui-là*) are used here to represent paradigms which also contain the corresponding feminine and plural forms. For more information, see Buridant (2000) and Grevisse-Goosse (2007).

(ii) The demonstrative forms *ce* and *celui* no longer express differences in distance by themselves; therefore, already in Middle French, *ici* and *là* were added to express these distinctions. Subsequently, both forms have weakened again and have been transformed into the suffixes *-ci* and *-là*, e.g. *ceci, cela, celui-ci, celui-là*.[18] Note that they no longer systematically indicate distance-related oppositions: *-là* does not necessarily imply that the referent is far away and functions as the unmarked form with respect to *-ci*; it refers to a generic space around the speaker and the hearer (Da Milano 2007: 30).[19] Thus, both the forms *ce* and *celui* and the linguistic items that were called upon to restore the demonstrative function (*ecce-* and *accu-*) or to indicate the deictic differences in distance (*-ci* and *-là*) have undergone coalescence and semantic weakening.

The changes thus confirm the idea of different degrees of grammaticalization between the three languages under study, French being more advanced with respect to the formation of unified paradigms for demonstrative pronouns and determiners than, respectively, Italian and Spanish (cf. the scale under (1) above). French can thus be said to be more grammaticalized than the other two languages, because (i) it has created separate paradigms for demonstrative determiners and pronouns, (ii) these demonstrative forms have undergone desemanticization and erosion, and (iii) both *ce* (as a determiner) and *celui* (which has to be followed by *-ci* or *-là* or other complements, such as a relative phrase) have lost their autonomy.

7. Conclusions

We have provided evidence from central areas of the grammar of three Romance languages that one of them, French, has reached a further stage of grammaticalization in these areas than Spanish and Italian. This raises several issues for further research.

From an empirical point of view, it needs to be investigated what the relation is between all the Romance languages, including those we have not taken into consideration, with respect to their degree of grammaticalization. More importantly, it must be verified whether data similar to those described here are known from other language families. Although facts have been pointed out that support the hypothesis for Romance in general (Loengarov 2006; Marchello-Nizia 2006a:

[18] Note once more that Italian seems to be evolving in the way French did: Sabatini (1985: 159) points out that in non-standard Italian the demonstrative pronouns *questo* and *quello* tend to be reinforced by *quí* 'here' and *là* 'there', being often replaced by *questo qui* and *quello là*.

[19] In fact, nowadays *là-bas* is added to the word to mark greater distance (Da Milano 2007: 30).

111) and for a similar cline regarding Germanic languages (Hüning et al. 2006; Mortelmans 2004; Van Haeringen 1956), much more typological evidence would be needed to strengthen our hypothesis.

On a theoretical level, the question arises whether examples from one or two language families are sufficient to raise the issue regarding different rates of grammaticalization in general. If it turns out that a comparable situation holds for other language families, one should wonder why this is so and which factors determine the rate of grammaticalization. We believe that the explanation lies in the combination of internal and external factors (language contact, frequency, the existence of structural patterns that can act as attractors (cf. section 2), etc.), which reinforce each other; but we have to leave this question too for further research.

CHAPTER 25

GRAMMATICALIZATION AND SEMANTIC MAPS

HEIKO NARROG
JOHAN VAN DER AUWERA

1. Semantic maps

1.1. Introduction

Semantic maps are a way to visualize regular relationships between two or more meanings or grammatical functions of one and the same linguistic form. By 'regular', it is meant that these relationships can either be observed cross-linguistically, in a language sample of a certain size,[1] or within one language with a certain number of markers or constructions which exhibit the same kind of form–meaning relationship. The first semantic map is usually attributed to Anderson (1982; 1986), who offered maps of the perfect and related categories and of evidentials.[2] It was only in the late 1990s, however, that this approach took hold. Recent research using

[1] Haspelmath (2003: 217) claims that a dozen of 'genealogically diverse' languages are sufficient. Wälchli (2010) shows that sample size has considerable influence on the outcome of a map, and argues in favour of large sample sizes. Note, though, that Haspelmath (2003) is referring to 'classical' maps (see below), while Wälchli (2009) is referring to statistically plotted maps.

[2] One can, of course, find predecessors. For the indefiniteness map of Haspelmath's (1997), for instance, one can go back to Aristotle and the Aristotelian Square of Oppositions (van der Auwera and Van Alsenoy forthcoming).

semantic maps includes Haspelmath (1997; 2003; 2004a) on indefinite pronouns, reflexives, dative functions, and coordinating constructions, Malchukov (2004) on adversatives, van der Auwera and Plungian (1998) on modality, van der Auwera and Malchukov (2005) on depictive adjectivals, and Narrog and Ito (2007) and Narrog (2009b; 2010b) on case, particularly the area of instrumentals and comitatives.

The evidence that is normally, but not necessarily, used as the basis for the construction of semantic maps is polysemy data. Consider a form which has three uses (functions or meanings). Since we are dealing with polysemy rather than with homonymy, the uses are related, but they are all related to each other either in a similar way, or one use is intermediate between the other uses. The two constellations are represented in Fig. 25.1 and both constitute semantic maps. The semantic links are symbolized by lines.

Of these two constellations the second one is the more interesting one. If use B is truly semantically intermediate, one would not expect there to be a form which has uses A and C, but not B. This is an empirically testable hypothesis. The strength of the hypothesis depends both on the plausibility of the semantic analysis positing B as semantically intermediate and on the linguistic evidence, typically cross-linguistic, showing that in language after language forms either have just one function or all three and if two, then either A and B or B and C but never A and C.

Fig. 25.2 gives a real example of what this kind of map may look like. The map says that there is a relationship of direct meaning extension between the meanings/functions connected by a line. It is also claimed that there is no relationship of direct meaning extension between meanings/functions not connected by a line. The map thus posits various implicational universals: for example, if a linguistic marker or construction has the functions of comitative and agent, it must also have the function of instrumental. The map can in principle also be construed deductively without cross-linguistic empirical evidence. One can think of a map of colour terms or of body-part terms, where some kind of conceptual space is already given from outside language (cf. Zwarts 2010), but a map can in principle also be a product of pre-empirical conceptual analysis, for example the famous network analysis for the English preposition *over* by Brugman and Lakoff (Lakoff 1987). However, ultimately the claims made in the map must be empirically testable. Thus, the validity of a map can always be challenged by bringing up

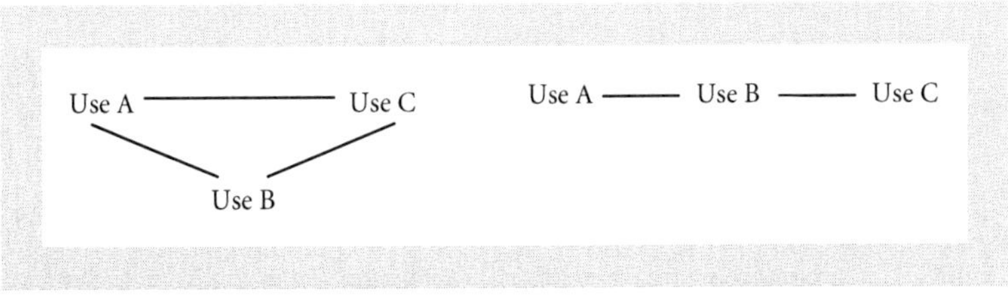

Fig. 25.1. Two maps with three uses of one linguistic form

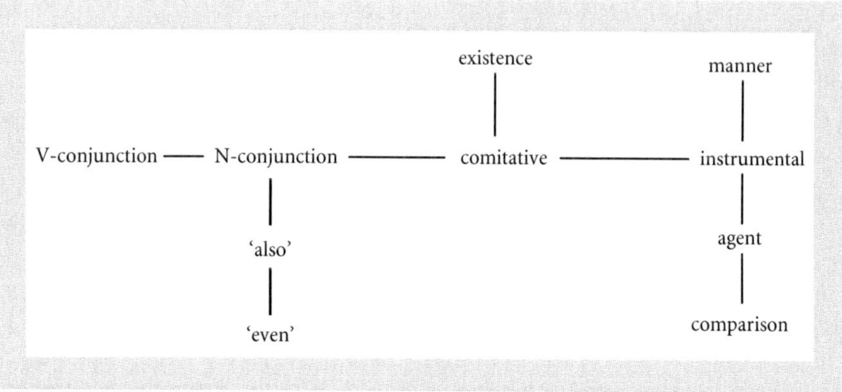

Fig. 25.2. A semantic map for conjunction and related functions (Haspelmath 2004a: 21)

examples of direct meaning extension not represented on the map, or by empirically rejecting the evidence that has been brought up in favour of a connection represented on the map.

1.2. Types of semantic map

The maps as in Figs 25.1 and 25.2 are not the only way to conceive of, or to draw a semantic map. At least the following distinctions can be made:

1) (a) maps which explicitly depict connections between meanings through lines vs. (b) maps that represent similarity between meanings by spatial adjacency;
2) (a) maps which are construed based on semantic analysis complemented by knowledge of cross-linguistic data vs. (b) maps that are plotted on the basis of data alone (usually on the basis of statistical methods), and do not involve semantic analysis.

The map in Fig. 25.2 is of type (1a). If, for example, the connecting lines are removed from it, the relationship between meanings/functions on this map would be represented exclusively by spatial adjacency, i.e. it would become a map of type (1b). Its properties would change. While in the map in Fig. 25.2 it is possible to place a meaning B relatively far from meaning A and still posit a connection, this would contradict the principles of a map based on spatial adjacency. But this example also shows that the borderlines between different types of maps are not impermeable. In the case of the map in Fig. 25.2, the connecting lines can be removed, and, because spatial adjacency happens to be observed in this map, it could also function as a map of type (1b). Furthermore, methodologically (2b) maps are basically a subset of (1b) maps. That is, maps of the (1b) type may or may not be statistical. Likewise, as argued in section 3, statistically plotted maps are not necessarily incompatible with connections between meanings/functions. Also, while the very process of generating the map automatically excludes semantic analysis as a factor in the construction of the map, the input can be manipulated in a manner that reflects the judgements of the researcher, for example by deleting apparently semantically infelicitous or ungrammatical instances from the input data.

In the kind of map making illustrated so far, which has the features of (1a) and (2a), and is called 'classical' (van der Auwera 2008), 'traditional' (Malchukov 2010), or 'implicational' (Wälchli 2010), the a priori analysis and the a posteriori analysis often go hand in hand. But the two are nevertheless independent. If, for example, in a map with the meanings A, B, and C, grammatical forms with only two of these meaning can have either A and B or B and C, but never A and C, the position of B still has to be semantically interpreted. This independence is very clear in statistical map-making. The statistical method usually employed is multidimensional scaling (MDS). Fig. 25.3 probably presents the first MDS semantic map that was produced and circulated, and eventually published in Croft and Poole (2008: 26).

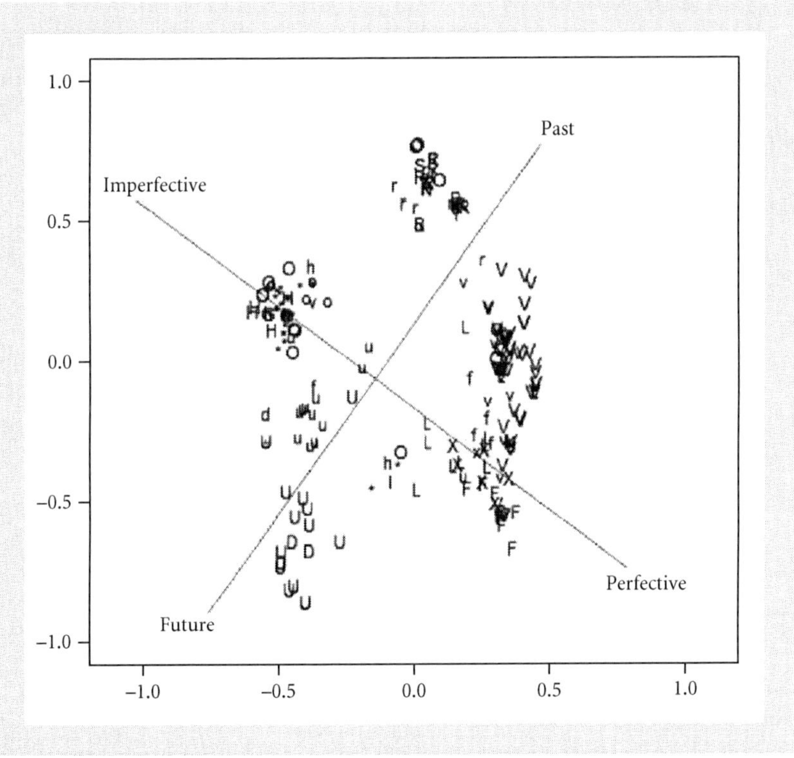

Fig. 25.3. Spatial model of tense and aspect with Dahl's prototypes (Croft and Poole 2008: 26)

It is not necessary to explain this map in any detail here, since this is done in the original paper. The letters stand for specific tense/aspect categories, e.g. U for future, D for predictive, V for perfective, and O for progressive. Each occurrence designates a context that is more (capital letter) or less (small letter) typical for the category in question. Thus, for example, typical future contexts cluster with typical predictive contexts in the lower left half of the figure. The two dimensions of this figure are not given a priori, nor are they set up by the researcher, but they are automatically calculated by the statistical programme. In contrast, the two axes and their labels (IMPERFECTIVE, PAST, etc.) are added by the researchers as a result of their interpretation of this spatial arrangement. Note that the map in Fig. 25.3 has no lines. Similarity is now only symbolized by spatial adjacency.

The biggest gain in this type of map is that spatial adjacency can now reflect similarity, in this case, of contexts, in a much more fine-grained way than in the classical maps, and we can see the new maps starting to join and possibly replace the classical ones, especially those that purely relied on the representation of similarity through proximity. Fig. 25.3 illustrates one further advantage. Statistically calculated maps can draw on a wide range of linguistic data, and are able to translate linguistic contexts directly into mappings. They are also not limited to the representation of meaning extension, i.e. polysemy.[3] Cysouw (2010: 70) has recently radically redefined maps of this kind as a 'metric on meaning'. In other words, any data that are calculable and that provide insight into the similarity of meanings/functions can be utilized for the construction of a semantic map. Cysouw (2010) provided examples himself, and explored data on the (degree of) formal similarity of transitive/intransitive verb pairs, thus resulting in a similarity map for transitive/intransitive verb pairs, which does not represent possible polysemies. Cysouw (2010) even combines a dimension calculated through MDS with metrics gained otherwise in a single graph. This approach opens up new avenues of research that have not yet been fully explored (see also Wälchli 2010). However, these maps are strictly confined to the representation of similarity. Implicational universals, for example, are not represented in such a map. Nor are these maps designed to reflect the analysis of the researcher, who checks for and features out factors that lead to quirky polysemies (cf. Malchukov 2010). Thus, Malchukov (pp. 178, 195) contrasts 'similarity maps' with traditional maps, which represent a 'semantic residue of the similarity map' and can be considered as 'an important tool for semantic analysis'.

[3] Arguably, classical maps are not restricted to polysemy mapping either. At least, the imperative map in van der Auwera, Dobrushina, and Goussev (2004) is not.

2. From grammaticalization paths to semantic maps

Most semantic maps have so far dealt with particular areas of grammar rather than of the lexicon (see Perrin 2010 for an exception), and only a few maps have integrated relationships between lexical and grammatical meanings and functions. Thus, if grammaticalization is strictly viewed as being confined to the pre-emption of erstwhile lexical units or constructions for grammatical functions, the potential overlap between grammaticalization research and semantic map research would be relatively small, but if change 'from already grammaticalized to more grammatical structures' (Heine, Claudi, and Hünnemeyer 1991: 148) is also understood as part of grammaticalization, as is usually the case, the overlap becomes much larger.

Decisively for the topic of this chapter, classical semantic maps can be 'dynamicized' by incorporating diachronic information. They can thus include information on semantic change, a central component of grammaticalization. Consider again the map on the right of Fig. 25.1. If a marker has each of three uses, use A could have been the original one, then use B developed, and then use C. This directionality of meaning extension, which is usually believed to be unidirectional (cf. also Heine 2003; Traugott and Dasher 2002) can be represented in the form of arrows in a classical map.

If two or more markers on a so-called 'grammaticalization path' are not taken to be synonymous (for example, as formally different expressions of the future), but as related, then these paths can already be conceived of as semantic maps, or at least as their building blocks[4] (cf. the grammaticalization paths in the area of possibility, as proposed by Bybee et al. (1994: 240), and shown in Fig. 25.5). On the other hand, it is assumed that most semantic maps 'cover' an area of related meanings and/or functions. This is an element obviously missing from many traditional grammaticalization paths. This difference is no obstacle for mutual relevance, though, for grammaticalization paths typically run through semantic space as well, even though the exhaustive description of the semantic space is not a condition for positing these paths. In Fig. 25.5, although no semantic space was labelled, it is clear that we deal with a semantic space of possibility.

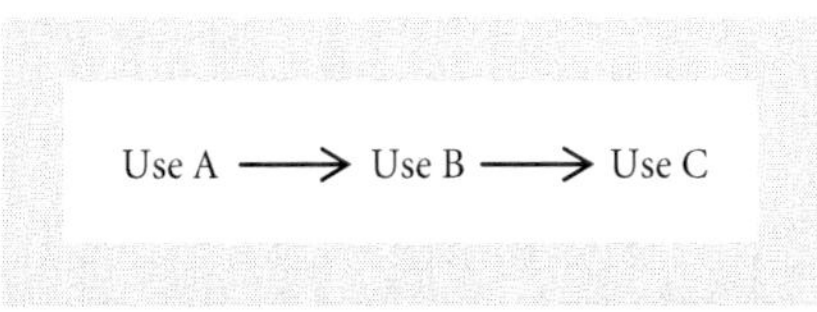

Fig. 25.4. The dynamicized semantic map

[4] For the term 'grammaticalization path' cf. Bybee, Pagliuca, and Perkins 1994: 12–13. Bybee et al. (1994) also speak more generally of 'paths of development'.

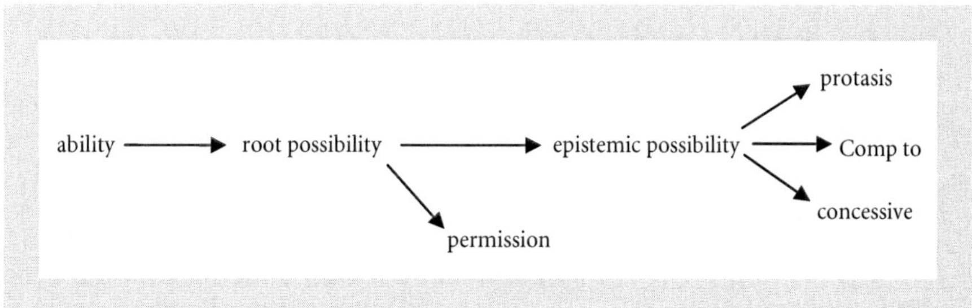

Fig. 25.5. Grammaticalization paths starting from ability (Bybee et al. 1994: 240)

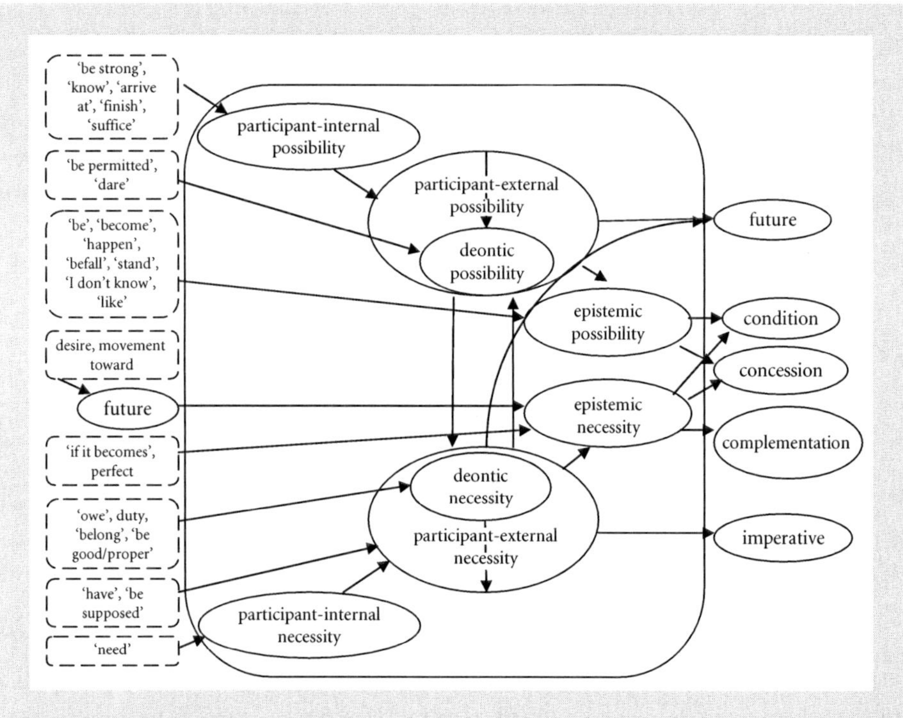

Fig. 25.6. Semantic map of modality (van der Auwera and Plungian 1998: 98, 100)

Van der Auwera and Plungian's (1998) map of modality, as reproduced in Fig. 25.6, stands out from previous semantic map research in a number of respects. It includes an account of connections between lexical and grammatical categories as well as connections between grammatical categories. It further represents the directionalities of these connections, and thus aims to represent an entire semantic area to the extent that this area is defined by the authors. It also shows how the addition of ovals allows the representation of specialization (from general participant-external possibility to its subtype of deontic possibility) and generalization (from the subtype of deontic necessity to general participant-external necessity).

This map incorporates the grammaticalization paths represented in Figure 25.5, thus illustrating the possibility of utilizing grammaticalization research for semantic maps. In principle, lexical source categories are placed on the left of the map, and grammatical categories to the right. Grammaticalization proceeds to the right, with the most grammaticalized categories at the right end.[5] Lexical categories do not normally occur to the right of grammatical ones, but this is not excluded, in which case one can speak of 'degrammaticalization'. One should stress that semantic maps in principle only involve representation of the semantic aspect of grammaticalization. In traditional 'grammaticalization paths' like those in Bybee et al. (1994), it is tacitly assumed that semantic change is the core of grammaticalization, optionally accompanied by a variety of phonological and morphosyntactic changes. For purely morphosyntactic (or phonological) changes, however, there is by definition no need for 'semantic' maps.

3. Future possibilities of semantic maps for grammaticalization research

Semantic maps and grammaticalization studies are both relatively young enterprises with rapidly expanding results. Concerning grammaticalization, the constant accumulation of knowledge about cross-linguistically recurring semantic changes into the area of grammar and within grammar is reflected in publications such as Heine and Kuteva (2002). Semantic map research, on the other hand, is providing information on the relationship of meanings and functions in core areas of grammar, and this at an increasing rate. Indefiniteness (Haspelmath 1997), tense–aspect (see above; also Croft and Poole 2008), modality (see above; and also van der Auwera, Kehayov, and Vittrant 2009; Boye 2010; De Haan 2010), mood (see van der Auwera, Dobrushina, and Gussev 2004), coordination (see above; Mauri 2010) and case (Luraghi 2001b; Narrog and Ito 2007, Malchukov and Narrog 2008; Narrog 2010b), and ditransitive constructions (Malchukov, Haspelmath, and Comrie to appear) have been covered, at least partially.

While only a small portion of the semantic map research has been concerned with diachronic issues, as was seen above in Figs. 25.5 and 25.6, one can in fact take any synchronic map and try to dynamicize it with results from grammaticalization work. Fig. 25.7 shows how diachronic directionalities can be added to most of the

[5] One category, future, is placed both to the left and the right of the modality area. This is the result of the decision to exclude future from modality (see Narrog 2005b: 712–13 for a discussion).

links on the conjunction map (the diachronic information is taken from Haspelmath 2004a: 24, Heine and Kuteva 2002, and Narrog 2010b).

Map 25.7 contains a number of diachronic hypotheses—for example, that a morpheme with comitative function may acquire instrumental function but not vice versa.[6] The hypothesized directionalities should ideally be backed up by historical evidence. The directionalities given in this particular map are in this respect relatively unproblematic. However, as the number of historically well-documented languages is rather limited, directionalities may also be posited on the basis of internal or comparative reconstruction, as is not uncommon in grammaticalization research (cf. Givón 2000).

Semantic maps are primarily a means of representation, but they can lead to new questions and they can illustrate where clarification is needed, both with respect to the semantic maps themselves and to grammaticalization. For example, if information on specific directionalities in a semantic map cannot be found in previous grammaticalization research, this can become a motivation to investigate those directionalities. This is for example the case for the relationship between 'also' and 'even' in Fig. 25.7. There is also the important question of apparent mismatches between semantic maps and empirical data. For example, contradicting the map in Fig. 25.7, a form X in language L may have the functions of N-conjunction and instrumental, but not comitative. Such a case can lead to the revision of a map. On the other hand, it may also be due to 'noise', for example, the historical loss of the comitative function of form X, due to the emergence of a new, more expressive,

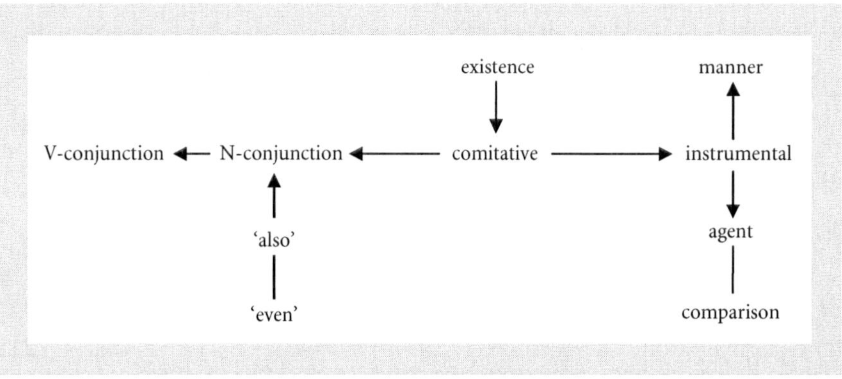

Fig. 25.7. A semantic map for conjunction and related functions (Haspelmath 2004a: 21) with added diachronic directionalities

[6] The directionality from comitative (source) to instrumental (target) is also a fine example that there can indeed be 'more' and 'less' grammaticalized functions within the area of grammar. As Stolz, Stroh, and Urdze (2006; ch. 10) found in a large language sample, in languages where comitatives and instrumentals are expressed distinctly, the comitative is almost always formally more complex than the instrumental. More complexity can be taken as a parameter of a lower degree of grammaticalization (cf. Lehmann 2002b: 4.2.1.).

morpheme Y in language L. Or the N-conjunction and instrumental function may have in fact different historical sources, which have come to resemble each other through phonological change, or other non-semantic reasons. Such cases are not uncommon; see discussions of more concrete examples in van der Auwera (2008), Malchukov (2010), and Narrog and Ito (2007). In this manner, it can be the semantic map itself which leads to question of how the synchronic polysemy of a specific form has come into being.

Another issue not fully explored yet is the compatibility of the representation of a diachronic dimension with statistical maps. The common assumption so far has been that they are incompatible with each other. Van der Auwera (2008) and Narrog (2010b) both present the easy integration of a diachronic dimension—and thus easy harmonization with grammaticalization research—as one of the important advantages of 'classical' maps. However, depending on the nature of the input data, there are some statistical maps where the points on the map are distinct enough, i.e. where there is no substantial overlap and clustering of points, to allow lines to be drawn and, consequently, directionalities to be represented (e.g. the map of indefinite pronoun functions in Croft and Poole 2008: 17).

It is also possible to formulate the following hypothesis. On a statistical map, the closer two meanings are placed to each other, the more likely that there is a diachronic relationship between them. Testing this hypothesis would involve the parallel construction, and then comparison, of classical-diachronic and statistical maps in a number of different semantic domains.

Acknowledgements

Narrog's work was supported by the Ministry of Education, Culture, Sports, Science, and Technology–Japan (Grant No. 20520346/0004). Van der Auwera's work was helped by the Belgian Federal Science Ministry Grant P6/44 (within the programme of inter-university attraction poles).

PART III

DOMAINS OF GRAMMATICALIZATION

CHAPTER 26

GRAMMATICALIZATION AND PROSODY

ANNE WICHMANN

1. Introduction

Despite the variety of approaches to grammaticalization in terms of its motivation and features, a common element of most accounts is the description of attrition of phonetic substance. Meillet (1912, cited in Hopper and Traugott 2003: 24) observes 'weakening of phonological form and of concrete meaning'. Later, Lehmann (1995c), for example, includes loss of phonological (and semantic) weight among his set of (paradigmatic) parameters (cited in Hopper and Traugott 2003: 31). In general, the phonological changes described are segmental, involving reduction and elision, and in some cases syllable loss, but I will argue that these are secondary consequences of underlying suprasegmental (prosodic) changes, and that the prosodic changes are primary. Furthermore, by focusing on prosody rather than on segments we are able to examine grammaticalization processes in languages that are typologically very diverse. While most of the evidence I present comes from English, I also report related work on Sinitic languages that suggests that my claims may have wider applicability. I shall show how the availability of recorded speech now allows us to explore synchronic data for evidence of prosodic change: such research has so far focused mainly on discourse markers and other items that have acquired, or are in the process of acquiring, a discourse function. Whether this process is appropriately described as grammaticalization will be addressed in section 5 below, together with some theoretical implications for the study of grammaticalization.

It is of course impossible, given our relatively recent capacity to make and store sound recordings, to conduct a historical study of pronunciation other than indirectly (e.g. through rhyming patterns in verse, changes in orthography, or metalinguistic comment). However, present-day prosodic realization, as I shall argue below, provides vital evidence to complement independent analyses of historical change. Most studies referred to here are based on data derived from spoken corpora (see Wichmann 2008), which allow an automatic search for lexical strings in the orthographic transcription. Items are generally chosen that are suspected of undergoing, or having undergone, grammaticalization, and a range of textual, contextual, and interactional evidence is used to shed light on their meaning or meanings. Prosodic evidence is more difficult to obtain. Some studies (e.g. Aijmer 2002) have based their analyses on an existing prosodic transcription, but most studies rely on the researchers' own auditory analysis of sound files, often complemented by acoustic analysis. This is made easier by the increased availability of speech analysis software that can easily be installed on a PC, so that the identification of prominence, pitch contours, and intonational phrases can now be supported by inspection of the waveform, spectrogram or fundamental frequency (F0)[1] curve.

2. Attrition: the role of prosody

One of the correlates[2] of semantic change is thought to be frequency of use, and this assumption underlies Bybee's (2001) account of phonological change. Her study is not restricted to grammaticalized expressions but describes in general the kinds of effects that frequency and repetition can have on the segmental realisation of certain items, many of which would be regarded as grammaticalized. She discusses language as a 'conventionalised, cultural object' (2001: 8), meaning that it is shaped by repetition. Repetition breeds familiarity and thus predictability, which then permits a reduction of form without impeding communication for the hearer. Bybee correctly describes reduction and other effects as the result of both temporal reduction (shortening of time spent on the item, causing the overlapping of articulatory gestures) and the reduction of magnitude of the gestures

[1] Fundamental frequency (F0) is the physical correlate of what is perceived as pitch.

[2] Frequency may be both the trigger for change and the consequence of change (see Fischer and Rosenbach 2000: 27).

themselves. Overlapping articulatory gestures can give the impression of deletion, even if instrumental analysis (e.g. electropalatography) can reveal the persistence of an apparently absent gesture. Assuming that language change may in part be auditively motivated, in that users repeat what they hear, there would be no motivation to acquire a gesture that is not audible. The reduced size of a gesture may also underlie consonant lenition and deletion, or vowel reduction in unstressed syllables. Such effects are, of course, language-specific and subject to phonotactic constraints, but are, according to Bybee, a universal feature of language that is constantly 'mutating under the dynamic forces of language use' (2001: 6). Quite independently of theories of semantic change, such phenomena are of course familiar as connected speech processes, varying in their occurrence according to situation, for example speech rate and degrees of informality, and according to the phonotactic constraints of the language concerned. Unlike situation-bound variation, in the process of grammaticalization, however, these phonological changes appear to become fixed—no longer optional variants of corresponding full forms, but the default realization of a new, shorter item.

The segmental attrition Bybee refers to is, I will argue, not the primary process, but a consequence of suprasegmental processes, first and foremost the loss of prosodic prominence (or stress), which may or may not lead to the segmental processes described above. Less often mentioned are the syntagmatic consequences—an item's formal status inside a prosodic domain. Speech is produced in phrases, variously known as Intonational Phrases (IPs), tone groups, or tone units. An IP in English must contain an accented syllable and an associated complete tonal contour: this is the obligatory 'nucleus' of the domain, which may be preceded by other accented syllables. The first accented syllable may be preceded by unstressed syllables (so-called 'prehead' syllables) and the nucleus may be followed by a 'tail' (any unstressed syllables following the nucleus up to the end of the intonation domain). The pitch contour associated with the nucleus, the nuclear tone, spreads from the nuclear syllable to the end of the domain, to include any unstressed post-nuclear syllables. The number of nuclear tones available in English is a matter of debate, but most models allow at least a falling, rising, and falling–rising contour (see e.g. Cruttenden 1997). In the Autosegmental model of intonation (see e.g. Ladd 1996), dynamic contours are expressed not holistically, as in the British system, but as the interpolation of pitch between individual high (H) and low (L) target points. The target associated with the accented syllable is additionally marked with an asterisk *. Thus a falling contour is the interpolation between H* and L, while a rise is represented by the sequence L* H.

Briefly, the paradigmatic elements of prosody are accent placement and choice of pitch contour, while the syntagmatic dimension is concerned with the status of a syllable within the structure of the intonation phrase. I shall deal first with studies that focus on paradigmatic features, and then move on to syntagmatic issues.

3. Paradigmatic relations: intonational meaning and prominence

3.1. Correlating semantic and prosodic weight

The perception of an accented syllable in English is due to various phonetic cues, some more perceptually important than others. These cues are principally duration, in that a stressed syllable is longer than the same syllable in unstressed position, and pitch excursion—a peak (or occasionally a trough) of F0, aligned with or closely associated with the accented syllable. Intensity (loudness) also plays a part, but it is thought to be perceptually less important. Duration and pitch are of course to be understood in relative terms: a stressed syllable in fast speech may in real terms be shorter than its unstressed counterpart in slow speech. Exact measurements of syllable length are therefore difficult to interpret, and are not a clear indication of the presence of stress unless normalised to reflect the overall articulation[3] rate of the stretch of speech. Pitch prominence is similarly perceived relative to its context. If the overall pitch range of an utterance is compressed, a pitch excursion that gives rise to the percept of stress may be very small in absolute terms, but is prominent in relation to its surroundings.

A theory of intonational meaning (Pierrehumbert and Hirschberg 1990) claims that for English there is a direct correlation between prosodic salience (accenting) and semantic weight. The least prominent is the unstressed syllable, of moderate salience is a rising contour (L* H), while a falling contour (H* L) is perceived as the most salient. This theory is consistent with the fact that closed-class grammatical words such as pronouns, prepositions, conjunctions, etc. are rarely given prosodic prominence, while open-class words carrying propositional meaning have much greater potential to be accented. It follows from this that if a word or expression has begun to lose some of its propositional meaning and to acquire a grammatical—or possibly discoursal—function, it is more likely to be deaccented, or if accented, to carry a low rather than a high pitch accent (L* vs. H*). In cases of 'layering' (Hopper 1991), where both lexical and grammatical forms coexist, the degree of prosodic prominence may contribute to the disambiguation of the two. The picture is of course more complex, as I will discuss below, but as a number of studies show, this is still a valid assumption to make. In the following I will briefly outline a number of studies that have focused on the prosodic features of grammaticalized or grammaticalizing expressions.

[3] Articulation rate is the speed of vocalisation excluding pauses, whereas speech rate is the speed including pauses. Both are measured in terms of words or syllables per unit of time.

3.2. Studies of prosodic realisation of discourse markers

In their study of *now* in American English, Hirschberg and Litman (1993) were motivated by practical rather than theoretical considerations. Their concern was to develop Automatic Speech Recognition (ASR) systems that could disambiguate between utterance-initial *now* as a time adverbial and as a discourse marker (or in their terms 'cue phrase'). They noted that discourse marker *now* was more likely to be deaccented, while most adverbial *now* tokens were accented. Although differences were not sufficient to allow automatic disambiguation in all cases, the trend observed is consistent with the view that greater semantic content will be associated with a greater potential for prosodic prominence. A more recent corpus-based study with similar findings is Wichmann, Simon-Vandenbergen, and Aijmer's (2010) study of *of course*. There is independent historical evidence that the meaning and syntactic function of the expression has changed over time in a manner consistent with grammaticalization. Lewis (2003) traces the historical development of *of course* and shows that its meaning derives from a structure containing the noun 'course' (French/Middle English *cours*) meaning 'the path taken e.g. by a river', and came to mean 'in the natural order of things', 'predictable', or 'to be expected'. It is variously classified as an adverb (Quirk et al. 1985) and as a pragmatic particle or marker (Holmes 1988; Simon-Vandenbergen and Aijmer 2003/4). Wichmann et al.'s study was based on the spoken section of ICE GB[4] (Nelson, Wallis, and Aarts 2002), a corpus of Southern British English. The corpus contained tokens of *of course* in its epistemic meaning of 'naturally, predictably', together with tokens that are derived from this meaning but now have the function of establishing common ground between speaker and hearer ('we/you know this'). As would be predicted, these different uses are reflected in prosody. There is a very strong association between meaning and accentual status: tokens of *of course* meaning 'naturally'/'predictably' are more likely to be stressed, and those meaning 'we/ you know this' are more likely to be unstressed.

A further illustration of the relationship between prosodic prominence and grammaticalized words and expressions is to be found in a corpus-based study of the word *sorry*. Wichmann (2009) found three distinct prosodic types that map onto three different, but overlapping, functions of *sorry* as identified by Aijmer (1996). As an apology or an expression of regret, *sorry* is accented, and carries a falling, rising or falling-rising tone: *I'm \so /sorry; I'm very \sorry; \/Sorry.*[5] As an attempt to elicit the repetition of an utterance, an isolated *Sorry?* is accented but exclusively with a rising contour: */sorry. Sorry* also occurs as a 'trouble marker' both

[4] ICE GB (International Corpus of English in Great Britain) contains 600,000 words of transcribed speech. The study described here was based on 200 tokens of *of course*.

[5] The symbols \ , / and \/ indicate a falling, rising and falling-rising tone respectively.

initially and finally in longer utterances, as in *Say that again sorry*, or *Sorry what did you say?* Here, the word *sorry* is always short and unstressed. As we would expect, the pragmatic particle—the 'trouble marker'—is prosodically the least salient.

Despite language-specific realizational differences, similar patterns of prominence variation are to be found in the realization of the French word *enfin*. A study of the historical development of *enfin* (Hansen 2005) shows that it has undergone a process of grammaticalization. It developed from a prepositional phrase (*à la fin, en la fin*) to a single word *enfin* as an adverb of time, referring to the end of a sequence of events in time, and also in a quasi-iconic way to refer to the ordering of events in a text. It can indicate the end of an enumeration of propositions, and also a synthesis of a list of propositions e.g. *Cédric est grand, beau, intelligent, spirituel, enfin parfait quoi!*[6] (example from Hansen 2005). There has thus been a shift of meaning from reference to temporal events to reference to the discourse itself. In present-day French, *enfin* is most commonly used as a particle, derived from its synthesizing use, as a repair strategy to interrupt one's own speech (roughly: 'I will not pursue that line of argument') and also as an interjection to interrupt others, expressing a sense of irritation or impatience, e.g. *Enfin! Ça va pas, ça!*[7] Against the background of this historical analysis, Bertrand and Chanet (2005) examined tokens of *enfin* in a corpus of spoken French and showed that these various functions are reflected in their prosodic realization. Non-particle use was of longer duration than particle use and was associated with a rising F0 contour high in the speaker's range, whereas *enfin* as a particle was realized with a falling F0 contour, shorter, and was also lower in the speaker's range. In contrast to the hierarchy of salience ascribed by Pierrehumbert and Hirschberg to falls and rises in English, Bertrand and Chanet ascribed more salience to rising contours than to falling contours. However, this can be ascribed to the difference between English and French phonology. Post (2000) suggests that while the location of stress in French is highly predictable, focal and non-focal accents 'have the same tonal structure but different degrees of prominence. The acoustic differences between the two are gradual rather than categorical... [a syllable] can be made more prominent in emphatic speech by increasing the height of the pitch peak, the duration and intensity of the segments, their voice quality etc.' (2000: 178). Thus, Bertrand and Chanet's assessment of contours high in a speaker's range as being more salient than those lower in the speaker's range suggests an increased emphasis or prominence on adverbial usage of *enfin*, and a much-decreased prominence on the particle, and as such is consistent with findings for English.

[6] Cedric is tall, handsome, intelligent, witty—just perfect really.

[7] Come on! That won't do!

3.3. Accenting of grammaticalized expressions: apparent contradictions

Despite the findings described above, we find numerous claims in the literature that, far from being downgraded prosodically, discourse markers are typically found to have tonic stress followed by a pause (e.g. Schiffrin 1987, cited by Aijmer 2002: 32), making them maximally prominent. These two contrasting patterns were observed by Halliday and Hasan: 'there is a general tendency in spoken English for conjunctive elements as a whole to be, phonologically, either tonic (maximally prominent) or reduced (minimally prominent) rather than anything in between' (1976: 271). Bolinger (1989) and Lam (2009) describe both unaccented and accented cases of *well.* Hirschberg and Litman (1993) found that the difference between accented and deaccented tokens was not sufficient to disambiguate functions of *now*, because many tokens with a clear discourse function *did* carry a pitch accent. Holmes (1988) claims that *of course* may be unstressed but may also carry a nuclear tone.

This presents problems for the reported relationship between grammaticalized items and loss of prosodic salience, since such observations appear to contradict the notion that grammaticalized items, having lost their referential meaning, are likely to be deaccented. But in fact there is no such contradiction: Halliday and Hasan point out that although 'cohesive elements' are normally non-prominent, 'if the cohesive element itself is brought into focus of attention, this is marked in the usual way by tonic prominence' (1976: 271). The same is true for conjunctions such as *and* and *but* when they have a cohesive function derived from, but not wholly distinct from, their grammatical function. By treating discourse markers that are accented and in a separate IP as a special case of focus, we can maintain the general correlation between semantic and prosodic weight.

3.4. Stress and segmental attrition

We now return to our point of departure: the account by Bybee of reasons for segmental attrition. I have claimed here that the primary effect of routinization is loss or 'erosion' of prominence. The speaker invests less effort in the production of the item and it becomes deaccented. It is well known that an unaccented item is shorter than the same item in accented position. The first effect of accent loss is therefore reduced duration, and thus a reduction of time available to complete or maximize articulatory gestures. This may, under certain circumstances, lead to segmental attrition for the reasons outlined by Bybee. This phenomenon is well documented in English and related languages: the particle *enfin* can be realized as *'fin* (Bertrand and Chanet 2005); *of course* can be reduced to *'course* in informal conversation (Wichmann et al. 2010). *Well* can be reduced to *w'll* and *w'* (Bolinger

1989); *sorry* as a 'trouble marker' can reveal a loss of /r/ colouring [soi] or even further reduction to [so] (Wichmann 2009). Note, however, that such reduced forms are a possible but not essential consequence of prosodic erosion. They occur particularly in fast, conversational speech but much less frequently in more formal speech such as broadcast interviews or political debates. Thus the segmental attrition seen as a typical feature of grammaticalization is a partial and secondary phenomenon, and, like normal connected speech processes, subject to contextual constraints.

If we are to claim any degree of universality for the primacy of prosody, however, we need evidence from typologically very different languages. Initial evidence of this kind comes from Ansaldo and Lim (2004), who report on isolating tonal languages (Mandarin, Cantonese, and Hokkien) in which phonotactic constraints prohibit the kind of syllable reductions observed in other languages. They offer evidence that these languages also exhibit features of phonological 'erosion' as a result of grammaticalization, but that these occur not at the level of segments but at the suprasegmental level, including tonal reduction or changes in duration and vowel quality. They suggest that 'the mechanism by which the reductions occur may be related to metrical structure. When grammaticalized morphemes typically occur next to syntactically salient, stressed units, they are assigned weak stress, the first step to the phonetic erosion process' (2004: 360).

4. Syntagmatic phenomena and grammaticalization

I pointed out at the beginning of this chapter that in English the paradigmatic phenomena of accent placement and contour choice have syntagmatic consequences. This is important because structural integration is assumed to be a feature of grammaticalization, and counterexamples, such as discourse markers, pose problems for grammaticalization theory. However, integration is always expressed in terms of morphology or syntax and never in terms of prosody. In the following, I will consider the relevance of prosodic structure in the grammaticalization process and show that, prosodically at least, apparent counterexamples are less problematic than they may seem.

Speech is divided into phrases which have an internal structure, an obligatory tonal contour, and are separated by boundaries. Unstressed syllables are not only non-salient but are by definition always a subordinate part of the tonal contour associated with the accented syllable. They are thus fully integrated into the tonal contour, in the sense that grammatical morphemes may be cliticized, either as part of a nuclear tail—post-nuclear unstressed syllables up to the right edge of the IP—or as a prehead—the unstressed syllables that precede the first or only accented syllable in the domain. A change of status from fully lexical to having a grammatical or deictic function (as with discourse markers) is highly likely, therefore, to have both paradigmatic and syntagmatic consequences—a downgrading of prosodic prominence, as has been illustrated above, and a concomitant loss of structural independence.

These structural consequences are described in different ways but are a feature of many of the studies reported above. Hirschberg and Litman (1993) noted that *now* as a 'cue phrase' was realized most frequently as the unstressed prehead in a larger IP. Holmes (1988), in her account of *of course*, finds both separate and prosodically integrated versions: a separate tone group containing a stressed syllable (rising or falling) or, in initial position, as an unstressed prehead. Unstressed *sorry* (Wichmann 2009) was realized most commonly as a prehead syllable and occasionally as a nuclear tail. Each of these descriptions has a syntagmatic dimension—a consequence of the loss of prosodic prominence that is symptomatic of the grammaticalization process. Two recent studies that have an explicit focus on phrasing—structural separation and integration—are corpus-based investigations of the syntax and prosody of comment clauses (CCs) e.g. *I think*, *I suppose* (Dehé and Wichmann 2010a; 2010b). While some CCs were found to be phrased separately, as one would predict on the basis of the syntactic disjunction between the host clause and the comment clause, by far the most occurrences were prosodically integrated, most commonly as a nuclear tail. While clearly of epistemic derivation, these unstressed tokens contribute little to the truth value of the proposition. They have been conventionalized as lexical items, and are no longer amenable to syntactic analysis but have a discoursal or interactional function similar to that of discourse markers.

In all these cases, the structural integration assumed to be criterial for grammaticalization, while it may be absent in syntactic terms, is clearly present in terms of prosodic structure. The theoretical implications of this are discussed below.

5. Theoretical implications

The prosodic analysis of discourse markers has a number of implications, not least for their classification in relation to other, more prototypical grammaticalized items. It is still a matter of debate whether discourse markers are the result of grammaticalization, or of a separate process of 'pragmaticalization'. Many aspects of the process of change are shared with grammaticalization, including semantic bleaching, subjectification, and decategorialization. Controversial is whether discourse markers are in fact 'grammatical', and views depend on how grammar is characterized. Traugott claims that discourse markers are the result of grammaticalization processes, arguing that grammar can encompass 'focusing, topicalization, deixis, and discourse coherence' (Traugott 2003: 626). Günthner and Mutz (2004), on the other hand, suggest that the development of pragmatic markers is problematic for grammaticalization theory because it 'contradicts classical features of grammaticalization' (2004: 85). In particular, they point out that discourse markers contravene Lehmann's criterion of scope, in that contrary to the tendency towards syntactic integration, assumed to be a feature of grammaticalization, they display a widening of scope and decreased clausal integration. However, I have shown above that in terms of prosodic structure the criterion of scope is upheld. While accented syllables can constitute an independent intonation phrase, unaccented items cannot melodically[8] stand alone and are thus necessarily integrated into the overall contour. Typically, a discourse marker, unless it is given special emphasis, is integrated as part of either the prehead of a tone group or the nuclear tail. Thus, if we express the process of change in terms of prosodic structure rather than syntactic structure, the observed process of increasing prosodic integration is entirely compatible with, rather than counter to, existing views of grammaticalization.

The paradigmatic features we have observed—loss of stress on grammaticalized items—are consistent with the view that semantic and prosodic weight are directly correlated. Pierrehumbert and Hirschberg's (1990) theory applies to English, but recent work in phonology by Gussenhoven (e.g. 2004) provides a possible explanation for why this tendency may be universal, by positing 'Biological Codes', i.e. communicative strategies that exploit physiological constraints on the human voice. Some aspects of human speech are biologically determined: the size of the larynx determines a person's pitch range, the physical effort needed for phonation determines the size of pitch excursion, and prosodic phrasing is subject to limitations of the breathing process. Nonetheless, within their biological limitations, speakers can and do actively control their voices, especially pitch variation, for a variety of reasons. Of relevance here is Gussenhoven's 'Effort Code',[9] which 'associates wider pitch excursions and a higher incidence of movements with greater effort' (2004: 79). In other words, there is a form–function relationship that is exploited for communicative purposes. How this is realized depends on the language involved, but it seems that apparent differences in effort, with

[8] This distinction is important because it is possible for an item to be separated by a pause but still melodically part of a larger unit.

[9] One of three Biological Codes, the others being the Frequency Code and the Production Code.

concomitant effects on prosodic prominence, may be exploited by speakers to distinguish between items carrying different semantic weight.

To summarize, the phonological phenomena associated with grammaticalization are clearly more diverse and complex than might appear. I have argued that the primary effect of frequency and habituation is not segmental but prosodic. Features described elsewhere are generally the consequence of prosodic erosion and are not universal, but depend on the language concerned. I hope to have shown in this chapter that grammaticalization involves not only (and not always) the attrition of phonetic substance but more importantly the loss of prosodic prominence with a concomitant loss of independence in intonational structure.

CHAPTER 27

THE GRADUAL COALESCENCE INTO 'WORDS' IN GRAMMATICALIZATION

MARTIN HASPELMATH

1. Historical background

It has long been known that morphologically complex forms often arise from earlier syntactic phrases. In particular, function words often become morphological affixes, as in the examples in (1).

(1) Old High German / Proto-Germanic (cf. Lahiri 2000)

Old High German		Proto-Germanic			
suoch-t-un	<	**sōki-dēd-un*	<	**sōki*	*dēd-un*
seek-PRET-3PL		seek-PRET-3PL		seek	do.PRET-3PL
'they sought'		'they sought'		'they did seeking'	

(2) Hungarian / Proto-Hungarian (cf. Korhonen 1996)

Hungarian		Proto-Hungarian	
ház-ban	<	**ház*	*bel-n*
house-INESS		house	guts-LOC
'in the house'		'inside the house'	

I am grateful to Bernard Comrie, a referee, and the editors for helpful comments on an earlier version of this chapter.

(3)

Spanish		Latin		
dár-me-lo	<	*dare*	*mihi*	*illud*
give.INF-me-it		give.INF	me.DAT	that.ACC
'to give it to me'		'to give me that'		

(4)

Swedish		Proto-Nordic		Proto-Germanic	
hest-en	<	**hest-r-in-n*	<	**hest-az*	*in-az*
horse-DEF		horse-NOM-DEF-NOM		horse-NOM	that-NOM
'the horse'		'the horse'		'that horse'	
				(cf. Faarlund 2009)	

The function words become 'glued' to a related content word, or 'agglutinated', to use a term originally introduced by Wilhelm von Humboldt (1822). In this chapter, I will use the term 'coalescence' for this diachronic process (cf. Jespersen 1922: 376; Lehmann 1995a[1982]: 148).[1]

Historical linguists have long been interested in coalescence. Until well into the 19th century, it was widely thought that historical-comparative linguistic reconstruction offered a window into the earliest human language, and the idea that complex morphological forms derive from the concatenation of primitive simple forms can be traced back to 18th-century enlightenment works or earlier (Lehmann 1995a: 1–2). The most prominent representative of this approach in the 19th century was Humboldt's protégé Franz Bopp (Bopp 1833; Stolz 1991), who presented the first comprehensive reconstruction of Proto-Indo-European and speculated extensively on earlier origins of reconstructed forms. For example, on the basis of Sanskrit *emi* 'I go', Greek *eĩmi* 'I go', and Lithuanian *eimi* 'I go', he reconstructed **ai-mi*, deriving from the earlier independent elements **ai* 'go' and **mi* 'I'.

In the last third of the 19th century, with the rise of truly modern linguistics, glottogonic speculation was abandoned, and at the same time linguists realized that morphological forms were subject not only to unifying syntagmatic changes (coalescence) but also to unifying paradigmatic changes (analogical change). Many complex words in Indo-European languages could be traced back to analogical transformations (cf. Paul 1920: §§242–3; Jespersen 1922: ch. 19), so the interest in diachronic agglutination dropped dramatically. Significantly, in Meillet's (1912)

1 One reason for preferring *coalescence* to *agglutination* for the diachronic process is that the latter is more commonly used for a synchronic type. (And see Haspelmath (2009) for serious doubts concerning the coherence of 'agglutination' as a typological concept, at least as traditionally understood. The traditional ingredients of 'agglutination', lack of stem alternation, lack of cumulation, and lack of affix suppletion, do not seem to be significantly correlated.)

famous article on grammaticalization, almost no reference is made to the evolution of synthetic morphological forms from earlier syntactic phrases; instead, Meillet concentrates on the rise of function words from content words, i.e. on periphrastic constructions. Moreover, the creation of grammatical forms was less and less thought of as a general typological issue, and increasingly as a specific diachronic development in specific cases.

However, the more recent tradition of grammaticalization research, which is often seen as beginning with Givón (1971), again focused on diachronic agglutination. The new development here was primarily that data from non-Indo-European languages were also brought to bear on the issue (see also Hodge 1970 on Egyptian-Coptic; Tauli 1966 on Uralic), and these did confirm the earlier impression that inflectional and derivational affixes often derive from earlier independent function words. Thus, grammaticalization research begins with diachronic agglutination in three different periods: in the 18th century (enlightenment speculation), in the early 19th century (beginning historical-comparative studies), and in modern typologically oriented research.

Over the last few decades, grammaticalization research has broadened considerably, and the semantic-pragmatic changes occurring in grammaticalization have become very prominent (e.g. Traugott 1982; Heine, Claudi, and Hünnemeyer 1991; Bybee, Pagliuca, and Perkins 1994; and much subsequent work). Still, current characterizations of grammaticalization usually invoke the change from independent word to affix, i.e. from syntactic to morphological combination. Grammaticalization is often characterized as a transition (or cline) that includes the change from "syntax/word" to "morphology/affix" as one segment:

(5) a. discourse > syntax > morphology > morphophonemics > zero (Givón 1979: 209)
  b. content item > grammatical word > clitic > inflectional affix (Hopper and Traugott 1993: 7)
  c. phrases or words > non-bound grams > inflection (Bybee et al. 1994: 40)
  d. unbound word > enclitic > inflectional affix > derivational affix (Harris and Campbell 1995: 337)
  e. lexical verb > vector verb > auxiliary > clitic > affix > zero (Fischer 2007: 182)

The present chapter thus focuses on one aspect of grammaticalization that is still considered important, even though it no longer occupies centre stage in grammaticalization research. While the question of the origin of morphological patterns has receded into the background, the question of general constraints on diachronic change, in particular directionality of change, is vigorously debated (e.g. Haspelmath 1999; 2004b; Idiatov 2008; Askedal 2008; Norde 2009a; Börjars and Vincent, chapter 14 above), and coalescence has played an important part in these debates.[2]

2. Coalescence and Reanalysis

One general point that has not been made so far is that the traditional notion of "glueing" function words to their hosts makes a highly problematic presupposition: that linguists have a consistent way of distinguishing between syntactic and morphological patterns—or, in other words, that we know how to tell phrases apart from complex words, and affixes from simple words. This presupposition pervades naive reflection on language, and it is also widespread in contemporary linguistics. In the days of structuralism, the word was widely considered a problematic notion, and linguists tried to avoid relying on this notion in their theories (cf. Schwegler 1990: ch. 2; Albrecht 2002; Robins 2002). In current linguistics, the word notion and the morphology/syntax division are usually presupposed and rarely argued for (an exception is Dixon and Aikhenvald 2002). In a recent paper (Haspelmath 2011), I have examined a fair number of criteria for distinguishing words from phrases and affixes, and I conclude that no single criterion and no set of criteria yield a consistent, cross-linguistically applicable word notion. As a result, we do not have a cross-linguistically applicable distinction between syntax and morphology. This is also the reason why the word 'word' is given in quotation marks in the title of this chapter.

So in this chapter, I will argue against the widespread simplistic view according to which the coalescence of phrases into complex words consists of an abrupt

(6) Hungarian
a ház beln > *a ház-ban* 'in the house'

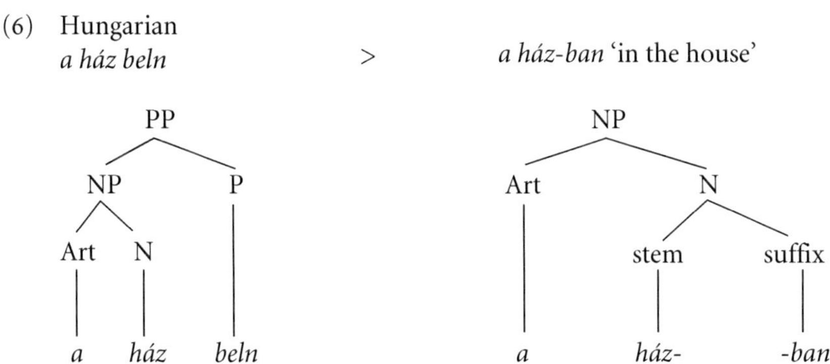

[2] Coalescence from function word to affix is also called 'morphologization' (cf. Joseph 2003). Joseph tries to dissociate it from grammaticalization, which he sees as much broader and not very closely related to morphologization.

reanalysis from the syntactic level to the morphological level, whereby lexical categories become affixal categories (cf. 6).

The reanalysis approach is consonant with what typical textbooks tell their readers (including Hopper and Traugott 1993: 40–48; Haspelmath 2002), but it is based on a highly simplified view of grammatical patterns that lacks any awareness of the difficulty of distinguishing between words and phrases. Instead, I argue that coalescence is a gradual increase in bondedness or tightness of combination, reflected in a variety of diverse changes that need not coincide perfectly. We will see some of these in the next section.

3. Ingredients of coalescence

The diachronic change by which independent function words become bound words (or clitics) and finally affixes involves many different aspects.[3] It is only the spelling that makes it appear that the affix/word distinction is a simple binary contrast (word vs. affix), or perhaps a ternary contrast (word, written with a space; clitic, written with an equals sign; affix, written with a hyphen). In this section, I review a number of different parameters that are generally implicated in the word/affix distinction, and in coalescence of combinations of function word plus host.

3.1. Loss of prosodic independence

A common process is the loss of prosodic independence, leading to an item's inability to form a prosodic word of its own. For example, in colloquial German clitic personal pronouns, the vowel changes to schwa, which is not allowed as the only vowel of a prosodic word:

(7) a. Older and standard German
wenn du sie siehst >
[du: zi:]
'if you see her' (lit. if you her see)

b. Colloquial German
wenn de se siehst
[də zə]
'if you see her'

[3] Since I do not think that words and affixes can be identified consistently across languages, I use the terms 'word', 'clitic', and 'affix' in a loose sense here, referring to the kinds of things that are generally separated in linguists' notations by spaces, equals signs, and hyphens, respectively. This is not satisfactory, but I cannot think of a better alternative for the purposes of this chapter.

While there are four prosodic words in (7a), there are only two in (7b) ([vɛn də zə] and [zi:st]). Syntactically, nothing changes in (7a, b), but prosodically, a reduction has taken place at the later stage.

Another example is provided by Hungarian monosyllabic postpositions, which are in the vowel harmony domain of their complement: *a ház ban* [the house in] 'in the house', *a kéz ben* [the hand in] 'in the hand'. The postposition *ban/ben* derives from an earlier prosodically independent form **beln* (Korhonen 1996). In Hungarian spelling, the monosyllabic postpositions are written as suffixes, perhaps because vowel harmony domains are always joined orthographically. But syntactically, these prosodically integrated postpositions are virtually[4] identical to other postpositions (e.g. *a ház mellett* 'beside the house'), so Creissels (2006) and Trommer (2008) have argued that they should not be regarded as suffixes, *contra* the representations in (2) and (6), which still follow the conventional (spelling-based) view (see also König, Chapter 41, below).

Loss of prosodic independence can take many different forms, and have segmental or just suprasegmental effects. Simplistically, it is often thought of as merger of two prosodic words into a single type of prosodic word, but it is important to recognize that languages need not have just one single prosodic word (as is often implied). Different phonological regularities may be sensitive to different phonological domains, so we cannot in general say that an element is either a separate prosodic word or not (cf. Schiering, Hildebrandt, and Bickel 2010). What all cases of prosodic grammaticalization share is that the function element becomes more dependent on its host.

Loss of prosodic independence is widely seen as independent of morphosyntactic change. That prosodic word domains are separate from morphosyntactic word domains is now generally recognized (e.g. Hall 1999). Grammaticalization involves both phonological and morphosyntactic changes, but these are not directly linked. It needs to be explained specifically why they tend to occur together.

3.2. Loss of positional variability

One often-cited difference between words and affixes is the fixed position of affixes, but of course many function words are not free in their positioning at all, so when they turn into affixes, nothing changes. Thus, articles (cf. (4) above) and postpositions (cf. (2) above) are almost always positionally fixed, and auxiliary verbs (cf. (1)) and subject and object pronouns (cf. (3)) are also very often rigidly positioned with respect to their host, even when there is otherwise no reason to say that they are affixes.

[4] A difference between monosyllabic harmonizing postpositions and polysyllabic non-harmonizing postpositions is noted in section 3.4 below.

But there are also many cases of positional freedom, and a widespread view is that positionally variable elements are clitics, which may become affixes once their position is fixed. In Portuguese, for example, object pronouns are positionally variable (cf. 8a, b), and in Polish, subject person markers (such as *-śmy*) are variable in the past tense (cf. 9a, b). (In both cases, the order of the elements is not free, but the specific factors play no role here.)

(8) Portuguese (Luís 2009: 19)

a. *Ele quer-os.*
he wants-them 'He wants them.'

b. *Acho que ele os quer.*
I.think that he them wants 'I think that he wants them.'

(9) Polish (Andersen 1987: 31)

a. *Nigdy tego nie myśleli-śmy.*
never that not thought-PST.1PL 'We never thought that.'

b. *Nigdy-śmy tego nie myśleli.*
never-PST.1PL that not thought 'We never thought that.'

In Spanish, positional variability of the kind shown in (8a, b) was found in the medieval language, but it has disappeared in the modern language. Thus, many linguists now say that the Spanish object person forms are prefixes (e.g. Bonet 1995).

However, even in Spanish, some positional variability is left: Object person forms normally precede the verb, but in infinitives, gerunds, and imperatives they follow it (*me lo dio* [me it gave] 'gave it to me', vs. *dár-me-lo* [give.INF-me-it] 'to give it to me', cf. (3) above). Moreover, object clitics can optionally 'climb up' to a higher verb (*Quiere dár-me-lo* 'He wants to give it to me', or *Me lo quiere dar*). Thus, the difference between Portuguese and Spanish is not as clear-cut as a reanalysis account would lead us to expect.[5]

In modern Polish, positional variability of subject person markers is greatly reduced compared to the situation in earlier Polish, as discussed in Andersen (1987). He notes that the frequency of the combination of the subject person markers with the verb increased gradually over the centuries. In modern Polish, the position on the verb (as in (9a)) is thus much more common, and there are clear signs that the placement of the person marker on other constituents (as in (9b)) is on its way out: non-adjacency of person marker and verb 'is more common in written than in spoken language, in speech more common in formal than in

[5] Moreover, as we will see in section 3.5, Portuguese object person forms sometimes show morphophonological idiosyncrasies in combination with different host shapes, which makes them look less clitic-like than the Spanish object person forms.

casual styles, and more usual in the speech of older than in that of younger people' (Andersen 1987: 30).

Such a gradual decrease in positional variability is hard to reconcile with the abrupt reanalysis scenario.

3.3. Loss of interruptibility

Another feature of affixes that distinguishes them from clitics is the immediate adjacency to their host. In modern French, object person forms are always immediately adjacent to the verb, whereas in Old French, object pronouns and verb were sometimes interrupted by other words, as illustrated in (10), where the word *plus* intervenes between the object pronoun *te* and the verb. Modern French would render this as *qu'il te fasse adorer plus.*

(10) Old French (*La vie de Saint Eustache* 335: de Kok 1985: 570)

ke	*il*	*te*	*plus*	*face*	*aorer*
that	he	you	more	make	adore

'that he make you adore more'

Thus, one would say that the increasing uninterruptibility of the combination shows that it has become an affix. Like positional variability, interruptibility can be a gradual matter: sometimes only very few items can intervene between a function word and a content word, and it is difficult to say at which point the transition to affixhood would have taken place. Such a scenario of a gradually decreasing set of intervening elements is not compatible with a reanalysis as in (6).

3.4. Loss of wide scope over coordination

Affixes are often said not to allow wide scope over coordination, as opposed to clitics (e.g. Lehmann 1995a: 150). (Alternatively, such patterns may be described by coordination ellipsis of the grammatical element.) For example, in French it is not possible for object person forms to have scope over coordinated verbs; Miller (1992) takes this as evidence for the affixal status of these pronouns, which have their origin in free personal pronouns in Latin:

(11) French (Miller 1992)
**Pierre les voit et écoute.* (OK: *Pierre les voit et les écoute.)*
'Pierre sees and hears them.'

Likewise, the German infinitive marker *zu* no longer allows coordination ellipsis. This was possible in earlier German (cf. Haspelmath 1989: 297):

(12) Early New High German (M. Luther, Ezekiel 19:6)

der gewonet auch die leute zu reissen und fressen
who learned also the people to catch and eat
'who learned to catch and devour the people'

In modern German, the infinitival marker must be repeated with each coordinand (*zu reißen und zu fressen*), so it behaves like a prefix.

Another well-known case of loss of coordination ellipsis concerns the adverb-forming suffix *-mente* in Romance languages. In Spanish, it can be ellipsed when two adverbs are coordinated, but in Italian, this is no longer possible.

(13) a. Spanish *dulce- y afectuosa-mente*
b. Italian **dolce- e affettuosa-mente* (OK: *dolcemente e affettuosamente*)
'sweetly and affectionately'

But sometimes, the evidence is contradictory. In Serbian, the future-tense marker can be ellipsed in coordination (cf. 14a, b), in contrast to the present-tense person marker (cf. (14c)). This is fully expected, as the future-tense marker was recently grammaticalized from an auxiliary meaning 'want'.

(14) Serbian (Milićević 2005: 45)

a. *Peva=ćemo i igra=ćemo.*
sing=1PL.FUT and dance=1PL.FUT
'We will sing and we will dance.'

b. *Peva=ćemo i igrati=Ø.*
sing=1PL.FUT and dance
'We will sing and we will dance.'

c. *Peva-mo i igra-mo.* (**Peva-mo i igra.*)
sing-1PL.PRS and dance-1PL.PRS
'We sing and dance.'

However, the future-tense marker behaves like an affix in that it affects the shape of the stem (cf. *igra=ćemo* in (14a), not **igrati=ćemo*).

In Hungarian, the monosyllabic postpositions (which, as we saw earlier, are within the vowel harmony domain of their host) do not allow coordination ellipsis:

(15) Hungarian (É. Kiss 2002: 184)

a. *a ház nál és a garázs nál*
the house at and the garage at
'at the house and at the garage'

b. **a ház és a garázs nál*

This might be taken as evidence for their affix status, but it conflicts with the observation that *nál* 'at' occurs with no preceding host when the complement is a pronoun suffix (*nál-am* 'at me', *nál-ad* 'at you', etc.).

Thus, while the loss of wide scope over coordination does seem to be a widespread concomitant of grammaticalization, we cannot derive the facts from a simple reanalysis scenario.

3.5. Acquisition of morphophonological idiosyncrasies

When clitics turn into affixes, one may expect them to develop morphophonological idiosyncrasies of a kind that is not found with combinations of words. For example, when English *not* fused with preceding verbs, it was not only reduced to *n't*, but also affected the shape of the verb stem in many cases: *do* vs. *don't*, *shall* vs. *shan't*, and so on (cf. Zwicky and Pullum 1983). And conversely, the shape of the grammaticalizing element is typically invariable as long as it is a clitic, but becomes subject to idiosyncratic alternations once it turns into an affix. For example, the Portuguese object person forms vary depending on the form of the verb that precedes them:

(16) *leva-o* 's/he takes him'
levam-no 'they take him'
levá-lo 'to take him'

In a simplistic view of the syntax/morphology difference, this could be derived from a reanalysis as in (6): "Lexical" phonological interactions are possible only in the morphological component, not in the syntactic component (see Anderson 1992 for such an architecture of the grammar). But grammatical systems are more complicated. The Portuguese object person forms in (16) do not behave like affixes in that their order is variable (cf. (8) above), so that they commonly precede the verb, and when they do, they may have wide scope over coordination, and certain other words may intervene between them and the verb (Luís 2009: 18–19). Similarly, the Bulgarian definite article, grammaticalized from a former demonstrative, shows quite a bit of morphophonological variability (determined by the properties of its host word). However, it occurs not only on nouns but sometimes on adjectives or quantifiers that precede the noun. According to Bermúdez-Otero and Payne (2011), the generalization is that it occurs on the head of the first immediate constituent within the NP.

(17) Bulgarian (Bermúdez-Otero and Payne 2011)
a. *knigi-te* 'the books'
b. *interesni-te knigi* 'the interesting books'
c. *mnogo-to interesni knigi* 'the many interesting books'
d. *tvărde interesni-te knigi* 'the very interesting books'

Thus, even though in general morphophonological idiosyncrasies mostly occur with grammaticalized elements that exhibit affix-like behaviour in all respects, there are some cases which do not conform to the simplest picture.

3.6. Conclusion

The different criteria by which clitics and affixes are normally distinguished do not always coincide perfectly. This means that the changes cannot be derived from a simple architectural bifurcation of grammar into syntax and morphology, as is often assumed. Viewing coalescence as an abrupt reanalysis from a syntactic pattern to a morphological pattern does not do justice to the full richness of the attested phenomena in grammaticalization. In fact, as I have argued in Haspelmath (2011), the non-coincidence of the various criteria for syntactic vs. morphological status makes the very idea of a syntax/morphology distinction highly doubtful. Combinations of signs have different degrees of tightness, and it is not at all clear that this continuum can usefully be divided into two parts (syntax vs. morphology) or three parts (free words vs. clitics vs. affixes).

4. Linearity and relevance

A crucial question that has not been raised so far is what kinds of elements coalesce in grammaticalization. Function words become affixes on content words that we call their hosts, but what are suitable hosts?

All linguists know that certain combinations of content words and grammatical formatives are very common, so much so that they rarely ask why this should be so. Consider the combinations in (18).

(18) a. Noun + number marker / case-marker / article / possessive index
b. Verb + voice marker / aspect marker / tense marker / mood marker / negation marker / argument index
c. Adposition + argument index

All of the cases of coalescence that we have considered so far have been of one of these types, and this is not due to the bias towards European languages. There are two reasons why the combinations in (18) are the most common ones:

(19) a. Linear Fusion Hypothesis: "items that are used together fuse together" (Bybee 2002: 112)
b. Relevance Hypothesis: "affixation is more likely when the stem and gram form a coherent semantic unit" (Bybee et al. 1994: 22)

Clearly, both hypotheses are correct at some level. In many cases, they apply simultaneously, and so their effect is reinforced. A general iconic principle requires elements that are relevant[6] to each other to occur next to each other, so number markers normally occur next to their nouns, and case markers, articles, and possessive indexes normally occur next to their noun phrases. Likewise, voice markers, aspect markers, and argument indices are expected to occur next to their verb. Tense, mood, and negation are somewhat different, because they concern a unit that is larger than the verb (a verb phrase, predication, or clause). Traditionally, the verb is regarded as the head of this unit, and this is often thought to be the reason why these grammatical markers tend to coalesce with the verb.

But Linear Fusion sometimes counteracts Relevance. When function words occur next to the most relevant content word, they may still fuse with a word on the other side. An example comes from English, where the aspect and modality auxiliaries *be, have,* and *will* (or rather their reduced forms *'m*, 's, *'re*, *'ve*, *'ll*) may fuse with the preceding subject rather than with the following verb. Zwicky and Pullum (1983) claimed that these are clitics with no idiosyncratic effects on their hosts, but this is not always so. The reduced future-tense marker *'ll* combined with the personal pronouns behaves differently from *'ll* combined with full NPs:

(20) a. *she'll do it* (*she'll* monosyllabic, rhymes with *fill*)
b. *Lee'll do it* (*Lee'll* disyllabic, rhymes with *real*)

Thus, *she'll, he'll, we'll,* etc. are coalesced units, not unlike person-TAM complexes in other languages such as Hausa or Wambaya:

(21) a. Hausa (Chadic; Newman 2000: 570)
Kaa *daawoo?*
2SG.M.COMPL return
'Have you returned?'

b. Wambaya (Australian; Nordlinger 1998: 138)
Ngajbi *ngi-ny-a.*
see 1SG.A-2.P-NONFUT
'I saw you.'

Such elements resemble auxiliaries, but in Hausa and Wambaya, all verb forms require such person-TAM complexes, and in English, one normally says that *will* is an auxiliary, not that *she'll* is an auxiliary. Anyway, these cases illustrate the effect of Linear Fusion where it goes against the expectation of Relevance. The auxiliary *(wi)ll* frequently cooccurs with a following verb, but also with a preceding subject, so it could fuse or coalesce with either. According to Relevance, one would expect it

[6] 'Relevance is the extent to which the meaning of a grammatical category affects the inherent meaning of the lexical stem with which it is associated' (Bybee et al. 1994: 22)

to fuse with the following verb (on the assumption that aspect and mood are more relevant to the verb than to the subject), but here it fuses with the preceding subject.[7] The importance of frequency of linear adjacency for coalescence has been emphasized by Krug (1998), who studied the rate of contraction of English auxiliaries with the subject, and found that more frequent combinations show more contractions.

Another case where Linear Fusion wins over Relevance is combinations of prepositions with articles in some Romance and Germanic languages, e.g. French (*de + le > du, à + le > au*), Italian (*in + il > nel, di + l > della*), and German (*zu + dem > zum, in + das > ins*, etc.). Here, too, it is particularly the most frequent combinations that coalesce (cf. Nübling 2005), and the Relevance Hypothesis would have predicted a coalescence with the noun, not with the article.

Coalescence of this type that defies Relevance is a challenge for the simple reanalysis scenario of (6), but for reasons that are different from the reasons we saw in section 3. At first sight, the hypothetical reanalysis in (22) looks similar to the reanalysis in (6).

(22) German

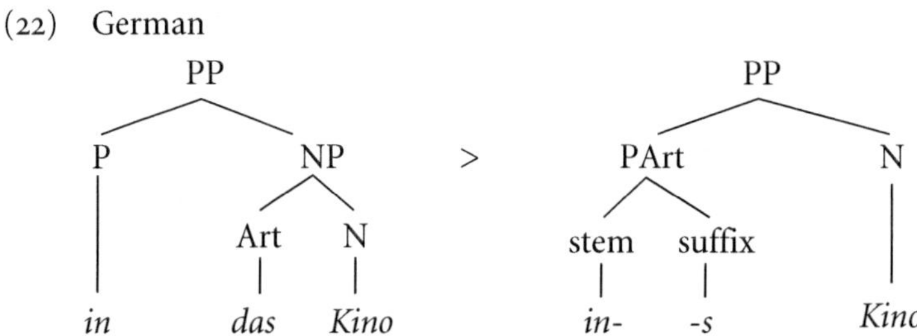

The problem here is of course that the tree on the right-hand side is not a syntactic tree that anyone would be happy to posit, because syntactic constituents are normally expected to match semantic constituents. To describe such patterns, a more powerful descriptive apparatus, where morphology and syntax are more independent of each other (e.g. Autolexical Syntax: Sadock 1991), would be required. The very fact that Linear Fusion can override Relevance shows that the simplest case, where formal tightness of combination correlates closely with semantic tightness of combination ('relevance'), is not the general case.[8]

[7] It is possible that for some reason, fusion of function words with a preceding host is generally preferred to fusion with a following host (Bybee et al. 1990; Hall 1992). However, it seems to me that the general 'suffixing preference' that was already observed by Greenberg (1957) is not as well-established as these authors assume, because much of the evidence for it comes from orthographic representations, and these could well be shaped by an orthographic suffixing bias of Western linguists (ultimately due to the fact that Latin had more suffixes).

[8] A reviewer suggests that coalescence may only be caused directly by frequency of occurrence, and that Relevance is just one of the factors behind frequency of occurrence.

The extent to which coalescence is determined by simple frequency of occurrence is not known yet. So far, too few studies of coalescence have examined corpus frequencies and correlated them with observed cases of fusing elements. This is difficult to do, because coalescence is not easy to observe in attested texts. We can often infer that coalescence must have taken place, but we rarely have large enough corpora from earlier periods to test specific hypotheses about the causes of coalescence. Thus, we will have to use more indirect methods for exploring the respective roles of Linear Fusion and Relevance.

5. Conclusion

Coalescence of function words with nearby content words is a widespread phenomenon in languages, and it is often assumed that most affixes ultimately have their origin in fused function words. This process was once at the centre of linguists' attention in grammaticalization studies, but as it is difficult to study in attested texts, it is less important in current empirical work. However, anyone who wants to understand the synchronic morphosyntactic patterns of languages needs to be aware of the general tendencies of coalescence, and we need a better understanding of them if we want to understand synchronic systems. Due to the influence of spelling and tradition, many linguists still think of morphosyntactic structure as strictly divided into morphology (internal structure of words) and syntax (structure of word combinations), but since we do not have a workable definition of the word as a general unit of languages, this is not helpful. There are various senses in which sign combinations can be more or less tight, and these do not correlate perfectly, either diachronically (as seen in section 3 of this chapter) or synchronically (as shown in Haspelmath 2011). Future research will have to investigate whether further constraints on the coalescence of linguistic elements can be found.

CHAPTER 28

GRAMMATICALIZATION AND WORD FORMATION

ILSE WISCHER

1. Introduction

If grammaticalization is a process by which linguistic elements change into constituents of grammar, or by which grammatical items become more grammatical in time, and on the other hand, if word formation processes, such as compounding, derivation, conversion, clipping, or blending, 'allow for the production of new lexical items' (cf. Brinton and Traugott 2005: 17), then one would have to propose that grammaticalization and word formation must be distinct processes, possibly even contradictory or mirror images. Nevertheless, especially in derivations, as one major type of word formation, the development of derivational affixes is often referred to as an example of grammaticalization, since these bound morphs find their origin in independent lexical units (cf. English *-dom* < Old English *dōm* 'judgement'; *-ly* < Old English *līc* 'body'; *a-* < Old English *on* 'on, in'; etc.) and, thus, progress along the cline from syntax to morphology. Furthermore they are subject to such processes that are often linked to grammaticalization as semantic bleaching, phonetic erosion, paradigmaticization, decategorialization, and fusion. On the other hand, the status of derivational affixes as grammatical categories is highly controversial (cf. Adams 2002[1973]: 12). Hopper and Traugott (2003: 4f.)

and Brinton and Traugott (2005: 63) even draw a distinction between lexical and grammatical derivational affixes. Consequently, there are diverging views on the origin of derivational affixes as the result of a grammaticalization or a lexicalization process.

Another controversial issue with respect to the relationship between grammaticalization and word formation involves the creation of new 'lexical' items with adverbial or discourse functions. For Meillet (1958[1912]: 138–9) the German temporal adverb *heute* 'today', which has its origin in a free syntactic combination **hiu tagu* (this–INSTRUMENTAL day–INSTRUMENTAL), is an example of grammaticalization, although it meets all requirements of what is traditionally called 'lexicalization': phonetic reduction, morphological demotivation, and loss of semantic compositionality. In terms of word formation we can call it a 'darkened phrasal compound'. Likewise, the archaic English discourse particle *methinks* 'I think' had derived from a once productively formed impersonal construction out of simple conventionalization, culminating in its fossilization and partly demotivation. Is this a particular type of word formation which has at the same time been grammaticalized (cf. Brinton and Traugott 2005: 67)?

Other processes of word formation, such as functional conversions like *the ups and downs* or hypostases like *an ism* are commonly quoted as examples of degrammaticalization. Thus, they serve as alleged counterexamples to the unidirectionality claim of grammaticalization.

The following sections will elucidate the relationship between grammaticalization and such processes of word formation as mentioned above. The focus will be on derivations and phrasal compounds.

2. Derivational affixes

Although the term 'grammaticalization' was coined by Meillet only in 1912, the concept that grammatical affixes develop through the agglutination of independent material words is much older. It is to be found as early as in Bopp (1975[1833]) and Humboldt (1822) and has since been widely accepted. While Bopp and Humboldt were more concerned about grammatical affixes, in later works of the 19th century, as in Whitney (1970[1875]), reference was already made to inflections and derivations with respect to suffixes like English *-ful*, *-less*, *-ly*, *-some*, *-ship*, *-dom*, and the English past marker *-ed*[1] or the French future inflection *-ai*:

[1] The idea that the Germanic weak past inflection (Engl. *-ed*) has descended from the past tense of the verb 'do' goes back at least to Bopp (1975[1816]) and is perhaps the most widely accepted

> These are some of the plainest among the numerous examples which might be brought forward, going to show that suffixes of derivation and inflection are made out of independent words, which, first entering into union with other words by the ordinary process of composition, then gradually lose their independent character, and finally come to be, in a more or less mutilated and disguised form, mere subordinate elements, or indicators of relation, in more elaborate structure. (Whitney 1970: 124)

Whitney does not draw a difference between the grammatical status of inflections and derivations, but treats them in the same manner with regard to their origin.

Today inflections are generally considered elements of grammar, since they only change the grammatical form of a lexeme, while derivational affixes make new words and are thus traditionally considered as 'bound lexical morphemes'.[2] Inflections are regularly used according to the grammatical rules of a language, so that the meaning of the complex word form can be accessed analytically on the basis of the knowledge of a grammatical rule. Derivational affixes, on the other hand, are less regular in their combinations and underlie certain lexical constraints. The meaning of the derived lexeme is often idiosyncratic and must be accessed holistically. Consequently, there arises the question of whether derivational affixes, if they are not elements of grammar, but of the lexicon, should ever be the result of a grammaticalization process at all.

This is indeed a disputable issue, especially since the status of derivational affixes as grammatical or lexical categories is not uniformly agreed upon (e.g. Adams 2002: 12; Hopper and Traugott 2003: 4f.; Brinton and Traugott 2005: 63).

Lehmann (1995a[1982]: 87) with regard to English *-ly* and Romance *-mente* states: 'Both of these suffixes are grammaticalizations of nouns which formerly served as the heads of the underlying adjectives.' In an earlier work (1989: 12) he called the process whereby an original lexical item becomes a derivational affix (OHG *haidus* 'shape' > MHG *-heit*) 'lexicalization'. The same can be found in Blank (2001: 1602f.) for OE *had* 'state' > ME *-hood.* He considers 'the turning of these words into affixes' as 'another clear case of lexicalization', although he admits: 'If, however, one prefers to see word-formation as the "grammaticalization of the lexicon" . . . the change of an autonomous word into an affix (and from free compounding into a rule-based process) is rather a kind of grammaticalization' (Blank 2001: 1603).

This problem can be solved, however, if one assumes a continuum between grammar and lexicon along which we can find more or less grammatical or lexical items, even if they are bound morphs. The synchronic degree of grammaticalization can then be determined according to the criteria shown in Fig. 28.1. So we can find

etymology of this affix today, although it is by no way uncontroversial; cf. the discussion in Lass (1993: 164–6).

[2] Cf. Kastovsky (1982: 73); Lipka (2002: 86f.); Kortmann (2005: 88). However, there are controversial opinions on the status of derivational affixes; cf. Adams (2002: 12); Bauer (2002[1983]: 39–41).

	Lexicon <·······························> Grammar
Semantic abstraction	low <·······························> high
Paradigmatic variability	high <·······························> low
Class	open <·······························> closed

Fig. 28.1. Criteria for bound lexical and grammatical categories

affixes that are situated closer to the lexical end of the grammar–lexis cline, which resemble elements of compounds, and at the other end, in the core area of grammar, there are inflections.

From a diachronic perspective, derivational affixes, as far as they arise from separate and independent lexical units,[3] run through similar processes as inflections: semantic abstraction, phonetic reduction, paradigmaticization, decategorialization, and fusion; hence their evolution has traditionally been characterized as a process of grammaticalization (e.g. Ramat 1992: 558n; Hopper and Traugott 1993: 41).[4]

On the grammaticalization cline (cf. Hopper and Traugott 1993: 7; 2003: 7), however, there is no stage of derivation:

content item > grammatical word > clitic > inflectional affix

Derivational affixes are situated, according to Hopper and Traugott (1993: 7), on a cline of lexicality:

a basket *full* (of eggs . . .) > a cup*ful* (of water) > hope*ful*
part of phrase > part of compound > derivational affix

This cline of lexicality is missing in the second edition of the book (cf. Hopper and Traugott 2003: 5). Instead, the authors draw a distinction between lexical and grammatical derivational affixes, with the former only modifying the meaning of the base without changing the word class (*happy* > ***un**happy; duck* > *duck**ling***), while the latter do not only add to the meaning of the base, but they serve to indicate the grammatical category (*swim* > *swimm**er**; happy* > *happi**ly***). We will see that such a distinction is not very useful.

[3] For other scenarios of their evolution see Wischer (2010).

[4] Although Hopper and Traugott (2003: 41) do not explicitly refer to the evolution of derivational suffixes like *-hood, -dom*, and *-ly* as a grammaticalization process, the reader can easily infer that this is meant by the authors when they use these examples to explain the concept of fusion as a type of reanalysis. It is interesting to note that these examples are missing in the 2nd edition of their book, where derivational affixes in the context of grammaticalization are treated with much more caution.

Kuryłowicz includes derivational affixes in his definition of grammaticalization:

> Grammaticalization consists in the increase of the range of a morpheme advancing from a lexical to a grammatical or from a less grammatical to a more grammatical status, e.g. from a derivative formant to an inflectional one. (1975[1965]: 69)

This implies that derivational affixes are less grammatical than inflections. Still the question remains whether there is indeed a grammaticalization path that turns derivational morphemes into inflections.

Although, as will be shown later, there may be rare examples of that kind, there is generally one major difference between the origin of inflections and that of derivational affixes. While the former develop directly from free grammatical words (e.g. prepositions, auxiliary verbs) in particular syntactic structures,[5] the latter do not have their origin directly in a free lexical element, but emerge via the stage of a compound. Derivational suffixes are former heads of compounds and prefixes are modifiers.[6] That means that derivational affixes arise from lexical elements which are already bound morphs within a lexical unit, and as such they usually remain in the lexicon even though they become more general in meaning and start to form paradigms, though not of the grammatical sort. These are lexical paradigms.

Here it becomes evident that a distinction between grammatical and lexical derivational affixes as suggested by Hopper and Traugott (2003: 5) or Brinton and Traugott (2005: 35, 92) cannot be adequate. The feature of marking a grammatical category cannot be a sufficient reason for the classification of a linguistic item as an element of grammar, since all heads of compounds also indicate the word class although they are clearly not grammatical units; cf. *call-**girl*** (V+N→N) or *play**ground*** (V+N→N). Moreover, grammatical markers do not usually change the word class at all; cf. plurality markers on nouns or aspectual markers on verbs, etc. Nevertheless, bound morphs can have a more or less grammatical status, in the same way as free morphs.[7] The decisive criteria, as listed above, are their degrees of semantic abstraction and of paradigmatic variability, together with the type of class that they belong to, whether it is rather open or rather closed.

Derivational affixes form semantic subsets in the lexicon, e.g. *un-* <contradiction>, *-ness* <state>, *-er* <agent>. These paradigms usually do not reach the quality of grammatical categories, as inflectional paradigms do.

In contrast to inflectional affixes, which:

1. are members of relatively closed classes (e.g. English past tense suffix *-ed* + a small list of exceptional forms);

[5] Cf. e.g. the French future or the Germanic weak past tense suffix.

[6] Of course, not each derivative is formed in that way, but the derivational affix as such has its origin in a compound; once it has been established as derivational affix, it is available for analogical use.

[7] Cf. Lehmann's (2002a: 8) distinction between lexical and grammatical prepositions.

2. can combine with (almost) any member of a word class, including newly borrowed or created words, to express the respective category;
3. have a very abstract, functional meaning;

derivational morphemes

1. also occur in relatively closed classes, which, however, are more open for new members to join the paradigm (cf. English markers of contradiction: *un-*, *a-*, *dis-*, *in-*, *non-*);
2. are subject to lexical constraints and thus not automatically combinable with (almost) any member of a word class (cf. *performance–*performation*, but: *reformation–*reformance*);
3. are semantically more complex, although there is a considerable variability (cf. *vice-president, nicely*).

It is, however, possible that a semantic subclass of derivational affixes turns into a grammatical category. In such a situation we can indeed speak of a grammaticalization of a derivational formative into an inflection, as mentioned by Kuryłowicz (cf. e.g. classifiers that can turn into gender markers, or verbal prefixes that can become aspectual markers), even if only few affixes seem to be suitable for such a change. They would have to be sufficiently abstract in meaning. Prefixes or suffixes which are semantically too specific (*sub-*, *-ful*, *-ish*) will hardly semantically erode so much that they come to denote a functional meaning.[8]

Furthermore, as mentioned above, it is extremely difficult to clearly distinguish between lexicon and grammar in this area. That is the reason why, for example, the status of Russian verbal prefixes as markers of Aktionsart (lexical) or aspect (grammatical) is a matter of dispute.[9]

3. Phrasal compounds and other types of word formation

Compounding is a central type of word formation which, like derivation, results in the formation of new lexemes. These complex linguistic items are often subject to idiomaticization and can thus be seen as lexicalized, since many scholars identify idiomaticization with lexicalization (cf. Brinton and Traugott 2005: 56).

[8] As Hopper and Traugott (2003: 101) state: 'the lexical meanings subject to grammaticalization are usually quite general . . . they are typically not selected from more specialized terms . . . '

[9] On the relationship between aspect and Aktionsart, see Wischer (2004).

While compounds are formed by combining free linguistic units according to certain language specific rules (N+N; V-*ing*+N; N+A; etc.), there are other complex words, which are the result of the conventionalization, and sometimes idiomaticization, of particular syntactic phrases or parts of phrases. The prototype of such 'phrasal compounds' are words like *forget-me-not* or *mother-in-law.* In this group I would also include phrasal verbs (*look up, write down*, etc.), composite predicates (*take a walk, have a drink*, etc.), and complex words like *a lot of, in front of, sort of*, etc. In some cases such complex words can fuse into one lexeme through a process of univerbation (German *heute* < *hiu tagu*; Early Modern English *methinks* < *me þynceþ*).

Some of these complex word formations have adopted a grammatical function and thus have joined a functional category, for example English indefinite pronouns (*everything, somebody*), prepositions (*apart from, instead of*), or subordinators (*as long as, in order that).* In such constructions, a lexical word has lost its original lexical meaning and has become an integral part of a new grammatical word. Thus, the formation of these complex words is rightly treated as grammaticalization. Yet, due to their univerbation and idiomaticization they are similarly subject to a lexicalization process.

Phrasal verbs have been lexicalized in a similar way, although the adverbial particle functions like a perfective aspectual marker. It can be compared to the verbal prefix to mark the perfective aspect in Russian. However, the degree of paradigmaticization, specialization, and obligatorification is much lower in English. Nevertheless, we can observe a lexicalization of complex words (phrasal verbs) by univerbation and idiomaticization and an incipient grammaticalization of the adverbial particle.

With composite predicates the situation is much more complicated. Brinton (2008a: 33) argues that some of them are 'lexicalizations, while others are better regarded as cases of grammaticalization'. I would agree with Brinton's distinction between composite predicates of the *lose sight of* types, which are to a high degree lexicalized and can thus be considered phrasal compounds in the widest sense, and those of the *take a look at* type, which are less lexicalized and whose schematic structure, consisting of a light verb and a verbal noun, expresses an aspectual meaning of perfectivity. Here we seem to have the case of an incipient grammaticalization of a schematic construction.

Finally, there are other types of word formation, like conversion or hypostasis,[10] which are sometimes considered mirror images of grammaticalization. When conversion occurs in examples like *the ups and downs* or *to off*, i.e. when a minor category (here an adverb) has been converted into a major category (a noun or

[10] 'Hypostasis relates to suffixes or suffix-like elements which through secretion or abstraction acquire the status of independent words, for example, *ana, ism(s), ists, ology,* and a group of recent coinages such as *burger, scape, teria*' (Stekauer 2000: 74); on hypostasis see also Pennanen (1966).

verb), this has been widely recognized as lexicalization or degrammaticalization (e.g. Ramat 1992; 2001; Newmeyer 1998; Traugott 2005). Here it could be argued that a conversion is possible because adverbs are not central grammatical categories and can therefore be consciously accessed by the speaker. What we are dealing with here is an abrupt, conscious word formation process, and not a reversal of a gradual, subconscious grammaticalization process.

Hypostasis is a very rare process of the reinterpretation and separation of an individual 'constituent' of a word, which is assigned a generalized or hyperonymic meaning. Examples would be English *-ism* as occurring in *imperialism, communism, descriptivism*, or German *-zig* as in *vierzig, fünfzig, sechzig*, in which a derivational suffix was separated and hypostatized. Hypostasis, however, is not restricted to genuine suffixes. Sometimes the separated element is the result of a reinterpretation and secretion,[11] as happened with English *burger*, from *hamburg-er*. The latter example could also be mentioned under the rubric of folk etymology. With this I hope to have shown that hypostasis, like conversion, is an abrupt conscious word formation process, which is possible because derivational suffixes are not core elements of grammar and can thus, albeit rarely, be consciously accessed by the speaker.

4. Summary

While inflectional affixes clearly have a grammatical status, derivational affixes are situated on a continuum between grammar and lexicon. With regard to their formation, they differ in that an inflection is obviously the result of a cliticization and/or fusion of a free element in a particular syntactic construction, while a derivational affix, as a rule, passes through the stage of a compound. Prefixes derive from former modifier elements and suffixes are former heads of compounds.

Although derivational affixes have a predominantly lexical status, they cannot be described as the result of a lexicalization process, if one agrees with Lehmann's (2002a: 13) position: 'Every monomorphemic unit is, by definition, already in the lexicon and therefore cannot be lexicalized. Only complex units may be lexicalized.'[12] What can be lexicalized is then the whole derivative, but not the derivational affix. The evolution of derivational affixes, if they have their origin in

[11] For the theory of secretion see Jespersen (1925: 384ff.; 1942: 352ff.); Koziol (1937: 140); Algeo (1991: 6).

[12] This understanding can also be found in all common definitions of lexicalization. It is always the whole complex linguistic item that turns into a lexical unit (cf. Brinton and Traugott 2005: 95–9).

independent lexemes, resembles in all its aspects a grammaticalization process, except for the intermediate compound stage and the fact that the result does not have the status of a grammatical category. Nevertheless, the respective linguistic unit has moved from the core area of the lexicon in the direction of grammar, possibly without ever reaching it completely. This leads me to the conclusion that derivational affixes, though they are not grammaticalized from a synchronic point of view, diachronically, however, as long as they have their origin in independent lexemes, have run through a process of grammaticalization.

Furthermore, under certain conditions it is possible that derivational affixes in the course of time may leave the lexical domain and move to the core area of grammar. This is the case when their meaning is further bleached and becomes so abstract as to express a grammatical function (e.g. aspect). In this process their productivity is increased, and at the same time the variability of forms from which the speaker can choose to express this abstract meaning is reduced, i.e. a specialization takes place. Finally, their use in the respective contexts becomes obligatory and the marked forms enter into opposition with unmarked forms in other contexts. The result is the change of a derivational affix into an inflection.[13]

Finally, the formation of phrasal compounds can be accompanied by a grammaticalization process, which may affect the whole construction or only part of it. Thus, some syntactic constructions can be lexicalized and as such immediately integrated into the paradigm of minor categories like prepositions, subordinators, or discourse markers. This is usually described as the grammaticalization of a construction (e.g. *in front of*, *methinks*). Other syntactic phrases may be lexicalized, whereby recurring elements in different phrasal compounds of a similar kind may be assigned a grammatical function (e.g. adverbial particles in phrasal verbs or light verbs in composite predicates).

As has been shown, word formation, though usually closely associated with the lexical domain of a language, is in various ways interrelated with processes of grammaticalization, the reason for which seems to lie in the fuzzy relationship between lexicon and grammar.

[13] Such a line of development from compounds to derivations to inflections has already been postulated by Meillet (1958) and Kuryłowicz (1975); today, however, it is disputed among scholars in grammaticalization theory (cf. Brinton and Traugott 2005: 86).

CHAPTER 29

GRAMMATICALIZATION AND SYNTAX: A FUNCTIONAL VIEW

SCOTT DELANCEY

GRAMMATICALIZATION theory plays a fundamental role in functional-typological syntax. The development of grammaticalization theory over the last generation has sometimes been misunderstood as an aspect of historical linguistics (e.g. Joseph 2004), but as an explanatory framework for common types of syntactic change it is not really anything new. The importance of the explosion of interest in and work on grammaticalization over the last 40 years is in the recognition of grammaticalization theory as a fundamental component of a functional theory of syntax. Grammaticalization theory is one of the two essential components of the functional-typological approach to syntax, the other being the interconnected theories of cognitive and pragmatic motivation. In the functionalist view, essentially shared with the Cognitive Linguistics school, all linguistic form above the level of morpheme, from word classes and affix categories to long-distance anaphora and control phenomena, originates in constructions and categories with transparent motivation (which I cannot devote any space to here; see e.g. Givón 1979; 1995; 2001; 2009; Bybee, Perkins, and Pagliuca 1994; Croft 2001; 2006; 2008; Heine 1993; 1997a; 1997b; Heine and Kuteva 2002; 2007). The role of grammaticalization theory is to explain how fixed, recurrent constructions develop from transparent, motivated concatenations of words. Since such syntactic, often synchronically arbitrary grammatical structure is characteristic of all but the very freshest pidgin proto-grammars, a theory of grammaticalization is essential to the functionalist programme.

1. Grammaticalization theory in functional-typological syntax

Functionalists do not see grammar as an abstract, logically coherent system organized in terms of predefined categories, but as 'an automated, streamlined, conventionalized, speeded-up language processing system' (Givón 2001: 15), a set of tools adapted by usage to particular tasks or sets of tasks. The specific processes by which 'automatization', 'conventionalization', or 'adaptation' come about are what we study under the rubric of grammaticalization. Thus the functionalist account of syntax has two components: an understanding of the functional imperatives—cognitive structures and problems of information management—that lead to the first creation of constructions, and an understanding of grammaticalization, the process by which motivated constructions then evolve into opaque grammatical structure. Grammaticalization is not simply a mechanism by which morphological structure develops; it is the constant, universal tendency of language out of which all structure arises.

Grammaticalization is, broadly speaking, the shift of a form or construction from one category to another. A formal approach to syntactic structure which assumes predefined, universal categories (or categories defined in terms of universal syntactic features) leads us to expect natural languages to have well-defined, discrete syntactic categories, which should be easily comparable across languages, and much syntactic research and theory assumes that this is the case. The gross structure of languages approximates this ideal closely enough to permit some progress in the classification of linguistic constructions. But any attempt to come to terms with the full range of morphosyntactic phenomena in any single natural language quickly founders on the flotsam and jetsam of fuzzy categorial boundaries, singleton 'categories', and intermediate constructions, the pervasive imprecision which is found throughout all languages.

One way of dealing with this universal aspect of syntax is to simply discard troublesome data by defining it as irrelevant 'peripheral' rather than theoretically interesting 'core' grammar. But any approach which leaves half the data unexplained obviously requires an additional theory to clean up its residue. Grammaticalization theory is perfectly suited to this task, and thus is a necessary component to any attempt to explain the syntactic structure of natural languages.

Grammaticalization theory traces all structure back—diachronically as well as logically—to simple combinations of nouns and verbs (Heine and Kuteva 2007 push this a step further and consider verbs to develop from nouns). We can describe the simplest forms of linguistic communication—early child language and undeveloped pidgin communication—in terms of a set of uncategorized symbols combined according to little more than Behaghel's principle that conceptual connection between concepts or referents is expressed by contiguity of the symbols which denote or refer to them. Using any lexicon, we can effectively describe a person who yells or is yelling by simply placing side by side a word which means 'person' and one which means 'yell'. We see grammar arising as soon as we can detect a fixed, recurrent construction, like *VERB-person*, which speakers can pull 'off the shelf' to refer to an agent or actor associated with a particular action. At the far end of the grammaticalization process, we may end up with a semantically light, phonologically reduced, probably morphologized affix which attaches to verbs to derive agent nominalizations, or perhaps simply nominalizations (see below).

This is the origin of all grammatical categories, including 'major' lexical categories like adposition and adjective as well as smaller categories such as nominalizer. All such categories arise through the same processes, and thus there is no theoretical need to maintain separate stories for 'major' and 'minor' categories. Indeed, all languages have unique forms or singleton categories, morphemes whose behaviour and distribution distinguishes them from all other morphemes in the language; a notorious example is English modal *better* (see below). Such a form may correspond, in function and behaviour, to what in other languages is a larger and more important category. For example, Klamath, a recently extinct Plateau Penutian language of Oregon, is an example of a language which lacks the adposition category (DeLancey 2005); the work which in most languages is done by adpositions is done in Klamath by elements of verbal or adverbial origin which are incorporated into the verb stem (DeLancey 1999a). However, there is one morpheme in Klamath which has essentially the behavior of a postposition, the associative *dola*:

(1) doscambli hoot sa ?at, sqel **c'asgaay-as dola.**
few.run-along-back that 3pl now Marten Weasel-OBJ with
'...now they ran back, Marten together **with Weasel.**'

Dola has the form of a verb in the simple indicative tense, and its syntactic behaviour is in many ways what one would expect of a Klamath verb. For example, it can govern object case, as in examples (1) and (2). The order of a Klamath verb and its arguments is quite free, and so with *dola*: it usually follows its argument, as in (1), but it can also precede it:

(2) q'ay honk s?aywakta kakni hoot sa kat **dola honk-s.**
NEG DEM know PL.REL that 3pl REL **with DEM-OBJ**
'. . . those who [were] **with him** did not know that.'

But *dola* is not a verb; the Klamath verb can occur in a wide range of inflected forms (DeLancey 1991), but *dola* occurs in only this form.

Thus *dola* has no obvious categorial assignment in Klamath, since there is no other morpheme with the same, or even very similar, behaviour and distribution. It acts very much like an adposition in a language like English, but where English *with* is a well-behaved member of a well-defined category of adposition, *dola* is a category of its own. There is ample reason to consider it to have originated as a serial verb, and then lost its verbal behaviour as it specialized into a more 'adpositional' function. Klamath *dola* is evidence that what is constant across languages is recurrent grammaticalization pathways, not universal categories. Klamath has followed the well-documented pathway from verb to something quite like an adposition, but shows no inclination to give the output of the process any very prominent place in its overall syntactic organization.

A great deal of research has been devoted to identifying and understanding the recurrent grammaticalization scenarios or 'universal pathways' which produce widely attested structures. I cannot deal with the origin of all widely attested grammatical structures in this limited space; for accounts going beyond the few examples discussed here see especially Givón (1995; 2001; 2009), Bybee (2007), Bybee, Perkins, and Pagliuca (1994), Bybee and Hopper (2001), Heine and Kuteva (2007), Bisang (1996; 2004). The essential point is that what I am presenting is not simply an account of how certain structures, of which one could make a list, develop within some sort of formal theory. Rather, it is an account of where all syntax comes from. Thus the limits and possibilities of syntax are defined by the range of possible motivated constructions and the phenomena of grammaticalization (see Heine and Kuteva 2007: 342ff.), not by constraints on the possible outputs of the process: there is no need, and no place, for a mystical 'syntactic theory' which deductively defines the possible outcomes. All categories arise through grammaticalization. Languages may have very idiosyncratic lowest-level categories, while higher-level categories are amalgamations of smaller ones into broader functional bundles (see Croft 2001).

Thus functional syntax expects a number of phenomena which many other syntactic frameworks have to stretch to accommodate. Cross-linguistic variation in the inventory and size of syntactic categories, and especially the ubiquity of singleton categories, is one kind of evidence that grammaticalization theory gives us a more adequate understanding of natural languages than any deductive formal theory. Another is the universal occurrence of forms and constructions with indeterminate, intermediate, or transitional categorial status. Grammaticalization is a gradual process: as a form grammaticalizes, it sheds its previous behaviours and acquires its new ones piecemeal, not all at once. Thus, contrary to what is often claimed in the generative literature (e.g. Newmeyer 2000), word classes in languages are fuzzy, and there is demonstrably such a thing as intermediate categorial status (Bolinger 1980; DeLancey 1997). We will see examples in the next section. Like singleton categories such as English modal *better* and Klamath associative *dola*, these find no easy place in a world of constructions defined in terms of preordained categories, but are a natural and inevitable outgrowth of the grammaticalization processes which also bring about larger and more universal categories.

2. The origin and nature of syntactic categories

Word classes and phrasal categories are mutually defining: morpheme classes are defined by the constructions in which their members can occur, and constructions are defined in terms of the categories of which they are constructed. So, the definition of an adposition is that it can be the head of an adpositional phrase; the definition of an adpositional phrase is that it is an adposition with a nominal argument. Languages generally allow a number of constructions in which another word is used to modify a noun; we have an adjective category when a particular set of words occur primarily in this function, in a specific construction which only they participate in. Thus the origin of word classes and that of phrase structure are the same story.

2.1. Where do grammatical categories come from? The rise of adpositions

Adposition is not a universal category (DeLancey 2003; 2005). There are two common sources: they arise either from verbs through serial verb constructions (e.g. Li and Thompson 1974a; Heine and Reh 1984; Lord 1993) or from nouns through relator noun constructions (Starosta 1985; DeLancey 1997; König, Chapter 41 below). Both these pathways represent a reanalysis of syntactic structure, thus placing the grammaticalizing element in a new construction and thereby changing its category.

The well-known serial verb source involves a lexical verb such as Mandarin *ná* 'take, pick up, hold in the hand' (ex. 3, from Li and Thompson 1974a), which, when it expresses background information in a serial verb construction, can be reinterpreted as an adverbial constituent of the second clause rather than an independent clause on its own (ex. 4):

(3) tā ná-zhe yī-běn shū
he hold-PROG one-CLASSIFIER book
'He is holding a book.'

(4) tā ná shànzi tiào le
she take fan dance PERF
'She took a fan and did/to do a dance.' OR 'She did a dance with a fan.'

Li and Thompson document at length the heterogeneous behaviour exhibited by these forms in Mandarin, where each has its own particular configuration of verbal constructions (tense/aspect marking, negation, etc.) in which it can and cannot participate.

The relator noun source is a very common construction in which a subcategory of nouns, often ill-defined, syntactically and functionally seems to fall somewhere in between fully-fledged nouns and true adpositions. These are variously named; following Starosta (1985) I will refer to them as relator nouns (RN). In English, these are the non-prepositional elements in constructions like *on **top** of, in **front** of, in **back** of,* and *on **behalf** of.* These are clearly noun stems, and are functioning as nouns in being the argument of one PP and the head noun modified by another. But they lack all other noun features. They cannot have articles, or pluralize: we can say:

(4) *in front of all the houses,*

but we cannot pluralize the relational noun:

(5) **in fronts of all the houses*

RNs cannot take any modifiers, and this, like presence or absence of an article, distinguishes a relator noun from the homophonous but not synonymous lexical noun:

(6) *in the very front of the hall*
(7) **in very front of the house*

RNs are certainly not prepositions, but they cannot do most of the things which we expect a lexical noun to do. As constructions like this grammaticalize further, they may coalesce into new adpositions, e.g. *on top of > atop, by side of > beside.* But a language can have a large set of intermediate forms which cannot be neatly categorized. In many Tibeto-Burman languages, such as Boro (spoken in Assam in northeast India), we occasionally see a fully-fledged RN construction, with genitive marking on the lexical noun and the RN as the syntactic argument of a postposition:

(8) *no-ni* *sigaŋ-ou*
house-GEN front-LOC
'in front of the house.'

But the full relator noun construction illustrated in (5) is not that common. Most relator nouns occur with only a locative or ablative postposition, but no genitive marking:

(9) *doŋphoŋ* *khathi-ou*
tree near-LOC
'near a tree'

One common locative postposition, the ablative *-niphrai*, is transparently an old genitive + RN construction, but most speakers think of it as an unanalysable unit. Even the locative *-ou* shows evidence of a similar origin. Noun phrases with human referents cannot take the *-ou* directly, but must be marked as genitive *-ni-ou*, often reduced to *-nao*:

(10) *aŋ* *nwŋ-thaŋ-ni-ou* *lazi-nai-bw* *mẃnw*
1SG 2SG-HON-GEN-LOC ashamed-NMZ-also get
'I'm ashamed before you, I'm shy in front of you.'

(11) *thá-laŋ-bai* *manswi-ni-ou*
stay-take-PERF person-GEN-LOC
'[It] stayed in the person.'

In these data we can see that adposition and RN are not coherent categories with strictly defined boundaries. Like adposition and serial verb in languages like Chinese, they are two poles of a diachronic process along which various morphemes are found, showing all possible combinations of categorial behaviours.

2.2. Grammaticalization and the gradience of categories

As noted above, one implication of the gradual nature of grammaticalization is that we should expect to find in any language a number of minor morphosyntactic categories and individual forms with unique and idiosyncratic morphosyntactic behaviour. This is indeed the case; we regularly find cases of grammaticalizing forms occupying intermediate categorial status. The analysis of a RN construction like (8) or (10) is problematic:

(10) in front of the house

It appears to be an adpositional phrase with the argument of the adposition modified by a dependent adpositional phrase. However, *front* and Boro *sigaŋ* are not fully-fledged nouns—they do not occur with modifiers or dependents. They have the position of head nouns with respect to the lexical noun, which is formally a genitive dependent. But they do not head a true noun phrase: unlike true nouns, they cannot take modifiers or complements other than the obligatory genitive modifier, and unlike ordinary noun phrases, they cannot occur in a determiner phrase (*front* in *in the front of the house* is the true noun, not the relator noun; note that *in front of the house* refers to a location outside of the house, *in the front of the house* to a location within it). Thus just as *front* and *sigaŋ* are not exactly nouns, so *front of the house* and *no-ni sigaŋ* are not exactly noun phrases.

And the problem is even worse. At least *front of the house* and *no-ni sigaŋ* look superficially like well-behaved N″, and so we can pretend that *in front of the house* and *no-ni sigaŋ-ou* are unproblematic adpositional phrases. But we cannot even do that with *doŋphoŋ khathi-ou* 'near the tree', to which we cannot assign a well-motivated phrase structure without creating a new subcategory for those relator nouns which, like *khathi*, do not accept genitive marking on the lexical noun.

A famous example of the phenomenon of gradient categoriality is the motley set of forms aspiring to auxiliary status in modern English such as *used to*, *want to*, *ought to* (Bolinger 1980). True auxiliaries in English can be identified by their participation in the subject-auxiliary inversion rule, while lexical verbs require *do* in constructions which call for subject-auxiliary inversion. In contemporary American English, forms like *used to* and *ought to* can do neither:

(11) **Do you ought to go along?*
(12) ?**Ought you to go along?*

Some of these have their own idiosyncratic question constructions; for example, in my speech the only possible question construction for ought to is (the negation is obligatory):

(13) *Hadn't you ought to go along?*

Compare the distinct but equally anomalous behavior of *usta*, with its defective tense distribution:

(14) *Did you usta go along?*
(15) **Do you usta go along?*
(16) **Used you to go along?*
(17) **Usta you go along?*

The most anomalous of the English not-quite-auxiliaries is 'modal' *better*, as in:

(18) *They better hurry.*
(19) *You better not pout.*

In slightly older forms of English, this typically occurred as *you'd better*, where the original verb can be recovered as *had* from the question construction *hadn't you better?* Currently in the U.S. the *'d* is rare, and younger speakers whom I have asked find the question construction archaic or even unrecognizable. In the modern construction, *better* occupies the position of an auxiliary. Like auxiliaries, it precedes the negative:

(20) *I may not tell him.*
(21) *I better not tell him.*

But unlike true auxiliaries, it cannot occur in the subject-auxiliary inversion construction:

(22) *May I tell him? / *Better I tell him?*

Although *better* is acquiring the functions and formal behaviours of an auxiliary, this is not a sudden, all-or-none process. The construction has lost the formal material which clearly distinguished it from the true auxiliaries. However, no English speaker would say or accept **Better we talk to him first?* Thus *better* has not acquired all the syntactic behaviours of an auxiliary. It's like serial verbs or relator nouns that have not yet developed into fully-fledged adpositions: its categorial status is intermediate and ambiguous.

Data such as these were accommodated in structuralist descriptive models, but are awkward, at best, for any theoretical framework which assumes that a language should be describable in terms of a predefined set of categories. This assumption is implicit in X′ theory (Kornai and Pullum 1990: 27), so that the undefined minor categories which are required for the adequate description of any language are a serious embarrassment to the X′ programme. Indeed, without an unambiguous account of the categorial status of forms like *ought to* and *better*, we cannot even provide a structural description for every sentence in the language, and thus cannot meet even the criterion of descriptive adequacy which is the first requirement of a formal theory of syntax. Grammaticalization theory tells us that we will never be able to provide an unambiguous account of either of the categorial status every form in a language, or the structural analysis of every construction, and thus that the fundamental aims of formal theory are in principle unachievable.

3. Complex constructions

More complex syntactic constructions such as complementation and relativization derive by the same processes from simple pragmatic constructions involving larger units. Although many languages have finite complement clause constructions, clearly the basic strategy for complementation, cross-linguistically, is nominalization. This is why complementizers are often etymologically definite articles or demonstratives (Noonan 2007; Heine and Kuteva 2002). Heine and Kuteva (2007) show the development of relative clause constructions from demonstrative and interrogative constructions, and Givón (2009) discusses more discourse-level sources for relative constructions such as clause chains and parenthetical side comments.

The simplest source of relative constructions is the nominalization strategy which we find in Sino-Tibetan and other languages. Relative clauses in these languages are simply nominalized clauses which can modify a head noun in the same way other nominals can, either as appositives or as genitive dependents. In Boro, a morpheme *-nai* nominalizes simple verb stems and clauses. Clauses nominalized with *-nai* function as full-fledged NPs:

(23) *tháŋ-nai-a mwzaŋ*
go-NMZ-SU good
'It would be good to go.'

(24) *dáosin-dáola bír-nai-a uhhhhh na bír-na hw-bai*
birds fly-NMZ-SU uhhhhh QUOT fly-NF give-PERF
'The birds' flying made a "uhhhh" sound.' (*Mirror*)

(25) *phipha thwidarlai-nai*
father die-NMZ
'one whose father had died' (*Mirror*)

And like other nominals, they can be used as modifiers of the head of a noun phrase. The argument of the modifying clause which is co-referential with the head noun is omitted.

(26) *mai ha-nai manswi-phwr*
paddy reap-REL person-PL
'the people who were harvesting rice'

(27) *aŋ gái-nai uwa*
yes 1SG plant-NMZ bamboo
'the bamboo which I planted'

While to describe the English translations of these examples we need to refer to several different constructions—adjectival modification, relative clause, headless relative clause, *to* infinitive, gerund construction—in Boro there is only one, a simple nominalization which is recruited to the function of modification.

In Tibetan we can see further developments in this process (DeLancey 1999b). All Tibetan dialects have a relative construction similar to that of Boro, involving an old nominalizer *-ba* which can be reconstructed as the earliest nominalization/relative construction in Tibetan. The Central dialects have innovated a set of newer, more specific nominalizers, including *sa*, a noun meaning 'earth, place', indicating an oblique argument, and *mkhan*, originally 'skilled or educated person', for agentive nominalizations. Since in Tibetan, as in Boro, modification is accomplished with nominal constructions, these nominalizations can be used as modifiers, and nominalized clauses as relative clauses:

(28) *stag gsod=mkhan*
tiger kill-NMZ
'one who killed a/the tiger, one who kills tigers, tiger-killer'

(29) *stag gsod=mkhan dmagmi*
tiger kill-NMZ soldier
'the soldier who killed a tiger/kills tigers'

In a more traditional instance of grammaticalization, in some dialects *mkhan* has displaced the other nominalizers and now marks all relative clauses, thus illustrating semantic bleaching and functional broadening, and categorial development to a relative clause marker. Thus we see syntax arising out of very simple source patterns.

Nominalization is one of the two basic processes which generate complex syntactic constructions: when a clause is treated as a nominal, it can then enter into simple syntactic relations with other constituents. It is not always necessary that the clause be formally nominalized: subordinating conjunctions, for example, are often simply adpositions, such as English *before* and *after*, taking a finite clause as their argument (Genetti 1991). The other major engine for the generation of syntactic constructions is verb serialization. For example, morphological valence-adjusting constructions such as causatives and applicatives (Givón 2009), arise through the grammaticalization of looser multiclausal constructions. The source construction can either be a complement construction in which one clause serves as an argument for another, usually a nominalization construction, or from a sequence of serialized verbs. It is common for a benefactive applicative to develop from a serialized verb 'give', as in Boro:

(30) *aŋ thwrsi-phwr-kho sú-bai*
1SG dish-PL-OBJ wash-PERF
'I washed the dishes.'

(31) *aŋ* ***bi-nw*** *thwrsi-phwr-kho sú-na* ***hw-bai***
1SG 3SG-DAT utensil-PL-OBJ wash-NF give-PERF
'I washed the dishes **for him/her**.'

In (31) the case marking of *aŋ*, *bi-**nw***, and *thwrsi-phwr-**kho*** identifies them as the three arguments of a ditransitive predicate, but that predicate is still formally a serial verb construction with *hw* 'give'.

4. Grammatical relations and alignment

Like all systematic grammatical structure, the means by which languages indicate the relations among a predicate and its arguments arise from simple pragmatic source constructions through grammaticalization. Functionalists see grammatical relations like Subject and Object as clusters of formal properties associated with clusters of functional properties, and pay close attention to the correlation between particular formal and functional properties (Givon 1995; Croft 2001). Thus languages do not simply 'have' a Subject relation; rather, a language develops a set of behaviours or constructions—syntactic pivot in various constructions, case marking, verb agreement, and so forth—which more or less (hardly ever completely) converge on one argument of the clause. Each of these behavioural properties develops independently through its own grammaticalization path. The idea that the subject relation, sometimes considered a universal core syntactic configuration, actually represents a grammaticalized topic construction has been a staple of functionalist syntax since its earliest days (Li and Thompson 1976; Givón 1979), but this is not a simple change. A topic NP will likely be a syntactic pivot, and thus have or easily acquire the syntactic behaviours associated with subjects in clause chaining, complement, and coordinating constructions, but verb agreement, for example, develops from a distinct topicalization construction with a repeated pronoun (Givón 1976).

These represent the primary type of pathway in the development of the kinds of construction which we take to define grammatical relations and alignment—reinterpretation of a marked pragmatic construction as the unmarked main clause structure. A common pathway of this type involves the reinterpretation of a nominalized clause, often with a finite copula, as a finite main clause construction. The pathway begins with a nominalized clause, often in construction with a copula, used as a pragmatically marked alternative to the simple finite clause. A well-studied example is the Japanese *no da/desu* construction (Kuno 1973 [1965]: 2223ff.):

(31) *kaze o* *hiita*
cold OBJ drew
'I've caught a cold.'

(32) *kaze o* *hiita no* *desu*
cold OBJ drew NMZ be
lit. 'It is that I've caught a cold.'

Some cross-linguistically common functions of the marked construction are prone to reinterpretation as main clause and thus finite status (Noonan 1997; 2008b; Bickel 1999), particularly grammatical functions such as tense/aspect, evidentiality/

mirativity, and stylistic functions such as formality. Among its other effects, such a reanalysis can produce constructions with new grammatical alignments. For example, the Kuki-Chin (Tibeto-Burman) languages of eastern Burma and northeast India, in a quite unusual pattern, have ergative case marking but nominative verb agreement, as in Mizo:

(33) *ui* *a = zuang*
dog 3SG = jump
'A dog is jumping.'

(34) *kei* *ka = zuang*
I 1SG = jump
'I am jumping.'

(35) *ui* *in* *mìi* *a = se*
dog ERG man 3SG = bite
'A dog bit a man.'

(36) *kei* *in* *còo* *ka = ei*
I ERG food 1SG = eat
'I am eating.'

Note the consistent ergative case marking: transitive A arguments in (34, 35) are marked with the instrumental postposition *in*. But the agreement proclitics attached to the verb always index the S argument, regardless of transitivity; 1st person in (33) and (35), 3rd person in (32) and (34). This represents a recent reorganization of the verbal system. The original finite clause construction (still retained as part of a mixed paradigm in one sub-branch) has been replaced by a nominalized verb stem; the agreement proclitics are identical with the possessive proclitics which attach to nouns, and they are attached to the finite verb because it was, historically, formally a nominal, originally apparently a marked stylistic form associated with formal or oratorical style (DeLancey to appear). The most topical argument of the nominalized verb was expressed as its possessor. When the rhetorical construction entered the core grammar as an unmarked finite clause, it added to the grammar a construction with subject–object alignment.

CHAPTER 30

GRAMMATICALIZATION AND WORD ORDER CHANGE

CHAOFEN SUN
ELIZABETH CLOSS TRAUGOTT

1. Introduction

Meillet included the 'syntacticization' of Latin 'free' word order in Romance among his examples of grammaticalization, the change that 'introduces categories that had no linguistic expression beforehand, transforms the system as a whole' (Meillet 1958 [1912]: 133). Since then there has been general agreement that word order change, construed as a major systemic process, whether a shift from discourse-prominent to syntax-prominent order, or from OV > VO, may result from and be a trigger for grammaticalization of morphosyntax. The development of obligatory subject in Romance and Germanic languages is regarded as a hallmark of grammaticalization construed as increased dependency (see Lehmann 1995a[1982]). In some cases like English there have also been typological shifts from largely synthetic to largely analytic morphology. However, word order change *per se* has not been regarded as a case of grammaticalization. For example, Heine and Reh (1984) consider it primarily as the outcome of grammaticalization, such as the erosion and loss of markers, and more recently Heine and König (2010: 117) argue that cross-linguistically linearization of recipient and rheme arguments in ditransitives 'is derivative of the grammaticalization of communicative strategies'. In the Minimalist framework Roberts and Roussou (2003) argue that grammaticalization is 'upward' in the functional hierarchy, whereas reanalysis of word order is 'downward' and has 'no interface effects' with lexical items, argument structure, etc. (p. 208). In this chapter we too take the position that word order change understood as linearization of word or constituent order alone is not grammaticalization. However, the two are so often intertwined that their interdependence deserves close attention.

'Word order change' is most often associated with shifts in constituent ordering in highly schematic patterns associated with S, O, and V, especially the ordering of head-modifier constituents such as determiners and nouns, auxiliaries, and main verbs (see Greenberg 1966; Hawkins 1983; Dryer 1992). While all logically possible orders of S, O, and V are attested in languages, the key issue is whether a language comes to be verb-final (OV) or not (VO). Most languages are not rigidly verb-final or verb-non-final, and local subparts of the grammatical systems may not match the constituent order patterns associated with these global word orders (e.g. English is VO, and the prepositional possessive as in *the book of John* is harmonic with VO, but the clitic genitive in *John's book* is not). Such mismatches may be due to a number of factors. Especially frequently mentioned are:

(a) Information structure and the tendency to start a sentence with old information (topic) (Givón 1983). This tendency may be disrupted by competing factors involved in the marking of topic and focus (Faarlund 1990; Lehmann 2008).
(b) Weight of constituents (e.g. Hawkins 1983; 1994; Siewierska 1993). There is a tendency to position 'light' elements leftward in the phrase, and heavy material in rightward position. This may be disrupted by changes in the weight of expressions when lexical items becomes grammaticalized and phonologically reduced.
(c) Contact (Fortescue 1993). Thomason and Kaufman (1988: 55) suggested that 'word order seems to be the easiest sort of syntactic feature to borrow or to acquire via language shift'. Matras and Sakel (2007), and Heine (2008) identify exploitation in contact situations of structures that match those in the speaker's repertoire; therefore borrowing usually results not in new order, but in selection and generalization of already available orders. By contrast, Harris and Campbell (1995: 137–44) discuss cases of word orders hypothesized to arise only through borrowing.

These three factors do not operate independently, and their role in any individual instance of word order change is often debated.

Order of elements within the verb phrase has been a topic of considerable interest ever since Bybee (1985) argued that cross-linguistically the linear ordering modal (epistemic) tense aspect in V-final languages (or its mirror image, aspect tense modal in V-non-final languages) is predictable from their 'relevance' to the verb (see also Bybee, Perkins, and Pagliuca 1994). There has also been extensive discussion of shift in the position of elements within the noun phrase, some of which we illustrate below. Highly local freezing of the order of constituents at different times may enable different kinds of grammaticalization. For example, in Latin finite verb and infinitive could occur in the orders *cantare habeo* 'to sing I have' and *habeo cantare* 'I have to sing'. By hypothesis, French *je chanterai* 'I will sing' developed when Latin was still predominantly OV, but *j'ai chanté* 'I have sung' after the shift to VO in Romance (Lehmann 1992; Roberts and Roussou 2003; see also Andersen 1987 on Polish).

Here we outline examples of three sites in which word order changes can be said to be closely tied to grammaticalization: clause structure, argument structure, and modifier structure within the NP. Our examples will be drawn mainly from English and Chinese. Since the Chinese data are less well known, these will be illustrated in more detail than those of English. Recurrent themes will be the roles of information structuring, understood primarily as topic-focus and as reference tracking, and of analogization (see Chapter 2 above).

2. Word order changes associated with clause structure

Information structure concerns packaging the content of propositions in terms of given and new—concepts which relate to identifiability and accessibility of referents. Prince (1992) distinguishes between speaker–new/old and hearer–new/old. Topic–focus, the domain of information structure most frequently cited in work on word order change, concerns speaker–new/old. By hypothesis, the functions of information structure do not change, but the link to syntax may (Lehmann 2008; Los 2009). Invoking Lambrecht's (1994: 185) 'Principle of the Separation of Reference and Role' ('Do not introduce a referent and talk about it in the same clause'), Lehmann argues that contrastive focus is often explicitly encoded as a cleft structure (2008: 212), but may become eroded through grammaticalization. In earlier French the cleft signalled contrastive focus; syntactically it was compositional, since the copula agreed with the focus NP. In contemporary French this construction is no longer contrastive (bleaching), and the copula is singular regardless of the number of the focus NP (loss of grammatical differentiation). Clefts are now the default for argument focus (1a) or for introducing new referents in presentational sentences (1b) (Lambrecht 1994):

(1) a. C'est les étudiants qui ont raison (Lehmann 2008: 213)
It is the students who have reason
'It is the students who are right.'

b. Y a le téléphone qui sonne (Lehmann 2008: 214)
There has the telephone which rings
'The telephone is ringing!'

Contemporary French questions with interrogative pronouns are also typically cleft as in (2a). They derive ultimately from biclausal focused structures as in (2b):

(2) a. C'est qui qui me parle? (Lehmann 2008: 222)
It is who who me speaks
'Who is speaking to me?'

b. Latin (Lehmann 2008: 221 [Cic. *Verr.*])
Quid est igitur quod fieri possit?
What is then which be.done can
'What can be done then?'

Such cleft structures may become monoclausal (see Harris and Campbell 1995: 152 and Heine and Kuteva 2005: 160–63 on the development of monoclausal focus constructions from clefts in Breton). Lehmann further hypothesizes that monoclausal topic–comment structures are grammaticalized and reduced forms of clefts, consistent with the reduction of complexity typical of grammaticalization. In languages where topic–comment occupy one clause, the 'various dichotomies of information-structure', which requires expression in 'at least two propositions' have been 'leveled out under grammaticalization' (2008: 227).

In recent papers on English, Los (2009) and van Kemenade (2009) put forward hypotheses about the interaction of word order change and information structure related to changes from Old to Middle English. Kemenade is concerned with restructuring of subordinate clauses, Los with the loss around 1400 of verb-second (V2) syntax. Here we outline Los's hypothesis. Old English word order was discourse-oriented, but, according to many analyses, basically OV (see Taylor and van der Wurff 2005). Main clauses typically attest to V2 ordering, which means that the finite verb follows a constituent, usually an adverb (3a), NP (3b), or adverbial phrase:

(3) a. Adverb – V – S (*c.*1000 Ælfric, *Lives of Saints*)
þa hloh Policarpus
then laughed Policarpus

b. S – V – IO (*c.*1000 Ælfric, *Homilies I*)
God bebead Abrahame þæt...
God commanded Abraham-DAT that...

The first constituent was 'multifunctional in that it could encode marked and unmarked topics, as well as marked focus; after its loss, these functions were divided between the subject (unmarked topic) and the presubject constituent (marked topic, marked focus)' (Los 2009: 99). In Early Middle English *c*.1200, VO became the dominant order (as (3b) suggests, V2 itself enabled the shift from OV to VO, because its effect is to make one NP in a transitive clause clause-final), and subject came to be obligatory. The loss of V2 after the rise of VO and syntacticization of subject, led to the development in the 15th century of new strategies for creating subject, including prepositional passives (e.g. *He was well thought of*), Exceptional Case Marking passives (e.g. *John was rumoured to be lying*), and Informative-presupposition IT-clefts (e.g. *It is with great pleasure that I present this award*). These changes all involve the regularization and extension of subject, and are therefore cases of grammaticalization that result from the word order changes.

3. Word order changes associated with argument structure

In the 1970s there was much interest in the role of serial verb constructions in the expression of argument structure (Li 1975). In a still widely cited paper Li and Thompson (1974b) showed that in Chinese the verb *bǎ* 'take' was grammaticalized into a preposition-like object marker of the following N. They hypothesized that this led to a shift from VO to OV word order in the ninth century. Both synchronic (Sun and Givón 1985) and diachronic studies (Sun 1997) found this hypothesized word order change in Chinese highly problematic, as the verb-final sequence makes up less than ten percent in both spoken and written texts in Modern Chinese. The BA construction appears to be specialized, and not generalizable to the system as a whole.

The formation of the Chinese BA construction that allegedly set off a V-final pattern results initially from grammaticalization involving argument structure in Middle Chinese (2nd–10th centuries CE) and further grammaticalization triggered by information structure in Early Modern Chinese (11th–18th centuries CE).

In Old Chinese a 'light verb' *yǐ* 'use, take' that occurred frequently in the initial V slot of a bi-clausal V (NP) V serial-verb construction can be ambiguously interpreted as a verb or a preposition 'with':

(4) 故以羊易之 (孟子3rd c. BCE)
gù yǐ yáng yì zhī
thus use sheep change it
'(Someone) therefore changed it with a sheep.'

Starting in Middle Chinese, *yǐ* and other synonymous light verbs such as *qǔ* 'get', *chí* 'hold', etc. that frequently occurred in this syntactic slot were substituted by *bǎ* 'take' and *jiāng* 'hold' (Cao and Long 2005) where they came to mark theme/patient (Sun 2008). In (5) the main predicate is a ditransitive *dùyǔ* 'give' with the *bǎ*-marked nominal *jīn-zhēn* 'gold needle' functioning as its theme:

(5) 莫把金針度與人 (朱子語類12th c. CE)
mò bǎ jīn-zhēn dùyǔ rén
NEG BA gold-needle give other
'Don't give the gold needle (secret) to the others.'

Sun hypothesizes that by the end of Middle Chinese *bǎ* became grammaticalized as a preposition marking theme/patient in a monoclausal structure with three arguments such as (5). However, the modern BA construction arose as the result of further grammaticalization of *bǎ* in other contexts. In Middle Chinese *bǎ* was also frequently used in a pattern that emerged in the period: a cause and effect relationship that is usually expressed in the order effect–cause. In this construction a focus-marker *lái* (< 'come') or *qù* (< 'go') marks the purpose/cause, e.g. in (6) *bǎ shēng-rén zhī yán* 'take the words of the sages' is the effect, and *lái qióngjiū* '(for the) purpose (of) study' is the cause/focus. In this pattern both effect and cause must be expressed by verbs, such as *bǎ* 'take' and *qióngjiū* 'study.'

(6) 把聖人之言來窮究 (朱子語類 12th c. CE)
bǎ shēng-rén zhī yán lái qióngjiū
take sacred-person GEN word come (purpose) study
'(Someone) take the words of the sages (for the) purpose (of) study.'

In Early Modern Chinese, further grammaticalization to prepositions disfavoured the use of *bǎ/jiāng* as effect Vs in this pattern, which declined from nearly 20 per cent in the 12th century (*Zhūzi yǔlèi*) to about 10 per cent (*Lǎoqǐdà* and *piáotōngshì yánjiě*) in the 14th and became almost completely extinct in 19th-century vernacular texts (*Érnǔyīngxióng zhuàn*) (Sun 2008). While *bǎ* fell into disuse in the effect–cause pattern in (6), its use increased in a resultative pattern where the predicate focus is expressed by two verbal morphemes implying cause–effect (in that order). In (7) *jié* 'cut' is the cause and *duàn* 'break' the effect. Here *bǎ* appears not to express effect but simply to mark a theme/patient:

(7) 相似把个利刃截斷 (朱子語類 12th c. CE)
xiāngsì bǎ ge lì rèn jié-duàn
appear BA CL sharp sword cut-break
'(It is) like break the sharp sword (into pieces).'

Co-occurrence of *bǎ* with the verb-final resultative increased dramatically from less than 40 per cent in the 12th century (*Zhūzi yǔlèi*) to nearly 80 per cent in present-day Standard Chinese (*Lǎoshě, Wang Shuò*) (Sun 2008).

In sum, the history of BA is a case of specialization. Of the several verbs with which the verb *bǎ* originally competed, it came to be restricted to constructions like (5) as a grammaticalized preposition. By analogy, further grammaticalization turned *bǎ* (and *jiāng*) into prepositions in other contexts (6), and therefore they could no longer function as verbs to express effect. As a result, the already available V-final V–V structure was preferred (7). The history of the BA construction underlines the importance of not expecting global, systemic word order changes, but rather localized changes based on individual constructions.

4. Changes in NP modifier structure

4.1. The development of numeral classifiers in Chinese

Information structure has also been suggested as relevant to changes within the domain of NP in Chinese (Campbell 2004). Specifically, the grammaticalization of the numeral classifier system (NU-CL) after the nominal head in Old and Middle Chinese interacts with focus resulting in a new NU-CL N word order in Early Modern Chinese:

(8) N NU-CL > NU-CL N

The examples in (9) illustrate the situation in early Old Chinese (three millennia ago). Numerals existed, but not a classifier system. The general word order is modifier N (9a). Takashima (1996) claims that if a numeral occurs prenominally, the focus is on the numeral (9b), but if it occurs postnominally, focus is on the N and numeral together (9c).

(9) a. 三白豕 (粹349)
sān bái shi
three white pig
'three white pigs'

b. 三百羌 (續2. 12. 3)
sān bǎi qiāng
three hundred Name
'three hundred Qiang (people)'

c. 白豕九 (粹79)
bái shǐ jiǔ
white pig nine
'nine white pigs'

Campbell (2004) observes that there is also an N NU N pattern at this time, exemplified by (10):

(10) 羌百羌 (粹190)
qiāng bǎi qiāng
Name hundred Name
'Qiang, one hundred of them'

This pattern makes up only 2 per cent of the oracle inscriptional texts (about 10th century BCE) in contrast to 85 per cent for NU N, and 13 per cent for N NU. Campbell argues that (10) is an exceptional case of compound focus carrying two operators resembling the two capitalized foci in the English sentence *Please bring some SANDWICHES, THREE of them.* In other words, in (10) *qiāng* is repeated to function as some kind of counting device. In Bronze inscription (*c.*5th century BCE) occurrences of this type dramatically increase to 20 per cent, suggesting that the grammaticalization of the numeral classifier system is under way as is the loss of the earlier focus structure in oracle texts. Some nominals that had clear semantic measure or shape content, as evidenced by their selectional restrictions with nouns of different kinds, grammaticalized into a semi-closed category of classifiers in an N NU-CL structure. In (11) *shù* 'bunch' and *péng* 'thing/person of the same kind, string' can be interpreted in their original measure/shape meanings, but *pǐ* 'one side of two parts of a scroll' has already been extended to function as a classifier for 'horse':

(11) 錫(賜)弓 、矢束、馬匹、貝五朋 (遺錄160) (5th c. BCE)
xī gōng shì shù mǎ pǐ bèi wǔ péng
award bow arrow CL horse CL shell five unit
'Award a bow, a bunch of arrows, a horse, and five strings of shells.'

Such a classifier system matures in Middle Chinese (2nd–10th centuries CE) (Liu 1965).

The numeral classifier system, which originated by grammaticalization of a numeral and a classifier after the head noun, started to interact with the general modifier N word order. In Old Chinese, a measure/shape N with abstract CL function can occur before the head provided there is no numeral, but the number 'one' is implied (12). For example in (12c) *pǐ* (CL) and *dān* (modifier) are in matching positions emphasizing singleness (Sun 2001). In (12b) *pǐ* and *shù*, which occur post-head in (11), occur in pre-head position.

(12) a. 匹馬只輪無反者 (左傳：僖公 *c.*5th c. BCE)
pǐ mǎ zhǐ lún wú fǎn zhě
CL horse CL wheel NEG return one
'Not a single horse, or a single wheel, returned.'

b. 用匹馬束絲 (两周83.96 *c.*5th c. BCE)
yòng pǐ mǎ shù sī
use CL horse CL silk
'Use a horse and a bundle of silk.'

c. 匹馬單槍突九重 (敦煌變文：張淮深 10th c. CE)
pī mǎ dān qiāng tū jiǔ chóng
CL horse single spear break nine layer
'To break through nine layers (of soldiers) all by oneself.'

Example (12a) illustrates the subjectification associated with the word order shift in its first stage: the pre-head classifiers, *pǐ* and *zhǐ* (< a particle meaning 'unclosed mouth'), express the speaker/writer's assessment that the failure was extreme.

By hypothesis, classifiers with implied numeral 'one' (12) were used in pre-nominal position on analogy with modifiers, and this enabled classifiers with unrestricted numerals to appear as modifiers, hence the development of numeral classifier order NU-CL N. Pre- and post-head numeral classifiers co-existed in late Old and Middle Chinese, and became more frequent in the latter period. The final stage of grammaticalization occurs after the 14th century CE, when practically no post-head NU CL can be found in vernacular texts any more (Sun 2001).

4.2. The shift of adjectives to post-determiner and determiner position in English

As we have seen, the Old Chinese and Contemporary Chinese NPs were rather different in structure. So were Old English and Contemporary English NPs. Although demonstratives could occur in the NP, there was no clearly definable category determiner in Old English. However, in Middle English from *c.*1200 on, the order of elements in the NP in English has been determiner–post-determiner–modifier–N. In some cases, an adjective functioning originally as a modifier has acquired post-determiner and even determiner uses.

Although it has long been observed that some adjectives which were originally descriptive modifiers became post-determiners and intensifiers with different, often more adverbial meaning and distribution, the first explicit account of such changes is Adamson (2000). Adamson shows how evaluative adjectives (Dixon 1982) like *lovely, pretty,* acquired scalar, degree modifying polysemies when used in post-determiner position, largely from the 17th century on. For example, in Old English *luflich* meant 'loving, amiable'. In Middle English it was also used to mean 'beautiful'. Both these meanings are descriptive. In the 17th century the affective, evaluative meaning 'excellent' begins to appear, and in that meaning *lovely* is used, like other affective adjectives in English, on the left of other modifiers. Compare *kind lovely woman* ('woman who is kind and beautiful') with *lovely kind woman* ('woman whom I like and who is kind'). Affective adjectives in some cases became intensifiers, cf. *a pretty/jolly ugly sofa, pure hard work.* Some of these polysemous expressions continue to retain the behavioural characteristics of an adjective (e.g., they can be preceded by articles and quantifiers). Others have become very marginal types of adjective (*mere,* which originally meant 'pure', *utter,* which meant 'outer'), and one has split entirely from its adjectival source: *very* (< *verrai* 'true', borrowed from French) (see Vandewinkel and Davidse 2008 on *pure*). A not unsimilar change in Chinese is *hǎo* 'good' as in *yī liǎng hǎo qìchē* 'a good car' > pre-NU-CL evaluative *hǎo* as in *hǎo yī liǎng qìchē* 'what a good car'.

Breban (2008) shows that adjectives of difference (*different, distinct, several*) underwent similar changes. Of these, *several,* which meant 'distinct' in the 18th century, as in *an open severall marke* 'an open distinct mark', initially became a post-determiner signaling individuated, distributed plurality, as in *He dismissed the legions to their several provinces,* and in the 20th century a quantifier (determiner), as in *several open marks, He stayed several days.* Breban argues that here we have grammaticalization of an attributive adjective to post-determiner marking distributivity, followed by further grammaticalization to fully quantificational meaning, accompanied by association of the expressions with different word order slots within the NP. Unlike the scaling set *(lovely, pretty, mere),* the adjectives of difference acquire information-structuring uses in their post-determiner functions, since they individuate, identify and make the referent of the N accessible. This is also true of the post-determiner use of *same.* As a post-determiner it signals anaphoric reference ('aforementioned'). This use is derived from the descriptive adjective 'identical' (Breban 2010).

In these cases, the more grammatical uses involve recruitment of adjectives to increasingly leftward positions in the NP. The word order itself does not change, but the position of the adjective does as a morphosyntactic correlate of grammaticalization. As in the case of the numeral classifiers, the shift involves analogization to an already extant position.

5. Some further issues

The types of change mentioned here are only a small subset of the kinds of word order change that interact with grammaticalization. An active area of research is on the role of left and right/initial and final periphery of the clause, and recruitment of expressions to them, e.g. in Japanese various contentful/lexical expressions have been recruited from clause-internal to clause-external position, where they serve connective, topic-changing, and attitudinal functions (Onodera and Suzuki 2007). Somewhat similar developments have occurred in French, although there is less intersubjective social marking than in Japanese (see e.g. Hansen 2008) (see Diewald, Chapter 36 below).

A key issue currently being debated is how the motivations for word order should be conceptualized. Does word order change, and most especially change in order of constituents, result primarily from constraints on performance and processing (e.g. Hawkins 2004), or from acquisition, Universal Grammar, and the asymmetry of phrases as conceptualized within X′ theory and its later developments (e.g. Kayne 1994)? While the answer might appear to depend on whether one regards change as change in use (Croft 2000) or in grammars (Kiparsky 1968), Whitman (2008) suggests that no one mode of explanation is or can be adequate. Both 'functionalist' and 'formal' approaches offer insights into the variable facts of word order change. He argues that cross-categorial generalizations about constituent order are most robust 'in just the case where grammaticalization is abundantly attested' (Whitman 2008: 241), and that 'cross-categorial markedness generalizations such as the Head Parameter are not statements about synchronic grammar, but rather products of language change' (p. 252).

As Meillet realized a century ago, research on the interface between grammaticalization and word order change is an exciting area of investigation. It can not only tell us about the complexities of change, but can help account for synchronic word order variation, especially the mismatches between individual constituent word orders and expected global patterns. Most importantly, systemic, 'global' word order changes tend to result from multiple local changes.

CHAPTER 31

GRAMMATICALIZATION AND SEMANTIC CHANGE

REGINE ECKARDT

1. Solving semantic equations

The meaning of natural language sentences obeys the principle of compositionality, i.e. the denotation of a sentence is determined by the meanings of its parts and the way in which they are combined. Since grammaticalization refers to language change in which words and constructions change their morphosyntactic status, we therefore expect that semantic composition will change as well, if only in the combination of items.

The principle of compositionality is also a driving force in grammaticalization. Turning points in language change are often defined by utterances (quotes) of a double-faced nature. Such quotes make sense in terms of the older language stage (= older literal sense), even if somewhat forced or incongruent. However, they also could convey a *new* message (i.e. not based on the older literal sense of words), not only for the modern reader but, plausibly, also for the contemporary audience. The new message can arise by pragmatic inferencing, generalization processes, but sometimes also simply situational 'guesswork'.

How were the contemporary hearers to make sense of these new messages? They, as we all do, trusted the principle of compositionality. Hence, they assumed that this new message came about by combining the meaning of the parts of the utterance in the regular way. They tried to figure out (a) which word or morpheme was most likely the carrier of the new pieces of meaning, and (b) what exactly this new piece of meaning must be. In brief, they had to solve a semantic equation with one unknown. Given that language changes occur without severely impeding communication, we can infer the following corollary version of the principle of compositionality:

Speakers (of one cultural/social community) will solve semantic equations in one unknown in a more or less uniform manner.

The results of solving the semantic equation can be denotations that are abstract in the sense that they could not be defined by ostension. This contrasts with typical denotations of (simple) lexical words. To define the meaning of *chair*, all you need is a chair to point at, but you cannot define the meaning of a past tense morpheme by pointing anywhere.

For this reason, meaning changes in grammaticalization should be investigated in a semantic framework that does justice to compositionality, at both the lexical and the grammatical level. Any framework that offers this feature will be suitable, but for various reasons I will base the discussion of micro-steps of semantic change in this chapter on truth-conditional semantics and its extensions into pragmatics. In the summary, I will relate them to macro-trends in grammaticalization that have been proposed in the literature, notably trends like bleaching, subjectification, enrichment, and pathways of change.

I will restrict attention to a small number of cases which will serve to illustrate the main types of semantic change. In the verbal domain, I will investigate the emergence of German passive *werden* + past participle, take a look at the Romance/Germanic perfect: *have* + past participle, and briefly review the classical example of English future *going to* + infinitive. Another classic in the field is the development of modals. The emergence of scalar degree modifiers shows how semantic reanalysis leads from concrete to abstract content. Loss of presuppositions is characteristic for the stages of negation particles along the Jespersen cycle. I will then argue that modal, emotive, and discourse particles also emerge by semantic reanalysis and hence show 'grammaticalization' in a semantic sense, even though they are more 'extragrammatical' in a morphosyntactic sense (see the parameters in Lehmann 1995a[1982]). Finally, I will take a look at paradigmatization from a pragmatic viewpoint.

2. Micro-steps of change

2.1. Argument structure

The emergence of the German passive *werdan* + $V_{\text{past.participle}}$ rests on a minimal semantic change in the choreography of tense and aspect indexicals *S* (speech time), *R* (reference time), and *E* (event time; Reichenbach 1947; Kamp and Reyle 1995; Klein 1994). I will use Behaghel's (1924: 199ff.) data record of the change. He reports that $werden_{\text{present}}$ + $V_{\text{past.participle}}$ regularly conveys futurate meaning in early OHG sources.

(1) *arslagan uuirdit Christ*
slaughtered become Christ = 'Christ will become (a) slaughtered (one)'
translates Lat. *occidetur* 'will be slaughtered'
Isidor 27,12 (8th c.); Behaghel (1924, II: 200) (*c.*636)[1]

Sentences in the Latin present passive are regularly *not* translated by the $werden_{\text{present}}$ + $V_{\text{past.participle}}$ construction but by more present-oriented constructions, notably the present tense active. So, for instance, Lat. *illud quaeritur* 'this is being searched' is translated as *dhaz suochant* '(they) search for this'.

In its older reading, *werdan* introduces its own referential argument. It refers to phases *E* of change between a state non-*p* and a state *p*. Tense/aspect locate *E* relative to the time of speech *S* and reference time *R*. Specifically, present tense asserts that $E = R = S$. A sentence like *Christ wirdit arslagan* hence denotes the proposition 'there is a phase of change *E* located at *S* which leads to the state $p =$ Christ is (a) slaughtered (man)'. It is open what kind of change *E* the speaker had in mind.

In the newer interpretation of such sentences, however, speakers specifically assumed that these pre-phases are phases where someone *<verb>-s <subject>* ('slaughters Christ'). The verb *werden* no longer introduces an event *e*. The complex [*werden* + $V_{\text{past.participle}}$] is interpreted as *the* finite verb of the sentence. The event argument of the sentence is described by $V_{\text{past.participle}}$. Specifically, present tense locates *E* at speech time *S*. Examples like the following mark the turning point. Being generic in character, they refer to a series of events *E* which might in part be in the future, in part at present, thus blurring the former future reference of *werden* + $V_{\text{past.participle}}$.

(2) *wirdit thaz ouh ana wan ofto in sambazdag gidan*
becomes this also without doubt often on Saturday done
'this is also, without doubt, often done on Saturdays'
Otfried III, 16,37; Behaghel (1924, II: 201) (863–71)

[1] Historical sources and dictionaries are referred to by the following abbreviations: Ælfric Gram. = Ælfric, *Grammar* (*c.*1000), ed. Zupitza, 1880; DW = J. Grimm and W. Grimm (eds), *Deutsches Wörterbuch* (Leipzig: S. Herzel, 1838); Fastnachtsp: Svarmus = *spvrca loqvens. ein kurtzweilige fasznacht-predig, vom doctor Schwarmen zu Hummelshagen, auff Grillenberg vnd Lappeneck* (16th c.), ed. T. G. v. Karajan (Vienna, 1851); H.v.Aue = Hartmann von Aue, *Erec* (*c.*1185), ed. A. Leitzmann (Tübingen: Niemeyer, 1963); Hel. = *Heliand* (*c.*850), ed. B. Taeger (Tübingen: Niemeyer, 1984); Isidor = *Der althochdeutsche Isidor* (*c.*636), ed. Hench, Strassburg, 1983; Keiserb = Geiler von Keiserberg, *Das Buch von den Sünden das Mundes* (Strassburg, 1518); Nib. C = Der Nibelungen Noth. Handschrift C (*c.*1230), Bibliotheca Augustana (http://www.hs-augsburg.de/~harsch/germanica/); Otfried = Otfrieds Evangelienharmonie (863–71), ed. P. Piper (Freiburg, 1882).

Final evidence for the shift is offered by the fact that 'true' future passives now get an extra future marking, e.g. by *sculan* (Behaghel 1924: 201).

(3) *than scal Judeono filu theses rîkeas suni berôbote uuerđen*
then shall Judes' son of-these kingdom his robbed become
'then the son of Judes will be robbed of his kingdom'
Hel. 2138, 2139 (*c.*850)

Our next case is the emergence of perfect. Perfect constructions in European languages mostly pattern after the Latin *habeo* + $V_{past.participle}$ construction (de Acosta 2006) which took its origin from small clause constructions of the form *Subj has* [Obj_{acc} $V_{past.participle}$]$_{SC}$. Such small clause constructions generally require some relational link between the matrix subject referent and the embedded small clause. (4) suggests a plausible link while (5) is harder to interpret. This difference is attested in all (living) languages that have the respective construction (# = semantically marked).

(4) *Joanna has her daughter living close to her.*
(5) *#Joanna has Mr Smith's daughter living close to him.*

Sæbø (2009) proposes that *have* can take small clause complements only if the meaning of the small clause offers an implicit parameter which is instantiated by the matrix subject. In an early stage of proto-perfect, this general pattern could be exploited by selecting the AGENT parameter of the participle verb for this implicit link. '*Joanna has* [*a mouse killed*]$_{SC}$' with the role of **Joanna** being that of the killer of the mouse. The resulting messages, however, could be derived more simply by morphosyntactic reanalysis and by regrouping *have* + $V_{past.participle}$ to one complex verb form, where the subject of the clause instantiates the highest argument of the verb. This type of morphosyntactic construction no longer requires the object DP as a hinge between matrix verb and small clause. The new composition therefore is also meaningful for the past participle form of intransitive verbs (*have smiled, have slept*...), which allows the pattern to spread. Sæbø (2009) devises a specific version of the intermediate step of what we might call 'fossilized parameter short-cutting' as part of his panchronic analysis of *have*.

The emergence of futurate *going* + *to* V_{inf} has been investigated more intensely than perhaps most other tense/aspect forms of English (e.g. Visser 1973; Hopper and Traugott 2003; Eckardt 2006). Authors agree that at a certain point, speakers/hearers saw reason to believe that a word string like:

(6) *A is going to see the king.*

no longer conveyed the (older) message: '*A* is presently moving (*e*) somewhere with the intention: *A* sees the king there.' Instead, they believed that the intended literal message was, more simply, '*A* will see the king soon.' Structural reanalysis led from a small clause construction to a simple clause with a complex verb form:

(6)a. i. *A is going [to see the king]*$_{\text{SmallClause}}$
ii. *A [is going to see] the king*

We face an avalanche of semantic changes: First, speakers lose the notion of a movement event *e*, namely the referential argument of the (former) verb *go*. This leaves the sentence with one event to report about, here: the *seeing* event. Tense and aspect information will refer to that event *E*. *E* is understood to happen in the future, but the message of the sentence is actually richer. Present tense still locates reference time at speech time *R*=*S*, but speakers understand that at *R*, subject *A* is already doing something which will lead to *E* almost certainly: '*A* is in a pre-phase *pre*(*E*) of *E*.' Taking up as much as possible of the older progressive message, the sentence is reanalysed to report that this pre-phase surrounds the reference time *R*. Thus *S*=*R* *R*>*pre*(*E*), and consequently, *S* precedes *E*. The *see* event *E* happens in the future. Taking this to be the literal message of (6), the speaker/hearer faces the task of identifying (possible) parts of this message as the literal meaning contribution of parts of the sentence (in the new chunking). The grammar of Modern English shows the equations that survived over time (Eckardt 2006).

(6)b. i. [[*going-to*]]: Takes a predicate *V* of events as its argument. States that reference time R is in a pre-phase of an event described by *V*.
ii. [[*be*]]: Carries the tense information. Present tense states that *R*=*S*, past and future tenses refer to *R*<*S* and *S*<*R* respectively.

Note that *going* is no longer interpreted as carrying progressive morphology, and *to* is no longer part of an embedded clause, hence phonological reduction '*gonna*' is possible.

2.2. Modals and modality

The previous cases illustrated reorganization of argument structure, loss of referential arguments (specifically of verbs, when they shift to an auxiliary status) and rearrangement of tense/aspect structure. These processes can also be diagnosed in the diachronic development of modals, but the case of modals is more intricate. Modals show an ever-increasing range of uses, ranging from the so-called root modals to more abstract, futurate, and epistemic readings. Clines like the two below are typical, as argued by Traugott (1989).

OE *sculon* ('owe') > *shall* (deontic) > *shall* (metaphysic)
OE *cunnan* ('have the physical ability to') > *can* (deontic) > *can* (epistemic)

Semantic analyses of modals treat them as quantifiers over possible options ('worlds': Lewis 1973). *Shall* generates a universal statement, whereas *can* makes an existential statement. *Must, will, ought to, need* pattern with *shall*, whereas *may, might* are analysed like *can*. The backbone of the analysis is as follows:

x shall VP: $\forall w$ (*w* is a relevant option $\rightarrow$ *x* does *VP* in *w*)
x can VP: $\exists w$ (*w* is a relevant option $\wedge$ *x* does *VP* in *w*)

Different modal flavours are attributed to different choices of what counts as a relevant option. Quantification over worlds where *x* behaves according to the law will create a deontic reading, worlds where *x* acts according to her desires will create a bouletic reading ('what *x* must do if she acts out her desires'), and so on. Choices are in part lexically restricted, in part driven by the conversational background (Kratzer 1981; for an introduction see Kaufmann, Condoravdi, and Harizanov 2004).

Hence, we find that the logical backbone of modals remained the same over time, but they were transferred from source domain to target domains. This view offers a beautiful link to Sweetser (1990), who argues that the development of modals should be viewed as *metaphoric extension.*

A closer look reveals that the most recent, epistemic readings generally rest on a speaker-subjective choice of relevant option. I will confine myself to one example.

(7) *Epistemic 'could': Granny could be home.*
Relevant options: *worlds w that are such that <u>I, the speaker, think</u> that they could be the real world where I actually live in*
Meaning:
$\exists w$ (*w* is such that I think it could be the real world
$\wedge$ in *w*: Granny is home)

Traugott and Dasher (2002) describe this final step as subjectification, a view which again coheres well with this analysis (see also Langacker, Chapter 7 above, and Nicolle, Chapter 32 below).

Yet the meaning of some modals underwent another, more serious reanalysis. The universal modal *must* emerged from OE/OHG *motan*, which meant 'may, is allowed to'.

(8) *'Licet' is alyfed is word: 'mihi licet' ic mot, 'nobis licet' we moton; 'tibi licuit' ðu mostest*
'Licet' is 'permitted': 'mihi licet' I 'mot', 'nobis licet' we 'moton'; 'tibi licuit' you 'mostest'; note: L 'licet' translates to ModE 'may, it is permitted'
Ælfric Gram. (St. John's Oxf.) 264. (*c.*1000)

Hence, an existential modal ('there are worlds . . . ') changed into a universal ('in all worlds . . . '). The opposite direction is also attested, in the case of German *dürfen.* OHG/MHG shows *darf* in the sense 'need (to have/to do)'.

(9) *mein herr der apt der* ***darf*** *dein*
my lord the Abbott he **needs** you.GEN
Fastnachtsp. 203, 14. (DB, 2; 1721,8) (16th c.)

In late MHG, the verb developed a second reading, 'may', in which it is exclusively used in ModHG. Hence, a universal modal changed into an existential. Traditional scholars favour the hypothesis that the change was initiated specifically in negated contexts (DW *dürfen*; OED *must*, v.[1]). The logical analysis of modals reveals the nature of the change. Negated universal statements are equivalent to existential negatives, and schematic paraphrases of the relevant type of example are as follows:

(10) Not all relevant worlds *w* are such that *p* holds true in *w*.
⇔There are relevant worlds *w* such that *not-p* holds true in *w*.
All relevant worlds *w* are such that *not-p* holds true in *w*.
⇔There isn't a relevant world *w* such that *p* holds true in *w*.

Here is the effect of this equivalence with *dürfen*. A negated statement like (11) can be the result of two different, semantically equivalent compositions.

(11) *in dem winter henkt man das fleisch hinausz daz es gefrier und mürb werd,*
('in winter, you hang the meat outdoors to freeze it and make it soft . . . ')
und man darf es nit salzen
and one 'darf' it not salt
'. . . and you needn't salt it'
Keiserb. 79b. (DB, 2; 1721,8) (1518)
i. Not [must (one salts the meat)]
ii. May [not (one salts the meat)]

Speakers who analysed (11) as in (ii) would assume the (newer) meaning 'may' for *dürfen*. Speakers who analysed (11) as in (i) would use the (older) meaning 'be obliged to'. What we see here is a particularly transparent case of semantic reanalysis, leading from universal to existential modal. This reanalysis can operate in both directions (see *must*), so it is not a unidirectional change.

2.3. From content to degree: reanalysis of particles

Semantic reanalysis can be more involved in that speakers reassess the divide between literal content of a sentence and inferred information. This is typical for numerous scalar particles. The adverb *sere* originally meant 'painfully'. This use is widely attested up to MHG.

(12) *so ist maniger geheilet, der nv vil sere wnd lit*
so is some/many healed who now very painfully wounded lies

many will be healed then (= at the time of a planned celebration) who lie painfully wounded now. (Nib. C, Av. 4, 258. (*c*.1230))

The combination with *vil* ('very') shows that *sere* is used in the sense 'painful' here. However, the verb 'wounded' (and others) denotes a gradable state, wounds can be more or less severe. Generally, severe wounds are also painful, and vice versa. Hence, speakers could perceive the overall information 'he was wounded severely, and it hurt' as coming about in two ways:

(13) i. lit.: 'he was wounded painfully' + inference: 'it was a severe wound'
ii. lit.: 'he was wounded to a high degree' + inference: 'it hurt'

Speakers who hypothesize semantic composition as in (ii) will assume that *sere* contributes the degree adverb 'high degree'. Later, and modern uses of *sehr* 'very' attest this reanalysis. In ModHG, *sehr* is a degree adverb and can instantiate the degree argument of a gradable predicate. Kennedy (1999) offers the details of an integrated analysis of gradable predicates and degree modifiers, including an analysis of *sehr* 'very' in its new sense. Semantic reanalysis starts from a lexically rich, functionally simple manner modifier ('it hurts') and leads to a modifier of an abstract functional nature.

Similar developments occur with high frequency. German *bloß* = 'naked, bare' underwent reanalysis to become a scalar particle like modern English *only*.

(14) *wan Êrec was Blôz als ein Wîp*
because Erec was bare(ly) like a woman
H.v.Aue, Erec, 103 (*c*.1185)
i. he went bare (= without any weapon) like a woman
ii. he went barely like an (unarmed) woman; this manner is inferior to other manners in which you could enter a fight (e.g. fully armed).

Earlier *bloß* denotes a simple quality. Analyses of modern *only/nur/bloß* particles can be found in Rooth (1992). These particles associate with focus and create rich scalar messages by combining presuppositions and assertions. A final example of a word that moved from 'physical effort' to 'low degree' is English *hardly* = 'with energy; vigorously' (OED, *hardly*, 1.).

(15) *hardly perceive something*
i. to perceive only with an effort
ii. not perceive very well at all; barely perceive

This example demonstrates that scalar particles can change their meaning from a high-degree adverb to a low-degree adverb. We see that the changes in question rest on the reanalysis of specific examples. They are not metaphorical shifts where degrees would be transferred from one domain to another.

2.4. Negation: as presuppositions come and go

Grammaticalization can also involve changes in presuppositions. Frequently, negation particles start as negative polarity items (NPIs: Ladusaw 1996). OE/OHG *wight*/*wiht* 'being, thing' in emphatic uses of the type 'not a THING, not a SOUL' (attested since Gothic *ni*... *waith*) can serve as illustration. Polarity sensitivity is caused by a new lexical requirement that the word be always used in so-called emphatic focus. The logic of emphatic focus reinforces the NPI licensing conditions; all utterances with $wight_{FOC}$ presuppose that the reported proposition is most surprising in a range of propositions that could have been uttered in its stead (for a detailed exposition see Krifka 1995; Eckardt 2006). At that stage, the negation-to-be can be used in downward-entailing contexts which include negated contexts but are more general. The data for this stage are sparse in Germanic languages, but the younger negation 'companions' of French (*point*, *personne*, *rien*) exhibit the full range of uses in downward-entailing contexts before they turn into negation particles (see the data record in Eckardt 2003).

Presupposition loss is a common process in language change. Over time, the requirement to interpret the (prospective) negation particles with an emphatic focus was lost. We find data where the former scalar undertone of sentences with *wight*/*wiht*, *ne-wight*/*n-iht* is relaxed. Speaker communities will usually retain a syntactic restriction on the use of the item, and restriction to the scope negation is one common choice. At that point, then, the particle gets syntactically tied to negation. If we return to our sample case, Germanic languages today have *nicht*/*not* or *it*/*et* (Alemannic) depending on whether negative concord was common in the crucial period (OE, OHG) or not (Alemannic).

The development of negative polarity items into negation has been in focus ever since Jespersen (1917). It may be worth noting that there are other ways in which polarity sensitive items can lose presuppositions and undergo reanalysis. Specifically, they become free choice pronouns ('any whatsoever' type) and universal quantifiers like *immer* 'always' = *je-mehr*. The latter has completely lost all presuppositions of the earlier polarity item *je*.

2.5. Guessing the speaker's mood: emotive particles

Words or constructions can require a rich conceptual background, based on what they contribute to the overall information of the sentence. When hearers are confronted with utterances where this background cannot easily be reconstructed, they reanalyse the word as conveying information in a shallower manner. One typical result of such a reanalysis are particles (discourse marking, speaker's attitude, speech act marking, etc.).

German *eigentlich* can be used as an adverb roughly synonymous to English *truly, in fact*. A detailed analysis reveals that *eigentlich* serves to create a contrast between some *true* state of affairs and an *apparent* state of affairs. Eckardt (2009) devises a uniform semantic value for *eigentlich* in adjectival and adverbial use, in questions and assertions. *eigentlich* in this sense expresses a rich conceptual background of the speaker (see also Schmitz and Schröder, 2004).

(16) *Eigentlich ist Peter klug.*
'eigentlich' is Peter clever
'In contrast to what matters may look like, Peter is really clever'

In addition, *eigentlich* is used as a discourse marker. In these uses, it cannot be stressed and fails to refer to a contrast between real/apparent. It conveys that 'the speaker, after some reflection, feels yet inclined to assert *p*', often with an undertone of good will. Hence, (17) in this sense is a friendly reply, whereas (18) with stressed *eigentlich* introduces a reproach.

(17) *Eigentlich hast Du recht.* 'After some reflection, I think that you're right'
(18) *EIGENTLICH hast Du recht.* 'In one sense you are right (but in another . . .)'

Unstressed, emotive *eigentlich* apparently gained its meaning in utterances with older *eigentlich* where contrasts were difficult to see, but the speaker's overall (compromising) attitude was understood by the speaker.

German speakers seem particularly prone to such reanalyses, but *let's* in English is a similar case (Hopper and Traugott 2003), and Brinton (1996) surveys particles in OE. Emotive and discourse particles emerge by semantic/pragmatic processes that are similar to those of our earlier cases, namely when hearers guess the meaning contribution of one word in an overall understood message. The result of this guesswork changes the grammatical status of the word (adverb > particle), along with its change in meaning.

2.6. Pragmatic competition and paradigmatization

Frequently, speakers can choose between two expressions that convey the same idea. Optimality theory in pragmatics has led to specific hypotheses about the competition processes that lead to an optimal lexical choice (Blutner 2000; Benz 2003). Levinson (2000) applies essentially the same ideas to grammaticalization. Unrolling the basics of Gricean pragmatics, he offers a pragmatic analysis of the emergence of the English *PRO-self/PRO* paradigm.

Levinson argues on psycholinguistic grounds that reflexive actions are perceived as more marked than actions of an agent on a third object. Hence, sentences that report the former ('*x did something to x*') carry a more marked message than sentences that report the latter ('*x did something to y*').

On basis of his neo-Gricean reformulation of the maxims of manner and quantity, Levinson predicts that, generally, marked expressions will be interpreted as reporting marked messages whereas unmarked expressions are interpreted as reporting on the normal case.[2]

The older intensifier *self* was increasingly used without lost rich presuppositions. Pro-forms like *him-self* could no longer sensibly be interpreted as intensifying constructions, and instead were perceived as a marked variant of the simpler pronoun *him*. (For a semantic/pragmatic analysis of intensifying *self*, *selber* see Eckardt, 2001; Keenan 2002 for comprehensive data.) At that stage, the pair *PRO*/*PRO-self* entered into pragmatic competition. In the long run, the more complex element was tied to the marked message (*coreference with the clausal subject*) whereas the simpler element regularly expressed the non-marked message (*reference to a different object*). Thus, complementary distribution was achieved as the result of pragmatic competition.

The link between bidirectional optimality theory and paradigmatization has hardly been explored so far. The paradigmatization of number terms and deictic pronouns into article systems could offer a fruitful field of research in this direction. Likewise, pragmatic competition could help to understand the change of the *be* + *V-ing* construction from an optional way to describe ongoing events to an obligatory progressive form.

3. Micro- and macro-changes

The above case studies in grammaticalization exemplify a wide variety of changes at the level both of semantics and of pragmatics. Grammaticalization can involve changes in the argument structure of predicates, including the loss of referential arguments (= event arguments of verbs, mostly), shifts from indirect instantiation to direct instantiation of arguments, and the restructuring of instantiation of tense/aspect indexicals.

The changes in content follow from semantic reanalysis, where the same overall proposition ('sentence message') is computed on basis of a new underlying structure. In more complex instances, the reanalysis is more far-reaching and affects the division between implied and asserted information (*going* future, scalar particles). The two sides—gain and loss—have been described in the literature under the term 'pragmatic enrichment' (Traugott 1988), more elaborately as 'generalized invited inferences' (Traugott and Dasher 2002), and 'bleaching' (since Meillet 1912).

[2] This is where Levinson (2000) and Blutner (2000) converge.

A particular kind of loss is the loss of presuppositions, i.e. the failure of speakers to observe the proper informational background that is specified in the lexical entry of a word. Presuppositions can indeed be violated, as long as the hearer is able to 'accommodate' them, i.e. take the missing information for granted. However, when the missing piece is too substantial, hearers will resort to new interpretations of utterances.

'Metaphoric transfer' can help to use words in new semantic domains without any intermediate uses for reanalysis. Apart from the single example discussed here, such transfers play a predominant role where spatial concepts shape our language for other relational concepts (explored in Heine 1997c; Levinson and Wilkins 2006).

'Subjectification' (Traugott 1989; 1995a) can be seen as a cover term for all those instances where the hearer reinterprets an expression as stating something about the speaker's attitude or perspective on the proposition expressed.

Regular pathways of change, finally, arise whenever words of similar meaning are also used in similar contexts which typically give rise to the same implicatures, opening the way for the same kinds of semantic reanalysis. In this chapter, I used scalar particles to illustrate such recurrent patterns. Surveys like Heine and Kuteva (2002) offer a survey over regular pathways of change, many of which recur in unrelated languages. This reveals that semantic reanalysis is another aspect of the universal human language faculty.

CHAPTER 32

PRAGMATIC ASPECTS OF GRAMMATICALIZATION

STEVE NICOLLE

1. Introduction

Much of the literature assumes that grammaticalization is motivated by extra-linguistic factors, in particular speaker-hearer interaction and 'the relationship between language and the contexts in which it is used' (Hopper and Traugott 2003: 75); this is the domain of pragmatics. Although there is disagreement over where exactly the boundary between pragmatics and semantics/grammar should be drawn, a common position equates pragmatics with those aspects of utterance (or text) construction and interpretation which depend on inference, as opposed to semantics and grammar which depend on convention. The expression 'pragmatic inference', therefore, refers to an inference which generates meaning from the use of a linguistic form in a particular context. Pragmatic meaning, i.e. meaning derived by inference, may be either truth-conditional or non-truth-conditional (Recanati 1989; Carston 2004), and so 'pragmatic' should not be equated with non-truth-conditional; correspondingly, grammaticalization need not involve a change from non-truth-conditional to truth-conditional meaning.

The aim of this chapter is to briefly describe and evaluate some recent accounts of pragmatic aspects of grammaticalization.[1] In evaluating these accounts, the following questions will be borne in mind:

1. Which inferences contribute to grammaticalization and what distinguishes them from the majority of inferences which have no lasting effect on language?
2. How does inferential (extralinguistic) meaning become encoded (linguistic) meaning?
3. What is the role of context in grammaticalization?
4. What are the limits of the contribution of pragmatic inference to grammaticalization?

2. Invited inferences and the role of context

Rather than trace the history of pragmatic approaches to grammaticalization,[2] I shall begin with what are probably the best known accounts of the inferences and contexts involved in grammaticalization. According to Traugott's Invited Inference Theory of Semantic Change (Traugott 1999b; 2002a), grammaticalization begins when a construction, used in a specific context, gives rise to an Invited Inference (IIN). An IIN is a 'particularized conversational implicature', i.e. a communicated proposition whose meaning is context-dependent rather than derived directly from the encoded information in the utterance/text. An important characteristic of IINs is that they 'are not stably associated with any linguistic form' (Traugott 2004: 547). The IINs that contribute to grammaticalization arise when the speaker/writer formulates her utterance/text in such a way that the addressee/reader feels invited to draw a particular inference, thereby ensuring that what is implied is understood as being part of what is communicated.

[1] Hopper and Traugott (2003: xv) define grammaticalization as 'the change whereby lexical items and constructions come in certain linguistic contexts to serve grammatical functions and, once grammaticalized, continue to develop new grammatical functions'. The first part of the definition, the change from lexical to grammatical status, is termed 'primary grammaticalization', whilst the second part, the development of further grammatical functions, is termed 'secondary grammaticalization' (Traugott 2002a: 26–7; Traugott and Dasher 2002: 81). Most studies of the role of pragmatics in grammaticalization have been concerned with primary grammaticalization, and this will be the focus of the current chapter. Henceforth, the term 'grammaticalization' will refer to primary grammaticalization.

[2] Historical overviews can be found in Heine, Claudi, and Hünnemeyer (1991: 238–41), Traugott (2004), Eckardt (2006: 22–58) and Fischer (2007: 58–61, 115–24).

If a construction gives rise to the same IIN often enough in a specific kind of context, it may become a Generalized Invited Inference (GIIN). A GIIN is an implicature which is normally associated with a certain linguistic form but which can still be cancelled by the addition of incompatible premises, without the utterance or text sounding self-contradictory. GIINs can thus be viewed as stereotype inferences (Traugott 2004: 552). As GIINs become 'widely understood, and often exploited' (Traugott 2002a: 33), they may become conventionalized, and the inference formerly associated with the construction will become part of its encoded meaning, or semantics. At this point the construction may be ambiguous between its original meaning and the newly grammaticalized meaning, or the original meaning may eventually be lost; in either case, when the new grammatical meaning is recovered, it is no longer cancellable.

Probably the best-known accounts of the role of context in grammaticalization are found in Heine (2002) and Diewald (2002). Heine (2002: 86) posits four contexts leading to the development of a new grammatical meaning: (i) unconstrained context, (ii) bridging context, which gives rise to an inference which prefigures a new meaning, (iii) switch context, which is incompatible with the source meaning, and (iv) conventionalization, at which point the new meaning no longer needs to be supported by the context that gave rise to it. Diewald (2002) has three contexts which differ slightly from Heine's: (i) untypical contexts resulting from expansion of the distribution of the item, (ii) critical context, which may involve changes in morphosyntactic distribution and 'invites several alternative interpretations, among them the new grammatical meaning' (2002: 103), and (iii) isolating context, which favours the grammatical meaning over the source meaning (or vice versa); the grammaticalizing item is now polysemous. Diewald (pp. 115–16) notes that once grammaticalization has occurred, 'the relevant contextual factors are no longer found in the syntagmatic context of the sentences containing the element under grammaticalization, but in the paradigmatic context constituted by the grammatical oppositions of the target category'; this is the situation in Heine's (iv).

In order to have some basis for evaluating the Invited Inference Theory of Semantic Change and Heine's and Diewald's models of relevant types of context, let us look at the development of the *like to* V construction as described in Kytö and Romaine (2005). Example (1), from contemporary Alabama English, is an 'avertive' construction (Kuteva 2001: 75–112), meaning roughly 'She was on the verge of having a heart attack, but did not have a heart attack' (Kytö and Romaine 2005: 1):

(1) She liketa had a heart attack.

The earliest instances of *like to* V as an avertive occur in the mid-15th century, but by the end of the 19th century the construction had become obsolete in Standard

English.[3] The original encoded meaning, illustrated in (2) below, was similar to Modern Standard English *be likely to* V; the voyage was likely and imminent, and nothing in the context suggests that it was abandoned:

(2) having a letter from my cozin Nicholas that our viage was lyke to hold, I prepared my self to be redye. (1582, Helsinki E2, Richard Madox, diary, p. 84) (Kytö and Romaine 2005: 14)

Avertive interpretations of *like to* V arose in very specific, highly constrained contexts, in which it is clear that although the event described by V was likely, it did not in fact occur. Such a context is provided in (3), where the past perfect form of the conditional clause 'yf hit hadde had his course' indicates that the main clause introduced by *lyke to* is counterfactual:

(3) by on of the mynsteris of the said Cathedrall Churche was set afire, and began to brenne, and yf hit hadde had his course lyke to have sette a fyre and brende the chief and grete parte of the citee (1447, Helsinki ME4, Letters and Papers of John Shillingford, p. 87)
'One of the minsters of the said Cathedral church was set afire and began to burn, and if it had had its course, would have come close to setting a fire and burning the chief and great part of the city.' (Kytö and Romaine 2005: 14)

Kytö and Romaine (pp. 24–5) found that between 1350 and 1550, explicit expressions of counterfactuality (e.g. conditional clauses and *but*) always occurred alongside avertive uses of *like to* V. From 1550 onwards, they found some examples in which non-linguistic context alone expressed counterfactuality, until from 1750 to 1850 counterfactual (i.e. avertive) interpretations of *like to* V were indicated solely by the context (without conditional clauses, *but*, or *almost*) as in (4):

(4) Boy, shut ye door, for I rem'ber this time 4 yeares we had like to have been killed by thunder & lightning. (1666, Corpus of Early American English, Danforth, diary p. 165) (Kytö and Romaine 2005: 5)

According to Kytö and Romaine (2005), contexts such as (3) provided the onset contexts for grammaticalization of the avertive meaning of *like to* V. Traugott (2004: 560) notes that new meanings 'are reinforced by juxtaposition with connectives that sharply constrain the implicatures. [. . . IINs] are initially recruited redundantly to extant linguistic contexts for discourse purposes.' In fact, contexts like (3) are so highly constrained that the invited inference cannot be cancelled by additional premises, only by removing the accompanying expressions of counterfactuality. The situation here seems to be not so much that of an IIN associated with *like to* V becoming a GIIN, as the counterfactual meaning associated with the

[3] The reason for this is not explained by Kytö and Romaine; possibly alternative expressions such as *almost* and *was/were going to* V took over the avertive function.

entire context (because of a conditional clause, or *but* in other examples) becoming associated with *like to* V. The original meaning of *like to* V (V is imminent and likely to occur) has not changed, but the additional avertive meaning is *added* to this original meaning.

Both Heine's 'bridging context' and Diewald's 'critical context' are 'characterised by multiple structural and semantic ambiguities' (Diewald 2002: 103), with the result that the grammaticalizing item becomes polysemous in the following stage. However, there is no evidence of ambiguous contexts in the grammaticalization of *like to* V, nor did the construction become polysemous.[4] In addition, both Heine (2002) and Diewald (2002) assume that at some point the source meaning must be incompatible with a 'switch' or 'isolating' context, and yet the context in (3) is not incompatible with the source meaning of *like to* V; the fact that a fire was not set is not incompatible with the likelihood of such an event. This may explain why such contexts occurred for 200 years without avertive meaning becoming encoded by the construction.

Thus in this case study, the grammatical meaning did not arise from a particularized conversational implicature but was explicit in the contexts in which *like to* V occurred. These contexts were neither ambiguous nor incompatible with the original meaning of *like to* V, and the avertive meaning did not replace the original meaning but was added to it as the construction underwent grammaticalization. This need not entail that Traugott's Invited Inference Theory of Semantic Change and Heine's and Diewald's models of relevant types of context are always wrong, but it does suggest that they do not account for every case of grammaticalization.

3. Relevance theory

I will now discuss an alternative approach based on relevance theory (Sperber and Wilson 1995[1986], Carston 2002), since this has become arguably the most influential pragmatic theory in recent years. According to relevance theory, all communication is (to a certain degree) inferential and context-dependent, and contexts are viewed as cognitive and created rather than objective and given. Communication is governed by the 'principle of relevance' according to which successful communication yields adequate cognitive effects (explicatures and implicatures) with minimal expenditure of inferential processing effort, a cost/benefit balance termed 'optimal relevance'. Relevance theoretic accounts of grammaticalization assume that

[4] Traugott (Ch. 2 above) also questions whether an ambiguous stage in grammaticalization is always necessary.

grammaticalization is a by-product of the principle of relevance, and therefore focus on the inferential process *per se*, including how the most relevant contexts are determined, rather than on distinguishing particular kinds of context.

As we have seen, it is not always the case that an Invited Inference is a particularized conversational implicature. Adopting the relevance theory perspective, Ariel (2008: 165–6) observes that invited inferences can be of various types: implicatures, metaphorical and metonymical inferences, broadening, narrowing, and so forth, any of which can potentially lead to grammaticalization. Rather than try to define specific types of inference or specific contexts which trigger grammaticalization, Ariel takes as her starting point the communicative intention of the speaker. Inferences which may give rise to grammaticalization she terms Privileged Interactional Interpretations (PIIs), defined as:

> the meaning which the speaker is seen as minimally and necessarily committed to, i.e. the one by which she is judged as telling the truth or being sincere. It is also the meaning which contains the message that the addressee should take to be the relevant contribution made by the speaker. (Ariel 2008: 299)

Relevance theory questions the need for a separate category of generalized conversational implicature, and instead distinguishes conversational implicatures from inferences which contribute to explicatures, i.e. propositions derived from the linguistic meaning of an utterance through a process of pragmatic enrichment. A PII may be either an implicature or an explicature, as either can serve as the basis for cognitive effects (Ariel 2008: 302, following Nicolle and Clark 1999). However, Ariel (2008: 305–6) claims that PIIs are more often explicatures than implicatures, and that therefore inferences leading to explicatures are more likely sources of grammaticalization than are implicatures.[5] Relevance theory also allows that an utterance may give rise to more than one explicature and/or implicature, and therefore there need not be only one PII.

Ariel's approach can, I propose, be fruitfully integrated with Nicolle (1998a), the earliest relevance theoretic account of grammaticalization. This account exploits the relevance-theoretic distinction between two basic kinds of linguistically encoded information: conceptual information, which contributes to the content of conceptual representations, and procedural information, which constrains the inferential processes which an addressee must perform in order to determine the speaker's intended meaning (Blakemore 1987). Lexical items, which form part of the source constructions in grammaticalization, are associated with concepts having logical and encyclopedic properties, whereas discourse markers, pronouns, and tense/aspect/modality markers, all of which are potential endpoints in

[5] Similarly, according to another relevance theoretic account (Berbeira Gardón 2008), grammaticalization results from the inferential process of ad hoc concept construction, which also entails that new inferred meanings are explicatures rather than implicatures.

grammaticalization, are not associated with concepts but rather constrain different inferential processes: discourse markers constrain the recovery of implicatures and higher-level explicatures, pronouns constrain reference assignment, tense markers constrain the determination of temporal reference, and so forth. Nicolle (1998a: 16) characterizes grammaticalization as follows:

> the semantic change driving grammaticalization (taken as a composite functional and formal development) is the addition of procedural information to the semantics of an expression, alongside the conceptual information already encoded. In other words a grammaticalizing expression comes to constrain the interpretation of the associated utterance in some way, whilst continuing to encode information with the potential to give rise to a conceptual representation.

Let us see how this accounts for the grammaticalization of *like to* V, discussed above. In the original uses of *like to* V, before the construction had acquired an avertive semantics, inference (highly constrained by the accompanying linguistic context) was required in order to determine whether the event associated with V did or did not in fact occur. This would have formed part of the PII, since whether or not V occurred clearly serves as the basis for the cognitive effects of the utterance. According to Nicolle (1998a: 23), the conventionalization of such inferences results in the addition of procedural information to the semantics of a construction. That is, the inferential process required to determine whether or not V did in fact occur became constrained by *like to* V, rather than by any accompanying linguistic context. Now, procedural information reduces processing effort by constraining inferential processes that an addressee would have to perform in any case; thus, the process of grammaticalization can be viewed as being motivated by the principle of relevance, according to which an optimally relevant interpretation is one which achieves adequate cognitive effects for minimal processing effort.

The claim that grammaticalization begins with the addition of procedural information to the meaning of a construction (subsequently adopted by De Mulder 2008 and Barbet 2010) has three specific consequences. First, since a construction either does or does not encode procedural information, and since conceptual and procedural information are discrete categories, the onset of grammaticalization is viewed as semantically immediate rather than gradual, as argued by Givón (1991b) with respect to the development of serial verb constructions. What is gradual, however, is actualization: the spread of a newly grammaticalized form through the grammatical system of the language and through the community of speakers of the language.

Second, the addition of procedural information to the meaning of a construction need not entail that the original conceptual information is lost. Nicolle (1998a: 23; 1998b: 233–4) notes that although the conceptual information encoded by a newly grammaticalized construction may no longer constitute the most important information in an utterance, it may nonetheless remain accessible; this is known as semantic retention[6] (Bybee and Pagliuca 1987; Bybee, Perkins, and Pagliuca 1994: 15–18) and corresponds to Hopper and Traugott's (2003: 94–5) claim that there is no loss of meaning in early stages of grammaticalization. Newly encoded procedural information is automatically recovered, since it provides an effort-reducing constraint on the inferential processing which the addressee would perform in any case. However, a grammaticalized construction's original conceptual information is only recovered if the addressee fails to derive adequate cognitive effects from the procedural information alone, since the retrieval and inferential enrichment of conceptual information increases processing effort and therefore reduces relevance unless offset by additional cognitive effects.

The third consequence of this approach is that whatever meaning is eventually lost from a grammaticalized expression should be conceptual rather than procedural, since procedural information by definition reduces processing effort and therefore always contributes to optimal relevance. A grammaticalized expression might undergo secondary grammaticalization (the development of further grammatical functions by an already grammaticalized construction), resulting in different procedural information being encoded, but it should not revert to encoding only conceptual information which would be a case of degrammaticalization (see Norde, Chapter 38 below). The theory thus predicts that grammaticalization should be unidirectional.

The conceptual information which is retained need not be the literal original meaning of a construction. For example, in the *be going to* construction, the retained conceptual information is intention and inevitability rather than physical movement. Eckardt (2006: 100), investigating the grammaticalization of *be going to* (between 1550 and 1650), notes that all the contexts which invited a future interpretation also conveyed the protagonists' intentions.[7] At this early stage, the meaning 'the subject intends to V' would have been a Privileged Interactional Interpretation (PII). Since this PII is a meaning derived from a combination of encoded and inferred information, it is an explicature. Through inference, intention gave rise to the notion of inevitability, which subsumes future time reference.[8]

[6] Hopper (1991: 28–30) uses the term 'persistence' but unlike Nicolle (1998a) equates persistence with polysemy.

[7] This entails that the future use of *be going to* developed with agentive subjects and subsequently spread to non-agentive subjects. In support this position, only 7 out of 218 occurrences of future uses of *be going to* V recorded between 1630 and 1780 (from the Diachronic Part of the Helsinki Corpus of English Texts and the Corpus of Late Modern English Texts) had non-human or non-agentive subjects.

[8] Bybee (2006) notes that the verb *go* was one of a number of verbs which could indicate intention when used in the construction type *be V-ing to*, and she invokes frequency to explain why the change of meaning from intention to future time reference arose with *be going to* but not with other verbs. Frequency alone does not cause grammaticalization (Lindquist and Mair 2004a: xiii), but a certain minimal frequency does seem to be required; the other verbs in the *be V-ing to* construction type simply did not occur frequently enough to grammaticalize.

Eckardt (2006: 119) treats inevitability (termed 'imminence') as a conventional implicature, whereas in relevance theory, it is an explicature just as intention is, since neither is cancellable, indicating that they are at least partly encoded (Nicolle 1998b).[9]

The relevance theory approach thus provides a principled account of why inferential meaning should become encoded, why elements of pre-grammaticalized meaning may remain, and why grammaticalization is unidirectional. However, as we will see below, although the addition of procedural information to the semantics of an expression is a sufficient criterion for a change to count as a case of grammaticalization, it is not a necessary criterion.

4. Subjectification

Relevance-theoretic accounts of grammaticalization focus on the inferential processes of utterance interpretation, with a consequent emphasis on the role of the addressee rather than the speaker. However, both have a role to play: addressees contribute to the routinization and conventionalization of inferential processes through their tendency to minimize processing effort, whilst speakers may use language to express more than is strictly encoded, including their own attitudes towards the situation being described. Traugott (1989; 1995a) observed that as meanings change during grammaticalization, they tend to increasingly express the speaker's subjective perspective on a situation. This tendency is called 'subjectification' (or 'subjectivization'), defined as 'the development of a grammatically identifiable expression of the Speaker's belief or Speaker's attitude towards what is said' (Traugott 1995a: 32).

Subjectification is illustrated by the way in which, between Middle and Early Modern English, '*supposing* gradually comes to be used almost exclusively to express the Speaker's attitude towards the proposition, i.e. its evaluation as hypothetical' (Visconti 2004: 179). Subjectification in this case involves a change from a high degree of commitment towards the truth of the proposition on the part of the subject of the matrix clause, as in (5), to a low degree of commitment towards the truth of the proposition on the part of the speaker/writer, as in (6), with a corresponding grammatical shift from verb to conjunction:

[9] A similar point is made by Nagy (2010) in relation to the grammaticalization of the Catalan periphrastic perfective past from GO + infinitive. She notes that the notion of intention inherent in the uses of the verb GO involved in grammaticalization cannot and never could be cancelled, hence intention is not a conventionalized implicature but originally formed part of the meaning of GO.

(5) The disciples, *supposing* that he had ben a fantasme, criden for drede. (*c.* 1430, *Love Mirror, Brsn e.9 144* Middle English Dictionary.)
'The disciples, believing he was a ghost, cried out in dread.'

(6) Or *supposing* that there is but one bishop; when he is sent into perpetual banishment, how must his Office be supply'd? (1692, Humphrey Hody, Lampeter Corpus) (Visconti 2004: 172)

Traugott's definition of subjectification is not the only one, however; the best known alternative is that of Langacker (1990; 1998; 2006).[10] For Langacker, 'subjectification' refers to a change in the way a situation is viewed or 'construed' rather than to a change in the semantic content of an expression. For example, according to Langacker (2006), the English modals have always expressed a force or potency. As main verbs in Old English, with meanings such as 'want' or 'be able', this force or potency originated in the subject of the clause; that is, the subject had the desire or ability to perform the action described by the infinitival complement of the verb. In Langacker's terminology, the verb 'profiled' the relation between the subject (or 'trajector') and the complement (or 'landmark'). In the epistemic and deontic uses of modern English modals, the force or potency no longer originates with the grammatical subject (hence the wider range of possible subjects) but with the speaker, for example in the form of her epistemic judgement of the event being described. Thus for Langacker, subjectification refers to a change in the way in which the modal force has been construed; the modal force is no longer 'the onstage focus of attention,' i.e. 'objectively construed', but is 'offstage and unprofiled,' i.e. 'subjectively construed' (Langacker 2006: 20). As Langacker (pp. 17–21) notes, his conception of subjectification is compatible with Traugott's but should not be confused with it. Whilst Langacker's approach focuses on the internal conceptual structure of expressions, Traugott's approach focuses on the uses to which expressions are put.

The development of epistemic modality has often been described in pragmatic terms as involving inference (see Barbet 2010: 32), suggesting that subjectification results from inference. However, Nicolle (2007; 2009) argues that, in certain constructions, subjectification (as defined by Langacker) can trigger the structural changes characteristic of grammaticalization independently of the conventionalization of inferential meaning. This is exemplified by the *go/come* V construction type:

(7) They give you a, a credit note and you, you **go put** them back.

(8) . . . then they **come serve** you with whatever you want.[11]

[10] Another use of the term is found in Verhagen (2005).

[11] Examples from BYU-BNC: The British National Corpus (available online at http://corpus.byu.edu/bnc).

In finite clauses, this construction type has undergone syntactic reanalysis, as *go/come* occupies the syntactic position otherwise occupied by tense or agreement features (Nicolle 2007: 55–7). Since there is nowhere else for tense or agreement features to occur, there can be no overt morphological inflection in the *go/come* V construction (compare (7) with **he goes puts*... and (8) with **they came served*...). The verbs *go* and *come* in the above examples have not undergone semantic change, and there is no obvious conventionalized inference expressed by these constructions. Neither is there a more general construction type which could serve as an analogical model for the grammaticalization of *go/come* V. Nicolle (2009: 203–4) notes that deictic expressions, like *go* and *come*, are inherently subjective in that they incorporate the perspective of the speaker. Used as main verbs, *go* and *come* profile the relation between a subject and a complement, but in the *go/come* V construction type there is no complement and therefore no objective relation to be profiled. Instead, *go/come* and the following verb represent a single event into which the subjective component of meaning is incorporated. Grammaticalization of *go/come* V therefore appears to be motivated by subjectification alone, and not by pragmatic inference.

5. Conclusion

This chapter began by listing four questions that accounts of pragmatic aspects of grammaticalization must address:

1. Which inferences contribute to grammaticalization, and what distinguishes them from the majority of inferences which have no lasting effect on language?
2. How does inferential (extralinguistic) meaning become encoded (linguistic) meaning?
3. What is the role of context in grammaticalization?
4. What are the limits of the contribution of pragmatic inference to grammaticalization?

The inferences, or interpretations, which contribute to grammaticalization are those which are intended by the speaker (Invited Inferences or Privileged Interactional Interpretations) and which are routinely associated with particular expressions. According to Traugott's Invited Inference Theory of Semantic Change, grammaticalization occurs when such inferences becomes conventionalized. In the RT account proposed above, grammaticalization occurs when a particular expression constrains the PII, rather than merely being associated with it. The expression now encodes procedural information, and this is the point at which inferential meaning becomes linguistic meaning in the RT account. The contexts involved in grammaticalization must constrain the inference process, but need not be ambiguous, inviting alternative interpretations of the grammaticalizing expression. In the RT account, contexts are constructed as part of the inferential utterance interpretation process, and so no attempt is made to identify a predetermined set of context types associated with grammaticalization. Finally, the relation between subjectification and grammaticalization, for example, in the development of the *go/ come* V construction, suggests that pragmatic inference is not always necessary for grammaticalization to occur.

CHAPTER 33

GRAMMATICALIZATION AND DISCOURSE

RICHARD WALTEREIT

1. The diachronic relation of grammar and discourse

We can think of grammar as part of the language's inventory of signs, and grammaticalization as the diachronic process that creates grammar. Taking discourse to be the discretionary use of these signs by speakers, we can ask what do they have to do with one another? The question can be raised at two levels.

First, it seems fairly obvious that items that have undergone grammaticalization were—or could have been, at an earlier stage of the language's history—stretches of discourse. For example, the English *going to*-future's diachronic predecessor—is of course the gerund of the lexical verb *to go* freely combined with the preposition *to*. Whenever we find a concatenation of two items *A* and *B* in speech (such as *going* and *to*), the question arises whether either *A* or *B* are mandated by the presence of the other one (or by a third item), or whether their presence is independent of each other. If the former, their concatenation would probably reflect rules of the language's grammar; if the latter, their concatenation would mean that the speaker chose so, i.e. they would pertain to discourse. At this level, then, grammaticalization simply means that a particular concatenation *A B*, or even just their particular order, shifts from the realm of discourse to the realm of grammar. I would like to refer to this level as the *historical* relation between grammaticalization and discourse.

Another question, however, is controversial: In the recruitment of *A B* to the grammar, what role, if any, does the fact play that *A B* was, in a previous stage of the language, a stretch of discourse? We could refer to this as the *diachronic* relation between grammaticalization and discourse. In a way, this question is the core issue of grammaticalization theory. Any answer to it implies a claim about the very nature of the grammaticalization process.

In generative work on grammaticalization, grammaticalization is typically located in first language acquisition, under the assumption that a child might acquire a grammar that does not exactly match the grammar underlying the input they are exposed to (e.g. van Gelderen 2004; Roberts and Roussou 2003). This reflects the long-standing notion that language change is the product of children making small mistakes in the acquisition of their first language. The real motivation for grammaticalization is then sought in principles relating to properties of caregivers' grammar, rather than in discourse. This assumption implies that there is no genuine diachronic relation between grammar and discourse. *A* and *B happen* to be adjacent in discourse as a product of the parents' grammar.

Functional theories of grammaticalization though, assuming by definition a strong link between usage and grammar, tend to give (adult) discourse greater weight in the recruitment process. A variety of theoretical approaches can be distinguished within this tradition. The most radical one is quite possibly Emergent Grammar (Hopper 1987), where grammar only ever emerges from discourse. In other words, grammar exists only as a one-off diachronic process arising from discourse, and hence has minimal synchronic stability.

A recent framework relating discourse and grammar is Construction Grammar (CG). While CG has long existed mainly as a synchronic model of grammatical representation, there is now a growing body of diachronic research (Traugott 2008a; Noël 2007; Trousdale 2008c). In CG, grammar and discourse are opposite endpoints of a continuum, defined by increasing schematicity. Highly schematic and abstract constructions are on the 'grammar' endpoint of that continuum, whereas one-off 'constructs' (Traugott 2008c) are at the 'discourse' end of the continuum. The key to the passage from discourse to grammar, in the constructional approach, is frequency (cf. Bybee 2002; 2007)—an increase in the occurrence of a particular sequence *A B* in discourse will move it towards the 'grammar' stage of the continuum. It has been pointed out that, on this account, grammaticalization as a diachronic process tends to merge with the diachronic rise of new constructions more widely (Noël 2007). Some researchers criticize this and point out that grammaticalization still has defining characteristics that set it apart from the rise of constructions pure and simple (Noël 2007), whereas others seem to embrace this tendency (Trousdale 2008a; Traugott 2008c). This would effectively mean that 'grammar' is essentially shorthand for whatever is routinized in language at a schematic level. While this seems a very attractive model, it does not, as such, provide an answer to the question why some items become more frequent over time, in other words why items move from discourse to grammar.

However, a third approach considers frequency merely as an effect, not a cause, of ongoing language change, thereby potentially giving an answer to that question. In this approach, inspired by Rudi Keller's 'Invisible Hand' theory of language change, grammar is the residue of strategic language use on the part of speakers (Keller 1990). Speakers prefer a construction over an essentially synonymous alternative because the former offers rhetorical or other advantages over the latter in communication (Traugott and Dasher 2002); through increasing adoption by other speakers, the new construction will be used more and more frequently, for the communicative advantages it affords; it will turn into a routinized technique and will thereby make it into the language's inventory of signs (Haspelmath 1998; Detges 2000; 2001; 2004; Detges and Waltereit 2002). The upshot of Keller's theory is that languages change because speakers, in their desire to communicate convincingly, 'tweak' the conventions of language, i.e. use forms not for their meaning but for the perceived advantages in communication that they may offer, at the risk of not entirely complying with their conventional meaning. To choose an example from lexical change: according to Keller, the prestige decline of the Old High German high-status noun *vrouwe* 'lady', which became the neutral *Frau* 'woman' in Modern German, was triggered by a politeness strategy where speakers tended to extend the usage of *vrouwe* also to address women of lower social status, thereby assuring themselves obvious advantages in the communication. Crucially, this implies that speakers make one-off innovations, i.e. decide to speak in a novel way. Again, the question arises then why some items, as the outcome of this process, end up as grammar and others, for example, as lexical items or discourse markers. This will be the focus of section 3 of this chapter.

2. What sets off grammaticalization?

2.1. Normal variability of speech?

Croft (2010) challenged the notion that change is set off by deliberate innovations. Based on an analogy with sound change, Croft suggests instead that morphosyntactic change, including grammaticalization, is triggered by natural variation of lexical choice in discourse. Research in acoustic phonetics has found that there is always variation in the production of any particular phonological representation (cf. Ohala 1989). Ohala argues that diachronic sound change may originate in this articulatory variation. In other words, sound change is the result of the selection of a variant out of the range of variation inherent in normal speech, rather than requiring any specific departure from the conventions underlying those representations. Croft suggests that morphosyntactic change comes about in the same way. In an experiment with a number of informants recounting the same animated cartoon, Croft noted that the variation in the expressions they chose often mirrored meaning changes in grammaticalization clines. For example, some people use the verb *to walk*, where others would use *to go* for the same state of affairs. This mirrors semantic change in light verbs—French *aller* 'to go', used as source construction for stems from Latin *ambulare* 'to walk'. In other words, synchronic variation as a result of speaker choice in verbalizing experience mirrors diachronic change. Just as phonetic change is claimed to be the outcome of essentially uncontrollable natural variation inherent in spontaneous speech, so would morphosyntactic change, including grammaticalization, be the outcome of essentially arbitrary speaker choice when verbalizing the same piece of experience. An important implication of this is that innovation appears to be rather ubiquitous rather than being rare.

However, the analogy between sound change and morphosyntactic change does not seem entirely felicitous. Natural variation in articulation reflects essentially a varying degree of perfection in individuals in meeting a particular *given target*: the phonological representation as prescribed by conventions of the language. This is, Croft suggests, presumably rooted in the fact that 'the level of neuromuscular control over articulatory gestures needed for identical (invariant) productions of a phoneme is beyond a speaker's control' (Croft 2010). Morphosyntactic variation, however, is normally compliant with the conventions of the language. Variability can easily be attributed to the fact that any state of affairs in the world is matched by a number of items and constructions of language. We would therefore expect there to be a certain amount of variation between individuals verbalizing the same experience. In other words, natural variation in articulation and natural variation in morphosyntax arise for different and essentially unrelated reasons.

2.2. How to recognize an innovation

While Croft's argument that grammaticalization is simply a by-product of natural variability in discourse is not convincing, the opposite view (inherent in Keller's theory) that language change, including grammaticalization, is entirely driven by individual acts of creativity replicated by a herd of followers may be too naive. Crucial here is the semantic relation between the lexical and the grammatical stage of the form.

From a semantic point of view, incipient grammaticalization represents either a metonymic or a taxonomic (semantic widening) change. Grammaticalization as recruitment of lexical items to the grammar instantiates metonymy; 'secondary' grammaticalization, i.e. the change from already grammatical to 'more grammatical', i.e. less marked, is semantic widening (Detges and Waltereit 2002). For example, the English *going-to* future tense is metonymically related to its source construction, the verb of movement *to go to [verb]*. Someone who moves towards a certain place in order to do something implies that they will perform that activity in the future. Turning to secondary grammaticalization, the Old French marked French negation *ne... pas* 'not at all', marked because the proposition needed to be activated in previous discourse (Hansen and Visconti 2009), has gradually turned into standard negation in Modern French. Now, standard negation logically includes marked negation—any instance of marked negation is also negation plain and simple. Hence the change is, in lexical semantic terms, semantic widening.

A type of semantic relation familiar from lexical change, but unattested in grammaticalization, is metaphor. The unavailability of metaphor for grammaticalization is important because what metonymy and semantic widening have in common, but do not share with metaphor, is a potential overlap of referents, with ensuing potential ambiguity in early stages (Koch 2004). For example, in the above case of the *going-to* future, early examples are often ambiguous between a lexical verb and a grammatical interpretation. But it is the very essence of metaphor that source and target meaning do not overlap (cf. Blank 1997). A metaphor cannot be ambiguous between its figurative and its literal meaning.

What referential overlap means specifically for innovations is that in the early stages it is not easy to recognize an innovation as such, since the construction in question could as well instantiate the 'old' meaning. The very concept of 'bridging context', i.e. a context that leads from one interpretation of a form to another (Heine 2002), relies on the availability of the two readings. In other words, an innovation based on metaphor as semantic relation can unequivocally be recognized as such, whereas an innovation based on metonymy or semantic widening/narrowing often cannot. This potential ambiguity makes it hard to observe any actual innovation in linguistic (or other) behaviour since unusual, i.e. potentially innovative, behaviour can often be accounted for in two different ways. Either it is unusual because the underlying circumstances are unusual and prompted action accordingly, but is in line with existing conventions; or it is unusual because conventions have not been applied in the way they were supposed to.

For example, one of the most notable features of Albert Camus's novel *L'Étranger* 'The Stranger' (1942) is the near-complete absence of the simple past (*passé simple*). Rather, Camus uses the compound past (*passé composé*), which at the time was already common for narrating past events in spoken language, but restricted to resultative, i.e. not genuinely temporal, uses in the written language of that time. Early literary and linguistic commentators of the novel tended to analyse this as an adroit stylistic move: the concatenation of resultatives created an impression of the sentences being almost unconnected stumbling blocks which cleverly reflected the protagonist's fragmentized experience; they suggested that the *passé composé* was the right tense to use because it reflected the underlying states of affairs. More recently, though, Camus's novel has tended to be viewed as spearheading a more and more widespread use of the narrative *passé composé* in writing (cf. de Saussure 2006: 106)—i.e. it now appears as an essentially linguistic, rather than stylistic, innovation. Camus's move has been classed as an innovation *retroactively*, because it was *followed* by similar behaviour. Thus, a relevant change in conventions can often be recognized as such only long after the event. Contemporary observers cannot be sure (except in the case of metaphor) whether they are witnessing a linguistic innovation or whether what the speaker says is unusual simply because what they talk about is unusual.

In sum, while language change may indeed ultimately rely on individual speakers' creative speech, we do not need to posit that innovative speakers deliberately and noticeably chose to depart from existing conventions. Rather, language change may be more of a collective process, and the respective roles of innovating vs. propagating members of the speech community could be less distinctly separate from one another than the classical references to these concepts in Coseriu (1957) and Weinreich, Labov, and Herzog (1968) suggest.

3. Discourse strategies resulting in language change: the French adverb *bien* 'well'

In the following I will describe the discourse-based model of grammaticalization and related types of language change proposed in Waltereit and Detges (2007) and Waltereit (forthcoming). This model essentially applies Keller's Invisible Hand theory to other-than-lexical change. Discussing three distinct diachronic successors of the same lexical base, we will be able to see how various ways of using a lexical item in discourse can create different diachronic pathways.

3.1. Various outcomes of the same lexical base

The French lexical adverb *bien* has undergone (at least) three changes: it has turned into a grammatical concessive conjunction *bien que*:

(1) J'y ai participé, <u>bien</u> que je sois conscient du risque.
'I took part, <u>even though</u> I am aware of the risk.'

In this function, its position is syntactically fixed at the left margin of a clause. Furthermore its scope is syntactically fixed as well to the clause. Moreover, it has a function at a propositional (ideational) level.

Another outcome for *bien* is its use as a discourse marker:

(2) GAS non le problème oui c'est c'est la politique d'immigration
CG voilà oui d'accord bien non parce que votre formule elle peut être ambiguë oui elle peut être interprétée hein y en a plein qui disent le problème c'est l'immigration
'GAS No the problem, yes, is the immigration policy
CG Right, I agree, well no, because what you say may be ambiguous: it may be read, well, many people say the problem is immigration itself' [CLAPI]

As a discourse marker, it is placed at the margin of the stretch of discourse it applies to, rather than in relation to a unit that could be described in terms of constituent structure. Concomitantly, the speaker is essentially free to extend its scope to what they choose to be the stretch of discourse relevant for it (cf. Waltereit and Detges 2007). On a semantic level, the discourse marker has a textual or interactional function.

The third variant under discussion here is *bien* as a modal particle in French. In this use it occupies an intermediate position between the grammatical item and the discourse marker (cf. Hansen 2008). In example (3), *bien* has an interactional function: it orientates the question towards a positive answer. Modal particles share their interactional function with a relevant subset of discourse markers. However, they also share important properties with grammatical items, namely their fixed syntactic position and the rigidity of their scope, which is identified with the clause.

(3) Vous avez bien reçu mon message?
'You got my message, didn't you ?'

Table 33.1 summarizes the differences and commonalities among the three forms.

Table 33.1. Diachronic outcomes of adverb *bien*

	Outcomes of adverb *bien*		
	Concessive conjunction	Modal particle	Discourse marker
Scope	Clause	Clause	Stretch of discourse
Syntactic position	Fixed	Fixed	Variable
Type of meaning	Propositional	Interactional	Metatextual/ interactional

The discourse-based model of grammaticalization accounts for these three outcomes by positing respectively different strategic uses of the adverb *bien* in discourse that yielded the three different forms. I will now deal with each of them in turn.

3.2. The rise of the modal particle *bien* from scalar argumentation

Hansen (1998b) has shown that the modal use of *bien* (as in (3)) incorporates, as part of its conventional meaning, an anticipation of hearer's stance. How does this relate to the lexical meaning of the adverb *bien* 'well'? Waltereit and Detges (2007) suggested that the relevant connection is the use of the adverb *bien* 'well' in *scalar argumentation*, as in (14):

(4) Et mesires Pierres respondi: 'Ba!', fist il, 'de n'avés vous oï comment Troies le grant fu destruite ne par quel tor ?—'Ba ouil !', fisent li Blak et li Commain, 'nous l'avons bien oï dire.' (Robert de Clari, *La Conquête de Constantinople* 106, early 13th c.)

'And Mylord Pierre answered: "Ba," he said, "haven't you heard about how Troy the great was destroyed and in which way this happened?"—"Of course," said Blak and Commain, "we heard clearly/a lot about it."'

Blak and Commain are countering the suggestion that they did not hear about Troy's destruction by stressing that they heard 'a lot' about it—i.e. in order to convey that a particular state of affairs is indeed the case (contrary to what the interlocutor expects), they claim that that state of affairs is the case *to a high degree.* By making the stronger point that they heard about it to a high degree, the weaker point is made by scalar implication. We can view this as 'overuse': speakers say more than they need to. Already in Old French, the modal use is conventionalized, as can be seen from uses with stative predicates:

(5) Ceste virge dont j' ai retraite Et rimee ceste matere Bien est de Dieu et de sa mere. (Gautier de Coinci, 1218)

'This virgin whose story I have told in rhymes is indeed from God and his mother'

As the scalar argumentation strategy relates propositions expressing states of affairs, it is natural that the resulting form (the modal particle) takes propositions in their scope. The syntactic position of the modal particle, i.e. immediately following the finite verb, reflects to a certain extent the underlying strategy, seeing that the latter focuses on the veracity of the assertion, which in turn is expressed in the finite verb form.

3.3. *Bien* in concessive complex sentences

Let us now turn to the concessive conjunction *bien que*, a genuinely grammatical item. The adverb *bien* 'well' was already used in Old French to concede a point in argumentation, without being part of an actual concessive conjunction:

(6) Dahez ait qui vos oï *onques*, Ne vit onques mes, que je soie! Bien puet estre, mes je pansoie, Que le gué me contredeïstes; Bien sachiez que mar me feristes. (Chevalier de la Charrette, 1177, TFA)
'Cursed be whoever saw or heard you, even if it's myself ! It is well possible that you forbade me the ford, but I was deep in thought. You should know well that you did me wrong.'

The speaker concedes that his interlocutor did not allow him to cross the ford, but dismisses this on the grounds that he 'was deep in thought'. The second proposition is introduced with *mes* 'but', a conjunction that has genuinely argumentative meaning. According to standard assumptions of argumentation theory (Anscombre and Ducrot 1977), *but* characterizes its proposition (q) as yielding an argument whose force outweighs the argumentative force of a previous proposition (p). Now, the proposition p, in this case, is marked with *bien*, which, as we have seen, makes it argumentatively stronger than it would be without that adverb. This, however, does not override the force of *mes* 'but' in proposition q. In other words, no matter how strong the force of p is on and by itself, it cannot outweigh q as long as the latter is marked by the conjunction *mes* 'but' (cf. e.g. Haspelmath and König 1998; Leuschner 2006). Waltereit (forthcoming) refers to this as 'implicature of irrelevance', which is based on the same scale as is the modal particle *bien*. *Bien* conveys that its host occupies a higher rung on the respectively relevant scale than the same proposition without *bien*.

An already grammaticalized use of this implicature in Old French is the conjunction *se bien* 'even if'.

(7) Le chevalier siudre n'osai, Que folie feire dotasse. Et, se je bien siudre l'osasse, Ne sai ge que il se devint. (Yvain, *c.*1180, TFA)
'I did not dare to follow the knight out of fear to do some folly. And even if I had dared to follow him I would not know what had become of him.'

Again, the formal features of the outcome match those of the underlying discourse strategy. The strategy underlying the grammaticalization of *se bien* has scope over a proposition, grammatically expressed by a clause, in the same way as the diachronic outcome, a conjunction, has scope over a clause.

3.4. The rise of *bien* as a discourse marker

The third outcome for *bien* is a discourse marker—a process often referred to a pragmaticalization (cf. Dostie 2004 and references cited therein). The adverb *bien* can be used, without requiring any change in its own semantic representation, as an interjection to express approval (positive evaluation). The first diachronic step to note is a metonymic change in the interjection use from 'positive evaluation' to 'agreement'.

(8) (Ha ! Vous voullez avoir plaisance ? Bien, vous l'aurez pour ung taudis, Mais gens qui prennent leur aisance Se retreuvent les plus mauldis. (La Chesnaye, 1508, FRANTEXT)

'Ha ! You want fun ? All right, you'll have it for a song, but people who take their freedom find themselves the most cursed ones.'

The interjection *bien* has come to be used, since the 17th century, as a genuine discourse marker, i.e. coordinating the joint construction of discourse rather than action in the wider sense:

(9) ROY. Tu cognoistras comment sans aucun artifice, Je te veux faire voir la volonté des Dieux.
CHRYSEIDE. Je sçay que cét Hymen leur est trop odieux.
ROY. Bien bien, nous le verrons, cependant prenons place Au plus prés de l'Autel où doit fondre ta glace. (Jean Mairet, 1630, FRANTEXT)
'R: You will see that I will let you see the Gods' will without any tricks.
C: I know they hate this nuptial bond.
R: Bien, bien, let's see, however let's take a seat next to the altar where you will lose your coldness.'

The features of the contemporary outcomes of *bien* are consonant with the discourse strategies they were arguably used for.

We have seen that discourse markers originate in expressions whose original purpose is to coordinate human action more widely. Essentially, they turn into discourse markers once they are specialized to the coordination of discourse. The scope of the original expressions is not necessarily constrained by grammatical boundaries, and will only incidentally coincide with them. Likewise, discourse markers, as the unintended outcome of those strategies, have variable scope over stretches of discourse, rather than being defined in terms of grammatical constituents. Additionally, they have (of course) a discourse-related, i.e. a textual or interactional, function rather than an ideational one.

To summarize, we see that an important subset of functional change is governed by the patterns of discourse that the relevant items are being used for rhetorically by speakers. Table 33.2 summarizes the scope of the underlying strategic use and the contemporary properties of the three outcomes of *bien* discussed in this chapter. In other words, lexical items, and constructions in general, have a certain potential for argumentative or otherwise strategic use in discourse. Speakers may take advantage of this, flouting existing conventions of language or conventions of use.

Table 33.2. Argumentation strategies and outcomes

		bien	
Scope of strategic use	Coordination of construction of discourse	Common ground	Proposition
Outcome	Discourse marker	Modal particle	Concessive conjunction

According to the nature of the argumentative/strategic use, the outcome can be grammaticalization, pragmaticalization, or other types of change.

4. Grammaticalization and Discourse

To return to the diachronic relation between grammar and discourse referred to in section 1, I have reported research that stresses the importance of patterns of argumentation in discourse for the emergence of grammar over time.

Detges (2001) argues that what is relatively straightforward in the case of lexical change, as argued by Keller (1990) and referred to in section 1, applies *mutatis mutandis* to grammatical change as well. To achieve their interactional goals in discourse, speakers may use items in a strategic way that, however slightly, deviates from their conventional meaning, thus changing that meaning over time. The pathway of that change and its eventual outcome depend on the original strategic use the item in question was put to. Grammaticalization is the unintended outcome of those strategies that have scope over a proposition. Discourse markers are the outcome of those strategies that relate to the coordination of the construction of discourse. Modal particles occupy an intermediate position between these two (Hansen 1998a).

Under this view, the diachronic relation between grammar and discourse is an extremely strong one. A sequence *A B* is eventually recruited to the grammar because it is used in discourse with a rhetorical purpose.

CHAPTER 34

GRAMMATICALIZATION AND CONVERSATION

ELIZABETH COUPER-KUHLEN

1. Introduction

The argument to be pursued in this chapter will not strike students of social interaction as particularly new or controversial, but for others it may be somewhat revelatory. In a nutshell it is this: many grammatical constructions—in particular bipartite ones—have grown out of, or emerged (Hopper 1987; 1998; Bybee 2006), from the sequential routines of mundane conversational interaction. First attested in early language acquisition and described as movement from vertical to horizontal construction (Scollon 1976),[1] this process is known today among conversation analysts and like-minded scholars as the trade-off between sequence organization and turn construction (Schegloff 2007). Put simply, what is on one occasion accomplished via a succession of (cross-speaker) actions can, on other occasions, be 'collapsed' into a single speaker's (expanded) turn. An example might be the conversational routine illustrated by:[2]

[1] Cf. also Ochs and Schieffelin (1983), whose observations concern above all the use of topic-comment structures for foregrounding referents.

[2] All examples used in the following are taken from recordings of naturally occurring social interaction.

(1) Summons-answer pre-sequence (adapted from Schegloff 2007: 51)

```
5  Car:  Vic(tor),
6  Vic:  Yeh?
7  Car:  Come here for a minute.
```

This summons routine can be collapsed into a single turn for the accomplishment of a related task, as in:

(2) Integrated summons + request (Schegloff 2007: 56n.)

```
Alvin,=can you come a bit closer to the ta:ble maybe even there?
```

Now if the collapsed form of a conversational routine is found to entail recurrent lexicosyntactic forms, as here (schematically): [Term of address]+[Request], then one might justifiably speak of a *construction*[3] which—viewed developmentally—has grammaticalized from the conversational routine. Diachronic evidence for such a claim is difficult to come by, given the absence of historical conversational records. But ample synchronic evidence can be found in conversation, particularly when the component parts of a putative construction appear in both 'independent' and 'integrated' form, and when the integrated forms can be shown to have specialized for specific purposes. Both 'layering' and 'specialization' are considered hallmarks of grammaticalization (Hopper 1991; Hopper and Traugott 2003). In the following, I discuss three case studies from present-day English conversation to substantiate this argument, before concluding with a critical evaluation of its implications.

2. Some case studies

The constructions to be discussed in this section all have in common that they are bipartite, i.e. consist in their integrated form of two components, and that their parts can be used independently to implement separate conversational actions. Although many of the labels commonly used for these constructions are misleading,[4] they have been retained here for their recognitional value: these are the names linguists will be familiar with. It must be stressed, however, that from a spoken-language perspective the integrated forms should not be thought

[3] 'Construction' is being used here in the sense of Traugott (2003).

[4] Both 'left-dislocation' and 'extraposition', for instance, imply negatively connoted departures from a norm where all the syntactic elements are 'in place'. But this norm is a written-language norm and not necessarily appropriate for spoken interaction.

of as the point of departure. Many are the product of a normativization associated with stylistic training at school (Hopper 2001) and have been reified through the written language bias in linguistics (Linell 2005).[5] Nor, in a spoken-language or conversational perspective, should the integrated forms be thought of as the endpoint along some putative line of linguistic or cognitive development. On the contrary: although the integrated forms coexist with the independent forms in conversation, they are often less frequent. The cognitive and interactional demands of online speech production in conversation actually appear to favour fragmentation rather than integration (cf. also Chafe 1982). It is these demands which are responsible for the 'back formation' of fragmented or independent forms from already integrated ones.[6] The integrated forms live their own lives in conversation; they can rarely be replaced by, or freely exchanged with, the independent forms in their context of occurrence. In conversation—as with all situated language use—the choice of independent vs. integrated form for the implementation of a particular action ultimately depends on the local context; it is a question of *recipient design*, i.e. the fitting of an action, or a format for accomplishing it, to the particulars of a given situation.

2.1. Left dislocation

The 'Left dislocation' construction has been described in its integrated grammatical form as follows: 'a noun phrase is positioned initially and a reinforcing pronoun stands 'proxy' for it in the relevant position in the sentence' (Quirk et al. 1985: 1310). Empirical studies of spontaneous discourse, however, have identified a larger and looser set of related constructions called [Referent] + [Proposition]: 'some referent is specified initially and is then followed by a proposition relevant in some way to this referent' (Ochs and Schieffelin 1976: 240). Yet it was Geluykens, working with a large corpus of conversational data, who first pointed out that the Left dislocation construction is 'the result of a (usually) three-stage, interactional process by which new referents are first introduced by the speaker, then acknowledged by the hearer, and finally elaborated upon by the speaker' (1992: 33). Left dislocation then originates in a conversational routine.

[5] As Hopper writes, 'Grammatical constructions (of the more complex type, EC-K) are normativized rationalizations of families of smaller and more fragmented quasi-lexical parts. They result from the grammaticalization of these fragments' (2001: 124).

[6] I am thinking here of the use of *because* and *although* as conjuncts rather than as subordinating conjunctions (Couper-Kuhlen 1996; Hopper and Traugott 2003: 209) or of the increased use of main-clause word order in German *weil* 'because' and *obwohl* 'although' clauses (Günthner 1996).

This routine has been called a 'recognition search sequence' in conversation analytic work (Sacks and Schegloff 1979).[7] Schegloff (2007) cites the following fragment as a typical case:

(3) Recognition search sequence (adapted from Schegloff 2007: 238)
Participants are engaged here in a round of storytelling about claims for insurance compensation due to property damage.

09→	She:	**Peter.**
10		(0.2)
11→	She:	**Legget?**
12		(0.5)
13	Kar:	[Oh yeah.]
14	She:	[(Y'know who) I'm tal]king about? Yeah. 'hh
15→		**He collected a fo:rtune for that.**
16→		**He claimed all k(h)i:nds of damages.**

With the isolated form 'Peter' in line 9, Sherry is monitoring for evidence from her interlocutor that the latter knows the person in question. At the same time she is projecting that she will have more to say about this person. Her choice of a personal name reflects the preference for achieving *recognition* of third party referents in conversation with a minimal form which makes maximal assumptions about the other's knowledge (Sacks and Schegloff 1979). If Karen recognizes the person in question, she can be expected to signal so in next turn. Lacking such a signal (as here in line 10), the referring speaker can use next turn to supply more information in the pursuit of recognition (as here in line 11). A number of such rounds can follow, if necessary. If recognition cannot be secured this way, the referring speaker may ultimately offer a *non-recognitional* description, e.g. *this guy I know from work*, in order to establish the non-known person as a referent for the projected telling. The recognition search sequence is terminated when the interlocutor signals recognition (as here in line 13) or when an unknown referent is established through a non-recognitional description.[8] At this point the referring speaker resumes the projected telling or informing (as in line 15 here), typically using an anaphoric form to index the now established referent.

Recipients need not always provide a verbal indication of recognition in a separate turn. A current speaker may simply pause following referent introduction, providing just enough space for the recipient to request elaboration if needed, but proceed with the telling if no request is forthcoming. Geluykens (1992) found this

[7] According to Sacks and Schegloff's (1979) description, the recognition search can be initiated either by the person doing the referring (e.g. through so-called 'try-marking', i.e. final high-rising intonation) or by the recipient of the referring form (e.g. through repair initiation in next turn).

[8] For more on person reference in conversation, see Enfield and Stivers (2007).

variant to be the most frequent in his materials.[9] In such cases, it is the absence of repair initiation by the recipient which confirms that recognition has been achieved or that a referent has been satisfactorily established.

On other occasions, the current speaker may not have any grounds for assuming that the interlocutor will recognize the referent and thus use a descriptive, non-recognitional form from the outset, before proceeding to the relevant telling:

(4) Quasi-integrated Left dislocation (adapted from Schegloff 2007: 274)
(Two erstwhile friends are reminiscing about some of their least favorite teachers at school.)

5.27→ Bee: **Well one I had, t! 'hhhh in the firs' term there,**
5.28→ **fer the firs' term of English, she die::d** hhuh-uhh ['hhh
5.29 Ava: [Oh:.
5.30 Bee: She died in the middle of the te:rm? mhhh!

Bee makes no pause here after supplying a description of the referent about whom she projects more talk (line 5.28). Instead, she proceeds to the telling right away, with a pronominal form pointing back to the referent. In Geluykens' study, 30 per cent of the left-dislocated structures identified were like this one, i.e. had no pause or intervening turn between the introduction of the referent and the following proposition (1992: 41).

Intriguingly, Geluykens' work shows that the majority of left dislocations without an intervening turn or a pause—those which are maximally integrated and can be said to be the most grammaticalized—are used not to introduce new referents in conversation, but have become specialized for other purposes, among them contrast and/or listing (1992: 83ff.). This is the case, for instance, in the following fragment, where Ros is giving instructions to an acquaintance about how to find her house:

(5) Integrated Left dislocation (SBL 010)

01 Ros: And the very first house after that corner is a
02 corner hou:se (0.7)
03 it's the corner of Victoria Parkway, h
04 Bea: m-hm,
05 Ros: and Willow Run. And that's my hou:se.
06 Bea: oh:.
07 Ros: mm hm [:.
08 Bea: [yes I know exactly where it i:s.=

[9] In over 47% of the left dislocation patterns in his corpus there was a pause between referent introduction and the subsequent proposition but no intervening turn (Geluykens 1992: 41).

Ros: =no:w the house has some: fruit tree:s on the corner,
(.) orange tree:s, °°(think it's the fir-)°° hh
it's the corner house. hh
first there's the corner house of Magnolia and Willow Run.
it has: geraniums and roses.
→ **a[nd then] the ne:xt house,=**
Bea: [m-hm,]
→ Ros: **=it's just a dri:veway**
and then there's a (0.4)
then you go on Willow Run ri:ght.
Bea: mm-hm
Ros: go straight (0.6)
uh there's a corner right away
and that corner house is mi:ne.

Ros is displaying concern here about several corner houses which could be confused with her own. She uses first a presentative *there*-construction (lines 12–13) and then a Left dislocation (lines 14+16) to describe the two that are not hers and contrast them with her own house (lines 21–2). These structures are not being used primarily to establish referents for some projected telling, but rather to line up already identified referents (*the corner house of Magnolia and Willow Run, the next house*) and contrast them with the target referent, her own house.

In sum, what grammarians like to call 'Left dislocation' can be thought of as the coalescence and entrenchment of a frequent and flexible conversational routine called a 'recognition search sequence'. It is encountered when speakers first establish referents about whom (or which), projectably, more will be said in subsequent talk. In their independent form, the two component parts, typically a freestanding noun phrase and a subsequent clause or set of clauses, carry out separate actions.[10] They are delivered in different turn-constructional units and are often separated from one another by intervening turns and/or opportunities for such. This is in the truest sense of the word an *inter-actional* pattern. Yet there are also 'collapsed' or coalesced forms attested in conversation, ones in which the two parts are more closely connected, i.e. not separated by a pause or intervening turn, and where they are analysably deployed as an integrated whole, in the service of a single action. These tend to be construction-like, and significantly they appear to have become specialized for particular purposes, such as listing and/or contrast.

[10] See Ono and Thompson (1994) and Thompson and Couper-Kuhlen (2005) for a discussion of independent NPs and clauses, respectively, as they function in interaction.

2.2. Concession

For most grammarians, concession is a semantic notion expressed first and foremost through an adverbial subordinate clause.[11] Concessive adverbial clauses are introduced by the conjunction *although* (or its more colloquial form *though*) and are said to be positioned as a rule before the main clause: *Although Britain considers itself an advanced country, it has a very old-fashioned system of measurements* (Quirk et al 1972: 749). Yet studies of conversation have found surprisingly few instances of concessive adverbial clauses with *although* (Ford 1993) and even fewer instances of preposed ones (Barth 2000). By contrast, they have found an abundance of concessive-like action sequences or conversational routines (Antaki and Wetherell 1999; Couper-Kuhlen and Thompson 2000; Barth-Weingarten 2003; Steensig and Asmuss 2005). One of the most frequent is a strategy for disagreeing with what an interlocutor has just said by first partially agreeing with it: conversation analysts call this the 'agreement + disagreement' strategy when it is situated within assessment sequences (Pomerantz 1984). Together with the interlocutor's prior turn, the 'agreement + disagreement' strategy is part of a fundamentally interactional routine, organized as follows:

(6) Cardinal Concessive routine (Couper-Kuhlen and Thompson 2000: 382)
Speaker A: States something or makes some point
Speaker B: Acknowledges the validity of this statement or point (i.e. provisionally agrees)
+
Claims the validity of a potential contrasting statement or point (i.e. disagrees)

It is the acknowledging action which is concessive-like, because it involves an admission that what the other has just said may indeed be (partially) true. At the same time this admission projects that the speaker will go on to make a contrasting claim.

The Cardinal Concessive represents a highly flexible conversational routine. In addition to the basic form shown in (6), it has a number of variants, one of which will be discussed below. Moreover, it permits a variety of different formal realizations. For instance, the concessive move can encompass a whole chunk of discourse:

(7) Agreement + disagreement sequence
(Dave Hatch, a radio studio anchorman, and his caller are discussing the relative merits of a penal system in which felons wear an electronic bleeper

[11] In one typical understanding, a concessive adverbial clause is said to 'imply a contrast between two circumstances; ie that in the light of the circumstance in the dependent clause, that in the main clause is surprising' (Quirk et al 1972: 745).

around their neck rather than go to prison. Mrs Etchalls is in favor of electronic bleepers.)

ETCH: everybody KNOWS,
whoever you SEE do:n't they,
they know you've done SOMEthing,
whereas (0.7) YOU know,
once you're- you're going awAy,
a lot of people could just think you've gone on a HOLiday
or something li:ke tha:t.
(0.4)
→ DAVE: **I suppose they COULD,**
→ **YES I suppose it would mean that you'd have to spend**
→ **quite a lot of time inDOORS,**
→ **or else you'd have to wear a large MUFFler all the time.**
→ **or pretend you had a stiff NECK,**
→ **and wear one of those big PINK things they give you.**
ETCH: yeah,
→ DAVE: **or something like THAT.**
(0.6)
DAVE: but i must say I THINK-
it's the one sort of opinion i HAVE on the matter,
i think i would rather THAT than go to prIson,
because (0.2) PRIson must be VERy soul destrOying.
don't you think,

Following Mrs Etchalls' statement that bleepers are a preferable sort of punishment due to their visibility (lines 01–07), Dave first stages a rather elaborate but conditional agreement by imagining how difficult it would be to hide an electronic bleeper (lines 09–16). This is the concessive move, which—together with the interlocutor's confirmation (line 15)—results in a small action sequence of its own. But Dave then follows up with a powerful argument against Mrs Etchalls' position and in favour of prison as punishment (lines 18–22). Concession here is thus part of a disagreement sequence.

On other occasions, the speaker's concessive move is more circumspect, being reduced to a single clause or phrase, as in the following excerpt (cited from Barth 2000: 413):

(8) Quasi-integrated preposed Concessive
(Betsy is about to travel to Australia and is asking her sister and brother-in-law for advice on where to exchange currencies. Wally has just suggested the bank but his wife objects.)

01	MOR:	.hhh but you dOn't get a very good rAte of exchAnge
02		at those (.) [those (.) banks.
03→	WAL:	**[nO too trUE you don't; no-**
04		but it w- i- it's bEtter than (.) [doing it at the bA:r;
05	BET:	[but whEn do you change
06		YOUR money;

Following Mora's objection that rates are not particularly good at the bank (lines 01–02), Wally briefly acknowledges this point (line 03), but then goes on to maintain that they are better than at the bar (line 04). With the concessive move reduced to an acknowledging clause or a phrase, as here, the resulting pattern begins to resemble the entrenched and grammaticalized Concessive construction: *yes (that's right/true/correct) but*... (Couper-Kuhlen and Thompson 2000: 389; Steensig and Asmuss 2005).

Another Concessive construction appears to have emerged from a variant of the Cardinal Concessive routine in (6). This construction has a postposed *although*-clause; in its proto-form, with independent parts, it has the reverse order 'disagreement + (partial) agreement':

(9) Disagreement + (partial) agreement sequence
(Charles and his friends are talking about a French friend Didier, whom Charles has described as 'a musician and kind of cabaret artist'.)

01	STE:	w'll i- dz– this guy's a CABaret artist,
02		i mean -
03		does [he perFORM in
04	CHA:	[well i- i don't think he does that proFESSional-
05→		**i mean he DOES -**
06→		**he: he's had like a COUPle of engagements,**

Following Steve's question as to where Didier performs (lines 01–03), Charles moves immediately to correct the misinterpretation that Didier is a professional: *I don't think he does that professional-* (line 04). But before completing this unit, he breaks off and proceeds to weaken the claim by contrastively acknowledging that Didier *has* had a *few* engagements, thereby suggesting that there may be a sense in which he is professional after all. Charles' conceding move in (9) could easily be paraphrased with *although*: 'I don't think he does that professionally, although he *has* had a *few* engagements.' This is a good indication that there is a close relation between the disagreement + (partial) agreement action sequence and the Concessive construction with a postposed *although*-clause (see also Barth 2000).

Interestingly, the postposed *although*-construction appears to have undergone further grammaticalization to yield the particle use of *though* (Barth-Weingarten and Couper-Kuhlen 2002). This use is documented in a case like the following:

(10) Integrated postposed Concessive (Couper-Kuhlen and Thompson 2000: 395f.)
(Laura has been talking about her frequent backaches. Ruth has reported her doctor's claim that everybody gets backaches because the backbone is 'built for an animal to walk on all fours'.)

	MOM:	ACtually,
		that HELPS,
		(-) when you have a backache.
	LAU:	really?
	MOM:	(--) is to -
		(-) to get down on your hands and KNEES,
		and walk aROU-
		and crawl aROUND,
	LAU:	oh,
		not crou-
→		not ALL the way DOWN **though**,
	MOM:	unhunh,

Here the concessive move, roughly the equivalent of 'although what you say is partially true', is reduced to *though* and cliticized onto the prior unit, where it appears as an unaccented final particle (line 11). In cases like this, what is analysably an instance of concession is not accomplished via an action sequence but has been collapsed into a single turn-constructional unit and a single action. Intriguingly, the final particle *though* appears to be currently specializing for the purpose of marking an incipient topic shift (Barth-Weingarten and Couper-Kuhlen 2002).

Formally speaking, Concessive constructions may seem to have little in common with the family of Left-dislocated constructions. Yet on a more abstract level the trajectory of their emergence is similar: a conversational routine involving a sequence of actions and turn-constructional units coalesces into a single action realized in a single turn-constructional unit. When lexico-syntactic forms recur, the coalesced pattern becomes entrenched as a grammaticalized construction for carrying out the action in question. Subsequently, the construction may specialize for particular purposes.[12]

2.3. Extraposition

The Extraposition construction is known to grammarians as a kind of postponement, the most common type being where 'the clausal subject is placed at the end of the sentence, and the nominal subject position is filled by the anticipatory pronoun *it*', e.g. *It's a pity to make a fool of yourself* (Quirk et al 1972: 963f.). Empirical studies of conversation have identified a forerunner of the Extraposition construction in the frequently employed strategy of providing a preface for an upcoming story or telling (Couper-Kuhlen and Thompson 2008). The conversational routine involves first giving a prospective assessment of the form *it's funny/ sad/amazing*..., where *it* refers to the upcoming telling and the assessing phrase to how the speaker evaluates it, and then launching the telling. Let us call this the 'evaluative preface + telling' routine. Using an evaluative preface of this sort serves to put interlocutors on notice that a story or telling will follow, allowing them to align as story recipients,[13] and at the same time signals what kind of evaluation will be relevant at its conclusion. Here is an example:

(11) Evaluative preface + telling routine
(Nan, who is middle-aged, is telling her friend Emma about the other students in her night-school psychology class.)

01	Nan:	they are so cute ↓yeah they really.
02		they were just (.) ve:ry .hhhhh very very sweet with me:
03→		a:nd **it was so funny**
04		in fact one of the kids came up to me;
05		(.) one of the young .hhhh fellas that (.)
06		Ra:lph's about twenty two:,
07	Emm:	mm h[m:¿]
08	Nan:	[a:]nd he had been,h in, (.)
09		one of my mi:cro groups right at the very beginning,
	((25 lines omitted))	
34	Nan:	.hhhhh en then afterwards Ra:lph
35		came up and he said (.)
36		I:'d like (.) Nancy? (0.2)

[12] Cf. also Couper-Kuhlen and Thompson (2005), who discuss the specialization of another type of concessive construction for use in self-repair.

[13] As story recipients they would e.g. be expected to refrain from talking themselves until the story project is brought to a recognizable conclusion (Sacks 1992).

37		he said I'd like to (0.2)
38		take you over to Shakey's and buy you a ↓bee:r. (.)
39	Nan:	uhhhh ↓huh [↓huh.h] hhh
40	Emm:	[h o: w] ↓cu::[te.

From the context it is clear that Nancy's assessment of *it* being *so funny* in line 03 does not refer to something she has already talked about, but is instead a prospective assessment of something she will talk about next. What follows is a rather circuitous story concerning one of the young men in her psychology class, who asked her out for a beer as a token of his admiration. The climax, presented as a stretch of reported speech in lines 36–8, is cued as funny by Nancy's laughter in line 39. Emma now signals her affiliation with *how cute* (line 40), taking up the term of assessment Nancy used at the outset (line 01).

The 'evaluative preface + telling' pattern illustrated in (11) is a conversational routine in the sense that it involves two separate actions: a prospective evaluation followed by a delivery of what it is that is being evaluated. These two actions are accomplished as independent actions in turn-constructional units with no syntactic link between them. On other occasions in conversation, however, we find similar prospectively evaluative phrases but with the assessable being expressed as a clause which is syntactically dependent on the prior unit. Typically, such a clause is a formulation not of a succession of events as in (11), but of a single situation. Here is an example:

(12) Integrated Extraposition
[Emma and her friend Nancy are talking about the amount of publicity in the aftermath of the Robert Kennedy assassination in Los Angeles.]

03	Emm:	[I won't even turn the tee vee o:n,h
04		(.)
05	Nan:	well I had turned it on when I first got u:p just to see:
06		how thin:gs were: progressi:ng but the thing was so sad and
07		all that horrible sad music they kept
08		(.)
09	Nan:	keep [playing] all the [time you] know,
10	Emm:	[oh:::::] [G*o:::d]
11	Emm:	they go on and o:n and o:[n with thi]:s
12	Nan:	[°y a: h,°]

```
13     Emm:  like yesterday showing them going in the chu- .hh I mean so
14           much I: know it's sa:d but my God let's don't throw it at
15           the public °constantl[y°
16→    Nan:                     [.t.hhh we:ll ↑I think it's sad
17→          that they don't uh:.h allo:w u-you know the families
18→          at least the decen[cy of hav]ing some privacy.
19     Emm:                     [e e y a h]
```

In response to Emma's assessment that the situation is *sad* (line 14), Nancy announces in line 16 that she too finds something sad. What this is, is now succinctly formulated in a single clause (lines 17–18) introduced by *that*, making it syntactically dependent on the prior unit.

The integrated form of 'prospective assessment + assessable' yields what linguists call Extraposition. As a comparison of (12) with (11) reveals, the integrated form can be seen as a coalescence and entrenchment of the more loosely organized 'evaluative preface + telling' conversational routine. Rather than two separate actions being carried out as a succession of independent turn-constructional units, they are now collapsed into one action and one turn unit. Often these collapsed structures are deployed for the specific purpose of proposing to close down the topic or sequence pursued thus far. They are in essence 'summary assessments' (Schegloff 2007: 186), allowing the speaker to both capture the gist of what has transpired so far and evaluate it in one single turn unit (see Couper-Kuhlen and Thompson 2008 for examples).

In sum, like Left dislocation and Concession, Extraposition is another case where the developmental trajectory extends from a conversational routine with two independent actions organized in a sequential fashion, to a bipartite grammatical construction with integrated and dependent components implementing a single action.

3. Conclusions and open questions

A path of grammaticalization from vertical to horizontal development like that hypothesized here for Left dislocation, Concession, and Extraposition appears all the more plausible when we consider that there is evidence of a similar development for other bipartite structures, including Conditionals (Haiman 1978), postposed Causal constructions (Ford 1993; Couper-Kuhlen 1996), and Right dislocations

(Geluykens 1987; Couper-Kuhlen and Ono 2007). These constructions have also been related to interactional sequences in discourse.

Yet for other bipartite constructions, a vertical-to-horizontal path of grammaticalization may appear less plausible: this is the case, for instance, with the Pseudo-cleft construction (Hopper 2004; Hopper and Thompson 2008) and so-called 'Projector' constructions such as '*the thing is*', including its equivalents in German (Günthner 2008). The problem here is that, although related patterns involving fragments and chunks of discourse are found in conversation, the projecting parts of these constructions invariably have dependent syntax: i.e. they are not attested as independent actions in conversation. It is thus more difficult to argue that their grammaticalized forms originate in interactional sequences of actions.

A number of questions pose themselves at the conclusion of this chapter. Do all dual-action (i.e. interactional) routines lend themselves to being 'collapsed' into a single bipartite structure? If there are bipartite structures which do not originate in dual-action conversational routines, where do they come from? And finally, how far can the vertical-to-horizontal developmental process argued for here plausibly be said to reach? Will it account for cases of grammaticalization which are not bipartite? All of these are open questions at the moment. It is to be hoped that this chapter will have contributed to stimulating an investigation of them.

CHAPTER 35

GRAMMATICALIZATION AND LEXICALIZATION

DOUGLAS LIGHTFOOT

1. Introduction

During the rise of scholarly activity on grammaticalization studies, particularly during the 1980s and 1990s, one was hard pressed to find complementary work in the related area of lexicalization studies. No doubt this stemmed from several causes, among them the fact that grammaticalization as a field (and with it, historical linguistics) underwent something of a popular revival, and thus attracted much of the scholarly attention; but it was also largely through the recognition of much language change phenomena associated with grammaticalization that scholars began to take more notice by the early years of the 21st century of the seemingly opposite or parallel type of change we call lexicalization. Grammaticalization research has thus served as a sort of gateway to lexicalization research, and it continues to do so. Another reason for the relatively recent and relatively sparse lexicalization agenda has its roots in the patchwork labelling landscape we have beheld for years. One cannot investigate a phenomenon if it is not clear what the object, or in this case, the entire (sub-)area of investigation is. Recent work, especially by Brinton and Traugott (2005), Himmelmann (2004), Hopper and Traugott (2003), and Lehmann (2002a) has assisted in narrowing and refining the notions of what lexicalization as a type of change entails.

This chapter begins with a partial overview of the study of lexicalization phenomena to date, necessarily in conjunction with grammaticalization. Various commonalities and differences between the two are examined. I then highlight certain problem areas raised in the research, with emphasis placed on the part–whole relationship of the structures under consideration, and the ongoing challenge of handling troublesome categorization such as derivational affixation. Examples are used for the most part from Germanic. I then conclude with suggestions for future pathways of investigation.

2. Competing notions and consensus on grammaticalization and lexicalization

Grammaticalization and lexicalization may both refer to synchronic and diachronic processes, as well as to theoretical frameworks. Traugott (2005: 1702) identifies the basic commonality between the two among most researchers as regarding '...the pairing of meaning and form, and the extent to which this pairing is systematic or idiosyncratic'. Major stumbling blocks in further determining the relationship between grammaticalization and lexicalization (a necessary step in understanding the two types of changes) have been the recognition among most that grammar and lexicon are not mutually exclusive categories, that in a sense the lexicon arguably entails all words and certain word parts, regardless of their being more grammatical/systematic or more lexical/idiosyncratic, and that linguists have too often mixed lexicalization with degrammaticalization. The following brief, two-part survey profiles how notions such as these of grammaticalization and lexicalization in the literature have varied, and how relatively recently more of a consensus exists.

2.1. Varying concepts of grammaticalization and lexicalization

Meillet (1958[1912]) and Kuryłowicz (1975[1965]) included types of change such as phrase > compound > derivation > inflection in their discussion of grammaticalization, though there is much debate as to how one would demarcate the area of the more lexical from the more grammatical here. Kuryłowicz (p. 52) also termed lexicalization a reverse process of grammaticalization, which perhaps added to the terminological uncertainty in recent times. Meillet (1912: 138–9) put forth the reconstructed Old High German form **hiu tagu* 'this day, today' yielding Modern German *heute* 'today' as an example of grammaticalization, though to many it appears a good candidate for lexicalization, since it is difficult to gauge the grammaticality accrued from an adverbial phrase changing to an adverb. At a time when some, excluding Lehmann, considered degrammaticalization to be similar in nature to lexicalization,[1] Lehmann (1995a[1982]: 19) writes: 'No cogent examples of degrammaticalization have been found.' Perhaps instead of inspiring researchers to seek out examples of degrammaticalization, or some sort of lexicalization, this comment was mistakenly accepted as conflating lexicalization with degrammaticalization by many and they more readily sought out instances of grammaticalization instead of (at the expense of?) evidence for lexicalization. While many have likewise viewed Bybee (1985) as a catalyst for work in this field, the notion there of a lexical–derivational–inflectional continuum may have led some to assume there is a cross-linguistic diachronic path proposed, but that full continuum was only meant to be a synchronic and typological tool, as noted by Brinton and Traugott (2005: 86). Thus a lack of clarity between lexicalization and grammaticalization has been on hand since the coinage of the term 'grammaticalization'.

As grammaticalization studies began to gain momentum in the 1980s and 1990s, the vast majority naturally held grammaticalization as the focus, and it was only at times that lexicalization might also receive mention. Lehmann (1995a) does not comment extensively on lexicalization, but he states, for instance, that a noun developing into a derivational affix is an example of lexicalization, which can be confusing considering the typical cline of grammaticalization indicating that words can develop into affixes (e.g. Heine, Claudi, and Hünnemeyer present the cline of discourse > syntax > morphology > morphophonemics > zero (1991: 13)). In Lehmann's later work (1989; 1995b), there is a sharper recognition that both processes entail a reductive component, that they may be on hand in parallel fashion, or that they proceed sequentially. A certain amount of ambiguity still exists in Lehmann (1989) in terms of the extent to which a given item may undergo one or both changes (see e.g. Lightfoot 2005), but this is one of the first works to deal with lexicalization as a full-fledged topic along with grammaticalization.

Heine et al. (1991) explicitly raise the issue of lexicalization several times in their handbook on grammaticalization, though they do not go in depth into the topic. They indicate that the issue is problematic and deserving of further attention (pp. 3, 26, 95), and interestingly note that most authors agree that 'when words belonging to an open class, like that of nouns, develop into closed class words such as adverbs, this constitutes an instance of grammaticalization' (p. 3). If lexicalization were to be an opposite notion, as many have thought, then this assertion runs counter to Hopper and Traugott (1993: 127), who state that closed-class to open-

[1] Ramat (1992: 549–51) refers to degrammaticalization as entailing lexicalization, and characterizes degrammaticalization as being 'the contrary' (p. 549) of grammaticalization. Thus one can construe lexicalization as being the opposite of grammaticalization.

class development (*to up the ante*) among other recruitment devices for the lexicon such as metalinguistic talk (German *duzen* and French *tutoyer* from *du* and *tu*, meaning 'to use the familiar form of address') and acronym usage (e.g. *scuba* 'self-contained underwater breathing apparatus') are just lexicalization. An explanation of the types of lexicalization is not on hand, however, which fairly easily leads to criticism of the unidirectionality hypothesis,[2] since at this point one can interpret closed-class items becoming open-class items as grammatical material becoming lexical material, as in *to up* and *to off*, and that is confusingly labelled as the opposite-sounding process from grammaticalization. Part of Hopper and Traugott's reasoning that the above sorts of lexicalization are not counterexamples to unidirectionality is that 'lexicalization is a process distinct from grammaticalization, is not unidirectional, and can recruit material of all kinds', and that this is some general notion of lexicon enrichment (1993: 127). Here one thus has the beginnings of the case that there must be various sorts of lexicalization, and somehow linguists need clearer distinctions of the types.

Oddly, it is only Heine, et al. (1991: 262, fn. 6) during this period who note Anttila's (1989: 151) claim that any new lexical item undergoes lexicalization, even if it is an open-class noun developing into a closed-class adverb. One would have expected this citation in the second edition of Hopper and Traugott (2003), as they continue to embrace the notion of multiple types of lexicalization, adding importantly that the type of lexicalization that is brought about abruptly is not to be considered related to grammaticalization at all, which itself is a gradual process (p. 134). Any such conversions (such as *ism* lexicalized to a noun and *up* lexicalized to a verb, metatalk, and acronym-like language) entail instantaneity, which rules them out from being considered somehow relational to grammaticalization. I infer that Hopper and Traugott do seem to associate gradual change with lexicalization arising from univerbation, regardless of whether the outcome is a lexical or grammatical item. They appear to present syntagmas and complex lexemes becoming a simple lexeme as examples of lexicalization, such as *gar* 'spear' plus *leac* 'leek' becoming *garlic* and *have to* becoming the modal-like *hafta*. Thus they are implicitly in harmony with Anttila above on any type of lexeme being the outcome of a kind of lexicalization, and they likewise acknowledge that lexicalization along with grammaticalization can be working together, as claimed in numerous works from this time (Hopper and Traugott 2003: 134–5).

Some of the works intertwining lexicalization and grammaticalization in the 1990s do not attempt to distinguish between types of lexicalization which are briefly noted in Hopper and Traugott (2003: 134). Giacalone Ramat (1998: 121) writes that she wishes to 'rethink the traditional view according to which grammaticalization and lexicalization are quite distinct, even opposite processes. Rather,

[2] Campbell (2001b) states: 'instances of conversion of grammatical material into lexical items are clearly against the unidirectionality claim' (p. 131).

they seem to be complementary or overlapping and processes of change such as loss of autonomy or univerbation are similar both in grammar and in the lexicon'. Van der Auwera (1999: 132–4) associates higher productivity with grammaticalized Dutch prefixes and non-productivity with lexicalized prefixes, but he also asserts that relevant meanings of prefixes can be both grammaticalized and lexicalized. Wischer (2000) makes a number of noteworthy comments regarding the nature of lexicalization[3] with respect to grammaticalization. She claims Early Modern English *methinks* underwent desyntacticization from Old English *me ðincð* 'it seems to me', and was then recognized as its own whole symbol, thus it was lexicalized. Like Bauer (1983), Wischer considers this type of lexicalization to be necessarily gradual, and thereby makes it a somewhat parallel process to grammaticalization. *Methinks* is also described as grammaticalizing after it became a collocation, since it developed immediately into an adverbial marker of evidentiality (Wischer 2000: 363–4). Wischer also associates demotivation with lexicalization, characterizes it differently from degrammaticalization, and gives a brief overview of varying representations of both lexicalization and grammaticalization. Mithun (2001) examines how a stative verb in Mohawk, *-kowanen* 'be large', changed into a derivational clitic, *=kó́wa*, to function as an augmentative nominalizer, thus differentiating 'cat' from 'panther', for example. She states that the proper context and routinization allowed first for gradual lexicalization, thus fading the semantics and setting the stage for a reanalysis of the item's grammatical structure into a nominalizer. Van der Auwera (2002) combines grammaticalization and lexicalization analyses, and treats both wide and narrow notions of degrammaticalization as separate from lexicalization, but lexicalization remains for him one broad concept (i.e. inclusive of conversions and all means of making of lexicon). Norde (2001: 237) also highlights that lexicalization should be considered separately from degrammaticalization, since there could be abrupt jumps along the cline of grammaticality from right to left, but her focus is not on what different processes may be involved in different types of lexicalization. Heine (2003: 166–7) likewise does not recognize abrupt changes like conversion to be tantamount to degrammaticalization, and situates them as belonging to a type of lexicalization unrelated to grammaticalization—a position in step with Hopper and Traugott (2003).

Important concepts to take from these preceding representative works are that they began to differentiate types of lexicalization, often from degrammaticalization. Degrammaticalization came to mean more that which is somehow an opposite process to grammaticalization, and thus began to free lexicalization from that oppositional sense. A recognition grew that there are broader and narrower notions of lexicalization, the broader one entailing anything entering the lexicon, and the narrower one excluding items such as acronyms, conversions, and metatalk

[3] The next good overview of lexicalization after Wischer is Brinton (2002).

on the grounds that those changes are inherently of a different nature due to being non-gradual. Just as many identify Christian Lehmann as a stimulus for the modern revival of grammaticalization studies in 1982, I see his work seven years later (Lehmann 1989) as being largely responsible for the still-growing research field of lexicalization (with respect to grammaticalization),[4] and thus it is fitting that his work continues into the next phase toward a conceptual consensus.

2.2. Toward a consensus

Lehmann (2002a) explicitly distinguishes a kind of broad lexicalization from a type of lexicality associated with meaning in terms of degree of concreteness (p. 14). But while Lehmann's version of broad lexicalization is supposed to encompass anything 'belonging to the inventory', he goes on to claim that 'lexicalization and grammaticalization are reductive processes' and that 'we may reasonably speak of lexicalization only with respect to complex units' (p. 15). This leaves one to wonder how conversion would be dealt with, such as the new English noun *ism*. Lehmann (1995b: 1256) treated such cases as degrammaticalization, but here it would seem not to fit a reductive instance which we would 'reasonably speak of', so perhaps Lehmann (2002a) is a harbinger of the position in Heine (2003) and Hopper and Traugott (2003), where conversions and the like are understood as a type of lexicalization unrelated to the changes associated with grammaticalization.

Lehmann (2002a) also explicitly expands the lens through which linguists examine language. Instead of focusing on a single element or a larger word to which it belongs grammaticalizing or lexicalizing, for example, Lehmann states: 'it is the construction of which the element is a constituent which may embark on either course. If this is so, then the grammaticalization of a construction does not entail the grammaticalization of any of its component elements' (p. 7). The author presents indirect discourse as an example to show that although sentence (1b) has a more complex and grammaticalized structure than (1a), no specific element underwent the change—it is the whole structure:

(1) a. Irvin apologized, he didn't hit me on purpose.
    b. Irvin said he didn't hit me on purpose.

Also worth mentioning is the inherent variation of degree of grammaticality and lexicality in word classes. Lehmann notes, for example, that 'there are more lexical and more grammatical adpositions' (2002a: 1), that there are lexical and

4 Criticism of the unidirectionality hypothesis has also fueled the research engines for lexicalization and degrammaticalization, especially (e.g. Norde 2001). Indeed, Fischer, Norde, and Perridon (2004: 2) rightly note that Campbell's edited issue of *Language Sciences* (2001a) 'threw up quite a bit of dust in the grammaticalization field.' Cowie (1995) also provided a constructive impetus in the form of criticism.

grammatical attributes in all word classes, and that 'it is not the case that the so-called minor parts of speech have something particularly grammatical about them' (p. 8).[5] Hopper and Traugott (2003: 5) profess the same belief, for example, in discussing 'lexical derivational morphemes' (such as *-ling* in *duckling*) as opposed to 'grammatical derivational morphemes' which change the grammatical category of a word (such as agentive *-er* in English).[6] This is noteworthy because previous work has not made strong claims on gradience in lexicality. Traugott (2005: 1711), in fact, puts forth in discussion on grammatical material becoming more grammatical, 'There does not appear to be anything comparable in the lexical domain.'[7] Her opinion has long since changed.

Himmelmann (2004) shares a number of stances with Lehmann (2002a), such as recognizing univerbation in both lexicalization and grammaticalization, and seeing the entire construction (syntagmatic context) as what undergoes grammaticalization. Thus Himmelmann states that the elements with which an item grammaticalizes tend to belong to a growing set, and terms this context expansion 'host-class expansion' (2004: 32). He also recognizes a broad type of lexicalization that can be fed by any type of linguistic material, but like Lehmann agrees that change entailing univerbation is the more interesting and prevalent type of lexicalization when compared with grammaticalization. Though Himmelmann does not see these two types of change as opposites, he finds an opposition with respect to host-class expansion. Grammaticalization has it, as elements are generalized so as to be paradigmatically or syntagmatically suitable for a growing number of contexts, while lexicalization tends to lead to a single context's instantiation of univerbation (p. 36). Himmelmann deviates from some of the recent literature by writing that lexicalization in terms of univerbation is abrupt (2004: 36). This blurs the line somewhat with respect to the broader (including abrupt instances) and more narrow (usually gradual and unmotivated) types of lexicalization described more and more in the field.

The current state of the field is best summarized by Brinton and Traugott (2005).[8] Their *Lexicalization and Language Change*, which is actually better put as 'Lexicalization and Grammaticalization', provides an extensive research survey, first portraying the vast variety of definitions associated with both types of change, then presenting case studies utilizing their proposed definitional framework, as well as suggestions for further work. They arrive at the following definitions:

[5] A similar conclusion comes from Mithun (1997), where she provides counter-evidence in the form of derivational affixation to the characterization of so-called closed classes having relatively few members. See also Brinton (2002), who discusses the relative lexicality of adjectives and adverbs.

[6] I do question, however, why the cline of lexicality is removed from the first chapter in Hopper and Traugott's (2003) second edition. Similar clines remain in ch. 5, though.

[7] The date on this work is deceptively late. By at least 2003, Traugott no longer held this view (Lightfoot 2005: 584).

[8] An opposing view is Fischer (2008: 355, 372 fn 10).

> Lexicalization is the change whereby in certain linguistic contexts speakers use a syntactic construction or word formation as a new contentful form with formal and semantic properties that are not completely derivable or predictable from the constituents of the construction or the word formation pattern. Over time there may be further loss of internal constituency and the item may become more lexical. (Brinton and Traugott 2005: 96)

Simple conversions and acronyms which are easily predictable are thus ruled out under this definition—a certain amount of opacity or non-literalness is called for. Common threads from previous work in the field here include: a non-instantaneous nature (i.e. gradualness of development), a relatively narrow version of lexicalization (since conversions are ruled out), and acceptance of degrees of lexicality, univerbation, and host-class reduction (or decrease in pattern productivity and possibly decrease in token productivity) (Brinton and Traugott 2005: 96–7). Above all, this process has material at its outcome that is understood as semantically contentful (p. 98).

As this narrow version of lexicalization is in terminological conflict with lexicalization as understood in general, non-grammaticalization-oriented linguistics (i.e. where any item enters the lexical inventory), I suggest we always qualify it as 'narrow lexicalization'.

Grammaticalization, on the other hand, is described in the following way:

> Grammaticalization is the change whereby in certain linguistic contexts speakers use parts of a construction with a grammatical function. Over time the resulting grammatical item may become more grammatical by acquiring more grammatical functions and expanding its host-classes. (Brinton and Traugott 2005: 99)

Similarities with narrow lexicalization thus include: gradualness, polar semantic fluctuation (toward either opacity or generalization); gradient shifting is typical,[9] and a tendency toward univerbation (pp. 99–100). These elements overlap with Brinton and Traugott's (p. 110) table.

Unlike lexicalization, Brinton and Traugott note, among other features, that the output of grammaticalization is of course an item of grammatical nature, and it has host-expansion (i.e. there is an increase in pattern and token productivity) (2005: 99–100).

Brinton and Traugott (2005) also discuss opposite types of phenomena, such as de- and anti-lexicalization, and de- and anti-grammaticalization, but I refer the reader to the relevant sections of this volume for those topics. The literature on lexicalization at this point makes it clear that narrow lexicalization is not the reverse change of grammaticalization, though confusion did exist earlier.

Finishing this non-exhaustive survey of lexicalization in relation with grammaticalization, I briefly mention the works of Haas (2007), Trousdale (2008b), and

[9] i.e. movement along the continuum between linguistic categories (Brinton and Traugott 2005: 27).

Table 35.1. Parallels between lexicalization and grammaticalization (Brinton and Traugott 2005: 110)

	Lexicalization	Grammaticalization
Gradualness	+	+
Unidirectionality	+	+
Fusion	+	+
Coalescence	+	+
Demotivation	+	+
Metaphorization/metonymization	+	+
Detcategorialization	–	+
Bleaching	–	+
Subjectification	–	+
Productivity	–	+
Frequency	–	+
Typological generality	–	+

+ characteristic of; - not characteristic of.

Fischer (2008). Haas's treatment of English *each other* conceives of (narrow) lexicalization and grammaticalization as being non-overlapping phenomena. (Narrow) lexicalization primarily entails univerbation and fossilization, while grammaticalization primarily entails semantic, pragmatic, and syntactic context expansion (2007: 34). Haas concludes that the development of *each other* involves simultaneous (narrow) lexicalization and grammaticalization. Trousdale (2008b) uses a Construction Grammar approach to conclude that increasingly schematic constructions allow for a more grammatical function, while an increasingly substantive construction tends to allow for a more lexical/referential function.[10] Changes in possessive constructions from Old English to Middle English were indicative of grammaticalization, and from Middle English onward they were indicative of (narrow) lexicalization (Trousdale 2008b: 171–2). Trousdale also interestingly asserts that the initial stages of both processes elicit the most similarity in terms of increased productivity, generality, and loss of compositionality (p. 173). And most recently Fischer (2008) takes issue broadly with the assumptions and methodology of much work in the field of grammaticalization. Fischer proposes using analogy in order to understand what appears to be grammaticalization and (narrow)

[10] Cf. Brinton and Traugott's (2005: 104) scales of grammaticalization (G1–G2–G3), with the highest degree (G3) being inflections, and (narrow) lexicalization (L1–L2–L3), with the greatest degree (L3) being contentful simplexes ("e.g., *neighbor* < Old English *neah-ge-bur* 'near + dweller' "; p. 96).

lexicalization.[11] When doing so, she finds much similarity in the two types of changes, with a principal difference being that lexicalization takes place on a concrete token level, and grammaticalization on a combined token–type level (Fischer 2008: 352).

3. Problems

The main problem is a dearth of consensus on our terminology concerning lexicalization. This may be somewhat remedied by the label 'narrow lexicalization' and by Brinton and Traugott (2005), but the discussion will continue due to problems such as deciding what level of a structure to focus upon, and considering what type of change best describes hybrid-like cases such as derivational affixation.

3.1 Parts or wholes?

Lehmann (2002a: 7) maintains it is not individual elements but rather a whole construction which undergoes either lexicalization or grammaticalization. This seems to be, however, a question of degree. He adds that though one considers (narrow) lexicalization in terms of complex units, 'grammaticalization concerns a complex unit and may simultaneously affect *in particular one of its constituents*' (2002a: 15, emphasis DL). But if word categories vary in their degrees of lexicality similarly to gradience found in grammaticality, and the mechanisms of narrow lexicalization and grammaticalization are so similar (Fischer 2008; Trousdale 2008a; 2008b), then can narrow lexicalization not also affect in particular one constituent? This seems quite clear in cases of reduction, such as Germanic compounds with *man* as the second constituent which undergoes more change. Early and late Old High German illustrate this in the compound *gomman(n)* 'husband, man', made up of Germanic **gom* 'man' and **man* 'man':

(2) Old High German (Tatian 7, 9, from Douglas Lightfoot 2006)
Anna . . . lebeta mit ira gommanne sibun iâr fon ira magadheiti
Anna lived with her husband seven years from her girlhood
'Anna lived with her husband seven years from (the time) of her girlhood.'

The man/husband word *gomman* displays the dative singular suffix *-e*, which vanishes with other declension by late Old High German in Notker:

[11] See Lehmann (2004: 160–62) for an opposing viewpoint.

(3) sô êrsámero cómen chíndo (Notker, II, 63, 11, from Douglas Lightfoot 2006)
such honourable man children
'of such honourable boys'

By Middle High German, *gomman* has virtually disappeared. In Modern German, *man* again undergoes affixation, as noted in standard references. Compare the reduction of stress and generalizing of meaning to 'person' in compound-like structures such as English *ombudsman* and *marksman.*

The point is: do we gain anything by considering these examples of reduction somehow in association with narrow lexicalization instead of simply as demorphologization? They are really one and the same, unless there is somehow also parallel or simultaneous grammaticalization taking place. And if there is an example of both narrow lexicalization and grammaticalization occurring, such as in Lehmann's (2004: 169) adverbial example *aufgrund* 'on the basis of', from the preposition *auf* and the noun *Grund*, how does one really keep the two processes' effects of reduction apart to say with certainty that first there is (narrow) lexicalization only and then there is grammaticalization?

3.2 Derivational affixation

The level focusing issue spills over into derivation, as noted by Norde (2009: 186) in discussion of Brinton and Traugott (2005): 'it is not always clear whether B&T are referring to the derivational affix per se (e.g. *-wise*), the derived form as a whole (e.g., *clockwise*), or the historical development of the suffix (... from a noun meaning "manner").' I would suggest that due to the in-between nature of derivation it deserves more attention. Some constructions with derivational affixation are poor examples of narrow lexicalization: they can be fairly productive (e.g. English *-wise*, German *-weise*), can become semantically generalized (e.g. Germanic **haid* 'way, appearance, person, position' > German *-heit* 'characteristic of, quality of'), can belong to somewhat open classes (recall footnote 5 and Mithun 1997), and can be componential (as attested in the literature on affixoids, e.g. Lightfoot 2005: 589–90). The larger construction, the suffix's co-constituent, and the suffix itself all need looking into in each instance for each language, with special care taken that morphosyntactic variants (i.e. heterosemy) are not confused in the given analysis (Brinton and Traugott 2005: 75). And if Heine et al. (1991) can point to 'source structures' as conceptual origins for grammaticalizing elements, can there not also be a similar phenomenon for grammatical derivation? Study of derivational suffixes' source structures are needed to help examine their relative grammatical status (Brinton and Traugott 2005: 35–6; Hopper and Traugott 2003: 5). And if one looks at a co-constituent, e.g. Germanic **gom* 'man', in a construction like Old High German *gomman* 'man', can one discern by extension something like a *co-source structure*? Early in their histories, a number of high frequency German suffixes (*-lich* -ly, *-heit* -hood, *-tum* -dom) had co-constituents of a person-oriented nature (see e.g. Douglas Lightfoot 2007: 69–70). One example is Middle High German *maget* + *tuom* 'girl' + 'status', or 'virginity'.

4. Conclusion

The challenge remains for examining narrow lexicalization in relation to grammaticalization, not the least of which is that we continue to try demarcating categories which we hold to be gradient and non-discrete (Fischer 2008). Brinton and Traugott (2005: chs 5, 6) articulate many points to work on, but I trust that the work outlined here helps to pave the way for continued fruitful research. Parts and wholes discernment and derivation are just two more areas requiring attention, but along the way to dealing with that and other issues is the greater problem of better defining the 'core notion of "grammar", "grammatical category", [and] "grammatical function"' (Diewald 2007: abstract).

CHAPTER 36

GRAMMATICALIZATION AND PRAGMATICALIZATION

GABRIELE DIEWALD

1. Introduction

The title of this chapter implies that processes of grammaticalization and pragmaticalization are interrelated in some relevant way. The following pages will explore in how far this assumption holds.

For several years the relation between grammaticalization and pragmaticalization has been discussed controversially in grammaticalization research, as both notions are associated with two linguistic concepts which are usually seen as strictly separated from each other: grammar on the one hand and pragmatics on the other. While grammar is taken to be the backbone of linguistic structure, strictly organized into paradigms, subject to rules and displaying abstract meanings which in many cases seem to be difficult to relate to pragmatic functions, pragmatics is typically seen as the domain motivated by the communicative needs of the participants of the linguistic interaction and subject to various types of idiosyncratic, hardly regular conditions and restrictions of language usage. Thus, it looks as if the two processes are diametrically opposed to each other from the conceptual point of view. Recent theoretical work in grammaticalization theory as well as the growing body of detailed case studies of grammaticalization, however, has led to the suspicion that grammar and pragmatics might not be as separate as assumed, and that it might be worthwhile to discuss the issue afresh. This is the motivating factor for this chapter.

Sections 2 and 3 attempt a terminological clarification of both terms independently from each other; section 4 explores their mutual relations. The basic hypothesis is that fundamental features of grammar itself are rooted in pragmatics, and that therefore there is reason to interpret pragmaticalization as an integral part of grammaticalization.

2. Grammaticalization and grammar

The term 'grammaticalization' is ambiguous, as it is used to refer to diachronic processes (i.e. development of grammatical functionality in an item) as well as to synchronic stages (i.e. degrees of grammatical functionality in synchronic items compared). As the target of the whole process of grammaticalization is usually referred to as 'grammar', it is important to define not only what is understood by grammaticalization but also what is understood by grammar.

2.1. The process: grammaticalization

The essence of grammaticalization is nicely summarized by Lehmann (2004: 155): 'Grammaticalization of a linguistic sign is a process in which it loses in autonomy by becoming subject to constraints of the linguistic system.' Grammaticalization in its dynamic, procedural aspects is known to be a complex, multifactorial type of language change, i.e. it does not consist of a single, homogeneous process but of a number of interacting processes: 'Grammaticalization is a process leading from lexemes to grammatical formatives. A number of semantic, syntactic and phonological processes interact in the grammaticalization of morphemes and of whole constructions,' Lehmann (1995a[1982]: p. v) Summing up the discussion of the last decades of the 20th century, Traugott (2003: 644) states that 'early grammaticalization can therefore be seen as a complex set of correlated changes', which she specifies as follows:[1]

> i. structural decategorialization; ii. shift from membership in a relatively open set to membership in a relatively closed one (i.e., from lexical category to syntactic operator category) in the context of a specific construction; iii. bonding (erasure of morphological boundaries) within a construction; iv. semantic and pragmatic shift from more to less

[1] Similar observations have been made by many others, e.g. Haspelmath (1999); Heine (2003: 579ff.).

referential meaning via invited inferencing [...] [and, in later stages] phonological attrition, which may result in the development of paradigmatic zero [...]. (Traugott 2003: 644)

Consequently, the distinctive and unique feature of grammaticalization is generally seen in its particular combination and serialization of several processes and stages, which—among other things—find their repercussion in grammaticalization scales and paths, and complex scenarios of successive contexts and constructions.

It should be noted that pragmatic factors and motives are major driving forces in the early stages of this complex process as well as in the dynamics of its progress. Some of these factors have been dealt with extensively in prior research: (i) the motives/factors of economy on one hand and explicitness/expressivity on the other, (ii) cognitive processes and rhetorical devices like metaphorical and metonymic transfer, and general pragmatic strategies like conversational implicature and invited inferencing, and (iii) contexts and constructions. As point (i) is generally discussed in studies on language change, it is not taken up here (cf. Diewald 2006). The same applies to (iii), which is the topic of many recent publications (see also Gisborne and Patten, Chapter 8 above). One aspect of (ii), however, though also broadly discussed in the past, must be briefly taken up here, as it touches on the issue of pragmaticalization. It is the notion of subjectification. In line with Traugott (1989; 1999a; Traugott and Dasher 2002), subjectification is seen here as a particular type of semantic change, i.e. as a semantic process which leads to a higher degree of speaker involvement encoded as an inherent semantic feature in the linguistic item, the lexeme, itself:

Subjectification is the semasiological process whereby SP/Ws [speakers/writers] come over time to develop meanings for Ls [lexemes] that encode or externalize their perspectives and attitudes as constrained by the communicative world of the speech event, rather than by the so-called 'real-world' characteristics of the event or situation referred to. (Traugott and Dasher 2002: 30)

Finally, the authors classify subjectification as a type of metonymy: 'And, most importantly, subjectification can be understood as a type of metonymy-association with SP/W in the strategic course of speaking/writing' (Traugott and Dasher 2002: 81). Subjectification or subjective meaning, i.e. speaker-based meaning, has a very close natural connection to pragmatics, as the concept of 'speaker' is the central feature of any pragmatic aspect of language (cf. sections 3 and 4).

To sum up this subsection, we may say that grammaticalization is a complex, multi-layered process which is motivated, triggered, and steered by pragmatic factors and which leads 'into grammar'.

2.2. The target: grammar

Though the target of the diachronic process of grammaticalization is grammar, the notion of grammar itself has received astonishingly little attention in grammaticalization studies. This shortcoming was deplored as early as 1992 by Himmelmann: 'Work in grammaticalization also hardly ever makes explicit the concept of grammar underlying a given investigation' (1992: 2).

The notion of grammar is typically treated as an unexplained and presupposed basic concept from which the term 'grammaticalization' is derived. Very often this amounts to circularity of the following type: 'Grammaticalization' is 'items becoming part of grammar', and 'grammar' is built up by 'items having undergone a process of grammaticalization' (see Diewald 2010 for extensive treatment). This lack of a definition of the fundamental concept of grammar is part of the difficulties one meets in the attempt to delimit the domains of grammaticalization and pragmaticalization.

Nevertheless, there is broad agreement that the following three features are essential ingredients for any definition of grammar:[2]

- obligatoriness;
- paradigmatic integration;
- relational meaning.

The first two features, the obligatoriness and paradigmaticity of grammatical signs, are closely linked to each other. The paradigmatic integration of a sign, or its paradigmaticity, refers to the fact that the members of a grammatical paradigm, which as a whole is constituted by a categorical value (i.e. the common semantico-functional denominator of the category in question, which in an abbreviating manner is expressed in category labels like 'tense' or 'voice'), are closely linked to each other, and often display intra-categorial sub-groupings (cf. e.g. Lehmann 1995a). 'Obligatoriness' refers to the fact that, if there is a paradigm encompassing a set of oppositive values, a choice has to be made between its members, and there is no way of omitting this information. The two notions of obligatoriness and paradigmaticity also figure prominently in Lehmann's grammaticalization parameters.

As is well known, neither 'obligatoriness' nor 'paradigmaticity' refers to absolute phenomena; instead, both notions are a matter of degree—which, however, even if an important issue, cannot be discussed here (see Wiemer and Bisang 2004; Himmelmann 1992; 2004; Lehmann 1995a; Plungian 1998; Diewald 2010). The third criterion, the relational meaning structure, is crucial to the discussion of grammaticalization and pragmaticalization. The specific relational meaning structure of grammatical signs has to do with their inherent indexicality,[3] which was first mentioned by Jespersen 1992[1924], Bühler (1982[1934]), and Jakobson (1971[1957]),

[2] For a detailed discussion on this issue see Diewald (2010), cf. also Bybee, Perkins, and Pagliuca (1994: 2); Dahl (2001); Plungian (1998); Mel'čuk (1976: 84).

[3] The term 'indexical' is taken here in the sense of Peirce to be a rough hypernym of all kinds of 'pointing processes'.

who dubbed indexical grammatical signs 'shifters'. Since then many other linguists have applied this notion (e.g. Anderson 1985: 172; Traugott and König 1991: 189; Diewald 1991; 2006: 414–16; Langacker 1985; 2002), which—somewhat reducing the complexity of the argumentation—may be summarized as follows: grammatical categories share as their common semantic denominator a relational structure which establishes a link between two points, namely, the linguistic element the category modifies and some other entity. This latter entity, the anchoring point of the relation, is the deictic *origo* or one of its 'derivatives'. The deictic *origo* is defined here with reference to Bühler as the source or zero point of the 'coordinate system of "subjective orientation", in which all partners in communication are and remain caught up' (1982[1934]: 118). It is an abstract point typically located in the speaker, but—again following Bühler—transferrable to other locations, i.e. other origos in other 'pointing fields', which though no longer truly deictic, still contain the relational structure, and thus can be traced back to their original pragmatic anchoring. As this issue will be dealt with in section 4, it may be noted here as a brief summary that the third defining feature of grammatical signs is their indexical potential, which enables them to link linguistic elements of varying size and function in relation to one another or to some relevant non-linguistic entity.

3. Pragmaticalization

The term 'pragmaticalization' was not introduced in its own right, but (to the best of my knowledge) was used to set off some types of change from grammaticalization (see Erman and Kotsinas 1993 for an early use of the term). To be more precise, the notion of pragmaticalization was employed to tackle problems arising in the diachronic development of discourse markers and modal particles. As the terms grammaticalization and pragmaticalization are the very focus of this contribution, it is necessary to take a closer look at this issue (see Diewald 2006; 2010).

Typically, the relevant studies are very reluctant to subsume the rise of particles and discourse markers under the heading of grammaticalization (see e.g. Zayzon 2009: 55). In her work on *I think*, Aijmer (1997) draws a sharp line between grammaticalization on the one hand and pragmaticalization on the other. In her view, the former process 'is concerned with the derivation of grammatical forms and constructions (mood, aspect, tense, etc.) from words and lexical structure', whereas 'pragmaticalized items', i.e. items having undergone a process of pragmaticalization, involve a 'speaker's attitude to the hearer' (p. 2). Therefore, Aijmer (pp. 6ff.) argues for a separate 'cline of pragmaticalization' in parallel to grammaticalization scales, without however providing clear criteria for distinguishing both processes. The criterion of non truth-conditionality, which is addressed by Aijmer as having 'overriding importance for distinguishing between grammatical(ized) and pragmatical(ized) elements' (Aijmer p. 3) is not 100 per cent selective, as there are categories like e.g. the active vs. passive distinction, which clearly are non-truth-conditional and at the same time grammatical in the conventional sense.

Günthner (1999: 437) considers it plausible to treat the fact that the functional domain in the development of German *obwohl* from conjunction to discourse marker shifts from 'purely grammatical functions' to 'conversational functions' as an argument in favour of a distinct process of pragmaticalization, but goes on to point out that the development of discourse particles in many formal and semantic aspects is indistinguishable from 'proper' grammaticalization processes, as defined in Lehmann's (1985) grammaticalization parameters.

In a similar line of reasoning, Barth-Weingarten and Couper-Kuhlen (2002), who treat the development of discourse functions in final *though* in English, suggest that pragmaticalization ought to be subsumed as a specific subtype under the broad heading of grammaticalization, which deviates in some aspects from prototypical cases of grammaticalization, but is too similar to it to be treated as 'a separate, independently definable process' (p. 357). Finally, Günthner and Matz highlight the dilemma:

> This type of change which leads to discourse and pragmatic markers, to elements which organize structure, and contextualize discourse with respect to discourse-pragmatic concerns and not with respect to sentence-grammatical concerns (e.g. congruence, binding), contradicts classical grammaticalization. (2004: 98)

That is, while in her paper of 1999 Günthner still tries to reconcile the conflicting observations, in the later paper this effort is abandoned. Despite the fact that the diachronic development of discourse markers in all relevant structural and semantic aspects is a paradigm example of grammaticalization, the authors state a 'contradiction' to grammaticalization. Without further qualifying how we should safely distinguish between 'sentence-grammatical concerns' and 'discourse-pragmatic concerns', the authors seem to regard the differentiation between these two areas as something that is given a priori, and as the cutting-edge criterion for subclassifying the field of language change under discussion.

This short survey of different suggestions on how to classify the diachronic development of discourse functions points to the fact that pragmatic meaning is generally not regarded to be part of grammar. The frontier line in this debate seems to run between 'true' grammatical function and 'merely' pragmatic function. It nicely illustrates the tendency of linguistics in general, and grammaticalization studies in particular, to regard the traditional set of familiar grammatical categories as the semantic-functional benchmark for judging grammatical categories on semantic-functional terms.

The common denominator of most of these studies is the following. As the diachronic processes creating those items are virtually indistinguishable from the diachronic processes leading to undisputable grammatical categories, it is an assumed difference in the direction of change, in the target domain, which is used to motivate the introduction of the notion of pragmaticalization. In other words, the term 'pragmaticalization' has been introduced into linguistic discussion to refer to the development towards a target domain, which usually is not thought of as being part of grammar, and therefore might be called a 'supposedly deviant target domain'. This state of affairs is set out in Figure 36.1, where the processes of grammaticalization and pragmaticalization are visualized as diverging into orthogonal directions. The arrow pointing towards the upper right-hand corner represents the process of grammaticalization in the narrow sense of the term, i.e. restricted to the traditionally accepted set of grammatical categories; the other arrow, pointing towards the lower right-hand corner, represents pragmaticalization, i.e. the development towards a target domain which is not usually included in the set of traditional grammatical categories, and therefore (to put it bluntly) might be called a 'deviant' target domain in contrast to the 'typical' target domain,

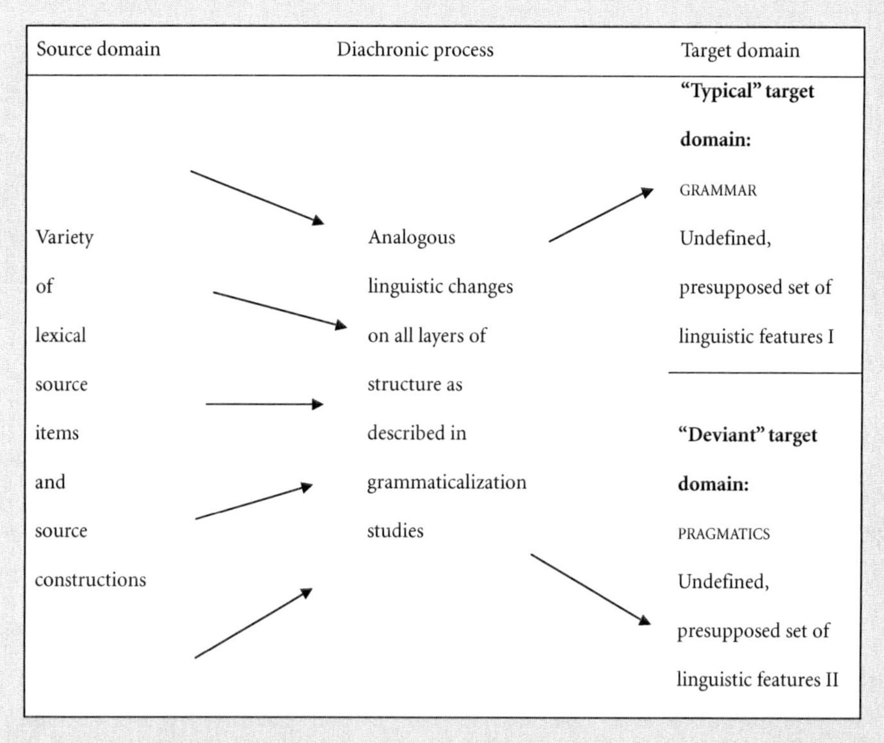

Fig. 36.1. Pragmaticalization understood as change towards a deviant target domain

which consists of the hitherto undisputed set of grammatical categories and distinctions (e.g. referred to in the quote by Günthner and Mutz 2004: 98).

An approach with a slightly different perspective is taken in a study on the development of Italian *tuttavia* from a temporal adverbial to a textual connective by Giacalone Ramat and Mauri (in press). The authors argue that this development is an instance of grammaticalization for functional and semantic reasons, although—as they demonstrate—those of Lehmann's parameters which refer to morphosyntactic processes are not distinctive in this case (see section 2 for a discussion of the grammaticalization parameters). In order to be able to subsume phenomena like the development of textual connectives and other 'pragmatic' markers under the heading of grammaticalization, the authors in a follow-up paper suggest distinguishing between standard and non-standard grammaticalization which they define as respectively displaying or not-displaying the reflexes of all grammaticalization parameters (Giacalone Ramat and Mauri 2009a). However, as not only the grammaticalization of 'pragmatic' markers but also the rise of other grammatical categories may display this behaviour and not show changes in all the six grammaticalization parameters, the distinction between nonstandard grammaticalization and standard grammaticalization does not indicate the border between the rise of pragmatic markers and other categories.[4]

Summarizing this discussion, it may be stated that the diachronic processes as they are observed in the large class of items which are usually called modal particles, discourse particles, and discourse markers are virtually indistinguishable from acknowledged cases of grammaticalization as far as their structural, semantic, and chronological features are concerned. The only difference lies in the fact that they lead to a supposedly 'deviant target domain', which is why the notion of 'pragmaticalization' was used to set these diachronic changes off from 'true' grammaticalization.

4. Pragmatic features of 'grammar'—or pragmaticalization as an integral part of grammaticalization

Taking up the issue of the definitional criteria of grammar (obligatoriness, paradigmatic integration, and relational meaning), which was briefly raised in section 2,

[4] Reactions in the complete set of all six grammaticalization parameters are typically found only in very old grammaticalization processes with a sufficiently long history of textual evidence.

this last part focuses on the notion of relational meaning. It lays out its deictic foundation and its major derivations, and, finally, ventures to suggest that pragmaticalization—if defined appropriately—may be seen as an integral part of grammaticalization.

The line of argument is as follows. Deictic signs (i.e. the prototypical instantiation of indexical signs) incorporate reference to the relevant communicative situation, in particular the respective current speaker. The current speaker functions as the anchoring point or *origo* from which the utterance emanates and to which the utterance is tied back by its deictic signs. In short; deictic signs locate the utterance or elements of it with respect to the speaker and thus, indisputably, are a core issue of pragmatics. If grammar (a grammatical sign) contains an indexical structure, it encodes 'pragmatic' information as part of its own inherent semantic structure. In other words; as grammar contains semanticized, schematized, and abstracted information about the localization of the utterance in the communicative situation, it is fundamentally rooted in pragmatics (cf. Givón 1979). To the extent that grammaticalization is the development of such an anchoring function in a linguistic item, it may be said that pragmaticalization is a sub-process of grammaticalization.

The following paragraphs give a more detailed account of the relational meaning of grammatical signs in their deictic, syntagmatic, and paradigmatic realizations, whereby the deictic realization is seen as the most prototypical, unmarked case, while the two latter realizations represent transferred or derived relational structures, in which the deictic anchoring is weakened or transformed from situational into syntagmatic or paradigmatic anchoring.

4.1. The deictic relation

As Jakobson (1971[1957]) has already shown, a large number of grammatical functions (e.g. tense, mood, nominal determination) are deictic in the strict sense of the term, i.e. they localize the linguistic entity they apply to with respect to the coordinates of the speaker, the deictic *origo* (Bühler 1982[1934]). In other words, a deictic relation is a relation between the actual speech situation, the deictic *origo*, and the linguistic utterance (or some part of it), i.e. a relation between the 'speech event' and the 'narrated event' in the sense of Jakobson (1971: 133). Thereby, the utterance is immediately linked to the communicative event. This link can be represented as a relational structure, i.e. a relation between a source via a path towards a goal (source → path → goal). A prototypical instance of deictic anchoring (a deictic process) displays a relational structure in which the speaker is the centre of the communicative universe, i.e. the deictic *origo* (i.e. the source and anchoring point) which is the point of departure of any cognitive and linguistic processing associated with a particular communicative event. Deictic signs, therefore, are defined as containing a directed relation between the *origo* and the denoted entity as part of their semantic content. The general meaning of this relational structure can be paraphrased as follows: 'the entity that is denoted with the help of this deictic sign is denoted in its relation to the actual speaker/the *origo*' (cf. Diewald 1991; Bühler 1982).

Deictic meaning—though not restricted to lexical elements—can be most conveniently illustrated by deictic local or temporal adverbials like the German local adverb *hier* 'here' in a sentence as *Die Katze liegt hier* ('The cat is lying here'). The deictic sign *hier* represents a directed relation between two elements of the situational context: the *origo*, which is the source, and the denoted entity, which is the goal of the deictic process, and which, due to further semantic features (i.e. dimension and distance), is specified as a local entity which is 'close' to the location of the speaker. Thus the meaning of *hier* can be paraphrased as a 'place that from the position of the speaker is regarded by the speaker as near, and is denoted as such'.

Deictic grammatical categories, like tense (which realizes the temporal perspectivization or localization of the scene described with respect to utterance time) and mood (which realizes a speaker-based factuality judgment of the scene described), instantiate a particular variation of the basic relational structure of deictic signs. A grammatical sign modifies another (lexical) sign by relating it to some other element, i.e. to some reference point lying outside both of them. That is, a grammatical sign establishes a link between the linguistic element it modifies and some other entity. A simple example, the grammatical category of preterite, may suffice here for illustration. The preterite (in languages like English or German) achieves the temporal perspectivization or localization of the scene described with respect to utterance time, i.e. the *origo*. In addition to this purely relational function, it also denotes a specific past value which encodes distance to the *origo* and contrasts with other values in the grammatical paradigm of temporal distinctions. Thus the function of the preterite in an example like *She wrote dozens of letters* is to give an instruction that might be paraphrased roughly as follows: 'Go to the deictic origo; from there interpret the narrated event as temporally distant.' The value of the preterite is in opposition to the unmarked value of the tense paradigm, the present tense, which in a parallel way can be paraphrased as: 'Go to the deictic origo; from there interpret the narrated event as temporally non-distant.'

Beyond grammatical categories displaying this type of clearly deictic relations, there are others which make use of a derived relational structure.

4.2. Derived indexical relations

In grammatical items the deictic relation very often is transferred from the genuinely deictic relation to the syntagmatic and paradigmatic plane of linguistic structure, thus producing different types of relational structure and layers of grammatical function. Although the derived relational structures are not deictic in the strict sense, they still represent the relevant relational structure of connecting the linguistic item which is modified by the grammatical sign in question to some other instance which in turn functions as the *origo*.

The transfer of that relational structure from the deictic to the syntagmatic plane leads for example to anaphoric and connective relations (e.g. anaphoric pointing devices, secondary tenses like pluperfect, markers of subjunctive relations, etc.). The transfer to the paradigmatic plane is slightly more complex and therefore needs some explanation.

The paradigmatic relation is not primarily concerned with single items (which figure prominently in Lehmann's grammaticalization parameters) but with the relations between the members of a paradigm, i.e. it is concerned with the paradigm as a relational structure where each member is defined by its relational meaning(s), which encode (nothing but) its position in the paradigm itself. A straightforward example is the closed-class paradigm of case distinctions in German, which expresses neither deictic relations like tense markers nor syntagmatic relations like conjunctions or concord markers. Instead, the meaning of each member of the paradigm consists of nothing but its position in relation to the other members, which is encoded as a derived relational structure. The nominative in languages like German represents the unmarked value and zero point of the dimension of case marking; the oblique cases encode a relational structure that localizes each of them with respect to that zero point, i.e. by 'pointing back' to the nominative and encoding the 'distance' from it.

Disregarding the enormous span of variation in paradigms (which requires thorough investigation beyond the scope of this chapter), we may still contend that there is one common criterion that makes for the paradigmatic relational structure of grammatical meaning, which can be described as follows:

> Grammatical meaning contains a relational structure that is anchored in paradigmatic organization. The stricter the paradigmatic organization, the more the relational meaning is converted into expressing the paradigmatic opposition between marked and unmarked members; it expresses intra-paradigmatic positional meaning.

The following overview assembles the three types of relational structure that are assumed to be relevant aspects of grammatical meaning. While the first one, the deictic relation, is the basic, non-derived prototype, the other two relational structures are—in the sense of Bühler (1982)—derived modes of pointing in derived planes.

Relational structures defining central features of grammar:

1. *Deictic relational structure.* The linguistic sign points to the deictic *origo* (zero point of subjective orientation) thereby connecting the narrated event to the communicative situation; it is the dominant relation in central grammatical categories like tense or mood.

2. *Syntagmatically interpreted relational structure.* The linguistic sign points to some entity in the linguistic syntagm (secondary, transferred *origo*) thereby establishing syntagmatic relations within the linguistic level; it is the dominant relation for the expression of textual meanings and functions (e.g. anaphoric relation, conjunctive and subjunctive relations, valency relations).
3. *Paradigmatically interpreted relational structure.* The linguistic signs point to the unmarked value of a paradigm (secondary, transferred *origo*), thereby encoding intra-paradigmatic oppositions; it is the dominant relation for the creation and realization of language internal obligatoriness of signs.

It is assumed here that these three relations are not mutually exclusive and may be present in a grammatical item to varying degrees. Thereby, the varying combinations account for different types of grammatical meaning and different types of grammatical categories with deictic categories representing the semantically richer, less grammaticalized stages and highly abstract, intra-paradigmatic oppositions representing older, more grammaticalized stages. As the basic relational structure, however, is deictic, grammar can be seen as pragmatically motivated.

5. Conclusion

This chapter has discussed the notions of grammaticalization (and grammar) and pragmaticalization both independently and in relation to each other. Grammaticalization has been defined as a complex, multi-layered process leading 'into grammar', i.e. into paradigmatic, obligatory structures, which as a common core display some type of relational meaning. The need to introduce the term 'pragmaticalization' has been shown to be the outcome of an attempt to preserve the domains of 'grammar' and 'pragmatics' as clearly distinct domains.

After arguing for a more comprehensive notion of 'grammar' which is broad enough to encompass the development of 'pragmatic' elements, it is suggested that the broader notion of grammar should be based on the recognition of the fact that grammatical signs always contain an indexical relation. This indexical relation, no matter in which modified and abstracted version it may appear, is finally based on a deictic relation and is thus deeply entrenched into pragmatics. In short: grammatical meaning is not only enriched by pragmatic components but the pragmatic foundation is one of its prototypical features. Grammar itself may be seen as frozen pragmatic anchoring, and grammaticalization as a complex process turning lexical items into grammatical ones (cf. Givón 1979), by inter alia providing them with an indexical anchoring, i.e. via a process which may be called pragmaticalization.

CHAPTER 37

ICONICITY VERSUS GRAMMATICALIZATION: A CASE STUDY

JOHN HAIMAN

1. Introduction

Among the universally acknowledged side-effects of economically motivated reduction in general and grammaticalization in particular is the loss of semantic transparency. In the course of formal erosion and the concomitant creation of a new grammatical category, the original link between the form and the meaning of any communicative expression may become obscure, resulting in a decrease of iconicity (The best general account of this trade-off is in the description of how iconic charades rapidly become a conventional sign language, in Bellugi and Klima 1976; another programmatic description of the same trajectory is given in Givón 1979: ch. 5. Compare also Haiman 1985: 195; Heine, Claudi, and Hünnemeyer 1991: 121.) In fact, this causal connection is recognized even by scholars who are sceptical about whether grammaticalization needs to be recognized as a separate kind of change at all (Fischer 1999: 349).

One striking example of the trade-off between transparency and compactness is offered by the relatively exotic grammatical category of medial verbs (specially marked verbs of non-final clauses in clause-chaining constructions), encountered in many Papuan languages. Originally, the medial verb was exactly like an independent verb, possibly followed by a coordinating conjunction, a situation still more or less reflected in Tauya (MacDonald 1990: 171).[1] In some languages, however, the personal endings of the medial verb have fused together with that conjunction to create a whole new opaque paradigm of medial endings into which the conjunction has disappeared (Haiman 1985: 191–4).

It has been a commonplace of grammaticalization theory at least since Heine and Reh (1984) that the reduction of biclausal structures to monoclausal ones through a reduction of either clause (desententialization or clause fusion) is a kind of grammaticalization (cf. Lehmann 1988a: 189–204). For an extended example of the conflict between iconicity and this particular kind of grammaticalization, we turn to a hitherto unstudied case of clause fusion—the reduction of the expression meaning 'why' from a separate clause meaning something like 'How does it come about that . . . ' to something like an embedded constituent of the second clause meaning something like 'for what' (cf. Heine et al. 1991: 58). The conflict is only visible in the relatively small number of languages in which 'why' is assigned a clause of its own, and where that clause is under assault from a variety of reduction processes.

In his valuable cross-linguistic survey of interrogative words, Michael Cysouw (2004) has pointed out that the *morphological* paradigmaticity of so-called '*wh*-words', taken so much for granted by students of Indo-European languages, is typologically quite rare, attested in his sample by only a handful of languages (Apalai, Ashenaca Arawakan, Kiliva, Desano, Tamil, Maybrat, and Thai) outside the Indo-European family. 'In most cases,' he notes, 'question words come from various [morphological] sources.'

With relatively few exceptions, however, the paradigm of interrogative words exhibit a striking *syntactic* uniformity, in languages all over the world. English may stand in for a large number of languages in which *wh*-words, regardless of their morphology, exhibit the same syntactic behaviour. However, 'why', whether expressing cause or purpose, and 'how' recurrently (albeit infrequently) seem to inhabit clauses of their own, while the other interrogative words typically do not. English may also exhibit this. In addition to 'why', there exists a colloquial variant 'how come', still a transparent reduction of 'How (does it) come (about that)' (an original cause clause) and another colloquial string 'what if', still a transparent reduction of the original result clause 'What (would happen) if . . . '. The latter are marked by their failure to induce subject–verb inversion (cf. König and van der Auwera 1988: 102–6 for inversion as a positive sign of clause integration in Germanic languages):

(1) a. *Why are we here?* (SV inversion, signaling embedding of 'why')
b. *How come we're here.* (no SV inversion)
c. *What if you were here?* (no SV inversion)

[1] The coordinate conjunction replaces, rather than simply follows, the verb-final mood marker.

In addition, of course, (1b) includes a verb: on the basis of the one-verb-per-clause hypothesis, 'how come' is a separate clause on two counts, while "what if" qualifies on only one count: that it fails to induce subject–verb inversion.

If every clause is a picture of reality, and if we conceptualize both the cause and the consequence of any given scenario as *another* scenario ('this situation caused another situation': cf. Kulikov and Sumbatova 1993: 327), then assigning to each scenario its own clause is diagrammatically iconic. Compare questions about causes in somewhat archaic (biblical or Shakespearean) English, which exhibit an *S1 (cause), that S2 (consequence)?* structure:

(2) a. *Who is this man, that even the wind and the sea obey him?*
    b. *Upon what meat does this our Caesar feed, that he is grown so great?*

With the exception of *how come* and *what if*, present-day English treats all interrogative pronouns in the same way with respect to both fronting and subject–verb inversion. There are many other languages like English in which all interrogative words are treated equally from a syntactic point of view, that is they are *equally* inside or outside the matrix clauses with which they occur. This pattern of equal treatment includes not only the familiar Indo-European languages, which pattern like English, but also French, Yoruba, and other African languages, or Breton and other Celtic languages in which *all* interrogative words are clefted to mark focus, and are hence all equally outside the matrix clause which they introduce (Heine and Reh 1984: 109–10, 147–82, 249–50; Campbell and Harris 1995: 152–61).

There are, however, some languages (not very many) in which the 'why' expressions (and to a lesser extent, the 'how' expressions) are routinely *separated from* other interrogatives and given a separate clause of their own. Call them 'how come' languages. Such languages seem to include Hua, Khmer, Semelai (Kruspe 2004: 176–83), Zapotec (Black 2000: 65–6), Japanese (Toshio Ohori, p.c.), Jarawara, Mandarin, Cantonese, Diegueño, Choctaw (Broadwell 2006: 108–11), Lao (Enfield 2007: 91–2), and Sanuma (Borgman 1990: 67–71).

It seems, moreover, that the distinction between 'why' and 'how come' strategies is not merely a static one. As suggested by English pairs like (1a,b) a 'why' language may plausibly become a 'how come' language (assuming that the upstart colloquial form ever completely supplants the inherited one), but the reverse is much more richly attested.

The (admittedly fragmentary) data from many 'how come' languages illustrate how the pressure for paradigmatic homogeneity (identical syntactic treatment for all interrogative pronouns) competes with iconicity (the assignment of special extra-clausal status for interrogative pronouns denoting cause and consequence). In such languages, 'how come', under assault from this pressure, is ground down to or replaced by a nominal constituent.

2. The iconic strategy

Our focus here will be on Hua (Papuan) and Khmer (Austroasiatic), two languages of which the author has first-hand knowledge.

2.1. Hua[2]

Interrogative words in Hua include:

(3)			
	aiga'	which	adjective (A)
	aigafu-	how is it?	verb (V)
	aigatoga	where	noun (N)
	aiga'auva	what kind of	A
	aituvita'	when	N
	da'auva na	what	N
	dakni'	how much, how many	N
	kzo'	who	N
	zahu-	do what	V

As in many non-Indo-European languages, there is no neat morphological symmetry, nothing like a paradigm of *wh*-words. There is admittedly some morphological overlap: **Da'*- occurs in both *dakni'* and *da'auva na*; **ai-* occurs in *aituvita'* and *aiga'* (and all of the latter's compounds: *aigafie*, *aigatoga*, and *aiga'auva*). There is no Q-word fronting. Hua is an SOV language, and interrogative *nominal* words generally occur in situ.

Unlike the other interrogative words listed in (3), the interrogative verb *zahu-* is not only a verb, but one capable of acting as a complete sentence, albeit one which is limited in various ways. For example, it cannot occur in any other tense than the aorist. But it can occur in both 2SG and 3SG forms:

(4) a. *Za-* *hane*
What do.2SG.
'What are you doing? How are you? What are you up to?'

b. *Za-* *hie*
What do.3SG.
'What's the matter?'

Zahu- in different-subject medial form means 'why'. In different-subject medial clauses, the verb stem is followed by a medial ending (Med.) *-ga-* ~ *-na* ~ *'ga* which agrees with the subject of that verb (the conjunction 'and' is reconstructible within this ending), and an anticipatory ending (Ant.) which agrees with the subject of the

[2] All data are taken from Haiman (1980: 275).

following verb. All cause clauses are therefore separate from the following final verb scenario, in which the result is described.

(5) a. *zahi-* *ga-* *na* *vie*
What.do 3SG.Med. 3SG.Ant. go.3SG.
'Why did s/he go?'

b. *zahi-* *ga-* *da* *visue*
what.do 3SG.Med. 1SG.Ant I.go.subjunctive
'Why should I go?'

2.2. Khmer[3]

Interrogative words in Khmer include:

(6)			
	(av)ej	anything, what	N
	na:	any, which	A
	ja:ng mec	how	A
	ja:ng na:	how	A
	(do:c) mdec	how	A
	nau: na:	anyone, who	N
	ponma:n	how much, how many	Q
	ponna:	how big	Q

Khmer is predominantly SVO, and Q-words occur in situ.

(7) a. *mwn deung cia tveu: ja:ng na:*
not know comp. do kind which
'[sc. Some subject] doesn't/didn't know what to do.'

b. *piak nih nwng piak nuh knoh knia ja:ng mec?*
word this and word that differ each other kind how
'How does this word differ in meaning from that one?'

c. *piak nisseut mian nej tha: mec?*
word nisseut have meaning say what
'What does the word 'nisseut' mean?'

Given a two clause scenario "S1 causes S2", the causal relationship is frequently expressed by S1 *ba:n cia* "get + complementizer (= CAUSE)" S2, as in:

(8) a. *tlaeum aeng thom ponna:* ba: n cia *ceut thom mleh?*
Liver you big how much get comp. heart big so much
'How big is your liver, that you are so arrogant?'

[3] All data from Haiman (in preparation).

b. *[niang nwng deung pi: lbeuc a:nj pi: mun haeuj]* <u>*ba:n cia*</u>
lady this know about trick I from before finish CAUSE

[mdaw:ng nih mwn prap a:nj]
once this not tell me
'The lady knew about my previous tricks and therefore she didn't tell me this time.'

c. *[Ja:ng nih haeuj] ba:n cia [juvacaun a:c aociarauh ci:va phiap*
kind this finish CAUSE youth can savor life

ba:n ciang mnuh rausial]
succeed exceed people afternoon
'And so this meant that the youth could savor life more than anyone else on that afternoon.'

The question word 'why' is rendered in 'formal' (cf. Huffman and Proum 1977) Khmer as the collocation:

(9) *het (av)ej ba:n cia [sentence]*
Cause what get comp.
'what cause brings it about that..'

as in:

(10) a. <u>*het ej ba:n cia*</u> *aju' 500 cnam haeuj mwn toan ngoap?*
why age 500 year already not yet croak
'How come he's 500 and hasn't croaked?'

b. <u>*het ej ba:n cia*</u> *ko:n srej knjom kaeut mau:k ceh ni'jiaj*
why child female I born come know speak
'How come my daughter was born knowing how to speak?'

c. <u>*het avej ba:n cia*</u> *neak cambac treuv krawlee:t meu:l a'dej-ta ka:l?*
why person necessary must glance look past time
'Why must we pay attention to the past?'

There are variations on this structure, but as long as the cause expression *X ba:n (cia)* has the verb *ba:n* 'cause, get' in it, it is going to have the same extra-clausal status:

(11) a. *[het ja:ng mec]* <u>*ba:n cia*</u> *[neak aeng jum?]*
cause kind how get be person you cry
'How come you are crying?'

b. *[het ej]* *ba:n* *[aopuk mda:j knjom ka:l dael*
cause what get father mother I time which

koat neuv rauh mian traup sawmbat 8 klang]
3 stay live have goods goods 8 shed
'How come my parents when they were alive had 8 storage sheds of goods?'

c. *[mec] ba:n cia [ju:r mleh kroan tae claw:ng spian ponneung?]*
how get be long so just cross bridge this much
'How come it's taking her so long just to cross the bridge?'

d. *[mec] ba:n [neak aeng kheu:nj botrej jeu:ng mau:k*
how get person you see daughter 1PL come

haeuj neak aeng mwn prau:m ciah cenj]
and person you not agree avoid exit
'How come you saw my daughter [the king is speaking, and using the royal we] coming and didn't get out of her way?'

e. *[awnjceung] ba:n [lo:k kru: cap ni'jiaj rwang pi: ta: baw:h]*
thus get monk teacher start relate story about hermit
'And so it was that the teacher started to relate a story about a hermit.'

f. [*awnceung] ba:n*[4] *[kla:c mnuh pial neung]*
thus get fear person ignorant that
'and that is why (I) am afraid of ignorant people.'

3. Assaults on the Iconic Strategy

3.1. Hua

The only phonetic signs of erosion or grammaticalization of *zahiga-*, the different-subject medial 'why' word in Hua, are: an irregular deletion of [hi] to [i] and the equally irregular reduction via lenition of the medial desinence *-ga-* to [ja]. Minor as they appear, these changes (*zahiga-* > *zaija*) were sufficient to render the morphology of the 'why' word temporarily opaque to at least one Hua learner,

[4] Incidentally, it is sentences like (11b,d,e,f) where *ba:n* occurs alone (that is without the following complementizer *cia*) which suggest that a plausible source for the prefixed causative morphemes *bVN-* and *p-* in Khmer (and Mon-Khmer generally) may be the 'get' verb, as argued in Haiman (1999). This is of course a frequent grammaticalization path for causative morphemes in general, and the phonological mechanism for the reduction *ba:n* > *bVN* > *p* is a very familiar one in Khmer.

back in 1971. Syntactically, *zahiga-* is a medial verb, but morphologically it is a frozen one. Medial verbs in this language generally occur in different forms (called 'coordinate' and 'subordinate') depending on whether their tense and mood are necessarily identical with that of the following clause. If they are necessarily identical, the 'coordinate' form is used; if they may be distinct, the subordinate one is. *Zahiga-*, with the medial ending *-ga* (cognate with the coordinate conjunction) is invariably 'coordinate' irrespective of the tense or mood of the following clauses. The 'subordinate' form would be **zahima-*, (with the medial ending *-ma*, cognate with the relative clause ending) but this simply does not occur.[5] So to this extent, the medial verb has undergone some decategorialization.

Moreover, the 'why' expression can occur within the S2 clause, a thing which cannot occur with other medial verbs in clause chains:

(12)

Ma	*demo*	*fumo*	*zahigaka*	*mine?*
This	man	pork	why	give.2SG

'Why did you give this man pork?'

3.2. Khmer

The entire unreduced 'Why' clause may occur within the matrix clause, so that it follows the subject:

(13)

aeng	*[mec*	*ba:n*	*cia]*	*hian si:*	*mun*	*lo:k*
you	how	get	be	dare chow down	before	monk

'Hey you, how do you dare chow down before the monks have eaten?'

Or it may be formally reduced (by total loss of the verb *ba:n*) without such clause-integration:

(14) a.

[het	*ej]*	*kaw:*	*aeng*	*mau:k*	*vwnj?*
Cause	what	so	you	come	back

'So how come you're back?'

b.

taeu	*[het*	*do:c*	*mdec]*	*niari:*	*dael*	*mian*	*pea'hana'*	*cia*	*mneak*	*sawmbo:*
Q	cause	like	how	lady	who	have	much	be	one.person	rich

daoj	*pho:k*	*traup*	*mau:k*	*teunj*	*sawmbot*	*tnak*	*lee:k*	*bej*
by	property	goods	come	buy	ticket	class	number	three

'How come a rich lady with lots of property would buy a third class ticket?'

Or it may be replaced by another expression:

[5] It is noteworthy that in the closely related Move dialect of Yagaria, the only recorded 'why' word has an impeccably nominal character as *da'-ouva gava'* 'what likeness kind' (Renck 1975: 70). It is unknown whether Move ever had a form like the DS medial verb exhibited in Hua.

(14) c. *coh* *neak* *aeng ni'jiaj* *awnjceung?*
What about person you speak thus
'Why do you speak thus?'

It may be that an intermediate stage in this development is a sentence in which *coh* (an interrogative marker glossed as 'what about?') redundantly (?) occurs on a noun phrase in the cause clause, and *ba:n cia* still separates the cause clause from the result clause:

(14) d. [*coh* *mae mae ceh* *cla:wng teuk* *ja:ng mec*]
what about mothers know cross water kind how

<u>*ba:n cia*</u> *mwn* *tauteuk* *sampawt*
get be not wet skirt
'Why do women know how to cross water in such a way that they do not wet their skirts?'

e. [*coh* *kmae* *jeu:ng mian pumnia* *pia* *kam ej* *kaw:*]
what about Khmer 1PL. have evil do evil act what so

ba:n cia [ve:tunia *awh* *mnuh muaj* *nawkau: i: ceung]*
get be famine exhaust people one city thus
'What evil deeds have we Khmer committed to bring it about that famine is killing off our people by the city in this fashion?'

It is not known to what extent the phenomena described in Khmer are typical of Mon-Khmer languages, or of Austroasiatic languages in general.[6]

The reduction processes in Hua and Khmer share a common outcome: the separate-clause origin of the 'why' expression is obscured.

4. The same tension in other languages

The 'why' expression may lose its extra-clausal status in at least two unrelated ways. First, it may cease to appear clause-marginally, as in both Khmer and Hua. Second, it may lose its verbal status, either through the loss of the verb entirely, as in Khmer,

[6] In Minor Mlabri, a related Mon-Khmer language, the 'why' word *tipiaa* is completely integrated into the matrix clause, and appears where all other adverbial expressions do, clause-finally.
'at *beer* *djak* *tipiaa*
The two go what
'Why did they go?' (Rischel 1995: 150).)

or through the partial or total loss of morphological verbal trappings on a neutral stem, as in Hua.

4.1. Loss of clause-marginal status

Clause integration in Germanic is marked, as noted, by the ability of a clause-initial Q-word to induce subject–verb inversion. A less dynamic form of clause integration is the ability of a clause-peripheral constituent (a priori a conceivable chunk of another clause) to occur *within* the clause it accompanies.[7] In many languages, 'why' alone can occur clause-peripherally. This seems to be the case in Semelai (Kruspe 2004: 176–83), where *mande* 'what' occurs in situ, but its homophone 'why' occurs clause-initially. This is also a distinguishing feature of the 'why' word in Chinese.

4.1.1. *Chinese*

4.1.1.1. Mandarin (all data from Li and Thompson 1980; 1984). In Mandarin, Q-words typically occur in situ. There are three 'why' expressions. The first, *zenme*, also means 'how':

(15) a. *ni* *zenme* *jiao* *youyong*
You how/why teach swim
'How/why do you teach swimming?' (Li and Thompson 1984: 51).

But, if *zenme* means 'why' (and only then) it may be disambiguated from 'how' by occurring clause-initially:

(15) b. *zenme* *ni* *bu* *qu shang-ke*
Why you not go ascend class
'Why aren't you attending class?' (Li and Thompson 1980: 523-4)

The second, *weishenme* 'for what', like *zenme* can also appear in both positions:

(16) a. *weishenme* *ta* *bu* *kaixin*
For what 3 not happy
'Why is s/he not happy?'

b. *ta* *weishenme* *bu* *kaixin*
3 for what not happy
'Why is s/he not happy?'

Finally, *ganma* 'do what' is treated as a serial verb which may either precede or follow the matrix verb:

[7] Parenthetical clauses (e.g. *He is, I'm afraid, wrong in this*) are marked by heavy pauses. There is no such prosodic evidence for the parenthetical nature of embedded 'why' expressions.

(17) a. *ni* *dai* *shoudianfong* *[ganma]*
You bring flashlight do what

b. *ni* *[ganma]* *dai* *shoudianfong*
you do what bring flashlight
'What did you bring a flashlight for?' (Li and Thompson 1980: 525)

4.1.1.2. Cantonese. In Cantonese, the 'why' of cause is rendered by the clause *dím gáai* 'how explain'. But this expression may occur either at the left margin of the matrix clause, or integrated into it, following the subject (Matthews and Yip 1994: 329):

(18) a. *dím* *gáai* *wúih* *gám* *gé*
How explain would this PRT
'Why is it like this?'

b. *léih* *dím* *gáai* *mh* *chēut* *sēng* *a*
you how explain not out voice PRT
'Why don't you say something?'

The 'why' of purpose is rendered by the purpose clause *jouh māt (yéh)* 'do what', 'what's the matter'. Again, this expression may occur either iconically (following the main clause) or integrated within the matrix clause where it follows the subject (Li and Thompson 1980: 330):

(19) a. *leih* *gam* *mang jang* *jouh* *mat* *a*
you so frustrated do what PRT
'What are you so frustrated about?'

b. *léih* *jouh* *māt* *gam* *gánjéung* *a*
you do what so nervous PRT
'What are you so nervous for?'

The colloquial *sái māt* 'need what' 'What's the point of' occurs clause-externally at the beginning, but when the matrix clause (rarely) occurs with an overt subject, it may also appear in the integrated post-subject position:

(20) a. <u>*sái*</u> <u>*māt*</u> *mahn* *kéuih* *jēk*
Need what ask him PRT
'Why ask him?'

b. *léih* <u>*sái māt*</u> *gam* *gēng* *a*
you need what so fear PRT
'What are you so afraid of?'

In both Mandarin and Cantonese, then, the clause-integration of the 'why' words is indicated by their ability to occur in post-subject position. Their status as a separate clauses, on the other hand, is reflected in their unique ability to occur clause-'initially' (='as a result of what prior cause') or clause-'finally' (= 'in order to achieve what goal').

4.2. Loss of verbhood

4.2.1. *Jamul Tiipay (Diegueño)*

Like Hua, Jamul Tiipay (Miller 2001: 176–9) is a clause-chaining, switch-reference marking language, in which the 'why' word is a separate verbal clause. In addition to the interrogative pronouns *me'a* 'where', *me'ap* 'who', *maayiich* 'what', the language has some interrogative verbs: *mu'yuu* 'be how', *ma'tri* 'do how', *ch*-'i* 'be how many', and *ch*-i* 'say what'. The 'why' word is generally the different-subject (DS) form of 'be how':

(21) *muuyuu- chm me-shally me-xyan m-wa-aa*
Be how DS 2-arm 2-hold in 2-sit-Q
'Why are you holding your arm?'

A same-subject (SS) form is also possible:

(22) *muuyuu- m- i- ch ii*m- akxap*
Be how 2 say SS 2 eject
'Why did you make him leave?'

But there also exists a totally uninflected form of *muuyu(u)* which can also serve as the 'why' word:

(23) *muuyuu me-patt me-yak*
Be how 2-lie 2-be.lying
'Why are you lying down?'

In (21) and (22), Jamul is a 'how come' language. In (23), by shedding the verbal affixes of the question word (person-marking or switch-reference marking), i.e. through decategorialization, it has become a 'why' language.

4.2.2. *Jarawara (Awara: Amazonian; data from Dixon 2004: 403–5)*

In addition to interrogatives *himata* 'what', *hibaka* 'who', which behave as nouns, the language has verbal interrogatives like *himata ebe* 'what happen', and the 'why' word is based on the latter:

(24) *inamatewe himata ebe ne ohi nara*
Child what happen aux.m. cry aux m. Q
'Why is the child crying?'

But there are also nominal forms *himata-ihi* 'due to what', *himata-ta-bijo* 'due to the lack of', and the invariable *himata-ba* 'why', whose etymology is uncertain:

(25) *himata-ba boko noko jojome tihine tirija*
Why boko seed eat (redup.) aux.2 aux. 2
'Why did you eat the boko seed?'

Again, if Jarawara is a 'how come' language in (24), it is a 'why' language in (25) through the loss of the cause verb *ebe* 'happen'.

5. Conclusion

The grammaticalization of causation is a well-known topic in grammatical typology, with erstwhile separate causal verbs getting ground down in some cases to auxiliary verbs or totally opaque causative affixes on matrix verbs (cf. Lehmann 1988a: 201–2). It is shown here with a handful of examples that a comparable reduction can affect the question word 'why' itself. Although sections (3) and (4) have spoken of 'tension' between iconic and paradigmatic pressures, it would seem that this is not a fair fight: iconicity is repeatedly swamped by the usage-induced pressures for formal reduction on the one hand, and standardization on the other. Not only are the languages in which 'why' has a clause of its own in a distinct minority as opposed to languages where some 'for what' paraphrase is the norm: even in those languages where the iconic expression of a separate clause is 'permitted', there exist either grammaticalized alternatives or the iconic form is itself subject to various degrees of reduction.

These facts are typical. Grammaticalization through everyday use is the constant, cunning, and patient adversary of iconicity.[8] The 9 to 5 civil servant performing the drudgery of his job triumphs in the same way over the weekend protest marcher—except, as we all know, under the extraordinary circumstances of a revolution, which do sporadically occur.

[8] As a Khmer proverb says, 'the heron [of iconicity] may on occasion forget about the trap [of grammaticalization], but the trap never forgets about the heron.'

CHAPTER 38

DEGRAMMATICALIZATION

MURIEL NORDE

1. Introduction

The status of degrammaticalization in grammaticalization studies has long been an uneasy one. The term was coined by Lehmann (Lehmann 1995a[1982]: 16) for a nonexistent phenomenon at a time when there was general consensus that there was only movement from lexicon to grammar, not vice versa. In the decades that followed however, an increasing body of evidence suggested that degrammaticalization does exist, and hence that 'a presumed absolute universal had to be weakened to a statistical universal' (Haspelmath 2004b: 23). In this chapter I will discuss the basic similarities and differences between grammaticalization and degrammaticalization (section 2), as well as outline a typology of degrammaticalization changes, based on Norde (2009a), arguing that there are three basic types, which I have termed 'degrammation' (section 3), 'deinflectionalization' (section 4), and 'debonding' (section 5). As a generic definition of all three types, I propose the following:

(1) Degrammaticalization is a composite change whereby a gram in a specific context gains in autonomy or substance on more than one linguistic level (semantics, morphology, syntax, or phonology). (Norde 2009a: 120)

2. Degrammaticalization and grammaticalization

2.1. Main similarities and differences between grammaticalization and degrammaticalization

The very term *de*grammaticalization suggests that it is derivative of grammaticalization—more precisely, that degrammaticalization is the reverse of grammaticalization. Indeed, grammaticalization and degrammaticalization are often seen as each other's mirror image, but the relation between the two is actually more complex than that. Basically, degrammation can be seen as the reverse of what Traugott has termed 'primary grammaticalization', and deinflectionalization and some cases of debonding can be seen as the reverse of 'secondary grammaticalization' (see Traugott 2002a: 26f. for discussion of the terms 'primary' and 'secondary' grammaticalization, as well as (2) below), but there are also crucial differences, which make it inappropriate to speak of 'mirror-image reversals'. In this section, I will give a bird's-eye view of the main similarities and differences between grammaticalization and degrammaticalization. The similarities between grammaticalization and degrammaticalization may be summarized as follows:

(i) Both are 'composite changes', i.e. the concurrence of 'primitive' changes on different levels (semantics, morphology, syntax, and/or phonology).[1] In most cases there are changes in both form (phonology, morphology, and/or syntax) and meaning, but there are also cases where there are only changes in form.[2]

(ii) Both grammaticalization and degrammaticalization are gradual, in the sense that they comprise a series of small changes (i.e. it is not necessarily the case that all primitive changes occur simultaneously).

[1] One issue that cannot be addressed here is the interrelation of the various primitive changes involved in a grammaticalization or degrammaticalization change. Suffice it to say that I do not agree with Newmeyer (1998: 235) that grammaticalization is 'essentially an epiphenomenal result of *independent* historical developments' (see Heine and Kuteva (2002: 3f.) and Heine (2003b: 579) for convincing arguments against Newmeyer's position).

[2] This, however, appears to be comparatively rare. Some examples of cliticization involve a change in form only, e.g. spoken Dutch proclitic *k=* voor *ik* 'I', as in *kheb* ([kɛp]) for *ik heb* 'I have'. This is only a change in form (phonological reduction, morphological bonding/univerbation, and syntactic restrictions, e.g. the impossibility of enclitic pronouns in comparisons: *hij heeft meer boeken dan ik heb/*kheb* 'he has more books than I have'). In most cases of cliticization however, there is some semantic reduction as well: English *=ll*, for example, as in *I'll do that*, cannot have a volitional reading, whereas *will* can, e.g. in *if you will*. In degrammaticalization, changes in form without changes in meaning appear to be rare as well, but some cases of debonding (section 5) may be examples of it.

(iii) Both result in novel grams or structures. Thus, in cases where grams can be shown to continue a less grammatical function that had always been around, however marginalized, the change will not qualify as a case of degrammaticalization.[3]

(iv) Both are context-internal changes, in the sense that 'the identity of the construction and the element's place within it are always preserved' (Haspelmath 1999: 1064). The (de)grammaticalization gram changes in function, but there is no change to the surface structure of the construction in which the gram appears, at least not initially.

Unsurprisingly, the principal difference between grammaticalization and degrammaticalization is the directionality of the primitive changes involved. For instance, where grammaticalization involves semantic attrition, degrammaticalization may involve semantic strengthening, or where grammaticalization involves syntactic fixation or morphological coalescence, degrammaticalization involves a decrease in bondedness or an increase in syntactic freedom. The second difference is frequency: grammaticalization is far more frequently attested, with far more cross-linguistic regularity, than is degrammaticalization. Finally, where several subsequent grammaticalization changes may form a chain, as in (2), degrammaticalization is not a chain phenomenon.

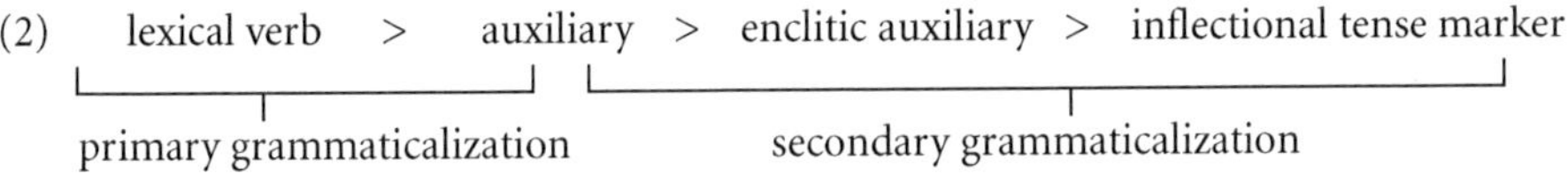

For instance, Old Swedish inflectional MASC.SG.GEN *-s* has degrammaticalized into the Modern Swedish enclitic *s*-genitive, but there is no evidence that the *s*-genitive is degrammaticalizing further into a free grammatical marker (e.g. a possessive pronoun). Further degrammaticalization is not precluded *per se*, but because degrammaticalization involves several primitive changes into a 'marked' direction, which is one of the reasons why it is so rare, chances that one and the same gram will degrammaticalize more than once are obviously low (see further Norde 2009a: 100ff.).

[3] An example of this kind of change, which has been termed 'retraction' in Haspelmath (2004b: 33ff.), is the history of English *man*. Originally a noun, *man* had grammaticalized into an indefinite pronoun 'one' (cf. German *man*), a usage that disappeared again at a later stage, and in PDE *man* can only be used as a noun. Crucially however, *man* had never ceased to be a noun, so this is not a novel lexical function that arose out of an earlier grammatical one, and hence I do not consider it a case of degrammaticalization.

2.2. A degrammaticalization typology

Degrammaticalization, unlike grammaticalization, is generally held to refer to changes that have little in common and lack cross-linguistic replication (e.g. in Heine 2003a: 175). While it is certainly true that degrammaticalization changes are for the most part unique tokens of change that are not found in any other language, a close examination of all known cases reveals some similarities nevertheless. In Norde (2009a) I have proposed a typology that is based on changes in the degree of bondedness. Thus the primary criterion has been morphological, since this appeared to yield the most plausible classification. A typology based on semantic criteria, for example, would have grouped together function words becoming lexical words and derivational affixes becoming lexical words, and since these types of change are otherwise so different in nature we would have a typology that seems less adequate than the one proposed here.

In order to classify grammaticalization and degrammaticalization changes, one needs to consider (the directionality of) all primitive changes involved, and to decide which primitive changes must be attested for a change to qualify as a given type of (de)grammaticalization. The classification proposed here is based on Lehmann's 'parameters of grammaticalization' (Lehmann 1995a: 121–78), which are used to identify primitive changes at different levels. In sections 3–5 I will discuss the three main types of degrammaticalization and explain on the basis of what criteria I have chosen to classify them in this way. For reasons of space Lehmann's parameters cannot be discussed in full (see Norde forthcoming for extensive discussion), so I will merely list the parameters and indicate which primitive changes are associated with them in degrammaticalization:

1. Integrity: *resemanticization* and *phonological strengthening* (gain in semantic and phonological substance respectively), as well as *recategorialization* (the acquisition of morphosyntactic features of members of major word classes; only to be found in degrammation and some instances of debonding).
2. Paradigmaticity: *deparadigmaticization*—(i) movement from a closed word class to an open word class (in degrammation), or (ii) 'discharge' from an inflectional paradigm (in deinflectionalization and debonding of inflectional affixes).
3. Paradigmatic variability: *deobligatorification*—increasing paradigmatic variability, or becoming optional in specific morphosyntactic contexts.
4. Structural scope: *scope expansion*—an increase in syntactic scope.[4]

[4] Scope is a particularly problematic parameter, since it does not appear to have a clear preferred directionality in either grammaticalization or degrammaticalization (see Norde in preparation for discussion), but it has been retained nevertheless to assess how scope changes in degrammaticalization.

5. Bondedness: *severance*—(i) transition to a 'less bound' morpheme type (in deinflectionalization), or (ii) transition from bound morpheme to free morpheme (in debonding).
6. Syntagmatic variability: *flexibilization*—increase in syntactic freedom (degrammation and debonding only).

I wish to note in advance, however, that classifications are inherently arbitrary and my classification of degrammaticalization changes is no exception. Other authors may want to use different combinations of primitive changes as criteria for classification. The advantage of using a rigid set such as Lehmann's criteria is, however, that the details of the change can be made explicit, which also leaves room for alternative classifications. For instance, if one considers resemanticization as a prerequisite for all degrammaticalization changes, some cases of debonding (see section 5) will fall outside such a definition of degrammaticalization.

3. Degrammation

3.1. Definition and examples

Degrammation[5] is a rare kind of context-induced change from grammatical word to lexical word. Examples are:

(3) a. preterite subjunctive of modal *welle* 'would' > full verb *wotte* 'to wish', in a variety of Pennsylvania German spoken in Waterloo County, Canada (Burridge 1998);
b. Chinese deontic modal *dĕi* > lexical verb meaning 'to need, require' (Ziegeler 2004);[6]
c. Old Church Slavonic *nĕčĭto* 'something' > Bulgarian *nešto* 'thing' (Willis 2007: 278ff.);
d. Welsh 3SG possessive pronoun *eiddo* 'his' > noun meaning 'property' (Willis 2007: 283ff.);

[5] Willis (2007) uses the term 'syntactic lexicalization' for this kind of change.

[6] More examples of verbs with both modal and lexical usages have been presented as degrammaticalization in the literature, but these will not be considered to be degrammation for various reasons (Norde 2009a: 121, 136ff.). For instance, English *dare* (Beths 1999) appears to be an example of retraction rather than degrammaticalization (cf. Traugott 2001). And in the case of Swedish *må* 'may; feel' (Van der Auwera and Plungian 1998), the lexical verb did not develop out of the modal, but both verbs have been shown to derive from an earlier lexical verb: Old Swedish *magha* 'to be strong' (Andersson 2007).

e. Middle Welsh preposition *yn ôl* 'after' > full verb *nôl* 'to bring' (Willis 2007: 292ff.).

Degrammation will be defined as follows:

(4) Degrammation is a composite change whereby a function word in a specific linguistic context is reanalysed as a member of a major word class, acquiring the morphosyntactic properties which are typical of that word class, and gaining in semantic substance. (Norde 2009a: 135)

In this definition, degrammation involves both semantic change (from grammatical content to lexical content) and morphosyntactic change (from minor to major word class, typically acquiring the inflection of that particular word class). Note, however, that degrammation is crucially different from conversions from function word to lexical item (*to down a drink, ifs and buts*) because in conversions grammatical items are 'recruited', as it were, as lexical items in entirely different contexts, whereas degrammation occurs in ambiguous contexts. One illustration of such an ambiguous context is the Welsh example in (5), where *aeth yn ol* can mean either 'went after' or 'went to fetch'; it was in such contexts that the preposition *yn ol* was reanalysed as a verb (which was later reduced to *nôl*). This shift thus involved the same type of pragmatic inferencing that is typically attested in grammaticalization, meaning that pragmatic inferencing is a bidirectional process (Willis 2007: 299).

(5) Yna yd **aeth** y gweisson **yn ol** y varch a 'e
then PART went the lads after his horse and his
arueu y Arthur
weapons for Arthur
'Then the lads went after/went to fetch his horse and his weapons for Arthur'

Degrammation is furthermore characterized by recategorialization, because its target categories, nouns and verbs, are generally richer in inflection than function words.[7] For instance, Pennsylvania German *wotte* 'to wish' was indeclinable as a modal form 'would', but as a full verb, it features inflected forms such as imperative *wott* or the past participle *gewott*. And when degrammation results in a noun it acquires morphosyntactic properties of nouns. For instance, the Bulgarian noun *nešto* 'thing' (from a pronoun meaning 'something') has regular neuter inflection (plural *nešta*, definite form *neštoto*, with enclitic definite article), and it can be modified by determiners and adjectives.

Probably the main reason why degrammation is so rare is that it involves a shift from minor word classes, with little or no inflection, to major word classes, which typically inflect. This implies that in order for a grammatical element to degrammaticalize into a major lexical category it has to have a form which can plausibly be

[7] This does not hold for Chinese *děi*, however (example (3b), since Chinese is an isolating language.

reanalysed as an inflected form (Willis 2007: 303), which evidently becomes progressively difficult the more inflections a language possesses.

3.2. Degrammation in terms of Lehmann's parameters

The defining parameter in degrammation is integrity. In all cases discussed in this section, the grams gain in semantic substance (resemanticization) and morpho-syntactic properties (recategorialization). The one exception to this general pattern of enrichment is Welsh *nôl*, which is phonologically reduced from *yn ol*. Yet this reduction is not sufficient to dismiss this example as a valid case of degrammation (see further Norde forthcoming for discussion). As regards the other parameters and their associated primitive changes (in italics) we observe the following:

Paradigmaticity (*deparadigmaticization*). In degrammation, deparadigmaticization entails that a gram moves into a major word class. This is attested in all cases, which develop into (lexical) verbs or nouns.

Paradigmatic variability (*deobligatorification*). In degrammation, a decrease in obligatoriness is obvious, as lexical items are less obligatory than grammatical items.

Structural scope (*scope expansion*). In degrammation, the evidence is inconclusive. In Pennsylvania German *wotte* scope is expanded because as a full verb ('wish'), *wotte* may take scope over a clause, whereas it only took scope over a VP when it is used as a modal verb ('would'). But in other cases (e.g. Welsh *eiddo* and *nôl*) it is not evident that there has been a change in scope at all.

Bondedness (*severance*). Bondedness is not a relevant parameter in degrammation, because function words are free morphemes already.

Syntagmatic variability (*flexibilization*). Flexibilization is always found in degrammation, because the prototypical target categories of debonding, nouns and verbs, are more flexible syntactically than function words such as modal verbs and prepositions.

4. Deinflectionalization

4.1 Definition and examples

Of all three types of degrammaticalization distinguished in Norde (2009a), deinflectionalization is by far the least common, but it includes one of the most discussed examples, the *s*-genitive. Examples of deinflectionalization are:

(6) a. MASC/NEUT.SG.GEN -(*e*)s > enclitic *s*-genitive in English (Jespersen 1894), Danish (Herslund 2001), Norwegian (Johannessen 1989), and Swedish (Norde 1997; 2006a).[8]
b. Old Swedish MASC.SG.NOM *-er* > Modern Swedish derivational nominalization suffix *-er* (Norde 2002: 53ff.).
c. Old Swedish NEUT.PL.NOM/ACC *-on* > Modern Swedish derivational 'berry-suffix' *-on* (Norde 2002: 55f.).
d. Kwaza (an isolated language spoken in Brazil) inflectional exhortative marker *-ni* > derivational causational marker *-nĩ* (Van der Voort 2002).

Deinflectionalization is the least attested type of degrammaticalization, and is defined as follows:

(7) Deinflectionalization is a composite change whereby an inflectional affix in a specific linguistic context gains a new function, while shifting to a less bound morpheme type. (Norde 2009a: 152)

Deinflectionalization is a subtle kind of degrammaticalization, because it involves a shift from one type of bound morpheme (an inflectional affix) to another (a derivational affix or a clitic). This evidently raises the question of which bound morphemes are 'less grammatical' than others. I will argue that inflectional affixes are 'more grammatical' than both clitics and derivational affixes. As regards clitics, these are considered 'less grammatical', for instance because they are less bound (both morphologically and phonologically) and do not form paradigms.[9] And the main reason why derivational affixes are considered 'less grammatical' is that they are not grammatically obligatory (Bybee 1985: 81). For a more extensive account of the grammatical status of bound morphemes, see Norde (2009a: 152ff.).

Apart from a shift to a less bound type of morpheme, deinflectionalization entails a gain in function. The *s*-genitive in both English and Mainland Scandinavian gains the function of determiner (while continuing its possessive function); the two Swedish inflectional suffixes that become derivational (examples (6b,c) gain the function of nominalizer (e.g. *en dummer* 'a stupid one') or 'berry-suffix' (e.g. *hallon* (litt. 'slopeberry') 'raspberry'). In the Kwaza case, an inflectional exhortative marker has become a derivational marker of causativity. Obsolescent or marginal inflections appear to be particularly prone to deinflectionalization: Old Swedish *-s* and *-er*, originally inflections to mark the genitive case and the

[8] An alternative approach to the *s*-genitive is a construction-based analysis, according to which the *s*-genitive construction is an instance of grammatical constructionalization, because, as a determiner, it becomes more schematic on the constructional level (Trousdale 2008a; Norde and Trousdale 2009). This analysis is not incompatible with the one presented here, because on the morpheme-level, the history of the *s*-genitive is a clear case of degrammaticalization.

[9] A second problem, which cannot be discussed here, regards establishing the grammatical status of the *s*-genitive. For a recent discussion on this problem in Swedish see Börjars (2003) and Norde (2006a).

nominative with some nouns and adjectives, degrammaticalized when the Old Swedish case system collapsed, and Old Swedish *-on* was a very marginal plural marker which only survives in two Modern Swedish nouns (*ögon* 'eyes', *öron* 'ears').

4.2. Deinflectionalization in terms of Lehmann's parameters

For deinflectionalization, the defining parameter is paradigmaticity, because what is most characteristic of these cases, as we have seen in the preceding section, is that inflectional suffixes cease to form part of inflectional paradigms (deparadigmaticization). As far as the other parameters are concerned, I note the following:

Integrity (*resemanticization*): In deinflectionalization, grams do not acquire lexical meaning, but a new function. For instance, in the case of the *s*-genitive, the new function (DETERMINER) is added to the original one (GENITIVE), but the case of Swedish *-er*, the original function (NOMINATIVE) has disappeared and been replaced by the new function (NOMINALIZER meaning 'person who is (associated with) X'; where 'X' is the noun or adjective to which derivational *-er* is attached); (*phonological strengthening*): there is mostly no change at the phonological level, with the exception of Kwaza *-nĩ*, where a phonetic feature (nasality) has been added; (*recategorialization*): deinflectionalized grams do not recategorialize, because they do not join a major word class.

Paradigmatic variability (*deobligatorification*): In deinflectionalization, grams can be said to become less obligatory, because inflectional case markers are always obligatory in case-marking languages such as Old Swedish, whereas clitics or derivational markers may be substituted by other expressions.

Structural scope (*scope expansion*): Scope is an inconclusive parameter in deinflectionalization (cf. also note 4), because it may involve either expansion (scope of the *s*-genitive is expanded from the word level to the phrase level), reduction (in the Kwaza case, scope is reduced from the proposition to the VP), or no change in scope at all (both Old Swedish MASC.SG.NOM *-er* and Modern Swedish derivational *-er* are attached to a single word).

Bondedness (*severance*): In deinflectionalization, severance implies a shift to a 'weaker' type of morpheme boundary (e.g. from stem–affix boundary to host–clitic boundary in the case of the *s*-genitive).

Syntagmatic variability (*flexibilization*): In deinflectionalization, flexibilization cannot occur by definition, because the deinflectionalized grams remain bound and hence fixed in a specific morphological slot.

5. Debonding

5.1. Definition and examples

The final group of degrammaticalization changes involve a shift from bound morpheme to free morpheme, a type which I will term debonding:

(8) Debonding is a composite change whereby a bound morpheme in a specific linguistic context becomes a free morpheme. (Norde 2009a: 186)

Debonding is a relatively common type, but it is also the most heterogeneous one, because its source grams can be inflectional, enclitic, or derivational.

Debonding inflectional suffixes and clitics are some of the most-cited degrammaticalization changes, such as Northern Saami *haga* (abessive suffix > abessive postposition; Nevis 1986), or Irish *muid* (1PL. verb suffix > personal pronoun 'we'; Doyle 2002), exemplified in (9):

(9) a. molfa-**maid** Early Modern Irish
praise-FUT.1PL

b. molfaid **muid** Contemporary Connemara Irish
praise-FUT we
'we will praise'

Another example is from Hup (Epps in preparation), a polysynthetic Amazonian language with a complex verb template with multiple slots for grammatical formatives. Some of these formatives (which according to Epps are inner suffixes) may become enclitic, even to a nonverbal predicate.

What all examples of debonding inflectional affixes have in common is that they continue the grammatical function they had as affixes.[10] The same is true of debonding clitics. Examples of this type of debonding are the following:

(10) a. Infinitival markers in English (Fischer 2000; Fitzmaurice 2000) and Norwegian (Faarlund 2007): from proclitic to free morpheme.
b. Japanese adverbial subordinator *-ga* 'although' > free linker *ga* 'but' (Matsumoto 1988).

Of these examples, (10b) is questionable, because the Japanese particle involves a shift towards increasing subjectivity (Matsumoto 1988: 347f.), a change normally associated with grammaticalization, not degrammaticalization. The infinitival markers appear to be valid examples, however, because earlier evidence suggests

[10] Irish *muid* is an exception, as a pronoun can be said to be slightly less abstract than a verbal suffix.

that the infinitival markers were inseparable from the infinitive (see (11a)), whereas split infinitives (11b) and coordination reduction in contemporary English and Norwegian show that they are clearly free morphemes.

(11) a. Traust och bescherming **at**forswara Early Modern Norwegian
trust and safety to.defend
'to defend trust and safety'

b. *eg skal lova å ikkje seia noko* Modern Norwegian
I shall promise to not say anything
'I promise not to say anything'

Debonding of derivational affixes is different from the two types discussed above, even though it is generally acknowledged that there is no strict demarcation between clitics and inflectional affixes on the one hand and derivational affixes on the other (Brinton and Traugott 2005: 132ff.); but for the present purpose it suffices to say that, unlike clitics and inflectional affixes, derivational affixes usually do not have a grammatical function but are used to derive a new meaning. As a consequence, debonding derivational affixes do not continue a grammatical function (as do inflectional affixes and clitics) but expand their semantic substance. Examples of this subtype of debonding are the following:

(12) a. Dutch/Frisian/German *tig/tich/zig* '*-ty*' > quantifier 'dozens' (Norde 2006b).
b. Northern Swedish prefix *bö-* > full verb *bö* 'to need' (Rosenkvist 2008).
c. English *-ish* (as in *boyish*) > free adverb *ish* 'kind of' (Kuzmack in preparation).
d. Tura *-lá* '(approx.) anywhere' > separable derivational marker with the additional function of focalizer (Idiatov 2008).

This type of debonding is often confused with the lexicalization of derivational affixes such as *isms* and *ologies* (Brinton and Traugott 2005: 60), but is crucially different from it. Words such as *isms* and *ologies* can be seen as 'delocutive word formation' (Haspelmath 2004b: 29ff.), a metalinguistic usage of affixes as a hypernym of all derivations containing that affix (e.g. 'all ideologies ending in *-ism*'), and this kind of change is not construction-internal. A debonded affix such as Dutch *tig*, on the other hand, is not a hypernym of all numerals between 20 and 90, but has a meaning of its own, and appears in the same quantifying constructions as numerals ending in *-tig*.

5.2. Debonding in terms of Lehmann's parameters

The defining parameter in debonding is bondedness, because in all three subtypes, bound morphemes (inflectional, enclitic, or derivational), become free morphemes (severance). As regards the other parameters, the subtypes may differ slightly:

Integrity (*resemanticization*): When derivational affixes debond, they gain in semantic substance, but with debonding inflectional affixes and clitics this is usually not the case; in Japanese *ga* there is even a 'counterdirectional' change in meaning (increasing subjectivity), which makes *ga* a problematic example; (*phonological strengthening*): there is mostly no change at the phonological level, with the exception of Dutch *tig*, which is pronounced ([tɩx]), whereas the suffix from which it derives is pronounced [təx]; (*recategorialization*): with inflectional affixes and clitics, there is usually no recategorialization, with the exception of Irish *muid* which has an emphatic form *muide* (Norde 2009a: 206), but debonding derivational affixes (except English *ish*) do recategorialize, because they acquire verbal morphology (Northern Swedish *bö* and Tura *lá*), or superlative and comparative forms (Dutch *tig*; see Norde forthcoming for examples).

Paradigmatic variability (*deobligatorification*): In some cases there is no decrease in obligatoriness (infinitival markers, for example, remain obligatory; English *ish* remains non-obligatory), in others there is (e.g. the Northern Saami postposition *haga* may be substituted by other abessive elements; Ylikoski 2008: 106f.; Tura *lá* is not longer obligatory as a free morpheme, because it can often be replaced by a free morpheme with similar function).

Structural scope (*scope expansion*): In debonding, scope expansion is generally attested, as evidenced, for example, by the rise of split infinitives and coordination reduction with infinitival markers, or the ability to take scope over entire phrases, as with Dutch *tig*.

Syntagmatic variability (*flexibilization*): In most cases of debonding grams gain in syntactic freedom, as they become free morphemes.

6. Concluding remarks

Paradoxically, the very existence of the degrammaticalization changes both challenges and confirms the so-called unidirectionality hypothesis (e.g. Hopper and Traugott 2003: 99ff.), which says that lexical items may become grammatical, but not vice versa, and grammatical items may become 'more grammatical' (in terms of Lehmann's parameters), but not less so. Degrammaticalization challenges this hypothesis because change in the 'reverse' direction is evidently possible, but at the same time, the relatively low number of attested degrammaticalization changes confirms that there exist strong directional tendencies in grammatical change. These tendencies, in turn, are fed by directional preferences of the primitive changes involved (Norde 2009a: 66ff.)—for instance, desemanticization is far more common than resemanticization, and univerbation is far more common than severance. The cumulative effect of those preferences is that degrammaticalization is rarer still, as degrammaticalization is defined as involving counterdirectional primitive changes on more than one level. This naturally begs the question of why there are directional preferences in the first place. The most plausible explanation, in my view, is that since grammaticalization typically involves attrition on all levels, grams (particularly affixes) have little possibility of gaining substance on any of these levels. For instance, once the semantics of a gram have been substantially bleached, little semantic substance remains to infer new meanings or functions from (in ambiguous contexts, which I consider the locus of (de)grammaticalization change). Such pragmatic inferencing seems most viable in grams that form the source of degrammation, because these are less bleached semantically than, for example, case suffixes. But degrammation is hindered by the fact that its target categories (nouns and verbs) inflect, so that in order for an ambiguous context to arise, the function word needs to be morphologically identical to an inflected noun or verb form. A common denominator for most cases of deinflectionalization is that the deinflectionalizing gram was either part of an obsolescent morphological category such as case (Old Swedish MASC/NEUT.SG.GEN *-s*, MASC.SG.NOM *-er*), or was very marginal (Old Swedish NEUT.PL.NOM/ACC *-on*, which only occurred in a handful of nouns). Debonding of clitics and inflectional affixes is often facilitated by changes elsewhere (particularly in syntax), but this does not seem relevant in debonding of derivational affixes, many cases of which originate in emphatic constructions (e.g. Dutch *tig* 'dozens' or English *ish*).

PART IV

GRAMMATICALIZATION OF FORM CLASSES AND CATEGORIES

CHAPTER 39

THE GRAMMATICALIZATION OF AGREEMENT

ELLY VAN GELDEREN

Givón (1971; 1978), arguing that agreement markers arise from pronouns, says: 'agreement and pronominalization . . . are fundamentally one and the same phenomenon' (1978: 151). In this chapter, I show that emphatic and demonstrative pronouns as well as nouns can be reanalysed as subject pronouns, which in turn can be reanalysed as agreement and later be lost. I refer to this series of changes as the Subject Agreement Cycle or Subject Cycle. Subject agreement is frequent, as Bybee's (1985) estimate of 56 per cent verbal agreement with the subject shows and Siewierska's (2008) of 70 per cent. Subjects aren't the only arguments involved in this kind of a cycle; object pronouns can also become agreement markers, as I will show.

The outline of this chapter is as follows. In section 1, I briefly discuss the linguistic cycle in general and the question whether subject and object cycles are the most relevant to the typology of a language. Section 2 provides examples of the subject cycle and section 3 of the object cycle. These sections also pay attention to where the cycles start and how the subjects and objects are renewed. Section 4 examines possible explanations for why subject and object cycles exist.

My thanks to Olga Fischer, Bernd Heine, and Heiko Narrog for helpful suggestions.

1. Early work on the linguistic cycle

When linguists use 'THE linguistic cycle', as for example Hodge (1970) does, they mean the change from analytic to synthetic and back. Subject and object cycles are of course crucial in determining the degrees of analyticity and syntheticity.

There are early advocates of the view that language change is cyclical, such as de Condillac (1746), von Humboldt (1822), and Bopp (1975 [1816]). The oft-cited passage in von der Gabelentz (1901[1891]: 256) uses 'spiral' to indicate new cycles are not identical to the old ones:

(1) immer gilt das Gleiche: die Entwicklungslinie krümmt sich zurück nach der Seite der Isolation, nicht in die alte Bahn, sondern in eine annähernd parallele. Darum vergleiche ich sie der Spirale. (von der Gabelentz 1901: 256)[1]

Both words, 'cycle' and 'spiral', emphasize the unidirectional nature of linguistic change: the change is not one from synthetic to analytic forms and then back, but to ever different forms.

Hodge (1970), in 'The Linguistic Cycle', shows, using the history of Egyptian, that it has gone through a few cycles. He uses lower and upper case to give a visual representation of full cycles from synthetic (sM), with little s(yntax) and more m(orphology) to analytic (Sm) and to another synthetic stage. His representation is provided in Table 39.1.

Hodge's stages mainly concern marking of the arguments on the verb (synthetic) or independently (analytic). However, Heine, Claudi, and Hünnemeyer (1991: 246) argue that there is 'more justification to apply the notion of a linguistic cycle to individual linguistic developments'. I take them to mean that arguing for a negative or aspect cycle is more feasible than arguing for a cycle from one language type to another, i.e. analytic to synthetic to analytic and so on.

Table 39.1. Developments in Egyptian (from Hodge 1970: 5)

Proto-Afroasiatic	*Sm
Old Egyptian	sM
Late Egyptian	Sm
Coptic	sM

[1] '[A]lways the same: the development curves back towards isolation, not in the old way, but in a parallel fashion. That's why I compare them to spirals' (my translation).

Sapir (1921: 128) says 'that the terms [analytic and synthetic] are more useful in defining certain drifts than as "absolute counters"'. Languages can be in one stage for agreement and in another for TMA markings and negation. The often-cited Chinese language is analytic in that mood, negation, and aspect are expressed as separate words but might be becoming more synthetic because, for instance, the perfective marker *-le* cannot be on its own and has grammaticalized from the verb *liao* meaning 'to complete' among other meanings (Sun 1996). Modern English cannot be characterized as a completely analytic language since futures and negatives are becoming less independent, as in (2).

(2) *I* ***shouldna*** *done that* Colloquial English
'I should not have done that.'

This shows that it is really hard to give a precise definition of synthetic and analytic and therefore of the cyclical stage a language is in. Looking at cycles provides some insight into the mechanisms. If one thinks of head-marking patterns (the marking of subject and object on the verb) as crucial to the analyticity/ syntheticity of a language, they are the most important.

2. The subject cycle[2]

The oft-noted cline expressing that pronouns can be reanalysed as clitics and agreement markers is given in (3).

(3) a. demonstrative > third person pronoun > clitic > agreement > zero
b. noun/oblique/emphatic > first/second person pronoun > clitic > agreement > zero

For instance, the Latin demonstrative *ille* 'that' is reanalysed as the French 3rd person subject pronoun *il* 'he', in accordance with (3a), as is the 3rd person object pronoun *le* 'him'. First and 2nd person agreement markers frequently develop from nouns rather than demonstrative, as shown in (3b). As we will see later, the French 3rd person masculine singular pronoun *il* is on its way to becoming an agreement marker. The originally oblique emphatic 1st and 2nd person pronouns *moi* 'me' and *toi* 'you' are becoming 1st and 2nd person pronoun subjects, respectively. The differences between (3a) and (3b) reflect the well-known views of Benveniste (1966b) that 1st and 2nd person pronouns and 3rd person ones function differently: the former have their own reference, while the latter need to refer. I will argue that

[2] The examples in this section are taken from van Gelderen (2009: ch. 2).

this means the 3rd person has either deictic or gender features, whereas 1st and 2nd person are pure person-features.

The changes in (3) have been studied extensively. According to Tauli (1958: 99, based on Gavel and Lacombe 1929–37), the Basque verbal prefixes *n-*, *g-*, *z-* are identical to the pronouns *ni* 'I', *gu* 'we', and *zu* 'you.' Givón (1978: 157) assumes that Bantu agreement markers derive from pronouns. As early as the 19th century, Proto-Indo-European verbal endings *-mi,- si, -ti* are considered to arise from pronouns (e.g. Bopp 1816). Hale (1973: 340) argues that in Pama-Nyungan, inflectional markers are derived from independent pronouns: 'the source of pronominal clitics in Walbiri is in fact independent pronouns.' Likewise, Mithun (1991) claims that Iroquoian agreement markers derive from Proto-Iroquoian pronouns, and Haugen (2008) argues that Nahuatl agreement markers derive from earlier forms. Fuß (2005) cites many additional examples.

Marking subject and object arguments on the verb may constitute polysynthesis. I will not discuss that aspect here but will just focus on the mechanism of pronoun to agreement.

The traditional agreement cycle can be represented as having a demonstrative/ pronominal source. In many languages, the agreement affix resembles the emphatic pronoun and derives from it. The best-known case is French subject pronouns. The subject was optional in earlier stages of French. The optional emphatic subject *je* 'I' is reanalysed from emphatic pronoun in (4a) to subject pronoun in (4b). The latter shows an additional emphatic *moi*. *Je* in (4a) is different from that in (4b) in that it need no be adjacent to the verb and is not contracted.

(4) a. *Se je meïsme ne li di* — Old French
If I myself not him tell
'If I don't tell him myself.' (Franzén 1939: 20, Cligès 993)

b. *Moi, j'ai vu ça.* — Colloquial French
me I-have seen that
'I've seen that.'

Currently, *je* is regarded by many (Lambrecht 1981; Zribi-Hertz 1994) as an agreement marker, e.g. (5a) and (5b) show that the subject marker is obligatory and (5c) that it must immediately precede the verb. The same is true for the 2nd person and in many dialects even for 3rd person.

(5) a. *Je lis et j'écris* — Colloquial French
I read and I-write

b. **Je lis et écris*
I read and write

c. **Je probablement ai vu ça*
I probably have seen that

If the subject pronouns are being reanalysed as agreement markers on the verb, how can this happen where other clitics also precede the verb in Standard French, such as the negative and object in (6)?

(6) *mais je ne l'ai pas encore démontré* — Standard French
but I NEG it-have NEG yet proven
'... but I haven't yet proved that'
(*Annales de l'institut Henri Poincaré*, 1932: 284; Google search)

It turns out that sequences such as in (6) are very rare in Colloquial French. As is well known, the negative *ne* is fast disappearing and object clitics are being replaced by *ça*, as in (7).

(7) *j'ai pas encore démontré ça* — Colloquial French
I-have NEG yet proven that
'I haven't yet proved that.'

So we see French go from a stage with an optional emphatic *je* to one where *je* is an agreement marker on the verb. The subject is renewed by an oblique *moi*. This reanalysis is really far advanced with 1st and 2nd person. Third person pronouns are agreement markers in very colloquial French (see e.g. Zribi-Hertz 1994).

In Indo-European languages, it is clear where the cycle starts. In Old English, a moderate pro-drop language, the 3rd person pronoun is dropped more often than 1st or 2nd person pronouns. This means that 1st and 2nd person pronouns are the first to be reanalysed as arguments, shown in Table 39.2. In Italian dialects, a similar split appears. As (8) and (9) show (both from Poletto 2004), the 2nd person is 'ahead' of the 3rd to have obligatory subject agreement (i.e. *te* in (8)).

Table 39.2. Null versus overt subject in four Old English manuscripts (from van Gelderen 2000, based on Berndt 1956)[3] (percentages in brackets)

1S	9/212 (96)	9/656 (99)	6/191 (97)	21/528 (96)
1P	0/53 (100)	1/120 (99)	1/44 (98)	2/100 (98)
2S	16/103 (87)	22/308 (93)	12/90 (88)	22/226 (91)
2P	10/206 (95)	21/428 (95)	20/168 (89)	62/302 (83)
3S	445/116 (21)	1,292/225 (15)	223/246 (54)	995/186 (16)
3P	263/108 (29)	618/154 (20)	130/141 (52)	528/124 (19)

[3] A reviewer points out that the figures include pro-drop in coordinated sentences. This is true but seems as frequent (Berndt 1956: 72) with 1st as with 3rd person pronouns.

(8) *Ti te magni sempre* Venice
you you eat always
'You always eat.'

(9) *Nane (el) magna* Venice
John he eats
'John eats.'

Indefinites and quantifiers are the last to show 'doubling', as (10) shows, where the quantifier *nissun* cannot appear with the pronoun *el*. When they do occur together, the earlier pronoun has been reanalysed as agreement marker, because the quantifier cannot double with real arguments, unlike topicalized elements.

(10) *Nissun (*el) magna* Venice
Nobody he eats
'Nobody eats.' (all from Poletto 2004)

In many non-Indo-European languages, the verbal paradigm shows a split between 1st and 2nd person on the one hand and 3rd person on the other. For example, in Algonquian languages, such as Cree, 1st and 2nd person agreement is a prefix and 3rd person agreement is a suffix, as in (11).

(11) a. *ni-nēhiyawān* Cree
1s-speak.Cree
'I speak Cree.'

b. *ki-nēhiyawān* Cree
2s-speak.Cree
'You speak Cree.'

c. *nēhiyaw-ēw* Cree
speak.Cree-3s
'S/he speaks Cree.'
(Mithun 1991: 87, data from Monica Brown)

Mithun (1991: 87) provides other data that North American languages 1st and 2nd person have different grammaticalization patterns from 3rd person pronouns, and argues that there is 'evidence of the special antiquity of first and second person forms' in that they are considerably more fused.

Many 1st and 2nd person pronouns derive from nouns (see Cysouw 2003; Babaev 2008): Dutch *jullie* 'you-P' has its origin in *je lieden* 'you people', and Indonesian *saya* 'I' originates in 'servant, slave', but is now the regular 1st person, as in (12). Thai is reported to have over 20 1st and 2nd person markers, all derived from nouns. In (13), also from Indonesian, the 2nd person still has the lexical meaning of 'father.'

(12) *Saya tinggal di Bali* Indonesian
I live at Bali
'I live in Bali.'

(13) *Bapak tinggal di sini* Indonesian
Father live at here
'Do you-honorific live here?' (Sneddon 1996: 162)

Demonstratives and nouns provide sources of person and number features, but other features are bleached out when this reanalysis takes place.

In conclusion, the reanalysis of a subject pronoun to an agreement marker is a frequent occurrence. First and 2nd person lead the way in becoming clitics and then agreement markers. Indefinite subjects are the last.

3. Examples of Object Cycles[4]

Like subject pronouns, independent object pronouns can attach to verbs to become dependent heads. They can subsequently be reanalysed as agreement markers and disappear. This increase and decrease in head marking can be represented as the Object Cycle. The phenomenon is widely attested in the Afro-Asiatic, Bantu, Dravidian, and Indo-European language families. In this chapter, I will discuss examples from Indo-European and Athabascan.

In Standard Spanish, personal pronouns are 'doubled' through clitics, as (14) shows. That is not the case with full NPs, as (15) shows.

(14) *lo vimos a él* Standard Spanish
him 1P-saw OM him
'We saw him.'

(15) a. *Vimos la casa de Maria* Standard Spanish
1P-saw the house of Maria
b. **La vimos la casa de Maria*
it 1P-saw the house of Maria
'We saw Maria's house.'

In other varieties of Spanish, names are doubled, as in (16) and (17), and in some even indefinite NPs are, as in (18).

4 The examples in this section are taken from van Gelderen (2009: ch. 3).

(16) *Pedro* ***lo*** *vió* ***a*** ***Juan*** River Plate Spanish
Pedro him 3S-saw OM Juan
'Pedro saw Juan.'

(17) *De repente* ***la*** *vió* ***a*** ***Grimanesa*** *bajando las escaleras* Limeño
Suddenly her saw OM Grimanesa descending the stairs
'Suddenly, s/he saw Grimanesa coming down the stairs.' (Mayer 2003: 21)

(18) ***lo*** *trae* ***un*** ***chiquihuite*** Malinche Spanish
it he-brings a basket
'He brings a basket.' (Hill 1987: 74)

Thus, the varieties of Spanish show how an object cycle operates. In standard Spanish the object is still a full pronoun, whereas in Malinche Spanish it has been reanalysed as agreement marker.

In South Slavic, various languages double the object. Macedonian doubles definite objects, as in (19) and (20), but not indefinite objects, as in (21).

(19) *Daniela* ***go*** *poznava nego* Macedonian
Daniela 3MS knows him
'Daniela knows him.'

(20) *Daniela* ***ja*** *kupi knigata* Macedonian
Daniela 3FS bought book-the
'Daniela bought the book.'

(21) *Daniela kupi* ***edna kniga/knigi*** Macedonian
Daniela bought one book/books.
'Daniela bought a book/books.'
(Daniela Kostadinovska and Victorija Todorovska, p.c.)

Northern Athabascan languages, such as Ahtna, Slave, and Dogrib, display complementary distribution between the nominal objects in (22a) and verbal affixation in (22b).

(22) a. *sú* ***tuwele*** *k'ágoweneli* Slave
Q soup 2S.taste
'Have you tasted the soup?'

b. *sú* ***be-****k'ágoweneli* Slave
Q 3S-2S.taste
'Have you tasted it?' (from Jelinek 2001)

Babine-Witsuwit'en, a northern Athabascan language, has only indefinite DPs, as in (23a), in complementary distribution with verbal agreement (Gunlogson 2001;

Jelinek 2001); the definite ones can be doubled, as in (23b). This fact points to a change towards a more polysynthetic stage.

(23) a. *dinï hida nilh'ën* Babine-Witsuwit'en
man moose at.3.look
'The man is looking at **a moose**.'

b. *hida* ***dinï*** *yi-nilh'ën* Babine-Witsuwit'en
moose man 3-at.3.look
'The moose is looking at **the man**.'
(Gunlogson 2001: 374)

The innovative southern languages have an obligatory agreement marker with all objects, as is shown in the Navajo example in (24). This object marker is at the periphery but, as more material is added to the verbal complex, it may be eroded.

(24) *('atoo') yí-ní-dlą́ą́'-ísh* Navajo
soup 3S-2S-eat-Q
'Did you eat the soup?'

The start of the object cycle is much less clear than that of the subject cycle where 1st and 2nd person are the ones first reanalysed. For the object cycle, it is human objects or definite objects, as is the case in Spanish and Macedonian; and in Athabascan, it may be definite human objects. Since 1st and 2nd person are the most definite arguments, they lead the way in Swahili (see Wald 1979), and possibly in Albanian, Marshallese, and Uto-Aztecan (see van Gelderen 2009).

4. Towards an explanation?

In Givón's (1976) account, topicalized nominals turn into subjects. This is sometimes called the NP-detachment hypothesis: agreement markers develop from resumptive pronouns in topicalized constructions, such as (25a). The topic is then reanalysed as subject, as in (25b).

(25) a. That man, **he** shouldn't be…
↓
b. That man he-shouldn't be…

Ariel (2000: 211) and Fuß (2005: 9–10), among others, argue against Givón's account. Fuß suggests that Givón would predict the changes starting in the 3rd person, which is not the case. Ariel examines the stages in Hebrew and argues that they do not show many topicalized nominals. She also cites evidence from Celtic, Swahili, and Australian languages where pronouns and agreement are in complementary distribution, which one would not expect in Givón's account.

Ariel (1990; 2000) argues for an Accessibility Theory. A (simplified) Accessibility Hierarchy is provided in (26): agreement and pronouns represent different points on a continuum of accessibility marking. A speaker chooses between these on the basis of the mental accessibility of what is referred to.

(26) zero < poor agreement < rich agreement < clitics < unstressed pronouns < stressed pronouns < demonstratives < full name
(part of the accessibility scale: Ariel 2000: 205)

A personal pronoun is more accessible in the speaker's mind than a noun is. Ariel suggests that 1st and 2nd person are more accessible than 3rd person and can therefore be marked by agreement rather than a full pronoun. Third persons are less accessible and therefore marked by either pronouns or nouns. This need for 3rd persons to be additionally marked also explains the use of demonstratives for 3rd persons, a more marked form for a less accessible person, and the use of topic-drop for (highly accessible) 1st person in English (*Hope to see you soon.*) She concludes that 'first and second person referents are consistently highly accessible, but third person referents are only extremely accessible when they happen to be the continuing discourse topic(s)' (Ariel 2000: 221).

There are, of course, counterexamples from languages that have 3rd person agreement but not 1st or 2nd. Ariel mentions English 3rd person singular present marking. In English, 1st and 2nd person pronouns were historically used as subjects before 3rd person ones (Berndt 1956; van Gelderen 2000: ch. 3). The same is true of German (van Gelderen 2000: 136; Axel 2005).

Another account of the person differences is the frequency-driven one, espoused by several scholars. Siewierska (2004: 266–8) provides a brief review and points out that the frequency of certain pronouns is so dependent on text type that it is hard to use this to explain person differences. Spoken narratives contain a lot of 3rd person subjects (and objects) but regular dialogue has a lot of 1st and 2nd person. I will therefore turn to other explanations and look at the problem through a Minimalist lens.

Poletto's explanation of the person hierarchy involves feature checking. First and 2nd person marking involves more features than 3rd person. Therefore, in the case of 1st and 2nd person, the verb has too many features to check and a clitic pronoun appears as an auxiliary element, i.e. it 'is a sort of substitute for a verb' (2000: 147). Poletto argues, that rather than having the verb check all the features in separate functional categories, the clitics or agreement markers do this more economically. She claims that pronoun doubling is more frequent with those elements that have more functional information, and that the number of features to be checked causes the doubling. She explains the Definiteness Hierarchy by a universal order of checking domains: 1st and 2nd below 3rd, below plural, etc. I will also use features, but argue something different.

Elsewhere (e.g. van Gelderen 2008), I have claimed that there is a cognitive principle, Feature Economy, assisting the acquisition process, and that DPs and other elements are analysed by the language learner with as few semantic features as is compatible with the data. Within Minimalism, lexical items have several kinds of features: (pro)nouns have interpretable person features because person is something inherent to them whereas verbs need to 'receive' person features from a nominal. The features on the verb are uninterpretable because they are not relevant to the meaning, only to keeping the computation going (i.e. to make sure elements connect to form a sentence).

(27) The cycle of person (and number) features

noun >	emphatic subject > pronoun >	agreement >	Zero
[semantic]	[interpretable]	[uninterpretable]	

During grammaticalization, a pronoun loses its interpretable features and, as an agreement marker, ends up with uninterpretable features in a functional position. The consistency with which certain interpretable features disappear first, i.e. are reanalysed as uninterpretable, needs to be explained. I suggest (*contra* Déchaine & Wiltschko 2002) that 1st and 2nd person are pure phi-features (person and number), whereas 3rd person has additional features and is therefore not incorporated as easily. A longer account of this can be found in van Gelderen (2009: ch. 2).

5. Conclusion

Pronouns are often reanalysed as agreement markers. In this chapter, I have provided a few examples and also suggested some of the explanations given by people for where the cycles start and how the reanalysed pronouns are renewed.

CHAPTER 40

ADVERBIAL GRAMMATICALIZATION

PAOLO RAMAT

1. Definition of adverb

Though not present in all languages, the linguistic category adverb (ADV) may be given a universally valid definition which applies to all languages that have adverbs. We have to distinguish between definition and implementation of categories, but a categorial definition cannot be language-bound (see Ramat 1999).[1] From a functional point of view, the ADV category presents a wide range of values which go from manner to time, space, degree, and modifies other categories (see next paragraph). As we shall see below, some values are more grammaticalizable than others: in Turkish and Malay, for example, reduplication of an adjective (ADJ) or, respectively, a verb (VB) to form the corresponding manner ADV is grammaticalized, and produces a real category change: Turk. *derin derin* 'deeply' (*derin* 'deep') with ADJ → ADV, Malay *diam-diam* 'silently' (*diam* 'to be silent') with VB → ADV).[2]

[1] For further reading on the subject of the present chapter, see Cuzzolin, Putzu, and Ramat (2006), Ramat (1996; 2006; 2008), and Ramat and Ricca (1994; 1998).

[2] Dealing with grammaticalization processes we have of course to distinguish between repetition as a regular morphological means and occasional repetition: in Afrikaans we find *Dis beter dat sulke mense liever stil-stil verwyn* 'it is better that such people rather disappear quietly' (*stil*$_{ADJ}$ 'quiet') and also *Hy skop-skop*$_{VB}$ *die grond van die dooie gestig af*, lit. 'He kick-kick the soil from the dead face off', i.e. 'He removes the soil from the dead face by kicking movements', where the repetition does not produce an adverbial value and just indicates a repeated action (Conradie 2003).

Here is a viable definition of adverb: ADV is a grammatical category of invariable lexemes which are syntactically dispensable (cf. *The news she had just received deeply surprised her* and *The news she had received surprised her*: the second sentence is absolutely grammatical).

ADV is a lexical element which cannot represent a sentence by itself, unless it is used in a conversational answer turn.[3] From the semantic-functional point of view it is clear that *just* and *deeply* modify the sense of the sentence. Hence we can say that ADV is a modifier of predicates (*just received, deeply surprised*), other modifiers (e.g. *rather deeply*), NPs (*even the (Prime) Minister was surprised*) or even higher syntactic units (*Unfortunately, he missed the goal*): see Ramat and Ricca (1994). Haser and Kortmann (2006: 67) find counterexamples to the morphosyntactic features that according to Ramat and Ricca (1994) characterize prototypical adverbs, namely (i) adverbs are invariable, (ii) they are optional, (iii) they can be modified by other adverbs, (iv) they can modify other word categories except nouns. For instance, it is true that, contrary to (ii), certain verbs, in some languages like English, require the presence of adverbs: *The job paid us handsomely* vs. **The job paid us.* As for (iv), it has to be specified that ADVs cannot modify nouns, but they do modify NPs: **even Minister was surprised* is ungrammatical, but *even [the (Prime) Minister]*$_{\text{NP}}$ *was surprised* is fine. The point is, however, that an adverb can well lack one of the above four features, but, if so, it is not a prototypical ADV.

Note that this definition does not include adverbial phrases such as *in principle, in my opinion*, etc., which represent an open class that can always be extended. For practical reasons, the definition considers just monorhematic expressions (i.e. one-word expressions), though many adverbial phrases behave just like monorhematic ADVs. Moreover, formulaic phrases such as *in/to the eyes of* are complex prepositions obligatorily introducing an NP, or a clause.

There is a lively discussion about modal particles ('*Modalpartikeln*') such as Engl. *indeed*, Germ. *eben*, etc. Do they belong to the ADV category or not? Actually, they do not modify other lexemes of the sentence. Their function seems to be different and syntactically they are not bound to other lexemes in the sentence; they express a particular discourse intention/strategy of the speaker: cf. Germ. *Deutsch ist eben schwer* 'German is really difficult', where the modal particle is pointing to the fact that the speaker has already expressed his/her opinion about the difficulty of German and now is iterating his/her statement with a pragmatic effect (see Diewald and Ferraresi 2008: 79). Modal particles could be considered to be similar to utterance ADVs which qualify the speaker's attitude toward what (s/)he's going to

[3] E.g. Question: *Have you been heavily surprised by the news?* Answer: (*very*) *heavily*. A restricted number of adverbs may be used as predicates in sentences like *You'll get well soon*, Fr. *Je ne me sens pas bien*, Germ. *Mir geht es nicht gut*, Bulg. е съм добре (not добьíр$_{\text{MASC}}$ / добрá$_{\text{FEM}}$ / добрó$_{\text{NTR}}$) lit. 'Not I.am well', i.e. 'I'm not feeling well'. But one cannot say **You'll get happily soon* nor **Je ne me sens pas heureusement* instead of *Je ne me sens pas heureux*. Generally speaking, adverbs cannot be used as predicates when they are derived from adjectives: *heureux* > *heureusement* (see below).

say (e.g. *Frankly, I do not believe you*) but *Really/Frankly/Honestly, German is a difficult language* has not the same meaning as *Deutsch ist eben schwer* where *eben* has a cohesive function and does not depend on clause-internal constituents. (cf. *? *Eben Deutsch ist schwer*)). Abraham (2000: 333), in the frame of the minimalist theory, distinguishes between 'modal particles' and the original full lexical homonyms they derive from, as they have a completely different distribution (see e.g. *bloß* in *Sei bloß ruhig*! 'Be quiet, for God's sake!'). In what follows I will not consider modal particles.

2. Cognitive and linguistic categories

It is necessary to distinguish between linguistic categories like NOUN, VERB, ADJECTIVE, ADVERB, etc. (the traditional parts of speech, with their morphosyntactic implementations) and congnitive categories like TENSE, EVIDENTIALITY, OPTATIVITY, etc.—and also ADVERBIALITY (which can even lack autonomous lexical and/or morphosyntactic expression). There exist languages such as Yidiŋ (Australia, Pama-Nyungan) or Palau (Philippines, Micronesia) where the adverbial function is expressed not by autonomous lexemes but by other means. In Yidiŋ 'adverbs' are inflected exactly as the verb they modify. Palau makes use of a relator *-r* with adverbial function both with verbs and NPs (see Hagège 1985). In Avar some "adverbs" agree with the NP that appears in the same phrase but they don't agree with the verb they semantically modify (Anderson 1985: 200ff.). Givón (1984: 80f.) notes that '[i]n some languages, noun, verb or adjective stems may become **incorporated** into the verbal word when functioning as manner adverbs'. Many other instances of ADVERBIALITY expressed by means other than ADV could be quoted (see Cuzzolin et al. 2006). The consequence is that it is not always easy to morphologically distinguish between adverbs and nouns or adjectives, or between adverbs, prepositions, and conjunctions (Haser and Kortmann 2006: 68). In the so-called flexible languages (see Hengeveld 1992) the same lexeme may be used as ADV, ADJ, or ADP. Lexical items can be used with different functions without any superficial modification of their form (see the transcategorization of German *schön*$_{\text{ADJ}}$: *sie ist schön* 'good looking' and *sie singt schön*$_{\text{ADV}}$ 'in a nice way', Turkish *güzel*$_{\text{ADJ}}$ *sanatlar* 'fine arts' and *siz güzel*$_{\text{ADV}}$ *konuşuyorsunuz* 'you (PL) speak good'; cp. Ježek and Ramat 2009). According to the constructional approach, it has to be noted that the syntactic function of a lexeme is often defined by its position within a construction and its semantics is determined by a combination of its own lexical meaning plus the meaning contributed to it by the function of the position within the construction (Bisang in press).

3. Adverbial formations

Case and mood markers can be used to express adverbial circumstantials. Lat. *certē* 'surely', *apertē* 'clearly', etc. reflect an old instrumental that disappeared in classical Latin (see below) and Finnish, along with the suffix *-sti*, added to ADJs to form ADVs (*hauska* 'nice' > *hauskasti* 'nicely'), has also an element *-in* (e.g. *hyvin* 'well' < *hyvä* 'good', *harvoin* 'rarely' < *harva* 'rare'): *-in* is the plural (*-i-*) ending of the instructive (instrumental) case *-n*, used almost always in plural even when referring to a single object. Hungarian has a host of specialized suffixes to build ADVs: 1. from ADJs (*V*)+*n* (which is connected with the superessive case): *keserü* 'bitter' > *keserüen* 'bitterly'; 2. The suffix *-ul/ül* is used for ADJs ending in *-t(a)lan/-t(e)len* that have a negative meaning: *szokatlan* 'unusual' > *szokalatanul* 'unusually'; 3. ADJs based on nouns may form ADVs by using a suffix *-lag/-leg*:[4] *gyakorlat* 'practice' > *gyakorlati* 'practical' > *gyakarlati-lag* 'practically'; *elmélet* 'theory' > *elméleti* 'theoretical' > *elméletileg* 'theoretically'.

The phenomenology of forming adverbs could be easily extended. But the aim of this chapter is not to enumerate all the possible strategies. We just notice that Nahuatl has ADV+NOUN compounds: *nen* 'fruitlessly' + *tlaca-tl* 'man' > *nentlacatl* 'a person who can do nothing'. The head of this compound is the noun, whereas in prototypical adverbs the head is the adverbial ending, originally a noun which became a suffix: German *glücklicher-weise*, French *heureuse-ment* 'fortunately'. *-weise* 'way, manner'[5] and *-ment* < Lat. *mente* 'mind' are feminine nouns; hence the adjectival feminine agreement (not **glücklichemweise* nor **heureuxment*). English *-ly* adverbs have had the same development: Old English *bealdlīce* > *baldly*, *swētlīce* > *sweetly* where *-līce* derives from Germanic **likom* 'body, form' (Gothic *leik*, Old English *līc*). Thus *friendly* (< **frijondlīka*) meant 'having the form/aspect of a friend'. In German the *-weise* adverbs originally implied the existence of a corresponding *-lich* adjective: *glück* > *glücklich* 'happy' (thus, originally, 'having the form/aspect of *glück*, good luck'), but in English *-ly* could be attached immediately to simple adjectives, as in *bealdlīce* and *swētlīce*.[6] A similar technique for building adverbs is

[4] *-lag/-leg* (already found in late Old Hungarian) is formed by the Ablative suffix *-l* (cp. *-ul* /*-ül*). *-g* is unclear but could be a lative suffix (**-k*) as in terminative *-ig* 'up to'. Thanks are due to my colleague Guido Manzelli for checking the Finno-Ugric data.

[5] Thus, literally 'in a happy manner'.

[6] However, not all *-ly*-lexemes are adverbs: see *likely* 'probable'. Cf. Chao (2007).

found in Chinese: *shēng* 'to be born, to be by nature' is compounded with *hăo* 'good', giving *hăoshēng* 'well' (lit. 'what is good by nature'; cf. Banfi 2008: 67).

4. The grammaticalization of adverbs

In these adverbs we encounter a clear grammaticalization process: we start out with a phrase-level construction (*glücklicher weise*) which gradually passes on to the word level as a compound. The second member of the nominal compound becomes a word formation suffix which may apply to different lexemes (e.g. *seltsamerweise* 'rarely', *notwendigerweise* 'necessarily', also from nouns: *beispielsweise* 'for instance', *ausnahmsweise* 'exceptionally', etc.). Phonetic erosion may reduce or cancel the transparency of the compound: no English speaker recognizes in *-ly* the second member of a compound (Old English *līc* < Germanic **likom*).

Thus, grammaticalization causes the existence of many adverbial suffixes whose etymology is not clear. Turkish may form adverbs by agglutinating *-le* to a noun: *dikkat* 'care' > *dikkatle* 'carefully', *tereddüt* 'hesitation' > *tereddütle* 'hesitantly', and Ancient Greek had a suffix *-ως* for deriving ADVs from ADJs and NOUNS: *ἄδικος* 'unjust' > *ἀδίκως* 'unjustly', *ἀδέσποτος* 'without master, free' > *ἀδεσπότως* 'freely'. The etymological source of *-le* and *-ως* is not clear.[7] On the other hand, Turkish *-in*, used for temporal adverbs such as *yaz-ın* 'in the summer', *kışın* 'in the winter', derives from an old instrumental case, just as Homeric Greek *-φι* in the stereotyped expression like *ἶφι* 'with force, strongly' (see above for the development Case → ADV). These suffixes are no longer productive and the adverbs formed with them are a closed class of frozen forms.[8]

We thus have to distinguish between:

(a) productive word formation rules (WFRS), which are the usual way for building new adverbs (an open class);[9]

[7] Remember that, being a language with noun and adjective declension, Greek grammarians already considered the adverbs ending in *-ως* as the sixth case. This implicitly underlines the difficulty of drawing a neat borderline between inflection and word-formation rules. See below also the discussion of German *nachts*.

[8] As an anonymous peer review observes, it would be interesting to inquiry whether the adverb–verb agreement we find in languages such as Yidiŋ or the Avar adverb–NP agreement (see section 2) can be considered as a case of grammaticalization. There is no doubt that agreement is a grammatical strategy. The point is whether, when analysing Yidiŋ and Avar, we can really speak of lexemes that belong to the ADV category. In the frame of the present chapter I can but allude to the problem.

[9] Even if the WFRS cannot be mechanically applied: we have *philosophical-ly, cynical-ly* from the adjectives *philosophical, cynical,* but also *linguistically* (not **linguistic-ly* like *public-ly, frantic-ly* (arch.)), although the adjective is *linguistic* and not **linguistical.* Analogical processes are evidently at work.

(b) WFRs that have been productive but synchronically are no longer productive;
(c) lexical items which cannot be explained according to known WFRs.

The boundaries between (a), (b), and (c) are not clear-cut. No doubt that the -(*e*)*s* German suffix is the genitive marker (: *Auftrag-*(*e*)*s* 'of the task', *Wein-*(*e*)*s* 'of the wine'), but in space and time adverbials such as *unterwegs* 'on the way', *links* 'to the left', *nachts* 'during the night',[10] *sonntags* 'on Sunday' the -*s* is no longer a productive adverbial suffix, and one cannot say **Kirchens* 'in the church' nor **Wochens* 'during the week'. *Unterwegs* etc. belong clearly to the (b) type.

At the (b) -level there may be two competing forms, an older and a new one: Ancient Greek ὅκοι 'at home', Lat. *dom(u)i*, same meaning, are remnants of the locative case; but we may find instead the new prepositional phrases ἐν οἴκῳ, *in domo*.[11]

But how should we judge adverbs like *tomorrow*, *today*, or *tonight* vs. **toweek* 'this week' or **tomonth* 'this month'? *Morrow* (cf. German *der Morgen* 'the morning') is an archaic word, rarely used. On the other hand *yester-day* has a quite usual word as second element of the compound, whereas *yester* exists just in the other, rare, temporal adverb *yesteryear* (but not **yesterweek*). Both the *tomorrow* and *yesterday* types are non-productive, and only partially transparent. They are between (b) and (c): see Traugott's discussion (1994) about monomorphemic or bimorphemic adverbs like *today* and *tonight*.

Finally we have adverbs of the (c) type, such as Ancient Greek χθές 'yesterday' whose etymology and formation are by no means clear. χαμαί 'in the earth' is an old locative (like Latin *humī*), but the noun *χάμα does not exist in Greek, so that χαμαί is completely opaque. Moreover, as we already said, the locative case disappeared very early, both in Greek and Latin, leaving behind just a handful of frozen forms. To be included in (c) are also adverbs which are no longer transparent, even if their etymology is clear. No one recognizes in Italian *oggi*, Spanish *hoy* 'today' the Latin NP *hoc die* 'in this day'. In *oggi*, *hoy* we have univerbation—via phonetic attrition—of a previously transparent NP. *Oggi* and *hoy* represent the final stage of a continuum which goes from full descriptivity to full labelling (see Seiler 2008: 99–108). *Tomorrow* and *yesterday* represent an intermediate step along this continuum. Italian *sta-mani* 'this morning' (archaic *stamane*) is less transparent than *sta-mattina* (same meaning: *sta-* is the shortening of *questa*$_{\text{FEM}}$ 'this') since *mattina* 'morning' is a usual word of contemporary Italian, whilst *mane* (< Lat. *mane* 'morning') is an archaic word, no longer in use.

[10] Cp. Dutch *'s nachts* where the *'s* is the clear trace of the genitive of the article *des*. The genitive used to express time is typical of ancient Indo-European languages: cp. Greek νυκτός 'during the night'. Germanic languages continue the Indo-European use of cases to express circumstantials (that later became frozen adverbs).

[11] Note that according to the definition of ADV adopted above ("a grammatical category of invariable lexemes which are syntactically dispensable") *links*, *sonntags*, etc. are true adverbs (of space and time, respectively), although they do not have adverbial counterparts in English (and *homely* does not correspond to Greek ὁκοι 'at home': it is an ADJ, as in *a homely lady*).

Clearly, as already observed above, grammaticalization of adverbs concerns, from a synchronic point of view, the (a) type: new adverbs may be created according the WFRs of the language, whereas in cases like *oggi* and *tomorrow* we can speak of isolated lexicalizations of previous NPs and, respectively, PPs. Latin NPs such as *clara mente, aperta mente, sincera mente* underwent desemanticization ('semantic bleaching') of the second element and univerbation. *Apertis*$_{\text{PLUR}}$ *mentibus*$_{\text{PLUR}}$ 'with open minds' would have been possible in Latin if referred to a plurality of persons. But an invariable *-mente* became in the Romance languages a suffix capable of building new adverbs (neologisms) of every possible semantic kind: Italian *atomicamente, linguisticamente, automobilisticamente, tennisticamente*, etc.

5. Grammaticalization and Lexicalization

In the literature, lexicalization and grammaticalization are often discussed together and sometimes even blended. But, even if it is difficult to draw sharp dividing lines along the continuum previously alluded to, they have in principle to be kept apart. To give two clear examples of lexicalization and grammaticalization, respectively: the already quoted *oggi, hoy* are new lexical items created via univerbation, but they have no impact on the morphological system of Italian and Spanish. The *will/shall* forms of the English future, by contrast, have lost their original meaning and serve as grammatical means to build a form of the verbal paradigm. Chen (2008) has studied the development of four adverbs of quantification in Mandarin Chinese: *zhong, lau, duo,* and *shao* underwent a semantic change from concreteness to abstractness. For instance, the ADJ *lau* originally denotes a long life span (*wo <u>lau</u> le* 'I (am) old') but comes to denote an adverbial quantification of a dynamic process along the time axis (*wo shou bu liao ta <u>lau</u> chou yan*, lit. 'I cannot bear he always smoke', i.e. 'I cannot bear his regularly smoking habits'). *Lau* is still an autonomous word which can qualify many verbs or situations ('states of affairs') like English *always* or Spanish *siempre.* Accordingly, *lau* is not on a par with English *-ly* or French *-ment.* Similarly, we cannot consider *always* and *siempre* as grammaticalized elements: independently of their etymology they are and remain lexical items, which do not enter into any paradigmatic system. In conclusion, *lau* belongs to the same level as *schön* in the above-quoted German example, and we can speak of *lau* as an item which can undergo transcategorization.

Imbert and Grinewald (2008) have examined the grammaticalization and/or lexicalization of 'relational preverbs', i.e. a category of verbal prefixes which are grammaticalized from postpositions. Rama, a Chibchan language spoken in Nicaragua, and Homeric Greek are typologically comparable under this point of view. Greek ἀπο 'off', κατα 'down', etc. (the accent is movable) may occur as ADV (with stress on the final syllable: ἀπό, κατά, etc.), ADP (mainly POST with stress retraction ἄπο κάτα or complete cliticization to the verb), or as PREV (see Cuzzolin et al. 2006). For a similar development of adverbial elements to PREVS—and particles—in Hittite and more generally in ancient Indo-European, see Luraghi 2001a).

We have seen that:

- The function ADVERBIALITY is present everywhere (mainly as expression of circumstantials).
- ADV is a linguistic category (part-of-speech) whose boundaries vis-à-vis other categories are not watertight (see above the German example of *schön*).
- Diachronically we have to distinguish between three types of ADVS (see above (a–c)).
- Some adverb types are easier to grammaticalize according to regular WFRs than others (e.g. manner ADVS, like German *glücklicher-weise*, Fr. *heureuse-ment*, when compared with time ADVS, like German *gestern*, French *hier* 'yesterday'). This means that the WFRs for manner ADVS apply to a larger set of words than time ADVS (see Fr. *vachement* 'very' < *vache* 'cow': *un film vachement rigolo* 'a very amusing movie').

6. Place of the adverbs

A final point to be underlined is the place of the adverbial marker. According to a general principle of 'natural morphology', derivational suffixes occur before inflectional suffixes. They represent the unmarked case (see e. g. *driv-er-s*, where *-er-* is a derivational suffix, whereas *-s* is the plural marker). Polish has an ADJ *ładny* 'nice' and the ADV *ładnie* 'nicely' with the derivative adverbial suffix *-e* (in some cases we may also have *-o*); its comparative is *ładni-ej* 'nicer', where the morphological mark of comparison comes after the derivational suffix *-e*. Basque, as the majority of languages, has the same order ADJ+ADV marker+COMPAR marker (examples from Ricca 1998: 461):

(1) *errex* 'easy' and *errex-*<u>*ago*</u>$_{\text{COMPAR}}$ 'easier'.
(2) *errex-ki*$_{\text{ADV}}$ 'easily' and *errex-*<u>*ki*</u>$_{\text{ADV}}$-<u>*ago*</u>$_{\text{COMPAR}}$ 'more easily'.

On the other hand, Hungarian has the reverse order ADJ+COMPAR marker+ADV marker. (3) has the same order as (2):

(3) *rend-*<u>*es*</u>$_{\text{ADJ}}$ 'tidy, well ordered' and *rend-*<u>*es*</u>$_{\text{ADV}}$-<u>*ebb*</u>$_{\text{COMPAR}}$ 'tidier'.

But in (4) we have:

(4) *rend-<u>es-en</u>*ADV 'orderly' and *rend-<u>es-ebb</u>*COMPAR-*<u>en</u>*ADV 'more orderly' lit. 'order-ly-er'.

Comparing (1) and (2), usually labelled 'adverb comparative', with (3) and (4), which can be considered as 'adverb of the comparative adjective', Ricca suggests that ADV and COMPAR should be seen as belonging to the same morphological process: either derivation or inflection.[12]

7. Conclusions

I have presented a survey of ways in which adverbs can come into existence: via affixation, via case suffixes, by conversion, by 'simple meaning change' (as in Chinese), by change of status (e.g. manner→discourse adverbials), and with true grammaticalized derivators (*-mente*, etc.).

Not every process that produces an adverb is *per se* a grammaticalization process. As we have seen in the previous sections, ADV is a linguistic category which shows very different morphological behaviours. Also, there are languages which have no morphological expression for such a category, or may use lexemes that by default belong to other categories for expressing the adverbial function (see section 2, with the example of German *sie singt schön*). In non-Indo-European languages, adverbs may be inflected and may agree with other elements of the sentence (see the cases of Yidiŋ, Palau, and Avar quoted above). This contradicts one of the basic properties stated at the beginning of this chapter: that ADV is a grammatical category of invariable lexemes. The difficulty of clearly defining what ADV is has led some linguists to deny the existence of such a category and to consider 'adverb' a kind of wastebasket in which to throw all the linguistic material which is difficult to classify (cp. Pottier 1962: 53). This is not the place to reopen the discussion on parts of speech. What we have seen in this chapter is that it makes sense to speak of grammaticalization of adverbs in those languages where there exists the ADV category (see section 4).[13]

[12] There are also languages where COMPAR and ADV are cumulated in a single morpheme. See Polish *słab-y* 'weak' ~ *słab-sz-y* 'weaker' and *słab-o* 'weakly' ~ *słab-iej* 'more weakly'; Lithuanian ger-*as* 'good' ~ *ger-esn-is* 'better' and *ger-ai* 'well' ~ *ger-iau* 'more well'.

[13] The anonymous reviewer observes that there seem to be recurring source constellations which produce adverbs, e.g. the pathway 'instrumental + something → adverb' recurs several times and in various guises. Likewise, there seems to be a trend for full phrases to reduce to adverbial material. It might indeed be worthwhile to study which are the most frequent pathways which lead to ADV. This point opens the way to a typological approach to the study of ADV: are there linguistic types which are easier than other to 'adverbialize'?.

CHAPTER 41

THE GRAMMATICALIZATION OF ADPOSITIONS AND CASE MARKING

CHRISTA KÖNIG

1. Introduction

The behaviour of case in grammaticalization has been discussed in detail in previous chapters in the present handbook series (Kulikov 2008; Heine 2008); the present chapter therefore is restricted mainly to issues that have been treated more peripherally in those contributions.

There is no clear cut borderline between a case language and a non-case language; as with other categories, the transition is fluid. It depends, among other things, on the definition of the means employed for expressing case functions. Case markers commonly develop out of nouns or verbs via an intermediate stage of adpositions, and it is frequently unclear at what stage they can in fact be viewed as being case markers proper (see the discussion on Hungarian below).

2. Features

2.1. Common sources

As observed above, nouns and verbs are the most common sources for case markers, in particular of case markers encoding peripheral participants. Tables 41.1 and 41.2 present some of the frequent pathways from nouns to case markers and from verbs to case markers, respectively, as presented by Heine (2008; see also Kahr 1975; 1976; Kulikov 2006).

Table 41.1. Some common de-nominal sources of case markers (Heine 2008)

Nominal meaning	Case function	Typical English gloss of case function
'back', 'buttock'	locative	'behind'
'flank', 'side'	locative	'beside', 'next to'
'ground', 'reason'	cause	'because'
'head', 'eye', 'front', 'breast'	locative	'in front of'
'hand', 'comrade'	comitative	'(together) with'
'house', 'home'	locative, possessive	'at', 'of'
'middle', 'center'	inessive	'in'
'place', 'area'	locative	'at', 'around'
'soil', 'ground'	locative	'below', 'underneath'
'stomach,' 'guts'	inessive	'in'
'top', 'head', 'sky'	superessive	'on'

Table 41.2. Some common de-verbal sources of case markers (Heine 2008)

Verbal meaning	Case function	Typical English gloss of case function
'come from', 'leave'	ablative	'from'
'be at'	locative	'at'
'go to', 'come to', 'reach', 'arrive at'	allative	'to'
'give'	benefactive, dative	'for', 'to'
'meet', 'join', 'follow'	comitative, instrumental	'with'
'take'	patient, object case	–
'pass'	perlative, pergressive, path	'through', 'along'

Case markers may come into existence via the extension of the function of another case marker. Table 41.3 gives an overview of some common pathways from one case function to another. This is one of the ways in which also core cases, such as nominative, accusative, and ergative, emerge. As can be seen in Table 41.3, an ergative marker can be derived in particular from a locative or comitative, an accusative being an extension, for example, of a dative, the nominative by the extension from A case to S case.

For the rise of an ergative case marker, the following sources are mentioned in the literature (see in particular Narrog 2008):

(i) instruments, as in Hittite, Sanskrit, Avar, Dyirbal, Mangarayi (Lehmann 1983: 368; 1988b: 63; 2002b: 73; Heine and Kuteva 2002: 180; Palancar 2002: 234);
(ii) source, as in Tauya, Dani, Athpare (see Palancar 2002: 234);
(iii) agents expressed as peripheral participants in passive clauses, as in Tibetan, Dyirbal, Avar, Tiriyo (see Givón 2001: 263; Hopper and Traugott 2003: 171; Lehmann 2002b: 98; Palancar 2002: 242; Heine 2008);
(iv) locatives, as in Australian languages (Heine 2008);
(v) genitive/partitives, as in Lak, Eskimo, Sherpa (see Lehmann 1988b: 63; 2002b: 98; Heine 2008);
(vi) nominatives, as in Päri, Jur Luwo, Anywa (see König 2008).

These case markers may be further grammaticalized to nominatives, as in Sherpa, Georgian, Mingrelian, Wappo (Givón 2001: 263; Lehmann 1988b: 63; 2002b: 98; Heine 2008; Li, Thompson, and Sawyer 1977).

The list above is far from exhaustive. Strikingly, there seem to be some back and forth developments at work, since ergatives may grow out of nominatives but also the other way round. This is not necessarily a violation of the unidirectionality

Table 41.3. Common patterns of extension from one case function to another (Heine 2008)

From	To
A	S
ablative	cause, possessive, partitive, instrumental
allative	benefactive, dative, accusative/O, purposive
benefactive	purposive
comitative	instrumental, ergative, manner, possessive
dative	accusative/O
instrumental	ergative, manner
locative	comitative, agent, ergative, instrumental

principle, as we are dealing here with different items and different kinds of process; it would in fact be a violation if one and the same marker developed in both ways.

2.2. Definiteness and case

There is a pronounced interrelationship between case and definiteness. First, case may develop out of a definiteness marker. Instances of such a development are possible, but rare. The ergative case *-ma/m* in Georgian has been grammaticalized out of a demonstrative pronoun *man* 'that, he' (see Harris and Campbell 1995: 341, and esp. Kulikov 2006: 29–30). In the West Nilotic languages Päri, Anywa, and Jur-Luwo, spoken in the Republic of Sudan and adjacent areas, an earlier definite marker *-Cɪ* has developed into a (marked) nominative and further into an ergative (König 2006; 2008), hence:

definiteness marker > marked-nominative case marker > ergative case marker

In addition, definiteness may shape case as a split condition for case systems, or as the starting or terminal point of development of a case inflection. The following generalizations seem to hold cross-linguistically: (i) If a language has case inflections then definite elements are most likely to be among them. (ii) If a language shows a case inflection with definite elements only, such as personal pronouns, then that may either mark the first stage of the development of case or its final stage (see below on Berber).

Aikhenvald (1995) argues that the Berber languages have experienced a rise and fall of case marking. With regard to case, Berber languages show an intricate behaviour in that some languages have lost all case inflections while others have fully-fledged case systems, and others again have defective systems, where case inflections occur in certain domains only. Table 41.4 shows the historical development of case in Berber, i.e. the rise and fall of a nominative in a marked-nominative system. Language examples are given in the last row. The development of a nominative which itself developed out of a definite marker (Maarten Kossmann, p.c.) started with definite nouns (stage 2) and spread to indefinite nouns

Table 41.4. Rise and fall of case in Berber

Stage 1		Stage 2		Stage 3		Stage 4
No case	>	Marked nominative with definite nouns	>	Marked nominative with all nouns	>	No case
Proto-Berber, East Numidian, Guanche		Ait Ziyan		Kabyle, Tashelhiyt, Tuareg		Wargla

(stage 3). At stage 1, there was no marked-nominative case system. Aikhenvald therefore concludes that Proto-Berber had no marked-nominative system, the latter being a later development.

Other well-known examples for the loss of case are English and the Romance languages. Old English still had four cases: a nominative, accusative, genitive, and dative plus a vestigial instrumental; Modern English has retained the genitive plus some case inflections in its pronouns (Allen 1995; Blake 2001). With the transition from Latin to Romance languages, the latter lost case as well. Due to phonological changes, Vulgar Latin already lost some of the case inflections of Classical Latin. In modern Romance languages, the functions of the old case suffixes were taken over by prepositions (see Ledgeway, Chapter 59 below; Blake 2001).

2.3. Case inflected elements

Typically, case shows up in nouns. A closer look suggests the following hierarchy of case inflected elements, particularly in nominative–accusative languages:

pronouns	>	definite nouns	>	indefinite nouns	>	kinship terms	>	proper nouns

Elements which are inherently definite show no homogeneous behaviour: whereas pronouns are most likely to be case inflected, proper nouns often are not.

Apart from nouns and pronouns, case inflections may show up in nominal modifiers such as adjectives, determiners, and numerals. Due to grammaticalization and the widening of the scope of case functions, it is possible that other elements of the language can be case-inflected as well, at least to a certain extent. An extreme example is Ik, a Kuliak language spoken in northeastern Uganda, where nearly all elements of the language can be inflected for case, including adverbials, conjunctions, and verbs (see König 2005).

Two case inflections, the dative and the copulative, have become part of verbal inflection: The dative has been grammaticalized to a subjunctive marker (cf. example 1). Ik is a language where the case paradigm includes pragmatic markers such as the copulative, a case suffix which has grammaticalized out of a copula, which itself is mainly used as a focus marker, and which has further been grammaticalized to a narrative marker (cf. (1)), i.e. an inflectional category of the verbal paradigm. In example (1), the source concepts are presented in the third line placed below the target concepts. The subjunctive has developed out of a dative; the narrative out of a copula. The copula itself grammaticalized to a case marker, called copulative, mainly used for focus constructions. The grammaticalization chains can be graphed as follows:

copula	>	focus	>	narrative
dative	>	subjunctive		

(1) Ik (Kuliak, Northern Uganda)

na	ay-uɗót-ike	tulú-ɛ́ɛ́n-á	riʝ-é	ʝɛʝ-ío	ɗiw-íke
when	ripe-AND-SBJV.	rabbit-PEE.SG-NOM	field-GEN	remain-NAR.	red-SBJV.
Source:	DAT			COP	DAT

'While [the garden of the elephant] had ripened [well], the rabbit's garden remained red.'

The ablative *-o* and the dative *-ik*[e] in Ik have been grammaticalized to the extent that both are used in a wide range of different functions (up to twelve). The ablative encodes source, sender, locative, instrument, partitive, cause, manner, time, the agent in passive clauses, the possessor in verbal possession, and the standard in comparative expressions (see König 2005).

2.4. From adposition to case affix

A well-described pathway leads from noun or verb to adpositon to case suffix (see e.g. Heine, Claudi, and Hünnemeyer 1991; Blake 2001):

noun, verb (> adverb) > adposition > case affix > loss

Grammaticalization processes may lead to a situation where scholars debate whether a particular system can count as using case affixes or adpositions. Discussions about the number of cases that a particular language distinguishes may also be triggered by the ambiguous status of elements combining features of nouns, adpositions, and case affixes. Hungarian is a good example of such discussions. The range of cases that Hungarian should have varies between 17 (18 in Kiefer 1987; 2000: 580; 22 in Moravcsik 2003: 117) and 28, but there is also the conclusion that Hungarian has no case but rather 'fused postpositional portmanteaus', as argued for by Spencer (2008).

Spencer (2008) proposes a profound analysis of Hungarian, his conclusion being that Hungarian has no case (system). Nevertheless, Spencer uses the term *case* constantly in the same paper (compare pp. 44 and 54). This inconsistency may reflect the dilemma which is a crucial feature of systems where case has been grammaticalized out of nouns. On the pathway from noun to case affix, the ambiguous element still shows features of an adposition and already features of a case affix. Hungarian covers the intermediate stage from adposition to case affix, and some elements even exhibit a second grammaticalization cycle where a noun plus adposition is taken as the base for a new development of the same kind. Such a phenomenon is found in other case languages as well, it tends to be referred to as case compounding.

Hungarian has affixes which have adverbial functions, at least to some extent, and are more derivational than inflectional. Features of such items are:

Group one. Some of them behave like adverbs (less case-like)—the noun itself needs an additional postposition, *kívül* is an example of this group:

(2) Hungarian

ez-en	a	ház-on	kívül
this-superessive	the	house-superessive	beside

'beside the house' (Spencer 2008: 40)

Spencer argues that elements like *kívül* show what may be called a limited amount of case-like features, since they can only be added to an already inflected 'case' noun, like the superessive in example (2). The cases listed in Table 41.5 present the few cases which are essentially grammatical in function.

Group two. A second subclass consists of postpositions which show a higher degree of case behaviour. A comparison of examples (2) and (3) illustrates the difference:

(3)

e	mögött	a	ház	mögött
this	behind	the	house	behind

'behind the house' (Spencer 2008: 40)

Unlike *kívül* 'beside', it is possible for *mögött* to be attached to the noun directly where no additional case-like element is needed. The basic form of the noun, like *ház* 'house' in (3), assuming a case analysis, has the status of the morphologically unmarked nominative.

A language may develop several rounds of this same process, which leads to what has been referred to as 'derivational case compounding'. The latter is defined by Austin (1995) as a situation whereby case A serves as the 'basis' form for another case B where B does not occur independent of A. In Tocharian, nine cases are distinguished, only two of them not being instances of case compounding: the nominative and the accusative. The remaining ones are based on the accusative

Table 41.5. Hungarian case forms of *ember* 'person' (Spencer 2008: 38)

nominative	*ember*
accusative	*ember-t*
dative	*ember-nek*

Table 41.6. Origin of case markers in Bodic languages (Noonan 2008a: 134)

Stage 1	[Na-GEN] Nb-LOCc	genitival modification of the locative-marked N
Stage 2	[Na] Pb(-LOCc)	locative-marked postposition
Stage 3	Na-LOCb (-LOCc)	(compound) locative case clitic

(historically *-in* for singular and *-is* for plural). Former postpositions fused with the historical accusative, which governed these postpositions.

Noonan claims for Bodic (Tibeto-Burman) a historical development of cases as summarized in Table 41.6, being the result of derivational case compounding. The source construction (stage 1) consists of a noun modified by a genitive with a locative case marker; at stage 2 usually the genitive is lost, the former locative noun grammaticalizes to a postposition, which often has lost its locative case marker; and at stage 3 the former adposition has become a case clitic. One example is the Proto-Bodic noun *s-*naŋ(* 'interior', which has developed into a comitative. In the Tamangic languages (Bodic) all stages, noun, adposition, and case marker are attested; see (4–7) (Noonan 2008a: 135):

(4) stage 1: Chantyal
tɦim-ye nɦaŋ-ri
house-GEN interior-LOC
'to/in the house's interior'

(5) stage 2: Thakali (Georg 1996)
tim naŋ-ri
house inside-LOC
'inside the house'

(6) Chantyal
tɦim nɦâŋ
house inside
'inside the house' (Noonan 2008a: 135)

(7) stage 3: Chantyal
tɦim nɦari
house INESSIVE
'inside the house' (Noonan 2008a: 135)

2.5. Means of case encoding

The means by which case is encoded can shape a system. Case expressed by adpositions or adpositional elements may result in case systems with large inventories (as in Hungarian or Finnish). Case expressed exclusively by tone usually results in case systems with small inventories, typically two. Such systems are found in Surmic, Nilotic, and Cushitic languages of East Africa. Case expressed by portmanteau morphemes, simultaneously encoding gender, number, and case, may result in a system where there is no zero form, but all cases tend to be derived. There is an area in southeast Ethiopia where Highland East Cushitic and West Omotic—particularly Ometo languages are of this type—all being marked-nominative languages (see König 2008).

Peripheral cases expressed by suffixes may result in derivational case compounding. In the Ometo language Maale (Afroasiatic), the ablative is an instance of derivational case compounding with three cases. The ablative *-ppa* is attached to the locative *-ídda*, which itself is attached to the accusative *-ó*. The case which is nearer to the stem is taken as the basis for the following case marker.

(8) Maale (South Ometo, West Omotic, Afroasiatic)
máár-ó-ídda-ppa
house-ACC-LOC-ABL
'from the house' (Amha 2001: 69)

2.6. Case and information structure

There exists a well-documented relationship between topic and subject case, which is nominative; and focus and object case, which is accusative. A topic marker can be grammaticalized to a nominative (e.g. in Highland East Cushitic (Afroasiatic), or in Umbundu and Ngangela (both Bantu)); and a focus marker can be grammaticalized to an accusative (e.g. in Khoekhoe, and Khwe (former Central Khoisan); see König 2008).

If a language has a grammaticalized topic marker and a nominative, it may show complex behaviour of the following kind: (i) Topic is the source for a case marker: for instance, topic can be grammaticalized to become a subject marker, or a nominative marker, as in the W2 dialect of !Xun of what is traditionally called the Northern Khoisan family. In the northern !Xun dialects, the particle *má* is used as a productive topic marker which has become an obligatory subject marker particularly in the W2 dialect, where the subject of declarative main clauses requires a postposed *má*. The fact that *má* has become an obligatory subject marker in certain contexts, and that it can be used twice per clause, to encode topic and subject, are reasons to argue that in W2 *má* has been grammaticalized to a case marker for subject arguments.

(9) !Xun, W2 dialect

m̀hm̀	má	djòqɛ̀.
1.PL.INC	TOP	happy

'We are happy.'

(10)

mí	má	hŋ́	hà̰.
1.SG	TOP	see	N3

'I see him.'

(ii) If the language has developed both a topic and a nominative marker, the question arises how the two interact. They may exclude each other, as in Japanese, where topic and subject are marked by different particles and the nominative *ga* and the topic marker *wa* do not co-occur on the same noun. Similarly, a topicalized object can also not be inflected with the accusative *o*: they exclude each other—they may appear within the same clause only on different elements. This means that the topic marker *wa* in Japanese has already built a paradigmatic bond with case markers—an indication that it has grammaticalized beyond its pure pragmatic force, or that the case marker also exhibits some pragmatic value (see Ogawa 2008).

(11) Japanese (Komori 2009: 1)

ame	ga	futte	iru
rain	NOM	rain	be

'Rain is falling.'

(12)

ame	wa	futte	iru	ga	yuki	wa	futte	inai.
rain	TOP	fall	be	but	snow	TOP	fall	be.NEG

'Rain is falling but snow isn't.'

2.7. Split conditions

Case inflections often do not operate homogeneously in a given language: there may be areas where case inflections are neutralized, or where a different case system is at work. These systems are called split systems. The conditions which trigger the split can be of the following kind. Clause types (main vs. subordinate clauses, focus clauses, relative clauses, certain conjunctions, questions), personal deixis (1st and 2nd person versus 3rd person; e.g. in Datooga, Ik: see Kiessling 2007; König 2005), or tense–aspect distinctions. According to Harris (1981), Georgian and Laz have an active pattern in the past tense, but in the present tense Georgian has a nominative–accusative system. Hindi-Urdu, Marathi, Punjabi, and some Iranian languages such as Pashto and Kurdish are described as having ergative only in the perfect (Blake 2001). Ik shows a person split of 1st and 2nd person vs. 3rd person, where in the former the case system is neutralized. The West Nilotic languages Päri, Anywa, and Jur-Luwo have a split with regard to clause types. Basically, in Päri it is the main clause having an ergative system whereas the remaining clause types show a marked-nominative system (see König 2008). These split conditions are reflexes of different grammaticalization processes, a frozen history which still bears witness to contrasting grammaticalization pathways. Definiteness is a common split condition for case systems, meaning that case inflection appears with definite nouns only (e.g. in Amharic and other Semitic languages of Ethiopia: Tosco 1994).

3. Conclusions

As this chapter may have shown, there is synchronic evidence for determining relative degrees of grammaticalization. The behaviour of case, or case systems, synchronically is shaped by features the language has developed in other areas such as definiteness, topic, focus, or means of case coding.

Case exclusively expressed by tone results most probably in a system with a relatively small inventory of cases being distinguished, whereas case expressed by adpositions may typically lead to case systems with a relatively large inventory of cases. Case as a syntactic tool typically shows overlaps with pragmatic categories such as topic and focus with regard not only to their diachronic source but also to the way the two systems interact synchronically in a language (e.g. in Japanese). Definiteness shapes case or case systems on various levels, either being the source for grammaticalization, a restriction, or an indicator of the first or final stage of grammaticalization.

CHAPTER 42

THE GRAMMATICALIZATION OF DEFINITE ARTICLES

WALTER DE MULDER

ANNE CARLIER

1. Introduction

The concept of definiteness is by no means exclusively expressed by articles. As has been shown by Krámsky (1972), various other grammatical phenomena can contribute to mark definiteness, amongst which word order, case inflection, verb agreement, and stress or intonation. Definiteness as a nominal feature has been considered as the analogue of the perfective aspect in the verbal domain: both convey the grammatical function of quantification (Leiss 2000; 2007).

From a typological viewpoint, the grammatical category of the articles is rather uncommon. According to Dryer (1989), articles would be attested in only one third of the languages of the world. Only 8 per cent would have both a definite and an indefinite article. Moreover the spread of this phenomenon is geographically very unequal, with a high incidence in (western) European languages (for an overview, see Himmelmann 1997: 195–207; Bauer 2007; Dryer 2008). From a historical viewpoint, it is established with respect to the European languages, for which written records enable us to observe long-term evolutions, that, apart from Greek, the grammatical category of articles is a recent phenomenon. Hence, the existence of this category is not a feature inherited from Indo-European. On the contrary, a Semitic influence has been hypothesized for the Mediterranean area (Putzu and Ramat 2001). As to Romance, although the grammaticalization process is initiated in Late Latin (Selig 1992; Putzu and Ramat 2001), fully-fledged definite articles appear only in the first vernacular texts, from the 9th century on. In Germanic languages, they occur in Middle High German and Middle English around the 11th century.[1] According to Heine and Kuteva (2006), the Romance and Germanic model is replicated and spreads from West to East, affecting also non-European languages like Finnish. They observe that the influence is more important in the southern part of Europe (Albanian, Macedonian, Bulgarian) than in the north (Russian, Ukrainian, Belorussian). Schroeder (2006) shows that there is geographical continuum: in western European languages, the definite article is formally distinct from the demonstrative (e.g. English, Spanish, French); in central Europe, the definite article has the same form as the demonstrative pronoun (e.g. German); some eastern European languages have a demonstrative but no definite article (e.g. Russian) or only an incipient article use of the demonstrative, limited to certain registers or used by younger speakers (e.g. Finnish; cf. Laury 1997).

Even though the grammatical category of articles as such is far from being universal, the grammaticalization process that leads to its development exhibits cross-linguistic regularities: in the majority of cases, the definite article originates from a weakened demonstrative, mostly the distal demonstrative or the 3rd person demonstrative, whereas the indefinite article derives from the unity numeral 'one'. Other sources are exceptional:

- From a formal viewpoint, definite articles originating from verbal or nominal lexemes are attested. The verbs involved are 'say' (e.g. Middle French *ledit* 'the said' described by Mortelmans 2008, and the Proto-Chadic demonstratives/ anaphors analysed by Frajzyngier 1996b: 192) and 'see' in its ostensive use (e.g. Sissala *ná:* Lyons 1999: 331; cf. French *voici* /*voilà* 'see here/see there' and Latin *ecce* prefixed to demonstratives). Frajzyngier (1996b: 179) also mentions the article derived from the nominal lexeme 'hand' in the Chadic language Gidar, with a similar ostensive meaning.
- Semantically, definite articles can be derived from anaphoric markers, without deictic meaning. This is the case for the definite article derived from the verb 'say' mentioned above. Another instance of anaphoric marker having an article-like behaviour is the identity marker *ipse* in Late Latin (Selig 1992), which has been selected as the origin of the definite article in some Romance languages (varieties), amongst which Sardinian (Aebischer 1948).

[1] There is, however, some discussion about the exact moment of their appearance. Cf. Philippi (1997); Leiss (2000); Abraham (2007).

The definite article is more widespread than the indefinite article. On the basis of the empirical data of Moravcsik (1969), Heine (1997b) argues that a language that has a grammaticalized indefinite article is likely to have also a definite article, while the reverse does not hold. Even if there are exceptions (e.g. Turkish), this inference is valid in 95 per cent of the languages of the sample.

In line with this typological generalization, we can expect that, from a historical viewpoint, definite articles tend to emerge earlier than indefinite articles. In this context, it is interesting to consider French, which has a very complete article paradigm. Besides the definite article *le*, derived from the Latin distal demonstrative *ille*, and the indefinite singular article *un*, whose source is the Latin unity numeral *unu(m)*, there is also a non-singular indefinite article, called the partitive article, originating from the contraction of the preposition *de* and the definite article (*de le* > *del* > *deu* > *du*).[2] The use of the articles is generalized to the point that zero determination, which was very common in Old French, has become exceptional. The emergence of the different articles and the progressive spread to new contexts of use can be accounted for in terms of the scale of individuation, as proposed in Fig. 42.1.

The use of the article is older and more systematic when the entity referred to is highly individuated, and is more recent and more fluctuating when the entity referred to is low on the scale of individuation. Eventually, the presence of an article is generalized to all common nouns and the article tends to become a noun marker

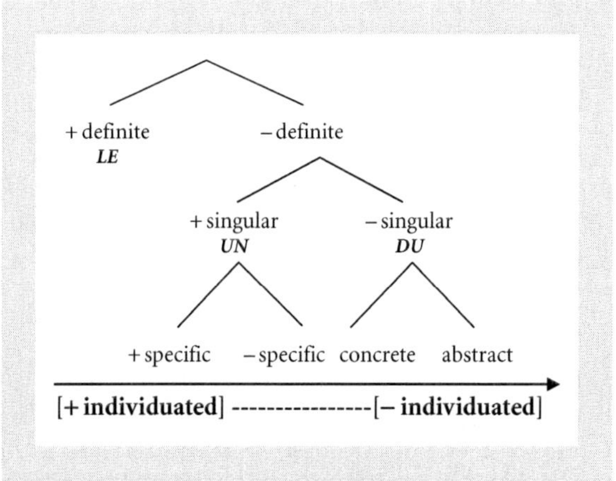

Fig. 42.1. Scale of individuation

[2] The indefinite non-singular or 'partitive' article, where *de* has completely lost its prepositional status (Carlier 2007), should be distinguished both from the preposition *de* contracted with the definite article (e.g. *le chien du berger* 'the dog of the shepherd') and from *de* within the scope of negation, which is unmarked as to number (*je n'ai pas de chat /de chats/de pain* 'I don't have a cat/cats/ bread' (lit.: of cat/of cats/of bread).

or a noun phrase marker, indicating the left boundary of the NP. There is, however, frequently a residual domain of article-less nouns: the article may not be used in combination with nouns determined intrinsically (proper nouns), by their anchorage within the speech situation (vocative), or by another determiner (possessives, demonstratives, quantifiers, etc.).

According to the hypothesis of Greenberg (1978), the article derived from the demonstrative evolves along the following grammaticalization path:

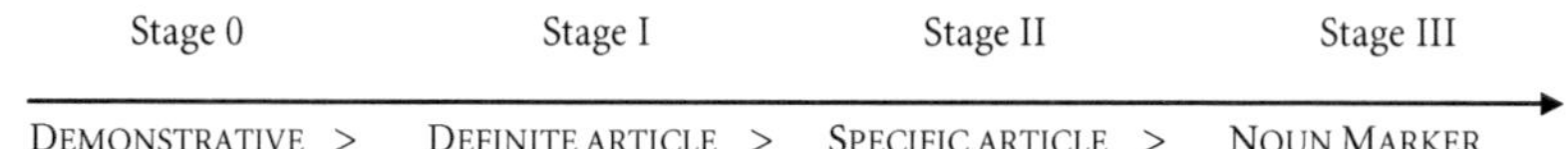

Fig. 42.2. The cycle of the definite article according to Greenberg (1978)

The gradual spread of the article to new contexts according to Greenberg's model can also be conceived as a progress on the scale from more individuated (Stage 0 Demonstrative) to less individuated (Stage III Noun Marker). The specific or so-called 'non-generic' Stage II article encompasses the first contexts of use of the indefinite singular article and seems to occur in languages without an indefinite article coexisting with the definite article (Greenberg 1991: n. 5). At Stage III, the article extends to all common nouns and becomes a marker of nominality. This grammaticalization path will structure this chapter, although it will be refined and complemented on some points.

Cross-linguistically, articles can be characterized both semantically and morphosyntactically. From a semantic viewpoint, articles encode definiteness or specificity. Definiteness, which occupies a higher position in the individuation hierarchy in Fig. 42.1 above, is typologically the most widespread feature, but specificity is, for instance, common in the Austronesian and in some Bantu languages. From a morphosyntactic viewpoint, articles are adnominal and are different in this respect from pronouns. They appear in a fixed position with respect to the nominal expression (either to the right or to the left) and can sometimes have the status of affixes. As such, they can function as noun markers or noun phrase markers. Whereas the semantic dimension is predominant in the first stages of the grammaticalization process, it can progressively fade out, which is reflected in a spread to new contexts where the articles convey neither definiteness nor specificity. The morphosyntactic role of noun marker or noun phrase marker becomes more important as grammaticalization proceeds, and goes along with routinization and extension of the conditions of use.

2. From demonstrative (Stage 0) to definite article (Stage I)

2.1. The hypothesis of semantic loss

How does the demonstrative evolve into a definite article? The demonstrative signals that the identity of the referent should be established by making reference to the speech situation or the immediate context of utterance. It typically conveys a deictic meaning component, indicating the location of the referent in terms of distance with respect to the speaker or in terms of association with the 1st, 2nd, and 3rd person. It is commonly assumed that the exophoric or situational use of the demonstrative, referring to entities in the extralinguistic situation, is the basic use, giving rise to endophoric or intralinguistic uses, among which the anaphoric use (Diessel 1999: 109–11). Definite articles would be derived from adnominal anaphoric demonstratives.

A somewhat different view of the grammaticalization path is proposed by Lyons (1999: 161, 332). He argues that the shift from demonstrative to definite article is initiated in two types of uses: in the exophoric use, when the referent is directly perceived in the physical surroundings, and in the anaphoric use, where the referent is straightforwardly recalled from the preceding discourse. Deictic information is redundant in these two contexts of use because the referent is immediately accessible. Hence, in the English example (1), the definite article and the distal and proximal demonstratives alternate to refer to an entity visible in the immediate situation. In the Late Latin examples (2a,b), the distal and the proximal demonstrative can be equally used to resume a referent introduced in the previous context.

(1) Pass me *the/this/that bucket.* (Hawkins 1978: 111)

(2) a. *Lucca castrum dirigunt, atque funditus subvertunt, custodes* **illius castri** *capiunt* (Fredegarius, *Continuations* §25, ed. John Michael Wallace-Hadrill)
'They go to the fort of Loches, they raze it to the ground and take prisoner the guardians of ***that fort***.'

b. *Radulfus haec cernens, castrum lignis monitum in quodam montem super Vnestrude fluvio in Toringia construens, exercitum undique quantum plus potuit collegens, cum uxorem et liberis in* **hunc castrum** *ad se definsandum stabilibit.* (Fredegarius, §87)
'Observing this, Radulf put up a fort protected with a wooden stockade on a rise above the banks of the Unstrut, in Thuringia, and when he had assembled from everywhere an army as big as he could, he established himself with his wife and children within ***this fort*** to withstand a siege.'

These may act as 'critical contexts' (Diewald 2002) or 'bridging contexts' (Evans and Wilkins 2000; Heine 2002), where the deictic meaning component of the demonstrative can weaken, yielding the shift from demonstrative to definite article. The new definite article would first be restricted to these contexts and spread to other contexts later on.

In the framework of these two hypotheses, several facts remain nevertheless unexplained (Himmelmann 1997: 96–8).

(i) In some languages, there exists a demonstrative which has an exclusively anaphoric function and is devoid of deictic meaning (e.g. *is* in Latin). Given the hypothesis deriving the definite article from the anaphoric use of the demonstrative, how can we explain that this type of demonstrative does never develop into a definite article, as noted by Himmelmann (1997: 98)?

(ii) From a typological perspective, the most common source of the definite article is the distal demonstrative or the 3rd person demonstrative (Greenberg 1978: 61; Himmelmann 1997: 96–8). If we admit, with Lyons (1999), that the shift from demonstrative to definite article is initiated in contexts of use that allow free alternation between proximal and distal demonstratives, how can we account for this widespread tendency?

(iii) It is widely accepted that the characteristic context of use of the definite article is the associative anaphor (Himmelmann 1997), where the definite article gives the instruction to retrieve the referent *indirectly*, by activating a frame of accessible knowledge which the referent is associated with in a univocal way (Hawkins 1978; 1991; Kleiber 1992; Epstein 2002). The demonstrative, by contrast, typically focuses the hearer's attention on the referent *directly*, without considering its structural links with a frame of accessible knowledge. Even if these structural links exist, the use of the demonstrative instead of the definite article deactivates them, as is illustrated by the following couple of examples, quoted from Charolles (1990).

(3) a. *We arrived in a village.* ***The church*** *was on a hill.*
b. *We arrived in a village.* ***That church****, really, how awful!*

Neither Lyons' hypothesis nor the hypothesis deriving the definite article from an anaphoric demonstrative referring to a previously mentioned discourse participant accounts for this meaning shift from direct reference to indirect reference, which is crucial in the development of the definite article.

Moreover, empirical research on several languages (e.g. Laury 1997 for Finnish, Epstein 1993 for Old French and Jamul Diegueño, Trager 1932, Selig 1992, Vincent 1997b, and Carlier and De Mulder 2010 for Late Latin, Faingold 2003 for the evolution from Latin to Spanish, Portuguese, and Romanian) has shown that the emergent definite article derived from the demonstrative is not merely a neutral tool for taking up previously mentioned referents, but has a strong textual function: it is used exclusively for important participants of a narrative, in particular when they are not currently in the focus of attention. The reasons of the pragmatic impact of the use of the definite article in its initial state are twofold. In a language stage where zero determination is the rule, the use of a determiner as such is significant. This highlighting effect is even stronger in the case of the incipient definite article, because it still owns the demonstrative force of its origin and attracts attention to the referent.

Although it is true that the grammaticalization of the definite article involves at some point a weakening of the demonstrative force of its source, more attention should be paid to the pragmatic factors that set off the grammaticalization process to understand the evolutionary pathway from distal demonstrative to definite article. According to Hopper and Traugott (2003), the early stages of a grammaticalization process have to be conceived in terms of pragmatic strengthening, and meaning loss or 'bleaching' occurs only at later stages, as grammaticalization continues and forms become more routinized. In this perspective, it can be assumed that the incipient definite article, although it extends to new textual uses, is still endowed with a demonstrative meaning. We will take advantage of this hypothesis in order to understand the crucial meaning shift from direct reference to indirect reference (iii). In the light of this hypothesis, we will also take up the question of why the distal demonstrative is cross-linguistically the most common source for the definite article (ii).

2.2. Pragmatic and semantic definiteness

Some languages have an opposition between two definite articles: a strong and less grammaticalized article, on the one hand, and a weak and more grammaticalized article, on the other. This is, for instance, the case in some Germanic languages. In standard German, the opposition between the strong and the weak article is visible in certain prepositional phrases (Hartmann 1982; Löbner 1985): the weak article is enclitic with respect to the preposition (*zu der* > *zur, in das* > *ins, bei dem* > *beim, für das* > *fürs*), whereas the strong article keeps in the same context its phonological integrity. There are moreover several German dialects, amongst which the Rhineland dialect (Heinrichs 1954) and the Mönchen Gladbach dialect (Hartmann 1982), which have a systematic formal opposition between the strong and the weak definite article. This is also the case in a North Frisian dialect, Fehring (Ebert 1971).

On the meaning side, the opposition between the strong definite article (*di/det*) and the weak definite article (*a*) is independent from the distinction between exophoric and endophoric reference. It can rather be described in terms of pragmatic *vs* semantic definiteness (Löbner 1985). The strong article, less grammaticalized, expresses pragmatic definiteness: it is used when the identification of the referent relies on the specific context of utterance; the weak article, more grammaticalized, conveys semantic definiteness: the referent of the definite expression is identified independently of the specific context of utterance. In the North Frisian dialect Fehring, the strong article is used in the following cases:

- to refer to an entity perceivable in the immediate situation:

(4) *Smatst' mi ans* **det pokluad** *auer?*
Throw me once **the pencil** over here?

- to resume a referent previously mentioned, with the same denomination (5) or by means of a different denomination (6), which can add new information (7):

(5) *Peetje hee jister an kü slaachtet. Jo saai,* **det kü** *wiar äi sünj.*
'Peetje has slaughtered a cow yesterday. It is said that **the cow** was not healthy.'

(6) Matje *hee al wäler an näi bridj.* **Di gast** *kön a nöös uk wel äi fol fu.*
'Matje has again a girlfriend. **That guy** cannot get enough of it.'

(7) *Heest dü wat faan* Teetje *hiard ? Je,* **di idioot** *hee uunrupen an saad dat hi äi kem wul ?*
'Did you hear something about Teetje ? Yes, **that idiot** called me to say he won't come.

- to refer to a proposition (discourse deixis):

(8) A jongen smeed me malmarter efter dön lööpern, wat uun an re för't lööperhool laai. **Det spal** *käand ik noch äi.*
'The kids threw with marbles to marbles aligned before the marble hole. I didn't know **that play.**'

- in first mention, in combination with a relative clause:

(9) *Rooluf hee* **det klook** *wechsleden, wat hi faan san uatlaatj fingen hee.*
'Rolf lost **the watch** that he received from his grandfather.'

The weak article appears in the following cases:

- to refer to a referent retrievable by its structural links with the immediate situation (10),
- for associative anaphor (11),
- to refer to unique entities within the discourse universe (12/13),
- for generic reference (14).

(10) **A hünj** *as auerkeerd würden.*
'**The dog** got run over.' (for instance the speaker's dog)

(11) *Üüs wi bi* det hüs *uunkam, wiar diar ab seedel bi-d-***a döör.**
'When we came to the house, there was a message at **the door.**'

(12) **A san** *skiinjt.*
'**The sun** shines.'

(13) **A köning** *kaam tu bischük.*
'**The king** came for a visit.'

(14) **A kaater** *klesi.*
'**Cats** scratch.'

The question arises whether the article expressing pragmatic definiteness should be considered as a weak demonstrative (as argued for by Himmelmann 1997: 55) rather than a strong definite article. In the case of the Late Latin *ille*, the exact status of the pragmatic definiteness marker—demonstrative or definite article—has led to much discussion. It is doubtful that this discussion is relevant, however, since the grammaticalization process from demonstrative to definite article is continuous rather than subdivided into discrete steps. More interesting is the observation that the range of uses of the pragmatically definite article corresponds to the uses of the emerging definite article. In particular, when the noun is determined by a relative clause, the use of the demonstrative becomes regular and the distal demonstrative is preferred to the proximal demonstrative. As has been shown by Himmelmann (1997), it is in this syntactic configuration that the distal demonstrative can take a recognitional interpretation. In the next section, we will show that the recognitional use of the distal demonstrative offers the key to understanding the transition from pragmatic to semantic definiteness or, in other words, to the status of full-fledged definite article.

2.3. From pragmatic to semantic definiteness

In order to comprehend the nature of the transition between demonstrative and definite article, we have to explain why the distal demonstrative in locative systems or the 3rd personal demonstrative in person-oriented systems is typologically the most common source for the definite article.

The distal demonstrative differs from the proximal demonstrative(s) in the following respect: whereas a proximal demonstrative, e.g. *this book*, denotes a referent that is wholly identified via elements in the context of its occurrence, the distal demonstrative, e.g. *that book*, signals that the referent cannot be identified solely on the basis of the immediate context of utterance (Vuillaume 1980; Kleiber 1987). In this way, the distal demonstrative can be understood as an invitation addressed to the hearer to mobilize previous knowledge in order to retrieve the referent. This pragmatic inference is activated in the recognitional use and can be made explicit (cf. example (16), *you know / I talked to you about her*).

(15) English
I couldn't sleep last night. **That dog** *(next door) kept me awake* (Gundel et al. 1993)

(16) French
Cette personne, *tu sais, Mlle E... dont je t'ai parlé, avec qui je devais prendre le thé dans la quinzaine chez Mme Chesneau qui la connaît, eh bien, j'ai appris hier qu'elle a un amant, un grand banquier de Paris, qui ne veut pas l'épouser.* (Villiers de L'Isle-Adam, *Correspondance générale*)

'**That person**, you know, Ms E . . . I talked to you about her, with whom I had to have tea within two weeks in the house of Mrs Chesneau who knows her, well, I heard yesterday that she has a lover, an important banker of Paris, who doesn't want to marry her.'

(17) Late Latin
Hic sunt carctas de illi thellenio de **illo mercatho** (*Les diplômes originaux des Mérovingiens*, éd. Ph. Lauer and Ch. Samarin, quoted by Selig 1992: 166)
Here are the documents of the toll of ***the*** (lit. ***that***) ***market*** (=of our market, of the well-known market organized on the day of the patron saint).

With respect to the other uses of demonstratives, the recognitional use of the distal demonstrative has a distinctive feature: the referent is not mentioned in the preceding context or present in the current discourse situation (Himmelmann 1997: 61; 2001; Diessel 1999). It points to 'specific, presumably shared' knowledge of speaker and hearer (Himmelmann 2001: 833)—often based upon a common experience—that has to be activated by the hearer in order to identify the referent.

Hence, contrary to the proximal demonstrative, the distal demonstrative is able to denote a referent that is not fully identified or even not accessible within the immediate context of its occurrence. In order to achieve the identification of this referent, the distal demonstrative can mobilize specific knowledge shared by speaker and hearer. Because of these two features, the distal demonstrative is the appropriate candidate to be recruited as the source of the definite article.

As the distal demonstrative in its recognitional use, the definite article can denote a referent that is not accessible in the immediate context of utterance. The distal demonstrative becomes a definite article when the anchorage in the speech situation is lost and the use of article no longer requires specific knowledge shared by speaker and hearer to be activated in order to identify the referent of the noun phrase. Rather, the definite article conveys the instruction that the descriptive content of the NP allows the identification of the referent in a univocal way, by virtue of its structural links with a frame of accessible knowledge, these links being often of a stereotypical nature (Löbner 1985; Hawkins 2004: 85).

By this shift from pragmatic definiteness to semantic definiteness, the definite article extends its use to contexts in which a demonstrative would be inappropriate:

(i) to refer to a referent retrievable by its structural links with the immediate situation, e. g. *Close* ***the door****. Beware of* ***the dog*** ('the door of the room we are in at the moment, the dog of the house we are approaching');
(ii) for associative anaphor, e.g. *We arrived in a village.* ***The church*** *was on the hill*;
(iii) to refer to unique entities within the discourse universe: *the sun, the king*;
(iv) for generic reference: ***Les chats*** *aiment le lait. /* ***The dog*** *is a domesticated form of the wolf.*

This analysis does not preclude other factors from contributing to the emergence or the extension of the articles. Leiss (2007) argues that there is a trade-off between verbal aspect and nominal determination, since they partake of the same grammatical function of quantification: aspect languages such as Russian tend to be article-less, whereas article languages tend to avoid aspect marking. In the light of this hypothesis, the emergence of the definite article in German has been explained as the result of the gradual disappearance of aspect marking (Abraham 1997; Philippi 1997; Leiss 2000; 2007). For Romance languages, it has been hypothesized that the extension of the definite article is correlated to the erosion of nominal inflectional marking of case and number.

3. From definite article (Stage I) to 'specific' article (Stage II)

At Stage II of Greenberg's cycle of the definite article, the article is no longer restricted to semantically definite contexts but spreads to indefinite specific contexts. It thus includes contexts of use that in other languages would be reserved to the indefinite article derived from the unity numeral, such as the introduction of new referents in the discourse universe. An example of this stage of the grammaticalization is the Tagalog specific article *ang* (Himmelmann 1997: 103):

(18) Doón ay na-kita nilá ***ang*** isa-ng ma-lakí-ng higante
DIST.LOC PM REAL.STAT-see 3.PL.POSS SPEC one-LK IRR.STAT-big-LK giant
'There they saw a great giant . . . '

On the other hand, non-articulated forms still occur when there is neither definite nor specific reference.[3]

The progress in the grammaticalization process involves not only an increase of the contexts of use but also semantic erosion. The following excerpt, quoted by Epstein (2002: 368), offers an example of a 'critical context' where definiteness may be reinterpreted as specificity.

(19) The film's setting and the story both have a mythic simplicity. In the aftermath of a drought that leaves most people surviving by selling themselves into lifelong servitude, a farmer and a weaver escape and set up residence in a desert ghost town. Their only contact with the outside world is a trader who keeps them in debt to him while also keeping them supplied with essentials.

[3] For more details, see Greenberg (1978: 64–9), Schuh (1983), and Rijkhoff (2002: 92–7).

> Then **the woman** arrives, like a fleeing animal. Her family has been killed in a flood. She doesn't ask to stay, but they feel guilty after they rebuff her ('our first sin' they call it) and invite her to share their refuge. And so begins the slow spiral toward a disaster as ineluctable, no doubt, as the eternal cycles of drought and flood.
> (*Spectator*, Raleigh, North Carolina, 14 Feb. 1996, 11–12)

By using the definite article, the author indicates that *the woman* has a definite reference by association with a frame of accessible knowledge. However, the definite article does not provide any information about the nature of this frame of accessible knowledge and leaves it to the interpretative ability of the hearer/reader to reconstruct this frame. Since the reconstruction of the associative frame can be an open-ended process, this frame can fade out. The NP *the woman* will then acquire the interpretation of referring to a specific but unidentified woman.

This evolution can be described as a further step in the semantic erosion at work in the grammaticalization process. The distal demonstrative of Stage 0, in contrast to the proximal demonstrative, indicates that the referent is not plainly identified within the immediate context of its occurrence and can activate specific knowledge shared by speaker and hearer in order to achieve the identification of the referent. This anchorage in the speech situation is lost in the following stage: the definite article of Stage I implies that a frame of knowledge is accessible, which no longer needs to be specific to speaker and hearer and by means of which the referent can be identified as in a univocal way. For the specific article of Stage II, no frame of accessible knowledge is supposed to allow the identification of the referent, so that the referent need not be pragmatically or semantically definite, but can be conceived as discursively new.

Himmelmann (1997: 107) suggests that Stage II specific articles could evolve directly from pragmatically definite used demonstratives, without passing through an intermediate Stage I definite article. In line with this hypothesis, Diessel (1999: 139) proposes analysing the indefinite use of the English proximal demonstrative *this*, first identified by Prince (1981), as a specific marker.

(20) There was *this guy* in my class last quarter.

4. From 'specific' article (Stage II) to noun (phrase) marker (Stage III)

The progressive spread to new contexts of use eventually leads to a situation where the articulated form becomes the normal form of the noun. The article will then have reached Stage III of Greenberg's cycle: it is a marker of nominality or gender, with no synchronic connection to definiteness or specificity (Greenberg 1978: 69).

5. Conclusion and perspectives

The distinction between different stages of grammaticalization should not obscure the fundamentally continuous nature of the grammaticalization process (Greenberg 1978: 61). In this context, it should be mentioned that the syntactic dimension of the article as a noun marker or a noun phrase marker, which is salient in Stage III, is already present in the early stages of the grammaticalization process. Indeed, among the first attestations of the Stage I article we find the use of the article as a nominalization marker of adjectives. The syntactic structure of the noun phrase and the morphosyntactic categorization of determiners and nouns are strengthened as the definite article develops. Himmelmann (1997) argues convincingly that, as this structure becomes more frequent and more entrenched, the use of the article may become routine, and may expand outside the contexts where it was initially justified for semantic and pragmatic reasons.

Moreover, the definite article might not necessarily go through all the stages described above. In this respect, it should be examined to what extent the existence of other articles may slow down the grammaticalization process. For instance, does the existence of an indefinite article deriving from the unity numeral have an influence on the possible transition from the definite Stage I article to the specific Stage II article? Harris (1980b: 83) has argued that the French deictically neutral demonstrative *ce* is on the point of becoming a fully-fledged Stage I definite article, in the same way as the Latin demonstrative *ille* gave rise to the Old French definite article *li*. Can we expect the same evolution for the Modern French demonstrative *ce* given the existence of the definite article *le* (De Mulder and Carlier 2006)?

Finally, the general tendencies sketched here do not exclude idiosyncratic evolutions in some languages. For instance, the definite articles in some Romance languages acquire already in an early stage, from the 12th century on, a generic interpretation in contexts where this is still impossible for English, German, and Dutch (e.g. English (**The*) *Whales are mammals* vs French *Les baleines sont des mammifères*). This could possibly be explained by an early widening of the frame of accessible knowledge contributing to the identification of the referent, since in the generic meaning this frame coincides with the universe.[4]

[4] On the notion of widening of the knowledge frame and its role in the progression of the evolution of the definite article towards generic interpretation, see Renzi (1976) and Hawkins (2004).

CHAPTER 43

THE GRAMMATICALIZATION OF PASSIVES

BJÖRN WIEMER

1. Range of phenomena

Structurally, the notion 'passive' comprises morphologically marked devices by which the highest-ranking (= most agent-like, Actor) or single argument of a predicate is syntactically demoted, while a lower-ranking (= more patient-like, Undergoer) argument can be promoted to a syntactically privileged position, usually called 'subject'.[1] Derived constructions with a promoted Undergoer are subsumed as 'foregrounding passive' (henceforth FP); if promotion is lacking we use the term 'backgrounding passive' (BP, often called '(subject) impersonal'). Promoted Undergoers trigger number agreement on the inflected verb and, in languages with case morphology, they are coded with the nominative. The demoted argument is either omitted altogether or expressed by an oblique NP or a PP

[1] 'Actor' and 'Undergoer', used in the tradition of Role & Reference Grammar as generalizations over specific case roles (Van Valin 2005), are better suited as notions than 'agent' or 'patient', since not every argument undergoing demotion or promotion can reasonably be considered as 'agentive' or 'patientive'. For the need to use these generalized notions with respect to passives, cf. Keenan (1985: 261), Kazenin (2001), Wiemer (2004: 305–307), Toyota (2008: 9f.).

(outside the core),[2] but it is always implied. Another, rare type of FP is the so-called 'recipient (or dative, indirect) passive'. It is characterized by the promotion of a core argument which in the active voice is coded with the dative (see 2.2.3).

Thus passives here are understood narrowly since they only change the coding hierarchy of arguments in the syntax, not the verb's propositional semantics (Haspelmath 1990: 26f., 45f.; Kazenin 2001: 899, 903). This distinguishes the passive from related categories like decausatives as well as from object-oriented resultatives (in the sense of Nedjalkov 1988; cf. Wiemer 2004: 286–8), with which they often remain homonymous (see 2.1.3 for predicative past participles).

In contrast to the FP, the BP can be (and usually remains) based on intransitive, one- or two-place verbs; if it becomes extended to transitive verbs, transitivity relations do not change. BPs in many languages are restricted to predicates whose highest-ranking argument denotes a human being; compare German:

(1) a. *Es* ***wurde*** *den ganzen Abend* ***getanzt*** *und* ***gelacht.***
it PASS.PST.3.SG the whole evening.ACC dance.PTCP and laugh.PTCP
lit. 'The whole evening it **was danced** and **laughed.**'
'The whole evening there was dancing and laughing.'

b. *Man* ***tanzte*** *und* ***lachte*** *den ganzen Abend.*
IMPERS dance.PST.3.SG and laugh.PST.3.SG the whole evening.ACC
lit. 'One **danced** and **laughed** the whole evening.'
'People were dancing and laughing the whole evening.'

(2) a. ?*Es* ***wurde*** *den ganzen Tag* ***gequakt.***
it PASS.PST.3.SG the whole day.ACC croak.PTCP
lit. 'The whole day it **was croaked.**'/'There was croaking all the day.'

b. ?*Man* ***quakte*** *den ganzen Tag.*
IMPERS croak.PST.3.SG the whole day.ACC
lit. 'One **croaked** the whole day.'/'Some people/somebody croaked all the day.'

Sentences (2a,b) can be interpreted only as metaphorically describing sounds uttered by people. In some languages, equivalent, pronoun-like indicators of the pragmatically demoted (often unknown) argument are used, e.g. Germ. *man* (< *Mann* '(hu)man'; see ex. (1b), Fr. *on* (< *homme* '(hu)man'). However, pronoun-like *man* etc. do not themselves signal any restructuring of semantic arguments in the syntax, nor are they accompanied by morphological changes in the predicate. Therefore they are outside the scope of passives as defined above.

[2] Languages differ as to whether they allow for the expression of the demoted argument or block its expression altogether.

In most languages, FP and BP are etymologically related, since they are marked by the same morphemes;[3] several attempts have been made to explain them as successive stages on a grammaticalization cline (see section 3). It turns out that passives are 'parasitic' on other form:function distinctions; they arise as constructions consisting of various components each of which has been subject to its individual evolution. As a rule, only convergent diachronic change of two or more components leads to passive constructions. The following components need to be taken into consideration (Wiemer 2004):

- morphology on the lexical verb (inflectional or derivational, e.g. participles);
- auxiliaries (or serial verbs, e.g. in isolating languages);
- oblique expression of the highest-ranking semantic argument (Actor-phrase).

In the following we will look separately at each of these 'ingredients'. Identity of lexical meaning (= argument structure) between active and passive voice is usually a late result of the complex interaction of (probably independent) diachronic morphosyntactic changes accompanied by analogical expansion of marking techniques, often also by the establishment of inherent diathetic orientation of deverbal adjectives (becoming participles of transitive verbs) and by competition among paradigmatically interrelated adjunct phrases (as candidates of oblique Actors); cf. Wiemer (2004).

2. The components and grammaticalization paths

Passive morphemes (affixes, auxiliaries, serial verbs) have been suggested to derive in some languages from verbs meaning 'be', 'become', 'reach', 'get/receive', 'give', 'hit/touch', 'see', 'go (away)', 'eat', 'fall', 'suffer' (Haspelmath 1990: 29; Heine and Kuteva 2002: 122, 133, 145f., 270, 284).

In the following I will refer to grammaticalization paths leading to passives which were surveyed in Haspelmath (1990, esp. the table on p. 54). This section is structured according to the kinds of units which serve as 'input' of the components of passives mentioned above.

[3] For exceptions (e.g. in Welsh) see Keenan (1985: 258f.), Kazenin (2001: 905) with further references.

2.1. Morphology on the lexical verb

We can distinguish three types of morphology; the first two yielding synthetic passives, the third partaking in the formation of analytical passives.

2.1.1. *Bound or stem-internal morphology*

According to Haspelmath (1990: 28), the most widespread type of passive morphology in general is affixes added directly to or inside the stem; e.g., Quechua (cited from Keenan 1985: 255):

(3) *Čuku apa-**ka**-rqa-n*
hat take-PASS-PST-3
'The hat was taken.'

Such cases count as classical examples of grammaticalization: free morpheme > clitic > agglutinated > bound (flexion). Sometimes passive affixes result from the coalescence of former auxiliaries or inactive verbs ('be' etc., e.g. Turkish *-il* and Japanese *-ar(e)*) with the stem they modify (Haspelmath 1990: 39, 41).[4] In Manchu-Tungusic languages, a morpheme (*-bu-*) deriving from the verb 'give' has been agglutinated closely to the verb stem. Notice that the same holds for the causative interpretation of this morpheme (Nedjalkov 1993: 194) which, according to known grammaticalization chains (see 2.2.1), must have preceded its passive function. Thus coalescence of this originally autonomous lexeme is not conditioned by the establishment of a passive marker as such, but occurs earlier. This parallels passives coded by reflexive markers (see 2.1.2).

In isolating languages, equivalent lexical morphemes are serialized with other morphemes (Keenan 1985: 261); see 2.2. For instance, Thai *thùuk* and analogous morphemes in some East and Southeastern Asian languages have apparently undergone meaning changes along the cline 'to touch, hit on the point' > 'to undergo (an unfavourable experience)' > adversative passive > non-adversative passive (with intermediate steps of modalized meanings). The shift from adversative to neutral passive is accompanied by tightening: virtually no element can nowadays intervene between *thùuk* and the modified verb (Prasithrathsint 2006). Considerably less frequent are sound replacements (like root-internal vowel alternation in Semitic) and differential agreement inflections as, e.g., with the Latin passive paradigm based on *-r*.

[4] Generally it remains to be checked whether such constructions should not better count as resultatives whose passive function rises under favourable context conditions (e.g. Korean *ji-* in Haspelmath 1990: 39), and thus have not fully grammaticalized.

2.1.2. *Clitics and agglutinated morphemes*

Agglutinated or clitic reflexive-anticausative markers are a frequent source of passive morphology in European languages; agglutinated morphemes correspond to Haspelmath's (1990: 29f.) 'extra-inflectional affix'. They derive from (and can remain homonymous with) pronominal reflexive markers (RM) (Heine and Kuteva 2002: 44, 253). However, if phonological reduction of that marker occurs, it is usually *not* conditioned by a change from anticausative to passive; instead, the latter change should be characterized as a mere reinterpretation of argument structure. Consequently, such cases cannot be considered paradigm examples of grammaticalization (Wiemer 2004: 280f.). It is interesting to note that passives thus marked often betray traces of anticausatives (or other Actor-demoting diatheses) from which they derive. Consequently, they are more reluctant to accept oblique Actors than analytic passives (see 2.3).

Non-pronominal particles cliticized to the verb are rare. Haspelmath (1990: 29) adduces only Margi (Chadic) *kə́r*, probably the reduction of a reflexive noun originally meaning 'head'. Provided this reconstruction is correct it would illustrate the path ('head'/'body' >) 'self'/reflexive > anticausative > passive.

2.1.3. *Participles and other non-finite verb forms*

Derivational morphology rendering participles frequently constitute the core of analytic passives (e.g. English *The article* ***was written*** *quickly*). However, the evolution of analytic passives rests not only on the productive derivation of deverbal adjectives, but also on a subsequent process whereby participles of two-place verbs start being unanimously oriented toward the lowest-ranking argument (cf. Wiemer 2004: 286–8).

Celtic languages abound with deverbal agent nouns (*nomina actionis*) used as direct objects of transitive 'get' (similarly Mayan; cf. Keenan 1985: 259); compare e.g. Welsh (by courtesy of Ranko Matasović):

(4) *Pan oedd yr holl bobl yn <u>cael</u> eu* ***bedyddio***
when were ART all people PTC get.VN their baptize.VN
'When all the people were being **baptized**...' (lit. '...were <u>getting</u> their **baptizing**') (Bible: Luke 3:11).

The crucial turning point toward a genuine passive is reached when the construction ['get' + deverbal noun] loses its originally adversative overtones (see 2.1.1) and admits corresponding lexical input (deverbal nouns), as in (4). Again, grammaticalization does not consist in 'morphologization' alone, but in the loosening of collocational restrictions between the elements of a construction that preserve the lexical meaning with respect to a corresponding unmarked voice.

In analytic passives the complementary counterpart to non-finite verb forms are auxiliaries, to which we now turn.

2.2. Auxiliaries

Auxiliaries differ from 'ordinary verbs': they lack arguments of their own, but share them with lexical verbs, and they are usually deficient with respect to verbal categories of the given language. Like affixes, they convey grammatical functions and, depending on the morphology of a given language, it can be difficult (or senseless) to distinguish them from bound or juxtaposed ('serialized') morphology of the kind treated in 2.1.1 and 2.1.2.

Passive auxiliaries can derive from intransitive or from transitive source verbs, all of which can be characterized as inactive, i.e. non-agentive verbs (Haspelmath 1990: 38ff.). In addition, the source verbs can be divided into:

(i) stative verbs: 'be', 'remain' (> 'become'), attested in some European languages (see 2.2.2), 'suffer' dominating in Southeastern Asia (Keenan 1985: 260; Yap and Iwasaki 2003; cf. also Chappell and Peyraube, Chapter 65 below for these and more lexical sources in Sinitic);

(ii) verbs with inchoative or change-of-state meanings (see 2.2.2): 'get/receive' (e.g. ancient Chinese), 'become' (e.g. German *werden*, Persian *šod*), 'reach/ get into (> become)' (e.g. Latvian *tikt*), 'become' (< 'remain') (e.g. Polish *zostać*, Italian *rimanere*), 'undergo' (Southeastern Asian languages) (Keenan 1985: 257f; Haspelmath 1990: 38–42; Heine and Kuteva 2002: 145f.; Wiemer 2004: 297–305); 'meet with, touch' seems to be restricted to East Asia (Prasithrathsint 2006; Chapter 65 below);

(iii) other: 'eat' in Sinhala (Sri Lanka; Keenan 1985: 259) and a small number of Hunan dialects of Chinese and in earlier stages of Chinese (Hilary Chappell and Alain Peyraube, p.c.).

A subgroup of (ii), prominent in Indo-Iranian and in the 'Alpine passive' (Ramat 1998: 227f.) are motion verbs: 'come' ('Alpine passive'), 'go (away)' (e.g. Urdu *jānā*). Similar cases are attested in Scottish Gaelic (MacAulay 1992: 177f.), Maltese, and Quechua. Cf. the systematic overview in Majsak (2005: 179–81, 215f., 382f.). Only in Quechua does the respective morpheme seem to have become an affix (*ri-* < 'go'; Majsak 2005: 181).

2.2.1. 'Get'- and 'give'-passives

Adversative overtones in passives derived from 'get' or 'give' often retain a trait of control, or responsibility, on the part of the subject's referent. This is atypical for other kinds of passive, but can be explained on the assumption that 'get'- and 'give'-passives develop via (reflexive) causatives or benefactives (cf. however Chapter 65 below). In English ('get')[5] and West Slavic ('give') this pattern is well attested with participles.

[5] Notice that the residual adversative meaning arises only due to this combination and is not simply a result of semantic bleaching of 'get/give' (cf. Toyota 2008: 173f. for English).

One part of the 'story' consists in semantic changes of the transitive verb, which for English *get* can be summarized as follows (Givón and Yang 1994; Toyota 2008: 174–82):

(5) 14th–16th c.: semantic changes of 'get' (= 'obtain'), 'take possession of X'
> (i) 'obtain/take X for oneself' (reflexive-benefactive)
> (ii) 'obtain/take X for another person' (benefactive)
> (iii) 'take/move X toward another person' (causative-locative)
> (iv) 'take/move X toward another thing'.

Based on this account, *get* entered grammaticalization as a transitive verb and subsequently 'bleached out'.

The other part of the story again boils down to the loosening of categorial restrictions, on the side of *get*, and to a clear diathetic orientation of participles: *get* was used with adjectives earlier (from the end of the 15th century) than with genuine participles (e.g. *got acquainted with*, 1652). Thus *get* + participle evolved as an extension of *get* + adjective, which, in turn, implies that participles in *-ed* were stripped of their adjectival semantics.

In parallel, the benefactive construction (see (5.ii)) began to be extended by purposive complements (cf. modern English *He gets her some words <u>to say</u>*) as did the causative construction (cf. *He gets her <u>to clean</u> the room*). Such verbal complements made the construction biclausal. Only subsequently did they undergo an extension toward adjectives and passive participles. The latter were often accompanied by a 'be'-copula, but this was dropped later so that, again, the whole structure became monoclausal. During the whole period, 'causative constructions had their respective reflexive variants' (Givón and Yang 1994: 132). A rather late example from Sterne (quoted from Givón and Yang 1994: 131) is the following:

(6) ... *he had* ***got*** *<u>himself</u> so gallantly <u>arrayed</u>. I scarcely knew him* ...

The final step consisted in simplifying reflexive causatives by dropping the reflexive marker (and the 'be'-copula). Notice that, aside from the change biclausal > monoclausal, this 'loss' turns out to be the only place in the history of the 'get'-passive in which structural reduction (erosion) occurs. At all preceding stages, semantic generalization of 'get' itself and analogical extension into complement types and word classes in syntactic positions played the decisive role.

Basically, all these observations also hold true for permissive and reflexive-permissive constructions centering around 'give'-verbs in West Slavic. See the cline in (7) and an example from Polish (8) illustrating the probably most grammaticalized stage (with realized possibility; cf. von Waldenfels 2008: 283f.):

(7) lexical 'give' > permissive > reflexive-permissive > modal passive > passive.

(8) *Otwór* *wyglądał* *na lisią norę,* *lecz*
opening.NOM.SG.M look_like.IPFV:PST.3.SG.M on fox_den.ACC.SG.F but
pokruszony *łupek* *łatwo* ***dał*** *się* *rozkopać.*
crumble.PTCP slate.NOM.SG.M easily give.PFV:PST.3.SG.M REFL dig_out:PFV.INF
'The hole looked like a fox's den, but the crumbled slate **could** easily be dug out.' [= '. . . let itself easily dig out' ⊃ 'was dug out']

However a 'real' passive void of additional modal or adversative 'nuances' still occurs extremely rarely in both Polish and Czech (cf. von Waldenfels 2008; also Wiemer, Chapter 61 below).

A chain analogous to (7) (with omission of the modal passive) has been observed with 'give'-verbs in some East and Southeastern Asian languages. Classical Manchu, Evenki, and Chinese (different varieties) have 'run through' it completely, Malay and Thai (as well as Akan, West Africa) only partly so. The critical point in this chain is reached when causative 'give' starts taking non-agentive subjects or when the subject (= causer) has less control than the causee ('unwilling permission'). The same holds for 'let'-passives (Yap and Iwasaki 2003) and for the agglutinated CAUS/PASS-marker *-ki-* (< 'make, do') of Trans-Eurasian languages (Robbeets 2007), which, for instance in Korean, has likewise become void of adversative overtones (Keenan 1985: 262).

2.2.2. *'Become'-passives*

Auxiliaries deriving from non-motional inchoative verbs seem to be attested only in German (*werden* < Old High German *uuerdan*), Swedish (*bliva*), Latvian (*tikt*), Polish (*zostać*), and Late Latin, which demonstrates the convergence of *fieri* 'to become' and *facere* 'to make, do' into aspectually complementary passive auxiliaries (Cennamo 2006). Contemporary Italian *rimanere* shows first signs of a passive auxiliary (Schwarze 2003). The Polish and Italian auxiliaries derive from verbs originally meaning 'remain, stay'. All verbs mentioned started as copula, which expanded their collocatability with predicative nominals to participles which, in turn, lost adjectival semantics. The auxiliation process was finished by the semantic tightening of the entire phrase and the loss of erstwhile restrictions to participles of telic verbs and similar aspectual restrictions. This was accompanied by a loss of an exclusively inchoative, i.e. telic, meaning for all lexemes mentioned except the Polish one (cf. Vogel 2006: part II for German). Pol. *zostać* differs: after the shift 'remain > become', throughout its history it has not altered its aspectual default function. As a passive auxiliary it has remained inchoative and punctual; consequently, the *zostać*-passive can never refer to processes or states. Furthermore, auxiliation of *zostać* has not led to categorial defectivity (cf. Wiemer 2004: 300–303; Chapter 61 below).

2.2.3. *'Recipient passive'*

German and all West Slavic languages except Polish show a passive construction whose auxiliary has evolved from a ditransitive 'receive'-verb (e.g. Germ. *bekommen, kriegen,* Czech *dostat*); the subject of this passive corresponds to the dative object of the lexical verb which can name a recipient, an addressee or a beneficient/ maleficient:

(8) *Peter hat seinen Computer (von seinem Bruder)*
Peter.NOM have.PRS.3.SG his computer.ACC by his brother.DAT
repariert bekommen.
fix/repair.PTCP get.PTCP
'Peter got his computer fixed (by his brother).'

Like the plain passive (with *werden*), the recipient passive allows for an Actor-phrase (see ex.(8)), but unlike the former it always needs a subject (i.e. it does not have a backgrounding equivalent). The stages of its development have been sketched inter alia: by Askedal (2005), Vogel (2006: 213–15). Lately, it has started to appear even with intransitive verbs (see ex.(9)). Such usage, however, is not (yet) accepted by many native speakers:

(9) ?*Sie bekamen applaudiert / geschimpft / geholfen.*
they.NOM get.PST.3.SG applaud.PTCP / rebuke.PTCP / help.PTCP
lit. 'They got applauded / rebuked / helped.'

2.3. Oblique expression of the demoted highest-ranking semantic argument

Although 'there seems to be a general correlation between the degree of grammaticization of a passive and its ability to cooccur with an agent phrase' (Haspelmath 1990: 56), it is arguable whether, among the components of passives, it is oblique Actors that are the latest to develop.[6] Although in many languages with passive morphology, oblique Actors are impossible (or highly unusual), diachronic syntax gives us examples with oblique Actors even in BPs (see section 3). The evolution of Actor-phrases taken in isolation can only be considered as instances of semantic extension (bleaching). There are hardly any cases in which such phrases do not serve other functions as adjuncts in the unmarked voice; an exception is monofunctional Hebrew *al yedei* (lit. 'on the hands') marking only an oblique Actor in the passive and in nominalizations (Keenan 1985: 252, 265; Israel Tal, p.c.).

[6] Notice e.g. that with 'give'-passives the dative-marked Actor is diachronically primary, since the dative belongs to the earlier permissive construction (see 2.2.1). If reflexive-permissives develop into modal passives (as in Polish and Czech), the former causee can no longer be expressed as oblique Actor (von Waldenfels 2008).

Among the sources of oblique Actors[7], adverbial markers predominate, i.e. various case markers and adpositional phrases indicating:

(a) The instrument, means or natural force, e.g. the Russian instrumental. Among morphological cases this represents the most widespread type of semantic role conflation.
(b) Cause or reason, as in Tzeltal (Mayan) *yu'un* 'because' (Keenan 1985: 259) or Sotho (Niger-Congo) using a prefix (Palancar 2002: 152).
(c) Location, e.g. adessive as with dialectal Russian *u* + genitive, but also English *by* (a cognate of Germ. *bei* 'at') and some Celtic varieties (Keenan 1985: 275; MacAulay 1992: 177f.).
(d) Direction:
(d.i) Ablative, e.g. Latin *ā(b)*, Modern Greek *apó* (Old Greek *hüpó* had a more specific meaning 'from under'), Romance continuations of Latin *dē*, descendents of Common Slavic *otъ* (see Old Polish, Czech, Croatian/Serbian), German *von* and Old English *from*, Hungarian *-tól* (rather an essive marker), Western Greenlandic *-mit* (cf. Palancar 2002: 156).
(d.ii) Perlative (often associated with intermediary and causee; see below); e.g. Old English *þurh*, German *durch*, Polish *przez*, Old Greek *diá*. Oblique agents with this etymology are attested only in Indo-European languages, almost all of them spoken in Europe (Palancar 2002: 187).

More rarely, oblique Actors are derived from comitative PPs (arguably via an intermediary instrumental stage) and morphemes with an original meaning 'hand' (arguably via perlative 'through' or after a synecdochic transfer 'hand' → 'person'); cf. Heine and Kuteva (2002: 80, 165f.).

In some languages (e.g. Turkic, Tungusic, Gujarati, Greenlandic Inuit), causees of causative constructions have functionally expanded toward oblique Actors. Obviously such an extension occurs only if the respective agentive referent (= causee) already occupies a syntactically peripheral position (including the dative; Palancar 2002: 187–91); this implies pragmatic demotion. Noticeably, causee>Actor shifts involving originally perlative PPs ('through') predominate with analytic (participial) passives; with 'reflexive' passives (see 2.1.2), they are less felicitous and restricted to referents ranking low on the animacy scale (cf. Palancar 2002: 187 for Spanish).

Genitival and other possessive Actor-phrases are considerably rarer (Palancar 2002: 174) and betray their adnominal origin. The Lithuanian *genetivus auctoris*, for example, results from a reanalysis of dependency relations by which a possessive pronoun or a noun in the genitive gets used outside its NP, whereby it starts modifying the predicate (Wiemer 2004: 310–13). A similar case is known from classical Armenian (Benveniste 1966a: 180–83). The genitival actor in Malagasy is

[7] For a detailed overview see Palancar (2002: chs 11, 12).

slightly different: it is cliticized on the verb as a possessor is on a NP. This peculiar marking technique correlates with the nominal origin of verbal morphology (Keenan 1985: 259). In any case, what is crucially involved with genitival Actor-phrases is not grammaticalization proper, but syntactic reanalysis combined with semantic extension.

2.4. Object>subject-reanalysis and reinterpretation of pronouns or personal desinences

Omission of a plural-subject NP (e.g. Russian *Menja*.1.SG.ACC *uvolili*.PFV:PST.3.PL 'They have dismissed me') or the use of unspecific 3.PL subjects (e.g. *They have fired me*) are a widespread device of 'Actor suppression' (Heine and Kuteva 2002: 235f.). These techniques cannot count as passives, since no morphological changes are involved. They can, however, develop into FPs if 3.PL-affixes lose their participant-coding status and an oblique Actor-phrase can be added; a former object NP can then be reinterpreted as subject. This has happened in Kimbundu (Niger-Congo) with a 3.PL-affix in a construction with an original object-topic; afterwards, by analogy, the 3.PL-affix must have been extended to other members of the verbal paradigm (Givón 1979: 188, 211). Such a process seems to have been attested only with original 3.PL-affixes, not with specialized generalized morphemes of the *man*-type. It is particularly common in Africa (Heine and Kuteva 2002: 236f.).[8]

3. On the diachronic relation between foregrounding and backgrounding passive

Diachronic syntax gives us examples with oblique agents in BPs. This raises the question of whether BPs have always been the first to develop and to precede an FP. So far, different observations have yielded a contradictory picture. Apparently the direction depends on the etymological or structural basis on which passives evolve. The development BP > FP is possible if the BP emerges from the reanalysis of a

[8] A similar extension to BP or FP has been attested for the 1.PL.INCL-affixes *-an*, *-a* in Ainu (Shibatani 1985: 823f.). Here semantic (or referential) bleaching occurs. But it remains questionable whether this property alone makes this case a clear instance of grammaticalization, at least on account of the unidirectionality hypothesis: the converse development BP > 1.PL-marker is known for Florentine Italian (Stefanini 1982: 98f.), as is the change indefinite pronoun > 1.PL for French and colloquial Finnish (Liukkonen 1995).

topicalized object+3.PL-construction (see 2.4). In Celtic and Mayan, the diachronic primacy of BPs (together with oblique Actors) is conditioned by the specific structure of nominalizations from which they derive (see 2.1.3). On the other hand, in the history of 'become'-passives (see 2.2.2) and other passives based on inactive verbs, BPs appeared only after the first steps toward auxiliation of the 'become'-verb had been taken. The same seems to hold for passives based on RMs (see 2.1.2); cf. Vogel (2006: 96–107). This generalization is corroborated by the fact that in West Slavic languages, the development reflexive-permissive > modal passive agreeing constructions precedes the appearance of constructions without an agreeing subject (von Waldenfels 2008: 284ff.). Furthermore, data available for historically attested periods of Italo-Celtic suggest that the direction BP > FP can be reversed (Kemmer 1993: 177–80 for Romance; Wehr 1995: 30f. for Latin).

CHAPTER 44

AUXILIARIES AND GRAMMATICALIZATION

MANFRED KRUG

1. Towards a definition of auxiliaries

The present chapter illustrates the relationship between auxiliaries and grammaticalization and tries to shed light on two major issues: how does grammaticalization impact on discussions and definitions of auxiliaries? And how can auxiliaries contribute to a better understanding of grammaticalization? Building on crosslinguistic empirical and theoretical work such as Bybee, Perkins, and Pagliuca (1994), Heine (1993), and Kuteva (2001), this chapter takes a typologically informed, functional approach towards defining and describing auxiliary verbs. Like these, and like formal cross-linguistic work (Steele et al. 1981), this chapter assumes a universal category of auxiliaries. Unlike synchronic analyses, however, a treatment of auxiliaries and grammaticalization must consider the history of auxiliaries. The aim of this chapter, then, is not to criticize or even falsify detailed and descriptively adequate accounts of language-*specific* auxiliary verbs. The focus is simply different: a discussion of the relationship between auxiliaries and grammaticalization necessitates a broader, i.e. functional and panchronic approach to auxiliarihood, as has been shown by previous work. Compare Heine's scepticism

Thanks for comments on an earlier version are due to Johan van der Auwera, Martin Haspelmath, Julia Schlüter, the editors, and two anonymous reviewers. The usual disclaimers apply.

regarding purely synchronic approaches and Kuteva's dynamic definition of the *development* of auxiliaries:

> Any explanatory model that does not take the dynamics of linguistic evolution into consideration is likely to miss important insights into the nature of auxiliaries. (Heine 1993: 129)

> [T]he development of auxiliaries can be said to involve a morphosyntactic change whereby the lexical structure (1) *verb–complement* turns into the grammatical structure (2) *grammatical marker–main verb*. . . . It is this process of complex lexical verb structures developing over time into auxiliary grammatical structures, with all its accompanying semantic, morphosyntactic and phonological changes, that I will refer to as *auxiliation*. (Kuteva 2001: 1–2)

Despite the cross-linguistic starting point, exemplification in this chapter will come primarily from Indo-European languages, with English serving as the main source, since the histories of some Indo-European languages and the developmental paths of their auxiliary verbs are the best documented to date. In particular, the research situation for English (with many diachronic written records, historical grammars, the *Oxford English Dictionary*, and a number of historical corpora) is unparalleled, and the rise of the auxiliary category in English had been scrutinized and debated in the literature on historical change (cf. Lightfoot 1979; Plank 1984; Warner 1993) even before grammaticalization studies began to flourish in the 1990s. Studies of English auxiliaries have, then, served as central input for work on grammaticalization and thus considerably advanced research and theory in the field, which has shifted its focus somewhat, however, from modals like *can* or *should* to auxiliary constructions like *going to/gonna, want to/wanna* or *promise to*—partly due to radical and rapid changes on the levels of phonology, morphosyntax, semantics, and discourse pragmatics (cf. Traugott 1989; 1997a; Hopper and Traugott 2003; Krug 2000; Ziegeler 2008). English therefore offers many examples to illustrate the relationship between auxiliaries and grammaticalization and thus the nature of auxiliarization or, for short, auxiliation.

From a typological but synchronic perspective, prototypical characteristics of auxiliaries can be identified in terms of form and meaning. The most frequently cited properties are given below (for more exhaustive lists and discussion, see Heine 1993: in particular Ch. 1; for a justification of a prototype approach to auxiliaries, see Heine 1993: Chs 2.6, 3.4):

(i) On the formal level (understood as involving syntactic, phonological, and morphological structure), auxiliaries are generally characterized as free grammatical morphemes that bear structural resemblance with lexical verbs but do not occur independently; as their complements auxiliaries take nonfinite verb forms which are part of the same clause.

(ii) On the semantic level, auxiliaries are generally defined as contributing to the grammatical expression of tense, aspect, and modality (TAM). Many descriptions add sentence type (e.g. interrogative vs. declarative vs. imperative), diathesis (e.g. passive), and negation markers.

Some of the characteristics given in (i) and (ii) stem from rather traditional accounts of auxiliaries. The remainder of the chapter will exemplify the listed properties and centre on definitional problems, many of which turn out to be of theoretical relevance to the study of grammaticalization. From this discussion, which tries to accommodate synchronic, diachronic, and dialectal variation, it should become clearer why a panchronic approach to auxiliaries is necessary for the present purposes.

2. Auxiliaries and Grammaticalization: A Panchronic Approach

2.1. Auxiliaries as verbs or deverbal entities

On a traditional account, *auxiliaries* are defined as free morphemes and equated with *auxiliary verbs*, because they tend to resemble main verbs structurally and distributionally. In other words, auxiliaries tend to occur in the same position in the sentence as lexical verbs and have a similar morphological structure. However, auxiliaries typically lose some of their verbal characteristics in the course of auxiliation. Grammaticalization thus contributes to categorial indeterminacy because auxiliary uses often split from the original lexical verbs. This may happen by functional streamlining, in which case one of two near-synonyms remains a lexical verb, while another grammaticalizes, as in (main verb) Spanish *ser* from the Latin copula *ess(er)e* 'be', which contrasts with auxiliary *estar* from Latin *stare* 'stand', which in turn is used in the expression of progressives and for transitory states:

(1) Es una lástima. vs. Está cantando.
3SG.be a pity 3SG.be GND.sing
'It's a pity.' 'She/He is singing.'

Alternatively, auxiliary functions may develop and coexist with a homonymous main verb (though often the auxiliary will be phonetically reduced), as can be witnessed for the English primary verbs DO, BE, and HAVE. These have developed auxiliary functions for the expression of interrogatives and negation (DO), passives and progressives (BE), present and past perfect (HAVE). Compare some English auxiliary constructions with their lexical source verbs (for more exhaustive cross-linguistic lists of auxiliaries, see Appendix B in Bybee et al. 1994: 316ff.). Auxiliaries are italicized in the examples below.

(2)	She *didn't* read. {past + negation}	vs. She did her homework.
(3)	I *DO* know him. {emphasis}	vs. I'll do the dishes.
(4)	She*'s/is* reading. {progressive}	vs. She is at home/an architect/clever.
(5)	He *was/got* beaten. {passive}	vs. He was at home/got ('received') a letter.

Many similar cases exist in non-Indo-European languages. The Ewe progressive, for instance, is similar to the corresponding English construction (Heine 1993: 121). Furthermore, functional differentiation between two near-synonyms, as in (1) above, and functional split of an individual verb can occur side by side. This can be seen from the Spanish copula *ser*, which has in addition to the main-verb use exemplified in (1) also an auxiliary use in passive constructions. Compare:

(6) (El) era invitado (por . . .)
he was invited (by . . .)

To consider the effects of auxiliation, let us next contrast an English lexical verb and a member of another central subcategory of auxiliaries, the modal auxiliary *must*:

(7) He saw/sees her brother.
(8) He must do it.

Example (7) features a lexical verb inflected for tense or person, while the modal auxiliary *must* in (8) apparently does not inflect for 3rd person singular in the simple present tense (as *sees*) or for past tense (as *saw*), and *must* takes an infinitival complement rather than a noun phrase. Historically, however, *must* was a past-tense form and contrasted with present-tense *mot*, a tense contrast which survives in High German (*muss* 'has to' vs. *musste* 'had to').

English *must* is by no means an exception in losing past time reference. While Shakespeare could still say *I would* ('wanted to') *speak to him* to express a desire, modern speakers cannot.[1] Moreover, this was not the first time that these verbs had lost their ability to refer to past time. Almost all Germanic modal verbs—for example English *can, may, shall*—go back to so-called preterite present verbs, which had lost their potential to refer to past events in pre-Old English times. And because they were preterite presents, they lacked the 3rd person marking from the start. In other words, they had a special morphology, which became even more special over time, particularly in English, whose central modals constitute probably the most highly grammaticalized verb class in Germanic, if not the languages of the

[1] A note on volition may be indicated here. While some accounts exclude volition from modal meanings and thus from auxiliary status, this one does not. One of the reasons is that volitional modals are in many languages structurally parallel to other modals; another is that volitional modals shade into and often develop into intention and future markers (see section 2.4).

world (for a list of distinctive auxiliary and modal criteria in contemporary English, see Quirk et al. 1985: 137).

Through grammaticalization, the historical past tense forms *must, might, would, could, should, ought (to)* also largely lost their potential to refer to past events in most contexts by late Modern English (Warner 1993; Plank 1984). The language developed new and unambiguously deontic and dynamic modal constructions that can be tense-marked, like *wanted to, was able to, was obliged to,* and *had to.* This continual renewal of grammatical functions leads to the coexistence of older and newer instantiations of the same grammatical morpheme; it is a common phenomenon in grammaticalization, which was ascribed principle status and called 'layering' by Hopper (1991). The meanings of the above-mentioned older inventory of the English core modal verbs shifted from past-time marking to other, usually more abstract grammatical domains such as hypotheticality and irrealis (*would; should* in conditional clauses) or politeness (*would, could*). And those that still retain the possibility of referring to a past event are either unusual and need contextual clues, as *could* in (9), or have survived only in a special grammatical niche, as habitual *would* (*OED s.v. will*) in (10).

(9) I could ('was able to') swim when I was a kid. I can't swim any more.
(10) We would often go for a swim when we were kids.

Such traces of their past-tense meaning suggest that another principle of grammaticalization, that of 'persistence', is valid not only for the transition from a lexical to a grammatical item, as formulated in Hopper (1991: 22), but also for the transition from one grammatical marker to another. A related argument could be made for many of the semantic paths identified in Bybee et al. (1994), which demonstrate how the study of auxiliaries can contribute to a better understanding of the nature of grammaticalization.

2.2. Complements of auxiliaries

Auxiliaries are generally assumed to take as complements a non-finite verb form. Exceptions are contexts that can be interpreted as elliptical, as in:

(11) He can swim and she can too. ~ He can swim and so can she.
(12) She is swimming and he is too. ~ She is swimming and so is he.
(13) They can ride a bike, can't they?
(14) Will he go? He will not/won't.
(15) Did he go? He did not/didn't.

Due to the effects of grammaticalization, even closely related languages differ in this respect. A good example is the contrast between German and English. German still licenses structures like:

(16) Er kann/darf/wollte das
he can/may/would that (OBJ)
'he can/may/wanted to do that'

where a modal verb apparently takes a direct object. (An alternative interpretation in terms of ellipsis would be to supply *tun* 'do' or *haben* 'have'.) English, too, allowed such structures until the early modern period but, as mentioned above, has pursued the grammaticalization of its set of modals further. These have split from lexical verbs on the one hand by retaining older characteristics—like NOT negation and inversion in interrogatives (cf. example (14) above), two syntactic contexts in which main verbs require auxiliary DO, as exemplified in (15)—and by acquiring new restrictions. To the latter belongs the loss of nominal complements and of nonfinite forms (hence the modern English double modal constraint in standard dialects: **I might can*; **I had might*). Modern English auxiliaries permit ellipsis of the verbal complement only in contexts where the understood main verb complement is easily recoverable, as in (11–15) above.

Which kinds of nonfinite complement are taken by auxiliaries is another field of debate. Traditionally, auxiliaries are seen to govern infinitives, present participles, or past participles. Examples include:

(17) I should be-INF home by ten {MODAL}
(18) I am leaving-PRES.PART {PROGRESSIVE}
(19) He was raised-PAST.PART by his uncle {PASSIVE}

In the area of modal verbs, many accounts still stipulate that only those that take bare, i.e. unmarked infinitives should be granted full membership in the auxiliary category—a position which is probably due to a focus on Germanic preterite present verbs. From a functional perspective, which takes into account typical concomitants of grammaticalization, such a stance seems flawed for a number of reasons. Some verbs (such as *dare, need, ought*), for instance, have long vacillated between bare and *to*-marked infinitives (Krug 2000; Brinton and Traugott 2005: 75; Schlüter to appear). Following a purely morphosyntactic definition, the same grammatical word would belong to two different functional categories, depending solely on the presence or absence of the infinitival marker *to*:

(20) I oughtn't go ~ I oughtn't to go

Labels that are often resorted to for those English constructions that take *to*-infinitives are 'peripheral' or 'marginal modals', 'quasi-modals', or 'semi-auxiliaries' (see Quirk et al. 1985; Bolinger 1980 for an overview). Such approaches are useful from a language-specific descriptive perspective that aims at maximally homogeneous morphosyntactic categories. They are not useful from the typologist's onomasiological bird's eye perspective, however, because functional equivalents like deontic *should* and *ought to* would then be treated as members of different syntactic categories. Compare:

(21) I shouldn't go ~ I oughtn't to go.

From a typological perspective, an often-quoted statement by Bolinger (1980: 297) is a first step in the right direction, since it does not specify whether or not an infinitive is marked or unmarked:

(22) The moment a verb is given an infinitive complement, that verb starts down the road of auxiliariness.

It is often overlooked that an important clue to auxiliary complementation patterns lies in the grammaticalization period, i.e. the contemporary linguistic context when a new functional layer grammaticalizes. The older set of English modals, for instance, grammaticalized at a time when NOT negation and Subject–Verb inversion in questions were available for all verbs, and when *to*-infinitives were infrequent. It is probably due to frequency effects that auxiliary–negator sequences like *cannot, should not, is not, have not, do not* became entrenched, thus closely bonded and then reduced to *can't, isn't*, etc. Such entrenched sequences did not take part in the later grammaticalization of DO periphrasis that applied to lexical verbs (cf. Bybee, Chapter 6 above; Krug 2003 for statistical detail).[2]

Contractions like *wanna, gonna, gotta, hafta* exhibit further effects of grammaticalization that result in definitional problems. Due to the bondedness arising from high frequencies of co-occurrence with the preceding verb, the infinitival marker *to* is obscured and fused, and this blurs the distinction between bare and *to*-infinitival complements. The issue is not only a phonetic one, as contracted and uncontracted forms show differences in syntactic behaviour as well (see Krug 2000 for detail). Regarding bare infinitives as criterial and thus classifying *want to* as a main verb while granting the contraction *wanna* auxiliary status, however, would be mistaken from a panchronic grammaticalization point of view, because the diachronic relationship and the synchronic variation of the construction would be left unexplained.

Layering in (auxiliary) verb complementation in the history of English is not limited to the spread of marked, i.e. *to*-infinitives since Middle English (on which see Los 2005). Over the past centuries there seems to have occurred a new historical drift from *to*-infinitives towards *-ing* forms, a development of the past 500 years or so, which has been labelled the 'Great Complement Shift' (Vosberg 2006) and which is still going on. Affected by this development, although to different extents, are verbs like *start, begin, avoid*, or *stop* (Vosberg 2006; Mair 2006: ch. 4). Consider

[2] The fact that some low-frequency auxiliaries in English (like *shall*) behave like their high-frequency category members (like *will*) and unlike high-frequency lexical verbs (like *go*) is best explained by analogy and the cognitive relatedness of auxiliaries. In addition, some auxiliaries that are low-frequency in modern English were high-frequency in older stages, and decreased in frequency of occurrence because of semantic changes or the emergence of new competitors in the field.

the variation in present-day English (see sections 2.3 and 2.4 below for a discussion of ingressive as an auxiliary notion):

(23) He started to kick the ball.
(24) He started kicking the ball.

The complement *kicking* in example (24) allows for two equally plausible syntactic interpretations, either as a present participle or as a gerund. Their meaning is identical in this construction and thus the ambivalent terms '*-ing* participle' or '*-ing* form' seem preferable (cf. Quirk et al. 1985: 137–47, 1189–90). On a narrow definition, *start* with the more nominal gerund complement would be denied auxiliary status, while *start* when followed by a present participle would be categorized as auxiliary. This is not convincing, as even the gerund still exhibits verbal traits: It takes an object complement (*the ball*). Semantic subtleties between *to*-infinitives and *-ing* complements apart (on which see Vosberg 2006), we are most likely dealing with a new layer of auxiliary complementation that should not have a bearing on the classification of auxiliary status. What we are dealing with are different complementation patterns of auxiliary constructions. Closer examination of the notion of finiteness and cross-linguistic illustration of the issues raised in this section is provided in Anderson (2006), Hansen (2009), and Krug (forthcoming).

2.3. Auxiliaries as free morphemes

On a traditional analysis, auxiliaries are free grammatical morphemes, but this is not without problems (cf. Haspelmath, Chapter 27 above). For obvious reasons, this definition cannot work for functional equivalents across languages. The same grammatical morpheme may be an affix in one language (as inflectional mood or ingressive *-sc-* in classical Latin) but a grammatical word or even a complex construction in another language (cf. the English modals or inchoative *begin* or *start to do*). Such categorization depends not on the function of the morpheme but solely on where synchronically a grammatical marker is on the well-known grammaticalization path (Hopper and Traugott 2003: 7), which is sometimes referred to as the 'cline of grammaticality' and whose focal points are given in (25):

(25) content item > grammatical word > clitic > inflectional affix

Language-internally, the matter is not clear-cut either: A free-morpheme analysis works for auxiliary DO in present-day English in the following grammatical constructions:

(26) He doesn't (< does not) know. {negation}
(27) Do you know him? {interrogative}
(28) He DID know. {emphasis}

As expected, the boundaries in (25) above are fuzzy. Are clitics (more) free or (more) bound morphemes? This is not a marginal problem, as cliticization of auxiliaries is a pervasive phenomenon in the languages of the world. English too has a whole range of clitics like *'d* (< *would*) or *'s* (<*is/has*). But excluding the same grammatical morpheme as in (27) from auxiliarihood only because it can occur in a clitic form as in (27)′ below would be a serious descriptive loss:

(27)′ D'you know him?

Let us go one step further and look at the final stages of the cline of grammaticality. The preterite suffix in the Germanic languages, as in English *jumped* or German *spielte* ('played'), which is taken to derive from a Proto-Indo-European form meaning 'did', does clearly not qualify as an auxiliary today, but would have done so during its development. The problem of free vs. bound morpheme status is aggravated by the facts that writing may not be a proper reflection of the phonetic and syntactic facts, and that many languages and dialects are not even documented in written form. Hence, the question of whether a grammatical morpheme is a grammatical word, clitic, or affix remains a vexing one, in particular because synchronic variants of one and the same morpheme will often belong to more than one focal point on the cline of grammaticality. Kuteva (2001) therefore includes, rightly in my view, the evolution of TAM affixes among auxiliation processes.

An all-encompassing view of auxiliaries is not without problems, though. For the cross-linguistic comparison of linguistic forms, for instance, it is necessary to establish a workable synchronic distinction between auxiliaries and clear cases of inflection. I shall therefore adopt the position that an auxiliary needs to have a synchronic allomorph that is either a free form or a clitic. Excluded from auxiliarihood are, in addition, person and number marking, which often derive etymologically from pronouns and numerals and may therefore with some justification be considered more 'nominal' categories.

A related question is whether or not to exclude multi-word constructions that are followed by nonfinite verb forms from auxiliarihood. Typically, more and less fused variants of constructions coexist synchronically, and the fused ones develop from periphrastic ones. Some well-known examples are (for details, see Hopper and Traugott 2003: 9, 24):

(29) Latin *cantare habemus* > French *chanterons* vs. Italian *canteremo*
sing-INF we have 'we will sing' 'we will sing'
'we will sing'

(30) Greek (transliterated from θελω < ινα)
thelô (h)ína > *thena* > *tha*
I wish that contracted form grammatical word (future marker)

The development of the modern Greek future morpheme *tha*, already mentioned by Meillet (1912), is derived from classical Greek *thelô hína* ('I wish—that'; cf. the discussion of finiteness in Krug forthcoming). It has gone through the intermediate stages *thelô na* and *thena*. The decision as to when a construction achieves auxiliary status is therefore to some extent arbitrary, especially when one considers the fact that newer and older layers of a construction coexist synchronically, as in the case of English modal constructions. Compare:

(31) I want to go ~ I wanna go
(32) I have to go ~ I hafta go
(33) I have got to go ~ I've got to go ~ I got to go ~ I gotta go
(34) I am going to go ~ I'm going to go ~ I'm gonna go ~ [a:nə gəʊ]

It goes without saying that for each example above there exist further intermediate and more reduced forms (see Krug 2000). Most important for a discussion of auxiliaries is that, on a traditional account that excludes constructions composed of several free morphemes, the sequence *want to* in (31) would be a main or catenative verb, while the phonologically reduced but functionally identical *wanna* in the same line would be an auxiliary verb. Just how arbitrary such decisions are becomes clearer from looking at examples (32) and (33), where the variants given may be identical phonetically but would be rendered in writing differently by different authors, depending solely on stylistic considerations. (33) and (34) finally show that the presence or absence of an additional auxiliary within a larger auxiliary construction—HAVE and BE in HAVE *got to* and BE *going to*, respectively—is variable, and while for HAVE deletion in (33) semi-conventionalized forms exist in standard varieties, there are none for BE deletion in (34). It is for reasons like these, inter alia, that most recent accounts subsume multi-word constructions under discussions of auxiliaries. Further reasons include: (i) typically entire constructions undergo grammaticalization and not the individual constituents of the construction; (ii) the distinction between a biclausal (verb–complement, i.e. main verb) analysis and a monoclausal (i.e. auxiliary verb) analysis is often difficult to justify on semantic or structural grounds.

2.4. Meaning and function of auxiliaries

Almost all functional accounts include in their definitions of auxiliaries those elements that contribute to the grammatical expression of TAM: tense, aspect (including Aktionsart, cf. Sasse 2006), and modality. Many accounts include in addition periphrastic expressions of diathesis (notably passives), negation, emphasis, and sentence type (like interrogative vs. declarative vs. imperative/prohibitive), irrealis, adhortative, or optative, although some of these additional uses can be subsumed under modality (cf. Palmer 2003; van der Auwera 2006; Krug 2009; Narrog and van der Auwera, Chapter 25 above).

As has been pointed out, research has shown that entire constructions undergo grammaticalization rather than the auxiliary alone (Heine 1998; Traugott 2002). Nevertheless, the semantic contribution of auxiliaries in such constructions seems to fall into two major classes: those auxiliaries which have lost their original lexical meaning almost entirely and taken on abstract, grammatical meaning contrast with semantically more weighty auxiliaries. Tense, aspect, negation, and passive markers typically belong to the former, while modal markers tend to have more concrete meaning and are thus, semantically, closer to lexical verbs. This aspect partly accounts for why English *want to* is more often classified as a main verb than *get* in passive constructions.

Abstractness, however, comes in shades and ambiguous cases are the norm rather than the exception. Consider the semantic field of future/prediction, intention, and volition with such coexisting constructions as *will, want to, wish to, intend to, plan to, plan on -ing*. While the English *will*-future at first glance seems to be a clear case of tense marking, futures often arise out of volition and intention markers, as is indeed also true of English *will*. And the widespread 'movement-towards'-based futures (like English *be going to*; see Bybee et al. 1994: chs 6, 7 for ample cross-linguistic exemplification) complicate matters as they go through an intention-marking stage on their path to the future.

3. Conclusion

The preceding discussion suggests that a panchronic approach can best accommodate different structures across many languages, and describe the effects of grammaticalization in the auxiliary domain. It therefore lends further support to Heine's conclusions that auxiliaries indeed constitute a universal functional category if a prototype perspective is adopted, and that an auxiliary is 'a linguistic item covering some range of uses along the Verb-to-TAM chain' (Heine 1993: 70). If this perspective is adopted, all items from affix to complex constructions that are phonologically, morphologically, and syntactically motivated and explainable as developments from verbal sources on their path to a tense, aspect, or modality marker will qualify as auxiliaries. Harking back to the typical property bundles of auxiliaries given at the beginning of this chapter and the subsequent discussion, a somewhat more specific functional definition—i.e. one which combines form and meaning, but one which can at the same time account for more notions than TAM—would include:

(i) An auxiliary is a (de)verbal entity with scope over a (de)verbal complement which is less than fully finite.
(ii) An auxiliary has a synchronic allomorph in the form of a free morpheme or clitic.
(iii) An auxiliary helps form a grammatical construction for the expression of crosslinguistically recurrent meanings beyond person, number, and case marking.

While properties (ii) and (iii) appear universally applicable, property (i) reflects the present focus on auxiliary verbs, which was adopted because verbs are the most common sources of auxiliaries and serve well to illustrate the workings of auxiliation. The definition of an auxiliary as a 'verbal or deverbal entity' broadens the perspective slightly, as it is meant to include etymologically opaque items with verblike behaviour. Critics might still argue that 'verbal origin' or 'verblike behaviour' of auxiliaries are inadequate remnants of a Standard Average European perspective, and that a comprehensive and truly onomasiological approach to auxiliaries and grammaticalization must include TAM markers deriving from adverbs and nouns like *tomorrow*, *yesterday*, or *stick* (cf. Anderson 2006; Hilpert 2006). Such an all-encompassing view, even though only shared by a minority of researchers at present, would certainly have its merits; but the relevant phenomena would have exceeded what can reasonably be treated within the limits of this chapter. Even following the above definition will mean for many languages a considerable increase in the range of items to be treated under the label of auxiliaries, and will therefore meet with scepticism among many grammarians. It should be noted, though, that the above definition does not mean that previous morphosyntactic accounts become invalid: one could simply introduce more subclasses of auxiliaries. Descriptive successes of the past, then, need not be discarded, and potential losses of descriptive simplicity, like binary syntactic classifications for individual languages, would be counterbalanced by gains in historical and crosslinguistic adequacy.

Among the most important theoretical aspects that concern the relevance of auxiliation for the nature of grammaticalization is the fact that many developmental paths—semantic, phonological, and functional—have contributed to our understanding of unidirectionality in language change (cf. Traugott, Chapter 2 above). A second important insight is the regularity with which certain changes affect a great number of unrelated languages, for this has led researchers to identify internal, cognitive mechanisms that govern language change rather than rely on external or language-specific ad hoc explanations. A third area which has recently received a great deal of attention is frequency (cf. Hopper and Traugott 2003: ch. 5.6). While considerable progress has been made in this field, it remains a promising research area for investigating the relationship between auxiliaries and grammaticalization.

CHAPTER 45

THE GRAMMATICALIZATION OF COMPLEX PREDICATES

LAUREL J. BRINTON

1. Introduction

A 'complex predicate' is a construction consisting of a 'light verb', typically *do*, *give*, *have*, *make*, or *take* in English, in combination with a deverbal noun, for example, *give a push*, *make a vow*, *have a bite*, *take a stroll*, or *do a study*. This construction—variously termed a 'composite predicate', an 'expanded predicate', a 'verbo-nominal construction', and a 'complex verb'—has been extensively studied in Present-day English (see e.g. Olsson 1961; Live 1973; Wierzbicka 1982; Cattell 1984; Akimoto 1989; Stein 1991; Algeo 1995; Allerton 2002) and is increasingly the focus of diachronic study (see Brinton and Akimoto 1999c; Claridge 2000; Iglesias-Rábade 2001; Moralejo-Gárate 2001; Bergs 2005: 210–45; Brinton 2008a; Matsumoto 2008; cf. also Visser 1970: 138–41). What construction types are encompassed by the designation complex predicate (henceforth ComPred) is a matter of debate (section 2). Following a survey of the history of the ComPred in English (section 3), this chapter will examine what makes this construction in English interesting for grammaticalization studies: its existence 'somewhere near the middle of the magnetic field of language . . . where grammar and lexis meet' (Algeo 1995: 203), and the fact that its development has been treated as lexicalization by some scholars and as grammaticalization by others (section 4.1). The conclusion arrived at in this chapter is that the ComPred must be understood as encompassing at least two construction types, one arising through grammaticalization and the other through lexicalization (sections 4.2 and 4.3).

2. Definition of the complex predicate

The ComPred has a tripartite structure consisting of (1) a light verb, (2) an article (*a, the*, Ø), and (3) a deverbal noun. The light verb is seen as auxiliary-like, carrying little meaning and serving a primarily connective function. Some ComPreds allow interchangeability of light verbs with little semantic significance, e.g. *have/take a bath, have/take a drink, make/do a study*, whereas for others, the substitution of one light verb for another may effect a change in meaning, especially from stative to dynamic reading (*have* vs. *take pity*) (see e.g. Huddleston and Pullum 2002: 295; Matsumoto 2008: 27–8).[1] The typical ComPred includes an indefinite article (*do a sketch, give a shout, have a chat, make a call*, or *take a swim*), but some ComPreds have an obligatory Ø article (*give advice, have knowledge, make use, take pity*) while others more rarely have a definite article (*give the lie to*; *give the slip to*). The 'lexical center' (Algeo 1995: 203–4) of the ComPred is the deverbal noun, which carries the eventive sense of the predicate. In prototypical ComPreds, the deverbal noun is formally identical to the verb, i.e. it is a zero derivation, as in *do a dive, give a cheer, pay a visit*, but the deverbal noun may also be formed by the addition of a derivational suffix, as in *give encouragement, take action, have an argument*, or be otherwise etymologically related to the verb, as in *take a breath, give advice*. Those constructions with a following prepositional phrase, as in *make a fuss over, have a try at, do a drawing of, give encouragement to*, are usually classified as ComPreds as well.[2]

ComPreds show a range of syntactic behaviour. Most ComPreds allow adjectival modification of the deverbal noun (e.g. *make a harsh comment, take a last look at*), but some do not (e.g. *catch (?first) sight of, make a (?sincere) application*). Occa-

[1] British English, in which dynamic *have* is more advanced than in North American English, has a preference for *have*-ComPreds (*have* vs. *take a {bath, look, bite}*) (see Trudgill, Nevalainen, and Wischer 2002: 7; cf. Algeo 1995: 215–16).

[2] However, Akimoto (2009: 231–2) argues that only those with optional PPs should be included, while those with obligatory PPs, such as *make mention of, catch sight of, make a mockery of, give consideration to*, are not ComPreds proper.

sionally the deverbal noun of a ComPred can be pluralized (*make corrections to*), though normally it cannot be (**give jumps*, **have needs of*, **take notices*). Some ComPreds allow passivization and topicalization (*an adjustment was made yesterday, an adjustment he made yesterday*) whereas others do not (?*a guess was taken*). For those ComPreds occurring with a following PP, the passive presents a number of options: both 'inner' and 'outer' passive may be possible (*advice was given to her/she was given advice*), only an inner passive may be allowed (*thought was given to the design*, but not **the design was given thought*), or only an outer passive is allowed (*she was given a pat (on the back)* but not **a pat (on the back) was given to her*). Finally, *give* ComPreds may or may not allow indirect object movement (*give help to him/give him help* vs. *give birth to her/*give her birth*). Because of their syntactic flexibility, ComPreds would thus seem to belong to the class of forms that Nunberg, Sag, and Wasow (1994: 496–7) call 'idiomatically combining phrases' rather than more fully lexicalized 'idiomatic phrases'.

The degree to which ComPreds are syntactically variable and semantically non-compositional is reflective of their degree of idiomaticity and ultimately of their status as free, grammatical constructions or fixed, lexical items, as is discussed in section 4.

3. History of the complex predicate in English

In English, the ComPred is of native origin and arose in Old English, but was less frequent, less idiomaticized (more transparent semantically), and less unified and fixed than in Present-day English (see Brinton and Akimoto 1999b). A typical Old English ComPred is the following:

(1)

þæt	se	ealda	feond	him	ne	mæge
so that	the	old	devil.NOM.SG.M	him.DAT.SG.M	not	may.3.PRS.IND

eft	on	ðam	ytemestan	dæge	his lifes	**ænige**
again	on	the	last.SUPL	day.DAT.SG.M	his life.GEN.SG.N	any

gedrecednesse	**don**
harm.ACC.SG.F	do.INF

(HomM 7 (KerTibC 1) B3.5.7; DOEC)
'so that the old devil may not again to him on the last day of his life do any harm'

ComPreds are formed with *don* 'do', *habban* 'have', *niman* 'take', *sellan* 'give', and later *macian* 'make', with *niman* being replaced by *take* and *sellan* by *give* (both borrowings from Old Norse) in early Middle English. Thus, we see the same semantic set of light verbs being used throughout the history of English (on the continuity of forms, see Brinton 2008a: 47).

For the ComPred, as for many other aspects of English grammar, it was during the Middle English period that 'the crucial steps in their evolution were taken ... forming the basis for further syntactic and semantic refinement and especially for numerical expansion' (Claridge 2000: 95). Increased productivity and frequency in Middle English is in part due to deverbal nouns borrowed from French (e.g. *bataille, deliberacioun, force, promyse, querele*), but ComPreds remain somewhat restricted syntactically: predominately they occur without an article, modification is limited to a restricted set of adjectives (e.g. *good, grete, muchel, strang*), and the construction is rarely passivized. Semantically, ComPreds in Middle English are generally transparent in meaning; they show a 'loose degree of fixedness' (Moralejo-Gárate 2001: 150), falling more to the non-fixed (free) rather than to the fixed (idiomatic) end of the continuum. Two typical Middle English ComPreds are the following:

(2) a. He **gaf** hem **answere** a-gayn, þat god it him sent. (a1375 *WPal.*(KC 13) 395; *MED*)
'He gave him the answer again that god sent it to him.'
b. If he may **done no labour** For elde or sykenesse ... Or for his tendre age also, Thanne may he yit a-begging go. (a1425(?a1400) *RRose* (Htrn 409) 6723; *MED*)
'if he may do no labour on account of age or sickness or because of his tender age also, then he may yet go begging.'

Based on the frequency of ComPreds in Early Modern English and their semantic range, Claridge concludes that the construction is fully established (2000: 174). However, as the forms in (3) attest, the ComPred has still not reached the stage of development characteristic of Present-day English: ComPreds with a zero-article (cf. 3c) are still the majority form (see Kytö 1999: 185; Claridge 2000: 137–40):

(3) a. after the Death of his Wife he had **made a Resolution** never to marry again; (1696 Anon., *Alcander and Philocrates*, p. 106 (105); EEPF)
b. wherefore I **took a** firm **Resolution**, never to make known to any one soever the least thing that concerns such Tricks and Cheats: (ca. 1683 Anon., *The London Jilt*, p. 128 (120); EEPF)
c. she reflected with some indignation, to have her Labours defeated, and however **took resolution** within her self, not to see so fair an opportunity utterly lost. (1685 Anon., *Nicerotis*, p. 96 (90); EEPF)

In a corpus of Early Modern English dramatic and poetic texts, Hiltunen (1999: 144–5) finds that 70 per cent of *do/give/have/make/take* ComPred tokens have a zero-article (see Fig. 45.1). According to Claridge (2000: 137–40, 145, 157–8, 161), modification of the deverbal noun is 'surprisingly low' in Early Modern English, the meaning of the construction is 'overwhelmingly' transparent, and passives are rare.

The almost obligatory appearance of the indefinite article in the ComPred in the Late Modern English period has the consequence that the ComPred comes to be associated with individuated, countable situations. This association of ComPreds with the expression of verbal aspect is widely (though not universally) recognized: ComPreds are said to denote a single occurrence rather than the continuous or the iterative (Live 1973: 34), they have an 'antidurative' effect in limiting an activity in time (Wierzbicka 1982: 757, 759), or they denote 'a segment of an activity ... cut out from an activity that has no boundaries' (Stein 1991: 17–18). Most cogently, Prince (1972: 413, 418) argues that the ComPred contains a 'semelfactive predicate' with the meaning '(be) a bounded activity'. In contrast to the simplex verb, which perspectivizes the situation as an activity (e.g. *walk*), the ComPred perspectivizes the situation as an accomplishment or an achievement (e.g. *take a walk*), denoting one single completed action. The ComPred becomes a exponent of telic aspect: it adds an intended endpoint to a situation, an endpoint which varies with the nature

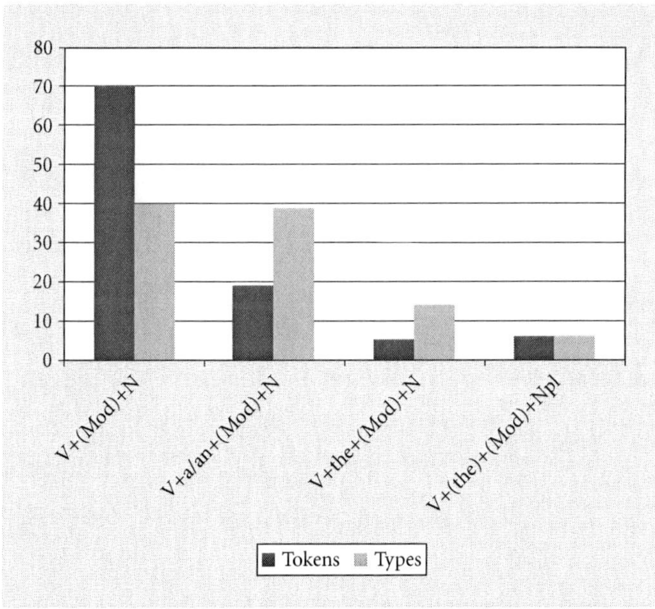

Fig. 45.1. Percentage of ComPreds in Early Modern English with zero-articles, indefinite articles, and definite articles (figures from Hiltunen 1999: 144–5)

of the situation; for example, with a situation of unlimited duration such as sleeping, the ComPred *have a sleep* denotes a sleep of some limited length of time, while with an incremental situation such as moving, the ComPred *make a move* isolates one increment of the situation (see further Brinton 2008a: 46–9).

During earlier periods of the language, aspectual meaning is not systematic in the ComPred (see Claridge 2000: 245–6; Moralejo-Gárate 2001: 142; Iglesias-Rábade 2001: 159), but in the Late Modern English period—a period in which the ComPred 'develops rapidly', according to Strang (1970: 101)—the expression of aspectual meaning comes to the fore. The aspectual function is particularly noticeable with ComPreds introduced by *have*, which in its non-light verb uses is stative:

(4) a. Some Demon whisper'd, L----, **have a taste**! (1821–22 Hazlitt, *Table Talk*; CLMET)
b. He, somewhat to my discomfort, enticed her from the room to **have a run** in the hall (1848 A. Brontë, *Tenant of Wildfell Hall*; CLMET)
c. Isabella ceased speaking, and **took a drink** of tea (1847 E. Brontë, *Wuthering Heights*; CLMET)

Also in the Late Modern period the grammatical distinction between certain *have* and *give/take/make* ComPreds, in which the former expresses stative meaning and the latter dynamic meaning (as in *have/make a wish*, *have/give an answer*), becomes more entrenched (see above, section 2):[3]

(5) a. although he **had an answer** at the veriest tip of his tongue (1797 Inchbald, *Nature and Art*; CLMET)
b. I will look it over to-night, and **give** you **an answer** tomorrow (1812 Smith and Smith, *Rejected Addresses*; CLMET)

During this period the construction is also extended to deverbal phrasal verbs, e.g. *make a comeback, have a breakdown, give a handout, do a make-over* (Stein 1991: 9), and to so-called *give*-gerund constructions, e.g. *give a thrashing to, give a kicking to, give a talking to,* dating from the mid-19th century (see Trousdale 2008b: 48–51).

(6) a. You must keep moving all night . . . or else you goes to a twopenny-rope shop and **gets a lie down** (1850 Kingsley, *Alton Locke* I. v. 80; *OED*)
b. I shall **give** him **a good scolding** after dinner. (1875 Hayward, *Love agst. World* 38; *OED*, cited in Trousdale 2008b: 50)

[3] Note that not all such pairs express the stative/dynamic contrast, e.g. *have/take a shower, walk, nap*, etc.

4. Grammaticalization and/or Lexicalization

4.1. Previous approaches

While many synchronic studies treat ComPreds as lexicalized, some recognize the intermediate status of ComPreds between unitary predicates and free formations. Allerton (2002: 8) points out that simply listing ComPreds in the lexicon would not bring out their 'evident regularity of syntactic patterning' (17). Huddleston and Pullum see ComPreds as grammatically productive (2002: 290–96), but at the same time classify certain ones as 'verbal idioms' which are more or less 'fossilised' (288–9). Quirk et al. discuss ComPreds first as productive prepositional verbs (1985: 1158–9, 1211–12) but later point out that phrasal lexical items such as *lose sight of*, though exhibiting some degree of separateness, are at the same time characterized by fusion; they thus illustrate the 'gradience between grammar and lexicon, including a gradience in lexicalization' (1530n).

In historical studies, ComPreds have usually been treated as instances of (attenuated) lexicalization. Claridge speaks of the 'lexicalization' or 'institutionalization' of verb-nominal combinations, though she too sees this as a matter of 'degree' (2000: 73, 78, 140, 157, 161). Traugott (1999c: 259) concludes that historically the development of composite predicates is 'best construed as lexicalization followed by idiomatization', and for Bergs (2005: 218), historical changes result in a 'gradience in lexicalization and idiomatization'. In contrast, Brinton and Akimoto (1999a: 17) point out that aspects of the development of ComPreds, such as decategorialization of the noun and its increasing fusion with the verb, loss of syntactic variability, syntactic reanalysis of the construction, and acquisition of discourse meanings, resemble changes characteristic of grammaticalization.

4.2. Lexicalization

If we understand lexicalization in its broadest sense as 'adoption into the lexicon' (see Brinton and Traugott 2005: 18), the historical overview (given in section 3) would point to ComPreds undergoing a process of lexicalization. ComPreds show a tendency toward fusion—both syntactic and semantic—into a lexical unit that is stored in the 'inventory' (the lexicon) and is accessed holistically (Lehmann 2002a). Over time, individual ComPred constructions become progressively more fixed or fossilized, especially in acquiring an indefinite article and restricting the deverbal noun to the singular. Although there is some syntactic freedom (e.g. many ComPreds can be used in the passive or take adjectival modifiers), the constructions are for the most part fixed. Evidence of lexical unity may be provided by the increase of the outer passive since the 18th century (e.g. *she was given help* but not **help was given to her*) (Akimoto 2002: 14). The outer passive seems to confirm the coalescence of the light verb and the deverbal noun into a coherent whole, into 'a phonetic and semantic unit or a kind of compound verb' (Visser 1973: 2163).[4]

The development of ComPreds would also seem to be consistent with lexicalization understood as idiomatization and loss of compositionality (Brinton and Traugott 2005: 54–7). Many ComPreds acquire meanings that are not entirely predictable from the meanings of the parts (e.g. *pay attention to* = 'consider', *take care of* = 'attend to') and seem to be idiosyncratic, one-off developments rather than following general and predictable patterns of change.

4.3. Lexicalization and grammaticalization

That said, the apprehension of ComPreds as entirely lexicalized is brought into question by the continued syntactic independence and flexibility of the ComPred, which reveals itself in two ways:

- the intervention of an adjective between the light verb and deverbal noun;
- the possibility of separating the light verb and deverbal noun in passive constructions, especially in the inner passive, which promotes the deverbal noun to subject position and thus separates it from its collocated light verb (e.g. *mention was made of his exploits*).

For example, Claridge notes that even highly 'institutionalized' and internally cohesive ComPreds such as *take place in, make use of, find fault with* may have rather extensive modification and commonly occur in the inner passive (2000: 157–8, 161, 164).

The mixed behavior of ComPreds is thus evidence for identifying two categories that differ in respect to lexicalization and grammaticalization.

(a) The first category—the *lose sight of* type—includes ComPreds formed with a variety of light verbs and generally with no indefinite article.
(b) The second category—the *have a look (at)* type—includes ComPreds formed with a restricted set of light verbs and typically containing an indefinite article.

4.3.1. Lose sight of *types: lexicalization*

In the first category are ComPreds formed with a wide variety of verbs, often having a high degree of semantic specificity:

[4] Akimoto (2002) also points out that outer passives are more common with ComPreds containing zero-affixed nouns, which because of their less 'nouny' character enter more readily into idiomatic structures.

curry/find favour with	*get access to*	*pay tribute to*
cast doubt on	*grab attention*	*provide support for*
inflict shame on	*lay hold of*	*put trust in*
bear witness to	*lose sight of*	*raise objections to*
catch sight of	*pay heed*	*show preference*

Some ComPreds of this type are completely non-productive (e.g. *open fire on, seize control of, keep track of*), while others show minimal productivity (e.g. *lose sight/count/track of*). Over time, the possibilities of collocation have been reduced; neither the deverbal noun nor the light verb can be altered; e.g. *lose sight of* allows permutation neither to **lose vision of* nor to **forfeit sight of*. Thus, these ComPreds have the highly specified semantic content and the low pattern productivity ('host-class reduction') characteristic of lexicalization (see Himmelmann 2004: 36–7; cf. Brinton and Traugott 2005: 96–7). Furthermore, these ComPreds overwhelmingly occur without an indefinite article. The zero-article in ComPreds has been associated with idiom formation (see e.g. Kytö 1999: 186; Claridge 2000: 137–40; Akimoto 2002: 12).[5] These ComPreds often have non-compositional or highly idiomaticized meaning (e.g. *lose sight of* 'forget about, not keep fresh in one's mind', *pay court to*, 'pay courteous attention to', or *curry favour with* 'behave ingratiatingly to'). We can think of ComPreds of this type as instances of phrasal constructions that have become fossilized and less compositional; they are lexical (or lexicalized) items that fall between partially fixed phrases and complex, semi-idiomatic forms on the scale of lexicality (Brinton and Traugott 2005: 94).

4.3.2. Take a look (at) *type: grammaticalization*

In contrast, ComPreds consisting of the light verbs *make, take, give, have*, and *do* exhibit changes characteristic of grammaticalization:

- The continuity in the semantic set of light verbs from Old English to the present and their meaning are consistent with the semantic generality of the input of grammaticalization (see Brinton and Traugott 2005: 99).
- Although the set of light verbs remains stable, the number of deverbal objects expands over time. Romance borrowings swell the set of deverbal nouns, so that by Early Modern English they predominate in the ComPred construction (Claridge 2000: 136). These ComPreds thus exhibit what Himmelmann (2004: 32) calls 'host-class expansion', where a grammaticalizing form increases its range of collocations with members of the relevant category.
- The ComPred construction is also expanded to new (morpho)syntactic forms, the gerund (see Trousdale 2008b: 55) and the phrasal verb. This shows the

[5] Trousdale (2008b: 57) argues that the absence of articles or restriction on articles in ComPreds is evidence of decategorialization of the verbal nominal (cf., however, Brinton and Traugott 2005 who restrict decategorialization to grammaticalization).

characteristic expansion of syntactic context found in grammaticalization (Himmelmann 2004: 32).

- The light verbs in this ComPred type are highly productive in forming new ComPreds (see e.g. the lists of *make-* and *take-* complex predicates cited by Nunberg et al. 1994: 532–4). Such as increase in type and token frequency is likewise characteristic of grammaticalization (Brinton and Traugott 2005: 100).

However, what argues most strongly for the grammaticalization of the *give/take* ComPred type is the 'semantic-pragmatic expansion' (Himmelmann 2004: 33) it undergoes. As a result of the emergence of an obligatory indefinite article in the ComPred, the meaning of the construction has been enriched with aspectual meaning (telic Aktionsart, stative/dynamic contrast) added to its eventive meaning. The ComPred construction acquires grammatical (aspectual) meaning not found in the simplex verb. In constructional terms, the ComPred undergoes a change from less to more schematic as meso-constructions (*have* ComPred Construction, *give* ComPred Construction, etc.). Elements within these meso-constructions acquire grammatical properties: 'As the meso-construction entrenches, the light verb functions increasingly as a marker of a particular grammatical category (here as an aspectual marker)' (Trousdale 2008b: 60). Strictly speaking, it is not the light verb but the entire construction that is grammaticalized.

Thus, we can think of ComPreds of this type as instances of grammaticalized phrasal constructions. Were these phrasal constructions to be further grammaticalized, one would expect the light verb of move in the direction of becoming a grammatical (derivational) prefix (not unlike the verbal aspectual prefixes of Slavic). But another possible scenario is that these grammaticalized constructions could suffer a loss of their semantic compositionality and become lexicalized, e.g. *give it a shot* 'try', *take a gander* 'look at', *take a dim view of* 'disapprove of', *make short work of* 'put an end to quickly', *make a hit with* 'be successful with', *take stock of* 'reckon'; Trousdale (2008b) argues that this is the case with many of the *give*-gerunds that he has examined.

5. Conclusion

This chapter has argued that in its development and syntactic behaviour the English ComPred presents evidence for a gradience view of lexicality and grammaticality. Aspects of fusion make clear that we are dealing with forms with some (but not a complete) degree of coalescence. ComPreds in English do not seem to constitute a unified class historically, but develop differently along lines of grammaticalization and lexicalization, understood as complementary, not opposing diachronic processes. Some ComPreds exhibit the high degree of fossilization, loss of compositionality, and lack of productivity characteristic of lexicalization. Others, especially those consisting of the 'light' verbs *make*, *have*, *take*, *give*, and *do*, are productive and have acquired grammatical functions while remaining relatively transparent in meaning, thus becoming highly grammaticalized. Lexicalization and grammaticalization represent mutually reinforcing processes that lead to grammatical variation. '[S]peakers have available a number of stored, or lexicalized, collocations and constructions of differing levels of abstraction and productivity—including fixed expressions . . . as well as ones with open slots . . . ' (Torres Cacoullos and Walker 2009b: 348). While grammaticalized ComPreds may undergo further fossilization and decompositionality and become lexicalized collocations, lexicalized ComPreds may come to occupy particular niches and thus, rather than standing apart from the development, interact with and shape the grammaticalization path followed by the more generalized ComPred construction and lead to the distribution of grammaticalized and lexicalized forms found in English.

CHAPTER 46

NEGATIVE CYCLES AND GRAMMATICALIZATION

MAJ-BRITT MOSEGAARD HANSEN

1. Introduction

It is plausible to assume that negation must be a universal feature of language. Indeed, according to Miestamo (2005: 5), 'no languages without negation have been found'. Yet, unlike its conceptual counterpart affirmation, which is normally left implicit, negation appears to invariably receive overt expression in language (cf. Greenberg 1966: 50). Formally, then, negation is clearly the marked pole of the affirmative-negative opposition.[1]

In this chapter, the term 'negation' will henceforth be used to refer to what Payne (1985: 198) calls 'standard' negation, viz. the form of clause negation that is considered most basic in a given language, which applies productively in declarative main clauses, and which does not involve quantifiers. Thus, to take English as an example, standard negation is expressed in that language by the particle *not*, frequently taking the form of an enclitic *n't* on the finite verb, usually in combination with *do*-support, as in (1). English has a variety of other ways of negating states

[1] Many scholars have argued that negation is likewise conceptually marked with respect to affirmation. For reasons of space, the present chapter will not enter into that particular debate, but see Horn (1989: 45ff.) for an overview.

of affairs (some of them exemplified in (2–4)), but while this is true of many languages, such additional constructions will not be discussed here.

(1) John didn't sing.
(2) For John not to have sung is surprising.
(3) Nobody sang.
(4) That song remained unsung.

It is a salient feature of standard negation that its formal expression tends to evolve and change over time. Of particular interest in the context of grammaticalization is the fact that, cross-linguistically, the relevant changes appear very frequently to follow cyclical patterns. Two such patterns have been identified in the literature, the more widely known of the two being the so-called Jespersen Cycle (so dubbed by Dahl 1979: 88, but originally described by Jespersen 1917), while the other—identified and discussed by Croft (1991b)—takes the form of a negative-existential cycle. Jespersen's Cycle, along with possible explanations for it and its link to grammaticalization, will be discussed in section 2 below, followed by a brief treatment of Croft's Cycle along similar lines in section 3. Given that Croft's Cycle is not only of significantly more recent formulation, but also narrower in scope than Jespersen's, there is—unsurprisingly—a vastly more extensive literature on the latter. The structure of the present chapter, and the relative amplitude of the discussion devoted to each of the two cycles, reflect that fact.

2. Jespersen's Cycle

This pattern of evolution pertains to a number of languages which express negation through one or more markers of an adverbial nature. Jespersen (1917: 4) describes the cycle as follows:

> [t]he original negative adverb is first weakened, then found insufficient and therefore strengthened, generally through some additional word, and this in turn may be felt as a negative proper and may then in the course of time be subject to the same development as the original word.

Schematically, the complete sequence can be illustrated using French (in an extended sense, including its mother language Latin at one end, and French-based Creoles at the other) as Table 46.1.[2]

[2] Note that Louisiana French Creole represents an expected future development of Standard French only insofar as a cyclical development in the strict sense is envisaged (whereby movement of the postverbal marker to preverbal position is a precondition for the cycle to repeat itself in a formally

Table 46.1. The evolution of French clause negation (sample sentence: 'I do not say...')

Stage 0 (Classical Latin)	*non dico*	The negator is preverbal
Stage 1	*je ne dis*	The preverbal negator is phonetically reduced
Stage 2	*je ne dis (pas)*	The preverbal negator is optionally complemented by a postverbal element
Stage 3	*je ne dis pas*	The postverbal element grammaticalizes as part of a discontinuous negator embracing the verb
Stage 4	*je (ne) dis pas*	The original preverbal negator becomes optional
Stage 5 (future French?)	*je dis pas*	The negator is postverbal
Stage 6 (Louisiana French Creole)	*mo pa di*	The previously postverbal negator migrates to preverbal position

With respect to Stage 5, it must be noted that no variety of French has fully reached this stage yet, in terms of having completely abandoned the use of *ne*. Nevertheless, conversational registers of Québecois and Swiss French, in particular, come very close, showing rates of *ne*-retention of only 1.5 per cent and 2.5 per cent, respectively (Sankoff and Vincent 1977: 252; Fonseca-Greber 2007: 256).

A number of other languages, particularly (but not exclusively) of European origin, appear to have gone through some or all of the stages set out in Table 46.1; for instance Afrikaans (Biberauer 2009), Bantu (Devos and van der Auwera 2009), Brazilian Portuguese (Schwegler 1988; Schwenter 2006), Catalan (Espinal 1993), Dutch (Burridge 1983), English (Frisch 1997; van Kemenade 2000; Wallage 2008), German (Abraham 2003), Greek (Kiparsky and Condoravdi 2006), and Italian (Bernini and Ramat 1996; Zanuttini 1997; Hansen and Visconti 2009).

Although, superficially, the similarities among these various languages in terms of how negation has evolved are quite striking, the reality is—as one might expect—somewhat more complex than Jespersen's original formulation would suggest.

For one thing, the different stages are not necessarily as neatly ordered as Table 46.1 suggests. For instance, Schwenter (2006) shows that in Brazilian Portuguese negation can be expressed by a plain preverbal *naõ* or by an embracing *naõ ... naõ* construction (cf. (5)), which seems to suggest that the language is currently at Stage

similar way). It is entirely possible that the actual evolution of French negation will not go beyond Stage 4 or 5 as represented in Table 46.1, and that it may instead take a slightly different direction, such as adding an additional postverbal marker. Accordingly, van der Auwera (2009), taking a broader view of the notion of 'cycle', explicitly argues for the existence of a variety of Jespersen Cycles.

2 of Jespersen's Cycle. However, speakers also have the option of using a plain sentence-final *naõ* (cf. (6)), which would be indicative of Stage 4. Stage 3 appears not to (have) be(en) instantiated at all, insofar as the embracing construction is still considered non-canonical:

(5) A. *O João não foi à festa.* B. *Não foi não.*
'A. João didn't go to the party. B. He didn't go.' (Schwenter 2006: (11))

(6) A. *Você gostou da palestra da Maria?* B. *Gostei não.*
'A. Did you like Maria's talk? B. I didn't.' (Schwenter 2006: (12))

Furthermore, once a language has reached Stage 3, Stage 4 is in fact not the only possible next step. Thus, the language may instead add an obligatory or optional third negative marker, as in (7) below. This has happened in some Bantu languages (Devos and van der Auwera 2009) and in Lewo (van der Auwera (2009: 57):

(7) Laadi (Devos and van der Auwera 2009: (69))

ka	*-na*	*-tim-uny*	*-áâni*	*-ko*
NEG1	-1SG.TM	-dig-N	-NEG3	-NEG2

'I hadn't dug.'

At stages 2–4 of the cycle, the relative status of the pre- vs. postverbal negative element may be unclear or controversial. Even when the forms appear identical from one stage of the cycle to the next, their morphosyntactic and semantic status may have changed. Thus, Rowlett (1998) and Wallage (2008) have argued cogently that in French and English, respectively, the preverbal marker—*ne* in both cases—was the principal negator only so long as the postverbal marker (*pas* and *not*, respectively) remained optional. However, once the latter was fully grammaticalized and could no longer be left out, i.e. once these languages reached Stage 3, the evidence points to it being the principal negator, while the preverbal element became more akin to an agreement marker (Rowlett 1998: 134; Wallage 2008: 673). It is perhaps significant in this connection that, according to Frisch (1997: 32), Stage 3 never became properly entrenched in English. In other words, the language may in fact have passed directly from Stage 2 to Stage 4.[3]

The property of being a sufficient exponent of negation must, of course, be transferred from the pre- to the postverbal marker before the transition to Stage 4 (i.e. loss of the preverbal marker) can take place. In contradistinction to English and French, Biberauer (2009) shows that, in contemporary Afrikaans, the postverbal marker is phonetically, semantically, and categorially weak compared to the original preverbal marker, in as much as only the latter can be modified, reinforced by other elements, and stressed, while only the former can felicitously be omitted.

[3] Indeed, the same may be true of conversational spoken French, to the extent that, from the time postverbal *pas* became obligatory, there is sporadic evidence in the literature that *ne*-deletion was taking place in informal discourse (Martineau and Mougeon 2003: 129).

She concludes that this language appears to remain stably at Stage 3, with no signs of dropping its preverbal negator.

Finally, in languages that appear to have reached Stage 4, where the postverbal negator is strong enough to appear on its own, but is still in competition with the bipartite form, the use of the postverbal negator alone may differ pragmatically from bipartite negation.[4] According to Schwenter (2006), Brazilian Portuguese postverbal *naõ* in (6) above differs from the embracing *naõ... naõ* construction exemplified in (5) by being felicitous only in dialogic contexts. Fonseca-Greber (2007), on the other hand, suggests that bipartite *ne... pas* seems, in conversational Swiss French at least, to have developed a new function of expressing emphasis, in contrast to the by now pragmatically neutral postverbal *pas*. If this is also true of colloquial French as spoken in France, then such a new contrast may prevent French from eventually reaching Stage 5 of Jespersen's Cycle.[5]

2.1. Explaining Jespersen's Cycle

As pointed out by van der Auwera (2010), Jespersen's account focuses exclusively on the formal properties of negation, and essentially explains the negative cycle as being triggered by the phonetic weakening of the original preverbal marker (i.e. in the case of French, the weakening of Latin NŌN to Old French *ne*). According to Kiparsky and Condoravdi (2006: 4), however, the evidence of such phonetic weakening is not very strong across languages.[6] Moreover, as mentioned above, contemporary Afrikaans appears to be one language where it is the innovative postverbal marker that is phonetically weaker (cf. Biberauer 2009).

Observing that Latin NŌN itself is assumed to represent the univerbation of IE **ne* + OENUM ('one'), Jespersen's contemporary Antoine Meillet proposed instead (without reference to Jespersen) that pragmatics may be the driving force in the negative cycle:

Les langues suivent ainsi une sorte de développement en spirale: elles ajoutent des mots accessoires pour obtenir une expression intense; ces mots s'affaiblissent, se dégradent et tombent au niveau de simples outils grammaticaux; on ajoute de nouveaux mots ou des

[4] Stage 2 may, of course, likewise be characterized by pragmatic differences between the competing modes of expression. That possibility will be discussed in greater depth in section 2.1 below.

[5] At Stages 2 and 3, at least, a language may also have competing postverbal elements, possibly with pragmatic differences between them: thus, in medieval French, the adverbs *pas*, *mie*, and to a lesser extent *point* and *go(ut)te* (which was restricted to a very small number of verbs), were in competition for the postverbal slot, while Classical and Modern Standard French show variation between *ne... pas* and *ne... point*. A pilot study by Hansen (forthcoming) suggests that, in medieval French, the precise choice of postverbal marker may have affected the speech act expressed by the negated clause.

[6] Even French is not a fully convincing case, given that *ne* only lost its ability to carry stress towards the end of the Middle French period (16th c.), i.e. approximately half a millennium after the language entered stage 2 of Jespersen's Cycle (Martineau and Mougeon 2003: 123f.).

mots différents en vue de l'expression; l'affaiblissement recommence, et ainsi sans fin. (Meillet 1912: 140)

'Languages thus undergo a sort of spiral development: they add extra words to obtain an intensified expression; those words weaken, wear out, and are reduced to the level of simple grammatical tools; new or different words are added for expressive purposes; the weakening process begins anew, and so on without end'. (My translation.)

There are a number of reasons to believe that Meillet's account may be more accurate, and certainly, from the point of view of grammaticalization theory, we would expect the formal changes that characterize the cycle to be driven by the meanings attached to different constructions rather than the other way around.

Thus, neither the transition from a simple preverbal negator to bipartite negation nor the transition from bipartite negation to a simple postverbal negator is achieved abruptly: as Table 46.1 suggests, both these transitions are characterized by periods of variation between the older and the more recent strategy, represented by Stages 2 and 4. Given that, in at least some cases, these stages last for centuries and appear quite stable, it is plausible to assume that the competing strategies may, at least initially, differ not just in form, but also in aspects of their meaning.

Observed differences in contemporary Stage 4 languages were briefly touched upon above. With respect to Stage 2 languages, contemporary descriptions do, indeed, frequently treat the bipartite construction as pragmatically different from the plain preverbal negator. Such differences would be inexplicable if the reinforcing element had been introduced simply to compensate for the formal reduction of the original negator.

At an intuitive level, the pragmatic difference in question seems to have to do with somehow emphasizing—or, to use Meillet's term, 'intensifying'—negation. Now, far from being contingent on the canonical negator having been formally weakened, the ability to express negative emphasis would appear to be a universal feature of languages (Schwegler 1988: 36; Kiparsky and Condoravdi 2006: 7), and it is moreover a category which is commonly formally marked by the addition of a particle-like expression.

Indeed, frequent etymological sources for reinforcing postverbal markers have in common that they are elements which naturally lend themselves to the expression of emphasis. Thus, we find negative reinforcers derived from quantitative expressions denoting minimal amounts, i.e. expressions which either are negative polarity elements or have NPI-like properties (Israel 2001). Saliently, this is the case with French *pas* (< Latin PASSU(M) 'step') and its principal medieval competitors, *mie* (< MICA(M) 'crumb') and *point* (< PUNCTU(M) 'point'), as well as similar or cognate expressions in other Romance languages (e.g. Catalan *pas*, Italian *mica*). Alternatively, postverbal markers can be based on negative interjections, presumably originally added as emphatic tags. This appears to be the case, for instance, in Brazilian Portuguese (Schwegler 1988: 38) and in Afrikaans (Biberauer 2009).

All of this points to the weakening and ultimate loss of the original preverbal negator in Jespersen's Cycle being, in fact, the consequence rather than the cause of increasingly frequent use of the new postverbal marker.

If we accept this, can we be more precise about the exact nature of the perceivedly more 'emphatic' forms of negation expressed by bipartite structures at Stage 2? For, as Schwenter (2006) points out, emphasis is a rather ill-defined notion in itself.

Several studies have suggested that the use of bipartite Stage 2 negation in various Romance languages is subject to discourse-functional constraints linked to the presupposed or otherwise given nature of the negated proposition or its underlying positive counterpart (e.g. Bernini and Ramat 1996; Espinal 1993; Schwegler 1988; Zanuttini 1997; Schwenter 2006; Hansen and Visconti 2009; Hansen 2009). According to Zanuttini (1997: 61), for instance, in Italian only (9) below would constitute a felicitous exchange with the addition of *mica*, whereas (8) would not:

(8) A. *Chi viene a prenderti?*
B. *Non so. Ma Gianni non a (*mica) la macchina.*
'A. Who's coming to pick you up?
B. I don't know. But Gianni doesn't [*NEG2] have the car.'

(9) A. *Chi viene a prenderti—Gianni?*
B. *Non so. Ma Gianni non a mica la macchina.*
'A. Who's coming to pick you up—Gianni?
B. I don't know. But Gianni doesn't [NEG2] have the car.'

Schwenter (2006) suggests that Brazilian Portuguese *naõ . . . naõ* only appears in propositions that are already activated in the short-term memory of the hearer, while Hansen and Visconti (2009) and Hansen (2009b) propose that medieval French clauses negated by *ne . . . mie/pas* were constrained to be either already activated in the short-term memory of the hearer or inferable (i.e. accessible to activation) based on other propositions thus activated. In all the relevant Romance languages, the plain preverbal markers, on the other hand, are compatible with propositions conveying information that is entirely new to the discourse.

We may speculate that if French, unlike Italian, Catalan, and Brazilian Portuguese, has proceeded to Stage 3, this may perhaps be attributable to the fact that the bipartite negator in medieval French could mark propositions which were merely inferable. A pragmatic constraint including inferable propositions may be more easily loosened to embrace pragmatically neutral negation than one which includes only directly activated propositions.

The gradual loss of the preverbal marker in Stages 4 and 5 is perhaps explained by the typologically strongly marked nature of discontinuous negation (Bernini and Ramat 1996: 44): Stage 3 negation may be inherently unstable due to its discontinuous form.

2.2. Jespersen's Cycle and grammaticalization

The question must now be asked to what extent the individual developments that together make up Jespersen's Cycle are actually instances of grammaticalization.

Phonological reduction of the preverbal negative marker, insofar as it plays a role in the Cycle at all, is not in and of itself a matter of grammaticalization. Where phonological reduction is evidence of cliticization, however, as in the case of the English *n't* contraction, and the loss of stress in French *ne*, for instance, secondary grammaticalization (defined as the evolution of an already grammatical item towards an even greater degree of grammaticalization, cf. Brinton and Traugott 2005: 76f.) is clearly involved.

Nor is the initial insertion of postverbal 'emphatic' elements, so long as these retain their original meaning (as is the case with Latin MICA(M), exemplified in (10)), as such a matter of grammaticalization:

(10) *quinque dies aquam in os suum non coniecit, non micam panis* (Petronius, Satyricon, 1st c. AD)
'for five days he didn't put any water in his mouth, not a crumb of bread'

Once such elements become bleached of their literal meanings, however, and become general-purpose NPIs, capable of appearing with semantically non-harmonious verbs, as in (11), and subsequently acquire actual negative meaning, as evidenced by their ability to occur alongside NPIs (cf. (12)), they can be considered to have undergone grammaticalization, as evidenced by context expansion (Himmelmann 2004):

(11) *Tut seie fel, se jo mie l'otrei!* (*Chanson de Roland*, v. 3897, *c.*1080)
'May I be a complete traitor, if I grant it in the least!'

(12) *Tuit vos Franceis ne valent pas meaille.* (*Li coronemenz Loois*, v. 2433, *c.*1150)
'All your Frenchmen aren't [NEG2] worth a dime.'

Assuming that bipartite constructions are pragmatically marked at Stage 2, the 'unmarking' that must take place before the transition to Stage 3 can occur represents further bleaching and context expansion, which together with the obligatorification of the postverbal marker that characterizes Stage 3 represents secondary grammaticalization.

The gradually increasing deletion and eventual loss of a redundant preverbal marker in Stages 4 and 5 is, of course, not grammaticalization.[7] Finally, ulterior word order changes that result in the erstwhile postverbal marker taking preverbal position in the clause may be attributable to analogical change, Stage 5 speakers

[7] If Fonseca-Greber's (2007) analysis, briefly mentioned above, is correct, and the loss of Stage 4 French *ne* is being halted by its developing a new function as a marker of emphasis, then such a development would qualify as a case of exaptation (Lass 1990), and regrammaticalization.

taking the lexical rather than the finite verb as their point of reference (Schwegler 1988: 50f.); cf. (13):

(13) *J'* *ai* *pas* *dit* *ça*
1sg.s FIN.AUX NEG LEX DEM
'I haven't said that/I didn't say that.'

3. Croft's Cycle

Croft (1991b) identifies a different type of negative cycle, involving the interaction of negation with existential predicates. This cycle involves three synchronic language types and has three stages, each consisting in the transition from one type to another.

Type A languages use the regular verbal negator to negate existential predicates, e.g. (14):

(14) Tzutujil (Croft 1991b: 7, (3))
ma *ko* *ta* *jaay*
NEG EX IRR house
'There aren't any houses.'

Type B languages, on the other hand, employ a special negative existential predicate, as in (15):

(15) Amharic (Croft 1991b: 9, (17))
səkk^{w}aryälläm
sugar NEG.EX.3SG
'There is no sugar.'

Type C languages, finally, feature a polysemous marker which is both a regular verbal negator and a negative existential, cf. (17), from the Australian Aboriginal language Nunggubuyu, whose verbal negator *wa:='ri* is one of the 3.SG forms of the negative existential verb exemplified in (16):

(16) Nunggubuyu (Croft 1991b: 11, (31))
aŋga: = *'ri* *ana-lha:wu*
it.B = NEG.EX words
'There must be no words.'

(17) Nunggubuyu (Croft 1991b: 11, (32))
wa: = *ri* *ŋa* = *ŋadugumbi:-ni* *ŋaŋ* = *jama:-'*
it.A = NEG(ex) I.fished I.did.thus
'I didn't fish like that.'

Croft's Cycle then consists in successive (though possibly overlapping) shifts from A to B, from B to C, and from C back to A. A > B comes about via univerbation (phonological fusion) of the regular verbal negator and the existential predicate, resulting in a new predicate with an added element of meaning. This might suggest that the diachronic process involved in this shift is lexicalization; but as the change brings about a new paradigmatic contrast between a positive and a negative existential predicate, both of which have functional rather than content meaning, it can legitimately be regarded as a case of grammaticalization (cf. Brinton and Traugott 2005: 100).

B > C involves the semantic bleaching of the existential meaning of the negative existential, resulting in context expansion of the new regular verbal negator. This represents a clear case of grammaticalization. There is an interesting overlap with Jespersen's Cycle here, inasmuch as Croft (1991b: 13f.) suggests that this shift is triggered by the use of the negative existential as a marker of emphasis (cf. (18)):

(18) Mara (Croft 1991b: 14, (41))

ganagu	*wu-nayi*	*maluy*
NEG	3SG/3SG-saw	NEG.EX/EMPH

'He didn't see him at all/He saw nobody'

In the C > A change, the negative existential reading of the polysemous marker is lost and the purely negative reading derived from it is used in combination with positive existentials. This implies constructional analogy, which in and of itself does not make this development an instance of grammaticalization. There is, however, further context expansion—and hence increased grammaticalization—of the already grammaticalized negative marker.

Croft (1991b: 22f.) explains the sequencing of changes by suggesting, first, that the initial fusion of the verbal negator and the existential predicate (i.e. A > B) probably has to take place before the negative existential can be used emphatically, to avoid creating a sequence of two predicates. The value of this explanation is not quite clear, however, as ['Normal' Predicate + Negation + Existential Predicate] seems to be no more nor no less a sequence of two predicates than ['Normal' Predicate + Negative Existential Predicate]. Indeed, Croft himself observes that certain strongly isolating languages constitute exceptions to the general pattern by progressing directly from Type A to Type C.

Secondly, that Type C must be derived from Type B is explained by the logical requirement that the negative existential undergo weakening before syntactic analogy can take place. Finally, Type C is said to be inherently unstable, in so far as the equation between negative existential and verbal negator makes it appear as if the existential predicate is simply absent when negated, leading to the introduction of the positive existential in these constructions.

CHAPTER 47

THE GRAMMATICALIZATION OF TENSE AND ASPECT

KEES HENGEVELD

1. Introduction

This chapter considers the processes of grammaticalization that involve tense and aspect markers from the perspective of a layered, hierarchical approach to grammatical categories. After a brief introduction to the notion of hierarchical layering and the predictions that follow from it as regards grammaticalization processes in section 2, I look at grammaticalization processes leading to aspect in section 3, processes leading away from aspect in section 4, processes leading to tense in section 5, and processes leading away from tense in section 6. The chapter is rounded off with a schematic summary in section 7.

I am grateful to Enoch Aboh, Guglielmo Cinque, Peter Harder, an anonymous referee, and the participants in the Amsterdam FDG Colloquium for their comments on an earlier version of this chapter.

2. Grammaticalization and Layering

2.1. Layering

The idea that grammatical categories are organized in layers[1] arose in the 1980s in a variety of grammatical frameworks: in Role & Reference Grammar (Foley and Van Valin 1984), in Usage-Based Grammar (Bybee 1985), in Functional Grammar (Hengeveld 1989), and in Generative Grammar[2] (Pollock 1989). A major difference between these approaches is that Bybee (1985) and Hengeveld (1989) define layers in semantic terms, while Foley and Van Valin (1984) and Pollock (1989) define them in positional terms. The approaches converge in that the semantic ones predict that grammatical elements will be ordered according to their semantic scope, while the syntactic approaches start from the order and labels the resulting categories in terms of their semantics. The results arrived at through these two procedures are remarkably similar.

The basic idea may be illustrated with the following examples from Hidatsa (Matthews 1965):

(1) Wíra i ápáari ki stao ski.
tree it grow INGR REM.PAST CERT
'The tree must have begun to grow a long time ago.'

In this example the relative order of the tense, mood, and aspect (TMA) markers with respect to the predicate is ingressive–remote past–certainty. Semantic approaches to layering would interpret this as a result of the fact that there are differences in scope between them: ingressive, specifying the internal temporal structure of the event, is within the scope of remote past, specifying the external temporal structure of the event. Both are in the scope of certainty, which qualifies the content of the message as a whole. These scope relations may be indicated as in (2):

(2) certainty (remote past (ingressive (predicate+arguments)))

It is not the absolute linear order but the relative order with respect to the predicate that is predicted to correlate with scopal layers. Thus, the order of the relevant TMA markers in the English translation of example (1) is the mirror-image of the one in the Hidatsa original.

Syntactic approaches would interpret the order in (2) such that the more removed a grammatical element is from the verb, the higher the corresponding

[1] For a detailed comparison between various approaches to layering see Narrog (2009a).

[2] The layered approach to grammatical categories in Government and Binding theory was more fully developed in the 1990s as the Cartographic Approach. See Cinque and Rizzi (2011) for an overview.

functional node is in the syntactic representation of the sentence involved (see e.g. Cinque 1999).

2.2. Layering in Functional Discourse Grammar

Any prediction following from a layered approach depends on how exactly the scope relations between categories are defined. I will follow here the classification of TMA categories in terms of their scope offered in Hengeveld and Mackenzie (2008; 2010) in the context of Functional Discourse Grammar. Table 47.1 summarizes this classification.

Scope relations are defined here in terms of five different semantic layers. Working inside out, the predicate designates a *property* that applies to one or more participants in a state-of-affairs; the *situational concept* is a description of a set of possible states-of-affairs; a *state-of-affairs* is the situated real or hypothesized situation the speaker has in mind; the *episode* is a thematically coherent combination of states-of-affairs that are characterized by unity or continuity of time, location, and participants; the *proposition* is the mental construct entertained about a state-of-affairs.

Tense, mood, and aspect are not unified categories in their application to these layers of semantic organization, but fall into different subcategories according to their scope. Aspect is subdivided into two categories, separating quantitative aspectual distinctions (such as habitual and distributive), which quantify over states-of-affairs as a whole, from qualitative aspectual distinctions (such as imperfective and resultative), which affect the internal temporal organization of a state-of-affairs. Tense is subdivided into absolute tense distinctions (such as past and

Table 47.1. TMA categories in Functional Discourse Grammar

<table>
<tr><th></th><th>Propositional content</th><th>Episode</th><th>State-of-affairs</th><th>Situational concept</th><th>Property</th></tr>
<tr><td>Aspect</td><td></td><td></td><td>event quantification</td><td>phasal aspect (im)perfectivity</td><td rowspan="4">predicate</td></tr>
<tr><td>Tense</td><td></td><td>absolute tense</td><td>relative tense</td><td></td></tr>
<tr><td>Evidentiality</td><td>inference</td><td>deduction</td><td>event perception</td><td></td></tr>
<tr><td>Mood</td><td>subjective modality</td><td>absolute (ir)reality</td><td>relative (ir)reality</td><td>participant-oriented modality</td></tr>
</table>

future), which locate (a series of) states-of-affairs in time with respect to the moment of speaking, and relative tense distinctions (such as anterior and posterior), which locate a single state-of-affairs in time relative to another one. Evidentiality splits up into inference distinctions (such as supposition), which indicate how the propositional content follows from the speaker's existing knowledge, deduction distinctions (such as visual evidence), which indicate how an episode can be deduced from observable facts, and event perception distinctions (such as witnessed and non-witnessed), which concern the direct perception of a state-of-affairs by the speaker. The widest range of subcategories is found in the area of Mood, where we find subjective modality distinctions (such as certainty and doubt), which indicate the speaker's attitude toward a propositional content; absolute (ir)reality distinctions (as expressed in e.g. conditions), which set a frame of interpretation for a series of states-of-affairs; relative (ir)reality distinctions (as expressed in e.g. purpose clauses), which characterize a single state-of-affairs; and participant-oriented modality distinctions (such as ability and intention), which express a relation between a participant in a state-of-affairs and the realization of that state-of-affairs.

2.3. Grammaticalization

Hengeveld (1989: 142) hypothesizes that diachronic developments in the field of TMA expressions will go from lower to higher scope, and not the other way round.[3] This means for the TMA categories listed in Table 1 that there will be scope increase over time along the following scale:

(3) situational concept > state-of-affairs > episode > propositional content

The history of English *will* may serve as a first illustration of this scale (Bybee, Pagliuca, and Perkins 1991). *Will* started out as a lexical verb before becoming an expression of obligation/intention (participant-oriented modality, situational concept), then developed into a posterior marker (relative tense, state-of-affairs), then into a future (absolute tense, episode), and finally acquired suppositional readings (epistemic modality, propositional content). I will explore the hypothesis in (3) further in the following sections.[4]

[3] This ties in rather well with Traugott's (1982) hypothesis that grammaticalization is from 'less personal' to 'more personal' and with Bybee's (1985) hypothesis that grammaticalization is from 'more relevant' to 'less relevant' to the verb.

For a comparable approach in a generative framework see Roberts and Roussou (2003)

[4] See Boland (2006: 187–96), itself partly based on Bybee, Perkins, and Pagliuca (1994), and Olbertz (1998) for applications of this hypothesis.

3. The origin of aspect

3.1. Introduction

As Table 47.1 shows, and in the light of the general prediction given in (3), the only possible origins for aspectual expressions are predicates. These predicates may be verbal (3.2) or nonverbal (3.3) in nature.

3.2. Verbal predicates

Evident lexical origins for aspectual categories are phasal verbs such as *begin* and *end* that may grammaticalize into ingressive and egressive aspect markers. A case in point is Spanish *empezar* 'begin', which, in combination with a verb in the infinitival form, grammaticalized into an ingressive periphrastic construction, as illustrated in the following example (Olbertz 1998: 96):[5]

(4) Empiez-an a pas-ar cosa-s.
begin-PRES.3.PL to happen-INF thing-PL
'Things began to happen.'

The grammaticalized nature of this construction shows up in the fact that *empezar* has an inanimate subject in (4), while the transitive lexical use of this verb requires an animate one.

A further verbal lexical origin for aspectual categories is somewhat less straightforward, in that it involves the metaphorical or metonymical extension of the original meaning of the lexical verb. A well-known example of this is the prospective aspectual auxiliary *go to* in English, as in the following example from Bybee and Dahl (1989: 92):

(5) The ladder is going to fall.

This construction will only be used, as Bybee and Dahl (1989: 92) observe, if the ladder is already in an unstable position at the reference time, so that it may be classified as a prospective construction in the use illustrated here. The grammaticalized nature of the construction shows up, among other things, in the fact that there is an inanimate subject not capable of going anywhere by itself. The prospective interpretation is a result of the metaphorical extension of the meaning of forward movement in space in the direction of an object, to the meaning of forward movement in time in the direction of an event.

[5] See Heine (1993: 57) for the comparable development of an egressive aspect marker in Swahili.

Another rather typical example of aspectual categories that arise through metaphorical extension is illustrated in the ingressive periphrastic construction from Brazilian Portuguese (Marize Hattnher, p.c.) illustrated in (6):

(6) A máquina desatou a guspir dinheiro.
DEF.SG.F machine break.PST.PF.3.SG to spit money
'The machine (suddenly) started to spit out money.'

The momentaneous meaning of *desatar* 'break' in its lexical sense, which involves a sudden change of one state into another of a concrete object, is extended here to a sudden change of one state-of-affairs to another one, hence the ingressive interpretation, which can be paraphrased as 'The machine broke into spitting out money'. The grammaticalized nature of the construction is evident from, among other things, the fact that there is an inanimate subject incompatible with the lexical interpretation of the verb.

3.3. Non-verbal predicates

Both constructions based on a primary and on a secondary non-verbal predicate may be the source of an aspectual category (see Hengeveld 1992: ch. 11).

Constructions based on a primary non-verbal predicate may or may not contain a copular verb. The latter situation obtains in Turkish. Consider the following examples (Lewis 1967: 96, 159):

(7) gel-ecek haber
come-POST news
'news to come'

(8) Gel-eceğ=im.
come-POST=1.SG
'I am about to come.'

(9) Güzel=im.
beautiful=1.SG
'I am beautiful.'

Turkish has a posterior participle ending in *-ecek/-eceğ*. This participle is of an adjectival nature, as shown in example (7), in which it is used attributively. The same participle may, however, also be used predicatively, as is illustrated in (8). In this case it is directly followed by an enclitic element that is used with other non-verbal predicates as well, as shown in (9), and that derives from a former inflected copula. The aspectual reading of (8) is of a prospective nature, and it may be paraphrased as 'I have the property (now) that I will come later'.

A slightly different strategy is exhibited by languages in which modifiers cannot be used predicatively. In these languages equative constructions may develop into aspectual constructions. Consider the following examples from Mandarin Chinese (Li and Thompson 1981: 587, 148, 590):

(10) Tā (shì) zuótiān lái de.
3.SG (COP) yesterday come NR
'He arrived yesterday.'

(11) Zhāngsān (shì) yi-ge hùshì.
Zhangsan (COP) one-CLFR nurse
'Zhangsan is a nurse.'

(12) Tā zuótiān lái le.
3.SG yesterday come PF
'He came yesterday.'

In Mandarin Chinese the copula *shì* is used optionally with nominal predicates only. By nominalizing the clause 'he came yesterday', a nominal constituent 'one who arrived yesterday' is obtained, which is then used as a nominal predicate in (10), giving rise to a construction that is parallel to any other construction based on a nominal predicate, as a comparison of (10) and (11) shows. Sentence (10) is resultative in nature and may be paraphrased as 'He is someone (now) characterized by his arriving yesterday'. As noted by Li and Thompson (1981: 590), it would be an appropriate answer to the question 'Why couldn't he speak English?'. Its non-resultative counterpart in (12) could be used as an answer to a question like 'Has he arrived yet?'.

A third construction based on a primary non-verbal predicate that may be the source of aspectual categories is the locative non-verbal predication type (Heine and Reh 1982). The shift to an aspectual interpretation arises in this case through metaphorical extension. This may be illustrated by means of the Basque examples (13) and (14) (Lafitte 1944: 263, 215), each containing the locative marker *-n* and a copula:

(13) Etche-a-n d-a.
house-SG-LOC 3.SG.ABS-COP.PRES
'He is at home.'

(14) Ibil-tze-n d-a.
walk-INF-LOC 3.SG.ABS-COP.PRES
'He is walking.'

The progressive interpretation of (14), which may be paraphrased as 'He is in walking', arises through the conceptualization of the subject being located within (the time span) of the state-of-affairs rather than within a concrete location (13).

In a second group of non-verbal predications that may give rise to aspectual constructions, the non-verbal predicate is secondary, the main verb being one of existence or possession. An example of an existential construction developing into an aspectual construction comes from Tamil (Asher 1982: 52, 178, 40):

(15) Kannan iru-kkar-aar-aa.
Kannan EX-PRES-3.SG.HON-INT
'Is Kannan in?'

(16) Coll-i(y)=iru-kkar-een . . .
say-ADVR-EX-PRES-1.SG
'I have said . . . '

(17) Skaatlantukku pooy-i aaŋkilam paticcaan.
Scotland.DAT go-ADVR English study.PAST.3.SG.M
'Having gone to Scotland he studied English.'

The verb *iru* 'to be present, to exist' can be used as a main predicate in Tamil, as illustrated in (15). The same verb combines with an adverbial participle to form a resultative construction, as in (16). The adverbial nature of this participle is evident from its appearance in constructions such as (17). An appropriate paraphrase of the lexical origin of (16) is therefore one in which the non-verbal predicate is a secondary predicate that combines with a primary verbal predicate, as in 'I exist in the circumstance of having said . . . '.

Secondary non-verbal predication in combination with a lexical predicate also characterizes aspectual constructions based on a verb of possession. A common path of development is given schematically in the following series of examples:

(18) a. I have [a read book] attribution
b. I have [a book] [read] secondary predication
c. I [have read] a book primary predication

(19) a. I have [a book to read] attribution
b. I have [a book] [to read] secondary predication
c. I [have to read] [a book] primary predication

The participial construction *read* in (18) and the infinitival one *to read* in (19) in a first stage pass from attribution to secondary predication. In the resulting situation, the combination of the temporal reference of the main clause and the anterior/posterior reference of the participle gives rise to respectively resultative and prospective meaning. In a further stage of development (see below), the possessive verb grammaticalizes and the secondary predicate becomes primary.

3.4. Some generalizations

All the constructions that may give rise to aspectual categories have in common that they are bi-predicational in nature. Each of the two predications has its own temporal orientation, generally absolute in the main predication and relative in the dependent predication. The combination of two temporal reference points then gives rise to a specific aspectual interpretation. A prospective interpretation arises from the combination of the temporal orientation of the main predication with the posterior specification of the dependent predication; a progressive interpretation arises from the combination of the temporal orientation of the main predication with the simultaneous specification of the dependent predication; and the resultative interpretation arises from the combination of the temporal orientation of the main predication with the anterior specification of the dependent predication. Thus the aspectual interpretations exist by virtue of a temporal clash. When the predicate of the main predication grammaticalizes into an auxiliary and the construction as a whole thus becomes mono-predicational, this effect is lost and the construction is generally reinterpreted as a (relative) temporal one. This will be the topic of section 4.4.

4. The destination of aspect

4.1. Introduction

It follows from the prediction in (3) in combination with Table 47.1 that aspectual categories may potentially develop into categories of (i) event quantification, (ii) event perception, and (iii) relative tense. These are frequent destinations of aspectual categories. Furthermore, relative tense categories may develop into absolute tense categories by moving up one further scopal layer.

4.2. From aspect to event quantification

As noted by Bybee and Dahl (1989), it is common for progressives to develop into more general imperfectives that can also be used to refer to habitual or repeated activities, both categories of event quantification. An example is the use of the English progressive to refer to repeated activities, as in the following example (Bybee and Dahl 1989: 82):

(20) He is working on his book every day.

This involves a change in meaning from the ongoingness of a single state-of-affairs to the ongoingness of a series of states-of-affairs. A similar situation obtains in, for example, Spanish, a language in which the past imperfective covers both types of ongoingness.

4.3. From aspect to evidentiality

A further well-attested development (Bybee and Dahl 1989: 73; Boland 2006: 190) is one in which resultative aspectual expressions evolve into expressions of event perception, an evidential category. Such a development took place in, for example, Turkish, as illustrated in the following examples (Lewis 1967):

(21) Kar yağ-tı-ø.
snow fall-VIS.PST-3.SG
'Snow has fallen.' (I saw it happen)

(22) Kar yağ-mış-ø.
snow fall-NONVIS.PST-3.SG
'Snow has fallen.' (I didn't see it happen)

In the past tense, Turkish makes a distinction between states-of-affairs witnessed by the speaker (21) and those not witnessed by the speaker (22). The verbal ending *-mış*[6] used in the latter case is identical in form to the past participial ending, which does not carry evidential meaning, illustrated in (23) (Kornfilt 1997: 416).

(23) ağaç-ten yer-e düş-müş bir elma
tree-ABL ground-DAT fall-ANT INDEF apple
'an apple fallen from the tree to the ground'

The step from resultative (the current situation reveals a past state-of-affairs) to non-witnessed (lack of direct perception of a state-of-affairs) is not difficult to envisage.

4.4. From aspect to tense

As anticipated in section 3, aspect markers frequently develop into tense markers. On the basis of Table 47.1 and the general hypothesis in (3), one would expect that aspect markers develop into relative tense markers before they develop into absolute tense markers, and the available evidence suggests that this is indeed the case. The general development can be sketched as follows for three different pathways of change:

[6] The shape of this suffix is sensitive to vowel harmony.

(24) Resultative–Anterior–Past

```
            E                    R
Stage 1     ------------------ •     Resultative
            E                    R
Stage 2     •------------------      Anterior
            E                    S
Stage 3     •------------------      Past
```

In a resultative construction the focal point of information[7] (•) is the state-of-affairs at reference time (R) that is the result of a previous state-of-affairs (E). An anterior relative tense interpretation arises when the focal point of information becomes the previous state-of-affairs (E) itself, seen from the perspective of the reference time (R). An absolute past-tense interpretation arises when the reference time is restricted to the speech moment (S). An example of this development is Spanish *haber*, to be discussed below.

(25) Progressive–Simultaneous–Present

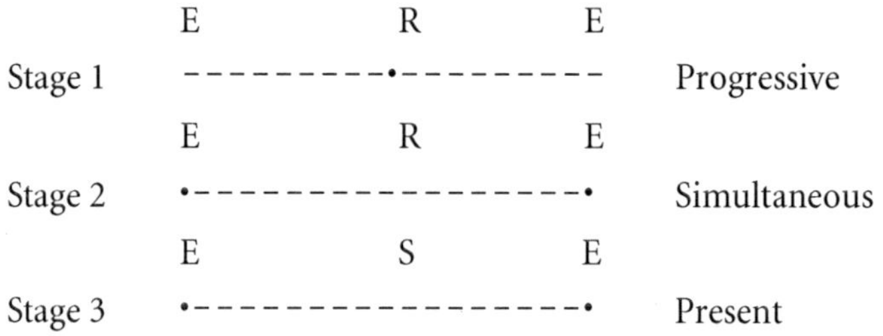

```
             E         R         E
Stage 1      ---------•---------      Progressive
             E         R         E
Stage 2      •------------------•     Simultaneous
             E         S         E
Stage 3      •------------------•     Present
```

In a progressive construction the focal point of information (•) is the state-of-affairs at reference time (R) which co-occurs with a another state-of-affairs (E). A simultaneous relative-tense interpretation arises when the focal point of information becomes the concurrent state-of-affairs (E) itself, seen from the perspective of the reference time (R). An absolute present-tense interpretation arises when the reference time is restricted to the speech moment (S). An example of this development is the English Progressive, which has reached the third phase in (25) as it expresses the non-habitual absolute present with dynamic verbs.

[7] For the role of focal information in grammaticalization processes see Harder and Boye (Ch. 5 above).

(26) Prospective–Posterior–Future

	R		E	
Stage 1	•------------------			Prospective
	R		E	
Stage 2	------------------•			Posterior
	S		E	
Stage 3	------------------•			Future

In a prospective construction, the focal point of information (•) is the state-of-affairs at reference time (R) which precedes another state-of-affairs (E). A posterior relative-tense interpretation arises when the focal point of information becomes the later state-of-affairs (E) itself, seen from the perspective of the reference time (R). An absolute present-tense interpretation arises when the reference time is restricted to the speech moment (S). General evidence for this development is provided in Fleischman (1982).

To give just one example of the general development sketched here, consider the Spanish *haber* 'have' + past participle construction.[8] This construction started out as a true resultative construction, in which a verb of possession cooccurred with an adjectival participle. In present-day Spanish this construction has been replaced by the combination of *tener* 'have, hold' + past participle, as in (27):

(27) Tengo prepara-d-a una cena fenomenal.
have.PRES.1.SG prepare-ANT-F.SG INDEF.SG.F meal(F) terrific
'I have a terrific meal ready (for you).'

This construction, as its predecessor, is appropriately used when the meal is actually ready, corresponding to stage 1 in (24). Note that the past participle agrees with the patient argument, thus showing the properties of a secondary non-verbal predicate (see 3.3).

The construction with *haber* then evolved into a perfect, i.e. a relative anterior tense. The relative nature of the construction is evident from the fact that the construction itself can be used in all absolute tenses:

(28) Había / he / habré preparado
have.PST.1.SG / have.PRES.1.SG / have.FUT.1.SG prepare-ANT
una cena fenomenal.
INDEF.SG.F meal(F) terrific
'I had/have/will have prepared a terrific meal.'

[8] For a detailed and insightful discussion of the history of this construction see Olbertz (1993).

Reference is now to the anterior event that occurs previous to but within the time span defined by the absolute tense carried by the auxiliary and potential adverbial modifiers, and with current relevance at reference time, corresponding to stage 2 in (24). The past participle no longer shows agreement, but occurs in a fixed form, showing that this is no longer a case of secondary predication. The past participle is the main predicate, and the former possessive verb is auxiliarized, as is apparent (among other things) from the fact that it can be used with intransitive verbs as well.

In most Spanish dialects the construction has evolved further into an absolute tense expressing recent past. Kuteva (2001: 37), citing Schwenter (1994: 93–4), provides the following examples from Alicante Spanish:

(29) a.

Cuénta=me	tu	día	hoy.
tell=1.SG.DAT	your	day	today

'Tell me about your day today.'

b.

Me	he	levanta-do	a	las	siete.
1.SG.REFL	AUX.PRES.1.SG	get.up-PST.PRTCPL	at	the	seven

'I got up at seven o'clock.'

Me	he	duchado.
1.SG.REFL	AUX.PRES.1.SG	take.shower-PST.PRTCPL

'I took a shower.'

Hemos	ido	a-l	banco	para
AUX.PRES.1.PL	go-PST.PRTCPL	to-DEF.SG.M	bank(m)	to

sacar	dinero.
withdraw-INF	money

'We went to the bank to withdraw money.' . . . etc.

This use of *haber* + participle is in competition with a simple perfective past, as reference is made to states-of-affairs that have been completed at a moment prior to the moment of speaking, corresponding to stage 3 in (24).

5. Further origins of tense

Applying the hypothesis in (3) to Table 47.1 again, the prediction is that potential sources for tense markers are aspect markers and markers of participant-oriented modality. The creation of tense markers from aspect markers was discussed in the previous section, so I will restrict myself to modal sources here. And indeed the development from participant-oriented modality to tense is well attested, in the sense that often the sources for posterior and future tenses are volitional or deontic modal markers, as synchronically observable in examples such as (31), taken from Bybee and Dahl (1989: 63):

(30) It looks like it wants to rain.

Fleischman (1982) shows for Romance and English that in this development the erstwhile modal expression, as predicted by the hypothesis, first acquires a (relative) posterior meaning, before acquiring an (absolute) future meaning.

6. The destination of tense

To round off the picture, let me briefly consider the potential destinations of tense markers according to the hypothesis in (3). As Table 47.1 shows, these are inferential evidentiality and subjective modality. Data from few languages are available to verify whether this development is a general one, but the data that are available indicate that this is indeed a possible pathway. A well-known development is from future tense to supposition (Fleischman 1982), a form of inference, as in (31):

(31) He will be in Paris by now.

Table 47.2. Attested developments in the grammaticalization of tense and aspect

	Propositional content	Episode	State-of-affairs	Situational concept	
Aspect			event quantification	phasal aspect (im)perfectivity	
Tense		absolute tense	relative tense		predicate
Evidentiality	inference	deduction	event perception		
Mood	subjective modality	absolute (ir)reality	relative (ir)reality	participant-oriented modality	

7. Summary

Table 47.2 summarizes the paths of grammaticalization involving tense and aspect that have been discussed in the previous sections.[9]

The overall conclusion that may be drawn is that developments in the domain of tense and aspect may be fruitfully interpreted in terms of scope increase along hierarchically organized layers of semantic organization.

[9] Further pathways may be attested, but these involve modal categories not dealt with in the current chapter.

CHAPTER 48

THE GRAMMATICALIZATION OF MODALITY

DEBRA ZIEGELER

1. Introduction

It is difficult to discuss any topic on grammaticalization without reference to the area of modality, as was clearly implied by Plank (1984) when he described the development of the English modals as 'a paradigm case of grammaticization' (p. 308). Since that time, in the past 25 years, a multitude of literature focusing on the grammaticalization of modality has emerged, for example, Abraham (1998), Abraham and Leiss (2008), Aijmer (1985), Bybee (1985; 1998b), Bybee and Fleischman (1995), Bybee, Pagliuca, and Perkins (1991), Bybee, Perkins, and Pagliuca (1994), Fleischman (1982; 1989), Frawley (2006), Givón (1994), Goossens (1982; 1987; 1999; 2000), Heine (1993), Horn (1989; 2001), James (1986), Kuteva (2001), Narrog (2005a; 2005b), Nordlinger and Traugott (1997), Nuyts (2000; 2001), Sweetser (1990), Traugott (1989), Traugott and Dasher (2002), Van der Auwera and Plungian (1998), and Ziegeler (2000; 2006), to name just some relevant works. The reader is advised to refer to such works for a comprehensive coverage of some of the principal arguments that have arisen in relation to modality and grammaticalization. In the present chapter, however, the grammaticalization of modality will be discussed first in relation to its diachronic sense, using as an example the evolution of English modal verbs (since this area has provided a wealth of research over the past two decades) and then to its sense referring to the diverse synchronic representation of mood across languages today. Thus, two main areas of research will be discussed: (i) the pragmatic issues of the diachronic development of English modal verbs, and (ii) the problems of defining the synchronic grammaticalization of modal categories in present-day typology.

2. Terminological matters

For a simple working definition, Palmer (2003: 6) discusses modality as relating to the degree of speaker assertion in the intended illocution. Similar definitions have been provided by Bybee et al. (1994: 181), Lyons (1995: 253–4) and Nuyts (2006: 17), who all refer to modal meanings as related to speaker commitment to a proposition. The grammaticalized expression of modality is manifest in a range of linguistic devices cross-linguistically, including a broad spectrum of formal categories not restricted to modal verbs (both auxiliaries and main verbs), but also including modal adverbs, particles, discourse elements, and periphrastic constructions (see e.g. De Haan (2006) for a typological overview). Such formal devices may be employed to cover a range of modal functions, from deontic and epistemic verbal modality to clause-related moods such as the imperative, subjunctive, optative, as well as conditional and counterfactual constructions, and future time reference. The category of modal verbs provides one area for a wide range of terminological variety. Earlier standard references to English terminology can be found in works such as Lyons (1977) and Palmer (1986[2001]), which also discuss issues such as the presence or absence of subjectivity in the modal verb meanings (see below). Studies such as Van der Auwera and Plungian (1998) have revised the earlier distinctions of Palmer's deontic/epistemic/dynamic classes to refer more to the roles of participants in the modal expression; for example, deontic functions are seen as 'participant-external' modalities (e.g. *must* and *may* in *You may/must not smoke in this building*), and dynamic (e.g. *can* or *will*, as in, *John can speak Italian*) as 'participant-internal' modalities (Ziegeler 2001 labelled the latter 'characterizing' functions; such types have also been associated with 'facultative' functions by Goossens 1987). There was little disagreement, though, on the classification of epistemic meanings, expressing the judgements and evaluations of the speaker, e.g. for *must* in examples like *It must be raining*.

Coates (1983), as well as Sweetser (1990) and Talmy (1988) before Sweetser, had labeled all non-epistemic modal verbs as having 'root' meanings, while Nuyts (2001a: 25) found that such a term was too general as it failed to encompass the distinctions between modalities imposed on the subject by an external force and those originating in the subject. Many early accounts had tried, therefore, to distinguish modal types on the basis of subject roles or modal source. Bybee (1985), Heine (1995), and Bybee et al. (1994) referred to the presence of a non-epistemic category of 'agent-oriented' modality, as distinct from 'speaker-oriented' modality, but the distinctions are not always that clear. Bybee et al.'s category of speaker-oriented modality includes illocution types such as imperatives, prohibitives, optatives, hortatives, and admonitives, but also includes permission, as expressed by deontic modal verbs such as *can*. Other deontics, such as *should* and *must*, are attributed to agent-oriented modality. The term 'agent-oriented', also, may lead to a misunderstanding of the notion of sentence roles in relation to modality: the subject of a modal verb is, in most cases, an Experiencer role (see e.g. Diewald 2001), and an Experiencer role is a dual-orientation subject role, both a goal and a source of the modal force. The dual orientation of the subject participant underlies the classifications of Van der Auwera and Plungian (1998) and their allusions to a directional path from participant-internal to participant-external modality. In the area of non-epistemic modality, though, it is possible that no single classification can cover all the meaning differences available, as intimated by Van der Auwera and Plungian (p. 80). An alternative means of classifying non-epistemic modal types uses time reference relating to the realization of the modal proposition; this is discussed in Ziegeler (2006), which distinguishes 'future-projecting' from epistemic modality ('generic' modality referring to Goossens's 1987 facultative types). These terms will be referred to again in the present chapter.[1]

3. Diachronic grammaticalization

The importance of terminological distinctions is obvious in studies of diachronic grammaticalization, as early accounts (e.g. Goossens 1982; Shepherd 1982; Bybee 1985; Traugott 1989) had pointed to a development of epistemic functions from non-epistemic ones. Shepherd's (1982) study had shown parallels between the acquisitional routes of the grammaticalization of modals (in Antiguan Creole) and the historical routes that modals were held to have followed, from deontic to epistemic uses. Sweetser (1990: 49) had observed that there were polysemies in

[1] Bybee et al. (1994: 184) restrict the notion of future-projection primarily to modal meanings of obligation, meanings of possibility being considered less capable of future-projecting time reference. Ziegeler (2006) uses participant referentiality as a determining feature.

modal meanings across a number of unrelated languages (e.g. Indo-European, Semitic, and Philippine languages), and described the differentiation of semantic functions in modal expressions in terms of forces and barriers based on analogies with relationships of causativity as described by Talmy (1988), and treating the relationships as diachronically ordered. The main focus of Sweetser's work was that it indicated a metaphorical relation between the deontic modality of social-physical forces and barriers and that of the epistemic world of barriers and forces to reasoning and judgment, as in the following (1990: 61):

(1) a. Deontic: John **may** go
Interpreted as: 'John is not barred by (my or some other) authority from going.'
b. Epistemic: John **may** be there
Interpreted as: 'I am not barred by my premises from the conclusion that he is there.'

Sweetser's work, like that of many others of her time, had used mainly English data and extended the generalizations made on the basis of such data to non-English languages. It did, however, leave a number of questions unanswered, especially those relating to the modal verbs which are not so easily perceived as having meanings controlled by underlying causative inferences (e.g. *will*, *would*, *can*, and *could*). It also left open the question of certain ambiguities, e.g. *John must go to all the department parties* (1990: 64), which presuppose that the two poles of modal meanings are interlinked—a possibility that is inconsistent with a metaphorical analysis, since metaphor does not allow for contiguity of conceptual meaning. This type of ambiguity will be discussed below.

Sweetser's hypotheses were attacked by Gamon (1993), amongst others, on the basis that they could not account for intermediate stages of development, such as the wide-scope deontic modality expressed by the ancestors of *must*, with predicates referring to the inevitability of an event (such as dying, arriving, etc.). The spread of the early modal form to such environments (Achievements in Vendler's 1967 categories) was an indication of the gradual loss of potential control available in the subject: Achievements refer to punctual or dynamic states of affairs, but unlike most non-epistemic modals, the subject role could be attributed with a reduced potentiality for control over the predicated event. Similar examples were also outlined by Traugott (1989) and Traugott and Dasher (2002), and such intermediate environments suggest that the grammaticalization of modality cannot accommodate the abruptness of a metaphorical shift—something that was emphasized in much of Traugott's work and which became a focal point of much dispute at the time.

Traugott's (1989) seminal work on the development of epistemic meanings in English had laid the groundwork for the more fine-grained, pragmatic analysis of later work (Traugott and Dasher 2002) developing the earlier Gricean analysis into a fully-fledged theoretical application to historical change in general (the Invited Inferences Theory of Semantic Change—IITSC). Her earlier study had concentrated on the aspects of gradualness that accompanied change, providing the diachronic aspect with a plausible viewpoint in terms of actuation. It was proposed that modal functions change through the pragmatic shifts of the conventionalization and strengthening of conversational implicatures over time, and involved a process more closely associated with metonymy and incrementation of meaning aspects within a single conceptual domain than metaphor, which involves the linking of unrelated meanings across distant conceptual domains. Traugott's (1989) study had traced the development of *shall* (**sculan*), *will* (**willan*), and *must* (**motan*), from their origins as main verbs in Old English (which she dates from 600 to 1125 AD). Her main claim was that epistemic meanings were later developments and were questionable in Old English at the time; for example, *must* was believed not to contain strong epistemic meanings (without a reinforcing adverb such as *nedes* 'needs') until the 17th century, e.g. (1989: 42):

(2) the fruit **muste** be delicious, the tree being so beautiful (1623 Middleton, *Spanish Gipsie* 1, i.16)

Traugott and Dasher (2002: 121), though, on the basis of further data, pre-date the epistemic meanings to the 14th century. *Motan*, the predecessor of *must*, had a meaning of ability and permission originally, and this was believed to supply the appropriate pragmatic conditions for the extension of meaning via Gricean Quantity 2 implicatures ('say no more than you must') in that a declaration of permission could be extendable to meanings of obligation or expectation—meanings which were associated with it by around the 11th century, according to Traugott and Dasher (2002: 121). Their principle criticism of Sweetser's (1990) metaphor hypothesis was founded in the provision of an alternative, more plausible one of semantic inferencing over an extended time period. Like Gamon (1993), they pay particular attention to the emergence of meanings of inevitability, also discussed by Goossens (1999; 2000), which seem to provide the linking stages necessary for a functional shift to epistemic meanings, permitting either a deontic interpretation or an epistemic one. Traugott and Dasher (2002: 136) suggest that such indeterminacy is a sum of the inextricable linking of meanings of deontic requirement and epistemic truth in expressing meanings of predestination. An example of such uses appears already in Old English (Traugott and Dasher 2002: 127):

(3) Ealle we **moton** sweltan
All we must die
'We must all die.' ?8th c. *Exodus*, 12.33 (cited in Warner 1993: 162)

Nordlinger and Traugott (1997), though, had extended the findings of Gamon's (1993) proposal for a wide-scope deontic modality; i.e. one in which the grammaticalization of epistemic meanings from deontic was intercepted by a stage in which a scope increase was found, from a narrow scope first attributable to the subject alone, to a later, wider dimension applying to the entire proposition. Included amongst such wide-scope deontics were examples of modals co-occurring with agentless passives, in which the subject is often inanimate, but also possible are those described by Verstraete (2001: 1508) in which the deontic modal source is unknown:

(4) But to reach orbit an object **must** accelerate to a speed of about 17.500 miles per hour . . . and it **must** reach an altitude of more than 100 miles (160 kilometres) in order to be clear of the atmosphere. (ICE-GB: W2B-035#39:1)

Since the modal subject in (4) in both cases is inanimate, there is ambiguity in such examples between deontic necessity derived from an imposing source and a necessity attributable to the situation as a whole, being devoid of any agency. The 'inevitability' readings of *must* illustrated in (4) share the same characteristics of wide (propositional) scope. What such examples have in common is the fact that, although they contain dynamic or event-related predicates, they are bordering on epistemic readings (perhaps less subjectified ones), and such intermediate stages are essential to illustrate evidence of gradual change in grammaticalization.

Traugott's work, in addition, had pointed to the factor of increasing speaker-subjectification in the development of the modal meanings; i.e. that epistemic meanings carried with them the nuances of the speaker's evaluative commitment to the nature of the proposition; this is also outlined in Traugott and Dasher (2002: 40) as concomitant with the increase in scope over the proposition, as shown above. Narrog (2005a) argues that there is no necessary correlation between subjectivity and modality, and subjectivity can be found in a number of non-modal constructions as well. However, this does not suggest that modality cannot be found without some kind of speaker-subjective overtone: the association of epistemic modality with subjectified meaning is unavoidable in that it involves the evaluations of the speaker (see e.g. Gamon 1993: 147). Traugott's claims were for an increased role for the speaker in the modal expression, which is a natural outcome of the loss of potential subject control or a shift in the 'locus of potency' (shown by Goossens (2000: 157–8), using Langacker's description (1991: 269–71).

Such changes were found to be consistent with those outlined in Ziegeler (2006) for the development of the periphrastic modal *be supposed to* and the core modal *will*. In both such cases, the modality appeared to originate in a generic source form, the modality co-occurring with nonspecific subjects, or expressing characteristics, attributes, or habits belonging to the subject. The modal *could* was also found to be associated mainly with generic senses in Old English (Ziegeler 2001: 298):

(5) ... forðon hie **cuðon** on horsum ealra folca feohtan betst & ærest
'... because they of all people knew how to fight best on horseback'[2]
(850–950, Alfred's *Orosius*, ed. H. Sweet, p. 112)

The same generic meanings predominated the early stages of the development of *will*, in an example also cited in Traugott (1989: 39) as appearing in Old English:

(6) elpendes hyd **wile** drincan wæter
'elephant's hide will absorb water' *Orosius* 230.26.

Both examples (5) and (6) are generic by virtue of their non-referring subjects or characterizing senses. Thus, the study of the development of modality cannot avoid taking into consideration the entire construction in which the modal verb is located; modality is a composite feature of the grammars that grammaticalize it, not just an inherent characteristic of certain verb forms. The same sentiments have been voiced by Bybee (1998b: 264).

Ziegeler (2006) proposed a three-tiered chronology of modality, based on historical evidence, into Generic > Future-Projecting > Epistemic, relying on the characteristics of the lexical aspect of the main predicate as a guideline for determining the modal meaning, the mechanisms of grammaticalization being via pragmatic inferencing as earlier studies had suggested. Thus, the Future-Projecting category was a natural progression from early generic uses, in which the modal verb combined with non-referential subjects and referred to events or circumstances with no anchorage in time or space (thus yielding optimum preconditions for the development of predictive modal inferences). The common shared meaning factor cutting across other non-epistemic modal categories was that they referred to actions taking place later than the time of speaking (see also Heine 1995); hence, the use of the term Future-Projecting, rather than root or deontic. The loss of subject control which accompanies this gradual transition is also discussed in Heine and Miyashita (2008b).

4. Cross-linguistic studies

As mentioned above, diachronic studies in languages with long recorded histories represent only one perspective of research into the grammaticalization of modality, and in the mid-1990s there emerged a spate of publications discussing the

[2] The translations for Alfred's *Orosius* from Giles (ed.) (1969[1858]), read: 'they were known to be the best of all people in horsemanship', though the original citation is from the Sweet edn, as found in the Helsinki Corpus. (It was felt that Giles' gloss was not sufficiently close to the intended meaning.)

representational aspects of the grammaticalization of modality in languages with perhaps less available diachronic evidence. Bybee et al. (1994), in a comprehensive survey of some 76 different languages, undertook a pioneering study of tense, aspect, and modal forms in which it was clearly demonstrated that the meanings familiar to more readily documented languages with historical evidence could be seen to be grammaticalized using the same pool of lexical source concepts in an extensive range of typologically unrelated languages, and were grammaticalized along similar pathways showing intermediate stages of development. For example, lexical sources for the grammaticalization of ability and possibility were most frequently found to be derived from verbs meaning 'know', just as is illustrated above in the lexical source for English *could* in (5). The verb *diba* in Motu (Papua-Austronesian) expresses ability meaning 'can', as well as 'know'; Danish *kunne* ('can') also referred to mental ability ('know'), and Tok Pisin has *kæn* (from English 'can') and *savi* is another lexical source for ability modality, deriving from the Portuguese verb meaning 'know' (Bybee et al. 1994: 190). From ability meanings, grammaticalization paths were shown to lead to functions such as expressing permission, epistemic possibility, and concession, as shown in (7) (adapted from Bybee et al. (1994: 240):

(7) a. ability > root possibility > epistemic possibility > protasis
> complement to 'think' verbs
> concessive uses

b. ability > root possibility > permission

Bybee et al. had relied to some extent on the use of English as a comparative benchmark for the defining of modal categories cross-linguistically; however, Chung and Timberlake (1985: 241–3) before them had referred to the need to consider classical Indo-European categories of mood as not always relevant to many of the world's languages. In other languages, modality could be seen as simply a binary distinction between what is real and what is unreal. Mithun (1995: 375) had also discussed modality (expressed by verbal suffixes) in languages such as Central Pomo (Hokan) and Amele (Trans New Guinea) as grammaticalizing a distinction between what is actual and what is in the realm of thought. However, she found differences cross-linguistically in areas such as imperative marking, which are marked for unreality in Central Pomo and Amele but not in other languages such as Maricopa (Yuman, Arizona)—a difference she attributes to factors such as social politeness.

The terms 'realis' and 'irrealis' began to be associated with binary features of modality in such languages at this time, though it was soon evident that such terms could not be generalized to account for a common set of semantic features by which the distinction could be universally defined. Studies such as Chafe (1995) had found subtle differences in the encoding of realis and irrealis in the interrogative domain in languages such as Caddo (North Iroquoian), in which the realis/irrealis distinction is encoded by a pronominal prefix, *bahw*: *yes/no* interrogatives were marked as irrealis and *wh*-interrogatives were marked as realis, expressing either the presence or absence of the speaker's presupposed knowledge backing the question (Chafe 1995: 353–4). In the same language, future time reference is grammaticalized as realis, while in many other languages the modal verbs which signal irrealis meaning are frequently the source for the expression of future time, for example, verbs expressing desire, in languages such as Danish, Inuit, and Tok Pisin (Bybee et al. 1994: 254).

Bybee et al. (1994) had provoked much discussion by referring to the elusiveness of the category 'irrealis' across their database, and the fact that it could never occur with any consistency as a binary category; in their original words, this 'binary distinction is not crosslinguistically valid' (p. 238). Their frustrations were due to the prevalence of so much variation in what the term characterized across different languages, as shown above. Habitual aspect was typically found to be another area of vacillation cross-linguistically between realis and irrealis, as shown by Cristofaro (2004), e.g.:

West Greenlandic (Eskimo-Aleut)

(8) a. mulu-guni tiki-**ssa**-aq atisa-I
Stay.away-4SG:COND come-FUT-3SG:INDIC clothes-his:PL
ataniiruti-vis-sima-llu-tik
be.without.connection-really-PERF-4-CONT
'(After) staying away for ages he would arrive home, his clothes all falling apart.' (Fortescue 1984: 280-81)

b. inna-ja-**ssa**-atit
go.to.bed-early-shall-2SG:INDIC
'You must go to bed early.' (Fortescue 1984: 292)

In this language, past habitual is marked as irrealis, using the same verbal affix, *ssa*, for expressing obligation modality and future. However, Cristofaro finds that generally, it is past habituals that are marked as irrealis, while present-tense habituals are often marked by forms used to encode actualized events.

Givón (1994) also found functional incoherence in the use of the categories of realis/irrealis, preferring instead to assign cross-linguistic modal meanings to the two broad modal cluster groups of deontic and epistemic modality, as discussed in Ziegeler (2005). Narrog (2005a: 183) objects to the realis/irrealis distinction for its lack of definition, suggesting that it does not sort out what is real from what is factual, and that it basically assigns all modality to either an indicative or subjunctive category. He also maintains that the terms are specialized to languages of a particular geographical area (e.g. North America). However, one could argue that the distinction may still have a usefulness in describing certain distinctions in creoles and mixed language varieties (see e.g. Ho and Platt 1993; Bickerton 1981, who demonstrate a consistent overlap between such categories and aspectual meanings of completion or realization of an event).

Thus, although the grammatical distinctions imposed by European languages may be too fine to be extended to other languages, the definitions of modality suggested in section 2 as referring to the degree of speaker commitment to the truth of a proposition may be found to be useful in referring to a variety of languages: the grammaticalization of modality not only embraces the truth conditions of a proposition, but is found, cross-linguistically, to express the speaker's *assertion* of such truth conditions, as emphasized by Bybee et al. (1994: 239), and this may vary from one language to another.

5. Concluding remarks

Grammaticalization studies over the past twenty years have contributed much to the understanding of modality across languages, due to the evidence available not only from historical approaches but also from previously unrecorded languages. The present chapter highlights the contrast in trends between 'real-time' studies of a diachronic nature, in which grammaticalization pathways may be closely observed to emerge step-wise through the mechanism of pragmatic inferencing, and 'apparent-time' studies, in which the same diachronic pathways can be hypothesized to emerge on the basis of data regarding common lexical source material and existing evidence. Space does not permit full coverage of a range of other topics of particular current interest, such as evidentiality, a field closely associated with (epistemic) modality but perhaps most succinctly described, as De Haan (2006: 59) has recently done, as 'propositional deixis' rather than a modality.[3] The questions surrounding such issues, and many others, are better left to a review of broader scope than is possible here.

[3] See Fitneva (2001), Lazard (2001), and Nuyts (2001), cited in Ziegeler (2006: ch. 5) for further arguments against the alignment of evidentiality and epistemic modality.

CHAPTER 49

THE GRAMMATICALIZATION OF EVIDENTIALITY

ALEXANDRA Y. AIKHENVALD

1. Evidentiality and information source

Evidentiality is a grammatical category with source of information as its primary meaning—whether the speaker saw the event happen (known as *visual* evidential), or heard it but didn't see it (*non-visual* evidential), or made an inference based on general knowledge or visual traces (*assumed* evidential and *inferential* evidential respectively), or was told about it (known as *reported*, *secondhand*, or *hearsay* evidential). Languages may distinguish just first-hand and non-first-hand information, or have a special marker just for reported evidentiality. Non-first-hand evidential as a separate category typically covers inferential and reported meanings (but is not a subtype of either inferential or reported evidential). In larger evidential systems, first-hand or visual evidential may contrast with non-visual, inferred, assumed, and reported.[1]

[1] A systematic analysis of evidentials across the world is found in Aikhenvald (2004; 2006) (see references there). Johanson and Utas (2000) contain case studies of smaller evidential systems. Jacobsen (1986) is a fine summary of work on, and recognition of, this category. French linguists sometimes employ the term 'mediative' (see Guentchéva 1996).

Evidentiality is a verbal category in its own right. It does not bear any straightforward relationship to the expression of speaker's responsibility, or attitude to the statement. Neither is evidentiality a subcategory of modality or a tense.[2]

The relationship between information source and grammatical evidentiality is comparable to that of time, as a category in the real world, and tense, as grammaticalized location in time. Evidentials as a separate grammatical category are found in about a quarter of the world's languages. As Boas (1938: 133) put it, 'while for us definiteness, number, and time are obligatory aspects, we find in another language [...] source of information—whether seen, heard, or inferred—as obligatory aspects.'

In contrast, every language has ways of expressing how one knows things. This may be accomplished with lexical means—verbs referring to reports, claims, or perception, with adverbs, parentheticals, or with prepositional phrases. Speech report constructions indicate that the speaker knows something from someone else.

Alternatively, a non-evidential category may acquire a secondary meaning relating to information source. Conditionals may acquire overtones of uncertain information obtained through a non-first-hand source. This is the case in a number of Romance languages (see Squartini 2008 for a general pan-Romance perspective). In many Iranian languages, forms of past tense and perfect aspect develop overtones of a non-first-hand information source.

Participles and nominalizations may develop connotations of non-first-hand information. Passive participles in Lithuanian have overtones of hearsay or inference (see Wiemer 2007; Gronemeyer 1997). Past participles in Mansi, from the Ob-Ugric branch of Finno-Ugric, have overtones of non-first-hand evidentials (Perrot 1996: 158).

For each of these forms, information source is just one of their meaning extensions, a 'side-effect'. Categories and forms which have additional meanings to do with information source are known as 'evidentiality strategies'. Over time, the evidential meaning of an evidentiality strategy may become its primary sense. Evidentiality strategies are a frequent source for developing bona-fide evidential forms.

Grammaticalization of evidentials follows two general paths. Markers of evidentiality may develop out of grammaticalizing a lexical item: a verb, or, less frequently, a noun becomes a grammatical marker of information source within a closed system of choices.[3] Alternatively, an evidential may evolve out of an evidentiality strategy, acquiring the status of a grammatical system in its own right.

[2] See criticism and further discussion in Aikhenvald (2004; 2008), and also De Haan (1999), Lazard (1999; 2001).

[3] A partial and now outdated account of grammaticalization of evidentials is in Willett (1988).

2. From a lexical item to a grammatical evidential

Evidentials may come from grammaticalized verbs (section 2.1), locative and deictic markers (2.2), or members of other word classes (2.3).

2.1. From a verb to an evidential

Different evidential specifications come from (A) verbs of speech, (B) verbs of perception, and, less frequently, (C) verbs of other semantic groups.

(A) Verbs of speech are a frequent source for markers of reported and of quotative evidentials. The reported evidential *-ti-* in Tsafiki, a Barbacoan language from Ecuador, is transparently related to the verb *ti-* 'say' (Dickinson 2000). Other evidentials in Tsafiki are visual, inferred, and assumed. The adverbial reported particle *unnia* in West Greenlandic is derived from verb stem *unnir-* 'say (that)' (Fortescue 2003: 301). The reported evidential suffix *-lda* in Lezgian, a Northeast Caucasian language, is the result of grammaticalization of *luhuda* '(one) says' (Haspelmath 1993: 148).[4] The reported evidential *di* in Kham, a Tibeto-Burman language from Nepal, is connected to a verb of speech (Watters 2002: 296–300).

A verb of speech can be grammaticalized as a reported speech marker in the form of a 3rd person form. The quotative particle *h°a* in Abkhaz is an archaic past absolutive of the verb 'say' (Chirikba 2003: 258–9; see also examples from Georgian in Harris and Campbell 1995: 168–72).

An evidential can come from a derivation based on a verb of speech. In Udihe, a Tungusic language (Nikolaeva and Tolskaya 2001: 461), one of the variants of the reported evidential, *gum(u)*, could be an old passive form of the verb *gun* 'say'. Another variant, *gun-e-i*, is a habitual present participle of the same verb.

Reported evidentials hardly ever come from grammaticalized verbs other than speech verbs (they can come from other sources, as we will see below).

(B) Verbs of perception give rise to markers of visual and non-visual sensory evidentiality. In Maricopa, a Yuman language (Gordon 1986), the visual evidentiality suffix has developed from the lexical verb 'see'. In Wintu (Schlichter 1986: 49; Pitkin 1984: 148), the non-visual sensory evidential *nt^hEr* goes back to a passive form based on the verb 'hear' (followed by the inferred evidential). Non-visual marker *-mha* in Tariana goes back to the verb *-hima* 'hear, feel', while the present visual *-nuka, -naka* is related to the first person singular form of the verb *-ka* 'see'.

[4] For further examples see Heine and Kuteva (2002: 267–8) and Aikhenvald (2004).

A verb of perception may give rise to a quotative evidential. In Biansi (Tibeto-Burman) the past non-finite form of *run* 'cause to hear' marks quoted speech (Trivedi 1991: 26). In Shibacha Lisu (Yu 2003) all evidentials come from grammaticalized verbs: the visual evidential comes from the verb 'see', the non-visual and the reported come from the verb 'hear' (following different paths of phonological change), and one inferred evidential comes from the verb 'listen'. This is an example of an etymologically heterogeneous system.

(C) Verbs of other semantic groups can develop into various evidentials. The non-visual evidential in Hupda and in the closely related Yuhup (both from the Makú family) is the result of grammaticalization of the verb 'produce sound' (Epps 2005: 628).

Verbs meaning 'seem, be perceived, feel' often participate in developing non-visual evidentials in East Tucanoan languages (see Aikhenvald 2003). Desano uses a compounded verb *kari-* 'seem' to indicate 'that the speaker obtained his information from senses other than the visual' (Miller 1999: 65). According to Malone (1988: 132), the Tuyuca non-visual present marker could have evolved from 'a relic auxiliary verb' 'seem' or 'be perceived'. In all these cases, grammaticalization must have taken place in compounded verbs.

Verbs referring to location and existence may give rise to inferred and assumed evidentials. The inferred evidential *ʔel* in Wintu (Schlichter 1986: 52) goes back to a verbal element meaning 'exist' (cf. section 3, on the development of copulas into evidential markers). In Hupda, one inferred evidential comes from a grammaticalized verb meaning 'be located inside something else', and the other comes from the verb 'exist' (Epps 2005: 632, 638–40).

Grammaticalization of a verb as an evidential may involve a change in its status, from main to secondary verb, rather than transforming it into a bound morpheme. The secondary verb *awine/awa* 'seem' in Jarawara now marks inference as part of a complex predicate. It is likely to go back to a biclausal construction involving the verb *-awa-* 'see, feel', which later on fused into one predicate (Dixon 2003: 184–5).

2.2. From a deictic or a locative to an evidential

The source of evidence is established by the speaker at a specific time and place. This is similar to tense, which can be present, past, or future in relation to the time of speaking. Just like tense, evidentials can be considered deictic in character (as shown by Jakobson 1971[1957]). It is thus hardly surprising that primarily deictic elements may evolve into evidentials. The source for the 'assumed experiential' evidential *-ʔel* in Wintu is the proximal demonstrative root *-ʔE* 'this' and a derivational suffix *-l* (Pitkin 1984: 175). The primarily hearsay, or reported, particle *rɛ́* or *ɛ́* in Sissala, a Gur (Voltaic) language spoken in Burkina Faso, developed from the locative demonstrative *rɛ́* 'here', 'this' (Blass 1989: 303). In Hakha Lai

(Sino-Tibetan:Peterson 2003: 416), inferred evidentials go back to demonstrative pronouns. A similar example from Lega, a Bantu language, was discussed by Botne (1995).

Locative and directional markers also give rise to evidentials. The inferential *-ləm* in Meithei is an erstwhile directional suffix (Chelliah 1997: 224). Its directional meaning, lost from modern Meithei, survives in many other Tibeto-Burman languages. This suffix comes from the grammaticalization of a Proto-Tibeto-Burman noun **lam* 'road, way'. The auditory evidential marker *-ke* in Euchee, an isolate from North America, is cognate with the locative suffix *ke* meaning 'yonder', 'way over there' (Linn 2000: 318). According to Linn, the semantic connection between the two has to do with distance: 'the action is so far away that it can only be heard and not seen.'

2.3. Nouns, and other word classes, as sources for evidentials

Grammaticalized nouns may give rise to evidentials. In Xamatauteri, a Yanomami variety (Ramirez 1994: 170), the reported evidential *hora* comes from an erstwhile incorporated noun meaning 'noise'. The reported evidential *-hima-* in Piro, an Arawak language from Peru, comes from a noun meaning 'sound' (Matteson 1965: 127). The marker of the non-visual sensory evidential in Northern Samoyedic languages Nganasan, Nenets, and Enets goes back to a noun meaning 'voice'. The reported particle *omen* in Basque also occurs as a noun meaning 'rumour, fame, reputation' (Jacobsen 1986: 7).

Members of other word classes can be reinterpreted and reanalysed as evidentiality markers. The reported adverb 'they say' in Paumarí, an Arawá language, is likely to have developed out of the noun meaning 'news'—a cognate adverb subsequently grammaticalized as a 'reported' verbal suffix in the Madi dialect complex which includes Jarawara (Dixon 2003: 180).

Adverbial morphemes with epistemic meanings may develop into evidentials. The reported evidential in Wintu probably came from a morpheme meaning 'maybe, potentially' (Schlichter 1986: 50). In West Greenlandic, the inferential suffix *-gunar-* derives from a Proto-Eskimo morpheme meaning 'probably' (Fortescue 2003: 292, 299).

The process of grammaticalizing a verb, a noun, a demonstrative, or a directional into an evidential involves change of categorial status of the form, and also crystallization of a meaning of information source as the primary sense. A similar process is at work when evidentiality strategies give rise to evidentials.

3. Evidentiality strategies as sources for evidentials

Evidential extensions of non-evidential categories (or evidentiality strategies) share their meanings with grammatical evidentials. Typical meanings of evidentiality strategies cover hearsay, inference, assumption, and non-first-hand evidence. The development of evidentiality as a grammatical category out of essentially non-evidential forms involves reanalysis and reinterpretation, as corollaries of grammaticalization.

Non-indicative modalities may develop overtones of uncertain and non-firsthand information, as does the conditional in French. They may then develop into non-first-hand evidentials. In Cree/Montagnais/Naskapi, an Algonquian language from Canada, conjunct dubitative forms have developed non-first-hand evidential meanings in contexts which prohibit the non-first-hand markers proper, for instance, under negation (see James, Clarke, and MacKenzie 2001: 230, 254–7). Since the non-first-hand meaning 'has become conventionalized as a new meaning for dubitative suffixes in appropriate contexts', we hypothesize that an erstwhile evidential strategy is on its way towards becoming an evidential proper.

The development of a non-first-hand evidential may involve future, which—by its nature—is close to a non-indicative modality. A future clause typically includes an element of prediction concerning something unwitnessed and of subsequent lack of certainty. It can easily come to be associated with a description of events which the speaker has not witnessed personally, and of which they can only talk on the basis of an educated guess, an inference, an assumption, or hearsay. The non-first-hand evidential in Abkhaz and Circassian, two Northwest Caucasian languages, goes back to the future marker (Chirikba 2003: 262–4). The 'indirect' evidential in Hill Patwin, *-boti/-beti* (Whistler 1986: 69–71) comes from a combination of the auxiliary *bo/be* 'be (locational)' followed by the definite future suffix. Along similar lines, two non-sensory evidentials in Akha, a Tibeto-Burman language, developed from future markers: 'assumptive' future and 'speculative' future (Thurgood 1986: 221–2).[5]

Declarative and indicative modality markers may give rise to direct and visual evidentials. In Shipibo-Konibo, the direct evidential *-ra* may have come from the declarative-indicative marker reanalysed as an evidential at a later stage of language evolution (Valenzuela 2003: 43). In Tariana, an erstwhile declarative

[5] According to Metslang and Pajusalu (2002: 101), the reported evidential marker *-na-* in South Estonian originates in the potential mood.

marker *-ka* (which survives in this function in closely related Arawak languages) was reanalysed as recent past visual evidential (Aikhenvald 2003).[6]

PERFECT, RESULTATIVE, PAST TENSES and other forms with a completive meaning can acquire an additional, meaning of non-first-hand information. As Friedman (2003: 209) put it, 'both Balkan Slavic languages and Albanian developed evidential strategies using native past forms, and as the contextual variant meanings became invariant the strategies became grammaticalized'. The non-first-hand evidential in Turkic, Iranian languages, and in many Finno-Ugric languages originates in anterior and perfect forms (Johanson 2003: 287 and further references in Aikhenvald 2004: 279–80). The non-first-hand evidential marker *-shapan* in Cree/Montagnais/Naskapi goes back to a Proto-Algonquian perfect (James et al. 2001: 247). Complex resultative constructions (involving perfective converbs and a copula 'be') gave rise to non-first-hand evidentials in Dargwa and Archi (Tatevosov 2001: 460–61).

The connection between perfect (or anterior) in its resultative meaning and a non-first-hand evidential is a typologically widespread tendency. The result of an action or state, or of an action or state viewed as relevant for the moment of speech, is reinterpreted as having the meaning of an inference based on visible traces and on other non-first-hand sources, such as assumption and hearsay. Once this range of non-first-hand meanings become the main meaning of the form, it can be considered an evidential.

There is some evidence of perfectives or resultatives giving rise to evidentials in larger systems. The Tuyuca non-visual present marker may have evolved from an older perfect aspect construction (Malone 1988: 132). The emergence of the inferred evidential in Tariana involved the reanalysis of the anterior aspect marker *-nhi* accompanied by the visual evidential. Several past tenses may develop into different evidentials. In Kamaiurá, *je* 'reported' and *rak* 'attested' have clear cognates in past tense markers in other Tupí-Guaraní languages: the 'attested' evidential goes back to a recent past marker and the 'reported' to a remote past marker (Seki 2000: 344).

PARTICIPLES AND OTHER DEVERBAL NOMINALIZATIONS are often used as evidentiality strategies, with the meaning of non-first-hand or reported evidential. In Nenets (Perrot 1996) the non-first-hand ('auditive') forms come from nominalizations. The non-first-hand past in Komi is based on a past participle (Leinonen 2000: 421). In Lithuanian, the reported evidentials developed out of active participles (Gronemeyer 1997: 93).

SPEECH COMPLEMENTS are another frequent source for evidentials. The development of an evidentiality marker out of a complementation strategy involves 'de-subordination' of an erstwhile subordinate clause. That is, a complement clause of a verb of saying acquires the status of a main clause. Then, if the verb in such a dependent clause had a special form, this form takes on the status of a reported

[6] See also McLendon (2003), for a putative link between 'indicative', 'factual', and 'direct' (or 'visual') evidentials in Pomoan languages.

evidential. This scenario has been reconstructed for present reported evidentials in Standard Estonian (see Harris and Campbell 1995: 99; Wälchli 2000: 194–6).[7] The original construction consisted of the main verb of speech or perception and an active participle in partitive form. Once the main verb is systematically omitted, what was a nonfinite verb form occurs in a main clause. The only indication that the information comes from someone else is the present participle in partitive case. This form is now a reported evidential.

Copula constructions can develop into evidential markers. In Patwin (Whistler 1986) the auxiliary (locational 'be') marks a 'direct' sensory evidential. In Jamul Tiipay (Yuman: Miller 2001: 193), the non-first-hand evidential derives from an auxiliary construction involving the verb 'be'. In Akha (Thurgood 1986: 218–21), 'nonsensorial' evidential particles developed from copulas. The reported enclitic *-guuq* in West Greenlandic probably arose from verbalizing affix *-(ng)u-* 'it is so that' and 3rd person singular indicative inflection, i.e. 'be it so that' (Fortescue 2003: 301). The emergence of an evidentiality system in Lhasa Tibetan appears to have resulted from a variety of diachronic processes including reanalysis of the tense–aspect system and reanalysis of an original copula as an evidential marker: *'dug*, an erstwhile existential copula, now marks 'actual visual knowledge' (DeLancey 1986: 205).

4. Grammaticalizing information source: a summary

Evidentials evolve from a variety of sources, including

- forms from open classes (mostly verbs, more rarely nouns) and from closed classes (deictic markers, pronouns, locationals); and
- reinterpretation and reanalysis of evidentiality strategies, whereby what was a secondary meaning for a grammatical device becomes its major meaning.

Language contact and areal diffusion provide a major motivation for developing an evidentiality system. This is the reason why grammaticalized evidentials are a feature of many linguistic areas, including the Balkans and the Vaupés River Basin.

Grammaticalization is a gradual process. In numerous varieties of Latin American Spanish, expressions involving *diz que*, literally, 'says-that', are on their way towards becoming a reported evidential with overtones of doubt and inference, similar to non-first-hand evidential in Turkic or Iranian languages. Travis (2006)

[7] For similar developments in Latvian and Lithuanian, see Wälchli (2000: 194–5).

describes partial grammaticalization of *diz que* in Colombian Spanish, where this expression partly maintains the status of a verb followed by a complementizer. In contrast, in Mexican Spanish, *dizque* is a grammatical particle with the meaning of reported speech and unreliable, non-first-hand information (Olbertz 2007).[8] This grammaticalization in progress is also—at least partly—motivated by contact with indigenous languages, past and present.

[8] A similar development of *dizque* in Amazonian Portuguese is discussed by Aikhenvald (2002); also see Olbertz (2005) for Ecuadorian Spanish, and Babel (2009) for the Spanish of southern Bolivia.

CHAPTER 50

THE GRAMMATICALIZATION OF DISCOURSE MARKERS

NORIKO O. ONODERA

1. Introduction

In this chapter, first, a theoretical outline of discourse markers is given (section 2). I will then give an overview on how the development of discourse (or pragmatic) markers has recently been treated in the study of language change—i.e. as grammaticalization or as something else (section 3). Based on this controversial issue of the grammaticalization status of the development of discourse markers, I will look at the new reformulated model of grammaticalization. In section 4, this new model and its traditional counterpart are briefly reviewed. Then in section 5, the initial position, an essential feature of discourse markers, will be exemplified. This feature may lead to scope expansion in the development of the markers. After the brief

My deepest gratitude goes to Heiko Narrog, Bernd Heine, Elizabeth Traugott, and an anonymous reviewer for their invaluable comments on the earlier versions of this chapter.

sketch of other examples in languages of the world (section 6), the issue of periphery will be discussed in section 7.

2. What are discourse markers?

Since the publication of Deborah Schiffrin's groundbreaking volume, *Discourse Markers* (1987), discourse markers have been approached both synchronically and diachronically. In the 1980s, against the backdrop of the expanding field of spoken language analysis, 'discourse analysis' and 'conversation analysis', numerous synchronic analyses were made. In the 1990s, diachronic analyses of discourse markers also began.

According to Schiffrin's 'operational definition', discourse markers are 'sequentially dependent elements which bracket units of talk' (1987: 31–41). Because of the deliberate ambiguity of 'units' in this definition, it is applicable to the analysis of units of various types and sizes (speech acts, tone units, etc.). 'Sequential dependence' and 'bracketing' provide the qualifying features of markers (see also Onodera 2004: 16). A discourse marker signals the speaker's view/attitude/judgement with respect to the relationship between the chunks of discourse that precede and follow it, typically in the sentence (utterance)-initial positions. Discourse markers do not solely occur at the beginning of the utterance (initial position), but also may appear at the end of the utterance (final position) (see also sections 5 and 7).

As 'contextual coordinates', which is Schiffrin's 'theoretical definition' of discourse markers (1987: 40, 326–7; Onodera 2004: 16–17), markers index the current utterance in relation to context, which here includes participants and text. Hence, the markers work as both 'participation coordinates' and 'textual coordinates'. Each marker indexes the utterance to 'proximal' or 'distal' context. In terms of 'participation', proximal equals the speaker and distal, the hearer. In 'textual' terms, proximal refers to the prior text and distal to the upcoming text. Since markers are 'brackets' (Goffman 1974) which both initiate and terminate units of talk, discourse markers occur in both utterance-initial and final positions. However, the focus is often on the predominance of initiating brackets (see also section 5).

Another statement which helps clarify the function of markers is by Traugott (1995b: 6): 'What DMs do is allow speakers to display their evaluation not of the content of what is said, but of the way it is put together, in other words, they do metatextual work.'

3. Grammaticalization of discourse markers: the controversy

3.1. Three perspectives

There seem to be three perspectives on the issue of whether the development of the discourse marker is a case of grammaticalization. The first perspective regards it to be so (Traugott 1995b; Onodera 1995; Brinton 1996; Tabor and Traugott 1998; Suzuki 1998; Stenström 1998). Traugott (1995b: 1) argues that the development of English *indeed, in fact,* and *besides* as utterance-initial discourse markers should be considered a case of grammaticalization. They are argued to exemplify a cluster of long-attested structural characteristics of early grammaticalization and more recently recognized characteristics, pragmatic strengthening and subjectification, although such a development shows increase in syntactic freedom and scope.

Other researchers have followed suit in categorizing various discourse markers as having undergone grammaticalization. Brinton (1996) argues for grammaticalization for several English pragmatic markers, such as *hwæt, anon, bifel,* and *I gesse,* in her diachronic study. Onodera (1995) supports this view in her study of the development of the Japanese clause-final concessive subordinator *-temo* which shifted to the utterance-initial discourse marker *demo.* Likewise for Suzuki (1998), in her study on the shift of the Japanese lexical noun *wake* (reason) to an utterance-final particle, and for Stenström (1998) for the itinerary from the causal subordinator *because* to an initial discourse marker.

Here it should be noted that whether the development in question counts as a case of grammaticalization or not depends on the result of close analysis of the item's history or process of change itself. So, the same thing cannot be concluded for the development of one whole linguistic group or category (e.g. conjunctions, discourse markers) even within the same language. For example, if it is true that two discourse or pragmatic markers (particles) undergo grammaticalization, each grammaticalization process may differ to some extent: e.g. there is scope expansion in the development of the marker *demo* (Onodera 1995), while in the case of the utterance-final particle *wake* having evolved from a lexical item (Suzuki 1998), scope expansion is not involved. Thus, even within the same language, pragmatic elements that are often categorized similarly have undergone somewhat different structural changes. (I will return to the issue of 'periphery' in section 7.)

The second perspective considers the development of discourse markers as a case of pragmaticalization (Aijmer 1996; Erman and Kotsinas 1993). One reason for this evaluation seems to be that the markers are regarded to be outside of the core grammar. Pragmaticalization here refers to the process where discourse markers come to involve the speaker's attitude toward the hearer. In this perspective, pragmatic elements are judged to be optional in the sentence while grammaticalized forms are an obligatory part of the grammatical 'core' (Aijmer 1996: 3).

The third perspective (Barth-Weingarten and Couper-Kuhlen 2002) views the developmental change of similar pragmatic elements/markers as 'borderline phenomena' (Giacalone Ramat and Hopper 1998: 1). Barth-Weingarten and Couper-Kuhlen (2002) reports that the development of *though* as an utterance-final discourse marker of concession or a topic shifter is neither grammaticalization nor pragmaticalization. Their proposal of a 'more attractive solution' (p. 357) to the issue of the grammaticalization status of discourse markers is to 'treat ... the notion of grammaticalization as a[n] ... instance of prototypicality'. This stance brings no necessary change in terms of the analysis of markers. However, what differs from the first two perspectives is the judgement of grammaticalization status. This perspective gives us the advantage of explaining why in some cases only some of Lehmann's traditional grammaticalization criteria are met. It also releases us from the necessity of making a binary decision as to whether a particular case is to be counted as a grammaticalization or not.

3.2. Background for the first perspective

With these three perspectives in mind, I will now explain how the first (grammaticalization as expansion) came into being. It was the proposal which includes 'structural scope expansion' in the grammaticalization phenomena (Tabor and Traugott 1998) that made it possible to encompass several 'borderline' examples of discourse markers in the category of grammaticalization. This reformulation of 'scope size' seems to have been motivated more or less by diachronic studies of discourse markers in different languages.

Traugott (1995b) describes how the developments of 'indeed', 'in fact', and 'besides' all show well-known structural features of early grammaticalization: decategorization, phonological reduction, generalization, and more recently discussed features such as pragmatic strengthening and subjectification. Rather than matching the typical features of grammaticalization, the changes undergone by these discourse markers and the suggested cline (ibid), 'Clause-internal Adverbial > Sentence Adverbial > Discourse Particle', involve increased syntactic freedom and scope (Onodera 2004: 202).

In Onodera (1995), the development of Japanese utterance-initial *demo* and *dakedo* gained a new morphosyntactic status. And this developmental process seemed also to qualify as grammaticalization according to the following definition of grammaticalization:

> The dynamic, unidirectional historical process whereby lexical items in the course of time acquire a new status as grammatical, morpho-syntactic forms, and in the process come to

code relations that either were not coded before or were coded differently. (Traugott and König 1991: 189)

The morphosyntactic shift in *demo* type connectives (*d* connectives) is from the 'clause-final connecting device *de* + *mo*' (the gerundive form of a copula *da* + an adversative clause-final particle *mo*) to an intersentential syntactic connective. This shift is also accompanied by clear pragmatic strengthening, more specifically, subjectification. However, this case also follows the enlargement of scope and decrease in bondedness. The same tendency opposite to the traditional features of grammaticalization was also reported in Matsumoto's (1988) analysis of the development of utterance-initial (intersentential) connective *ga*.

Tabor and Traugott (1998: 265) then proposed that 'structural unidirectionality (in any formulation) is not an appropriate presupposition at this stage in the development of the field' because 'structural compacting, including scope-reduction, has been vaguely articulated up to now' as seen in the above analyses. Unidirectionality here refers to one-way hypothesized paths that are explanatory to the extent that they predict frequently attested directions of change, whether at the semantic or morphosyntactic level (cf. Traugott and Dasher 2002: 86).

Brinton (1996; 2001) even more clearly claims that the development of pragmatic markers is a case of grammaticalization. In Brinton (2001), she examined *look*-forms ((*now*) *look* (*here*), *lookyou*, *lookee*, *lookahere*, and *look it*) and reported that their development displays most, if not all, of the characteristic signs of grammaticalization: 'decategorization', 'coalescence' (i.e. 'increase in morphological bondedness' (Lehmann 1995a[1982]: 147–57)) as seen in *lookye/lookyou*, 'phonological attrition', 'desemanticization', 'increase in pragmatic meaning', 'pragmatic strengthening' (Hopper and Traugott 1993: 75–7), 'subjectification', and 'divergence' (Brinton 2001: 193).

Nonetheless, admitting that 'there are ways in which the development of *look*-forms is not characteristic of grammaticalization as it is commonly understood' (p. 194), Brinton lists three relevant features uncharacteristic of grammaticalization. First, pragmatic markers violate the 'condensation' (Lehmann 1995a: 143–7) principle, 'because in acquiring pragmatic (textual and expressive) meanings, they expand rather than shrink in scope' (Brinton 2001: 194). Secondly, the markers also infringe the syntactic 'fixation' criterion (Lehmann 1995a: 158–60). Thirdly, *look*-forms began 'life as syntagms, or full constructions, rather than as individual lexical items' (Brinton 2001: 194), which is contrary to the characteristic of grammaticalization as traditionally defined.

In conclusion, what Brinton (2001) suggests seems to be that the similarities between the development of pragmatic markers and grammaticalization prevail over the differences.

4. Two current views of grammaticalization

As reviewed above, the surge of interest in the development of discourse markers appears to have become a trigger for the new and somewhat '"extended" view of grammaticalization' (Traugott forthcoming, a: 1; Traugott forthcoming, b: 5) in addition to the 'traditional', 'prototype' (Traugott forthcoming, a: 1, Traugott forthcoming, b: 1) or 'narrow' (Traugott forthcoming, a: 1) view of grammaticalization.

4.1. Traditional view of grammaticalization

The current two views of grammaticalization are only briefly presented here. The traditional or narrow view includes the shifts toward 'increase in bondedness (dependency)', 'decrease in scope', or 'functional element from content word' in grammaticalization. Lehmann's (1995a: ch. 4) 'parameters of grammaticalization' are often considered criterial features, and they are 'integrity, paradigmaticity, paradigmatic variability, structural scope, bondedness, syntagmatic variability' (p. 164). The traditional view sees the change from a lexical to a grammatical, or from a less grammatical to a more grammatical, element as grammaticalization, which has been articulated in early works on grammaticalization. Recently, however, the question of how linguistic typology fits in to this traditional view of grammaticalization has arisen. The following is one such concern: 'examples in English, French, Japanese, and some other languages typically have disjoint syntax and prosodic patterns, and therefore do not fit a model of grammaticalization as increased dependency' (Traugott forthcoming, b: 7).

4.2. Extended view of grammaticalization

The second view of grammaticalization is the one which allows scope expansion. Such expansion has been exemplified by the developmental processes of discourse markers, such as English 'indeed', 'in fact', and 'besides' and Japanese *demo*, *dakedo*, and *ga* in 3.2. This view seems to have emerged after the appearance of diachronic analyses of such elements as pragmatic markers (as illustrated in section 3) and speech-act verbs (Traugott 1989). In the past two decades, the diachronic analysis or meaning changes of pragmatic/discourse markers has attracted linguists. Such diachronic studies have been done in a diversity of languages, including English, French, German, Spanish, and Japanese, and these interests continue to spread. Then, the issue of whether or not the developments of these pragmatic markers were grammaticalization became a controversial topic. And here emerged the problem of whether the structural changes in different languages with inherent typological differences (such as different word order) can be discussed in the hitherto proposed structural unidirectionality.

In the extended view of grammaticalization, exclusion of 'structural unidirectionality (in any formulation)' (Tabor and Traugott 1998: 265) from the criterial features of grammaticalization has been suggested as a solution to this typological problem.

5. Initial position of discourse markers

Although I allow the appearance of markers at both initial and terminal ends of talk units as brackets (Goffman 1974: 255), the predominance and symbolism of the initial position must be clarified. The initiating brackets not only open an episode but also form a slot for signals defining what kind of transformation is to be made of the materials within the episode (Goffman 1974). Because of this distinctive feature of the initial position, I used the following criterial condition (originally suggested by Schiffrin) for judgement of whether an expression is a discourse marker or not (e.g. Onodera 2004): '[a discourse marker] has to be commonly used in initial position of an utterance' (Schiffrin 1987: 328). This feature, the markers' prominent appearances in the initial positions, holds in languages even with quite different typological characteristics; for example, the markers occur utterance-initially in English and Japanese with different basic word order (English SVO, Japanese SOV). In this section, I propose that the initialness of discourse markers is universal, and that this feature supports the extended view of grammaticalization (section 4.2).

The required initialness also holds for other types of markers, such as traffic signs. In traffic, there are signs in both opening and terminating positions; however, the distinctiveness and dominance of the opening position still remains. For instance, signs that mark the speed limit of '80 km/h' typically stand at the entrance of a street rather than the end. It is required for the target of the information, here the drivers, to be given the information in the initiating position.

The distinctive feature of the initialness of discourse markers is demonstrated in the following three examples; English *anyway* (1), German *obwohl* (2), and Japanese *demo* (3). (1) shows that the discourse marker *anyway* indicates a frame-shift in an English conversational narrative.

(1) (Ann's narrative continues in a conversation between her and Noriko who are at the entrance stairs.) (from Onodera 1998: 20–21)

1	Ann:	I called her back,
2		and I said, 'Could I',
3		. . . Can you hear me well enough?
4	Noriko:	Wow. [A cicada starts to sound just above Ann and Noriko, and
5		interrupts the conversation. Noriko laughs.]
6		Oh.
7	Ann:	Um.
8	Noriko:	. . . . So close.
		p
9	Ann:	. . . . /?/
10	Noriko:	. . . Yeah.
11	Ann:	. . . *Anyway*, I said 'Could I . . . u:m . . . come out and look at the dog? /?/
12		We drove out,
		[narrative continues]

In this excerpt of Ann's narrative 'how she first got her dog', *Anyway* in line 11 marks her resumption of story-telling. This marker designates the frame-shift;[1] a shift from an 'unexpected interruption (by a cicada chirp)' back to 'story-telling' (Onodera 1998: 20–22). Hearing *anyway*, the hearer Noriko perfectly understood the speaker's resumption of story-telling. Ann's repetition, 'I said "Could I . . . " ', in lines 2 and 11 clearly shows the speaker's return to the original point in her story. The marker *anyway* uttered in a later position would not work as a frame-shift marker here. It must appear in the opening of the new frame.

Example (2) comes from Günthner (2000), examining a newly found German discourse marker, *obwohl*. Günthner explains that in today's German interaction, the originally concessive subordinator *obwohl* is frequently used utterance-initially as in (2), which is from a South German dialect. It is analysed as a newly developed discourse marker.

(2) Green Tea (Günthner 2000: 447)

44 Eva:	*willsch*	*mal*	*proBIERe?*							
	want-you	once	try							
45 Hans:	*hm.*	*Ich*	*MAG*	*kein*	*grünen*	*tee.*				
	uu.	I	like	no	green	tea				
46	(0.5)									
47 Hans:	*obwohl*	*GEB*	*mir*	*doch*	*mal*	*ne (-)*	*h'HALBE*	*tasse*	*voll.*	
	though	give	me	nevertheless	once	DET	half	cup	full	

[1] Here, the 'frame' (Tannen and Wallat 1993[1987]) refers to 'types of speech activity that the speakers think they are engaged in' (Onodera 1998: 2).

'44 Eva: you wanna try some?
45 Hans: hm. I don't like green tea.
46 (0.5)
47 Hans: although pour me half a cup.'

Such use of *obwohl* in line 47 with main-clause syntax is 'treated as ungrammatical by traditional German grammar' (Günthner 2000: 439). Günthner states that this use of *obwohl* works like 'discourse deixis' (Levinson 1983: 85–8) which indicates 'the relationship between an utterance and the prior discourse' (p. 87). This is similar to Fraser's (1990: 383) definition of discourse markers. The *obwohl*-clause 'corrects the validity of the preceding speech act (Hans' refusal)' (Günthner 2000: 447). In this case, *obwohl* takes over the role of a discourse marker designating an upcoming correction or disagreement (p. 439). (See also section 6.)

The third and last example to show the distinctive initialness of the marker is (3) (from Onodera 2004: 79). This is an excerpt from a casual Japanese conversation among three female graduate students in Washington, DC. When the three women came to the student hall and sat down on the sofa, Mari 'kicked off' the whole conversation:

(3)	Mari:	a. *Demo,*	nihon	ni	kaettara	tanoshimi	desu	ne.
		But	Japan	to	go.back	fun	COP	FP
		b. Minasan.	Oishii	mono	ippai	tabete	kite	
		Guys.	Delicious	food	much	eat	come	
		c. kudasai.						
		give						

'But, it will be fun, won't it, when you go back to Japan [for a vacation], guys? Eat a lot of delicious food.'
[conversation continues] (Onodera 2004: 79)

In terms of functions and distribution, the discourse marker *demo* is equivalent to English *but.* Hearing *demo* in (a), the hearers, Midori and Noriko, clearly heard Mari's intention of opening a conversation, with *demo* indexing back to some point in the prior talk (plans for the upcoming summer). *Demo* indexes the current utterance to a particular point in prior discourse, thanks to the pro-predicate function ('replacing function') of *d* (in *demo*), which was originally a copula. The utterance-initial *demo* seems to have developed from a clause-connecting concessive *V-te* + *mo.* In the initial position, as a discourse-connecting conjunction and a discourse marker, there remains no meaning of the original copula *d.* Such use of *demo* as in (a) is labelled as the discourse marker use 'opening a conversation'.[2]

[2] Among the discourse markers, some seem to carry grammatical functions. For example, *demo* and *ga* (Matsumoto 1988) are adversative coordinate conjunctions in Japanese as well as discourse

In this case again, *demo* must be used at the initiation of the whole conversation in order to fulfil its function as a discourse marker.

The brief overview of the three cross-linguistic examples of markers shows the prominence of the utterance-initialness of the discourse markers. A marker must appear before what is to be informed. This is what the marker highlights, and it is the upcoming speaker's intention/action/subjective strategy. In the three examples, the appearance of each marker in the 'utterance-final' counterpart does not function at all (in such cases as (1) and (3)), or if it does, its effect is in a more reduced or obscure way (in such a case as (2)). In all the cases, there is a separate intonational contour over the initial discourse marker.

As for the discourse marker, the initial position means the sentence- (or utterance-) initial position. I would suggest that this is the universal site for discourse markers to function most efficiently. Returning to the diachronic development of the markers, and to the 'issue of structural scope'—as long as this feature is retained, the items do not shrink but expand in scope.

6. Development of discourse markers in languages of the world

I will now present a few more works on the development of discourse markers in different languages, other than those illustrated above. In English, Traugott and Dasher (2002: ch. 4) and Traugott (1995b) demonstrate that *indeed* and *in fact* have undergone the process; summarily full lexical noun > epistemic > initial DM, and *actually* has also partially undergone a similar history. Stenström (1998) reveals that the causal subordinator *because* has developed to be used as an utterance-initial 'typical discourse marker' (p. 143) *cos*. The recent marker use of *cos* indicates the speaker's intention of 'take-off for further talk' (p. 134) or continuation. Stenström (1998: 144) concludes that this evolutionary process 'should be explained in terms of grammaticalization rather than pragmaticalization'.

As well as the discourse marker use of *obwohl* in German (see section 5), the rise of discourse pragmatic functions of Italian modifying suffixes such as *-ino, -etto, -uccio,* and *-one* have been analysed as 'according to Traugott, examples of grammaticalization' (Günthner and Mutz 2004: 97). They also represent counterexamples to classical features of grammaticalization (Lehmann 1995a). Günthner

markers. Also in English, *and, but,* and *or* are analysed as both coordinate conjunctions and discourse markers (Schiffrin 1987: ch. 6).

and Mutz (p. 99) concludes that their observed pragmatic changes 'can only be addressed within an extended model of grammaticalization'.

7. The issue of periphery

One unsolved assignment is the issue of periphery (cf. Onodera and Suzuki 2007).[3] What kind of expressions in terms of structure and meaning occur in initial and final positions? The relationship among (1) the shift of expression to the initial position (left periphery) or to the final position (right periphery) in its development, (2) the type of function, and (3) the typological structural differences in languages seems to be an intriguing and important issue for the future. The examples illustrated above seem to deserve attention.

[3] This issue was first evoked in E. Traugott's comments at the panel *Historical Changes in Japanese: Subjectivity and Intersubjectivity* (the Ninth International Pragmatics Conference, Italy, 2005). K. Horie's comment on my presentation at the Eleventh International Pragmatics Conference (Melbourne, 2009) also made me pay further attention to this issue.

CHAPTER 51

GRAMMATICALIZATION OF REFERENCE SYSTEMS

ZYGMUNT FRAJZYNGIER

1. The notion of grammaticalization

The term 'grammaticalization' is understood here as the coding of a function within the grammatical system of the language. This definition is broader than the frequent definition of the change from lexical item to a grammatical morpheme. Grammaticalization as understood in the present study may include a variety of forms and have a variety of sources.

2. The notion of reference

The domain of reference can have two types of expressions in its scope: the identity of a nominal expression or the nature of a proposition. For nominal expressions, the reference could be in the real world, in a hypothetical world, or in the domain

I would like to thank Erin Shay for the careful reading of several versions of this article and numerous substantial and editorial comments. I am also very grateful to Toshio Ohori for the critical comments and most useful suggestions. I have implemented all of them. I alone am responsible for any errors of fact or interpretation.

of discourse. For propositions, the reference could be in the domain of reality or in the hypothetical domain. The domains of reference for propositions are usually described in discussions of modality. The present chapter therefore deals only with the reference of nominal expressions. The grammaticalization of the following formal means is discussed: independent deictic markers; pronouns; determiners; agreement systems; and gender and nominal class systems. The chapter discusses grammaticalization of the following functional domains: deixis; previous mention; the domains *de dicto* and *de re*; coreference and switch reference; logophoricity; definiteness; indefiniteness; the category known; and the category of deduced reference.

3. State of the Art

Reference systems remain one of the least studied areas of language structure. Very few grammars discuss reference systems in their totality. Most describe elements of reference systems, such as definiteness, indefiniteness, pronouns, and agreement, but this is done in isolation from other elements of the reference systems. A notable exception is Bosch (1983). In the generative tradition, only one aspect of the reference system was studied thoroughly: binding conditions and their application in defining lexical nouns, pronouns, and anaphors. The presence or absence of definite and indefinite articles remains the most studied question within the domain of reference (Lyons 1999; Dryer 2005). Hagège (1982: ch. 4) is one of the few works in which the system of reference is treated as a separate domain.

The aim of the present chapter is to describe the range of functions within the domain of reference and the means of coding those functions. The interest of reference systems for grammaticalization theory is that a very small number of lexical sources, mainly deictic elements, are exploited for the coding of a large number of functions. This variety is achieved by combining these lexical sources with each other or with linear order, affixation, full nouns, or the absence of overt coding. Deictic elements are also the sources of grammatical morphemes in many domains other than reference, including complementation, topicalization, focusing, and the formation of verbless predications.

Studies of the grammaticalization of reference systems usually concentrate on the sources of various coding means rather than on the evolution of the whole system, but it is the structure of the whole system that determines the functions of the individual means. The question of the grammaticalization of reference systems as a whole—i.e. why some languages have grammaticalized some functions but not others—remains open.

4. DEIXIS

Deixis involves reference to elements in the surrounding reality rather than in discourse. Common distinctions within the deictic system are person/entity deixis, space deixis, and time deixis. Deixis can be coded by different lexical categories, such as deictic demonstratives ('this', 'that'), verbs ('come', 'depart'), nouns corresponding to compass directions ('east', 'west'), adverbs of place and time ('here', 'there', 'now', 'later') (see Fillmore 1975; Anderson and Keenan 1985).

Deictic lexical items can be combined with each other to code additional functions. Independent deictic lexical items may become determiners of other lexical items or of other deictics, e.g. Polish *tamten* 'that', composed of the remote locative deictic *tam* 'there' and the entity deictic *ten* 'this'. Some languages may use repetition of the same determiner to code degrees of distance. In Hdi (Central Chadic) a noun can be preceded and/or followed by up to two deictic elements:

(1) *ká xəŋ mántsá* ***nà ná*** *kɗíx* ***ná ná****, kɗíx-á xìyá yà*
COMP 3PL thus DEM DEM donkey DEM DEM donkey-GEN guinea corn COP
'They said, "This donkey here is the donkey of guinea corn."' (Frajzyngier and Shay 2002)

Some languages code reference to three deictic persons—the speaker, the addressee, and the 3rd person—while other languages (French, Hausa: Newman 2000) have four persons: the speaker, the hearer, the 3rd person specified, and the 3rd person unspecified. In many languages the 3rd person referent cannot be deictic. Bhat (2005) considers only the 1st and 2nd person markers to be pronouns; the 3rd person he considers to be a demonstrative (cf. also the review of Bhat by Cysouw 2006). For thorough discussions of the category person, see Cysouw (2003) and Siewierska (2004).

The unspecified person in the subject role is sometimes referred to as the 'impersonal passive'. Some languages distinguish between the unspecified person that may include the speaker (English 'one' as subject, in some varieties) and the unspecified subject that excludes the speaker (English 'they' and the 3rd person plural in many other languages):

(2) **One** (inclusive) would say for example it's not worth reading. (London–Lund Corpus)
(3) I think **they** (exclusive) are grooming him for quite a responsible job. (London–Lund Corpus)

Although pronouns are often derived from deictics, they belong to categories where the principle of indirect means applies. The principle of indirect means is a trigger of frequent replacements (Frajzyngier and Jirsa 2006). For lexical sources of various pronouns see Heine and Kuteva (2002). Some languages distinguish between the 1st person inclusive, which includes the addressee, and the 1st person exclusive, which excludes the addressee. Although reference to the 2nd person is usually considered to be deictic, Pero (West Chadic) distinguishes between the addressee of current discourse and the addressee of reported discourse. The addressee of reported discourse is thus an anaphoric element for the listeners of the reported speech.

Direct discourse:

(4) *ɗóe* *ma-tà-táppó-n* *tí* *ràm* *dàmbáŋ-ì* *mà-n-ɗúngò* *córì*
all 2PL-FUT-gather PREP field *damban*-DEF 2PL-SEQ-start dance
'You all will gather on the field of *damban* and start dancing.'

Reported discourse:

(5) *péemè* *wóccò* *tí* *cákkà* *tà* *mágánì*
2-REP.PL leave PREP 3M FUT teach sense
'You leave that for him and he will teach him sense.' (Frajzyngier 1989a)

For the categories space and time, languages often distinguish proximate, remote, and sometimes intermediate distance. With respect to space deixis, in some languages the point of reference in deixis is the speaker. Other languages can have both the speaker and the listener as the point of reference, as is the case in Japanese and Korean and in Hausa (Jaggar 2001). Deixis may have elements of speech in its scope:

(6) Listen to this... What's the point of talking to a group?
(http://sethgodin.typepad.com/seths_blog/2006/10/listen_to_this.html)

Deictic markers often become determiners that modify a noun, and they may eventually become definite markers (Diessel 1999). Determiners, however, do not necessarily have functions in the domain of reference. They are often markers of topicalized or focused constituents.

5. Gender and class systems

The fundamental function of gender and nominal class systems is to code reference in discourse (Martinet 1967; Frajzyngier and Shay 2003). For different views on the role of gender and noun classes, see Aikhenvald (2000) and Craig (1986a). For a review of gender in typological perspective, see Corbett (1991; 1994). The evidence that gender markers code reference is provided by the fact that when gender systems disappear as a result of phonological reduction they are replaced by other means of coding reference, such as articles.

Gender markers are usually derived from demonstratives (Greenberg 1978). The sources of nominal class markers in languages such as Bantu remain to be discovered.

6. The domains *de dicto* and *de re*

Some languages distinguish between the domains *de dicto* and *de re* (Frajzyngier 1991). The domain *de dicto* designates reference to entities that are introduced in speech but have no independent existence in reality. Referents in the domain *de re* are entities that exist in reality. The difference between the two domains may involve the use of different markers to code similar functions in the two domains, or it may involve coding different types of distinctions in the two domains. Thus, if the language distinguishes gender and number in the domain *de re*, the distinction(s) may be neutralized in the domain *de dicto*. Mupun (West Chadic) distinguishes gender in the 2nd and 3rd person singular. In the description of a hypothetical situation, i.e. a situation in the domain *de dicto*, the masculine pronoun is used even if the referent can only be female:

(7)

gaskiya,	*get*	*kadan*	***ka***	*kə*	*ak*	*ɓe*	*ba*	*də*	*mo*	*pə*	*ɪal*
truly (H.)	past	if (H.)	2M	with	pregnancy	SEQ	NEG	PAST	3PL	PREP	

ɗik	*n-ka*
marry	PREP-2m

'Truly, in the past if you (masc.) were pregnant they wouldn't marry you.' (Frajzyngier 1993: 88)

German distinguishes gender in the 3rd person singular in the domain *de re* but does not necessarily make this distinction in the domain *de dicto*:

(8)

Die	*Menstruation*	*ist*	*bei*	***jedem***	*etwas*	*anders*
DEF:F	menstruation	is	for	everybody (M)	a little bit	different

'Everybody has a slightly different menstruation.' (Pusch 1984).

7. Previous mention

Some languages have grammaticalized the category previous mention. This is the case in Mupun for both entity and locative reference:

(9) a. *wu wa sə́*
3M come there (deictic)
'He came from there.' (only deictic)

b. *wu wa ɗi*
3M come there (anaph)
'He came from there.' (only anaphoric)

The evidence that the category involved is previous mention rather than definiteness or the category known is that previous-mention markers are distinct from deictic markers and that a previous-mention marker is used only when the noun it determines has been mentioned before. Also, the previous-mention marker can be used with a proper noun:

(10) *yaksə mu dəm ɗi n-**Germany** nə*
then 1PL go there PREP-Germany PM
'Then we went to Germany.' (Frajzyngier 1993)

8. Category known

Frisian (Germanic) makes a distinction between the anaphoric and known categories coded by different definite markers:

	M	F/N	PL
Known	a	at	a
Anaphoric	di	det	dö(n)

Known:

(11) a. Jister skiinjd **a** san an wi wiar üütj bi't weeder
yesterday shine DEF sun and we were out water
'Yesterday the sun shone and we were out on the water.'

Anaphoric:

(11) b. Ik haa wüf faan Berlin bi strun meet. **Det** wüf saad,
1SG have woman from Berlin on beach meet DEF woman said
'I met a woman from Berlin on the beach. And the woman said...'
(Karen Ebert, p.c.)

9. The domain of deduced referent

The deduced reference marker instructs the listener to identify the referent using knowledge from various sources, including the listener's cognitive system, the speech environment, and previous discourse, but not through previous mention of the same referent. Mina (Central Chadic) has a subdomain of deduced reference that is marked by the form *ta* (phrase-internal form *tə*; phrase-final form *tàŋ* or *táŋ*). The marker *tá* explicitly tells the listener that the referent is not the noun marked by *tá* but some other referent associated with that noun:

(12) *tíl á nd-á á r báy tàŋ*
go 3SG go-GO PRED PREP chief DED
'He went to the chief's [court].' (not to the chief) (Frajzyngier, Johnston, and Edwards 2005)

10. Category definite

The category definite, because of its presence in Romance and Germanic languages, has been the object of numerous descriptive and cross-linguistic studies. In Dryer's (2005) study, only 188 of the 566 languages examined are listed as having no definite or indefinite articles or affixes coding definiteness. The functions of morphemes categorized as 'definite article' may be quite different even in closely related languages. In English, the definite marker instructs the listener to identify the referent in any way possible, whether through previous mention, the presence of the entity in the environment of speech, or common knowledge. The definite article in English cannot be used with proper names. Definite articles in Romance and Germanic languages code gender and number of nouns they determine and can, at least to some extent, be used with proper names. Of the 566 languages in Dryer's study, 56 have definite articles that are identical with demonstratives. If the definite article is grammaticalized from a demonstrative, it appears that it is more frequently the remote rather than the proximate demonstrative that is the source of the definite marker (Frajzyngier 1992). For a proposed grammaticalization of the definite article in Finnish, see Juvonen (2000).

Definiteness of the noun can be coded by affixes to constituents other than the noun. In Gidar (Central Chadic), definiteness of the object is coded by inflectional markers on the verb, the high tone central vowel *ə́*:

(13) a. *tə̀-nzád-ə́-k* *ɗə̀fá*
3F-cure-3M-PRF man
'She cured the man.' (the man is known)

Unknown object does not have the high tone on the epenthetic central vowel:

(13) b. *tə̀-nzád-ə̀k* *ɗə̀fá*
3F-cure-PRF man
'She cured somebody.' (Frajzyngier and Shay 2003: 165)

11. Indefinite

The category referred to as 'indefinite' in many languages codes an unspecified member of a set of entities having one or more features in common. Indefiniteness can be coded by pronouns corresponding to 'who', 'what' that often serve also as interrogative pronouns. The indefinite/unspecified word for a human referent often has the equivalent of 'man, person' as its source (e.g. French *on* from Latin *homo*). The indefinite word for a non-human, non-animate referent may have the equivalent of the noun 'thing' as its source (e.g. Italian *cosa*).

One means of marking a noun as indefinite is the use of an indefinite article. While many languages have both definite and indefinite articles, 41 out of 251 languages in Dryer's (2005) sample have indefinite but not definite articles. Indefinite articles in many languages are derived from lexical items designating the numeral 'one', but this is not the only source of indefinite articles. In the 181 languages that have indefinite articles, 91 have an indefinite article identical with the numeral 'one' and 90 have other indefinite markers (see also Heine and Kuteva 2007). In some languages, the marker of indefinite reference is the verb of existence:

(14) *áŋkwà* *gdzà* *dáwalè* *à* *də̀* *kàtà* *gyáalè*
exist young boy 3SG SEQ want girl
'A certain boy wanted to marry a girl.' (Wandala, Central Chadic; Frajzyngier field notes)

12. Coreference and switch reference

The term 'coreference' or 'same reference' designates the interpretation of an argument as having the same referent as an argument in the preceding proposition. The term 'switch reference' or 'different reference' refers to the interpretation of a referent as distinct from the one in the preceding proposition.

In many languages, coreference is the default reading and is unmarked (cf. Comrie 1998), while switch reference is the marked category. In languages that code the subject on the verb ('agreement'), such coding implies coreference. The marked means, such as the use of a subject pronoun or a demonstrative that agrees in person, gender, and number with the subject coded on the verb, often implies switch reference (Frajzyngier 1997):

(15) *A* *wuni* *muvjili,* *że* ***wuni*** *maju* *dosydź*
CONJ 3PL say:PAST:3PL COMP 3PL have:PRES:3PL enough
żyvności *kedy* *xlebam* *stfylaju*
food when bread:INSTR shoot:PRES:3PL
'And they$_1$ said that **they$_2$** have enough food if they$_2$ use bread for shooting.'
(Polish; Nitsch 1960: 245, transcription slightly simplified)

While switch reference most often has the subject in its scope, there are languages that have the object in the scope of switch reference. This system obeys the principle that coreference is the unmarked case and switch reference is the marked case. In Mupun, the 3rd person direct object is not marked in the perfective aspect:

(16) *n-sin* *takarda* *n-ha* *nə* *a* *la* *a* *ta*
1SG-give book PREP-2M COMP 2M take 2M read
'I gave you a book so that you can take [it] and read [it] (the book).'

If the verb has a direct object pronoun, the pronoun is not bound by the object of the preceding clause:

(17) *da* *komtak* *dəm* *ɓe* *wu* *baa* *k* *la* *duu* *fin* *ɓwet* ***nə***
M fellow went SEQ 3M swing PREP DIMIN stick 3M hit ANAPH
'The fellow went, swung the stick, and hit it.' (not the stick, something else)

Languages may encode the distinction between coreference and switch reference through means other than pronouns. In Hua (Papuan: Haiman 1983) and Choctaw (Muskogean), switch reference is coded through affixes to the verb. Choctaw uses one affix to code the same subject (SS) and another affix to code the different subject (DS) of the embedded clause:

(18) *John-at* *abiika-haatokoo-**sh*** *ik-iiy-o-tok.*
John-NOM sick-because-SS III-go-NEG-PT
'Because John$_1$ was sick, he$_1$ didn't go.'

John-at *abiika-haatokoo-**n*** *ik-iiy-o-tok.*
John-NOM sick-because-DS III-go-NEG-PT
'Because John$_1$ was sick, he$_2$ didn't go.' (Broadwell 1997: 32, PT-past)

13. Logophoricity

The term 'logophoric' (Hagège 1974) refers to pronouns that are coreferential with the subject of the matrix clause whose predicate is a verb of saying. Logophoric pronouns have been described for large number of African languages, including Adamawa languages (Cloarec-Heiss 1969; Hagège 1974), Bantu (Hyman and Comrie 1981), Kwa (Clements 1975), and some Chadic languages (Frajzyngier 1985; 1989b; 1993; 1997).

Frajzyngier (1997) proposed, with respect to complements of verbs of saying, that if a language codes the distinction between coreference and switch reference, through the pronoun system, use of the same pronoun in the same syntactic position codes switch reference, while use of a different pronoun, or the same pronoun in a different syntactic position, codes coreference. The importance of this hypothesis is that it partially explains two elements in the taxonomy of pronouns: pronouns that are bound within a sentence and pronouns that are not bound within a sentence. This hypothesis contradicts the central intuition of Fiengo and May that 'if an expression is repeated, it follows that the two occurrences have the same semantic value, in the cases at hand, its reference' (1995: 794).

Logophoric pronouns, i.e. pronouns indicating coreferentiality, are usually different from matrix clause pronouns, while pronouns coding switch reference are the same as matrix clause pronouns. This is the case in Mupun:

(19) *wu/wa/mo sat n wu/wa/mo ta ɗee n-jos*
he/she/they say COMP he/she/they stop stay PREP-Jos
'He$_1$/She$_1$/They$_1$ said that he$_2$/she$_2$/they$_2$ stopped over in Jos.' (Frajzyngier 1993: 108)

In other languages, the distinction between coreferentiality and switch reference with the subject of the matrix clause is coded by the position of the subject pronoun in the embedded clause. This is the case in Lele (East Chadic):

(20) *yàá-dú ná bòy-**dú** kójò kò-tó*
say-3F COMP break-3F hoe GEN-3F
'She$_1$ said that she$_2$ broke her$_{1/2}$ hoe.'

(21) *yàá-dú ná **dú** bòy kójò kò-tó*
say-3F COMP 3F break hoe GEN-3F
'She$_1$ said that she$_1$ broke her$_{1/2}$ hoe.' (Frajzyngier 2001)

14. Conclusions

One of the interesting aspects of the grammaticalization of reference is that a large variety of functions are coded by the same lexical sources: deictic markers, which often become determiners and pronouns; numeral 'one'; equivalents of the verb 'to say'; existential verbs; unspecified referent markers equivalent to 'who', 'what', 'man, person', 'thing'; and also nouns marked for gender. The wide variety of functions coded in the domain of reference is made possible by combining these lexical sources with linear order, affixation, the use of full nouns, or the absence of any overt coding (Comrie 1998).

CHAPTER 52

THE GRAMMATICALIZATION OF SUBORDINATION

TOSHIO OHORI

1. Introduction

Subordination has occupied an important place in grammaticalization studies, because complex structures tend to arise from simple structures and hence the origin and development of subordinate constructions can often be reconstructed (for the grammaticalization of coordination, see Mithun 1988). Major overviews of grammaticalization (e.g. Heine, Claudi, and Hünnemeyer 1991; Lehmann 1995a [1982]; Hopper and Traugott 2003) all include more than passing discussions of the grammaticalization of subordination.

Generally, subordination is defined as a relation in which a clause has a function equivalent to that served by a word in a simple clause. Thus when a clause functions as either a subject or an object of another clause, it is called a complement clause. When a clause modifies a noun, as an adjective does, it is a relative clause, and when a clause occupies an adjunct position modifying another clause, it is an adverbial clause. The last category is less homogeneous than the other two both structurally and semantically, and the border between adverbial subordination and coordination may be viewed as a continuum, mediated by such constructions as converbs and clause-chaining. In what follows, after surveying the general tendencies of the grammaticalization of subordination, some selected cases of the development of the three types of construction will be reviewed. At the same time, attention will be paid to the fates of subordinate constructions.

2. General tendencies

Building on a wide range of well-documented cases, several tendencies have been established regarding the grammaticalization of subordination. Some salient ones are reviewed below (see also Cristofaro 2003 for an in-depth study).

First, in terms of the semantic category of grammatical morphemes, the hierarchy (1) proposed in Heine et al. (1991) is well established. Besides, they identify the pathway SPACE > DISCOURSE, as illustrated in (2).

(1) PERSON > OBJECT > PROCESS > SPACE > TIME > QUALITY

(2) Kenya Pidgin Swahili (Heine et al. 1991: 184)
kila *mtu* *ile* *na-ambi-wa* *mambo* *hii* *na-shangaa*
each person REL NF-tell-PASS matter this NF-be.surprised[1]
'Everybody who was told this story was surprised.'

In (2), the morpheme *ile*, originally a distal demonstrative, is used as a relative clause marker. The extension from the SPACE category (whether location or motion) to subordinate markers is cross-linguistically very common (cf. section 5).

While (1) is a scenario of semantic development via metaphorical extension, the metonymic and context-induced change of meaning (3) is proposed by Traugott (1982). Later, in Traugott (1989) and Traugott and Dasher (2002), among others, the terms 'subjectification' and 'intersubjectification' were introduced to designate the overall trend past the rise of textual meanings. A parade example is English *while* which developed from a complex temporal marker expressing simultaneity (4) to a monomorphemic marker (5) providing pragmatic background for the main clause situation, and then to a concessive marker (6).

(3) Propositional > Textual > Expressive

(4) Old English (Traugott and König 1991: 200)
& *wicode* *þær* *þa* *hwile* *þe* *man* *þa* *burg*
and camped there that time that one that fortress
worhte *&* *getimbrede*
worked-on and built
'and camped there while the fortress was worked on and built'
(ChronA (Plummer) 913.3)

(5) Middle English (p. 201)
Thar mycht succed na female, Quhill foundyn mycht be ony male
'No female was able to succeed while any male could be found.'
(1375 Barbour's Bruce 1.60 (*OED*))

[1] NF stands for *non-future* in this chapter.

(6) Early Modern English (p. 201)
Whill others aime at greatnes boght with blod, Not to bee great thou stryves, bot to bee good
'While others aim at greatness that is bought with blood, you strive to be not great but good.'
(1617 Sir W. Mure Misc. Poems xxi.23 (*OED*))

Some might wonder if the semantic/pragmatic change of the kind outlined in (3) qualifies as a case of grammaticalization. But if we take grammar broadly as embracing those subsystems of language that are responsible for encoding intersubjective meanings (call it the interaction-centred view of grammar), the development of such subsystems is definitely a proper object of grammaticalization inquiry.

On the structural side, the general tendency that dominates the grammaticalization of subordination is given in a nutshell as 'less to more clause integration'. For example, Lehmann's (1988a) typological framework provides such scales as downgrading of subordinate clauses, syntactic level, desententialization, grammaticalization of main predicate, interlacing, and explicitness of linking, which taken together define the degree of clause integration (see also Givón 1995). Thus a loosely juxtaposed paratactic linkage may change to an asymmetrical hypotaxis; a clause-level linkage may change to a core-level linkage (e.g. VP subordination); a subordinate clause may be nominalized or lose such properties as tense and mood; an explicit phrasal conjunctive expression may be reduced to a simple morpheme (cf. (4–6)) and then to zero.

3. Complement clauses

Heine and Kuteva (2002) cite the following sources as commonly identified for the grammaticalization of the complement construction: ALLATIVE, DEMONSTRATIVE, MATTER, W-QUESTION, RELATIVE, RESEMBLE, SAY, and THING. Among these, one particularly well-known source is demonstratives, as seen in many Indo-European languages, for example English *that*. Another commonly found source is for verbs of saying to develop into complementizers (e.g. Lord 1976; 1993; Frajzyngier 1991; 1996a). Examples are taken from Lord (1993: 185), with slight regularization.

(7) Ewe
a. *me-bé* *me-wɔ-e.*
I-say I-do-it
'I said "I did it."' or 'I said that I did it.'

b. *me-gblɔ* *bé* *me-wɔ-e.*
I-say (say) I-do-it
'I said, "I did it."' or 'I said that I did it.'

According to Lord (1993), the morpheme *bé*, originally meaning 'to say', is obligatory in the quotative construction (7b). It can also be used in combination with verbs other than those for reported speech. In (8), *bé* is used as a marker for a desire complement (from Lord 1993: 189).

(8) Ewe
me-dí *bé* *má-fle* *awua* *ɖewó*
I-want (say) I.SBV-buy dress
'I want to buy some dresses.'

The verb meaning SAY may develop into other related grammatical categories, for example Mandarin *de hùa* 'GEN/Linker story' > condition. In Japanese, the SAY verb does not undergo this kind of change, but nominal complements are marked by *to iu* (quotative 'say'), as in *[intai-suru]-to iu happyoo* ([retire-do]-COMP announcement) 'an announcement that (X) will retire' (compare: **[intai-suru] happyoo*).

The grammaticalization from MATTER and RESEMBLE to complementizers can be illustrated by Japanese *koto* 'matter; thing'> marker of propositional and factive complements and *yoo* 'way; manner' > marker of irrealis (e.g. optative, jussive, and comparison) complements, respectively. Both are originally nouns, and can be modified by demonstratives like *kono* 'this' in modern Japanese as well, as in *kono koto/yoo* (cf. also examples of complements with *tokoro* 'place' discussed by Ohori 2001). Another commonly used complementizer in Japanese is *no* (see Horie 1998; 2000), often glossed as nominalizer. In classical Japanese, the complement clause predicate was marked by the particular ending, which is called *rentaikei* (noun-modifying or more precisely nominalized form).

(9) Japanese (10th c.)
kono *okina-wa* *Kaguyahime-no* *yamome-naru-wo*
this old.man-TOP Kaguyahime-GEN unmarried-COP-ACC
nagekasi-kere-ba, . . .
deplore-PFV-CONJ
'Since this old man had deplored Kaguyahime's being unmarried, . . .'
(*Taketori Monogatari*, p. 27, Iwanami Bunko edition)

In this example, the complement of the verb *nagekasi-* 'to deplore', marked by the accusative case, is in the nominalized form *naru* (as opposed to the finite form *nari*), and no overt complementizer is present. *Koto*-complements are also present in the same period as (9), conditioned by the type of the matrix predicate. Later, due to the restructuring of the verbal paradigm in Middle Japanese, the merger of the nominalized form and the finite form occurred. This change was accompanied by the attachment of the particle *no* (nominalizer and genitive marker) at the end of the complement clause. Thus in the 18th-century texts we find instances of *no*-marked complement clauses, though the problem of dialectal diversity would need to be considered for a fuller account.

Finally, complement constructions themselves feed into the process of grammaticalization. Heine and Kuteva (2002) cite COMPLEMENTIZER > PURPOSE, while they admit that it is yet to be known how universal this pathway is. Further cases of the fates of complement constructions involve what Evans (2007) calls 'insubordination' (a.k.a. 'suspended clauses': Ohori 1995). An example from Japanese is given below. As mentioned earlier, *to iu* is a grammaticalized form of the quotative plus the verb of saying.

(10) Japanese
dare-mo *tasuke-nai-to iu*
who-even help-NEG-COMP
'(the story is) nobody helped (me)'

Here, a complement clause (which would otherwise be headed by a noun like *wake* 'story; reason') stands alone as an independent clause, and *to iu* is shifting to an utterance-final pragmatic particle, with what might be called an 'anti-evidential' function, i.e. the speaker is relating his/her own direct experience with a detached stance. Each language may develop different pragmatics, but this is a rather common change complement clauses may undergo.

Another fate of complement clauses is modal markers, as shown by Thompson and Mulac (1991) based on the data from spoken English. In their study, Thompson and Mulac show that the matrix clause of the complement construction *I think* takes on an epistemic meaning, comparable to that of *maybe*, without the complementizer *that*. This sort of functional shift, accompanied by changes in form, is also common across languages.

4. Relative clauses

Compared with complement clauses, languages draw upon a narrower range of source categories for relative clauses. The common sources for relative clause markers according to Heine and Kuteva (2002) are: DEMONSTRATIVE, HERE, and W-QUESTION.

As this list implies, the same morpheme can be used for both complement and relative clauses. English *that* (< DEMONSTRATIVE) and French *que* (< W-QUESTION) are such examples. Also, in languages where the dominant relative clause construction is the head-internal type, the two constructions look alike, often taking the form of a nominalized clause. Classical Japanese is one such language where there was no formal distinction between the two, and the relative construction took the form exactly as (9), the difference being merely the semantics of the matrix predicate. In this sense, NOMINALIZER may be added as an immediate source for a relative clause construction, though it remains to be further examined to what extent the head-internal relative clause really qualifies as a relative clause.

Nominalizers were used as relativization strategies in Classical Chinese too, resulting in what appear to be headless relatives. The subject nominalizer was 者 *zhě* 'V-er', and the object nominalizer was 所 *suǒ* 'V-ee' (both are in the modern Mandarin transcription, and so are the following examples). Originally the former means 'person; one' while the latter means 'place'. Examples are from Pulleyblank (1995: 67 for (11) and 16 for (12); glosses are supplemented by TO).

(11) Chinese (4th c. BC)
Niǎo shòu zhī hài rén zhě xiāo (鳥獸之害人者消)
bird beast GEN harm man NMZ disappear
(*Mèngzi* 3B/9)
'The birds and beasts that had injured people disappeared.'

(12) Chinese (4th c. BC)
Sǒu zhī suǒ zhī yě (叟之所知也)
senior.man GEN NMZ know PRT
(*Mèngzi* 1A/7)
'It is what your reverence well knows.'

In modern Mandarin, *de* is employed instead as an enclitic to a clause modifying a noun (thus functioning as a marker for a head-external relative construction). However, its precise etymology is not certain (Chao 1968: 253) and its grammaticalization path is opaque.

Yet another source for the relative clause marker, which Frajzyngier (1996a: 450) identifies for several Chadic languages, is ASSOCIATIVE markers.

(13) Hausa (Frajzyngier 1996a: 451, taken from Kraft and Kirk-Greene 1973: 107)
yaarò-n dà Audù ya aikàa
boy-DEF REL Audu 3M send
'the boy that Audu sent'

The morpheme *dà* is used not only in the comitative meaning followed by a referential noun, but can be followed by an attribute noun expressing a property concept, resulting in e.g. *dà saurii* 'ASSC speed' > 'fast'. Frajzyngier speculates

(1996a: 453): 'Since the relative clause is an attributive element for the head noun, it is quite natural for the speakers of the language to use with it the device that is already used to mark a property concept as an attributive element.'

Whereas the primary motivation for the grammaticalization of the complement clause is conceptual-semantic, in that the construal of an event as an entity is at the root of the construction, discourse-pragmatic motivations have a high profile in the grammaticalization of the relative clause: besides encoding an attributive relation between two clausal units, relativization involves an establishment of a coreferential relation between the two NPs that belong to the linked clauses. Unlike in the case of complementation, it is not required to construe an event as an entity in the relative clause construction. According to Langacker (1991: 433), '[t]he essential feature of relativization is . . . a particular kind of clause linkage based on correspondence: the same conceived entity . . . figures simultaneously in the situations described by both component clauses.' As such, relativization does not involve conceptual recategorization, and this may be why the immediate sources for the relative clause marker are rather limited: DEMONSTRATIVE and HERE are clearly referential, and W-QUESTION also has the property of indefinite reference. In the latter case, the relative clause construction provides means for spelling out the referent of an indefinite question. NOMINALIZER seems to be widespread in pro-drop languages, where coreference need not be marked by any overt referential expression. ASSOCIATIVE is probably the only source with clear conceptual-semantic ground, because here the attribution of some property by a clausal unit is the primary motivation.

The fate of relative clauses is also limited. Heine and Kuteva (2002) mention only RELATIVE > COMPLEMENTIZER, though the languages being cited are diverse both areally and genetically.

5. ADVERBIAL CLAUSES

Since adverbs themselves form a heterogeneous category, we shall proceed by listing some commonly identified semantic types without defining adverbial clauses categorically (see Kortmann 1997 for a European perspective). For the semantic relations such as time, place, and cause/reason, their origins are often straightforward. One possibility is to use nouns denoting these relations in combination with complement clauses. Another is to use case markers, especially oblique ones, as clause linking particles. The first pathway tends to be highly transparent. In some cases, however, interesting semantic shifts take place, as in the following Japanese example using *kuse* originally meaning 'bad habit'.

(14) Japanese

okane-ga *nai* *kuse-ni* *zeetaku-suru*
money-NOM be.not bad.habit-DAT luxury-do
‘Even though (X) has no money, (s/he) is enjoying a luxurious life.’

This shift in meaning may remotely remind the reader of the development of English *(de)spite*, for nouns having negative evaluation lead to concessive or adversative markers in both languages.

The second pathway for the rise of adverbial clauses, namely the functional extension of case markers, is also widespread across the languages of the world (see e.g. Moravcsik 1972; Austin 1981; Genetti 1986; 1991; Croft 1991a; Ohori 1996). Some salient ones are: ABLATIVE > CAUSE, ALLATIVE > PURPOSE, DATIVE > PURPOSE, LOCATIVE > CIRCUMSTANCE/CONDITION, INSTRUMENTAL > CAUSE, ERGATIVE > CAUSE, and COMITATIVE > CIRCUMSTANCE. Of these, examples of ERGATIVE/INSTRUMENTAL > CAUSE and ABLATIVE > CONDITION are given below.

(15) Tauya

a. *ʔasu-ni* *fai-e-ʔa*
knife-ERG cut-1/2-IND
‘I cut (it) with a knife.’ (MacDonald 1990: 128)

b. *fanu* *ne-pi* *ʔumu-a-te-ni* *wamasi* *mene-a-ʔa*
man 3S-GEN die-3S-DS-ERG widow stay-3S-IND
‘Her husband died so she’s a widow.’ (MacDonald 1990: 237)

(16) Digueño

a. *‘i:kwic+pu+c* *‘wil^y+k* *w+yiw*
man+DEM+SUBJ rock+ABL 3+come
‘The man came from the rock.’ (Gorbett 1974: 95) 25)

b. *‘+m+c+l^{y}ayp+x* *‘+ma:w+pu+k,* *‘+suw+x* *‘+ma:w*
1+work-PLUR+IRR 1+NEG+DEM+ABL 1+eat-PLUR+IRR 1+NEG
‘If we don’t work, we don’t eat.’ (Gorbett 1974: 95)

In what follows, we will limit ourselves to the grammaticalization of conditional clauses and purpose clauses. For the former, there are diverse sources besides case markers. For example, Traugott (1985: 299) gives MODALITY, COPULA, GIVEN, INTERROGATIVE, TEMPORAL, and CAUSAL, the last two of which are closely associated with the notion of source, cf. (16). To this list could be added SAY (Heine and Kuteva 2002)—cf. Mandarin *de hùa* mentioned earlier. COPULA develops into a conditional marker especially when combined with irrealis MODALITY, as in Japanese *nara(ba)* which comes from the irrealis form of a copula used in the classical period. The now optional *ba* (which should be represented as *(r)eba* in Modern Japanese due to reanalysis) itself is a conditional marker which is supposed to be related to the topic marker *wa* (< *pa*), indicating a connection to GIVEN.

In addition, the grammaticalization of negative conditional markers (with the meaning 'if not') in English provides an interesting case history (cf. Traugott 1997b). In Old English, this meaning was expressed by *butan*, which originally meant 'to exclude', and *nefne* < *ne efne* 'not exactly'. With both words, the intended meaning was something like 'excluding the state of affairs being talked about', thus suggesting EXCLUSION as a source concept for negative conditions. In Middle English, these markers became obsolete, and in late Middle English *on less that* was introduced (the first citation in *OED* being 1431) by the calque from French *à moins que*. *Than* and *that* disappeared by the end of the 16th century. According to *OED*, the last citation of the form with *than* is 1530 and that with *that* is 1596. The first citation of the form without either is 1509 (often spelled *onlesse*). Assuming a scalar model of meaning, the development from COMPARISON to conditional can be summarized as follows. Ordinary assertions have upper-bounding conventional implicatures (e.g. *I exercise for six hours* implicates *I exercise for five, four, three... hours*). Conditionals reverse this bounding effect and produce lower-bounding implicatures (e.g. *if you exercise for six hours* implicates *if you exercise for seven, eight, nine... hours*). But then negation reverses this effect again (e.g. *if you don't exercise for six hours* implicates *if you don't exercise for five, four, three... hours*). Consequently, the part of the scale denoted by the negative condition is equivalent to the range of possibilities expressed by the comparative *less* (e.g. *on less than six hours of exercise*). This pragmatic equivalence can be seen as the motivation for the development of *unless* as a negative conditional marker (note, in addition, that *un-* is not a negative prefix but comes from a locative preposition).

Next, purpose clauses have an equally wide range of sources. Heine and Kuteva (2002) give ALLATIVE, BENEFACTIVE, COME TO, COMPLEMENTIZER, GIVE, GO TO, MATTER, and SAY. English *to* is an example of ALLATIVE > COMPLEMENTIZER > PURPOSE, combined with BENEFACTIVE in the form *for to* which was common in Middle English. A dramatic case is supplied from Rama (Craig 1991), in which the morpheme *ba(ng)*, originally meaning 'to go', fed into the chain which spread to a postposition for goal, a preverb, and a prospective aspect marker, besides subordinator for purpose.

Of the source categories for purpose mentioned above, ALLATIVE, COME TO, and GO TO are motivated by the localist model of event structure: Purpose is conceptualized as spatial goal. GIVE and BENEFACTIVE also fit this model. MATTER and SAY are associated with COMPLEMENTIZER and may not have their own semantic component that would develop into purpose. A pragmatic motivation for the grammaticalization of SAY, however, might be a folk model that by uttering something, the speaker commits him/herself to its realization, and the utterance is taken to be a statement of purpose (cf. Hewitt 1987: 27, who says of Georgian 'a colloquial method of expressing purpose utilises perhaps the favourite method of speech-reporting, namely direct quotation').

Looking at Japanese data, purpose is expressed by either of the following, putting aside more periphrastic expressions: (i) DATIVE case attached to a verb stem; (ii) relational noun *tame* 'cause/BENEFACTIVE' complemented by a clause; (iii) suffixation of *beku* 'should' to the purpose clause (as in *katudoo-o tudukeru-beku nokot-ta* (activity-ACC continue-should remain-PST) '(X) remained in order to continue activity'); and (iv) relational noun *yoo* 'manner/way' complemented by a clause. Of these, only the last one permits switching of the subject, resembling English *so that.* (i) and (ii) fit the already mentioned pathways. (iii) is an example of the use of mood for marking purpose, and (iv) is seen as a development from RESEMBLE to COMPLEMENTIZER, and then to purpose.

Given their heterogeneity, the fate of adverbial clauses is not easy to ascertain systematically. One notable case is PURPOSE > INFINITIVE identified by Haspelmath (1989). In Japanese, conditional expressions have been conventionalized in a variety of ways, giving rise to markers of modality, conjunction, and adverbials (see Narrog and Ohori, Chapter 64 below, on Japanese). Also, insubordination of adverbial clauses is fairly common (see Ohori 1995; 2000; Higashiizumi 2006 for Japanese), exhibiting a particularly interesting case of (inter)subjectification.

CHAPTER 53

THE GRAMMATICALIZATION OF QUOTATIVES

GUY DEUTSCHER

1. Quotative what?

Few things occur as frequently in natural speech as the reporting of speech itself. The extreme frequency of reported speech constructions in discourse, coupled with their formulaic nature, makes them a prototypical locus for grammaticalization. Indeed, the grammaticalization of so called 'quotatives' has been one of the most frequently and intensely discussed areas in the study of grammaticalization. Even a very partial list of publications would vastly exceed the confines of this chapter. While African languages have dominated the discussion, languages from South and East Asia have also been particularly prominent (most notably Tibeto-Burman, Indo-Iranian, Dravidian, Tai-Kadai, Austronesian, Japanese), and the phenomenon has also been studied in a plethora of other languages, including ancient Indo-European and Semitic languages, Caucasian, Kartvelian, and creoles. (For many examples, see Heine and Kuteva 2002, and for a thorough review of the literature, see most recently Güldemann 2008, especially chapters 4, 5.)

However, the profusion of studies has not always translated into increasing clarification of all the issues. In particular, the term 'quotative' itself has been applied to different types of elements, and this has had pernicious effects on the understanding of the core issues in the process of grammaticalization itself. 'A quotative' is not an altogether happy deadjectival coinage. Its presumed meaning is 'a quotative something', but a quotative what: verb, construction, particle, inflection, evidentiality marker? The problem goes beyond the superficial level of terminological inconsistency. Since some of the elements above are typical *sources* of grammaticalization and others are typical *targets*, and since grammaticalization is crucially concerned with the diachronic changes in the semantic and morphosyntactic status of certain elements, the use of the same label for both sources and targets has obscured the analysis of certain processes. A particular case in point, as I will argue below, is the alleged 'quotative *like*' in English.

This chapter concentrates on the grammaticalization of direct speech constructions, and in particular on the emergence of quotative particles introducing direct speech. The distinction, or sometimes lack thereof, between direct and indirect reported speech will not be addressed here. The final section briefly surveys the further development of quotative markers into other grammatical functions.

2. Speech introducing clauses and quotative markers

Speech verbs like 'say' are frequently called 'quotative verbs' in the literature, when they serve to mark the presence of reported speech, as in (1) below. It would be unusual, however, to call such verbs 'quotative markers', since the term 'marker' invokes the expectation of a grammaticalized element, whereas 'said' in (1) is a completely normal verb, used in its literal lexical sense, and serving in its canonical syntactic role as the predicate of a full clause.

(1) She definitely said: 'I'll be back by 3 o'clock.'

For reasons that will become clear below, I suggest that the term 'quotative verb' should be abandoned, and that the term 'quotative' be reserved for *grammatical* markers (or at least, for elements that are in the process of becoming grammatical markers). In this chapter, verbs like 'say' in (1) will be called 'speech verbs' when their lexical content is meant, and a construction such as 'she definitely said: ... ' will be called a Speech Introducing Clause (SIC), that is, a clause whose function it is to indicate that an adjacent utterance is reported.

The term Quotative Marker (QM) will be used to refer to *grammatical* particles such as the Korean *la* in (2) below, which has no independent clausal status, and which serves 'redundantly' in addition to a SIC.

(2) Nami nun RS la malhay-ess-ta
Nami P RS QUOT say-PAST-P
'Nami said: "RS".' (Korean: Sohn 2001[1999]: 325)

The difference between the SIC 'Nami said' and the QM *la* seems simple enough in cases such as (2). But the waters become a little muddied when the SIC does not consist of canonical speech verbs. As is well known, various non-speech verbs, particularly motion verbs such as 'come' and 'go' and action verbs like 'do' or 'make' are often used instead of speech verbs in SICs, as in (3–5):

(3) and she goes 'I'm coming in a minute'
(4) och så kom han då 'Vad vill ni?'
and so came he then "what do you want?"' (Swedish: Romaine and Lange 1991)
(5) az hi osa li 'ma ata roce me-ha-xayim sheli?'
then she 3FSG.do 1SG.DAT 'what you want from-the-life mine?'
'So she does to me: "what do you want from my life?"' (Modern Hebrew)

In these examples, the verbs function syntactically as entirely normal predicates of entirely normal clauses. The only difference from (1) and (2) above is that in (3–5), the verbs in the SIC are not used in their core lexical sense. As there is no hint that these verbs are assuming a grammatical role, however, and as there is no reduction in their morphosyntactic status (although there may be a change in their argument structure), they should not be regarded as QMs in the sense defined above. Indeed, the SICs in (3–5) cannot be viewed as the result or the target of any grammaticalization process at all.

So far, this analysis is rather uncontroversial. But now consider (6) below. The SIC *she's like* is a normal English clause of the type 'X is like Y'. It is fully independent and follows the canonical structure of English copular clauses. In its syntactic status, the predicate *be like* is fully equivalent to the predicate *say* in (1). (In both cases, the reported speech can be viewed as the complement that is missing from the SIC.) And yet, while there seems to be widespread agreement that verbs like *say* in (1) or even *go* in (3) are not grammaticalized QMs, it is very common in the literature to refer to the element *like* in (6) as a quotative marker. Indeed, ever since Romaine and Lange's (1991) seminal discussion, it is usual to refer to *like* in (6) as the result of a process of grammaticalization.

(6) she's like 'I'm coming in a minute'

It seems to me that analysing *like* in (6) as a QM is misleading, because it obfuscates the close parallels between the SIC in (6) and the SICs in (1) and (3–5). The predicate *is like* in (6) is fully equivalent in status to the predicate *goes* in (3), for instance, and *goes* is surely not a grammaticalized QM but rather a full verb that serves as the predicate of a SIC. So, just as it would be unjustified to extract one element from the SIC in (3) and call it a QM, it is unjustified to extract the element *like* from the SIC in (6) and treat it as a QM. Of course, the SIC in (6) may well be a source for the grammaticalization of a QM (see more on this process below), but it is not the target of such a process. If *like* comes to be used in constructions such as *she said like*..., i.e. if it comes to be used as a syntactically reduced marker *in addition* to a SIC, then there would be justification for talking about its grammaticalization as a QM. But as long as this is not the case, extracting one element out of the SIC *X is like*... and labelling it a QM seems arbitrary.

3. Non-canonical SICs

The discussion so far has assumed a clear-cut binary opposition between fully independent SICs on the one hand and fully grammaticalized and dependent 'redundant' QMs on the other hand. Of course, such a division does not represent the complexities of the situation in reality. Indeed, since SICs are the grammaticalization *sources* of QMs, and since grammaticalization is a *gradual* process, we can expect to find various intermediary stages between fully independent SICs and fully grammaticalized QMs.

In addition, since SICs occur so frequently in natural discourse, and since they have such a formulaic nature, their internal structure can often be reduced, or at least assume idiosyncratic syntactic form, even when they still function externally as fully independent clauses. For example, in (7) below, the SIC *und er so* does not have the full internal structure of a canonical German clause, as it lacks a verb. And yet, the coordinator *und* clearly shows that in terms of its external status, the SIC *und er so* functions as a fully independent clause which encapsulates the meaning 'and he said (as follows)':

(7) Ich sagte ihm, dass er gehen muss. Und er so: ich werde es mir überlegen.
I told him that he go must And he so: I'll think about it.
(German: Heine and Kuteva 2002: 274)

Another example of a SIC with a synchronically opaque internal structure can be seen in Old Akkadian, the earliest attested stage (2500–2000 BC) of the Akkadian language. The construction '*enma* SPEAKER (*ana* ADDRESSEE)' in (8) and (9) below is highly unusual from the point of view of the synchronic grammar of the language. It does not fit any obvious clause type, neither verbal (which would require verb-final order) nor nonverbal. The word *enma* itself has no secure etymology and is used only in this particular SIC (see discussion in Deutscher 2000: 69). Indeed, the construction must have been opaque already to the speakers at the time, and was used as a fossilized idiom. Nevertheless, regardless of its internal structure, the construction as a whole serves as a fully independent SIC, and it encapsulates the meaning '(this is what) SPEAKER says/said/should say (to ADDRESSEE)', as examples (8) and (9) demonstrate. (All examples from Akkadian are from Deutscher 2000: 69ff.)

(8) ašma-ma aḫ̮tadu enma anāku-ma 'RS'
1SG.heard-P 1SG.rejoiced enma I-P 'RS'
'I heard (it) and rejoiced. This is what I say: "RS".'

(9) šībūtum šūt maḫ̮ar-šunu enma X ana Y 'RS'
witnesses REL in_front_of-them enma X to Y 'RS'
'witnesses that in front of them X said to Y: "RS"'

The typology of the internal structure of SICs is discussed by Güldemann (2008) (but with different terminology) and will not be elaborated here, since—as will be argued in the following section—what determines the process of grammaticalization is not the internal structure of the clause, but its use as a SIC.

4. Grammaticalization from SIC to QM

The lexical sources that have been quoted most often in the literature as the origins of grammaticalized QMs are verbs of saying. Güldemann (2008), on the basis of a sample of about forty African languages, argues that the importance of speech verbs in this respect has been exaggerated, and that the sources of QMs are just as likely to be verbs of motion, action, equation, similarity, inchoativity, or manner, as well as nonverbal elements such as presentation particles, pronominal elements marking the speaker, and other pronominal and nominal elements. To what extent the African frequencies represent the situation in other areas of the world remains to be investigated. However, for reasons already touched upon above, it seems to me misleading to discuss the lexical sources of QMs in isolation from their role within a SIC. Speech verbs or any other elements do not turn into QMs in isolation, but only by virtue of their use in a SIC. Of course, in the syntax of some languages, a SIC can consist of just one word (e.g. a 'say' verb). But as explained in Deutscher (2000: 70), as a point of principle, it is a whole SIC that undergoes grammaticalization, not any individual elements within it. Indeed, even a reduced QM can often betray traces of more than one element from the original SIC. For example, the Georgian QM *metki* (Harris and Campbell 1995: 169) is a reduction of an original SIC *me v-tkv-i* (I 1SG-say-AORIST.IND), so the reduced QM still incorporates elements from both the pronoun *me* and the speech verb *vtkvi*.

In short, the general path of grammaticalization leading to a QM should not be described as 'say' ⇒ QM, nor as 'like' ⇒ QM, nor as 'go' ⇒ QM, but rather as SIC ⇒ QM. The lexical sources are only relevant in as far as they are used inside a SIC. Any element that tends to appear within a SIC can end up contributing to the form of a grammaticalized QM.

The actual passage from a SIC to a QM can involve all the aspects of reduction that are typically associated with the process of grammaticalization: erosion in form, reduction in morphosyntactic variability, loss of syntactic independence, and loss of semantic features (most importantly the loss of the ability to mark the identity of speaker). The process of grammaticalization can be schematized very roughly in (10). The typical constellation in which an original SIC can start the process of reduction is when it appears after another SIC in parataxis (as exemplified in 10a) or alternatively in some sort of dependent relation (as in 10b).

(10)	SIC_1	SIC_2	'RS' ⇒	SIC_1	QM 'RS'
a.	he answered	he said:	'RS'	he answered	QM 'RS'
b.	he answered,	saying:	'RS'	he answered	QM 'RS'

It seems that the initial motivation for juxtaposing two SICs as in (10) is either purely for emphasis, or in contexts where the first SIC represents a more specific type of speech reporting (e.g. answer, command, request), and the need is then felt to buttress this with a more general SIC, e.g. one with a generic speech verb 'say'. In the majority of languages in which the grammaticalization of QMs has been discussed, the details of this process need to be reconstructed from synchronic layering. There are few exceptions, however, where one can actually follow the details of the process historically. One of them is the grammaticalization of a QM in Akkadian over a period of two millennia. It is worthwhile to summarize the main stages of this process as a paradigm case for the grammaticalization of a QM, since the diachronic evidence reveals some aspects that are not easily reconstructible from synchronic variability.

5. From SIC to QM in Akkadian

Examples (8) and (9) above show the starting point for the Akkadian SIC '*enma* X (*ana* Y)'. Until 2000 BC, this construction was used only as a fully independent SIC. It did not normally follow other SICs, but rather appeared on its own to introduce the meaning 'this is what X said/says/should say (to Y)'.

The form of this SIC undergoes some phonological and morphological changes after *c.*2000 BC: *enma* changes to *umma*, and the ability to append the addressee Y is lost. Instead, an emphatic particle *-ma* is added to the speaker X, so the form of the construction becomes *umma* X-*ma*. The most important development, however, is that the *umma* X-*ma* clause now starts appearing frequently in parataxis after another SIC. Example (11) below, from shortly after 2000 BC, demonstrates this stage. (All examples below are from the Babylonian dialect of Akkadian.) Here a conversation is reported. In the first line, the *umma* X-*ma* clause follows another SIC with a more specific speech related verb, 'write'. But in the second line, which represents the continuation of the reported conversation, the *umma* X-*ma* clause continues to bear the load of introducing speech on its own:

(11) ašpurak-kum umma anāku-ma 'RS'
1SG.wrote-2MSG.DAT umma I-P
'I wrote to you (and this is what) I said: "RS".'

umma atta-ma 'RS'
umma you-P
'You said: "RS".'

The juxtaposition SIC$_1$ + *umma* X-*ma* + RS, as in the first line of (11), becomes increasingly frequent when SIC$_1$ represents specific speech-related situations, such as answer, write, send a message, complain, and so on. Initially, this juxtaposition is not found when SIC$_1$ contains the generic speech verb *qabûm* 'say'. But a little later in the second millennium, we start finding the *umma* X-*ma* clause appearing also after 'say'. The earliest examples are clearly of emphatic nature, and also have a marked structure. As can be seen in (12) from the 19th century BC, *umma* X-*ma* and the say-SIC bracket the RS from two sides:

(12) umma anāku-ma atta lū bēl-ī-ma anāku lū warad-ka
umma I-P you EMPH lord-my-P I EMPH servant-your
aqbi-šum
I.said-to him
'I said: "You really are my lord and I really am your servant" I said to him.'

From the 18th century BC onwards, *umma* X-*ma* appears regularly also after the generic verb 'say', in contexts which are no longer emphatic, and where *umma* X-*ma* no longer brackets the RS, but is simply juxtaposed to the first SIC, as in (13). The frequency of this construction is a clear sign of semantic reduction.

(13) ana Y aqbi-ma umma anāku-ma '(reported speech)'
to Y I.said-P umma I-P
'I said to Y: "(reported speech)".'

However, one interesting stage in the process of reduction that is not always easily reconstructed from synchronic layering is that there is quite a long period of a one-sided, or asymmetric, reduction in the syntactic and semantic status of *umma* X-*ma*. On the one hand, throughout the first half of the second millennium, *umma* X-*ma* does not lose the ability to introduce RS on its own, and is frequently found without any preceding SIC, as in (14) below. On the other hand, the grammaticalization of the *umma* X-*ma* clause is evident from the fact that it becomes extremely common after other SICs (including the unmarked speech verb *qabûm*), in fact almost obligatory. In other words, while the *umma* X-*ma* clause does not lose its ability to serve as a sole SIC for a few centuries, other SICs lose the ability to introduce speech without the mediation of *umma* X-*ma*. (Or at least, RS without *umma* X-*ma* becomes extremely rare, except in poetic texts.)

(14) pīqat umma X-ma
perhaps umma X-P
'Perhaps X might say "…"'

In the second half of the second millennium BC, the asymmetry is balanced, as the obligatorification of *umma* X-*ma* after other SICs finally leads to the expected reduction in both form and syntactic independence. After 1500 BC, the marking of the speaker disappears from the *umma*-clause, and the sequence *umma* X-*ma* is reduced to an invariable *ummā*:

(15) X ana mārti-šu išappara ummā šumma mimma iqtabû-nikki
X to daughter-his 3MSG.write ummā if anything 3PL.say-2FSG.DAT

qibī ummā amāt-a ana šarr-i našāku
say.IMP.FSG ummā matter-ACC to king-GEN 1SG.bring.STATIVE
'X wrote to his daughter: "if they say anything to you, say: 'I am bringing the matter to the king'".'

With the loss of the marking of the speaker, *ummā* has now lost the ability to function as a SIC without any preceding clause, and it can no longer appear in constructions such as (14) above. Syntactically, therefore, *ummā* is no longer a clause, but can now be regarded as dependent. In other words, we may now call *ummā* a grammaticalized QM.

Notice, however, that although *ummā* has lost its syntactic independence, it has not entirely lost its semantic content in all contexts: while in the second line of (15) above, *ummā* may be an entirely 'redundant' QM, in other contexts it can still be the only bearer of the speech meaning, as it serves to extend non-speech clauses into a speech situation, as in (16) below. (Indeed, *ummā* does not lose this ability to extend non-speech clauses into a speech situation even in later stages of the language.)

(16) eql-a ana X ittadin ummā 'RS'
field-ACC to X 3SG.gave ummā
'He gave the field to X, saying "RS".'

In fact, *ummā* retains the ability to serve in constructions such as (16) not only in the second millennium, but also in the first, until the death of the language around 500 BC. Nevertheless, in the first millennium, we see further signs of reduction in both form and status. In form, *ummā* is reduced to *umma* in the Babylonian dialect and to a mere *ma* in the Assyrian dialect. And as evidence for further syntactic reduction (in both Assyrian and Babylonian), the particle now starts appearing not just once before the whole reported speech, but is frequently repeated before every new clause within the reported speech, as in (17):

(17) šarru iqtabi umma lā tapallaḫ umma rēška anašši
king 3MSG.said umma NEG 2MSG.fear umma I will summon you
'The king said: "don't be afraid, I will summon you."'

In summary, the evidence from Akkadian shows how slow and gradual the process of grammaticalization of an erstwhile SIC into a QM can be. Over a period of nearly two millennia, we can see how a fully independent SIC, with an opaque internal structure but with full syntactic independence and with the clear meaning 'This is what X said', gradually loses its syntactic independence and its clausal status through its frequent juxtaposition after other SICs, and turns into a grammaticalized, obligatory, and 'redundant' QM.

6. Further development of QMs to other grammatical functions

Quotative markers are themselves often the starting point of further changes into other grammatical functions. The most common (or, at least, most commonly reported) first step in such a development is the extension of QMs from the restricted function of introducing reported speech to be used as complementizers with a much wider range of complement-taking verbs. It seems that QMs may be extended in the first instance to non-speech verbs that are nevertheless conceptually closely associated with speech situations, for example 'hear' (one hears [it said] . . .), 'think' (which in many languages is represented as speaking to oneself), or 'fear' (one fears [saying to oneself]: . . .). Cognition verbs, on the other hand, which are conceptually further away from speech situation, seem to be only a later phase in the extension. In Akkadian, for example, the QM *umma* was extended in the first millennium to the verbs 'hear' and 'fear', but was never extended beyond these to be used with 'know'. A similarly modest extension can be observed in the Biblical Hebrew QM *lē'mōr* (literally 'to-say.INF').

There is, however, evidence from numerous languages of QMs that have been extended to all types of complement taking verbs (and beyond, to other syntactic roles). This process has been shown for many African languages by Lord (1993: 184ff.), for Austronesian languages by Klamer (2000), and recently for Sinitic languages by Chappell (2008). The theoretical aspects of this development are also discussed in depth by Heine and Kuteva (2007: 236–40). Nonetheless, one typical example is given from Ewe (18), where the QM *bé* (originally from 'say') is used as a complementizer with the verb 'know', and with a wide range of complement-taking verbs.

(18) me-nyá bé e-li
1.SG-know QUOT 2.SG-exist
'I know that you are there.' (Ewe: Heine and Kuteva 2007: 237)

QMs may also develop in another direction and turn into evidentiality markers of various types, as discussed by Aikhenvald (2004: 272ff.). The Akkadian example in (17) above, for instance, while clearly not having reached the status of an evidentiality marker, nevertheless hints at the way in which such a development may progress, as the repeated use of a QM for every reported clause can naturally lead to its reinterpretation as a clause-internal marker of reported-evidentiality.

Finally, a QM may be extended into a wide range of discourse-pragmatic functions in various syntactic configurations, as is shown by Suzuki (2007) for the Japanese QM *tte*.

CHAPTER 54

THE GRAMMATICALIZATION OF COORDINATING INTERCLAUSAL CONNECTIVES

ANNA GIACALONE RAMAT
CATERINA MAURI

1. The notion of interclausal connective

Two clauses can be linked in a number of different semantic relations either by being simply juxtaposed or by means of explicit linking devices. This distinction is commonly referred to as the opposition between asyndetic (1) and syndetic (2) constructions, respectively (cf. Lehmann 1988a: 210).

This work is the result of a continuous exchange of ideas between the two authors. However, Anna Giacalone Ramat is responsible for the writing of sections 2.1, 2.2, and 3.3, Caterina Mauri is responsible for the writing of sections 1, 3.1 and 3.2.

(1) Parengi (Mithun 1988: 334)
noʔn kuy alung ir-ru, din-ruʔ
he well inside jump-PST die-PST-UNDERGOER
'He jumped inside the well and died.'

(2) *Mary washed the dishes* **and** *Peter dried them.*

As Kortmann (1997: 46) and Mithun (1988: 357) point out, explicit linking devices are especially frequent in written language. In spoken discourse the situational context (intonation, extra-linguistic cues, etc.) helps in defining the nuances that language may miss, but in written texts language is the only tool available to establish and infer interclausal relations (cf. also Meillet 1958[1921]). The aim of this chapter is to analyse the rise and grammaticalization of a specific subtype of interclausal linking devices, namely coordinating connectives.

Interclausal connectives have been referred to as 'conjunctions' in the European tradition, mainly denoting free and invariable morphemes (cf. Lang 2002: 636). The term 'conjunction', however, is here restricted to the expression of combination ('and') relations and will thus not be adopted in the European traditional sense.

Coordinating interclausal connectives are characterized by their ability to establish alone (i.e. further cooccurring connective elements are optional, not obligatory) a coordination relation between two clauses. Following Mauri (2008b: 41), we will consider as coordination relation between two clauses any relation established between functionally equivalent states of affairs, having the same semantic function and autonomous cognitive profiles and being both coded by utterances characterized by the presence of some illocutionary force (cf. also Haspelmath 2004a: 34).

A major distributional criterion for identifying coordinating connectives is provided by Dik (1968: 34–7), who assumes that 'two members can never be coordinated by more than one coordinator'. Such a method however has some intra-linguistic and cross-linguistic limits, first of all because interclausal coordinating connectives do not show the same properties in all languages, and because markers may show different degrees of grammaticalization (Haspelmath 2007: 48).

Both Haspelmath (2007) and Mauri (2008b) highlight that the category of coordinating connectives does not have sharp boundaries and should be best described in terms of a cline or a continuum. Therefore, the markers included in this analysis as coordinating connectives will be identified on the basis of their function, rather than on the basis of their morphosyntactic and distributional properties.

2. The grammaticalization of coordinating connectives: general properties

2.1. Intra-linguistic variation, renewal, and borrowability

Two coordinated states of affairs can stand in different conceptual relations. Three main relation types have been recognized in the literature on clause coordination: conjunction ('and'), disjunction ('or'), and adversativity ('but'). There are crucial differences among the interclausal connectives encoding these three types of coordination, which group conjunctive and disjunctive connectives apart from adversative ones.

First of all, adversative connectives show a higher intra-linguistic variation than conjunctive and disjunctive connectives. In other words, in the same language there are usually a number of adversative connectives, partially overlapping in their functions, whereas such variation is not frequently attested in the expression of combination and alternative relations. Take for instance French, which only shows *et* for conjunction and *ou* (*ou bien*) for disjunction, but a number of different connectives for contrast relations, e.g. *toutefois*, *mais*, *par contre*, *alors que*, *pourtant*.

Secondly, adversative connectives are more easily and quickly renewed than conjunctive and disjunctive ones, which instead seem more stable over time. Romance languages provide clear examples of such a difference in pace: as pointed out by Meillet (1958: 171–2), of the original Latin inventory, Romance languages have preserved *et* for conjunction (> Fr. *et*, It. *e*, Sp. *y*) and *aut* for disjunction (> French *ou*, Italian, Spanish *o*), while none of the Latin adversative connectives (*sed*, *tamen*, *at*, etc.) has survived. Besides, in some cases the development of adversative markers occurred only in very recent times, as is the case of It. *però*, whose adversative value was conventionalized during the 16th century.

Finally, adversative connectives are more easily borrowed than disjunctive and conjunctive ones. An implicational hierarchy (see (3)) has been suggested by Matras (1998b: 301–5), according to which in bilingual contexts languages replacing combination markers also replace alternative (disjunctive) markers, and languages replacing alternative markers also replace contrast (adversative) markers:

(3) 'but' > 'or' > 'and'

According to Matras, this implication mirrors the different degrees of 'intensity with which the speaker is required to intervene with hearer-sided mental processing activities' (Matras 1998b: 305–25) in establishing the relations of combination, alternative, and contrast. The more the relation implies a contrast, the more the speaker has to maintain assertive authority despite the denial of the addressee's expectations. To do so, bilingual speakers tend to adopt connectives of the pragmatically dominant language.

In our view, the explanation provided by Matras for the hierarchy in (3) points to the deeply intersubjective function of adversative connectives, which may also play a role in motivating the differences described above with respect to the grammaticalization of conjunctive and disjunctive connectives. Adversative connectives are crucial to the expressive potential of speakers, and therefore speakers are constantly in search of new and expressive ways of conveying contrast, determining a high synchronic intra-linguistic variation and a quicker renewal. Conjunctive and disjunctive connectives, on the other hand, are rather connected to the organization/description of the linked states of affairs and are thus characterized by a lesser degree of intersubjectivity, which in turn determines a less urgent need for expressivity and renewal.

2.2. Documentation and diachronic methodology

The differences highlighted in the preceding section lead to some methodological considerations. The direct consequence of the different paces in the renewal of coordinating connectives is that in a well-documented family such as the Indo-European one, the grammaticalization of adversative connectives is more likely to be attested in historical texts, thus allowing for the identification of the successive stages of the diachronic process (see Diewald 2002). By contrast, the diachronic analysis of conjunctive and disjunctive connectives is often limited to the etymological reconstruction of the diachronic sources, without the possibility of following their grammaticalization steps in texts. This, of course, does not hold for languages with a recent system of connectives, where their diachronic origins are still morphologically transparent (see Mithun 1988: 351–6). However, such languages are usually also characterized by a scarce written tradition, which makes it rather difficult to follow the diachronic path back in time. In such cases, the attested synchronic variation is the best tool to identify the critical contexts and functions where the diachronic process began.

The availability of written documentation and the dating of the change thus crucially determine the methodology that may be employed in the diachronic analysis. Sections 3.1, 3.2, and 3.3 will discuss data according to different levels of depth. Section 3.1 focuses on the diachronic sources of coordinating connectives, basically from an etymological perspective. Section 3.2 then examines the attested paths under the lens of the traditional criteria for grammaticalization identified by Lehmann (1995a [1982]). Section 3.3, on the other hand, takes into account the factors, the stages and contexts characterizing the paths at issue, analysing the occurrences in texts.

Table 54.1. Diachronic sources for conjunctive connectives

Source meaning	Examples
1. Spatial and temporal meanings of linear succession 'in front', 'after, before, then'	I.E. **hanti, hant-* 'in front' > O.Saxon *ant-*, Goth. *and(a)-* 'in front' [cognate to Lat. *ante* 'in front, before', Gr. *antí* 'in front, against', Hit. *ánti*] > Engl. *and*, Germ. *und* (cf. Traugott 1986: 141, Kluge and Seebold 1989: 179, 749)
2. Focal additive particles 'also, too'	I.E. **eti* 'also, too' > Lat. *et* 'also, and', Gr. *éti* 'furthermore'; Slavic *i*: 'also' > 'and' (Meillet 1958: 165, cf. also Mithun 1988)
3. Paragraph linking strategies, particles and adverbs 'besides', 'moreover', 'and then'	Mohawk (Northern Iroquoian) *tahnu'*: 'besides' > 'and' (Mithun 1988: 347)
4. Comitative markers	Sarcee (Athapaskan) *mih* 'with' > 'and' (Mithun 1988: 349; see also Stassen 2001)
5. Verbs meaning 'go', 'bring' in narrative contexts	Hdi (Chadic) *là* 'to go' > 'and then' (Frajzyngier and Shay 2002: 428–31); Tetun (Austronesian) *hodi* 'to bring' > 'and then' (van Klinken 2000: 354–7)
6. Pronominal roots	I.E. 'proximal stem' **tó* > Hittite *ta* 'and' (Luraghi 1990: 65–70), OCS *ta, to, ti* 'and', Ukr. *ta* 'and'

Table 54.2. Diachronic sources for disjunctive connectives

Source meaning	Examples
1. Distal meaning 'that, other'	Dan. Nor. Swe. *eller* 'or' < Proto-Germanic **alja-*, **aljis-* 'other' (Falk and Torp 1910: 187); I.E. **au-* 'other, that' > Lat. *aut* (**auti*) 'or', *autem* 'but' > It. Sp. Cat. *o*, Fr. Port. *ou*
2. Interrogative particle	Instrumental form of Common Slavic **ch'to* 'what' > Cz. Pol.: *czy*, Bel. *ci* 'choice-aimed or'
3. Free choice verbs	Lat. *vel* 'want'> 'simple or', Fr. *soit... soit* 'be it' > 'either... or'
4. Dubitative particles 'perhaps'	Kuuk Thaayorre (Pama-Nyungan) =*okun* 'DUB' > 'or' (Gaby 2006: 323–4); Rus., Bulg., S-Cr.: *i* ('and') + *li* (dubitative particle) > *ili* 'or'
5. Negative particles	Nakanai (Oceanic) *(ou)ka* 'NEG' > *ka* 'or' (Johnston 1980: 239)
6. Denied conditional clause 'if not', 'if it is not so'	Cavineña (Tacanan) *jadya=ama ju-atsu* 'thus=NEG be-ss' (lit. being not thus, if it is not so) > 'or' (Guillaume 2004: 114); Lezgian *tax̂ajt'a* 'or' < conditional form of the negated aorist participle of *x̂un* 'be', meaning 'if it is not' (Haspelmath 1993: 332); Italian *sennò* 'otherwise' < *se* 'if' + *no*

Table 54.3. Diachronic sources for adversative connectives

Source meaning	Examples
1. Spatial meaning of *distance* (separation), *closeness* (same place), or *opposition*	OE *be utan* 'at (the) outside' > Engl. *but* (cf. Traugott 1986: 143); OE *in stede* 'in the place' > *instead*; *whereas* < 'in the place where'; Lat. *ante* > It. *anzi*; German *sondern* 'separate' > 'but rather'
2. Temporal meaning of overlap, simultaneity 'while'	Eng. *while*; It. *mentre* 'while, until' > 'whereas'; Fr. *alors que* 'when' > 'whereas', *ce pendant* 'during this' > *cependant* 'whereas'
3. Temporal meaning of continuity 'always'	It. *tuttavia*, Fr. *toutefois* 'always, continuously' > 'nonetheless' (Giacalone Ramat and Mauri 2009b); Eng. *still* 'constantly' > 'nonetheless'
4. Causal (and resultive) meaning	It. *però*, Fr. *pourtant* 'therefore' > 'nonetheless' (cf. Giacalone Ramat and Mauri 2008); Germ. *dafür* 'for that' > 'on the other hand'
5. Comparative meaning 'more', 'bigger'	Lat. *magis* > It. *ma* (Marconi and Bertinetto 1984), Fr. *mais*; Old Serbian *veće* 'bigger' > Serbian *već* (Meillet 1958)
6. Emphatic reinforcing of the 2nd clause	Eng. *in fact*, It. *bensi* 'but rather'

3. Diachronic sources and paths of change

3.1. Recurrent diachronic sources of coordinating connectives

Tables 54.1–54.3 show a far from exhaustive list of the recurrent diachronic sources attested across languages for conjunctive, adversative, and disjunctive connectives, providing examples and references for each diachronic path.

Conjunctive connectives often develop from spatio-temporal adverbs and prepositions (Table 54.1, item 1) typically indicating a linear succession in time 'before, after' or a linear organization in space 'in front, beside'. Such diachronic paths involve a metaphorical process of abstraction from concrete to more abstract, logical notions (Traugott 1986: 137). Further frequent sources for conjunctive connectives are focal additive particles meaning 'also, too' (item 2) and paragraph-linking strategies or discourse markers of the type 'moreover, and then' (item 3).

In both cases, the source denotes an addition to some previously mentioned entity but on different syntactic levels. Focal additive particles usually precede or follow elements at the lower levels, and typically start their grammaticalization path as connectives between NPs (Mithun 1988: 340); paragraph-linking and discourse markers, on the other hand, grammaticalize at the higher levels as connectives between clauses. Comitative markers (item 4), too, grammaticalize as connectives at the NP level (Stassen 2001; Haspelmath 2007), by virtue of sharing with conjunction the joint involvement of two participants, and may eventually extend to the coordination of higher-level entities (e.g. *mih* in Sarcee: Mithun 1988: 349). Verbs with a dislocative meaning, such as 'go' or 'bring' (item 5), may develop into conjunctive connectives in narrative contexts, where they frequently occur between successive events, the second of which requires a dislocation, thus triggering their reanalysis as clause linkage devices. Finally, as exemplified by Indo-European languages, the diachronic source for conjunctive connectives may consist of pronominal roots (item 6), whose anaphoric use may easily develop into an interclausal connective function.

Table 54.2 shows a list of frequent diachronic sources for disjunctive connectives. Distal elements meaning 'that, other' may acquire a disjunctive meaning (item 1) by virtue of the inherent duality and exclusivity that characterizes both the notion of alternative and the notion of 'otherness'.

Items 2–6 all instantiate a further inherent semantic property of disjunction: the irrealis potential status of the two alternatives, which cannot be presented as facts, but need to be overtly indicated as *possibilities* (see Mauri 2008a). The following diachronic sources mirror the potential nature characterizing the notion of alternative and belong to the so-called 'irrealis realm' (see Elliott 2000). Interrogative markers (2) typically develop into disjunctive connectives in contexts where the speaker asks for a choice between two equivalent possibilities, i.e. in questions. Free choice constructions (3), on the other hand, grammaticalize as connectives in declarative sentences, where each alternative is overtly stated as a possible choice for the hearer. Dubitative epistemic markers (4) and conditional constructions (6) encode the speaker's doubt on the actual occurrence of the two alternatives, which cannot be certain until a choice is made. Finally, negative markers (5) develop into disjunctive connectives in contexts where one of the two alternatives is overtly denied in order for the second one to be proposed.

Diachronic sources for adversative connectives are exemplified in Table 54.3. While disjunctive connectives link potential (non-co-occurring) alternatives, both conjunctive and adversative connectives denote co-occurring events. This may explain why languages with a restricted set of connectives often employ the same strategy both for combination and contrast relations (cf. !Xun, Northern Khoisan, *te*)[1] and why conjunctive and adversative connectives frequently share the same diachronic sources. For instance, spatio-temporal meanings may grammaticalize into both conjunctive and adversative connectives through metaphorical processes of increasing abstraction (compare Table 54.1, path 1 to Table 54.3,

[1] We would like to thank the editors of this volume for bringing this case to our attention.

paths 1–3). Spatial sources (Table 54.3, item 1) may denote a wide set of relations, ranging from closeness to distance, and the adversative meaning arises when the differences existing between the linked clauses are foregrounded, at the expenses of their respective spatial location. A similar mechanism is at work for diachronic sources denoting temporal values, such as the relation of simultaneity 'while' (2) and the meaning of continuity 'always' (3). In both cases, the coexistence over time of two events comes to be perceived as surprising, as a consequence of the fact that the antonymic differences existing between the two events are foregrounded at the expense of their temporal relation.

Further diachronic sources for adversative connectives are, somehow unexpectedly, causal ones (4), the reanalysis of which typically occurs in negative contexts. As pointed out by Giacalone Ramat and Mauri (2008), the denial of an expected causal sequence ('not for that') may be easily reanalysed as a construction overtly encoding the (counter-expectative) contrast deriving from such denied expectation. The grammaticalization of comparative markers into adversative ones is exemplified in (5). This path is motivated by the inherent asymmetry that characterizes both contrast and comparison, at the logical and at the informational level. Finally, adversative connectives may also derive from strategies expressing an emphatic reinforcement of the second clause, on which a special focus is given as opposed to the preceding one (6).[2]

3.2. The grammaticalization of coordinating connectives under the lens of traditional parameters

The grammaticalization of coordinating connectives shows some recurrent properties, which may be described with reference to the parameters identified by Lehmann (1995a) for grammaticalization processes. Phonological reduction and univerbation are often attested in the first stages of the diachronic paths under examination (cf. OE *be utan* > Engl. *but*). However, the opposite can also be observed, since it is not infrequent to notice processes of strengthening due to the cyclical need for expressivity that characterizes the use of connectives (Meillet 1958: 161; cf. also Italian *o pure* 'or also' > *oppure* 'or').

[2] Adversative connectives share with concessive connectives the ability to encode a contrast between two clauses, and this might lead one to hypothesize that these two types of connectives may derive from similar diachronic sources, although the former encode a coordination relation while the latter a subordination relation. However, the comparison of our data with the diachronic sources of concessive connectives discussed by König (1988) reveals several differences, which cannot be examined here in detail for questions of space. Briefly, the diachronic paths attested for adversative and concessive connectives partially overlap as far as originally temporal values are concerned, but tend to diverge in the remaining cases.

Among the criteria identified by Lehmann (1995a), there are three that prove problematic in the description of the development of interclausal connectives: namely obligatorification, paradigmaticization, and scope reduction. The problems in applying these criteria can be explained by the function and morphosyntactic properties that are typical of interclausal connectives as such.

Being clause linkers, coordinating connectives typically show a wide scope over the two linked clauses; therefore a scope reduction would be inconsistent, if not incompatible, with their syntactic function (cf. Traugott 2003: 643). Secondly, unless the connective itself takes part in an inflectional paradigm (as in e.g. Japanese *-te* 'and', Korean *-ko* 'and', *-kena* 'or', in which the connectives are verbal suffixes), coordinating connectives need not be obligatory in the same way as inflectional morphemes are, as witnessed by the alternation between syndesis and asyndesis even in languages having a well developed system of connectives. Along the same line, connectives need not take part in a paradigm as, say, number or gender inflections do, because, although they constitute a closed set, different connectives may happen to co-occur and are not necessarily mutually exclusive (see section 1).[3] For these reasons, obligatorification, paradigmaticization, and scope reduction cannot be taken as indicators of the degree of grammaticalization of interclausal connectives.

Furthermore, the grammaticalization of coordinating connectives is characterized by an increase in abstraction, developing relational, grammatical meanings from adverbs, verbs, nouns, prepositional phrases, and particles with more concrete reference. In the case of adversative connectives, this process of abstraction is typically associated with an increase in subjectivity (see Hopper and Traugott 2003), involving a shift from objective functions to functions based in the speaker's attitude to what is said.

3.3. Factors at play and gradualness in morphosyntactic and semantic change

The recurrent paths presented so far share common factors which are significant for the grammaticalization process. Together with widely accepted hypotheses on the subject, we will also discuss some theoretical considerations based on a corpus study on the grammaticalization of adversative connectives in Italian (see Mauri and Giacalone Ramat in press, 2009 on the development of *mentre*, *tuttavia*, and

[3] In languages where the interclausal connective belongs to an inflectional system (e.g. languages expressing interclausal coordination by means of converbs, serial verb constructions and switch-reference strategies: see Haspelmath 2004a), the connective can be argued to be both obligatory and part of a paradigm. As far as its scope is concerned, on the other hand, although in such cases the connective is inflectional in nature, its scope remains necessarily interclausal.

però, based on texts from the 13th to the 20th centuries). Although the analysis was restricted to a few Italian connectives, the model elaborated seems suitable and generalizable for understanding the diachronic paths under examination.

As pointed out by Heine (2002) and Diewald (2002), the different contexts in which a form is attested play a crucial role in grammaticalization processes, to the point that it is possible to analyse the successive stages along which the diachronic change occurs based on the analysis of the types of contexts. The grammaticalization of connectives typically starts in contexts that are semantically and syntactically ambiguous between the original meaning and the connective role, i.e. 'critical' contexts according to Diewald's terminology. In such contexts speakers activate pragmatic inferences concerning the presence of an interclausal relation of combination, contrast, or alternative, without specifically reassigning a connective function to the form at issue. An instance of critical context is exemplified in (4) from Old Italian, where the complex sentence is ambiguous between two readings: (i) an asyndetic juxtaposition of two conflicting clauses, the second of which starts with the temporal adverb *tuttavia* 'always'; (ii) and a syndetic adversative construction in which *tuttavia* works as interclausal connective meaning 'nonetheless'.

(4) Palamedès pis., *c.*1300 (part 2, ch. 25; see Mauri and Giacalone Ramat in press)
[...] *chè noi mangiamo sì poveramente in questo luogo, u*
because we eat.1PL so poorly in this place where
voi mi vedete, che a grande pena ne possiamo sostenere
you me see.2PL that to great difficulty it.GEN can.1PL bear
nostra vita; né non 'sciamo giammai di qua entro
our life nor NEG go.out.1PL never from here inside
***tuttavia** ci dimoriamo sì come noi lo possiamo fare* [...]
always there dwell.1PL so as we it.ACC can.1PL do
'[...] because we eat so poorly in this place, where you see me, that with a great difficulty we manage to bear our lives; nor we go out of here; **always (nonetheless)** we dwell in this place as we can do [...]'

In (4) *tuttavia* may be reinterpreted as having scope over both the clause in which it occurs and the preceding clause, thus being ambiguous between a narrow scope (clause-internal, 'always') and wide scope (clause-external, 'always, *including the case mentioned before*') reading. In a critical context such as (4), speakers activate a conversational inference of coherence with what precedes, so that *tuttavia* is interpreted as referring not only to the clause that follows, but also anaphorically to the specific situation mentioned in the preceding one (Mauri and Giacalone Ramat in press).

The occurrence of a given form in critical contexts, however, is not a sufficient condition for the change to happen. As pointed out by Bybee (2006), it is also necessary that critical contexts significantly increase in frequency, in order for the critical construction to be processed as a single unit and for the form to be reinterpreted as having an interclausal connective function. Quantitative evidence supporting the identification of a restricted critical period, during which the frequency of critical contexts significantly increases, was found in our data: in the development of *però* 'therefore' > 'nonetheless', critical contexts increase during the 15th and 16th centuries, reaching 25 per cent of the total number of occurrences; in the development of *tuttavia* 'always' > 'nonetheless', the peak frequency of critical contexts reaches 23 per cent of the total number of occurrences during the 14th century. If critical contexts do not significantly increase, the new meaning may not become conventionalized and the form is likely to keep its original value (as happened in the case of *pertanto* 'therefore' in Italian, which was never reanalyzed as adversative despite its early occurrences in critical contexts).

The critical stage can be followed by a phase in which the old meaning and the new connective one co-exist in complementary syntactic distribution. For instance, in the case of *però*, during the 17th and 18th centuries the original resultive meaning 'therefore' systematically occurred in initial position and after *e* 'and' (5), while the new adversative meaning systematically occurred in postposed position and after a wide scope negation (6).

(5) Vincenzo Monti, Epistolario ('A Girolamo Ferri—Longiano', 9 Aug. 1774; see Mauri and Giacalone Ramat in press)

Ella	*forse*	*può*	*essere*	*a giorno*	*del*	*prezzo*	*che*	*ha*
You.POL	perhaps	may	be	updated	of.DEF	price	REL	has

al	*presente*	*questo*	*libro,*	*e*	***però***	*la*	*prego*
at	present	this	book	and	**therefore**	you.POL.ACC	pray

aver	*la*	*bontà*	*di*	*avvisarmi*
to.have	DEF	kindness	of	let.know:me

'You (POLITE) may perhaps be well informed on the price that this book has at the moment, and **therefore** I ask you to be so kind as to let me know [. . .]'

(6) Vincenzo Monti, Epistolario, ('All'ab. [Cesare Monti]—[Fusignano]', 15 Sept. 1790; see Mauri and Giacalone Ramat in press)

Non	*sono*	*solito*	*di*	*scrivervi*	*mai*	*le*	*nuove*	*di*
NEG	be.1SG	used	of	write:2PL.DAT	never	DEF	news	of

Roma;	*questa*	*volta*	***però***	*ve*	*ne*	*voglio*	*dare*
Rome	this	time	**however**	2PL.DAT	3.GEN	want.1SG	give

una	*che*	*non*	*è*	*piccola [. . .]*
one	REL	NEG	is	small

'I'm not used to writing to you news from Rome; this time **however** I want to tell you one that is not little [. . .]'

During the stage of syntactic and semantic specialization, the form occurs in what Diewald calls isolating contexts, namely contexts that are incompatible with the original meaning, as in (6), where the resultative interpretation of *però* is excluded. Such contexts reveal that the form–function reanalysis through which the connective function has been conventionalized has taken place. The stage of syntactic specialization may not occur if the diachronic source already shows the morphosyntactic properties of the target function, i.e. if the source is already an interclausal connective and simply undergoes a semantic shift (e.g. *mentre* in Italian, which develops its adversative function from an original simultaneity one).

Finally, the new value may extend to all the morphosyntactic contexts, including those that were associated to the original meaning during the stage of syntactic specialization. Such an extension usually entails the gradual disappearance of the source function, as in the development of *però* and *tuttavia*, although layering situations are also possible. A condition of layering, i.e. coexistence of old and new meanings, is attested in such cases as Italian *mentre*, English *while*, and Russian *i* ('too' and 'and', Zeevat and Jasinskaja 2007: 324–5).

The factors at play in the successive stages of the paths just described, namely pragmatic inferences activated by the context, frequency, and specific syntactic distributions, are mirrored at the synchronic level in an intra-linguistic gradience, which is itself a crucial prerequisite for the gradualness of change in grammaticalization processes.

CHAPTER 55

THE GRAMMATICALIZATION OF FINAL PARTICLES

SANDRA A. THOMPSON
RYOKO SUZUKI

1. Introduction

In this chapter on the grammaticalization of final particles, we consider several attested pathways by which final particles arise, bringing data from case studies in Japanese and English. We restrict our investigation to contemporary synchronic data rather than historical data, and we focus on the crucial interactional and prosodic factors involved in the emergence of final particles.

Our working characterization of 'final particle' is:

> a final particle is a discourse marker that occurs at the end of an interactional unit, whether a turn, a turn unit, or a prosodic unit, and indexes certain pragmatic stances... (Mulder and Thompson 2008: 183)

Final particles are common in conversation in many genealogically unrelated languages; some languages, such as Japanese, the Sinitic languages, and Thai, are well known for their rich use of final particles. But they are also abundant in many other languages, including Finnish and the Germanic languages German, Dutch, and English, for example.

In this chapter we will survey three very different pathways in the 'final particleization' process. This will be followed by a brief discussion of the factors involved in the development of final particles.

2. Case studies

2.1. English final particles *but* and *though*

The frequent occurrence of English connectives such as *and, but, because, so,* and *or* which occur at the beginning of a prosodic unit is well known. The term 'syntactic conjunctionals' was introduced by Jefferson (1980) to include these words when they occur at the end of a conversational turn.

Mulder and Thompson (2008) and Mulder, Thompson, and Williams (2009) investigate the grammar, prosody, and sequential organization of *but* in turn-final position, as illustrated from an American English conversation:

(1) SBC0008 ('Tell the Jury that') 1303.52–1309.90[1],[2]

1 RICKIE: I don't think he would do anythi=ng,
2 ... when people are around.
3 REBECCA: [right].
4 RICKIE: [you know],
5 down at the other seat [or <X in] back X>,
6 REBECCA: [right].
7 RICKIE: I could scream **but**,
8 .. (H)
9 REBECCA: yeah.

[1] The American English data cited here come from the Corpus of Spoken American English (John W. Du Bois et al., 2000–2005. Santa Barbara Corpus of Spoken American English, Parts 1–4. Philadelphia: Linguistic Data Consortium. http://www.ldc.upenn.edu).

[2] For our spoken examples, we follow the transcription system described in Du Bois et al. (1993). Noteworthy conventions include these: each numbered line one intonation unit; = lengthening; .. / ... very brief pause/audible pause; [ ] overlapped speech; <VOX ... VOX> marked voice quality; <F> louder than surrounding talk (*forte*); <P> softer than surrounding talk (*piano*); <X> uncertain hearing; (H) inhalation; (Hx) exhalation; @ laughter; - / -- truncated syllable / truncated intonation unit; % glottal stop.

Mulder and Thompson show that in their American English data, this turn-final *but* carries an unstated contrasting implication, what we call a 'hanging implication'. Here Rickie's arrowed turn ending with *but* implies that, while she could have screamed, it wouldn't have done any good. Prosodically this turn is treated as indeterminate as to its completion, but evidence that Rickie has finished her turn can be seen in the fact that it is followed by a pause (..) and an inhalation ((H)) at line 8. Evidence that Rebecca also takes Rickie's turn as having come to completion is her *yeah*, indicating her affiliation with Rickie's implication that screaming wouldn't have done any good.

Mulder and Thompson suggest that in comparing synchronic conversational data from the United States and Australia, a cline of 'turn-finality' emerges, as shown in Table 55.1. That is, prosodic-unit-initial *but* occurs at the beginning of a prosodic unit (as in both occurrences of *but* in (2)), 'Janus-faced' *but* occurs at the end of a prosodic unit but the speaker continues ((3)), and turn-final *but* ends a turn (as in (1) above).

(2) Another radio [SBC0006 ('Cuz') 55.43–59.23]
1 ALINA: so he got another radi[o this] summer,
2 LENORE: [(H)=]
3 ALINA: **but** of course that got ripped off also.
4 <VOX **but** never mind VOX>.

(3) Switcharound [SBC0014 ('Bank Products') 1192.84–1208.05]
1 JIM: .. we would charge (H) % .. five-hundred fifty dollars on ac- on an account,
2 it would be five-hundred dollars,
3 it's really kind of a switch around **but**.
4 (H) what .. what that would--
5 .. I think it would be good for (H) .. the five or six of us,
6 (H) to have Galino down here,

Table 55.1. A cline of 'turn-finality'

initial *but*	>Janus-faced *but* >	final *but*
[prosodic-unit-initial *connective*]		[turn-final *final particle*]
least final ——————————————→		most final

Mulder and Thompson note that in their American conversational data, turn-final *but* seems to always carry an implication left 'hanging', as in (1). In their Australian data, however, there is abundant evidence that *but* has progressed 'all the way' to becoming a final particle with no hanging implication, as shown in (4) and (5).

(4) Opals [S1A-067:217–223][3]

Patricia, Jess, and another female speaker are looking at photos and opals from Jess's recent visit to an opal-mining area.

1 JESS: but,
2 if you ever go there,
3 it's good like,
4 you don't stay there for too long **but**.
5 PATRICIA: so [you] --
6 JESS: [<F> we on]ly stayed <F> there for three days.
7 PATRICIA: you haven't got any other photos.

In lines 1–4 of (4), Jess is reporting that the opal-mining area they went to is worth a visit, even though one wouldn't want to stay there for too long.

(5) Pounding Things [S1A-031:21–25]

Four tennis players are discussing how various players respond when they get upset on the court.

1 ANDREW: I think [Lenore] gets a bit agro,[4]
2 JILL: [yeah].
3 REBECCA: does she?
4 SHARON: <P> Leah <P>,
5 REBECCA: Lenore? oh yea:h,
6 ANDREW: not,
7 you know,
8 this pounding [thing] like we do **but**.
9 SHARON: [yeah].

In line 1 of (5), Andrew identifies Lenore as one tennis player who gets 'a bit aggravated' on the court. Then in lines 6–8, he qualifies this statement by conceding that when she gets upset she doesn't pound on things like 'we' do, though.

In other words, what differentiates the American final *but* from the Australian final *but* is that in Australian English *but* has fully developed as a final particle,

[3] Our Australian data come from the conversational part of the Australian component of the International Corpus of English (ICE-AUS) <http://www.ucl.ac.uk/english-usage/ice/iceaus.htm>.

[4] *Agro* in Australian English = 'aggravated'.

Table 55.2. Connective to final particle (Pathway 1)

prosodic-unit-initial connective	>>>	final particle with hanging implication	>>>	final particle with no hanging implication, and only retrospective contrastive meaning

parallel to the development of *though* (Barth-Weingarten and Couper-Kuhlen 2002). While both American English and Australian English have Final Hanging *but*, only Australian English has Final Particle *but*. That is, in both (4) and (5) from our Australian data, final *but* has progressed far enough to be considered a 'true' final particle. Not only is it uttered with final prosody, but instead of leaving an implication 'hanging', the semantically contrastive material is supplied in the intonation unit ending with the final *but* particle, supporting the claim that in Australian English *but* has become a fully developed final particle marking contrastive content.

We can speculate that American English will also begin to show uses of final particle *but* with no hanging implication in the near future. We can also speculate that other connectives currently used with hanging implications may also be starting to be used as fully-fledged final particles with no hanging implication, such as *so*, *and*, *because*, and *or*.

What Mulder and Thompson and Barth-Weingarten and Couper-Kuhlen show for the development of both *but* and *though* from an intonation-unit-initial connective to a final particle to a final particle with only retrospective contrastive meaning, then, instantiates one pathway giving rise to final particles.

In the next section we will outline two other pathways by which final particles can emerge with the stories of Japanese *kara* and *tte*.

2.2. Japanese *kara* and *tte*

2.2.1. *Kara*

Kara is known as a causal connective particle, often translated into English as 'because'. In Japanese grammar books, and also in spoken data, the most frequent linguistic context involving *kara* is [Clause *kara*, 'Main Clause'].[5] In stark contrast to English, in Japanese (as in many other languages with predicates occurring at the

[5] We are using the term 'main clause' in single quotes here simply to identify the clause (a) which follows the *kara*-clause in this constructional schema and (b) for which the *kara*-clause provides a reason. We remain agnostic as to any distinction between 'main' and 'subordinate' status for these clauses.

end of clauses and turns) (Tanaka 1999), connectives also occur clause- and turn-finally, as shown in (6):

(6) Zeitaku ('Luxurious life')[6]

1	K:	*maa,* well	K: well,
2		*ima saisho da* ***kara,*** now beginning COP KARA	because it's the beginning (of the semester),
3		*yooryoo wakannai shi=,* efficiency know:NEG and	(I) don't know how to coordinate well,
4	M:	*n=,*	M: mm,
5		*maa nee.*	(I) see.

Speaker K produces a *kara*-clause (line 2), providing the reason for the state of affairs described in the following 'main clause' (line 3).

In conversation, we also find a *kara*-marked clause providing a reason for a state of affairs after the speaker presents this state of affairs (e.g. Higashiizumi 2006; Mori 1999a; 1999b), as in (7):

(7) Broccoli

1	A:	*kore,*	A: won't this (book) be
2		*waribiki ni naran no ka na=.*	on discount (I wonder)?
3	B:	*... naranai desho.* be:NEG COP:PRESUMPTIVE	B: it will not (I guess).
4		*kaitenai nda* ***kara.*** write:NEG NMZ:COP KARA	because it is not written, so.
5		*... muri yuccha ikan.*	(you) should not say (such) an impossible thing.

Notice that speaker B's assertion in line 3 is followed by her statement of justification in line 4. Mori (1999a: 176–8), in her analysis of *kara*, observes that placement of causal clauses after an assertion is remarkably frequent, and further states that *kara*-clauses do not always occur immediately adjacent to the initial assertion: the production of a *kara*-clause is locally managed in response to recipients' feedback, so several pieces of talk can occur between the assertion and the *kara*-clause.

[6] Japanese data come from the collections of audio conversations called JPN/PacRim corpus, which include approximately 5 hours worth of about 30 conversations. We thank Tsuyoshi Ono for making the data available. The rough translations of utterances (which are not necessarily line-by-line translations) are shown in the right column. Due to space limitations, the morpheme-by-morpheme glosses are added only for the lines that are directly relevant to our discussion. The abbreviations we use are these: CNT continuative; COP copula; NEG negative; NMZ nominalizer; NOM nominative; PASS passive; PRT particle; PST past; Q question; STAT stative; TOP topic.

We have seen that the clause-final particle *kara* can indicate either forward linkage, as in (6), or backward linkage, as in (7). Prosodically, and not surprisingly, *kara* with forward linkage is frequently associated with continuing intonation, as indicated by the comma (line 2 in (6)), while *kara* with backward linkage tends to be pronounced with final intonation, indicated by a period (line 4 of (7)).

In conversation, there are also a fair number of instances of *kara*-clauses which occur without any 'main clause' associated with them in terms of either grammar or content. In extract (8), for example, W (wife) and S (husband), both academics, are discussing female researchers trying to balance house chores (such as cooking) and time to spend on their own research. Earlier in the conversation, W wonders if one's (her) research creativity is used up by cooking day after day:

(8) Kurieitibitii ('Creativity')

1	W:	*... atashi yappari,*	W:	am I trying to
2		*yokubari na no ka na=.*		do too much (I wonder)?
3		*... soko made mo,*		(I) don't get to that point (i.e. like some
4		*naranain da yo ne.*		women academics who give up cooking for their family in order to do their own research)
5	S:	... (Hx) ... *maa dakara,*	S:	well, so,
6		*ryoohoo dekin no wa sa,*		if (one) can do both,
7		*ichiban,*		that would be
8		*ii kedo sa* [=].		the best but.
9	W:	[*n*]=.	W:	yeah.
10	S:	.. *yappari sorya,*	S:	well,
11		... *kyapashitii tteiu no ga,* capacity called NMZ NOM		there is a limit (to how much one can
12		*aru* ***kara*** *ne=.* exist KARA PRT		handle) so ...
13	W:	.. *de ne=,*	W:	and
14		*ryoohoo dekite,*		(people) might think
15		*toozen da=,*		(women) are supposed to handle
16		*mitaini,*		both (i.e. family chores and research)
17		*omou no ka mo shirenai kedo sa=.*		naturally but.

In line 12, S produces a *kara* clause, where *kara* is combined with an alignment-seeking final particle *ne* (lengthened), which occurs with final intonation. There is no explicit corresponding 'main clause', but there is a 'hanging implication' that it is difficult to do both house chores and research. Both the pause and W's taking the next turn are indications that W treats S's previous turn as being complete. W goes on further to present the commonly held view that women should be able to handle both chores and research, a view which contrasts with the hanging implication. Prosodic and pragmatic characteristics, then, together with the absence of an explicit 'main clause', can be viewed as an indication of *kara* moving from a connective particle and towards becoming a final particle.[7]

Another example of an 'independent' *kara*-clause is given in (9), which is the concluding sentence in a blog, addressed to the blogger's niece and nephew who had refused to travel to Alaska with her. Just as in (8), *kara* in (9) is also followed by a final particle *ne* and a period, indicating prosodic finality. Syntactically, there is no 'main clause' following this *kara*-clause since this is the final sentence in the blog. Furthermore, the fact that the *kara*-clause is preceded by a concessive clause marked by *temo* 'although' (becoming *demo* after a nasal) makes this *kara*-clause itself a 'main clause', reflecting a common utterance-final use of *kara*: to convey the social action of warning. The fact that *kara* is here joined by the final particle *ne* to form the final-particle complex *kara ne* provides further support for our claim that the connective *kara* has grammaticized as a final particle:

(9) A blog (http://chirohamu.exblog.jp/11625564/)

atode	*donnani*	*kuyandemo*	*shiranai*	***kara***	*ne.*
later	how.much	regret:though	know:NEG	KARA	PRT

'No matter how much you regret later, I won't care (about you guys).'

In addition to warnings, we see a range of pragmatic functions of independent *kara*-clauses. In our conversational data for example, we find a speaker also using an independent *kara*-clauses in the context of complaining. Ohori (1995: 210–11) provides a constructed example of an independent *kara*-clause used to give an excuse for refusing an invitation.

What we've seen, then, are three examples illustrating a pathway for *kara*'s grammaticization: extract (7) shows a 'post-main' *kara*-clause; extract (8) shows a *kara*-clause with no explicit 'main clause', but a 'hanging implication' (as with English *but*, illustrated in (1)); and in extract (9), we see an instance of a *kara*-clause with neither an explicit 'main clause' nor a clear 'hanging implication'. Rather, the *kara*-clause itself functions as an independent clause expressing an assertion/warning. Its prosodic ('punctuational' in the case of (9)) and pragmatic characteristics, its affinity with final particles, as well as its syntactic independence, point to the fact that *kara* is turning into a final particle (Higashiizumi 2006).

In our conversational data, final *kara* is more frequently pronounced with final intonation than continuing intonation, and we also see long-established final

[7] Lines 8 and 17 show a clause marked by *kedo*, another connective particle indicating contrast, typically translated as 'but, although'. Some scholars suggest that *kedo* is also becoming a final particle (e.g. Nakayama and Ichihashi-Nakayama 1997; Mori 1999b; and Ohori 1995).

Table 55.3. Connective particle to final particle (Pathway 2)

clause-final connective >>>	clause-final connective >>>	turn-final particle
• pre-'main clause'	• post-'main clause'	• post-independent clause (with possible hanging implications)
• continuing prosody	• final prosody	• final prosody
		• *kara* commonly combined with other final particles

particles commonly occurring after them, e.g. *kara ne* and its lengthened version *kara ne=*. We take these two facts to further support our argument that *kara* is well on its way to being a final particle.

Table 55.3 summarizes the pathway of *kara* shifting from a connective particle to a final particle.

2.2.2. *Tte*

Okamoto (1995) observes that the complementizers *koto, no, to, tte* also function as 'sentence-final particles' with 'pragmatic force'. This subsection focuses on the way *tte*, a casual-style quotative complementizer (cf. the more formal *to*), is becoming a final particle in naturally occurring conversations.

In textbooks, and very commonly in conversations, the quotative *tte* follows reported speech, and precedes the verb of saying (and, less frequently, verbs of thinking and writing). Example (10) below illustrates this use. Speaker U recounts a dialogue between his physical education teacher and himself back in his high-school days. Focusing on the *tte* in lines 3–6, we see that the teacher's utterance (*juudoo ni hairu ki wa nai ka* 'Don't (you) want to join the judo team?') precedes the quotative *tte*, and the passive past tense form of the verb *iu* 'say' (*iwareta*) immediately follows *tte*:

(10) Bukatsu ('Club activity')

1	U: *ikinari sa,*	U: all of a sudden,
2	M: .. *un.*	M: uh-huh.
3	U: . . . *juudoo ni,* judo.team to	U: 'aren't (you)
4	*hairu ki wa,* join interest TOP	interested in joining
5	*nai ka,* NEG Q	the Judo team?'
6	*tte iwareta* <X *wake* X>. TTE say:PASS:PST PRT	(I) was asked (by the teacher).

In our data, there are other tokens of *tte* occurring at the end of a clausal intonation unit, but their functions are not to index reported speech. Example (11) is one such case of *tte*, functioning as a final particle and indicating an insistent attitude by the speaker:

(11) Surprise (K is discussing a surprise party for Satoko and describing how to handle the phone call to Marvin's and Satoko's house)

1	K:	<Q *Maabin kore wa ne,*	K:	'hey Marvin,
2		(HH) *eto,*		uh,
3		*satoko ni,*		we are calling (you),
4		(HH) *iwanai de,*		without telling
5		(HH) *keikaku shiteru nda kedo* Q>,		Satoko',
6		*tte ieba ii ja nai.*		why don't we tell (him) that.
7		*nan=kai ka,* several.times or		if we try several times,
8		*kaketeru aidani,* call:CNT:STAT while		there will be a chance (that he'll answer and we can tell him that), for sure, you see.
9		*zettai chansu ga aru* ***tte.*** definitely chance NOM exist TTE		
10	M:	(HH) *nan=kai ka ttatte,*	M:	even though (you say we could call)
11		*kake- --*		'several times', (we) don't actually
12		*kakeru yoo de,*		call them as often
13		<H *kakenai deshoo* H>,		as we think we do
14		*nakanaka=.*		(you know).

In line 9, we find a *tte* which is different from quotative *tte* discussed above (or in line 6 of this excerpt), since what precedes *tte* (i.e. *nankai ka kaketeru aida ni zettai chansu ga aru* 'if we try several times, there will be a chance (that he'll answer and we can tell him that)') is not reported speech but K's opinion. We argue that utterance-final *tte* here functions as a final particle of insistence, further endorsing K's opinion, and not as a quotative marker. The fact that M presents her reservation in the subsequent turn supports our claim that K's previous turn is formulated and treated as an opinion.

The next example shows the use of *tte* in utterance-final position in a joking context. It comes from the same conversation as (11), in which M and K are planning a surprise party for Satoko in San Francisco by driving there.

(12) Surprise

1	M:	*moo ikkai itta kara,* already once go:PST KARA	M:Since (I) drove (all the way to San Francisco) once already,
2		*doraibu niwa* driving for:TOP *jishin mo tsuiteru @shi tte?* confidence also have:CNT:STAT PRT TTE	(I) have confidence in my driving, (just kidding).[8]
3		[@@@]	<laughter>
4	K:	[*abunai @na=*].	K: how scary.
5		(HH) *datte masako,*	because Masako, (you) undergo a
6		(HH) *san furanshisuko ni hairu to,*	personality change as you drive into
7		*seikaku kawaru n da mon.*	San Francisco.

As noted in R. Suzuki (2007: 230), in line 2, speaker M first presents her positive evaluation of her own driving skills. By attaching *tte* at the end, with rising intonation and laughter, M transforms her comment, making it as if it were uttered by someone else, and hence detaches herself from her own statement that she has confidence in her driving. M's self-detachment, accomplished by utterance-final *tte* and laughter, is quickly aligned to by K in line 4 through an overlap in laughing voice quality and a negative assessment of M's driving skills. We can see, therefore, that M produces her statement as a joke, and it is treated by K as a joke. This 'joking *tte*' occurs utterance-finally with a rising intonation contour distinct from the 'insisting *tte*', which has a low pitch. We suggest that the tokens of *tte* exemplified in (11) and (12) are functioning, not as quotative complementizer, but as final particles, and that their prosody correlates with their pragmatic effect.

Like *kara*, *tte* also attracts other morpheme(s) and forms final-particle complexes. For example, R. Suzuki (1999; 2007) argues that the sequence of *n* + *da* + *tte* (nominalizer *no* plus the copula *da* plus *tte*) functions as a unitary hearsay marker. S. Suzuki (1999) discusses another combination of utterance-final *da* + *tte* (copula *da* plus *tte*), which she characterizes as a marker showing that a speaker views the just-heard utterance as unanticipated or unexpected.

These examples show that even though the earlier, and still the most frequent, function of *tte* is that of a quotative complementizer, as in (10), we also find *tte* doing other types of pragmatic work utterance-finally. Final *tte* and its derived particle complexes enable speakers to treat the preceding *tte*-final utterance as

[8] The translation 'just kidding' is intended here to convey the feel of this jokingly produced utterance, in which *tte* plays a role together with prosody in this context.

Table 55.4. Complementizer to final particle (Pathway 3)

quotative complementizer	>>>	turn-final particle
• pre-'main verb/clause' (e.g. *iu* 'to say)		• post-independent clause
• continuing prosody		• distinct prosody

Table 55.5. Three pathways to 'final particle-ization'

English	*but*	[prosodic-unit-initial connective >> final particle]
Japanese	*kara*	[prosodic-unit-final connective >> final particle]
Japanese	*tte*	[complementizer >> final particle]

something that s/he wants the recipient to agree with (insistence), to laugh at (joking), as something not directly accessible to the recipient (hearsay), or as something unanticipated. Each of these uses has its own distinct morphological and prosodic shape, suggesting that each use of final *tte* has started a life of its own. Broadly speaking, we suggest that *tte* seems to be further down the path toward 'final particle-ization' than *kara*.

In this section, then, we have discussed another pathway taken by present-day final particles, as shown in Table 55.4.

3. Summary of Pathways to Final Particle-hood

We have illustrated three different pathways by which grammatical or lexical forms can become final particles, as schematized in Table 55.5.

4. Discussion and Conclusion

Arguing from Japanese and English conversational data, we have outlined three attested pathways by which final particles can develop. Our discussion has shown that at least four factors must be taken into consideration in our endeavour to understand the grammaticization of these fascinating and highly interactional forms:

- Language typology:
  The much-discussed word-order differences between Japanese and English allow us to see how both clause-initial (in English) and clause-final (in Japanese) morphemes can become final particles.
- Lexical categories:
  Final particles can develop from connectives and complementizers.[9]
- Prosody:
  The prosody of the turn-unit in which the item occurs and of the item itself is critical to determining its function.
- Sequential and interactional factors:
  The organization of the interactional sequences in which the forms are used plays a major role in the way they contribute to meaning-making.

[9] Indeed, much research (e.g., Ohori 1995; Okamoto 1995; R. Suzuki 1999) has shown that there is an even richer array of pathways leading to final particles than we are able to show here; R. Suzuki 1999, for example, provides evidence for low-content nouns becoming final particles in Japanese.

PART V

THE DIFFERENT FACES OF GRAMMATICALIZATION ACROSS LANGUAGES

CHAPTER 56

GRAMMATICALIZATION IN SIGN LANGUAGES

ROLAND PFAU

MARKUS STEINBACH

1. Introduction

Sign languages (SLs) are languages in the visual-gestural modality, as opposed to spoken languages, which make use of the auditive-oral modality. The linguistic study of SLs is a comparably young research field (for Sign Language of the Netherlands (NGT) see Tervoort 1953; for ASL Stokoe 1960). It is now a well-established fact that the SLs used by the members of deaf communities are natural languages with complex grammatical structures on all levels of linguistic description (Sandler and Lillo-Martin 2006). Still, we also find interesting modality-specific properties which result from the use of different articulators, the use of the signing space for grammatical purposes, and the iconic potential afforded by the visual modality (Meier forthcoming).

Given that language change is a crucial property of all natural languages, it is not surprising that SLs also undergo diachronic changes—and that they do so for internal (Frishberg 1975) and external (Battison 1978; Schermer 2003) reasons. In this chapter, we focus on a type of internal change, namely grammaticalization. In section 2, we

For sharing their sign language expertise with us, we are indebted to Andrea Kaiser, Joni Oyserman, Pamela Perniss, Josep Quer, Wendy Sandler, Jutta Warmers, and an anonymous reviewer. Moreover, we wish to thank Bernd Heine and Tania Kuteva for invaluable feedback.

start our investigation with some comments on the methodological challenges diachronic SL research is faced with. In section 3, we describe selected grammaticalization phenomena that we take to be modality-independent. Even more interesting are, of course, modality-specific instances of grammaticalization; these will be addressed in section 4. Here, our focus will be on the grammaticalization of gestures.

2. Methodology: Internal Reconstruction

In the area of linguistic reconstruction, the comparative method is widely acknowledged to be the most reliable of the available methods. This option, however, is not available for languages which have no written form, as is the case with SLs. The oldest available sources for diachronic SL research are usually dictionaries or pamphlets that contain sketchy illustrations or photographs of signs. From the early 20th century on, filmed material may also be available, but this material is scarce.

In the absence of written (or filmed) records of a language, it may still be possible to make statements about its historical development. The method of linguistic reconstruction commonly used under these circumstances is internal reconstruction (IR), 'the exploitation of patterns in the synchronic grammar of a single language or dialect to recover information about its prehistory' (Ringe 2003: 244). Obviously, IR is only of limited use in historical linguistics, since diachronic changes may eliminate language structures in unrecoverable ways. Therefore, IR is generally less reliable than the standard comparative method.

With few exceptions, the data reported in this chapter were compiled by means of IR. Given (i) that the lexical and the grammatical item are phonologically similar, (ii) that grammaticalization is usually unidirectional, and (iii) that we do know about common grammaticalization paths from the study of languages for which written records do exist, we may make inferences about grammaticalization processes on the basis of synchronic data—albeit with due caution. After all, in the absence of historical data, the possibility of an anomalous development (e.g. degrammaticalization) can never be excluded. We must therefore acknowledge the possibility that some of the data are over-interpreted.

3. From lexical to grammatical element

We will begin our investigation by discussing a number of grammaticalization pathways that parallel those described for spoken languages. Grammaticalization is known to proceed in two steps: first, from lexical element to free grammatical marker (type 1), and subsequently, from free grammatical marker to grammatical affix (type 2). We will see that most grammaticalization phenomena described to date for SLs are of the former type.

3.1. Grammaticalization of aspectual and tense markers

While verbs in SLs do not usually inflect for tense, SLs are known to have complex systems of aspectual marking. Aspectual modification is either realized by changing the movement properties of a verb stem—be it by means of stem-internal changes and/or reduplication—or by using free aspectual markers (Klima and Bellugi 1979; Rathmann 2005).

The development of aspectual markers from verbs and adverbs is probably the best-known instance of grammaticalization in SLs. For the sake of illustration, we will discuss examples from Italian Sign Language (LIS).[1] Zucchi (2003) identifies two different aspectual uses of the LIS verb FATTO ('finish/done'—as in 'Gianni finished his homework'). In (1a), this sign—now glossed as FATTO-1—is used as a marker of completion, locating the event within the time indicated by the time adverbial. Note that the lexical verb FATTO appears in preverbal position, while FATTO-1 follows the verb. Moreover, FATTO (FATTO-2) can also mark temporal precedence, as in (1b). In this use, Zucchi (2003) analyses it as a present perfect marker.[2]

(1) a. YESTERDAY GIANNI HOUSE BUY **FATTO-1** [LIS]
'Yesterday Gianni bought a house.'
b. YESTERDAY AT-3 GIANNI EAT **FATTO-2**
'Gianni had already eaten yesterday at 3.'

Besides being the source for aspectual markers, lexical verbs may also develop into tense markers. Janzen and Shaffer (2002: 203f.) argue that the ASL future tense marker FUTURE has developed from the verb sign GO-TO.

(2) JOHN **FUTURE**$_{tns}$ BUY HOUSE [ASL]
'John will buy a house.'

Fig. 56.1(a) shows that GO-TO is articulated slightly above waist height, the shoulder being the primary joint involved in the movement. When used as a grammatical

[1] Similar phenomena have been described for ASL (Fischer and Gough 1972[1999]; Sexton 1999), Israeli SL (Meir 1999), and Greek SL (Sapountzaki 2005). In Israeli SL and Greek SL, however, the source of the marker is an adverb ('already') or adjective ('ready').

[2] Notation conventions: SL examples are glossed in small caps. Subscript numbers ($_1$SIGN$_3$) refer to locations in the signing space used in verbal agreement and pronominalization (see Fig. 56.2); signs glossed as INDEX are pointing signs targeting these locations. Lines above the glosses indicate the scope of a particular non-manual marker, e.g. '$\overline{hs}$' for a negative headshake.

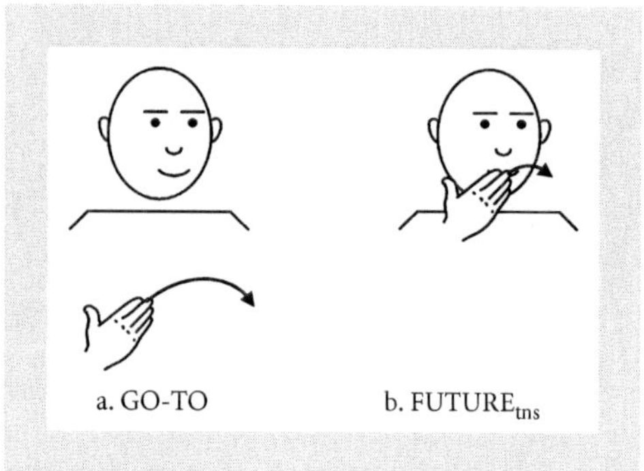

Fig. 56.1. From verb to tense marker in ASL

marker expressing future tense, as in (2) (Neidle et al. 2000: 79), the sign is phonologically reduced: it is executed with a much shorter forward movement near the cheek, the wrist being the primary joint involved (cf. Fig. 56.1(b)).

Clearly, this ASL example exemplifies a well-documented grammaticalization path, whereby a temporal term is derived metaphorically from a spatial term, such as a movement verb (Bybee, Perkins, and Pagliuca 1994).

3.2. Grammaticalization of complementizers

Nouns and verbs are common sources for the grammaticalization of complementizers. The Noun-to-Comp chain, for instance, is attested in German Sign Language (DGS), where the noun REASON has developed into a complementizer introducing adverbial clauses (3). This grammaticalization process probably involves structural reanalysis of a multi-clausal structure, such as 'I am sad. The reason is: my dog died.' Note, however, that there is no prosodic break between REASON and the following sign in (3). Moreover, the inherent repetition present in the lexical sign tends to be omitted in the grammaticalized form, i.e. the sign is phonologically reduced.

(3) INDEX$_1$ SAD **REASON** POSS$_1$ DOG DIE [DGS]
'I'm sad because my dog died.'

The Verb-to-Comp chain can be illustrated by an example from ASL. Fischer and Lillo-Martin (1990) argue that the ASL verb UNDERSTAND is the source of a complementizer introducing adverbial clauses and roughly meaning 'provided that'.

3.3. Grammaticalization of agreement auxiliaries

For a number of genetically unrelated SLs, the development of a special type of auxiliary has been described. These auxiliaries differ from spoken language auxiliaries in two respects. First, they are introduced to express subject and object agreement, whereas the main function of spoken language auxiliaries is to express tense, aspect, and modality (Steele 1978). Second, while spoken language auxiliaries usually develop from verbs (Heine 1993), the SL auxiliaries are grammaticalized from a wider variety of sources: verbs, nouns, and pronouns. In this section, we focus on agreement auxiliaries which developed from lexical sources; auxiliaries that developed from pronouns will be discussed in section 4.1.

Agreement in SLs is locus agreement (Meir 2002; Sandler and Lillo-Martin 2006). Many SLs have verbs that can be modulated such that the beginning and end point of the movement trajectory coincide with the location of the subject and object, respectively. These locations are either the locations of referents present in the discourse (e.g. the signer and the addressee) or locations that were previously established for non-present referents in the signing space in front of the signer (cf. Fig. 56.2). The verb GIVE could, for instance, move from location 2 towards location 1, thereby expressing the meaning 'you(SG) give to me'.

For the most part, agreement auxiliaries find use with verbs that cannot be modulated to express agreement (plain verbs). For Taiwan Sign Language (TSL), Smith (1990) describes two auxiliaries that developed from verbs. One of the two is similar in form to the verb SEE, the other one is derived from the verb MEET (see Fig. 56.3(a)). Example (4) illustrates the use of the latter auxiliary, which Smith glosses as AUX-11 (Smith 1990: 222). In this example, the dominant hand moves from location 1 towards the non-dominant hand, which is held stationary at location 3. Clearly, the auxiliary is void of the semantic content of the source verb.

(4) $\overline{\text{THAT VEGETABLE,}}^{\text{top}}$ INDEX$_1$ $_1$**AUX-11**$_3$ NOT-LIKE [TSL]
'I don't like that dish.'

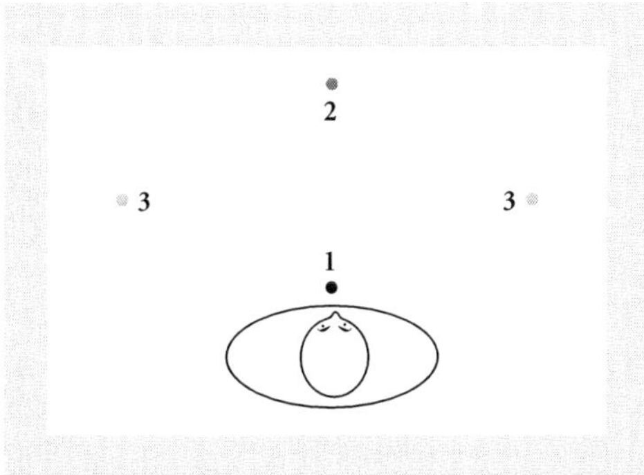

Fig. 56.2. Localization of referents in signing space

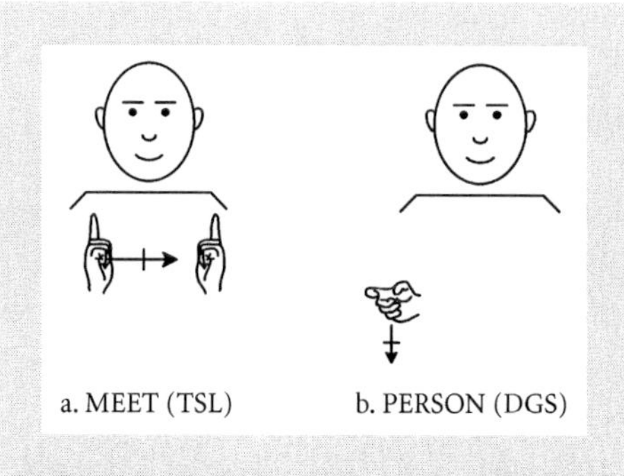

Fig. 56.3. Sources for auxiliaries in TSL (a) and DGS (b)

According to Sapountzaki (2005), Greek Sign Language (GSL) has an agreement auxiliary which developed from the lexical verb GIVE and functions as a marker of a causative change of state.[3]

As opposed to TSL and GSL, in DGS the source for the auxiliary is not a verb but rather the noun PERSON (Fig. 56.3(b)). Example (5) illustrates the auxiliary use of this sign, which, following Rathmann (2000), we gloss as PAM (*Person Agreement Marker*). PAM combines with the plain verb LIKE and again realizes agreement by means of path movement from the location introduced for MOTHER towards the location of the addressee.

(5) MOTHER INDEX_3 INDEX_2 LIKE $_3\text{PAM}_2$ [DGS]
'(My) mother likes you.'

It is noteworthy that cross-linguistically, the N-to-Aux chain attested in DGS is highly unusual if not nonexistent. Kuteva (2001: 22) states that 'all lexical sources for auxiliary verb constructions involve verb meanings which are relatively concrete and basic to human experience'. In the light of this generalization, the N-to-Aux chain attested in DGS constitutes a highly remarkable pattern.[4]

3.4. Type 2 grammaticalization

All the phenomena discussed so far involve the grammaticalization of free grammatical morphemes from lexical elements, i.e. type-1 grammaticalization. In SLs, the development of affixes from free morphemes appears to be rare. As a matter of

[3] For spoken languages, Heine (1993) identifies a number of event schemas that are common sources for auxiliaries grammaticalized from verbs. The TSL auxiliary AUX-11 belongs to the Motion Schema, while the GSL auxiliary GIVE-AUX can be subsumed under the Action Schema.

[4] Auxiliaries that developed from lexical sources are also attested in Catalan SL and NGT (Bos 1994). See Steinbach and Pfau (2007) for a detailed discussion and comparison of agreement auxiliaries. For a detailed description of further grammaticalization phenomena, we refer the reader to Pfau and Steinbach (2006) and references cited therein.

fact, affixational (sequential) morphology is uncommon in SLs in general. Aronoff, Meir, and Sandler (2005) attribute the paucity of affixation to two factors: the youth of SLs and the fact that SLs exploit other, modality-specific means for the morphological modification of signs. Since the phonological primitives of signs—handshapes, movements, locations, and non-manual elements—may all function as morphemes, various stem-internal changes may apply simultaneously to a single sign.

Still, some instances of sequential affixation have been reported in the literature. Aronoff et al. (2005) discuss a few ASL and Israeli SL affixes which they claim to originate from lexical signs. One of their examples is the ASL negative suffix ZERO, which attaches to verbs to express the meaning 'not at all' (e.g. SEE^ZERO). The source of this one-handed affix, which tends to fuse phonologically with the verbal stem, is the two-handed sign NOTHING, i.e. once again, we observe phonological reduction of the source.

4. The grammaticalization of gestures

Let us now turn to what we take to be the modality-specific side of grammaticalization, i.e. the grammaticalization of co-speech gestures. Wilcox (2004) distinguishes two different grammaticalization paths from gesture to sign. The first path begins with a gesture developing into a lexical element, which may then further develop into a functional element. Since the second process begins with a lexicalized gesture, this pathway does not crucially differ from grammaticalization in spoken languages. The only difference lies in the gestural origin of the lexical source. Examples include the ASL tense marker FUTURE (see section 3.1) and some ASL modal verbs such as CAN and SHOULD/MUST, which can be traced back to lexical signs that originated in gestures commonly used by non-signers (Janzen and Shaffer 2002; Wilcox 2004). By contrast, in the second path, grammaticalization proceeds directly from a gestural source to a functional element, skipping the intermediate lexicalization stage. Hence, this path crucially differs from grammaticalization in spoken language. In the following, we first consider manual gestures (sections 4.1 and 4.2). In section 4.3, we then turn to bound non-manual gestures. Some supporting evidence from young and emerging SLs is finally presented in section 4.4.

4.1. From gesture to pronoun

Cross-cultural studies suggest that pointing is a universal human behaviour attested in cultures around the world. In fact, it can be considered a foundational building block of human communication (Kita 2003). Interestingly, in SLs, pointing to locations in space can assume various grammatical functions, amongst which are locative and nominal uses.[5] In the following, we will focus on pointing signs involving the 1-handshape (index finger extended).[6]

For pointing signs in SLs, Pfau and Steinbach (2006) suggest the grammaticalization pathway in Fig. 56.4. Based on the fact that pointing to locations is concrete and therefore appears closest to its gestural root, they propose that pointing entered the grammar of SLs as a marker of location (step ①; also see section 4.4).

In spoken languages, demonstratives commonly develop from locative adverbs (Heine and Kuteva 2002). Pfau and Steinbach (2006) therefore tentatively claim that in SLs, the demonstrative use of the pointing sign also developed from its locative use (step ②). In principle, however, an alternative scenario might be suggested according to which both the locative and the demonstrative developed from the pointing gesture. In fact, subtle phonological differences notwithstanding, the locative and demonstrative use of pointing signs are not easily distinguished, as is illustrated in (6a).

(6) a. PETER DECIDE HOUSE **INDEX**$_3$ BUY [DGS]
'Peter decided to buy that house / the house over there.'

b. **INDEX**$_1$ THINK **INDEX**$_3$ TRUST $_3$PAM$_2$ [DGS]
'I think that he trusts you(SG).'

c. THAT FEMALE $_3$**AUX-1**$_1$ NOT-LIKE [TSL]
'That woman doesn't like me.'

Additionally, INDEXes may also fulfil the function of personal pronouns (step ③), as shown in (6b). Once again, we are dealing with a diachronic process that is well attested in spoken languages: the development of personal pronouns from demonstratives (Diessel 1999). It has to be noted, however, that in spoken languages, only 3rd person pronouns are grammaticalized from demonstratives. By contrast, all SL pronouns have a common source, i.e. a pointing gesture.

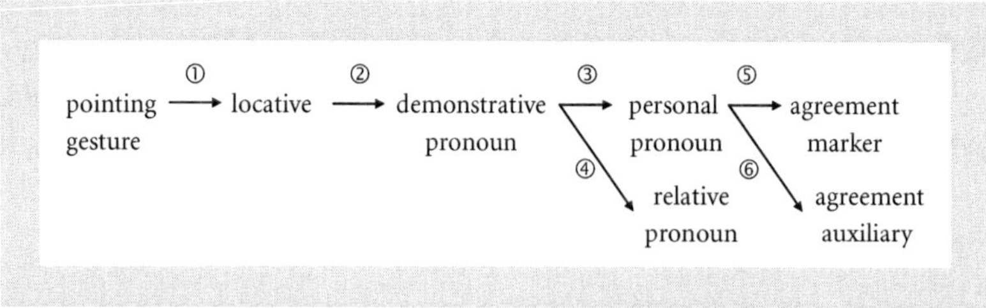

Fig. 56.4. Suggested grammaticalization path for the pointing gesture

[5] Here we adopt the assumption that pointing signs are indeed part of the grammatical system of SLs; for a different view, see Liddell (2003).

[6] See Kendon (2004: ch. 11) and Pfau (2011) for functions associated with other handshapes.

Finally, we want to turn to step ⑥ in Fig. 56.4, the development of agreement auxiliaries from pronouns. Besides the lexical sources discussed in section 3.3, agreement auxiliaries may also develop from concatenated pronouns. In the TSL example in (6c), the 1-hand performs a swift movement between two locations in signing space, thereby expressing subject and object agreement (Smith 1990: 217).[7] To the best of our knowledge, a process whereby two pronouns combine and form one prosodic word that functions as an auxiliary is unattested in spoken languages. We are thus left with a grammaticalization chain in which only step ①, from gestural source to locative adverb, and step ⑥, from pronouns to agreement auxiliary, are modality-specific. All other steps can be considered modality-independent grammaticalization phenomena.[8]

4.2. From gesture to classifier

In most SLs investigated to date, some verbs (verbs of motion and location) can undergo handshape changes depending on certain semantic or physical properties of one of their arguments. These handshapes are commonly referred to as 'classifiers', on a par with classifier morphemes in spoken languages (Supalla 1986). Here, we only consider the so-called Handle classifiers, which specify the way the object of a transitive predicate is handled.[9] In (7), for instance, the verb GIVE combines with the classifier handshape for long and thin objects, the so-called F-handshape (see left picture in Fig. 56.5). If the manipulated object was a cup, then the verb would surface with a C-handshape (right picture).

(7) WOMAN INDEX$_3$ FLOWER $_3$GIVE:CL(**long/thin**)$_1$ [DGS]
'The woman is giving me a flower.'

Handle classifiers are iconically motivated, and they are therefore strikingly similar across SLs. Also, they are clearly related to gestures used in the hearing community. There is good evidence, however, that classifiers are part of the grammatical system of (at least some) SLs: they are obligatory on certain verbs and they form a closed paradigmatic set comparable to spoken-language noun class systems. Consequently, classifiers can be seen as grammaticalized gestures which enter the language system at the morphology stage as bound morphemes.

[7] The use of such an auxiliary has also been described for GSL (Sapountzaki 2005), Indopakistani SL (Zeshan 2003), and Japanese SL (Fischer 1996).

[8] We refer the reader to Pfau and Steinbach (2006) for discussion of steps ④ and ⑤ in Fig. 56.4 and for further examples of free grammatical morphemes that developed from co-speech gestures (e.g. question particles).

[9] Other important classifier types are Bodypart and Entity classifiers which reflect shape characteristics of (agentive or non-agentive) subjects of intransitive predicates (e.g. a person walking, a car moving).

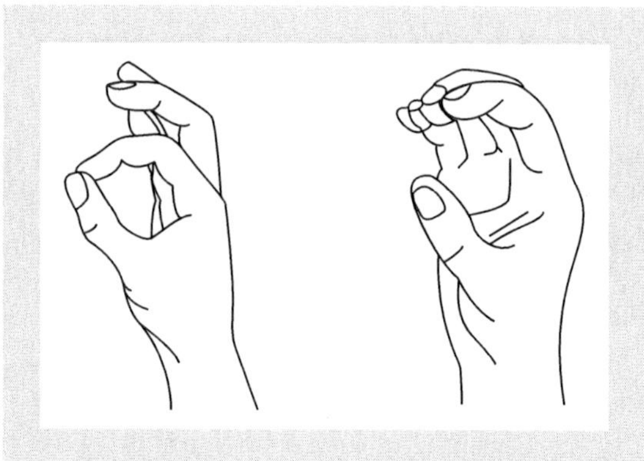

Fig. 56.5. Handle classifiers

In fact, Glück and Pfau (1998) and Zwitserlood (2003) argue that classifier handshapes in DGS and NGT are (gender) agreement markers. Crucially, Handle classifiers are not grammaticalized from nouns. The DGS noun FLOWER, for instance, does not involve the F-handshape. In contrast, in spoken languages, classificatory systems often result diachronically from noun incorporation (Mithun 1984).

4.3. Non-manual gestures

In all SLs investigated to date, non-manual markers (facial expressions, head and body movements) constitute an integral part of the grammar in that they are capable of distinguishing sentence types and of providing clues about the information structure (Pfau and Quer 2010). Most of these syntactic non-manual markers originate from communicative gestures used in the hearing population. Here, we focus on negation and topic marking.

The side-to-side headshake is a commonly used, though culture-specific co-speech gesture (McClave 2000). In many SLs, a headshake can fulfil a linguistic function in that it can be the sole marker of sentential negation, as shown in the DGS example (8), in which the headshake (hs) only accompanies the verb.

```
                          hs
(8)  WOMAN FLOWER BUY                 [DGS]
```

'The woman does not buy a flower.'

Crucially, when used as a grammatical marker, the scope of the headshake is linguistically constrained relative to the manual sign(s) it accompanies. Moreover, its exact distribution is subject to language-specific rules. In ASL transitive clauses, for instance, it is impossible to have headshake on the verb only (Neidle et al. 2000). In addition, in some SLs (e.g. LIS, Hong Kong SL), the use of a manual negative particle is obligatory, i.e. clauses cannot be negated by headshake only (Zeshan 2004). Consequently, we consider the negative headshake a grammaticalized gesture the distribution of which is constrained by language-specific grammatical principles (Pfau 2008; Pfau and Quer 2002).

Note finally that in geographical areas in which a backwards head tilt is used as a co-speech gesture signalling negation, the same gesture is also commonly found as a grammatical marker in the respective local SL (e.g. GSL, Turkish SL).

Janzen (1999) proposes another grammaticalization pathway that also began with a non-manual gesture—an eyebrow raise—and resulted in a grammaticalized non-manual marker (9). In many, if not most, SLs this conventionalized signal has become the obligatory yes/no question marker.

(9) communicative questioning gesture → yes/no question → topic constituent

The same eyebrow raise commonly accompanies topicalized constituents. According to Janzen, the use of the same marker is motivated by the fact that topics imply the question *Do you know X?* Again, the distribution of the non-manual marker is not random: the eyebrow raise always co-occurs with a specific syntactic constituent. Janzen concludes that eyebrow raise is a highly grammaticalized gesture expressing various discourse functions in SLs.[10]

4.4. Evidence from young and emerging sign languages

Admittedly, some of the scenarios argued for above, in particular, the pathway depicted in Fig. 56.4, are somewhat speculative. There is, however, evidence from recent studies on young and emerging SLs that suggests that at least some of the proposals made here are on the right track. In a sense, these SLs allow us to witness grammaticalization phenomena in fast motion.

In Nicaragua, a new SL emerged when deaf children came together in a centre for special education, established in 1977 in the capital, Managua. All of these kids brought with them individual homesign systems, which eventually converged into a single common system (Senghas 1995; Polich 2005). Children who entered the school later were thus exposed to a more established system. This social situation led to an unusual language community, in which the most fluent signers are the youngest members. Over the years, a more conventionalized and more complex SL emerged: Nicaraguan Sign Language (NSL) (Kegl, Senghas, and Coppola 1999).

[10] It has been argued that some non-manual markings are prosodic, i.e. they function as intonational contours (Sandler and Lillo-Martin 2006; Pfau and Quer 2010). Gussenhoven (2004) suggests that similarly, spoken languages have the potential to grammaticalize paralinguistic (emotional) meanings of intonation (i.e. acoustic gestures).

By comparing the language use of signers from different cohorts, the development of grammatical categories can be reconstructed. To that end, Coppola and Senghas (2010) compared the use of pointing signs in narratives retold by homesigners and signers from three cohorts.[11] Their data clearly show that all signers, irrespective of cohort, make frequent use of locative points. Interestingly, a comparable number of locative points was attested in the gesture systems used by the homesigners (*c.*6.7 per cent). From this, we may conclude that pointing gestures, once they enter the language system, do indeed start out as locative points, as indicated in Fig. 56.4 (step ①).

In contrast, the use of nominal points increased dramatically across cohorts, from approx. 1.4 per cent (cohort 1) to 3.2 per cent (cohort 2) to 6.7 per cent (cohort 3). Coppola and Senghas distinguish between nominal points that combine with nouns (e.g. POINT BIRD) and nominal points that combine with verbs (e.g. POINT CLIMB), where the former would likely fulfil a demonstrative function and the latter a pronominal function. They found that only the combination of nominal points with verbs increased across cohorts, in particular between cohorts 2 and 3. It therefore appears that the demonstrative use of nominal points, which remained constant across cohorts, is the more basic one, available to signers at an earlier stage in the development of the language. The fact that cohort 3 signers frequently use nominal points instead of nouns suggests that we witness the grammaticalization of personal pronouns from demonstratives. In other words: the NSL data provide evidence for step ③ in Fig. 56.4.[12]

The emergence of prosodic structure, involving the systematic use of non-manual markers, has been described for Al-Sayyid Bedouin Sign Language (ABSL), an indigenous SL which, due to spread of genetic deafness, emerged in a Bedouin community in the Negev desert in the past 75 years. In a study on second-generation ABSL signers, Sandler et al. (to appear) find that only the younger signers use non-manual prosodic cues consistently to mark syntactically complex utterances (e.g. conditionals). The relevant non-manual markers tend to be synchronized with prosodic/syntactic constituents, just like the non-manual markers described in section 4.3. While this does not imply that a fully regular prosodic system has developed within only one generation, it does suggest that these non-manuals, which may originate from gestures used in the community, gradually develop into grammatical markers.

[11] First cohort: children who arrived in the late 1970s and early 1980s; second cohort: children who arrived in the mid- to late-1980s; third cohort: children who arrived in the 1990s.

[12] Given the grammaticalization chain in Fig. 56.4, one would further expect that the use of personal pronouns precedes the spatial modulation of verb signs for the expression of agreement. Indeed, Senghas and Coppola (2001) found that cohort membership had an influence on the frequency of spatially modulated verb forms, but their study included only first- and second-cohort signers, i.e. signers who, in the later study, made only infrequent use of pronominal pointing signs.

5. Conclusion

Clearly, grammaticalization in SLs is by no means an uncommon phenomenon. With few exceptions, the attested pathways from lexical to grammatical element are modality-independent. In addition, we also described two general properties of grammaticalization that appear to be modality-specific. First, SLs only show little evidence of type 2 grammaticalization. Second, they have the unique possibility of grammaticalizing manual and non-manual gestures.

It has to be acknowledged, however, that this outcome may, to some extent, result from the methodology used. After all, internal reconstruction is not an ideal tool for detecting modality-specific grammaticalization phenomena. Hence, continuing research efforts are necessary to either confirm or disconfirm claims concerning modality independence.

CHAPTER 57

GRAMMATICALIZATION IN AFRICAN LANGUAGES

BERND HEINE

1. Introduction

While grammaticalization studies have a tradition of over 200 years (see Heine, Clandi, and Hünnemeyer 1991: 6–11), in their modern format they can be traced back to Givón's (1971) study of an East African language, where a new approach to understanding language structure was proposed. Givón's work inspired other students of African languages to search for regularities in grammatical evolution, with the effect that already by 1982 a first monograph on grammaticalization processes in African languages was available (Heine and Reh 1982). In this tradition, the present chapter aims at providing an overview of grammatical developments in African languages; it goes without saying that it is hardly possible to provide an appropriate treatment of the several hundred grammaticalization

I wish to express my gratitude to Marianne Mithun for highly valuable comments on an earlier version of this chapter. Furthemore, my gratitude is also due to Professor Osamu Hieda and the Tokyo University of Foreign Studies, as well as to Professor Kyung-An Song and the Korean Ministry of Education, Science, and Technology for generously having sponsored the research leading to this paper within its World Class University programme (Grant No. R33–10011).

processes that have been identified so far in the nearly 2,000 languages of Africa (cf. Heine and Reh 1984; Heine and Kuteva 2002; Heine 1997a; Güldemann 2003).

Grammaticalization is defined as the development from lexical to grammatical forms, and from grammatical to even more grammatical forms.[1] Since the development of grammatical forms is not independent of the constructions to which they belong, the study of grammaticalization is in the same way concerned with constructions, and with even larger discourse segments (see Traugott and Heine 1991a; 1991b; Heine et al. 1991; Bybee, Perkins, and Pagliuca 1994; Lehmann 1995a [1982]; Heine and Kuteva 2002; Hopper and Traugott 2003 for details). A wide range of criteria have been proposed (see esp. Lehmann 1995a); in our model it is the four parameters listed in (1) that need to be distinguished, and henceforth we will rely on these parameters, using them as a tool for identifying and describing instances of grammaticalization (see Heine and Kuteva 2002: ch. 1, for more details).

(1) Parameters of grammaticalization
   a. extension, i.e. the rise of new grammatical meanings when linguistic expressions are extended to new contexts (context-induced reinterpretation),
   b. desemanticization (or 'semantic bleaching'), i.e. loss (or generalization) in meaning content,
   c. decategorialization, i.e. loss in morphosyntactic properties characteristic of lexical or other less grammaticalized forms, and
   d. erosion ('phonetic reduction'), i.e. loss in phonetic substance.

Each of these parameters concerns a different aspect of language structure or language use; (1a) is pragmatic in nature, (1b) relates to semantics, (1c) to morphosyntax, and (1d) to phonetics. Except for (1a), these parameters all involve loss in properties. But the process cannot be reduced to one of structural 'degeneration': there are also gains. As linguistic items undergoing grammaticalization lose in semantic, morphosyntactic, and phonetic substance, they also gain in properties characteristic of their uses in new contexts—to the extent that in some cases their meaning and syntactic functions may show little resemblance to their original use.

The ordering of these parameters reflects the diachronic sequence in which they typically apply: grammaticalization tends to start out with extension, which triggers desemanticization, and subsequently decategorialization and erosion. Erosion is the last parameter to come in when grammaticalization takes place, and in a number of the examples presented below it is not (or not yet) involved. Paradigm instances of grammaticalization involve all four parameters but, as we will see below, there are as well cases where not all of the parameters play a role.

[1] For a fairly comprehensive list of definitions that have been proposed for grammaticalization, see Campbell and Janda (2001).

2. Noun phrase categories

A prominent characteristic of many African languages can be seen in the presence of noun class systems, be they of the nature-based type in the Niger-Congo languages or of the sex-based type in Afroasiatic languages or the Khoe languages of southwestern Africa (Heine 1982). However, not much information is available on the genesis and the development of these systems. Much the same applies to the case systems of African languages: our knowledge of the grammaticalization of case marking is severely limited (see König 2005). But there are other areas of the noun phrase for which there is more information on grammaticalization, and the present section will give an overview of research in these domains.

One of these domains is spatial orientation and the structure of adpositional phrases. Perhaps the most common conceptual source leading to the rise of adpositions (i.e. prepositions or postpositions) is provided by body-part terms. In specific contexts they can be reinterpreted as spatial concepts and give rise to grammatical categories of location, cf. English *in front of*, *in back of*. Most if not all African languages have developed one or more adpositions via the grammaticalization of nouns, whereby terms for specific parts of the body were extended to contexts where their lexical semantics was backgrounded (desemanticization) and some spatial schema foregrounded. Example (2) from the Dhaasanac language of southern Ethiopia and northern Kenya illustrates this kind of combining. The body-part noun delimits or specifies the location of the first noun, turning into a postpositional head of the preceding noun.

(2) Dhaasanac (East Cushitic, Afroasiatic; Tosco 2001: 240–44)

kúo	ɓíl	ʔaf	taalliʔ
2.SG.S	house	mouth	stand.PERF

'Were you (standing) in front of the house?'

As Table 57.1 shows, a whole set of nouns in this language have been grammaticalized in this way, and out of the ten nouns that have given rise to postpositional units in this Cushitic language, eight denote body parts. These Dhaasanac examples are, however, not in every respect typical of what can be observed in African languages. First, it is not only body parts that have developed into adpositions. There are other sources in addition, in particular nouns denoting environmental landmarks. And second, while it is in fact mostly nouns meaning 'back' that have given rise to adpositions for 'behind', the spatial concept 'in front' is more likely to be derived from nouns for 'eye', 'face', or 'breast' than for 'head'. 'Head' is perhaps a more common source for 'above, on top of' rather than 'in front of' in African languages (see Heine 1989; 1997b).

In the contexts in which this process took place, the body part nouns concerned lost most of the morphosyntactic characteristics of nouns (decategorialization),

Table 57.1. The grammaticalization of body part nouns to adpositions in Dhaasanac (East Cushitic, Afroasiatic; Tosco 2001: 240–44)

Form	Meaning	Literal meaning
?afu	in front of	mouth
bál	next to	chest
mé	in front of	head
sugu	behind	back
?él	behind, back	back
géere	inside	belly
?innu	around, amidst, between	eyes
tóomo	between	waist

such as the ability to take modifiers or inflections and derivations, and acquired the properties of function-specific grammatical heads of noun phrases. But there may remain some nominal properties that bear witness to the nominal origin of the adpositions. In the following example from the Kuliak language So of northeastern Uganda, the preposition *sú* 'behind' has retained the ablative (ABL) case suffix *-o* of nouns, which suggests that the preposition is historically derived from the body-part noun *sú* 'back':

(3) So (Kuliak, Nilo-Saharan; own data)

nɛ́kɛ	yóG	sú-	o	sóG
be.at	people	behind-	ABL	hill

'There are people behind the hill.'

Another noun phrase domain showing conservative behaviour is that of personal pronouns, and person markers in general, which belong to the most stable parts of language; most can be traced back to the earliest form of a language family. Nevertheless, there are a number of examples where new personal pronouns have emerged in African languages. These are primarily new 3rd person pronouns, which were created via the grammaticalization of demonstrative pronouns (much as in Romance languages, where the distal demonstrative *ille* of Latin developed into 3rd person pronouns), but in some languages also by extending the use of generic nouns for 'person(s)' or 'man/men' (see Heine and Song forthcoming). For example, the Central Sudanic language Lendu has suppletive forms for the noun for 'man': the singular stem *ke* 'man' changes to *ndrú* or *kpà* 'people' in the plural, and this suppletion has been retained in the grammaticalization from noun to personal pronoun: the 3rd person singular pronoun is *ke*, and the 3rd person plural pronouns are *ndru* or *kpa*.

(4) Lendu (Central Sudanic, Nilo-Saharan; Tucker 1940: 392)

ma- zhi **ndru.** **ke** zhi **kpa**

1.SG- love 3.PL 3.SG love 3.PL

'I love them.' 'He loves them.'

In a number of African languages yet another kind of process can be observed, leading from a noun for 'persons' or 'people' to a 1st person plural pronoun ('we').[2] Examples of this pathway of grammaticalization can be found in three of the four African language phyla: The Niger-Congo family is represented with languages such as Kono, Susu, and the Cangin languages, Nilo-Saharan with Ngiti and some Western Nilotic languages, and Khoisan with !Xun (Heine and Song forthcoming). The following example is taken from the Labwor language of northeastern Uganda, where there is an inclusive first person plural pronoun *jɔ̀* 'we (including you)', historically derived from the noun *jɔ̀* 'people'. This pronoun is weakly grammaticalized, meaning that in many contexts it is ambiguous between its nominal and pronominal uses; it is never used as a subject pronoun and only occasionally as an object pronoun (5a) or as a possessive pronominal modifier (5b).

(5) Labwor (Western Nilotic, Nilo-Saharan; own data)

a. ɛ́n ɔ́nɛ̀nɔ̀ jɔ̀

3.SG see.PFV.3.SG people

'He has seen us all.'

b. ɛ̀thínɔ̀ jɔ̀ 'our children (including yours)'

children people

Another process that can be observed widely in Africa concerns reflexive and reciprocal pronouns. The former are most commonly derived historically from nouns for 'body', as in example (6). In this process, the noun gives up its lexical meaning in appropriate contexts (extension, desemanticization) in favor of a referential function, and it also loses most of the morphosyntactic properties that it had as a noun (decategorialization).

(6) Yoruba (Kwa, Niger-Congo; Awoyale 1986: 4)

Nwosu rí **ara** rɛ

Nwosu saw body his

'Nwosu saw himself.'

The example in (6) illustrates the clearly predominant type to be found in Africa, as is suggested by the figures in Table 57.2, based on a small sample of African languages from all major genetic groupings and regions of the continent. But this

[2] Much the same process has also taken place outside Africa; e.g. in both European and Brazilian Portuguese, the phrase *a gente* 'the people' developed into a pronoun for 'we' (Merlan 2006: 233). But there are many more examples of this process in Africa than elsewhere in the world.

Table 57.2. Nominal sources of reflexive markers in African languages (Heine 2000; Schladt 2000)

Nominal source	Africa		Worldwide	
	Frequency	%	Frequency	%
'body'	25	61.0	71	79.8
'head'	6	14.6	13	14.6
Other body parts	10	24.4	5	5.6
Total	41	100	89	100

table also shows that the situation does not seem to be dramatically different in other parts of the world.

In many African languages, the process from body-part noun to reflexive marker constitutes only the first step of a more extensive development leading on the one hand to reciprocal markers and on the other to intransitivers, anticausatives, and sometimes also to passive markers. The following example from the Central Sudanic language Ma'di illustrates such an extensive chain of grammaticalization, where in addition to the lexical source of the chain, namely the noun *rū*[3] 'body', there are reflexive, reciprocal, and passive functions (see Heine and Miyashita 2008a for a more detailed discussion).

(7) Ma'di (Central Sudanic, Nilo-Saharan; Blackings and Fabb 2003: 93, 117–20)

a. má má ʔà **rū** dʒɛ̀ — Noun/Reflexive
1.SG 1.SG POSS body/REF wash
(i) 'I am washing my body.'
(ii) 'I am washing myself.'

b. ɔ́pí ō- dʒè **rū** rá — Reflexive
Opi 3- wash REF AFF
'Opi has certainly washed himself.'

c. ká kɨ̌ **rù** dʒè — Reflexive/Reciprocal
3 PL REF wash
(i) 'They are washing themselves.'
(ii) 'They are washing each other.'

d. èɓī ɔ̄- ɲā rʊ̄ rá nì — Passive
fish 3- eat REF AFF FOC
'It is fish that has certainly been eaten of all the things.'

[3] The form *rū* exhibits several different phonetic shapes.

But reciprocal categories are more commonly derived historically from certain nouns whose meanings imply some reciprocal relation, such as 'comrade', 'mate', 'companion', 'friend', 'fellow', or 'neighbour', typically used as verbal object complements. In the following example from the Mande language Tigemaxo, reciprocal meanings are expressed by the erstwhile noun *bɔlɔ* 'comrade':

(8) Tigemaxo (Mande, Niger-Congo; Blecke 1996: 245)
ye ye taŋa bɔlɔ te
3.PL 3.PL measure REC POST
'They tried each other out.'

Another common grammaticalization process affecting the noun phrase concerns the development from a noun for 'child' to a diminutive marker, which has taken place in some form or other in hundreds of African languages (cf. Heine and Kuteva 2009). For example, when extended as a head noun in endocentric compounds to contexts where the first constituent (i.e. the modifier) denotes an inanimate concept (extension), the relational noun *mà* '(own) child' of !Xun lost its lexical semantics (desemanticization). It is used productively as a diminutive suffix (9), which can be added to virtually any noun, having lost virtually all morphosyntactic properties of a noun (decategorialization).

(9) !Xun (W2 dialect, Northern Khoisan; Heine and König forthcoming)
tc'āō 'tooth' tc'āō-**mà** 'small tooth'
n!āō 'house' n!āō-**mà** 'small house'

3. Verb phrase categories

One of the most conspicuous lines of grammaticalization to be observed in African languages can be seen in the constant growth of new forms for tense, aspect, and modality (see Poulos 1986, and Bybee et al. 1994 for a worldwide survey). Perhaps most commonly this involves a process leading from a structure like (10a) to one like (10b): a verb (V_1) taking a nonfinite verb as a complement (in most cases an infinitival verb) gradually develops into an auxiliary, losing part or all of its lexical semantics in favour of some grammatical function (desemanticization), and many of its morphosyntactic properties, such as the ability to select the sentence subject or to take adverbial modifiers (decategorialization). In the same way that V_1 acquires properties of an auxiliary, so too does the verbal complement gain properties of a new main verb (V_2). Since part of the old morphosyntactic structure tends to be retained, at least for a long time, the result is a somewhat peculiar structure where inflections typically associated with a verbal word are coded on the auxiliary while the main verb appears in a nonfinite, invariable form.

(10) The grammaticalization of auxiliary constructions (auxiliation)
a. main verb (V_1) (nonfinite verb) complement
b. auxiliary main verb (V_2)

But the process may proceed further, in that the auxiliary undergoes further decategorialization by losing its independent word status and turning into a clitic of the new main verb. In extreme cases it may turn into a verbal affix, and it also may be subject to erosion, being reduced to a monosyllabic grammatical affix, as the example of the Swahili future tense in (11) shows: Swahili has grammaticalized a verb of volition to a future tense marker (English *will* provides a similar example).

Example (11a) illustrates the lexical use of the verb *-taka* 'want', and (11b) its use as a future tense marker in relative clauses. In main clauses, the future marker was reduced to *-ta-* (cf. (11c)). Originally a lexical verb requiring human subject referents, as in (11a), the use of this item was extended to contexts involving inanimate subjects (extension). Desemanticization had the effect that the lexical meaning of the verb was 'bleached out'. In accordance with its use as a tense marker, *-taka* underwent decategorialization: it lost its status as an independent word as well as most other verbal properties and became a prefix of the main verb. Finally, *-taka* underwent erosion, being phonologically reduced to *-ta-* in main clauses (11c), but retaining its original full form in relative clauses (11b)[4].

(11) Swahili (Bantu, Niger-Congo; own data)

a. a- **taka** ku- ja
C1.PRES[4]- want INF- come
'He wants to come.'

b. a- **taka**- ye ku- ja Desemanticization, decategorialization
C1- FUT- C1.REL infinitive- come
'he who will come'

c. a- **ta**- ku- ja Erosion
C1- FUT- INF- come
'He will come.'

Instead of the grammaticalization scheme presented in (10), the grammaticalization of tense, aspect, and modality may involve other morphosyntactic templates such as verb serialization. This applies especially but not only to the isolating-analytic languages along the West African coast (Lord 1993). Consider the following example from the Ewe language of Ghana and Togo, where a completive aspect is expressed simply by juxtaposing the aspectual verb *vɔ* 'be finished' to the main verb:

[4] The item *a-* in (11a) is a portmanteau morpheme consisting of the noun class 1 marker *a-* (C1) plus the tense marker *-a-*.

Table 57.3. Common pathways leading to markers for tense, aspect, and modality in African languages

Lexical source	Grammaticalization 1	Grammaticalization 2	Grammaticalization 3
'want', 'go to', 'come to'	Intention	Future	Epistemic modality
'come from'	(Immediate) past		
'want', 'be near to'	Proximative ('be about to')		
'be at' (location), 'do', 'be with'	Progressive	Imperfective, present	(Default tense)
'(re)turn'	Iterative		
'finish', 'end'	Completive	Resultative, perfect	Perfective, past
'be able'	Deontic modality, possibility	Epistemic modality	

(12) Ewe (Kwa, Niger-Congo; own field notes)

a. é vɔ
it be.finished
'It is over.'

b. é vá vɔ
he come be.finished'
'He has come (already).'

The pool of verbs that tend to be selected for auxiliation is fairly small. Table 57.3 provides a list of the types of verbs most commonly recruited. For more examples of verbs, see Bybee et al. (1994) and Heine and Kuteva (2002).

4. Clause subordination

In analysing patterns of clause combining in a range of languages of worldwide distribution, Heine and Kuteva (2007) argue that there are two main diachronic pathways leading to the growth of complex sentences, either via clause expansion or via clause integration. The relevant processes are sketched in (13).

(13) The two main channels in the rise of clause subordination

a. S [NP] > S_1 [S_2] Expansion

b. $S_1 + S_2$ > S_1 [S_2] Integration

Clause expansion is based on a conceptual strategy whereby clausal (propositional) participants are treated like nominal participants. The strategy has the effect that—over time—nominal structures acquire the properties of subordinate clauses. Still, there tend to be some nominal properties that survive this process and bear witness to the nominal origin of the subordinate clause. These are markers of subordination that resemble a grammatical form associated with noun phrase structure, such as case, gender, definiteness markers, or nonfiniteness markers on the subordinate verb, such as a nominalization, participial, or infinitival marker. Thus, in the following example from the Namibian Khwe language, the presence of the accusative clitic *'à* in (14b) suggests that the complement clause preceding the clitic has arisen via expansion from nominal to clausal structure (see Heine 2009 for discussion).

(14) Khwe (Central Khoisan, Khoisan; own data)

a. doá- m̀ 'à |x'ún- á- hān
kudu- M.SG ACC kill- JUNC- PERF
'(They) killed a kudu antelope.'

b. xàcí tcà- á- tè 'à tí |x'ân qāámà- à- tè
she be.sick- JUNC- PRES ACC I very regret- JUNC- PRES
'I am very sorry that she is sick.'

In clause integration, by contrast, two coordinate clauses are reinterpreted as a new construction where one of them has the function of a subordinate clause of the other. Among the many patterns of integration leading to the rise of new markers and structures of complement clauses, the one sketched in (15) appears to be particularly common in Africa.

(15) Main stages in the evolution from verb for 'say' to clause subordinator

a. Speech act verb 'say'.
b. 'Say' as a quotative marker.
c. Complementizer of object clauses headed by speech-act, perception, and cognition verbs.
d. Complementizer of subject clauses.
e. Subordinator of purpose clauses.
f. Subordinator of cause clauses.

The Ewe example in (16a) illustrates the lexical use of a speech act verb, nowadays highly restricted in the contexts in which it can occur, while (16b) shows the quotative use preceding direct-speech clauses, and (16c) the use of *bé* as an object complementizer after a cognition verb.

(16) Ewe (Kwa, Niger-Congo; own data)

a. e **bé?**
2.SG say
'What are you saying? (Did I understand you correctly?)'

b. é gblɔ **bé:** 'ma- á- vá etsɔ̀'
3.SG say bé 1.SG- FUT come tomorrow
'He said: "I'll come tomorrow."'

c. me- nyá **bé** e- li
1.SG- know *bé* 2.SG- exist
'I know that you are there.'

A second very common pathway of grammaticalization, in Africa and elsewhere, leads from demonstrative pronouns to relative clause markers, and sometimes further to complementizers (cf. English *that*; see Heine and Kuteva 2007: ch. 5). The following examples from the Ik language of northeastern Uganda may illustrate this pathway. The proximal demonstrative *na* 'this', plural *ni* 'these' is exemplified in (17a) and (17b), while (17c) and (17d) illustrate the relative construction of Ik. Note that, unlike its English counterpart *that*, the Ik item is less decategorialized in that it has retained its number distinction.

(17) Ik (Kuliak, Nilo-Saharan; König 2002)

a. cek- a **ná**
woman- NOM DEM.PROX
'this woman'

b. kʊrʊɓáa **ní**
things.NOM DEM.PROX.PL
'these things'

c. cek- a **na** wicé- á bɛɗ^{a} bíraa
woman- NOM REL.SG children- ACC like be.not
nɛɛ́ n^{a}
here.DAT DEM
'The woman whom the children like is not here.'

d. ena na kʊrʊɓaɗi- a **ní** ɪlíɓ- at^{a}
see ENC things- ACC REL.PL be.green- 3.PL
'He sees things which are green.'

For a more detailed discussion of clause subordination, see Ohori (Chapter 52 above).

5. Conclusions

The observations made in this chapter were meant to show that grammaticalization theory not only offers a means of reconstructing earlier states in the history of African languages but can also be of use for explaining structural characteristics of these languages. For example, the fact that in a number of African languages there are reflexive forms or adpositions that resemble nouns, or subordinating conjunctions that resemble verbs or demonstratives in their form, can be accounted for in a principled way by means of grammaticalization theory, using the parameters listed in (1) for deriving the former from the latter. Furthermore, a number of African languages have a distinction between an inclusive and exclusive 1st person plural in their system of personal pronouns, which can be explained as being the result of the grammaticalization of a noun for 'persons' or 'people', as we saw in our Labwor example of section 2.

At the same time, the discussion in this chapter may have shown that grammaticalization is a universal phenomenon. The processes discussed in the preceding sections are not restricted to Africa but can also be observed in other parts of the world. These processes are hypothesized to be unidirectional; thus, nouns may develop into prepositions, or demonstratives into relative clause markers or complementizers, while it is unlikely that a preposition will turn into a body-part noun or a complementizer into a demonstrative pronoun. To be sure, a few examples contradicting the unidirectionality principle have been identified (see esp. Newmeyer 1998). However, the vast majority of cases of grammatical change that have been documented are in accordance with the principle, and so far, not a single case of complete reversal of a grammaticalization process has been identified.

CHAPTER 58

GRAMMATICALIZATION IN GERMANIC LANGUAGES

MARTIN HILPERT

1. Genetic and structural characteristics

The Germanic languages represent a branch of the Indo-European language family that is traditionally traced back to a common ancestor, Proto-Germanic, which was spoken around 500 BC in the southern Baltic region (Henriksen and van der Auwera 1994). Three sub-branches, East, West, and North Germanic, are recognized; of these, only the latter two survive in currently spoken languages. The now-extinct East Germanic branch included Burgundian, Gothic, and Vandalic. The North Germanic branch is represented by Danish, Faroese, Icelandic, Norwegian, and Swedish. West Germanic, which is less clearly identifiable as a single branch than North Germanic, has given rise to Afrikaans, Dutch, English, Frisian, German, and Yiddish. The living Germanic languages have an extremely wide geographical distribution beyond the Proto-Germanic territory; besides colonial varieties (Afrikaans) and emigrant varieties (Texas German), many non-native varieties (Indian English) and creoles (Tok Pisin) are based on Germanic languages.

Structurally, the Germanic languages are characterized by a pervasive loss of Proto-Indo-European inflectional categories. In comparison, English and

Afrikaans exhibit the lowest degree of inflection, whereas Faroese, German, and Icelandic retain categories such as case, gender, and number on nouns and adjectives. The Germanic languages share a morphological distinction between present and preterite in the verbal domain. Here, an older system of strong verbs, which form the past tense through ablaut (*sing–sang*), contrasts with a newer system of weak verbs that have a past tense suffix containing an alveolar or dental stop (*play–played*). Generally, suffixation is much more common than prefixation. All Germanic languages exhibit derivational suffixes that allow the formation of new words from nominal, verbal, and adjectival stems. Some of these, such as English *-ly*, *-ship*, or *-some* go back to a common Proto-Germanic origin.

A syntactic commonality is the so-called V2 (verb-second) order. As a default, the Germanic languages exhibit SVO word order in declarative main clauses (German: *Ich trinke Kaffee—I drink coffee*). However, if a constituent is fronted for the purpose of topicalization, the subject will follow the verb rather than precede it (*Kaffee trinke ich nie—Coffee I never drink*). As can be seen from the last gloss, English deviates from the other Germanic languages in this respect. However, V2 used to exist even in English and is retained in a few stylistically marked constructions (*Into the room walked Noam Chomsky*). In alignment with the characteristic of SVO order, the Germanic languages exhibit prepositions rather than postpositions. Also, they share a large inventory of clause-initial adverbial subordinators (Kortmann 1997). Another common syntactic feature of the Germanic languages is the expression of *yes*/*no* questions by means of word order rearrangements, specifically the fronting of the verb. Again, English assumes a special role, since the pattern of *do*-support (Culicover 2008) complicates the picture.

2. Historical Documentation and Research Methodology

The history of the Germanic languages is preserved rather well; at least for all national languages, substantial written materials from early stages onwards are available. The main research methodology is thus the philological study of texts from different historical periods. Comparisons of this kind can show when and how a linguistic structure underwent qualitative changes in form and meaning. For instance, it can be determined when approximately during its grammaticalization English *can* lost its infinitive form or ceased to take direct objects.

Many historical materials have recently been made available in electronic format, thus facilitating corpus-based investigations into grammaticalization phenomena

(Mair, Chapter 19 above). This development has created an additional research focus on quantitative changes. Accounts of grammaticalization phenomena now commonly report frequency developments. To take another example from English, aspectual *keep V-ing* has increased both in absolute frequency and in relative frequency, i.e. in comparison to the lexical verb *keep*. At the same time, the grammaticalization of *keep V-ing* is evident in the occurrence of more and different verbs in the gerund slot, which suggests semantic broadening (Hilpert to appear). By tracking frequency changes over time, corpus-based studies can be especially useful in scenarios of incipient grammaticalization. Their main potential, however, lies in the empirical assessment of theoretical claims about grammaticalization. If a hypothesis is operationalized in terms of corpus frequencies, then even gradual differences can corroborate or disconfirm it. For instance, if the claim is that a given grammaticalizing form becomes more productive, this can be verified by applying quantitative measures of productivity (Baayen 2008) to diachronic corpus data.

Another important research strategy is the synchronic comparison of grammaticalized forms across the Germanic languages (cf. De Mulder and Lamiroy, Chapter 24 above). In many grammatical domains, structurally analogous forms are found across different languages. Examples include *wh*-clefts, the perfect with *have*, or verb-initial conditional clauses (*Had I known this, I wouldn't have come*). These may differ cross-linguistically in their relative degree of grammaticalization, thus affording comparisons between different developmental stages. They can also show how the same grammaticalization path can give rise to quite different language-specific developments (Hilpert 2008). To summarize, the rich data available is useful both for the exploration of grammaticalization phenomena in Germanic and for the examination of hypotheses about grammaticalization in general.

3. Language contact

The languages of Europe exhibit many structural affinities that reflect deep-seated patterns of mutual contact and exchange (Heine and Kuteva 2006). Some of the grammaticalization phenomena discussed in section 4 can be viewed as 'Euroversals', representing areal commonalities rather than genetic ones. The role of language contact, both between languages within the branch itself and with languages from other families, is thus of major importance. Crucial features, such as heavy mutual borrowing of lexis or the decline of inflectional complexity, are often argued to represent direct outcomes of intensive contact (Trudgill 1989; McWhorter 2002; cf. Thomason 2010 for a different view). However, contact is not equally important to all members of the branch. Unlike languages such as English or German, Faroese and Icelandic have remained largely in isolation, and these languages show greater retention of older grammatical features and a lower ratio of borrowed lexis. Among the Germanic languages that have been shaped by contact situations, English stands out as a dramatic example, as it has been substantially influenced by Latin, Scandinavian, and French. At the global level, language contact is of further importance, as many of the world's creoles are Germanic-based.

4. Examples of grammaticalization in the Germanic languages

4.1. Passive inflection

In the North Germanic languages, an inflectional passive (cf. Wiemer, Chapter 61 below) has grammaticalized out of the Proto-Germanic reflexive pronoun **sik*. On the formal side, the development is characterized by phonological reduction of the pronoun and simultaneous univerbation with the preceding verb. In present-day Faroese and Icelandic, the form of the suffix is *-st*; in the languages of the mainland it has reduced further to *-s*.

(1) a. Icelandic *Úrið* *tyndi-st*
watch lost-PASS
'The watch got lost.'

b. Swedish *Ingenting* *hörde-s*
nothing heard-PASS
'Nothing could be heard.'

The semantic development of the pronoun first followed the cross-linguistically common path from reflexive to mediopassive, which describes a process of semantic broadening. The process turns the erstwhile reflexive pronoun into a verbal affix that encodes low distinguishability both of the participants that are involved in an action and of the sub-events of those actions (Kemmer 1993). Analogous mediopassive constructions with *sich*, without univerbation, are found in German, but neither in Dutch nor in English. The Old Norse mediopassive could express reflexivity (*geymask* 'hide oneself'), reciprocity (*berjask* 'fight one another'), anticausativity (*andask* 'die'), and passive (*synjask* 'be denied') at the same time (Heltoft 2006); passive is believed to be a late addition. In the modern Scandinavian languages, the passive remains a productive pattern, whereas reflexivity is obligatorily expressed with a full reflexive pronoun and the other meanings are retained only in a number of reciprocal or deponent verbs (e.g. Swedish *brottas* 'wrestle', *skämmas* 'feel shame'). Besides the inflectional *s*-passive, the Scandinavian languages have developed a periphrastic passive, so that for instance Danish *myrdes* 'be murdered' is alternatively expressed as *blive myrdet.* Factors favouring the morphological variant include the absence of a concrete agent and the presence of a modal auxiliary, but the dynamics between competing passive constructions exhibit subtle cross-linguistic differences (Engdahl 1999).

4.2. Suffixed definite articles

Another example from Scandinavian concerns definite articles (cf. De Mulder and Carlier, Chapter 42 above). The North Germanic languages express definiteness both with suffixed articles and, in the case of attributive constructions, with free-standing articles. As shown in (2), there are different forms for the two genders (utrum, neutrum), and adjectives inflect for definiteness.

(2)	a. Swedish	*en bil*	*bil-en*	*den fin-a*	*bil-en*
		a car	car-DEF	the nice-DEF	car-DEF
		'a car'	'the car'	'the nice car'	
	b. Swedish	*ett hus*	*hus-et*	*det stor-a*	*hus-et*
		a house	house-DEF	the large-DEF	house-DEF
		'a house'	'the house'	'the large house'	
	c. Danish	*et hus*	*hus-et*	*det stor-e*	*hus*
		a house	house-DEF	the large-DEF	house
		'a house'	'the house'	'the large house'	

The examples further show a difference between Danish and Swedish. Whereas Danish keeps the autonomous and the suffixed articles in complementary distribution, depending on the presence of an attributive adjective, Swedish allows their co-presence in what is called 'double determination'. Despite the vexing similarity of the indefinite autonomous article and the suffixed definite article, the origins of the latter are disputed. Two main hypotheses are being entertained in the current literature (Börjars and Harries 2008: 295), both of which hold that a post-nominal demonstrative, Old Norse *(h)inn*, underwent univerbation with the preceding noun. The difference between these hypotheses concerns the question whether the critical context for grammaticalization was a postposed adjectival modification, comparable to a phrase such as 'Erik the holy', or if it was merely a postposed demonstrative by itself. These alternatives are shown in (3).

(3)	a. NOUN	(h)inn	ADJ	>>	NOUN-inn	ADJ
	b. NOUN	(h)inn		>>	NOUN-inn	

4.3. Auxiliaries

All Germanic languages have grammaticalized a set of auxiliary verbs (Heine 1993). These can be defined as verbal elements that have defective paradigms, cannot function as the main predicate of a clause, take not fully finite verbal complements, and carry grammatical meanings from domains such as tense, aspect, modality, and voice. The core auxiliaries of Present-Day English form a group that is clearly distinguishable on morphosyntactic grounds (the NICE properties: Quirk et al. 1985); in other Germanic languages the patterning of auxiliaries is more heterogeneous.

The Germanic auxiliaries strongly represent the domain of modality (Krug, Ziegeler, Chapters 44 and 48 above). Lexical verbs of ability, desire, and obligation have developed into auxiliaries with dynamic, deontic, epistemic, and interpersonal meanings. Functions of tense and aspect are also covered by auxiliaries. For instance, future time reference is conveyed by English *will*, Dutch *zullen*, Swedish *ska*, and German *werden*, while all of these also have modal functions and are frequently viewed as core modal auxiliaries. Aspectual functions are found in perfect constructions and in cases of posture verb auxiliation, as is discussed below.

(4) a. Danish *Netværket vil omfatte flere virksomheder.*
network.DEF will include.INF several activities
'The network will comprise several activities.'

b. Dutch *Hij moet volgende week terugkomen.*
he must following week return.INF
'He has to return next week.'

c. Yiddish *Keyner darf zikh keynmol nit ayln.*
no one must self never not hurry.INF
'No one should ever hurry.'

Besides auxiliaries that take bare infinitives as complements, several lexical verbs have come to be used with marked infinitival complements. These include verbs of movement, possession, and cognition, but also aspectualizers ('begin', 'continue', 'stop'), as well as the copula in certain collocations ('be about to').

(5) a. Swedish *Bensin kommer att bli dyrare.*
gasoline comes to become-INF more.expensive
'Gasoline will become more expensive.'

b. Icelandic *Ég kann að syngja.*
I know to sing.INF
'I am able to sing.'

c. Faroese *Hann er um at fara.*
he is about to go.INF
'He's about to go.'

A further functional domain of the Germanic auxiliaries is the passive. Here, lexical verbs of becoming (Swedish *bliva*, German *werden*) or receiving (German *bekommen*, *kriegen*, English *get*), along with the copula, are complemented by a past participle.

(6) a. Danish *Huset* *blev* *solgt.*
house-DEF become.PST sell.PPART
'The house was sold.'

b. German *Sie* *bekommt* *den* *Führerschein* *entzogen.*
she gets the driving.license revoke.PPART
'Her driving license is being revoked.'

c. English *I was paid./I got paid.*

A European feature of the Germanic languages is the grammaticalization of a perfect auxiliary from a verb of possession, which is shared with Greek and the Romance languages, but with few languages elsewhere (Heine 1997c). The constructions consist of a present tense form of a possession verb and a participle of a lexical verb, which can either be prefixed (Afrikaans), suffixed (Danish, English), or circumfixed (German).

(7) Afrikaans *Sy* *het* *ge-werk.*
Danish *Hun* *har* *arbejd-et.*
German *Sie* *hat* *ge-arbeit-et.*
English *She* *has* *work-ed.*

The Germanic languages vary to the extent that the perfect alternates between a possession verb and the copula 'be' as an auxiliary. Forms such as English *I have been* correspond to Afrikaans *ik es gewees* or German *ich bin gewesen*. Split auxiliary systems involving verbs meaning 'have' and 'be' have been suggested as a Euroversal (Heine and Kuteva 2006: 11).

Historically, the Germanic perfect constructions are thought to have been calqued from a corresponding Latin structure (Giacalone Ramat 2008). Latin *habere* grammaticalized into a perfect marker in the context of a resultative construction. The direct object of that construction was followed by a participle denoting the resultant state, thus roughly corresponding to an English sentence such as *I have the book finished.* The crucial step in the grammaticalization process was the reanalysis by which the participle was reinterpreted from a characteristic of the object ('I have the book, in a finished state') towards a completed action of the subject ('I just finished the book'). The Germanic perfect constructions show developments that signal further grammaticalization, i.e. increases in frequency, loss of agreement on the participle, changes in placement of the participle, etc.

A long-term and still-current development of the European perfects is its ousting of the preterite in German, French, and Italian, especially in dialectal varieties (Heine and Kuteva 2006). As a corollary of its replacing the preterite, the German perfect has given rise to a reduplicated perfect construction of the kind shown in (8). It is, however, unclear whether this construction takes over the former function of the present perfect, functions as a pluperfect, or represents an autonomous renewal of a construction with past time reference.

(8) German *Das hab ich schon gemacht gehabt.*
that have I already make.PPART have.PPART
'I've already done that.'

A special type of auxiliation can be observed in Dutch and the North Germanic languages. Here, verbs of general posture ('sit', 'stand', 'lie') have come to express aspectual meanings, chiefly in the categories of durative or progressive aspect (Kuteva 1999; Lemmens 2005). The examples below illustrate constructions that have developed from lexical verbs meaning 'sit', as is still transparent.

(9) a. Dutch *Ze zit te studeren.*
she sits to study.INF
'She's studying'.

b. Faroese *Vi sótu og prátaðu.*
we sat and chatted
'We were chatting.'

The Dutch construction instantiates the common pattern of an auxiliary followed by a marked infinitive; the North Germanic pattern involves a conjunction and is known as pseudo-coordination. While in many cases the posture verb might be taken to literally indicate the posture that a human being assumes during a particular activity, this need not always be the case, as shown by the examples below.

(10) a. Dutch *Onze ploeg stond lamlendig te hockeyen.* (Lemmens 2005: 185)
our team stood sluggishly to hockey.INF
'Our team was playing hockey sluggishly.'

b. Danish *Han ligger og kører rundt hele natten.* (Braunmüller 1991: 103)
he lies and drives around all night
'He is driving around all night long.'

Besides such qualitative evidence, there are also quantitative indicators for ongoing grammaticalization. Hilpert and Koops (2008) use corpus data to contrast a lexical and a grammaticalized variant of the Swedish posture verb *sitta* 'sit'. The two variants differ, amongst other things, with regard to their typical argument structure. While lexical *sitta* is often elaborated with a locative adverbial, such elaboration is substantially less frequent in the grammaticalizing construction.

Regarding the overall process of posture verb grammaticalization, Kuteva (1999) suggests that these verbs become available as a source once they are established as unmarked markers of location. In Dutch and the North Germanic languages, verbs meaning 'sit' can be used to point out the location of an inanimate object. As a result of their wider applicability, posture verbs are thus thought to increase in frequency and undergo a process of semantic bleaching that facilitates their development into grammatical markers.

4.4. Discourse markers

A common grammaticalization path in Germanic is the development of discourse markers out of conjunctions (cf. Waltereit, Onodera, Chapters 34, 50 above). Other typical sources are adverbs (*really*), imperatives (*look*), or prepositional phrases (*in fact*). Discourse markers can be defined as elements that are largely restricted to the spoken modality and that are typically found in the periphery of turns (Auer and Günthner 2005). Their primary function lies in the organization of talk-in-interaction. Discourse markers may thus initiate a turn, indicate a topic change, or signal the beginning or continuation of a narrative, amongst other functions. Examples of the development from conjunction to discourse marker include English *although*, *because*, and *so*. One example from Swedish is the coordinating conjunction *men* 'but', which has come to be used turn-initially, often in combination with *ja* 'yes' or *nej* 'no', to signal emotional involvement.

(11) a. Swedish *jag har hört din röst men jag har inte sett dej*
I have heard your voice but I have not seen you
'I have heard your voice but I haven't seen you.'

b. Swedish *nej men god dag god dag Kalle*
no but good day good day Kalle
'Well hello hello Kalle!'

A German example is the subordinating concessive conjunction *obwohl* 'although', which has acquired a corrective function as a discourse marker. In the dialogue below, speaker B first makes a statement, then pauses and takes it back with an utterance preceded by *obwohl* (example from Günthner 1999).

(12) a. German *Sie kommt heute, obwohl sie krank ist.*
she comes today, although she sick is
'She will come here today, although she is sick.'

b. German A: *brauchst du noch en Kissen?*
need you still a pillow
'Do you need another pillow?'

B: *hm ne das reicht (pause) obwohl des isch doch*
hm no this suffices although this is still
unbequem
uncomfortable
'Hm, no, it's okay. No, it's still uncomfortable.'

In examples such as these, conjunctions come to be used outside their typical syntactic context, thus undergoing decategorialization, which also shows itself in the development of independent intonation, strong restrictions on the initial or final position, and a replacement of earlier grammatical meanings with discourse-pragmatic functions.

4.5. Germanic examples of degrammaticalization

Surveys of putative counterexamples to the unidirectionality of grammaticalization (Janda 2001; Norde, Chapter 38 above) typically include several prominent examples from the Germanic languages. These include the formation of lexical verbs from prepositions (*to down a drink*) or the development of the *s*-genitive in English and North Germanic from a case marker to a clitic (Rosenbach 2004; Norde 2006a; cf. Börjars 2003 for a different view). This section briefly reviews two examples of degrammaticalization that have been proposed.

Burridge (1998) discusses the verb *wotte* 'wish' from Pennsylvania German (also known as Pennsylvania Dutch). Norde (Chapter 38 above) classifies this as a case of 'degrammation'—a lexical verb appearing to derive from a modal auxiliary *welle* 'want to'. The latter shows multiple signs of advanced grammaticalization, such as the preference for nonfinite verbal complements and the inability to form the passive. The form *wotte* goes back to the past subjunctive of that modal (*wette*). Unlike its source, it is unable to take infinitival complements. It does however occur with sentential complements. The verb conveys a fully lexical meaning that can be modified adverbially. These examples appear to reverse processes that the modal *welle* underwent in its grammaticalization.

(13) a. PA German **Ich wott kumme.*
I want come.INF
'I want to come.'

b. PA German *Ich wott, du kennscht frieher kumme.*
I wish you could earlier come
'I wish you could come sooner.'

b. PA German *Wott mal hart fer sell.*
wish MP hard for that
'Wish hard for that.'

Burridge suggests a sociocultural explanation for the apparent developmental U-turn of *wotte*. The Mennonite lifestyle that is maintained by the speakers of Pennsylvania German greatly values modesty, thus creating a functional need for a detached, uninvolved marker of preference. The preterite form of *welle* exhibited the right characteristics to be co-opted for such a purpose.

Another putative counterexample from the domain of modality concerns the Swedish auxiliary *må* 'may, be permitted' (van der Auwera 2002), which is argued to have given rise to a lexical verb meaning 'feel'.

(14) a. Swedish *Du må säga vad du vill, han lyssnar ändå inte.*
you may say what you want he listens anyway not
'You can say whatever you want, he is not going to listen.'

b. Swedish *Hunden mår inte bra.*
dog.DEF feel.PRS not good
'The dog does not feel well.'

Andersson (2008) challenges this interpretation by showing that the lexical meaning is in fact already attested in the earliest written sources in Swedish, and that corresponding examples exist in Old Norse, Old English, and Old High German. As an alternative to the degrammaticalization scenario, Andersson proposes that both the modal and the lexical verb originate from a Proto-Germanic verb with the meaning 'be strong, have power'. Such a meaning allows conceptual extension to modal meanings of possibility and permission, as well as to a lexical meaning of psychological constitution.

CHAPTER 59

GRAMMATICALIZATION FROM LATIN TO ROMANCE

ADAM LEDGEWAY

1. Introduction

With the expansion of Roman domination, Latin, a member of the 'Italic' branch of the *centum* Indo-European dialects (Coleman 1987), gradually established itself over the entire Italian territory and beyond, coming to be spoken in much of Europe and the Mediterranean. The survivors of these spoken varieties of Latin in the Iberian Peninsula, Gaul, Italy, Istria, and Dacia, often diverging quite significantly from each other and especially from the classical language, began to emerge from 9 AD (Wright 1983: 7) as the early Romance vernaculars which we today associate with the standard Romance languages and the many non-standard languages and dialects of the Romània (see entries in Price 2000).

Not only do we have extensive knowledge and rich textual documentation of Latin from as early as 6 BC, but we can also trace the evolution of the descendant Romance languages and dialects through a wealth of medieval and modern Romance texts (Malkiel 1974) and, since the beginning of the 20th century, the recordings of the dialect geographers. The sum of these sources reveals an unparalleled wealth of diachronic, diatopic, and diastratic variation, in short a fertile testing ground for assessing and shaping new ideas and perspectives about language change, structure, and variation in grammaticalization.

Nonetheless, the role of grammaticalization within historical treatments of Romance has tended to be eclipsed by, and hence subsumed within, a tradition which has, somewhat simplistically, viewed the principal morphosyntactic differences between Latin and Romance as two opposite poles of a syntheticity–analyticity continuum (Schlegel 1818; Harris 1978: 15–16; Schwegler 1990), often interpreted as the surface reflex of a change in the basic ordering of head and dependency (Harris 1978: 16; Renzi 1985: 131–7; Vincent 1988: 55–6, 62–3; Bauer 1995; Oniga 2004: 52; Ledgeway 2011: §5) according to a well-known typological distinction from which many other basic properties are said to follow (Greenberg 1963; Lehmann 1974). However interpreted, all presumed cases of analytic development or right-branching head-modifier order in Romance can be independently subsumed within the general theory of grammaticalization (Hopper and Traugott 1993: 52). In particular, the analytic developments witnessed in the history of Romance are not in any way exclusive to the Romance family, but simply exemplify a cross-linguistic tendency for synthetic structures, once weakened through phonetic erosion or other forces within the system, to be progressively replaced by new competing structures which 'given the nature of syntactic change, cannot help but be analytic' (Vincent 1997a: 101). A much-discussed case in point is the replacement of the classical Latin synthetic future (**DABIS** 'give:FUT;2SG') with an (original modal) infinitive+HABERE 'have' periphrasis (**DARE+HA(BE)S** 'give:INF+**have**:**PRS.2SG**'; Fleischman 1982; Pinkster 1987; Hopper and Traugott 1993: 42–4; Adams 1991), now fully synthesized in the modern languages (cf. 7th-c. *daras* 'give:FUT;2SG' from *Fedregar's Chronicle*; Valesio 1968) and itself frequently rivalled by a new periphrastic GO-future (Fr. *tu* ***vas*** *donner* 'you **go:PRS.2SG** give:INF'; Hopper and Traugott 1993: 9–10).

2. Overview of Grammaticalization in Romance

There is general recognition among Romanists of all theoretical persuasions (see Harris 1978: 5–6; Bauer 1995: 5; La Fauci 1997: 11–12) that, in the passage from Latin to Romance, the morphosyntax of the emerging languages underwent significant changes in three fundamental areas of the grammar, readily observable at a superficial level in:

(i) the gradual reduction and/or eventual loss of the case system and rise of the articles with increased use of prepositions (**REGIS** **FILIA** 'king:**GEN.M.SG** daughter:**NOM.F.SG**' vs Sic. ***a*** *figghia* ***du*** *re* '**the** daughter **of:the** king');

(ii) the profusion of auxiliary structures (Occ. present perfect *ai dormit* 'I.have slept', Srd. continuous aspect *so kredende* 'I.am believing');
(iii) the gradual shift from unmarked (S)OV order (PAULUS LIBROS SCRIPSIT 'Paul: NOM.M.SG book:ACC.M.PL wrote') towards a fixed (S)VO (/V(S)O) order (Sp. *(Pablo) escribió (Pablo) libros*) via an intermediate V2 order.

As a concomitant of these changes in the passage from Latin to Romance, the left edge of the nominal, verbal, and sentential domains develops a dedicated position for functional elements, namely DET(erminers), AUX(iliaries), and COMP(lementizers), the latter also hosting the finite verb in V2 contexts. This reflects the traditional intuition popularized within syntheticity–analyticity and head-directionality approaches, which highlights the emergence in Romance of articles and clitics, auxiliaries, and a whole host of finite and nonfinite complementizers, all generally absent from Latin. In current theory (see van Gelderen, Chapter 4 above), grammatical elements of this type are generally considered to head their own functional projections DP, I(nflectional)P, and CP providing the locus of grammatical information for the nominal group, verbal group, and the sentence, respectively. On this view, one of the most significant generalizations of the traditional synthesis–analysis and head–parameter approaches can now be insightfully and elegantly rephrased in terms of the emergence of these functional categories (Vincent 1997a: 105; 1997b: 149; Lyons 1999: 322–3) and, significantly for our purposes, the grammaticalization of a number of corresponding functional elements that lexicalize these positions, a small selection of which we shall now briefly review (for a fuller treatment, see Ledgeway 2011: §3.3).

2.1. Nominal group

Quintilian's oft-quoted observation 'NOSTER SERMO ARTICULOS NON DESIDERAT' ('our language does not require articles') can be taken to mean not simply that Latin lacked articles, but more fundamentally, a dedicated position for articles and other determiners (Lyons 1999: 155). Consequently, the emergence of a DP can be seen to provide the relevant (in)definiteness marking of its associated NP, and in some Gallo-Romance varieties like French the accompanying determiner is not simply a spell-out of (in)definiteness, but also now a quasi-obligatory element as the sole exponent, in most cases, of number and gender (Harris 1980a: 67).

2.1.1. *Articles*

The clearest evidence for the rise of DP structure in Romance comes from the universal appearance in all varieties of the indefinite and definite articles (see also De Mulder and Carlier, Chapter 42 above). The former continues a weakened form of the Latin numeral for 'one' UNUM/-AM (M/F) (> Cat./It./Sp. *un/una*, Fr. *un/une*, Pt. *um/uma*, Ro. *un/o*), and in some varieties formally contrasts with the fuller forms of the numeral (Cal. *unu/una* vs. *nu/na* + *guagliune/-a* 'one:M/F' vs 'a:M/F' + 'boy/girl'). Unlike the early emergence and grammaticalization of the definite article (3–8 AD: Lyons 1999: 333), systematic usage of the indefinite article does not emerge until around the 14th century (Pozas-Loyo 2008; Maiden 1995: 121). Before then the indefinite article is reserved for particularized new referents, presumably a residue of its numeral origin, whereas bare NPs are employed for non-particularized referents (Price 1971: 118–19; Lapesa 1974: 453; Parry and Lombardi 2007: 91–2). For example, in the French 11th-century *Vie de St Alexis* the article is not employed in the prayer of a childless couple in their request to God ***Enfant** nos done* 'child us= give.IMP.2SG', since the meaning of the NP is 'any child'. When, however, God blesses them with a child, a specific individual, this is reported with the indefinite article: ***Un fi** lor donet* 'a son to.them= he.gives'. In the modern languages, by contrast, indefinite NPs, whether particularized or not (witness the indicative/subjunctive alternation in the following example), require the article: Cat. *busco **una minyona** que em neteja/netegi la casa* 'I.look.for.PRS a maid that me= cleans.IND/SBJV the house').

Turning now to the definite article, this continues a weakened form of the Latin distal demonstrative ILLE (> Cat./Sp. *el/la*, Fr./Occ. *le/la*, It. *il/la*, Pt./SItR. *o/a*, Ro. *-(u)l/-a*) or, more rarely, the Latin intensifier IPSE '-self' (> Bal./Costa Brava Cat. *es/sa*, Srd. *su/sa*; Aebischer 1948: 193). In many late Latin texts both ILLE and IPSE frequently (co-)occur in contexts where their spatial deictic function is considerably weakened, and their principal role is limited to marking definiteness (Renzi 1985: 144–7; Nocentini 1990; Vincent 1997b; 1998), a precursor to the modern article famously termed by Aebischer (1948) an 'articloid'. Traditionally, then, the principal question has been whether the latter is a demonstrative with a much-increased frequency (Herman 2000: 84–5) or an article, but with a still-limited range of uses (Lyons 1999: 333). Clearly, there are elements of truth in both positions, which should be seen as the start and the end points in an unresolved and ongoing process of grammaticalization. In terms of their distribution, Renzi (1976), Selig (1992), and Zamboni (2000: 116) argue that IPSE was predominantly used anaphorically in conjunction with second-mention items (*Peregrinatio Aetheriae*: MONTES ILLI ... FACIEBANT **UALLEM** INNITAM ... **UALLIS AUTEM IPSA** INGENS EST UALDE 'th(os) e mountains ... formed an endless **valley** ... **The** (= aforementioned) **valley** is indeed truly huge'), whereas ILLE could be used both anaphorically and cataphorically with first-mention items (**MONTES ILLI**, INTER QUOS IBAMUS, APERIEBANT '**the mountains**, between which we were going, opened out'). To this picture Vincent (1997b) adds that IPSE, unlike ILLE, performed a topic-marking function, only picking out informationally prominent second-mention items (hence unsuitable for the object clitic paradigm).

In early Romance the definite article displays considerable attenuation of its original deictic force, increasingly coming to mark shared cognition between speaker(s) and addressee(s). Nonetheless, it still retained considerable identifying force—witness its exclusion in early texts with unique, abstract, and generic referents (Parry and Lombardi 2007: 83–4; OGsc. *leichatz estar* ***ypocresie*** 'let:IMP;2PL be:INF **hypocrisy**'), a usage often fossilized in modern proverbs and set expressions (Cat. *parar/desparar* ***taula*** 'to lay/clear (the) **table**'; Fr. ***noblesse*** *oblige*). In the modern languages, by contrast, shared cognition between speaker(s) and addressee(s) assumes increasing importance, such that the article is now generally required with unique, abstract, and generic referents (Ro. *dreptatea este lumina vieții* 'justice=**the.NOM.F.SG** is light=**the.NOM.F.SG** life.**the.GEN.F.SG**'), as well as inalienable possessa (It. *mi ruppi* ***la*** *gamba* 'me.DAT= I.broke **the** leg'). Catalan varieties have moved the furthest in this direction (Wheeler, Yates, and Dols 1999: 67–8), developing a specialized paradigm for proper names variously blending ILLE-derived forms (***la*** *Joana* 'Jane') with clitic reflexes of DOMINUS/-A 'master/mistress' > *en/na* (***en*** *Joan* 'John').

2.1.2. *Other determiners*

With the rise of the DP, other categories with determiner-like properties which in Latin had adjectival status undergo grammaticalization under attraction to the D position. The main categories involved are demonstratives and possessives. In both cases we find that some Romance varieties preserve two complementary paradigms, one related to the adjective and the other to the determiner. For example, in Occitan demonstratives canonically behave like determiners, lexicalizing the prenominal D position and hence in complementary distribution with the article (e.g. Occ. ***aqueste*** *(*lo) brave ome* 'this= (the=) good man'). However, their original adjectival status has not been entirely jettisoned, as they may still occur in the canonical postnominal adjectival position, in which case the D position is filled with the article (e.g. ***lo*** *brave ome* ***aqueste*** 'the= good man this').

Similarly, in some varieties the possessive shows a formal contrast between a tonic adjectival paradigm (postnominal in Spanish and Romanian, pre- and postnominal in Occitan and Catalan) and a clitic determiner paradigm generally limited to the singular persons (prenominal in all but Romanian; Lyons 1986; Lombardi 2007). In all cases, the clitic forms are inherently definite on account of their lexicalization of the D position (Cat. ***ton*** *cosí* > 'your= cousin'), whereas the tonic forms are underspecified for definiteness and co-occur with a determiner (*un/aquell cosí* ***teu*** 'a=/that= cousin your').

2.2. Verbal group

One of the most salient developments of the verb system from Latin to Romance has been the large-scale transferral of many verb-related inflectional categories to preverbal auxiliaries (see also Krug, Chapter 44 above), the overt realization of a functional category Infl(ection). The emergence of an IP projection thus correlates directly with the grammaticalization of a number of originally lexical verbs to produce a wide range of auxiliaries—a process whose effects are not uniformly mapped onto the semantic, phonological, morphological, and syntactic structures of the various Romance languages, which not only show considerable differences in relation to otherwise similar constructions (Green 1987; Pountain 1982; Vincent 1987), but which individually also display considerable variation from one auxiliary construction to another (Pottier 1961; Jones 1988; Alboiu and Motapanyane 2000: 14–20). While acknowledging the absence of a discrete class of Romance auxiliaries, we may identify a number of general cross-linguistic properties or parameters of auxiliation (see Heine 1993), which characterize to varying degrees those Romance verbs which realize verb-related categories such as tense, aspect, mood, and voice.

In accordance with well-attested cross-linguistic pathways of auxiliation (Heine 1993: 45–8), the core Romance verb-related grammatical categories are thus derived from original lexical predicates indicating location (Sp. stative/dynamic passive *el pantalón* ***estaba/era*** *planchado* 'the trousers were (<STARE 'stand')/were being (<ESSE 'be') ironed'; Pountain 1982), motion (Srs. future ***vegnel*** *a lavá* 'I will (<UENIRE 'come') wash'), possession (Vnz. perfect *el* ***ga*** *invecià tanto* 'he has (<HABERE 'have') aged much'; Vincent 1982; La Fauci 1988: 46–50; Ledgeway 2011: §6.2.1.1), volition (Frl. future ***voj*** *parti* 'I will (<*UOLERE 'want') leave') and obligation (Srd. future ***den*** *éssere thuccatos* 'they will (<DEBERE 'must') have left').

In the area of morphosyntax, Romance auxiliation is clearly visible in the process of decategorialization, whereby the emergent auxiliary progressively jettisons the typical morphosyntactic properties of its erstwhile lexical status such as the ability to select its own arguments (cf. Harris and Campbell's (1995: 193) 'Heir-Apparent Principle'). Other reflexes include:

(i) the emergence of gaps in the verb paradigm, including the lack of an imperative for the reflex of perfective HABERE 'have' (Fr. ****aie*** *fini la tâche avant midi!* 'have.IMP.2SG finished the task by midday!') or the incompatibility of Italian progressive *stare* 'stand' + gerund with the preterite (***sta***/***stette studiando* 'he.stands/he.stood studying');

(ii) the inability to form passives (cf. infelicity of Sp. progressive aspectual periphrasis *andar* 'walk' + gerund in the passive ***los precios han sido* ***andados*** *aumentando* 'the prices have:PRS.3PL be:PTCP walk:PTCP.3PL increasing');

(iii) the inability to take a nominal complement, as exemplified by Pt. perfective *haver* 'to have' (***hei dois filhos* 'I have two children'), now replaced by a reflex of TENERE 'hold' (*tenho dois filhos*);

(iv) the reduction and loss of verb inflection, as exemplified by the fossilization of *UOLE(T) 'want:PRS.3SG' > *o* in the Romanian colloquial future construction *o* + *să* (COMP.SBJV) + subjunctive (*o să laud/lauzi/laude/lăudăm/lăudaţi/laude* 'I/you.SG/(s)he/we/you.PL/they will praise'), and the southern Apulian progressive marker *sta* 'stand:PRES.3SG' now used in all six grammatical persons

(Lec. *sta* + *pperdu/pperdi/pperde/pperdimu/pperditi/pperdenu* 'I am/you.SG are/(s)he is/we/you.PL/they are losing'; Ledgeway 2008b).

With increased semantic integration and grammatical dependency between auxiliary and verbal complement ([VP]+[VP] ⇒ [AUX+VP]), the construction comes to license a range of 'local' syntactic phenomena generally assumed to hold exclusively of monoclausal constructions (Cinque 2004), including the attraction of negators and clitic pronouns to the auxiliary (It. ***non mi** ha* (****non**) *visto*(****mi**) 'not me= he.has (not) seen(=me)') and, in Ibero-Romance, the impossibility of intervening adverbs between perfective auxiliary and participle (Sp. *ya había* (***ya*) *llorado* 'already he.had (already) cried').

In many cases, this increased integration is translated in the creation of morphologically specialized (and often synchronically irregular) auxiliary paradigms displaying phonologically reduced (typically clitic) forms, which, in certain cases, contrast with morphophonologically regular and full paradigms preserved for the original lexical meaning of the same verb (cf. UADO 'I.go' > Cal. *ve* (+ *rapu*) 'I'm gonna (open up)' vs *vaju* (+ *a ra casa*) 'I go (home)'). Exemplary in this respect is Ro. *(a) avea* 'have', which *qua* perfective auxiliary has developed specialized, reduced forms in a number of persons (***am** mâncat* 'we.have eaten' vs. ***avem** un dicţionar* 'we.have a dictionary'). Similarly, Catalan (Juge 2006) and Sardinian (Jones 1988) contrast a regular, full lexical paradigm for 'go' (*anar*) and 'owe' (*dévere*), respectively, with a morphophonologically specialized paradigm of the same now employed as preterite and future auxiliaries (Cat. ***anem** al mercat* 'we.go to.the market' vs. ***va(re)m** anar al mercat* 'we.go go:INF (= we went) to.the market'; Srd. *mi **devet** meta vinu* 'me= he.owes much wine' vs. ***det** próere* 'must.3SG (= it will) rain:INF').

Table 59.1. Morphophonological specialization in Romance auxiliary paradigms

Ro. *Avea*		Cat. *Anar*		Srd. *Dévere*	
Lexical	Aux	Lexical	Aux	Lexical	Aux
am	*am*	*vaig*	*và(re)ig*	*devo*	*devo*
ai	*ai*	*vas*	*va(re)s*	*deves*	*des*
are	*a*	*va*	*va*	*devet*	*det*
avem	*am*	*anem*	*và(re)m*	*devímus*	*demus*
aveţi	*aţi*	*aneu*	*và(re)u*	*devítes*	*dedzis*
au	*au*	*van*	*va(re)n*	*deven*	*den*

2.3. The sentence

In the same way that the heads D and Infl constitute the spell-out of grammaticalized categories related to their associated NP and VP complements, the sentential core too, now formally represented by IP, came to be embedded within a further layer of functional structure CP. In the passage from Latin to Romance, exploitation of this C(omplementizer) position most noticeably surfaces in the grammaticalization of verb fronting in main clauses as part of a V2 syntax (see section 2.3.1). However, it also surfaces indirectly in the loss of the accusative and infinitive construction, one of the most notable causalities of the widespread development of CP structure, which increasingly in the postclassical period was replaced by a finite complement clause introduced by the complementizers QUOD and QUIA, a usage finally consolidated as the core complementation pattern in vulgar texts after the fall of the Empire (Herman 1989; 2000: 88–9; Zamboni 2000: 119–20).

A further area highlighting the consolidation of the CP projection is evidenced by the emergence in Romance of nonfinite complementizers derived from the prepositions DE 'of' and AD 'to' introducing infinitives (Cat. *digues-li* ***de*** *venir* 'tell=him of.COMP come:INF'), which to all intents and purposes parallel the use of finite complementizers derived from QUOD(/QUID) and QUIA (*digues-li* ***que*** *vingui* 'tell=him that he.come.SBJV'; see also Ohori, Chapter 52 above). Evidence like this has led many researchers investigating the structure of the left periphery in Romance to propose a split C-domain (Rizzi 1997; Alboiu and Motapanyane 2000: §4.2; Benincà and Poletto 2004; Cruschina 2009; Ledgeway 2010), hierarchically articulated into several functional fields consisting of a series of grammaticalized positions whose simplified linearization can be summarized as C_{Force} > Top > Foc > $C_{\text{Fin(iteness)}}$ (cf. the relative position of topicalizations and complementizers in It. *so la data* ***di*** *averla sbagliata* 'I.know the date.TOP **of.COMP**$_{\text{Fin}}$ have:INF=it mistaken' and *so* ***che*** *la data l'ho sbagliata* 'I.know **that**$_{\text{Force}}$ the date.TOP it=I.have mistaken'). Indeed, some Romance varieties such as Romanian (Alboiu and Motapanyane 2000: §4.2) and many southern Italian dialects (Ledgeway 2005) present dual finite complementizer systems which appear to exploit both the higher and lower complementizer positions within the left periphery (Sal. *ticu* ***ca*** *lu libbru lu kkattu* 'I.say **that**$_{\text{Force}}$ the book.TOP it= I.buy' vs *ojju lu libbru* ***cu*** *lu kkattu* 'I.want the book.TOP **that**$_{\text{Fin}}$ it= I.buy'), sometimes simultaneously (Ro. *vreau* ***ca*** *mâine* ***să*** *meargă* 'I.want **that**$_{\text{Force}}$ tomorrow.FOC **that**$_{\text{Fin}}$ he.go.SBJV'). Apparently unique within Romance is Gascon, where the [+finite] feature of root declaratives has been exceptionally grammaticalized in the obligatory lexicalization of the lower Fin-C(omplementizer) position with *que* 'that' (Bec 1967: 47–8: *auèi* ***que*** *hè calor* 'today.TOP **that**$_{\text{Fin}}$ it.makes heat (= today it's hot)').

2.3.1. *Grammaticalized word orders*

Although unmarked order in Classical Latin is predominantly, but not uncontroversially, considered to be SOV (see Ledgeway 2011: §3.2.1), word order was nonetheless considerably 'free', albeit pragmatically conditioned. Grammatical functions within the Latin sentence could not therefore necessarily be read off surface linear order, but were typically identified by the morphological form of individual items. Thus, given a simple transitive sentence such as 'the boy calls the girl' (PUER: 'boy.NOM.M.SG', UOCAT 'calls', PUELLAM 'girl:ACC.F.SG'), all six possible permutations are possible. Contrary to the nominal and verbal groups, which already display significant signs of increasing contiguity and rigidification of their constituent parts in late Latin, the sentence continues to exhibit considerable freedom (Herman 2000: 85–7). Such continued freedom in the positioning of the subject and object was no doubt made possible by the survival of distinct core case inflections in the nominative and accusative for a number of centuries. On this point, Herman (2000: 86) perceptively concludes: 'Statistically, the characteristic feature of late Latin texts seems to be to have the verb between the two noun phrases [. . .] that is, either SVO or OVS.'

Significantly, it is precisely this predominant verb-medial order identified by Herman that, under the more usual label of V2, has been frequently claimed to constitute the transitional phase between original Latin SOV and modern Romance SVO (Harris 1978: 20–1; Renzi 1985: 267–75; Vincent 1998: 422–3). This V2 syntax is particularly well preserved in medieval varieties (Skårup 1975; Vanelli, Renzi, and Benincà 1985; Fontana 1997; Roberts 1993b; Benincà 2006; Salvi 2004; Ledgeway 2008a), especially, though not exclusively, in Gallo-Romance and Raeto-Romance. During this V2 stage sentences consist of two principal parts, a sentential core with fixed S V O ADV order, and a left edge consisting of a C(omplementizer) position to which the finite verb is raised in root clauses, where it is preceded by one or more elements fronted from the sentential core to be assigned a pragmatically salient (focused/topicalized) reading (OFr. [$_{\text{LeftPeriphery}}$ *autre chose* *ne* ***pot*** [$_{\text{Core}}$ *li roi* t_V *trouver* t_O]] 'other thing.FOC not= **could** the king find:INF'). Examples like this illustrate an early stage in the passage from Latin to medieval Romance where, as in Latin, word order is free, though pragmatically conditioned, in the left edge, but is grammatically fixed, as in modern Romance, within the sentential core.

On account of the high frequency of subject fronting to the sentential left edge as the default topic within the older V2 system, preverbal subjects were progressively reanalysed as occupying a non-derived position within the sentential core: [$_{\text{LeftPeriphery}}$ S_{Topic} V_{finite} [$_{\text{Core}}$ t_S t_V X]] ⇒ [$_{\text{LeftPeriphery}}$ Ø [$_{\text{Core}}$ S V_{finite} X]] (see also Sun and Traugott, Chapter 30 above). The result is the grammaticalization of modern Romance unmarked SV(O), where all but UNDERGOER subjects are now licensed in a dedicated position within the sentential core (Pt. ***o João*** *abriu a janela* '**João** opened the window' vs. *abriu-se* ***a janela*** 'opened=itself **the window**').

In many Gallo-Romance varieties grammaticalization of this dedicated preverbal subject position has run its full course, with fronting of even UNDERGOER subjects (Fr. ***Jean** a ouvert la fenêtre* vs. ***la fenêtre** s'est ouverte*), thereby erasing an earlier reflex of an active/stative distinction (La Fauci 1988; 1997; Ledgeway 2011: §6), and with the reanalysis of weakened preverbal subject pronouns as (obligatory) subject clitics functioning as I(nfl)-related agreement markers (Gen. ***a*** (< ILLA 'that.one: NOM.F.SG') *vegne* 'she comes'; Harris 1980a: 73–4; Hopper and Traugott 1993: 16–17; Poletto 1995; 2000).

Oversimplifying somewhat and putting aside some minor exceptions, Romance sentential word order can be said then to have converged in the modern languages towards a grammaticalized SVO order (e.g. Ro. *Ana înțelege problema* 'Ana understands problem=the.F.SG'), in which the grammatical functions of subject and object are unambiguously marked by their respective positions to the left and the right of the verb. In short, the Romance sentence provides dedicated grammaticalized positions for the verb, its arguments, and any accompanying adjuncts, whose linear structural template can be summarized as S (AUX) V (*ADV) (O) (IO) (*ADV).

CHAPTER 60

GRAMMATICALIZATION IN BRAZILIAN PORTUGUESE

MÁRIO EDUARDO T. MARTELOTTA
MARIA MAURA CEZARIO

THE goal of this chapter is to present a broad view of grammaticalization phenomena in Brazilian Portuguese. We make a concise analysis of a number of different clines of grammaticalization, focusing on the development of pronouns, auxiliaries, and connectives. The clines we present here are interesting because, although some of them seem very typical of Portuguese, they reflect the same trends present in the literature on grammaticalization. One example is the development of *a gente* (NP formed by the definite article *a* followed by the noun *gente*) into *a gente* (first person plural pronoun).[1] Some other clines can be seen in Portuguese and several other languages, like the development of *ir* (full verb meaning *to go*) into an auxiliary used as a future marker. Since the focus of this chapter is Brazilian Portuguese, we only mention European Portuguese when necessary.

The theoretical framework used in these studies follows the proposals presented in recent work on grammaticalization that highlight the intersection between grammaticalization theory and construction grammar (Traugott 2003; 2007; Noël

[1] Literally, the NP *a gente* originally means *the people* and it undergoes grammaticalization into the pronoun *a gente*, sharing with *nós* the function of indicating the 1st person plural pronoun.

2006; Bybee 2006). These proposals are in accordance with the definition of grammaticalization as a framework, proposed in Hopper and Traugott (2003: 1), which is concerned with issues such as 'how lexical items and constructions come in certain linguistic context to serve grammatical function or how grammatical items develop new grammatical functions'. According to this approach a construction with a particular item in a discursive-pragmatic context becomes grammaticalized, instead of an item itself. That is, discourse is characterized by the high use of conventionalized word sequences that gradually undergo semantic demotivation (Brinton and Traugott 2005), losing compositionality. In the case of grammaticalization, the output is a procedural element which reflects the speaker's attitude regarding the relationship between parts of his/her discourse and the relationship between discourse and its pragmatic context.

Two major mechanisms usually associated with grammaticalization are metaphorization and metonymization (Traugott and Dasher 2005). Metaphorization is an analogical principle that involves a linkage between different conceptual domains that requires a specific context to take place. We have adopted the concept of invited inference, a conceptual and discursive metonymization that comes from implicatures associated with linguistic material in syntagmatic space, due to its usage in particular contexts.

The parameters of grammaticalization proposed by Heine and Kuteva (2007) are also important to the analysis we develop here. They specify a group of phenomena that characterize the expressions that undergo grammaticalization: extension (the rise of new grammatical meaning when linguistic expressions are extended to a new context), desemanticization (the loss of part of the original meaning of the expression that is incompatible with the new context), decategorization (the loss of morphosyntactic characteristics of an original form), and erosion (phonetic reduction, coalescence).

These parameters give rise to gradual changes which can be described in terms of a three-stage model, called the overlap model (Heine: 2003): A > A/B > (B). According to this schema, any change involves not only the simple replacement of A by B, but also an intermediate stage of ambiguity that precedes the eventual development of B.

1. The development of pronouns

The historical evolution of Portuguese shows some changes of deictic and/or lexical items that became either personal pronouns or pronouns of address. This happened, for instance, to the Latin demonstrative pronoun *ille*, which became the 3rd person pronoun *ele*. This change, a well-known instance of grammaticalization, can be interpreted as being part of the more general process of DEM PRON > 3rd person PRON > clitic PRON > verb agreement (Heine and Kuteva 2002). In fact, the subject pronoun *ele* (and its inflections) has had its use extended to that of the object pronoun:

(1) Eu encontrei *ele* ontem instead of Eu encontrei-*o* ontem[2]
I met he yesterday I met him yesterday
'I met him yesterday.' 'I met him yesterday.'

In this case *ele* remains a tonic pronoun, but it is employed in the place of the clitic *o*, which is now used exclusively in written discourse or in contexts of very formal interaction.

1.1. The case of *você*

The item *você* provides another instance of grammaticalization that leads to pronominal forms. This pronoun indicates the 2nd person singular or plural (*você/vocês*), but when it is the subject of the sentence it is used with the 3rd person verb form, probably due to its origin as a pronoun of address. *Vossa Mercê* was used until the 15th century to address the king. In that century, the general courteous form of address, *vós*, was replaced by several forms of address made up of nominal elements. According to Cintra (1972), the use of *Vossa Mercê* was extended to include a larger number of hierarchical levels in society. From this point on, the king started to be addressed as *Vossa Alteza*.

In their study of a corpus of theatre plays written in the 19th and 20th centuries, Lopes and Duarte (2003) noticed that within a few years *vossa mercê* was being used more frequently, ultimately becoming a polite form of address for any person, regardless of their title or position. The impact of this high frequency led to phonological reduction: *vossa mercê* > *vossamecê* > *vossemecê* > *vosmecê* > *você* and, in certain contexts, *ocê* or *cê*. The pronominalization of *você* probably began at the end of the 18th century, although it was only in the 20th century that it replaced *tu*, the 2nd person pronoun, almost everywhere in Brazil (Lopes 2003).[3]

The *você* form is reduced to *ocê* and *cê* in informal speech. Vitral and Ramos (2006) show that *cê* is more restricted in its use than *ocê*, whose syntactic distribution is relatively similar to *você*. *Cê*, for instance, only appears as a subject in the preverbal position and cannot act as an object:

[2] Except for the sentences collected from historical texts, we use invented examples.

[3] It is still possible to find the current use of the pronoun *tu* in certain specific interactional settings with the verb in the 3rd person singular, as with *você*.

(2) a. *V(ocê)* chegou cedo. / *Cê* chegou cedo.
you arrived early
'You arrived early.'

b. Eu amo *v(ocê)*. / *Eu amo *cê*.
I love you
'I love you.'

c. *V(ocê)* foi o culpado. / *Cê* foi o culpado.
you were the guilty
'You were to blame.'

d. Foi *v(ocê)* o culpado. / *Foi *cê* o culpado
were you the guilty
'It was you who were to blame.'

Vitral and Ramos propose that the uses of *cê* reflect a process of cliticization, based on the fact that clitics are preverbal in Brazilian Portuguese, unlike in Portugal, where clitics appear after the verb. They argue that *cê*:

(i) cannot be topicalized or focused:

(3) a. *V(ocê)* ele não viu mas viu a turma toda.
you he not saw but saw the group all.
/ **Cê* ele não viu mas viu a turma toda.
'He didn't see you but he saw everyone else.'

b. Só *v(ocê)* estava lá. / *Só *cê* estava lá.
Only you were there
'You were the only one there.'

(ii) cannot be preceded by a preposition:

(4) Eu *falei* com *v(ocê)* / *Eu falei com *cê*
I talked to you
'I talked to you.'

(iii) cannot be in a coordinate structure with a tonic item:

(5) Ele e *v(ocê)* chegaram juntos. / *Ele e *cê* chegaram juntos.
He and you arrived together
'You both arrived together.'

1.2. The case of *a gente*

Another instance of grammaticalization concerning the development of pronouns is *a gente*, which is a pronoun currently used as the 1st person plural in Brazil

(Lopes 2003). Nevertheless, if it is the subject of the sentence, it takes the singular 3rd person verb form, as in example (6):

(6) a. *A gente* trabalha-ø aqui.
We work-3SG here
'We work here.'

According to Lopes (2003), *a gente*[4] was also used in the plural until the 16th century to make reference to groups of people, as in:

(7) E suas gentes forom logo juntas com el[5]
And their people went immediately together with him
'And their people went together with him at once.'

The plural form gradually disappeared and in the 20th century and the singular form became categorical. As it was used in contexts that imply that the speaker is included in the group, *a gente* was reanalysed as a 1st person plural pronoun. This implicature became conventionalized, and in the 1970s *a gente* definitively entered the table of Brazilian Portuguese pronouns, coexisting with the pronoun *nós*, which is still widely used.

Although the 'correct' form of writing is *a gente*, it is arguable that in oral discourse a demorphologization occurs. The morpheme *a* loses its grammatical value and becomes part of the construction as a whole, retaining its phonological substance (Brinton and Traugott 2005). This process is noticeable in the written production of high school students, where the form *agente* is common.

Since both *você* and *a gente* are used with the 3rd person verb form, some scholars argue that Brazilian Portuguese is moving towards a uniform verbal system:

1SG *Eu falava*[6]
2SG *Você falava*
3SG *Ele falava*
1PL *A gente falava*
2PL *Vocês falavam*
3PL *Eles falavam*

In view of this fact, some researchers propose that Brazilian Portuguese, unlike European Portuguese, is becoming a language with obligatory subjects, i.e. it develops gradually from a pro-drop into a non-pro-drop language.

[4] The word *gente* still exists in Portuguese, but nowadays when someone uses *a gente* without any modifier of the noun, it means that the speaker is necessarily included.

[5] From Crônica de D. João, a 15th century text apud Lopes 2003)

[6] Verb *falar* 'to speak' conjugated in the imperfect tense.

2. The development of auxiliary verbs

According to Heine (1993), the formation of auxiliaries has to do with some basic cognitive schemas, such as location ('X is at Y'), motion ('X moves to/ from Y'), volition ('X wants Y'), action ('X does Y'), and possession ('X has Y'). Verbs that codify these schemas are good candidates to become auxiliaries. Several instances of development of auxiliaries in Brazilian Portuguese follow the basic event schemas proposed in Heine (1993). In this section we focus on two of them: the motion and volition schemas.

2.1. The motion schema

In the course of the 20th century, the Portuguese verb *ir* 'go' grammaticalized into a future marker in the context of *ir* + INF periphrasis, along the same lines as *go* in English and *aller* in French:

(8) Eu *vou-ø* viaja-r.
I go-PRS travel-INF
'I'm going to travel.'

The following examples indicate different moments in the cline full verb > auxiliary:

(9) a. Eu *vou-ø* para casa fala-r com Pedro.
I go-PRS to home talk-INF to Pedro
'I'm going home to talk to Pedro.'

b. Eu *vou-ø* fala-r com Pedro.
I go-PRS talk-INF to Pedro
'I'm going to talk to Pedro.'

c. *Vai-ø* chove-r.
go-PRS rain-INF
'It's going to rain.'

As Hopper and Traugott (2003) noticed in the grammaticalization of *be going to*, we can say that the auxiliary *ir* also has its source in a purposive directional construction with nonfinite complements (as in example (9a)) and the idea of futurity is an inference from the idea of purpose. At the beginning of the process only animate subjects were used, but now inanimate subjects and contexts without subjects (as in (9c)) are both common. The context that presumably triggered the invited inference is presented in example (9b), which does not show the directional adverbial phrase and creates ambiguity between the meaning of motion and the idea of futurity.

The use of *ir* as an auxiliary probably developed in the 19th century, becoming the ordinary future marker in oral discourse and presenting relatively high frequency in written discourse, too. In other words, the old way of expressing the future (with the morphemes *-rá/-re*) has gradually been replaced in oral speech and informal texts.

2.2. The volition schema

This schema is responsible for the grammaticalization of the full verb *querer* 'to want' into an auxiliary that expresses the proximative aspect, when it is used in the periphrasis formed by *estar* + *querer*:GER + infinitive:

(10) a. Ele está *quere-ndo* fala-r.
He is want-GER speak-INF
'He wants to speak.'

b. João está *quere-ndo* fica-r gripado.
João is want-GER get-INF a cold
'John is about to get a cold.'

c. O tempo está *quere-ndo* muda-r.
The weather is want-GER change-INF
'The weather is about to change.'

d. Está *quere-ndo* chove-r.
Is want-GER rain-INF
'It is about to rain.'

In example (10a), the verb keeps its original lexical meaning, related to will, and requires an animate subject. The proximative use, however, does not require an animate subject, as in (10b): it is possible to use this same construction with an inanimate subject, as in (10c) (the weather), or with a null subject, as in (10d). Even when the subject is human, as in (10b), the meaning is that of a proximative ('be about to or on the verge of') rather than of a lexical verb of volition. We may state that the proximative periphrasis with *querer* is restricted to some verbs, though more studies on the subject are still needed. It seems that the use of a proximative *querer* is limited to non-human subjects or to human subjects of clauses expressing the possibility of getting sick. Thus, the periphrasis with *querer* is located in the third stage of the four-stage model of context-induced reinterpretation proposed in Heine and Kuteva (2007), since the invited inference leading to the new proximative meaning is only usual in specific contexts.

3. The development of connectives

Brazilian Portuguese displays a variety of connectives of different origins. Only a few of the Latin connectives have survived in Portuguese, and words from other word classes are used to express this conjunctional function. The adverbial category is one of the most productive of such sources.

We will present here two different clines of grammaticalization from adverbs to connectives. In both cases we find a transfer from sensory-motor experiences in the concrete world to more abstract concepts of the world of discourse. The first is very productive in Portuguese and represents a cross-linguistically widespread phenomenon: the grammaticalization space > time > text. The second one, less productive, shows a change from adverbs of manner to temporal connectives.

3.1. The cline space > time > text

In several languages, spatial items are sources for the expression of grammatical concepts used for structuring texts. Since in some cases the polysemy implies a temporal use, we follow Heine, Claudi, and Hünnemeyer (1991) and Heine (2007) to in adopting the following schema (Fig. 60.1).

The following examples show the polysemy:

(11) a. A igreja fica *depois* da praça.
The church is after the square.
'The church is behind the square.'

b. João chegou *depois* das 7 horas.
João arrived after 7 o'clock
'João arrived after 7 o'clock.'

c. Eu não quero trabalhar e *depois* eu não preciso.
I not want work:INF and after I not need
'I don't want to work. Besides, I don't need to.'

Example (11a) exhibits *depois* with a spatial meaning, since it locates the church after the square according to the speaker's perspective. Example (11b) illustrates *depois* with a temporal meaning: it locates João's arrival at some point in time: after

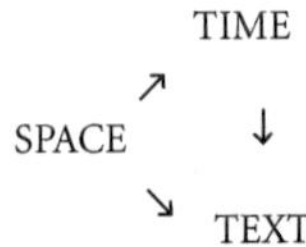

Fig. 60.1. Schema for space as a source

7 o'clock. Example (11c) is different because *depois* locates some information in the sequence of the text, presenting a meaning similar to the English connective *besides*.

According to Heine et al. (1991), distance in discourse does not imply temporal distance, i.e. it may be derived directly from spatial deixis. In Portuguese, demonstrative pronouns provide examples of transfer to the world of discourse. Pronouns such as *isso*/*isto* 'this' placed at the beginning of the clause have anaphoric functions and provide discursive continuity, subsequently developing a connective function.

(12) a. Eu não sei matemática. *Isso* é um problema.
I don't know mathematics. This is a problem
'I don't know mathematics. This is a problem.'

b. Eu não sei matemática, *por isso* eu não passei
I don't know mathematics for this I didn't pass
no teste.
the exam
'I don't know mathematics; that's why I didn't pass the exam.'

This cline reflects the *overlap model* (Heine 2003). At some point in time, the item *isso* in the construction *por isso* has presumably become ambiguous between the original anaphoric value and the connective function. With its high frequency, the construction has begun to lose compositionality, and has started to be reanalysed as a connective. This process is probably still clear to speakers of Portuguese, since it does not indicate a high degree of grammaticalization.

This is quite different from what happens with *porém*, an ancient conclusive connective formed by the preposition *por* 'for' and *ende* 'this', a spatial adverb coming from the Latin word *inde* that was used in anaphoric contexts. In archaic Portuguese, the construction *por ende*/*porende*/*porém*/*porẽ* was used to function, among other things, as a conclusive connective that was very similar to *por isso*.

(13) O coraçõ ham fero e deseio bestial, e *porẽ*
The heart have ferocious and desire bestial and hence
som muy enclinados pera luxuria.[7]
are very inclined to lust
'They have a feral heart and bestial desires, thus they are much inclined to lust.'

In the Renaissance period, *porém* developed the adversative value that it shows in present-day Portuguese. Gradually, the ancient meaning corresponding to English

[7] From *Orto do Esposo*, a text from archaic Portuguese (Maler 1956).

connectives like *hence* and *therefore* was replaced by a new one, similar to the English connective *but*:

(14) Ele é pobre *porém* sua irmã é rica.
He is poor but his sister is rich
'He is poor but his sister is rich.'

Said Ali (1971: 187) proposes that the archaic use of *porém* developed the new adversative value in one specific kind of contexts in which it could be inferred, namely in negative sentences. So he describes a kind of change characterized by Traugott and Dasher (2005) as invited inference, according to which both speaker and hearer negotiate meaning in an interactive way. One of the author's examples of this context is reproduced below:

(15) a. E ainda que quando o levaram diante d'el-rei
and although when him they take in front of the King
desmaiou, não desfalleceu *porem* em sua firmeza, mas
he fainted not weakened for that in his firmness but
foi um natural pejo.
was a natural shyness
'And although he fainted when they took him before the King, his firmness wasn't weakened for that reason, but was, in fact, a natural shyness.'

There are several other cases of this cline that we can characterize as *deictic* > *anaphoric* > *connective* in Portuguese. Correlative intensifiers such as *então* 'then', *entretanto* 'however' provide good examples. They can all be used in anaphoric contexts, tend to occur at the beginning of the sentence, and can be used as connectives. *Então* has developed a consecutive value, whereas *entretanto* (originally 'meanwhile') has developed a contrastive meaning, and became an adversative connective.

3.2. The cline manner adverbs > connectives

We can see this cline in the polysemy of the adverbs *bem* 'well, in a good/proper manner', *mal* 'wrongly, in a bad/improper manner', and *apenas* 'only', from the phrase *a penas* (originally 'with difficulty'). *Mal* and *bem* developed the function of temporal conjunctions meaning immediate time in the 19th century:

(16) a. *Mal* cheguei em casa, ele começou a reclamar.
badly I arrived home, he began to complain
'Hardly had I got home then he began to complain.'

b. *Nem bem* cheguei em casa, ele começou a reclamar.
Not well I arrived home, he began to complain
'Hardly had I got home then he began to complain.'

In these cases, the notion related to *do something badly* develops into a notion of rapidity. The case of *apenas* is similar. Formed by the preposition *a* and the plural noun *penas* (suffering, affliction), the construction meant '*with difficulty/with suffering*' in the 16th century. In the 17th century the item developed an emphatic value:

(17) Ele *apenas* veio para ver você.
He only came to see you
'He only came to see you.'

In present-day Portuguese, besides the use exemplified above, we can find structures such as (18):

(18) *Apenas* cheguei em casa, ele começou a reclamar.
Only I arrived home, he began to complain
'Hardly had I got home that he began to complain.'

As we can see, much like *mal* and *nem bem*, *apenas* has undergone grammaticalization, developing the function of an immediate temporal connective. The original expression meaning 'with difficulty' was reanalysed as a focus particle with a notion of restriction, and then as a connective that expresses immediate sequence in time.

4. Conclusion

We have attempted to present a broad view of grammaticalization phenomena in Brazilian Portuguese, in order to provide instances of the process in a language which is not usually covered in the main works on grammaticalization. All of them reflect general trends, although they take on their own specific features in Portuguese. We have shown how the grammaticalization of two pronominal forms—*você* and *a gente*—can be related to a simplification of the verbal system in Brazilian Portuguese. We have also demonstrated the development of some auxiliaries that reflects cross-linguistic clines, following the basic event schemas proposed in Heine (1993). Finally, we have presented some instances of development from adverbs into connectives. We hope this group of phenomena concisely presented here contributes to a better understanding of the phenomenon of grammaticalization.

CHAPTER 61

GRAMMATICALIZATION IN SLAVIC LANGUAGES

BJÖRN WIEMER

1. Scope of the chapter and general developmental lines

By and large, the Slavic language group shows a comparatively conservative morphosyntax. According to accepted areal divisions, we can say that the northern group (= East + West Slavic) has practically retained the Common Slavic (CS)[1] case system, which in some languages has become even more differentiated and which is involved in marking animacy in almost all Slavic languages. Conversely, Balkan Slavic, i.e. the eastern part of South Slavic, has lost the entire case system but retained the inherited system of past tenses (aorist, imperfect, perfect), which in turn has been abandoned in North Slavic (with the partial exception of Sorbian) and within South Slavic deteriorates in the northwest direction. These developments represent types of change other than grammaticalization in a narrow sense

[1] CS is a reconstructed stage of Slavic before more considerable dialectal diffusion started (beginning from the 6th c. AD). CS must be distinguished from Old Church Slavonic (OChS), which is a documented language (starting in the late 8th c. AD), actually, the first written variant of Slavic.

understood (after Meillet) as a cline on which originally lexically autonomous items become morphosyntactically dependent on other items.

The functions of the past tenses lost in northern Slavic are only partially covered by the younger opposition of perfective (PFV) vs. imperfective (IPFV) aspect. The latter has evolved in entire Slavic and, despite its unusual way of grammaticalization, will be included here (section 3.1.1) for its crucial role in verb morphology and its intricate interaction with other grammaticalized categories in Slavic. Apart from the PFV/IPFV opposition, the most important innovations in the tense-aspect system reflected in new morphological forms or constructions involve two gram types: future and resultative (3.1.2–3.1.3). Another clear case of grammaticalization is the establishment of modal auxiliaries in all Slavic languages (3.1.4).

As concerns changes relevant to the noun phrase, the only new classes of morphemes that arose in some sub-areas of Slavic are the definite and the indefinite article, both with preliminary, not-yet-grammaticalized stages in some more Slavic varieties[2] (2.2). The rise of a new adjectival declension (with pronominal endings) can be considered another salient case of grammaticalization proper (2.1).

In sum, in Slavic grammaticalization, phenomena have occurred predominantly in the realm of verbal categories; only very few phenomena are related to the noun phrase. In the subsequent exposition, 'nouny' categories (section 2) are firstly explored, then verbal categories (section 3), finally phenomena on the borderline between morphology and syntax (section 4) and from syntax (section 5). Cases of incipient or 'halfway' proceeded grammaticalization on all levels mentioned are numerous; for lack of space they will, however, be omitted.

2. Grammaticalization relevant to the noun phrase

2.1. Pronominal declension of adjectives

Originally CS did not make a clear-cut distinction between noun and adjective stems until 3rd person enclitics were attached to the latter, so that a sort of definite/indefinite distinction was introduced in NPs (Townsend and Janda 2003: 138–42). This opposition vanished almost totally, but since the pronominal forms and the earlier noun endings merged into new suffixes, a distinct adjectival paradigm

[2] For a recent overview see Heine and Kuteva (2006: 119–33), Wiemer and Hansen (to appear: 2.7).

(so-called 'long forms') arose. Compare the dative singular masculine/neuter (simplified schema):

(1) **dobr-u+jemu* 'good.DAT+him.DAT'
> *dobr-u-umu* > *dobr-umu* > *dobr-omu* (East Slavic, Serbian/Croatian)
> *dobr-emu* (West Slavic, Slovene)
(vs. *stol-u* 'table.M.DAT', *dom-ovi* 'house.M.DAT').

The pronominal forms have continually been ousting the ancient nominal ('short') forms.[3] Morphological coalescence—accompanied by phonological erosion and analogical levelling—has gone hand in hand with an increase in abstractness: 3rd person pronoun > declensional marker (case+number +gender).

2.2. Articles

Only colloquial Upper Sorbian (CUS) has developed both definite and indefinite articles, Molise Slavic (MSL) only has an indefinite article, Bulgarian only a definite one, as does Macedonian, where *eden* 'one' has not yet developed into a fully-fledged indefinite article. All these articles distinguish gender and number, in CUS and MSL also cases. The definite articles derive from a deictically neutral demonstrative (< CS/OChS[4] *tъ*), only Macedonian adds articles which continue to distinguish near and distal deixis (< CS/OChS *ovъ*, *onъ*).

The extent to which grammaticalization involves morphological coalescence and syntactic tightening varies. The Balkan Slavic definite article is an enclitic phrase marker attached to the first word (prepositions excepted) of the NP. In CUS, the definite article is still basically restricted to pragmatic definiteness (anaphoric, associative-anaphoric) but has begun to extend into semantic (inherent) definiteness (for reference to absolutely or relatively unique objects and in generic usage) as well; cf. Breu (2008: 84f.; to appear: 6.1.2), Scholze (2008: 157–81; to appear).

The indefinite article of CUS and MSL derives from the numeral 'one' (< CS/OChS *edinъ*) and remains a free morpheme preposed to the entire NP (Breu 2008; to appear). Reduced forms exist only in MSL for the nominative and accusative inanimate.

[3] Apart from lexicalized forms, the nominal paradigm has been abandoned in West and East Slavic (except standard Russian and Czech, where these forms are restricted to predicative use); they are still 'healthy' in South Slavic.

[4] See note 1.

3. Grammaticalization relevant to the verb and the verb phrase

3.1. TMA oppositions (paradigms)

The functional shift perfect > general past of the *l*-periphrasis and the loss of the aorist–imperfect opposition experienced by most Slavic languages (see section 1) stands in no apparent causal relation to the rise of a new opposition of derivational aspect which has become the most pervasive and crucial verbal category in every Slavic language.

3.1.1. *Opposition of perfective/imperfective aspect*

The rise of the perfective/imperfective (PFV/IPFV) aspect opposition is peculiar insofar as it is based on stem derivation, with suffixation being the predominant productive (although not exclusive) device. For this reason, the PFV/ IPFV opposition is not restricted to some finite verb forms (e.g. Romance past tenses) but present in any form including nonfinite ones. The gist of the 'grammaticalization story' of Slavic aspect resides in a development whereby stems related by morphological derivation can eventually substitute each other as lexical synonyms, but with complementary grammatical functions (see Table 61.1). This has amounted to a tendency toward 'the maximum distributional extension of affixes with aspectual functions' (V. Lehmann 2004: 174), whereby lexical concepts coded by verbal stems acquire a partner opposed with respect to a clearly defined set of functions (Wiemer 2001).

The core functions conform to those cross-linguistically identified with functional oppositions typical of aspect distinctions (singular event vs. process/state, bounded vs. unbounded); these are identical for all Slavic languages. Aspect choice conditioned by other functions, like reference to singular vs. iterated (habitual etc.) actions, varies among Slavic languages; so does aspect choice in sentences with temporal or conditional clauses, in modal contexts or for certain illocutive

Table 61.1. Evolution of patterns of aspect derivation

I. Productive affixation:	
(i) Simplex stem ⇒ prefixed stem	(ii) Prefixed stem ⇒ (secondarily) suffixed stem
II. Reinterpretation as functional opposition of lexically identical stems with complementary distribution of grammatical functions:	
(i) Imperfective/perfective stem (pair)	(ii) Perfective/imperfective stem (pair)

purposes. The contemporary diversification of aspect choice among Slavic presumably reflects different stages of grammaticalization (Wiemer 2008).[5] It is essential to realize that this case of grammaticalization has to be understood not in terms of bleaching or erosion, but as process of gradual tightening of functional oppositions (tendency toward complementary distribution of virtual synonyms), tightening of paradigmatic restrictions in interaction with other verbal categories (see below), and the rise of syntagmatic restrictions (e.g. with phasal verbs) for verbs each belonging to one of two classes (PFV vs. IPFV).

3.1.2. Future

CS did not have any inflected or analytic future. Futures whose evolution has involved morphological coalescence and erosion exist only in South Slavic and Ukrainian; for the former the lexical source is CS *xъtěti*[6] 'to want'. In Serbian/Croatian this morpheme is an inflected enclitic (2), whereas in Macedonian and Bulgarian it comes as an uninflected proclitic (3 and 6a). In both cases it combines with stems of either PFV or IPFV aspect:

Croatian

(2) a. *U subotu* *će* *stići* *Ivo.*
in Saturday.ACC.SG.F FUT.3.SG arrive:PFV.INF Ivo.NOM
'Ivo **will arrive** on Saturday.'

b. *U subotu* *ću* *stići.*
in Saturday.ACC.SG.F FUT.1.SG arrive:PFV.INF
'I **will arrive** on Saturday.'

Bulgarian

(3) a. *Skoro šte* ***dojde*** *poštenskij razdavač.*
soon FUT come:PFV.PRS:3.SG postman
'The postman **will come** soon.'

b. *Skoro šte* ***dojda.***
soon FUT come:PFV.PRS:1.SG
'I **will come** soon.'

[5] An important phenomenon that has accompanied the continued development of the PFV/IPFV opposition consists in the conventionalization of the shift of present tense forms of PFV verbs toward a PFV future. This shift has been accomplished in all North Slavic languages, whereas in South Slavic present tense forms of PFV verbs have continually been experiencing restrictions to subordinate (mostly temporal or conditional) clauses; this tendency increases from northwest (Slovene) to southeast (Bulgarian, Macedonian).

[6] Here and in the following, CS forms that were preserved in OChS will be rendered in accordance with the latter and, consequently, without an asterisk.

This morphological difference in the contemporary state corresponds to different stages on a cline, here simplified (cf. Kuteva 2001: 125–8):

(4) autonomous lexeme *xъtěti*: present tense 3.SG *xъšte* → volition, only animate subjects
> *xъšte* + infinitive: loss of volitional meaning → intention → future (prediction)
> *šta* + infinitive
> *šta* + shortened infinitive > *šta* + *da*.COMP + finite verb[7]
/ inanimate subjects become possible
> *šte* + finite verb (any subjects).

Slovene has not participated in this development and morphologically follows the North Slavic pattern by using the auxiliary *bom*.1.SG < **bodo* (see below).

The only contemporary North Slavic language with a synthetic future based on coalescence is Ukrainian. The lexical source verb has, until recently, been considered to be 'have' (CS/OChS *imati, iměti*). Danylenko (to appear) has shown this view to be untenable (primarily in view of facts from diachronic dialect geography together with involved sound changes). Instead, the source was most plausibly the etymologically closely related CS verb **jęti* 'take' in its ingressive ('start to V') meaning whose present tense forms were agglutinated to the infinitive: *sijaty-**mu***.1.SG, *sijaty-**meš***.2.SG, etc. 'I, you (etc.) will sow'. Contrary to Serbian/Croatian (see above), these forms cannot be separated from the verb stem and they occur only as an alternative to the usual North Slavic way of marking IPFV future by *budu* (see below).

A further difference compared to South Slavic is that Ukrainian *-mu, -meš*... can be attached only to IPFV stems. This corresponds to the ingressive etymology, and corroborates the assumption that the Ukrainian synthetic IPFV future can be considered as a remnant of a disrupted development of concurrent ingressive periphrases marking futurity. Probably since CS times, besides *xъtěti* and *imati/iměti*, several inchoative or ingressive verbs (OChS *stati* 'to become, to start', *začęti*, *načęti* 'to begin', etc.) were used to refer to future (posterior) events (cf. Večerka 1993: 174–85 on OChS, Vlasto 1986: 162–5 on 16th-18th-c. Russian) until they were overridden by another 'rival', namely *budu*.1.SG[8] (< **bodo*.1.SG), which has been reconstructed as an inchoative root alternation of the existential-copular verb *byti* 'to be'. *Budu* has become the marker of the analytic future in entire North Slavic, where it combines only with IPFV stems. It is also the only future marker in Slovene, where, however, it combines with verbs of either aspect.[9] If *budu*'s

[7] This complex structure was a consequence of the general loss of the infinitive. As for the complementizer, see section 5.2.

[8] Since this verb does not have any infinitive, it is commonly referred to by its 1.SG-form.

[9] In all North Slavic languages *budu* combines with the infinitive; only in Polish does it occur alternatively and in Slovene exclusively with the *l*-participle (identical to the former perfect). This collocation reflects its putative former status as a periphrastic perfect in the future (*futurum exactum*).

Table 61.2. Slavic resultatives (without inherited *l*-participle + *byti* 'be')

Suffix	-*n*-/-*t*-		-*vši*, non-agreeing	-*l*, agreeing
	Agreeing	Non-agreeing	Originally active	
+ ESSE, *byti*	practically everywhere in Slavic	NW Russian	NW Russian (southern part), northern Belarusian	West Slavic
+ HABĒRE, *imati, iměti*	West Slavic (W. Ukrainian)	Macedonian	–	Hanakian Czech, Cassubian

morphological and semantic reconstruction is correct, it demonstrates bleaching but no erosion nor morphosyntactic tightening.

3.1.3. Resultatives

In some Slavic-speaking areas resultatives have emerged. They centre around anteriority participles (mostly of PFV aspect) which combine either with a 'have'- or a 'be'-verb whose degree of auxiliation differs.
Object-oriented resultatives systematically interfere with analytic passives; only modern Standard Polish distinguishes between both by auxiliary choice (see section 4.1) and the aspect of the participle.

Grammaticalization is not accompanied by coalescence. Hardly ever does it manifest itself in morphosyntactic tightening insofar as rules of pragmatic word order have not been restricted anywhere. Nor is grammaticalization conditioned by erosion: in certain NW Russian dialect groups (5), loss of agreement marking on the participle is a side-effect of loss of gender distinctions in general whereas in Macedonian lack of agreement—and choice of the neuter as default gender (6)—can indeed be interpreted as the result of loss of object agreement with concomitant tightening of the auxiliary–participle bond in an originally possessive construction:

(5) NW Russian dialects

a. *Oni* *uexa-n-o.*
they.NOM go_away-N/T-NEUT
'They are gone.'

b. *Trav-a* *skoše-n-Ø.* or (c) *Trav-a* *skosi-vši*
grass:NOM.F mow-N/T-M grass:NOM.F mow-VŠI.INDECL
'The grass is mowed.'

(6) a. Macedonian
Denes ***imam*** ***dojde-n-o*** *za važna rabota, drug pat*
today have-PRS.1.SG come-N/T-N for important work other time
ќe zboruvame.
FUT talk:IPFV.1.PL
'Today I **have come** for an important job, we will talk some other time.'

b. *Cel vek go nemam vide-n-o.*
whole long_time him.ACC NEG-have:PRS-1.SG see-N/T-NEUT
'I haven't seen him for ages.'

The signs of grammaticalization generalizable over Slavic resultatives are to be seen in

(i) an aspectual shift toward (eventive) perfects.[10] Such a shift has occurred only with the three Macedonian constructions (even with HABĒRE as in 6b; cf. Graves 2000). Elsewhere resultative→perfect shifts have remained a negligible quantity.[11]
(ii) the degree to which anteriority participles have given up their diathetic (subject- vs. object-oriented) restrictions and expanded their lexical input. This has happened with Macedonian (see ex. (6a)), NW Russian dialects (see ex. (5c)), Czech (Hanakian) dialects, Cassubian, the rest of West Slavic only to a very limited extent; see note 10.

The restriction to PFV participles is occasionally loosened in the Macedonian and NW Russian constructions, elsewhere only exceptionally.

3.1.4. Modals

Slavic modal auxiliaries arose in historic time as an almost entirely new category (Hansen 2001; 2004). It consists of a few central and a slightly more numerous group of peripheral members, which, unlike Germanic, do not show any morphonological signs of grammaticalization. Their degree of grammaticalization can be determined only on:

- the lexical level: core modals do not retain any lexical meaning, but have at least two modal functions (dynamic, deontic, epistemic); e.g. Russian *moč'* 'can' (< CS **mogti* 'be mighty, capable');

[10] For the relation between resultative and perfect see Breu (1988), Nedjalkov (1988), Tommola (2000).
[11] For details concerning North Slavic see Wiemer and Giger (2005).

- the semantics–syntax interface: loss of argument structure;
- the syntactic level: they combine only with an infinitive (or its substitute in Balkan Slavic; see section 5.2) with which they share arguments;
- the paradigmatic (categorial) level: most of them are deficient with respect to the PFV/IPFV aspect opposition and to mood distinctions (no imperative), although they themselves can develop into new mood markers (see section 3.1.5).

3.1.5. Mood distinctions

CS possessed a conditional construction consisting of the *l*-participle + clitic auxiliary *bi-* inflected for person and number. This auxiliary, in turn, derived from the optative of *byti* 'to be' (< **b^hu-ī*). We may thus assume syntactic tightening during the CS period. Subsequently, the conditional developed into a subjunctive and *bi-* underwent analogical levelling so that forms of the aorist and the present stems were mixed up; compare modern Czech: *by-ch*.1.SG, *by-s*.2.SG, *by-Ø*.3.SG/PL, *by-chom*.1.PL, *by-ste*.2.PL vs. modern Polish: *by-m*.1.SG, *by-ś*.2.SG, *by-Ø*.3.SG/PL, *by-śmy*.1.PL, *by-ście*.2.PL.[12] This coalescence of two grammatical morphemes must have preceded their agglutination *in toto* to verb stems; otherwise one could hardly explain why only the entity as a whole can be detached from stems (see section 3.2).

This most ancient period of morphologization must be distinguished from a later one during which modals started indicating mood functions. This happened only rarely, for example with Polish *mieć* 'to have'. From a root modal it has acquired the function of a conditional marker (compare English *should*). At least during the 16th century it was also used as a subjunctive marker; this function, however, has not survived (Hansen 2001: 319f.; 2004: 254–6). The Serbian/Croatian possibility modal *moći* 'can' under negation together with the infinitive of the lexical verb has become a prohibitive marker; e.g. *nemoj*.2.SG *pjevati*.INF 'Don't sing!' (optionally to the regular negated imperative: *nepjevaj*). This pattern was attested already in OChS, which, in addition, used negated *xъtěti* in the same vein. A 'positive' equivalent to this analytic 'want'-imperative existed in Polish until about 100 years ago (Hansen 2004: 258f.).

Polish uses *niech(aj)* + present tense form (mostly PFV) as a sort of analytic hortative (or permissive). *Niech* is the truncated imperative of the now obsolete *niechać* 'to let'. The same holds for Russian *pust'* / *puskaj* (< *pustit'*.PFV / *puskat'*.IPFV 'to let (through)').

12 In East Slavic the desinences were lost altogether.

3.1.6. *Evidentials*[13]

Bulgarian and Macedonian have extended their inherited perfect series to express indirect (inferential and reportive) evidentiality. This extension probably rests on the conventionalization of a metonymic shift from reference to situations anterior to some reference interval toward reference to situations inferred as consequences of anterior situations, and thence to hearsay. The paradigmatic distinction from the indicative perfect is weak since many forms coincide.[14] However, the evidential perfect does not consist solely in this functional shift but can be marked by an innovation of stem-internal morphemic distribution encountered only in Macedonian and Bulgarian: the *l*-suffix can now be combined with the imperfect stem. Compare Bulgarian *pišel (bil)* as evidential counterpart to both imperfect *pišeše* 's/he was writing, used to write' and present *piše* 's/he writes, is writing'. Notice that no morphemes have evolved from former autonomous lexemes.

Evidential extensions of deontic modals meaning 'have' are attested to occur in all West Slavic languages (Polish *mieć*, Czech *mít*, Slovak *mat'*, Upper Sorbian *měć*). The extension pertains only to a reportive, not to an inferential function. This specific semantic pattern can be explained as a result of polysemy copying from the German modal *sollen*, which shows the same functional distribution.[15]

3.2. Person

Partial grammaticalization of personal desinences can be claimed to have occurred only in the northwest and southwest parts of Slavic; it has accompanied (though it has certainly not been conditioned by) the functional shift from perfect (*l*-participle + 'be'-copula) to general past tense (see section 3.1).[16] The former copula was dropped altogether in East Slavic (as a consequence, no personal endings in the past tense have evolved), whereas Polish shows an intermediary stage between cliticization and agglutination: only under certain circumstances can the person marker[17] still behave like a Wackernagel clitic and move away from the verb stem (see example (8a) vs. (8b)). The same applies to the subjunctive marker, itself consisting of two agglutinated morphemes *by*+person-number (see section 3.1.6; cf.

[13] For a general overview, see Wiemer (2010: 2.1–2.3).

[14] The 'copula criterion' (presence of the 3.SG-copula implies indicative perfect, its absence implies evidential meaning), often stated in textbooks and grammars of Bulgarian, does not hold empirically. In Macedonian it is not relevant at all, since the copula is generally absent in the 3rd person forms of the perfect.

[15] Sorbian speakers have been exposed to German influence much more than communities speaking other West Slavic languages.

[16] Note that no remarkable signs of coalescence with an auxiliary (copula) have resulted from this shift.

[17] This marker also redundantly indicates number (see (8a)).

example (8c)). The rest of West Slavic (as well as South Slavic) still treats these person–number markers as clitics; compare, for instance, Czech (in 9)[18] with (7, 8):[19]

(7) Russian

ja, ty, on *pe-l-Ø* / *ja, ty, ona* *pe-l-a* /
1.SG, 2.SG, 3.SG.M sing-PST-SG.M 1.SG, 2.SG, 3.SG.F sing-PST-F
my, vy, oni *pe-l-i*
1.PL, 2.PL, 3.PL sing-PST-PL
'I, you(SG), he sang / I, you(SG), she sang / we, you(PL), they sang.'

(8) a. Polish

(ja) śpiewa-ł-<u>em</u> / *śpiewa-ł-**a-m*** (comp. 2b) / *(my) śpiewa-l-i-**śmy***
1.SG sing-PST-1.SG.M / sing-PST-1.SG.F / 1.PL sing-PST-PL-1.PL
'I(M) sang / I(F) sang / we sang.'

*(ty) śpiewa-ł-**eś**,* *śpiewa-ł-a-**ś*** / *(vy) śpiewa-l-i-**ście***
2.SG sing-PST-2.SG.M / sing-PST-2.SG.F 2.PL sing-PST-PL-2.PL
'You(M) sang / you(F) sang / you(PL) sang.'

(on) śpiewa-ł-Ø / *ona śpiewa-ł-**a***
3.SG.M sing-PST-3.SG.M / 3.SG.F sing-PST-3.SG.F

*(oni) śpiewa-l-**i**, (one) śpiewa-ł-*y
3.PL.VIR sing-PST-PL.VIR 3.PL.NONVIR sing-PST-PL.NONVIR
'He / she / they(VIR vs. NONVIR) sang.'

b. *Gdy-**m**,* *Gdy-**ś*** *śpiewa-**ł**-Ø/* *śpiewa-**ł**-**a***
when-CONJ-1.SG when-CONJ-2.SG sing-PST-3.SG.M sing-PST-3.SG.F
'When I, you(SG) was singing (M vs. F) . . . '

c. *Gdy-**by-śmy** / Gdy-**by-ście** śpiewa-**l-i**,* *to . . .*
if-CONJ-1.PL / if-CONJ-2.PL sing-PST-PL SO
'If we / you(PL) sang (sing), then . . . '

(9) Czech

***jsem, jsi,** Ø* *zpíva-l-Ø* / *zpíva-l-a*
1.SG, 2.SG, 3 sing-PSTPST-3.SG.M / sing-PST-3-SG-F
'I, you(SG), s/he sang.'
***jsme, jste,** Ø* *zpíva-l-i* / *zpíva-l-y*
1.PL, 2.PL, 3 sing-PST-PL.VIR / sing-PST-PL.NONVIR
'We, you(PL), they(VIR vs. NONVIR) sang.'

[18] Serbian/Croatian and Slovene differ from Czech only in that (i) they rigidly abide by the Wackernagel Law, and (ii) they do not omit the copula in the 3rd person.

[19] Cf. Andersen (1987), Tommola (2000: 443–5).

4. Grammaticalization on the Edge between Morphology and Syntax

4.1. Passive

Slavic passives are marked either with a clitic or with an agglutinated reflexive marker (RM), which is highly polyfunctional as a general device of semantic or syntactic argument reduction. Or they are formed by the *n/t*-participles mentioned in section 3.1.3 and regularly overlap with object-oriented resultatives. The differentiation of these two passive types has been strengthened by an increased intersection with the aspect opposition: East Slavic allows for the RM-passive only with IPFV verbs, whereas the participial passive occurs practically only with PFV verbs; compare Russian:

(10) *Dorog-a* *peregoraživa-et-**sja*** *(derev'j-ami).*
road-NOM.SG.F partition:IPFV-PRS.3.SG-**RM** tree-INS.PL
'The road is (being) blocked (by trees).'

(11) *Dorog-a* *peregorože-**n**-a* *(derev'j-ami).*
road-NOM.SG.F partition:**PFV-N/T-NOM.SG.F** tree-INS.PL
'The road is (has been) cut / blocked (by trees).'

Other Slavic languages show this distribution only as a strong tendency. Polish differs in that (i) it eventually abandoned the RM-passive during the 19th century, (ii) uses *n/t*-participles of both aspects to distinguish aspect functions, and (iii) has established a 'become'-auxiliary (*zostać*:PFV / *zostawać*:IPFV) opposed to *być* 'be'. As a consequence, Polish not only shows a morphological distinction between resultative (static passive) and passive proper, but its passive paradigm has become richer than the active voice paradigm. Slavic passives permit oblique Actor phrases marked either by the bare instrumental (East Slavic, Czech/Slovak) or by various prepositional phrases (perlative *przez* in Polish, ablative *ot/od* in Czech/Slovak, South Slavic, adessive *u* 'at' in NW Russian dialects). For details and references see Wiemer (2004; Chapter 43 above).

A 'dative (recipient) passive' centring around the verb 'to get, receive' has grammaticalized in Czech (*dostat*), Slovak (*dostat'*), and Sorbian (Upper Sorbian *dóstać*, Lower Sorbian *krydnuś*); cf. Giger (2003). Its grammaticalization path more or less follows the German model with *bekommen/kriegen*, although in West Slavic it still does not show the same degree of grammaticalization ('measured' in terms of loss of diathetic restrictions and restrictions on lexical input).

4.2. Causative, permissive

All West Slavic languages have developed an analytic reflexive-causative construction based on an auxiliarized 'give'-verb marked with the RM. This construction has further evolved into a modal passive and is on the verge of becoming a fully-fledged passive according to the cline:

(12) lexical 'give' > permissive > reflexive-permissive > modal passive > passive

The Russian equivalent has stopped 'half-way', since it has developed only to the reflexive-permissive stage (cf. Podlesskaja 2005; von Waldenfels 2008).

5. Grammaticalization of syntactic phenomena

5.1. Converbs (gerunds)

Converbs (understood as markers of adverbial subordination) arose in Slavic only in historical time as petrified forms from the paradigm of nominally inflected participles. This process has involved syntactic tightening but no erosion. It resulted from the syntactic reanalysis of conjunctions which coordinated nominative forms of nominal participles and finite verbs with an identical subject referent (13a). Eventually, the subject NP was detached from the participle, which could no longer syntactically express its highest-ranking argument, and attracted to the finite verb; however, the requirement of its referential identity with the subject of the finite verb has remained (13b). (14) illustrates the starting situation (13a) from an East Slavic version of OChS, (15) is the modern Russian equivalent illustrating (13b):

(13) a. $NP_{nom/i}$—$participle_{nominal.nom}$—$Ø_i$ $verb_{finite}$
b. > $Ø_i$ $gerund_{indecl}$—$NP_{nom/i}$—$verb_{finite}$

(14) *Oleg*$_i$ ***nesja*** *zlato,* $Ø_I$ *priide* *k* *Kievu*
O.NOM carry:IPFV.NOM.SG.M gold.ACC come.AOR.3.SG to Kiev.DAT
lit. 'Oleg **bringing** gold, came to Kiev.'

(15) $Ø_i$ ***Nesja*** *zoloto,* *Oleg*$_i$ *priexal* *v* *Kiev.*
bring:IPFV.GER gold.ACC O.NOM come:PFV.PST.3.SG to Kiev.ACC
'**Bringing** gold, Oleg came to Kiev.'

Again, an increase in tight correlations with the aspect opposition can be observed: 'simultaneous' gerunds derive from IPFV verbs (see ex. (17)), 'anterior' gerunds from PFV verbs.[20] For details and references see Wiemer (to appear: 2.2.1–2.2.2).

5.2. *Da*: from connective to complex predicates

Balkan Slavic makes extensive use of the connective *da* introducing complements; for comparison, its Russian cognate is used only as coordinative conjunctive and a reply particle ('yes'). The development toward a subordination marker in South Slavic has proceeded even further since *da* started being used as part of finite substitutes of the lost or heavily receded infinitive. As a consequence, *da* is used now not only as a complementizer, for example of sentential arguments of control verbs but even after all sorts of auxiliaries; compare e.g. Serbian *Xoćemo*.PRS.1.PL *da idemo*.PRS.1.PL 'We want to go', Macedonian *Možam*.PRS.1.SG *da čitam*.PRS.1.SG *kirilica* 'I can read the Cyrillic alphabet'. Thus *da* developed into an inextricable component of complex predicates.

5.3. Counterfactual conditional (Russian)

Russian can use the fronted form of the seeming imperative singular as the expression of the protasis in a conjunction-less irrealis (Fortuin 2008: section 6):

(16) ***Soobraz-i*** *on / oni* *ran'še,* *on / oni* *by* *vsë*
grasp:PFV-IMP.SG he/they.NOM earlier, he/they.NOM SBJV all
uspe-l-Ø/ uspe-l-i.
manage:PFV-PST.SG.M/PL
'If he/they **had understood** (it) earlier, he/they would have managed (to do it).'

In very rare cases this construction can also express potential events; the entire protasis has to precede the apodosis. In any case, categorial reduction is involved, since the form of the singular is used irrespective of the number of the grammatical subject (see the example). It is still unclear whether this form etymologically corresponds to the imperative or derives from the extinct 3.SG.aorist. In the latter case, this development would amount to exaptation.

[20] The suffix of the anterior gerund {vši} is etymologically identical to the non-agreeing resultative on {vši} in NW Russ. dialects (see Table 61.2).

CHAPTER 62

GRAMMATICALIZATION IN TURKIC LANGUAGES

LARS JOHANSON

1. Introduction

The following comments are intended to provide examples of typical grammaticalization processes observed in Turkic languages. The present-day members of this language family can be divided into six branches:

Southwestern Turkic including Turkish, Gagauz, Azeri, Turkmen;
Northwestern Turkic including Noghay, Kazakh, Kirghiz, Tatar, Bashkir, Karachay-Balkar, Kumyk, Karaim;
Southeastern Turkic including Uzbek, Uyghur;
Northeastern Turkic including Yakut, Khakas, Tuvan, Tofan, Dukhan;
Chuvash (Volga region);
Khalaj (central Iran)

Older written languages, East Old Turkic (Orkhon Turkic, Old Uyghur, Karakhanid), Chaghatay, and Ottoman, will occasionally be cited. Examples will mostly be rendered in a unified broad phonetic transcription. Only Turkish examples will be quoted in the official orthography. Capital letters will be used to indicate morphophonemes, and bracketed signs to indicate segments that only occur in certain environments. Whenever possible, reference will be made to the types of grammaticalization paths established by Heine and Kuteva (2002).

2. Unknown sources

There have been numerous speculative attempts to trace core case suffixes, plural markers, primeval postpositions, aspect and mood markers, etc. back to originally independent words.

A grammaticalization path from a concept 'near(ness)' to the dative marker -KA has been suggested (Doerfer 1977; 1987). The possible source element might be a Proto-Turkic root **ḳa* 'nearness, unity', present in *ḳat* 'side', *ḳat-* 'to join (tr.)' and in the Old Turkic noun *ḳa:* 'family' (Clauson 1972: 578a).

Though core case markers may have developed from postpositions, this is impossible to prove. Not even the primeval Turkic postpositions have clear etymologies. The old prodessive postposition *üčün*, signalling benefactivity, reason, purpose, etc. ('for the sake of', 'because of', 'in order to'), has been subject to etymological speculations (Sevortjan 1974: 642–3). It has been connected with *u:ǰ* 'extremity', 'end', 'tip', which causes phonetic problems, with a reconstructed Altaic verb **ič-* 'to look' (Ramstedt 1957: 93), etc. It is present in most languages, e.g. Turkish *için*, Azeri *üčün*, Turkmen *üči:n*, Tatar *ŭčŭn* («өчен»), Bashkir *ŭsŭn* («өсөн»), Noghay *üšin*, Uzbek *ŭčŭn*, Uyghur *üčün*. It has given rise to the Chuvash clitic marker -*šĂn* 'for'. Ottoman Turkish displayed a bound variant, the clitic *-(y)čin/-(y)čün*, which was, however, given up in modern Turkish in favour of the free form.

Though relatively simple markers in present-day languages may have developed from less grammaticalized structures, the sources are seldom known. Markers of the types *-mIš* and *-GAn*, which signal a post-terminal (perfect-like) aspect, are of unknown origin, but may have developed from lexemes. Thus *-mIš* might go back to a form of a verb *bïš-* 'to ripen, to mature' (Clauson 1972: 376b–377a), while -GA*n* has developed from a form of *ḳa:n-* 'to be satisfied, satiated' (Clauson 1972: 632a).

3. Nonverbal sources

3.1. Adjectives as sources

Adjectives meaning 'other' have developed into elements meaning 'except', 'excluding', 'without'. One type is *bašḳa*, derived from *baš* 'head', e.g. Turkish *başka*, Azeri *bašġa*, Kumyk *bašγa*, Karachay-Balkar *bašxa*, Tatar *bašḳa*, Noghay, Kazakh *basḳa*, Chuvash *puś-nɛ*. The other type is *özgɛ*, derived from *ö:z* (section 3.2), e.g. Chaghatay *özgɛ*, Turkmen *ö:δγɛ*, Tuvan *öskɛ*. Adjectives meaning 'firm', 'solid', 'stable' have developed into adverbs meaning 'very', e.g. Turkish *pek* 'very' < *bɛrk* 'strong, stable'. Adverbs such as Tofan *dikka* 'very' derive from *tik* 'straight, upright, firm'.

3.2. Nouns as sources

Many nouns have developed into grammatical markers by virtue of certain salient semantic properties. Only relatively recent processes can be identified as such.

A clear case is the development of *ki:b* 'mould, model, shape' (Clauson 1972: 686b) plus a 3SG possessive suffix into an equative postposition expressing qualitative comparison ('as', 'like'), e.g. *altun kibi* 'like gold'. Modern forms include Turkish *gibi*, Azeri *kimi(n)*, Uzbek *kȧbi*. The Northwestern branch exhibits variants such as *kibik*. Forms such as Old Ottoman *bigi* and Chuvash *pɛk* are metathetic. The old noun *sïŋa:r* 'side' ('one of two sides', Clauson 1972: 840b–841a) is the source of a similar equative, e.g. Uzbek *siŋȧri* 'like'.

Nouns denoting 'amount' have developed into equative markers of quantitative comparison ('as much as', 'up to'), e.g. Turkish *kadar*, Azeri *ġɛdɛr*, Karachay-Balkar *ḳadar*, Uzbek *ḳadȧr*, a loanword of ultimately Arabic origin. (Cf. Heine and Kuteva 2002: 304–8.)

The noun *soŋ* 'end' is the source of postpositions meaning 'after' (temporal), e.g. Chaghatay *üč kündin soŋ* 'after three days', represented by Karaim *son*, Tatar *sŭŋ* («соң»), Bashkir *huŋ* («һуң»), Kumyk, Uzbek, Kazakh *soŋ*, Turkmen *θoŋ*, Khalaj *soy*, etc. The type *soŋra* 'after', with a fossilized directive marker, functions as adverbs and postpositions in many languages. Cf. Heine and Kuteva (2002: 134), where Turkish *son* 'end' is, however, taken to be a verb ('to end').

Generic nouns meaning 'thing', e.g. *šɛy*, and 'person', e.g. *za:t* (both ultimately of Arabic origin), have developed into indefinite pronouns, e.g. Turkish *bir şey* 'something', Kumyk, Karachay-Balkar *bir zat* 'something'. (Cf. Heine and Kuteva 2002: 208–9, 295–6.)

Nouns meaning 'side' have developed into adverbs and postpositions meaning 'in the direction of', 'towards'. The noun *sïŋ:ar* 'side' (see above) is the source of contracted forms, e.g. Chaghatay *sarï*, Azeri *sarï*, Uzbek *sari*, Khalaj *sa:ru*, Turkmen *θa:rï* (Clauson 1972: 840b, 844b.) The nouns *taraf* and *tama:n* 'side' have undergone similar developments, e.g. Azeri, Khalaj *tɛrɛf*, Uzbek *tåmån* 'towards'.

The noun *ḳaršï* 'opposite place' has developed into adverbs and postpositions meaning 'against' and 'contrary to', e.g. Chaghatay *ḳaršu*, Azeri, Turkmen *ġaršï*, Chuvash *xirĕś;* (cf. Clauson 1972: 663b–664a.)

A noun *ta:nɛ* 'grain', 'seed', 'piece' (from Persian *da:na*) has developed into a classifier in some languages, e.g. Turkish *iki tane yumurta* 'two eggs' (cf. 'piece' > classifier in Heine and Kuteva 2002: 238). The Uzbek combination with *bir* 'one' has developed into an indefinite article, e.g. *bittȧ ḳiz* 'a girl'. For the development of *bir* 'one' into an indefinite article see Heine and Kuteva (2002: 220–21).

Nouns denoting body parts have often developed into grammatical markers. The noun *bo:ð* 'stature', 'size', 'body', 'build', 'stretch' has given rise to reflexive pronouns ('self', 'own') in the Northeastern branch, e.g. *BOT*, *BOS*, *BOY* (cf. 'body' > reflexive in Heine and Kuteva 2002: 58–60). Most languages use the noun *ö:z* 'essence', 'spirit' (Clauson 1972: 278a) as a reflexive pronoun. Turkish *kendi* < *kɛndü* is of unknown origin; combinations such as *kɛndü öz*, *kɛndözi* occur in older languages.

A number of markers that go back to words for body parts express deictic location. Thus *öŋ* means 'front' and 'before' (place and time), in Old Uyghur also 'east'. The corresponding Chuvash *um* also means 'breast', which might indicate the path of grammaticalization (cf. 'breast' > 'front' in Heine and Kuteva 2002: 62).

Words for 'nose', *burun*, *murun*, are often used as 'before', 'formerly', 'prior to', 'previous', 'long ago'. Clauson describes the grammaticalization path as follows: 'nose' > 'a protruding natural feature, headland, peak (of a mountain)' > metaphorically 'in front', 'preceding' > 'preceding in time, previous' (1972: 366b). It can be compared to *ilk* 'first (in space or time)', 'before', 'formerly'; Old Uyghur, Ottoman, etc. *ilk*, Tatar *ĭlĭk* («элек»), Chuvash *ĭlĭk* («ĕлĕк»). Yakut *ilik* occurs in converbial constructions expressing actions that have not yet taken place, e.g. *kɛl-ɛ ilik-pin* 'I have not yet arrived' ('I am before arriving').

3.3. Secondary postpositions

The postpositions dealt with above are 'primary' postpositions, which govern the case (nominative, genitive, dative, or ablative) of their complements. As noted, some of them can be traced back to nouns. 'Secondary' postpositions all clearly go back to nouns. They are morphologically nominal forms, declinable as nouns, bearing possessive suffixes that agree with their complements, and various case suffixes. A postpositional phrase such as Turkish *ev-in ön-ün-de* <house-GENITIVE front-POSSESSIVE.3SG-LOCATIVE> 'in front of the house' is structured as a noun phrase like *ev-in bahçe-sin-de* 'in the garden of the house'. One difference is that complements of secondary postpositions sometimes stand in the nominative, e.g. *ev ön-ün-de.*

Secondary postpositions typically express spatial relations. Nouns denoting 'place', e.g. *yer*, *orin*, have developed into expressions for 'instead of', e.g. Turkish *yer-in-e*, Uzbek *orn-i-gȧ* <place-POSSESSIVE.3SG-DATIVE> (cf. Heine and Kuteva 2002: 239–40.) Azeri *ġabaγ-ïn-da* 'in front of' is based on *ġabaġ*, which has undergone the development 'pumpkin' > 'target' > 'front side' (Clauson 1972: 582b). Nouns for 'side' are used to express agent markers ('by') in passive sentences, e.g. Turkish *taraf-ın-dan*, Uzbek *tåmån-i-dȧn*. (Cf. Heine and Kuteva 2002: 199–200.)

The sources are frequently nouns denoting body parts. In Siberian languages, various contracted forms of *baγïr* 'liver, intestines' serve to express 'front part', e.g. *ba:r-ï* 'its front part' (Radloff 1911: 1451; Clauson 1972: 317a–b). The noun *ḳaš* 'eyebrow' is sometimes used for 'presence', 'nearness', e.g. *ḳaš-ïm-da* <eyebrow-POSSESSIVE.1SG-LOCATIVE> 'in my presence', 'near me' (Clauson 1972: 669a–b); compare the use of English *brow* for 'summit'. Nouns of the type *bet* 'human face' express 'this side of' > 'in front of' (Clauson 1972: 296b; cf. Heine and Kuteva 2002: 130–31.) Nouns of the type *ḳat* 'layer' express 'in the presence of', 'at', 'by', 'beside', e.g. Chaghatay *ata ḳat-ï-γa* <father presence-POSSESSIVE.3SG-DATIVE> 'to the father' (Clauson 1972: 593; Doerfer 1967: 419). Nouns such as *yan* 'side' express 'presence' > 'beside', 'at', 'to', e.g. Uzbek *yån-i-gȧ* <side-POSS.1SG-DATIVE>, 'to him / her / it'. Nouns going back to *bo:δ* 'stature' (section 3.2), can express 'in accordance with', e.g. Uzbek *ḳånun boy-i-čȧ* <law accordance-POSSESSIVE.3SG-EQUATIVE> 'in accordance with the law'.

4. Verbal sources

4.1. Verbal stems as sources

Verbs have often served as grammaticalization sources. An old verbal stem *sa:-* 'to think', 'to reckon', 'to count', 'to desire' has developed into a denominal desiderative suffix *-sA*, e.g. Old Uyghur, Karakhanid *suβ-sa-* 'to desire water', 'to be thirsty', *kör-üg-sɛ-* 'to want to see'. It has also given rise to the conditional marker *-sA*, whose older form *-sA-r* bears the old present suffix (Johanson 1995: 336).

The stem *art-* 'to increase' is the source of the type *art-uḳ* 'additional', 'extra amount', 'excessive(ly)', 'abundant', 'more than', 'superfluous', 'too much', e.g. Turkish *art-ık*, Karachay-Balkar *art-ïḳ*, Khalaj *art-uḳ*.

The old stem *ḳa:la:-* 'to heap up', still alive in Uzbek (Clauson 1972: 617b), has developed into markers of repeated, frequent, systematically, or periodically performed action. One type is *-GIlA*, e.g. Crimean Tatar *kɛs-kɛlɛ-* 'to cut continuously', Turkmen *baθ-γïla-* 'to suppress' (*baθ-* 'to press'), Bashkir *kil-gilɛ-* 'to arrive several times', Khakas *pas-xla-* 'to write repeatedly', Tuvan *biži-gilɛ-* 'to write repeatedly'. There may be detensive nuances: 'now and then', 'for a while', 'here and there', e.g. Tuvan *nomču-γala-* 'to read a little here and there', Chuvash *kul-kala-* 'to laugh for a while'.

4.2. Converbs as sources

Turkic converbs have often developed into postpositions (Johanson 1995). Forms based on 'to see' are the sources of postpositions meaning 'in view of', 'with respect to', 'according to', 'on account of', 'considering', 'because of', 'to judge from', e.g.

Chaghatay *kör-ɛ*, Turkish *gör-e*, Kumyk *gör-ɛ*, Karachay-Balkar *kör-ɛ*, Tatar, Bashkir *kür-ɛ*, Uzbek *kȯr-ȧ*, Uzbek *kȯr-ȧ*, Chuvash *kur-a*.

Forms based on 'to look' have become markers of 'in the direction of', 'towards' (spatial), e.g. Turkmen *baḳ-a*, Bashkir *ḳara-y*, Noghay, Uyghur *ḳara-p*, Uzbek *ḳarȧ-b*. The negative forms mean 'although', 'in spite of', e.g. Uzbek *ḳarȧ-mȧ-y*, Chuvash *păx-ma-sărax*.

Converbs of verbs for 'to reach' have given rise to markers of 'until', 'up to', 'as far as', e.g. Turkish *değin*, Kazakh *dɛyin*. (Cf. Heine and Kuteva 2002: 46.) Note that these forms cannot have developed further into *dɛk*, e.g. Turkish *-dek*, as sometimes claimed.

Converbs of verbs for 'to count' have produced expressions of 'every' or 'throughout', e.g. East Old Turkic *sa:-yu* (Clauson 1972: 858b–859a), Uzbek *yil sayin* 'every year', Chuvash *śul-sɛrɛn* 'every year', Noghay *yïl sayïn* 'the whole year'.

Converbs of verbs for 'to put down' have developed into markers of 'down (wards)', 'under', 'below', e.g. East Old Turkic *ḳo:δï* 'downwards' (< *ḳo:δ-*), Chaghatay *ḳoyï*, Tuvan *kudu*, Dukhan *ġodi*.

Converbs of *bi:r-lɛ-* 'to unite', derived from the numeral *bi:r* 'one', have yielded comitative and instrumental postpositions of the type *bir-lɛ* (Clauson 1972: 364b–365a), e.g. Turkmen *bilɛ(n)*, Uzbek *bilȧn*, Tuvan *bilɛ*, Kirghiz *mɛn(ɛn)*, Khakas *mïnan* (cf. Schönig 1998). The Chuvash comitative case marker *-pA(lA)* may have the same origin (Benzing 1959: 726).

Converbs of *boy-la-* 'to extend', derived from *bo:δ* 'stature' (sections 3.2 and 3.3), have developed into postpositions meaning 'comprising the distance or period of', 'along' (spatial and temporal), 'throughout', e.g. Uzbek *boy-lȧ-b*.

Converbs of verbs of the types *bašla-* 'to begin' and *al-* 'to take' have developed into abtemporal markers ('from . . . on', 'since'), e.g. Noghay *basla-p*, *al-ïp*, Uzbek *bååšlȧ-b*, *ål-ip*.

4.3. Postverbal constructions

Turkic languages have developed systems of postverbal constructions, consisting of converb markers attached to stems of lexical verbs and immediately following auxiliary verbs (Johanson 2002: 91–7).

The converb markers are usually of two types. Type A ends in a vowel, e.g. Turkish *gel-e* 'coming' (*gel-* 'to come'), whereas type B ends in a labial stop, e.g. Turkish *gel-ip*. In some varieties, e.g. Khakas, type B is dropped after consonant stems, e.g. *kil-ĭp* > *kil* (identical with the verbal stem). The converb marker and the auxiliary verb sometimes fuse to form one grammatical suffix. Occasionally, a finite form is used instead of the converb.

The constructions are created with a limited set of auxiliary verbs going back to lexical verbs: motion verbs such as 'to go', 'to come', 'to go away', 'to go out', 'to proceed', postural verbs such 'to stand', 'to remain', 'to sit', 'to lie', phasal verbs such as 'to begin', 'to finish', and verbs denoting various activities such as 'to do', 'to put', 'to occur', 'to place', 'to throw', 'to send', 'to give', 'to take'. Though the grammatical functions of the constructions are relatively similar across languages, they are not entirely predictable on the basis of the lexical meaning of the source verbs.

Postverbal constructions express semantic modifications of the action indicated by the lexical verb, expressing potentiality, attempt, phase specification, direction, version, etc.

4.3.1. *Potentiality*

Potentiality is expressed by constructions with verbs of the types 'to take', 'to know', and 'to become'. Verbs of the type *al-* 'to take', 'to get' have developed to express physical and mental ability (Heine and Kuteva 2002: 143–4, 148–9), mostly also permissiveness and epistemic possibility (2002: 27–9), e.g. Karachay-Balkar *kör-ɛ al-*, *kör-al-* 'to be able to see', Karaim *bar-al-* 'to be able to go', Bashkir *yaδ-a al-* 'to be able to write', Kirghiz *bɛr-ɛ al-* 'to be able to give'. Chuvash *-Ay-* represents the same type.

The Southwestern branch prefers constructions based on *bil-* 'to know', e.g. Azeri *gör-ɛ bil-* 'to be able to see', Crimean Tatar *at-a bil-* 'to be able to throw', Bashkir *yüδ-ɛ bĭl-* 'to be able to swim', Khalaj *kɛl-i-bil-* 'to be able to come'. Most constructions of this type indicate ability, permissiveness, and epistemic possibility, e.g. the Turkish potential marker *-(y)A-bil-*. Gagauz *-(y)A-bil-*, however, does not express epistemic possibility.

East Old Turkic used the now obsolete verb *u:-* 'to be able, powerful'. The regular negative forms of some later languages go back to its negative form *u:-ma-*, e.g. Old Ottoman *bul-ï-ma-* 'to be unable to find', Turkish *ver-e-me-* 'to be unable to give', Crimean Tatar *at-a-ma-* 'to be unable to throw', Khalaj *var-um-* 'to be unable to go' < *bar-u u:-ma-*.

4.3.2. *Attempted action*

Postverb constructions based on 'to see' and 'to look' express effort and care to carry out the action ('to make sure to do', 'to take care to do') or attempt to carry it out ('to try to do'). A + *kör-* is used in older languages, e.g. Chaghatay *al-a kör-* 'to try to get'. Another option is B + *kör-*, e.g. Uzbek *ye-b kȯr-* 'to try to eat', 'to taste', Uyghur *tɛt-ip kör-* 'to taste', Khakas *pas kör-* 'to try to write', *kis kör-* 'to try on (clothes)'. Uyghur also uses *baḳ-* 'to look, to watch' to express attempted action, e.g. *yɛ-p baḳ-* 'to try to eat', 'to have a taste'.

4.3.3. *Directionality*

Postverbal constructions often denote the direction of the action. Motion verbs meaning 'come' and 'go away' and verbs meaning 'give' and 'take' serve to express whether the action is directed away from or towards a deictic centre.

Venitive (cislocative) constructions indicate 'coming' by means of the type *kɛl-* e.g. Old Uyghur *ün-ɛ kɛl-* 'to come forth', Tatar *al-ïp kil-* 'to bring', Noghay *uš-ïp kɛl-* 'to fly here (to this place)', Khakas *al kil-* 'to bring'.

Andative (translocative) constructions indicate 'going away' by means of the types *bar-* and *kɛt-*, e.g. Old Uyghur *öl-üp bar-* 'to pass away', Tatar *ül-ịp kɛt-* 'to pass away', Noghay *uš-ïp bar-* 'to fly there (to that place)' (cf. Heine and Kuteva 2002: 155).

4.3.4. *Version*

Postverbal constructions may also express that the action is performed to the advantage of the performer or somebody else. Constructions based on 'to take' express subject version, i.e. that the action is intended for the performer ('to do for oneself, in one's own interest'), e.g. Tatar *tŭt-ïp al-* 'to grasp for oneself', Uyghur *yez-iw al-* 'to write down for oneself', Khakas *id-ĭp al-* 'to do for oneself'. Constructions based on 'to give' express object version, i.e. that the action is intended for some other person ('to do for, for the benefit of somebody'), e.g. Tatar *tab-ïp bir-* 'to find for somebody', Khakas *pas pir-* 'to write for somebody' (cf. 'benefactive' in Heine and Kuteva 2002: 149).

4.3.5. *Actional modification*

Postverbal constructions are mostly markers of actionality, modifying the intrinsic actional value (Aktionsart) of the lexical verb, specifying its qualitative or quantitative properties, the way the action is carried out, 'modes of action'. They may imply durativity, continuity, intensity, or sudden, involuntary, unintentional action, etc., mostly effects of their use to specify the internal phase structure.

For the description of aspect-sensitive actional meanings, the basic classificatory criterion is transformativity. An actional content is transformative if it has a natural evolutional turning point, a crucial initial or final limit. A non-transformative actional content does not imply any such limit. As transformativizers and non-transformativizers, postverbal constructions can recategorize the internal phase structure, specifying one inherent phase of the action (Johanson 2000: 66–76). Many auxiliaries, such as those going back to postural verbs, may also give additional information on the physical position in which the action is performed.

Transformativizing postverbal constructions operate on actionally ambiguous contents, highlighting a dynamic (initial or final) phase of the action. They are based on verbs meaning 'to send', 'to put', 'to throw', 'to go away', 'to come', 'to go out', 'to fall', etc.

Khakas examples:

'to send': *čĭ-bĭs-* 'to eat up', *odïr-ïbïs-* 'to sit down'; cf. Noghay *kül-ip yibɛr-* 'to burst out laughing', Kumyk *oxu-p yibɛr-* 'to start reading';

'to put': *xas sal-* 'to dig up', *pas sal-* 'to write down', *či-p sal-* 'to eat up'; cf. Tatar *ḳurḳĭt-ĭp ḳuy-* 'to frighten';
'to go out': *ïrla-p sïx-* 'to start singing', *toɣïn sïx-* 'to start to work';
'to go away': *usxun par-* 'to wake up', *sïn par-* 'to get broken';
'to throw' *pas tasta-* 'to write down'.

One semantic effect may be 'suddenness', e.g. Khakas *kĭr-ɛ sal-* 'to enter suddenly'.

The processes can be compared to the developments of 'to put', 'to leave', 'to let', 'to throw' into 'completive' markers (Heine and Kuteva 2002: 248, 297).

Certain constructions are non-transformativizers, highlighting the statal, non-dynamic phase of an action. They are based on postural verbs meaning 'to stand', 'to remain', 'to sit', 'to lie' and motion verbs meaning 'to proceed', 'to move'.

Constructions based on the type *tur-* 'to stand' thus block limit-oriented interpretations, e.g. Tatar *awïr-ïp tŭr-* 'to be ill', not 'to get ill', *ḳara-p tŭr-* 'to look', not 'to catch sight', *tŭt-ïp tŭr-* 'to hold', not 'to grasp', Kumyk *aša-p tur-* 'to eat', not 'to begin to eat' or 'to eat up', *oxu-p tur-* 'to read', not 'to start reading' or 'to read and finish reading', *yuxla-p tur-* 'to sleep', not 'to fall asleep', Karachay *oltur-ub tur-* 'to sit', not 'to sit down'. They can also denote 'continuity', e.g. Tatar *yaz-a tŭr-* 'to keep writing', Turkish *içedur-* 'to keep drinking'. Serial reinterpretations are possible, e.g. Kumyk *oxu-p tur-* 'to read repeatedly, habitually', Karachay-Balkar *yibɛr-ip tur-* 'to send repeatedly', Karachay *tig-ib tur-* 'to sew repeatedly, habitually', Khakas *kil tur-* 'to arrive repeatedly', *ïrla-p čör-* 'to sing repeatedly'.

The processes can be compared to the developments of 'to stand', 'to stay', 'to remain', 'to sit', 'to lie', 'to move' into continuous, habitual, durative, iterative markers (Heine and Kuteva 2002: 157–8, 193–4, 196–7, 254–6, 276–9, 280–82). Meanings or those kinds derive from the nontransformativizing function.

4.4. Viewpoint aspect markers

Certain postverbal constructions have, combined with present markers, developed into viewpoint aspect operators to renew the expression of intra-terminality (presents and imperfectives). These grammaticalization processes are based on verbs meaning 'to be', 'to stand', 'to move', 'to sit', 'to lie'. In written language, the constructions may be ambiguous between actional and aspectual meanings, whereas this ambiguity is dispelled by prosodic means in spoken language.

The type A + *tur-ur* evolved in the Northwestern and Southeastern branches, e.g. *yaz-a-tur-ur* ('stands writing'). The forms underwent strong phonetic erosion: fusion of the converb marker with the auxiliary and partial or total loss of *tur-ur*, e.g. > *yaz-a-dïr* > *yaz-a* 'is writing' (Johanson 1976). Some contructions are based on 'to sit', e.g. Kirghiz *ištɛ-p otur-mun* 'I am working'. The Turkish suffix *-(I)yor* evolved from a construction with a verb 'to move', e.g. *gel-iyor* 'comes, is coming' < *gɛl-ɛ yorï-r* ('moves coming') (Johanson 1971).

These items originally expressed high degrees of focality, focusing on the orientation point in the sense of progressives ('is just now doing'), and eventually turned into items of lower focality: simple presents and imperfects. This led to further renewals of high focality by means of the verb _yat-_ 'lie' in constructions of the type B + _yat-ïr_ 'lies'), e.g. Khakas _kör-čɛ_ 'is seeing, sees' < *_kör-üp yat-ïr_. The Uzbek focal present _yåz(a)yapti_ 'is writing' goes back to _yaz-a yat-ib tur-ur_ ('to write' + A + 'to lie' + B + 'stands').

Constructions with B + _turur_ developed into viewpoint aspect operators renewing the expression of post-terminality (resultatives, perfects, constatives), e.g. _yaz-ïp turur_ ('stands having written'). They underwent phonetic erosion, fusion of the converb marker with the auxiliary, and partial or total loss of _tur-ur_, e.g. > _yaz-ïp-dïr_ > _yaz-ïp_ 'has written' (on evidential meanings, see Johanson 2003.) They originally expressed high degrees of focality in the sense of resultatives ('is in the state of having done'), but later turned into items of lower focality, which led to further renewals of high focality by means of _yat-_ 'to lie', e.g. Khakas _uzu-p-čat-xan_ 'has slept' < *_uδï-p yat-ḳan_.

CHAPTER 63

GRAMMATICALIZATION IN KOREAN

SEONGHA RHEE

1. Introduction

Korean is one of the world's major languages, with approximately 78 million speakers, mostly residing in the Korean peninsula. It was formerly written in three systems using Chinese characters pronounced in the Korean way either taking the phonetic value or the semantic value of the character. Therefore, how a particular word or phrase in the literature dating from the 6th to 11th centuries written in these systems should be read is often controversial. In 1443 a national writing system, called Hangeul, was developed by King Sejong the Great. Designed on the phonemic principle, Hangeul is an alphabetical system written in a syllable-based block. It is written with inter-lexical spaces, unlike other neighboring languages. The historical significance of Hangeul is that its invention enabled uncontroversial documentation of Korean from the 15th century.

The genealogical classification of Korean is debated. Some linguists (e.g. Ramstedt 1939) place it in the Altaic language family since it has such linguistic properties as vowel harmony, agglutination, avoidance of certain sounds in onset, etc., while others consider it a language isolate because of a lack of convincing evidence linking Korean to other languages (Song 2005; Sohn 2001[1999]). It is an agglutinative language in its morphology and has an SOV word order.

Situated in a peninsula, Korea's linguistic contact was largely limited to its bordering country, China. Chinese heavily influenced Korean vocabulary from its supposed introduction in the second century BC. It is supposed that about 60 per cent of the vocabulary is of Chinese origin (Sohn 2001: 13), but a considerably lower percentage of Sino-Korean words is used in daily life. Many words of Japanese origin entered the Korean lexis during the early 20th century when Japan occupied Korea, but a nationwide effort eliminated much of the Japanese linguistic influence after the occupation ended. More recently, with the growing importance of English as the world's lingua franca coupled with English-friendly language policies, a large number of English words are also in use. However, the effect of the language contact with these languages is largely confined to the lexis, and the grammatical influence is nearly nonexistent.

2. Grammaticalization

2.1. Grammaticalization studies in history

Grammaticalization studies were begun in Korea in the 1950s by historical linguists who termed the phenomenon *hesa-hwa* 'the process whereby words become empty' (Yu 1962: 201). This nomenclature seems to have been inspired by Chinese scholars, who contrasted the functional items (*xūcí: hesa* 'empty word' in Korean) with lexical items (*shící: silsa* 'content word' in Korean).

Early discussion of grammaticalization often resorted to such notions as weakening and loss, corresponding to the bleaching model (Heine, Claudi, and Hünnemeyer 1991) in the western tradition. Up until the 1980s most grammaticalization studies addressed emergence of grammatical forms from the existence verb (Lee 1956; Yu 1962), nominative markers (K. Lee 1958; S. Lee 1958), postpositions (Kim 1975; Lee 1976; An 1983; Lee 1987), and tense–aspect–modality markers (Huh 1987, Han 1986).

The 1990s saw a sharp increase in interest in grammaticalization studies. Much research was carried out in the grammaticalization framework. Notable doctoral dissertations in this period include Ko (1995) and Rhee (1996), who addressed grammaticalization of verbs, Lee (1991) and Oh (1998), who presented a comprehensive description of tense–aspect–modality markers, as well as Chung (1993) and Ahn (1996), who addressed the grammaticalization of nouns. In the following decades research continued in sentence-final markers (also often called 'sentential endings'), postpositions, and auxiliary verbs, and such important works as Jung

(2001), Kang (2001) and numerous others contributed to the grammaticalization scholarship.

2.2. Domains of grammaticalization

2.2.1. *Morphophonological change*

Phonological erosion is a common concomitant to grammaticalization. Erosion of sounds may eventually lead to loss of morphemes. Unlike isolating and inflectional languages Korean morphology is quite complex because of its agglutinating nature. Agglutinated morphemes often lose phonologically or semantically non-salient elements in them. The Korean light verb is a paradigm example of how the erosion of a word can cause a large-scale change in grammar (Rhee 2009c).

The light verb *ha-* was polysemous in Middle Korean with the two meanings of 'do' and 'say'. By virtue of being 'light' in semantics, and being an utterance verb, known for its susceptibility to grammaticalization across languages, it came to be used in many grammatical constructions of diverse functions. These periphrastic constructions, being subject to high frequency, came to lose the light verb that was pivotal in the creation of the constructions. The loss was largely due to the lack of phonological and semantic prominence of *ha-* and increased inter-morphemic bonding. This erosion often triggered the erosion of other morphemes that occurred near it.

An initial consequence of the loss is the awkward situation where a constellation of multiple linguistic forms in a word cannot be appropriately analysed through traditional morphosyntactic rules. This situation triggers reanalysis whereby the remnants are construed as single grammatical units and as carrying the function that is morphosyntactically amenable. This invisibility of the light verb triggers a wholesale morphophonological change that affected hundreds of formerly periphrastic constructions. Some of the dramatic examples of massive erosion are the genesis of the identificational topic marker *-lan* and declarative adnominalizer *-tan*, as shown below:

(1) a. *-la-ko-ha-nun-kes-un* > *-lan*
SF-CONN-say-ADN-thing-TOP TOP

b. *-ta-ko-ha-nun* > *-tan*
SF-CONN-say-ADN ADN

(2) a. *hakkyo-lan kongpwuha-nun kos-i-ta*
school-TOP study-ADN place-be-DECL
'A school is a place where (you) study.' (< A thing that (people) call a school is . . .)

b. *keki* *ka-keyss-tan* *mal* *ha-n* *cek* *eps-ta*
there go-FUT-ADN word say-ADN time not.exist-DECL
'I didn't say that I would go there.' (< I didn't say the word that I would . . .)

An implication of this grammatical change is that it triggered the emergence of diverse paradigms of grammatical morphemes, a process whereby newly emerging forms create multiple layers of grammatical forms within a paradigm. In this layering, different forms of the same origin enter into functional division of labour, and some identical forms show functional divergence between semantically more conservative and more innovative functions, the latter being more subjective.

2.2.2. *Syntagmatic change*

Since grammaticalization occurs in a local context where linguistic forms create a construction with increased inter-lexical bonding, the construction often undergoes a reanalysis whereby a string of multiple linguistic forms is treated as a single unit. In Korean, as is common among agglutinating languages, such functional reanalyses often lead to reductive formal changes involving creation of portmanteau morphs.

One of the most common types of syntagmatic change observed in Korean is the emergence of auxiliaries derived from serial verb constructions (see section 2.3.3 for examples). In a serial verb construction, where two verbs are serialized by means of a nonfinite marker, the construction originally refers to two events that occur in sequence e.g. *ccic-e-peli-* 'tear and throw away,' *pilli-e-cwu-* 'lend and give'. Since language users tend to pay more attention to one of the two events, typically the first one (i.e. 'tearing' and 'lending'), the second event tends to be interpreted in a more abstract way, thus making it subsidiary to the first event. Therefore the construction with two main verbs becomes a construction with one main verb and one auxiliary, with the functional reinterpretation of *-e-peli-* as completive marker, and *-e-cwu-* as benefactive marker in the above examples.

Another paradigm example of syntagmatic reanalysis involves the genesis of tense markers. For instance, Modern Korean has two future tense markers: *-keyss-* and *-ul-kes-i-*. The emergence of the monomorphemic *-keyss-* is the result of a massive syntagmatic reduction of a periphrasis, *-key-hay-e-iss-* 'MODE-do-NF-exist-' (Huh 1982: 38; Rhee 1996: 109–10). The periphrastic *-ul-kes-i-* '-PROS.ADN-thing-be-' is formally transparent in terms of its internal structure, whose meaning can be rendered as 'x is a thing that y is prospectively z' but its semantic cohesion is such that it is construed simply as a futurity marker. One notable aspect of this change is syntactic upgrading whereby the subordinate clause becomes the matrix clause and the predicate of the original matrix clause becomes a part of the constellation of the sentence-final markers in what is now the matrix clause, as illustrated in (3).

(3) *pi-ka* *o-l* *kes-i-ta*
rain-NOM come-PROS.ADN thing-be-DECL
'It will rain.' (< Lit: It is (the) thing (in which) the rain comes prospectively.)

2.2.3. *Paradigmatic change*

Grammaticalization can effect a significant change by triggering a large-scale reorganization of an existing paradigm or creating an entirely new paradigm. This is well observed in Korean in recent studies on sentence-final markers, complementizers, and conditionals.

Korean has a large number of sentence-final markers, both ultimate and penultimate, depending on the sentence types, formality levels, politeness, and speaker's stance in addition to tense, aspect, and modality. An ongoing language change is a shift of certain connectives into sentence-final markers (Sohn 1995; Lee and Park 1999; Sohn and Park 2002; Jung 2001, Rhee 2002). For instance, *-ketun*, which formerly functioned as a conditional connective, now also functions as a sentence-final marker for speaker-orientedness, discourse-background, and turn-transition. Similarly, *-myense*, *-nikka*, *-untey*, *-nuntey*, *-key*, etc. formerly functioned as connectives but now function in addition as sentence-final markers.

Another category is the complementizers that developed in the 18th and the 19th centuries (Rhee 2008; 2009b). The construction involved in this development was a string of a sentence-final marker, a locution verb, and a connective, from which the locution verb disappeared as a result of phonological erosion, as shown in (4).

(4) *-ta/-la* 'DECL.SF' + *ha* 'say' + *-ko* 'CONN' > *-tako/-lako* 'COMP'
-la 'IMP.SF + *ha* 'say' + *-ko* 'CONN' > *-lako* 'COMP'
-nya 'INT.SF' + *ha* 'say' + *-ko* 'CONN' > *-nyako* 'COMP'
-ca 'HORT.SF + *ha* 'say' + *-ko* 'CONN' > *-cako* 'COMP'

A historical survey suggests that the declarative-based complementizer *-tako* came into being first, and then others followed its course. This suggests that grammaticalization may be actuated by a structural analogy whereby members of an entire paradigm may follow the one member that leads the grammaticalization process, thus creating a whole new paradigm in a short period.

Interestingly, these complementizers also become sentence-final markers through their frequent use in the elliptical structure where the matrix clause is missing. Again, with structural analogy all members quickly developed into sentence-final markers. Still more intriguing is the fact that a group of similar constructions, i.e. those with the conditional marker *-myen* in place of the connective *-ko* of the source constructions of the complementizers, have been developing into a new sub-paradigm of conditional markers (Koo and Rhee 2008; Koo 2009). These innovative conditionals carry a higher level of hypotheticality and intersubjectivity.

All these instances point to the facts that structural analogy can trigger grammaticalization; that grammaticalization based on structural analogy can affect the entire paradigm; and that the primary subcategory of a paradigm may lead the grammaticalization of the other subcategories within the paradigm (Koo and Rhee 2008). They are noteworthy in that these are instances of paradigm-based, *contra* exemplar-based, grammaticalization.

2.2.4. *Semantico-pragmatic change*

The extent of grammaticalization may be fundamentally constrained by the limit of pragmatics. One intriguing category in Korean showing the crucial role of pragmatics involves the use of silence, i.e. ellipsis. Rhee (2002a) illustrates how grammaticalization of pragmatic forces of exophoric (i.e. situational) ellipsis in discourse can bring about drastic changes in grammar. Many sentence-final markers in Modern Korean historically evolved from connective markers (Lee and Park 1999; Koo and Rhee 2001) as listed and exemplified in part as follows.

(5)

Marker	Connective function	Sentence-final function
-*ketun*	conditional	topic presentation/reason
-*nikka*	reason/cause	addressee-confirmation/contingency
-*myense*	concurrence	addressee-confirmation/challenge/derisive
-*ntey*	adversative	surprise / reluctance / reason
-*key*	mode	exhortative

(6) a. *ku-ka o-ketun i ton-ul cwu-ela*
HE-NOM come-CONN this money-ACC give-IMP
'If he comes, give this money to him.'

a′. *ku-ka onul yeki o-ketun*
he-NOM today here come-SF
'(Guess what!) He is coming here today.' 'It's because he is coming here today.'

b. *nwun-i o-nikka mwuchek chwup-ta*
snow-NOM come-CONN very cold-DECL
'As it's snowing, it's very cold.'

b′ A: [Do you really have no money?]
B: *eps-ta-nikka.*
not.exist-DECL-SF
'I don't. (Didn't I say that?)'

c. *ku-nun kongpwuha-myense nolay-lul tut-nun-ta*
he-TOP study-CONN song-ACC listen.to-PRS-DECL
'He listens to music while studying.'

c′. A: [I will help you.]
B: *ney il-to mos ha-myense?*
your work-even not do-SF
'While you cannot finish your own work? (Mind your own work!)'

The connective function of these forms still survives, rendering the utterance ambiguous between the two opposing functions of connecting clauses and ending sentences (cf. Ohori's (1995) 'suspended clause'; Evans's (2007) 'insubordination'). From a discourse perspective, what seems more interesting is that the mechanism of change operative in all these cases is pragmatic inferences in discourse, where the speaker chooses the strategic ellipsis of the intended utterance, i.e. the speaker employs omission of the main clause, thus leaving only the subordinate clause still marked with a connective at the end of the utterance. This intentional ellipsis gives the speaker certain benefits: utterance economy, relief from commitment to the elided proposition, and the addressee's enriched interpretation from the subordinate clause.

On the other hand, this intentional ellipsis exerts a strong challenging effect on the addressee. An utterance ended in a connective places the addressee in a quandary as the linguistic signal, i.e. use of a connective, forces the expectation of a main clause, while the suprasegmental information, e.g. intonation, clearly signals the completion of the utterance. It is at this stage that the addressee actively seeks the elided information in the missing main clause. In this process diverse meanings are pragmatically inferred. These new meanings form certain patterns depending on the available inference types derived from the semantics of the connective markers. These inference patterns in turn become conventionalized in the utterance-final markers. From this discourse strategy comes the syntactic change, i.e. the emergence of new sentence types with new sentential-end markers. This phenomenon is an example of the pragmatic inferences shaping the routes of semantic changes in grammaticalization (cf. Heine et al. 1991).

2.3. Grammaticalization and functional categories

2.3.1. *Nominalizers*

Over the years, the large number and variable status of Korean nominalizers have led to controversy over the exact number of nominalizers in Korean. Nominalization has long attracted the attention of grammaticalization scholars. Notable research includes Park (1999) and Rhee (2008; in press). Prior to the 15th century, six nominalizers, i.e. *-l*, *-m*, *-n*, *-i*, *-ki*, and *-ti*, were attested. Of these nominalizers, *-l*, *-n*, and *-i* ceased to function as nominalizers early, and *-l* and *-n* exclusively function as adnominalizers in Modern Korean. The lexical origins of the primary nominalizers are as follows (Rhee 2008; in press):

(7)

Nominalizer	Lexical source	
-ti, -ki, -ci	'place'	(Rhee 2008)
kes	'thing, skin, surface'	(Hong 1983; Park 1999)
-i	'this'	(Ryu 1990; Kang 1993)
-m	'regard, consider'	(Hong 1957; Kang 1993)

Nominalizers carry diverse functions. Primarily they have referring functions for the first-order entities, i.e. spatial entities such as individuals, things, and places, second-order entities, i.e. temporal entities such as actions, processes, and states, and third-order entities, i.e. propositions. They also have expressive functions such as sentence-final markers for notices, bullet-point listing, etc. Furthermore, they carry stance-marking functions for encoding addressee confirmation, feigned/exaggerated friendship, approval or suggestion-giving, self-assurance, prediction, determination, exclamation, conjecture, etc. (Rhee in press). The emergence of such stance-marking functions appears to have followed paths that can be characterized by subjectification and intersubjectification.

2.3.2. *Postpositions*

Korean is a postpositional language, and a large number of postpositions developed from primary category words such as nouns and verbs (Rhee 2002b). Korean has an elaborate system of postpositions for specifying fine-grained motional notions such as ascension, descension, ingression, egression, and reversion, as well as others that specify the manners and the features of the local geography involved in motions (Rhee 2002b). The richness and the systematicity of this system of motional expressions is fundamentally due to the meticulous lexicalization pattern and to the syntactic idiosyncrasy in Korean that makes use of verb serialization which is compositional and, in principle, unlimited. Some of the postpositions and lexical sources are as shown in (8) and the use of *-neme* 'over' as a postposition is exemplified in (9).

(8)	Postposition	Meaning/function	Lexical source
	-neme	'over'	'go over'
	-eytayko	'to' (allative)	'touch'
	-pwuthe	'from' (ablative)	'adhere'
	-eytaka	'to' (allative)	'draw near'
	-cocha	'even' (NPI)	'follow'
	-ttala	'on' (adversative)	'follow'

(9) *san-neme* *cak-un* *maul-ey* *han* *noin-i* *sa-n-ta*
hill-over be.small-ADN village-at one old.man-NOM live-PRS-DECL
'There lives an old man in a village over the hill.' (< If (you) go over the hill, there . . .)

Nouns are also a common source of grammaticalization. Since nouns tend to be embedded in a construction and lose salience before the entire construction grammaticalizes, postpositions from nominal sources undergo a process whereby a fully-fledged noun becomes a defective noun. Ahn (1996) sets up three developmental phases each of which can be characterized by the emergence of (1) defective nouns, (2) clitics, and (3) endings, postpositions and particles. Likewise, Kang

(2001) presents an analysis of the predicates involving such nouns as *pep* 'law', *moyang* 'shape', *kes* 'thing', and *the* 'ground' which eventually grammaticalized into markers that signal the speaker's modal stances, such as uncertainty, probability, certainty, etc.

2.3.3. *Auxiliaries*

In the development of auxiliaries, Korean recruits lexemes from diverse grammatical categories, but the primary source is the verb category. Rhee (1996) and Oh (1998) discuss the grammaticalization of verbs into auxiliaries. Rhee (1996) illustrates the development of verbs in the existence, action, and deictic movement categories. These auxiliaries come into grammar by way of serial verb constructions (see section 2.2.2), where predominantly the nonfinite marker *-e* is used. Unlike other nonfinite markers, *-e* is known to have a consolidating force facilitating reinterpretation of two events as one. A partial list of the verbs and auxiliaries thus developed is as follows (NB *-kotul- and -koancass-* use the nonfinite marker *-ko*):

(10)

Auxiliary	Meaning/function	Lexical source
-eka-	continuative, change-of-state	'go'
-eo-	continuative, change-of-state	'come'
-eci-	passive	'fall'
-eppaci-	viewpoint of deterioration	'fall into'
-etul-/-kotul-	ingressive, viewpoint of imprudence	'enter'
-ena-	inchoative, completive, ampliative	'exit'
-etay-	intensifier	'touch'
-koancass-	viewpoint of contempt	'sit'

(11) a. *icey cip-ey ta o-eka-n-ta*
now home-at all come-CONT-PRS-DECL
'Now (we) are almost home.' (< Lit.: Now we almost come home and go.)

b. *chayk-i ccic-eci-ess-ta*
book-NOM tear-PASS-PST-DECL
'The book is torn.' (< Lit.: The book tore and fell.)

2.3.4. *Discourse markers*

Discourse markers constitute one of the major categories of grammaticalized forms. Among the most common forms of discourse initiators are *Issci?* 'Look!' (< Lit. Does it exist?) and *Isscanha?* 'Look!' (< Lit. Doesn't it exist?). In addition to these regular discourse markers, an interesting type of discourse markers is observed in Rhee (2004). Certain discourse markers make use of rhetorical questions, i.e. questions asked without the intent of soliciting answers, in their development. Some examples follow:

(12)

Marker	Function	Source meaning
eti?	emphatical	'Where?'
mwelalkka?	pause filler	'What should (I) say?'
ettehsupnikka?	attention attracter	'How is (it)?'
NP-*inka?*	attention attracter	'Is (it) NP?'
kukey Q-*nyamyen*	topic presenter	'If you ask who/what..it is'
way NP-*isscanha?*	topic presenter	'Why, doesn't NP exist?'

One peculiarity is that some of these are templates with a slot that allows insertion of a range of items in the same paradigm (such as an interrogative pronoun in place of Q and a noun phrase for NP in the above examples). They seem to be regular sentences in form, but they can be used discourse-initially, and the extreme suddenness associated with these forms without contextual cues of what is being referred to in such literal questions as 'How is (it)?' or 'Is (it) X?' produces an engaging effect on the addressee. The development of these discourse markers shows the strategic use of prefabricated constructions for topic management in discourse.

3. Conclusion

Grammaticalization studies in Korean began in the 1960s, but it was not until the 1990s that serious research in this field truly began. During the past two decades remarkable progress has been made in grammaticalization scholarship. There are two aspects that make the study of grammaticalization in Korean particularly interesting.

First, for its agglutinating nature, Korean has a rich inventory of particles and endings that await grammaticalization analyses. For instance, a dictionary of particles and verbal endings by Lee and Lee (2001) contains about 2,240 entries. Each of these grammatical forms has its own history of grammaticalization. Many of them are in the process of grammaticalization right before our eyes.

Second, since the use of Korean was largely restricted to the Korean peninsula without much language contact until about a century ago, grammaticalization processes in this language were inevitably language-internal changes. Therefore, grammaticalization studies in Korean should offer an insight as to the extent of non-contact-induced, language-internal grammaticalization. With increasing contact with foreign languages in recent times, what types of grammatical features from other languages are susceptible to replication and what their limits are, in the view of Heine and Kuteva (2005), should be intriguing research questions.

It is to be noted that many of the grammatical forms currently in use, especially those whose origins go beyond the Late Middle Korean, do not show their clear lexical origins, and it is hard for linguists to establish their entire trajectories of historical change. This is largely due to the fact that the record of Korean written in Hangeul has less than 600 years of historical depth. Therefore, despite much progress in the studies of pre-Hangeul Korean records, more research is needed in this area to better understand the Korean language from the grammaticalization perspective.

CHAPTER 64

GRAMMATICALIZATION IN JAPANESE

HEIKO NARROG
TOSHIO OHORI

1. The Japanese language and its historical profile

Japanese has been a strictly head-final SOV language with nominative–accusative alignment, and with frequent omission of argument NPs, throughout its documented history. Genetically, it has been most often linked with the Altaic hypothesis, but the debate over its origin is not yet settled. From the 8th century until the present, relatively large amounts of texts are available with small intermissions. Japanese is thus known as one of the historically best-documented non-Indo-European languages. The situation is nevertheless not straightforward with respect to research on grammaticalization and language change because there have been shifts in the geographic centre of cultural activity, the social strata involved in writing, and the documented genres of writing. Therefore the dialects, sociolects, and styles of the available texts from each period of history vary considerably. Likewise, the accessibility of texts for non-specialists also varies period by period (the 'classical' period (10th–12th centuries), with numerous outstanding literary works, is the most accessible),[1] and no comprehensive historical corpora have been published yet (see, however, the University of Virginia's Japanese Text Archive, http://etext.lib.virginia.edu/japanese/). Consequently, a considerable portion of research on grammaticalization has been carried out from a synchronic Modern Japanese perspective.

Japanese was heavily influenced by Chinese in older periods, and especially from the 19th century a steady influx of loanwords from Western languages started. In both cases, due to the indirect nature of the contact, the influence mostly came through the channel of writing and has been mainly focused on the lexicon. Under such circumstances, an impact on grammar is observed primarily (i) where a phrase in an original language is translated (=calqued) partially deviating from the native idiom, and (ii) where the lexicon and grammar interact, with an introduction of new lexical categories. The first type of contact-induced grammaticalization includes, for example, the rise of complex postpositions (see section 2.4.1). The most salient example of the latter is exemplified by the growing vocabulary of Sino-Japanese verbal nouns with their characteristic ambiguous morphosyntactic behaviour (cf. Uehara 1998). See sections 2.4.2 and 2.5 below for examples of Sino-Japanese adverbs, adnominals, and nominal affixes. In contrast, in the spoken language there are only few genuine examples of grammatical influence due to language contact.

2. Grammaticalization

2.1. Overall tendencies

Morphologically, Japanese is agglutinating, and given the head-final nature of the language, clear cases of grammaticalization typically lead to the suffixation of formerly independent morphemes (i.e. lexemes). Prefixation is much less common, confined to a small number of categories, mostly honorification and negation (cf. section 2.4.2). Morpheme boundaries are usually clear, but as can be expected with concatenative structures (see Bickel and Nichols 2007: 181), assimilation and some fusion between stem and affixes is not uncommon. Concerning suffixes, one can distinguish three distributional classes: (i) inflections (only on verbs and adjectives), (ii) particles, and (iii) derivative suffixes (see Rickmeyer 1995 for details). Particles are clitic-like in being more loosely bound to stems than the other two classes. Derivational suffixes are not necessarily word-class-changing but simply derive enlarged stems. Particles and derivational suffixes can inflect themselves (in this case, traditional school grammar classifies them as *jodōshi* 'auxiliary verbs'). Based on historical evidence, the following cline of grammaticalization between these morpheme classes can be posited.

(1) word/construction > (particle) > suffix > inflection

'Particle' is put into parentheses because this step can be (and frequently is) skipped. Two salient accompanying tendencies are, first, loss of inflection with inflecting words, and, second, loss of phonological substance (attrition). Furthermore, frequently two or more morphemes merge into one (examples will be provided below). However, grammaticalization does not always lead to suffixation. There are many cases where a noun or verb exhibits a continuum from lexical to grammatical uses, and the grammatical use cannot be clearly classified as a suffix. Also, there are cases where periphrastic structures persist, especially in the verbal complex (see section 2.4.1).

Semantically, cases of grammaticalization in Japanese generally follow the well-known path from concrete to abstract domains, including temporal, speaker-oriented, interpersonal, and textual domains, which we will see below (cf. also Hino 2001; 2006).

2.2. Grammaticalization in Japanese: a showcase

Let us examine an excerpt of a Modern Japanese text from the viewpoint of grammaticalization.

(2) 1 *'Kore-kara NihoNbasi-no sit-te-'ru kurabu-e ik-u-N-da-kedo,*
this-ABL (PN)-GEN know-GER-be-NPS club-ALL go-NPS-NMZ-COP-AVS

2 *issyo-ni uti-mas-eN-ka. Naani, meNbaa-wa amai-des-u-yo.*
together-ADV play-POL-NEG-QUE INJ member-TOP easy-COP-NPS-ILL

3 *Reeto-wa koko-yori sukosi ooki-i-kedo.'*
rate-TOP here-ABL a.little large-NPS-AVS

4 *Watasi-wa naNtonaku unazui-ta. Atarasi-i sigoto-ba-wa*
I-TOP vaguely nod-PST new-NPS work-place-TOP
hosi-kat-ta tokoro-da.
want-VBZ-PST place COP

5	*Simizu-wa*	*siro-i*	*oovaakooto-o*	*haori,*	*soto-e*
	Shimizu-TOP	white-NPS	overcoat-ACC	wear	outside-ALL
	der-u-to		*sugu-ni*		
	go.out-NPS-CON		soon-ADV		
6	*riNtaku-o*	*tukamae-ta.*			
	pedicab-ACC	catch-PST			

'Now I'm going to a mahjong club in Nihonbashi that I know; won't you play with me? The members are easy to deal with. The rate, though, is a little higher than here.'

I vaguely nodded. I was looking for a new area to exploit. Shimizu put on a white coat and went outside, where he soon caught a pedicab.' (Asada Tetsuya, *Maajan Hoorooki* 1 [The Mahjong Roamer 1], 1969)

Several instances of grammaticalization can be immediately identified. The politeness auxiliary *-mas-* (citation form *-masu*) in line 1 comes from the verb *mawirasu* 'to serve; present'. Another instance of auxiliation is *-Te'ru* (citation form *-Te iru*) in line 1, glossed STA, which comes from the combination of the nonfinite verbal suffix *-Te* and a verb meaning 'to be (originally, 'sit')'. The past morpheme (lines 4, 6) *-Ta* is derived from the Old Japanese resultative *-tari* which in turn goes back to *-te ari* < *-te* 'gerund'+ *ari* 'to be; exist'. On the nominal side, the allative case particle *e* 'to' (lines 1 and 5) originates from a lexical noun meaning 'vicinity'. *Tokoro da* in line 4, glossed 'place COP', indicates a state, as the translation indicates. These are clear instances of grammaticalization as defined in section 2.1. As for conjunctive particles, *kedo* (adversative/contrastive) (lines 1, 3) is known to be a reduced form of *keredo* < *kere* conditional inflection of adjectives + *do* concessive particle. The immediate source for *to* indicating a temporal sequence (line 5) could be the noun conjunction/comitative *to*, but there is no clear historical evidence establishing this relationship between them. Finally, if we expand our perspective, the uses of *kedo* above represent a further type of grammaticalization, namely (inter-)subjectification. We will return to these issues in section 2.7.

2.3. Grammaticalization in the verbal and adjectival complex

'Adjectival' in this title refers to the class of 'real' adjectives as opposed to nominal adjectives (cf. Uehara 1998). By 'verbal and adjectival complex' we mean verbs and adjectives augmented by morphological and periphrastic material. The 'real' adjectives are verb-like rather than noun-like in Japanese, and their morphology intertwines with verbal morphology, so they are treated together here. The following categories are grammaticalized in the Japanese verbal complex, roughly in the order from 'inside' to 'outside' the verbal complex (Narrog 2010a): benefactives (periphrastics), voice (suffixes), referent honorification (prefixes, suffixes, periphrastics), negation (inflections, suffixes), aspect (inflections, periphrastics, compound verbs), modality (suffixes, particles, periphrastics), tense (inflections), mood (inflections), addressee honorification (prefixes, suffixes, particles), illocutionary force modulation (particles).

Examples of morphological grammaticalization include, (a) *-(a)m-* (LOJ 'future', suffix) > *-(y)oo* (MJ 'future' (inflection)), (b) *mawi-ir.as-* (OJ 'let come', lexical compound with suffix) > *-mas-* (MJ addressee honorific; suffix, cf. (2) line 2), (c) *de gozai.mas-* (Late MidJ 'be' (humble, polite); case particle + verb + suffix) > *des-* (MJ addressee honorific; particle verb, cf. (2), line 2).

Two particularly common types of periphrastic construction in the verbal complex have given rise to grammaticalization. In one type, the verb with grammatical functions follows the gerund *-Te*-form of the main verb. The most important aspectual marking in Modern Japanese, the stative *-Te i-* (*i-* = 'be'), is formed in this way (cf. (2), line 1), as are the benefactive markers such as *-Te kure/age-*, and some minor aspectual and directional constructions such as *-Te ik-* (inceptive or 'to move away from the deictic centre'). The second type is a conditional construction, which is, for example, responsible for the expression of the majority of non-epistemic modal marking, e.g. *-(a)na.kereba nar.ana-* (lit. 'if one doesn't do X, it will not become (as we expect)'; strong necessity). Hanazono (1999) offers a study on the degree of grammaticalization of these constructions.

Further, so-called 'formal nouns' are found in the verbal complex as well, mainly in modal functions; e.g. *hazu* 'notch; exact fit' for epistemic modality, and *yoo* 'appearance' for inferential evidentiality. 'Formal nouns' usually have a dual nature as lexical nouns and grammatical markers (cf. e.g. Fujii 2000 for *mono* 'thing' in its various functions), with some items more grammaticalized than others.

Lastly, compound verbs also play an important role in Japanese vocabulary and grammar. This is an area which is primarily associated with lexicalization rather than grammaticalization, but some verbs such as *hazime-* 'begin' and *tuduke-* 'continue' can be productively added to a large range of other verb stems in aspectual function, as in *tabe-hazime-* 'to begin to eat'. These verbs have grammatical functions, but are not morphologically grammaticalized, as there is little reason to classify them as suffixes rather than lexemes (i.e. compounds).

While most grammatical elements in the verbal complex are ultimately derived from lexical items, markers of one grammatical category can also extend their functional range to another category. The following directionalities of change have been attested:

(3) Voice > modality (*-(r)are-* spontaneous/passive > *-(r)are-* potential)
Referent honorification > addressee honorification (*mawiras-* humilitive > *-mas-* politeness; and situation awareness)

Aspect > tense (-*tari* resultative/perfective > -*Ta* past; -*t*- perfective > -*t*- past)
Aspect > mood (-*tari* resultative/perfective > -*Ta* imperative)
Modality > mood (-*(a)m*- future/intention > -*(y)oo* hortative)[2]
Modality > illocutionary force modulation (*daroo* epistemic > *daroo* request for confirmation)

2.4. Grammaticalization in the nominal complex

Nouns in Japanese bear considerably less grammatical marking than verbs. Definiteness and gender are not expressed at all, while plural marking is optional and only common with animate nouns. Instead, Japanese has case- and topic/focus-marking particles, postpositions, and a rich array of noun classifiers and many other nominal suffixes.

2.4.1. *Particles and postpositions on nouns*

Modern Japanese has a set of eight case particles (nominative *ga*, accusative *o*, dative *ni*, essive *de*, genitive *no*, allative *e*, ablative *kara* (or *yori*), and comitative *to*), and a number of particles that mark information structure (e.g. topic *wa*, focus *mo*, *sae*) and extent (*made* for limit and extent, *dake*, *bakari*, *kurai*, *hodo*, *nomi* for amount). Nominative *ga* was originally a genitive particle, and its reanalysis as nominative was facilitated by the loss of distinction between nominalized clauses (with genitive subjects) and non-nominalized clauses due to the reorganization of the verbal paradigm, completed in the 16th century. Concerning other case particles, the origins can be traced for only some of them, and in such cases they are related to nouns (most of the following etymologies are based on the *Nihon Kokugo Daijiten*, 2000–2002). The allative particle *e* goes back to an Old Japanese noun *pye* 'vicinity, direction' (cf. (2), lines 1 and 5), and the ablative particle *kara* most likely to the noun *kara* 'nature, origin' (cf. (2), line 1). *Dake* 'only' is derived from *take* 'height, length'. *Bakari* 'nothing but' is presumably originally the nominalized form of the verb *hakaru* 'measure, weigh', *hodo* 'as much as' goes back to Old Japanese *podo* 'space, period of time', and *kurai* 'about' to *kurawi* 'rank'.

In addition, Japanese has developed deverbal postpositions, which are a set of grammaticalized verbs, some of them of Sino-Japanese origin. They are either in the base form or in the gerundive -*Te* form, governing a noun phrase with a specific case particle, mostly *ni* or *o*. An example is *Kono teiaN-ni taisite/o megutte* this proposal-DAT face(v.)-GER/ACC go.around-GER 'against/concerning this proposal' (*tais*- is Sino-Japanese while *megur*- is a native Japanese verb). With respect to grammaticalization, they are of particular interest for two reasons. First, at least some of them entered the grammar of Japanese, or assumed their functions, through

[2] -am.u > au > OO > oo after consonant stem; -m.u > u > o > (y)oo after vowel stems in analogy; /y/ is a glide inserted after vowels.

the translation of Chinese writing from LOJ on (cf. Chen 2005), i.e. presumably through language contact instead of language-internal grammaticalization. Many of them still belong to a formal style. Second, compared to case and information structure particles, they form a relatively open class with gradient membership, comparable to emergent participial prepositions in English (cf. Matsumoto 1998 for the criteria of their grammaticalization).

2.4.2. *Nominal affixes*

Nominal affixes may be divided into (a) noun classifiers, and (b) others. The first are usually suffixed to numerals and used for counting nominal referents, e.g. *yubi ni-hoN* 'two fingers', but in some cases they may also modify (i.e. count the eventualities denoted by) verbal and adjectival predicates *iti-do taberu* 'eat once'. More than a hundred of them can be distinguished, while only about twenty are actually regularly used (cf. Downing 1996: ch. 3). In a few cases where the lexical source can be identified, it is usually a noun or nominalized verb, e.g. *kasira* 'head' for counting shrimps, or *hari* 'spread' for mosquito nets. Most frequently, however, classifiers are derived from Chinese vocabulary. Then they either have no lexical use or they have a quite different meaning when used as an independent word, e.g. *mai* for two-dimensional flat things (not used as a noun) and *hoN* for long things (meaning 'book' as a noun). A comparison of Modern Japanese with Middle Japanese (Rodriguez 1976[1604]; vol. 3) suggests two tendencies: the gradual replacement of Japanese classifiers by Sinitic classifiers (e.g. Modern Japanese *-hoN* instead of *-suzi* for threads, ropes, or hair), and a general simplification through loss of diversity of classifiers.

Concerning other nominal affixes, some of them derive nouns from verbs (e.g. V+*te* 'doer of V' or V+*kata* 'manner of V-ing'), while others modify nouns (e.g. N+*ryoku* 'force of N' or N+*gai* 'outside N'). Again, morphemes of Sinitic origin which have no lexical usage in Japanese abound, but where a native lexical source is known, it is usually another noun, e. g. *-te* from *te* 'hand', and *-kata* from *kata* 'form'. Japanese also has a small number of prefixes on nouns, mostly for honorification, e.g. *o-* as in *o-namae* 'name (elevated)' and negation, e.g. *hu-* (Sino-Japanese) as in *hu-sizen* 'unnatural'. In one case, part of the lexical origin is known. The most common honorific prefix *o-* goes back to *opo-mi* ('big' + (unknown)).

2.5. Grammaticalization of adverbs and adnominals

Adverbs are regularly derived from adjectives through the adverbial inflection *-ku* (e.g. *haya-* 'quick' > *haya-ku* 'quickly'), and from nominal adjectives (mostly Sinitic) with the adverbial particle *ni* (e.g. *geNki* 'vigour' > *geNki ni* 'vigorously'). In the latter case, *ni* is sometimes lost, or it becomes optional (e.g. *aNgai* 'unexpectedly). There are other adverbs outside these productive patterns which either come from Chinese, e.g. *gazeN* 'suddenly', or are indigenous onomatopoetica, e.g. *doNdoN* 'without hesitation; determinedly' and *zitto* 'firmly; still'. A minority of adverbs can be traced back to verbs and nouns. Concerning the former, a number of adverbs is derived from the gerundive *-Te* form of the verb, e.g. *kessite* ('decide'-GER) 'by no means' (negative polarity item), while adverbs derived from nouns are rare, e.g. *wariai* 'relatively' from *wariai* 'share'.

The most prominent adnominals, the demonstratives of the *ko-so-a-do* paradigm, have no known lexical origin. Other members of the semi-open class of adnominal words include those from non-lexical Chinese morphemes (e.g. *yaku* 'about'), and some with lexical roots in classical Japanese adnominal verb forms (e.g. *kitaru* 'coming; next', *iwayuru* 'so-called'). In addition to the direct borrowings from Chinese, the written language knows many 'pseudo-Japanese' adverbs, adnominals, and conjunctions whose meanings or very existence are due to their use in translations of Chinese (e.g. *sude ni* 'already' *oyobi* 'in addition; and'; cf. Yamada 1935).

2.6. Grammaticalization of complex sentences

This is an area of grammaticalization in Japanese which is relatively well documented in the Japanese grammaticalization literature (cf. also Chapter 52 above on subordination for further examples).

There are two major sources of markers of subordination in Japanese, both of which are also well known cross-linguistically (see Thompson, Longacre, and Hwang 2007). First, in many cases nouns function as the heads of complement clauses and adverbial clauses. *Koto* 'thing' is an example of the former, while *baai* ('case', marks a conditional), *tame* ('reason', marks a reason or purpose clause), *toki* ('time', temporal clause 'when'), and *ato* ('back', temporal clause 'after') are examples of the latter, in which case an adverbial clause is formed by clausal modification of a relational noun. Interestingly, *tokoro* 'place' has two faces, participating in both complement and adverbial constructions (see Ohori 2001 for details). Second, throughout the history of the language, case markers have often served as markers of adverbial subordination. Thus, *ga* 'and/but' goes back to the genitive/nominative particle *ga*. Concessive and earlier circumstantial clauses have been marked with dative *ni*, contrastive and circumstantial clauses with accusative *(w)o*, and causal clauses with ablative *kara*.

Other sources of complex constructions are as follows. The frequently used complement marker *no* comes from the genitive/nominalizing particle *no* with no clear lexical etymology (see Horie 1998 on the spread of its functional range). The most frequently used adverbial (or more precisely 'chaining') marker of Modern Japanese, the gerund *-Te*, is derived from the adverbial form of the perfective suffix verb *-t-*. Regarding conditionals, there is a hypothesis that *ba* in the Modern Japanese conditional inflection *-(r)eba* (from Old and Late Old Japanese *-(ur)e=ba*) is derived from the topic marker *wa* (OJ *pa*), while there is an alternative account that they have some common source. Ohori (1998a) examines this relationship on the basis of functional commonalities. Further, Ohori (1992; 1994), in an in-depth study of the development of conditional *-(ur)e=ba*, showed the development from looser to tighter clause integration, and the loss of switch-reference function. For a fully-fledged study of the diachrony of conditionals in Japanese, see Kobayashi (1996).

Conjunctions in Japanese do not form a morphosyntactically homogeneous word class. Examples include adverbs such as *mata* 'also' and combinations of anaphoric demonstratives or other 'formal' nouns with case particles (e.g. *sore kara* 'then', lit. 'from this'; *tokoro de* 'by the way', lit. 'at the place'). Still others are derived from particles indicating interclausal relationships, usually added to a copula, e.g. *dakara* 'therefore' from copula *da* and causal (original ablative) *kara* 'because'. The last case constitutes a case of change from a dependent to an independent morpheme, and thus of morphosyntactic degrammaticalization (cf. Matsumoto 1988).

2.7. Grammaticalization in discourse

A fine classic study of grammaticalization in context can be found in Ishigaki (1955), who analyzed in detail the conditions for the grammatical change of the genitive particle *ga* to nominative and clause-connecting particle.

A number of Japanese scholars publishing in English have been concerned with grammaticalization and pragmaticalization of morphemes which are typical of spoken language. Onodera (2004; 2007; Chapter 50 above) has investigated the particles/interjections *ne*, *na* and the conjunctive adverbs *demo* and *dakedo*. She showed their functions in conversation, the relationship between their functions and positions in the sentence, and their gradual subjectification and intersubjectification. Suzuki (2007; 2008) has worked on the development of the quotative particle *tte*, which extended its use to a topic-marking and eventually sentence-final particle. The uses of *kedo* in (2), lines 1 and 3, also instantiate (inter-)subjectification in that what is formally a concessive clause gives a reason for the speaker's speech act.

On the nominal side, Suzuki (1998) and Fujii (2000) deal with the pragmaticalization of nouns and their functions in discourse. Onodera (2007) has also brought a social dimension to her analysis by associating intersubjective conversational uses with the fulfilment of social norms.

2.8. Cases of morphosyntactic counterdirectionality in grammaticalization

The best-known example of counterdirectionality in Japanese was cited at the end of section 2.6 (Matsumoto 1988). Other cases are mentioned in Narrog (2004;

2005c; 2007a). The uninflecting negation suffix -*(a)nai* of Middle Eastern Japanese acquired inflection in Early Modern Japanese, probably in analogy to the negative adjective *na-*. The same is happening currently to the uninflecting evidential particle *mitai* in spoken discourse, which speakers are reanalysing as a (particle) adjective (e.g. *mita-ku*). The reanalysis of the lexicalized ending -*(a)s-* as the productive causative suffix -*(s)as-*, and the reanalysis of the lexicalized ending *-e-* of (intransitive) middle verbs as a potential morpheme in Middle Japanese, are examples of exaptation (i.e. a revival of already fossilized and functionally opaque material). These cases furthermore involve an accretion instead of attrition of phonological material. Very similar cases of accretion of phonological material can also be found colloquially in Modern Japanese, where the potential morpheme -*e-* is lengthened to -*ere-* by younger speakers (e.g. *ik-ere-ru* 'can go' instead of *ik-e-ru*), and the causative morpheme -*(a)se-* is lengthened to -*(a)sase-* (e.g. *ik-asase-ru* 'let go' instead of *ik-ase-ru*). This is not yet accompanied by any functional change, and simply makes the expression more explicit. All these cases exhibit morpho-syntactic rather than semantic or functional counterdirectionality.

3. What is special about grammaticalization in Japanese?

In conclusion, the following points can be recapitulated which make the study of grammaticalization in Japanese particularly interesting.

- Japanese is, despite various difficulties, one of the historically best-documented non-Indo-European languages. This makes it a good testing ground for hypotheses about grammaticalization in general.
- Grammaticalization is reflected structurally in Japanese in relatively straightforward and transparent ways (viz. by agglutination), compared to languages that have little or mostly fusional morphology.
- There are some areas of grammar which are particularly well grammaticalized in Japanese, offering particularly rich material for study. Such areas include primarily interpersonal relations, including honorification (cf. Dasher 1995; Traugott and Dasher 2002; Nagata 2006) and illocutionary modification, but Japanese also serves as a testing ground for the study of cross-linguistically common categories such as aspect, modality (see Narrog 2007b), and clausal subordination.
- It is generally assumed (and correctly so) that grammaticalization normally arises from spoken language, i.e. in conversation. Japanese, however, provides

a number of examples where grammaticalization was triggered by written language, sometimes through translation. This situation presumably arose in Middle Japanese when a larger proportion of the population started to participate in reading and writing (cf. the grammaticalization of postpositions as loan translations discussed in section 2.4.1 above). Another set of examples came in the late 19th–early 20th Meiji era, when the new standard was created for written language. Some of the grammatical elements of this new style that were borrowed from Sino-Japanese and pseudo-classical writing eventually made it into the spoken language through formal registers (e.g. *beki* for deontic necessity, *rasii* for inferential evidentiality). Extended uses of the passive and more frequent subject marking in Modern Japanese are also attributed to the influence of translations from European languages (see Kinsui 1992, who traces the *ni yotte*-passive entirely to translational style).

CHAPTER 65

GRAMMATICALIZATION IN SINITIC LANGUAGES

HILARY CHAPPELL
ALAIN PEYRAUBE

1. Introduction

While it is generally accepted that the word 'grammaticalization' was used for the first time by Antoine Meillet in 1912, the process of grammaticalization has been a well-known phenomenon for many centuries in China, at least from the 14th century, when Zhou Boqi, a Chinese scholar of the Yuan dynasty (1279–1368) stated that 'today's empty words are all former full words' (*jīn zhī xū zì jiē gǔ zhī shí zì* 今之虛字皆古之實字). The process was later called *xūhuà* 虛化 'voiding', before the term 'grammaticalization' (*yǔfǎhuà* 语法化) was coined in standard Mandarin in the 1980s. In fact, the tradition of dividing all the words of the Chinese language into two main categories, full words (*shící* 實詞 or full lexical items) and empty words (*xūcí* 虛詞 or functional grammatical morphemes), is still in current use.[1]

In this chapter, the topics to be discussed are the evolution of the disposal or object marking constructions, passive and causative constructions, and classifiers. They have been chosen to represent some of the special features of

[1] For a definition of empty words and full words, as well as for a standard classification of these two categories, see Zhu (1982). See also Cao (1995) for Medieval Chinese.

grammaticalization pathways, typical of Sinitic. Apart from classifiers, the three clause types have all arisen out of serial verb constructions, creating new forms with complex predicates.

The model of grammatical change used in the following sections will refer to two main mechanisms: analogy and reanalysis; the former includes so-called degrammaticalization, while the latter includes both grammaticalization and exaptation processes.[2] In this article, the definition of grammaticalization proposed by Hopper and Traugott (2003: 213) is adopted: 'a robust tendency for lexical items and constructions to be used in certain linguistic contexts to serve grammatical functions, and once grammaticalized, to be used to further develop new grammatical functions'.

2. Disposal constructions

2.1. Historical sketch

What is known as the 'disposal form' (*chŭzhìshì*) or the *bă* 把 -construction in Chinese has the following syntactic configuration: $NP_{1(Agent)}$ – Object Marker – $NP_{2(Patient)}$ – VP, where the object marker is a preposition. This marker is typically *bă* in contemporary Standard Mandarin Chinese, while an array of other forms is found in the other main dialect groups belonging to Sinitic (see section 2.2 below). This construction creates a strong contrast to one of the basic word orders in Chinese languages of S–V–O; the same applies for its constructional meaning which expresses high transitivity. This is manifested by the requirement for a clearly interpretable change of state for the referential object NP (describing how it has been 'disposed of' and hence the label in Chinese linguistics).

The disposal markers seen in vernacular texts of the Medieval Chinese period (2nd–13th centuries) are typically deverbal prepositions based on the V_1 position in serial verb constructions of the form: (NP_0[SUBJECT]) – V_1[TAKE] – NP_1 – V_2 – (NP_2). They first began to appear in the Late Han period (1st–3rd) and included *qŭ* 'to take' 取, *jiāng* 將 'to guide, lead, take', *bă* 把 'to grasp, hold', *chí* 持 'to grasp, hold', and *zhuō* 捉 'to clutch, hold, seize'. Thus, the morphological forms used to mark the direct object all derive from verbs of taking, a classical source for adpositional direct object markers (see Lord 1993; Heine and Kuteva 2002). Two

[2] For definitions and a detailed discussion concerning analogy, reanalysis, grammaticalization, exaptation, and degrammaticalization, see Peyraube (2005).

examples follow of these serial verb constructions, source of the disposal forms: (1) contains a second postverbal object NP_2, while (2) does not:

(1) *qŭ yī dà hăishuĭ jiāoguàn qí shēn*
take one big seawater pour 3SG body
'(He) took a large amount of seawater to pour over his body.'
(*Zēng Yī Ā Hán Jīng*, 4th-c. sutra)

(2) *zuì bă zhūyú zĭxì kàn*
drunk take dogwood carefully look
'Drunk, (he) took the dogwood (and) looked (at it) carefully.'
(*Jiŭ Yuè Lán Tián Cuī Shì Zhuāng*, 8th-c. poem by Du Fu)

The direct object of V_2 coded by NP_2 in (1) could later be omitted in cases where it coded the identical referent to NP_1, as Peyraube has argued (1989a), providing examples such as (3) where the NP_2 is a pronoun coreferential with NP_1:

(3) *rŭ jiāng cĭ rén ānxu shā* ***zhī*** *wú sŭn pī roù*
2SG take DEM man careful kill **3SG** NEG damage skin flesh
'Take this man (and) kill him carefully without damaging (his) skin and flesh.'
(*Fó Shuō Cháng Ā Hán Jīng*, 4th–5th-c. sutra)

The process which then played a crucial role in the development of these disposal constructions was the grammaticalization from V > Preposition, producing examples of the type given in (4) or (5), where *jiāng* or *bă* can no longer be interpreted as verbs meaning 'to take':

(4) *shí zhū bĭqiū jiāng cĭ băi Fó*
at.that.time PL monk OM DEM tell Buddha
'At that time, the monks narrated this to Buddha.'
(*Fó Bĕn Xíng Jí Jīng*, 6th-c. sutra)

(5) *xián cháng bă qín nòng*
leisure often OM lute play
'In (my) spare time (I) often played the lute.'
(*Jì Dù Shí Yí*, 8th-c. poem by Ren Hua)

This occurred after the synchronic derivation had taken place involving omission of a coreferential NP_2. To summarize, the synchronic change:

(i) $(NP_0) - V_1(\text{TAKE}) - NP_1 - V_2 - NP_2 \rightarrow (NP_0) - V1(\text{TAKE}) - NP_1 - V_2$
where $NP_2 = NP_1$ and TAKE = any verb in this semantic field

was followed by the diachronic change:

(ii) $(NP_0) - V_1(\text{TAKE}) - NP_1 - V_2 > (NP_0) - \text{Preposition}_{(<\text{TAKE})} - NP_1 - V.$

Other processes may have played a role in the birth of this disposal construction: an analogical process with certain ditransitive constructions,[3] involving the preposition *yǐ* 以 in Classical Chinese and verbs of giving (*yǐ* – $NP_{1(\text{direct object})}$ – $V_{(\text{GIVE})}$ – $NP_{2(\text{indirect object})}$), and, as has been argued recently in an intriguing new and original hypothesis by Cao and Yu (2000), the influence of Late Han Buddhist texts translated from Sanskrit using the verb *qǔ* 取 'to take' as a real disposal marker, as in (6):

(6) NP_1 – *qǔ* – $NP_{2(\text{Object})}$ – VP
zhū rénmín qǔ wǒ wǎng shā
PL people OM 1SG unjust sentence.to.death
'All the people unjustly sentenced me to death.'
(*Zēng Yī Ā Hán Jīng*, 4th-c. sutra)

2.2. Sources for disposal markers in contemporary Sinitic languages

On the basis of available synchronic descriptions of Sinitic languages, three main lexical domains as sources for disposal markers can be discerned, testifying to great diversity in terms of their hyponyms. These are:

(i) Verbs of taking and holding > object markers, e.g. cognates and synonyms of *bǎ* 把 'to take' as in Standard Mandarin; *jiāng* 將 'to take, lead' used in formal registers of Hakka, Southern Min, and Cantonese; *nɔ*[53] 拿 'take, hold' in Shanghainese (Wu); *na*[2] 拿 and *laq*[7] 搦 in Gan dialects.

(ii) Verbs of giving and helping > object markers, e.g. cognates and synonyms of *gěi* 給 'to give' as in Southwestern Mandarin; *bāng* 幫 'to help' in many Wu, Hui, and Xiang dialects, *dei*[11] 代 'to help' in Wenzhou (Wu).

(iii) Comitatives > object markers, e.g. cognates and synonyms of *kā(ŋ)* 共 in Min dialects, *t'ung*[11] 同 and *lau*[11] 摎 in Hakka dialects, *tseʔ*[45] 則 in Shaoxing (Wu); *gēn* 跟 in non-standard Mandarin and Wu dialects, all serving as the comitative 'with', itself evolved from verbs meaning 'to share, to gather', 'to mix' or 'to accompany'.

As can be readily perceived, the first lexical domain with verbs of taking and holding is the only one which corresponds to the common source identified in the documented history of Chinese. As described above, the stages of grammaticalization have been analysed for this pathway in detail. Regarding the two additional sources of *give/help* verbs and comitatives, Chappell (2006a; 2007) proposes that grammaticalization into object markers proceeds via a dative/beneficiary stage for both. The case of the comitative receives additional support from the earliest known historical documents for Chinese dialects, namely 16th-century Southern Min materials which permit identification of the dative/beneficiary role as the site

[3] See Mei (1990), Wei (1997), Wu (2003) for detailed discussions.

for reanalysis, having first passed through an intermediary stage as a generalized oblique marker (Chappell, Peyraube, and Wu forthcoming). Three main pathways of grammaticalization are thus proposed for each of the lexical domains represented above:

(i) TAKE/HOLD > direct object marker
(ii) GIVE/HELP > beneficiary/dative > direct object marker
(iii) VERB > COMITATIVE > oblique → beneficiary/dative > direct object marker

For (ii), it is well known that verbs of giving develop into markers of the dative or beneficiary (Peyraube 1988). In the former V_1 position of a serial verb construction, they are realized as prepositions marking the beneficiary 'for' or dative 'to' in Sinitic languages, from whence they develop into direct object markers. Although this does not appear to be a common pathway, it is reminiscent of the closely related semantic change from DATIVE > ACCUSATIVE in Indo-European languages, described in Heine and Kuteva (2002).

Comitatives used as markers of direct objects are even more rare cross-linguistically. They have not been generally described as being able to develop into accusative or object markers (Heine and Kuteva 2002). Sinitic languages therefore provide evidence for a special pathway, apparently not yet attested elsewhere. In written Mandarin, the use of *gēn* < 'to follow' as a comitative preposition can only be first detected in 18th-century literature (see Liu and Peyraube 1994), suggesting that its synchronic dialectal use as an object marker is likely to be a quite recent development, possibly only from the 19th-century. In contrast to this, the use of comitative *kā(ŋ)* in Southern Min as an object marker may be much earlier, with fledgling examples found in typical bridging contexts[4] of 16th-century literature (Chappell et al. in preparation).

3. Passives, causatives, and verbs of giving

3.1. Historical sketch

Syntactic passives in Sinitic generally share the basic form of $NP_{1(PATIENT)}$–$Preposition_{(<V1)}$–$NP_{2(AGENT)}$–VP_2. Three groups of prepositional passive markers can be discerned in the history of Chinese which correspond to several of the lexical

[4] See Heine (2002) for a definition of 'bridging context' whereby a specific context allows for a new inference to be made while keeping the original meaning.

domains listed as sources by Heine and Kuteva (2002), including *suffer*, *get*, *see*, and causative verbs.[5]

(i) Archaic (11th–2nd BC) and Pre-Medieval Chinese (1st BC–1st AD)
preposition *yú* 于 'at, by', verb *wéi* 為 'be, become', verb *jiàn* 見 'see'

(ii) Medieval Chinese (2nd–13th AD)
bèi 被 'suffer', *ái* 挨 'suffer', *zāo* (*shòu*) 遭 (受) 'suffer', *mèng* 蒙 'cover' and *shòu* 受 'receive', *yǔ* 與 (与) 'give', *jiāo* 教 'instruct'

(iii) Modern Mandarin (13th–present)
qǐ 乞 'give', *zhuó* 着 / 著 'suffer', *ràng* 讓 'let', *jiào* 叫 'tell, order', *gěi* 給 'give', and *bèi* 被 'suffer' in formal and written registers.

The earliest passive structure, VERB + *yú* 於 + AGENT was formed with a postverbal PP containing the preposition *yú* 'at', 'by', 'to', and was in common use throughout the Archaic period (11th–2nd BC). It was later superseded by two new competing agentless forms with *jiàn* 見 –VERB < 'to see' and *wéi* 為 –VERB < 'be, become' during the Late Archaic period (5th–2nd BC), both of which occupied first position in a V_1–V_2 series. They subsequently grammaticalized into preverbal auxiliaries. Only *wéi* developed a variant with an agent noun. They remained in common use until the Early Medieval period (2nd–6th AD). An example of the agentive variant of the *wéi* passive is given below:

(7) *dào shū jiāng wéi tiānxià liè*
dao doctrine FUT PASS world tear.in.pieces
'The doctrine of the *dao* will be torn into pieces by the world.'
(*Zhuāngzǐ: Tiān Xià*, 4th BC)

Another new form, the *bèi* 被 passive (<'suffer'), began to emerge in the Pre-Medieval period as an agentless form. The following example serendipitously includes two parallel V_1–V_2 structures with both the *bèi* and the *jiàn* (<'see') passives:

(8) *bèi* (auxiliary verb)–VERB:
Zēngzǐ jiàn yí ér yín, Bó Qí bèi zhú ér gē
Zengzi PASS suspect but recite.poem Bo Qi PASS exile but sing
'Zengzi recited poems when he was suspected, Bo Qi sang when he was exiled.'
(*Lùn Héng: Gǎn Xū Piān*, 2nd AD)

In Peyraube's view (1989b), there are essentially two different developments for this verb, one for its serial verb use in V_1(*bèi*) + V_2, and the other for its use in V_1(*bèi*) – $NP_{(AGENT)}$–V_2 (– C) where C is another constituent. A process of grammaticalization

[5] See Peyraube (1989b) for a definition of the passive and for more details on the Chinese types of construction. We note in passing that it is not uncommon for languages to accumulate a large number of morphological markers of the passive over time, as is the case in Chinese and in English.

affects only this second use, with reanalysis of the verb, *bèi*, as a preposition introducing the agent being completed by the end of the Early Medieval period, that is, towards the end of 6th century AD. This new agentive form of the *bèi* passive, modelled on the *wéi* construction (another case, probably of analogical change), subsequently became the dominant one during the Tang dynasty (618–907) in Late Medieval Chinese.

(9) *Pídài* *bèi* *zéi* *dào* *qù*
leather:bag: PASS thief steal grab
'The leather bag was stolen by bandits.'
(*Cháo Yě Jiăn Zài*, poem by Zhang Zhuo 660–740)

During the Modern period from the 13th century onwards, *bèi* became relegated more and more to the written language.

3.2. Sources of passive markers in contemporary Sinitic languages

The six principle sources of passive markers in Sinitic languages comprise the lexical domains of the following verbs: (i) *give*; (ii) *suffer*; (iii) *touch, be in contact with*; (iv) causative verbs including *tell, call, let*; (v) *wait* and (vi) *get/obtain, take.* The majority of Sinitic languages use a highly diverse group of markers based on verbs of giving to introduce the agent NP. In the northern zones for Mandarin dialects, the use of causative verbs is prevalent, particularly *jiào* 'tell, make' but also *ràng* 'let', while *zhuó* 'to suffer' is the typical marker for the majority of Southwestern Mandarin dialects (L. Li 2006). The basic form for these passive constructions, both agentive and adversative in nature, is:

$NP_{1(\text{PATIENT})}$–$\text{Preposition}_{\text{PASSIVE}}(<V_{1(\text{GIVE})}$)–$NP_{2(\text{AGENT})}$–V_2
exemplified by the Hengshan dialect of the Xiang group (Hunan):

(10) *tʰ*a^{33} *tiəŋ*^{33} *ɳi*^{24} *fu*^{34} *tæ*^{24} *tʰ*a^{45} *ia*^{11} *ma*^{34}
3SG today will PASS$_{(<\text{ 'give'})}$ 3SG father blame
'He will be blamed by his father today.' (Mao 1999: 267)

To account for the reanalysis of *give* verbs into both dative and passive prepositions, we have proposed that there are at least two different pathways of grammaticalization (Chappell and Peyraube 2006):

(i) V $_{[+\text{ GIVE}]}$ > dative marker
(ii) V $_{[+\text{ GIVE}]}$ > causative verb > passive

First, the syntactic configuration for the datives is different from that for the passive and causative constructions in most Sinitic languages: prototypical dative markers follow the main verb, whereas the causative verbs and passive exponents precede it. Second, this hypothesis appears to conform to available historical data which show that the causative use of these verbs appeared prior to the passive one. Third, causative verbs from sources other than verbs of giving similarly develop into passive markers (but not into dative prepositions). This applies, for example, to *jiào* 'tell, make' or *ràng* 'let' used as passive markers in contemporary Standard Mandarin Chinese.[6]

Cross-linguistically, there is ample evidence for the association between verbs of giving and dative prepositions or verbs of giving and causative verbs (Newman 1996). However, it is somewhat rare to find verbs of giving directly developing into passive markers. Apart from Sinitic languages, in this region of the world only a small number of Southeast Asian languages use this pathway, such as certain peninsular Western Malay dialects in their colloquial form but also certain Altaic languages (Evenki, Classical Manchu) (Zhang 2000; Yap and Iwasaki 2007). Interestingly, Wiemer (Chapter 61 above) gives examples of this same pathway in West Slavic languages, including Polish, though the passive use is as yet only an incipient development and quite rare.

Since the development directly from a verb of giving into a passive marker is not attested, while it is quite common to find passive markers directly grammaticalized from causatives, we propose the following implicational universal:

(11) *If a language has a passive marker whose origin is in a verb of giving, then it necessarily has a causative verb, realized by the same form, which has its source in the same verb of giving.*
[PASSIVE MARKER < GIVE] ⊃ [CAUSATIVE < GIVE]

4. Classifiers

A classifier (CLF) in Sinitic languages is a word which theoretically must occur after a demonstrative and/or number (NUM), or some other quantifiers, and before a noun (N):

(12) *(zhèi) sān běn shū*
(this) three CLF book
'(these) three books'

[6] See L. Jiang (1999) and S. Jiang (2002).

This definition does not say anything, however, about the semantic role of the CLF; nor does it allow the important distinction to be made between a CLF and a measure word (MW).

Measure words can indicate: (i) standards for length, weight, volume, and area; (ii) collectives; (iii) containers; (iv) parts of wholes. They are probably a universal feature of languages, while classifiers are not.

Chinese classifiers did not appear earlier than the Former Han period, *c.*2nd century BC, increasing in use during the Early Medieval (2nd–6th), before becoming prominent under the Late Medieval period (7th–13th).

Seven patterns, with either measure words or classifiers, are attested throughout the different stages of Chinese, from the Pre-Archaic period (14th–11th BC) to the Late Medieval period: (i) NUM–N, (ii) N–NUM, (iii) N_1–NUM–N_2, (iv) N–NUM–MW, (v) N–NUM–CLF, (vi) NUM–MW–N, and (vii) NUM–CLF–N.

In the oracle bone inscriptions of Pre-Archaic Chinese (14th–11th), the pattern NUM–N is by far the most common pattern and is probably also the oldest. Patterns (ii), (iii), and (iv) are also attested.[7]

(13) *yǒu* *yī* *niú* *Zǔ* *Yǐ*
sacrifice one bovine Ancestor Yi
'(One should) sacrifice one bovine to Ancestor Yi.'
(*Bìng Biàn* 120.8, 14th–11th BC)

By the time of Late Archaic Chinese (5th–2nd), the N–NUM–MW pattern has grown in importance, while NUM–N has the highest frequency. The most interesting development in this period is undeniably the appearance of the prenominal measure word NUM–MW–N, which did not exist in Early Archaic.

(14) *yóu* *yǐ* *yī* *bēi* *shuǐ* *jiù* *yī* *chē* *xīn* *zhī* *huǒ* *yě*
be.like with one $glass_{MW}$ water rescue one $cart_{MW}$ firewood LIG fire PRT
'It is like fighting a fire in a cartful of firewood with a glass of water.'
(*Mèngzǐ: Téng Wén Gōng: Xià*, 4th BC)

The following word order change must thus have occurred during Late Archaic Chinese of N–NUM–MW > NUM–MW–N where the predicate NUM–MW in pattern (iv) (N–NUM–MW) is reanalysed as the modifier of the head noun in pattern (vi) (NUM–MW–N). In Pre-Medieval Chinese (Han dynasty: 1st BC–1st AD), this pattern steadily gains ground.

The most important issue for the Pre-Medieval period is in fact to ascertain whether individual classifiers had come into existence or not. This indeed appears to be the case with regard to the postnominal structure, N–NUM–CLF:

[7] Examples such as *Qiāng yī Qiāng* 'one Qiang (person)' are also found in the Oracle Bone Inscriptions but do not involve 'echo classifiers' as the second occurrence is used as a noun, and not as a classifier in any operation of enumeration (see Peyraube 1998 for the relevant argumentation).

(15) *jīzǐ* *wǔ* *méi*
egg five CLF
'five eggs'
(Han Dynasty Bamboo Strips Collection S15, 10.12; *c.*1st AD)

A close examination of the Han inscriptions on bamboo or wood tablets—which represent a rich corpus excavated from ruins at a border garrison in northwest China—does in fact reveal that classifiers were not rare at this time (see Drocourt 1993). It is well known that there is a division among the world's languages between those with morphologically marked plurals and no classifiers on the one hand, and those with classifiers but no plural markers on the other. Peyraube (1998) suggested that the appearance of true classifiers in China might have been triggered by the loss of a plurality marker in Archaic Chinese, realised as infix '*-r*' (for the reconstruction of such an infix, see Sagart 1993).

Every classifier has its own history, but they all derive from nouns (or verbs in a very few cases) through a process of grammaticalization which bleaches them of their full lexical meaning. For instance, the classifiers *méi* 枚, *kǒu* 口, *tóu* 头, already attested under the Han, come from nouns meaning 'tree trunk', 'mouth', and 'head' respectively and were used as a general classifier in the first case, and mainly for animals in the case of the two others.

By the Early Medieval period (2nd–6th), the classifiers are not yet obligatory when used in quantified NPs, even though the increase in their use dates from this period. Moreover, they continued to be used in the postnominal position. It is only in the Late Medieval period (7th–13th) that the prenominal NUM–CLF–N pattern becomes widespread, with 70 per cent of quantified NPs involving the systematic use of classifiers.

(16) *chéng* *yī* *duǒ* *hēi* *yún*
ride one CLF black cloud
'(They) rode on a black cloud.'
(*Hán Qín Hǔ*, *c.* 9th–10th)

Note also that by this time *méi* is no longer the general classifier. It has been replaced by *gè* 个 which has an extended use with all kinds of nouns, especially abstract ones, but also persons, as in:

(17) *jiāoxué* *bā* *wàn* *gè* *tǔdì*
teach eight ten.thousand CLF disciple
'(He) taught eighty thousand disciples.'
(Buddhist Transformation text, *c.*9th–10th)

Finally, besides being used in NPs involving numerals, some classifiers (mainly *gè*) can also be used in the prenominal pattern with a demonstrative, a new development, beginning in the 10th century: DEM–CLF–N.

(18) *cǐ* *gè* *dìyù-zhōng* *yǒu* *yī* *Qīngtí* *fūrén* *yǐ* *fǒu*
DEM CLF hell-in there.be one Qingti madam yes no
'Is there a Madam Qingti in this hell?'
(*Dà Mù Qián Lián Míng Jiān Qiú Mǔ*, 9th–10th)

The change in word order proposed above for measure words of N–NUM–MW > NUM–MW–N, ensuing upon reanalysis of predicative NUM–MW as a noun modifier, also took place for the classifiers:

N–NUM–CLF > NUM–CLF–N

Thus, exactly like the form containing a prenominal MW, already dominant for many centuries, the NUM–CLF was similarly reanalysed as a modifier of the head noun (for details, see Peyraube 1998).

From Late Medieval to the Modern period (19th century), classifiers diversified and, besides their role in quantification, also took on the function of qualification or classification. Interestingly, in certain dialects of Northern Chinese, there is a new tendency to lose this latter function, due to a process of lexical unification of all classifiers into just one: *gè*.

Acknowledgements

This research has been supported by funding from both the European Research Council (ERC Advanced Grant Project FP-7 'Sinotype' 230388) and the Programme blanc of the Agence Nationale de la Recherche, France (ANR-08-BLAN-0174 'Diamin'). We express our gratitude to both these organizations.

References

Aaron, Jessi E. (2006). 'Variation and change in Spanish future temporal expression', doctoral dissertation, University of New Mexico.

Abraham, Werner (1991). 'The grammaticalization of the German modal particles', in Traugott and Heine (1991b: 331–80).

——(1993). 'Einleitung zum Thema dieses Bandes. Grammatikalisierung und Reanalyse: Einander ausschließende oder ergänzende Begriffe?', *Folia Linguistica Historica* 13.1–2: 7–26.

——(1997). 'The interdependence of case, aspect and referentiality in the history of German: the case of the verbal genitive', in van Kemenade and Vincent (1997: 29–61).

——(1998). 'The aspectual source of the epistemic-root distinction of modal verbs', in H. W. Boeder, C. Schröder, K. H. Wagner, and W. Wildgen (eds), *Sprache in Raum und Zeit, in Memoriam Johannes Bechert*, Band 2: *Beitrage zur Empirischen Sprachwissenschaft.* Tübingen: Narr, 231–49.

——(2000). 'Modal particles in German: word classification and legacy beyond grammaticalisation', in Petra M. Vogel and Bernard Comrie (eds), *Approaches to the Typology of Word Classes.* Berlin: Mouton de Gruyter, 321–50.

——(2003). 'Autonomous and non-autonomous components of "grammaticalization": economy criteria in the emergence of German negation', *Sprachtypologie und Universalienforschung* 56.4, 325–65.

——(2004). 'The grammaticalization of the infinitival preposition: toward a theory of "grammaticalizing reanalysis"', *Journal of Comparative Germanic Linguistics* 7.2: 111–70.

——(2007). 'The discourse-functional crystallization of DP from the original demonstrative', in Stark et al. (2007: 241–56).

——and Leiss, Elisabeth (eds) (2008). *Modality–Aspect Interfaces: Implications and Typological Solutions.* Amsterdam: Benjamins.

Adams, J. N. (1991). 'Some neglected evidence for Latin *habeo* with infinitive: the order of the constituents', *Transactions of the Philological Society* 89: 131–96.

Adams, Valerie (2002[1973]). *An Introduction to Modern English Word-Formation.* London: Longman.

Adamson, Sylvia (2000). 'A lovely little example: word order options and category shift in the premodifying string', in Olga Fischer, Anette Rosenbach, and Dieter Stein (eds), *Pathways of Change: Grammaticalization in English.* Amsterdam: Benjamins, 39–66.

Aebischer, Paul (1948). 'Contribution à la protohistoire des articles *ille* et *ipse* dans les langues romanes', *Cultura Neolatina* 8: 181–203.

Ahlqvist, Anders (ed.) (1982). *Papers from the Fifth International Conference on Historical Linguistics.* Amsterdam: Benjamins.

Ahn, Joo Hoh (1996). 'A study of the phenomena of grammaticization in the Korean noun'. PhD dissertation, Yonsei University, Korea.

Aijmer, Karen (1985). 'The semantic development of *will*', in J. Fisiak (ed.), *Historical Semantics and Historical Word-Formation*. Berlin: Mouton de Gruyter, 11–21.

——(1996). *Conversational Routines in English*. London: Longman.

——(1997). '*I think*: an English modal particle', in Toril Swan and Olaf Jansen Westvik (eds), *Modality in Germanic Languages: Historical and Comparative Perspectives*. Berlin: Mouton de Gruyter, 1–47.

——(2002). *English Discourse Particles*. Amsterdam: Benjamins.

——(2004). 'The semantic path from modality to aspect: *be able to* in a cross-linguistic perspective', in Lindquist and Mair (2004a: 57–78).

Aikhenvald, Alexandra Y. (1995). 'Split ergativity in Berber languages', *St Petersburg Journal of African Studies* 4: 39–68.

——(1996). 'Areal diffusion in northwest Amazonia: the case of Tariana', *Anthropological Linguistics* 38: 73–116.

——(2000). *Classifiers: A Typology of Noun Categorization Devices*. Oxford: Oxford University Press.

——(2002). *Language Contact in Amazonia*. Oxford: Oxford University Press.

——(2003). 'Mechanisms of change in areal diffusion: new morphology and language contact', *Journal of Linguistics* 39: 1–29.

——(2004). *Evidentiality*. Oxford: Oxford University Press. (Paperback, with revisions, 2006.)

——(2006). 'Evidentiality in grammar', in Keith Brown (ed.), *Encyclopedia of Language and Linguistics*, 2nd edn, vol. 4. Oxford: Elsevier, 320–25.

——(2008). 'Information source and evidentiality: what can we conclude?', *Rivista di linguistica* 19: 207–27 (dated 2007, published 2008).

——and Dixon, R. M. W. (eds) (2001). *Areal Diffusion and Genetic Inheritance: Problems in Comparative Linguistics*. Oxford: Oxford University Press.

————(eds) (2003). *Studies in Evidentiality*. Amsterdam: Benjamins.

————(eds) (2006). *Grammars in Contact: A Cross-Linguistic Typology*. Oxford: Oxford University Press.

Aitchison, Jean (1991). *Language Change: Progress or Decay?* Cambridge: Cambridge University Press.

Akimoto, Minoji (1989). *A Study of Verbo-Nominal Structures in English*. Tokyo: Shinozaki Shorin.

——(2002). 'Two types of passivization of "V + NP + P" constructions in relation to idiomatization', in Teresa Fanego, María José López-Couso, and Javier Pérez-Guerra (eds), *English Historical Syntax and Morphology*. Amsterdam: Benjamins, 9–22.

——(2009). Review of *Lexicalization and Language Change*, *Studies in English Literature* 50: 226–34.

Alanne, Eero (1972). 'Zur Rolle der syntaktischen Interferenz der verwandten und unverwandten Sprachen', *Neuphilologische Mitteilungen* 73: 568–74.

Alba, Matt (2008). 'Ratio frequency: insights into usage effects on phonological structure from hiatus resolution in New Mexican Spanish', *Studies in Hispanic and Lusophone Linguistics* 1: 247–86.

Alboiu, Gabriela, and Motapanyane, Virgina (2000). 'The generative approach to Romanian grammar: an overview', in Gabriela Alboiu and Virginia Motapanyane (eds), *Comparative Studies in Romanian Syntax*. Amsterdam: Elsevier, 1–48.

Albrecht, Jörn (2002). 'Das Wort im europäischen Strukturalismus', in D. A. Cruse, Franz Hundsnurscher, Michael Job, and Peter Rolf Lutzeier (eds), *Lexicology: An International Handbook on the Nature and Structure of Words and Vocabularies*, vol. 1. Berlin: de Gruyter, 138–43.

Algeo, John (1991). 'Introduction', in John Algeo (ed.), *Fifty Years among the New Words. A Dictionary of Neologisms, 1941–1991.* Cambridge: Cambridge University Press, 1–16.

——(1995). 'Having a look at the expanded predicate', in Bas Aarts and Charles F. Meyer (eds), *The Verb in Contemporary English.* Cambridge: Cambridge University Press, 203–17.

Allen, C. L. (1995). *Case Marking and Reanalysis: Grammatical Relations from Old to Early Modern English.* Oxford: Oxford University Press.

Allen, Cynthia (1977). 'Topics in diachronic English syntax'. PhD, University of Massachusetts.

Allerton, D. J. (2002). *Stretched Verb Constructions in English.* London: Routledge.

Amha, Azeb (2001). *The Maale Language.* Dordrecht: Foris.

An, Hyo-pal (1983). 'Hesahwauy Yenkwu' [A study of the formation of empty words]. MA thesis, Kyungnam University, Korea.

Andersen, Henning (1973). 'Abductive and deductive change', *Language* 49.4: 765–93.

——(1987). 'From auxiliary to desinence', in Martin B. Harris and Paolo Ramat (eds), *Historical Development of Auxiliaries.* Berlin: Mouton de Gruyter, 21–51.

——(2001). 'Actualization and the (uni)directionality', in Henning Andersen (ed.), *Actualization: Linguistic Change in Progress.* Amsterdam: Benjamins, 225–48.

——(2005). 'On the *Handbook of Historical Linguistics*', *Diachronica* 22: 155–76.

——(2006). 'Grammation, regrammation, and degrammation: tense loss in Russian', *Diachronica* 23.2: 231–58.

——(2008). 'Grammaticalization in a speaker-oriented theory of change', in Thórhallur Eythórsson (ed.), *Grammatical Change and Linguistic Theory: The Rosendal Papers.* Amsterdam: Benjamins, 22–44.

Anderson, Gregory D. S. (2006) *Auxiliary Verb Constructions.* Oxford: Oxford University Press.

Anderson, Lloyd B. (1982). 'The "perfect" as a universal and as a language specific category', in Paul J. Hopper (ed.), *Tense–Aspect: Between Semantics and Pragmatics.* Amsterdam: Benjamins, 227–64.

——(1985). 'Inflectional morphology', in Shopen (1985: iii.50–201).

——(1986). 'Evidentials, paths of change, and mental maps: typologically regular asymmetries', in Wallace Chafe and Marianne Mithun (eds), *Evidentiality: The Linguistic Coding of Epistemology.* Norwood: Ablex, 273–312.

——(1992). *A-Morphous Morphology.* Cambridge: Cambridge University Press.

——and Keenan, Edward L. (1985). 'Deixis', in Shopen (1985: ii.259–308).

Andersson, Peter (2007). *Modalitet och förändring: En studie av* må *och* kunna *i fornsvenska.* Göteborg: Institutionen för Svenska Språket.

——(2008). 'Swedish *må* and the (de)grammaticalization debate', in López-Couso and Seoane (2008: 15–32).

Ansaldo, Umberto, and Lim, Lisa (2004). 'Phonetic absence as syntactic prominence: grammaticalization in isolating tonal languages', in Fischer et al. (2004: 345–62).

Anscombre, Jean-Claude, and Ducrot, Oswald (1977). 'Deux mais en francais?', *Lingua* 43: 23–40.

Antaki, Charles, and Wetherell, Margaret (1999). 'Show concessions', *Discourse Studies* 1.1: 7–27.

Anttila, Raimo (1989[1972]). *Historical and Comparative Linguistics*, 2nd revised edn. Amsterdam: Benjamins.

——(2003). 'Analogy: the warp and woof of cognition', in Joseph and Janda (2003: 425–40).

Antzakas, Klimis (2006). 'The use of negative head movements in Greek Sign Language', in U. Zeshan (ed.), *Interrogative and Negative Constructions in Sign Languages*. Nijmegen: Ishara Press, 258–69.

Arbib, Michael A. (2005). 'From monkey-like action recognition to human language: an evolutionary framework for neurolinguistics', *Behavioral and Brain Sciences* 28.2: 105–24.

Ariel, Mira (1990). *Accessing NP Antecedents*. London: Croom Helm.

——(2000). 'The development of person agreement markers', in Michael Barlow and Suzanne Kemmer (eds), *Usage-Based Models of Language*. Stanford, CA: CSLI, 197–260.

——(2008). *Pragmatics and Grammar*. Cambridge: Cambridge University Press.

Arlotto, Anthony (1972). *Introduction to Historical Linguistics*. Boston: Houghton.

Aronoff, Mark, Meir, Irit, and Sandler, Wendy (2005). 'The paradox of sign language morphology', *Language* 81: 301–44.

Ashby, William J. (1981). 'The loss of the negative particle *ne* in French: a syntactic change in progress', *Language* 57.3: 674–87.

——(2001). 'Un nouveau regard sur la chute du *ne* en français parlé tourangeau: s'agit-it d'un changement en cours?', *French Language Studies* 11: 1–22.

Asher, Ronald E. (1982). *Tamil*. Amsterdam: North-Holland.

Askedal, John O. (2005). 'Grammatikalisierung und Persistenz im deutschen "Rezipienten Passiv" mit *bekommen/kriegen/erhalten*', in Torsten Leuschner (ed.), *Grammatikalisierung im Deutschen*. Berlin: Mouton de Gruyter, 211–27.

——(2008). '"Degrammaticalization" versus typology: reflections on a strained relationship', in Thórhallur Eythórsson (ed.), *Grammatical Change and Linguistic Theory: The Rosendal Papers*. Amsterdam: Benjamins, 45–77.

Auer, Peter, and Günthner, Susanne (2005). 'Die Entstehung von Diskursmarkern im Deutschen: ein Fall von Grammatikalisierung?', in Torsten Leuschner and Tanja Mortelsmans (eds), *Grammatikalisierung im Deutschen*. Berlin: de Gruyter, 335–62.

Aureli, Massimo (2003). 'Pressione dell'uso sulla norma: le relative non standard nei giudizi degli utenti', *Studi italiani di linguistica teorica e applicata* 32.1: 45–67.

Austin, Peter (1981). 'Switch-reference in Australia', *Language* 57: 309–34.

——(1995). 'Double case marking in Kanyara and Mantharta languages: Western Australia', in Plank (1995: 363–79).

Awoyale, Yiwola (1986). 'Reflexivization in Kwa languages', in Gerrit Jan Dimmendaal (ed.), *Current Approaches to African Linguistics*, vol. 3. Dordrecht: Foris, 1–14.

Baayen, R. Harald (2008). 'Corpus linguistics in morphology: morphological productivity', in A. Lüdeling, M. Kytö, and T. McEnery (eds), *Handbook of Corpus Linguistics*. Berlin: de Gruyter, 1–52.

Babaev, Kirill (2008). 'Personal pronoun origins', *LinguistList* 19.2.

Babel, Anne (2009). '*Dizque*, evidentiality and stance in Valley Spanish', *Language in Society* 38: 487–511.

Baker, Mark (1985). 'The Mirror Principle and morphosyntactic explanation', *Linguistic Inquiry* 16.3: 373–415.

——(1988). *Incorporation: A Theory of Grammatical Function Changing*. Chicago: University of Chicago Press.

——(2008). *The Syntax of Agreement and Concord*. Cambridge: Cambridge University Press.

BAKKER, PETER (2006). 'The Sri Lanka Sprachbund: the newcomers Portuguese and Malay', in Y. Matras, A. McMahon, and N. Vincent (eds), *Linguistic Areas: Convergence in Historical and Typological Perspective*. Basingstoke: Palgrave Macmillan, 135–59.

BALL, CATHERINE N. (1991). 'The historical development of the *it*-cleft', PhD dissertation, University of Pennsylvania.

——(1994). 'The origins of the informative-presupposition *it*-cleft', *Journal of Pragmatics* 22: 603–28.

BANFI, EMANUELE (2008). 'Sul suffisso i.e. *-*(V)nt*-: tra dati storico-linguistici e fatti di proto-grammaticalizzazione', in Romano Lazzeroni, Emanuele Banfi, Giuliano Bernini, Marina Chini, and Giovanna Marotta (eds), *Diachronica et synchronica*. Pisa: ETS, 53–70.

BAO, ZHINMIN (2005). 'The aspectual system of Singapore English and the systemic substratist explanation', *Journal of Linguistics* 41: 237–67.

BARBET, CÉCILE (2010). 'Le verbe modal *devoir* en français médiéval et contemporain: hypothèses pragmatiques sur le changement sémantique', in B. Combettes et al. (eds), *Le changement en français: études de linguistique diachronique*. Berne: Lang, 19–41.

BARLOW, MICHAEL, and KEMMER, SUZANNE (2000). *Usage-Based Models of Language*. Stanford, CA: CSLI.

BARON, NAOMI S. (1977). *Language Acquisition and Historical Change*. Amsterdam: North-Holland.

BARTH, DAGMAR (2000). '*That's true, although not really, but still*: expressing concession in spoken English', in Elizabeth Couper-Kuhlen and Bernd Kortmann (eds), *Cause, Condition, Concession, and Contrast: Cognitive and Discourse Perspectives*. Berlin: Mouton de Gruyter, 411–37.

BARTH-WEINGARTEN, DAGMAR (2003). *Concession in Spoken English: On the Realisation of a Discourse-Pragmatic Relation*. Tübingen: Narr.

——and COUPER-KUHLEN, ELIZABETH (2002). 'On the development of final *though*: a case of grammaticalization?', in Wischer and Diewald (2002: 345–61).

BATTISON, ROBBIN (1978). *Lexical Borrowing in American Sign Language*. Silver Spring, MD: Linstok Press.

Battye, Adrian, and Roberts, Ian (eds) (1995). *Clause Structure and Language Change*. Oxford: Oxford University Press.

BAUER, BRIGITTE (1995). *The Emergence and Development of SVO Patterning in Latin and French*. Oxford: Oxford University Press.

——(2002[1983]). *English Word Formation*. Cambridge: Cambridge University Press.

——(2007). 'The definite article in Indo-European: emergence of a new category', in Stark et al. (2007: 103–40).

BAUER, LAURIE (1983). *English Word-Formation*. Cambridge: Cambridge University Press.

BEC, PIERRE (1967). *La langue occitane*. Montpellier: PUF.

BECKNER, CLAY, and BYBEE, JOAN (2009). 'A usage-based account of constituency and reanalysis', *Language Learning* 59, Suppl. 1 (December), 29–48.

BÉGUELIN, MARIE-JOSÉ (2000). 'Des clauses impersonnelles aux constituants phrastiques: quelques axes de grammaticalisation', in P. Seriot and A. Berrendonner (eds), *Le paradoxe du sujet: les propositions impersonnelles dans les langues slaves et romanes. Cahiers de l'ILSL* 12: 25–41.

Behaghel, Otto (1924). *Deutsche Syntax*, vol. 2. Heidelberg: Winter.

Bellugi, Ursula, and Klima, Edward (1976). 'Two faces of the sign: arbitrary and abstract', in S. Harnad, H. Steklis, and J. Lancaster (eds), *Origins and Evolution of Language and Speech*. New York: New York Academy of Sciences, 514–43.

Benincà, Paola (2006). 'A detailed map of the left periphery of medieval Romance', in Raffaella Zanuttini, Héctor Campos, Elena Herberger, and Paul Portner (eds), *Crosslinguistic Research in Syntax and Semantics: Negation, Tense, and Clausal Architecture*. Washington, DC: Georgetown University Press, 53–86.

——and Poletto, Cecilia (2004). 'Topic, focus, and V2: defining the CP sublayers', in Luigi Rizzi (ed.), *The Structure of CP and IP: The Cartography of Syntactic Structures*, vol. 2. Oxford: Oxford University Press, 52–75.

Bennis, Hans, Pica, Pierre, and Rooryck, Johan (eds) (1997). *Atomism and Binding*. Dordrecht: Foris.

Benveniste, Emile (1958). 'Les verbes délocutifs'. Reprinted in Benveniste (1966b: 277–85).

——(1966a). 'La construction passive du parfait transitif', in Benveniste (1996b: 176–86).

——(1966b). *Problèmes de linguistique générale*. Paris: Gallimard.

Benz, Anton (2003). 'Learning and diachronic laws for partial blocking', in Paul Dekker and Robert van Rooij (eds), *Proceedings of the 14th Amsterdam Colloquium*, Amsterdam: 75–80.

Benzing, Johannes (1959). 'Das Tschuwaschische', in J. Deny, K. Grønbech, H. Scheel, and Z. V. Togan (eds), *Philologiae Turcicae Fundamenta*, vol. 1. Wiesbaden: Steiner, 695–751.

Berg, Thomas (1998). *Linguistic Structure and Change: An Explanation from Language Processing*. Oxford: Clarendon Press.

Berbeira Gardón, José Luis (2008). 'Hacia un estudio léxico-pragmático de la gramaticalización: convencionalización de inferencias y conceptos *ad hoc*', in M. L. Mora Millán (ed.), *Cognición y lenguaje: estudios en homenaje a José Luis Guijarro Morales*. Cádiz: Univesidad de Cádiz, 19–44.

Bergs, Alexander (2005). *Social Networks and Historical Sociolinguistics: Studies in Morphosyntactic Variation in the Paston Letters (1421–1503)*. Berlin: Mouton de Gruyter.

Bermúdez-Otero, Ricardo, and Payne, John (2011). 'There are no special clitics', in Alexandra Galani, Glyn Hicks, and George Tsoulas (eds), *Morphology and Its Interfaces*. Amsterdam: Benjamins, 147–86.

Berndt, Rolf (1956). *Form und Funktion des Verbums im nördlichen Spätaltenglischen*. Halle: Niemeyer.

Bernini, Giuliano, and Ramat, Paolo (1996). *Negative Sentences in the Languages of Europe: A Typological Approach*. Berlin: Mouton de Gruyter.

Bertrand, Roxane, and Chanet, Catherine (2005). 'Fonctions pragmatiques et prosodie de *enfin* en français spontané', *Revue de Sémantique et Pragmatique* 17: 101–19.

Beths, Frank (1999). 'The history of *dare* and the status of unidirectionality', *Linguistics* 37.6: 1069–1110.

Bhat, D. N. S. (2005). *Pronouns*. Oxford: Oxford University Press.

Biber, Douglas (2004). 'Historical patterns for the grammatical marking of stance: a cross-register comparison', *Journal of Historical Pragmatics* 5.1: 107–36.

——Johansson, Stig, Leech, Geoffrey, Conrad, Susan, and Finegan, Edward (1999). *Longman Grammar of Spoken and Written English*. London: Longman.

Biberauer, Theresa (2009). 'Jespersen off course? The case of contemporary Afrikaans negation', in van Gelderen (2009: 91–130).

Bickel, Balthasar (1999). 'Nominalization and focus in some Kiranti languages', in Y. Yadava and W. Glover (eds), *Studies in Nepalese Linguistics*. Kathmandu: Royal Nepal Academy, 271–96.

——and Nichols, Johanna (2007). 'Inflectional morphology', in Shopen (2007: iii.169–240).

Bickerton, Derek (1981). *Roots of Language*. Ann Arbor, MI: Karoma.

——(1984). 'The language bioprogram hypothesis', *Behavioral and Brain Sciences* 7.2: 173–221.

——(1990). *Language and Species*. Chicago: University of Chicago Press.

——(1995). *Language and Human Behavior*. Seattle: University of Washington Press.

Bisang, Walter (1992). *Das Verb im Chinesischen, Hmong, Vietnamesischen, Thai und Khmer*. Tübingen: Narr.

——(1996). 'Areal typology and grammaticalization: processes of grammaticalization based on nouns and verbs in East and mainland South East Asian languages', *Studies in Language* 20.3: 519–97.

——(1998). 'Grammaticalisation and language contact: constructions and positions', in A. Giacalone Ramat and P. J. Hopper (eds), *The Limits of Grammaticalization*. Amsterdam: Benjamins, 13–58.

——(1999). 'Classifiers in East and Southeast Asian languages: counting and beyond', in Jadranka Gvozdanovic (ed.), *Numeral Types and Changes Worldwide*. Berlin: Mouton de Gruyter, 113–85.

——(2004). 'Grammaticalization without coevolution of form and meaning: the case of tense-aspect-modality in East and mainland Southeast Asia', in Walter Bisang, Nikolaus P. Himmelmann, and Björn Wiemer (eds), *What Makes Grammaticalization? A Look From its Fringes and its Components*. Berlin: Mouton de Gruyter, 109–38.

——(2006). 'South East Asia as a linguistic area', in Keith Brown (ed.), *Encyclopedia of Language and Linguistics*, vol. 11. Oxford: Elsevier, 587–95.

——(2008a). 'Transcategoriality and argument structure in Late Archaic Chinese', in Jaakko Leino (ed.), *Constructional Reorganization*. Amsterdam: Benjamins, 55–88.

——(2008b). 'Grammaticalization and the areal factor: the perspective of East and mainland Southeast Asian languages', in López-Couso and Seoane (2008: 15–35).

——(2009). 'On the evolution of complexity: sometimes less is more in East and mainland Southeast Asia', in Geoffrey Sampson, David Gil, and Peter Trudgill (eds), *Language Complexity as an Evolving Variable*. Oxford: Oxford University Press, 34–49.

Black, Cheryl (2000). *Quiegolani Zapotec*. Dallas, TX: Summer Institute of Linguistics.

Blackings, Mairi, and Fabb, Nigel (2003). *A Grammar of Ma'di*. Berlin: Mouton de Gruyter.

Blake, Barry J. (2001). *Case*. Cambridge: Cambridge University Press.

Blakemore, Diane (1987). *Semantic Constraints on Relevance*. Oxford: Blackwell.

Blank, Andreas (1997). *Prinzipien des lexikalischen Bedeutungswandels dargestellt an romanischen Sprachen*. Tübingen: Niemeyer.

——(2001). 'Pathways of lexicalization', in Martin Haspelmath, Ekkehard König, Wulf Oesterreicher, and Wolfgang Raible (eds), *Language Typology and Language Universals: Ein internationales Handbuch*. Berlin: de Gruyter, 1596–1608.

Blass, Regina (1989). 'Grammaticalization of interpretive use: the case of *ré* in Sissala', *Lingua* 79: 299–326.

Blecke, Thomas (1996). *Lexikalische Kategorien und grammatische Strukturen im Tigemaxo (Bozo, Mande).* Cologne: Köppe.

Blutner, Reinhard (2000). 'Some aspects of optimality in natural language interpretation', *Journal of Semantics* 17: 189–216.

Boas, Franz (1938). 'Language', in Franz Boas (ed.), *General Anthropology.* Boston: Heath, 124–45.

Boland, Annerieke (2006). *Aspect, Tense and Modality: Theory, Typology, Acquisition.* Utrecht: LOT.

Bolinger, Dwight (1980). '*Wanna* and the gradience of auxiliaries', in Gunter Brettschneider and Christian Lehmann (eds), *Wege zur Universalienforschung: Sprachwissenschaftliche Beiträge zum 60. Geburtstag von Hansjakob Seiler.* Tübingen: Narr, 292–9.

——(1989). *Intonation and its Uses.* London: Arnold.

Bolonyai, Agnes (1998). 'In-between languages: language shift/maintenance in childhood bilingualism', *International Journal of Bilingualism* 2: 21–43.

Bonet, Eulàlia (1995). 'Feature structure of Romance clitics', *Natural Language and Linguistic Theory* 13.4: 607–47.

Booij, Geert, Lehmann, Christian, Mugdan, Joachim, and Skopeteas, Stavros (eds) (2004). *Morphology: A Handbook on Inflection and Word Formation,* vol. 2. Berlin: de Gruyter, 1190–1202.

Bopp, Franz (1833). *Vergleichende Grammatik des Sanskrit, Zend, Griechischen, Lateinischen, Litauischen, Altslawischen, Gothischen und Deutschen,* vol. 1. Berlin: Dümmler.

——(1975[1816]). *Über das Conjugationssystem der Sanskritsprache in Vergleichung mit jenem der griechischen, lateinischen, persischen und germanischen Sprache.* Hildesheim: Olms (reprint of the 1816 edn, Frankfurt/Main: Andreäische).

Boretzky, Norbert (1983). *Kreolsprachen, Substrate und Sprachwandel.* Wiesbaden: Harrassowitz.

——(1989). 'Zum Interferenzverhalten des Romani', *Zeitschrift für Phonetik, Sprachwissenschaft und Kommunikationsforschung* 42.3: 357–74.

——Enninger, Werner, and Stolz, Thomas (eds) (1989). *Beiträge zum 5. Essener Kolloquium über 'Grammatikalisierung: Natürlichkeit und Systemökonomie',* vol. 1. Bochum: Brockmeyer.

Borgman, Donald (1990). 'Sanuma', in D. Derbyshire and G. Pullum (eds), *Handbook of Amazonian Languages,* vol. 2. Berlin: Mouton de Gruyter, 15–248.

Börjars, Kersti (2003). 'Morphological status and (de) grammaticalisation: the Swedish possessive', *Nordic Journal of Linguistics* 26.2: 133–63.

——and Harries, Pauline (2008). 'The clitic–affix distinction, historical change, and Scandinavian bound definiteness marking', *Journal of Germanic Linguistics* 20.4: 289–350.

Boroditsky, Lera (2000). 'Metaphoric structuring: understanding time through spatial metaphors', *Cognition* 75: 1–28.

Bos, Helen (1994). 'An auxiliary verb in sign language of the Netherlands', in I. Ahlgren, B. Bergman, and M. Brennan (eds), *Perspectives on Sign Language Structure.* Durham: ISLA, 37–53.

Bosch, Peter (1983). *Agreement and Anaphora: A Study of the Role of Pronouns in Syntax and Discourse.* New York: Academic Press.

Botha, Rudolf P. (2003). *Unravelling the Evolution of Language.* Amsterdam: Elsevier.

Botne, Robert (1995). 'The pronominal origin of an evidential', *Diachronica* 12: 201–21.

Bowerman, Melissa (1985). 'What shapes children's grammars?', in Dan I. Slobin (ed.), *The Crosslinguistic Study of Language Acquisition*, vol. 2: *Theoretical Issues*. Hillsdale, NJ: Erlbaum, 1257–1319.

Boye, Kasper (2010). 'Semantic maps and the identification of cross-linguistic generic categories', *Linguistic Discovery* 8.1: 4–22.

——and Harder, Peter (2007). 'Complement-taking predicates: usage and linguistic structure', *Studies in Language* 31.3: 569–606.

————(2009). 'Evidentiality: linguistic categories and grammaticalization', *Functions of Language* 16: 9–43.

————(submitted). 'A usage-based theory of grammatical status and grammaticalization'.

Boyland, Joyce T. (1996). 'Morphosyntactic change in progress: a psycholinguistic approach', Dissertation, University of California, Berkeley.

Braine, Martin D. S. (1963). 'The ontogeny of English phrase structure: the first phase', *Language* 39: 1–14.

Braunmüller, Kurt (1991). *Die skandinavischen Sprachen im Überblick*. Tübingen: Francke.

Breban, Tine (2008). 'Grammaticalization, subjectification, and leftward movement of adjectives of difference in the noun phrase', *Folia Linguistica* 42: 259–306.

——(2010). 'Reconstructing paths of secondary grammaticalization of *same* from emphasizing to phoric and nominal-aspectual postdeterminer uses', *Transactions of the Philological Society* 108.1: 68–87.

Breitbarth, Anne (2009). 'A hybrid approach to Jespersen's Cycle in West Germanic', *Journal of Comparative Germanic Linguistics* 12: 81–114.

Brems, Lieselotte (2007). 'The grammaticalization of small size nouns: reconsidering frequency and analogy', *Journal of English Linguistics* 35: 293–324.

Breu, Walter (1988). 'Resultativität, Perfekt und die Gliederung der Aspektdimension', in Jochen Raecke (ed.), *Slavistische Linguistik 1987*. Munich: Sagner, 42–74.

——(1994). 'Der Faktor Sprachkontakt in einer dynamischen Typologie des Slavischen', in Hans Robert Mehlig (ed.), *Slavistische Linguistik 1993*. Munich: Sagner, 41–64.

——(1998). 'Romanisches Adstrat im Moliseslavischen', *Die Welt der Slaven* 43: 339–54.

——(1999). 'Die Komparation im Moliseslavischen', in René Métrich, Albert Hudlett, and Heinz-Helmut Lüger (eds), *Des racines et des ailes: théories, modèles, expériences en linguistique et en didactique*. Nancy: ANCA, 37–63.

——(2003a). 'Der indefinite Artikel in slavischen Mikrosprachen: Grammatikalisierung im totalen Sprachkontakt', in Holger Kuße (ed.), *Slavistische Linguistik 2001*. Munich: Sagner, 27–68.

——(2003b). 'Bilingualism and linguistic interference in the Slavic–Romance contact area of Molise (southern Italy)', in Regine Eckardt, Klaus von Heusinger, and Christoph Schwarze (eds), *Words in Time: Diachronic Semantics from Different Points of View*. Berlin: Mouton de Gruyter, 351–73.

——(2003c). 'Impersonales Neutrum im Moliseslavischen', in Sebastian Kempgen, Ulrich Schweier, and Tilman Berger (eds), *Rusistika, Slavistika, Lingvistika*. Munich: Sagner, 57–71.

——(2004). 'Der definite Artikel in der obersorbischen Umgangssprache', in Marion Krause and Christian Sappok (eds), *Slavistische Linguistik 2002*. Munich: Sagner, 9–57.

Breu, Walter (2008). 'Razvitie sistem artiklej v slavjanskix mikrojazykax v absoljutnom jazykovom kontakte', in Sebastian Kempen, Karl Gutschmidt, Ulrike Jekutsch, and Luger Udolph (eds), *Deutsche Beiträge zum 14, internationalen Slavistenkongress, Ohrid 2008.* Munich: Sagner, 75–88.

——(to appear). 'The grammaticalization of an indefinite article in Slavic micro-languages', in Björn Wiemer, Björn Hansen, and Bernard Wälchli (eds), *Grammatical Replication and Grammatical Borrowability in Language Contact.* Berlin: Mouton de Gruyter.

Brinton, Laurel J. (1988). *The Development of English Aspectual Systems: Aspectualizers and Post-verbal Particles.* Cambridge: Cambridge University Press.

——(1996). *Pragmatic Markers in English: Grammaticalization and Discourse Functions.* Berlin: Mouton de Gruyter.

——(2001). 'From matrix clause to pragmatic marker: the history of *look*-forms', *Journal of Historical Pragmatics* 2.2: 177–99.

——(2002). 'Grammaticalization versus lexicalization reconsidered: on the "late" use of temporal adverbs', in Teresa Fanego, Maria Jose Lopez-Couso, and Javier Perez-Guerra (eds), *English Historical Syntax and Morphology.* Amsterdam: Benjamins, 67–97.

——(2004). 'Subject clitics in English: a case of degrammaticalization?', in Lindquist and Mair (2004a: 227–56).

——(2008a). '"Where grammar and lexis meet": composite predicates in English', in López-Couso and Seoane (2008: 33–53).

——(2008b). *The Comment Clause in English: Syntactic Origins and Pragmatic Development.* Cambridge: Cambridge University Press.

——and Akimoto, Minoji (1999a). 'Introduction', in Brinton and Akimoto (1999c: 1–20).

————(1999b). 'The origin of the composite predicate in Old English', in Brinton and Akimoto (1999c: 21–58).

————(eds) (1999c). *Collocational and Idiomatic Aspects of Composite Predicates in the History of English.* Amsterdam: Benjamins.

——and Traugott, Elizabeth Closs (2005). *Lexicalization and Language Change.* Cambridge: Cambridge University Press.

Broadwell, Aaron (1997). 'Binding theory and switch-reference', in Bennis et al. (1997: 31–49).

——(2006). *A Choctaw Reference Grammar.* Lincoln: University of Nebraska Press.

Bromhead, Helen (2009). *The Reign of Truth and Faith: Epistemic Expressions in 16th and 17th Century English.* Berlin: Mouton de Gruyter.

Browman, Catherine P., and Goldstein, Louis M. (1992). 'Articulatory phonology: an overview', *Phonetica* 49: 155–80.

Brunet, Jacqueline (2006). *Grammaire critique de l'italien,* vol. 15: *Le verbe* 3: *Les subordonnées, suite et fin.* Paris: Presses universitaires de Vincennes.

Bruyn, Adrienne (1996). 'On identifying instances of grammaticalization in Creole languages', in P. Baker and A. Syea (eds), *Changing Meanings, Changing Functions.* London: University of Westminster Press, 29–46.

Bühler, Karl (1982 [1934]). *Sprachtheorie: Die Darstellungsfunktion der Sprache. Mit einem Geleitwort von Friedrich Kainz.* Stuttgart: Fischer.

——(1990). *Theory of Language: The Representational Function of Language.* Translated by Donald Fraser Goodwin. Amsterdam: Benjamins. (Translation of Bühler 1934.)

Buridant, Claude (2000). *Grammaire nouvelle de l'ancien français.* Paris: SEDES.

Burling, Robbins (2005). *The Talking Ape: How Language Evolved.* Oxford: Oxford University Press.

Burridge, Kate (1983). 'On the development of Dutch negation', in Hans Bennis and W. U. S. van Lessen Kloeke (eds), *Linguistics in the Netherlands 1983*. Dordrecht: Foris, 31–40.

——(1993). *Syntactic Change in Germanic: Aspects of Language Change in Germanic with Particular Reference to Middle Dutch.* Amsterdam: Benjamins.

——(1995). 'From modal auxiliary to lexical verb: the curious case of Pennsylvania German *wotte*', in Richard M. Hogg and Linda van Bergen (eds), *Historical Linguistics 1995*, vol. 2: *Germanic Linguistics.* Amsterdam: Benjamins, 19–33.

——(1998). 'From modal auxiliary to lexical verb: the curious case of Pennsylvania German *wotte*', in Richard M. Hogg and Linda van Bergen (eds), *Historical Linguistics 1995*, vol. 2: *Germanic Linguistics.* Amsterdam: Benjamins, 19–33.

Butler, Christopher S. (2003). *Structure and Function: A Guide to Three Major Structural-Functional Theories.* Amsterdam: Benjamins.

Bybee, Joan (1985). *Morphology: A Study of the Relation Between Meaning and Form.* Amsterdam: Benjamins.

——(1998a). 'The emergent lexicon', *Chicago Linguistic Society* 34: 421–35.

——(1998b). 'Irrealis as a grammatical category', *Anthropological Linguistics* 40: 257–71.

——(2000). 'Lexicalization of sound change and alternating engironments', in Michael B. Broe and Janet Pierrehumbert (eds), *Laboratory V: Language Acquisition and the Lexicon.* Cambridge: Cambridge University Press, 250–68.

——(2001). *Phonology and Language Use.* Cambridge: Cambridge University Press.

——(2002). 'Sequentiality as the basis of constituent structure', in Talmy Givón and Bertram F. Malle (eds), *The Evolution of Language out of Pre-language.* Amsterdam: Benjamins, 109–34.

——(2003). 'Mechanisms of change in grammaticization: the role of frequency', in Joseph and Janda (2003: 602–23).

——(2006). 'From usage to grammar: the mind's response to repetition', *Language* 82.4: 711–33.

——(2007). *Frequency of Use and the Organization of Language.* Oxford: Oxford University Press.

——(2008). 'Grammaticization: implications for a theory of language', in Jianshing Guo et al. (eds), *Crosslinguistic Approaches to the Psychology of Language: Research in the Tradition of Dan Isaac Slobin.* London: Taylor & Francism 345–56.

——(2009). 'Language universals and usage-based theory', in Morten H. Christiansen, Christopher Collins, and Shimon Edelman (eds), *Language Universals.* Oxford: Oxford University Press, 17–39.

——(2010). *Language, Usage and Cognition.* Cambridge: Cambridge University Press.

——and Beckner, Clay (2009). 'Usage-based theory', in Bernd Heine and Heiko Narrog (eds), *Handbook of Linguistic Analysis.* Oxford: Oxford University Press, 827–55.

——and Dahl, Östen (1989). 'The creation of tense and aspect systems in the languages of the world', *Studies in Language* 13.1: 51–103.

——and Fleischman, Suzanne (eds) (1995). *Modality in Grammar and Discourse.* Amsterdam: Benjamins.

——and Hopper, Paul J. (eds) (2001). *Frequency and the Emergence of Linguistic Structure.* Amsterdam: Benjamins.

BYBEE, JOAN, and PAGLIUCA, WILLIAM (1987). 'The evolution of future meaning', in A. G. Ramat, O. Carruba, and G. Bernini (eds), *Papers from the 7th International Conference on Historical Linguistics.* Amsterdam: Benjamins, 109–22.

————and PERKINS, REVERE (1990). 'On the asymmetries in the affixation of grammatical material', in William Croft, Keith Denning, and Suzanne Kemmer (eds), *Studies in Typology and Diachrony.* Amsterdam: Benjamins, 1–42.

——————(1991). 'Back to the future', in Traugott and Heine (1991b: 17–58).

——PERKINS, REVERE, and PAGLIUCA, WILLIAM (1994). *The Evolution of Grammar: Tense, Aspect, and Modality in the Languages of the World.* Chicago: University of Chicago Press.

——and SLOBIN, DAN I. (1982). 'Why small children cannot change language on their own: suggestions from the English past tense', in Ahlqvist (1982: 29–37).

——and TORRES CACOULLOS, RENA (2009). 'The role of prefabs in grammaticization: how the particular and the general interact in language change', in Roberta L. Corrigan, Edith A. Moravcsik, Hamid Ouali, and Kathleen Wheatley (eds), *Formulaic Language*, vol. 1: *Distribution and Historical Change.* Amsterdam: Benjamins, 187–217.

CAMPBELL, LYLE (1987). 'Syntactic change in Pipil', *International Journal of American Linguistics* 53.3: 253–80.

——(ed.) (2001a). *Grammaticalization: A Critical Assessment*, special issue of *Language Sciences* 23.2–3.

——(2001b). 'What's wrong with grammaticalization?', in Campbell (2001a: 113–61).

——and HARRIS, ALICE (1995). *Historical Syntax in Cross-linguistic Perspective.* Cambridge: Cambridge University Press.

——KAUFMAN, TERRENCE, and SMITH-STARK, THOMAS C. (1986). 'Meso-America as a linguistic area', *Language* 62.3: 530–70.

——and JANDA, RICHARD (2001). 'Introduction: conceptions of grammaticalization and their problems', in Campbell (2001a: 93–112).

CAMPBELL, ROD (2004). 'Focus, classifiers, and quantificational typology: a brief acccount of cardinal expressions in Early Inscriptional Chinese', in Ken-ichi Takashima and Shaoyu Jiang (eds), *Meaning and Form: Essays in Pre-modern Chinese Grammar.* Munich: Lincom: 19–42.

CANALE, W. M. (1978). 'Word order change in Old English: base reanalysis in generative grammar', doctoral dissertation, University of Toronto.

CAO, GUANGSHUN (1995). *Jindai hanyu zhuci* [Particles in modern Chinese]. Beijing: Yuwen Chubanshe.

——and LONG GUOFU (2005). 'Zaitan zhonggu hanyu de chuzhishi' [On the MiddleChinese disposal construction again], *Zhongguo Yuwen* 4: 320–32.

——and YU, HSIAO-JUNG (2000). 'Zhonggu yijing zhong de chuzhishi' [Disposal constructions in medieval Chinese Buddhist transformation texts], *Zhongguo Yuwen* 6: 555–63.

CAREY, KATHLEEN (1995). 'Subjectification and the development of the English perfect', in D. Stein and S. Wright (eds), *Subjectivity and Subjectivisation: Linguistic Perspectives.* Cambridge: Cambridge University Press, 83–102.

CARLIER, ANNE (2007). 'From preposition to article: the grammaticalization of the French partitive', *Studies in Language* 31: 1–49.

——and DE MULDER, WALTER (2010). 'The emergence of the definite article in Late Latin *ille* in competition with *ipse*', in H. Cuyckens, L. Van de Lanotte, and K. Davidse (eds), *Subjectification, Intersubjectification and Grammaticalization.* The Hague: Mouton de Gruyter, 241–76.

Carston, Robyn (2002). *Thoughts and Utterances: The Pragmatics of Explicit Communication*. Oxford: Blackwell.

——(2004). 'Truth-conditional content and conversational explicature', in Claudia Bianchi (ed.), *The Semantics/Pragmatics Distinction*. Stanford, CA: CSLI, 65–100.

Cat, Cécile de (2005). 'French subject clitics are not agreement markers', *Lingua* 115: 1195–1219.

——(2007). *French Dislocation*. Oxford: Oxford University Press.

Cattell, Ray (1984). *Composite Predicates in English*. Sydney: Academic Press.

CEEC = The Corpus of Early English Correspondence.

Cennamo, Michela (2006). 'The rise and grammaticalization of Latin *fieri* and *facere* as passive auxiliaries', in Werner Abraham and Larisa Leisiö (eds), *Passivization and Typology: Form and Function*. Amsterdam: Benjamins, 311–36.

Chafe, Wallace (1982). 'Integration and involvement in speaking: writing and oral literature', in Deborah Tannen (ed.), *Spoken and Written Language: Exploring Orality and Literacy*. Norwood, NJ: Ablex, 35–53.

——(1994). *Discourse, Consciousness, and Time: The Flow andd Displacement of Conscious Experience in Speaking and Writing*. Chicago: University of Chicago Press.

——(1995). 'The realis–irrealis distinction in Caddo, the northern Iroquoian languages, and English', in Bybee and Fleischman (1995: 349–65).

——and Nichols, Johanna (eds) (1986). *Evidentiality: The Linguistic Coding of Epistemology*. Norwood, NJ: Ablex.

Chambers, J. K. (1995). *Sociolinguistic Theory: Linguistic Variation and its Social Significance*. Oxford: Blackwell.

Chang, Franklin (2008). 'Implicit learning as a mechanism of language change', *Theoretical Linguistics* 34: 115–22.

Chao, Milagros (2007). 'Adjectives in *-ly* and their homomorphic adverbs: measuring the productivity of adjectival *-ly*', *Proceedings of the 30th International AEDEAN Conference. Huelva* (CD-ROM).

Chao, Yuen-Ren (1968). *A Grammar of Spoken Chinese*. Berkeley: University of California Press.

Chapman, Don, and Skousen, Royal (2005). 'Analogical modeling and morphological change: the case of the adjectival negative prefix in English', *English Language and Linguistics* 9: 333–57.

Chappell, Hilary (2006a). 'From Eurocentrism to Sinocentrism: the case of disposal constructions in Sinitic languages', in Felix Ameka, Alan Dench, and Nicholas Evans (eds), *Catching Language: The Standing Challenge of Grammar Writing*. Berlin: Mouton de Gruyter, 441–86.

——(2006b). 'Language contact and areal diffusion in Sinitic languages: problems for typology and genetic affiliation', in Aikhenvald and Dixon (2006: 328–57).

——(2007). 'Hanyu fangyan de chuzhi biaoji de leixing' [A typology of object-marking constructions: a pan-Sinitic view], *Yuyanxue Luncong* 36: 183–209.

——(2008). 'Variation in the grammaticalization of complementizers from *verba dicendi* in Sinitic languages', *Linguistic Typology* 12: 45–98.

——and Peyraube, Alain (2006). 'The analytic causatives of Early Modern Southern Min in diachronic perspective', in Dah-an Ho, H. Samuel Cheung, Wuyun Pan, and Fuxiang Wu (eds), *Linguistic Studies in Chinese and Neighboring Languages*. Taipei: Academia Sinica, 973–1011.

Chappell, Hilary, Peyraube, Alain, and Wu, Yunji (forthcoming). 'A comitative source for object markers in Sinitic disposal constructions: *gēn* in the Waxiang language of western Hunan', *Jounal of East Asian Linguistics.*

Charolles, Michel (1990). 'L'anaphore associative: problèmes de délimitation', *Verbum* 13: 119–48.

Chelliah, Shobhana L. (1997). *A Grammar of Meithei.* Berlin: Mouton de Gruyter.

Chen, Chenju (2008). 'A case study on the grammaticalization of adverbs of quantification in Mandarin Chinese', paper from the conference 'New Reflections on Grammaticalization 4', Leuven, July.

Chen, Chun-Hui (2005). 'Bunpōka to shakuyō: nihongo ni okeru dōshi no chūshikei o fukunda kōchishi o rei ni' [Grammaticalization and borrowing: postpositions derived from verbs in the base form as an example], *Nihongo no Kenkyū* 1.3: 123–38. Chinese', in Jakko Leino (ed.), *Constructions.* Amsterdam: Benjamins.

Chirikba, Vjacheslav (2003). 'Evidential category and evidential strategy in Abkhaz', in Aikhenvald and Dixon (2003: 243–72).

Chomsky, Noam (1957). *Syntactic Structures.* The Hague: Mouton.

——(1965). *Aspects of the Theory of Syntax.* Cambridge, MA: MIT Press.

——(1975). *Reflections on Language.* Cambridge, MA: Pantheon.

——(1988). *Language and Problems of Knowledge.* Cambridge, MA: MIT Press.

——(1995). *The Minimalist Program.* Cambridge, MA: MIT Press.

——(2004). 'Beyond explanatory adequacy', in Adriana Belletti (ed.), Structures and Beyond. Oxford: Oxford University Press, 104–31.

——(2005). 'Three factors in language design', *Linguistic Inquiry* 36.1: 1–22.

——(2007). 'Approaching UG from below', in Uli Sauerland et al. (eds), *Interfaces + Recursion = Language.* Berlin: Mouton de Gruyter, 1–29.

——and Halle, Morris (1968). *The Sound Pattern of English.* Cambridge, MA: MIT Press.

Christiansen, Morten H., and Chater, Nick (2008). 'Language as shaped by the brain', *Behavioral and Brain Sciences* 31.5: 489–508.

Chung, Jae-young (1993). 'A study on the grammaticalization of dA syntagma in Middle Korean', PhD dissertation, Hankuk University of Foreign Studies, Korea.

Chung, Sandra, and Timberlake, Alan (1985). 'Tense, aspect and mood', in Shopen (1985: 202–58).

Cinque, Guglielmo (1999). *Adverbs and Functional Heads: A Cross-linguistic Perspective.* Oxford: Oxford University Press.

——(2004). '"Restructuring" and functional structure', in A. Belletti (ed.), *Structures and Beyond,* Cambridge: Cambridge University Press, 132–91.

——and Rizzi, Luigi (2011). 'The cartography of syntactic structures', in Bernd Heine and Heiko Narrog (eds), *The Oxford Handbook of Linguistic Analysis.* Oxford: Oxford University Press, 51–65.

Cintra, Luiz F. Lindley (1972). *Sobre formas de tratamento na língua portuguesa.* Lisbon: Livros Horizonte.

CLAPI: Corpus de langues parlées en interaction: http://clapi.univ-lyon2.fr

Clark, Eve V., and Carpenter, Kathie L. (1989). 'The notion of source in language acquisition', *Language* 65: 1–30.

Clark, Herbert H. (1996). *Using Language.* Cambridge: Cambridge University Press.

Claridge, Claudia (2000). *Multi-word Verbs in Early Modern English.* Amsterdam: Rodopi.

CLAUSON, SIR GERARD (1972). *An Etymological Dictionary of Pre-Thirteenth-Century Turkish.* Oxford: Clarendon Press.

CLEMENTS, GEORGE N. (1975). 'The logophoric pronoun in Ewe: its role in discourse', *Journal of West African Languages* 10: 141–77.

CLMET: Corpus of Late Modern English Texts. Compiled by Hendrik de Smet. http://perswww.kuleuven.be/~u0044428

CLOAREC-HEISS, FRANCE (1969). *Les modalités personnelles dans quelques langues oubanguiennes: discours direct–discours indirect.* Paris: SELAF (Société des Études Linguistiques et Anthropologiques de France).

CLOSS, ELIZABETH (1965). 'Diachronic syntax and generative grammar', *Language* 41.3: 402–15.

CLYNE, MICHAEL (1967). *Transference and Triggering.* The Hague: Mouton.

COATES, JENNIFER (1983). *The Semantics of Modal Auxiliaries.* London: Croon Helm.

COATES, RICHARD (1987). 'Pragmatic sources of analogical reformation', *Journal of Linguistics* 23: 319–40.

COCA= Corpus of Contemporary American English.

COLEMAN, ROBERT (1987). 'Latin and the Italic languages', in B. Comrie (ed.), *The World's Major Languages.* Oxford: Oxford University Press, 180–202.

COLLINGE, NEVILLE (1985). *The Laws of Indo-European.* Amsterdam: Benjamins.

COMRIE, BERNARD (1976). *Aspect: An Introduction to the Study of Verbal Aspect and Related Problems.* Cambridge: Cambridge University Press.

——(1998). 'Reference tracking: description and explanation', *Sprachtypologie und Universalienforschung* 52.1: 335–46.

CONRADIE, C. JAC (2003) 'The iconicity of Afrikaans reduplication', in Müller and Fischer (2003: 203–24).

COPPOLA, MARIE, and SENGHAS, ANN (2010). 'Getting to the point: the emergence of deixis in Nicaraguan signing', in D. Brentari (ed.), *Sign Languages: A Cambridge Language Survey.* Cambridge: Cambridge University Press, 543–69.

CORBETT, GREVILLE (1991). *Gender.* Cambridge: Cambridge University Press.

——(1994). 'Gender and gender systems', in R. Asher (ed.), *The Encyclopedia of Language and Linguistics.* Oxford: Pergamon Press, 1347–1353.

——and Noonan, Michael (eds) (2008). *Case and Grammatical Relations.* Amsterdam: Benjamins.

Corpus of Early English Correspondence (1998). Compiled by Terttu Nevalainen, Helena Raumolin-Brunberg, Jukka Keränen, Minna Nevala, Arja Nurmi, and Minna Palander-Collin at the Department of English, University of Helsinki.

Corrigan, Roberta L., Moravcsik, Edith A., Ouali, Hamid, and Wheatley, Kathleen (eds) (2009). *Formulaic Language,* vol. 1: *Distribution and Historical Change.* Amsterdam: Benjuamins.

COSERIU, EUGENIO (1957). *Sincronía, diacronía e historia: el problema del cambio lingüístico.* Madrid: Gredos.

COUPER-KUHLEN, ELIZABETH (1996). 'Intonation and clause combining in discourse: the case of *because*', *Pragmatics* 6.3: 389–426.

——and ONO, TSUYOSHI (2007). '"Incrementing" in conversation: a comparison of practices in English, German and Japanese', *Pragmatics* 17.4: 513–52.

——and THOMPSON, SANDRA A. (2000). 'Concessive patterns in conversation', in Elizabeth Couper-Kuhlen and Bernd Kortmann (eds), *Cause, Condition, Concession, and Contrast: Cognitive and Discourse Perspectives.* Berlin: Mouton de Gruyter, 381–410.

Couper-Kuhlen, Elizabeth, and Thompson, Sandra A. (2005). 'A linguistic practice for retracting overstatements: "concessive repair"', in A. Hakulinen and M. Selting (eds), *Syntax and Lexis in Conversation: Studies on the Use of Linguistic Resources in Talk-in-Interaction.* Amsterdam: Benjamins, 257–88.

————(2008). 'On assessing situations and events in conversation: "extraposition" and its relatives', *Discourse Studies* 10.4: 443–67.

Cowie, Claire (1995). 'Grammaticalization and the snowball effect (review of *Grammaticalization* [1993])', *Language and Communication* 15.2: 181–93.

Craig, Colette (1986a). 'Introduction', in Craig (1986b: 1–10).

——(ed.) (1986b). *Noun Classes and Categorization: Proceedings of a Symposium on Categorization and Noun Classification, Eugene, Oregon, October 1983.* Amsterdam: Benjamins.

——(1991) 'Ways to go in Rama: a case study in polygrammaticalization', in Traugott and Heine (1991b: 455–92).

——and Hale, Kenneth (1988). 'Relational preverbs in some languages of the Americas', *Language* 64: 312–44.

Creissels, Denis (2006). 'Suffixes casuels et postpositions en hongrois', *Bulletin de la Société de Linguistique de Paris* 101.1: 225–72.

Crippen, James (2010). 'Lingít Yoo X̱'atángi: a grammar of the Tlingit language', MS.

Cristofaro, Sonia (2003). *Subordination.* Oxford: Oxford University Press.

——(2004). 'Past habituals and irrealis', in Lander et al. (2004: 256–72).

Croft, William (1991a). *Syntactic Categories and Grammatical Relations: The Cognitive Organization of Information.* Chicago: University of Chicago Press.

——(1991b). 'The evolution of negation', *Journal of Linguistics* 27: 1–27.

——(1995). 'Autonomy and functionalist linguistics', *Language* 71: 490–532.

——(2000). *Explaining Language Change: An Evolutionary Appproach.* London: Longman.

——(2001). *Radical Construction Grammar: Syntactic Theory in Typological Perspective.* Oxford: Oxford University Press.

——(2006). 'The relevance of an evolutionary model to historical linguistics', in Ole Nedergård Thomsen (ed.), *Different Models of Linguistic Change.* Amsterdam: Benjamins, 91–132.

——(2008). 'Evolutionary linguistics', in W. Durham, D. Brenneis, and P. Ellison (eds), *Annual Review of Anthropology,* vol. 37. Palo Alto, CA: Annual Reviews, 219–34.

——(2010). The origins of grammaticalization in the verbalization of experience', *Cognitive Linguistics* 48: 1–48.

——and Cruse, D. A. (2004). *Cognitive Linguistics.* Cambridge: Cambridge University Press.

——and Poole, Keith T. (2008). 'Inferring universals from grammatical variation: multidimensional scaling for typological analysis', *Theoretical Linguistics* 34: 1–37.

Cruschina, Silvio (2009). 'Discourse-related features and the syntax of peripheral positions: a comparative study of Sicilian and other Romance languages', doctoral thesis, University of Cambridge.

Cruttenden, Alan (1997). *Intonation,* 2nd edn. Cambridge: Cambridge University Press.

Culicover, Peter (2008). 'The rise and fall of constructions and the history of English *do*-support', *Journal of Germanic Linguistics* 20.1: 1–52.

Cuzzolin, Pierluigi, Putzu, Ignazio, and Ramat, Paolo (2006). 'The Indo-European adverb in diachronic and typological perspective', *Indogermanische Forschungen* 111: 1–38.

Cysouw, Michael (2003). *The Paradigmatic Structure of Person Marking*. Oxford: Oxford University Press.

——(2004). 'Interrogative words: an exercise in lexical typology'. Typescript.

——(2006). Review of Bhat (2005). *Journal of Linguistics* 42.3: 697–703.

——(2010). 'Semantic maps as metrics on meaning', *Linguistic Discovery* 8.1: 70–95.

Da Milano, Federica (2007). 'Demonstratives in the languages of Europe', in P. Ramat and E. Roma (eds), *Europe and the Mediterranean as Linguistic Areas: Convergences from a Historical and Typological Perspective*. Amsterdam: Benjamins, 25–47.

Dahl, Östen (1979). 'Typology of sentence negation', *Linguistics* 17: 79–106.

——(1985). *Tense and Aspect Systems*. Oxford: Blackwell.

——(ed.) (2000). *Tense and Aspect in the Languages of Europe* (Empirical Approaches to Language Typology, Eurotyp, 20–6). Berlin/New York: Mouton de Gruyter.

——(2001). 'Grammaticalization and the life cycles of constructions', *Rask Colloquium*, Odense, supplement 14: 91–133.

——(2004). *The Growth and Maintenance of Linguistic Complexity*. Amsterdam: Benjamins.

——(2008). 'Grammatical resources and linguistic complexity: Sirionó as a language without NP coordination', in Matti Miestamo, Kaius Sinnemäki, and Fred Karlsson (eds), *Language Complexity: Typology, Contact, Change*. Amsterdam: Benjamins, 153–63.

——(2009). 'Two pathways of grammatical evolution', in Givón and Shibatani (2009: 239–48).

Danylenko, Andrii (to appear). 'Is there any inflectional future in East Slavic? A case of Ukrainian against Romance reopened', in Östen Dahl, Bridget Drinka, Lujan Martinez, and Eugenio Ramon (eds), *Dating Dialectal Changes in Grammatical Categories in Indo-European*.

Darwin, Charles (1968[1859]). *The Origin of Species*. London: Penguin.

Dasher, Richard B. (1995). 'Grammaticalization in the system of Japanese predicate honorifics', PhD, Stanford University.

Dawkins, R. M. (1916). *Modern Greek in Asia Minor*. Cambruidge: Cambridge University Press.

Deacon, Terrence W. (1997). *The Symbolic Species: The Co-evolution of Language and the Brain*. New York: Norton.

de Acosta, D. (2006). 'have + perfect participle in Romance English: synchrony and diachrony', dissertation, Cornell University.

Déchaine, Rose-Marie, and Wiltschko, Martina (2002). 'Decomposing pronouns', *Linguistic Inquiry* 33.3: 409–42.

de Condillac, Etienne Bonnot (1746). *Essai sur lórigine des connaissances humaines*. Paris.

De Haan, Ferdinand (1999). 'Evidentiality and epistemic modality: setting boundaries', *Southwest Journal of Linguistics* 18: 83–102.

——(2006). 'Typological approaches to modality', in Frawley (2006: 27–69).

——(2010). 'Building a semantic map: top-down versus bottom-up approaches', *Linguistic Discovery* 8.1: 102–17.

Dehé, Nicole, and Wichmann, Anne (2010a). 'The multifunctionality of epistemic parentheticsl in discourse: prosodic cues to the semantic-pragmatic boundary', *Functions of Language*.

Dehé, Nicole, and Wichmann, Anne (2010b). 'Sentence-initial *I think (that)* and I believe (that): prosodic evidenc for use as main clause, comment clause and discourse marker', *Studies in Language.*

de Kok, Ans (1985). *La place du pronom personnel régime cojoint en français: une étude diachronique.* Amsterdam: Rodopi.

DeLancey, Scott (1986). 'Evidentiality and volitionality in Tibetan', in Chafe and Nichols (1986: 203–13).

——(1991). 'Chronological strata of suffix classes in the Klamath verb', *International Journal of American Linguistics* 57: 426–45.

——(1997). 'Grammaticalization and the gradience of categories: relator nouns and postpositions in Tibetan and Burmese', in Joan Bybee, John Haiman, and Sandra A. Thompson (eds), *Essays on Language Function and Language Type.* Amsterdam: Benjamins, 51–69.

——(1999a). 'Lexical prefixes and the bipartite stem construction in Klamath', *International Journal of American Linguistics* 65.1: 56–83.

——(1991b). 'Relativization inTibetan', in Yogendra Yadava and Warren Glover (eds), *Studies in Nepalese Linguistics.* Kathmandu: Royal Nepal Academy, 231–49.

——(2003). 'Location and direction in Klamath', in Erin Shay and Uwe Seibert (eds), *Motion, Direction, and Location in Languages.* Amsterdam: Benjamins, 59–90.

——(2005). 'Adposition as a non-universal category', in Zygmunt Frajzyngier et al. (eds), *Linguistic Diversity and Language Theories.* Amsterdam: Benjamins, 185–202.

——(to appear). 'Finite structures from clausal nominalization inTibeto-Burman', in F. H. Yap and J. Wrona (eds), *Nominalization in Asian Languages: Diachronic and Typological,* vol. 1: *Sino-Tibetan and Iranian Languages.* Amsterdam: Benjamins.

De Mulder, Walter (2008). 'Grammaticalization, métonymie et pertinence', in J. Durand, B. Habert, and B. Laks (eds), *Congrès Mondial de Linguistique Française.* Paris: Institut de Linguistique Française, 359–65.

——and Carlier, Anne (2006). 'Du démonstratif à l'article défini: le cas de *ce* en français moderne', *Langue française* 152: 96–113.

De Smet, Hendrik (2009). 'Analysing reanalysis', *Lingua* 119: 1728–55.

——(forthcoming). 'Grammatical interference: subject marker *for* and phrasal verb particles *out* and *forth*', in Elizabeth Closs Traugott and Graeme Trousdale (eds), *Gradualness, Gradience and Grammaticalization.* Amsterdam: Benjamins, 75–104.

Detges, Ulrich (1999). 'Wie entsteht Grammatik? Kognitive aund pragmatische Determinanten der Grammatikalisierung von Tempusmarkern', in J. Lang and I. Neumann-Holzschuh (eds), *Reanalyse und Grammatikalisierung in der romanischen Sprachen.* Tübingen: Niemeyer, 31–52.

——(2000). 'Time and truth: the grammaticalization of resultatives and perfects within a theory of subjectification', *Studies in Language* 24.2: 345–77.

——(2001). 'Grammatikalisierung: Eine kognitiv-pragmatische Theorie', habilitation thesis, University of Tübingen.

——(2004). 'How cognitive is grammaticalization? The history of the Catalan *perfet perifràstic*', in Fischer et al. (2004: 211–27).

——(2006). 'The passé composé in Old French and the old Spanish perfecto compuesto', in K. Eksell and T. Vinther (eds), *Change in Verbal Systems: Issues on Explanation.* Berlin: Lang, 47–71.

——and Waltereit, Richard (2002). 'Grammaticalization vs. reanalysis: a semantic-pragmatic account of functional change in grammar', *Zeitschrift für Sprachwissenschaft* 21: 151–95.

Deutscher, Guy (2000). *Syntactic Change in Akkadian: The Evolution of Sentential Complementation.* Oxford: Oxford University Press.

——(2005). *The Unfolding of Language: An Evolutionary Tour of Mankind's Greatest Invention.* New York: Metropolitan Books.

Devos, Maud, and van der Auwera, Johan (2009). 'Jespersen Cycles in Bantu: double and triple negation'. MS.

Dickinson, Connie (2000). 'Mirativity in Tsafiki', *Studies in Language* 24: 379–421.

Diessel, Holger (1999). *Demonstratives: Form, Function, and Grammaticalization.* Amsterdam: Benjamins.

——(2004). *The Acquisition of Complex Sentences.* Cambridge: Cambridge University Press.

——(in press). 'Where do grammatical morphemes come from? On the development of grammatical markers from lexical expressions, demonstratives, and question words', in Kristin Davidse, Tine Breban, Lieselotte Brems, and Tanja Mortelmans (eds), *New Reflections on Grammaticalization.* Amsterdam: Benjamins: http://www.holger-diessel.de/

——and Tomasello, Michael (2001). 'The acquisition of finite complement clauses in English: a corpus-based analysis', *Cognitive Linguistics* 12: 97–141.

Diewald, Gabriele (1991). *Deixis und Textsorten im Deutschen.* Tübingen: Niemeyer.

——(2001). 'A basic semantic template for lexical and grammaticalized uses of the German modals', *Belgian Journal of Linguistics* 14 (special issue, *Modal Verb in Germanic and Romance Languages*', ed. Johan van der Auwera and Patrick Dendal), 23–41.

——(2002). 'A model for relevant types of contexts in grammaticalization', in Wischer and Diewald (2002: 103–20).

——(2006). 'Discourse particles and modal particles as grammatical elements', in Kerstin Fischer (ed.), *Approaches to Discourse Particles.* Amsterdam: Elsevier, 403–25.

——(2007). 'On some problem areas in grammaticalization theory—and a suggestion how to tackle them', paper presented at the conference 'What's New in Grammaticalization?', Free University Berlin, 11–12 May.

——(in press). 'On some problem areas in grammaticalization theory', in Ekkehard König, Elke Gehweiler, and Katerina Stathi (eds), *What's New in Grammaticalization?* Amsterdam: Benjamins.

——and Ferraresi, Gisella (2008). 'Semantic, syntactic and constructional restrictions in the diachronic rise of modal particles in German: a corpus-based study in the formation of a grammaticalization channel', in López-Couso and Seoane (2008: 77–110).

Dik, Simon (1968). *Coordination: Its Implications for the Theory of General Linguistics.* Amsterdam: North-Holland.

Dixon, R. M. W. (1982). *Where Have All the Adjectives Gone?* Berlin: Mouton de Gruyter.

——(2003). 'Evidentiality in Jarawara', in Aikhenvald and Dixon (2003: 165–88).

——(2004). *The Jarawara Language of Southern Amazonia.* Oxford: Oxford University Press.

——and Aikhenvald, Alexandra Y. (eds) (2002). *Word: A Cross-linguistic Typology.* Cambridge: Cambridge University Press.

DOEC: Dictionary of Old English Web Corpus, ed. Antonette diPaolo Healey: http://www.doe.utoronto.ca/pub/webcorpus.html

Doerfer, Gerhard (1967). *Türkische und mongolische Elemente im Neupersischen unter besonderer Berücksichtigung älterer neupersischer Geschichtsquellen, vor allem der Mongolen- und Timuridenzeit*, 3. Wiesbaden: Steiner.

——(1977). 'Zu türkisch bana "mir", sana "dir"', *Central Asiatic Journal* 21: 208–14.

——(1987). 'Eine sonderbare Stelle bei Maḥmūd al-Kāšgarī', *Central Asiatic Journal* 31: 199–208.

Dostie, Gaétane (2004). *Pragmaticalisation et marqueurs discursifs: analyse sémantique et traitement lexicographique.* Brussels: De Boeck–Duculot.

Downing, Pamela (1996). *Numeral Classifier Systems: The Case of Japanese.* Amsterdam: Benjamins.

Doyle, Aidan (2002). 'Yesterday's affixes as today's clitics: a case-study in degrammaticalization', in Wischer and Diewald (2002: 67–81).

Drachman, Geberell (1978). 'Child language and language change: a conjecture and some refutations', in Jacek Fisiak (ed.), *Recent Development in Historical Phonology.* Berlin: Mouton de Gruyter, 123–44.

Dreer, Igor (2007). *Expressing the Same by the Different: The Subjunctive vs the Indicative in French.* Amsterdam: Benjamins.

Drocourt, Zhitang (1993). 'Analyse syntaxique des expressions quantitatives en chinois archaïque', *Cahiers de Linguistique—Asie Orientale* 22.2: 217–37.

Dryer, Matthew S. (1989). 'Article–noun order', *Chicago Linguistic Society* 25: 83–97.

——(1992). 'The Greenbergian word order correlations', *Language* 68: 81–138.

——(2005). 'Definite articles', in Haspelmath et al. (2005: 154–7).

——(2008). 'Negative morphemes', in Haspelmath et al. (2008 online: ch. 112).

Du Bois, John W., Schuetze-Coburn, Stephan, Cumming, Susanna, and Paolino, Danae (1993). 'Outline of discourse transcription', in Jane A. Edwards and Martin D. Lampert (eds), *Talking Data: Transcription and Coding Methods for Discourse Research.* Hillsdale, NJ: Erlbaum, 45–89.

Dyer, Nancy Joe (1972). 'A study of the Old Spanish adverb in *-mente*', Hispanic Review 40: 303–8.

É. Kiss, Katalin (2002). *The Syntax of Hungarian.* Cambridge: Cambridge University Press.

Ebert, Karen H. (1970). 'Referenz, Sprechsituation und die bestimmten Artikel in einem nordfriesischen Dialekt', dissertation, Kiel, Bräist/Bredstedt, Nordfriisk Institut.

——(1971). *Referenz, Sprachsituation und die bestimmten Artikel in einem nordfriesischen Dialekt.* Bredstedt: Nordfriisk Instituut, Studien und Materialen 4.

——(1998). 'Genussynkretismus im Nordseeraum: die Resistenz des Fering', in Wilfried Boeder et al. (eds). *Sprache in Raum und Zeit*, vol. 2. Tübingen: Narr, 269–81.

Eckardt, Regine (2001). 'Reanalysing *selbst*', *Natural Language Semantics* 9: 371–412.

——(2003). 'Eine Runde im Jespersen-Zyklus', University of Konstanz: http://www.ub.uni-konstanz.de/kops/volltexte/2003/991

——(2006). *Meaning Change in Grammaticalization: An Enquiry into Semantic Reanalysis.* Oxford: Oxford University Press.

——(2008). 'Concept priming in language change', *Theoretical Linguistics* 34: 123–34.

——(2009). 'The real, the apparent, and what is *eigentlich*', in B. Behrens and C. Fabricius Hansen (eds), *Structuring Information in Discourse: The Explicit/Implicit Dimension*. University of Oslo.

——(in preparation). 'APO: Avoid Pragmatic Overload', in Maj-Britt Mosegaard-Hansen and Jacqueline Visconti (eds), *Current Trends in Diachronic Semantics and Pragmatics*. Bingley: Emerald.

EEPF: Early English Prose Fiction, ed. Holger Klein, David Margolies, and Janet Todd (Chadwyck-Healey): http://collections.chadwyck.com/home/home_eepf.jsp

Ellegård, Alvar (1953). *The Auxiliary* do: *The Establishment and Regulation of its Use in English*. Stockholm: Almqvist & Wiksell.

Elliott, Jennifer R. (2000). 'Realis and irrealis: forms and concepts of the grammaticalisation of reality', *Linguistic Typology* 4: 55–90.

Ellis, Nick C. (1996). 'Sequencing in SLA: phonological memory, chunking and points of order', *Studies in Second Language Acquisition* 18: 91–126.

Elsig, Martin, and Poplack, Shana (2009). 'Synchronic variation in diachronic perspective: question formation in Québec French', in Andreas Dufter, J. Fleischer, and G. Seiler (eds), *Describing and Modeling Variation in Grammar*. Berlin: Mouton de Gruyter, 255–70.

Enfield, Nicholas James (2003). *Linguistic Epidemiology: Semantics and Grammar of Language Contact in Mainland Southeast Asia*. London: Routledge Curzon.

——(2007). *A Grammar of Lao*. Berlin: Mouton de Gruyter.

——and Stivers, Tanya (eds) (2007). *Person Reference in Interaction: Linguistic, Cultural and Social Perspectives*. Cambridge: Cambridge University Press.

Engdahl, Elisabet (1999). 'The choice between *bli*-passive and s-passive in Danish, Norwegian and Swedish', *NORDSEM Report* 3: http://www.ling.gu.se/~engdahl/passiv-w

Epps, Patience (2005). 'Areal diffusion and the development of evidentiality: evidence from Hup', *Studies in Language* 29: 617–50.

——(in preparation). 'On directionality in language change: the case of productive deaffixation in Hup'.

Epstein, Richard (1993). 'The definite article: early stages of development', in J. van Marle (ed.), *Historical Linguistics*. Amsterdam: Benjamins, 111–34.

——(2002). 'The definite article, accessibility, and the construction of discourse referents', *Cognitive Linguistics* 12: 333–78.

Erman, Britt and Kotsinas, Ulla-Britt (1993). 'Pragmaticalization: the case of *ba*' and *you know*', *Studier i Modernspråkvetenskap* 10. Stockholm: Almqvist & Wiksell, 76–93.

——and Warren, Beatrice (2000). 'The idiom principle and the open choice principle', *Text* 20: 29–62.

Espinal, Maria-Teresa (1993). 'The interpretation of *no-pas* in Catalan', *Journal of Pragmatics* 19: 353–69.

Evans, Nicolas (2007). 'Insubordination and its uses', in Irina Nikolaeva (ed.), *Finiteness: Theoretical and Empirical Foundations*. Oxford: Oxford University Press, 366–431.

——and Wilkins, David (2000). 'In the mind's ear: the semantic extensions of perception verbs in Australian languages', *Language* 76: 546–92.

Evans, Vyvyan, and Green, Melanie (2006). *Cognitive Linguistics: An Introduction*. Edinburgh: Edinburgh University Press.

Faarlund, Jan Terje (1990). *Syntactic Change: Toward a Theory of Historical Syntax*. Berlin: Mouton de Gruyter.

FAARLUND, JAN TERJE (2000). 'Reanalysis in word order stability and change', in Rosanna Sornicola, Erich Popper, and Ariel Shisha-Halevy, with Paola Como (eds), *Stability, Variation and Change of Word-Order Patterns over Time*. Amsterdam: Benjamins, 119–32.

——(2007). 'Parameterization and change in non-finite complementation', *Diachronica* 24, 1: 57–80.

——(2009). 'On the history of definiteness marking in Scandinavian', *Journal of Linguistics* 45.3: 617–39.

FAGERLI, OLE TORFINN (2001). 'Malefactive by means of GIVE', in Hanne Gram Simonsen and Rolf Theil Endresen (eds), *A Cognitive approach to the Verb: Morpholoogical and Constructional Perspectives*. Berlin: Mouton de Gruyter, 203–22.

FAINGOLD, EDUARDO D. (2003). *The Development of Grammar in Spanish and the Romance Languages*. Basingstoke: Palgrave Macmillan.

FALK, HJALMAR, and TORP, ALF (1910). *Norwegisches–Dänisches etymologisches Wörterbuch*. Heidelberg: Winter.

FARACLAS, NICHOLAS G. (1987). 'Creolization and the tense-aspect-modality system of Nigerian Pidgin', *Journal of African Languages and Linguistics* 9.1: 45–59.

FAUCONNIER, GILLES, and TURNER, MARK (2002). *The Way We Think: Conceptual Blending and the Mind's Hidden Complexities*. New York: Basic Books.

FIENGO, ROBERT, and MAY, ROBERT (1994). *Indices and Identity*. Cambridge, MA: MIT Press.

————(1995). 'Response to William's review of *Indices and Identity*', *Language* 71: 794–801.

FILLMORE, CHARLES J. (1975). *Santa Cruz Lectures on Deixis*. Bloomington: Indiana University Linguistics Club.

FIORENTINO, GIULIANA (1999). *Relativa debole: sintassi, uso, storia in italiano*. Milan: Angeli.

FISCHER, OLGA (1999). 'On the role played by iconicity in grammaticalization processes', in Max Nänny and Olga Fischer (eds), *Form Miming Meaning*. Amsterdam: Benjamins, 345–74.

——(2000). 'Grammaticalisation: unidirectional, non-reversable? The case of *to* before the infinitive in English', in Olga Fischer, Anette Rosenbach, and Dieter Stein (eds), *Pathways of Change: Grammaticalization in English*. Amsterdam: Benjamins, 149–69.

——(2007). *Morphosyntactic Change: Functional and Formal Perspectives*. Oxford: Oxford University Press.

——(2008). 'On analogy as the motivation for grammaticalization', *Studies in Language* 32.2: 336–82.

——(2009). 'Grammaticalization as analogically driven change?', *VIEW[Z]: Vienna English Working Papers* 18.2: 3–23.

——and ROSENBACH, ANETTE (2000). 'Introduction', in Olga Fischer, Anette Rosenbach, and Dieter Stein (eds), *Pathways of Change: Grammaticalization in English*. Amsterdam: Benjamins, 1–37.

——Norde, Muriel, and Perridon, Harry (eds) (2004). 'Introduction', in *Up and Down the Cline: The Nature of Grammaticalization*. Amsterdam: Benjamins, 1–16.

FISCHER, SUSAN (1996). 'The role of agreement and auxiliaries in sign language', *Lingua* 98: 103–20.

——and GOUGH, BONNIE (1972[1999]). 'Some unfinished thoughts on FINISH', *Sign Language and Linguistics* 2: 67–77.

——and Lillo-Martin, Diane (1990). '*Understanding* conjunctions', *International Journal of Sign Linguistics* 1: 71–80.

Fitneva, Stanka A. (2001). 'Epistemic marking and reliability judgements: evidence from Bulgarian', *Journal of Pragmatics* 33: 401–20.

Fitzmaurice, Susan (2000). 'Remarks on de-grammaticalization of infinitival *to* in present-day American English', in Olga Fischer, Anette Rosenbach, and Dieter Stein (eds), *Pathways of Change: Grammaticalization in English*. Amsterdam: Benjamins, 171–86.

Fleischman, Suzanne (1982). *The Future in Thought and Language: Diachronic Evidence from Romance*. Cambridge: Cambridge University Press.

——(1989). Temporal distance: a basic linguistic metaphor. *Studies in Language* 13.1: 1–50

——(1995). 'Imperfective and irrealis', in Bybee and Fleischman (1995: 519–51).

Flores Farfán, José Antonio (2004). 'Notes on Nahuatl typological change', *Sprachtypologie und Universalienforschung* 57: 85–97.

Foley, William A., and Van Valin, Robert D., Jr (1984). *Functional Syntax and Universal Grammar*. Cambridge: Cambridge University Press.

Fonseca-Greber, Bonnibeth Beale (2007). 'The emergence of emphatic *ne* in conversational Swiss French', *Journal of French Language Studies* 17: 249–75.

Fontana, Josep (1997). 'On the integration of second position phenomena', in van Kemenade and Vincent (1997: 207–49).

Ford, Cecilia E. (1993). *Grammar in Interaction*. Cambridge: Cambridge University Press.

Fortescue, Michael (1984). *West Greenlandic*. London: Croom Helm.

——(1993). 'Eskimo word order variation and its contact-induced perturbation', *Journal of Linguistics* 29: 267–89.

——(2003). 'Evidentiality in West Greenlandic: a case of scattered coding', in Aikhenvald and Dixon (2003: 291–306).

Fortuin, Egbert (2008). 'Polisemija imperativa v russkom jazyke', *Voprosy jazykoznanija* 1: 3–23.

Fox, Barbara A., and Thompson, Sandra A. (2007). 'Relative clauses in English conversation: relativiizers, frequency, and the notion of construction', *Studies in Language* 31: 293–326.

Frajzyngier, Zygmunt (1985). 'Logophoric systems in Chadic', *Journal of African Languages and Linguistics* 7: 23–37.

——(1989a). *A grammar of Pero*. Berlin: Reimer.

——(1989b). 'Three kinds of anaphors', in Isabelle Haïk and Laurice Tuller (eds), *Current Progress in African Linguistics*. Dordrecht: Foris, 194–216.

——(1991). 'The *de dicto* domain in language', in Traugott and Heine (1991a: 219–51).

——(1993). *A grammar of Mupun*. Berlin: Reimer.

——(1996a) *Grammaticalization of the Complex Sentence: A Case Study in Chadic*. Amsterdam: Benjamins.

——(1996b). 'On sources of demonstratives and anaphors', in B. Fox (ed.), *Studies in Anaphora*. Amsterdam: Benjamins, 169–203.

——(1997). 'Pronouns and agreement: systems interaction in the coding of reference', in Bennis et al. (1997: 115–40).

——(2001). *A Grammar of Lele*. Stanford, CA: CSLI.

——(in press). *Grammar of Wandala*. Berlin: Mouton de Gruyter.

——and Jirsa, Bill (2006). 'The principle of indirect means in language use and language structure', *Journal of Pragmatics* 38.4: 513–42.

Frajzyngier, Zygmunt, and Johnston, Eric, with Edwards, Adrian (2005). *A Grammar of Mina.* Berlin: Mouton de Gruyter.

——and Shay, Erin (2002). *A Grammar of Hdi.* Berlin: Mouton de Gruyter.

————(2003). *Explaining Language Structure through Systems Interaction.* Amsterdam: Benjamins.

FRANTEXT: Frantext: http://www.frantext.fr

Franzén, Torsten (1939). *Etude sur la syntaxe des pronoms personnels sujets en ancien français.* Uppsala: Almqvist & Wiksell.

Fraser, Bruce (1990). 'An approach to discourse markers', *Journal of Pragmatics* 14: 383–95.

Frawley, William (ed.) (2006). *The Expression of Modality.* Berlin: Mouton de Gruyter.

Fried, Mirjam (2008). 'Constructions and constructs: mapping a shift between predication and attribution', in A. Bergs and G. Diewald (eds), Constructions and Language Change. Berlin; Mouton de Gruyter, 47–79.

Friedman, Victor A. (2003). 'Evidentiality in the Balkans with special attention to Macedonian and Albanian', in Aikhenvald and Dixon (2003: 189–218).

Fries, Charles C. (1940). 'On the development of the structural use of word-order in Modern English', *Language* 16: 199–208.

Frisch, Stefan (1997). 'The change in negation in Middle English: a NEGP licensing account', *Lingua* 101: 21–64.

Frishberg, Nancy (1975). 'Arbitrariness and iconicity: historical change in American Sign Language'. *Language* 51: 696–719.

Fujii, Seiko (2000). 'Incipient decategorialization of mono and grammaticalization of speaker attitude in Japanese discourse', in Gisle Andersen and Thorsten Fretheim (eds), *Pragmatic Markers and Propositional Attitude.* Amsterdam: Benjamins, 85–117.

Fub, Eric (2005). *The Rise of Agreement.* Amsterdam: Benjamins.

Gaby, Rose (2006). 'A grammar of Kuuk Thaayorre', PhD thesis, University of Melbourne.

Gachelin, Jean-Marc (1997). 'The progressive and habitual aspects in non-standard Englishes', in Edward Schneider (ed.), *Englishes Around the World.* Amsterdam: Benjamins, 33–46.

Gamon, David (1993). 'On the development of epistemicity in the German modal verbs *mögen* and *müssen*', *Folia Linguistica Historica* 14.1–2: 125–76.

Gavel, Henri, and Lacombe, Georges (1929–37). *Grammaire Basque I et II.* Bayonne: Imprimerie de la 'Presse'.

Gelderen, Elly van (1993). *The Rise of Functional Categories.* Amsterdam: Benjamins.

——(2000). *A History of English Reflexive Pronouns.* Amsterdam: Benjamins.

——(2004). *Grammaticalization as Economy.* Amsterdam: Benjamins.

——(2008). 'Where did Late Merge go? Grammaticalization as feature economy', *Studia Linguistica*: 287–300.

——(ed.) (2009). *Cyclical Change.* Amsterdam: Benjamins.

——(2011). *The Linguistic Cycle.* Oxford: Oxford University Press.

Gell-Mann, Murray (1994). *The Quark and the Jaguar: Adventures in the Simple and the Complex.* London: Little, Brown.

Geluykens, Ronald (1987). 'Tails (right-dislocations) as a repair mechanism in English conversation', in J. Nuyts (ed.), *Getting One's Words into Line.* Dordrecht: Foris: 119–29.

——(1992). *From Discourse Process to Grammatical Construction: On Left-Dislocation in English.* Amsterdam: Benjamins.

Genetti, Carol (1986). 'The development of subordinators from postpositions in Bodic languages', in Vassiliki Nikiforidou et al. (eds), *Proceedings of the Twelfth Annual Meeting of the Berkeley Linguistic Society, February 15–17*, 387–400.

——(1991) 'From postposition to subordinator in Newari', in Traugott and Heine (1991a: 227–55).

Georg, S. (1996). *Marphatan Thakali.* Munich: Lincom.

Geurts, Bart (2000a). 'Explaining grammaticalization (the standard way)', *Linguistics* 38.4: 781–98.

——(2000b). 'Function or fashion? Reply to Martin Haspelmath', *Linguistics* 38.6: 1175–80.

Giacalone Ramat, Anna (1998). 'Testing the boundaries of grammaticalization', in Anna Giacalone Ramat and Paul Hopper (eds), *The Limits of Grammaticalization.* Amsterdam: Benjamins, 107–27.

——(2008). 'Areal convergence in grammaticalization processes', in López-Couso and Seoane (2008: 129–67).

——and Hopper, Paul J. (1998). 'Introduction', in Anna Giacalone Ramat and Paul J. Hopper (eds), *The Limits of Grammaticalization.* Amsterdam: Benjamins, 1–11.

——and Mauri, Caterina (2008). 'From cause to contrast: a study in semantic change', in Elisabeth Verhoeven et al. (eds), *Studies on Grammaticalization.* Berlin: Mouton de Gruyter, 303–21.

————(2009a). Introduction to the workshop 'Grammaticalization Between Semantics and Pragmatics', Pavia, February. MS.

————(2009b). 'Dalla continuità temporale al contrasto: la grammaticalizzazione di tuttavia come connettivo coordinativo', in A. Ferrari (ed.), *Sintassi storica e sincronia dell'italiano: subordinazione, coordinazione, giustapposizione.* Florence: Cesati, vol. 1, 449–470.

————(in press). 'Dalla continuità temporale al contrasto: la grammaticalizzazione di tuttavia come connettivo avversativo', in *Proceedings of the SILFI (Società di Linguistica e di Filologia Italiana)*, July, Basel.

Giger, M. (2003). 'Die Grammatikalisierung des Rezipientenpassivs im Tschechischen, Slovakischen und Sorbischen', in P. Sériot (ed.), *Contributions suisses au XIIIe congrès mondial des slavistes à Ljubljana, août 2003.* Bern: Lang, 79–102.

Gil, David (2009). 'How much grammar does it take to sail a boat?', in Sampson et al. (2009): 19–33.

Giles, J. A. (ed.) (1969[1858]). *The Whole Works of King Alfred the Great*, vols 1 and 2. New York: AMS Press.

Gisborne, Nikolas (2010). *The Event Structure of Perception Verbs.* Oxford: Oxford University Press.

Givón, Talmy (1971). 'Historical syntax and synchronic morphology', *Chicago Linguistic Society Proceedings* 7: 394–415.

——(1973). 'The time-axis phenomenon', *Language* 49: 890–925.

——(1975). 'Negation in language: pragmatics, function, ontology', *Working Papers on Language Universals* 18: 59–116.

——(1976). 'Topic, pronoun, and grammatical agreement', in Li (1976: 151–88).

——(1978). 'Negation in language', in Peter Cole (ed.), *Pragmatics.* New York: Academic Press, 69–112.

——(1979). *On Understanding Grammar.* New York: Academic Press.

——(1982). 'Tense-aspect modality: the creole proto-type and beyond', in P. J. Hopper (ed.), *Tense-Aspect: Between Semantics and Pragmatics*. Amsterdam: Benjamins, 115–63.

——(1983). *Topic Continuity in Discourse: An Introduction*. Amsterdam: Benjamins.

——(1984). *Syntax*, vol. 1. Amsterdam: Benjamins.

——(1991a). 'The evolution of dependent clause morpho-syntax in Biblical Hebrew', in Traugott and Heine (1991b: 257–310).

——(1991b). 'Serial verbs and the mental reality of "event": grammatical versus congnitive packaging', in E. C. Traugott and B. Heine (eds), Approaches to Grammaticalization, vol. 1. Amsterdam: Benjamins, 81–127.

GIVÓN, TALMY (1994). 'Irrealis and the subjunctive', *Studies in Language* 18: 265–337.

——(1995) *Functionalism and Grammar*. Amsterdam: Benjamins.

——(2000). 'Internal reconstruction: as method, as theory', in Spike Gildea (ed.), *Reconstructing Grammar: Comparative Linguistics and Grammaticalization*. Amsterdam: Benjamins: 107–59.

——(2001). *Syntax*, vol. 1, 2nd edn. Amsterdam: Benjamins.

——(2002). *Bio-linguistics: The Santa Barbara Lectures*. Amsterdam: Benjamins.

——(2009). *The Genesis of Syntactic Complexity*. Amsterdam: Benjamins.

——and Malle, Bertram F. (eds) (2002). *The Evolution of Language out of Pre-language*. Amsterdam: Benjamins.

——and Shibatani, Masayoshi (eds) (2009). *Syntactic Complexity: Diachrony, Acquisition, Neuro-Cognition, Evolution*. Amsterdam: Benjamins.

——and YANG, LYNNE (1994). 'The rise of the English GET-passive', in Barbara Fox and Paul J. Hopper (eds), *Voice: Form and Function*. Amsterdam: Benjamins, 119–49.

GLARE, P. (1977). *Oxford Latin Dictionary*. Oxford: Oxford University Press.

GLÜCK, SUSANNE, and PFAU, ROLAND (1998). 'On classifying classification as a class of inflection in German Sign Language', in T. Cambier-Langeveld, A. Lipták, and M. Redford (eds), *Proceedings of ConSole 6*. Leiden: SOLE, 59–74.

GOFFMAN, ERVING (1974). *Frame Analysis*. Cambridge, MA: Harvard University Press.

GOŁĄB, ZBIGNIEW (1956). 'The concept of isogrammatism', *Buletin Polskiego Towarzystwa Jezykoznawczego* 15: 1–12.

GOLDBERG, ADELE (1995). *Constructions: A Construction Grammar Approach to Argument Structure*. Chicago: University of Chicago Press.

——(2006). *Constructions at Work*. Oxford: Oxford University Press.

GOOSSENS, LOUIS (1982). 'On the development of modals and of epistemic function in English', in Ahlqvist (1982: 74–84).

——(1987). 'The auxiliarization of the English modals: a functional grammar view', in Martin Harris and Paolo Ramat (eds), *Historical Development of Auxiliaries*. Berlin: de Gruyter, 111–43.

——(1999). 'Metonymic bridges in modal shifts', in Klaus-Uwe Panther and Günter Radden (eds), *Metonymy in Language and Thought*. Amsterdam: Benjamins, 193–210.

——(2000). 'Patterns of meaning extension, "parallel chaining", subjectification, and modal shifts', in A. Barcelona (ed.), *Metaphor and Metonymy at the Crossroads: A Cognitive Perspective*. Berlin: Mouton de Gruyter, 149–69.

GORBETT, LARRY (1974) *A Grammar of Digueño Nominals*. New York: Garland.

GORDON, LYNN (1986). 'The development of evidentials in Maricopa', in Chafe and Nichols (1986: 75–88).

Gotti, Maurizio, Dossena, Marina, Dury, Richard, Facchinetti, Roberta, and Lima, Maria (2002). *Variation in Central Modals: A Repertoire of Forms and Types of Usage in Middle English and Early Modern English.* Bern: Lang.

Goyens, Michèle, Lamiroy, Béatrice, and Melis, Ludo (2002). 'Déplacement et repositionnement de la préposition 'à' en français', *Linguisticae Investigationes* 25.2: 275–310.

Graves, Nina (2000). 'Macedonian: a language with three perfects?', in Östen Dahl (ed.), *Tense and Aspect in the Languages of Europe.* Berlin: Mouton de Gruyter, 479–94.

Green, David (1998). 'Mental control of the bilingual lexico-semantic system', *Bilingualism: Language and Cognition* 1: 67–81.

Green, John (1987). 'The evolution of Romance auxiliaries: criteria and chronology', in Martin Harris and Paolo Ramat (eds), *The Historical Development of Auxiliaries.* Berlin: Mouton de Gruyter, 255–67.

Greenberg, Joseph H. (1957). *Essays in Linguistics.* Chicago: University of Chicago Press.

——(1963). 'Some universals of grammar with particular reference to the order of meaningful elements', in *Universals of Languages.* Cambridge, MA: MIT Press, 58–90.

——(1966). *Language Universals, with Special Reference to Feature Hierarchies.* The Hague: Mouton.

——(1978). 'How does a language acquire gender markers?', In Joseph H. Greenberg, Charles A. Ferguson, and Edith A. Moravcsik (eds), *Universals of Human Language,* vol. 3: *Word Structure.* Stanford, CA: Stanford University Press, 47–82.

——(1991). 'The last stages of grammatical elements: contractive and expansive desemanticization', in Traugott and Heine (1991a: 301–14).

Grevisse-Goosse, André (2007). *Le Bon Usage.* Brussels: Duculot–De Boeck.

Grice, H. Paul (1957). 'Meaning', *Philosophical Review* 66: 377–88.

——(1975). 'Logic and conversation', in Peter Cole and Jerry L. Morgan (eds), *Speech Acts.* New York: Academic Press, 41–58.

Gries, Stefan, and Stefanowitsch, Anatol (2004). 'Extending collostructional analysis: a corpus-based perspective on "alternations"', *Journal of Corpus Linguistics* 9: 97–129.

Gronemeyer, C. (1997). 'Evidentiality in Lithuanian', *Working Papers* 46: 93–112, Lund University, Department of Linguistics.

Gsell, Otto, and Wandruszka, Ulrich (1986). *Der romanische Konjunktiv.* Tübingen: Niemeyer.

Guentchéva, Zlatka (ed.) (1996). *L'Énonciation médiatisée.* Louvain: Peeters.

Guillaume, Antoine (2004). 'A grammar of Cavineña, an Amazonian language of northern Bolivia', PhD thesis, La Trobe University.

Güldemann, Tom (2003). 'Grammaticalization', in Derek Nurse and Gérard Philippson (eds), *The Bantu Languages.* London: Routledge, 182–94.

——(2008). *Quotative Indexes in African languages: A Synchronic and Diachronic Survey.* Berlin: Mouton de Gruyter.

Gundel, J. K., Hedberg, N., and Zacharski, R. (1993). 'Cognitive status and the form of referring expressions in discourse', *Language* 69: 274–307.

Gunlogson, Christine (2001). 'Third person object prefixes in Babine-Witsuwit'en', *International Journal of American Linguistics* 67.4: 365–95.

Günthner, Susanne (1996). 'From subordination to coodination? Verb-second position in German causal and concessive constructions', *Pragmatics* 6.3: 323–71.

——(1999). 'Entwickelt sich der Konzessivkonnektor *obwohl* zum Diskursmarker? Grammatikalisierungstendenzen im gesprochenen Deutsch', *Linguistische Berichte* 180: 409–46.

——(2000). 'From concessive connector to discourse marker: the use of *obwohl* in everyday German interaction', in Bernd Kortmann and Elizabeth Couper-Kuhlen (eds), *Cause—Condition—Concession —Contrast.* Berlin: Mouton de Gruyter, 439–68.
——(2008). '"Die Sache ist . . . ": eine Projektorkonstruktion im gesprochenen Deutsch', *Zeitschrift für Sprachwissenschaft* 27.1: 39–72.
——and MUTZ, KATRIN (2004). 'Grammaticalization vs. pragmaticalization? The development of pragmatic markers in German and Italian', in Walter Bisang, Nikolaus P. Himmelmann, and Björn Wiemer (eds), *What Makes Grammaticalization?A Look from its Fringes and its Components.* Berlin: Mouton de Gruyter, 77–107.
GUSSENHOVEN, CARLOS (2004). *The Phonology of Tone and Intonation.* Cambridge: Cambridge University Press.
HAAS, FLORIAN (2007). 'The development of English *each other*: grammaticalization, lexicalization, or both?', *English Language and Linguistics* 1.1: 31–50.
HAASE, MARTIN (1992). *Sprachkontakt und Sprachwandel im Baskenland: die Einflüsse des Gaskognischen und Französischen auf das Baskische.* Hamburg: Buske.
HAGÈGE, CLAUDE (1974). 'Les pronoms logophoriques', *Bulletin de la Société de Linguistique de Paris* 69.1: 287–310.
——(1982). *La structure des langues.* Paris: Presses Universitaire de France.
——(1985). *Les catégories de la langue palau (Micronésie), une curiosité typologique.* Munich: Fink.
HAIMAN, JOHN (1978). 'Conditionals are topics', *Language* 54: 564–89.
——(1980). *Hua: A Papuan language of the Eastern Highlands of New Guinea.* Amsterdam: Benjamins.
——(1983). 'On some origins of switch reference marking', in John Haiman and Pamela Munro (eds), *Switch Reference and Universal Grammar.* Amsterdam: Benjamins. 105–128.
——(1985). *Natural Syntax.* Cambridge: Cambridge University Press.
——(1994). 'Ritualization and the development of language', in Pagliuca (1994: 3–28).
——(1999). 'Auxiliation in Khmer: the case of *baan*', *Studies in Language* 23.1: 149–72.
——(in preparation). *A Grammar of Khmer.* Amsterdam: Benjamins.
——and Thompson, Sandra A. (eds) (1988). *Clause Combining in Grammar and Discourse.* Amsterdam: Benjamins.
HALE, KEN (1973). 'Person marking in Warlbiri', in Stephen Anderson and Paul Kiparsky (eds), *A Festschrift for Morris Halle.* New York: Holt, Rinehart & Winston, 308–44.
——(2001). 'Navajo verb stem position and the bipartite structure of the Navajo conjunct sector', *Linguistic Inquiry* 32.4: 678–93.
HALE, MARK (1998). 'Diachronic syntax', *Syntax* 1: 1–18.
HALL, CHRISTOPHER J. (1992). Morphology and Mind: A Unified Approach to Explanation in Linguistics. London: Routledge.
HALL, TRACY A. (1999). 'The phonological word: a review', in Tracy A. Hall and Ursula Kleinhenz (eds), *Studies on the Phonological Word.* Amsterdam: Benjamins, 1–22.
HALLAN, NAOMI (2001). 'Paths to prepositions? A corpus-based study of the acquisition of a lexico-grammatical category', in Bybee and Hopper (2001: 91–120).
HALLE, MORRIS (1962). 'Phonology in generative grammar', *Word* 18: 54–72.
HALLIDAY, MICHAEL, and HASAN, RUQAIA (1976). *Cohesion in English.* London: Longman.
HAN, TONG-WAN (1986). 'A diachronic study on the Korean past tense *-ess*', *Journal of Korean Linguistics* 15: 217–48.

Hanazono, Satoru (1999). 'Jōkenkei fukugō yōgen keishiki no nintei' [The acknowledgement of complex predicate forms based on conditionals], *Kokugogaku* 197: 39–53.

Hansen, Björn (2001). *Das slavische Modalauxiliar (Semantik und Grammatikalisierung im Russischen, Polnischen, Serbischen/Kroatischen und Altkirchenslavischen).* Munich: Sagner.

——(2004). 'Modals and the boundaries of grammaticalization: the case of Russian, Polish and Serbian–Croatian', in Walter Bisang, Nikolaus P. Himmelmann, and Björn Wiemer (eds), *What Makes Grammaticalization? A Look from its Fringes and its Components.* Berlin: Mouton de Gruyter, 245–70.

——(2009). 'Modals/Modalauxiliare', in Sebastian Kempgen, Peter Kosta, Tilman Berger, and Karl Gutschmidt (eds), *The Slavic Languages: An International Handbook of Their History, Their Structure and Their Investigation.* Berlin: Mouton de Gruyter, 468–83.

Hansen, Anna Berit, and Malderez, Isabelle (2003/4). 'Le ne de négation en région parisienne: une étude en temps réel', *Langage et société* 107: 5–30.

Hansen, Maj-Britt Mosegaard (1998a). 'La grammaticalisation de l'interaction, ou, Pour une approche polysémique de l'adverbe "bien"', *Revue de Sémantique et Pragmatique* 4: 111–38.

——(1998b). *The Function of Discourse Particles: A Study with Special Reference to Spoken Standard French.* Amsterdam: Benjamins.

——(2005). 'From prepositional phrase to hesitation marker', *Journal of Historical Pragmatics* 6.1: 37–68.

——(2008). *Particles at the Semantics/Pragmatics Interface: Synchronic and Diachronic Issues. A Study with Special Reference to the French Phasal Adverbs.* Bingley: Emerald.

——(2009). 'The grammaticalization of negative reinforcers in Old and Middle French: a discourse-functional approach', in Maj-Britt Mosegaard Hansen and Jacqueline Visconti (eds), *Current Trends in Diachronic Semantics and Pragmatics.* Bingley: Emerald.

——(forthcoming). 'A pragmatic approach to historical semantics, with special reference to markers of clausal negation in Medievel French', in Kathryn Allan and Justyna Robinson (eds), *Current Methods in Historical Semantics.* Berlin: Mouton de Gruyter.

——and Visconti, Jacqueline (2009). 'On the diachrony of "reinforced" negation in French and Italian', in Corinne Rossari, Claudia Ricci, and Adriana Spiridon (eds), *Grammaticalization and Pragmatics: Facts, Approaches, Theoretical Issues.* Bingley: Emerald, 137–71.

Harris, Alice C. (1981). *Georgian Syntax: A Study in Relational Grammar.* Cambridge: Cambridge University Press.

——and Campbell, Lyle (1995). *Historical Syntax in Cross-linguistic Perspective.* Cambridge: Cambridge University Press.

Harris, Martin (1978). *The Evolution of French Syntax: A Comparative Approach.* London: Longman.

——(1980a). 'Noun phrases and verb phrases in Romance', *Transactions of the Philological Society* 78: 62–80.

——(1980b). 'The marking of definiteness in Romance', in J. Fisiak (ed.), *Historical Morphology.* The Hague: Mouton, 141–56.

——(1982a). 'The "past simple" and the "present perfect" in Romance', in N. Vincent and M. Harris (eds), *Studies in the Romance Verb.* London: Croon Helm, 42–70.

——(1982b). *The Evolution of French Syntax: A Comparative Approach.* London: Longman.

Hartmann, Dietrich (1982). 'Deixis and anaphora in German dialects: the semantics and pragmatics of two definite articles in dialectal varieties', in J. Weissenborn and W. Klein (eds), *Here and There: Cross-Linguistic Studies on Deixis and Demonstration*. Amsterdam: Benjamins, 187–207.

Haser, Verena, and Kortmann, Bernd (2006). 'Adverbs', in Keith Brown (ed.), *Encyclopedia of Language and Linguistics*, 2nd edn. Oxford: Elsevier.

Haspelmath, Martin (1989). 'From purposive to infinitive: a universal path of grammaticalization', *Folia Linguistica Historica* 10: 287–310.

——(1990). 'The grammaticization of passive morphology', *Studies in Language* 14.1: 25–72.

——(1993). *A Grammar of Lezgian*. Berlin: Mouton de Gruyter.

Haspelmath, Martin (1997). *From Space to Time: Temporal Adverbials in the World's Languages*. Munich: Lincom Europa.

——(1998). 'Does grammaticalization need reanalysis?', *Studies in Language* 22: 315–51.

——(1999). 'Why is grammaticalization irreversible?', *Linguistics* 37: 1034–68.

——(2000). 'The relevance of extravagance: a reply to Bart Geurts', *Linguistics* 38: 789–98.

——(2003). 'The geometry of grammatical meaning: semantic maps and cross-linguistic comparison', in Michael Tomasello (ed.), *The New Psychology of Language*, vol. 2. Mahwah, NJ: Erlbaum, 211–43.

——(2004a). 'Coordinating constructions: an overview', in Martin Haspelmath (ed.), *Coordinating Constructions*. Amsterdam: Benjamins, 3–39.

——(2004b). 'On directionality in language change with particular reference to grammaticalization', in Fischer et al. (2004: 17–44).

——(2007). 'Coordination', in Shopen (2007: 1–51).

——(2009). 'The agglutination hypothesis: a belated empirical investigation', in Sergio Scalise, Elisabetta Magni, and Antonietta Bisetto (eds), *Universals of Language Today*. Berlin: Springer, 13–29.

——(2011). 'The indeterminacy of word segmentation and the nature of morphology and syntax', *Folia Linguistica* 45.1: 31–80.

——Dryer, Matthew S., Gil, David, and Comrie, Bernard (eds) (2005). *The World Atlas of Language Structures*. Oxford: Oxford University Press. Also published byMax Planck Digital Library (Munich, 2008).

——and König, Ekkehard (1998). 'Concessive conditionals in the languages of Europe', in Johan van der Auwera (ed.), *Adverbial Constructions in the Languages of Europe*. Berlin: Mouton de Gruyter, 563–640.

Haugen, Einar (1950). 'The analysis of linguistic borrowing', *Language* 26: 210–31.

——(1982). *Scandinavian Language Structures: A Comparative Historical Survey*. Minneapolis: University of Minnesota Press.

Haugen, Jason (2008). *Morphology at the Interfaces*. Amsterdam: Benjamins.

Hawkins, John A. (1978). *Definiteness and Indefiniteness: A Study in Reference and Grammaticality Prediction*. London: Croom Helm.

——(1983). *Word Order Universals*. New York: Academic.

——(1991). 'On (in)definite articles: implicatures and (un)grammaticality prediction', *Journal of Linguistics* 27: 405–42.

——(1994). *A Performance Theory of Order and Constituency*. Cambridge: Cambridge University Press.

——(2004). *Efficiency and Complexity in Grammars*. Oxford: Oxford University Press.

Hay, Jennifer (2001). 'Lexical frequency in morphology: is everything relative?', *Linguistics* 39: 1041–70.

Heath, Jeffrey (1984). 'Language contact and language change', *Annual Review of Anthropology* 13: 367–84.

Heine, Bernd (1982). 'African noun class systems', in Hansjakob Seiler and Christian Lehmann (eds), *Apprehension: Das sprachliche Erfassen von Gegenständen*, part 1: *Bereich und Ordnung der Phänomene*. Tübingen: Narr, 189–216.

——(1989). 'Adpositions in African languages', *Linguistique Africaine* 2: 77–127.

——(1992). 'Grammaticalization chains', *Studies in Language* 16: 335–68.

——(1993) *Auxiliaries: Cognitive Forces and Grammaticalization*. Oxford: Oxford University Press.

——(1994). 'Grammmaticalization as an explanatory parameter', in Pagliuca (1994: 255–87).

——(1995). 'Agent oriented vs. epistemic modality: some observations on German modals', in Bybee and Fleischman (1995: 17–53).

——(1997a). 'Grammaticalization theory and its relevance for African linguistics', in Robert K. Herbert (ed.), *African Linguistics at the Crossroads*. Cologne: Köppe, 1–15.

——(1997b). *Cognitive Foundations of Grammar*. Oxford: Oxford University Press.

——(1997c). *Possession: Sources, Forces, and Grammaticalization*. Cambridge: Cambridge University Press.

——(1998). 'On explaining grammar: the grammaticalization of *have*-constructions', *Theoretical Linguistics* 24.1: 29–41.

——(2000). 'Polysemy involving reflexive and reciprocal markers in African languages', in Zygmunt Frajzyngier and Traci S. Curl (eds), *Reciprocals: Forms and Functions*. Amsterdam: Benjamins, 1–29.

——(2002). 'On the role of context in grammaticalization', in Wischer and Diewald (2002: 83–101).

——(2003a). 'On degrammaticalization', in Barry Blake and Kate Burridge (eds), *Historical Linguistics 2001*. Amsterdam: Benjamins, 163–79.

——(2003b). 'Grammaticalization', in Joseph and Janda (2003: 575–601).

——(2005). 'On reflexive forms in creoles', *Lingua* 115: 201–57.

——(2007). 'Grammaticalization space > time > text', handout distributed at the workshop on 'Grammaticalization of the Discourse and Grammar Research Group', Universidade Federal do Rio de Janeiro.

——(2008). 'Grammaticalization of cases', in Malchukov and Spencer (2008: 458–79).

——(2009). 'Complexity via expansion', in Givón and Shibatani (2009: 23–51).

——Claudi, Ulrike, and Hünnemeyer, Friederike (1991). *Grammaticalization: A Conceptual Framework*. Chicago: University of Chicago Press.

——and König, Christa (2010). 'On the linear order of ditransitive objects', *Language Sciences* 32: 87–131.

————(forthcoming). *The !Xun Language: A Dialect Grammar*. Cologne: Köppe.

——and Kuteva, Tania (2002). *World Lexicon of Grammaticalization*. Cambridge: Cambridge University Press.

————(2003). 'On contact-induced grammaticalization', *Studies in Language* 27: 529–72.

————(2005) *Language Contact and Grammatical Change*. Cambridge: Cambridge University Press.

———(2006). *The Changing Languages of Europe.* Oxford: Oxford University Press.

———(2007). *The Genesis of Grammar: A Reconstruction.* Oxford: Oxford University Press.

———(2009). 'The genesis of grammar: on combining nouns', in Rudie Botha and Henriette de Swart (eds), *Language Evolution: The View from Restricted Linguistic Systems.* Utrecht: LOT (Netherlands Graduate School of Linguistics), 139–77.

——and Miyashita, Hiroyuki (2008a). 'The intersection between reflexives and reciprocals: a grammaticalization perspective', in Ekkehard König and Volker Gast (eds), *Reciprocals and Reflexives: Theoretical and Typological Explorations.* Berlin: Mouton de Gruyer, 169–223.

Heine, Bernd, and Miyashita, Hiroyuki (2008b). 'Accounting for a functional category: German *drohen* "to threaten"', *Language Sciences* 30.3: 53–101.

——and Narrog, Heiko (2010). 'Grammaticalization and linguistic analysis', in Bernd Heine and Heiko Narrog (eds), *The Oxford Handbook of Linguistic Analysis.* Oxford: Oxford University Press, 401–23.

——and Reh, Mechthild (1982). *Patterns of Grammaticalization in African Languages.* Institut für Sprachwissenschaft, Universität zu Köln.

———(1984). *Grammaticalization and Reanalysis in African Languages.* Hamburg: Buske.

——and Song, Kyung-An (2010). 'On the genesis of personal pronouns: some conceptual sources', *Language and Cognition* 2.1: 117–48.

———(forthcoming). 'On the grammaticalization of personal pronouns', *Journal of Linguistics.*

Heinrichs, Heinrich M. (1954). *Studien zum bestimmten Artikel in den germanischen Sprachen.* Giessen: Schmitz.

Heltoft, Lars (2006). 'Grammaticalisation as content reanalysis: the modal character of the Danish S-passive', in Ole N. Thomsen (ed.), *Competing Models of Linguistic Change: Evolution and Beyond.* Amsterdam: Benjamins, 268–88.

Hengeveld, Kees (1989). 'Layers and operators in Functional Grammar', *Journal of Linguistics* 25.1: 127–57.

——(1992). *Non-verbal Predication: Theory, Typology, Diachrony.* Berlin: Mouton de Gruyter.

——(2004). 'Mood and modality', in Booij et al. (2004: ii.1190–1202).

——and Mackenzie, J. Lachlan (2008). *Functional Discourse Grammar: A Typologically-Based Theory of Language Structure.* Oxford: Oxford University Press.

———(2010). 'Functional Discourse Grammar', in Bernd Heine and Heiko Narrog (eds), *The Oxford Handbook of Linguistic Analysis.* Oxford: Oxford University Press, 367–400.

Henriksen, Carol, and van der Auwera, Johan (1994). 'The Germanic languages', in Ekkehard König and Johan van der Auwera (eds), *The Germanic Languages.* London: Routledge, 1–18.

Herman, József (1989). '*Accusativus cum infinitivo* et subordonné à *quod, quia* en latin tardif: nouvelles remarques sur un vieux problème', in G. Calboli (ed.), *Subordination and Other Topics in Latin.* Amsterdam: Benjamins, 133–52.

——(2000). *Vulgar Latin.* University Park: Pennsylvania State University Press.

Herslund, Michael (2001). 'The Danish s-genitive: from affix to clitic', *Acta Linguistica Hafniensia* 33: 7–18.

Hewitt, Brian George (1987). *The Typology of Subordination in Georgian and Abkhaz.* Berlin: Mouton de Gruyter.

Higashiizumi, Yuko (2006). *From a Subordinate Clause to an Independent Clause: A History of English* because-*Clause and Japanese* kara-*Clause.* Tokyo: Hituzi Syobo.

Hill, Jane (1987). 'Spanish as a pronominal argument language: the Spanish interlanguage of Mexicano speakers', *Coyote Papers* 6: 68–90.

Hilpert, Martin (2006). 'Auxiliaries in spoken Sinhala', *Functions of Language* 13.2: 259–83.

——(2007). 'Germanic future constructions: a usage-based approach to grammaticalization', PhD thesis, Rice University.

——(2008). *Germanic Future Constructions: A Usage-Based Approach to Language Change.* Amsterdam: Benjamins.

——(to appear). 'Diachronic collostructional analysis: how to use it, and how to deal with confounding factors', in Kathryn Allan and Justyna Robinson (eds), *Current Methods in Historical Semantics.* Berlin: Mouton de Gruyter.

——and Koops, Christian (2008). 'A quantitative approach to the development of complex predicates: the case of Swedish pseudo-coordination with *sitta* "sit"', *Diachronica* 25.2: 242–61.

Hiltunen, Risto (1999). 'Verbal phrases and phrasal verbs in Early Modern English', in Brinton and Akimoto (1999c: 133–65).

Himmelmann, Nikolaus P. (1992). *Grammaticalization and Grammar.* Institut für Sprachwissenschaft, Universität zu Köln.

——(1997). *Deiktikon, Artikel, Nominalphrase: zur Emergenz syntaktischer Struktur.* Tübingen: Niemeyer.

——(2001). 'Articles', in M. Haspelmath, E. König, and W. Oesterreicher (eds), *Language Typology and Language Universals.* Berlin: Mouton de Gruyter, 831–41.

——(2004). 'Lexicalization and grammaticization: opposite or orthogonal?', in Walter Bisang, Nikolaus P. Himmelmann, and Björn Wiemer (eds), *What Makes Grammaticalization? A Look from its Fringes and its Components.* Berlin: Mouton de Gruyter, 21–42.

Hino, Sukenari (2001). *Keishikigo no Kenkyū. Bunpōka no Riron to Ōyō* [Research on formal words: grammaticalization theory and its application]. Fukuoka: Kyūshū Daigaku Shuppankai.

——(2006). 'Keishikigo no ima-mukashi' [Past and present of formal words]. *Nihongogaku* 25.12: 46–61.

Hirschberg, Julia, and Litman, Diane (1993). 'Empirical studies on disambiguation of cue phrases', *Computational Linguistics* 19: 501–30.

Hjelmslev, Louis (1966[1943]). *Omkring sprogteoriens grundlæggelse.* Copenhagen: Københavns Universitet.

Ho, Mian Lian, and Platt, John T. (1993). *Dynamics of a Contact Continuum.* Oxford: Clarendon Press.

Hodge, Carleton (1970). 'The linguistic cycle', *Linguistic Sciences* 13: 1–7.

Hoefler, Stefan, and Smith, Andrew D. M. (2008). 'Reanalysis vs. metaphor: what grammaticalisation can tell us about language evolution', in Andrew D. M. Smith, Kenny Smith, and Ramon Ferrer I Cancho (eds), *The Evolution of Language (EVOLANG) 7,* Rome. World Scientific: 163–70.

————(2009). 'The pre-linguistic basis of grammaticalisation: a unified approach to metaphor and reanalysis', *Studies in Language* 33.4: 883–906.

Hoffmann, Sebastian (2005). *Grammaticalization and English Complex Prepositions: A Corpus-Based Study.* London: Routledge.

Hofstadter, Douglas (1995). *Fluid Concepts and Creative Analogies.* New York: Basic Books.

Hoijer, Harry (1945). 'The Apachean verb, part I: verb structures and pronominal prefixes', *International Journal of American Linguistics* 11.4: 193–204.

——(1971). 'Athapaskan morphology', in Jesse Sawyer (ed.), *Studies in American Indian Languages.* Berkeley: University of California Press, 113–47.

Hollmann, Willem (2003). 'Synchrony and diachrony of English periphrastic causatives: a cognitive perspective', PhD thesis, University of Manchester.

——and Siewierska, Anna (2007). 'A construction grammar account of possessive constructions in Lancashire dialect: some advantages and challenges', *English Language and Linguistics* 11: 407–24.

Holmes, Janet (1988). '*Of course*: a pragmatic particle in New Zealand women's and men's speech', *Australian Journal of Lingusitics* 2: 49–74.

Holyoak, Keith J., and Thagard, Paul (1995). *Mental Leaps: Analogy in Creative Thought.* Cambridge, MA: MIT Press.

Hong, Jongseon (1983). 'Myengsahwa Emiuy Pyenchen' [Historical change of nominalizing particles], *Journal of Korean Language and Literature* 89: 31–89.

Hong, Ki-Moon (1957). *Cosenelyeksamwunpep* [Historical linguistics of Korean]. Pyongyang: Kwahakwen.

Hopper, Paul (1987). 'Emergent grammar', *Proceedings of the 13th Annual Meeting of the Berkeley Linguistics Society*, 139–57.

——(1991). 'On some principles of grammaticization', in Traugott and Heine (1991a: 17–35).

——(1998). 'Emergent grammar', in Michael Tomasello (ed.), *The New Psychology of Language: Cognitive and Functional Approaches to Language Structure.* Mahwah, NJ: Erlbaum, 155–75.

——(2001). 'Grammatical constructions and their discourse origins: prototype or family resemblance?', in M. Pütz, S. Niemeier, and R. Dirven (eds), *Applied Cognitive Linguistics*, vol. I: *Theory and Language Acquisition.* Berlin: de Gruyter, 109–29.

——(2004). 'The openness of grammatical constructions', *Chicago Linguistic Society* 40: 239–56.

——and Thompson, Sandra A. (2008). 'Projectability and clause combining in interaction', in Ritva Laury (ed.), *Crosslinguistic Studies of Clause Combining: The Multifunctionality of Conjunctions.* Amsterdam: Benjamins, 99–123.

——and Traugott, Elizabeth Closs (1993). *Grammaticalization.* Cambridge: Cambridge University Press.

————(2003). *Grammaticalization*, 2nd edn. Cambridge: Cambridge University Press.

Horie, Kaoru (1998). 'On the polyfunctionality of the Japanese particle *no*: from the perspectives of ontology and grammaticalization', in Toshio Ohori (ed.), *Studies in Japanese Grammaticalization: Cognitive and Discourse Perspectives.* Tokyo: Kurosio Syuppan, 169–92.

——(2000). 'Core–oblique distinction and nominalizer choice in Japanese and Korean', *Studies in Language* 24: 77–102.

Horn, Laurence R. (1989). *A Natural History of Negation.* Chicago: University of Chicago Press.

——(2001). *A Natural History of Negation.* Stanford, CA: CSLI.

Hruschka, Daniel J., Christiansen, Morten H., Blythe, Richard A., Croft, William, Heggart, Paul, Mufwene, Salikoko S., Pierrehumbert, Janet, and Poplack, Shana.

(2009). 'Building social cognitive models of language change', *Trends in Cognitive Sciences* 13.11: 464–9.

Huddleston, Rodney, and Pullum, Geoffrey K. (2002). *The Cambridge Grammar of the English Language.* Cambridge: Cambridge University Press.

Hudson, Richard (2007). *Language Networks.* Oxford: Oxford University Press.

Huffman, Franklin, and Proum, Im (1977). *English–Khmer Dictionary.* New Haven, CT: Yale University Press.

Huh, Woong (1982). 'Hankwukmal Ttaymaykimpepuy Keleon Palcachwi' [The path of the Korean tense system], *Hankul* 178: 3–51. Reprinted in Huh (1987: 197–245).

——(1987). *Kwuke Ttaymaykimpepuy Pyencheonsa* [A developmental history of the Korean tense system]. Seoul: Saem.

Humboldt, Wilhelm von (1822). *Über die Entstehung der grammatischen Formen und ihren Einfluss auf die Ideenentwicklung. Abhandlungen der Akademie der Wissenschaften zu Berlin.* (Reprinted 1972, Darmstadt: Wissenschaftliche Buchgesellschaft.)

——(1985). *Über die Sprache: Ausgewählte Schriften*, ed. Jürgen Trabant. Munich: Deutscher Taschenbuch.

Hundt, Marianne (2001). What corpora tell us about the grammaticization of voice in *get*-constructions', *Studies in Language* 25: 49–88.

Hüning, Matthias, Vogl, Ulrike, Van der Wouden, Ton, and Verhagen, Arie (2006). *Nederlands tussen Duits en Engels: Handelingen van de workshop aan de Freie Universität Berlin.* Leiden: Stichting Neerlandistiek Leiden.

Hurford, James R. (2007). 'The origin of noun phrases: reference, truth and communication', *Lingua* 117.3: 527–42.

Hyman, Larry M., and Comrie, Bernard (1981). 'Coreference and logophoricity in Gokana', *Studies in African Linguistics*, Supplement 8: 69–72.

ICE-GB: The International Corpus of English, Great Britain. Survey of English Usage Project, University College, London. Director: Bas Aarts.

Idiatov, Dmitry (2008). 'Antigrammaticalization, antimorphologization and the case of Tura', in López-Couso and Seoane (2008: 151–69).

Iglesias-Rábade, Luis (2001). 'Composite predicates in Middle English with the verbs *niman* and *taken*', *Studia Neophilologica* 73: 143–63.

Ijbema, Aniek (2002). 'Grammaticalization and infinitival complements in Dutch', dissertation, Leiden University.

Imbert, Caroline, and Grinewald, Colette (2008). 'Twenty years of relational preverbs: a grammaticalization account', paper presented at the conference 'New Reflections on Grammaticalization, 4', Leuven, July.

Ishigaki, Kenji (1955). *Joshi no Rekishiteki Kenkyū* [A historical study of particles]. Tokyo: Iwanami.

Israel, Michael (1996). 'The way constructions grow', in Adele Goldberg (ed.), *Conceptual Structure, Discourse and Language.* Stanford, CA: CSLI, 217–30.

——(2001). 'Minimizers, maximizers and the rhetoric of scalar reasoning', *Journal of Semantics* 18: 297–331.

Itkonen, Esa (2005). *Analogy as Structure and Process.* Amsterdam: Benjamins.

Ito, Rika, and Tagliamonte, Sali A. (2003). '*Well weird, right dodgy, very strange, really cool*: layering and recycling in English intensifiers', *Language in Society* 32, 257–279.

Jackendoff, Ray (2002). *Foundations of Language: Brain, Meaning, Grammar, Evolution.* Oxford: Oxford University Press.

Jacobsen, William H., Jr (1986). 'The heterogeneity of evidentials in Makah', in Chafe and Nichols (1986: 3–28).

Jäger, Agnes (2008). *History of German Negation*. Amsterdam: Benjamins.

Jäger, Gerhard, and Rosenbach, Anette (2008a). 'Priming and unidirectional language change', *Theoretical Linguistics* 34: 85–113.

————(2008b). 'Priming as a testing ground for historical linguists? A reply to Chang, Eckardt and Traugott', *Theoretical Linguistics* 34: 143–56.

Jaggar, Phillip J. (2001). *Hausa*. Amsterdam: Benjamins.

Jake, Janice L., and Myers-Scotton, Carol (1997). 'Relating interlanguage to code-switching: the composite matrix language', *Proceedings of Boston University Conference on Language Development*. 21: 319–30.

Jakobson, Roman (1971[1957]). 'Shifters, verbal categories, and the Russian verb', in Roman Jakobson (ed.), *Selected Writings*, vol. 2: *Word and Language*. Berlin: Mouton de Gruyter, 130–47.

James, Deborah (1982). 'Past tense and the hypothetical: a cross-linguistic study', *Studies in Language* 6.3: 375–403.

——Clarke, Sandra, and Mackenzie, Marguerite (2001). 'The encoding of information source in Algonquian: evidentials in Cree/Montagnais/Naskapi', *International Journal of American Linguistics* 67: 229–63.

James, Francis (1986). *Semantics of the English Subjunctive*. Vancouver: University of British Columbia Press.

Janda, Richard D. (2001). 'Beyond "pathways" and "unidirectionality": on the discontinuity of language transmission and the counterability of grammaticalization', *Language Sciences* 23: 265–340.

Janse, Mark (2009). 'Watkins' Law and the development of agglutinative inflections in Asia Minor Greek', *Journal of Greek Linguistics* 9: 93–109.

Janzen, Terry (1999). 'The grammaticization of topics in American Sign Language', *Studies in Language* 23: 271–306.

——and Shaffer, Barbara (2002). 'Gesture as the substrate in the process of ASL grammaticization', in R. P. Meier, K. A. Cormier, and D. G. Quinto-Pozos (eds), *Modality and Structure in Signed and Spoken Languages*. Cambridge: Cambridge University Press, 199–223.

Jefferson, Gail (1980). 'On a failed hypothesis: "conjunctionals" as overlap vulnerable: two explorations of the organization of overlapping talk in conversation', *Tilburg Papers in Language and Literature* 28: 1–37.

Jelinek, Eloise (1984). 'Empty categories, case, and configurationality', *Natural Language and Linguistic Theory* 2: 39–76.

——(2001). 'Pronouns and argument hierarchies', paper presented at 'Perspectives on Aspect', Utrecht, December.

Jenner, Philip N., and Pou, Saveros (1980/81). *A Lexicon of Khmer Morphology*. Honolulu: University Press.

Jespersen, Otto (1894). *Progress in Language. With Special Reference to English*. London: Swan Sonnenschein.

——(1917). 'Negation in English and other languages', *Historisk-filologiske Meddeleser* 1.

——(1922). *Language: Its Nature, Origin and Development*. London: Allen & Unwin.

——(1925). *Die Sprache: Ihre Natur, Entwicklung und Entstehung*. Heidelberg: Winter.

——(1942). *A Modern English Grammar on Historical Principles*, part 6: *Morphology*. London: Allen & Unwin.

——(1992[1924]). *The Philosophy of Grammar. With a new introduction and index by James D. McCawley*. Chicago: University of Chicago Press.

JEŽEK, ELISABETTA, and RAMAT, PAOLO (2009). 'On parts-of-speech transcategorization', *Folia Linguistica* 49: 391–416.

JIANG LANSHENG (1999). 'Hanyu shiyi yu beidong jianyong tanyuan' [On Chinese causatives and passives], in *Jindai Hanyu tanyuan* [Issues in Modern Chinese]. Beijing: Shangwu Yinshuguan, 221–36.

JIANG SHAOYU (2002). 'Gei ziju, jiao ziju biao beidong de laiyuan' [Origin of the passives in *bei* and in *jiao*], *Yuyanxue Luncong* 26: 59–177.

JOHANNESSEN, JANNE BONDI (1989). 'Klitika: en avgrensning', *Norsk lingvistisk tidsskrift* 2: 117–47.

JOHANSON, LARS (1971). *Aspekt im Türkischen: Vorstudien zu einer Beschreibung des türkeitürkischen Aspektsystems*. Uppsala: Almqvist & Wiksell.

——(1976). 'Zum Präsens der nordwestlichen und mittelasiatischen Türksprachen', *Acta Orientalia* 37: 57–74.

——(1992). 'Strukturelle Faktoren in türkischen Sprachkontakten', *Sitzungsberichte der Wissenschaftlichen Gesellschaft an der Johann Wolfgang Goethe-Universität Frankfurt am Main* 29.5: 169–299.

——(1995). 'On Turkic converb clauses', in M. Haspelmath and E. König (eds), *Converbs in Cross-linguistic Perspective: Structure and Meaning of Adverbial Verb Forms—Adverbial Participles, Gerunds*. Berlin: Mouton de Gruyter, 313–47.

——(2000). 'Viewpoint operators in European languages', in Östen Dahl (ed.), *Tense and Aspect in the Languages of Europe*. Berlin: Mouton de Gruyter, 27–187.

——(2002). *Structural Factors in Turkic Language Contacts* (with an introduction by Bernard Comrie). London: Curzon.

——(2003). 'Evidentiality in Turkic', in A. Y. Aikhenvald and R. M. W. Dixon (eds), *Studies in Evidentiality*. Amsterdam: Benjamins, 273–290.

——and UTAS, BO (eds) (2000). *Evidentials: Turkic, Iranian and Neighbouring Languages*. Berlin: Mouton de Gruyter.

JOHANSSON, SVERKER (2005). *Origins of Language: Constraints on Hypotheses*. Amsterdam: Benjamins.

JOHNSTON, RAYMOND LESLIE (1980). *Nakanai of New Britain: The Grammar of an Oceanic Language*. Canberra: Pacific Linguistics.

JONAS, DIANNE, WHITMAN, JOHN, and GARRETT, ANDREW (eds) (forthcoming). *Grammatical Change: Origins, Nature, Outcomes*. Oxford: Oxford University Press.

JONES, MICHAEL (1988). 'Auxiliary verbs in Sardinian', *Transactions of the Philological Society* 86: 173–203.

JOSEPH, BRIAN D. (2001). 'Is there such a thing as "grammaticalization"'?, *Language Sciences* (special issue, *Grammaticalization: A Critical Assessment*, ed. L. Campbell) 23.2–3: 163–86.

——(2003). 'Morphologization from syntax', in Joseph and Janda (2003: 472–92).

——(2004). 'Rescuing traditional (historical) linguistics from grammaticalization theory', in Fischer et al. (2004: 45–71).

——(2006). 'How accommodating of change is grammaticalization? The case of "lateral shifts"', *Logos and Language* 6.2: 1–7.

——and Richard D. Janda (eds) (2003). *The Handbook of Historical Linguistics.* Oxford: Blackwell.

Jucker, Andreas (1993). 'The discourse marker *well*: a relevance-theoretical account', *Journal of Pragmatics* 19.5: 435–53.

Juge, Matthew (2006). 'Morphological factors in the grammaticalization of the 'go' past in Catalan', *Diachronica* 26: 313–39.

Jung, Yonhee (2001). 'Grammaticalization of Korean clause connectives', PhD dissertation. Hankuk University of Foreign Studies.

Jurafsky, Daniel, Bell, Alan, Gregory, Michelle, and Raymond, William (2001). 'Probabilistic relations between words: evidence from reduction in lexical production', in Bybee and Hopper (2001: 229–54).

Juvonen, Päivi (2000). *Grammaticalizing the Definite Article: A Study of Definite Adnominal Determiners in a Genre of Spoken Finnish.* Department of Linguistics, Stockholm University.

Kahr, Joan Casper (1975). 'Adpositions and locationals: typology and diachronic development', *Working Papers on Language Universals* (Stanford) 19: 21–54.

——(1976). 'The renewal of case morphology: sources and constraints', *Working Papers on Language Universals* (Stanford) 20: 107–51.

Kamp, Hans, and Reyle, Uwe (1995). *From Discourse to Logic.* Dordrecht: Kluwer.

Kang, Eun-Kook (1993). *Cosene Cepmisauy Thongsicek Yenkwu* [A diachronic study of Korean suffixes]. Seoul: Sekwanghakswulcalyo.

Kang, So-Yeong (2001). 'A study on the process of grammaticalization in Korean nouns', PhD dissertation, Ewha Woman's University.

Kari, James (1975). 'The disjunct boundary in the Navajo and Tanaina verb prefix complexes', *International Journal of American Linguistics* 41: 330–45.

——(1989). 'Affix positions and zones in the Athapaskan verb complex: Ahtna and Navajo', *International Journal of American Linguistics* 55: 424–54.

Kärkkäinen, Elise (2003). *Epistemic Stance in English Conversation: A Description of Its Interactional Functions, with a Focus on 'I think'.* Amsterdam: Benjamins.

Karlsson, Keith (1981). *Syntax and Affixation: The Evolution of* mente *in Latin and Romance.* Tübingen: Niemeyer.

Karmiloff, Kyra, and Karmiloff-Smith, Annette (2001). *Pathways to Language: From Fetus to Adolescent.* Cambridge, MA: Harvard University Press.

Karttunen, Frances (1976). 'Uto-Aztecan and Spanish-type dependent clauses in Nahuatl', paper presented at 'Parasession on Diachronic Syntax', *Chicago Linguistic Society*: 150–58.

Kastovsky, Dieter (1982). *Wortbildung und Semantik.* Düsseldorf: Schwan-Bagel.

Kaufmann, Stefan, Condoravdi, Cleo, and Harizanov, Valentina (2006). 'Formal approaches to modality', in Frawley (2006: 71–106).

Kay, Paul, and Fillmore, Charles J. (1999). 'Grammatical constructions and linguistic generalizations: the *What's X Doing Y?* construction', *Language* 75: 1–33.

Kayne, Richard (1994). *The Asymmetry of Syntax.* Cambridge, MA: MIT Press.

Kazenin, Konstantin I. (2001). 'The passive voice', in Martin Haspelmath, Ekkehrd König, Wulf Oesterreicher, and Wolfgang Raible (eds), *Language Typology and Language Universals: An International Handbook*, vol. 2. Berlin: de Gruyter, 899–916.

Keenan, Edward L. (1985). 'Passive in the world's languages', in Shopen (1985: i.243–81).

——(2002). 'Explaining the creation of the reflexive pronouns in English', in D. Minkova and R. Stockwell (eds), *Studies in the History of the English Language: A Millennial Perspective*. Berlin: Mouton de Gruyter, 325–54.

——and Comrie, Bernard (1977). 'Noun phrase accessibility and universal grammar', *Linguistic Inquiry* 8: 63–99.

Keesing, Ronald M. (1988). *Melanesian Pidgin and the Oceanic substrate*. Stanford, CA: Stanford University Press.

——(1991). 'Substrates, calquing and grammaticalization in Melanesian Pidgin', in Traugott and Heine (1991a: 315–42).

Kegl, Judy, Senghas, Ann, and Coppola, Marie (1999). 'Creation through contact: sign language emergence and sign language change in Nicaragua', in M. DeGraff (ed.), *Language Creation and Language Change: Creolization, Diachrony, and Development*. Cambridge, MA: MIT Press, 179–237.

Keller, Rudi (1990). *Sprachwandel: Von der unsichtbaren Hand in der Sprache*. Tübingen: Francke.

Kemenade, Ans van (1999). 'Functional categories, morphosyntactic change, grammaticalization', *Linguistics* 37: 997–1010.

——(2000). '"Jespersen" Cycle revisited: formal properties of grammaticalization', in Susan Pintzuk, George Tsoulas, and Anthony Warner (eds), *Diachronic Syntax: Models and Mechanisms*. Oxford: Oxford University Press, 51–74.

——(2009). 'Discourse relations and word order change', in Roland Hinterhölzl and Svetlana Petrova (eds), *Information Structure and Language Change: New Approaches to Word Order Variation and Change in the Germanic Languages*. Berlin: Mouton de Gruyter, 91–118.

——and Vincent, Nigel (eds) (1997). *Parameters of Morphosyntactic Change*. Cambridge: Cambridge University Press.

Kemmer, Suzanne (1993). *The Middle Voice*. Amsterdam: Benjamins.

Kendon, Adam (2004). *Gesture: Visible Action as Utterance*. Cambridge: Cambridge University Press.

Kennedy, Chris (1999). *Projecting the Adjective*. New York: Garland.

Kiefer, Ferenc (1987). 'The cases of Hungarian nouns', *Acta Linguistica Adacemiae Scientarum Hungaricae* 37: 93–101.

——(2000). *Strukturális magyar nyelvtan III: Morfológia*. Budapest: Akadémiai Kiadó.

Kiessling, Roland (2007). 'The "marked nominative" in Datooga', *Journal of African Languages and Linguistics* 28.2: 149–91.

Kim, Minju (2003). 'Discourse frequency and the emergence of grammar: a corpus-based study of the grammaticalization of the Korean existential verb is(i)-ta', dissertation, University of California, Los Angeles.

Kim, Moon-Woong (1975). 'Kwukeuy Hesa Hyengsengey Kwanhan Yenkwu' [A study on the formation of empty words in Korean], MA thesis, Kyungpuk National University, Korea.

King, Robert (1969). *Historical Linguistics and Generative Grammar*. New York: Prentice Hall.

Kinsui, Satoshi (1992). 'Ōbunyaku to judōbun. Edo jidai o chūshin ni' [Western translations and the passive: focus on the Edo period], in Bunka Gengogaku Henshū Iinkai (eds), *Bunka Gengogaku: Sono Teigen to Kenchiku*. Tokyo: Sanseidō, 1–15.

Kiparsky, Paul (1965). 'Phonological change', PhD dissertation, Massachusetts Institute of Technology.

——(1968). 'Linguistic universals and linguistic change', in Emmon Bach and Robert T. Harms (eds), *Universals in Linguistic Theory.* New York: Holt, Rinehart & Winston, 171–202.

——(forthcoming). 'Grammaticalization as optimization', in Diane Jonas and John Whitman (eds), *Grammatical Change: Origins, Nature, Outcomes.* Oxford: Oxford University Press.

——and CONDORAVDI, CLEO (2006). 'Tracking Jespersen's Cycle', in Mark Janse, Brian D. Joseph, and Angela Ralli (eds), *Proceedings of the 2nd International Conference of Modern Greek Dialects and Linguistic Theory.* Mytilene: Doukas. Downloaded from: http://www.stanford.edu/~kiparsky/Papers/lesvosnegation.pdf

KITA, SOTARO (ed.) (2003). *Pointing: Where Language, Culture, and Cognition Meet.* Mahwah, NJ: Erlbaum.

KLAMER, MARIAN (2000). 'How report verbs become quote markers and complementisers', *Lingua* 110: 69–98.

KLEIBER, GEORGES (1987). 'L'opposition *cist/cil* en ancien français ou comment analyser les démonstratifs?', *Revue de linguistique romane* 51: 5–35.

——(1992). 'Article défini, unicité et pertinence', *Revue Romane* 27: 61–89.

KLEIN, WOLFGANG (1994). *Time in Language.* London: Routledge.

KLIMA, EDWARD (1965). 'Studies in diachronic transformational syntax', PhD, Harvard University.

——and BELLUGI, URSULA (1979). *The Signs of Language.* Cambridge, MA: Harvard University Press.

KLUGE, FRIEDRICH, and SEEBOLD, ELMAR (1989). *Etymologisches Wörterbuch der deutschen Sprache.* Berlin: de Gruyter.

KO, YOUNG-JIN (1995). 'A study of the processes of grammaticalization in Korean predicates: from syntactic constructions to morphological constructions', PhD dissertation, Yonsei University.

KOBAYASHI, KENJI (1996). *Nihongo Jōken Hyōgenshi no Kenkyū* [A study in the history of conditional expressions in Japanese]. Tokyo: Hituzi Syobo.

KOCH, PETER (2001). 'Metonymy: unity in diversity', *Journal of Historical Pragmatics* 2: 201–44.

——(2004). 'Metonymy between pragmatics, reference and diachrony', in: *metaphorik*.de 07, 6–54. http://www.metaphorik.de

KOMORI, YOSHIHIRO (2009). 'Disambiguating between "wa" and "ga" in Japanese': http://www.sccs.swarthmore.edu/users/03/yoshi/jpn.pdf

KÖNIG, CHRISTA (2002). *Kasus im Ik.* Cologne: Köppe.

——(2005). 'Case in Africa: on categorial misbehaviour', in Erhard Voeltz (ed.), *Studies in African Linguistic Typology.* Amsterdam: Benjamins, 195–207.

——(2006). 'Marked nominative in Africa', *Studies in Language* 30.4: 655–732.

——(2008). *Case in Africa.* Oxford: Oxford University Press.

KÖNIG, EKKEHARD (1988). 'Concessive connectives and concessive sentences: cross-linguistic regularities and pragmatic principles', in John A. Hawkins (ed.), *Explaining Language Universals.* Oxford: Blackwell, 145–66.

——and VAN DER AUWERA, JOHAN (1988). 'Clause integration in German and Dutch conditionals, concessive conditionals, and concessives', in Haiman and Thompson (1988: 101–34).

Koo, Hyun Jung (2009). 'Fused paradigms: grammaticalization in extension of conditional markers', paper presented at the 19th International Conference on Historical Linguistics, 10–14 August, Radboud University.

——and Rhee, Seongha (2001). 'Grammaticalization of a sentential end marker from a conditional marker', *Discourse and Cognition* 8.1: 1–19.

————(2008). 'Manipulated hypotheticality in conditionals: a journey in search of strength and diversity', paper presented at 'New Reflections on Grammaticalization IV', 16–19 July, Catholic University of Leuven.

Korhonen, Mikko (1996). 'Typological drift in the Finno-Ugrian languages with special reference to the case system', in Tapani Salminen (ed.), *Typological and Historical Studies in Language by Mikko Korhonen*. Helsinki: Finno-Ugrian Society, 195–206.

Kornai, András, and Pullum, Geoffrey (1990). 'The X-bar theory of phrase structure', *Language* 66: 24–50.

Kornfilt, Jaklin (1997). *Turkish*. London: Routledge.

Kortmann, Bernd (1997). *Adverbial Subordination: A Typology and History of Adverbial Subordinators Based on European Languages*. Berlin: Mouton de Gruyter.

——(2004a). '*Do* as a tense and aspect marker in varieties of English', in Bernd Kortmann (ed.), *Dialectology Meets Typology: Dialect Grammar from a Cross-Linguistic Perspective*. Berlin: Mouton de Gruyter, 245–75.

——(2004b). 'Synopsis: morphological and syntactic variation in the British Isles', in Kortmann et al. (2004: ii.478–95).

——(2005). *English Linguistics: Essentials*. Berlin Cornelsen.

——(in preparation). *World Atlas of Varieties of English*. Berlin: Mouton de Gruyter.

——and König, Ekkehard (1992). 'Categorial reanalysis: the case of deverbal prepositions', *Linguistics* 30: 671–97.

——and Schneider, Edgar (2006). *Varieties of English*. Berlin: Mouton de Gruyter. Online material available at: http://www.varieties.mouton-content.com

————in collaboration with Burridge, Kate, Mesthrie, Raj, and Upton, Clive (eds) (2004). *A Handbook of Varieties of English*. 2 volumes + 1 CD-ROM. Berlin: Mouton de Gruyter.

——and Szmrecsanyi, Benedikt (2011). 'Parameters of morphosyntactic variation in World Englishes: prospects and limitations of searching for universals', in Peter Siemund (ed.), *Linguistic Universals and Language Variation*. Berlin: Mouton de Gruyter, 257–83.

Kouwenberg, Silvia, and LaCharité, Darlene (2004). 'Echoes of Africa: reduplication in Caribbean Creole and Niger-Congo languages', *Journal of Pidgin and Creole Languages* 19: 285–331.

Kövecses, Zoltán (2002). *Metaphor: A Practical Introduction*. Oxford: Oxford University Press.

Koziol, Herbert (1937). *Handbuch der englischen Wortbildungslehre*. Heidelberg: Winter.

Kraft, Charles H., and Kirk-Greene, A. H. M. (1973). *Hausa*. London: Hodder & Stoughton.

Krámsky, Jiří (1972). *The Article and the Concept of Definiteness in Language*. The Hague: Mouton.

Kratzer, Angelika (1981). 'The notional category of modality', in H. J. Eikemeyer and H. Rieser (eds), *Words, Worlds and Contexts*. Berlin: de Gruyter, 38–74.

Krauss, Michael (1965). 'Eyak: a preliminary report', *Canadian Journal of Linguistics* 167–87.

——(1973). 'Na-Dene', in Thomas Sebeok (ed.), *Current Trends in Linguistics* 10. The Hague: Mouton, 903–78.

KRIFKA, MANFRED (1995). 'The semantics and pragmatics of polarity items', *Linguistic Analysis* 25: 209–57.

KRUG, MANFRED (1998). 'String frequency: a cognitive motivating factor in coalescence, language processing, and linguistic change', *Journal of English Linguistics* 26: 286–320.

——(2000). *Emerging English Modals: A Corpus-Based Study of Grammaticalization*. Berlin: Mouton de Gruyter.

——(2001). 'Frequency, iconicity, categorization: evidence from emerging modals', in Bybee and Hopper (2001: 309–36).

——(2003). 'Frequency as a determinant in grammatical variation and change', in Günter Rohdenburg and Britta Mondorf (eds), *Determinants of Grammatical Variation in English*. Berlin: Mouton de Gruyter, 7–67.

——(2009). 'Modality and the history of English adhortatives', in Raphael Salkie, Pierre Busuttil, and Johan van der Auwera (eds), *Modality in English: Theory and Description*. Berlin: Mouton de Gruyter, 315–47.

——(in preparation). 'Towards a panchronic definition of auxiliaries', MS, Bamberg.

KRUSPE, NICOLE (2004). *A Grammar of Semelai*. Cambridge: Cambridge University Press.

KULIKOV, LEONID (2006). 'Case systems in a diachronic perspective: a typological sketch', in Leonid Kulikov, Andrej Malchukov, and Peter de Swart (eds), *Case, Valency and Transitivity*. Amsterdam: Benjamins, 23–47.

——(2008). 'Evolution of case systems', in Malchukov and Spencer (2008: 439–57).

KULIKOV, LEONID, MALCHUKOV, ANDREJ, and DE SWART, PETER (eds) (2006). *Case, Valency and Transitivity*. Amsterdam: Benjamins.

——and SUMBATOVA, NINA (1993). 'Through the looking glass and how causatives look there', in B. Comrie and M. Polinsky (eds), *Causatives and Causativity*. Amsterdam: Benjamins, 327–41.

KUNO, SUSUMU (1973[1965]). *The Structure of the Japanese Language*. Cambridge: MIT Press.

KURYŁOWICZ, JERZY (1975[1965]). 'The evolution of grammatical categories', *Esquisses linguistiques* 2: 38–54. (*Diogenes* 1965: 55–71.)

KUTEVA, TANIA A. (1999). On "sit"/"stand"/"lie" auxiliation', *Linguistics* 32.2: 191–213.

——(2001). *Auxiliation: An Enquiry into the Nature of Grammaticalization*. Oxford: Oxford University Press.

KUZMACK, STEFANIE (in preparation). '*Ish:* a new case of antigrammaticalization', MS, University of Chicago.

KYTÖ, MERJA (1991). *Variation and Diachrony, with Early American English in Focus*. Frankfurt am Main: Lang.

——(1999). 'Collocational and idiomatic aspects of verbs in Early Modern English: a corpus-based study of MAKE, HAVE, GIVE, TAKE, and DO', in Brinton and Akimoto (1999c: 167–206).

——and ROMAINE, SUZANNE (2005). '"We had like to have been killed by thunder & lightning": the semantic and pragmatic history of a construction that like to disappeared', *Journal of Historical Pragmatics* 6: 1–35.

LA FAUCI, NUNZIO (1988). *Oggetti e soggetti nella formazione della morfosintassi romanza*. Pisa: Giardini.

——(1997). *Per una teoria grammaticale del mutamento morfosintattico: dal latino verso il romanzo*. Pisa: ETS.

Labov, William (1969). 'Contraction, deletion, and inherent variability of the English copula', *Language* 45: 715–62.
——(1972a). *Language in the Inner City.* Philadelphia: University of Pennsylvania Press.
——(1972b). *Sociolinguistic Patterns.* Philadelphia: University of Pennsylvania Press.
——(1984). 'Field methods of the Project on Linguistic Change and Variation', in John Baugh and Joel Sherzer (eds), *Language in Use.* Englewood Cliffs, NJ: Prentice Hall, 28–53.
——(1994). *Principles of Linguistic Change*, vol. 1: *Internal Factors.* Oxford: Blackwell.
——(2001). *Principles of Linguistic Change*, vol. 2: *Social Factors.* Oxford: Blackwell.
Ladd, D. Robert (1996). *Intonational Phonology.* Cambridge: Cambridge University Press.
Ladusaw, William (1996). 'Negation and polarity items', in S. Lappin (ed.), *The Handbook of Contemporary Semantic Theory.* Oxford: Blackwell, 321–41.
Lafitte, Pierre (1944). *Grammaire Basque: Navarro-labourdin littéraire.* Bayonne: Librairie 'Le Livre'.
Lagerqvist, Hans (2009). *Le subjonctif en français moderne.* Paris: Presses de l'Université Paris-Sorbonne.
Lahiri, Aditi (2000). 'Hierarchical restructuring in the creation of verbal morphology in Bengali and Germanic: evidence from phonology', in Aditi Lahiri (ed.), *Analogy, Levelling, Markedness: Principles of Change in Phonology and Morphology.* Berlin: Mouton de Gruyter, 71–123.
Laitinen, Mikko (2007). *Agreement Patterns in English: Diachronic Corpus Studies in Common-Number Pronouns.* Helsinki: Société Néophilologique.
Lakoff, George (1987). *Women, Fire and Dangerous Things.* Chicago: University of Chicago Press.
——(1990). 'The invariance hypothesis: is abstract reason based on image-schemas?', *Cognitive Linguistics* 1: 39–74.
——and Johnson, Mark (1980). *Metaphors We Live By.* Chicago: University of Chicago Press.
Lakoff, Robin (1969). *Abstract Syntax and Latin Complementation.* Cambridge, MA: MIT Press.
Lam, Phoenix (2009). 'What a difference the prosody makes: the role of prosody in the study of discourse particles', in D. Barth-Weingarten, N. Dehé, and A. Wichmann (eds), *Where Prosody Meets Pragmatics.* London: Emerald.
Lambrecht, Knud (1981). *Topic, Antitopic, and Verb Agreement in Non Standard French.* Amsterdam: Benjamins.
——(1994). *Information Structure and Sentence Form: A Theory of Topic, Focus, and the Mental Representations of Discourse Referents.* Cambridge: Cambridge University Press.
Lamiroy, Béatrice (1999). 'Auxiliaires, langues romanes et grammaticalisation', *Langages* 135: 33–45.
——(2001). 'Le syntagme prépositionnel en français et en espagnol: une question de grammaticalisation', *Langages* 143: 91–106.
Lander, Y. A., Plungian, Vladimir A., and Urmanchieva, Anna Yu (eds) (2004). *Irrealis and Irreality.* Moscow: Gnosis.
Lang, Ewald (2002). 'Die Wortart "Konjunktion"', in D. A. Cruse et al. (eds), *Lexicology: Ein Internationales Handbuch zur Natur und Struktur von Wörtern und Wortschätzen.* Berlin: de Gruyter, 634–41.
Langacker, Ronald W. (1977). 'Syntactic reanalysis', in Li (1977: 57–139).

——(1981). Review of Talmy Givón, *On Understanding Grammar, Language* 57: 436–45.

——(1985). 'Observations and speculations on subjectivity', in John Haiman (ed.), *Syntax: Proceedings of a Symposium on Iconicity in Syntax.* Amsterdam: Benjamins, 109–50.

——(1987). *Foundations of Cognitive Grammar,* vol. 1: *Theoretical Prerequisites.* Stanford, CA: Stanford University Press.

——(1990). 'Subjectification', *Cognitive Linguistics* 1: 5–38.

——(1991). *Foundations of Cognitive Grammar,* vol. 2: *Descriptive Application.* Stanford, CA: Stanford University Press.

——(1995). 'Raising and transparency', *Language* 71: 1–62.

——(1998). 'On subjectification and grammaticization', in J.-P. Koenig (ed.), *Discourse and Cognition.* Stanford, CA: CSLI, 71–89.

——(1999a). 'Assessing the cognitive linguistic enterprise', in Theo Janssen and Gisela Redeker (eds), *Cognitive Linguistics: Foundations, Scope, and Methodology.* Berlin: Mouton de Gruyter, 13–59.

——(1999b). *Grammar and Conceptualization.* Berlin: Mouton de Gruyter.

——(2000). 'A dynamic usage-based model', in Michael Barlow and Suzanne Kemmer (eds), *Usage-Based Models of Language.* Stanford: CSLI, 1–63.

——(2002). 'Deixis and subjectivity', in Frank Brisard (ed.), *Grounding: the Epistemic Footing of Deixis and Reference.* Berlin: Mouton de Gruyter, 1–27.

——(2003). 'Constructional integration, grammaticization, and serial verb constructions', *Language and Linguistics* 4: 251–78.

Langacker, Ronald W.(2005a). 'Construction grammars: cognitive, radical, and less so', in Francisco J. Ruiz de Mendoza Ibáñez and M. Sandra Peña Cervel (eds), *Cognitive Linguistics: Internal Dynamics and Interdisciplinary Interaction.* Berlin: Mouton de Gruyter, 101–59.

——(2005b). 'Integration, grammaticization, and constructional meaning', in Mirjam Fried and Hans C. Boas (eds), *Grammatical Constructions: Back to the Roots.* Amsterdam: Benjamins, 157–89.

——(2005c). 'Dynamicity, fictivity, and scanning: the imaginative basis of logic and linguistic meaning', in Diane Pecher and Rolf A. Zwaan (eds), *Grounding Cognition: The Role of Perception and Action in Memory, Language and Thinking.* Cambridge: Cambridge University Press, 164–97.

——(2006). 'Subjectification, grammaticization, and conceptual archetypes', in Angeliki Athanasiadou, Costas Canakis, and Bert Cornillie (eds), *Subjectification: Various Paths to Subjectivity.* Berlin: Mouton de Gruyter, 17–40.

——(2008a). *Cognitive Grammar: A Basic Introduction.* New York: Oxford University Press.

——(2008b). 'Sequential and summary scanning: a reply', *Cognitive Linguistics* 19: 571–84.

——(2009a). *Investigations in Cognitive Grammar.* Berlin: Mouton de Gruyter.

——(2009b). 'Constructions and constructional meaning', in Vyvyan Evans and Stéphanie Pourcel (eds), *New Directions in Cognitive Linguistics.* Amsterdam: Benjamins, 225–67.

——(2010). 'How not to disagree: the emergence of structure from usage', in Kasper Boye and Elisabeth Engberg-Pedersen (eds), *Language Usage and Language Structure.* Berlin: Mouton de Gruyter, 107–44.

Lapesa, Rafael (1974). 'El sustantivo sin actualizador en español', in R. Cano and M. T. Echenique (eds), *Estudios de morfosintaxis histórica.* Madrid: Gredos, 436–54.

LaPolla, Randy J. (2006). 'On grammatical relations as constraints on referent identification', in Tasaku Tsunoda and Taro Kageyama (eds), *Voice and Grammatical Relations*. Amsterdam: Benjamins, 139–51.

Larsen-Freeman, Diane (1997). 'Chaos/complexity science and second language acquisition', *Applied Linguistics* 18: 141–65.

Lass, Roger (1990). 'How to do things with junk: exaptation in language evolution', *Journal of Linguistics* 26: 79–102.

——(1993). *Old English: A Historical Linguistic Companion*. Cambridge: Cambridge University Press.

——(2000). 'Remarks on (uni)directionality', in O. Fischer, A. Rosenbach, and D. Stein (eds), *Pathways of Change*. Amsterdam: Benjamins, 207–27.

Laury, Ritva (1997). *Demonstratives in Interaction: The Emergence of a Definite Article in Finnish*. Amsterdam: Benjamins.

Lazard, Gilbert (1999). 'Mirativity, evidentiality, mediativity, or other?', *Linguistic Typology* 3: 91–110.

——(2001). 'On the grammaticalization of evidentiality', *Journal of Pragmatics* 33: 359–67.

Ledgeway, Adam (2005). 'Moving through the left periphery: the dual complementiser system in the dialects of southern Italy', *Transactions of the Philological Society* 103: 336–96.

——(2008a). 'Satisfying V2: *sì* clauses in Old Neapolitan', *Journal of Linguistics* 44: 437–40.

——(2008b) 'The grammaticalisation of progressive and andative aspect in the dialects of Apulia', paper presented at 4th Oxford–Kobe Linguistics Seminar, 'The History and Structure of the Romance Languages', April.

——(2010). 'The clausal domain CP structure and the left periphery', in R. D'Alesssandro, A. Ledgeway, and I. Roberts (eds), *Syntactic Variation: The Dialects of Italy*. Cambridge: Cambridge University Press, 38–51.

——(2011). 'Syntactic and morphosyntactic typology and change', in M. Maiden, J. C. Smith, and A. Ledgeway (eds), *The Cambridge History of the Romance Languages*. Cambridge: Cambridge University Press, 382–471, 724–34.

Lee, Hee-Ja, and Lee, Jong-Hee (2001). *Emi Cosa Sacen* [A dictionary of endings and particles]. Seoul: Hankook.

Lee, Hee-Seung (1956). 'Concaysa "issta"ey Tayhaye: Ku Hyengthayyosolouy Palceney Tayhan Kochal' [On the verb of existence *issta*: its development into a morpheme]. *Seoul National University Journal* 17.

Lee, Hyo Sang (1991). 'Tense, aspect, and modality: a discourse-pragmatic analysis of verbal affixes in Korean from a typological perspective', PhD dissertation, University of California, Los Angeles.

——and Park, Yong-Yae (1999). 'Grammaticalization of the Korean connective *nunte/(u) nte*: a case of grammaticalization of figure–ground relation', paper presented at 'New Reflections on Grammaticalization I', Potsdam, June.

Lee, Ji Won (2008). 'On the development of *because*: a corpus-based study', in Amano Masachiyo, Michiko Ogura, and Masayuki Ohkado (eds), *Historical Englishes in Varieties of Texts and Contexts*. Frankfurt: Lang, 325–34.

Lee, Ki-Baek (1958). 'Cwukyekcosa "I"ey Tayhan Yenkwu' [A study on nominative *-i*], *Language and Literature* 2: 94–124.

Lee, Sungnyong (1958). 'Cwukyek "ka"uy Paltalkwa Ku Haysek' [The development of nominative marker *-ka* and its interpretation], *Journal of Korean Language and Literature* 19: 53–7.

——(1976). 'On the development of the doublet *is-ta / si-ta* in the 15th century Korean', *Journal of Korean Linguistics* 4: 1–23.

LEE, TAEYEONG (1987). 'A study on the grammaticalization of Korean', PhD dissertation, Chonbuk National University.

LEHMANN, CHRISTIAN (1983). 'Rektion und syntaktische Relationen', *Folia Linguistica* 17: 339–78.

——(1985). 'Grammaticalization: synchronic variation and diachronic change', *Lingua e stile* 20: 303–18.

——(1988a). 'Towards a typology of clause linkage', in Haiman and Thompson (1988: 181–225).

——(1988b). 'On the function of agreement', in Michael Barlow and Charles A. Ferguson (eds), *Agreement in Natural Language: Approaches, Theories, Descriptions*. Stanford, CA: CSLI, 55–65.

——(1989). 'Grammatikalisierung und Lexikalisierung', *Zeitschrift für Phonetik, Sprachwissenschaft und Kommunikationsforschung* 42: 11–19.

——(1992). 'Word order change by grammaticalization', in Marinel Gerritsen and Dieter Stein (eds), *Internal and External Factors in Syntactic Change*. Berlin: Mouton de Gruyter, 395–416.

——(1993). 'Theoretical implications of grammaticalization phenomena', in William A. Foley (ed.), *The Role of Theory in Language Description*. Berlin: Mouton de Gruyter, 315–40.

LEHMANN, CHRISTIAN (1995a[1982]). *Thoughts on Grammaticalization*. Munich: Lincom Europa (revision of *Thoughts on Grammaticalization: A Programmatic Sketch*, 1 (1982), Arbeiten des Kölner Universalienprojekts 49).

——(1995b). 'Synsemantika', in Joachim Jacobs, Arnim von Stechow, Wolfgang Sternefeld, and Theo Vennemann (eds), *Syntax: Ein Internationales Handbuch Zeitgenösischer Forschung*. Berlin: de Gruyter, 1251–66.

——(1995c). 'Grammaticalization: synchronic variation and diachronic change', *Lingua e stile* 20.3: 303–18.

——(2002a). 'New reflections on grammaticalization and lexicalization', in Wischer and Diewald (2002: 1–18).

——(2002b). *Thoughts on Grammaticalization*, 2nd rev. edn. Erfurt: Seminar für Sprachwissenschaft der Universität.

——(2004). 'Theory and method in grammaticalization', *Zeitschrift für Germanistische Linguistik* 32.2: 152–87. Repr. in Gabriele Diewald (ed.), *Grammatikalisierung*. Berlin: Mouton de Gruyter, 152–87.

——(2005). *Thoughts on Grammaticalization*. Munich: Lincom.

——(2008). 'Information structure and grammaticalization', in Lopez-Couso and Seoane (2008: 207–29).

LEHMANN, VOLKMAR (2004). 'Grammaticalization via extending derivation', in Walter Bisang, Nikolaus P. Himmelmann, and Björn Wiemer (eds), *What Makes Grammaticalization? A Look from its Fringes and its Components*. Berlin: Mouton de Gruyter, 169–86.

LEHMANN, WINFRED (1974). *Proto-Indo-European Syntax*. Austin: University of Texas Press.

LEINONEN, M. (2000). 'Evidentiality in Komi Zyryan', in Johanson and Utas (2000: 419–40).

LEISS, ELISABETH (2000). *Artikel und Aspekt: die grammatischen Muster von Definitheit*. Berlin: Mouton de Gruyter.

——(2007). 'Covert patterns of definiteness/indefiniteness and aspectuality in Old Icelandic, Gothic, and Old High German', in Stark et al. (2007: 73–102).

Lemmens, Maarten (2005). 'Aspectual posture verb constructions in Dutch', *Journal of Germanic Linguistics* 17: 183–217.

Lenker, Ursula, and Meurman-Solin, Anneli (eds) (2007). *Connectives in the History of English.* Amsterdam: Benjamins.

Leuschner, Torsten (2006). *Hypotaxis as Building-Site: The Emergence and Grammaticalization of Concessive Conditionals in English, German, and Dutch.* Munich: Lincom.

Levinson, Stephen C. (1983). *Pragmatics.* Cambridge: Cambridge University Press.

——(2000). *Presumptive Meanings: The Theory of Generalized Conversational Implicature.* Cambridge, MA: MIT Press.

——and Wilkins, David P. (eds) (2006). *Grammars of Space: Explorations in Cognitive Diversity.* Cambridge: Cambridge University Press.

Lewis, Charlton, and Short, Charles (1879). *A Latin Dictionary.* Oxford: Oxford University Press.

Lewis, David (1973). *Counterfactuals.* (Revised edn 1986.) Oxford: Blackwell.

Lewis, Diana (2003). 'Rhetorical motivations for the emergence of discourse particles, with special reference to English *of course*', in T. van der Wouden, A. Foolen, and P. Van de Craen (eds), *Particles*, special issue of *Belgian Journal of Linguistics* 16: 79–91.

Lewis, G. L. (1967). *Turkish Grammar.* Oxford: Oxford University Press.

Li, Charles N. (ed.) (1975). *Word Order and Word Order Change.* Austin: University of Texas Press.

——(ed.) (1976). *Subject and Topic.* New York: Academic Press.

——(ed.) (1977). *Mechanisms of Syntactic Change.* Austin: University of Texas Press.

——and Thompson, Sandra A. (1974a). 'Coverbs in Mandarin Chinese: verbs or prepositions?', *Journal of Chinese Linguistics* 2.3: 257–78.

————(1974b). 'An explanation of word order change', *Foundations of Language* 12: 211–14.

————(1976). 'Subject and topic: a new typology of language', in Li (1976: 457–89).

————(1980). *Mandarin Reference Grammar.* Berkeley: University of California Press.

————(1981). *Mandarin Chinese.* Berkeley: University of California Press.

————(1984). 'Mandarin', in W. Chisholm (ed.), *Interrogativity.* Amsterdam: Benjamins, 47–61.

————and Sawyer, Jesse O. (1977). 'Subject and word order in Wappo', *International Journal of American Linguistics* 43.2: 85–100.

Li, Lan (2006). 'Zhuo zi shi de beidong ju de gongshi fenbu yu leixing chayi' [Synchronic distribution and typological differences for passive constructions formed with *zhuo*], *Zhongguo Fangyan Xuebao* 1: 1–9.

Li, Xuping, and Bisang, Walter (forthcoming). 'Classifiers in Sinitic languages: from atomization to (in)definiteness marking'. University of Mainz.

Lichtenberk, Frantisek (1991a). 'On the gradualness of grammaticalization', in Traugott and Heine (1991a: 37–80).

——(1991b). 'Semantic change and heterosemy in grammaticalization', *Language* 67.3: 475–509.

Liddell, Scott K. (2003). *Grammar, Gesture, and Meaning in American Sign Language.* Cambridge: Cambridge University Press.

Lightfoot, David (1974). 'The diachronic analysis of English modals', in J. M. Anderson and C. Jones (eds), *Historical Linguistics*. Amsterdam: North-Holland, 219–49.

——(1979). *Principles of Diachronic Syntax*. Cambridge: Cambridge University Press.

——(1991). *How to Set Parameters*. Cambridge, MA: MIT Press.

——(1999). *The Development of Language: Acquisition, Change, and Evolution*. Oxford: Blackwell.

——(2000). 'The spandrels of the linguistic genotype', in James R. Hurford, Chris Knight, and Michael Studdert-Kennedy (eds), *The Evolutionary Emergence of Language: Social Function and the Origins of Linguistic Form*. Cambridge: Cambridge University Press, 231–47.

——(2006). *How New Languages Emerge*. Cambridge: Cambridge University Press.

Lightfoot, Douglas (2005). 'Can the lexicalization/grammaticalization distinction be reconciled?', *Studies in Language* 29.3: 583–615.

——(2006). 'Aspects of the rise and fall of the compound *gomman* in Tatian', *Leuvense Bijdragen* 95: 71–86.

——(2007). 'Co-source structures of the suffix *-tum* in German', *Southern Journal of Linguistics* 31.1: 63–79.

Lindblom, Björn, MacNeilage, Peter, and Studdert-Kennedy, Michael (1984). 'Self-organizing processes and the explanation of language universals', in Brian Butterworth, Bernard Comrie, and Östen Dahl (eds), *Explanations for Language Universals*. Berlin: de Gruyter, 181–203.

Lindquist, Hans, and Mair, Christian (eds) (2004a). *Corpus Approaches to Grammaticalization in English*. Amsterdam: Benjamins.

Lindquist, Hans and Mair, Christian (2004b). 'Introduction', in Lindquist and Mair (2004a: 9–14).

Linell, Per (2005). *The Written Language Bias in Linguistics: Its Nature, Origins and Transformations*. London: Routledge.

Linn, Mary (2000). 'A grammar of Euchee (Yuchi)', PhD dissertation, University of Kansas.

Lipka, Leonhard (2002). *English Lexicology: Lexical Structure, Word Semantics, and Word Formation*. Tübingen: Narr.

Liu, Jian, and Peyraube, Alain (1994). 'History of some coordinative constructions in Chinese', *Journal of Chinese Linguistics* 22.2: 179–201.

Liu, Shiru (1965). *Weijin Nanbeichao Liangci Yanjiu* [A study on the classifiers in the Wei and Jin dynasties]. Beijing: Zhonghua Shuju.

Liukkonen, K. (1995). '*Jo būta*', *Linguistica Baltica* 4: 209–10.

Live, Anna H. (1973). 'The *take-have* phrasal in English', *Linguistics* 95: 31–50.

Löbner, Sebastian (1985). 'Definites', *Journal of Semantics* 4: 279–326.

Loengarov, Alexander (2005). '*Le fait que*... et la question du subjonctif: la directionnalité de la grammaticalisation', *Cahiers Chronos* 12: 67–81.

——(2006). 'L'alternance indicatif/subjonctif dans les langues romanes: motivation sémantico-pragmatique et grammaticalisation', PhD dissertation, University of Leuven (KUL).

Lohndal, Terje (2009). 'Spelling out parametric variation', talk, Arizona State University.

Lombardi, Alessandra (2007). 'Definiteness and possessive constructions in medieval Italo-Romance', in A. L. Lepschy and A. Tosi (eds), *Histories and Dictionaries of the Languages of Italy*. Ravenna: Longo, 99–118.

London–Lund Corpus: see Svartvik.

Longobardi, Guiseppe (2001). 'Formal syntax, diachronic minimalism, and etymology', *Linguistic Inquiry* 32.2: 275–302.

Lope-Blanch, Juna Manuel (1990). 'Algunos usos de indicativo por subjuntivo en oraciones subordinadas', in I. Bosque (ed.), *Indicativo y subjuntivo.* Madrid: Taurus, 180–82.

Lopes, Célia Regina dos Santos (2003). *A inserção de a gente no quadro pronominal do português.* Madrid: Iberoamericana.

——and Duarte, Maria Eugênia Lamoglia (2003). 'De Vossa Mercê a você: análise da pronominalização de nominais em peças brasileiras e portuguesas setecentistas e oitocentistas', in S. F. Brandão and M. A. Mota (eds), *Análise contrastiva de variedades do português: primeiros estudos*, vol. 1. Rio de Janeiro: In-Folio, 61–76.

López-Couso, Maria José, and Seoane, Elena (eds) (2008). *Rethinking Grammaticalization.* Amsterdam: Benjamins.

Lord, Carol (1976). 'Evidence for syntactic reanalysis: from verb to complementizer in Kwa', in Sanford B. Steever, Carol A. Walker, and Salikoko S. Mufwene (eds), *Papers from the Parasession on Diachronic Syntax*, 22 April, Chicago Linguistic Society, 179–91.

——(1993) *Historical Change in Serial Verb Constructions.* Amsterdam: Benjamins.

Los, Bettelou (2005). *The Rise of the* to-*Infinitive.* Oxford: Oxford University Press.

——(2009). 'The consequences of the loss of verb-second in English: information structure and syntax in interaction', *English Language and Linguistics* 13: 97–125.

Luís, Ana R. (2009). 'Patterns of clitic placement: evidence from "mixed" clitic systems', in Patience Epps and Alexandre Arkhipov (eds), *New challenges in Typology: Transcending the Borders and Refining the Distinctions.* Berlin: de Gruyter, 11–34.

Lunkenheimer, Kerstin (in press). 'Tense and aspect', in Raymond Hickey (ed.), *Areal Features in the Anglophone World.* Berlin: Mouton de Gruyter.

Luraghi, Silvia (1990). *Old Hittite Sentence Structure.* London: Routledge.

——(2001a). 'The development of local particles and adverbs in Anatolian as a grammaticalization process', *Diachronica* 18.1: 31–58.

——(2001b). 'Syncretism and the classification of semantic roles', *Sprachtypologie und Universalienforschung* 54.1: 35–51.

Lyons, Christopher (1986). 'On the origin of the Old French strong–weak possessive distinction', *Transactions of the Philological Society* 84: 1–41.

——(1999). *Definiteness.* Cambridge: Cambridge University Press.

Lyons, John (1977). *Semantics.* 2 vols. Cambridge: Cambridge University Press.

——(1995). *Linguistic Semantics: An Introduction.* Cambridge: Cambridge University Press.

Macaulay, Donald (1992). 'The Scottish Gaelic language', in Donald MacAulay (ed.), *The Celtic Languages.* Cambridge: Cambridge University Press, 137–248.

Macaulay, Ronald K. S. (2005). *Talk that Counts: Age, Gender, and Social Class Differences in Discourse.* Oxford: Oxford University Press.

——(2006). 'Pure grammaticalization: the development of a teenage intensifier', *Language Variation and Change* 18: 267–83.

MacDonald, Lorna (1990). *A Grammar of Tauya.* Berlin: Mouton de Gruyter.

Maiden, Martin (1995). *A Linguistic History of Italian.* London: Longman.

Mair, Christian (1997). 'The spread of the *going-to*-future in written English: a corpus-based investigation into language change in progress', in Raymond Hickey and Stanisław Puppel (eds), *Language History and Linguistic Modelling.* Berlin: Mouton de Gruyter, 1537–43.

——(2004). 'Corpus linguistics and grammaticalisation theory', in Lindquist and Mair (2004a: 121–50).

——(2006) *Twentieth Century English: History, Variation and Standardization*. Cambridge: Cambridge University Press.

——(forthcoming). 'Using "small" corpora of written and spoken English to document ongoing grammatical change: the case of specificational clefts in 20th century English', in Manfred Krug and Julia Schlüter (eds), *Research Methods in Language Variation and Change*. Cambridge: Cambridge University Press.

Majsak, Timur A. (2005). *Tipologija grammatikalizacii konstrukcij s glagolami dviženija i glagolami pozicii*. Moscow: Jazyki slavjanskix kul'tur.

Malchukov, Andrej L. (2004). 'Towards a semantic typology of adversative and contrast marking', *Journal of Semantics* 21.2: 177–198.

——(2010). 'Analyzing semantic maps: a multifactorial approach', *Linguistic Discovery* 8.1: 176–98.

——Haspelmath, Martin, and Comrie, Bernard (to appear). 'Ditransitive constructions: a typological overview', in Andrej Malchukov, Martin Haspelmath, and Bernard Comrie (eds), *Studies in Ditransitive Constructions*. Berlin: Mouton de Gruyter.

——and Narrog, H. (2008). 'Case polysemy', in Malchukov and Spencer (2008: 518–35).

——and Spencer, Andrew (eds) 2008. *The Oxford Handbook of Case*. Oxford: Oxford University Press.

Maler, Bertil (ed.) (1956). *Orto do esposo. Texto inédito do fim do século XIV ou começo do XV. Edição crítica com introdução, anotações e glossário*. Rio de Janeiro: Instituto Nacional do Livro.

Malkiel, Yakov (1974). 'Distinctive traits of Romance linguistics', in F. Hymes (ed.), *Language in Culture and Society: A Reader in Linguistics and Anthropology*. New York: Harper & Row, 671–88.

Malone, Terrell (1988). 'The origin and development of Tuyuca evidentials', *International Journal of American Linguistics* 54: 119–40.

Mao, Bingsheng (1999). 'Hengshan fangyan (Qianshan hua) de jieci' [Coverbs in the Hengshan Qianshan dialect], in Wu Yunji (ed.), *Hunan fangyan de jieci* [Coverbs in Hunan dialects]. Changsha: Hunan Shifan Daxue Chubanshe, 264–77.

Marchello-Nizia, Christiane (1995). *L'évolution du français: ordre des mots, démonstratifs, accent tonique*. Paris: Armand Colin.

——(2006a). *Grammaticalisation et changement linguistique*. Bruxelles: De Boeck.

——(2006b). 'From personal deixis to spatial deixis: the semantic evolution of demonstratives from Latin to French', in M. Hickmann and S. Robert (eds), *Space in Languages*. Amsterdam: Benjamins, 103–20.

——(2009). 'Word order from Latin to French: a case of grammaticalization or of typological coherence?', *Studies in Pragmatics* 5: 1–18.

Marconi, D., and Bertinetto, P. M. (1984). 'Analisi di *ma*', *Lingua e stile* 19: 223–58, 475–509.

Martineau, France, and Mougeon, Raymond (2003). 'A sociolinguistic study of the origins of *ne* deletion in European and Quebec French', *Language* 79.1: 118–52.

Martinet, André (1967). 'Que faut-il entendre par "fonction des affixes de classe"?', in *La classification nominale dans les langues négro-africaines*. Paris: CNRS, 15–25.

Matlock, Teenie (2001). 'How real is fictive motion?', doctoral dissertation, University of California, Santa Cruz.

Matras, Yaron (1994). *Untersuchungen zu Grammatik und Diskurs des Romanes-Dialekt der Kelderaša/Lovara.* Wiesbaden: Harrassowitz.

——(1996). 'Prozedurale Fusion: Grammatische Interferenzschichten im Romanes', *Sprachtypologie und Universalienforschung* 49.1, 60–78.

——(1998a). 'Convergent development, grammaticalization, and the problem of "mutual isomorphism"', in W. Boeder, C. Schroeder, and K.-H. Wagner (eds), *Sprache in Raum und Zeit.* Tübingen: Narr, 89–103.

——(1998b). 'Utterance modifiers and universals of grammatical borrowing', *Linguistics* 36.2: 281–331.

——(2002). *Romani: A Linguistic Introduction.* Cambridge: Cambridge University Press.

——(2009). *Language Contact.* Cambridge: Cambridge University Press.

——and Sakel, Jeanette (2007). 'Investigating the mechanism of pattern replication in language convergence', *Studies in Language* 31: 829–65.

Matsumoto, Meiko (2008). *From Simple Verbs to Periphrastic Expressions.* Bern: Lang.

Matsumoto, Yo (1988). 'From bound grammatical markers to free discourse markers: history of some Japanese connectives', in Shelley Axmaker et al. (eds), *Proceedings of the Fourteenth Annual Meeting of the Berkeley Linguistic Society, February 13–15, 1988. General Session and Parasession on Grammaticalization,* 340–51.

——(1998). 'Semantic change in the grammaticalization of verbs into postpositions in Japanese', in Toshio Ohori (ed.), *Studies in Japanese Grammaticalization.* Tokyo: Kuroshio, 25–60.

Matteson, Esther (1965). *The Piro (Arawakan) Language.* Berkeley: University of California Publications in Linguistics.

Matthews, George Hubert (1965). *Hidatsa Syntax.* The Hague: Mouton.

Matthews, Peter (2001). *A Short History of Structural Linguistics.* Cambridge: Cambridge University Press.

Matthews, Stephen, and Yip, Virginia (1994). *Cantonese: A Comprehensive Grammar.* London: Routledge.

Mauri, Caterina (2008a). 'The irreality of alternatives: towards a typology of disjunction', *Studies in Language* 32.1: 22–55.

——(2008b). *Coordination Relations in the Languages of Europe and Beyond.* Berlin: Mouton de Gruyter.

——(2010). 'Semantic maps or coding maps? Towards a unified account of the coding degree, coding complexity and coding distance of coordination relations', *Linguistic Discovery* 8.1: 210–32.

——and Giacalone Ramat, Anna (2009). 'The grammaticalization of interclausal connectives: the case of adversatives', talk presented at the 19th International Conference on Historical Linguistics, Nijmegen, 10–15 August.

————(submitted). 'The development of adversative connectives: stages and factors at play'.

Mayer, Elisabeth (2003). 'Clitic doubling in Limeño'. Australian National University.

Mazzon, Gabriella (2004). *A History of English Negation.* Harlow: Pearson Education.

McClave, Evelyn Z. (2000). 'Linguistic functions of head movements in the context of speech', *Journal of Pragmatics* 32: 855–78.

McDonough, Joyce (2000). 'The bipartite structure of the Navajo verb', in Theodore Fernald and Paul Platero (eds), *The Athabaskan Languages: Perspectives on a Native American Language Family.* Oxford: Oxford University Press, 139–66.

McLendon, Sally (2003). 'Evidentials in Eastern Pomo with a comparative survey of the category in other Pomoan languages', in Aikhenvald and Dixon (2003: 101–30).

McMahon, April M. S. (1994). *Understanding Language Change.* Cambridge: Cambridge University Press.

——(2006). 'Restructuring Renaissance English', in L. Mugglestone (ed.), *The Oxford History of English.* Oxford: Oxford University Press, 147–77.

McWhorter, John H. (2001). 'The world's simplest grammars are creole grammars', *Linguistic Typology* 5.2–3: 125–66.

——(2002). 'What happened to English?', *Diachronica* 19: 217–72.

MED: Middle English Dictionary (2001), ed. Hans Kurath, Robert E. Lewis, et al. Ann Arbor: University of Michigan Press.

Mehler, Jacques, Peña, Marcela, Nespor, Marina, and Bonatti, Luca (2006). 'The "soul" of language does not use statistics: reflections on vowels and consonants', *Cortex* 42: 846–54.

Mei, Tsu-lin (1990). 'Tang-Song chuzhishi de laiyuan' [Origin of the disposal form in the Tang and Song periods], *Zhongguo Yuwen* 3: 191–216.

Meier, Richard (forthcoming). 'Language and modality', in R. Pfau, M. Steinbach, and B. Woll (eds), *Sign Language.* Berlin: Mouton de Gruyter.

Meillet, Antoine (1912). 'L'évolution des formes grammaticales', *Scientia* (*Rivista di scienza*) 12.6: 384–400. Repr. in Meillet (1958: 130–48).

——(1915–16). 'Le renouvellement des conjonctions', *Annuaire de l'École Pratique des Hautes Études.* Repr. in Meillet (1958: 159–74).

——(1958[1921]). *Linguistique historique et linguistique générale.* Paris: Champion.

Meir, Irit (1999). 'A perfect marker in Israeli Sign Language', *Sign Language and Linguistics* 2: 43–62.

——(2002). 'A cross-modality merspective on verb agreement', *Natural Language and Linguistic Theory* 20: 413–50.

Mel'čuk, Igor A. (1976). 'On suppletion', *Linguistics* 170: 45–90.

Merlan, Aurelia (2006). 'Grammatikalisierungstendenzen im Portugiesischen und Rumänischen: von Nominalsyntagmen zu Pronomina', in Jürgen Schmidt-Radefeldt (ed.), *Portugiesisch kontrastiv gesehen und Anglizismen weltweit.* Frankfurt: Lang, 221–40.

Metslang, Helle, and Pajusalu, Karl (2002). 'Evidentiality in South Estonian', *Linguistica Uralica* 2: 98–109.

Meulleman, Machteld (in press). *Les localisateurs dans les constructions existentielles. Approche comparée en espagnol, en français et en italien.* Tübingen: Niemeyer.

Mey, Jacob L. (2001). *Pragmatics: An Introduction*, 2nd edn. Oxford: Blackwell.

Michaelis, Laura (2004). 'Type shifting in construction grammar: an integrated approach to aspectual coercion', *Cognitive Linguistics* 15: 1–67.

Miestamo, Matti (2005). *Standard Negation: The Negation of Declarative Verbal Main Clauses in a Typological Perspective.* Berlin: Mouton de Gruyter.

——Sinnemäki, Kaius, and Karlsson, Fred (2008). *Language Complexity: Typology, Contact, Change.* Amsterdam: Benjamins.

Migge, B., and Winford, Donald (2007). 'Substrate influence on the emergence of the TMA systems of the Surinamese creoles', *Journal of Pidgin and Creole Languages* 22: 73–99.

Milićević, Jasmina (2005). 'Clitics or affixes? On the morphological status of the future-tense markers in Serbian', in Wolfgang Dressler, Dieter Kastovsky, Oskar E. Pfeiffer, and

Franz Rainer (eds), *Morphology and its Demarcations: Selected Papers from the 11th Morphology Meeting, Vienna, February 2004.* Amsterdam: Benjamins, 39–52.

Miller, Amy (2001). *A Grammar of Jamul Tiipay.* Berlin: Mouton de Gruyter.

Miller, Marion (1999). *Desano grammar.* Arlington, TX: Summer Institute of Linguistics and University of Arlington Publication in Linguistics.

Miller, Philip (1992). 'Postlexical cliticization vs. affixation: coordination criteria', *Chicago Linguistic Society* 28: 382–96.

Milroy, James, and Milroy, Lesley (1985). 'Linguistic change, social network and speaker innovation', *Journal of Linguistics* 21: 339–84.

Milroy, Lesley (1999). 'Standard English and language ideology in Britain and the United States', in Tony Bex and Richard J. Watts (eds), *Standard English: The Widening Debate.* London: Routledge, 173–206.

Mithen, Steven (2005). *The Singing Neanderthals: The Origins of Music, Language, Mind and Body.* London: Weidenfeld & Nicolson.

Mithun, Marianne (1984). 'The evolution of noun incorporation', *Language* 60: 847–94.

——(1988) 'The grammaticization of coordination', in Haiman and Thompson (1988: 331–59).

——(1991). 'The development of bound pronominal paradigms', in Winfred Lehmann and Helen-Jo Jakusz Hewitt (eds), *Language Typology 1988.* Amsterdam: Benjamins, 85–104.

——(1995). 'On the relativity of irreality', in Bybee and Fleischman (1995: 367–88).

——(1997). 'Lexical affixes and morphological typology', in Joan Bybee, John Haiman, and Sandra Thompson (eds), *Essays on Language Function and Language Type.* Amsterdam: Benjamins, 357–71.

——(2001). 'Lexical forces shaping the evolution of grammar', in Laurel J. Brinton (ed.), *Historical Linguistics 1999.* Amsterdam: Benjamins, 241–52.

——(2008). 'The extension of dependency beyond the sentence', *Language* 83: 69–119.

Moore, Colette (2007). 'The spread of grammaticalized forms: the case of *be+supposed to*', *Journal of English Linguistics* 35.2: 117–31.

Moralejo-Gárate, Teresa (2001). 'Composite predicates and idiomatisation in Middle English: a corpus-based approach', *Studia Anglica Posnaniensia* 36: 171–87.

Moravcsik, Edith A. (1969). 'Determination', *Working Papers on Language Universals* 1: 63–98.

——(1972). 'On case markers and complementizers', *Working Papers on Language Universals* 8: 151–52.

——(2003). 'Inflectional morphology in the Hungarian noun phrase: a typological assessment', in Frans Plank (ed.), *Noun Phrase Structure in the Languages of Europe.* Berlin: Mouton de Gruyter, 113–252.

Mori, Junko (1999a). *Negotiating Agreement and Disagreement in Japanese: Connective Expressions and Turn Construction.* Philadelphia: Benjamins.

——(1999b). '"Well I may be exaggerating but . . . ": self-qualifying clauses in negotiating of opinions among Japanese speakers', *Human Studies* 22: 447–73.

Mortelmans, Jesse (2008). 'Grammaticalisation analogue de marqueurs de focalisation en latin tardif et en moyen français', *L'information grammaticale* 118: 44–8.

Mortelmans, Tanja (2004). 'Grammatikalisierung und Subjektivierung: Traugott und Langacker revisited', *Zeitschrift für germanistische Linguistik: deutsche Sprache in Gegenwart und Geschichte* 32: 188–209.

Mortier, Liesbeth (2007). 'Perspectives on grammaticalization and speakers' involvement: the case of progressive and continuative periphrases in French and Dutch', PhD dissertation, University of Leuven (KUL).

Mowrey, Richard, and Pagliuca, William (1995). 'The reductive character of articulatory evolution', *Rivista di linguistica* 7.1: 37–124.

Mufwene, Salikoko (2008). *Language Evolution: Contact, Competition and Change.* London: Continuum.

Mulder, Jean, and Thompson, Sandra A. (2008). 'The grammaticization of *but* as a final particle in English conversation', in Ritva Laury (ed.), *Crosslinguistic Studies of Clause Combining: the Multifunctionality of Conjunctions.* Amsterdam: Benjamins, 179–204.

————and Williams, Cara Penry (2009). 'Final *but* in Australian English conversation', in Pam Peters, Peter Collins, and Adam Smith (eds), *Comparative Grammatical Studies in Australian and NewZealand English.* Amsterdam: Benjamins, 337–58.

Müller, Wolfgang G., and Fischer, Olga (2003). *From Sign to Signing: Iconicity in Language and Literature* 3. Amsterdam: Benjamins.

Myhill, John (1988). 'The grammaticalization of auxiliaries: Spanish clitic climbing', *Berkeley Linguistics Society* 14: 352–63.

Nagata, Takashi (2006). *A Historical Study of Referent Honorifics in Japanese.* Tokyo: Hituzi Syobo.

Nagy, Katalin (2010). 'The pragmatics of grammaticalisation: the role of implicatures in semantic change', *Journal of Historical Pragmatics* 11: 67–95.

Nahkola, Kari, and Saanilahti, Marja (2004). 'Mapping language changes in real time: a panel study on Finnish', *Language Variation and Change* 16: 75–92.

Nakayama, Toshihide, and Ichihashi-Nakayama, Kumiko (1997). 'Japanese *kedo*: Discourse genre and grammaticization', in Ho-min Sohn and John Haig (eds), *Japanese Korean Linguistics* 6. Stanford: CSLI, 607–19.

Narrog, Heiko (2004). 'From transitive to causative in Japanese: morphologization through exaptation', *Diachronica* 21.2: 351–92.

——(2005a). 'On defining modality again', *Language Sciences* 27: 165–92.

——(2005b). 'Modality, mood, and change of modal meanings: a new perspective', *Cognitive Linguistics* 16.4, 677–731.

——(2005c). 'Nihongo no bunpōka no keitaiteki sokumen' [The morphological aspect of grammaticalization in Japanese], *Nihongo no Kenkyū* 1.3: 108–22.

——(2007a). 'Exaptation, grammaticalization, and reanalysis', *California Linguistic Notes* 32.1: 1–26.

——(2007b). 'Modality and grammaticalization in Japanese', *Journal of Historical Pragmatics* 8.2: 269–94.

——(2009a). *Modality in Japanese: The Layered Structure of the Clause and Hierarchies of Functional Categories.* Amsterdam: Benjamins.

——(2009b). 'Varieties of instrumental', in Malchukov and Spencer (2009: 593–601).

——(2010a). 'The order of meaningful elements in the Japanese verbal complex', *Morphology* 20 (special issue on affix ordering): 205–237.

——(2010b). 'A diachronic dimension in maps of case functions', *Linguistic Discovery* 8.1: 233–54.

——and Ito, Shinya (2007). 'Reconstructing semantic maps: the comitative-instrumental area', *Sprachtypologie und Universalienforschung* 60.4: 273–92.

Nau, Nicole (1995). *Möglichkeiten und Mechanismen kontaktbewegten Sprachwandels- unter besonderer Berücksichtigung des Finnischen.* Munich: Lincom.

Nedjalkov, Igor' V. (1993). 'Causative-passive polysemy of the Manchu-Tungusic *-bul-v(u)*', *Linguistica Antverpiensa* 27: 193–202.

Nedjalkov, Vladimir P. (ed.) (1988). *Typology of Resultative Constructions.* Amsterdam: Benjamins.

Neidle, Carol, Kegl, Judy, MacLaughlin, Dawn, Bahan, Ben, and Lee, Robert G. (2000). *The Syntax of American Sign Language: Functional Categories and Hierarchical Structure.* Cambridge, MA: MIT Press.

Nelson, Gerald, Wallis, Sean, and Aarts, Bas (2002). *Exploring Natural Language: Working with the British Component of the International Corpus of English.* Amsterdam: Benjamins.

Nevalainen, Terttu (1997). 'The processes of adverb derivation in Late Middle and Early Modern English', in Matti Rissanen, Merja Kytö, and Kirsi Heikkonen (eds), *Grammaticalization at Work: Studies of Long-Term Developments in English.* Berlin: Mouton de Gruyter, 145–90.

——(2008). 'Social variation in intensifier use: constraint on *-ly* adverbialization?', *English Language and Linguistics* 12.2: 289–315.

——and Raumolin-Brunberg, Helena (2003). *Historical Sociolinguistics: Language Change in Tudor and Stuart England.* London: Pearson Education.

————and Mannila, Heikki (2011). 'The diffusion of language change in real time: progressive and conservative individuals and the time-depth of change', *Language Variation and Change* 23.1.

Nevis, Joel A. (1986). 'Decliticization and deaffixation in Saame: abessive *taga*', in Brian D. Joseph (ed.), *Studies on Language Change* (= *Ohio State University Working Papers in Linguistics*) 34: 1–9.

Newman, John (1996). *Give: A Cognitive Linguistic Study.* Berlin: Mouton de Gruyter.

——(ed.) (2002). *The Linguistics of Sitting, Standing, and Lying.* Amsterdam: Benjamins.

Newman, Paul (2000). *The Hausa Language: An Encyclopedic Reference Grammar.* New Haven, CT: Yale University Press.

Newmeyer, Frederick J. (1998). *Language Form and Language Function.* Cambridge, MA: MIT Press.

——(2000). 'The discrete nature of syntactic categories: against a prototype-based account', in Robert Borsley (ed.), *The Nature and Function of Syntactic Categories.* San Diego, CA: Academic Press, 221–50.

——(2001). 'Deconstructing grammaticalization', *Language Sciences* 23.2–3 (special issue, *Grammaticalization: A Critical Assessment*, ed. Lyle Campbell): 187–230.

——(2006). 'What can grammaticalization tell us about the origins of language?', in Angelo Cangelosi, Andrew D. M. Smith, and Kenny Smith (eds), *The Evolution of Language,* Proceedings of the 6th International Conference (EVOLANG6), Rome. World Scientific, 484–5.

Nicolle, Steve (1998a). 'A relevance theory perspective on grammaticalization', *Cognitive Linguistics* 9: 1–35.

——(1998b). '*Be going to* and *will*: a monosemous account', *English Language and Linguistics* 2: 223–43.

——(2007). 'The grammaticalization of tense markers: a pragmatic reanalysis', in L. de Saussure, J. Moeschler, and G. Puskas (eds), *Tense, Mood and Aspect: Theoretical and Descriptive Issues.* Amsterdam: Rodopi, 47–65.

——(2009). '*Go-and*-V, *come-and*-V, *go*-V and *come*-V: a corpus-based account of deictic movement verb constructions', *English Text Construction* 2: 185–208.

——and Clark, Billy (1999). 'Experimental pragmatics and what is said: a response to Gibbs and Moise', *Cognition* 69: 337–54.

Nihon Kokugo Daijiten [Great dictionary of Japanese], 2nd edn, 2000–2002. Tokyo: Shogakukan.

Nikolaeva, Irina, and Tolskaya, Maria (2001). *A Grammar of Udihe.* Berlin: Mouton de Gruyter.

Nitsch, Kazimierz (1960). *Wybór polskich tekstów gwarowych*, 2nd edn. Warsaw: Państwowe Wydawnictwo Naukowe.

Nocentini, Alberto (1990). 'L'uso dei dimostrativi nella *Peregrinatio Egeriae* e la genesi dell'articolo romanzo', in *Atti del convegno internazionale sulla Peregrinatio Egeriae.* Arezzo: Accademia Petrarca di Lettere e Arti e Scienze, 137–58.

Noël, Dirk (2005). 'The productivity of a "source of information" construction: or, where grammaticalization theory and construction grammar meet', paper given at the Fitigra Conference, Leuven, February.

——(2006). 'Diachronic construction grammar vs. grammaticalization theory', *Preprints of the Department of Linguistics* 255. Leuven: Department of Linguistics.

——(2007). 'Diachronic construction grammar and grammaticalization theory', *Functions of Language* 14.2: 177–202.

Noonan, Michael (1997). 'Versatile nominalizations', in Joan Bybee, John Haiman, and Sandra A. Thompson (eds), *Essays on Language Function and Language Type.* Amsterdam: Benjamins, 373–94.

Noonan, Michael (2007). 'Complementation', in Shopen (2007: 52–150).

——(2008a). 'Case compounding in the Bodic languages', in Corbett and Noonan (2008: 127–48).

——(2008b). 'Nominalizations in Bodic languages', in López-Couso and Seoane (2008: 219–37).

Norde, Muriel (1997). 'The history of the genitive in Swedish: a case study in degrammaticalization', PhD thesis, University of Amsterdam.

——(2001). 'Deflexion as a counterdirectional factor in grammatical change', *Language Sciences* 23.2–3: 231–64.

——(2002). 'The final stages of grammaticalization: affixhood and beyond', in Wischer and Diewald (2002: 45–65).

——(2006a). 'Demarcating degrammaticalization: the Swedish s-genitive revisited', *Nordic Journal of Linguistics* 29.2: 201–38.

——(2006b). 'Van suffix tot telwoord tot bijwoord: degrammaticalisering en (re)grammaticalisering van *tig*', *TABU* 35.1–2: 33–60.

——(2009a). *Degrammaticalization.* Oxford: Oxford University Press.

——(2009b). Review of Brinton and Traugott, *Lexicalization and Language Change*, *Language* 85.1: 184–86.

——(forthcoming). 'Lehmann's parameters revisited', in Tine Breban, Liselotte Brems, Kristin Davidse, and Tanja Mortelmans (eds), *Grammaticalization and Language Change: Origins, Criteria, and Outcomes.* Amsterdam: Benjamins.

——and Trousdale, Graeme (2009). 'Morpheme-based and construction-based approaches to degrammaticalization', paper presented at International Conference on Historical Linguistics 19, Nijmegen.

Nordlinger, Rachel (1998). *A Grammar of Wambaya, Northern Territory (Australia).* Canberra: Pacific Linguistics.

——and Traugott, Elizabeth Closs (1997). 'Scope and the development of epistemic modality: evidence from *ought to*', *English Language and Linguistics* 1: 295–317.

Nørgård-Sørensen, Jens, Heltoft, Lars, and Schøsler, Lene (eds) (2011). *Connecting Grammaticalisation: The Role of Paradigmatic Structure.* Amsterdam: Benjamins.

Nübling, Damaris (2005). 'Von *in die* über *in'n* und ins bis *im*: die Klitisierung von Präposition und Artikel als "Grammatikalisierungsbaustelle"', in Torsten Leuschner, Tanja Mortelmans, and Sarah De Groodt (eds), *Grammatikalisierung im Deutschen.* Berlin: de Gruyter, 105–31.

Nunberg, Geoffrey, Sag, Ivan A., and Wasow, Thomas (1994). 'Idioms', *Language* 70: 491–538.

Nurmi, Arja (1999). *A Social History of Periphrastic* do. Helsinki: Société Néophilologique.

——(2002). 'Does size matter? The *Corpus of Early English Correspondence* and its sampler', in Helena Raumolin-Brunberg, Minna Nevala, Arja Nurmi, and Matti Rissanen (eds), *Variation Past and Present.* Helsinki: Société Néophilologique, 173–84.

——Nevala, Minna, and Palander-Collin, Minna (eds) (2009). *The Language of Daily Life in England (1450–800).* Amsterdam: Benjamins.

Nuyts, Jan (2001a). *Epistemic Modality, Language, and Conceptualization: A Cognitive-Pragmatic Perspective.* Amsterdam: Benjamins.

——(2001b). 'Subjectivity as an evidential dimension in epistemic modal expressions', *Journal of Pragmatics* 33.3: 383–400.

——(2006). 'Modality: overview and linguistic issues', in Frawley (2006: 1–26).

Ochs Keenan, Elinor, and Bambi Schieffelin (1976). 'Foregrounding referents: a reconsideration of left dislocation in discourse', *Proceedings of the Berkeley Linguistics Society* 2: 240–57.

OED: *Oxford English Dictionary* (2000–). 3rd edn online, editor-in-chief John Simpson. Oxford: Oxford University Press.

Ogawa, Akio (2008). 'Case in a topic-prominent language: pragmatic and syntactic functions of cases in Japanese', im Malchukov and Spencer (2008: 779–88).

Oh, Sang-suk (1998). 'A syntactic and semantic study of Korean auxiliaries: a grammaticalization perspective', PhD dissertation, University of Hawaii at Manoa.

Ohala, John J. (1984). 'An ethological perspective on common cross-language utilisation of Fo in voice', *Phonetica* 41: 1–16.

——(1989). 'Sound change is drawn from a pool of synchronic variation', in Leiv Egil Breivik and Ernst Håkon Jahr (eds), *Language Change: Contributions to the Study of its Causes.* Berlin: Mouton de Gruyter, 173–98.

Ohori, Toshio (1992). 'Diachrony in clause linkage and related issues', PhD, University of California, Berkeley.

——(1994). 'Diachrony of clause linkage: te and ba in Old through Middle Japanese', in Pagliuca (1994: 135–49).

——(1995). 'Remarks on suspended clauses: a contribution to Japanese phraseology', in Masayoshi Shibatani and Sandra A. Thompson (eds), *Essays in Semantics and Pragmatics in Honor of Charles J. Fillmore.* Amsterdam: Benjamins, 201–18.

——(1996). 'Case markers and clause linkage: toward a semantic typology', in Eugene Casad (ed.), *Cognitive Linguistics in the Redwoods: The Expansion of a New Paradigm in Linguistics*. Berlin: Mouton de Gruyter, 693–712.

——(1998a). 'Polysemy and paradigmatic change in the Japanese conditional marker *ba*', in Ohori (1998b: 135–62).

——(1998b). *Studies in Japanese: Grammaticalization. Cognitive and Discourse Perspectives.* Tokyo: Kurosio Syuppan.

——(2000). 'Framing effect in Japanese non-final clauses: toward an optimal grammar–-pragmatics interface', in Matthew L. Juge and Jeri L. Moxley (eds), *Proceedings of the Twenty-third Annual Meeting of the Berkeley Linguistic Society, February 14–17, 1997: General Session and Parasession on Pragmatics and Grammatical Structure*, 471–80.

——(2001). 'Clause integration as grammaticalization: a case from Japanese *tokoro*-complements', in Kaoru Horie and Shigeru Sato (eds), *Cognitive-Functional Linguistics in an East Asian Context*. Tokyo: Kurosio Syuppan, 279–301.

Okamoto, Shigeko (1995). 'Pragmaticization of meaning in some sentence-final particles in Japanese', in Masayoshi Shibatani and Sandra A. Thompson (eds), *Essays on Semantics and Pragmatics*. Amsterdam: Benjamins, 219–46.

Olbertz, Hella (1993). 'The grammaticalization of Spanish *haber* plus participle', in Jaap van Marle (ed.), *Historical Linguistics 1991: Papers from the 10th International Conference on Historical Linguistics*. Amsterdam: Benjamins, 243–63.

——(1998). *Verbal Periphrases in a Functional Grammar of Spanish*. Berlin: Mouton de Gruyter.

——(2005). '*Dizque* en el español andino ecuatoriano: conservador e innovador', in Hella Olbertz and Pieter Muysken (eds), *Encuentros y conflictos: bilingüismo y contacto de lenguas en el mundo andino*. Madrid: Iberoamericana, 77–94.

Olbertz, Hella (2007). 'Dizque in Mexican Spanish: the subjectification of reportative meaning', *Rivista di linguistica* 19: 151–72.

Olofsson, Arne (1990). 'A participle caught in the act: on the prepositional use of *following*', *Studia Neophilologica* 62: 23–35, 129–49.

Olsson, Yngve (1961). *On the Syntax of the English Verb, with Special Reference to 'have a look' and Similar Complex Structures*. Göteborg: Elanders Boktryckeri Aktiebolag.

Oniga, Renato (2004). *Il latino: breve introduzione linguistica*. Milan: Angeli.

Ono, Tsuyoshi, and Thompson, Sandra A. (1994). 'Unattached NPs in English conversation', *Berkeley Linguistics Society* 20: 402–19.

Onodera, Noriko Okada (1995). 'Diachronic analysis of Japanese discourse markers', in Andreas H. Jucker (ed.), *Historical Pragmatics*. Amsterdam: Benjamins, 393–437.

——(1998). 'Frame-shift markers in English: an analysis of *so* and *anyway*', in College of Literature, Aoyama Gakuin University (ed.), *Bungakubu Kiyoo* [Bulletin for College of Literature] 40. Tokyo: College of Literature, Aoyama Gakuin University, 13–26.

——(2004). *Japanese Discourse Markers: Synchronic and Diachronic Discourse Analysis*. Amsterdam: Benjamins.

——(2007) 'Interplay of (inter)subjectivity and social norms', *Journal of Historical Pragmatics* 8.2: 269–94.

——and Suzuki, Ryoko (eds) (2007). *Historical Changes in Japanese: Subjectivity and Intersubjectivitiy. Journal of Historical Pragmatics* 8.2 (special issue).

Pagliuca, William (ed.) (1994). *Perspectives on Grammaticalization*. Amsterdam: Benjamins.

PALANCAR, ENRIQUE L. (2002). *The Origin of Agent Markers*. Berlin: Akademie.

PALANDER-COLLIN, MINNA (1999). *Grammaticalization and Social Embedding: I THINK and METHINKS in Middle and Early Modern English*. Helsinki: Société Néophilologique.

——(2009). 'Variation and change in patterns of self-reference in Early English correspondence', *Journal of Historical Pragmatics* 10.2: 260–85.

PALMER, FRANK R. (1986[2001]). *Mood and Modality*. Cambridge: Cambridge University Press.

——(2003) 'Modality in English: theoretical, descriptive and typological issues', in Roberta Facchinetti, Manfred Krug, and Frank Palmer (eds), *Modality in Contemporary English*. Berlin: Mouton de Gruyter, 1–17.

PARK, JOO YOUNG (1999). 'A study of grammaticalization of *kut*', MA thesis, Sangmyung University.

PARRY, MAIR, and LOMBARDI, ALESSANDRA (2007). 'The interaction of semantics, pragmatics and syntax in the spread of the articles in the early vernaculars of Italy', in A. L. Lepschy and A. Tosi (eds), *Histories and Dictionaries of the Languages of Italy*. Ravenna: Longo, 77–97.

PATTEN, AMANDA L. (2010a). 'Grammaticalization and the *it*-cleft construction', in Graeme Trousdale and Elizabeth Traugott (eds), *Gradualness, Gradience and Grammaticalization*. Amsterdam: Benjamins.

——(2010b). 'Cleft sentences, construction grammar and grammaticalization', PhD thesis, University of Edinburgh.

PAUL, HERMANN (1920). *Prinzipien der Sprachgeschichte*, 5th edn. Halle: Niemeyer.

PAYNE, JOHN R. (1985). 'Negation', in Shopen (1985: 197–242).

PENNANEN, ESKO V. (1966). *Contributions to the Study of Back-Formation in English*. Tampere: Yhteiskunnallinen Korkeakoulu.

PERRIN, LOÏC-MICHEL (2010). 'Polysemous qualities and universal networks, invariance and diversity', *Linguistic Discovery* 8.1: 259–80.

PERROT, J. R. (1996). 'Un médiatif ouralien: l'auditif en Samoyède Nenets', in Guentchéva (1996: 157–68).

PETERS, ANN M. (1985). 'Language segmentation: operating principles for the perception and analysis of language', in Dan I. Slobin (ed.), *The Crosslinguistic study of Language Acquisition*, vol. 2: *Theoretical Issues*. Mahwah, NJ: Erlbaum, 1029–67.

PETERSON, DAVID A. (2003). 'Hakha Lai', in Graham Thurgood and R. J. LaPuta (eds), *The Sino-Tibetan Languages*. London: Routledge, 409–26.

PEYRAUBE, ALAIN (1988). *Syntaxe diachronique du chinois: évolution des constructions datives du 14ème siècle avant J.-C. au 18ème siècle*. Paris: Collège de France.

——(1989a). 'Zaoqi "ba" ziju de jige wenti' [Several issues regarding early *ba* sentences], *Yuwen Yanjiu* 1: 1–9.

——(1989b). 'History of the passive construction until the 10th century', *Journal of Chinese Linguistics* 17.2: 335–71.

——(1998). 'On the history of classifiers in Archaic and Medieval Chinese', in B. T'sou (ed.), *Studia Linguistica Serica*. Hong Kong: Hong Kong University Press, 39–68.

——(2005). 'Leitui, yufahua, quyufahua yu gongneng gengxin: disan jie Hanyu yufahua wenti yantaohui' [Analogy, grammaticalization, degrammaticalization and exaptation], paper presented at Third Conference on Chinese Grammaticalization Issues, Luoyang, 27–8 November.

PFAU, ROLAND (2008). 'The grammar of headshake: a typological perspective on German Sign Language negation', *Linguistics in Amsterdam* 1: 37–74.

——(2011). 'A point well taken: on the typology and diachrony of pointing', in D. J. Napoli and G. Mathur (eds), *Deaf Around the World*. Oxford: Oxford University Press, 144–63.

——and QUER, JOSEP (2002). 'V-to-Neg Raising and negative concord in three sign languages', *Rivista di Grammatica Generativa* 27: 73–86.

————(2010). 'Non-manuals: their prosodic and grammatical roles', in D. Brentari (ed.), *Sign Languages*. Cambridge: Cambridge University Press, 381–402.

——and STEINBACH, MARKUS (2006). 'Modality-independent and modality-specific aspects of grammaticalization in sign languages', *Linguistics in Potsdam* 24: 3–98.

PHILIPPI, JULIA (1997). 'The rise of the article in the Germanic languages', in van Kemenade and Vincent (1997: 62–93).

PIATTELLI-PALMARINI, MASSIMO (1989). 'Evolution, selection and cognition: from "learning" to parameter setting in biology, and in the study of language', *Cognition* 31.1: 1–44.

PIERREHUMBERT, JANET (2001). 'Exemplar dynamics: word frequency, lenition and contrast', in Bybee and Hopper (2001: 137–58).

——and HIRSCHBERG, JULIA (1990). 'The meaning of intonational contours in the interpretation of discourse', in P. R. Cohen, J. Morgan, and M. E. Pollack (eds), *Intentions in Communication*. Cambridge, MA: MIT Press, 271–311.

PIETSCH, LUKAS (2009). 'Hiberno-English medial-object perfects reconsidered: a case of contact-induced grammaticalisation', *Studies in Language* 33: 528–68.

PINKER, STEVEN (1994). *The Language Instinct: How the Mind Creates Language*. New York: Morrow.

——and BLOOM, PAUL (1990). 'Natural language and natural selection', *Behavioral and Brain Sciences* 13: 707–84.

PINKSTER, HARM (1987). 'The strategy and chronology of the development of future and perfect tense auxiliaries in Latin', in Martin Harris and Paolo Ramat (eds), *The Historical Development of Auxiliaries*. Berlin: Mouton, 193–223.

——(1990). *Latin Syntax and Semantics*. London: Routledge.

PINTZUK, SUSAN, TSOULAS, GEORGE, and WARNER, ANTHONY (2000). 'Syntactic change: theory and method', in Susan Pintzuk, George Tsoulas, and Anthony Warner (eds), *Diachronic Syntax*. Oxford: Oxford University Press, 1–22.

PITKIN, HARVEY (1984). *Wintu Grammar*. Berkeley: University of California Press.

PLAG, INGO (2002). 'On the role of grammaticalization in creolization: a reassessment', in G. G. Gilbert (ed.), *Pidgin and Creole Linguistics in the 21st Century*. New York: Lang, 229–46.

PLANK, FRANS (1984). 'The modals story retold', *Studies in Language* 8: 305–66.

——(1993). 'Entgrammatisierung: Spiegelbild der Grammatisierung?', in N. Boretzky, W. Dressler, T. Orešnik, and W. Wurzel (eds), *Beiträge zum internationalen Symposium über 'Natürlichkeitstheorie und Sprachwandel' an der Universität Maribor vom 13.5.–15.5.1993*. Bochum: Brockmeyer, 199–219.

——(ed.) (1995). *Double Case: Agreement by Suffixaufnahme*. Oxford: Oxford University Press.

——(2005). 'Delocutive verbs, crosslinguistically', *Linguistic Typology* 9: 459–91.

Plungian, Vladimir A. (1998). 'Грамматические категории, их аналоги и заместители. Диссертация на соискание ученой степени доктора филологических наук' [Grammatical categories, their analogues and alternatives], Habilitationsschrift, Moscow.

Podlesskaja, Vera I. (2005). '"Give"-verbs as permissive auxiliaries in Russian', *Language Typology and Universals* 58.1: 124–38.

Poletto, Cecilia (1995). 'The diachronic development of subject clitics in northern eastern Italian dialects', in Battye and Roberts (1995: 295–324).

——(2000). *The Higher Functional Field.* Oxford: Oxford University Press.

——(2004). 'Dialectology from a language internal perspective'. MS.

Polich, Laura (2005). *The Emergence of the Deaf Community in Nicaragua.* Washington, DC: Gallaudet University Press.

Pollock, Jean-Yves (1989). 'Verb movement, Universal Grammar, and the structure of IP', *Linguistic Inquiry* 20: 365–424.

Pomerantz, Anita (1984). 'Agreeing and disagreeing with assessments: some features of preferred/dispreferred turn shapes', in J. M. Atkinson and J. Heritage (eds), *Structures of Social Action: Studies in Conversational Analysis.* Cambridge: Cambridge University Press, 57–101.

Poplack, Shana (1980). 'Sometimes I'll start a sentence in Spanish y termino en español', *Linguistics* 18.7/8: 581–618.

——(2001). 'Variability, frequency and productivity in the irrealis domain of French', in Bybee and Hopper (2001: 405–28).

——Bourdages, Johanne S., and Dion, Nathalie (2009). 'Normes et variation: l'école a-t-elle une influence?', paper presented at the annual meeting of the Association canadienne de linguistique appliquée/Canadian Association of Applied Linguistics.

——and Dion, Nathalie (2009). 'Prescription vs praxis: the evolution of future temporal reference in French', *Language* 85.3: 557–87.

——and Malvar, Elisabete (2007). 'Elucidating the transition period in linguistic change', *Probus* 19.1: 121–69.

——and St-Amand, Anne (2007). 'A real-time window on 19th century vernacular French: *The Récits du français québécois d'autrefois*', *Language in Society* 36.5: 707–34.

——and Tagliamonte, Sali (1996). 'Nothing in context: variation, grammaticalization and past time marking in Nigerian Pidgin English', in Philip Baker and Anand Syea (eds), *Changing Meanings, Changing Functions: Papers Relating to Grammaticalization in Contact Languages.* London: University Press, 71–94.

————(2001). *African American English in the Diaspora.* Oxford: Blackwell.

——and Turpin, Danielle (1999). 'Does the FUTUR have a future in (Canadian) French?', *Probus* 11.1: 133–64.

——Walker, James A., and Malcolmson, Rebecca (2006). 'An English "like no other"? Language contact and change in Quebec', *Canadian Journal of Linguistics* 51: 185–213.

Posner, Rebecca (1996). *The Romance Languages.* Cambridge: Cambridge University Press.

Post, Brechtje (2000). 'Tonal and phrasal structures in French intonation' (PhD thesis). The Hague: Academic Graphics.

Post, Mark W. (2007). 'Grammaticalization and compounding in Thai and Chinese: a text frequency approach', *Studies in Language* 31: 117–75.

Pottier, Bernard (1961). 'Sobre el concepto de "verbo auxiliar"', *Nueva revista de filologia hispánica* 15: 325–31.

——(1962). *Sémantique des éléments de relation.* Paris: Klincksieck.

——(1969). *Grammaire espagnole.* Paris: PUF.

Poulos, George (1986). 'Instances of semantic bleaching in South-Eastern Bantu', in Gerrit Jan Dimmendaal (ed.), *Current Approaches to African Linguistics*, vol. 3. Dordrecht: Foris, 281–96.

Pountain, Christopher (1982). '*essere/stare as a Romance phenomenon', in Nigel Vincent and Martin Harris (eds), *Studies in the Romance Verb.* London: Croom Helm, 139–60.

Pozas-Loyo, Julia (2008). 'On the evolution of *un* in medieval and classical Spanish', paper presented at the 36th Romance Linguistics Seminar, Trinity Hall, Cambridge.

Prasithrathsint, Amara (2006). 'Development of the *thùuk* passive marker in Thai', in Werner Abraham and Larisa Leisiö (eds), *Passivization and Typology: Form and Function.* Amsterdam: Benjamins, 115–31.

Price, Glanville (1971). *The French Language: Present and Past.* London: Arnold.

——(2000). *Encyclopedia of European Languages.* Oxford: Blackwell.

Prince, Ellen (1972). 'A note on aspect in English: the *take a walk* construction', in Senta Plötz (ed.), *Transformationelle Analyse.* Frankfurt: Athenäum, 409–20.

——(1981). 'On the inferencing of indefinite-*this* NPs', in A. K. Aravind et al. (eds), *Elements of Discourse Understanding.* Cambridge: Cambridge University Press, 231–50.

——(1992). 'The ZPG letter: subjects, definiteness, and information-status', in William C. Mann and Sandra A. Thompson (eds), *Discourse Description: Diverse Analyses of a Fundraising Text.* Amsterdam: Benjamins, 295–325.

Pulleyblank, Edwin G. (1995) *Outline of Classical Chinese Grammar.* Vancouver: University of British Columbia Press.

Pulvermüller, Friedemann (2002). *The Neuroscience of Language: On Brain Circuits of Words and Serial Order.* Cambridge: Cambridge University Press.

Pusch, Luise F. (1984). *Das Deutsche als Männersprache: Aufsätze und Glossen zur feministischen Linguistik.* Frankfurt am Main: Suhrkamp.

Pustet, Regina (2008). 'Discourse frequency and the collapse of the adposition vs. affix distinction in Lakota', in López-Couso and Seoane (2008: 269–92).

Putzu, Ignazio, and Ramat, Paolo (2001). 'Articles and quantifiers in the Mediterranean languages: a typological-diachronic analysis', in Walter Bisang (ed.), *Aspects of Typology and Universals.* Berlin: Akademie, 99–132.

Quirk, Randolph, Greenbaum, Sidney, Leech, Geoffrey, and Svartvik, Jan (1972). *A Grammar of Contemporary English.* London: Longman.

————————(1985) *A Comprehensive Grammar of the English Language.* London: Longman.

Radloff, Wilhelm (1911). *Versuch eines Wörterbuchs der Türk-Dialekte*, 4. St Petersburg: Kaiserliche Akademie der Wissenschaften.

Ramat, Paolo (1992). 'Thoughts on degrammaticalization', *Linguistics* 30: 549–60.

——(1996). '"Allegedly John is ill again": stratégies pour le médiatif', in Guentchéva (1996: 287–98).

——(1998). 'Typological comparison and linguistic areas: some introductory remarks', *Language Sciences* 20.3: 227–40.

——(1999). 'Linguistic categories and linguists' categorizations', *Linguistics* 37: 157–80.

——(2001). 'Degrammaticalization or transcategorialization?', in Chris Schaner-Wolles, John Rennison, and Friedrich Neubarth (eds), *Naturally! Linguistic Studies in Honour of Wolfgang Ulrich Dressler*. Turin: Rosenbach & Sellier, 393–401.

——(2002). 'Die monolexikalischen Adverbien in den alten indoeuropäischen Sprachen', in F. Schmöe (ed.), *Das Adverb: Zentrum und Peripherie einer Wortklasse*. Vienna: Praesens, 17–24.

——(2006). 'Marginalia sulla grammaticalizzazione', in R. Bombi et al. (eds), *Studi linguistici in onore di Roberto Gusmani*, vol. 3, Alessandria: Edizioni dell'Orso, 1435–43.

——(2008). 'Les adverbes latins du point de vue de l'indo-européen', in M. Fruyt and S. Van Laere (eds), *Adverbes et évolution linguistique en latin*. Paris: L'Harmattan, 13–24.

——and Ricca, Davide (1994). 'Prototypical adverbs: on the scalarity/radiality of the notion of ADVERB', *Rivista di linguistica* 6: 289–326.

————(1998). 'Sentence adverbs in the languages of Europe', in Johan van der Auwera (ed.), *Adverbial Constructions in the Languages of Europe*. Berlin: Mouton de Gruyter, 187–285.

Ramirez, Henri (1994). 'Le parler Yanomami des Xamatauteri', PhD dissertation, University of Provence.

Ramisch, Heinrich (1989). *The Variation of English in Guernsey/Channel Islands*. Frankfurt: Lang.

Ramstedt, Gustaf John (1939). *A Korean Grammar*. Helsinki: Suomalais-Ugrilainen Seura.

——(1957). *Einführung in die altaische Sprachwissenschaft*, 1: *Lautlehre*. Helsinki: Suomalais-Ugrilainen Seura.

Rand, David, and Sankoff, David (1990). *Goldvarb 2.1: A Variable Rule Application for the Macintosh*. Montreal. Centre de Recherches Mathématiques, University of Montreal. Version 2: http://www.crm.umontreal.ca/~sankoff/GoldVarb_Eng.html

Rathmann, Christian (2000). 'The optionality of agreement phrase: evidence from signed languages', master's thesis, University of Texas at Austin.

——(2005). 'Event structure in American Sign Language', PhD dissertation, University of Texas at Austin.

Raumolin-Brunberg, Helena (1994). 'The development of the compound pronouns in *-body* and *-one* in Early Modern English', in Dieter Kastovsky (ed.), *Studies in Early Modern English*. Berlin: Mouton de Gruyter, 301–24.

——(2005). 'Language change in adulthood: historical letters as evidence', *European Journal of English Studies* 9.1 (thematic issue on letters and letter writing, ed. Minna Nevala and Minna Palander-Collin): 37–51.

——(2006). 'Leaders of linguistic change in Early Modern England', in Roberta Facchinetti and Matti Rissanen (eds), *Corpus-Based Studies of Diachronic English*. Frankfurt am Main: Lang, 115–34.

——(2009). 'Lifespan changes in the language of three early modern gentlemen', in Nurmi et al. (2009: 165–96).

Rayfield, Joan Rachel (1970). *The Language of a Bilingual Community*. The Hague: Mouton.

Recanati, François (1989). 'The pragmatics of what is said', *Mind and Language* 4: 295–329.

Reichenbach, Hans (1947). *Elements of Symbolic Logic*. London: Macmillan. Repr. 1980 (Dover).

Renck, Gunther (1975). *A Grammar of Yagaria.* Canberra: Pacific Linguistics.

Renzi, Lorenzo (1976). 'Grammatica e storia dell'articolo italiano', *Studi di grammatica italiana* 5: 5–42.

——(1985). *Nuova introduzione alla filologia romanza.* Bologna: Il Mulino.

Renzi, Luigi, and Salvi, Giampaolo (eds) (1991). *Grande grammatica di consultazione.* Bologna: Il Mulino.

Rhee, Seongha (1996). 'Semantics of verbs and grammaticalization: the development in Korean from a cross-linguistic perspective', PhD dissertation, University of Texas at Austin.

——(2002a). 'From silence to grammar: grammaticalization of ellipsis in Korean', paper presented at the 'New Reflections on Grammaticalization II' conference, 3–6 April, University of Amsterdam.

——(2002b). 'Grammaticalization of postpositionoids from movement verbs in Korean', paper presented at the International Conference on Adpositions of Movement, 14–16 January, Catholic University of Leuven.

——(2004). 'From discourse to grammar: grammaticalization and lexicalization of rhetorical questions in Korean', *LACUS Forum* 30: 413–23.

——(2008). 'Subjectification of reported speech in grammaticalization and lexicalization', *Harvard Studies in Korean Linguistics* 12: 590–603.

——(2009a). 'On the rise and fall of Korean nominalizers', in López-Couso and Seoane (2008: 239–64).

——(2009b). 'Through a borrowed mouth: reported speech and subjectification in Korean', *LACUS Forum* 34: 201–10.

——(2009c). 'Consequences of invisibility: paradigm creation from an eroded light verb', paper presented at the 19th International Conference on Historical Linguistics, 10–14 August, Radboud University.

——(in press). 'Nominalization and stance marking in Korean', in Foong Ha Yap, Karen Grunow-Hårsta, and Janick Wrona (eds), *Nominalization in Asian Languages: Diachronic and Typological Perspectives*, vol. 2: *Korean, Japanese and Austronesian Languages.* Amsterdam: Benjamins.

Ricca, Davide (1998). 'La morfologia avverbiale tra flessione e derivazione', in G. Bernini et al. (eds), *Ars linguistica.* Rome: Bulzoni, 447–66.

Rice, Keren (1993). 'The structure of the Slave (northern Athapaskan) verb', in Sharon Hargus and Ellen Kaisse (eds), *Issues in Lexical Phonology.* San Diego, CA: Academic Press, 145–71.

——(1998). 'Slave (Northern Athapaskan)', in Andrew Spencer and Arnold Zwicky (eds), *The Handbook of Morphology.* Oxford: Blackwell, 648–89.

——(2000). *Morpheme Order and Semantic Scope: Word Formation in the Athapaskan Verb.* Cambridge: Cambridge University Press.

Richards, Marc (2008). 'Two kinds of variation in a minimalist system', *Linguistische Arbeitsberichte* 87: 133–62. http://www.uni-leipzig.de/~asw/lab/lab87/LAB87_richards.pdf.

Rickmeyer, Jens (1995). *Japanische Morphosyntax.* Heidelberg: Groos.

Ridruejo, Emilio (2000). 'Modo y modalidad: el modo en las subordinadas sustantivas', in I. Bosque and V. Demonte (eds), *Gramática descriptiva de la lengua española.* Madrid: Espasa-Calpe, 3206–51.

Rijkhoff, Jan (2002). *The Noun Phrase.* Oxford: Oxford University Press.

RINGE, DON (2003). 'Internal reconstruction', in Joseph and Janda (2003: 244–61).
——(2006). *From Proto-Indo-European to Proto-Germanic.* Oxford: Oxford University Press.
RISCHEL, JOERGEN (1995). *Minor Mlabri.* Copenhagen: Museum Tusculaneum.
Rissanen, Matti, Kytö, Merja, and Heikkonen, Kirsi (eds) (1997). *Grammaticalization at Work: Studies of Long-Term Developments in English.* Berlin: Mouton de Gruyter.
RIZZI, LUIGI (1982). *Issues in Italian Linguistics.* Dordrecht: Foris.
——(1997). 'The fine structure of the left periphery', in L. Haegeman (ed.), *Elements of Grammar.* Dordrecht: Kluwer, 281–337.
ROBBEETS, MARTINE (2007). 'The causative-passive in Trans-Eurasian languages', *Turkic Languages* 11.2: 235–78.
ROBERTS, IAN (1993a). 'A formal account of grammaticalization in the history of Romance futures', *Folia Linguistica Historica* 13: 219–58.
——(1993b). *Verbs and Diachronic Syntax: A Comparative History of English and French.* Dordrecht: Kluwer.
——and ROUSSOU, ANNA (1999). 'A formal approach to grammaticalization', *Linguistics* 37: 1011–41.
————(2003). *Syntactic Change: A Minimalist Approach to Grammaticalization.* Cambridge: Cambridge University Press.
ROBINS, R. H. (2002). 'The word in American structuralism', in D. A. Cruse, Franz Hundsnurscher, Michael Job, and Peter Rolf Lutzeier (eds), *Lexicology: An International Handbook on the Nature and Structure of Words and Vocabularies,* vol. 1. Berlin: de Gruyter, 138–43.
RODRIGUEZ, JOÃO (1976[1604]). *Arte da Lingoa de Iapam.* Tokyo: Benseisha.
ROHLFS, GERHARD (1966–9). *Grammatica storica della lingua italiana e dei suoi dialetti.* 3 vols. Turin: Einaudi.
ROMAINE, SUZANNE, and LANGE, DEBORAH (1991). 'The use of *like* as a marker of reported speech and thought: a case of grammaticalization in progress', *American Speech* 66.3: 227–79.
ROOTH, MATS (1992). 'A theory of focus interpretation', *Natural Language Semantics* 1: 75–116.
ROSCH, ELEANOR, MERVIS, CAROLYN B., GRAY, WAYNE D., JOHNSON, DAVID M., and BOYES-BRAEM, PENNY (1976). 'Basic objects in natural categories', *Cognitive Psychology* 8.3: 382–439.
ROSENBACH, ANETTE (2004). 'The English *s*-genitive: a case of degrammaticalization?', in Fischer et al. (2004: 73–96).
ROSENKVIST, HENRIK (2008). 'A case of degrammaticalization in Northern Swedish', paper presented at the 'Continuity and Change in Grammar' workshop, University of Cambridge, March.
ROSS, MALCOLM D. (1996). 'Contact-induced change and the comparative method: cases from Papua New Guinea', in Mark Durie and Malcolm D. Ross (eds), *The Comparative Method Reviewed: Regularity and Irregularity in Language Change.* New York: Oxford University Press, 180–217.
——(2001). 'Contact-induced change in Oceanic languages in North-West Melanesia', in Aikhenvald and Dixon (2001: 134–66).
ROWLETT, PAUL (1998). *Sentential Negation in French.* Oxford: Oxford University Press.

RUBBA, JO (1994). 'Grammaticization as semantic change: a case study of preposition development', in Pagliuca (1994: 81–101).

RYU, RYUL (1990). *Cosenmallyeksa* [A history of Korean] 1. Pyongyang: Sahoykwahak.

SABATINI, FRANCESCO (1985). 'L' "italiano dell'uso medio": una realtà tra le varietà linguistiche italiane', in G. Holtus and E. Radtke (eds), *Gesprochenes Italienisch in Geschichte und Gegenwart*, Tübingen: Narr, 155–84.

SACKS, HARVEY (1992). *Lectures on Conversation*, vol. 2. Oxford: Blackwell.

——and SCHEGLOFF, EMANUEL (1979). 'Two preferences in the organization of reference to persons in conversation and their interaction', in George Psathas (ed.), *Everyday Language: Studies in Ethnomethodology.* New York: Irvington, 15–21.

SADOCK, JERROLD M. (1991). *Autolexical Syntax: A Theory of Parallel Grammatical Components.* Chicago: University of Chicago Press.

SÆBØ, KJELL JOHAN (2009). 'Possession and pertinence: the meaning of *have*', *Natural Language Semantics* 17.4: 369–97.

SAGART, LAURENT (1993). 'L'infixe -r- en chinois archaïque', *Bulletin de la Société Linguistique de Paris* 88.1: 261–93.

SAID ALI, MANUEL (1971). *Gramática histórica da língua portuguesa.* Rio de Janeiro: Livraria Acadêmica.

SALVI, GIAMPAOLO (2004). *La formazione della struttura di frase romanza: ordine delle parole e clitici dal latino alle lingue romanze antiche.* Tübingen: Niemeyer.

Sampson, Geoffrey, Gil, David, and Trudgill, Peter (eds) (2009). *Language Complexity as an Evolving Variable.* Oxford: Oxford University Press.

SANDLER, WENDY, and LILLO-MARTIN, DIANE (2006). *Sign Languages and Linguistic Universals.* Cambridge: Cambridge University Press.

——MEIR, IRIT, DACHKOVSKY, SVETLANA, PADDEN, CAROL, and ARONOFF, MARK (forthcoming). 'The emergence of complexity in prosody and syntax', *Lingua.*

SANKOFF, DAVID (1988). 'Sociolinguistics and syntactic variation', in Frederick J. Newmeyer (ed.), *Linguistics: The Cambridge Survey*, 4: *Language: The Socio-cultural Context.* Cambridge: Cambridge University Press, 140–61.

SANKOFF, DAVID, TAGLIAMONTE, SALI, and SMITH, ERIC (2005). *GoldVarb X: A Variable Rule Application for Macintosh and Windows.* Department of Mathematics, University of Ottawa, and Department of Linguistics, University of Toronto.

SANKOFF, GILLIAN (1990). 'The grammaticalization of tense and aspect in Tok Pisin and Sranan', *Language Variation and Change* 2.3: 295–312.

——and VINCENT, DIANE (1977). 'L'emploi productif de *ne* dans le français parlé à Montréal', *Le français moderne* 45: 243–56.

SAPIR, EDWARD (1921). *Language.* New York: Harcourt, Brace.

SAPOUNTZAKI, GALINI (2005). 'Free functional elements of tense, aspect, modality and agreement as possible auxiliaries in Greek Sign Language', PhD dissertation, University of Bristol.

SASSE, HANS-JÜRGEN (2006). 'Aspect and Aktionsart', in Keith Brown (ed.), *Encyclopedia of Language and Linguistics*, 2nd edn. Oxford: Elsevier, 535–8.

SAUSSURE, FERDINAND DE (1916). *Cours de linguistique générale.* Paris: Payot.

SAUSSURE, LOUIS DE (2006). *Temps et pertinence: éléments de pragmatique cognitive du temps.* Brussels: De Boeck–Duculot.

SCHEGLOFF, EMANUEL A. (2007). *Sequence Organization in Interaction: A Primer in Conversation Analysis*, vol. 1. Cambridge: Cambridge University Press.

Schermer, Trude (2003). 'From variant to standard: an overview of the standardization process of the lexicon of Sign Language of the Netherlands over two decades', *Sign Language Studies* 3: 469–86.

Schiering, René (2006). 'Cliticization and the evolution of morphology: a cross-linguistic study on phonology and grammaticalization', PhD dissertation, University of Constance.

——Hildebrandt, Kristine, and Bickel, Balthasar (2010). 'The prosodic word is not universal, but emergent' *Journal of Linguistics* 46: 657–709.

Schiffrin, Deborah (1987). *Discourse Markers.* Cambridge: Cambridge University Press.

Schladt, Mathias (2000). 'The typology and grammaticalization of reflexives', in Zygmunt Frajzyngier and Traci S. Curl (eds), *Reflexives: Forms and Functions.* Amsterdam: Benjamins, 103–24.

Schlegel, August Wilhelm von (1818). *Observations sur la langue et la littérature provençales.* Paris: Librairie grecque-latine-allemande.

Schlichter, Alice (1986). 'The origin and deictic nature of Wintu evidentials', in Chafe and Nichols (1986: 46–59).

Schlüter, Julia (to appear). '*To dare to or not to*: is auxiliarization reversible?', in Kristin Davidse, Jean-Christophe Verstraete, and An van Linden (eds), *Grammaticalization and Grammar.* Amsterdam: Benjamins.

Schmidtke-Bode, Karsten (2009). '*Going-to-V* and *gonna-V* in child language: a quantitative approach to constructional development', *Cognitive Linguistics* 20: 509–38.

Schmitz, Hans-Christian, and Schröder, Bernhard (2004). 'Updates with *eigentlich*', *Sprache und Datenverarbeitung* 28.1: 87–96.

Schoesler, L. (2006). 'Grammaticalisation et dégrammaticalisation: étude des constructions progressives en français du type *Pierre va/vient/est chantant*', *Cahiers Chronos* 16: 91–119.

Scholze, Lenka (2008). *Das grammatische System der obersorbischen Umgangssprache im Sprachkontakt.* Bautzen: Domowina.

——(to appear). 'On the grammaticalization of the definite article in Colloquial Upper Sorbian (CUS)', in Björn Wiemer, Björn Hansen, and Bernhard Wälchli (eds), *Grammatical Replication and Grammatical Borrowability in Language Bontact.* Berlin: Mouton de Gruyter.

Schönig, Claus (1998): 'Suffixartige und postpositionelle Ausdrücke für instrumentales und komitatives "mit" im Türkischen', in K. İmer and L. Uzun (eds), *Doğan Aksan Armağanı.* Ankara: Ankara Üniversitesi Dil ve Tarih-Coğrafya Fakültesi, 145–54.

Schroeder, Christophe (2006). 'Articles and article systems in some languages in Europe', in G. Bernini and Marcia L. Schwartz (eds), *Pragmatic Organization of Discourse in the Languages of Europe.* Berlin: Mouton de Gruyter, 545–601.

Schuh, Russell (1983). 'The evolution of determiners in Chadic', in E. Wolf and H. Meyer-Bahlburg (eds), *Studies in Chadic and Afroasiatic Languages.* Hamburg: Buske, 157–210.

Schwarze, Christoph (2003): '"Bleiben" und "werden": zur Polysemie von it. *rimanere*', in A. Blank and P. Koch (eds), *Kognitive romanische Onomasiologie und Semasiologie.* Tübingen: Niemeyer, 19–32.

Schwegler, Armin (1988). 'Word-order changes in predicate negation strategies in Romance languages', *Diachronica* 6.1–2: 21–58.

——(1990). *Analyticity and Syntheticity: A Diachronic Perspective with Special Reference to Romance Languages.* Berlin: Mouton de Gruyter.

Schwenter, Scott A. (1994). 'The grammaticalization of an anterior in progress: evidence from a peninsular Spanish dialect', *Studies in Language* 18.1: 71–112.

——(2006). 'Fine-tuning Jespersen's Cycle', in Betty J. Birner and Gregory Ward (eds), *Drawing the Boundaries of Meaning: Neo-Gricean Studies in Pragmatics and Semantics in Honor of Laurence R. Horn*. Amsterdam: Benjamins, 327–44.

——and Torres Cacoullos, Rena (2008). 'Defaults and indeterminacy in temporal grammaticalization: the perfect road to perfective', *Language Variation and Change* 20: 1–39.

Scollon, Ron (1976). 'Types of construction', in *Conversations with a One Year Old: A Case Study of the Developmental Foundation of Syntax*. Honolulu: University of Hawai'i Press, 149–74.

Seiler, Hansjakob (2008). *Universality in Language Beyond Grammar: Selected Writings 1990–2007*. Bochum: Brockmeyer.

Seki, Lucy (2000). *Gramática do Kamaiurá, língua Tupí-Guaraní do Alto Xingu*. Campinas: Unicamp.

Selig, Maria (1992). *Die Entwicklung der Nominaldeterminanten im Spätlatein*. Tübingen: Narr.

Senghas, Ann (1995). 'Children's contribution to the birth of Nicaraguan Sign Language', PhD dissertation,Massachusetts Institute of Technology.

——and Coppola, Marie (2001). 'Children creating language: how Nicaraguan Sign Language acquired a spatial grammar', *Psychological Science* 12: 323–8.

Seoane, Elena, and López-Couso, María José (eds) (2008). *Theoretical and Empirical Issues in Grammaticalization*. Amsterdam: Benjamins.

Sevortjan, Ėrvand V. (1974). *Ėtimologičeskij slovar' tjurkskix jazykov*, 1. Moskva: Nauka.

Sexton, Amy L. (1999). 'Grammaticalization in American Sign Language', *Language Sciences* 21: 105–41.

Sharma, Devyani (2009). 'Typological diversity in New Englishes', *English World-Wide* 30: 170–95.

Shepherd, Susan C. (1982). 'From deontic to epistemic: an analysis of modals in the history of English, creoles, and language acquisition', in Ahlquist (1982: 316–23).

Shibatani, Masayoshi (1985). 'Passives and related constructions: a prototype analysis', *Language* 61: 821–48.

Shopen, Timothy (ed). (1985/2007). *Language Typology and Syntactic Description*. Cambridge: Cambridge University Press. 2nd edn 2007.

Siewierska, Anna (1993). 'Syntactic weight vs, information-structure and word order variation in Polish', *Journal of Linguistics* 29: 233–65.

——(2004). *Person*. Cambridge: Cambridge University Press.

——(2008). 'Verbal person marking', in Haspelmath et al. (2008: ch. 102): http://wals.info/feature/102.

Simon-Vandenbergen, Anne-Marie, and Aijmer, Karin (2003/4). 'The expectation marker *of course*', *Languages in Contrast* 4.1: 13–43.

Simpson, Andrew, and Wu, Xiu-Zhi Zoe (2002). 'Agreement shells and focus', *Language* 78.2: 287–313.

Skårup, Povl (1975). *Les premières zones de la proposition en ancien français*. Copenhagen: Akademisk.

Slobin, Dan I. (1985). 'Cross-linguistic evidence for language-making capacity', in Dan I. Slobin (ed.), *The Cross-linguistic Study of Language Acquisition*, vol. 2: *Theoretical Issues*. Hillsdale, NJ: Erlbaum, 1157–1249.

——(1994). 'Talking perfectly: discourse origins of the present perfect', in Pagliuca (1994: 119–33).

——(1997). 'The origins of grammaticizable notions: beyond the individual mind', in D. I. Slobin (ed.), *The Crosslinguistic Study of Language Acquisition*, vol. 5: *Expanding the Contexts*. Mahwah, NJ: Erlbaum, 265–323.

——(2002). 'Language evolution, acquisition and diachrony: probing parallels', in Talmy Givón and Bertram F. Halle (eds), *The Evolution of Language and Pre-language*. Amsterdam: Benjamins, 375–392.

Smith, Andrew D. M. (2006). 'Semantic reconstructibility and the complexification of language', in Angelo Cangelosi, Andrew D. M. Smith, and Kenny Smith (eds), *The Evolution of Language*, Proceedings of the 6th International Conference (EVOLANG6), Rome. World Scientific, 307–14.

——(2008). 'Protolanguage reconstructed', *Interaction Studies* 9.1: 100–116.

——(forthcoming). 'The cognitive origins of linguistic complexity', in Michelle Aldridge and June Luchjenbroers (eds), *Conceptual Structure and Linguistics Research*, vol. 2: *Cognitive Linguistics Applied Across Contexts of Use*. Amsterdam: Benjamins.

Smith, K. Aaron (2001). 'The role of frequency in the specialization of the English anterior', in Bybee and Hopper (2001: 361–82).

Smith, Kenny (2006). 'Cultural evolution of language', in Keith Brown (ed.), *The Encyclopedia of Language and Linguistics*. Oxford: Elsevier, 315–22.

——and Kirby, Simon (2008). 'Cultural evolution: implications for understanding the human language faculty and its evolution', *Philosophical Transactions of the Royal Society of London, series B: Biological Sciences*, 363: 3591–3603.

Smith, Wayne H. (1990). 'Evidence for auxiliaries in Taiwanese Sign Language', in S. Fischer and P. Siple (eds), *Theoretical Issues in Sign Language Research*, vol. 1: *Linguistics*. Chicago: University of Chicago Press, 211–28.

Sneddon, James (1996). *Indonesian*. London: Routledge.

Sohn, Ho-min (2001[1999]). *The Korean Language*. Cambridge: Cambridge University Press.

Sohn, Sung-Ock (1995). 'On the development of sentence-final particles in Korean', *Japanese/Korean Linguistics* 5: 219–34.

——and Park, Mee-Jeong (2002). 'Discourse, grammaticalization, and intonation: an analysis of *ketun* in Korean', *Japanese/Korean Linguistics* 10: 306–19.

Solta, Georg R. (1980). *Einführung in die Balkanlinguistik mit besonderer Berücksichtigung des Substrats und des Balkanlateinischen*. Darmstadt: Wissenschaftliche Buchgesellschaft.

Song, Jae Jung (2005). *The Korean Language: Structure, Use and Context*. New York: Routledge.

Speas, Margaret (1984). 'Navajo prefixes and word structure typology', in Margaret Speas and Richard Sproat (eds), *Papers from the January 1984 Massachusetts Institute of Technology Workshop in Morphology*. Cambridge, MA: MIT Working Papers in Linguistics 7, 86–109.

——(1990). *Phrase Structure in Natural Language*. Dordrecht: Kluwer.

——(1991). 'Functional heads and the Mirror Principle', *Lingua* 84: 181–214.

Spencer, Andrew (2008). 'Does Hungarian have a case system?', in Corbett and Noonan (2008: 35–56).

Sperber, Dan, and Wilson, Deirdre (1995[1986]). *Relevance: Communication and Cognition.* Oxford: Blackwell.

Squartini, Mario (1998). *Verbal Periphrases in Romance: Aspect, Actionality and Grammaticalization.* Berlin: Mouton de Gruyter.

——(2008). 'Lexical vs. grammatical evidentiality in French and Italian', *Linguistics* 46: 917–47.

Stampe, David (1969). 'The acquisition of phonetic representation', *Chicago Linguistics Society* 5: 443–54.

Stark, Elisabeth, Leiss, Elisabeth, and Werner, Abraham (eds) (2007). *Nominal Determination: Typology, Context Constraints, and Historical Emergence.* Amsterdam: Benjamins.

Starosta, Stanley (1985). 'Relator nouns as a source of case inflection', in V. Acson and R. Leed (eds), *For Gordon Fairbanks.* Honolulu: University of Hawai'i Press, 111–33.

Stassen, Leon (2001). 'Noun phrase coordination', in Martin Haspelmath et al. (eds), *Language Typology and Language Universals: An International Handbook.* Berlin: Mouton de Gruyter, 1105–11.

Steele, Susan M. (1978). 'The category AUX as a language universal', in J. J. Greenberg (ed.), *Universals of Human Language*, vol. 3: *Word Structure.* Stanford, CA: Stanford University Press, 7–45.

——Akmajaian, A., Demers, R., Jeliniek, E., Kitagawa, C., Oehrle, R., and Wasow, T. (1981). *An Encyclopedia of AUX: A Study in Cross-Linguistic Equivalence.* Cambridge, MA: MIT Press.

Steensig, Jakob, and Asmuss, Birte (2005). 'Notes on disaligning "yes but" initiated utterances in German and Danish conversations: two construction types for dispreferred responses', in A. Hakulinen and M. Selting (eds), *Syntax and Lexis in Conversation: Studies on the Use of Linguistic Resources in Talk-in-Interaction.* Amsterdam: Benjamins, 349–73.

Stefanini, R. (1982). 'Reflexive, impersonal, and passive in Italian and Florentine', in M. MacAulay et al. (eds), *Proceedings of the Eighth Annual Meeting of the Berkeley Linguistic Society*: 97–108.

Stein, Gabriele (1991). 'The phrasal type "to have a look" in Modern English', *International Review of Applied Linguistics in Language Teaching* 19: 1–29.

Steinbach, Markus, and Pfau, Roland (2007). 'The grammaticalization of auxiliaries in sign languages', in P. Perniss, R. Pfau, and M. Steinbach (eds), *Visible Variation: Cross-linguistic Studies on Sign Language Structure.* Berlin: Mouton de Gruyter, 303–39.

Stekauer, Pavol (2000). *English Word-Formation: A History of Research, 1960–1995.* Berlin: Narr.

Stenström, Anna-Brita (1998). 'From sentence to discourse: *cos (because)* in teenage talk', in Andreas H. Jucker and Yael Ziv (eds), *Discourse Markers: Descriptions and Theory.* Amsterdam: Benjamins, 127–46.

Stephany, Ursula (1986). 'Modality', in Paul Fletcher and Michael Garman (eds), *Language Acquisition.* Cambridge: Cambridge University Press, 375–400.

Stokoe, William C. (1960). 'Sign language structure: an outline of the communication systems of the American deaf'. *Studies in Linguistics, Occasional Papers* 8. University of Buffalo (Reissued 1978, Linstok Press, Silver Spring, MD.)

Stolz, Thomas (1991). 'Agglutinationstheorie und Grammatikalisierungsforschung: einige alte und neue Gedanken zur Entstehung von gebundener Morphologie', *Zeitschrift für Phonetik, Sprachwissenschaft und Kommunikationsforschung* 44.3: 325–38.

——Stroh, Cornelia, and Urdze, Aina (2006). *On Comitatives and Related Categories. A Typological Study with Special Focus on the Languages of Europe.* Berlin: Mouton de Gruyter.

Strang, Barbara M. H. (1970). *A History of English.* London: Methuen.

Sun, Chaofen (1996). *Word-Order Change and Grammaticalization in the History of Chinese.* Stanford, CA: Stanford University Press.

——(1997). 'Ambiguity in context-induced semantic changes: the history of the Chinese BA construction', *Journal of Chinese Linguistics Monograph* 10: 225–56.

——(2001). 'Semantically conditioned shifts in Chinese', *Cahiers de linguistique Asie Orientale* 30: 133–78.

——(2008). 'Zhuguanhua yu xiandai hanyu "ba"ziju yanjiu' [A study of subjectification and the Modern Chinese "ba" construction], in Yang Shen and Shengli Feng (eds), *Dandai yuyanxue lilun he hanyu yanjiu* [Contemporary linguistic theories and related studies on Chinese]. Beijing: Commercial Press, 375–93.

——and Givón, Talmy (1985). 'On the so-called SOV order in Mandarin Chinese: a quantified text study and its implications', *Language* 61: 329–51.

Sundgren, Eva (2009). 'The varying influence of social and linguistic factors on language stability and change: the case of Eskilstuna', *Language Variation and Change* 21: 97–133.

Supalla, Ted (1986). 'The classifier system in American Sign Language', in Craig (1986: 181–214).

Suzuki, Ryoko (1998). 'From a lexical noun to an utterance-final pragmatic particle: *wake*', in Toshio Ohori (ed.), *Studies in Japanese Grammaticalization.* Tokyo: Kurosio Syuppan, 67–92.

——(1999). 'Grammaticization in Japanese: a study of pragmatic particle-ization', PhD dissertation, University of California, Santa Barbara.

——(2007) '(Inter)subjectification in the quotative *tte* in Japanese conversation: local change, utterance-ness and verb-ness', *Journal of Historical Pragmatics* 8.2: 207–37.

——(2008). 'Quoting and topic-marking: some observations on the quotative *tte* construction in Japanese', in Ritva Laury (ed.), *Crosslinguistic Studies of Clause Combining.* Amsterdam: Benjamins, 233–46.

Suzuki, Satoko (1999). 'Marker of unexpected statements: an analysis of the quotative particle *datte*', *Journal of the Association of Teachers of Japanese* 33.1: 44–67.

Svartvik, Jan (ed.), *London–Lund Corpus of Spoken English* (LLC).

Swan, Toril (1988). *Sentence Adverbials in English: A Synchronic and Diachronic Investigation.* Tromsø: University of Tromsø.

——(1997). 'From manner to subject modification: adverbialization in English', *Nordic Journal of Linguistics* 20: 179–95.

Sweetser, Eve E. (1982). 'Root and epistemic modals: causality in two worlds', *Proceedings of the Annual Meeting of the Berkeley Linguistics Society* 8: 484–507.

——(1990). *From Etymology to Pragmatics: Metaphorical and Cultural Aspects of Semantics Structure.* Cambridge: Cambridge University Press.

Szmrecsanyi, Benedikt (2006). *Morphosyntactic Persistence in Spoken English: A Corpus Study at the Intersection of Variationist Sociolinguistics, Psycholinguistics, and Discourse Analysis.* Berlin: Mouton de Gruyter.

——and Kortmann, Bernd (2009). 'Vernacular universals and angloversals in a typological perspective', in Markku Filppula, Juhani Klemola, and Helli Paulasto (eds), *Vernacular Universals and Language Contacts: Evidence from Varieties of English and Beyond.* London: Routledge, 33–53.

Tabor, Whitney, and Traugott, Elizabeth Closs (1998). 'Structural scope expansion and grammaticalization', in Anna Giacalone Ramat and Paul J. Hopper (eds), *The Limits of Grammaticalization.* Amsterdam: Benjamins, 229–72.

Tagliamonte, Sali (2002). 'Comparative sociolinguistics', in J. K. Chambers, Peter Trudgill, and Natalie Schilling-Estes (eds), *Handbook of Language Variation and Change.* Oxford: Blackwell, 729–63.

——(2003). 'Every place has a different toll: determinants of grammatical variation in cross-variety perspective', in Günter Rohdenburg and Britta Mondorf (eds), *Determinants of Grammatical Variation in English.* Berlin: Mouton de Gruyter, 531–54.

——(2004). '*Have to, gotta, must*: grammaticalisation, variation and specialization in English deontic modality', in Lindquist and Mair (2004a: 33–55).

——(2006). *Analysing Sociolinguistic Variation.* Cambridge: Cambridge University Press.

——and D'Arcy, Alexandra (2007). 'Frequency and variation in the community grammar: tracking a new change through the generations', *Language Variation and Change* 19: 199–217.

————(2009). 'Peaks beyond phonology: adolescence, incrementation, and language change', *Language* 85.1: 58–108.

——and Smith, Jennifer (2006). 'Layering, competition and a twist of fate: deontic modality in dialects of English', *Diachronica* 23.2, 341–80.

Takashima, Ken-ichi (1996). 'Language and palaeography', in Michiharu Itō and Ken-ichi Takashima (eds), *Studies in Early Chinese Civilization: Religion, Society, Language and Palaeography,* part 2. Hirakata: Kansai Gaidai University Press.

Tallerman, Maggie (2007). 'Did our ancestors speak a holistic protolanguage?', *Lingua* 117.3: 579–604.

Talmy, Leonard (1983). 'How language structures space', in Herbert L. Pick and Linda P. Acredolo (eds), *Spatial Orientation: Theory, Research, and Application.* New York: Plenum, 225–82.

——(1988). 'Force dynamics in language and cognition', *Cognitive Science* 12: 49–100.

Talmy, Leonard (1996). 'Fictive motion in language and "ception"', in Paul Bloom et al. (eds), *Language and Space.* Cambridge, MA: MIT Press, 211–76.

——(2000). *Toward a Cognitive Semantics,* vols 1 and 2. Cambridge, MA: MIT Press.

Tanaka, Hiroko (1999). *Turn-Taking in Japanese Conversation: A Study in Grammar and Interaction.* Amsterdam: Benjamins.

Tannen, Deborah, and Wallat, Cynthia (1993[1987]). 'Interactive frames and knowledge schemas in interaction: examples from a medical examination/interview', in Deborah Tannen (ed.), *Framing in Discourse.* New York: Oxford University Press, 57–76. (Originally appeared in *Social Psychology Quarterly* 50.2: 205–16 (1987).)

Tatevosov, Sergei G. (2001). 'From resultatives to evidentials: multiple uses of the perfect in Nakh-Daghestanian languages', *Journal of Pragmatics* 33: 443–64.

Tauli, Valter (1958). *The Structural Tendencies of Languages.* Helsinki: Finnish Academy of Sciences.

——(1966). *Structural Tendencies in Uralic Languages.* The Hague: Mouton.

TAYLOR, ANN, and VAN DER WURFF, WIM (eds) (2005). *Aspects of OV and VO Order in the History of English.* Special issue, *English Language and Linguistics* 9.

TAYLOR, JOHN R. (1995). *Linguistic Categorization: Prototypes in Linguistic Theory.* Oxford: Oxford University Press.

TERVOORT, BERNARD T. M. (1953). *Structurele Analyse van Visueel Taalgebruik Binnen een Groep Dove Kinderen.* Amsterdam: Noord-Hollandse Uitgeversmaatschappij.

TFA: Textes de Français Ancien: http://www.lib.uchicago.edu./efts/ARTFL/projects/TLA

THOMASON, SARAH GREY (2001). *Language Contact: An Introduction.* Washington, DC: Georgetown University Press.

——(2010). 'Contact explanations in linguistics', in Raymond Hickey (ed.), *The Handbook of Language Contact.* Oxford: Blackwell, 31–47.

——and KAUFMAN, TERRENCE (1988). *Language Contact, Creolization, and Genetic Linguistics.* Berkeley: University of California Press.

THOMPSON, SANDRA A. (2002). '"Object complements" and conversation: towards a realistic account', *Studies in Language* 26: 125–64.

——and COUPER-KUHLEN, ELIZABETH (2005). 'The clause as a locus of grammar and interaction', *Discourse Studies* 7: 481–505.

——LONGACRE, ROBERT E., and HWANG, SHIN JA J. (2007). 'Adverbial clauses', in Shopen (2007:, ii.237–300).

——and MULAC, ANTHONY (1991). 'A quantitative perspective on the grammaticization of epistemic parentheticals in English', in Traugott and Heine (1991b: 313–29).

THURGOOD, GRAHAM (1986). 'The nature and origins of the Akha evidentials system', in Chafe and Nichols (1986: 214–22).

TIMBERLAKE, ALAN (1977). 'Reanalysis and actualization in syntactic change', in Li (1977: 141–77).

TOBLER, ALFRED, and LOMMATZSCH, ERHARD (1925–2002). *Altfranzösisches Wörterbuch.* Berlin: Weidmann and Wiesbaden: Steiner.

TOMASELLO, MICHAEL (2003). *Constructing a Language: A Usage-Based Theory of Language Acquisition.* Cambridge, MA: Harvard University Press.

——(2008). *Origins of Human Communication.* Cambridge, MA: MIT Press.

——CARPENTER, MALINDA, CALL, JOSEP, BEHNE, TANYA, and MOLL, HENRIKE (2005). 'Understanding and sharing intentions: the origins of cultural cognition', *Behavioral and Brain Sciences* 28: 675–735.

TOMLIN, RUSSELL S. (1990). 'Functionalism in second language acquisition', *Studies in Second Language Acquisition* 12: 155–77.

TOMMOLA, HANNU (2000). 'On the perfect in North Slavic', in Östen Dahl (ed.), *Tense and Aspect in the Languages of Europe.* Berlin: Mouton de Gruyter, 441–78.

TORRES CACOULLOS, RENA (1999). 'Variation and grammaticalization in progressives: Spanish *-ndo* constructions', *Studies in Language* 23.1: 25–99.

——(2000). *Grammaticization, Synchronic Variation, and Language Contact: A Study of Spanish Progressive '-ndo' Constructions.* Amsterdam: Benjamins.

——(2001). 'From lexical to grammatical to social meaning', *Language in Society* 30: 443–78.

——(2006). 'Relative frequency in the grammaticization of collocations: nominal to concessive *a pesar de*', in T. Face and C. Klee (eds), *Selected Proceedings of the 8th Hispanic Linguistics Symposium.* Somerville, MA: Cascadilla Proceedings Project, 37–49.

——(2009). 'Variation and grammaticisation: the emergence of an aspectual opposition', in Stavroula Tsiplakou, Marilena Karyolemou, and Pavlos Pavlou (eds), *Studies in Language Variation: European Perspectives II*. Amsterdam: Benjamins, 215–24.

——(in press). 'Variation and grammaticalization', in M. Diaz Campos (ed.), *The Handbook of Hispanic Sociolinguistics*. Oxford: Blackwell.

——and Schwenter, Scott A. (2005). 'Towards an operational notion of subjectification', *Berkeley Linguistics Society* 31: 347–58.

——and Walker, James A. (2009a). 'On the persistence of grammar in discourse: a variationist study of *that*', *Linguistics* 47: 1–43.

————(2009b). 'The present of the English future: grammatical variation and collocations in discourse', *Language* 85: 321–54.

Tosco, Mauro (1994). 'On case marking in the Ethiopian language area (with special reference to the subject marking in East Cushitic', in Vermondo Brugnatelli (ed.), *Sem, Cam, Iafet: Atti della 7a Giornata di Studi Camito-Semitica e Indeuropei*. Milan: Centro studi camito-semitici, 225–44.

——(2001). *The Dhaasanac Language: Grammar, Texts, Vocabulary of a Cushitic Language of Ethiopia*. Cologne: Köppe.

Townsend, Charles E., and Janda, Laura A. (2003). *Gemeinslavisch und Slavisch im Vergleich: Einführung in die Entwicklung von Phonologie und Flexion*. Munich: Sagner.

Toyota, Junichi (2008). *Diachronic Change in the English Passive*. Basingstoke: Palgrave Macmillan.

Trager, George (1932). *The Use of the Latin Demonstratives (Especially Ille and Ipse) up to 600 A.D., as the Source of the Romance Article*. New York: Institute of French Studies.

Trask, R. Larry (1996). *Historical Linguistics*. London: Arnold.

——(2000). *The Dictionary of Historical and Comparative Linguistics*. Edinburgh: Edinburgh University Press.

Traugott, Elizabeth Closs (1972). *A History of English Syntax*. New York: Holt, Rinehart & Winston.

——(1982). 'From propositional to textual and expressive meanings: some semantic-pragmatic aspects of grammaticalization', in Winfred P. Lehmann and Yakov Malkiel (eds), *Perspectives on Historical Linguistics*. Amsterdam: Benjamins, 245–71.

——(1985) 'Conditional markers', in John Haiman (ed.), *Iconicity in Syntax*. Amsterdam: Benjamins, 289–307.

——(1986). 'On the origins of "and" and "but" connectives in English', *Studies in Language* 10: 137–50.

Traugott, Elizabeth Closs (1988). 'Pragmatic strengthening and grammaticalization', in S. Axmaker, A. Jaisser, and H. Singmaster (eds), *Proceedings of the 14th Annual Meeting of the Berkeley Linguistic Society*, 406–16.

——(1989). 'On the rise of epistemic meanings in English: an example of subjectification in semantic change', *Language* 65: 31–55.

——(1992). 'Syntax', in Richard M. Hogg (ed.), *The Cambridge History of the English Language*, vol. 1: *The Beginnings to 1066*. Cambridge: Cambridge University Press, 168–289.

——(1994). 'Grammaticalization and lexicalization', in R. E. Asher (ed.), *Encyclopedia of Language and Linguistics*. Oxford: Pergamon Press.

——(1995a). 'Subjectification in grammaticalization', in Dieter Stein and Susan Wright (eds), *Subjectivity and Subjectivisation*. Cambridge: Cambridge University Press, 31–54.

——(1995b). 'The role of discourse markers in a theory of grammaticalization', paper presented at the 12th International Conference on Historical Linguistics, Manchester, August.

——(1997a). 'Subjectification and the development of epistemic meaning: the case of *promise* and *threaten*', in Toril Swan and Olaf Westvik (eds), *Modality in Germanic Languages: Historical and Comparative Perspectives.* Berlin: Mouton de Gruyter, 185–210.

——(1997b). '*Unless* and *but* conditionals: a historical perspective', in Angeliki Athanasiadou and René Dirven (eds), *On Conditionals Again.* Amsterdam: Benjamins, 145–68.

——(1999a). 'The rhetoric of counter-expectation in semantic change: a study in subjectification', in Andreas Blank and Peter Koch (eds), *Historical Semantics and Cognition.* Berlin: Mouton de Gruyter, 177–96.

——(1999b). 'The role of pragmatics in semantic change', in J. Verschueren (ed.), *Pragmatics in 1998: Selected Papers from the 6th International Pragmatics Conference,* vol. 2. Antwerp: International Pragmatics Association, 93–102.

——(1999c). 'A historical overview of composite predicate types', in Brinton and Akimoto (1999c: 239–60).

——(2001). 'Legitimate counterexamples to unidirectionality', paper presented at Freiburg University: www.stanford.edu/~traugott/papers/Freiburg.Unidirect.pdf

——(2002a). 'From etymology to historical pragmatics', in Donka Minkova and Robert Stockwell (eds), *Studying the History of the English Language: Millennial Perspectives.* Berlin: Mouton de Gruyter, 19–49.

——(2002b). 'Regrammaticalization, exaptation and legitimate counterexamples to grammaticalization', paper presented at conference on 'Global Perspectives on Human Language: Scientific Studies in Honor of Joseph H. Greenberg', 25–7 April, Stanford University.

——(2003). 'Constructions in grammaticalization', in Joseph and Janda (2003: 624–47).

——(2004). 'Historical pragmatics', in L. R. Horn and G. Ward (eds), *The Handbook of Pragmatics.* Oxford: Blackwell, 538–561.

——(2005). 'Lexicalization and grammaticalization', in Alan Cruse, Franz Hundsnurscher, Michael Job, and Peter Rolf Lutzeier (eds), *Lexikologie/Lexicology,* vol. 2. Berlin: Mouton de Gruyter, 1702–12.

——(2007). 'The concepts of constructional mismatch and type-shifting from the perspective of grammaticalization', *Cognitive Linguistics* 18.4: 523–57.

——(2008a). '"All that he endeavoured to prove was . . . ": on the emergence of grammatical constructions in dialogic contexts', in Robin Cooper and Ruth Kempson (eds), *Language in Flux: Dialogue Coordination, Language Variation, Change and Evolution.* London: Kings College, 143–77.

——(2008b). 'Testing the hypothesis that priming is a motivation for change', *Theoretical Linguistics* 34: 135–42.

——(2008c). 'The grammaticalization of *NP of NP* patterns', in Alexander Bergs and Gabriele Diewald (eds), *Constructions and Language Change.* Berlin: Mouton de Gruyter, 23–46.

——(2010a). 'Grammaticalization', in Andreas H. Jucker and Irma Taavitsainen (eds), *Handbook of Historical Pragmatics.* Berlin: De Gruyter Mouton, 97–126.

——(2010b). 'Grammaticalization', in Silvia Luraghi and Vit Bubenik (eds), *A Continuum Companion to Historical Linguistics.* London: Continuum, 269–83.

——(forthcoming). 'The status of onset contexts in analysis of micro-changes', in Merja Kytö (ed.), *English Corpus Linguistics: Crossing Paths*. Amsterdam: Rodopi.

——and Dasher, Richard (2002). *Regularity in Semantic Change*. Cambridge: Cambridge University Press.

——and Heine, Bernd (eds) (1991a). *Approaches to Grammaticalization*, vol. 1. Amsterdam: Benjamins.

————(eds) (1991b). *Approaches to Grammaticalization*, vol. 2. Amsterdam: Benjamins.

——and König, Ekkehard (1991). 'The semantics-pragmatics of grammaticalization revisited', in Traugott and Heine (1991a: 189–218).

——and Trousdale, Graeme (2010). 'Gradience, gradualness and grammaticalization: how do they intersect?', in Elizabeth Closs Traugott and Graeme Trousdale (eds), *Gradience, Gradualness and Grammaticalization*. Amsterdam: Benjamins, 19–44.

Travis, Catherine (2006). '*Dizque*: a Colombian evidentiality strategy', *Linguistics* 44: 1269–97.

Trivedi, G. M. (1991). *Descriptive Grammar of Byansi, a Bhotiya Language*. Calcutta: Anthropological Survey of India, Government of India, Ministry of Human Resource Development, Department of Culture.

Trommer, Jochen (2008). '"Case suffixes", postpositions, and the phonological word in Hungarian', *Linguistics* 46.2: 403–37.

Trousdale, Graeme (2008a). 'A constructional approach to lexicalization processes in the history of English: evidence from possessive constructions', *Word Structure* 1, 156–77.

——(2008b). 'Constructions in grammaticalization and lexicalization: evidence from the history of a composite predicate construction in English', in Graeme Trousdale and Nikolas Gisborne (eds), *Constructional Approaches to English Grammar*. Berlin: Mouton de Gruyter, 33–67.

——(2010). 'Issues in constructional approaches to grammaticalization in English', in Katerina Stathi, Elke Gehweiler, and Ekkehard König (eds), *Grammaticalization: Current Views and Issues*. Amsterdam: Benjamins.

——(forthcoming). 'Grammaticalization, constructions, and the grammaticalization of constructions', in Tine Breban, Lieselotte Brems, Kristin Davidse, and Tanja Mortelmans (eds), *Proceedings of NRG 4 (New Reflections on Grammaticalization 4)*. Amsterdam: Benjamins.

Trudgill, Peter (1989). 'Contact and isolation in linguistic change', in Leiv Egil Breivik and Ernst Håkon Jahr (eds), *Language Change: Contributions to the Study of its Causes*. Berlin: Mouton de Gruyter, 227–37.

Trudgill, Peter (2009). 'Vernacular universals and the sociolinguistic typology of English dialects', in Markku Filppula, Juhani Klemola, and Helli Paulasto (eds), *Vernacular Universals and Language Contacts: Evidence from Varieties of English and Beyond*. London: Routledge, 304–22.

——Nevalainen, Terttu, and Wischer, Ilse (2002). 'Dynamic *have* in North American and British Isles English', *English Language and Linguistics* 6: 1–15.

Tucker, Archibald N. (1940). *The Eastern Sudanic Languages*, vol. 1. London: Oxford University Press.

Uchida, Mitsumi (2002). 'From participles to conjunctions: a parallel corpus study of grammaticalization in English and French', in Toshio Saito, Junsaku Nakamura, and Shunji Yamazaki (eds), *English Corpus Linguistics in Japan*. Amsterdam: Rodopi, 131–46.

Uehara, Satoshi (1998). *Syntactic Categories in Japanese: A Cognitive and Typological Introduction.* Tokyo: Kurosio Syuppan.

Valenzuela, Pilar (2003). 'Evidentiality in Shipibo-Konibo, with a comparative overview of the category in Panoan', in Aikhenvald and Dixon (2003: 33–62).

Valesio, Paolo (1968). 'The Romance synthetic future pattern and its first attestations', *Lingua* 20: 113–61.

van der Auwera, Johan (1999). 'Dutch verbal prefixes: meaning and form, grammaticalization and lexicalization', in Lunella Mereu (ed.), *Boundaries of Morphology and Syntax.* Amsterdam: Benjamins, 121–36.

——(2002). 'More thoughts on degrammaticalization', in Wischer and Diewald (2002: 19–29).

——(2006). 'Why languages prefer prohibitives', *Journal of Foreign Languages* 161: 2–25.

——(2008). 'In defense of classical semantic maps', *Theoretical Linguistics* 34.1: 39–46.

——(2009). 'The Jespersen Cycles', in van Gelderen (2009: 35–71).

——(2010). 'On the diachrony of negation', in Laurence R. Horn (ed.), *The Expression of Negation.* Berlin: Mouton de Gruyter, 73–109.

——Dobrushina, Nina, and Goussev, Valentin (2004). 'A semantic map for imperative-hortatives', in Dominique Willems, Bart Defrancq, Timothy Colleman, and Dirk Noël (eds), *Contrastive Analysis in Language: Identifying Linguistic Units of Comparison.* Basingstoke: Palgrave Macmillan, 44–66.

——Kehayov, Petar, and Vittrant, Alice (2009). 'Modality's semantic map revisited: acquisitive modals', in Lotte Hogeweg, Helen De Hoop, and Andrej Malchukov (eds), *Cross-linguistic Studies of Tense, Aspect, and Modality.* Amsterdam: Benjamins, 271–302.

——and Malchukov, Andrej (2005). 'A semantic map for depictive adjectivals', in Nikolaus P. Himmelmann and Eva Schulze-Berndt (eds), *Secondary Predication and Adverbial Modification.* Oxford: Oxford University Press, 393–421.

——and Plungian, Vladimir A. (1998). 'Modality's semantic map', *Linguistic Typology* 2.1: 79–124.

——and Van Alsenoy, Lauren (2011). 'Indefiniteness maps: problems, prospects and "retrospects"', in Eliza Kitis, Nikolaos Lavidas, Nina Topintzi, and Tasos Tsangalidis (eds), *Selected Papers from the 19th International Symposium on Theoretical and Applied Linguistics.* Thessaloniki: Monochromia, 1–14.

Van der Voort, Hein (2002). 'The quotative construction in Kwaza and its (de-)grammaticalisation', in Mily Crevels, Simon van de Kerke, Sérgio Meira, and Hein van der Voort (eds), *Selected Papers from the 50th International Congress of Americanists in Warsaw and the Spinoza Workshop on Amerindian Languages in Leiden.* Leiden: Research School of Asian, African and Amerindian studies (CNWS), 307–28.

Van Haeringen, Coenraad Bernardus (1956). *Nederlands tussen Duits en Engels.* The Hague: Servire.

van Klinken, Catharina (2000). 'From verb to coordinator in Tetun', *Oceanic Linguistics* 39.2: 350–63.

van Valin, Robert D., Jr (2005). *Exploring the Syntax–Semantics Interface.* Cambridge: Cambridge University Press.

Vandewinkel, Sigi, and Davidse, Kristin (2008). 'The interlocking paths of development to emphasizer adjective "pure"', *Journal of Historical Pragmatics* 9: 255–87.

Vanelli, Laura, Renzi, Lorenzo, and Benincà, Paola (1985). 'Typologie des pronoms sujets dans les langues romanes', in *Actes du XVIIe congrès international de linguistique et philologie romanes*, vol. 3: *Linguistique descriptive, phonétique, morphologie et lexique*. Aix-en-Provence: Université di Provence, 163–76.

Večerka, Radoslav (1993). *Altkirchenslavische (altbulgarische) Syntax* II: *Die innere Satzstruktur*. Freiburg i.Br.: Weiher.

Vendler, Zeno (1967). *Linguistics in Philosophy*. Ithaca, NY: Cornell University Press.

Verhagen, Arie (2005). *Constructions of Intersubjectivity: Discourse, Syntax, and Cognition*. Oxford: Oxford University Press.

Verschueren, Jef and Bertuccelli-Papi, Marcella (eds) (1987). *The Pragmatic Perspective*. Amsterdam: Benjamins.

Verstraete, Jean-Christophe (2001). 'Subjective and objective modality: interpersonal and ideational functions in the English modal auxiliary system', *Journal of Pragmatics* 33: 1505–28.

Vihman, Marilyn May (1980). 'Sound change and child language', in Elizabeth Closs Traugott, R. Labrum, and S. Shepherd (eds), *Papers from the Fourth International Conference on Historical Linguistics*. Amsterdam: Benjamins, 303–20.

Vincent, Nigel (1980). 'Iconic and symbolic aspects of syntax: prospects for reconstruction', in Paulo Ramat (ed.), *Linguistic Reconstruction and Indo-European Syntax*. Amsterdam: Benjamins, 47–68.

Vincent, Nigel (1982). 'The development of the auxiliaries *habere* and *esse* in Romance', in Nigel Vincent and Martin Harris (eds), *Studies in The Romance Verb*. London: Croom Helm, 71–96.

——(1987). 'The interaction of periphrasis and inflection: some Romance examples', in Martin Harris and Paolo Ramat (eds), *The Historical Development of Auxiliaries*. Berlin: Mouton, 237–56.

——(1988). 'Latin', in Martin Harris and Nigel Vincent (eds), *The Romance Languages*. London: Routledge, 26–78.

——(1997a). 'Synthetic and analytic structures', in M. Maiden and M. Parry (eds), *The Dialects of Italy*. London: Routledge, 99–105.

——(1997b). 'The emergence of the D-system in Romance', in van Kemenade and Vincent (1997: 149–69).

——(1998). 'Tra grammatica e grammaticalizzazione: articoli e clitici nelle lingue (italo)-romanze', in P. Ramat and E. Roma (eds), *Sintassi storica: atti del XXX congresso internazionale della Società di linguistica italiana*. Rome: Bulzoni, 411–40.

——and Börjars, Kersti (2010). 'Grammaticalization and models of language', in Elizabeth Closs Traugott and Graeme Trousdale (eds), *Gradience, Gradualness and Grammaticalization*. Amsterdam: Benjamins, 279–99.

Visconti, Jacqueline (2004). 'Conditionals and subjectification: implications for a theory of semantic change', in Fischer et al. (2004: 171–90).

Visser, Frederikus T. (1970). *An Historical Syntax of the English Language*, 1: *Syntactical Units with One Verb*. Leiden: Brill.

——(1973). *An Historical Syntax of the English Language*, 3.2: *Syntactical Units with Two or More Verbs*. Leiden: Brill.

Vitral, Lorenzo, and Ramos, Jânia (2006). *Gramaticalização: uma abordagem formal*. Rio de Janeiro: Tempo Brasileiro.

Vlasto, Alexis P. (1986). *A Linguistic History of Russia to the End of the Eighteenth Century*. Oxford: Clarendon Press.

Vogel, Petra M. (2006). *Das unpersönliche Passiv: eine funktionale Untersuchung unter besonderer Berücksichtigung des Deutschen und seiner historischen Entwicklung*. Berlin: de Gruyter.

von der Gabelentz, Georg (1901[1891]). *Die Sprachwissenschaft, ihre Aufgaben, Methoden und bisherigen Ergebnisse*, 2nd edn. Leipzig: Weigel.

von Fintel, Kai (1995). 'The formal semantics of grammaticalization', *North East Linguistics Society* 25: 175–90.

von Waldenfels, Ruprecht (2008). 'The grammaticalization of "give" with infinitive complement in Russian, Polish and Czech', PhD thesis, Regensburg.

Vosberg, Uwe (2006). *Die große Komplementverschiebung: Außersemantische Einflüsse auf die Entwicklung satzwertiger Ergänzungen im Neuenglischen*. Tübingen: Narr.

Vuillaume, Marcel (1980). 'La deixis en allemand', PhD thesis, Paris-Sorbonne.

Wälchli, Bernhard (2000). 'Infinite predication as marker of evidentiality and modality in the languages of the Baltic region', *Sprachtypologie und Universalienforschung* 53: 186–210.

——(2010). 'Similarity semantics and building probabilistic semantic maps from parallel texts', *Linguistic Discovery* 8.1: 331–71.

Wald, Benji (1979). 'The development of the Swahili Object Marker', in Talmy Givón (ed.), *Syntax and Discourse*. New York: Academic Press, 505–24.

Walker, James A. (2007). ' "There's bears back there": plural existentials and vernacular universals in (Quebec) English', *English World-Wide* 28: 147–66.

Wallage, Philip (2008). 'Jespersen's Cycle in Middle English: parametric variation and grammatical competition', *Lingua* 118: 643–74.

Waltereit, Richard (2006). 'The rise of discourse particles in Italian: a specific type of language change', in Kerstin Fischer (ed.), *Approaches to Discourse Particles*. Oxford: Elsevier, 61–76.

——(forthcoming). 'On the origins of grammaticalization and other types of language change in discourse strategies', in Kristin Davidse, Hubert Cuyckens, and Lieven Vandelanotte (eds), *Selected Papers from the 4th New Reflections on Grammaticalization Conference Leuven 2008*.

——and Detges, Ulrich (2007). 'Different functions, different histories: modal particles and discourse markers from a diachronic point of view', *Catalan Journal of Linguistics* 6: 61–80.

Wandruszka, Ulrich (2001). 'Frasi subordinate e congiuntivo', in L. Renzi and G. Salvi (eds), *Grande grammatica italiana di consultazione*. Milan: Il Mulino, 415–81.

Wang, Chueh-chen (2006). 'Grammaticalization of connectives in Mandarin Chinese: a corpus-based study', *Language and Linguistics* 7: 991–1016.

Wanner, Dieter (2006). *The Power of Analogy: An Essay on Historical Linguistics*. Berlin: Mouton de Gruyter.

Warner, Anthony (1993). *English Auxiliaries: Structure and History*. Cambridge: Cambridge University Press.

——(2005). 'Why *do* dove: evidence for register variation in Early Modern English negatives', *Language Variation and Change* 17: 257–80.

Watters, David E. (2002). *A Grammar of Kham*. Cambridge: Cambridge University Press.

Wehr, Barbara (1995). *SE-Diathese im Italienischen*. Tübingen: Narr.

Wei, Pei-chuan (1997). 'Lun gudai Hanyu zhong jizhong chuzhishi zai fazhan zhong de fen yu he' [On merger and separation in the development of several disposal constructions in Ancient Chinese], *Chinese Languages and Linguistics* 4: 555–94.

Weinreich, Uriel (1964[1953]). *Languages in Contact.* The Hague: Mouton.

——Labov, William, and Herzog, Marvin I. (1968). 'Empirical foundations for a theory of language change', in W. P. Lehmann and Yakov Malkiel (eds), *Directions for Historical Linguistics: A Symposium.* Austin: University of Texas Press.

Wheeler, Max, Yates, Alan, and Dols, Nicolau (1999). *Catalan: A Comprehensive Grammar.* London: Routledge.

Whistler, Kenneth W. (1986). 'Evidentials in Patwin', in Chafe and Nichols (1986: 60–74).

Whitman, John (2008). 'The classification of constituent order generalizations and diachronic explanation', in Jeff Good (ed.), *Linguistic Universals and Language Change.* Oxford: Oxford University Press, 232–52.

Whitney, William D. (1889). *Sanskrit Grammar.* Cambridge, MA: Harvard University Press.

——(1970[1875]). *The Life and Growth of Language.* Hildesheim: Olms.

Wichmann, Anne (1998). 'Using intonation to create conversational space: projecting topics and turns', in Antoinette Renouf (ed.), *Explorations in Corpus Linguistics.* Rodopi: Amsterdam, 217–32.

Wichmann, Anne (2008). 'Speech corpora', in Anke Lüdeling, Merja Kytö, and Tony McEnery (eds), *Corpus Lingustics: An International Handbook.* Berlin: Mouton de Gruyter, 187–207.

——(2009). 'Sorry: prosodic evidence for grammaticalization in progress', in Rhonwen Bowen, Mats Mobärg, and Sölve Ohlander (eds), *Corpora and Discourse—and Stuff.* Acta Universitatis Gothoburgensis.

——Simon-Vandenbergen, Anne-Marie, and Aijmer, Karin (2010). 'How prosody reflects semantic change: a synchronic case study of *of course*', in Kristin Davidse, Lieven Vandelanotte, and Hubert Cuyckens (eds), *Subjectification, Intersubjectification and Grammaticalization.* Berlin: Mouton de Gruyter.

Wiemer, Björn (2001). 'Aspektual'nye paradigmy i leksičeskoe značenie russkix i litovskix glagolov (Opyt sopostavlenija s točki zrenija leksikalizacii i grammatikalizacii)', *Voprosy jazykoznanija* 2001–2: 26–58.

——(2004). 'The evolution of passives as grammatical constructions in Northern Slavic and Baltic languages', in Walter Bisang, Nikolaus P. Himmelmann, and Björn Wiemer (eds), *What Makes Grammaticalization? A Look from its Fringes and its Components.* Berlin: Mouton de Gruyter, 271–331.

——(2007). 'Lexical markers of evidentiality in Lithuanian', *Rivista di linguistica* 19: 173–208.

——(2008). 'Zur innerslavischen Variation bei der Aspektwahl und der Gewichtung ihrer Faktoren', in Sebastian Kempgen, Karl Gutschmidt, Ulrike Jekutsch, and Ludger Udolph Ludger (eds), *Deutsche Beiträge zum 14, internationalen Slavistenkongress, Ohrid 2008.* Munich: Sagner, 383–409.

——(2010). 'Hearsay in European languages: toward an integrative account of grammatical and lexical marking', in Gabriele Diewald and Elena Smirnova (eds), *Linguistic Realization of Evidentiality in European Languages.* Berlin: Mouton de Gruyter, 59–129.

——(to appear). 'Umbau des Partizipialsystems', in Tilman Berger, Karl Gutschmidt, Sebastian Kempgen, and Peter Kosta (eds), *Slavische Sprachen: ein internationales Handbuch zu ihrer Struktur, ihrer Geschichte und ihrer Erforschung*. Berlin: Mouton de Gruyter, ch. 249.

——and BISANG, WALTER (2004). 'What makes grammaticalization? An appraisal of its components and its fringes', in Walter Bisang, Nikolaus P. Himmelmann, and Björn Wiemer (eds), *What makes Grammaticalization? A Look from its Fringes and Components*. Berlin: Mouton de Gruyter, 3–20.

——and GIGER, MARKUS (2005). *Resultativa in den nordslavischen und baltischen Sprachen: Bestandsaufnahme unter arealen und grammatikalisierungstheoretischen Gesichtspunkten*. Munich: Lincom.

——and HANSEN, BJÖRN (to appear). 'Assessing the range of contact-induced grammaticalization in Slavonic', in Björn Wiemer, Björn Hansen, and Bernhard Wälchli (eds), *Grammatical Replication and Borrowability in Language Contact*. Berlin: Mouton de Gruyter.

WIERZBICKA, ANNA (1982). 'Why can you *have a drink* when you can't **have an eat*?', *Language* 58.4: 753–99.

——(2006). *English: Meaning and Culture*. Oxford: Oxford University Press.

WILCOX, SHERMAN (2004). 'Gesture and language; cross-linguistic and historical data from signed languages', *Gesture* 4: 43–73.

WILLETT, THOMAS (1988). 'A cross-linguistic survey of the grammaticization of evidentiality', *Studies in Language* 12: 51–97.

WILLIAMS, LAWRENCE (2009). 'Sociolinguistic variation in French computer-mediated communication: a variable rule analysis of the negative particle *ne*', *International Journal of Corpus Linguistics* 14.4: 467–91.

WILLIS, DAVID (2007). 'Syntactic lexicalization as a new type of degrammaticalization', *Linguistics* 45.2: 271–310.

WISCHER, ILSE (2000). 'Grammaticalization versus lexicalization: "methinks" there is some confusion', in Olga Fischer, Anette Rosenbach, and Dieter Stein (eds), *Pathways of Change: Grammaticalization in English*. Amsterdam: Benjamins, 355–70.

——(2004). 'Old English prefixed verbs and the question of aspect and Aktionsart', in Christoph Bode, Sebastian Domsch, and Hans Sauer (eds), *Anglistentag 2003, München, Proceedings*. Trier: Wissenschaftlicher Verlag, 71–84.

——(2010). 'Sekretion und Exaptation als Mechanismen in der Wortbildung und Grammatik', in Rüdiger Harnisch (ed.), *Prozesse sprachlicher Verstärkung: Typen formaler Resegmentierung und semantischer Remotivierung*. Berlin/New York: De Gruyter, 29–40.

Wischer, Ilse, and Diewald, Gabriele (eds) (2002). *New Reflections on Grammaticalization*. Amsterdam: Benjamins.

WOLFRAM, WALT (2004). 'The grammar of urban African American Vernacular English', in Kortmann et al. (2004: 111–32).

WRAY, ALISON (2000). 'Holistic utterances in protolanguage', in Chris Knight, Michael Studdert-Kennedy, and James R. Hurford (eds), *The Evolutionary Emergence of Language: Social Function and the Origins of Linguistic Form*. Cambridge: Cambridge University Press, 285–302.

WRIGHT, ROGER (1983). 'Unity and diversity among the Romance languages', *Transactions of the Philological Society* 81: 1–22.

WU, FUXIANG (2003). 'Zai lun chuzhishi de laiyuan' [On the origin of the disposal constructions], *Yuyan Yanjiu* 3: 1–14.

WU, ZOE (2004). *Grammaticalization and Language Change in Chinese.* London: Routledge Curzon.

WÜLLNER, FRANZ (1831). *Über Ursprung und Urbedeutung der sprachlichen Formen.* Münster: Theissingsche Buchhandlung.

XU, LIEJIONG (2004). 'Manifestation of informational focus', *Lingua* 11: 277–99.

YAMADA, YOSHIO (1935). *Kanbun no Kundoku ni Yorite Tutaeraretaru Gohō* [Word usage transmitted through Japanese translation of Chinese writing]. Tokyo: Hōbunkan.

YAP, FOONG HA, and IWASAKI, SHOICHI (2003). 'From causatives to passives: a passage in some East and Southeast Asian languages', in Eugene H. Casad and Gary B. Palmer (eds), *Cognitive Linguistics and Non-Indo-European Languages.* Berlin: Mouton de Gruyter, 419–45.

——(2007). 'The emergence of 'GIVE' passives in East and Southeast Asian languages', in Mark Alves, Paul Sidwell, and David Gil (eds), *Proceedings of the Eighth Annual Meeting of the Southeast Asian Linguistic Society (1998).* Canberra: Pacific Linguistics, 193–208.

YLIKOSKI, JUSSI (2008). 'Non-finites in North Saami'. MS, University of Oulu: http://cc.oulu.fi/~jylikosk/080216.pdf

YOUNG, ROBERT (2000). *The Navajo Verb System:An Overview.* Albuquerque: University of New Mexico.

——and MORGAN, WILLIAM (1987). *The Navajo Language: A Grammar and Colloquial Dictionary,* 2nd edn. Albuquerque: University of New Mexico.

YOUNG, ROBERT and MORGAN, WILLIAMwith MIDGETTE, SALLY (1992). *Analytical Lexicon of Navajo.* Albuquerque: University of New Mexico.

YU, CHANG-DON (1962). *Kwukepyenchensa* [A history of Korean]. Seoul: Tongmunkwan.

YU, DEFEN (2003). 'Evidentiality in Shibacha Lisu', paper presented at 36th International Conference on Sino-Tibetan Languages and Linguistics, Melbourne.

ZAMBONI, ALBERTO (2000). *Alle origini dell'italiano: dinamiche e tipologie della transizione dal latino.* Rome: Carocci.

ZANUTTINI, RAFFAELA (1997). *Negation and Clausal Structure: A Comparative Study of the Romance Languages.* Oxford: Oxford University Press.

ZAYZON, REKA (2009). 'Funktionswandel deiktischer Stämme im Nganasanischen: Grammatikalisierung, Lexikalisierung, Pragmatikalisierung', *Acta Linguistica Hungarica* 51.1–2: 171.

ZEEVAT, H., and JASINSKAJA, K. (2007). '*And* as an additive particle', in M. Aurnague, K. Korta, and J. M. Larrazabal (eds), *Language, Representation and Reasoning.* Donostia-San Sebastián: University of the Basque Country Press, 315–40.

ZESHAN, ULRIKE (2003). 'Indo-Pakistani Sign Language grammar: a typological outline', *Sign Language Studies* 3: 157–212.

——(2004). 'Hand, head, and face: negative constructions in sign languages', *Linguistic Typology* 8: 1–58.

ZHANG, MIN (2000). 'Yufahua de leixingxue ji renzhi yuyanxue kaoliang: cong shiyi yu beidong biaoji jianyong xianxiang tanqi' [Grammaticalization in typological and historical linguistics: on the causative and passive markers], paper presented at 9th Conference on Modern Chinese, Wenzhou.

ZHU, DEXI (1982). *Yufa jiangyi* [Lessons on grammar]. Beijing: Shangwu yinshuguan.

ZIEGELER, DEBRA (1997). 'Retention in ontogenetic and diachronic grammaticalization', *Cognitive Linguistics* 8: 207–41.

——(2000). *Hypothetical Modality: Grammaticalization in an L2 Dialect.* Amsterdam: Benjamins.

——(2001). 'Past ability modality and the derivation of complementary inferences', *Journal of Historical Pragmatics* 2: 273–316.

——(2003). 'Redefining unidirectionality: insights from demodalisation?', *Folia Linguistica Historica* 24.1–2: 225–66.

——(2004). 'Redefining unidirectionality: is there life after modality?', in Fischer et al. (2004: 115–35).

——(2005). 'Mood and modality in grammar', in Keith Brown (ed.), *Encyclopedia of Language and Linguistics*, 2nd edn. Oxford: Elsevier, 259–267.

——(2006). *Interfaces with English Aspect: Diachronic and Empirical Studies.* Amsterdam: Benjamins.

——(2008). 'Grammaticalisation under control: towards a functional analysis of same-subject identity-sharing', *Folia Linguistica* 42.2: 401–51.

Zilles, Ana M. S. (2005). 'The development of a new pronoun: the linguistic and social embedding of *a gente* in Brazilian Portuguese', *Language Variation and Change* 17.1: 19–53.

Zribi-Hertz, Anne (1994). 'La syntaxe des clitiques nominatifs', *Travaux de Linguistique et Litterature*: 131–47.

Zucchi, Sandro (2003). 'The semantics of fatto', paper presented at the 14th Amsterdam Colloquium, December.

Zwarts, Joost (2010). 'Semantic map geometry: two approaches', *Linguistic Discovery* 8.1: 377–95.

Zwicky, Arnold M., and Pullum, Geoffrey K. (1983). 'Cliticization vs. inflection: English n't', *Language* 59.3: 502–13.

Zwitserlood, Inge (2003). *Classifying Hand Configurations in Nederlandse Gebarentaal.* Utrecht: Landelijke Onderzoekschool Taalwetenschap.

Name Index

Language Index

Subject Index